ATLANTIC CRUISING CLUB'S

GUIDE TO
LONG ISLAND SOUND
MARINAS

Powered by Datastact™

Written by Elizabeth Adams Smith
Edited by Richard Y. Smith

Jerawyn Publishing Inc.

www.AtlanticCruisingClub.com

Atlantic Cruising Club's
Guide to Long Island Sound Marinas

SEVENTH EDITION

Copyright © 2004 Jerawyn Publishing Inc.

ISBN Number: O-9664028-4-7
Library of Congress Catalog Number: 2003101654

Front Cover Photo by James Kirkikis
Back Cover Photos by Beth Adams Smith & Irina C. Adams

Front Cover: Mystic River, Mystic, CT
Back Cover: Britannia Yachting Center, Northport, NY
                Liberty Landing Marina, Jersey City, NY
                Old Lyme Dock, Lyme, CT

Senior Editor — Irina C. Adams
Executed Cover Design — Jessica Williams, Spark Design
Initial Cover Design — Rob Johnson
Book Design — Spark Design
Book & CD-ROM Programming — Dot Com Infoway Exports
Maps — Kasim Khan
Printed by Edwards Brothers, Ann Arbor, MI.

The publishers and editors of the Seventh Edition of the *Atlantic Cruising Club's Guide to Long Island Sound Marinas* have made reasonable efforts to ensure that the information contained herein is accurate and complete. The information in the Marina Reports is gathered and updated from marina questionnaires, personal site visits, telephone contacts, interviews, marina literature, reader comments and other sources. However, the Atlantic Cruising Club, its parent company, Jerawyn Publishing Inc., and the publishers and editors make no representation or warranty regarding accuracy and completeness.

None of the information contained herein, including chart schematics, latitude/longitude and reported water depths, is intended for use in navigation and may not be relied upon for such purposes. Readers should consult current NOAA charts and Notices to Mariners.

Ratings and reviews are, by their nature, subjective and subject to change at any time. They are not intended to be statements of fact. The Atlantic Cruising Club, the publishers and editors, and Jerawyn Publishing Inc. disclaim any responsibility for errors or omissions and do not assume any liability for claims or damages that might arise from use or publication of the *Guide*.

Bulk purchase discounts are available to yacht clubs, rendezvous organizers, boat manufacturers and other nautical groups for any of the Atlantic Cruising Club's Guides to Marinas. Please contact Guide@AtlanticCruisingClub.com or call 888-967-0994.

Atlantic Cruising Club's Guide to Long Island Sound Marinas
is written, compiled, edited and published by the Atlantic Cruising Club, an imprint of:

Jerawyn Publishing Inc.
PO Box 978; Rye, New York 10580

Table of Contents

To ensure objectivity, ACC neither solicits nor accepts marina advertising and there is absolutely no charge to marinas or boating facilities for their inclusion in the *Atlantic Cruising Club's Guides*. ACC reviewers have visited every Marina included in the Guides at least once — often several times. All ACC reviewers and personnel pay for their dockage and other marina services and, if arriving by boat, do not identify themselves until the conclusion of a marina stay.

Preface

Welcome to the Seventh Edition of the *Atlantic Cruising Club's Guide to Long Island Sound Marinas*. This volume covers 232 Long Island Sound region marinas from Block Island, RI to Cape May, NJ. It is one of six regional volumes covering the U.S. East and Gulf Coasts and two volumes covering the U.S. West Coast that will be published over the next year. Together they will describe about 1,800 "big boat" transient marinas. The other East Coast volumes cover New England (Maine to Rhode Island), the Chesapeake Bay, the Mid-Atlantic (including the ICW, Carolina Sounds and Bermuda), Florida's East Coast (including the Keys) and the Gulf Coast (Florida to Texas). The West Coast volumes cover the Pacific Northwest and the California Coast. Most of the research for these volumes is complete, and they'll be published as quickly as is practical.

▸ **A Little Background:** To us, cruising is one part fun, one part character building, one part enlightenment, one part food, one part adventure, and one part reading — with a little bit of stress thrown in just to keep us on our toes. So, at the end of the day, we often want to just tie up, kick back and relax in a slip or on a mooring. That usually means we need to find a marina. Easier said than done. A marina stay can be expensive — sometimes as expensive as a nice hotel room — and a lot harder to leave when it's not what you expected.

After years of trying to guesstimate what we'd find, based on the cruising guides' summary grids and marina ads or by quizzing dockmasters over the phone, we discovered a handy little loose-leaf Marina Guide covering about 250 East Coast marinas that was published by the Atlantic Cruising Club. The information was invaluable — it was objective, specific and even included rates along with the ACC Reviews and Ratings. The Guide provided details that weren't available anywhere else and all marinas included had been personally visited by ACC. We acquired the Atlantic Cruising Club in 1996, took it digital, added over a hundred Marina Reports and, a year and a half later, published the first publicly available Atlantic Cruising Club's Guide to East Coat Marinas — Book and CD-ROM. Since then, with the help of the ACC reviewers, we've visited more than 2,000 marinas (most of them several times), revised the original Marina Reports, and added more than 1,500 new ones. We've also built a library of well over 20,000 photographs and compiled more than 300 items of information on every significant transient facility along the East, Gulf and West Coasts.

▸ **Which Marinas Are Included?** The Guides attempt to include all facilities that can accommodate cruising boats 30 feet or longer and offer overnight transient dockage or moorings. Yacht Clubs which extend courtesies to all boaters without requiring reciprocity are also included. Transient accommodations do not need to be dedicated; many of the included dockage or mooring facilities welcome transients on a space-available basis. We have given priority in this edition to those facilities in the major cruising grounds or on the most frequented passage routes. Over time, ACC's reviewers will head farther up the rivers and expand into less visited — but potentially more interesting — areas.

▸ **Geographic Organization:** The ACC's *Guide to Long Island Sound Marinas* is organized into fourteen "sub-regions." Each sub-region corresponds to the gray tabs on the edge of the Guide's pages, to the graphic maps at the beginning of each section, and to the Geographic Marina List that follows this introduction. Within each sub-region, marinas are ordered, generally, from North to South or, for rivers or harbors, from mouth to source. We have attempted to arrange the Reports in the order a boater would encounter the marinas in a cruise from Block Island to Cape May.

▸ **The Enclosed CD-ROM:** The CD-ROM contains all the Marina Reports included in the print edition plus up to nine full-color photographs of each facility. Users can search on over 100 of the information items in the Marina Report, which makes it easy to cull through the roughly 70,000 pieces of data in each volume to find exactly the right marina. Installation is easy — just insert the CD into your computer's CD-ROM drive and the installation program will begin.

▸ **The Atlantic Cruising Club's Website:** The Atlantic Cruising Club's new, greatly expanded, website (www.AtlanticCruisingClub.com) will house all the Marina Reports, report updates, a forum for readers to communicate with ACC and with each other, boating and cruising links and other items of interest to our fellow cruisers. Please check it often for the most current information regarding marinas included in the Guide.

Preparing this *Guide* has really been a lot of fun. We've learned a great deal and we're looking forward to expanding ACC's marina coverage with additional volumes. On the drawing board, after the East, Gulf, and West Coasts, are: the Bahamas & the Caribbean and the Great Lakes. We hope that the newly expanded format, the extensive use of photos and more detailed Marina Reports and Ratings will point you to the right facility with the most appropriate services and surroundings for your cruising needs. We also hope that you will log-on to the ACC WebSite (or email us) with any changes, inaccuracies, new services or facilities you discover. Finally, we hope that you will share your marina impressions and general experiences with us and with your fellow cruisers.

Fair winds and happy cruising,

Beth and Richard Smith

Beth@AtlanticCruisingClub.com
Richard@AtlanticCruisingClub.com

ACC's Guide to Long Island Sound Marinas' Fourteen Sub-Regions

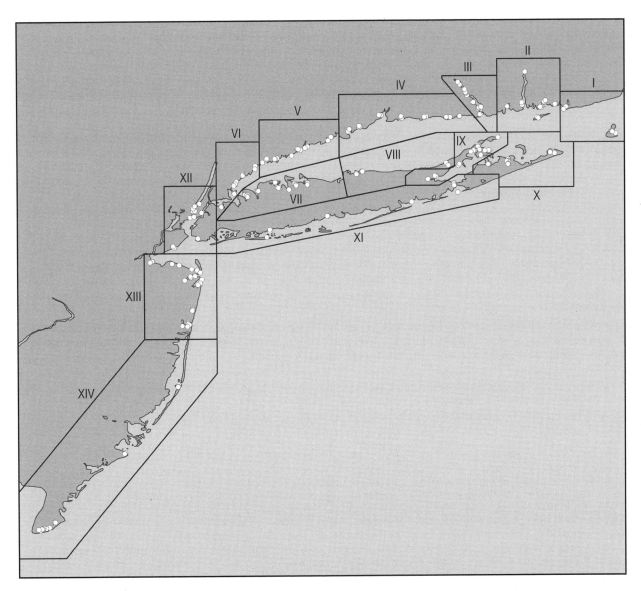

	STATE & SUB-REGION	PAGE		STATE & SUB-REGION	PAGE
I.	**Rhode Island** — *Block Island Sound*	21	VIII.	**New York** — *Eastern Long Island's North Shore*	151
II.	**Connecticut** — *Fishers Island Sound*	29	IX.	**New York**— *Long Island's North Fork*	161
III.	**Connecticut** — *Connecticut River*	51	X	**New York** — *Long Island's South Fork*	183
IV.	**Connecticut** — *Eastern Long Island Sound*	73	XI.	**New York** — *Long Island's South Shore Inlets*	205
V.	**Connecticut** — *Western Long Island Sound*	93	XII.	**New York/New Jersey** — *New York Harbor*	217
VI.	**New York** — *Western Long Island Sound*	111	XIII.	**New Jersey** — *Upper Atlantic Inlets*	231
VII.	**New York** — *Western Long Island's North Shore*	127	XIV.	**New Jersey** — *Lower Atlantic Inlets*	257

Atlantic Cruising Club's Ratings

 The Bell Ratings generally reflect the services and amenities available for the captain and crew rather than the services available for the boat. By their nature, ratings are subjective and may also reflect certain biases of the writers, editors and other reviewers. It is important to note that a five-bell marina will not always be a boater's best choice. There tends to be a correlation between higher bell ratings and higher overnight transient rates. Many of the resort-type amenities available at four- and five-bell marinas may be of little interest to boaters arriving late in the day and planning an early start the next morning. Similarly, a facility which has a one- or two-bell rating, good security, convenient transportation and a service-oriented staff, may be the best place to "leave the boat" for a period of time between legs of a longer cruise.

 The Boatyard Ratings, on the other hand, are less subjective. They simply indicate the extent of the boatyard services and the size of yachts that the facility can manage. To receive a boatyard rating at all (one-travelift), a facility must have a haul-out mechanism — a travelift or marine railway (or, in some cases, a heavy-duty crane or forklift) plus, at a minimum, a standard array of basic boatyard services. To receive a two-travelift rating, a facility will generally have haul-out capacity in excess of 70 tons and a full complement of all possible boatyard services.

 The Sunset Rating is the most subjective rating of all. This symbol indicates remarkable, special places like a pristine, untouched mooring field with no other facilities in sight, a marina that is, itself, so exquisitely turned out that it is truly beautiful, a skyline or distant vista that is simply breathtaking, or a marina that offers the possibility of a unique experience. A Sunset means that, in our view, there is more here than the first two ratings can convey — and only you can determine if the additional notation is valid for you and your crew. We'd be very interested in hearing your collective views.

The Bell Ratings

Outlined below are some of the facilities and amenities one might generally find at a marina or boating facility within a given Bell-Rating category. Please note that some marinas within a particular category may not have all of the facilities listed here and some may have more. (The word "Marina" is used generically here, and throughout the *Guide*, to denote all types of marine facilities.)

One Bell: The marina comfortably accommodates vessels over thirty feet in length, accepts overnight transients at docks or on moorings, and generally has heads. These are the "basic requirements" for ACC inclusion. Most facilities that are strictly mooring fields with a dinghy dock or basic docks without power pedestals or other services fall into this category.

Two Bells: In addition to meeting the basic ACC requirements, the marina generally has docks with power pedestals or a mooring field served by a launch (or a "dinghy loaner"). It has a dedicated marina staff, takes reservations, offers docking assistance, monitors the VHF radio, holds mail, and has an available fax machine. There are heads, showers, and, perhaps, a laundry. It likely has dock carts, a picnic area and grills.

Three Bells: With attractive and convenient facilities, the marina significantly exceeds basic requirements in many physical and operational categories. In addition to the two-bell services described above, the docks will usually have finger piers, and there will usually be a restaurant onsite or adjacent. A pool, beach, or major recreational amenity (i.e. a sport fishing center or a museum or a nature preserve) may also be nearby. The marina usually offers docking assistance and other customer-oriented services, a ships' store, cable TV, some kind of data port accessibility, and, hopefully, a pump-out facility.

Four Bells: Worth changing course to visit, the marina significantly exceeds requirements in most physical and operational categories and offers above average service in well-appointed, appealing, and thoughtfully turned-out facilities. In addition to the three-bell services described above, it will have a restaurant onsite, as well as a a pool or beach and other significant amenities like tennis courts, sport fishing charter, or historic or scenic sites. The marina will generally offer concierge services and have a particularly inviting environment.

Five Bells: A renowned, "destination" facility, the marina is worth a special trip. It has truly superior facilities, services and atmosphere. A five-bell marina is located in a luxurious, impeccably maintained environment and provides absolutely everything a cruising boater might reasonably expect, including room service to the boat. It offers all that is promised in a four-bell marina, plus outstanding quality in every respect.

Bell ratings reflect both subjective judgment and objective criteria. The ratings are intended to reflect the overall boater experience and are significantly impacted by a marina's setting and general ambiance. An ACC bias is discovering interesting and distinctive waterfront destinations which may not have all the standard marina services, but which provide a unique experience. These may be given ratings higher than their facilities would suggest. Similarly, maritime museums, which most boaters find particularly compelling, are usually given a "Sunset" to indicate that they offer maritime buffs more than just services. Ratings are also geographically specific and reflect the general level of available services in a given region. In other words, a five-bell marina in Florida (with a year-round season) will usually offer significantly more services and facilities than a five-bell marina in Maine (with a four-month season).

A Tour of a Marina Report

Photo: One for each marina in the printed Marina Report, up to 9 in full-color on the enclosed CD-ROM. Most were taken by ACC personnel during periodic visits. They are intended to provide a non-commercial, visual sense of each facility.

Ratings: Bells (1 - 5) reflect the quality of onsite marina facilities plus location, recreation, dining, lodgings, etc. Travelifts (1 - 2) indicate the extent of the boatyard services. A Sunset notes a particularly beautiful, special, unique, or interesting place.

Top Section: Facts, facts and more facts, including VHF channels, phone numbers, e-mail/ website addresses, number of slips, moorings, power options (rates for all), and much more. The format of this section is identical for every Marina Report for easy reference and comparison.

Middle Section: What's available, where and how to find it. Marine Services & Boat Supplies, Boatyard Services (including rates), Restaurants and Accommodations, Recreation and Entertainment, Provisioning and General Services, Transportation and Medical Services, all classified by distance — OnSite, Nearby, Within 1 mile, 1-3 miles or beyond. Names, phone numbers, price ranges and more.

Sub-Regions: The Long Island Sound Edition includes 14 sub-regions. For quick reference, these sub-region tabs are visible on the outside page edges. In each sub-region, Marina Reports are ordered North to South.

Marina Name: 232 marina and marine facilities included in the Long Island Sound Edition.

Photos on CD: Indicates the number of full-color photos of this facility that are on the CD-ROM.

Bottom Section: The "Setting" commentary portrays a sense of the marina's surroundings. "Marina Notes" provides important and interesting facts about the marina and its operations that may not have been covered in either of the earlier sections. "Notable" addresses anything the writers/reviewers feel is noteworthy about this facility, from special events or services to interesting side trips and/or local lore.

Harbor: Harbor or major body of water on which the marina resides.

Marina Report (sample)

East Hampton Point Marina and Boatyard

NY - LONG ISLAND SOUTH FORK

Navigational Information
Lat: 41°01.215' Long: 072°10.850' Tide: 3 ft. Current: 2 kt. Chart: 13209
Rep. Depths (MLW): Entry 8 ft. Fuel Dock 7 ft. Max Slip/Moor 7 ft./-
Access: Follow the channel into the harbor, just past Maidstone Marina

Marina Facilities (In Season/Off Season)
Fuel: Gasoline, Diesel
Slips: 57 Total, 12 Transient Max LOA: 110 ft. Max Beam: n/a
Rate (per ft.): Day $3.75* Week n/a Month n/a
Power: 30 amp $5, 50 amp $10, 100 amp $20, 200 amp n/a
Cable TV: Yes, $5 /night Dockside Phone: No
Dock Type: Fixed, Floating, Short Fingers, Pilings, Alongside
Moorings: 0 Total, 0 Transient Launch: Yes, Dinghy Dock ($10/day)
Rate: Day n/a Week n/a Month n/a
Heads: 4 Toilet(s), 4 Shower(s) (with dressing rooms), Hair Dryers
Laundry: 2 Washer(s), 2 Dryer(s) Pay Phones: Yes
Pump-Out: OnSite, OnCall, Full Service Fee: Free Closed Heads: Yes

Marina Operations
Owner/Manager: Tim Treadwell Dockmaster: Same
In-Season: May-Oct, 8am-5pm Off-Season: Nov-Apr, 9am-5pm
After-Hours Arrival: Contact Dockmaster
Reservations: Yes Credit Cards: Visa/MC, Amex
Discounts: None
Pets: Welcome Handicap Access: Yes, Heads, Docks

Marina Services and Boat Supplies
Services - Docking Assistance, Concierge, Boaters' Lounge, Security (On site), Dock Carts Communication - Phone Messages, Fax in/out, Data Ports, FedEx, AirBorne, UPS, Express Mail (Sat Del) Supplies - OnSite: Ice (Block, Cube), Ships' Store Near: Propane (Three Mile Harbor Boatyard 324-1320) 1-3 mi: Ice (Shaved), Bait/Tackle (Sams 324-8686), Live Bait

Boatyard Services
OnSite: Travelift (38T), Forklift, Crane, Engine mechanic (gas, diesel), Electrical Repairs, Electronics Repairs, Hull Repairs, Rigger, Bottom Cleaning, Brightwork, Air Conditioning, Refrigeration, Inflatable Repairs, Painting, Yacht Broker, Total Refits OnCall: Divers, Compound, Wash & Wax, Propeller Repairs, Woodworking, Upholstery, Metal Fabrication Dealer for: Yanmar Diesel. Member: ABYC Yard Rates: $75/hr., Haul & Launch $8/ft. (blocking incl.), Power Wash $3/ft., Bottom Paint $15/ft. (paint incl.) Storage: On-Land Winter $29.75 / $65 Indoor

Restaurants and Accommodations
OnSite: Restaurant (East Hampton Point 329-2800, L $7-15, D $20-40), Condo/Cottage (Individual townhouse cottages $295-495) Near: Restaurant (Riccardo's 324-0000, D $18-30) Under 1 mi: Restaurant (Michaels at Maidstone 324-0725), (Bostwicks 324-1111, D $10-24), Pizzeria (Pizza & Things 324-7974), Inn/B&B (Getaway House 324-9024) 1-3 mi: Inn/B&B (Mill House Inn 324-9786, $150-650)

Recreation and Entertainment
OnSite: Heated Pool, Picnic Area, Grills, Playground, Tennis Courts, Fitness Center, Fishing Charter (Fly fishing) Under 1 mi: Beach (Maidstone Park).

Video Rental Springs Video 324 5980 , Museum (Marine Museum's E.H. Boat Shop 324-6393, 267-6544) 1-3 mi: Golf Course (East Hampton G.C. 267-2100) 3+ mi: Horseback Riding (Stony Hill 267-3203, 4 mi.), Bowling (EH Bowl 324-1950, 4 mi.), Movie Theater (EH Cinema 324-0448, - 4 mi.), Cultural Attract (John Drew Theater 324-4050, 4 mi.)

Provisioning and General Services
OnSite: Copies Etc. Near: Convenience Store, Wine/Beer, Green Grocer (Round Swamp 324-4438) Under 1 mi: Market (Maidstone 329-2830), Gourmet Shop (Food & Co 329-3777), Delicatessen (Damarks 324-0691), Bakery, Beauty Salon (Springs 329-3129) 1-3 mi: Liquor Store (Franeys 324-0322), Bank/ATM, Post Office, Protestant Church, Dry Cleaners, Pharmacy (CVS 324-8587) 3+ mi: Supermarket (Waldbaum's 324-6215, 4 mi.), Health Food (Mother Natures 329-4745, 4 mi.), Fishmonger (Citeralla 329-1004, 4 mi.), Catholic Church (5 mi.), Synagogue (5 mi.), Library (324-0222, 4 mi.), Bookstore (Book Hampton 324-4939, 4 mi.), Hardware Store (Village 324-2456, 4 mi.)

Transportation
OnSite: Courtesy Car/Van OnCall: Rental Car (Enterprise 324-5050), Taxi (East End 324-8800), Airport Limo (East Hampton 324-5466) Near: Local Bus 3+ mi: InterCity Bus (Hampton Jitney 283-4600, 5 mi.), Rail (LIRR to NYC, 5 mi.) Airport: East Hampton/Islip (4 mi./60 mi.)

Medical Services
911 Service OnCall: Ambulance 1-3 mi: Doctor (EH Prime Care 907-9086), Dentist (Nelson 324-6800), Chiropractor, Holistic Services, Veterinarian (Disunno 324-0089) Hospital: Southampton 726-8200 (13 mi.)

East Hampton Point
PO Box 847; 295 Three Mile Harbor Rd.; East Hampton, NY 11937
Tel: (631) 324-8400 VHF: Monitor 9 Talk 10
Fax: (631) 324-3751 Alternate Tel: (631) 324-9191
Email: marina@easthamptonpoint.com Web: www.easthamptonpoint.com
Nearest Town: East Hampton (4 mi.) Tourist Info: (631) 324-0362

Setting -- On the east side of Three Mile Harbor is luxuriously appointed East Hampton Point. This very pleasant, upscale resort -- all beautifully maintained by a service-oriented staff -- is a destination in itself. The recreational facilities and cottages are nestled in a woodland setting away from the water.

Marina Notes -- *$135 per ft. seasonal. Full service marina and boatyard - second largest travelift in the Harbor. Excellent dockage - many single slips with some alongside. High end quarry tile heads with private dressing rooms and saunas. A TV lounge for the kids. All recreational facilities are an easy walk from the docks and available free to marina guests. Fully equipped, handsomely decorated, rental "cottages" are two-story, one or two bedroom townhouse units with kitchens, dining and living areas. Onsite East Hampton Point Restaurant has five dining "rooms" and a bar. Fine dining in the elegant indoor main room or adjacent porch and casual outdoor dining on one of The Decks or at the Bar (which sports a full size, dressed, wooden sail boat). The upstairs room and deck serves private functions. All promise breathtaking sunsets. This was formerly Wings Point and acquired by the current owners in the early nineties.

Notable -- A guest of the marina is a guest of the resort. Between the docks and Three Mile Harbor Road is a beautifully landscaped and well manicured long, fairly narrow mini resort. Shrubbery secludes the inviting pool which is surrounded by chaises, tables and chairs, and market umbrellas. The tennis courts, almost to the road, sport comfortable shaded seating. In between, closeted in greenery, are the cottages. A courtesy van makes regular runs to the beach and to the East Hampton shopping district -- block after block of high-end shops, boutiques, restaurants, gourmet shops and every service you might need.

THREE MILE HARBOR | 194

PHOTOS ON CD-ROM: 9

The Marina Reports

Individual Marina Reports are presented in a one page, easy-reference format to make the *Guide* as user-friendly as possible.

Each Report provides over 300 items of information, grouped into the following sections and categories:

TOP SECTION

MIDDLE SECTION

BOTTOM SECTION

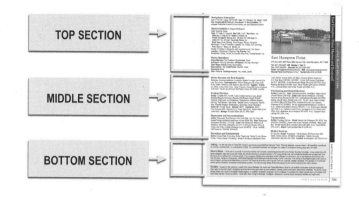

TOP SECTION

Name	Primary & Toll-Free Phone numbers	VHF channels — Talk & Monitor	Nearest Town (distance)
Address	Alternate Phone — after-hours	E-mail address	Tourist Office Phone
	Fax number	Web URL	

Navigational Information

Harbor (*bottom of page*)	Tidal Range & Maximum Current	Access — General Directions	Entry & Fuel Dock Depths
Latitude/Longitude	Chart Number	MLW Depths (*Reported by the marinas*)	Deepest Slip/Mooring

Marina Facilities (In Season/Off Season)

Fuel: Availability and Brand
　Diesel or Gasoline
　Slip-Side or OnCall Fueling
　High-Speed Pumps
Maximum Boat LOA & Beam
Slips: Number of Total/Transient
　Rates: Daily, Weekly, Monthly
　Power (Availability & Rates):
　30amp, 50 amp, 100 amp, 200 amp
　Cable TV: Availability, Terms, Rates
　Dockside Phone: Terms, Rates

Dock Type
　Fixed or Floating
　Alongside
　Short or Long Fingers, Pilings
Dock Material
　Wood, Concrete, Vinyl,
　Aluminum or Composite
Moorings: Total/Transient
　Rates: Daily, Weekly, Monthly
　Launch Service — Terms and Fees
　Dinghy Dock — Terms and Fees

Heads:
　Number of Toilets
　Number of Showers
　Dressing Rooms
　Hair Dryers & Other Amenities
Laundry:
　Number of Washers & Dryers
　Irons and Ironing Boards
　Book Exchange
　Pay Phones
Services to Anchored Boats

Pump-out Availability & Fees
　OnSite or OnCall
　Full Service or Self Service
　Number of Central Stations
　Number of Portable Stations
　In-Slip Dedicated Units
　Pump-Out Boats

Closed Head Requirements

The number of transient slips or moorings does not necessarily mean dedicated transient slips or moorings. Many facilities rent open slips and moorings to transient cruisers when their seasonal tenants are not in port. The number of Transient Slips/Moorings indicated is the facility's guesstimate, based on past experience, of the number generally available at any given time. In-Season and Off-Season rates are listed as $2.50/1.75. The parameters of those seasons are outlined in "Marina Operations" — Dates and Hours. If rates are complicated, which is becoming the norm, then the daily rate for a 40-foot boat is selected, followed by an asterisk, and a complete explanation of the rate structure is given in the "Marina Notes" section. The availability of 300 amp, European Voltage and 3-Phase is listed under "Marina Services and Boat Supplies." If there is alongside dockage, rather than individual slips, then the total number of alongside feet is divided by an average boat length of 40 feet and that number is displayed next to the Total/Transient Slips heading — followed by another asterisk. Dock Type is then listed as "Alongside" and the specifics are explained in "Marina Notes." The lack of finger piers — long or short — may signal a "Stern-To, Med-Mooring" approach. Since this can be a critical factor in choosing a marina, this will be highlighted in "Marina Notes." Since Book Exchanges or Lending Libraries, along with Pay Phones, are traditionally in the laundry room, these are itemized in the Laundry section. If there is Launch Service, the hours are usually included in Marina Notes, too.

A discussion of Closed Harbors, Pump-Out Facilities and the current Federal and State Regulations pertaining to Rhode Island, Connecticut, New York and New Jersey can be found in the Addendum.

Marina Operations

Marina Owner/Manager	After Hours Arrival Procedure	Discount Programs	Credit Cards Accepted:
Harbormaster	Reservation Policies	Boat-US, Nautical Miles, Safe/Sea	Visa, MasterCard, Discover,
Dockmaster	Pets: Welcome?	Dockage Fuel & Repair Discounts	Diners Club, American Express
Dates & Hours of Operation	Dog Walk Area, Kennel	Handicap Accessibility	

For municipal facilities the Harbormaster is listed under "Marina Owner/Manager" with the designation "(Harbormaster)" following his/her name. Dates and Hours for both in-season and off-season are provided and indicate the requisite time frames for the In-season and Off-season rates. In-season precedes off-season, separated by a (/) slash.

MIDDLE SECTION

Most of the information in this section is classified by "Proximity" — the distance from the marina to the service or facility, as follows:

OnSite — at the marina

OnCall — pick-up, delivery or slipside service

Nearby — up to approximately 4/10 of a mile — a very easy walking distance

Within 1 mile — a reasonable, though more strenuous, walking distance

1 – 3 miles — a comfortable biking distance, a major hike or a cab ride

3+ miles — a taxi, courtesy car or rental car distance — generally included is the approximate distance from the marina

(FYI: In this section, telephone area codes are included only if they are different from the area codes in the marina's contact information.)

Marina Services and Boat Supplies

General Services:	*MegaYacht Services:*	*Communications:*	*Supplies: (Listed by Proximity)*
Docking Assistance	Additional Power Options:	Mail and Package Hold	Ice — Block, Cubes, Shaved
Dock Carts	300 Amps	Courier Services	Ships' Stores — Local Chandlery
Trash Pick-up	Three-Phase	FedEx. Airborne, UPS	West Marine, Boat-U.S.,
Security — Type & Hours	European Voltage	Express Mail, Saturday Delivery	Boaters World,
Concierge Services	Crew Lounge	Phone Messages	Other Marine Discount Stores
Room Service to the Boat		Fax In and Out — Fees	Bait & Tackle
		Internet Access/Data Ports	Live Bait
		Type, Location & Fees	Propane & CNG

Under Services are additional power options beyond the basic amperage covered in the "Marina Facilities" section. Under Communications, is a list of the couriers that service the Marina's local area. This does not imply that the marina will manage outgoing courier services (unless, of course, they specifically offer concierge services); that process would be up to the individual boater. Communications also covers Internet access and data port availability with additional information provided in "Marina Notes." A brief discussion of Wi-Fi wireless Internet access systems is included in the Addendum. Under Supplies are resources for galley fuel – propane and CNG. As those of you who rely on CNG know, it is becoming harder and harder to find — if you discover any resources that we have not listed, please share them. Note, too, that West Marine has recently purchased all the Boat-U.S. stores. As of our publication date, they are planning to continue operating them under the Boat-U.S. name — so we have listed them separately.

Boatyard Services

Nearest Boatyard (If not onsite):		Metal Fabrication	*Yard Rates:*
Travelift (including tonnage)	Air Conditioning	Divers	General Hourly Rate
Railway	Refrigeration	Bottom Cleaning	Haul & Launch (Blocking included)
Forklift	Rigger	Compound, Wash & Wax	Power Wash
Crane	Sail Loft	Inflatable Repairs	Bottom Paint (Paint included?)
Hydraulic Trailer	Canvas Work	Life Raft Service	*Boat Storage Rates:*
Launching Ramp	Upholstery	Interior Cleaning	On Land (Inside/Outside)
Engine Mechanics — Gas & Diesel	Yacht Interiors	Yacht Design	In the Water
Electrical Repairs	Brightwork	Yacht Building	*Memberships & Certifications:*
Electronic Sales	Painting	Total Refits	ABBRA — No. of Cert. Techs.
Electronic Repairs	Awlgrip (or similar finish)	Yacht Broker	ABYC — No. of Cert. Techs.
Propeller Repairs	Woodworking	*Dealer For:* (Boats, Engines, Parts)	Other Certifications
	Hull repairs		

If the facility does not have a boatyard onsite, then the name and telephone number of the nearest boatyard is provided. In most cases, the services listed as "Nearby" or "Within 1 mile" will be found at that facility. "Dealer For" lists the manufacturers that the Boatyard services and its Authorized Dealerships. "Memberships and Certifications" refers to the two maritime trade organizations (ABBRA — American Boat Builders & Repairers Association & ABYC — American Boat and Yacht Council) which have programs that train and certify boatyard craftspeople and technicians. Several of the other professional maritime organizations and many manufacturers also offer rigorous training and certification on their particular product lines. These are included under "Other Certifications." A brief description of ABBRA and ABYC, and their certification programs, as well as the other major marine industry organizations is provided in the Addenda section.

Restaurants and Accommodations

Restaurants	Snack Bars	Fast Food	Motels
Seafood Shacks	Coffee Shops	Pizzeria	Inns/B&Bs
Raw Bars	Lite Fare	Hotels	Cottages/Condos

Since food is a major component of cruising, considerable attention has been given to both restaurants and provisioning resources. Eateries of all kinds are included (with phone numbers); full-service restaurants are listed simply as Restaurants. If delivery is available it is either noted or the establishment is listed as "OnCall." An attempt has been made to provide a variety of dining options and, whenever possible, to include the meals served Breakfast, Lunch, Dinner, Sunday Brunch (B, L, and/or D) plus the price range for entrées at each meal. If the menu is Prix Fixé (table d'hôte or one-price for 3-4 courses), this is indicated in the commentary. On rare occasion, if a restaurant has received very high marks from a variety of reviewers, that will be noted, too. If we are aware of a children's menu, the listing will indicate "Kids' Menu." Often the hours of onsite restaurants are included in "Marina Notes" or "Notable."

Price ranges have been gathered from menus, websites, site visits, marina notes and phone calls. Although these change over time, the range should give you an idea of the general price point. In large cities, the list generally consists of a handful of the closest restaurants — we expect that you will supplement this with a local restaurant guide. In small towns, the list provided may be "exhaustive" — these may be all there are and they may not be close.

Frequently, the need for local off-boat overnight accommodations arises — either for guests, crew changes, or just because it's time for a real shower or a few more amenities or a bed that doesn't rock. We have attempted to list a variety of local lodgings and, whenever possible, have included the room rate, too. The rates listed generally cover a 12-month range. So, if you are cruising in high season, expect the high end of the range. If the lodgings are part of the marina, then there is often a "package deal" of some sort for marina guests wishing to come ashore. We have asked the question about "package deals" and included the answers in "Marina Notes."

Recreation and Entertainment

Pools (heated or not)	Tennis Courts	Bowling	Park
Beach	Golf Course	Sport Fishing Charter	Museum
Picnic Areas & Grills	Fitness Center	Group Fishing Boat	Galleries
Children's Playground	Jogging Paths	Movie Theater	Cultural Attractions
Dive Shop	Horseback Riding	Video Rentals	Sightseeing
Volleyball	Roller Blade & Bicycle Paths	Video Arcade	Special Events

What there is to do, once you're tied up and cleaned up, is often a driving force in choosing a harbor or a particular marina. If you are choosing a facility to spend a lay-day or escape foul weather, the potential land-based activities become even more important. We have created a list of the possible major types of recreation and entertainment activities and have organized them, again, by proximity; if they are more easily reached by dinghy we note that, too.

A public golf course is almost always listed unless it is farther than 10 miles. Boat Rentals include kayaks, canoes and small sailboats. Group Fishing Boats are sometimes known as "head boats." Museums cover the gamut from art and maritime to historic houses and districts to anthropological and environmental. Cultural Attractions can range from local craft ateliers to aquaria to live theaters to all manner of musical concerts. Sightseeing can range from whale watching to historical walking tours. Special Events usually covers the major once-a-year local tourist extravaganzas — and almost all require significant advance planning (often these also appear in the "Notable" section). Galleries, both fine art and crafts, are listed under Entertainment rather than General Services since we view them more as opportunities for enlightenment than the shops that they really are. Admission prices are provided for both Adults and Children, when available, and are listed with the Adult price first, followed by the Children's price, i.e. $15/7. Occasionally, there is a family package price, which is also listed. Most entertainment and recreation facilities also offer Student and Senior Citizen pricing and other discounts; unfortunately, we don't have space to note them, but we do provide a phone number, so call and ask.

Provisioning and General Services

Complete Provisioning Service	Bakery	Houses Of Worship	Bookstore
Convenience Store	Farmers' Markets	Catholic Church	Pharmacy
Supermarket — usually major chain	Green Grocer	Protestant Church	Newsstand
Market — smaller, local store	Fishmonger	Synagogue	Hardware Store
Gourmet Shop	Lobster Pound	Mosque	Florist
Delicatessen	Meat Market	Beauty Salon	Retail Shops
Health Food Store	Bank/ATMs	Barber Shop	Department Store
Wine/Beer Purveyor	Post Office	Dry Cleaners	Copy Shops
Liquor/Package Store	Library	Laundry	Buying Club

As noted above, we think that most boaters travel on their stomachs, so knowing how to find local provisioning resources is very important. In addition, there is a fairly constant need for all kinds of services and supplies. When delivery is available for any of the provisioning resources or services, we've either noted that in the commentary or listed it as "OnCall."

For major provisioning runs, we have tried to identify the closest outlet for a regional supermarket chain. If a smaller, but fairly well supplied, market is close by, we include it as well as the more distant chain supermarket. Most people, we've discovered, really prefer to find interesting, local purveyors, so the presence of a Farmers' Market is notable. Usually these are a one or two-day-a-week events, so the exact days, times and locations are included. To differentiate Farmers' Markets from produce markets and farm stands, the latter are listed as Green Grocers. We've also tried to locate full Provisioning Services that will "do it all" and deliver dockside. And Fishmonger is just another name for fish sellers — these could be regular fish markets or directly "off-the-boat."

In the "General Services" category, we've included the nearest libraries because they can be wonderful sources of all kinds of "local knowledge," and can provide a welcome port on a foul weather day. They also usually have children's programs during the "season" and, with growing frequency, offer data ports or public Internet access on their own PCs. The Laundry in this section should not to be confused with the washers and dryers at the marina. Laundries are usually combination "do it for you" drop-off and self-service operations — and are frequently near restaurants or recreation or entertainment venues.

Transportation

Courtesy Car or Van	Rental Car — Local and Nat'l	Intercity Bus	Airport Limo
Bikes	Taxi	Rail — Amtrak & Commuter	Airport — Regional & Nat'l
Water Taxi	Local Bus	Ferry Service	

Once most cruisers hit land, they are on foot (except for those fortunate souls with sufficient on-board storage to travel with folding bikes). So transportation, in all its guises, becomes a very important consideration. We've divided transportation into two categories — getting around while in port and the longer-range issue of getting to and from the boat. If the marina or boatyard provides some form of courtesy car or van service, it's noted first. These services can include unlimited use of a car (very rare), scheduled use of a car (often 2 hours), an on-demand "chauffeured" van service, a scheduled van service, or a marina manager or employee willing to drive you to "town" at a mutually convenient time. The guests' use of this service is sometimes completely unrestricted; other times, it is reserved exclusively for provisioning or restaurant trips. If the details of this arrangement are simple, they are explained in the commentary; if complicated, they are explained in the "Marina Notes." Courtesy cars and/or vans are one of the most volatile of the marina services so, if this is important to you, call ahead to confirm that it's still available and to ask about the terms.

The Airport Limo services are either individual car services or vans. Rail covers Amtrak as well as commuter services that connect to a city, an Amtrak stop, or an airport. Local Buses also include the seasonal Trolleys that are becoming more common (and extraordinarily useful) in more tourist-oriented ports. Local, regional and inter-city ferry services are listed. Rates, when included, are usually for both Adults and Children, and indicate if one-way or round-trip; they are listed with the Adult price first, followed by the Children's price, i.e. $25/17RT. Note that there are usually Senior Citizen and Student prices but space has precluded their inclusion. Don't forget to ask.

For those of us cruising the coast less than full time, the logistics of going back and forth to the boat is often the stuff of nightmares. Rental cars have a variety of uses — local touring or long distance (back to where you left your car, to the airport or back home). We list local rental car agencies (for day rents), and regional ones (like Enterprise). We tend not to list the national ones (where pick-up and drop-off may be restricted to airports or downtown locations) because these are obvious and often very difficult to get to. Because Enterprise delivers and picks up — remembering that you have to return the driver to his/her office — we always include the nearest Enterprise office, if one exists, as "OnCall." (If another agency advertises pick-up/delivery, that information is included as "OnCall", too.)

Note that some franchise auto rentals, because the outlets are locally or regionally owned, seem to have a wide range of "drop-off" policies. Sometimes, if the region is large enough, it is possible to pick the car up at the current marina and drive to the marina where you left your own car, and leave the rental right there. When available, this service is just great. Call and check. The Airport listing often includes both the nearest regional and the nearest international. Because, as noted, long-distance, one-way car rentals are often based at airport locations, a marina's distance from an airport takes on a larger meaning than just catching a plane.

Medical Services

911 Service	Dentist	Holistic Service	Ambulance	Optician
Doctor	Chiropractor	Veterinarian	Hospital	

The data in this section is provided for informational purposes only and does not imply any recommendation. ACC is simply listing the nearest practitioner in each category. The first listing is the availability of 911 service; this service is surprisingly not ubiquitous — so it is important to know if dialing 911 will "work" in a given area. In the listings for Doctors, preference is given to walk-in clinics, then group practices and then general practitioners or internists. Dentists, Chiropractors, Veterinarians, and Holistic Services are also chosen in a similar fashion. A single practitioner is listed only if a "group" is not nearby. Holistic services will generally list massage therapists, but may also include acupuncturists, energy healers, and yoga classes when we find them. Hospital is usually the nearest major facility; if this is very far away and we are aware of a satellite, that will be noted — especially if there are no physicians nearby.

BOTTOM SECTION

Setting

This section provides a description of the location, environment and ambiance of each marina, boatyard or mooring field, including its views both landside and waterside, and any easily identifiable landmarks.

Marina Notes

Marina-specific information not included in the middle and top sections is detailed here. The source for this data includes interviews with marina staff, marina literature, marina comments provided to ACC, and surveyor/reviewer observations during site visits. If the rate structure is too complicated to detail in the "Facilities" section, a thorough explanation will be included here, preceded by an asterisk. Anything that is noteworthy or interesting about the facility is described in this paragraph. This includes history, background, recent changes, damage, renovations, new facilities, new management, comments on heads and showers (if they are, for instance, below par for the rating or particularly nice) and general marina atmosphere. If there is a restaurant or some form of lodging on-site, it is noted here, including any special deals for marina guests. If the marine services are part of a resort or a private yacht club with extensive recreation facilities, the level of access to those facilities is also detailed here or in "Notable." The facilities and services available to the visiting cruiser are also reflected in the rating.

Notable

This section focuses on additional items of interest related to the marina itself or the surrounding area. Details on special events, nearby attractions, the local community, ways of "getting around", the best beaches, special things to do, or other noteworthy facilities and/or services are listed here. Occasionally, there's also an elaboration of the onsite or nearby restaurants, amenities or accommodations.

The Data Gathering and Review Process

Collecting the data to create the Marina Reports is a multi-step process. A system of checks and balances keeps the information as accurate and as objective as possible. The intention is not to provide a promotional vehicle for marina and boatyard facilities — the intention is to provide a consumers' guide. Reasonable efforts have been made to confirm and corroborate the information. That does not mean that there won't be mistakes. The Marina Reports are a "snapshot in time" and things do change. It is also possible that, despite our best intentions, we just got it wrong. We hope that hasn't happened often, but a vehicle has been provided for you to tell us (and your fellow cruisers) if that is the case. Log-on to the ACC WebSite and add a Cruiser Note to the appropriate Marina Report (or send us an email). The data gathering and review process that ACC follows is outlined below:

▸ **Questionnaire:** A new marina, which has not been reviewed in an earlier edition, will be asked to fill out a very detailed four-page questionnaire — either before or after ACC's initial site visit and survey. The information provided is entered into ACC's proprietary database.

▸ **Site Visits:** Every facility included in the *Guide* is visited personally, at least once, by an ACC Reviewer who tours the marina or boatyard, walks the docks, pokes about the sheds, checks out the heads, showers and laundry, inspects the lounges, pool, beach, restaurants and hotel, and interviews the manager and/or dockmaster. The reviewer also takes photographs — one of which is included in each Marina Report in the Book and up to 8 more, in full-color, on the CD-ROM. The information that has been provided by the marinas is reviewed, confirmed, corrected and/or supplemented. If the reviewers arrive by boat, their affiliation with the Atlantic Cruising Club is not disclosed until the end of their stay. If they arrive by car, they introduce themselves before touring the facility. ACC pays in full for all services and refuses any complimentary accommodation, to maintain both the fact, as well as the perception of objectivity and impartiality. The ACC writers/editors have visited more than 2,000 facilities to provide a uniform basis for ratings, reviews and commentary. They have visited every facility included in the *Guide* at least once — in most cases, several times.

▸ **Data Confirmation Report:** After the completion of the Questionnaire and the Site Visit, each facility receives a Data Confirmation Report (DCR) that includes all the information in our database for that facility — up to 300 data points — with a request for updates and corrections. If there are significant changes, a new visit is scheduled as early as is practical.

▸ **Independent Research:** Information that is included in the final Marina Report is derived from many sources. In addition to the Site Visit, the Questionnaire and the DCR, independent data is also collected. Local tourist offices, chambers of commerce and websites are surveyed and interviewed. Independent researchers are assigned to gather specific data for the "Mid Section" — the "what is where" material. Forty categories have been selected as the most important for cruisers; independent researchers seek out names, phone numbers, rates and distances (from the marinas) for each of these. This data is used to supplement and/or corroborate the information from all the other sources.

▸ **The Photographs:** About 98% of the photographs in the book and on the CD-ROM have been taken by ACC Reviewers at the time of their site visits (in some cases the photographs will be from more than one visit). In a few cases, marinas have contributed aerial shots which provide a very useful overview. The photographs are not travel or tourism photos or even photojournalistic images. They are "location shots" or "snapshots." The intention is to show you what is there — as accurately as possible. The old saw "a picture is worth a thousand words" certainly applies here. We shoot what you would have seen had you arrived at the same time we did. The quality varies — the weather was not always perfect — but the sense of the place is usually correct.

We try to provide enough visual information so that you can both make an informed decision and recognize the place when you arrive. There's always a shot of the landside facility, of the view from the docks, and a close-up of a dock to show the quality of the slips and pedestals. And, finally, there are shots of the primary recreation facilities and restaurant, if they exist.

▸ **The Review and the Ratings:** As noted earlier, the ACC reviewers assign a three-part rating to each facility — A Bell Rating, a Boatyard Rating and a Sunset Rating. Then the Reviewers take all the material that has been gathered, including some subjective impressions, and write the bottom section's three-part Marina Review — "Setting," "Marina Notes" and "Notable."

▸ **The Draft Marina Report:** All of this material has been input into ACC's proprietary program called Datastract™, developed by the Atlantic Cruising Club's parent company, Jerawyn Publishing Inc. (JPI). The data is captured via a custom-designed multi-table input program which then collates, formats and outputs it as the single-page Marina Report. Every piece of data — including all the graphics and photographs — is placed in its precise position in the Marina Report by Datastract™. A Draft Report is sent to the marina facility for a final review for content accuracy before publication. Corrections are corroborated before the Marina Report is changed.

▸ **The Final Marina Report:** Datastract™ creates the final Marina Report, pulling all the corrected data and the photograph from the ACC database, and printing it to an Acrobat PDF file. The completed Marina Reports are then sent to the printer. Datastract™ replaces traditional publishing software resulting in a product that is more accurate and more timely.

▸ **The CD-ROM:** A very user-friendly version of the marina database resides on the enclosed CD-ROM. The CD-ROM permits users to select up to 100 of the 300+ possible data points as search criteria for querying the database for suitable marinas. The search engine will return a list of the facilities that meet the requested criteria. A "double-click" on a marina name will generate a color two-page Marina Report — with up to nine full-color photographs each. "Marina Reports" are created "on the fly" and can be viewed on the screen or printed out.

The Digital *Guide* on CD-ROM

The enclosed CD-ROM contains the *Atlantic Cruising Club's Digital Guide to Long Island Sound Marinas*; it includes all of the data and Marina Reports that are in this print version, but in full color, with more than 1,800 color photographs, all searchable on over 100 datafields.

▸ **Installation**
Simply insert the enclosed CD-ROM into the CD drive of your computer. The installation program starts automatically. If it doesn't, click Start/ Run and enter "d:\setup.exe" (assuming "d:" is the address of your computer's CD drive). During the installation process, you are asked to choose which of the three ACC Digital Guide components you wish to copy to your hard drive — this affects the amount hard disk space the program uses: Program (7.7 mb), Program and Database (24.2 mb), and Program, Database and Photos file (614.2 mb). If you have the hard disk capacity, it is best to install all of the components (Option 3) as the program will run considerably faster and you will not need to have the CD always at hand.

▸ **The Digital Guide is built around four screens:**

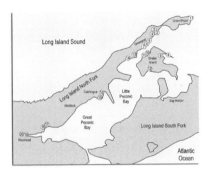

Region and Sub-Region Charts — Click on the "Charts" button to view a chart of the entire Long Island Sound Region with each of the 14 sub-regions outlined. Click on one of the outlines to access the chart for that particular Sub-Region. The locations of each of the marinas in that geographic area are displayed on the map. The location "points" and the marina names are "hot." Click on them to display the Marina Report for that marina. If you would prefer to add additional criteria to a marina search (or to skip the graphics interface entirely) the "search" button on the Long Island Sound Regional chart screen and on each of the Sub-Region chart screens, takes you directly to the Marina Search screen.

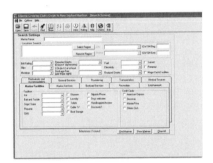

Marina Search Settings — This screen permits the user to enter up to 100 different search criteria—either singly or in combination. You may search for a particular marina by name (or part of name), for all of the marinas in a particular geographic region, city, or body of water, for marinas able to accommodate your vessel's LOA and draft, etc., etc., etc. If you arrived at this screen from one of the Sub-Region charts, then that Sub-Region is already entered in the "Location Search" box. You may add more sub-regions using the "Select Sub-Region" button. Once you have set the criteria for your search, click the "Find Marinas" button at the bottom of the screen (or the "Find" button in the toolbar). The search result (the number of marinas meeting your criteria) is indicated in the "Marinas Found" field. At this point, either refine your search to generate more or fewer marina choices or click the "Show Marinas" button to proceed to the next screen.

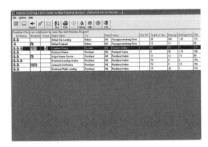

List of Selected Marinas — All of the marinas that meet your criteria are displayed on this screen. Next to each Marina Name are several items of information, including: bell, boatyard, and sunset ratings, city, state, and harbor. If, during the search, you set a criterion for "Slips," "Moorings," "LOA" or "Dockage Fee," a column for each selection also appears in the "List of Selected Marinas." The List may be sorted either geographically (default) or alphabetically. To view a full Marina Report for any of the marinas on the List, simply double-click on its name.

Marina Report — The Marina Reports in *ACC's Digital Guide* are identical to the Marina Reports in this printed version of the *Guide* but with some enhancements: The Reports are in color and each contains from 4 to 8 additional full-color marina photos. The Marina Reports Screen also lists the names of the other marinas that met your most recent search criteria. Clicking on one of those marina names displays its Marina Report. Finally, there is a box in the lower left hand corner of the Marina Report for you to enter your comments and observations about a given marina. This data is stored within the program and becomes part of the record for that marina. You can also print Marina Reports (and your comments, if you wish) using the Print command.

Note: For proper operation of the digital Guide, Internet Explorer 6.0 (or higher) must be installed on your computer. Each regional volume of the ACC Guides will automatically install into a separate, clearly labeled folder. Each will operate independently.

The Atlantic Cruising Club WebSite

As a reference work, *ACC's Guide to Long Island Sound Marinas* will be in a constant state of evolution. Its geographic coverage will be expanded as rapidly as time permits and Marina Reports will be modified as facts change and new information is received. As new marinas are added, and as substantive changes are discovered in the facilities of marinas already covered, updates will be posted on the Atlantic Cruising Club's WebSite: www.AtlanticCruisingClub.com

Please visit this site often. It's an easy way to keep your Guide updated and current. You'll also find useful cruising information, a community of cruisers sharing experiences and information, and a forum for your thoughts and comments on the facilities.

▸ **Cruisers' Comments:** A new section has been added to each on-line Marina Report to provide an opportunity for you to share your experiences and express your opinions. How was your visit at this facility? Is the rating fair or should it be adjusted? How did you find the general staff attitude toward transient boaters? Have the facilities, services, nearby restaurants or area resources changed? Please tell ACC and your fellow cruisers. A compilation of cruisers' comments can add another very useful dimension to the reviews.

You will find the Cruisers' Comments section divided into the same topic areas as the Marina Reports, so you can easily transfer any notes you may have made in the margins of your Guide into the comparable section on the ACC WebSite.

Please note: There is also a hard copy of the cruiser comments form at the end of this book which can be easily copied, then faxed or mailed.

Acknowledgments

The writers and editors would like to express their deep appreciation to a number of people who have contributed to the compilation and production of past and present editions of the Atlantic Cruising Club's Guides to Marinas:

Senior Editor: Irina C. Adams, for her tenacity and intelligence combined with her computer expertise, superb management and editorial skills, keen photographic eye — both as a photographer and editor — and her clear understanding of a complex process. **Associate Editor:** Kevin Chamberlain, for his diligence and his continuing commitment to the project. **Book and Page Design, Cover Execution, Back Cover Design and Execution:** Jessica Williams and Rupert Edson at Spark Design, for a wonderfully elegant book with a little edge — and for working with us all to figure out how to translate that perfectly designed page into 0s and 1s — they were truly the midwives of the Seventh Edition. **Programming:** Girish Ramdas and his team leaders R. Vijayakumar and V.M. Senthil Kumar at Dot Com Infoway Exports, for their creative code and tireless determination. **Cover Design:** Rob Johnson, for the original cover design, which we loved at first sight. **Icon Design:** Jennifer Grassmeyer, for the superb, bright and perfect new icons. **Maps/Charts:** Kasim Khan, for his combination of technical expertise and professionalism in developing the maps for both the book and the digital Guide. **Photo Retouching:** Michelle R. Averell, Belle Designs for creating over 1,800 lovely silk purses. **Photo Scanning:** Ian Watt, David Faranda and Michelle Laumeister, for their computer and graphic expertise.

And our very special thanks to:
Rick and Mary Ellen Adams, for discovering the original Atlantic Cruising Club and giving us our initial membership. We often cruised together and Rick, then the captain of *Elixir*, a Wilbur 38, was a fan of "tie up and plug in." Amanda Smith, one of ACC's most discerning and water-resistant reviewers, for her thorough investigations of the New Jersey Inlets and New York Harbor Marinas, her perceptive reports and great photos. Gary Joyce for the research he contributed on eastern Long Island marinas, his extensive "local knowledge" and the general boating expertise he brought to the project. Irina & Chris Adams for the many compelling photos taken from *Indian Summer* as they traveled along the Connecticut River and into harbors along Long Island Sound's northern shore. Ruth Jansson & Bette Conner, aboard *Annie B*, for the wonderful photos and commentary on Riverhead. Mystic Seaport, Southwestern Regional District Convention & Visitors Bureau, New York & Company, and many of the marinas for the images they graciously shared. Rick Huntley of the Connecticut Office of Long Island Sound Programs, the Long Island Sound division of the EPA, and Save the Sound for sharing their insights, information and expertise on these fragile waters. John and Betty Condon, for their contribution of notes and comments from their many sails along the Maine to Florida coast aboard their Tartan 41, *Second Wind*. John and Sue Scully, who cruise New England, LI Sound and the ICW in *Five Stars*, their Huckins 44, for their continuing encouragement. Jason C. Smith of Outsource Technology Group for his invaluable technical support. Rich Scholer of Park Lane Graphics, for sharing his decades of printing expertise — and helping us find the right "house." Original ACC Founder John Curry, and Editors Nancy Schilling and Jennifer Wise, for their impressive groundwork in developing the original Guide and the Sixth Edition Associate Editors Aimee Ganley and Jane Allison Havsey, for helping us take the first step.

The Members of the Atlantic Cruising Club, for their notes and emails describing their marina experiences. And, most important, the facilities' owners, managers and dockmasters who provided enormous quantities of detailed information on their marina and boatyard operations, along with aerial and ancillary photos (and reviewed ACC's interpretation at each step along the way), despite their discomfort with their inability to control the final Marina Report.

ATLANTIC CRUISING CLUB'S

GUIDE TO
LONG ISLAND SOUND MARINAS

THE
MARINA
REPORTS

Geographical Listing of Marinas

Marina Name	Harbor	City	Page No.
VII. NEW YORK — WESTERN LONG ISLAND'S NORTH SHORE			**127**
Brewer Capri Marina - East and West	Manhassett Bay	Port Washington	128
North Shore Yacht Club	Manhasset Bay	Port Washington	129
Toms Point Marina	Manhassett Bay	Port Washington	130
Manhasset Bay Marina	Manhassett Bay	Port Washington	131
North Hempstead Town Moorings	Manhasset Bay	Port Washington	132
Port Washington Yacht Club	Manhasset Bay	Port Washington	133
Hempstead Harbour Club	Hempstead Harbor	Glen Cove	134
Brewer Yacht Yard at Glen Cove	Hempstead Harbor/Glen Cove Creek	Glen Cove	135
The Jude Thaddeus Glen Cove Marina	Hempstead Harbor/Glen Cove Creek	Glen Cove	136
Oyster Bay Marine Center	Oyster Bay Harbor	Oyster Bay	137
Sagamore Yacht Club	Oyster Bay Harbor	Oyster Bay	138
Bridge Marina	Oyster Bay Harbor/Mill Neck Creek	Bayville	139
H & M Powles	Cold Spring Harbor	Cold Spring Harbor	140
Whaler's Cove Yacht Club	Cold Spring Harbor	Cold Spring Harbor	141
Wyncote Club	Huntington Harbor	Huntington	142
Huntington Yacht Club	Huntington Harbor	Huntington	143
Knutson's Marine	Huntington Harbor	Huntington	144
West Shore Marina	Huntington Harbor	Huntington	145
Coneys Marine	Huntington Harbor	Huntington	146
Willis Marine Center	Huntington Harbor	Huntington	147
Seymour's Boat Yard	Northport Harbor	Northport	148
Northport Village Dock	Northport Harbor	Northport	149
Britannia Yachting Center	Northport Harbor	Northport	150
VIII. NEW YORK — EASTERN LONG ISLAND'S NORTH SHORE			**151**
Port Jefferson Moorings & Launch Service	Port Jefferson Harbor	Port Jefferson	152
Danfords Marina & Inn on the Sound	Port Jefferson Harbor	Port Jefferson	153
Port Jefferson Town Marina	Port Jefferson Harbor	Port Jefferson	154
Ralph's Fishing Station & Marina	Mt. Sinai Harbor	Mount Sinai	155
Mount Sinai Yacht Club and Marina	Mt. Sinai Harbor	Mount Sinai	156
Old Man's Boat Yard	Mt. Sinai Harbor	Mount Sinai	157
Mattituck Inlet Marina & Shipyard	Mattituck Inlet/Mattituck Creek	Mattituck	158
Matt-A-Mar Marina	Mattituck Inlet/Mattituck Creek	Mattituck	159
IX. NEW YORK — LONG ISLAND'S NORTH FORK			**161**
Orient-By-The-Sea Marina	Gardiners Bay	Orient	162
Brewer Yacht Yard at Greenport	Stirling Basin	Greenport	163
Brewer Stirling Harbor Marina	Stirling Basin	Greenport	164
Townsend Manor Inn & Marina	Stirling Basin	Greenport	165
S.T. Preston & Son	Greenport Harbor	Greenport	166
Claudio's Marina	Greenport Harbor	Greenport	167
Greenport Moorings & Dock	Greenport Harbor & Stirling Basin	Greenport	168
Ram's Head Inn	Coecles Harbor	Shelter Island	169
Coecles Harbor Marina	Coecles Harbor	Shelter Island	170
Piccozzi's Dering Harbor Marina	Dering Harbor	Shelter Island Heights	171
Jack's Marine at True Value Hardware	Dering Harbor	Shelter Island Heights	172
The Island Boatyard & Marina	West Neck Harbor	Shelter Island	173
Brick Cove Marina	Sage Beach	Southold	174
Port of Egypt Marina	Southold Bay	Southold	175
New Suffolk Shipyard	Cutchogue Harbor	New Suffolk	176
Cutchogue Harbor Marina	Cutchogue Harbor	Cutchogue	177
Great Peconic Bay Marina	Flanders Bay	South Jamesport	178
Larry's Lighthouse Marina	Meetinghouse Creek	Aquebogue	179
Treasure Cove Marina Resort	Peconic River	Riverhead	180
Peconic Riverfront Marina	Peconic River	Riverhead	181

SEVENTH EDITION

SEVENTH EDITION

Marina Name	Harbor	City	Page No.
XIII. NEW JERSEY — UPPER ATLANTIC INLETS			**231**
Vikings Marina	Raritan Bay/Stump Creek	South Amboy	232
Lockwood Boat Works	Raritan Bay/Cheesequake Canal	South Amboy	233
Morgan Marina	Raritan Bay/Cheesequake Canal	Parlin	234
Lentze's Marina	Raritan Bay/Thorns Creek	West Keansburg	235
Monmouth Cove Marina	Raritan Bay/Belford Harbor	Port Monmouth	236
Atlantic Highlands Municipal Marina	Sandy Hook Bay	Atlantic Highlands	237
Sandy Hook Bay Marina	Sandy Hook Bay/Shrewsbury River	Highlands	238
Bahr's Landing Restaurant & Marina	Shrewsbury River	Highlands	239
Oceanic Marina	Navesink River	Rumson	240
Fair Haven Yacht Works	Navesink River	Fair Haven	241
Molly Pitcher Inn & Marina	Navesink River	Red Bank	242
Navesink Marina	Shrewsbury River	Sea Bright	243
Channel Club	Shrewsbury River	Monmouth Beach	244
Mariner's Emporium	Shrewsbury River	Long Branch	245
Shark River Yacht Club	Shark River	Neptune	246
Bry's Marine	Shark River	Neptune	247
Shark River Hills Marina	Shark River	Neptune	248
Belmar Marina	Shark River	Belmar	249
Hoffman's Marina	Manasquan River	Brielle	250
Brielle Marine Basin	Manasquan River	Brielle	251
Brielle Yacht Club	Manasquan River	Brielle	252
Southside Marina	Manasquan River	Point Pleasant	253
Clark's Landing Marina	Manasquan River	Point Pleasant	254
Crystal Point Yacht Club	Manasquan River	Point Pleasant Beach	255
XIV. NEW JERSEY — LOWER ATLANTIC INLETS			**257**
Lighthouse Marina	Barnegat Inlet	Barnegat Light	258
Marina at Barnegat Light	Barnegat Inlet	Barnegat Light	259
Barnegat Light Yacht Basin	Barnegat Inlet	Barnegat Light	260
Historic Gardner's Basin	Absecon Inlet/Gardner's Basin	Atlantic City	261
Les Kammerman's Atlantic City Marina	Absecon Inlet/Clam Creek	Atlantic City	262
Farley State Marina at Trump Resort	Absecon Inlet/Clam Creek	Atlantic City	263
Two Mile Landing Marina	Cape May Harbor/Lower Thorofare	Lower Township	264
Lighthouse Point Marina & Restaurant	Grassy Sound Channel	Wildwood	265
Schooner Island Marina	Grassy Sound Channel	Wildwood	266
Bree-Zee-Lee Yacht Basin	Cape May Harbor	Cape May	267
Canyon Club Resort Marina	Cape May Harbor/Cape May Canal	Cape May	268
Utsch's Marina	Cape May Harbor	Cape May	269
South Jersey Marina	Cape May Harbor	Cape May	270
Miss Chris Marina	Cape May Harbor/Spicer Creek	Cape May	271
Cape May Marine	Cape May Harbor/Spicer Creek	Cape May	272

I. Rhode Island: Block Island Sound

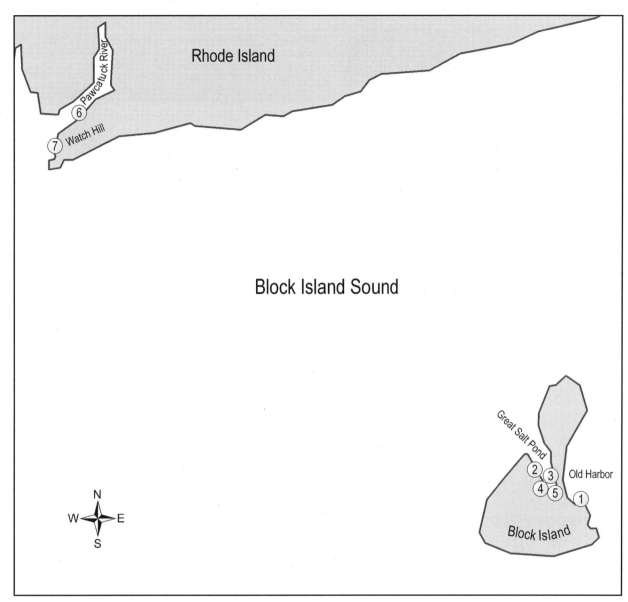

MAP	MARINA	HARBOR	PAGE	MAP	MARINA	HARBOR	PAGE
1	Old Harbor Dock	Old Harbor	22	5	Payne's New Harbor Dock	Great Salt Pond	26
2	Champlin's Marina	Great Salt Pond	23	6	Watch Hill Boatyard	Pawcatuck River	27
3	New Harbor Moorings	Great Salt Pond	24	7	Watch Hill Docks	Watch Hill Cove	28
4	Block Island Boat Basin	Great Salt Pond	25				

Navigational Information
Lat: 41°10.353' **Long:** 071°33.330' **Tide:** n/a **Current:** n/a **Chart:** 13215
Rep. Depths (*MLW*): **Entry** 15 ft. **Fuel Dock** n/a **Max Slip/Moor** 15 ft./-
Access: East side of Block Island, through breakwater at G3

Marina Facilities (*In Season/Off Season*)
Fuel: No
Slips: 60 Total, 60 Transient **Max LOA:** 65 ft. **Max Beam:** n/a
  Rate (*per ft.*): **Day** $2.75 **Week** n/a **Month** n/a
  Power: 30 amp Incl., 50 amp Incl., 100 amp n/a, 200 amp n/a
  Cable TV: No **Dockside Phone:** No
  Dock Type: Fixed, Wood
Moorings: 0 Total, 0 Transient **Launch:** n/a
  Rate: Day n/a **Week** n/a **Month** n/a
Heads: 2 Toilet(s), 2 Shower(s) (*with dressing rooms*)
Laundry: None **Pay Phones:** No
Pump-Out: OnSite, 1 Port **Fee:** Free **Closed Heads:** Yes

Marina Operations
Owner/Manager: Chris Willi (Harbormaster) **Dockmaster:** John Calhoun
In-Season: May 15-Oct 15, 7am-9pm **Off-Season:** Oct 16-May 14, Closed
After-Hours Arrival: Find a spot
Reservations: No **Credit Cards:** Cash / check
Discounts: None
Pets: Welcome, Dog Walk Area **Handicap Access:** No

Old Harbor Dock

PO Box 220; Water Street; Block Island, RI 02807

Tel: (401) 466-3235 **VHF: Monitor** 12 **Talk** 12
Fax: (401) 466-3219 **Alternate Tel:** (401) 466-3204
Email: n/a **Web:** n/a
Nearest Town: Old Harbor (*0 mi.*) **Tourist Info:** (401) 466-2982

Marina Services and Boat Supplies
Services - Docking Assistance **Supplies - Near:** Ice (*Cube*) **Under 1 mi:** Ships' Store, Bait/Tackle (*Orvis 466-5131*), Live Bait (*Twin Maples 466-5547*), Propane

Boatyard Services
OnCall: Engine mechanic (*gas, diesel*), Electrical Repairs, Rigger, Sail Loft, Divers, Propeller Repairs **Under 1 mi:** Travelift, Forklift, Launching Ramp.
Nearest Yard: A.H. Edwards Marine (401) 466-2655

Restaurants and Accommodations
OnSite: Restaurant (*Ballard's Main Room L $7-9, D $10-25*), Raw Bar (*Ballard's 11am-10pm, Sushi 2pm on*), Lite Fare (*Beachfront Café B, L, D*), Inn/B&B (*Ballard's 466-2231, $90-195*) **Near:** Restaurant (*Finns Seafood 466-2473, L $5-35, D $5-35*), (*Hotel Manisses Dining Room 466-2836, D $16-35*), (*Harborside D.R. L $10-20, D $20-30, Breakfast on weekends*), (*Gatsby Room 466-2836, D $14-29*), (*National Tap & Grille 466-2901, steak house*), (*Mohegan Café 466-5911, L $4-10, D $9-19*), Pizzeria (*Pizza Plous 466-9939*), Hotel (*National 466-2901, $80-250*), Inn/B&B (*Gothic 466-2918, $35-160*), (*Blue Dory Inn 466-5891, $65-295*), (*The 1661 Inn/Hotel Manisses 466-2421, $145-370*), Condo/Cottage (*Harborside Inn 466-5504, $70-210*)
Under 1 mi: Restaurant (*Atlantic Inn 466-5883, D $42, 4-Course Prix fixe*), Inn/B&B (*Atlantic Inn 466-5883, $100-210*)

Recreation and Entertainment
OnSite: Picnic Area, Grills, Fishing Charter (*5 including a 28' Harris Cuttyhunk, G. Willie Makit 466-5151*) **Near:** Beach (*Ballard's Beach*), Dive Shop (*Island Outfitters 466-5502*), Boat Rentals (*Oceans & Ponds Kayaking*

466-5131*), Movie Theater (*Empire 466-2555*), Video Rental, Museum (*BI Historical Society 466-2481 10am-5pm*) **Under 1 mi:** Playground, Jogging Paths, Roller Blade/Bike Paths, Park, Cultural Attract, Sightseeing (*Animal farm - Spring & High Sts.*) **1-3 mi:** Horseback Riding (*Rustic Rides 466-5060*)

Provisioning and General Services
OnSite: Lobster Pound (*John Grant 466-2997 4-6pm*) **Near:** Supermarket (*Seaside Market 466-5876*), Gourmet Shop (*Daily Market 466-9908*), Delicatessen, Health Food (*BI Depot 466-2403*), Wine/Beer, Liquor Store (*Red Bird Pkg. 466-2441*), Bakery, Farmers' Market (*Manisses Corner Wed 9-11am, Negus Park Sat 9-11am 466-2875*), Fishmonger (*Finn's 466-2102*), Meat Market, Bank/ATM, Post Office, Catholic Church, Protestant Church, Library (*466-3233 Dodge St.*), Beauty Salon, Laundry, Bookstore (*Book Nook 466-2993, Ship to Shore 466-5193*), Pharmacy (*Block Island Health 466-5825*), Clothing Store, Retail Shops **Under 1 mi:** Hardware Store (*Island Hardware & Supply 466-5831*), Florist, Copies Etc.

Transportation
OnSite: Ferry Service (*Pt. Judith, New London, Providence, Newport 783-4613*) **OnCall:** Taxi (*Minuteman 466-3131, Ladybird 466-3133*) **Near:** Bikes (*Old Harbor Bikes 466-2029, Island Bike & Moped 466-2700*), Rental Car (*Old Harbor Bike 466-2029*) **3+ mi:** InterCity Bus (*Adventure East to New York meets Ferry 847-8751, 20 mi.*) **Airport:** Block Island (*1 mi.*)

Medical Services
911 Service **OnCall:** Ambulance **Under 1 mi:** Doctor (*BI Medical Center 466-2974*) **Hospital:** South County 782-8010 (*20 mi.*)

Setting -- Set on the east side of Block Island, Old Harbor is a compact, man-made basin surrounded by rocks and reefs. The city has created a small transient marina for pleasure boats as well as for its seasonal working boats. Landside, it is also surrounded by BI's main "downtown" area. Virtually onsite is Ballard's "beach club" complex. Up the hill are most of Block Island's restaurants, shops and wonderful old inns.

Marina Notes -- Note: No Reservations. All med-style, stern-to or alongside dockage (no finger piers). Home to the Block Island Ferry to both Pt. Judith and New London -- so there is a lot of traffic and serious wakes coming and going. Shoreside are municipal heads and showers. Harbormaster's office is right on site. A $0.50 per head landing fee is assessed to support the development of better facilities. All of Block Island is "closed head" territory. A free pump-out service makes this very easy.

Notable -- There are at least 18 eateries -- from fine dining to casual restaurants, raw bars, and seafood shacks -- and 7 lovely inns or B&B's, all within easy walking distance. Ferries come from Pt. Judith (Galilee $8.50 1/way), New London ($15/1-way), and from Montauk (to New Shoreham - $20 1-way). Adventure East buses ($90 RT) go directly from New York City to Galilee docks, Westerly Airport or Newport - schedules timed to meet ferries. Greyhound Terminal in New London is next to the BI ferry dock, as is the Amtrak station. New England Air flies from Westerly airport to BI Airport ($75 RT). Taxis from TF Green airport to BI Ferry are approx $50 1/way - Best 800-231-2222. BI Seafood Festival & Chowder Cook-off 466-2982 3rd weekend in June.

Navigational Information
Lat: 41°11.000' **Long:** 071°34.958' **Tide:** 3 ft. **Current:** n/a **Chart:** 13215
Rep. Depths (*MLW*): **Entry** 18 ft. **Fuel Dock** 18 ft. **Max Slip/Moor** 18 ft./-
Access: Block Island Sound to Great Salt Pond

Marina Facilities (*In Season/Off Season*)
Fuel: Gasoline, Diesel, High-Speed Pumps
Slips: 240 Total, 200 Transient **Max LOA:** 195 ft. **Max Beam:** n/a
 Rate (*per ft.*): **Day** $3.25* **Week** Less 10% **Month** Less 15%
 Power: 30 amp $15, **50 amp** $30, **100 amp** n/a, **200 amp** n/a
 Cable TV: No **Dockside Phone:** No
 Dock Type: Fixed, Floating
Moorings: 0 Total, 0 Transient **Launch:** Yes (Free), Dinghy Dock
 Rate: **Day** n/a **Week** n/a **Month** n/a
Heads: 25 Toilet(s), 30 Shower(s)
Laundry: 20 Washer(s), 20 Dryer(s) **Pay Phones:** Yes
Pump-Out: OnSite, OnCall **Fee:** Free **Closed Heads:** Yes

Marina Operations
Owner/Manager: Joe Grillo **Dockmaster:** Seasonal
In-Season: May 15-ColDay, 7am-9pm **Off-Season:** ColDay-May 14, Closed
After-Hours Arrival: Call in advance
Reservations: Required for weekends **Credit Cards:** Visa/MC, Amex
Discounts: None
Pets: Welcome **Handicap Access:** No

Champlin's Marina

P.O. Drawer J; Block Island, RI 02807

Tel: (401) 466-7777; (800) 762-4541 **VHF: Monitor** 68 **Talk** 68
Fax: (401) 466-2638 **Alternate Tel:** n/a
Email: n/a **Web:** www.champlinsresort.com
Nearest Town: New Harbor **Tourist Info:** (401) 466-2982

Marina Services and Boat Supplies
Services - Docking Assistance, Concierge, Dock Carts **Communication -**
Mail & Package Hold, Phone Messages, Fax in/out, FedEx, Express Mail
Supplies - OnSite: Ice (*Block, Cube, Shaved*), Ships' Store, Bait/Tackle

Boatyard Services
OnSite: Compound, Wash & Wax **OnCall:** Engine mechanic (*gas, diesel*),
Electrical Repairs, Electronics Repairs, Hull Repairs **Nearest Yard:** A.H.
Edwards (401) 466-2655

Restaurants and Accommodations
OnSite: Restaurant (*Dockside Restaurant, Pier 76 D B $4-7, L $6-9, D $6-
25, 7am on*), Raw Bar, Snack Bar (*7am-midnight*), Hotel (*Champlin's Hotel
466-7777, $175-455, BI's only air conditioned hotel*) **Near:** Restaurant
(*Finns Seafood 466-2473*), (*The Oar 466-8820, B $2-7, L $3-12.50, D $5-14,
6:30am-1am, raw bar, too*), (*Dead Eye Dicks 466-2654, D $16-22, lunch Sat
& Sun*), (*Narragansett Inn*), (*Samuel Peckham Tavern 466-5458*), Pizzeria
(*Pizza Plus 466-9939*), Hotel (*Samuel Peckham 466-2231, $75-175*),
Inn/B&B (*Sullivan House 466-5020, $135-195*), (*Hygeia House 466-9616,
$65-235, a '99 total restoration of one of the Champlin family homesteads*)
Under 1 mi: Restaurant (*1661 Inn 466-2421, D $15-25, Al fresco Brunch on
the hill overlooking the ocean*), Hotel (*National 466-2901, $80-220*)

Recreation and Entertainment
OnSite: Pool, Beach, Picnic Area, Grills, Playground, Volleyball, Tennis
Courts, Fitness Center, Jogging Paths, Boat Rentals (*Aldo's at Champlin's
Marina 466-5811 kayaks, bumper boats, paddle boats, pontoon boats,
zodiaks*), Movie Theater (*240 seat Ocean West 466-2971 $5*), Video
Rental, Video Arcade (*9am-11pm*), Sightseeing **OnCall:** Horseback Riding
(*Rustic Rides 466-5060*), Fishing Charter **Near:** Park **1-3 mi:** Museum
(*North Light Maritime Museum*)

Provisioning and General Services
OnSite: Convenience Store (*Lighthouse Variety*), Bakery (*& ice cream
parlor, too 7am-11pm*), Laundry (*wash & fold service*), Newsstand, Copies
Etc. **OnCall:** Hardware Store (*Island Hardware & Supply 466-5831*)
Near: Delicatessen, Wine/Beer, Liquor Store (*Red Bird 466-2441*),
Lobster Pound, Bank/ATM, Pharmacy (*BI Health 466-5825*), Florist
Under 1 mi: Supermarket (*BI Grocery 466-2949; Seaside Market 466-5876,
BI Grocery 466-2949; Seaside Market 466-5876*), Gourmet Shop (*The Daily
Market 466-2949*), Health Food (*BI Depot 466-2403*), Farmers' Market
(*Manisses Corner Wed 9-11am, Negus Park Sat 9-11am 466-2875*),
Fishmonger, Post Office, Catholic Church, Protestant Church, Synagogue,
Library (*466-3233 Dodge St.*), Beauty Salon, Barber Shop, Bookstore
(*Book Nook 466-2993, Ship to Shore 466-5193*), Clothing Store, Retail Shops

Transportation
OnSite: Courtesy Car/Van, Ferry Service (*Viking to Montauk 631-668-5700
$40/20RT*) **OnCall:** Taxi (*Minuteman Taxi 466-3131*), Airport Limo (*Regal
Limousine 596-6570 on the mainland*) **Near:** Bikes (*Block Island Bike & Car
Rental 466-2297 & mopeds, too*), Rental Car (*Boat Basin Car & Rental 466-
5811*) **Airport:** Block Island (*1 mi.*)

Medical Services
911 Service **OnCall:** Ambulance **Under 1 mi:** Doctor (*Block Island Medical
Center 466-2974*) **Hospital:** South County 782-8010 (*20 mi.*)

Setting -- The Great Salt Pond's first facility to starboard is Champlin's, a complete resort with extensive facilities -- a self-contained, full-service destination
for cruising families. The atmosphere is very lively, particularly on weekends. Its 5000 feet of dockage fans out from the shore like a candelabra, and it's
frequently crowded with revelers. Champlin's extends its hospitality to the whole mooring field by providing free launch service.

Marina Notes -- *up to 30', $3.00/ft., 31-45' $3.25, 46-60' $3.50, 61-75' $3.75, 76-90' $4.00, over 90' $4.250/ft. 10% off for more than 7 days. 15-25% off for
more than 30 days. Rafting at the discretion of the dockmaster. Dockage rate includes shower facilities and pool. Bicycle & moped rentals are available. Future
reservations taken at any time. Only place for gas/diesel. Pump-out available to all boats. Note: Deposit required with reservation. Cancellations 14 days prior to
arrival date receive a full refund, less $35 administration fee. Cancellations less than 14 days forfeit half the deposit, no-shows forfeit all. Many boats spend the
season and their living quarters tend to "overflow" onto the docks. The Montauk Ferry lands here - expect arriving/departing crowds at 10:45am & 4:30pm.

Notable -- Onsite are: an Olympic size fresh water pool (with Tiki bar), tennis, volleyball, video game room, gift shop, a movie theater with 1st run features
every night and kids' matinees, brand new playground, boat rentals, of all kinds, a couple of eateries and a motel with air-conditioned rooms, suites, cable and
views of the Great Salt Pond and beyond. Dockside Restaurant, featuring Cajun cuisine, is open for B, L & D and also has a raw bar and great views across
the Pond. Consider a bike ride to the 19th century North Light(house), now a maritime museum (466-2982). House & Garden Tour 466-2982 every August.

New Harbor Moorings

P.O. Drawer 220; Block Island, RI 02807

Tel: (401) 466-3204 **VHF: Monitor** 12 **Talk** 12
Fax: (401) 466-3219 **Alternate Tel:** n/a
Email: n/a **Web:** n/a
Nearest Town: New Harbor **Tourist Info:** (401) 466-2982

Navigational Information
Lat: 41°11.091' **Long:** 071°34.776' **Tide:** 3 ft. **Current:** n/a **Chart:** 13215
Rep. Depths (*MLW*): **Entry** 14 ft. **Fuel Dock** n/a **Max Slip/Moor** -/50 ft.
Access: Block Island Sound to Great Salt Pond

Marina Facilities *(In Season/Off Season)*
Fuel: No
Slips: 0 Total, 0 Transient **Max LOA:** n/a **Max Beam:** n/a
  Rate *(per ft.)*: **Day** n/a **Week** n/a **Month** n/a
  Power: 30 amp n/a, 50 amp n/a, 100 amp n/a, 200 amp n/a
  Cable TV: No **Dockside Phone:** No
  Dock Type: n/a
Moorings: 90 Total, 90 Transient **Launch:** **Yes, Dinghy Dock
  Rate: Day $35-50/20* **Week** Inq. **Month** Inq.
Heads: 5 Toilet(s), 5 Shower(s)
Laundry: None **Pay Phones:** Yes, 1
Pump-Out: OnCall, Full Service, 3 Port **Fee:** Free **Closed Heads:** Yes

Marina Operations
Owner/Manager: Christopher Willi (Harbormaster) **Dockmaster:** Same
In-Season: Year-Round, 7am-9pm **Off-Season:** n/a
After-Hours Arrival: Call in advance
Reservations: Not Accepted **Credit Cards:** Cash or check
Discounts: None
Pets: Welcome, Dog Walk Area **Handicap Access:** No

Marina Services and Boat Supplies
Services - Docking Assistance, Dock Carts **Supplies - OnCall:** Ice *(Block, Cube)* **Near:** Ships' Store, Bait/Tackle *(Orvis 466-5131; Twin Maples 466-5547; B.I.Fish Works 466-5392)*, Live Bait, Propane

Boatyard Services
OnCall: Divers, Propeller Repairs, Woodworking **Near:** Travelift, Engine mechanic *(gas, diesel)*, Launching Ramp, Electrical Repairs, Electronic Sales, Rigger, Sail Loft, Bottom Cleaning. **Nearest Yard:** Block Island Marine (401) 466-2028

Restaurants and Accommodations
Near: Restaurant *(Samuel Peckham 466-5458)*, *(The Oar 466-8820, L $3-13, D $8-26, at B.I. Boat Basin)*, *(Dead Eye Dick's 466-2473, D $16-22, lunch Sat&Sun)*, *(Dockside 466-7777, B $4-7, L $6-9, D $6-25, at Champlin's, opens 7am)*, Pizzeria *(Pizza Plus 466-9939)*, Hotel *(Samuel Peckham's Inn 466-2439, $75-175)*, *(Champlin's 466-7777, $150-295)*, *(The Narragansett 466-2626, $95-125)*, Inn/B&B *(Hygeia House 466-9616, $65-235)* **Under 1 mi:** Restaurant *(Harborside 466-5504, L $10-20, D $20-30)*, *(Winfield's 466-5856, D $15-30)*, *(Hotel Manisses 466-2421, D $16-34)*, Hotel *(The National 466-2901, $80-220)*, Inn/B&B *(The Gothic 466-2918, $50-165)*

Recreation and Entertainment
OnCall: Fishing Charter *(Block Island Fishworks 466-5392 - fly fishing, charter boats, guide services)* **Near:** Beach *(Charlestown, Fred Benson)*, Picnic Area, Grills, Playground, Tennis Courts, Jogging Paths, Movie Theater *(Oceanwest at Champlin's 466-2971)*, Video Arcade *(Champlin's)*, Special Events *(Block Island Race Week)* **Under 1 mi:** Dive Shop *(Island Outfitters 466-5502)*, Horseback Riding *(Rustic Rides 466-5060)*, Boat Rentals *(Oceans & Ponds Kayaks 466-5131; Champlin's)* **1-3 mi:** Museum *(North Light Maritime Museum 466-2982)*, Sightseeing *(Mohegan Bluffs)*

Provisioning and General Services
OnCall: Bakery *(Aldo's, Ch.68 or listen for "Andiamo", his boat plies the harbor with pastries and baked goods; store within walking distance)*, Florist **Near:** Convenience Store *(Champlin's)*, Delicatessen, Lobster Pound, Meat Market, Bank/ATM, Post Office, Catholic Church, Library *(466-3233 Dodge St.)*, Hardware Store *(Island Hardware & Supply 466-5831)* **Under 1 mi:** Supermarket *(BI Grocery 466-2949, 466-5876, Seaside Market 466-9908 - in Old Harbor)*, Gourmet Shop *(The Daily Market 466-2949)*, Health Food *(BI Depot 466-2403)*, Wine/Beer *(Red Bird 466-2441)*, Liquor Store, Farmers' Market *(Manisses Corner Wed 9-11am, Negus Park Sat 9-11am 466-2875)*, Fishmonger, Bookstore *(Book Nook 466-2993, Ship to Shore 466-5193)*, Pharmacy *(BI Health 466-5825)*, Newsstand, Clothing Store, Retail Shops

Transportation
OnCall: Rental Car *(Boat Basin Car & Rental 466-5811)*, Taxi *(O.J. 741-0050)* **Near:** Bikes *(Block Island Bike & Car Rental 466-2297)*, Ferry Service *(to Montauk)* **Airport:** Block Island *(1 mi.)*

Medical Services
911 Service **OnCall:** Ambulance **Under 1 mi:** Doctor *(Block Island Medical Center 466-2974)* **Hospital:** South County 782-8010 *(20 mi.)*

Setting -- The Great Salt Pond, home to the Town of New Shoreham Mooring Field, provides a completely protected harbor surrounded by the simple beauty of Block Island's hills and beaches. The mooring field sits directly in front of two of the Pond's three transient marinas: Champlin's & the BI Boat Basin.

Marina Notes -- *to 39' - $35, 40-49' - $40, over 50' - $50. Mooring Balls are lime green (500 lbs. - up to 39') and orange (800 lbs. "H" - over 40'). Radio before taking an orange one. Weekends, moorings are generally taken by 10am. There's an anchorage on west side of channel (18-50' water). Stay within white buoys or gendarmes will call. Dinghies zip around mooring field from 8-11am looking for an opening. 2-boat maximum raft-up ($35 each). No limit on days. Can leave boat unoccupied if paid in advance. To save your mooring, leave dink or request official orange "Occupied" buoy. Check-out noon. Major turnover Sat & Sun. Harbor-master will stop by or pay at BI Boat Basin office (pick up a Harbor Guide). **Launch service from Old Port Launch or Champlin's Launch - both Ch.68 - (Note: Champlin's now offers free launch service to the mooring field). Or dinghy to BI Boat Basin (trash and recycling bins there, too). Efficient, high-speed pump-out - 3 boats monitor Ch.73. Free to all boats (tips appreciated). Heads & shower facilities are at the Fred Benson Beach Pavilion.

Notable -- Ice Deliveries Ch.72 8-10am daily, also 3-5pm weekends - cubes $4, block $3. Several restaurants, inns and a growing roster of services are in nearby New Shoreham; most of the island's shops and eateries are about a mile overland in Old Harbor. Dinghy dock is at B.I. Boat Basin. Note: the heads and showers at the B.I. Boat Basin are available only to their dockage customers. $0.50 per person landing fee assessed by town to improve B.I. facilities.

Navigational Information
Lat: 41°10.932' **Long:** 071°34.655' **Tide:** 3 ft. **Current:** n/a **Chart:** 13217
Rep. Depths (*MLW*): **Entry** 14 ft. **Fuel Dock** 10 ft. **Max Slip/Moor** 10 ft./-
Access: Block Island Sound to Great Salt Pond

Marina Facilities (*In Season/Off Season*)
Fuel: No
Slips: 100 Total, 85 Transient **Max LOA:** 110 ft. **Max Beam:** 24 ft.
 Rate *(per ft.)*: **Day** $2.75/Inq.* **Week** 7th night free **Month** Inq.
 Power: 30 amp Yes, **50 amp** Yes, **100 amp** n/a, **200 amp** n/a
 Cable TV: No **Dockside Phone:** No
 Dock Type: Floating
Moorings: 0 Total, 0 Transient **Launch:** Old Port Marine, VHF 68
 Rate: Day n/a **Week** n/a **Month** n/a
Heads: 6 Toilet(s), 8 Shower(s)
Laundry: None **Pay Phones:** Yes, 4
Pump-Out: OnSite, 1 Central **Fee:** Free **Closed Heads:** Yes

Marina Operations
Owner/Manager: Rally Migliaccio **Dockmaster:** Justin Lewis, Ben Edwards
In-Season: MemDay-LabDay, 7am-7pm **Off-Season:** n/a
After-Hours Arrival: n/a
Reservations: Suggested in Jul & Aug **Credit Cards:** Visa/MC
Discounts: None
Pets: Welcome, Dog Walk Area **Handicap Access:** No

Block Island Boat Basin

PO Box 369; West Side Road; Block Island, RI 02807

Tel: (401) 466-2631 **VHF: Monitor** 9 **Talk** n/a
Fax: (401) 466-5120 **Alternate Tel:** (401) 466-2632
Email: n/a **Web:** n/a
Nearest Town: New Harbor *(1 mi.)* **Tourist Info:** (401) 466-2982

Marina Services and Boat Supplies
Services - Docking Assistance, Trash Pick-Up, Dock Carts
Communication - Mail & Package Hold, Phone Messages, FedEx, AirBorne, UPS, Express Mail **Supplies - OnSite:** Ice *(Block, Cube)*, Ships' Store **Near:** Propane **Under 1 mi:** Bait/Tackle *(Twin Maples 466-5547)* **1-3 mi:** Live Bait

Boatyard Services
OnSite: Engine mechanic *(gas, diesel)*, Electrical Repairs **OnCall:** Rigger, Sail Loft *(Block Island Sail & Canvas 466-8981)*, Bottom Cleaning, Refrigeration **Nearest Yard:** A.H. Edwards Marine Repair (401) 466-2655

Restaurants and Accommodations
OnSite: Restaurant *(The Oar 466-8820, B $2-7, L $3-12.50, D $5-14, 6:30am-1am, raw bar, too)*, Snack Bar **Near:** Restaurant *(Narragansett Inn 466-2626, B $8, L $5-8, D $8-16, Breakfast buffet 7 days $8/4)*, *(Smuggler's Cove 466-7961)*, *(Aldo's 466-5871)*, Hotel *(The Narrangansett 466-2626, $95-125)*, *(Champlin's Hotel 466-7777, $150-295)*, *(Samuel Peckham 466-2231, $75-175)* **Under 1 mi:** Restaurant *(Finns Seafood 466-2473)*, *(Samuel Peckham Tavern 466-5458)*, *(Moneghan Café 466-5911, D $8-20)*, *(Winfield's 466-5856, D $15-30)*, *(Beachead 466-2249, L $10-$15, D $18-$27)*, Hotel *(National 466-2901, $80-220)*, Inn/B&B *(Blue Dory and Adrian Inns 466-5891, $85-365)* **1-3 mi:** Hotel *(Atlantic Inn 466-5883, $99-210)*

Recreation and Entertainment
OnSite: Picnic Area, Grills **OnCall:** Boat Rentals *(Oceans & Ponds 466-5131)*, Fishing Charter **Near:** Playground *(Lion's Playground)*, Roller Blade/Bike Paths, Movie Theater *(Oceanwest at Champlin's 466-2971)*, Video Rental, Video Arcade **Under 1 mi:** Beach *(Mosquito Beach on the Pond, Crescent Beach on RI Sound)*, Dive Shop, Jogging Paths **1-3 mi:** Tennis Courts, Horseback Riding *(Rustic Rides 466-5060)*, Museum *(Block Island's 1867 North Light 466-2982)*

Provisioning and General Services
OnSite: Convenience Store, Bank/ATM **OnCall:** Bakery *(Listen for Aldo's "Andiamo" - Champlin's also near)* **Near:** Hardware Store *(Island Hardware & Supply 466-5831)* **Under 1 mi:** Gourmet Shop *(The Daily Market 466-9908)*, Health Food *(BI Depot 466-2403)*, Farmers' Market *(Manisses Corner Wed 9-11am, Negus Park Sat 9-11am 466-2875)*, Post Office, Catholic Church, Library *(466-3233 Dodge St.)*, Beauty Salon, Barber Shop **1-3 mi:** Supermarket *(BI Grocery 466-2949, Seaside Market 466-9908 - in Old Harbor)*, Wine/Beer *(Red Bird 466-2441)*, Liquor Store, Fishmonger, Lobster Pound, Protestant Church, Synagogue, Laundry, Bookstore *(Book Nook 466-2993, Ship to Shore 466-5193)*, Pharmacy *(BI Health 466-5825)*, Newsstand, Clothing Store, Retail Shops

Transportation
OnSite: Rental Car *(Boat Basin Rental 466-5811)* **OnCall:** Water Taxi *(Oldport Launch)*, Taxi *(Mig's Rig 480-0493)* **Near:** Bikes *(Aldo's 466-5871)*, Ferry Service *(to Montauk, & at Old Harbor to Pt. Judith and New London - about 1.3 mi. walk)* **Airport:** Block Island *(1 mi.)*

Medical Services
911 Service **OnCall:** Ambulance **Under 1 mi:** Doctor *(Block Island Medical Center 466-2974)* **Hospital:** South County 782-8010 *(20 mi.)*

Setting -- The second - or middle - marina to starboard in the Great Salt Pond is the Block Island Boat Basin. It sits just a little to the right of the main channel and its docks form a wide double crossed "T" providing great views of the whole Pond. It's home to Oldport Launch and provides a dinghy dock for moored or anchored boats.

Marina Notes -- *$2.75 to 50', $3.00 over 50'. Six nights dockage, 7th night free. Individual slips - no rafting. Old Port Marine Launch, Ch.68 runs from the dock to boats anchored in the Pond. BI Boat Basin also hosts the dinghy dock for tenders (showers are for marina guests only). Moped and bike rentals onsite. Note: Reservations are necessary and require a deposit (accepted after Jan 1 for coming season). Cancellations: up to 14 days in advance, full refund; 2-13 days 50%, 2 days or less, forfeiture of deposit. Beware of the many local ordinances regarding trash removal and sewage pump-out - no used oil storage.

Notable -- Onsite Oar Restaurant (decorated with hundreds of oars of all sizes and shapes) serves breakfast, lunch, raw bar and dinner - inside or out -- all tables have great views. It's an easy mile walk to the shops and eateries of Old Harbor (marina has list of nearby restaurants). BI's east coast has two miles of spectacular beaches which are well worth a bike or dinghy ride -- the first heading north (off Corn Neck Road) is Crescent, then Scotch, then Mansion. Followed by the Clay Head Nature Trail. At the northernmost tip of the Island is Sandy Point and the 19thC North Light (house), now a museum. (An alternate approach is to beach your dinghy at Salt Pond's Mosquito Beach and walk across to Crescent Beach.) Heading south toward Old Harbor is more crowded Benson Beach.

Payne's New Harbor Dock

PO Box 646; Ocean Avenue; Block Island, RI 02807

Tel: (401) 466-5572 **VHF: Monitor** n/a **Talk** n/a
Fax: n/a **Alternate Tel:** (401) 466-5572
Email: n/a **Web:** n/a
Nearest Town: Block Island *(1 mi.)* **Tourist Info:** (401) 466-2982

Navigational Information

Lat: 41°10.936' **Long:** 071°34.493' **Tide:** 3 ft. **Current:** n/a **Chart:** 13215
Rep. Depths *(MLW):* **Entry** 12 ft. **Fuel Dock** n/a **Max Slip/Moor** 21 ft./-
Access: Blck Is. Sound to bell 23, into Great Salt Pond, then straight across

Marina Facilities *(In Season/Off Season)*

Fuel: Slip-Side Fueling, Gasoline, Diesel, High-Speed Pumps
Slips: 100 Total, 100 Transient **Max LOA:** 300 ft. **Max Beam:** n/a
  Rate *(per ft.):* **Day** $2.50/Inq.* **Week** $2.00 **Month** $2.00
  Power: 30 amp Incl., **50 amp** Incl., **100 amp** n/a, **200 amp** n/a
  Cable TV: No **Dockside Phone:** No
  Dock Type: Fixed, Floating
Moorings: 0 Total, 0 Transient **Launch:** n/a
  Rate: Day n/a **Week** n/a **Month** n/a
Heads: 8 Toilet(s), 8 Shower(s) *(with dressing rooms)*
Laundry: None **Pay Phones:** Yes, 3
Pump-Out: OnCall, Self Service, 1 Port **Fee:** Free **Closed Heads:** Yes

Marina Operations

Owner/Manager: Cliff Payne **Dockmaster:** Sands Payne
In-Season: Year-Round, 7am-1am **Off-Season:** n/a
After-Hours Arrival: Tie up anywhere
Reservations: No **Credit Cards:** Visa/MC
Discounts: None
Pets: Welcome, Dog Walk Area **Handicap Access:** Yes, Heads, Docks

Marina Services and Boat Supplies

Services - Docking Assistance, Boaters' Lounge, Trash Pick-Up, Dock Carts, Megayacht Facilities **Communication -** Mail & Package Hold, Phone Messages, FedEx, UPS *(Sat Del)* **Supplies - OnSite:** Ice *(Cube)*
Near: Ships' Store *(Block Island Marine Repair 466-2028)*, Bait/Tackle
Under 1 mi: Propane

Boatyard Services

Nearest Yard: Point Judith Marina

Restaurants and Accommodations

OnSite: Restaurant *(Narragansett Inn 466-2626, B $8/4, D $8-16, adjacent to Payne's, can land your dinghy on their beach)*, Snack Bar *(B $2-6.50, L $2-6.50, D $2-6.50)* **OnCall:** Pizzeria *(Pizza Plus 466-9939)*
Near: Restaurant *(The Oar 466-8820, B $2-7, L $3-12.50, D $5-14, at BI Boat Basin)*, *(Dockside B $4-7, L $6-9, D $6-25, at Champlin's)*, *(Samuel Peckham Tavern 466-5458)*, *(Dead Eye Dicks 466-2654, D $16-22, lunch Sat & Sun)*, Lite Fare *(Smuggler's Cove)*, Hotel *(Champlin's 466-7777, $150-395)*, *(The Narragansett 466-2626, $65-295)* **Under 1 mi:** Restaurant *(Finns Seafood 466-2473)*, *(Aldo's Place 466-5871)*, *(Hotel Manisses 466-2421, D $16-35)*, *(1661 Inn 466-2421, D $15-30, Sun Brunch on lawn)*, Hotel *(National 466-2901, $80-220)*, *(Harborside Inn 644-5504, $70-200)*, Inn/B&B *(Blue Dory and Adrian Inns 466-5891, $85-365)*

Recreation and Entertainment

OnSite: Picnic Area, Grills, Fitness Center, Boat Rentals, Fishing Charter
Near: Jogging Paths, Roller Blade/Bike Paths *(On the Island)* **Under 1 mi:** Movie Theater *(Champlin's)*, Video Rental, Video Arcade, Park, Sightseeing

1-3 mi: Beach *(small one is onsite, Mosquito is on Salt Pond, Crescent on RI Sound)*, Horseback Riding *(Rustic Rides 466-5060)*, Museum *(North Light Maritime)*

Provisioning and General Services

Near: Bakery *(Champlin's and Aldo's boat)*, Fishmonger, Clothing Store
Under 1 mi: Convenience Store *(Block Island Depot 466-2403)*, Supermarket *(BI Grocery 466-2949, Seaside Market 466-9908 - in Old Harbor)*, Gourmet Shop *(Daily Market 466-9908)*, Health Food *(Natural Grocery; Block Island Depot 466-2403)*, Wine/Beer, Liquor Store *(Red Bird Liquor 466-2441)*, Farmers' Market *(Manisses Corner 466-2875 Wed & Sat 9-11am)*, Lobster Pound *(at Old Harbor direct from boat)*, Meat Market, Bank/ATM, Post Office, Catholic Church, Protestant Church, Synagogue, Other, Library *(466-3233 Dodge St.)*, Beauty Salon, Barber Shop, Dry Cleaners, Bookstore *(Book Nook 466-2993, Ship to Shore 466-5193)*, Newsstand, Hardware Store *(Island Hardware & Supply 466-5831)*, Retail Shops **1-3 mi:** Pharmacy *(Block Island Health 466-5825)*

Transportation

OnCall: Taxi *(Rose 741-5598)* **Near:** Bikes *(Block Island Bike & Car Rental 466-2297)*, Water Taxi, Rental Car *(Block Island Bike & Car Rental)*, Ferry Service *(to Montauk, 1 mi. to Old Harbor for New London & Pt. Judith)*
Airport: Block Island *(1 mi.)*

Medical Services

911 Service **OnCall:** Ambulance **Near:** Holistic Services
Under 1 mi: Doctor *(Block Island Medical Center 466-2974)*, Chiropractor
Hospital: South Count 782-8010 *20 mi.*

Setting -- Payne's New Harbor Dock is the last transient facility in the Great Salt Pond, the least gentrified, and the closest to the restaurants, shops and services of Old Harbor. Amenities are quite limited, but there is a very basic yet appealing old fashioned atmosphere -- one that is becoming more and more difficult to find. Wonderful views of the moored boats and the green arms of the Pond enhance the rustic down-home ambiance.

Marina Notes -- Note: boats are docked stern-to, directly next to each other (almost rafted) and literally bow-to-bow -- there are no finger piers. If this is a problem, then the inside "ends" are the only solution. Watching the dockmaster maneuver a new load of boats into these quarters is an amazingly creative and instructive experience. The onsite snack bar (7am-6pm), souvenir, and marine supplies shop offers, among other things, clam cakes, chowder, lobster rolls, hot dogs, drinks, and taffy. *$2.50/ft a night to 50 feet; $3.00/ft 51 feet and over.

Notable -- The porches and rooms of the classic, beachy Narragansett Inn overlook Payne's docks. This quintessential BI Victorian Inn offers a lovely "all-you-can eat" breakfast buffet every morning ($7.95, $3.95 for kids), dinner Friday & Saturday, a turkey dinner on Sunday, and clean, airy rooms - some with shared bath, others with private. Narragansett's veranda is the perfect place for a quiet drink; land your dinghy on its sandy beach. Other restaurants, classic inns, and services are a reasonable one mile walk to Old Harbor. A perfect bike ride is southwest to 100 acre Rodman's Hollow Wildlife Preserve (off Cherry Road), then a picnic at Vail Beach, ending at Southeast Light atop 200 foot Monhegan Bluffs, which stand guard over the Atlantic.

Navigational Information
Lat: 41°19.458' **Long:** 071°50.712' **Tide:** n/a **Current:** n/a **Chart:** 12372
Rep. Depths (*MLW*): **Entry** 6 ft. **Fuel Dock** n/a **Max Slip/Moor** 5 ft./6 ft.
Access: Fishers Island Sound to Sandy Point, follow channel

Marina Facilities *(In Season/Off Season)*
Fuel: No
Slips: 55 Total, 2 Transient **Max LOA:** 40 ft. **Max Beam:** n/a
 Rate *(per ft.)*: **Day** $1.50/Inq. **Week** Inq. **Month** Inq.
 Power: 30 amp Incl., **50 amp** n/a, **100 amp** n/a, **200 amp** n/a
 Cable TV: No **Dockside Phone:** No
 Dock Type: Fixed, Floating, Wood
Moorings: 24 Total, 3 Transient **Launch:** None, Dinghy Dock
 Rate: Day $1.00/ft. **Week** n/a **Month** n/a
Heads: 2 Toilet(s), 1 Shower(s)
Laundry: None **Pay Phones:** No
Pump-Out: OnCall, 1 Port **Fee:** n/a **Closed Heads:** Yes

Marina Operations
Owner/Manager: James E. Long **Dockmaster:** Same
In-Season: May 15-Oct 15, 8am-4:30pm **Off-Season:** Oct 15-May 14, same
After-Hours Arrival: Call ahead
Reservations: Yes **Credit Cards:** Cash only, No credit cards
Discounts: None
Pets: Welcome, Dog Walk Area **Handicap Access:** No

Watch Hill Boatyard

21 Pasadena Avenue; Watch Hill, RI 02891

Tel: (401) 348-8148 **VHF: Monitor** 9 **Talk** 8
Fax: (401) 596-4711 **Alternate Tel:** n/a
Email: n/a **Web:** www.watchhillboatyard.com
Nearest Town: Westerly *(3 mi.)* **Tourist Info:** (401) 596-7761

Marina Services and Boat Supplies
Services - Trash Pick-Up, Dock Carts **Communication -** Mail & Package Hold, FedEx, AirBorne, UPS, Express Mail **Supplies - OnSite:** Ice *(Block, Cube)* **Near:** Live Bait **1-3 mi:** Ships' Store *(Hall's Marine Supply 348-9530)* **3+ mi:** West Marine *(860-536-1455, 6 mi.)*, Bait/Tackle *(Covedge Bait & Tackle 348-8888, 4 mi.)*, Propane *(Spicer Gas 596-6531, 4 mi.)*

Boatyard Services
OnSite: Crane, Launching Ramp, Rigger, Bottom Cleaning, Divers Electronic Sales, Electronics Repairs, Sail Loft, Propeller Repairs, Inflatable
OnCall: Repairs, Upholstery, Yacht Interiors

Restaurants and Accommodations
1-3 mi: Restaurant *(Maria's Seaside Café 596-6886, D $13-29, on the ocean)*, *(Olympia Tea Room 348-8211, L $10-12, D $20-28)*, *(Windjammer 322-9283)*, *(Seaside Grille 348-6333, L $8-17, D $18-30, inside or Veranda Deck or Patio at Watch Hill Inn)*, Motel *(Breezeway Resort 348-8953, $70-230)*, *(Andrea 348-8788)*, Inn/B&B *(Pleasant View Inn 348-6300)*, *(Narragansett Inn)*, *(Watch Hill Inn 348-8200, $100-500)*

Recreation and Entertainment
1-3 mi: Beach *(Watch Hill Beach)*, Movie Theater, Video Arcade, Park, Museum *(Lighthouse Museum 860-535-1440)*, Cultural Attract *(Flying Horse Carousel 348-6007)* **3+ mi:** Dive Shop *(Aqua Shop 348-8957, 4 mi.)*, Tennis Courts *(Pond View Racquet Club 322-1100, 4 mi.)*, Golf Course *(Elmridge Golf Course 860-599-2248, 4 mi.)*, Fitness Center *(New Attitude

Fitness 348-6288, 5 mi.)*, Horseback Riding *(Rainbow Stables 860-535-3411, 5 mi.)*, Bowling *(Alley Katz 596-7474, 4 mi.)*, Video Rental *(Visual Concepts 596-9555, 3.5 mi.)*

Provisioning and General Services
Under 1 mi: Catholic Church, Protestant Church **1-3 mi:** Convenience Store *(Linda's Landing 348-8144 snacks, coffee, ATM)*, Gourmet Shop *(Fras Italian Gourmet 596-2888)*, Delicatessen *(Bay St. Deli 596-6606)*, Health Food, Bakery, Green Grocer, Fishmonger, Bank/ATM, Post Office, Beauty Salon, Dry Cleaners, Laundry, Bookstore *(Mo Books N Art 348-0940)*, Florist, Clothing Store, Retail Shops **3+ mi:** Supermarket *(Ritaccos Mkt 596-1835, 5 mi.)*, Wine/Beer *(Cove Ledge Package 599-4844, 4 mi.)*, Liquor Store *(Warehouse Beer Wine Liquor 596-6160, 4 mi.)*, Library *(Westerly 596-2877, 4 mi.)*, Pharmacy *(Brooks 596-2901, 4 mi.)*, Hardware Store *(Big M Home Center 596-0302, 4 mi.)*, Copies Etc. *(Agjo Printing 599-3143, 4 mi.)*

Transportation
OnCall: Rental Car *(Enterprise 596-7847, Thrifty 596-3441)*, Taxi *(Eagle Cab 596-7300)*, Airport Limo *(King Charles Limousine 364-9999)*
Airport: Westerly/T.F. Green *(5 mi./40 mi.)*

Medical Services
911 Service **OnCall:** Ambulance **1-3 mi:** Doctor *(Giancaspro 596-2230)* **3+ mi:** Dentist *(Stadelmann & Gulino 596-0337, 4 mi.)*, Chiropractor *(Antonino Clinic 860-599-5551, 4 mi.)*, Veterinarian *(Westerly Animal Hospital 596-2865, 4 mi.)* **Hospital:** Westerly 348-3346 *(3 mi.)*

Setting -- Past the entrance to Watch Hill Cove to the mouth of the Pawcatuck River (just past Green 3), Watch Hill Boatyard dominates nicely protected, small, rural Colonel Willie Cove. The views waterside are pastoral; landside they are of a well maintained boatyard.

Marina Notes -- 81 slips for boats to 50'; 27 moorings for sailboats to 40'. Full service boatyard and marina. Closest full-service boatyard to Napatree Point and the reefs off Watch Hill. Most services and provisioning resources are in either Westerly to the north or Stonington to the west. The facility is nicely maintained, very quiet and family-oriented. Staff is focused on customer service. There is plenty of parking. Enterprise and several other auto rental agencies are nearby.

Notable -- The fishing right outside the river is reportedly great - especially for flounder, fluke, bass, and blues. It's about a 1.25 mile walk to the charming little village of Watch Hill. Antique shops, upscale clothing stores, gift shops, and eateries line the main street of this affluent, storied community. The town is known as an exclusive summer colony and for its beautiful, classic early 20thC shingle-style "cottages". Right next to the town dock is the famous Flying Horse Carousel, and beyond that is Watch Hill Beach. Walk a little bit farther to arrive at the beautifully preserved Napatree and Sandy Point Beaches with great bathing, surfing, and fishing.

Watch Hill Docks

Bay Street; Westerly, RI 02891

Tel: (401) 596-7807 **VHF: Monitor** 16 **Talk** 9
Fax: (401) 348-6090 **Alternate Tel:** (401) 348-8005
Email: n/a **Web:** n/a
Nearest Town: Watch Hill *(0 mi.)* **Tourist Info:** (401) 596-7761

Navigational Information
Lat: 41°18.616' **Long:** 071°51.499' **Tide:** n/a **Current:** n/a **Chart:** 12372
Rep. Depths *(MLW)*: **Entry** 7.5 ft. **Fuel Dock** n/a **Max Slip/Moor** 8 ft./-
Access: Fishers Island Sound to Sandy Point, follow Channel

Marina Facilities *(In Season/Off Season)*
Fuel: Gasoline, Diesel
Slips: 20 Total, 5 Transient **Max LOA:** 100 ft. **Max Beam:** n/a
 Rate *(per ft.)*: **Day** $2.50 **Week** $14 **Month** No Discount
 Power: 30 amp $6, **50 amp** Inq., **100 amp** n/a, **200 amp** n/a
 Cable TV: No **Dockside Phone:** No
 Dock Type: Fixed, Short Fingers, Pilings, Wood
Moorings: 0 Total, 0 Transient **Launch:** n/a, Dinghy Dock
 Rate: Day n/a **Week** n/a **Month** n/a
Heads: None
Laundry: None **Pay Phones:** Yes, 1
Pump-Out: OnCall, 1 Port **Fee:** n/a **Closed Heads:** Yes

Marina Operations
Owner/Manager: Frank Hall Boatyard **Dockmaster:** Seasonal
In-Season: MemDay-LabDay, 8am-8pm **Off-Season:** LabDay-Nov 15
After-Hours Arrival: Call in advance
Reservations: Yes **Credit Cards:** Visa/MC, Dscvr, Amex
Discounts: None
Pets: Welcome **Handicap Access:** No

Marina Services and Boat Supplies
Services - Docking Assistance, Trash Pick-Up **Communication -** FedEx, AirBorne, UPS, Express Mail **Supplies - Near:** Ice *(Cube)*, Ships' Store *(Hall's Marine Supply 348-9530)*, Bait/Tackle *(Watch Hill Fly Fishing 596-1914)* **3+ mi:** Propane *(Spicer Plus 596-6531, 6 mi.)*

Boatyard Services
OnCall: Electronic Sales, Electronics Repairs, Sail Loft, Propeller Repairs, Inflatable Repairs, Upholstery, Yacht Interiors **Under 1 mi:** Crane, Launching Ramp, Rigger, Bottom Cleaning, Divers. **Nearest Yard:** Watch Hill Boat Yard (401) 348-8148

Restaurants and Accommodations
Near: Restaurant *(Seaside Grille 348-6300, L $8-17, D $18-32, Part of Watch Hill Inn)*, *(Olympia Tea Room 348-8212, L $10-12, D $20-28, B, L, D)*, Snack Bar *(Bay Street Deli 596-6606, L $5-8)*, Lite Fare *(St. Claire Annex 348-8407, B, L 8am-10pm sandwiches & ice cream)*, *(Café Espresso II 348-0103)*, *(Linda's Landing 348-8144)*, Pizzeria *(Watch Hill Pizza 596-3663)*, *(Saki's 596-7239)*, Hotel *(Ocean House 348-8461, $125-260, Commanding Yellow Structure on the cliff - call to confirm they are open this season)*, Inn/B&B *(Watch Hill Court 348-8273, $70-250)*, *(Watch Hill Inn 348-8200, $100-265)*, *(Harbour House 596-7500)*

Recreation and Entertainment
Near: Beach *(Watch Hill Beach - right behind the carousel with lifeguard 348-6007; Napatree Beach - walk through the beach club parking lot or pull the dinghy up on the harbor side; or Ocean House Beach - in front of Ocean House Hotel, right of way off Bluff Avenue)*, Jogging Paths, Boat Rentals, Fishing Charter, Park, Cultural Attract *(Flying Horse Carousel 348-6007 $1 children only)*, Galleries *(Lilly Pad 596-3426; Puffins 596-1140)* **Under 1 mi:** Museum *(Watch Hill Lighthouse Museum Tue & Thu, 1-3pm, Jul-Aug)* **1-3 mi:** Tennis Courts *(Pond View Racquet Club 322-1100)* **3+ mi:** Golf Course *(Weekapaug Golf Club 322-7870, 5 mi.)*, Horseback Riding *(Manatuck Stables 860-535-3199, 5 mi.)*

Provisioning and General Services
Near: Convenience Store *(The Galley 348-8998, Linda's Landing 348-8144 snacks, coffee, ATM)*, Delicatessen *(Bay Street Deli 596-6606)*, Clothing Store *(Christinas - Lily Pulitzer heaven- is one of a dozen)*, Retail Shops **Under 1 mi:** Bookstore *(Book & Tackle Shop 596-0700, note no tackle! Mo Books N Art 348-0940)* **3+ mi:** Supermarket *(Stop & Shop 599-2433, 6 mi.)*, Liquor Store *(Warehouse-Beer Wine Liquor 596-6160, 5 mi.)*, Fishmonger *(McQuades 596-3474, 5 mi.)*, Catholic Church *(5 mi.)*, Protestant Church *(5 mi.)*, Library *(Westerly 596-2877, 4 mi.)*, Pharmacy *(CVS 348-2070, 5 mi.)*, Hardware Store *(McQuade's Ace Home Center 596-0302, 5 mi.)*

Transportation
OnCall: Rental Car *(Enterprise 596-7847)*, Taxi *(Eagle Cab 596-7300 from Westerly)* **Airport:** Westerly State Airport *(5 mi.)*

Medical Services
911 Service **OnCall:** Ambulance **3+ mi:** Doctor *(Seaside Internal Medicine 596-0328, 5 mi.)*, Chiropractor *(Antonino Clinic 860-599-5551, 5 mi.)*
Hospital: Westerly 348-3346 *(5 mi.)*

Setting -- Just past Watch Hill Yacht Club, this town facility is tucked into small, protected Watch Hill Cove -- in the heart of this pretty, Victorian, very affluent resort community. The cove is filled with classic yachts and vintage, beautifully restored sailboats along with more contemporary vessels. Ashore, the lanes are lined with large, impeccably maintained 19thC shingle-style and Queen Anne summer "cottages". Major services are in either Stonington or Westerly.

Marina Notes -- Deposit required with reservation. No landside services to speak of -- except, of course, charming Watch Hill. The town dinghy dock is available, free, to anchored boats. The Watch Hill Yacht Club, also in Watch Hill Cove, has several transient moorings available to members of reciprocating yacht clubs 596-4986, Ch.10 (launch plus heads & showers). The street side of their floats is available for dinghy tie-up by transients using Club moorings.

Notable -- Watch Hill's main street is about a quarter mile long and lined, in the season, with over a dozen preppy, beachy clothing boutiques plus eateries, gift shops and antique and art galleries. Adjacent is the famous Flying Horse Carousel; each horse, hand carved from a single block of wood, is beautifully embellished with a leather saddle, horse-hair mane and agate eyes (Jun15-LabDay, 1-9pm, children only). Watch Hill Inn, circa 1845, is across the street. Its Seaside Grille has a lovely main dining room plus an al fresco Veranda; upstairs a glass-walled banquet room accommodates 200 - all with breathtaking Harbor views especially at sunset. Spectacular Napatree Beach is an easy walk or dinghy ride (dogs forbidden because of Osprey nests). At the Point is Fort Mansfield, built for the Spanish American War. The Watch Hill Lighthouse, constructed in 1808, was replaced in 1856 with the white brick and granite tower.

II. Connecticut: Fishers Island Sound

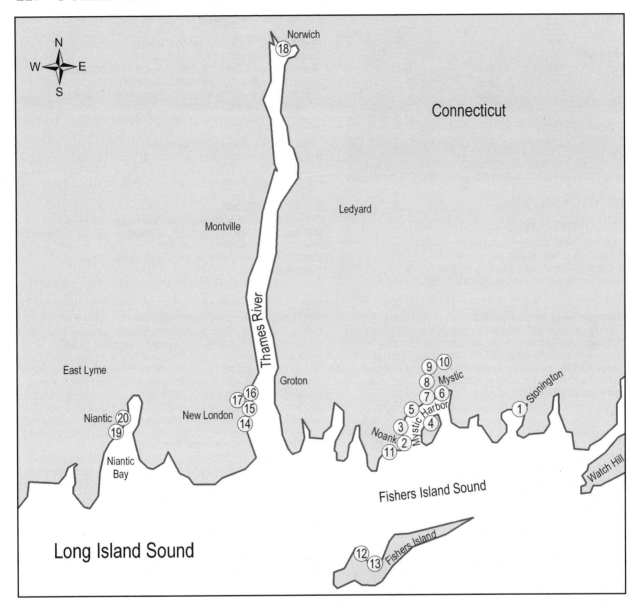

MAP	MARINA	HARBOR	PAGE	MAP	MARINA	HARBOR	PAGE
1	Dodson Boat Yard	Stonington Harbor	30	11	Spicer's Noank Marina	West Cove	40
2	Noank Shipyard	Mystic Harbor	31	12	Fishers Island Yacht Club	West Harbor, Fishers Island	41
3	Noank Village Boatyard	Mystic Harbor	32	13	Pirate's Cove Marine	West Harbor, Fishers Island	42
4	Mystic River Marina	Mystic Harbor	33	14	Thamesport Marina	New London Harbor	43
5	Mystic Shipyard	Mystic Harbor	34	15	Burr's Marina	New London Harbor	44
6	Brewer Yacht Yard at Mystic	Mystic River	35	16	New London Municipal Marina	New London Harbor	45
7	Fort Rachel Marine Services	Mystic River	36	17	Crocker's Boatyard	New London Harbor	46
8	John I. Carija & Son Boat Works	Mystic River	37	18	The Marina at American Wharf	Thames River/Norwich	47
9	Mystic Downtown Marina	Mystic River	38	19	Harbor Hill Marina & Inn	Niantic River	48
10	Mystic Seaport Museum & Docks	Mystic River	39	20	Port Niantic Marina	Niantic River	49

Dodson Boat Yard

CT - FISHERS ISLAND SOUND

Dodson Boat Yard

PO Box 272; 194 Water Street; Stonington, CT 06378

Tel: (860) 535-1507 **VHF: Monitor** 78 A **Talk** 78
Fax: (860) 535-2163 **Alternate Tel:** n/a
Email: dby@dodsonboatyard.com **Web:** www.dodsonboatyard.com
Nearest Town: Stonington *(0.1 mi.)* **Tourist Info:** (860) 572-9578

Navigational Information

Lat: 41°20.330' **Long:** 071°54.500' **Tide:** 2.5 ft. **Current:** n/a **Chart:** 13214
Rep. Depths *(MLW)*: **Entry** 8 ft. **Fuel Dock** 7 ft. **Max Slip/Moor** 8 ft./15 ft.
Access: Block Island, Fishers Island Sound to Stonington Harbor past R 10

Marina Facilities *(In Season/Off Season)*

Fuel: Gasoline, Diesel
Slips: 45 Total, 25 Transient **Max LOA:** 108 ft. **Max Beam:** n/a
  Rate *(per ft.)*: **Day** $2.75 **Week** Inq. **Month** Inq.
  Power: 30 amp Incl., 50 amp Incl., 100 amp n/a, 200 amp n/a
  Cable TV: No **Dockside Phone:** No
  Dock Type: Fixed, Floating, Long Fingers, Pilings, Alongside, Wood
Moorings: 118 Total, 25 Transient **Launch:** Yes (Free), Dinghy Dock (Inq.)
  Rate: Day $45* **Week** $210 **Month** Inq.
Heads: 8 Toilet(s), 6 Shower(s) *(with dressing rooms)*
Laundry: 2 Washer(s), 2 Dryer(s), Book Exchange **Pay Phones:** Yes, 2
Pump-Out: OnSite, Full Service, 1 Central **Fee:** $5 **Closed Heads:** Yes

Marina Operations

Owner/Manager: Bob Snyder **Dockmaster:** Ethan Grimes
In-Season: May-Aug, 7:30am-10pm **Off-Season:** Sep-Apr, 7:30am-4pm
After-Hours Arrival: Tie up at fuel dock
Reservations: Yes **Credit Cards:** Visa/MC, Dscvr, Amex
Discounts: None
Pets: Welcome, Dog Walk Area **Handicap Access:** Yes, Heads, Docks

Marina Services and Boat Supplies

Services - Docking Assistance, Concierge, Security (8 Hrs., 10pm-6am), Dock Carts, Megayacht Facilities **Communication -** Mail & Package Hold, Phone Messages, Fax in/out, FedEx, AirBorne, UPS, Express Mail *(Sat Del)* **Supplies - OnSite:** Ice *(Block, Cube)*, Ships' Store *(Well equipped)*, Propane, CNG **Near:** Bait/Tackle *(Buckys 599-5972/Don's Dock)*, Live Bait **1-3 mi:** West Marine *(536-1455)*

Boatyard Services

OnSite: Travelift *(35T)*, Forklift, Crane *(5T)*, Engine mechanic *(gas, diesel)*, Electrical Repairs, Electronics Repairs, Hull Repairs, Rigger, Sail Loft, Bottom Cleaning, Brightwork, Air Conditioning, Refrigeration, Divers, Compound, Wash & Wax, Interior Cleaning, Propeller Repairs, Woodworking, Painting, Awlgrip, Yacht Broker, Total Refits **OnCall:** Inflatable Repairs, Life Raft Service, Upholstery, Yacht Interiors, Metal Fabrication **Dealer for:** Westerbeke, Yanmar, Honda Outboards.

Restaurants and Accommodations

OnSite: Restaurant *(Boom 535-2588, L $5-13, D $15-23, 535-1381 Tue-Sat L11:30-2:30, D 5:30-9:30, Sun Brunch $7-17)* **OnCall:** Pizzeria *(Stonington Pizza 535-0886)* **Near:** Restaurant *(One South Café 535-0418)*, *(Noah's 535-3925, L $5-12, D $10-20)*, *(Water St. Café 535-2122, L $5-15, D $15-25, Sun Brunch)*, *(Skippers Dock 535-0111, L $8-15, D $25-35, 535-2000 - 500' dock)*, *(Mother's 535-0797)*, Lite Fare *(Water Street Deli 535-0797, L $4-8)*, Inn/B&B *(Inn at Stonington 535-2000, $135-295, 400' deepwater dock)*, *(Lasbury's Guest House 535-2681, $100-125)* **1-3 mi:** Restaurant *(Randall's Ordinary D $18-25)*, Motel *(Comfort Inn 572-8531)*, *(Sea Breeze 535-2843, $45-165)*, Inn/B&B *(Randall's Ordinary 599-4540, $130-270)*

Recreation and Entertainment

OnSite: Picnic Area, Grills, Boat Rentals **Near:** Playground, Tennis Courts *(Community Cntr. 535-2476)*, Jogging Paths, Park, Cultural Attract, Sightseeing *(Walk Water & Main Streets - 1780 Col. Amos Palmer House, Old Customs House, Portuguese Holy Ghost Society)* **Under 1 mi:** Beach *(DuBois)*, Fitness Center *(I Can 535-8064)*, Horseback Riding *(Rainbow Stables 535-3411)*, Museum *(Old Lighthouse Museum 535-1440 10am-5pm, Tue-Sat $4/2)* **1-3 mi:** Golf Course *(Pequot G.C. 535-1898)*, Roller Blade/Bike Paths, Movie Theater *(Westerly or Old Mystic)*, Video Rental

Provisioning and General Services

Near: Gourmet Shop *(Mystic Market East 572-7992)*, Liquor Store *(A&P Liquors 572-8446)*, Bank/ATM, Post Office, Catholic Church, Protestant Church, Library *(535-0658)*, Beauty Salon, Barber Shop, Bookstore *(Book Mart 535-0401)*, Newsstand, Clothing Store *(Fun! 535-2333, upscale outlet store)* **Under 1 mi:** Convenience Store *(Village Market 535-3512, delivers)* **1-3 mi:** Supermarket *(Stop & Shop 599-2433)*, Delicatessen *(Diamond 536-8565)*, Bakery, Farmers' Market, Pharmacy *(McQuades 536-4606)*, Florist

Transportation

OnSite: Courtesy Car/Van, Water Taxi **OnCall:** Rental Car *(Enterpr 536-6829)*, Taxi *(Yellow Cab 536-8888)* **1-3 mi:** Local Bus **3+ mi:** Rail *(Mystic, 5 mi.)* **Airport:** Westerly/TF Green *(8 mi./45 mi.)*

Medical Services

911 Service **OnCall:** Ambulance **1-3 mi:** Doctor *(Awwa 572-8834)*, Dentist, Chiropractor *(Antonino Clinic 599-5551)*, Veterinarian *(Stonington Veterinary Hospital 535-3011)* **Hospital:** Westerly RI 401-596-6000 *(6 mi.)*

Setting -- On the eastern shore of one of the most beautiful harbors on the East coast, in the delightful Borough of Stonington, is impeccably maintained, flower bedecked Dodson Boat Yard. The village boasts restored 17th/18th century houses, 5 restaurants and 20 antique stores, gift shops, and galleries.

Marina Notes -- *$45 + tax. Very accommodating, truly service-oriented staff. Family run - second generation of Snyders. Complimentary launch service 8am - 10pm, Ch.78 (if pre-arranged even later). Dinghy dock. Two mooring fields -- outer harbor can be a long dinghy ride. Docks are a mix of alongside, rafting and slips. Very well-equipped Ships' Store (has clothing as well) will meet West Marine prices on special orders. Loyal boatyard clientele from all over the Sound. 27 expert technicians on staff year-round. Mechanics, carpenters and riggers available weekdays and on-call on weekends. Heated Montek work building. All spars stored inside. Six spectacular, new "complete bathrooms" -- have service lights for customer to indicate "cleaning needed" (they are rarely used). Accommodates club cruises. Don Patrick's Carver Shop is onsite. Boom Kitchen is a lovely restaurant at the head of the docks.

Notable -- The best way to see Stonington is on foot. It's about a three-quarter mile stroll, along Water Street, from Dodson to the tip of the peninsula - DuBois Point - also the closest beach. There is excellent gallery gazing, antiquing, and gift shopping along the way. Five good restaurants within walking distance. Major supermarkets are a 10 minute drive. Capt. Nathaniel Palmer House, 535-8845 10am-4pm is within 1 mile. Mystic Seaport is a ten minute cab ride, as is Stonington Vineyards (535-1222) - wine tastings and an inviting picnic area. Blessing of the Fleet - last weekend June; Village Fair - 1st Sat August.

Navigational Information

Lat: 41°19.128' **Long:** 071°59.361' **Tide:** 3 ft. **Current:** n/a **Chart:** 12372
Rep. Depths (*MLW*): **Entry** 18 ft. **Fuel Dock** 14 ft. **Max Slip/Moor** 14 ft./6 ft.
Access: Fishers Island Sound to mouth of Mystic River

Marina Facilities (In Season/Off Season)

Fuel: *Hess* - Slip-Side Fueling, Gasoline, Diesel, High-Speed Pumps
Slips: 156 Total, 15 Transient **Max LOA:** 300 ft. **Max Beam:** n/a
  Rate (*per ft.*): **Day** $2.00 **Week** $12 **Month** $35
  Power: 30 amp $5, 50 amp $10, 100 amp n/a, 200 amp n/a
  Cable TV: Yes **Dockside Phone:** No
  Dock Type: Floating, Long Fingers, Alongside, Concrete
Moorings: 70 Total, 10 Transient **Launch:** Yes (Free), Dinghy Dock
  Rate: Day $45 **Week** $270 **Month** n/a
Heads: 6 Toilet(s), 4 Shower(s) (*with dressing rooms*)
Laundry: 2 Washer(s), 2 Dryer(s) **Pay Phones:** Yes, 4
Pump-Out: OnSite, Full Service, 1 Central **Fee:** $5 **Closed Heads:** No

Marina Operations

Owner/Manager: Dan & Kathleen Burns **Dockmaster:** n/a
In-Season: May-Sep, 7am-8pm **Off-Season:** Oct-Apr, 9am-5pm
After-Hours Arrival: Call in advance
Reservations: Yes, Preferred **Credit Cards:** Visa/MC, Dscvr, Amex
Discounts: Boat/US; Safe/Sea* **Dockage:** 10-25% **Fuel:** $0.10 **Repair:** In
Pets: Welcome, Dog Walk Area **Handicap Access:** Yes, Heads, Docks

Noank Shipyard

PO Box 9248; 145 Pearl Street; Noank, CT 06340

Tel: (860) 536-9651 **VHF: Monitor** 9 **Talk** 10
Fax: (860) 572-8140 **Alternate Tel:** (860) 536-9651
Email: noankship@aol.com **Web:** www.noankshipyard.com
Nearest Town: Mystic (*4 mi.*) **Tourist Info:** (860) 572-9578

Marina Services and Boat Supplies

Services - Docking Assistance, Dock Carts, Megayacht Facilities
Communication - Mail & Package Hold, Phone Messages, Fax in/out, Data
Ports (*Dock*), FedEx, AirBorne, UPS, Express Mail **Supplies - OnSite:** Ice
(*Block, Cube*), Ships' Store **Under 1 mi:** Bait/Tackle (*Wild Bill's 536-6648*)
1-3 mi: Marine Discount Store (*Sailing Specialties 536-4974*)

Boatyard Services

OnSite: Travelift (*70T*), Forklift, Crane, Engine mechanic (*gas, diesel*),
Electrical Repairs, Electronic Sales, Electronics Repairs, Hull Repairs,
Rigger, Bottom Cleaning, Brightwork, Air Conditioning, Refrigeration, Divers,
Compound, Wash & Wax, Interior Cleaning, Woodworking, Inflatable
Repairs, Metal Fabrication (*Mystic R. Metal Works*), Painting, Awlgrip, Yacht
Broker (*Y.B. Rodgers Yacht Sales/Seaport Yacht Sales*) **OnCall:** Propeller
Repairs, Life Raft Service, Upholstery, Yacht Interiors, Yacht Design, Yacht
Building, Total Refits **Under 1 mi:** Launching Ramp, Sail Loft. **Yard
Rates:** $60/hr., Haul & Launch $12-17.50/ft. (*blocking incl.*), Power Wash
Incl., Bottom Paint $14/ft. **Storage:** In-Water $21/ft., On-Land $35/ft.

Restaurants and Accommodations

OnSite: Seafood Shack (*Costello's 572-2779*) **Near:** Restaurant
(*Christine's Heart in Soul Café 536-1244, L $7-12, D $10-20, live entertainment Wed-Sun 9pm+ Cover $2-10*), Seafood Shack (*Abbott's 536-
7719, L $13-22, D $13-22*), Snack Bar (*Carson's*), Pizzeria (*Universal*)
Under 1 mi: Restaurant (*Seahorse 536-1670*), (*Drawbridge Inn 536-9653*)
1-3 mi: Hotel (*Harbour Inn 572-9253*), Condo/Cottage (*Shore Inne 536-
1180*) **3+ mi:** Hotel (*Seaport Motor Inn 536-2621, 4 mi.*), (*B.W. Sovereign
536-4321, $100-280, 3.5 mi.*), Inn/B&B (*Whaler's Inn 536-1506, 3.5 mi.*)

Recreation and Entertainment

OnSite: Picnic Area, Dive Shop, Fishing Charter **Near:** Playground,
Volleyball, Park **Under 1 mi:** Beach, Tennis Courts, Jogging Paths, Roller
Blade/Bike Paths **1-3 mi:** Fitness Center (*Mystic Comm Center 536-3575*),
Museum (*Mystic Aquarium, Noank Historical Society 536-3021*) **3+ mi:** Golf
Course (*Birch Plain G.C. 445-9918, 5 mi.*), Movie Theater (*4 mi.*), Video
Rental (*Videos 4 U 536-9899, 4 mi.*), Sightseeing (*Mystic Seaport, 5 mi.*)

Provisioning and General Services

OnCall: Florist **Near:** Convenience Store, Market (*Universal 536-0122*),
Delicatessen (*2 Sisters Deli 536-1244*), Liquor Store (*Universal 536-0122*),
Bakery (*Mystic River Baking Co.*), Fishmonger, Post Office, Protestant
Church **Under 1 mi:** Beauty Salon **1-3 mi:** Gourmet Shop (*Mystic Market
536-1500*), Bank/ATM, Catholic Church, Library (*Mystic/Noank 536-7721*),
Bookstore (*Bank Square Books 356-3795*), Pharmacy (*Fort Hill 445-6431*),
Newsstand, Hardware Store (*Servistar 448-1760*) **3+ mi:** Supermarket
(*A&P 572-8446, McQuades 572-3929, 5 mi.*), Farmers' Market (*Groton
Shopping Plaza Wed 2-6pm, Jun-Oct, 5 mi.*), Retail Shops (*3.5 mi.*)

Transportation

OnSite: Courtesy Car/Van **OnCall:** Rental Car (*Enterprise 536-6829*), Taxi
(*Yellow Cab 443-6230*) **Airport:** T.F. Green (*42 mi.*)

Medical Services

911 Service **OnSite:** Holistic Services (*Holistic Hands - Reflexology*)
Near: Veterinarian (*Noank-Mystic Vet 536-6656*) **1-3 mi:** Doctor (*Westerly
Hospital Mystic Medical 536-1666*) **3+ mi:** Chiropractor (*4 mi.*)
Hospital: Lawrence & Memorial 437-8101 (*10 mi.*)

Setting -- Right off the Sound, Noank Shipyard is the first facility to port at the mouth of the Mystic River. The marina is situated on a relatively undeveloped peninsula and its large blue work buildings stand out against the rural landscape. Views across the river from the docks are of unspoiled Mason's Island. The classic New England fishing village of Noank is a short walk away.

Marina Notes -- Courtesy car for transport to area attractions - at mutually convenient times. New floating concrete docks with full fingers and new pedestals; exterior docks act as wave attenuators that protect against the constant wakes of boats heading upriver. Monthly Power 30 amp $20/mo., 50 amp $25/mo. Liveaboards - $50/mo. Welcomes club cruises and other large groups and provides concierge service if needed. Low fuel prices. 900 ft. "T", 650 ft. fuel dock, and long piers easily accommodate large vessels. Full boatyard services with a 70T lift. Paint and fiberglass specialists. Boat US fuel discounts (10 cents). *SeaTow discounts as well. Very nice heads and showers, with private dressing rooms, are a bit of a hike from the docks.

Notable -- Costello's Clam Company is onsite - with an open deck and two floors of patio seating overlooking the boatyard, and famous Abbott's Lobster in the Rough is right next door. It's a short, pleasant walk to the charming village of Noank, which promises groceries, sundries, beaches, a village green, parks, and an old-fashioned ice cream parlor. Downtown Mystic is three miles by road -- somewhat closer by dinghy -- and Mystic Seaport is a couple of miles farther. 5 miles to A & P (572-8446). Foxwoods (800-FOXWOODS) and Mohegan Sun (888-226-7711) Casinos are a 20 minute ride and will send a pick-up van.

Noank Village Boatyard

Noank Village Boatyard

38 Bayside Avenue; Noank, CT 06340

Tel: (860) 536-1770 **VHF: Monitor** 72 **Talk** 72
Fax: (860) 536-2740 **Alternate Tel:** n/a
Email: hnvb@aol.com **Web:** www.noankvillageboatyard.com
Nearest Town: Noank *(0.3 mi.)* **Tourist Info:** (860) 572-9578

Navigational Information

Lat: 41°19.830' **Long:** 071°59.130' **Tide:** 3 ft. **Current:** n/a **Chart:** 13214
Rep. Depths *(MLW):* **Entry** 10 ft. **Fuel Dock** n/a **Max Slip/Moor** 10 ft./12 ft.
Access: Fishers Island Sound to Mystic River Channel, Can 19

Marina Facilities *(In Season/Off Season)*

Fuel: No
Slips: 51 Total, 12 Transient **Max LOA:** 125 ft. **Max Beam:** 24 ft.
Rate *(per ft.):* **Day** $2.00/Inq. **Week** Inq. **Month** Inq.
Power: 30 amp $5, **50 amp** $8, **100 amp** n/a, **200 amp** n/a
Cable TV: No **Dockside Phone:** Yes
Dock Type: Floating, Short Fingers, Pilings, Wood
Moorings: 150 Total, 25 Transient **Launch:** Yes (Free), Dinghy Dock
Rate: Day $1.00/ft. **Week** n/a **Month** n/a
Heads: 6 Toilet(s), 3 Shower(s) *(with dressing rooms)*
Laundry: 1 Washer(s), 1 Dryer(s) **Pay Phones:** Yes, 2
Pump-Out: OnSite, 2 Central, 1 Port **Fee:** $5-15* **Closed Heads:** No

Marina Operations

Owner/Manager: Bob Helbig **Dockmaster:** Ron Helbig (Yard Manager)
In-Season: Apr-Oct, 8am-7pm **Off-Season:** Nov-Mar, 8am-5pm
After-Hours Arrival: Tie up to dock
Reservations: Preferred **Credit Cards:** Visa/MC, Dscvr
Discounts: None
Pets: Welcome, Dog Walk Area **Handicap Access:** Yes, Heads, Docks

Marina Services and Boat Supplies

Services - Docking Assistance, Trash Pick-Up, Dock Carts, Megayacht Facilities **Communication -** Mail & Package Hold, Phone Messages, Fax in/out ($1/pp), Data Ports, Express Mail *(Sat Del)* **Supplies - OnSite:** Ice *(Block, Cube)* **Under 1 mi:** Ships' Store *(Noank Shipyard 536-6861)*, Bait/Tackle *(Wild Bills 536-6648)*, Live Bait **1-3 mi:** Propane **3+ mi:** West Marine *(536-1455, 6 mi.)*, CNG *(Brewer 536-2293, 4 mi.)*

Boatyard Services

OnSite: Travelift *(35T)*, Forklift, Engine mechanic *(gas, diesel)*, Electrical Repairs, Electronics Repairs, Hull Repairs, Rigger, Bottom Cleaning, Brightwork, Air Conditioning, Refrigeration, Divers, Compound, Wash & Wax, Interior Cleaning, Propeller Repairs, Woodworking, Metal Fabrication, Painting, Awlgrip, Yacht Design, Yacht Broker *(Gil Liepold)*, Yacht Building, Total Refits **OnCall:** Electronic Sales, Sail Loft, Inflatable Repairs
Near: Launching Ramp. **Yard Rates:** $70/hr., Haul & Launch $10/ft. *(blocking incl.)*, Power Wash $2/ft., Bottom Paint $14-16/ft. *(paint incl.)*
Storage: On-Land $33/ft. winter

Restaurants and Accommodations

Near: Seafood Shack *(Costello's Clam House by dinghy)*, *(Abott's Lobster 536-7719, L $13-22, D $13-22, by dinghy)*, Snack Bar *(Mystic River Bakery B $2, L $4-16)* **Under 1 mi:** Restaurant *(Fisherman 536-1717, L $5-8, D $8-15)* **1-3 mi:** Restaurant *(Capt. Daniel Packer Inne 536-3555, L $6-13, D $15-24)* **3+ mi:** Pizzeria *(Mystic Pizza 536-3700, L $6-16, D $6-16, 4 mi.)*, Motel *(Comfort Inn 572-8531, $50-150, 5 mi.)*, Hotel *(Mystic Hilton 572-0731, $85-250, 5 mi.)*, *(Best Western 536-4281, $60-170, 5 mi.)*, Inn/B&B *(Inne at Mystic 536-9604, $85-275, 4.5 mi.)*

Recreation and Entertainment

OnSite: Picnic Area, Grills, Fishing Charter **Near:** Playground, Dive Shop, Tennis Courts, Boat Rentals *(Anna R Sportfishing 536-0529)*, Park
Under 1 mi: Beach, Jogging Paths **1-3 mi:** Fitness Center *(Community Center 536-3575)*, Video Rental *(Mystic Video 572-0081)*, Sightseeing *(Mystic Aquarium* **3+ mi:** Movie Theater *(Village Cinema 536-4227, 4 mi.)*, Video Arcade *(5 mi.)*, Museum *(Mystic Seaport, 5 mi.)*

Provisioning and General Services

Near: Convenience Store *(Universal 536-0122)*, Delicatessen *(Carson's)*, Wine/Beer *(Universal)*, Bakery *(Mystic River)*, Meat Market, Newsstand
1-3 mi: Gourmet Shop *(Mystic Market 536-1500)*, Fishmonger, Lobster Pound *(Grossman's 356-1674)*, Post Office, Beauty Salon, Bookstore *(Bank Square 356-3795)*, Pharmacy *(Fort Hill 445-6431)*, Hardware Store *(Johnson's 448-1760)*, Copies Etc. *(Mystic Pub 536-2616)* **3+ mi:** Supermarket *(A&P, McQuades, 4 mi.)*, Farmers' Market *(Groton Shopping Plaza Wed 2-6pm, 4 mi.)*, Bank/ATM *(4 mi.)*

Transportation

OnCall: Rental Car *(Enterprise 536-6829)*, Taxi *(Mystic Cab 536-8888)*
1-3 mi: Bikes *(Rentals in town)* **3+ mi:** Rail *(Mystic Amtrak, 4 mi.)*
Airport: T.F. Green *(42 mi.)*

Medical Services

911 Service **OnCall:** Ambulance **Near:** Veterinarian *(Noank-Mystic 536-6656)* **1-3 mi:** Doctor *(Westerly Center 536-1666)* **3+ mi:** Dentist *(4 mi.)*, Chiropractor *(4 mi.)*, Holistic Services *(5 mi.)*
Hospital: Lawrence & Memorial 437-8101 *10 mi.*

Setting -- Noank Village Boatyard is on the port (western) side of the Mystic River, just outside Beebe Cove, hard by the railroad tracks. Landside, the marina has created an attractive, exceedingly well-maintained club-like atmosphere. The views across Mystic Harbor from the docks are of an active waterway. A contemporary, shingled, glass front building -- with steeply pitched-roof -- is one of its landmarks.

Marina Notes -- Knowledgeable and service-oriented staff. 50 new wood floating docks with new pedestals and finger piers create wider-than-normal slips. Extensive mooring field with complimentary club-quality launch service (complete with dog) - Ch.72. Gas grills with picnic area. *2 New pump-out facilities in 2001- self operated ($5) or yard-operated ($15). Nice tile heads. Several charter fishing boats make their home here. Family owned and operated since 1972. In 1997, founder Bob Helbig, Jeff Marshall, owner of Sailing Specialties, and two partners, bought Mystic Shipyard. They've combined the staff, facilities and services of all three to create Mystic Shipyard, LLC. Fairly recently, they also bought Mystic Cove Marina and renamed it Mystic Shipyard East.

Notable -- Quiet, historic Noank Village, a classic 19thC maritime community with some nicely restored houses, is an easy and pleasant walk. A couple of modest provisioning resources (Universal, Village Bakery, Carson's) are there, too. It's a reasonable dinghy ride to Downtown Mystic, which has a wide assortment of eateries and shops along Main Street on both sides of the bascule bridge. It's a considerably longer dinghy ride up the river to justly famous Mystic Seaport and Maritime Museum - suggest one of the local cabs. Antique boat parade - late July; Mystic Arts Festival - 1st weekend in August.

Navigational Information
Lat: 41°20.200' **Long:** 071°58.400' **Tide:** 4 ft. **Current:** n/a **Chart:** 13214
Rep. Depths (MLW): Entry 12 ft. **Fuel Dock** n/a **Max Slip/Moor** 12 ft./-
Access: Fishers Island Sound to Mystic River to Mason Island

Marina Facilities (In Season/Off Season)
Fuel: Texaco - Gasoline, Diesel
Slips: 160 Total, 25 Transient **Max LOA:** 150 ft. **Max Beam:** n/a
Rate (per ft.): **Day** $2.30 **Week** $11.90 **Month** Inq.
Power: 30 amp Incl., **50 amp** $5, **100 amp** Inq., **200 amp** n/a
Cable TV: Yes, Incl. **Dockside Phone:** No
Dock Type: Fixed, Floating, Long Fingers, Pilings, Wood
Moorings: 0 Total, 0 Transient **Launch:** n/a
Rate: Day n/a **Week** n/a **Month** n/a
Heads: 6 Toilet(s), 6 Shower(s)
Laundry: 2 Washer(s), 2 Dryer(s) **Pay Phones:** Yes
Pump-Out: OnSite, Full Service, 1 Central **Fee:** $5 **Closed Heads:** Yes

Marina Operations
Owner/Manager: R. J. Garbarino **Dockmaster:** David Hantman
In-Season: May-Oct, 8am-5pm **Off-Season:** Nov-Apr, 8am-4:30pm M-F
After-Hours Arrival: Call in advance
Reservations: Necessary **Credit Cards:** Visa/MC, Dscvr, Amex, Tex
Discounts: Annual contracts* **Dockage:** 7 Day **Fuel:** 250G **Repair:** n/a
Pets: Welcome, Dog Walk Area **Handicap Access:** Yes, Heads, Docks

Mystic River Marina

PO Box 66; 36 Quarry Road; Mystic, CT 06355

Tel: (860) 536-3123; (800) 344-8840 **VHF: Monitor** 9 **Talk** 11
Fax: (860) 536-0713 **Alternate Tel:** (860) 536-3123
Email: info@mysticrivermarina.com **Web:** www.mysticrivermarina.com
Nearest Town: Mystic (1.5 mi.) **Tourist Info:** (860) 572-9578

Marina Services and Boat Supplies
Services - Docking Assistance, Concierge, Security, Trash Pick-Up, Dock
Carts **Communication -** Mail & Package Hold, Phone Messages, Fax
in/out, FedEx, AirBorne, UPS, Express Mail (Sat Del) **Supplies - OnSite:**
Ice (Block, Cube), Ships' Store **Near:** Live Bait **Under 1 mi:** Marine
Discount Store (Sailing Specialties 536-4974), Propane **1-3 mi:** Bait/Tackle
(Shaffers Boat Livery 536-8713) **3+ mi:** West Marine (536-1455, 5 mi.)

Boatyard Services
OnSite: Travelift (50T, 35'), Forklift, Engine mechanic (gas, diesel), Electrical
Repairs, Electronics Repairs, Hull Repairs, Bottom Cleaning, Brightwork,
Refrigeration, Divers, Compound, Wash & Wax, Interior Cleaning, Propeller
Repairs, Woodworking, Painting, Awlgrip, Yacht Broker, Total Refits
Under 1 mi: Launching Ramp. **1-3 mi:** Electronic Sales, Air Conditioning,
Metal Fabrication. **Dealer for:** Interlux, Awlgrip, DuPont.
Yard Rates: $65/hr., Haul & Launch $10/ft. (blocking incl.), Power Wash
$2/ft., Bottom Paint $5.75/ft. **Storage:** On-Land $30/ft.

Restaurants and Accommodations
OnSite: Restaurant (Zavala 2, Mexican) **Near:** Seafood Shack
1-3 mi: Restaurant (Zhang's 572-5725), (S&P Oyster Co. 536-2674),
(Angie's & Pier 27 536-7300), (Sea Swirl Seafood 536-3452), (Steak Loft
536-2661, L $4-14, D $11-22), Pizzeria (Mystic Pizza 536-3700, L $6-16,
D $6-16), Motel (Seaport Motor Inn 536-2621, $50-150), Hotel (Mystic Hilton
572-0731, $85-205), (Best Western Sovereign 536-4281, $60-160), Inn/B&B
(Harbour Inn & Cottage 572-9253, $70-300)

Recreation and Entertainment
OnSite: Pool, Picnic Area, Grills, Playground, Special Events **Near:** Tennis
Courts, Jogging Paths, Boat Rentals, Roller Blade/Bike Paths, Park
Under 1 mi: Dive Shop, Sightseeing **1-3 mi:** Beach, Fitness Center
(Mystic Community Center 536-3575), Movie Theater, Video Rental (Mystic
Video 572-0081), Museum (Mystic Art Assoc. 536-7601), Cultural Attract
(Mystic Seaport) **3+ mi:** Golf Course (Pequot Golf Club 535-1898, 5 mi.)

Provisioning and General Services
OnSite: Newsstand, Clothing Store **Near:** Convenience Store, Gourmet
Shop (Mystic Market 536-1500), Delicatessen **Under 1 mi:** Bakery,
Fishmonger, Lobster Pound, Meat Market **1-3 mi:** Supermarket (A&P 572-
8446), Liquor Store (Blue Whale 572-6087), Farmers' Market (Thu 3-6pm
across from A&P), Bank/ATM, Post Office, Catholic Church, Library, Beauty
Salon (536-7721), Barber Shop, Dry Cleaners, Bookstore (Book Stop 572-
0003), Pharmacy (CVS 536-5628), Florist, Copies Etc. (Mystic Publications
536-2616) **3+ mi:** Hardware Store (Village 259-0425, 4 mi.)

Transportation
OnCall: Rental Car (Enterprise 536-6829, Avis, 6.5 mi. 445-8585), Taxi
(Yellow Cab 536-8888), Airport Limo (Stonington Limousine 535-4425)
Near: Local Bus (Mystic Trolley) **1-3 mi:** Bikes (Mystic Cycle 572-7433),
Rail (Amtrak) **Airport:** T.F. Green (42 mi.)

Medical Services
911 Service **1-3 mi:** Doctor (Jost 536-1666), Dentist, Chiropractor
(Dukehart 536-4007), Ambulance, Veterinarian
Hospital: Lawrence & Memorial 437-8101 (10 mi.)

Setting -- The first facility on the starboard side of Mystic Harbor, M.R.M. is on quiet, secluded Mason Island, in a protected area below the bridges. Its extensive network of docks radiates from a small peninsula that juts into the river, affording expansive views across and down the harbor.

Marina Notes -- *Discounts on dockage after 7 days, and on fuel over 250 gallons. Family owned and operated since 1957, the marina caters primarily to power boaters. The pool, surrounded by chain link fence, overlooks the river and docks. Nicely equipped and attractive ships' store. Extensive repair facilities, travelift, and brokerage onsite. Playground and picnic area with grills onsite. Zavala 2!, the new restaurant on the second floor, has views of the river and specializes in Mexican dishes and American seafood (BYOB).

Notable -- It's a short cab ride or longer dinghy trip up the river to Mystic Seaport, and a good mile and a half walk to the Mystic Amtrak depot and the Mystic Welcome Center (or take the dinghy). A quarter of a mile farther takes you to downtown Mystic. It's 2 miles directly upriver to Olde Mystick Village 536-4941, a colonial themed mall that looks like an 18thC village - with 60 shops and restaurants. Across the street are the Mystic Factory Outlets. There are 2 public dingy docks - at the downtown Mystic River Park - east bank below bridge - and at the Seaport's north gate. Or catch the trolley, which connects the marinas, Amtrak, Downtown, the Seaport, Aquarium, Mistick Village, McQuade's Supermarket and West Marine. Outdoor Art Fest second weekend in August. Antique and Wooden Boat Parade first weekend in September.

Mystic Shipyard

PO Box 201; 100 Essex Street; West Mystic, CT 06388

Tel: (860) 536-6588 **VHF: Monitor** 68 **Talk** 68
Fax: (860) 536-7081 **Alternate Tel:** (860) 536-6588
Email: info@mysticshipyard.com **Web:** www.mysticshipyard.com
Nearest Town: Mystic *(1 mi.)* **Tourist Info:** (860) 572-9578

Navigational Information
Lat: 41°20.616' **Long:** 071°58.435' **Tide:** 3.5 ft. **Current:** n/a **Chart:** 13214
Rep. Depths *(MLW)*: **Entry** 18 ft. **Fuel Dock** n/a **Max Slip/Moor** 15 ft./8 ft.
Access: Fishers Island Sound to Mystic River along Western shore

Marina Facilities *(In Season/Off Season)*
Fuel: No
Slips: 155 Total, 25 Transient **Max LOA:** 150 ft. **Max Beam:** 25 ft.
Rate *(per ft.)*: **Day** $2.25/$2.00 **Week** Inq. **Month** Inq.
Power: 30 amp $7, 50 amp $10, 100 amp n/a, 200 amp n/a
Cable TV: No **Dockside Phone:** No
Dock Type: Fixed, Long Fingers, Pilings, Wood
Moorings: 0 Total, 0 Transient **Launch:** n/a, Dinghy Dock
Rate: Day n/a **Week** n/a **Month** n/a
Heads: 10 Toilet(s), 10 Shower(s) *(with dressing rooms)*
Laundry: 4 Washer(s), 4 Dryer(s) **Pay Phones:** Yes, 3
Pump-Out: OnSite **Fee:** Free **Closed Heads:** No

Marina Operations
Owner/Manager: O: Jeff Marshall; M: Tim Porter **Dockmaster:** Glen Henry
In-Season: Year-Round, 8am-5pm **Off-Season:** n/a
After-Hours Arrival: Call ahead
Reservations: Yes, Preferred **Credit Cards:** Visa/MC, Dscvr
Discounts: Boat/US; 10% off parts **Dockage:** n/a **Fuel:** n/a **Repair:** n/a
Pets: Welcome, Dog Walk Area **Handicap Access:** Yes, Heads, Docks

Marina Services and Boat Supplies
Services - Docking Assistance, Boaters' Lounge, Security, Trash Pick-Up, Dock Carts, Megayacht Facilities **Communication -** Mail & Package Hold, Phone Messages, Fax in/out *($1)*, Data Ports, FedEx, AirBorne, UPS, Express Mail *(Sat Del)* **Supplies - OnSite:** Ice *(Block, Cube)* **OnCall:** CNG *(Brewer)* **Near:** Marine Discount Store *(Sailing Specialties 536-4974)* **1-3 mi:** Bait/Tackle *(Shaffers 536-8713)*, Propane **3+ mi:** West Marine *(536-1455, 5 mi.)*

Boatyard Services
OnSite: Travelift *(50T)*, Forklift *(5T)*, Engine mechanic *(gas, diesel)*, Electrical Repairs, Electronic Sales, Electronics Repairs, Hull Repairs, Rigger, Bottom Cleaning, Brightwork, Air Conditioning, Refrigeration, Divers, Compound, Wash & Wax, Interior Cleaning, Propeller Repairs, Woodworking, Awlgrip **OnCall:** Sail Loft, Inflatable Repairs, Life Raft Service, Upholstery, Metal Fabrication **Member:** ABBRA, ABYC - 3 Certified Tech(s), Other Certifications: Hunter, Mainship, Beneteau **Yard Rates:** $70/hr., Haul & Launch $15/ft. *(blocking incl.)*, Power Wash $2/ft., Bottom Paint $16/ft. *(paint incl.)* **Storage:** In-Water $32/ft., On-Land $32/ft.

Restaurants and Accommodations
Under 1 mi: Restaurant *(Zhang's 572-5725)*, *(Capt. Daniel Packer Inne 536-3555, L $6-13, D $15-24)*, *(Voodoo Grill 572-4422)*, *(Portuguese Fisherman 536-9300)*, Pizzeria *(Mystic Pizza 536-7688, L $6-16, D $6-16)*, Motel *(Comfort Inn 572-8531, $50-150)* **1-3 mi:** Restaurant *(41 Degrees North 536-9821)*, Seafood Shack *(Abbott's Lobster 536-7719, L $13-22, D $13-22, or dinghy)*, Inn/B&B *(Inn at Mystic 536-9604, $85-275)*, *(Harbour Inn & Cottage 572-9253, $70-300)*

Recreation and Entertainment
OnSite: Pool, Picnic Area, Grills **Under 1 mi:** Fitness Center *(Community Center 536-3575)*, Video Rental *(Videos 4 U 536-9899)*, Museum *(Mystic Art Assoc. 536-7601)*, Special Events *(Mystic Arts Fest - 1st weekend Aug; Taste of CT - weekend after LabDay)* **1-3 mi:** Playground, Dive Shop, Tennis Courts, Boat Rentals *(Small boats/kayaks)*, Fishing Charter, Cultural Attract *(Mystic Seaport)*, Sightseeing *(Mystic Aquarium, Mystic Village)* **3+ mi:** Golf Course *(Pequot G.C. 535-1898, 5 mi.)*, Movie Theater *(4 mi.)*

Provisioning and General Services
Near: Gourmet Shop *(Mystic Market 536-1500)*, Bakery *(Mystic Market)* **Under 1 mi:** Delicatessen, Liquor Store *(M.R. Wine and Spirits 536-9463)*, Fishmonger, Post Office, Library *(536-7721)*, Bookstore *(Bank Square Books 536-3795)* **1-3 mi:** Supermarket *(McQuades, A&P 536-5813)*, Health Food, Farmers' Market *(across from A&P, Thu 3-6pm)*, Bank/ATM, Beauty Salon, Barber Shop, Pharmacy *(CVS 536-5628)*, Hardware Store *(True Value 536-9601)*, Florist, Clothing Store, Copies Etc. *(Mystic Publications 536-2616)*

Transportation
OnCall: Rental Car *(Enterprise 536-6829 or Avis 445-8585, 6mi.)* **Near:** Local Bus *(Mystic Trolley)* **1-3 mi:** Bikes *(Mystic Cycle 572-7433)*, InterCity Bus *(SEAT Bus)*, Rail *(Amtrack)* **3+ mi:** Ferry Service *(Cross Sound Ferry, 10 mi.)* **Airport:** T.F. Green *(42 mi.)*

Medical Services
911 Service **OnCall:** Ambulance **1-3 mi:** Doctor *(Doron 536-2995)*, Dentist *(Curtiss 536-7447)*, Chiropractor, Veterinarian *(Noank-Mystic 536-6656)* **Hospital:** Lawrence & Memorial 437-8101 *(10 mi.)*

Setting -- Just below the railroad bridge, on the western shore of Mystic Harbor, the docks of Mystic Shipyard fan out from the tip of pretty Willow Point. The distinctive all-glass, semi-circular dormers of the contemporary club house are easily visible as you approach.

Marina Notes -- New riverfront pool with stone pavers on deck in 2001. South of all the bridges. The historic Mystic Shipyard first opened its doors in 1843, building schooners and iron-clad ships. At the turn of the century, after completing the last 5-masted 249 ft. coastal schooner, Jennie Dubois, it became a yacht building center. In the 1940's the Mystic Shipyard built sea sleds for recreational purposes and also as tenders for presidential yachts. Today, it's a full-service marina and boatyard providing complete shipwright, fiberglass, painting, mechanical and electrical services. Bought in 1997 by a consortium including Noank Village boatyard and Sailing Specialties, which embarked on a program of major upgrading. They also own former Mystic Cove, now renamed Mystic Shipyard East. The club house has a large and airy banquet facility with views of the marina and harbor. It accommodates up to 200; The Market provides catering.

Notable -- A mile walk to the heart of Downtown Mystic, a 1.75 mi. trolley ride to the Mystic Seaport and 2 mi. to the Aquarium. Alternatively, dinghy up the River to downtown's Mystic River Park (on the east side just below the bascule bridge), and then farther up, to Mystic Seaport (near the North Gate). The galleries and studios of the Mystic Art Association - 11am-5pm - are an easy walk (they're also available for special events). Downtown Mystic offers a plethora of shops, eateries, and things to do. Trolley service to Amtrak, Downtown, the Seaport, Aquarium, Mistick Village, McQuade's Supermarket and West Marine.

Navigational Information
Lat: 41°20.800' **Long:** 071°58.100' **Tide:** 3 ft. **Current:** 1.5 kt. **Chart:** 13214
Rep. Depths *(MLW):* **Entry** 15 ft. **Fuel Dock** 15 ft. **Max Slip/Moor** 15 ft./-
Access: Eastern shore of Mystic River, past Mason Island on Murphy Point

Marina Facilities *(In Season/Off Season)*
Fuel: Gasoline, Diesel
Slips: 220 Total, 5 Transient **Max LOA:** 150 ft. **Max Beam:** n/a
  Rate *(per ft.):* **Day** $2.00/$1.00 **Week** $14/Inq. **Month** $60/Inq.
  Power: 30 amp Incl., 50 amp Incl., 100 amp Incl., 200 amp n/a
  Cable TV: Yes, Incl. **Dockside Phone:** No
  Dock Type: Floating, Long Fingers
Moorings: 0 Total, 0 Transient **Launch:** n/a
  Rate: Day n/a **Week** n/a **Month** n/a
Heads: 12 Toilet(s), 9 Shower(s)
Laundry: 4 Washer(s), 4 Dryer(s), Book Exchange **Pay Phones:** Yes, 2
Pump-Out: OnSite, Self Service, 1 Central **Fee:** $0-5* **Closed Heads:** No

Marina Operations
Owner/Manager: Brewer Chain **Dockmaster:** Edward Ahlborn
In-Season: Summer, 8am-6pm **Off-Season:** Fall-Win-Sprg, 8am-4:30pm*
After-Hours Arrival: Contact office during day
Reservations: Required **Credit Cards:** Visa/MC, Dscvr, Amex
Discounts: Brewer Program **Dockage:** n/a **Fuel:** n/a **Repair:** n/a
Pets: Welcome, Dog Walk Area **Handicap Access:** No

Brewer Yacht Yard at Mystic

56 Roseleah Drive; Mystic, CT 06355

Tel: (860) 536-2293 **VHF: Monitor** 9 **Talk** 11
Fax: (860) 536-6560 **Alternate Tel:** (860) 536-2539
Email: info@brewermystic.com **Web:** www.brewermystic.com
Nearest Town: Mystic *(0.75 mi.)* **Tourist Info:** (860) 572-9578

Marina Services and Boat Supplies
Services - Docking Assistance, Boaters' Lounge, Trash Pick-Up, Dock Carts **Communication -** Mail & Package Hold, Phone Messages, FedEx, AirBorne, UPS, Express Mail **Supplies - OnSite:** Ice *(Block, Cube)*, Ships' Store, CNG **Near:** Propane **Under 1 mi:** Marine Discount Store *(Sailing Specialties 536-4974)* **1-3 mi:** Bait/Tackle *(Wild Bill's 536-6648)*
3+ mi: West Marine *(536-1455, 4 mi.)*

Boatyard Services
OnSite: Travelift *(35T)*, Forklift, Crane, Engine mechanic *(gas, diesel)*, Electrical Repairs, Hull Repairs, Bottom Cleaning, Brightwork, Air Conditioning, Refrigeration, Woodworking, Yacht Broker **OnCall:** Rigger, Divers, Compound, Wash & Wax, Interior Cleaning, Propeller Repairs, Inflatable Repairs, Life Raft Service, Upholstery, Painting, Awlgrip

Restaurants and Accommodations
OnSite: Lite Fare *(Eat at Joe's, formerly Mystic Riverboat Co., MemDay-LabDay)* **Near:** Restaurant *(Flood Tide 536-8140, B $7-12, L $11, D $22-36, Lounge $9-15, Sun Brunch $16 in The Inn at Mystic)*, *(Angies & Pier 27 of Mystic 536-7300)*, Inn/B&B *(Inn at Mystic 536-9604, $65-295, 15 acre resort with 1904 Colonial Revival Mansion on the River)*
Under 1 mi: Restaurant *(Captain Daniel Packer 536-3555, L $6-13, D $15-24)*, *(Johns Café 536-6700)*, Pizzeria *(Mystic 536-3700, L $6-16, D $6-16)*, Motel *(Seaport Motor Inn 536-2621, $80-170)*, *(Best Western 536-4281)*, Inn/B&B *(Taber Inn 536-4904, $130-165)*, *(Whalers Inn 536-1506)*, *(M.V. Valiant 97 ft. ship docked at Steamboat Inn - 5 staterooms)*
1-3 mi: Restaurant *(Copperfields 536-4281)*, *(Bravo Bravo 536-3228, D $15-23, at Whaler's Inn)*, Hotel *(Comfort Inn 572-8531, $90-170)*

Recreation and Entertainment
OnSite: Pool, Spa, Picnic Area, Grills *(charcoal)* **Near:** Roller Blade/Bike Paths **Under 1 mi:** Fitness Center *(Mystic Community Center 536-3575)*, Video Rental *(Mystic Video 572-0081)*, Museum *(Mystic Art Association 536-7601)* **1-3 mi:** Movie Theater *(Village Cinema 536-4227)*, Park, Sightseeing *(Mystic Seaport 572-0711 $17/9, Mystic Aquarium 572-5955 $16/11)*
3+ mi: Golf Course *(Pequot G.C. 535-1898, 4 mi.)*

Provisioning and General Services
OnCall: Wine/Beer **Near:** Convenience Store, Gourmet Shop *(Mystic Market 536-1500)*, Delicatessen *(Pasta Fresca 572-1245)*, Bank/ATM, Post Office, Bookstore *(Book Stop 572-0003)*, Pharmacy *(CVS 536-5628)*, Newsstand, Florist **Under 1 mi:** Supermarket *(McQuades or 1.5 mi to A&P 536-5813)*, Health Food, Liquor Store *(Mystic River 536-9463)*, Catholic Church, Protestant Church, Library *(Mystic & Noank 536-7721)*, Beauty Salon, Barber Shop, Dry Cleaners, Clothing Store, Retail Shops
1-3 mi: Bakery, Farmers' Market *(Thu 3-6pm across from A&P)*, Fishmonger, Hardware Store *(Village Hardware 259-0425)*, Copies Etc.

Transportation
OnCall: Rental Car *(Enterprise 536-6829)*, Taxi *(Yellow Cab 536-8888)*, Airport Limo **Near:** Local Bus *(Trolley)*, Rail *(Amtrack)* **1-3 mi:** Bikes *(Mystic Cycle 572-7433)* **Airport:** T.F. Green *(42 mi.)*

Medical Services
911 Service **OnCall:** Ambulance **Near:** Chiropractor **Under 1 mi:** Doctor *(Family Practice 536-9647)*, Dentist **1-3 mi:** Veterinarian *(Noank-Mystic 536-6656)* **Hospital:** Lawrence & Memorial 437-8101 *(10 mi.)*

Setting -- Situated on the eastern shore of Mystic Harbor, below both bridges, Brewer Yacht Yard surrounds the tip of Murphy Point - on the quieter Stonington side. An attractively landscaped raised pool area overlooks the parking lot on one side and the docks and river on the other. A picnic deck and covered seating area, perched above the marina, affords long views of the harbor, river and the traffic passing through the bridge.

Marina Notes -- *Pump-out is free to Brewer contract customers, $5 for others. *Off season 8am-4:30pm Mon-Fri, 9am-1pm Sat & Sun. Brewer Preferred Customer Program. Swimming pool and Jacuzzi open 7am-11pm. "Eat At Joe's" gourmet catering truck serves B&L on Sat & Sun; D on Fri & Sat. They'll pack food to go "out on the water". Picnic tables at the head of each dock. Charcoal for the grills at fuel dock and office. Wireless internet access available - contact Beacon Wi-Fi at (203) 762-2657. Other internet connections at the Visitors' Center and at Mystic-Noank Library - a 19thC neo-Romanesque building.

Notable -- Downtown Mystic is less than a mile walk - with restaurants, gift shops, and galleries. The trolley will get you to McQuade's Supermarket, West Marine, and the Aquarium. The Mystick River Park is just "around the corner" by dinghy; it's south of the bridge on the east bank. To get to the Mystic Seaport Museum (572-0711) dinghy upriver about one mile -- a good tender dock is at the north gate -- or take the trolley or a cab. Entrance fees: $17/9; check on specials. The Factory Outlets are about 2 miles upriver, and right across is the Olde Mistick Village (536-4941) -- with 60 shops and restaurants. Abbott's Lobster in the Rough (536-7719) is arguably the best on the Sound -- from Brewer's, go across the harbor and south, almost to the river's mouth.

Fort Rachel Marine Services

44 Water Street; Mystic, CT 06355

Tel: (860) 536-6647 **VHF: Monitor** 9 **Talk** 11
Fax: (860) 536-6647 **Alternate Tel:** n/a
Email: info@fortrachel.com **Web:** www.fortrachel.com
Nearest Town: Mystic *(0.25 mi.)* **Tourist Info:** (860) 572-9578

Navigational Information
Lat: 41°20.921' **Long:** 071°58.388' **Tide:** 3.5 ft. **Current:** n/a **Chart:** 13214
Rep. Depths *(MLW):* **Entry** 10 ft. **Fuel Dock** n/a **Max Slip/Moor** 8 ft./-
Access: Mystic River through railroad bridge, then directly to port

Marina Facilities *(In Season/Off Season)*
Fuel: No
Slips: 115 Total, 5 Transient **Max LOA:** 55 ft. **Max Beam:** 14 ft.
 Rate *(per ft.):* **Day** $2.50/$1.50 **Week** n/a **Month** n/a
 Power: 30 amp Incl., **50 amp** Incl., **100 amp** n/a, **200 amp** n/a
 Cable TV: Yes, Incl. Basic cable **Dockside Phone:** No
 Dock Type: Floating, Long Fingers, Alongside, Wood
Moorings: 0 Total, 0 Transient **Launch:** n/a
 Rate: Day n/a **Week** n/a **Month** n/a
Heads: 4 Toilet(s), 4 Shower(s) *(with dressing rooms)*
Laundry: None, Book Exchange **Pay Phones:** Yes
Pump-Out: OnSite, Full Service, 1 Port **Fee:** $20 **Closed Heads:** Yes

Marina Operations
Owner/Manager: David Hersant **Dockmaster:** Dutcha Slieker Hersant
In-Season: Apr-Nov, 8am-5pm **Off-Season:** Dec-Mar, 9am-4pm
After-Hours Arrival: Dock at "T-Dock" - with reservation & permission
Reservations: Yes, Required **Credit Cards:** Visa/MC, Amex
Discounts: None
Pets: Welcome, Dog Walk Area **Handicap Access:** Yes, Heads

Marina Services and Boat Supplies
Services - Docking Assistance, Boaters' Lounge, Dock Carts
Communication - Mail & Package Hold, Phone Messages, Fax in/out,
FedEx, AirBorne, UPS, Express Mail *(Sat Del)* **Supplies - OnSite:** Ice
(Block, Cube) **Under 1 mi:** Ships' Store *(Sailing Specialties 536-4974)*,
Bait/Tackle *(Wild Bill's 536-6648)*, Propane **1-3 mi:** West Marine *(536-1455)*

Boatyard Services
OnSite: Travelift *(35T)*, Forklift, Crane, Engine mechanic *(gas, diesel)*, Hull
Repairs, Sail Loft, Bottom Cleaning, Brightwork, Divers, Compound, Wash &
Wax, Interior Cleaning, Painting, Awlgrip **OnCall:** Electrical Repairs,
Electronic Sales, Electronics Repairs, Rigger, Air Conditioning, Refrigeration,
Propeller Repairs, Woodworking, Inflatable Repairs, Life Raft Service,
Upholstery, Yacht Interiors, Metal Fabrication **Near:** Launching Ramp,
Yacht Broker. **Yard Rates:** $75/hr., Haul & Launch $7-10/ft. *(blocking $80-160)*, Power Wash $2/ft., Bottom Paint $10/ft. **Storage:** In-Water $16-22/ft.,
On-Land $25-32/ft.

Restaurants and Accommodations
Near: Restaurant *(Capt. Daniel Packer 536-3555, L $6-13, D $15-24)*,
(Zhang's 572-5725), Raw Bar *(S & P Oyster Co 536-2674, L $6-18, D $6-18)*, Lite Fare *(Kitchen Little 536-2122, B $4-10, L $4-10)*, Pizzeria *(Mystic
Pizza 536-3700, L $6-16, D $6-16)*, Inn/B&B *(Steamboat & SV Valiant 536-8300, $120-295, 97 ft. ship w/ 5 staterooms)*, *(Whaler's 536-1506, $90-225)*
Under 1 mi: Inn/B&B *(Harbor Inne 572-9253)*, *(Inn at Mystic 539-9604,
$85-275)* **1-3 mi:** Snack Bar *(Steak Loft 536-2621, L $4-14, D 11-22)*,
Motel *(Comfort Inn 572-8531, $90-170)*, *(Seaport Motor 536-2621, $80-175)*

Recreation and Entertainment
OnSite: Picnic Area, Grills **Near:** Video Rental *(Mystic 572-0081)*, Museum
(Mystic Art Assoc. 536-7601) **Under 1 mi:** Fitness Center *(Mystic YMCA,
536-3575)*, Sightseeing *(Mystic Seaport 572-0711 $17/9)* **1-3 mi:** Movie
Theater *(Village 536-4227)*, Cultural Attract *(Mystic Aquarium 572-5955
$16/11)* **3+ mi:** Golf Course *(Pequot 535-1898, 4 mi.)*

Provisioning and General Services
Near: Library *(Mystic 536-7721)*, Beauty Salon, Bookstore *(Bank Square
536-3795)* **Under 1 mi:** Gourmet Shop *(Mystic Market 536-1500)*,
Delicatessen, Health Food, Wine/Beer *(Mystic River 536-9463)*, Liquor Store
(Free Delivery), Fishmonger, Lobster Pound, Bank/ATM, Post Office,
Protestant Church, Barber Shop, Dry Cleaners, Pharmacy *(CVS 536-5628)*,
Newsstand, Florist, Retail Shops, Copies Etc. *(Mystic Publ 536-2616)*
1-3 mi: Supermarket *(McQuades 536-4606)*, Farmers' Market *(Thu 3-6pm
across A&P)*, Catholic Church, Hardware Store *(Village 259-0425)*

Transportation
OnSite: Courtesy Car/Van **OnCall:** Rental Car *(Enterprise 536-6829)*, Taxi
(Mystic 536-8888), Airport Limo *(Stonington 535-4425)* **Near:** Local Bus
Under 1 mi: Bikes *(Mystic Cycle 572-7433)*, Rail *(Amtrak)*
Airport: T.F. Green *(42 mi.)*

Medical Services
911 Service **OnCall:** Ambulance **Near:** Doctor *(Jost 536-1666)*, Dentist
(Rege 572-8959) **Under 1 mi:** Chiropractor *(Dukehart 536-4007)*
1-3 mi: Veterinarian *(Noank-Mystic 536-6656)*
Hospital: Lawrence & Memorial 437-8101 *(10 mi.)*

Setting -- Immediately to port just past the railroad bridge, Fort Rachel Marine's docks are tucked into a cove off the Mystic River. The unique primary work building makes it easy to spot: a contemporary interpretation of a classic yard shed, it has enormous sliding doors - each constructed of a dozen windows.

Marina Notes -- Service oriented, welcoming facility catering primarily to sailboats. A pet-friendly marina. Limited courtesy transport available. Established in 1971, it acquired Mystic Harbor Marine in 1998, which greatly expanded the facilities. It is now a family-run, full-service boatyard that can handle boats up to 55 ft. 35T travelift onsite. Particularly inviting heads and showers with private dressing rooms. Ice is in the coffee lounge. Internet connections at the Mystic Library and Visitors' Center.

Notable -- The remains of Fort Rachel, which thwarted the British in the War of 1812, are at the foot of Water Street. It's a ten minute stroll to downtown Mystic, where shops, restaurants and services line Main Street on both sides of the bascule bridge. The surrounding streets are home to many early 19thC houses. Mystic Seaport is about a mile by land (a little shorter by dinghy - their dock is at the North Gate) Jul-Aug 9am-6pm, Apr-Jun, Sep-Oct 9am-5pm $17/9. The Mystic Marine Aquarium is about 2 miles away, Jul-Labor Day 9am-7pm, other 9am-6pm $16/11. The Mystic Trolley connects the marinas, Amtrak, Downtown, the Seaport, Aquarium, Mistick Village, McQuade's Supermarket and West Marine. Foxwoods (800-FOXWOODS) and Mohegan Sun (888-226-7711) Casinos will provide transportation.

Navigational Information

Lat: 41°20.997' **Long:** 071°58.308' **Tide:** 2.6 ft. **Current:** n/a **Chart:** 12372
Rep. Depths (*MLW*): **Entry** 10 ft. **Fuel Dock** n/a **Max Slip/Moor** 10 ft./-
Access: Mystic River, through railroad bridge, to port

Marina Facilities (*In Season/Off Season*)

Fuel: No
Slips: 16 Total, 1-2 Transient **Max LOA:** 80 ft. **Max Beam:** 20 ft.
 Rate (*per ft.*): **Day** $2.00 **Week** n/a **Month** n/a
 Power: 30 amp Incl., **50 amp** Incl., **100 amp** n/a, **200 amp** n/a
 Cable TV: No **Dockside Phone:** No
 Dock Type: Floating, Long Fingers, Wood
Moorings: 0 Total, 0 Transient **Launch:** n/a
 Rate: Day n/a **Week** n/a **Month** n/a
Heads: 1 Toilet(s), 1 Shower(s)
Laundry: None **Pay Phones:** No
Pump-Out: No **Fee:** n/a **Closed Heads:** No

Marina Operations

Owner/Manager: John I. Carija **Dockmaster:** Same
In-Season: Apr 15-Oct 15, 8am-5pm **Off-Season:** n/a
After-Hours Arrival: Make arrangements in advance
Reservations: Yes **Credit Cards:** Cash or checks
Discounts: None
Pets: Welcome **Handicap Access:** No

John I. Carija Boat Works

47 Water Street; Mystic, CT 06355

Tel: (860) 536-9440 **VHF: Monitor** n/a **Talk** n/a
Fax: (860) 536-3248 **Alternate Tel:** (860) 536-3186
Email: n/a **Web:** n/a
Nearest Town: Mystic (*0.2 mi.*) **Tourist Info:** (860) 572-9578

Marina Services and Boat Supplies

Supplies - Near: Ice (*Block*) **Under 1 mi:** Marine Discount Store (*Sailing Specialties 536-4974*), Bait/Tackle (*Shaffers Boat Livery 536-8713, Wild Bill's 536-6648*), CNG (*Brewer Yacht Yard*) **1-3 mi:** West Marine (*536-1455*)

Boatyard Services

OnSite: Brightwork **Near:** Travelift, Engine mechanic (*gas, diesel*), Hull Repairs, Bottom Cleaning, Air Conditioning, Divers.
Nearest Yard: Fort Rachel Marine (860) 536-6647

Restaurants and Accommodations

Near: Restaurant (*Bravo Bravo 536-3228, D $15-23*), (*Capt. Daniel Packer 536-2621, L $6-13, D $15-24*), (*41 Degrees North 536-9821*), (*Zhang's 572-5725*), Lite Fare (*Under Wraps 536-4042*), Pizzeria (*Mystic Pizza 536-3700, L $6-16, D $6-16*), Inn/B&B (*Six Broadway 536-6010, $195-225*), (*The Steamboat & SV Valiant 536-8300, $120-295, Inn + 97 ft ship with 5 staterooms*) **1-3 mi:** Restaurant (*Jamms 536-2683, L $5-12, D $11-19*), Fast Food (*Mc Donalds*), Motel (*Old Mystic Motor Lodge 536-9666, $50-180*), (*Days Inn 572-0574, $90-170*), (*Comfort Inn 572-8531, $90-170*), (*Seaport Motor Inn 536-2621, $80-170*)

Recreation and Entertainment

Near: Video Rental (*Mystic Video 572-0081*), Park **Under 1 mi:** Fitness Center (*Mystic Community Center 536-3575*), Museum, Sightseeing (*Mystic Seaport 572-0711 $17/9*) **1-3 mi:** Movie Theater (*Village Cinema 536-4227*), Cultural Attract (*Mystic Aquarium 572-5955 $16/11*) **3+ mi:** Golf Course (*Pequot Golf Club 535-1898, Four Seasons Golf 446-8799, 4 mi.*),

Horseback Riding (*Rainbow Stables 535-3411, 5 mi.*), Bowling (*Holiday Bowl 445-6500, 7 mi.*)

Provisioning and General Services

Near: Gourmet Shop (*Mystic Market 536-1500*), Health Food, Bakery, Fishmonger, Lobster Pound, Bank/ATM, Post Office, Catholic Church, Library (*Mystic & Noank Library 536-7721*), Beauty Salon, Barber Shop, Dry Cleaners (*Suburban Cleaners 536-7718*), Bookstore (*Bank Square Books 536-3795*), Pharmacy (*Seaport Pharmacy 536-8400*), Newsstand, Florist, Clothing Store, Retail Shops **Under 1 mi:** Convenience Store, Delicatessen, Wine/Beer, Liquor Store, Laundry, Copies Etc. (*Mystic Publications 536-2616*) **1-3 mi:** Supermarket (*McQuade's 536-4606, A&P 572-8446*), Farmers' Market (*Thu 3-6pm across from A&P*), Hardware Store (*True Value 536-9601*)

Transportation

OnCall: Rental Car (*Enterprise 536-6829*), Taxi (*Mystic Cab 536-8888*), Airport Limo (*Stonington Limo 535-4425*) **Near:** Local Bus (*Mystic Trolley*) **Under 1 mi:** Bikes (*Mystic Cycle 572-7433*), Rail (*Mystic*)
Airport: T.F. Green (*42 mi.*)

Medical Services

911 Service **Near:** Doctor (*Jost 536-1666*), Dentist (*Rege 572-8959*), Optician (*Optimystic Eyewear 536-1313*) **Under 1 mi:** Chiropractor (*Dukehart 536-4007*) **1-3 mi:** Veterinarian (*Noank-Mystic Vet 536-6656*)
Hospital: Lawrence & Memorial 437-8101 (*10 mi.*)

Setting -- The second facility to port after the railroad bridge, just north of Ft. Rachel, is the intimate and appealing John J. Carija & Sons marina. The slips peel out from a single dock that parallels the river bank. Large stone blocks bulkhead the shoreline and hold back a pleasant strip of grass, flowers and foliage. Classic, shingled buildings complete the traditional New England atmosphere.

Marina Notes -- Not intended to be a full service marina. Friendly, neat and clean, J.I.C. offers good, sturdy docks, with a useful complement of services, in a very, very convenient location with a most pleasant ambiance. Transients welcomed. Very nice head. Could easily be that elusive "private marina" in Mystic, a stone's throw from downtown. The surrounding streets - particularly High Street, West Mystic Ave, and Prospect St. -- are lined with houses dating from the late 18thC, including many belonging to sea captains. Pick up a walking tour from the Mystic River Historical Society. Internet connection is available at both the Mystic Visitor's Center in the old Amtrak depot and at the Mystic-Noank Library -- which is housed in an interesting 1894 neo-Romanesque building.

Notable -- Capt. Daniel Packer Restaurant is across the street and more restaurants are a short walk away. Downtown Mystic is just a few blocks north. Many services, shops, and some eateries can be found on Main Street on both sides of the rather unique bascule bridge. Famous Mystic Seaport is less than a mile walk or dinghy ride (their dock is at the north gate) and Mystic Aquarium is a little under two miles. Or take the trolley, which will also stop Downtown, at the Amtrak station, Mistick Village, McQuade's Supermarket and West Marine. The Mystic Art Association is on the way to the Mystic hub.

Mystic Downtown Marina

31 Water Street; Mystic, CT 06335

Tel: (860) 536-9980; (800) 536-9980 **VHF: Monitor** 8 **Talk** n/a
Fax: (860) 536-8411 **Alternate Tel:** (860) 536-6998
Email: n/a **Web:** www.ysm.cc
Nearest Town: Mystic *(0.1 mi.)* **Tourist Info:** (860) 572-9578

Navigational Information
Lat: 41°21.106' **Long:** 071°58.317' **Tide:** 3 ft. **Current:** 2 kt. **Chart:** 13214
Rep. Depths *(MLW):* **Entry** 16 ft. **Fuel Dock** n/a **Max Slip/Moor** 10 ft./-
Access: Mystic River, through railroad bridge, 3rd facility to port

Marina Facilities *(In Season/Off Season)*
Fuel: No
Slips: 29 Total, 6 Transient **Max LOA:** 40 ft. **Max Beam:** 25 ft.
  Rate *(per ft.):* **Day** $2.00 **Week** n/a **Month** n/a
  Power: 30 amp Incl., **50 amp** n/a, **100 amp** n/a, **200 amp** n/a
  Cable TV: No **Dockside Phone:** No
  Dock Type: Floating, Wood
Moorings: 0 Total, 0 Transient **Launch:** n/a
  Rate: Day n/a **Week** n/a **Month** n/a
Heads: 2 Toilet(s), 4 Shower(s) *(with dressing rooms)*
Laundry: 1 Washer(s), 1 Dryer(s) **Pay Phones:** Yes
Pump-Out: No **Fee:** n/a **Closed Heads:** No

Marina Operations
Owner/Manager: Dick Kerri **Dockmaster:** Same
In-Season: May 15-Sep 15, 8am-6pm **Off-Season:** Sep 16-May 14, 12-3pm
After-Hours Arrival: Call in advance to inquire if possible
Reservations: Yes, Preferred **Credit Cards:** Visa/MC, Cash
Discounts: None
Pets: No **Handicap Access:** No

Marina Services and Boat Supplies
Services - Docking Assistance, Dock Carts **Communication -** FedEx, AirBorne, UPS, Express Mail **Supplies - OnSite:** Ice *(Block, Cube)* **Near:** CNG *(Brewer Yacht Yard)* **Under 1 mi:** Ships' Store *(Sailing Specialties 536-4974)*, Bait/Tackle *(Wild Bill's 536-6648)*, Propane **3+ mi:** West Marine *(536-1455, 4 mi.)*

Boatyard Services
OnSite: Bottom Cleaning, Yacht Broker *(YSM)* **OnCall:** Rigger, Sail Loft, Air Conditioning, Refrigeration **Near:** Travelift *(75T)*, Engine mechanic *(gas, diesel)*, Launching Ramp, Hull Repairs, Metal Fabrication, Painting, Awlgrip, Yacht Building. **Under 1 mi:** Brightwork. **1-3 mi:** Electrical Repairs, Electronics Repairs, Woodworking, Inflatable Repairs. **Nearest Yard:** Fort Rachel Marine (860) 536-6647

Restaurants and Accommodations
Near: Restaurant *(Zhangs 572-5725)*, *(Anthony J's Bistro 536-0448, L $6-11, D $9-20)*, *(Bravo Bravo 536-3228, L $7-14, D $15-23)*, *(Captain Daniel Packer Inne 536-3555, L $6-13, D $15-24)*, *(Kitchen Little 536-2122, B $4-10, L $4-10, Even Gourmet took note)*, Pizzeria *(Mystic 536-3700, L $6-16, D $6-16)*, Inn/B&B *(The Whalers 536-1506, $135-225)*, *(The Steamboat 536-8300, $120-295)* **1-3 mi:** Restaurant *(Fisherman)*, Motel *(Comfort Inn 572-8531, $150)*, *(Seaport Motor Inn 536-2621, $80-180)*, Hotel *(Hilton 572-0731, $115-225)*, *(Marriott Residence 536-5150, $150-210)*

Recreation and Entertainment
OnSite: Picnic Area, Boat Rentals *(YSM Charters)*, Park, Sightseeing *(Mystic River Tours)* **Under 1 mi:** Fitness Center *(Community Center 536-3575)*, Roller Blade/Bike Paths, Video Rental *(Mystic Video 572-0081)*, Museum *(Mystic Art Assn. 536-7601, Seaport Marine Museum 572-0711 $17/9)* **1-3 mi:** Beach, Dive Shop, Jogging Paths, Fishing Charter, Movie Theater *(Village 536-4227)* **3+ mi:** Golf Course *(Pequot 535-1898, 5 mi.)*

Provisioning and General Services
Near: Green Grocer, Fishmonger, Lobster Pound, Bank/ATM, Post Office, Catholic Church, Protestant Church, Library *(Mystic & Noank Library 536-7721)*, Beauty Salon, Barber Shop, Dry Cleaners, Bookstore *(Bank Square Books 536-3795)*, Newsstand, Florist, Retail Shops **Under 1 mi:** Provsioning Service, Gourmet Shop *(Mystic Market 536-1500)*, Delicatessen, Liquor Store *(Mystic River Wine and Spirit 536-9463)*, Pharmacy *(CVS 536-5628)*, Copies Etc. *(Mystic Publications 536-2616)*
1-3 mi: Supermarket *(McQuade's 536-4606, A&P 572-8446)*, Bakery, Farmers' Market *(Thu 3-6pm across from A&P)*, Meat Market, Hardware Store *(True Value 536-9601)*

Transportation
OnCall: Rental Car *(Enterprise 536-6829, or Avis 445-8585, 6 mi.)*, Taxi *(Yellow Cab 536-8888)*, Airport Limo *(Stonington Limo 535-4425)* **Near:** Local Bus *(Trolley)* **Under 1 mi:** Bikes *(Mystic Cycle 572-7433)*, Rail *(Amtrak)* **3+ mi:** Ferry Service *(New London - Orient Point, 12 mi.)* **Airport:** T.F. Green *(42 mi.)*

Medical Services
911 Service **OnCall:** Dentist, Ambulance **Near:** Doctor, Chiropractor *(New London Chiro 442-8860)* **1-3 mi:** Veterinarian *(Noank-Mystic Vet 536-6656)* **Hospital:** Lawrence & Memorial 437-8101 *(10 mi.)*

Setting -- The last marina to port (after the railroad bridge but before the bascule bridge), Mystic Downtown Marina is the closest facility to the business district of Mystic. This nicely executed and well-groomed dockage-only facility is a fairly recent, and most welcome, addition to the Mystic marina scene. Its slips and alongside docks are near and around a small, attractively landscaped waterfront park. "Umbrellaed" picnic tables with views of the river and pots of flowers complete the scene. A handsomely renovated former factory flanks the northern end.

Marina Notes -- Managed and operated by Yacht Services of Mystic. YSM is also the New England distributor for Duffy Electric Boats, operator of Mystic River Tours (using Duffys) - 1.5 hrs., every hour starting at 1pm weekdays, 10am weekend, a yacht charter agency (bareboat or captained, 34-42 ft.), a yacht brokerage, and a yacht manager -- all located at the marina. Also a Certified Teaching Facility of the American Sailing Association. Mystic Jitney - 40 foot motorsailing tours. Note: there is a "No Pets" policy. Internet access is at the nearby Mystic Visitors' Association in the restored depot, and at the library.

Notable -- Downtown Mystic's restaurants, shops, galleries and attractions are a stone's throw away. Dozens of late 18thC and early 19thC houses line nearby streets (walking guide at Mystic Historical Society). Mystic Seaport is less than a mile north (the Seaport maintains a free dinghy dock at the north gate). The Mystic Aquarium's about a mile farther, as is Olde Mistick Village -- a 60 shop mall that is so nicely done as an early 19thC village that a visit might even appeal to committed non-shoppers. The Mystic Trolley connects the marinas with all the area attractions, shops and services.

Navigational Information
Lat: 41°21.605' **Long:** 071°57.798' **Tide:** 2.3 ft. **Current:** n/a **Chart:** 13214
Rep. Depths (*MLW*): **Entry** 12 ft. **Fuel Dock** n/a **Max Slip/Moor** 11 ft./-
Access: Mystic River, under both bridges, at G45 on starboard side

Marina Facilities (*In Season/Off Season*)
Fuel: No
Slips: 40 Total, 40 Transient **Max LOA:** 200 ft. **Max Beam:** n/a
  Rate (*per ft.*): **Day** $3.50* **Week** Inq. **Month** Inq.
  Power: 30 amp Incl., 50 amp Incl., 100 amp n/a, 200 amp n/a
  Cable TV: No **Dockside Phone:** No
  Dock Type: Fixed, Long Fingers, Pilings
Moorings: 0 Total, 0 Transient **Launch:** n/a
  Rate: Day n/a **Week** n/a **Month** n/a
Heads: 4 Toilet(s), 4 Shower(s)
Laundry: 1 Washer(s), 1 Dryer(s) **Pay Phones:** Yes
Pump-Out: OnSite, Self Service **Fee:** Free **Closed Heads:** Yes

Marina Operations
Owner/Manager: n/a **Dockmaster:** Dick Lotz
In-Season: May 10-LabDay, 9-5:30pm **Off-Season:** LabDay-Apr, 9am-5pm
After-Hours Arrival: Reservations only held until 5:15pm
Reservations: Necessary **Credit Cards:** Visa/MC, Amex
Discounts: None
Pets: Welcome **Handicap Access:** No

Mystic Seaport Museum & Docks

75 Greenmanville Avenue; Mystic, CT 06355

Tel: (860) 572-5391 **VHF: Monitor** 68 **Talk** 68
Fax: (860) 572-5344 **Alternate Tel:** (860) 572-0711
Email: n/a **Web:** www.mystic.org
Nearest Town: Mystic (*1 mi.*) **Tourist Info:** (860) 572-9578

Marina Services and Boat Supplies
Services - Docking Assistance, Security **Communication -** FedEx, UPS, Express Mail **Supplies - OnSite:** Ice (*Cube*) **Under 1 mi:** West Marine (*536-1455*), Bait/Tackle (*Shaffers Boat Livery 536-8713*), Propane, CNG (*Brewer Yacht Yard*) **1-3 mi:** Ships' Store (*Sailing Specialties 536-4974*)

Boatyard Services
Near: Bottom Cleaning. **Under 1 mi:** Launching Ramp, Electrical Repairs, Electronics Repairs, Hull Repairs, Rigger, Brightwork, Refrigeration.
Nearest Yard: Brewer Yacht Yard (860) 536-2293

Restaurants and Accommodations
OnSite: Restaurant (*Seamen's Inne 572-5303, L $6-11, D $15-23, 11:30am-2:30pm & 4:30-10pm, Sun Buffet 11am-2pm $10. Large party facility*), Lite Fare (*Schaefer Spouter Tavern L $6.50, 11am-4pm sandwiches*), (*The Galley Restaurant L $4-10, 9am-5pm, snacks, sandwiches, soups, salads, hot entrées*) **Near:** Pizzeria (*Avantis 536-6757*) **Under 1 mi:** Restaurant (*Flood Tide 536-8140, L $8-16, D $21-35*), (*Copperfields 536-4281*), Motel (*Seaport Motor Inn 536-2621, $70-170, across from Aquarium*), (*Whaler's Inn 536-1506*), Hotel (*Hilton 572-0731*), Inn/B&B (*Inn at Mystic 536-9604, $85-275*) **1-3 mi:** Motel (*Comfort Inn 572-8531, $90-170*)

Recreation and Entertainment
OnSite: Boat Rentals (*20 small "exact replica" wooden boats - Rowboats: Members - $5.25/half-hr, $8/hr, Non-Members $7/10.50; Sailboats: Mem--bers $10.50/hr, Non-Members $14/hr*), Park, Museum (*Exhibit and shop hours: 9am-5pm Apr-Oct, 10am-4pm Nov-Mar*), Sightseeing (*Antique steamboat cruises & carriage rides*)

Provisioning and General Services
Near: Fitness Center (*Mystic Community Center 536-3575*)
Under 1 mi: Beach, Movie Theater (*Village Cinema 536-4227*), Video Rental (*Videos 4 U 536-9899*), Cultural Attract (*Mystic Aquarium 572-5955, $16/11*)
3+ mi: Golf Course (*Pequot Golf Club 535-1898, 4 mi.*), Horseback Riding (*Rainbow Stables 535-3411, 5 mi.*), Bowling (*Holiday Bowl 445-6500, 6.5 mi.*)

Provisioning and General Services
OnSite: Bakery (*Bake Shop 8am-6pm*), Bookstore (*Mystic Seaport Stores 572-5386*), Retail Shops (*Museum Store, Variety Store*) **Near:** Copies Etc. (*Mystic Publications 536-2616*) **Under 1 mi:** Supermarket (*McQuade's or A&P 572-8446*), Gourmet Shop (*Mystic Market 536-1500*), Delicatessen, Liquor Store (*Mystic River 536-9463*), Farmers' Market (*Thu 3-6pm across from A&P*), Fishmonger, Lobster Pound, Meat Market, Bank/ATM, Post Office, Catholic Church, Library (*Mystic & Noank 536-7721, Internet*), Beauty Salon, Dry Cleaners, Laundry, Pharmacy (*CVS 536-5628*), Newsstand, Clothing Store **1-3 mi:** Hardware Store (*True Value 536-9601*)

Transportation
OnCall: Rental Car (*Enterprise 536-6829*), Taxi (*Yellow Cab 536-8888*), Airport Limo (*Stonington Limo 535-4425*) **Near:** Local Bus (*Mystic Trolley*) **Under 1 mi:** Bikes (*Mystic Cycle 572-7433 $15/day*), Rail (*Mystic Amtrak*) **Airport:** T.F. Green (*42 mi.*)

Medical Services
911 Service **OnCall:** Ambulance **Near:** Doctor (*Jost 536-1666*), Dentist (*Watts 536-6446*) **Under 1 mi:** Chiropractor (*Dukehart 536-4007*), Veterinarian (*Old Mystic Animal Clinic 536-4204*)
Hospital: Lawrence & Memorial 437-8101 (*10 mi.*)

Setting -- Seventeen waterfront acres, nearly 40 historic buildings and more than 480 vessels comprise this extraordinary museum - a living paean to 19th century New England seafaring life and all that has come after. Tall ships, classic wooden boats, fully furnished houses, a planetarium, large nautical gift shop, research library -- all artfully conceived and beautifully executed. Founded 1929, in the midst of the depression, Mystic Seaport is now the largest and most comprehensive maritime museum in North America. For anyone with a passion for "messing about with boats", this is worth a special trip.

Marina Notes -- *Rates: $3.50/ft. "Family Plus" Members $2.50/ft. "Sustaining Plus" Members $2.50/ft. & second night free once a season. Advance reservations required with $50 deposit - refundable up to 24hrs. in advance. (Reservations held until 5:15 pm; bridge opening without prior arrangement). Check-in after 1:15 bridge opening; check-out before 1:15. Monitors Ch.68 8am-7pm July-Labor Day, and phones 9am-4pm Mon-Fri, 9am-5pm daily Jul-Aug. Dockmaster's office at head of Dunton & Sabino Dock. Mystic Trolley to shopping, restaurants, attractions, Amtrak, etc. Dinghy to Downtown Mystic Park.

Notable -- A wonderful experience! Dockage includes admission for the whole crew (usually $17/9, Srs $16) and "after hours" the place is yours. Bell rating based on uniqueness of experience, not the facilities. Museum members ($40 & up) have access to the Members building with lounge, free beverages, quiet restrooms, shop and boat rental discounts, etc. "Family Plus" ($60) level or above a 25% dockage discount. Classes for kids, families, adults. Maritime scholars and buffs will find an extraordinary research collection and graduate-level courses. Demonstrations, kids' programs, exhibits - all day.

Spicer's Noank Marina

93 Marsh Road; Noank, CT 06340

Tel: (860) 536-4978 **VHF: Monitor** 68 **Talk** n/a
Fax: (860) 536-4406 **Alternate Tel:** n/a
Email: spicers@spicersmarina.com **Web:** www.spicersmarina.com
Nearest Town: Noank *(0.4 mi.)* **Tourist Info:** (860) 572-9578

Navigational Information
Lat: 41°19.360' **Long:** 071°59.625' **Tide:** 2.3 ft. **Current:** n/a **Chart:** 13214
Rep. Depths *(MLW):* **Entry** 7 ft. **Fuel Dock** n/a **Max Slip/Moor** 7 ft./7 ft.
Access: Day marked channel, just west of Mouse Island, past breakwater

Marina Facilities *(In Season/Off Season)*
Fuel: No
Slips: 410 Total, 25 Transient **Max LOA:** 50 ft. **Max Beam:** n/a
 Rate *(per ft.):* **Day** $2.50/Inq. **Week** Inq. **Month** Inq.
 Power: 30 amp Incl., **50 amp** n/a, **100 amp** n/a, **200 amp** n/a
 Cable TV: No **Dockside Phone:** No
 Dock Type: Floating, Long Fingers, Concrete
Moorings: 150 Total, 50 Transient **Launch:** Yes (Free), Dinghy Dock
 Rate: Day $2/ft. **Week** Inq. **Month** Inq.
Heads: 15 Toilet(s), 10 Shower(s) *(with dressing rooms)*, make-up counters
Laundry: 1 Washer(s), 1 Dryer(s) **Pay Phones:** Yes, 2
Pump-Out: Full Service, Self Service **Fee:** $0-20* **Closed Heads:** Yes

Marina Operations
Owner/Manager: Bill Spicer **Dockmaster:** John Gardiner
In-Season: Year Round, 8:30am-5pm **Off-Season:** n/a
After-Hours Arrival: Call ahead for instructions
Reservations: Yes, Preferred **Credit Cards:** Visa/MC, Dscvr
Discounts: Boat/US; Safe/Sea **Dockage:** 20-25% **Fuel:** 10% **Repair:** n/a
Pets: Welcome **Handicap Access:** No

Marina Services and Boat Supplies
Services - Docking Assistance, Trash Pick-Up, Dock Carts
Communication - Mail & Package Hold, Phone Messages, Fax in/out,
FedEx, AirBorne, UPS, Express Mail **Supplies - OnSite:** Ice *(Block, Cube)*,
Marine Discount Store, Bait/Tackle *(Wild Bill's Action Sports & Tackle 536-6648)* **1-3 mi:** Propane, CNG *(Brewer Yacht Yard 536-2293)*

Boatyard Services
OnSite: Travelift *(20T & 38T)*, Hydraulic Trailer, Engine mechanic *(gas, diesel)*, Launching Ramp, Electrical Repairs, Electronic Sales, Electronics Repairs, Hull Repairs, Rigger, Sail Loft *(Hood Sailmakers)*, Air Conditioning, Refrigeration, Compound, Wash & Wax, Propeller Repairs, Painting, Awlgrip, Yacht Broker *(Spicer's Sailboat Sales)* **OnCall:** Bottom Cleaning, Brightwork, Divers, Interiors **Dealer for:** Interlux, Cummins, Icom, Garmin, Raymarine, Yanmar, Autohelm, MerCruiser, Mercury, Westerbeke, Universal.
Yard Rates: $65-75, Haul & Launch $12-16/ft. *(blocking incl.)*, Power Wash Incl., Bottom Paint $13.50/ft. **Storage:** In-Water $23/ft.,
On-Land $30-33/ft.

Restaurants and Accommodations
OnSite: Restaurant *(Seahorse Tavern 536-1670, L $4-13,D $11-20, Kid's menu $4-7)* **Near:** Restaurant *(41 Degrees North 536-9821)*, *(Draw Bridge Inne 536-9653)*, *(Fisherman 536-1717)*, Lite Fare *(Christine's Heart 'n Soul Café 536-1244)* **Under 1 mi:** Seafood Shack *(Abbotts' Lobster 536-7719, L $13-22, D $13-22)*, *(Costello's Clam Shack 572-2779)*, Inn/B&B *(Shore Inne 536-1180)* **1-3 mi:** Restaurant *(Capt. Daniel Packer 536-2621, L $6-13, D $15-24)* **3+ mi:** Inn/B&B *(Harbour Inn & Cottage 572-9253, $45-250, 3.5 mi.)*, *(Whaler's Inn 536-1506, $100-220, 3.5 mi.)*

Recreation and Entertainment
OnSite: Fishing Charter *(Flying Fish 886-1838, Kingfisher 573-3614, Sarah J 536-6648, Magic 455-9942)* **Near:** Beach *(Palmer Cove or Esker Point)*, Picnic Area, Grills, Playground, Tennis Courts, Jogging Paths, Special Events *(Concerts at Carson's Fri. night)* **Under 1 mi:** Museum *(Noank Hist. Soc. 536-3021 by app't)* **1-3 mi:** Fitness Center *(Mystic Comm Ctr 536-3575)*, Sightseeing *(Mystic Seaport 572-0711 $17/9, Mystic Aquarium 572-5955 $16/8)* **3+ mi:** Golf Course *(Four Seasons 446-8799, 4 mi.)*

Provisioning and General Services
Near: Market *(Universal 536-0122)*, Delicatessen *(Carson's Variety 536-0059)*, Wine/Beer *(Universal)* **Under 1 mi:** Lobster Pound *(Ford's 536-2842, Abbott's, too)*, Barber Shop **1-3 mi:** Gourmet Shop *(Mystic Market 536-1500)*, Liquor Store *(Ackley's Package 445-0006)*, Pharmacy *(Fort Hill 445-6431)* **3+ mi:** Supermarket *(Stop & Shop 445-6796, 4 mi.)*, Library *(Mystic & Noank 536-7721, 4 mi.)*, Bookstore *(Bank Square Books 536-3795, 4 mi.)*, Hardware Store *(Village 259-0425, 4 mi.)*

Transportation
OnCall: Rental Car *(Enterprise 536-6829)*, Taxi *(Yellow Cab 536-8888)*, Airport Limo *(Executive 449-0038)* **1-3 mi:** Rail *(Mystic Amtrak)*
3+ mi: Bikes *(Mystic Cycle 572-7433, 4 mi.)* **Airport:** T.F. Green *(42 mi.)*

Medical Services
911 Service OnCall: Ambulance **Under 1 mi:** Veterinarian *(Noank-Mystic Vet 536-6656)* **1-3 mi:** Doctor *(Pequot Health Clinic 446-8265)*, Dentist, Chiropractor, Holistic Services *(Holistic Hands/Foot Reflexology 536-4128)*
Hospital: Lawrence & Memorial 437-8101 *(10 mi.)*

Setting -- Tucked comfortably behind a relatively recent 680 foot stone breakwater in West Cove (between Noank Peninsula's Morgan Point and Groton Long Point), this large, full-service marina and boatyard is easily accessible from Fishers Island Sound. The views of the surrounding area are rural and uncrowded; the views of the water are mostly of Spicer's well maintained docks and moorings, which fill most of the Cove.

Marina Notes -- Family owned and operated for over 60 years - currently third generation at the helm.. 38.5 ton BFM 19 ft. wide travelift with adjustable slings. Full service repair yard with a passion for "fixing things." Moorings inside and outside the breakwater. Complimentary launch service: Mon-Fri 10am-7pm Sat & Sun 9am-7pm. *Serviced pump-out $20, self-serve free. Three bath houses with particularly nice, comfortably large heads and showers include thoughtful mirrored make-up counters with plugs! Well-equipped marine store "competes with the catalogs". Wild Bill's Bait & Tackle is onsite, as is the Seahorse Tavern and Restaurant (for a lighter dinner alternative, the lunch menu is available all day in the Tavern). Home to a number of charter fishing boats.

Notable -- Spicer's provides an excellent base from which to explore the small-town charm of pretty Noank Village. It's about a 0.4 mile stroll to the village green. Many restored early 19thC houses and cottages line the streets, and there are a few shops and services -- a "frozen in the 50s" variety store with a soda fountain, a package & convenience store, post office and a church. It's a short dinghy ride (or a 0.3 mi. walk) to Palmer Cove Park -- there's a beach, a snack bar, and a lovely picnic area with grills, sitting in a grove of trees. Across the street from the park is the well-known Fisherman Restaurant.

Navigational Information

Lat: 41°15.958' **Long:** 072°00.701' **Tide:** 2.5 ft. **Current:** n/a **Chart:** 13214
Rep. Depths (*MLW*): **Entry** 9 ft. **Fuel Dock** n/a **Max Slip/Moor** 8 ft./-
Access: Fishers Island Sound to Fishers Island's West Harbor

Marina Facilities *(In Season/Off Season)*

Fuel: No
Slips: 50 Total, 15 Transient **Max LOA:** 125 ft. **Max Beam:** 30 ft.
 Rate *(per ft.)*: **Day** $2.50/Inq. **Week** Inq. **Month** n/a
 Power: 30 amp $5, 50 amp $10, 100 amp n/a, 200 amp n/a
 Cable TV: No **Dockside Phone:** No
 Dock Type: Fixed, Long Fingers, Pilings, Alongside, Wood
 Moorings: 0 Total, 0 Transient **Launch:** No, Dinghy Dock
 Rate: Day n/a **Week** n/a **Month** n/a
Heads: None
Laundry: None **Pay Phones:** Yes, 1
Pump-Out: No **Fee:** n/a **Closed Heads:** No

Marina Operations

Owner/Manager: John Evans **Dockmaster:** n/a
In-Season: n/a, 8am-6pm **Off-Season:** n/a
After-Hours Arrival: n/a
Reservations: Preferred **Credit Cards:** Visa/MC
Discounts: None
Pets: Welcome **Handicap Access:** No

Fishers Island Yacht Club

PO Box 141; Fishers Island, NY 06390

Tel: (631) 788-7036 **VHF: Monitor** 9 **Talk** 10
Fax: n/a **Alternate Tel:** (860) 536-9805
Email: marina@fiyc.net **Web:** www.fiyc.net
Nearest Town: New London **Tourist Info:** (631) 788-9638

Marina Services and Boat Supplies

Services - Docking Assistance, Trash Pick-Up, Dock Carts
Communication - UPS, Express Mail **Supplies - Near:** Ice *(Cube)*,
Propane *(Mobil Station)* **1-3 mi:** Ships' Store *(Pirate's Cove Marina 788-7528)*, Bait/Tackle *(Pirate's Cove)*

Boatyard Services

Under 1 mi: Travelift, Engine mechanic *(gas, diesel)*, Launching Ramp,
Electrical Repairs, Electronic Sales, Hull Repairs, Bottom Cleaning,
Brightwork, Divers, Compound, Wash & Wax, Interior Cleaning,
Woodworking, Inflatable Repairs, Painting, Awlgrip.
Nearest Yard: Pirate's Cove Marina (631) 788-7528

Restaurants and Accommodations

Near: Snack Bar *(Toppers ice cream)*, Lite Fare *(The News Café Light
Breakfast & Lunch Mon-Sat 7am-3pm, Sun 7am-2pm)* **Under 1 mi:** Lite
Fare *(Pequot Inn "Grille" 788-7247, D $3-13, late lunch and dinner)*, Inn/B&B
(Pequot Inn 788-7246, $100-125, 0.5 mi.)

Recreation and Entertainment

Near: Beach, Playground, Jogging Paths, Movie Theater *(Tue, Wed, Fri, Sun
night)*, Museum *(Henry L. Ferguson Museum 788-7239)*

Provisioning and General Services

OnCall: Lobster Pound *(check with Dockmaster)* **Near:** Convenience Store,
Bank/ATM, Post Office, Catholic Church, Protestant Church, Library, Beauty
Salon, Newsstand, Hardware Store, Retail Shops *(Picket Fence, Cano)*

Transportation

Near: Bikes *(Gold & Silver Shop)* **Under 1 mi:** Ferry Service *(to New
London 778-7463, 860-442-4471, or www.fiferry.com)*
Airport: T.F. Green *(50 mi.)*

Medical Services

911 Service **OnCall:** Ambulance **Under 1 mi:** Doctor
Hospital: Lawrence & Memorial in New London 442-0711 *45 min. via ferry*

PHOTOS ON CD-ROM: 6

Setting -- Location, Location! Location! Set in pretty and pristine West Harbor on very private Fishers Island, this small yacht club opens its docks (but not its club house) to all transient boaters -- from small sloops to mega yachts.

Marina Notes -- Very service-oriented staff. Dockmaster can help with directions to suppliers and repairs. Yacht club also has moorings in the harbor, which all are generally occupied by F.I.Y.C. members (although it doesn't hurt to ask). Can accommodate megayachts at the T-heads. Docks are a combination of slips with finger piers and alongside. Mobil Fuel dock adjacent. Lobstering is the main business of the permanent island residents and the dockmaster can often make arrangements to have lobsters delivered to your boat.

Notable -- A small beach is a short walk away. Fishing in the harbor, right off the rocks, is reportedly excellent. 4/10 of a mile to "town" which is a small collection of shops and services - museum, small women's clothing shop, a kids' store, bike rentals, ice cream parlor, cafe, and a movie theater. A tenth of a mile farther along is the Pequot Inn and Restaurant. The inn has 7 recently renovated rooms, each with private bath (2 with views of West Harbor). The Pequot Restaurant offers snacks and light fare -- pizza, hot and cold sandwiches, wraps, burgers, wings and salads -- plus a remarkable, international selection of beers. There's also a small dinner menu Mon-Fri 5-10pm, Sat & Sun 12:30-10pm. Pizza from 5-9:30pm -- call ahead for quick take-out (788-7247) -- and breakfast at 1am on Sat night/Sun morning. Entertainment Thu-Sat 10:30pm 'til closing. Billiards, too.

Pirate's Cove Marine

PO Box 365; 12 Peninsula Road; Fishers Island, NY 06390

Tel: (631) 788-7528 **VHF: Monitor** 9 **Talk** 10
Fax: (631) 788-7873 **Alternate Tel:** (631) 788-7245
Email: pcminc@fishersisland.net **Web:** n/a
Nearest Town: New London **Tourist Info:** (631) 788-9638

Navigational Information
Lat: 41°15.639' **Long:** 072°00.321' **Tide:** 2.5 ft. **Current:** n/a **Chart:** 13214
Rep. Depths (*MLW*): **Entry** 9 ft. **Fuel Dock** 9 ft. **Max Slip/Moor** 9 ft./10 ft.
Access: Fishers Island Harbor to SW corner to Inner Harbor

Marina Facilities (*In Season/Off Season*)
Fuel: No
Slips: 14 Total, 0 Transient **Max LOA:** 44 ft. **Max Beam:** n/a
 Rate (*per ft.*): **Day** n/a **Week** n/a **Month** n/a
 Power: 30 amp Yes, **50 amp** Yes, **100 amp** n/a, **200 amp** n/a
 Cable TV: No **Dockside Phone:** No
 Dock Type: Fixed, Floating, Long Fingers
 Moorings: 5 Total, 5 Transient **Launch:** No, Dinghy Dock
 Rate: Day $30/30 **Week** n/a **Month** n/a
Heads: None
Laundry: None **Pay Phones:** No
Pump-Out: No **Fee:** n/a **Closed Heads:** No

Marina Operations
Owner/Manager: Chip Dupont/Bill Wall **Dockmaster:** Same
In-Season: Year 'Round, 8am-4:30pm **Off-Season:** Same
After-Hours Arrival: No arrangements possible
Reservations: No **Credit Cards:** Visa/MC, Amex
Discounts: None
Pets: Welcome **Handicap Access:** No

Marina Services and Boat Supplies
Supplies - OnSite: Ships' Store, Bait/Tackle (*Pirate's Cove - fishing in harbor reportedly excellent*) **1-3 mi:** Ice (*Cube*)

Boatyard Services
OnSite: Travelift (*15T*), Engine mechanic (*gas, diesel*), Electrical Repairs, Electronic Sales, Hull Repairs, Bottom Cleaning, Brightwork, Divers, Compound, Wash & Wax, Interior Cleaning, Woodworking, Inflatable Repairs, Painting, Awlgrip **Near:** Launching Ramp. **Yard Rates:** $70/hr., Haul & Launch $8/ft. (*blocking $4.50/ft.*), Power Wash $3.75/ft. **Storage:** In-Water $4.85/ft./mo.

Restaurants and Accommodations
1-3 mi: Snack Bar (*Topper's*), Lite Fare (*Pequot Inn 788-7247, D $4-13, Mon-Fri 4:30pm-2am, Sat & Sun 2:30pm-4am*), (*News Café 788-7183, Light breakfast and lunch, Mon-Sat 7am-3pm, Sun 7am-2pm*), Inn/B&B (*Pequot Inn 788-7246, $100-125, May-Oct*)

Recreation and Entertainment
Near: Beach, Jogging Paths **1-3 mi:** Golf Course, Movie Theater (*Tue, Wed, Fri, Sun night*), Museum (*Henry L. Ferguson Museum 788-7239*)

Provisioning and General Services
1-3 mi: Convenience Store, Bank/ATM, Post Office, Catholic Church, Protestant Church, Library, Beauty Salon, Hardware Store, Retail Shops (*The Picket Fence, Cano, kids shop*)

Transportation
1-3 mi: Bikes (*Gold & Silver Shop*), Ferry Service (*Fishers Island Ferry District to New London 778-7463/860-442-4471; www.fiferry.com for current schedule and rates*) **Airport:** T.F. Green (*50 mi.*)

Medical Services
911 Service **OnCall:** Ambulance **1-3 mi:** Doctor **Hospital:** Lawrence & Memorial - New London 442-0711 (*45 min. via ferry*)

Setting -- Pirate's Cove is nestled in the nearly land-locked inner harbor accessed through a narrow passage in the southwest corner of Fisher Island's West Harbor. It maintains five transient moorings in the main harbor -- both locations are very pretty.

Marina Notes -- This is the only boat yard on the island. A family operation, begun in 1970, with on-site management and clear hands-on oversight. The inner harbor is the primary hurricane hole for the island. There's a dinghy dock on-site, but, because it's a bit far from the "village", many people prefer to land their dinghies at the Fisher's Island Yacht Club. A small ships' store can meet most basic needs. And a very active and well-supplied bait and tackle shop is also on the premises.

Notable -- Fishers Island is exceedingly private -- the whole eastern end is gated. The western end offers some interesting strolling destinations -- and a circumnavigation of the island by boat promises some truly spectacular house-browsing. In the village, there are very limited amenities: Pequot Inn consists of 7 recently renovated rooms, each with private bath (two with views of West Harbor). The Pequot Restaurant offers snacks and light fare -- pizza, hot and cold sandwiches, wraps, burgers, wings and salads -- plus a remarkable selection of international beers. There's also a small dinner menu Mon-Fri 5-10pm, Sat & Sun 12:30-10pm. Pizza from 5-9:30pm -- call ahead for quick take-out (788-7247) -- and breakfast at 1am on Sat night/Sun morning. Entertainment Thu-Sat 10:30pm 'til closing. Billiards, too. Toppers has ice cream, the Picket Fence gifts, and the News Cafe offers light breakfast and lunch.

Navigational Information
Lat: 41°20.028' **Long:** 072°05.840' **Tide:** 3 ft. **Current:** 3 kt. **Chart:** 12372
Rep. Depths (MLW): Entry 15 ft. **Fuel Dock** 12 ft. **Max Slip/Moor** 12 ft./14 ft.
Access: New London Ledge Light, 1 mile to Green's Harbor on port side

Marina Facilities (In Season/Off Season)
Fuel: Gulf - Gasoline, Diesel, High-Speed Pumps
Slips: 120 Total, 15 Transient **Max LOA:** 100 ft. **Max Beam:** 24 ft.
  Rate (per ft.): Day $1.72/Inq. **Week** $7.00 **Month** $15
  Power: 30 amp Incl., **50 amp** Incl., **100 amp** Incl., **200 amp** n/a
  Cable TV: No **Dockside Phone:** No
  Dock Type: Fixed, Long Fingers, Wood
Moorings: 12 Total, 6 Transient **Launch:** None
  Rate: Day $25 **Week** $105 **Month** $10/ft.
Heads: 2 Toilet(s), 2 Shower(s)
Laundry: None **Pay Phones:** No
Pump-Out: OnSite **Fee:** $5 **Closed Heads:** Yes

Marina Operations
Owner/Manager: Fred Paulos **Dockmaster:** Joe Strazzo
In-Season: Apr-Nov, 8am-8pm **Off-Season:** Dec-Mar, 9am-5pm
After-Hours Arrival: Take open slip
Reservations: Preferred **Credit Cards:** Visa/MC, Dscvr, Amex
Discounts: Boat/US **Dockage:** 25% **Fuel:** 10% **Repair:** 5%
Pets: Welcome **Handicap Access:** No

Thamesport Marina

260 Pequot Avenue; New London, CT 06320

Tel: (860) 437-7022; (800) 882-1151 **VHF: Monitor** 9 **Talk** 68
Fax: (860) 447-3342 **Alternate Tel:** (800) 442-2493
Email: thamesport@aol.com **Web:** connquest.com/thamesport/marina.htm
Nearest Town: Waterford (2 mi.) **Tourist Info:** (860) 444-2206

Marina Services and Boat Supplies
Services - Docking Assistance, Trash Pick-Up, Dock Carts
Communication - Data Ports, FedEx, AirBorne, UPS, Express Mail
Supplies - OnSite: Ice (Block, Cube) **Near:** Bait/Tackle (AW Marina 443-6076) **Under 1 mi:** Propane **1-3 mi:** West Marine (444-8755), CNG (Brewers) **3+ mi:** Boater's World (440-3658, 4 mi.)

Boatyard Services
OnSite: Divers, Interior Cleaning, Propeller Repairs **OnCall:** Engine mechanic (gas, diesel), Electrical Repairs, Electronic Sales, Electronics Repairs, Rigger, Sail Loft **Nearest Yard:** Burr's Marina (860) 443-8457

Restaurants and Accommodations
OnSite: Seafood Shack (Fred's Shanty 447-1701, L $2-12, D $2-12)
OnCall: Pizzeria (Pequot Pizza 442-2262, L & D $4-6) **Near:** Restaurant (Schooners 437-3801, L $7-12, D $13-20), (Gridlock Grille 442-7146, L $2-8, D $8-16), (Stash's Cafe & Bar 443-1095, live music and great people & motorcycle watching), (La Vie en Rose Bistro 555-8860), Pizzeria (Recovery Room 443-2619, L $5-15, D $5-15, no lunch weekends)
Under 1 mi: Restaurant (Lighthouse Inn 443-8411, D $14-20, Sun Brunch), Hotel (Lighthouse Inn 443-8411, $85-275, Soundfront Victorian mansion)
1-3 mi: Motel (Red Roof 444-0001, $45-95), Hotel (Holiday Inn 442-0631, $100-160), Inn/B&B (Queen Anne 442-0631, $90-185)

Recreation and Entertainment
OnSite: Fishing Charter (Lady Margaret 739-3687, Fish 739-3611, After You Too 537-5004, Atlantis 437-3662) **Near:** Beach (or "best in CT" Ocean Beach Park 2 mi.), Picnic Area, Grills, Dive Shop, Park (1839 massive

Fort Trumbull guards the entrance to the harbor - exhibits planned), Museum (Monte Cristo Cottage 443-0051 $5/0, readings, too; Submarine Force Museum 694-3174, Free - 5 mi.) **1-3 mi:** Bowling (Family Bowl 443-4232), Movie Theater, Cultural Attract (Eugene O'Neill Theater 443-5378)

Provisioning and General Services
Near: Convenience Store (Sams Food 442-5227), Delicatessen (R&B Cafe & Market Place 437-7712), Liquor Store (Grand Spirit 445-1044), Newsstand **Under 1 mi:** Catholic Church, Synagogue, Library (New London PL 447-1411), Beauty Salon, Barber Shop, Dry Cleaners, Laundry, Bookstore (Greene's Books & Beans 443-3312), Hardware Store (Schneider 442-5713), Florist, Copies Etc. (Sullivan Printing 443-5090) **1-3 mi:** Provisioning Service, Supermarket (Adams Super Food 443-8898, Stop & Save 442-7264), Gourmet Shop, Bakery, Farmers' Market (Jul-Oct at E. O'Neill Dr. & Pearl St., Tue & Fri, 9:30am-2pm 442-1530), Green Grocer, Meat Market, Protestant Church, Pharmacy (Brooks 443-5048), Clothing Store, Retail Shops, Department Store **3+ mi:** Buying Club (BJ's, 4 mi.)

Transportation
OnCall: Rental Car (Enterprise 442-8333), Taxi (Harrys 442-4054) **Near:** Local Bus (& NL Historic Trolley) **Under 1 mi:** InterCity Bus (Greyhound 447-3841) **1-3 mi:** Rail (Amtrak), Ferry Service (1.7 mi. to Block Island, Fishers Island, Orient Point) **Airport:** T.F. Green (50 mi.)

Medical Services
911 Service **OnCall:** Ambulance **Under 1 mi:** Doctor (Chaudhry 444-1292), Dentist, Chiropractor (Eastern Shore Chiropractic 444-6363), Holistic Services **Hospital:** Lawrence & Memorial 442-0711 (1 mi.)

Setting -- About one mile past the New London Ledge Light, tucked into Green's Harbor on the western bank of the very busy, commercial and semi-industrial Thames River, are two marinas catering to sport fishing boats and other seasonal and transient recreational vessels. The first is Thamesport Marina, a relatively new facility that is perched on the steep river bank.

Marina Notes -- In 1995, the original docks were removed and replaced, adding finger piers and new pedestals. 160 ft. fuel dock. Volume discount for 500, 1000, 1500 gals. Maintenance has been good and the upgrades have continued with new heads and showers; a laundry is coming soon. Clubhouse deck and picnic area. Onsite is Fred's Shanty, an open air seafood shack (10am-11pm daily in season, 10am-7pm off-season). Fred leased "Fred's" for decades; in the early 90's, he purchased both the marina and property across the road. Atlantic Dive Center is also onsite. Several charter boats make their home here - for local or off-shore fishing adventures. Note: the constant wash from the traffic could make it rolly.

Notable -- Just up the street is Monte Cristo Cottage, the restored boyhood home of Pulitzer and Nobel Prize winning playwright Eugene O'Neill - named for the role his father played for decades (MemDay-LabDay, Tue-Sat 10am-5pm, Sun 1-5pm, call for winter schedule; $5). The New London Historical Shuttle stops here. Up the hill is Michael's Ice Cream and Dairy. A couple of miles south is the Eugene O'Neill Theater Center - home to 5 institutes and 3 theaters. New London's downtown is 2 miles up river with many eateries plus ferry terminals and Union Station; a bus runs along Pequot Ave making it easy to get there.

Burr´s Marina

Burr's Marina

244 Pequot Avenue; New London, CT 06320

Tel: (860) 443-8457 **VHF: Monitor** 9 **Talk** 68
Fax: (860) 443-8459 **Alternate Tel:** n/a
Email: burrsmarina@juno.com **Web:** n/a
Nearest Town: New London *(2 mi.)* **Tourist Info:** (860) 444-2206

Navigational Information
Lat: 41°20.103' **Long:** 072°05.873' **Tide:** 3 ft. **Current:** 3 kt. **Chart:** 13213
Rep. Depths (*MLW***): Entry** 12 ft. **Fuel Dock** 9 ft. **Max Slip/Moor** 9 ft./9 ft.
Access: Channel 0.5 mi. to Hess tanks, then bear NW to Green's Harbor

Marina Facilities *(In Season/Off Season)*
Fuel: *Valvtec* - Gasoline, Diesel
Slips: 136 Total, 30 Transient **Max LOA:** 100 ft. **Max Beam:** n/a
 Rate *(per ft.)*: **Day** $2.50/1.65 **Week** $15/9 **Month** $23/14
 Power: 30 amp Incl., 50 amp Incl., 100 amp n/a, 200 amp n/a
 Cable TV: Yes, Incl. **Dockside Phone:** No
 Dock Type: Fixed, Short Fingers, Pilings
Moorings: 25 Total, 6 Transient **Launch:** Yes (Free)
 Rate: Day $1.65/ft. **Week** $9/ft. **Month** $14/ft.
Heads: 6 Toilet(s), 5 Shower(s) *(with dressing rooms)*
Laundry: 2 Washer(s), 2 Dryer(s), Book Exchange **Pay Phones:** Yes, 2
Pump-Out: OnSite, Full Service, 1 Central **Fee:** $5 **Closed Heads:** Yes

Marina Operations
Owner/Manager: Peter Bergamo **Dockmaster:** Adam Bergamo
In-Season: May-Sep, 8am-6pm* **Off-Season:** Oct 1-Oct 31, 8am-5pm
After-Hours Arrival: Take any unoccupied slip near fuel dock
Reservations: Yes, Preferred **Credit Cards:** Visa/MC, Dscvr, Amex, Tex
Discounts: Sea Tow **Dockage:** 10% **Fuel:** n/a **Repair:** n/a
Pets: Welcome, Dog Walk Area **Handicap Access:** No

Marina Services and Boat Supplies
Services - Docking Assistance, Concierge, Boaters' Lounge, Dock Carts
Communication - Mail & Package Hold, Phone Messages, Data Ports *(Office)*, FedEx, AirBorne, UPS *(Sat Del)* **Supplies - OnSite:** Ice *(Block, Cube)* **Near:** Bait/Tackle, Live Bait **Under 1 mi:** Ships' Store **1-3 mi:** West Marine *(444-8755)* **3+ mi:** Boater's World *(440-3658, 4 mi.)*

Boatyard Services
OnSite: Travelift *(20T)*, Forklift, Hull Repairs **OnCall:** Rigger, Divers
Near: Engine mechanic *(gas, diesel)*, Electrical Repairs, Electronic Sales, Electronics Repairs, Bottom Cleaning, Brightwork, Air Conditioning, Refrigeration, Compound, Wash & Wax, Interior Cleaning. **Yard Rates:** $70/hr., Haul & Launch $7/ft. *(blocking $7/ft.)*, Power Wash $3/ft.

Restaurants and Accommodations
OnSite: Restaurant *(Schooners 860-437-3801, L $7-12, D $13-20)*
OnCall: Pizzeria *(Ocean Pizza 443-0870)* **Near:** Restaurant *(La Vie en Rose Bistro 555-8860, prixe fixe menu plus Salsa Fri & Sat)*, Seafood Shack *(Fred's Shanty 447-1701, L $2-12, D $2-12)*, Pizzeria *(Recovery Room Café 443-2619, L $5-15, D $5-15)* **Under 1 mi:** Restaurant *(Lighthouse Inn 443-8411 D $14-20)*, Seafood Shack *(Captain Scott's Lobster Dock 439-1741)*, Lite Fare *(Tia Teresa's 444-8066)* **1-3 mi:** Restaurant *(Bulkeley House 443-5533)*, Motel *(Red Roof Inn 444-0001, $45-95)*, Hotel *(Lighthouse Inn, $85-275)*,*(Holiday Inn 442-0631, $100-160)*, *(Radisson 443-7000, $65-175)*

Recreation and Entertainment
OnSite: Pool, Picnic Area, Grills, Fishing Charter *('A Vanga 848-0170, White Lightening 739-6906)* **Near:** Beach *(or Ocean Beach Park 2 mi. 447-3031)*, Playground, Dive Shop, Park *(Ft. Trumbull)*, Museum *(Monte Cristo Cottage)*, Special Events *(Sail-fest mid-July)* **Under 1 mi:** Tennis Courts **1-3 mi:** Golf Course *(Shennecossett Municipal 445-6912)*, Bowling *(Family Bowl 443-4232)*, Movie Theater, Video Rental *(Video Galaxy 437-0096)*, Video Arcade *(Ocean Beach)*, Cultural Attract *(Gardes Arts, Eugene O'Neill Theater)*, Sightseeing *(Coast Guard Academy 444-8270 9am-5pm, Free)*

Provisioning and General Services
Near: Convenience Store *(Sams 442-5227)*, Delicatessen *(R&B Cafe & Market Place 437-7712)*, Health Food, Wine/Beer *(Hartlings Spirit 442-8244)*, Bank/ATM, Florist **Under 1 mi:** Lobster Pound *(Capt. Scott's)*, Beauty Salon, Barber Shop, Bookstore *(Greene's Books & Beans 443-3312)* **1-3 mi:** Supermarket *(Stop & Save 442-7264)*, Bakery, Fishmonger, Post Office, Catholic Church, Protestant Church, Synagogue, Library *(447-1411)*, Dry Cleaners, Pharmacy *(Brooks 443-5048)*, Newsstand **3+ mi:** Department Store *(Crystal Mall, 7 mi.)*, Buying Club *(BJ's, 4 mi.)*

Transportation
OnCall: Rental Car *(Enterprise 442-8333)*, Taxi *(Harrys 442-4054)*, Airport Limo *(A Touch Of Class 440-3898)* **Near:** Local Bus *(and New London Historic Shuttle)* **1-3 mi:** InterCity Bus *(Greyhound 447-3841)*, Rail *(Amtrak)*, Ferry Service *(Cross-Sound, Block Isl., Fishers Isl.)* **Airport:** T.F. Green/Bradley *(50 mi./60 mi.)*

Medical Services
911 Service **Near:** Doctor *(Frese 442-0290)*, Dentist **1-3 mi:** Chiropractor *(Eastern Shore Chiropractic 444-6363)*, Holistic Services, Veterinarian *(Mobile Clinic 443-2348)* **Hospital:** Lawrence & Memorial 442-0711 *(1 mi.)*

Setting -- The second set of docks on the western shore of the Thames, about a mile from its mouth, is Burr's Marina. The facility is built into the river bank with both a pool and restaurant overlooking the water and the docks. The surrounding residential area has a small-town atmosphere.

Marina Notes -- *8am-7pm Fri, Sat & Sun. Closed Nov-Apr. Owned/operated by the Bergamo Family since 1961. Helpful and service-oriented. Mega fuel dock. Several sportfish charter boats make their home here. An onsite 20T travelift, a fork-lift, and extensive on-call services make this the most easily Sound-accessible haul-out in the harbor. Onsite is Schooners, a well-known harbor-front surf & turf restaurant featuring very local, very fresh fish -- inside with table cloths or outside on the covered deck.

Notable -- The nearby neighborhood is home to some interesting vintage houses including the boyhood home of Eugene O'Neill - Monte Cristo Cottage. Two miles north is a major transportation hub -- 3 major ferry lines, local buses and the Amtrak Station all converge within a couple of blocks -- making this area an interesting candidate for "leaving the boat" or crew changes. Farther along is mile-square downtown New London. Ocean Beach Park (447-3031) is a little over 2 miles south. It has an old fashioned boardwalk along its spectacular crescent-shaped beach, plus picnic area, pool, video arcade, miniature golf, bathhouse, fabulous playground, water slide, nature walks, entertainment, and food concessions. It's open Mem-LabDay 9am-10pm - admission: $7 per vehicle ($10 weekends). The Coast Guard Academy is 3 miles north just above the I-95 bridge. 11 miles to Mohegan Sun Casino.

Navigational Information
Lat: 41°21.103' **Long:** 072°05.709' **Tide:** 3 ft. **Current:** 3 kt. **Chart:** 13213
Rep. Depths (*MLW*): **Entry** 15 ft. **Fuel Dock** n/a **Max Slip/Moor** 12 ft./15 ft.
Access: Thames River past the railroad bridge

Marina Facilities (*In Season/Off Season*)
Fuel: No
Slips: 4 Total, 4 Transient **Max LOA:** 200 ft. **Max Beam:** n/a
  Rate (*per ft.*): **Day** $1.00 **Week** n/a **Month** n/a
  Power: 30 amp n/a, 50 amp n/a, 100 amp n/a, 200 amp n/a
  Cable TV: No **Dockside Phone:** No
  Dock Type: Fixed, Floating, Alongside, Wood
Moorings: 15 Total, 15 Transient **Launch:** n/a
  Rate: Day $20 **Week** n/a **Month** n/a
Heads: 6 Toilet(s), 6 Shower(s) (*with dressing rooms*)
Laundry: 2 Washer(s), 2 Dryer(s) **Pay Phones:** No
Pump-Out: OnSite, Self Service **Fee:** n/a **Closed Heads:** Yes

Marina Operations
Owner/Manager: Bruce Hyde, Dev.Dir. **Dockmaster:** Dave Crocker, Hrbmstr
In-Season: Year Round, 9am-5pm **Off-Season:** n/a
After-Hours Arrival: Call in advance
Reservations: Yes **Credit Cards:** n/a
Discounts: None
Pets: Welcome **Handicap Access:** Yes, Heads, Docks

New London Municipal Marina

Foot of State Street; New London, CT 06320

Tel: (860) 447-1777 **VHF: Monitor** 9 **Talk** 10
Fax: n/a **Alternate Tel:** n/a
Email: n/a **Web:** n/a
Nearest Town: New London (*0 mi.*) **Tourist Info:** (860) 447-5201

Marina Services and Boat Supplies
Services - Megayacht Facilities **Supplies - Near:** Ice (*Block, Cube*), Ships' Store (*at Crocker's*), Bait/Tackle, Live Bait, Propane **1-3 mi:** West Marine (*444-8755*), Boater's World (*440-3658, Waterford*), CNG (*Brewer's*)

Boatyard Services
Nearest Yard: Crocker's Boatyard (860) 443-6304

Restaurants and Accommodations
Near: Restaurant (*Hughie's 442-4844*), (*Bankok City 442-6970, L $5-10, D $10-20*), (*Tony D's 439-1943, D $11-23*), (*Les Papillions 447-9489, D $13-25, 4-course degustation $40+; Jazz every night*), (*Anastacia's 437-8005, L $5-10, D $9-14*), (*Bank St. Lobster House 447-9398, L $6-10, D $12-20, closed Mon*), (*Bulkeley House 447-7753, D $17-23, L, too*), (*Northern Indian 437-3978*), (*Bank St. Roadhouse 443-8280*), (*Zavala 437-1891, Mexican; closed Tue*), (*Galley Bar & Grill 437-1113*), Pizzeria (*Captain's 447-2820, B $3-4, L $5-7, D $6-15*) **Under 1 mi:** Restaurant (*Nathaniel's 447-8777, B $3-8, L $6-8, D $13-23*), (*Aqua Grille B $7-9, L $8-10, D $11-20, in the Radisson*), Hotel (*Radisson 443-7000*), (*Holiday Inn 442-0631, $100-160*), Inn/B&B (*Queen Ann 447-2600, $90-185*)

Recreation and Entertainment
OnSite: Picnic Area, Park (*Waterfront Park*), Special Events (*Sat Market Jun-Aug 11am-4pm crafts, art, food*) **Near:** Museum (*Custom House 447-2501 $5/0; Nathan Hale School House*), Cultural Attract (*Garde Arts Center - Eastern CT Symphony, theater, dance*), Galleries (*Yah-Ta-Hey - Native American cratfs 443-3204*) **Under 1 mi:** Playground, Fishing Charter (*Reelin' Sportfishing 442-7519*) **1-3 mi:** Beach (*Ocean Beach - by bus*),

Golf Course (*Shennecossett Muni 445-6912*), Bowling (*Family Bowl 443-4232*), Video Rental (*Video Galaxy*), Sightseeing (*US Coast Guard Academy 444-8511, Daily 10am-5pm, Free; tours of training barque, the square-rigger USCG "Eagle" Fri-Sun afternoons*)

Provisioning and General Services
Near: Delicatessen (*Roz's 437-3010, B $4, L $4-8*), Wine/Beer, Liquor Store (*Globe Spirits 442-2743*), Bakery (*Roberto's 447-2102*), Bank/ATM, Library (*447-1411*), Bookstore (*Greene's Books & Beans 443-3312*), Copies Etc. (*Curry 442-2679*) **Under 1 mi:** Market (*Patsy's 443-5748*), Supermarket (*Stop & Save 442-7264*), Gourmet Shop (*Saeed's 440-3822,*), Farmers' Market (*E. O'Neill Dr. & Pearl St., Jul-Oct, Tue & Fri, 9:30am-2pm 442-1530*), Lobster Pound (*Capt. Scott's*), Dry Cleaners, Pharmacy (*CVS 443-5359*), Hardware Store (*Handy Store 444-7900*)

Transportation
OnCall: Rental Car (*Enterprise 442-8333, United 443-1164*), Taxi (*Yellow Cab 443-4321, Harry's 444-2255, Curtin 443-1655*) **Near:** Local Bus (*SEAT 886-2631, New London Historic Sites Shuttle 447-9202*), InterCity Bus (*Greyhound 447-3841*), Rail (*Amtrak & Shoreline East 800-255-7433*), Ferry Service (*to Block Isl. 442-7891, Fishers Isl. 443-6851, Orient Point 443-5281, Montauk Point 631-668-5700, Fox to casinos 888-SAILFOX*)
Airport: T.F. Green (*50 mi.*)

Medical Services
911 Service **OnCall:** Veterinarian (*4-Paws 235-6244*) **Near:** Holistic Services (*Back Stage*) **Under 1 mi:** Chiropractor (*N.L. 442-8860*), Optician (*Hyder 437-3937*) **Hospital:** Lawrence & Memorial 442-0711 (*0.5 mi.*)

Setting -- The new New London Municipal Marina is right in the heart of a revitalizing downtown. The first stages are complete - incorporated into the Waterfront Park on the Thames are a new pier, a few floating docks, a mooring field and an attractive boaters' amenities building. The new Waterfront Promenade starts at the railroad bridge and runs the full length of downtown to Union Station - in front of the marina it is sprinkled with picnic tables.

Marina Notes -- Designed for transient boaters and visiting tall ships. The granite, marble and stainless steel heads, showers and laundry are in a brand new building - this is not your typical municipal issue. The NL Police's onsite facility should alleviate security concerns. Additional moorings planned for a total of 35. SeaPony, a 149-passenger boat docks at the city pier (behind Union Station) - harbor tours $12/8 or private charter (440-2734). Delta Queen cruise ship docks here, too. Restored 19thC Union Station is a few blocks away. Amtrak to NY City, Providence and Boston. All major ferries are within blocks.

Notable -- Home to concerts and festivals throughout the summer. Nearby is the oldest continuously operating custom house in the country: 1883 Robert Mills Custom House (May-Dec, Tue-Sun 1-5pm). Many casual, seafood and ethnic restaurants are closeby along historic Bank Street. For a tour of historic sites, call 447-9202 or catch the trolley at E. O'Neill Drive. (Visitors' Info Center also located here.) A trolley ride away is O'Neill's Monte Cristo Cottage (443-0051) and Eugene O'Neill Theater (443-5378). Fort Trumbull, built in 1839, has hiking trails, a boardwalk, fishing pier, and interactive exhibits (8am 'til sunset, 444-7591). Submarine Force Museum and Nautilus 694-3174 (free) is across the river, north of the I-95 bridge - a long but worthwhile cab ride.

Crocker's Boatyard

56 Howard Street; New London, CT 06320

Tel: (860) 443-6304; (800) 870-1285 **VHF: Monitor** 9 **Talk** 10
Fax: (860) 443-0279 **Alternate Tel:** (860) 439-8668
Email: dcrocker@aol **Web:** www.crockersboatyardinc.com
Nearest Town: New London (0.4 mi.) **Tourist Info:** (860) 444-2206

Navigational Information
Lat: 41°20.885' **Long:** 072°06.002' **Tide:** 3 ft. **Current:** 0 kt. **Chart:** 13213
Rep. Depths (MLW): **Entry** 12 ft. **Fuel Dock** 12 ft. **Max Slip/Moor** 12 ft./-
Access: Past Ft.Trubull, then sharp turn to port

Marina Facilities (In Season/Off Season)
Fuel: Gulf - Gasoline, Diesel
Slips: 230 Total, 50 Transient **Max LOA:** 96 ft. **Max Beam:** 20 ft.
  Rate (per ft.): **Day** $2.00/1.50* **Week** $9.00 **Month** n/a
  Power: 30 amp Incl., **50 amp** Incl., **100 amp** Incl., **200 amp** n/a
  Cable TV: No **Dockside Phone:** Yes
  Dock Type: Floating, Short Fingers, Wood
Moorings: 0 Total, 0 Transient **Launch:** n/a, Dinghy Dock
  Rate: Day n/a **Week** n/a **Month** n/a
Heads: 8 Toilet(s), 8 Shower(s) (with dressing rooms), Hair Dryers
Laundry: None **Pay Phones:** Yes, 2
Pump-Out: OnCall, Full Service **Fee:** $5 **Closed Heads:** Yes

Marina Operations
Owner/Manager: Dave Crocker **Dockmaster:** Cyril Crocker
In-Season: Apr-Sep, 8am-5pm **Off-Season:** Oct-Mar, 8am-4:30pm
After-Hours Arrival: Call ahead
Reservations: Yes, Required **Credit Cards:** Visa/MC, Dscvr
Discounts: None
Pets: Welcome, Dog Walk Area **Handicap Access:** Yes, Heads, Docks

Marina Services and Boat Supplies
Services - Docking Assistance, Security (Card Keys), Trash Pick-Up, Dock Carts, Megayacht Facilities **Communication** - Mail & Package Hold, Phone Messages, Fax in/out (Free), Data Ports (Chandlery), FedEx, AirBorne, UPS, Express Mail (Sat Del) **Supplies - OnSite:** Ice (Block, Cube), Ships' Store **OnCall:** CNG **Near:** Bait/Tackle (Stalker Bait 444-7577), Propane **1-3 mi:** West Marine (444-8755), Boater's World (440-3658)

Boatyard Services
OnSite: Travelift (35T & 75T), Engine mechanic (gas, diesel), Electrical Repairs, Electronic Sales, Hull Repairs, Brightwork, Compound, Wash & Wax, Interior Cleaning, Propeller Repairs, Woodworking, Painting, Awlgrip, Yacht Broker (Hellier Yacht Sales) **OnCall:** Rigger, Sail Loft, Canvas Work, Bottom Cleaning, Air Conditioning, Refrigeration, Divers, Inflatable Repairs, Life Raft Service, Upholstery, Metal Fabrication **Dealer for:** Evinrude, Jphnson, MerCruiser, Volvo. **Member:** ABBRA, ABYC - 2 Certified Tech (s) **Yard Rates:** $75/hr., Haul & Launch $8/ft. (blocking $2/ft.), Power Wash $2.10/ft. **Storage:** In-Water $44.30/ft., On-Land Out $37/ft. In $6.25/sq.ft.

Restaurants and Accommodations
Near: Restaurant (Hughie's 443-6436), (Bulkeley House 443-5533, D $17-23), (Nathaniel's 447-8777, B $3-8, L $6-8, D $13-23, M-F 11-10, Sat 9am+, Sun 8am+, Early Bird - 2 for $17), Seafood Shack (Captain Scotts Lobster 439-1741), Lite Fare (Neon Chicken 444-6366, L, D $5-15), (Saeed's 440-3822), (Candy's Cozy Kitchen 444-6531), Pizzeria (Captain's 447-2820, L $5-7, D $6-15) **Under 1 mi:** Restaurant (Winthrop's 443-7000, L $5-15, D $15-25), (Bangkok 442-6970, L, D, $8-16), (Tony D's 439-1943, D $11-23), Hotel (Radisson 443-7000, $65-175), (Holiday Inn 442-0631, $100-160)

Recreation and Entertainment
OnSite: Pool, Picnic Area, Grills **Under 1 mi:** Jogging Paths, Roller Blade/Bike Paths, Fishing Charter, Movie Theater (Secret Theater 442-2787), Video Rental (Movie Gallery 437-0096), Cultural Attract (Garde Arts Center 444-7373), Galleries **1-3 mi:** Beach, Playground, Tennis Courts, Golf Course (Shennecossett Mun. 445-0262), Bowling (Family Bowl 443-4232), Museum (Lyman Allyn Art 443-2545; Submarine Force 694-3174)

Provisioning and General Services
OnSite: Wine/Beer (Grand Spirit 445-1044), Liquor Store (Harvest 443-4440), Fishmonger, Lobster Pound, Copies Etc. (Sir Speedy)
Near: Convenience Store (Mobil; Patsys 443-5748), Delicatessen (Shaw's Cove 442-3773), Health Food, Bakery, Catholic Church, Dry Cleaners, Laundry, Pharmacy (Brooks 445-7455), Hardware Store (Schneider 442-5713) **Under 1 mi:** Gourmet Shop, Bank/ATM, Post Office, Protestant Church, Synagogue, Library (447-1411), Bookstore (Greene's 443-3312), Florist, Retail Shops **1-3 mi:** Supermarket (Stop & Save 442-7264), Farmers' Market, Department Store (Crystal Mall), Buying Club (B.J.'s)

Transportation
OnCall: Rental Car (Enterprise 442-8333), Taxi (Harrys 444-2255), Airport Limo **Near:** Local Bus **Under 1 mi:** InterCity Bus (SEAT), Rail (Amtrak), Ferry Service (Cross-Sound, Fishers Is, Block Is) **Airport:** Groton (8 mi.)

Medical Services
911 Service OnCall: Ambulance **Near:** Holistic Services **Under 1 mi:** Doctor, Dentist, Chiropractor (New London 442-8860) **Hospital:** Lawrence & Memorial 444-4733 (1 mi.)

Setting -- This conveniently located boatyard/marina is tucked into Shaw's Cove -- a very quiet, almost land-locked basin behind a railroad draw bridge. A pool and flower-filled planters attempt, with some success, to soften the boatyard atmosphere and industrial views. Crocker's neighborhood is the beneficiary of the new riverfront park and boardwalk that runs from Union Station to Shaw's Cove, stopping at the far side of the railroad bridge - a 0.25 mile walk.

Marina Notes -- *Rates: $2/ft to 45', $3/ft 46-59'. A family operation since 1881, Crocker's has been servicing all manner of vessels - small, large, power and sail - ever since. Basin is very quiet with very little roll. The railroad swing bridge opens on request (unless train is imminent) - Ch.13 - from 5am-10pm, Apr-Nov - other times 8 hrs. notice needed. Several sport fishing charters make their home here including Brother's Too 447-8490 & M&M 437-3491. Good heads and showers and attractive 20 x 44 foot pool overlooking the docks and basin. Complete marine store onsite.

Notable -- Within a mile is a major transportation hub - ferries, Amtrak, intercity buses - making this a good place to leave the boat or change crews. Buses go to Foxwoods & Mohegan Sun Casinos. The quickly revitalizing New London downtown scene is close at hand -- all packed into one square mile. Farmers' Market at E. O'Neill Dr. & Pearl St., Jul-Oct, Tue & Fri, 9:30am-2pm 442-1530. Sail Fest - early July, Harvard-Yale Regatta - early June, Italian Fest - early Aug. The "Discover Historic New London Shuttle" tours a dozen sites Sat 10am-5pm & Sun 1-5pm, $5; it leaves from Trolley Building. (O'Neill Dr. & Golden St.) every 30 min. Project Oceanology & The Lighthouse Program offer fascinating tours and cruises on maritime history, ocean testing, lobstering $9-17 445-9007.

PHOTOS ON CD-ROM: 9

Navigational Information
Lat: 41°31.400' **Long:** 072°04.850' **Tide:** 3 ft. **Current:** n/a **Chart:** 12372
Rep. Depths *(MLW):* **Entry** 14 ft. **Fuel Dock** 14 ft. **Max Slip/Moor** 10 ft./-
Access: 12 mi. north of LI Sound, just past marker 53

Marina Facilities *(In Season/Off Season)*
Fuel: Gasoline, Diesel
Slips: 200 Total, 80 Transient **Max LOA:** 171 ft. **Max Beam:** n/a
 Rate *(per ft.):* **Day** $2.50* **Week** n/a **Month** n/a
 Power: 30 amp 7.25, **50 amp** 10.50, **100 amp** 17.95, **200 amp** n/a
 Cable TV: Yes, $4 **Dockside Phone:** No
 Dock Type: Floating, Concrete
Moorings: 0 Total, 0 Transient **Launch:** n/a
 Rate: **Day** n/a **Week** n/a **Month** n/a
Heads: 3 Toilet(s), 1 Shower(s) *(with dressing rooms)*
Laundry: 2 Washer(s), 2 Dryer(s) **Pay Phones:** No
Pump-Out: OnSite, 1 Central, 1 Port **Fee:** Free **Closed Heads:** No

Marina Operations
Owner/Manager: Ron Aliano/Valerie Aliano **Dockmaster:** Kurt Delaney
In-Season: Apr 1-Oct 31, 8am-5pm **Off-Season:** Nov 1-Mar 31, 10am-4pm
After-Hours Arrival: Dock and check in at office in the morning
Reservations: Yes, Preferred **Credit Cards:** Visa/MC, Dscvr, Amex
Discounts: Nautical Miles **Dockage:** 10% **Fuel:** $0.10 **Repair:** n/a
Pets: Welcome, Dog Walk Area **Handicap Access:** Yes, Heads, Docks

The Marina at American Wharf
One American Wharf; Norwich, CT 06360

Tel: (860) 886-6363; (888) 489-4273 **VHF: Monitor** 68 **Talk** 68
Fax: (860) 887-2467 **Alternate Tel:** (860) 886-6363
Email: dockmaster@ameri-group.com **Web:** www.americanwharf.com
Nearest Town: Norwich *(0 mi.)* **Tourist Info:** (860) 444-4257

Marina Services and Boat Supplies
Services - Docking Assistance, Security *(Gate enclosed)*, Dock Carts
Communication - Mail & Package Hold, Data Ports *(Office)*, FedEx,
AirBorne, UPS, Express Mail **Supplies - OnSite:** Ice *(Cube)*, Live Bait
Near: Ships' Store **3+ mi:** Boater's World *(10 mi.)*

Boatyard Services
OnCall: Canvas Work, Bottom Cleaning, Air Conditioning *(Mystic Yacht Restoration)* **Near:** Engine mechanic *(gas)*, Launching Ramp *(Public Launch Ramp)*, Electrical Repairs, Electronic Sales, Electronics Repairs.
Nearest Yard: Thayer's Marien (860) 887-8315

Restaurants and Accommodations
OnSite: Restaurant *(Americus On the Wharf 887-8555, L $8-15, D $8-28)*
OnCall: Lite Fare *(Liberty Tree 886-4465, B $3-6, L $3-10, D $6-10)*,
Pizzeria *(Dominos 887-4567)* **Under 1 mi:** Lite Fare *(D'Elia's Bakery & Grinder Shop 887-1062)*, Pizzeria *(Olympic 886-0196)* **1-3 mi:** Restaurant *(Bella Fiore 887-9030, L $6-12, D $12-25)*, *(Modestos L $12, D $25)*, *(Norwich Inn D $19-28, spa menu or "American")*, Motel *(Comfort Suites 892-9292, $100-140)*, Hotel *(Ramada 889-5201, $70-160)*, *(Marriot Courtyard 886-2600, $90-160)*, Inn/B&B *(Norwich Inn & Spa 886-2401, $130-375, major restoration in 1999 - probably the most elegant lodging in eastern CT including a world class spa)*

Recreation and Entertainment
OnSite: Pool, Picnic Area, Grills, Sightseeing *(Norwich Harbor Tours)*
Near: Park *(Award-winning Chelsea Harbor Park; Mohegan Park)*, Cultural Attract *(Donald Oat Theater, Spirit of Broadway)* **Under 1 mi:** Tennis Courts

(Mohegan Park), Jogging Paths *(Mohegan Park)*, Video Rental, Museum *(Slater Museum 887-2506 Tue-Fri 9-4, Sat&Sun 1-4 full-size replicas of the most famous statues of anient civilizations; Gaultieri Children's Gallery, too)*
1-3 mi: Fitness Center *(Norwich Inn & Spa - a full-service spa with 30+ treatment rooms 886-2401)*, Bowling *(Norwich Ten Pin)* **3+ mi:** Golf Course *(Norwich Municipal Golf Course, River Ridge Golf Course, 4 mi.)*, Fishing Charter *(Groton/Waterford, 10 mi.)*

Provisioning and General Services
Near: Convenience Store *(H & L)*, Bakery, Bank/ATM, Library *(Otis Library 889-2365)*, Bookstore, Newsstand **Under 1 mi:** Market *(P&M 886-9899)*, Liquor Store *(Square Package 887-2324)*, Green Grocer *(Sunshine Farms 823-1832)*, Post Office, Catholic Church, Protestant Church, Pharmacy *(CVS 887-7887)* **1-3 mi:** Supermarket *(Shop Rite 887-6088)*, Synagogue, Hardware Store, Florist, Retail Shops, Copies Etc. *(Staples)* **3+ mi:** Department Store *(Wal-Mart 889-7745, 4 mi.)*, Buying Club *(BJ's, 10 mi.)*

Transportation
OnSite: Courtesy Car/Van *(Courtesy van to casinos by reservation.)*
OnCall: Rental Car *(Enterprise 886-5603)*, Taxi *(Norwich 848-2227, Yellow 536-8888)* **Near:** Local Bus **3+ mi:** Rail *(New London, 10 mi.)*, Ferry Service *(Block Island, Orient Point, 10 mi.)*
Airport: Groton/Bradley *(10 mi./50 mi.)*

Medical Services
911 Service **OnCall:** Ambulance **1-3 mi:** Doctor *(West Side Medical 889-1400)*, Dentist, Holistic Services *(Norwich Inn 886-2401)*, Veterinarian *(North Stonington 535-3666)* **Hospital:** William Backus 889-3609 *(3 mi.)*

Setting -- Located at the head of the Thames River, 12 miles from the New London Ledge Light, The Marina at American Wharf is at the heart of the successful Norwich Harbor waterfront redevelopment plan. The multi-million dollar marina's classic, Jeffersonian-influenced architecture and grounds -- with its carefully tended flower borders, large swaths of perfect grass, and nicely maintained docks -- make this facility worth the trip.

Marina Notes -- * Weekends $2.75/ft. Holidays $3.25/ft. Built in 1987. Good heads & showers. Wonderful pool. Courtesy van to casino, shopping, hotels. Casino package - $75 plus dockage (min 2-nights): round trip trans. to Foxwoods, Match Play & Foxwood buffet coupons, cont. breakfast for 2, $50 gift certificate for Americus Restaurant, and electricity. The onsite, very pretty and petite all-glass Americus On the Wharf Restaurant offers inside/outside casual fine dining, 7 days, late Apr-early Nov. Extensive list of specials 2pm-midnight; $9.95 buffet lunch from 11:30am-2:30pm. Light menu also available for L/D.

Notable -- The picture-perfect New England town of Norwich sits at the confluence of the Thames, Yantic and Shetucket Rivers and has an abundance of 18th & 19thC structures (pick up walking tour brochure from the Tourist Office). Across the channel is Putts Up Dock, an unusual and wild 19-hole miniature golf course. The marina nearest to Foxwoods (800-FOXWOODS) and Mohegan Sun (888-226-7711) Casinos, and also to the truly amazing Mashantucket Pequot Museum & Research Center. The Mashantucket tracks the history of the Pequot Tribe with interactive, indoor/outdoor exhibits including a re-created 16thC village, computer simulations and 13 mini documentaries (Mem-LabDay daily 10am-7pm; off season 10am-6pm, closed Tue $12/8 800-411-9671).

The Marina at American Wharf

CT - FISHERS ISLAND SOUND

PHOTOS ON CD-ROM: 6

Harbor Hill Marina & Inn

Harbor Hill Marina & Inn

60 Grand Street; Niantic, CT 06357

Tel: (860) 739-0331 **VHF: Monitor** n/a **Talk** n/a
Fax: (860) 691-3078 **Alternate Tel:** (860) 673-4904
Email: info@innharborhill.com **Web:** www.innharborhill.com
Nearest Town: New London *(6 mi.)* **Tourist Info:** (860) 443-8332

Navigational Information
Lat: 41°19.520' **Long:** 072°11.230' **Tide:** 3 ft. **Current:** 2 kt. **Chart:** 13211
Rep. Depths *(MLW)*: **Entry** 10 ft. **Fuel Dock** n/a **Max Slip/Moor** 6 ft./-
Access: Niantic Bay through both bridges into Niantic River to western shore

Marina Facilities *(In Season/Off Season)*
Fuel: No
Slips: 70 Total, 5 Transient **Max LOA:** 48 ft. **Max Beam:** 17 ft.
 Rate *(per ft.)*: **Day** $2.50 **Week** n/a **Month** n/a
 Power: 30 amp Incl., **50 amp** n/a, **100 amp** n/a, **200 amp** n/a
 Cable TV: Yes, Incl. **Dockside Phone:** No
 Dock Type: Floating, Long Fingers, Wood
 Moorings: 0 Total, 0 Transient **Launch:** n/a
 Rate: Day n/a **Week** n/a **Month** n/a
Heads: 4 Toilet(s), 4 Shower(s) *(with dressing rooms)*
Laundry: None **Pay Phones:** No
Pump-Out: OnCall **Fee:** $5 **Closed Heads:** No

Marina Operations
Owner/Manager: Chuck Keefe **Dockmaster:** Ed Gottert
In-Season: Apr-Nov 1, 7am-7pm **Off-Season:** Closed
After-Hours Arrival: Call in advance
Reservations: Yes **Credit Cards:** Visa/MC, Amex
Discounts: None
Pets: Welcome, Dog Walk Area **Handicap Access:** Yes, Heads, Docks

Marina Services and Boat Supplies
Services - Docking Assistance, Security (7am-7pm, On premises), Trash Pick-Up, Dock Carts **Communication -** Mail & Package Hold, Phone Messages, Fax in/out ($1), FedEx, AirBorne, UPS, Express Mail *(Sat Del)* **Supplies - Near:** Ice *(Block, Cube)*, Ships' Store *(Boats Inc 739-6251)*, Bait/Tackle *(J&B 739-7419)* **1-3 mi:** Propane *(Amerigas 443-3591)*

Boatyard Services
OnSite: Launching Ramp **Nearest Yard:** Boats Inc. (860) 739-6251

Restaurants and Accommodations
OnSite: Inn/B&B *(Inn at Harbor Hill Marina 673-6485, $105-195)*
Near: Restaurant *(Constantine's 739-2848, L $4-10, D $8-20)*, *(Dad's of Niantic 739-2113)*, *(Morton House 739-9074)*, *(Seashell 739-6767)*, *(China May)*, Seafood Shack *(Skipper's 434-4852, L $2-13, D $2-13, weekdays 11-9, weekends 'til 10)*, Coffee Shop *(Dunkin Donuts)*, Lite Fare *(Hartford Grinder 739-3181)*, Pizzeria *(Family Pizza)*, Inn/B&B *(Niantic Inn 739-5451, $150)* **Under 1 mi:** Restaurant *(Unks 443-2717, L $10-12, D $12-20)*, *(Sunset Ribs 443-7427)* **1-3 mi:** Motel *(Days Inn 739-6921, $70-150)*

Recreation and Entertainment
OnSite: Picnic Area, Grills, Boat Rentals *(Kayaks)* **Near:** Beach *(Crescent Beach - dinghy, ask about beach passes)*, Playground, Fishing Charter, Movie Theater *(Niantic Cinema 443-5725)*, Museum *(Millstone Information & Science Center 691-4670 - focus on nucler energy; Childrens Museum of SE Conn. 691-1255 - 4mi.)* **Under 1 mi:** Group Fishing Boat *(Sunbeam-Capt John's 443-7259, Black Hawk)* **1-3 mi:** Fitness Center *(Waterford Athletic Center 447-2464)*, Park *(Harkness Memorial State Park 443-5725)*,

Cultural Attract *(Harkness summer concerts; Eugene O'Neill Memorial Theatre - 6 mi)* **3+ mi:** Golf Course *(Cedar Ridge 691-4568, 4.5 mi.)*, Horseback Riding *(Nob Hill Training Center 739-4727, 5 mi.)*, Bowling *(Family Bowl 443-4232, 5 mi.)*, Video Rental *(Video Galaxy 437-0096, 4 mi.)*, Special Events *(Lobsterfest-May, Sailfest-Jul, Outdoor Art Fest-Aug, 5 mi.)*

Provisioning and General Services
Near: Convenience Store *(Trax)*, Supermarket *(Adams 739-8136, Colonial)*, Delicatessen *(Sicilianas, Clubhouse 739-0222)*, Health Food *(Natural Food 739-9916)*, Wine/Beer *(Village Wine)*, Liquor Store *(Marina Spirit 739-2300)*, Bakery *(Village Bake 739-9638)*, Bank/ATM, Post Office, Catholic Church, Protestant Church, Other *(Baptist)*, Beauty Salon, Barber Shop, Dry Cleaners, Laundry, Bookstore *(Ada's Book Shelf 739-0308, Book Barn)*, Pharmacy *(Smiths 739-8930, CVS)*, Newsstand, Florist **Under 1 mi:** Market *(IGA)*, Farmers' Market, Fishmonger, Lobster Pound **1-3 mi:** Library *(East Lyme 739-6926)*, Hardware Store *(Follett Hardware 442-3142)*, Copies Etc. *(Presley Printing 739-0389)*

Transportation
OnCall: Rental Car *(Enterprise 442-8333)*, Taxi *(Yellow Cab 739-7775)* **3+ mi:** InterCity Bus *(Greyhound 447-3841, 7 mi.)*, Rail *(New London, 7 mi.)*, Ferry Service *(7 mi.)* **Airport:** Groton/Bradley *(7 mi./40 mi.)*

Medical Services
911 Service **OnCall:** Ambulance **Under 1 mi:** Holistic Services *(Natural Body Therapeutic Massage 739-5927; Abintra 739-0502)* **1-3 mi:** Doctor **3+ mi:** Chiropractor *(Chiropractic Center Of East Lyme 691-0434, 3.5 mi.)* **Hospital:** Lawrence & Memorial 442-0711 *(6.5 mi.)*

Setting -- On the western shore of the Niantic River-- in a sheltered cove, directly north of The Bar -- is this pretty, recently renovated, bed & breakfast and marina. Lovingly tended lawns and flower borders roll down to the carefully maintained docks. On the hill above the marina, lawn chairs and picnic tables, with sweeping views of the River and Bay provide a perfect place for a bite or a respite.

Marina Notes -- Comfortable slips with full finger piers radiate from a single floating dock. Launching ramp. Picnic tables and gas grills, located on the patio, are surrounded by flower gardens. Marina guests also have access to the wicker seating on the Inn's lovely front porch and to the easy chairs on the lawn. The large, clean boathouse has been recently renovated. The inn consists of 8 air-conditioned guest rooms with private baths, TV's and water views - some with balconies. Sportfishing charter onsite. Kayaks for guest use. Bay view meeting room for small gatherings. This part of the River is a very protected gunkhole. Bridges can be an issue: first bridge is an 11 ft. railroad bascule - open unless a train is imminent. The second is Rte. 156's 32 ft.- opens on request. Now pump-out boat onsite.

Notable -- A stone's throw are two seafood shacks: Skippers and Dad's. It's easy walking distance (0.2 mi.) to "downtown" Niantic - restaurants, shops, beaches, and two supermarkets. A dinghy ride across the river (or 0.7 mi. walk) will net another selection of restaurants. Nearby Millstone Info & Science Center has interactive exhibits on all kinds of energy - especially on nuclear reactors like the one whose towers are easily visible as you arrive (and from the beach).

Navigational Information

Lat: 41°19.578' **Long:** 072°11.208' **Tide:** 3 ft. **Current:** 2 kt. **Chart:** 13211
Rep. Depths (*MLW*): Entry 8 ft. **Fuel Dock** 7 ft. **Max Slip/Moor** 7 ft./-
Access: Niantic Bay, through both bridges, to western side of river

Marina Facilities *(In Season/Off Season)*

Fuel: *Mobil* - Gasoline, Diesel
Slips: 81 Total, 3 Transient **Max LOA:** 58 ft. **Max Beam:** n/a
  Rate *(per ft.):* **Day** $1.75/Inq. **Week** Inq. **Month** n/a
  Power: 30 amp Yes, 50 amp n/a, 100 amp n/a, 200 amp n/a
  Cable TV: Yes, Incl. **Dockside Phone:** No
  Dock Type: Floating, Long Fingers, Wood
Moorings: 0 Total, 0 Transient **Launch:** n/a
  Rate: Day n/a **Week** n/a **Month** n/a
Heads: 7 Toilet(s), 6 Shower(s)
Laundry: None **Pay Phones:** Yes, 1
Pump-Out: OnCall, 1 Port **Fee:** $5 **Closed Heads:** No

Marina Operations

Owner/Manager: Scott Bowden **Dockmaster:** n/a
In-Season: Apr 15-Oct, 8:30-4:30 **Off-Season:** Nov-Apr 14, 8:30-4:30
After-Hours Arrival: Call in advance
Reservations: Yes, Required **Credit Cards:** Visa/MC
Discounts: Boat/US **Dockage:** 25% **Fuel:** Inq. **Repair:** Inq.
Pets: Welcome **Handicap Access:** Yes, Heads, Docks

Port Niantic Marina

17 Smith Avenue; Niantic, CT 06357

Tel: (860) 739-2155 **VHF: Monitor** 9 **Talk** 11
Fax: (860) 739-4681 **Alternate Tel:** n/a
Email: port.niantic.inc@snet.net **Web:** www.portniantic.com
Nearest Town: New London *(6 mi.)* **Tourist Info:** (860) 443-8332

Marina Services and Boat Supplies

Services - Docking Assistance, Dock Carts **Communication -** Data Ports *(Office)*, FedEx, UPS, Express Mail **Supplies - OnSite:** Ice *(Block, Cube)*, Ships' Store **Near:** Bait/Tackle *(J & B Tackle 739-7419)* **1-3 mi:** Marine Discount Store *(Defenders)* **3+ mi:** Propane *(Amerigas 848-9277, 3.5 mi.)*

Boatyard Services

OnSite: Travelift *(35T)*, Electrical Repairs, Electronic Sales, Electronics Repairs, Hull Repairs, Rigger, Bottom Cleaning, Brightwork, Air Conditioning, Refrigeration, Divers, Compound, Wash & Wax, Interior Cleaning, Woodworking, Metal Fabrication, Painting, Awlgrip **OnCall:** Sail Loft, Propeller Repairs, Inflatable Repairs, Life Raft Service, Upholstery, Yacht Interiors **Near:** Engine mechanic *(gas, diesel)*, Launching Ramp.
Dealer for: Westerbeke, Sealand, Marine Power, Marine Air, Universal, Mercruiser, Marine Air, Algae-X, Max Power, Guardian, PSS Shaft.
Member: ABBRA, ABYC - 2 Certified Tech(s) **Yard Rates:** $65/hr., Haul & Launch $8/ft. *(blocking $5/ft.)*, Power Wash $2.75, Bottom Paint $12.30/ft.
Storage: In-Water L x Beam x $2.50/ft., On-Land L x Beam x $2.50/ft.

Restaurants and Accommodations

Near: Restaurant *(Morton House 739-9074, L & D)*, *(Constantines 739-2848, L $4-10, D $8-20)*, *(China May)*, Seafood Shack *(Skipper's 434-4852, L $2-13, D $2-13, 11am-9pm, to 10pm weekends)*, Lite Fare *(Dad's 739-2113)*, Pizzeria *(Seaview 739-4020)*, Inn/B&B *(Inn at Harbor Hill Marina 739-0331, $105-195)* **Under 1 mi:** Restaurant *(Unks 443-2717, L $10-12, D $12-20)*, *(Sunset Rib)*, *(LaCasa)*, Seafood Shack *(Angler's at Niantic Sport Fishing Dock)*, Fast Food *(Mc Donalds)*, Motel *(Niantic Inn 739-5451, $150)* **1-3 mi:** Motel *(Day's Inn 739-6921, $70-150)*, Hotel *(Holiday Inn 739-5483)*

Recreation and Entertainment

OnSite: Picnic Area, Grills, Fishing Charter *(Atlantic Flyway 442-6343)* **Near:** Boat Rentals, Group Fishing Boat, Movie Theater *(Niantic Cinema 443-5725)*, Video Rental, Museum *(Millstone Information & Science Center 691-4670; Children's Museum Of SE Conn. 691-1255 - 4mi.)* **Under 1 mi:** Beach, Playground, Park **1-3 mi:** Fitness Center *(Waterford Athletic Center 447-2464)*, Video Arcade, Cultural Attract *(Harkness summer concerts)* **3+ mi:** Golf Course *(Cedar Ridge 691-4568, 4.5 mi.)*

Provisioning and General Services

OnCall: Liquor Store *(Marina Spirit Shoppe 739-2300)* **Near:** Convenience Store, Supermarket *(Adams 739-8136, Colonial)*, Gourmet Shop, Delicatessen *(Hartford Giant Grinder 739-3181)*, Health Food *(Natural Food Store 739-9916)*, Bakery *(Niantic)*, Meat Market, Bank/ATM, Beauty Salon, Barber Shop, Bookstore *(Ada's Book Shelf 739-0308)*, Newsstand, Florist **Under 1 mi:** Fishmonger *(Angler at Niantic Sport Fishing)*, Lobster Pound, Post Office, Catholic Church, Protestant Church, Dry Cleaners, Laundry, Pharmacy *(Smiths 739-8930)* **1-3 mi:** Hardware Store *(Follett 442-3142)*

Transportation

OnCall: Rental Car *(Enterprise 442-8333)*, Taxi *(Yellow Cab 739-7775)* **3+ mi:** Rail *(New London, 7mi.)*, Ferry Service *(New London, 7 mi.)* **Airport:** Bradley *(40 mi.)*

Medical Services

911 Service **OnCall:** Ambulance **3+ mi:** Doctor *(4 mi.)*, Chiropractor *(Chiropractic Center of East Lyme 691-0434, 4 mi.)* **Hospital:** Lawrence & Memorial 442-0711 *(6.5 mi.)*

Setting -- A combination dry-stack storage operation and full-service boat-yard/marina, Port Niantic is the second set of docks on the western shore of the Niantic River above the draw bridges. It caters mostly to sportfishing boats and is clearly identifiable by its large storage shed.

Marina Notes -- In addition to the 81 deep, wide floating slips, there are 100 indoor racks with "valet" launch service. Pump out, repairs, haul-out, fuel, inside or outside winter storage, ice, heads and a small picnic area, all available onsite. Started in 1989, Port Niantic offers true inside winter storage home for power boats up to 30 tons on concrete floors. Small yard that promises personal attention and ABBRA certified technicians. J.B. Tackle shop is adjacent.

Notable -- Great fishing onsite or off-shore and good water skiing up the river. A quarter mile walk to town could well cover all possible provisioning and service needs -- including a large Adams Supermarket and a Colonial Market -- along with a number of eateries. Nearby Skippers specializes in fried clams. Dinghy across the river or walk the 0.7 mile footpath across the bridge for another assortment of eating opportunities. Angler's Seafood shack at the Niantic Sportfishing Docks, a lobster pound and fish market, Unk's, Sunset Rib, and LaCasa -- all full service waterfront restaurants. Niantic Sportfish is also home to a number of charter boats including Dot-E-Dee (739-7419) - half day $480, full day $600, evening $350. Ask at Port Niantic for recommendations of other sportfishing charters.

III. Connecticut: Connecticut River

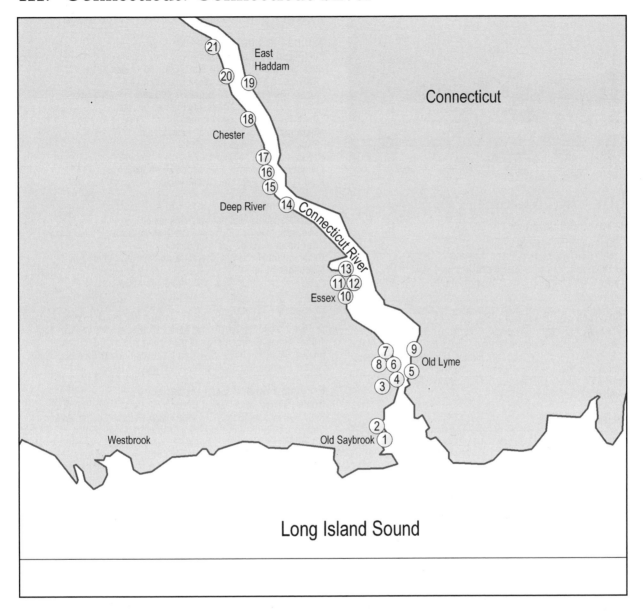

MAP	MARINA	HARBOR	PAGE	MAP	MARINA	HARBOR	PAGE
1	Harbor One Marina	Conn River/Saybrook Pt	52	12	Essex Island Marina	Conn River/Essex	63
2	Saybrook Point Inn	Conn River/Saybrook Pt	53	13	Brewer Dauntless Shipyard	Conn River/Essex	64
3	Ragged Rock Marina	Connecticut River	54	14	Brewer Deep River Marina	Connecticut River	65
4	Between the Bridges	Connecticut River	55	15	Chester Marina	Connecticut River	66
5	Old Lyme Dock Co.	Connecticut River	56	16	Castle Marina	Conn River/Chester Cr	67
6	Oak Leaf Marina	Connecticut River	57	17	Hays Haven Marina	Conn River/Chester Cr	68
7	Offshore East Marina	Conn River/Ferry Pt Basin	58	18	Chrisholm Marina	Connecticut River	69
8	Brewer Ferry Point Marina	Conn River/Ferry Pt Basin	59	19	Goodspeed Opera House	Connecticut River	70
9	Old Lyme Marina	Connecticut River	60	20	Andrews Marina at Harper's Landing	Connecticut River	71
10	The Chandlery at Essex	Connecticut River	61	21	Damar Ltd. / Midway Marina	Connecticut River	72
11	Essex Boat Works	Conn. River/Essex	62				

Harbor One Marina

Harbor One Marina

26 Bridge Street; Old Saybrook, CT 06475

Tel: (860) 388-9208 **VHF: Monitor** 9 **Talk** 9
Fax: (860) 342-0544 **Alternate Tel:** (860) 342-1085
Email: n/a **Web:** www.portlandboatworks.com/harbor1.htm
Nearest Town: Old Saybrook *(1.5 mi.)* **Tourist Info:** (860) 388-3266

Navigational Information
Lat: 41°16.920' **Long:** 072°21.080' **Tide:** 3 ft. **Current:** 3 kt. **Chart:** 12375
Rep. Depths *(MLW):* **Entry** 12 ft. **Fuel Dock** 10 ft. **Max Slip/Moor** 8 ft./-
Access: L.I. Sound to Connecticut R, 1 mile from main channel breakwater

Marina Facilities *(In Season/Off Season)*
Fuel: *Texaco* - Gasoline, Diesel
Slips: 86 Total, 5 Transient **Max LOA:** 100 ft. **Max Beam:** n/a
 Rate *(per ft.):* **Day** $2.00 **Week** Inq. **Month** Inq.
 Power: 30 amp Incl., **50 amp** Incl., **100 amp** Incl., **200 amp** n/a
 Cable TV: Yes, Incl. **Dockside Phone:** Yes, Incl.
 Dock Type: Fixed, Long Fingers, Pilings, Wood
Moorings: 0 Total, 0 Transient **Launch:** n/a
 Rate: Day n/a **Week** n/a **Month** n/a
Heads: 4 Toilet(s), 4 Shower(s)
Laundry: 2 Washer(s), 2 Dryer(s) **Pay Phones:** Yes, 1
Pump-Out: No **Fee:** n/a **Closed Heads:** No

Marina Operations
Owner/Manager: Paul Barton **Dockmaster:** n/a
In-Season: May-Oct, 8am-8pm **Off-Season:** Nov-Apr, 8am-6pm
After-Hours Arrival: Call in advance
Reservations: Preferred **Credit Cards:** Visa/MC, Amex, Tex
Discounts: None
Pets: Welcome, Dog Walk Area **Handicap Access:** No

Marina Services and Boat Supplies
Services - Docking Assistance, Concierge, Security, Trash Pick-Up, Dock Carts, Megayacht Facilities **Communication -** Mail & Package Hold, Phone Messages, Data Ports *(at slip on pedestal)*, FedEx, AirBorne, UPS, Express Mail **Supplies - OnSite:** Ice *(Cube)*, Ships' Store **Near:** Propane **1-3 mi:** Bait/Tackle *(Rivers End 388-2283)*, CNG *(Brewer Ferry Pt. 388-3260)* **3+ mi:** Boat/US *(399-3170, 4.5 mi.)*

Boatyard Services
OnSite: Electrical Repairs, Electronics Repairs, Hull Repairs, Brightwork, Refrigeration **Nearest Yard:** Between the Bridges (860) 388-1431

Restaurants and Accommodations
OnSite: Lite Fare *(By the C Cafe 388-0506, B $2-5, L $4-10)*
OnCall: Pizzeria *(Fiore 388-2699)*, *(Paesan's 399-8280)* **Near:** Restaurant *(Saybrook Pt. Dock & Dine 388-2010, L $6-13, D $13-25, 11:30am-10pm, Kids' menu)*, *(Terra Mar Grille 388-1111, B $6-13, L $8-15, D $23-31, 7-10am, 11:30-2, 6-9pm, Sun Brunch $26/16 11-2pm)*, Hotel *(Saybrook Pt Inn & Spa 395-2000, $180-330)* **1-3 mi:** Restaurant *(Bill's Seafood 399-1101)*, *(Main St Tavern 395-1094)*, *(Andriana's Italian Seafood 388-0408)*, Coffee Shop *(AM Cup 388-3309)*, Motel *(Comfort Inn 395-1414, $60-140)*, *(Liberty Inn 388-1777, $50-100)*, Inn/B&B *(Deacon Timothy Pratt 395-1229)*

Recreation and Entertainment
OnSite: Heated Pool, Picnic Area, Grills **Near:** Golf Course *(Fenwick 388-2516)*, Fitness Center, Jogging Paths, Fishing Charter *(Sea Sprite 669-9613)*, Park *(Ft. Saybrook Monument 388-2622, $2 donation)*, Sightseeing *(Old Saybrook Trolley 388-3266; African Queen 388-2007)*,

Galleries *(Saybrook Colony Artists* **Under 1 mi:** Beach *(Harvey's 395-3152 & Town)*, Video Rental, Cultural Attract *(Town Concerts Wed Jul-Aug)*
1-3 mi: Tennis Courts *(Old Saybrook Tennis 388-5115 $16/Court)*, Bowling *(AMF 388-3488)*, Museum *(Saybrook Walking Tour 388-3266)*, Special Events *(Arts & Crafts Fest - last weekend July)*

Provisioning and General Services
OnSite: Bakery *(Bagel Girls)* **Under 1 mi:** Convenience Store, Gourmet Shop, Fishmonger, Bank/ATM, Post Office, Catholic Church, Protestant Church, Library, Beauty Salon, Dry Cleaners, Laundry, Florist, Retail Shops **1-3 mi:** Supermarket *(Stop & Shop 388-6166)*, Delicatessen *(Saybrook Deli 395-0015)*, Wine/Beer, Liquor Store *(Old Colony 388-3820)*, Farmers' Market *(Cinema Plaza Sat, Old Saybrook Shopping Plaza Wed, 633-1067)*, Bookstore *(Harbor Books 388-6850)*, Pharmacy *(CVS 388-1045)*, Hardware Store *(Saybrook 388-3706)*, Copies Etc. *(Old Saybrook Print 388-1864)*

Transportation
OnSite: Local Bus *(Old Saybrook Trolley - 9am-10pm - Jul-Aug 7 days, May&Sep - Sat&Sun only $1 ride/$3 Day)* **OnCall:** Rental Car *(Enterprise 395-0758, Airways 399-5146)*, Taxi *(East Shore Cab 388-2819)*, Airport Limo *(Essex 767-2152)* **Near:** Bikes *(Saybrook Pt. Inn)* **Under 1 mi:** Rail *(Shore Line East 777-7433)* **Airport:** Bradley *(55 mi.)*

Medical Services
911 Service **Near:** Holistic Services *(Saybrrok Pt Spa 395-3245)*
Under 1 mi: Dentist, Ambulance **1-3 mi:** Doctor *(Community Health Center 388-4433)*, Chiropractor *(Yates 388-5781)* **3+ mi:** Veterinarian *(Saybrook 388-9681, 4 mi.* **Hospital:** Middlesex 358-3700 *(8 mi.*

Setting -- The first facility on the Connecticut River's western shore, just past South Cove, family oriented, quiet, professional Saybrook Point Marina provides a close and welcome respite. The slightly raised attractive pool, gazebo, and pool-house have long views of South Cove and across to Fenwick. Well-groomed grounds blend into the natural marsh and stands of sea oats. Across the River, bucolic Great Island's Roger Tory Peterson Wildlife area is a water fowl haven.

Marina Notes -- A wave fence -- which goes right to the bottom -- lessens some of the roll in a breeze. Separate megayacht dock with 3-phase power. Two sets of bath houses with 4 heads, 2 showers each. Home of Sea Tow. Cloud 9's By the C Café is located here, open 7 days, 7:30am-2:30pm. Right next door is Saybrook Point Inn; some of its facilities are available for a fee (One-day fitness & Pool Pass $15 with a treatment - $40 & up - 6am-10pm 395-3245). North Cove YC, Ch.9, may have moorings - reciprocal.

Notable -- The 18-hole Saybrook Point Miniature Golf (388-2407), Saybrook Pt. Park and Pavilion, Saybrook Dock & Dine, an ice cream stand, and the Saybrook Point Inn are close by. 1.5 miles to a large shopping center, discount mall, supermarket, six movie theaters and a summer stock theater. The Chamber of Commerce Trolley makes a 22-stop hourly loop through town, the RR station, the malls, and out to the beaches. Get the CofC 's self-guided 37-stop historic walking tour (www.oldsaybrook.com/ walktour). In town, is 1790 James Gallery & Soda Fountain (395-1406) ice cream, maritime art & concerts. The African Queen, the original steam launch from the movie, runs tours during Jul&Aug 388-2007. 400 antique dealers in 4 centers in a 2 mi. stretch.

Navigational Information
Lat: 41°17.000' **Long:** 072°21.000' **Tide:** 3 ft. **Current:** 3 kt. **Chart:** 12375
Rep. Depths (MLW): Entry 18 ft. **Fuel Dock** 18 ft. **Max Slip/Moor** 7 ft./-
Access: L.I. Sound to Connecticut R, 1 mile from main channel breakwater

Marina Facilities *(In Season/Off Season)*
Fuel: *Valvtect* - Gasoline, Diesel, High-Speed Pumps
Slips: 125 Total, 35 Transient **Max LOA:** 200 ft. **Max Beam:** n/a
  Rate *(per ft.)*: **Day** $3.50/Inq. **Week** $22.75 **Month** Inq.
  Power: 30 amp $9, 50 amp $18, 100 amp $35, 200 amp $50
  Cable TV: Yes, Incl. **Dockside Phone:** Yes, Inq.
  Dock Type: Fixed, Floating, Long Fingers, Short Fingers, Pilings
Moorings: 0 Total, 0 Transient **Launch:** n/a
  Rate: Day n/a **Week** n/a **Month** n/a
Heads: 20 Toilet(s), 10 Shower(s), Hair Dryers
Laundry: 2 Washer(s), 2 Dryer(s) **Pay Phones:** Yes, 4
Pump-Out: OnSite, Full Service, 1 Central **Fee:** Free **Closed Heads:** Yes

Marina Operations
Owner/Manager: Stephen Tagliatela **Dockmaster:** Jeff Howe
In-Season: May-Nov 14, 7:30am-Dusk **Off-Season:** Nov 15-Apr, 8am-6pm
After-Hours Arrival: Choose slip, register at the inn
Reservations: Yes, Preferred **Credit Cards:** Visa/MC, Dscvr, Din, Amex
Discounts: Boat/US **Dockage:** 10% **Fuel:** Inq. **Repair:** Inq.
Pets: Welcome, Dog Walk Area **Handicap Access:** Yes, Heads, Docks

Saybrook Point Marina

2 Bridge Street; Old Saybrook, CT 06475

Tel: (860) 395-3080 **VHF: Monitor** 9 **Talk** 11
Fax: (860) 388-1504 **Alternate Tel:** (860) 395-2000
Email: saybrook@snet.net **Web:** www.saybrook.com
Nearest Town: Old Saybrook *(1.5 mi.)* **Tourist Info:** (860) 388-3266

Marina Services and Boat Supplies
Services - Docking Assistance, Concierge, Security *(24 Hrs.)*, Trash Pick-Up, Dock Carts, Megayacht Facilities **Communication -** Mail & Package Hold, Phone Messages, Fax in/out, Data Ports *(at the Inn)*, FedEx, AirBorne, UPS, Express Mail *(Sat Del)* **Supplies - OnSite:** Ice *(Block, Cube)*, Ships' Store **Near:** Bait/Tackle, Live Bait **Under 1 mi:** Marine Discount Store **1-3 mi:** CNG *(Brewer Ferry Pt.388-3260)* **3+ mi:** Boat/US *(399-3170, 4.5 mi.)*, Propane *(Lagasse's 399-6996, 6 mi.)*

Boatyard Services
OnCall: Engine mechanic *(gas, diesel)*, Electrical Repairs, Electronics Repairs, Rigger, Sail Loft, Bottom Cleaning, Air Conditioning, Refrigeration, Divers, Compound, Wash & Wax, Interior Cleaning **Nearest Yard:** Oak Leaf Marina (860) 388-9817

Restaurants and Accommodations
OnSite: Restaurant *(Terra Mar Grille 388-1111, B $6-13, L $8-15, D $23-31, Sun Brunch $26/16)*, Hotel *(Saybrook Point Inn & Spa 395-2000, $180-330)* **OnCall:** Pizzeria *(Paesan's 399-8280)* **Near:** Restaurant *(Dock & Dine 388-2010, L $6-13, D $13-25)* **Under 1 mi:** Snack Bar **1-3 mi:** Restaurant *(Bills Seafood 399-5442)*, *(Lee & Eddies 388-3482)*, Fast Food *(Burger King)*, Motel *(Comfort Inn 395-1414, $60-140)*, *(Days Inn 388-3453)*, Inn/B&B *(Deacon Timothy Pratt 395-1229)*

Recreation and Entertainment
OnSite: Pool, Heated Pool, Spa, Grills, Playground, Fitness Center, Roller Blade/Bike Paths, Fishing Charter, Video Rental **Near:** Picnic Area, Golf Course *(Fenwick G.C. 388-2516)*, Jogging Paths, Boat Rentals, Park *(18 acre Ft. Saybrook 388-2622)*, Sightseeing, Galleries *(Saybrook Colony Artists)* **Under 1 mi:** Beach *(Harvey's & Town - dinghy)* **1-3 mi:** Tennis Courts *(Old Saybrook 388-5115 $16/Ct.)*, Bowling *(Amf 388-3488)*, Museum *(1767 Gen. Hart House 388-2622)*, Cultural Attract *(Village Green concerts Wed 7-8pm, Jul-Aug)*

Provisioning and General Services
OnSite: Laundry, Copies Etc. *(Business Center)* **OnCall:** Dry Cleaners **Near:** Newsstand **Under 1 mi:** Convenience Store, Health Food, Wine/Beer, Fishmonger, Lobster Pound **1-3 mi:** Supermarket *(Stop & Shop 388-6166)*, Delicatessen *(Saybrook Deli 395-0015)*, Liquor Store *(Old Colony 388-3820)*, Bakery, Farmers' Market *(Sat 9-12, Wed 10-2 633-1067)*, Bank/ATM, Post Office, Catholic Church, Protestant Church, Synagogue, Library, Bookstore *(Harbor Books 388-6850)*, Pharmacy *(CVS 388-1045)*, Hardware Store *(Saybrook 388-3706)*, Florist, Retail Shops

Transportation
OnSite: Courtesy Car/Van *(when available)*, Bikes *(free)*, Local Bus *(Trolley - 9am-10pm - Jul-Aug, $1 or $3/day pass)* **OnCall:** Rental Car *(Enterprise 395-0758, Thrifty 399-5146)*, Taxi *(Essex 767-7433)*, Airport Limo *(Essex 767-2152)* **1-3 mi:** Rail *(Shorline East 777-7433, Amtrak 800-USA-RAIL)* **Airport:** Groton/Bradley *(20 mi./55 mi.)*

Medical Services
911 Service **OnSite:** Holistic Services *(Spa)* **Under 1 mi:** Ambulance **1-3 mi:** Doctor *(MHS 395-1212)*, Chiropractor *(Connaughty 388-1654)* **3+ mi:** Dentist *(Clinic, 5 mi.)*, Veterinarian *(Saybrook 388-9681, 4 mi.)* **Hospital:** Middlesex 358-3700 *(8 mi.)*

Setting -- A state-of the-art, high-end resort at the mouth of the River, is the second facility to port with wide open vistas across to Great Island and out to L.I. Sound. The 700 ft breakwater, enclosed network of docks, and signature "lighthouse" dockhouse sit directly in front of the compact, luxurious resort.

Marina Notes -- 30-200 amp service. Concierge. Recycling bins. Indoor & outdoor heated pools, hot tub, steam bath & whirlpool, and fitness center - free for marina guests (Aquacize $8). Spa fees same as hotel guests: range $11-145. Hrs: Indoor Pool 5:30am-10pm, Outdoor (adjacent to slips) 9am-Dusk, Fitness Center 7am-10pm. Spa Tue-Thu 9-5, Fri-Sat 9-6, Sun-Mon 9-3. 80 Rooms, furnished in 18thC reproductions, many with fireplaces and water views - discount for marina guests. 9 function rooms for groups to 210. Third resort on this site - a country hotel, Pease House, built in 1870 was razed in the late 50's for the Gatsby-like Terra Mar resort, demolished in the early '80s. Current Inn opened in '89 with a new marina. Well-reviewed, elegant Terra Mar Grille - Break: M-Sat 7-10, Sun 8-10, Sun Br 11:30-2, Lunch: M-F 11:30-2, Sat 12-2:30, Dinner: Sun-Thu 5:30-9, Fri&Sat 'til 10. Lounge's light menu 11:30-9/10.

Notable -- Old Saybrook Trolley stops onsite - hourly access to 22 stops throughout the town. 1.5 miles to large shopping center, discount mall, supermarket, 6 movie/summer stock theaters. Private Fenwick C.C.'s golf course is nearby 388-2516. Superbly executed and maintained 18-hole Saybrook Pt Mini Golf adjacent., along with the Saybrook Pt. Park and Pavilion. Onsite fishing charters - Sea Sprite (669-9613) $525 full day/450 half. Across the river, Great Island's Roger Tory Peterson Wildlife Area is a water fowl haven and dinghy destination.

Navigational Information

Lat: 41°18.700' **Long:** 072°21.520' **Tide:** 4 ft. **Current:** 2 kt. **Chart:** 12375
Rep. Depths *(MLW):* **Entry** 5 ft. **Fuel Dock** n/a **Max Slip/Moor** 8 ft./-
Access: Western side of River, just past RR bascule bridge, long cut to basin

Marina Facilities *(In Season/Off Season)*

Fuel: No
Slips: 243 Total, 2 Transient **Max LOA:** 55 ft. **Max Beam:** n/a
  Rate *(per ft.):* **Day** $2.00/Inq. **Week** Inq. **Month** Inq.
  Power: 30 amp Incl., **50 amp** n/a, **100 amp** n/a, **200 amp** n/a
  Cable TV: Yes, Incl. **Dockside Phone:** No
  Dock Type: Floating, Long Fingers, Wood, Aluminum
Moorings: 0 Total, 0 Transient **Launch:** n/a
  Rate: Day n/a **Week** n/a **Month** n/a
Heads: 8 Toilet(s), 8 Shower(s), Hair Dryers
Laundry: 2 Washer(s), 2 Dryer(s) **Pay Phones:** Yes, 1
Pump-Out: OnSite, 1 Central **Fee:** $5 **Closed Heads:** Yes

Marina Operations

Owner/Manager: J. Van Epps & J. Champion **Dockmaster:** Keven Detoro
In-Season: Year-Round, 8am-5pm **Off-Season:** n/a
After-Hours Arrival: Call in advance
Reservations: Yes **Credit Cards:** Visa/MC, Dscvr
Discounts: None
Pets: Welcome, Dog Walk Area **Handicap Access:** Yes, Heads

Ragged Rock Marina

PO Box 860; 54 Ferry Road; Old Saybrook, CT 06475

Tel: (860) 388-1049 **VHF: Monitor** 16 **Talk** n/a
Fax: (860) 388-3050 **Alternate Tel:** (860) 388-1049
Email: n/a **Web:** n/a
Nearest Town: Essex *(1 mi.)* **Tourist Info:** (860) 388-3266

Marina Services and Boat Supplies

Services - Docking Assistance, Security *(8am - 5pm)*, Trash Pick-Up, Dock Carts **Communication -** Mail & Package Hold, Fax in/out, FedEx, AirBorne, UPS, Express Mail **Supplies - OnSite:** Ice *(Block, Cube)*, Ships' Store **Under 1 mi:** Bait/Tackle *(Rivers End Tackle 860-388-2283)*, CNG *(Brewer Ferry Pt.388-3260)* **3+ mi:** West Marine *(7 mi.)*, Boat/US *(399-3170, 5 mi.)*

Boatyard Services

OnSite: Travelift *(20T)*, Engine mechanic *(gas, diesel)*, Launching Ramp, Electrical Repairs, Hull Repairs, Rigger, Bottom Cleaning, Brightwork, Divers, Compound, Wash & Wax, Interior Cleaning **Under 1 mi:** Air Conditioning, Refrigeration. **1-3 mi:** Electronics Repairs, Sail Loft.

Restaurants and Accommodations

Near: Restaurant *(Saybrook Fish House 388-4836, L $5-10, D $12-22)*, *(Ship To Shore 395-0611, B $2-6, L $4-9, D $10-19, 7 days, 7am-9pm)* **Under 1 mi:** Motel *(Comfort Inn 395-1414, $60-140)*, *(Liberty Inn 388-1777)* **1-3 mi:** Restaurant *(Pat's Country Kit 388-4784, L $12, D $15)*, *(Wine & Roses 388-9646, L $12, D $15)*, Seafood Shack *(Johny's Ad's 388-4032)*, Pizzeria *(Pizza Hut 388-3437)*, Inn/B&B *(Saybrook Point Inn 395-2000, $180-330)* **3+ mi:** Motel *(Sandpiper 399-7973, $85-110, 4 mi.)*

Recreation and Entertainment

OnSite: Picnic Area, Grills, Playground **Near:** Roller Blade/Bike Paths **Under 1 mi:** Fishing Charter **1-3 mi:** Beach, Dive Shop, Tennis Courts, Golf Course *(Fenwick G.C. 388-2516)*, Fitness Center *(Saybrook Fitness & Aerobics 388-6303)*, Horseback Riding, Boat Rentals, Bowling *(Amf Saybrook 388-3488)*, Video Rental *(Variety Video 388-6313)*, Park, Sightseeing **3+ mi:** Museum *(Florence Griswold 434-5542, 4 mi.)*

Provisioning and General Services

OnSite: Newsstand **Near:** Fishmonger **Under 1 mi:** Delicatessen *(Cloud Nine 388-0800)* **1-3 mi:** Convenience Store, Supermarket *(Stop & Shop 388-6166)*, Gourmet Shop, Health Food, Wine/Beer, Liquor Store *(Genes Package Store 388-9549)*, Bakery, Farmers' Market *(Cinema Plaza Sat 9-12 & Old Saybrook Shopping Plaza Wed 10-2 633-1067)*, Green Grocer, Lobster Pound, Meat Market, Post Office, Catholic Church, Protestant Church, Synagogue, Other, Library, Beauty Salon, Barber Shop, Dry Cleaners, Bookstore *(The Happy Carrot 434-0380, Harbor Books 388-6850)*, Pharmacy *(CVS 388-1045)*, Hardware Store *(Christiansen Hardware 434-7053)*, Florist, Clothing Store, Retail Shops, Department Store, Buying Club, Copies Etc.

Transportation

OnCall: Rental Car *(Enterprise 395-0758)*, Taxi *(East Shore Cab 388-2819)*, Airport Limo *(Essex Limo)* **Near:** Local Bus *(Old Saybrook Trolley $1/$3 Day)* **1-3 mi:** InterCity Bus, Rail *(Old Saybrook Commuter)* **3+ mi:** Ferry Service *(New London, 20 min.)* **Airport:** Groton/Bradley *(17 mi./55 mi.)*

Medical Services

911 Service **Near:** Dentist, Chiropractor *(Connaughty 388-1654)* **1-3 mi:** Doctor *(Shoreline Family 434-1661)*, Holistic Services *(Essence 388-1002)*, Ambulance, Veterinarian *(Saybrook Vet 388-9681)* **Hospital:** Middlesex 767-3700 *(5 mi.)*

Setting -- Just past the railroad bascule bride, on the western shore is the entrance to the half-mile long channel that accesses Ragged Rock's extremely well-protected, deep, virtually enclosed basin. Once inside, the environment is quiet, rural and "boat yard"; views are of the surrounding marsh, with its stands of sea oats, and the basin which is literally filled with docks.

Marina Notes -- Two marina buildings anchor each side of the basin. Well-equipped ships store in east building along with one set of heads. West building houses second set of heads and has a play gym in front. Primarily a seasonal resident marina with some transit slips. Most boat yard services are available onsite. Established in 1973 by current owner Joan Van Epps. 2 sets of heads and showers - basic but the showers have dressing rooms. A four foot spot tends to shoal at the entrance, but is dredged regularly; check with the dockmaster before entering. Amtrak and the Connecticut Shoreline Commuter Rail runs along the "right of way" channel and across the end of the marina. The station is in downtown Old Saybrook.

Notable -- Other services and amenities are not easily at hand -- there's a small pub 0.3 mi. -- but the Chamber of Commerce's Old Saybrook Trolley makes all services, provsioning options, entertainment and recreation easily reachable. The Trolley loops hourly stopping at 22 places downtown, the railroad station, the historic district, the malls, and out to some of the marinas and beaches (9am-10pm - Jul-Aug 7 days, May&Sep - Sat&Sun only $1/$3 Day). The nearest stop is a short walk. The CofC also publishes a 37-stop historic walking tour of downtown.

Navigational Information
Lat: 41°18.960' **Long:** 072°21.040' **Tide:** 3 ft. **Current:** 1 kt. **Chart:** 12375
Rep. Depths *(MLW)*: **Entry** 15 ft. **Fuel Dock** 15 ft. **Max Slip/Moor** 15 ft./-
Access: Western shore of CT River, past bascule bridge and Ragged Rock

Marina Facilities *(In Season/Off Season)*
Fuel: *Texaco* - Gasoline, Diesel, High-Speed Pumps
Slips: 425 Total, 20 Transient **Max LOA:** 100 ft. **Max Beam:** n/a
  Rate *(per ft.)*: **Day** $2.50/$2.00* **Week** Inq. **Month** $25/15
  Power: 30 amp Incl., 50 amp Incl., 100 amp n/a, 200 amp n/a
  Cable TV: Yes **Dockside Phone:** Yes Direct tel.
  Dock Type: Floating, Long Fingers, Wood
Moorings: 0 Total, 0 Transient **Launch:** n/a
  Rate: Day n/a **Week** n/a **Month** n/a
Heads: 8 Toilet(s), 8 Shower(s) *(with dressing rooms)*
Laundry: 1 Washer(s), 1 Dryer(s) **Pay Phones:** Yes
Pump-Out: OnSite, Full Service **Fee:** $10 **Closed Heads:** No

Marina Operations
Owner/Manager: Fred Autorino/Mike Pendelton **Dockmaster:** Same
In-Season: May-Nov 15, 7am-8pm **Off-Season:** Nov 15-Apr
After-Hours Arrival: Call in advance
Reservations: Yes, Preferred **Credit Cards:** Visa/MC, Dscvr, Amex, Tex
Discounts: Boat/US **Dockage:** 25% **Fuel:** $0.10 **Repair:** n/a
Pets: Welcome, Dog Walk Area **Handicap Access:** No

Between the Bridges

142 Ferry Road; Old Saybrook, CT 06475

Tel: (860) 388-1431 **VHF: Monitor** 9 **Talk** n/a
Fax: (860) 395-3101 **Alternate Tel:** (860) 388-1431
Email: info@betweenthebridges.com **Web:** www.betweenthebridges.com
Nearest Town: Old Saybrook *(3 mi.)* **Tourist Info:** (860) 388-3266

Marina Services and Boat Supplies
Services - Docking Assistance, Concierge, Trash Pick-Up, Dock Carts
Communication - Mail & Package Hold, Phone Messages, Fax in/out,
FedEx, AirBorne, UPS, Express Mail **Supplies - OnSite:** Ice *(Block)*
Under 1 mi: Bait/Tackle *(Teds 388-4882)*, CNG *(Brewer Ferry Pt)*
3+ mi: Boat/US *(399-3170, 5 mi.)*, Propane *(Lagasse 399-6996, 6 mi.)*

Boatyard Services
OnSite: Travelift *(25T - 65T)*, Forklift *(20-45T)*, Crane *(40T)*, Engine
mechanic *(gas, diesel)*, Electrical Repairs, Hull Repairs, Bottom Cleaning,
Brightwork, Air Conditioning, Refrigeration, Compound, Wash & Wax, Interior
Cleaning, Woodworking, Awlgrip **OnCall:** Electronics Repairs, Rigger, Sail
Loft, Propeller Repairs, Metal Fabrication **Dealer for:** Volvo, Mercruiser,
PMC, Crusader, Detroit Diesel. Other Certifications: Volvo, Merc, PCM
Yard Rates: $70-80/hr., Haul & Launch $6.50-10/ft. *(blocking yes)*, Power
Wash $3/ft., Bottom Paint $1.50/sq.ft. *(paint incl.)* **Storage:** On-Land Inside
$65/ft., Outside $24/ft.

Restaurants and Accommodations
OnSite: Restaurant *(Ocean's 11 Martini Bar & Grill)*, Snack Bar **Under 1
mi:** Restaurant *(Ship To Shore 395-0611, B $2-6, L $4-9, D $10-19, 7 days,
7am-9pm)*, *(Saybrook Fish House 388-4836, L $5-10, D $12-22)*, Motel
(Comfort Inn 395-1414, $60-140), Inn/B&B *(Liberty Inn 388-1777, $50-100)*
1-3 mi: Restaurant *(Andrianas Seafood 388-0408)*, Fast Food, Pizzeria
(Pizza Works 388-2218), Hotel *(Saybrook Point 395-2000, $180-330)*

Recreation and Entertainment
OnSite: Pool, Picnic Area, Grills **OnCall:** Fishing Charter *(Eden - Capt

Retano 388-5897) **Near:** Jogging Paths, Roller Blade/Bike Paths **Under 1
mi:** Dive Shop, Tennis Courts **1-3 mi:** Beach, Golf Course *(Fenwick 388-
2516)*, Horseback Riding *(Saybrook Fitness 388-6303)*, Boat Rentals *(North
Shore Outfitters 388-5485)*, Video Rental *(Variety Video 388-6313)*, Park *(Ft
Saybrook Monument 388-2622 Don: $2)* **3+ mi:** Bowling *(Amf 388-3488, 4
mi.)*, Museum *(Griswold 434-5542, 4 mi.)*

Provisioning and General Services
OnSite: Newsstand, Hardware Store, Copies Etc. **Under 1 mi:** Delica-
tessen *(Cloud Nine 388-0800)* **1-3 mi:** Supermarket *(Stop & Shop
388-6166)*, Wine/Beer, Liquor Store *(Genes Package Store 388-9549)*,
Bakery *(Vanderbrooke 388-9700)*, Farmers' Market *(Cinema Plaza Sat 9-12
& Old Saybrook Shopping Plaza Wed 10-2 633-1067)*, Bank/ATM, Post
Office, Catholic Church, Protestant Church, Library, Beauty Salon, Barber
Shop, Dry Cleaners, Bookstore *(The Happy Carrot 434-0380)*, Pharmacy
(CVS 388-1045), Retail Shops, Department Store *(Wal-Mart 388-0621)*

Transportation
OnSite: Courtesy Car/Van, Local Bus *(Old Saybrook Seasonal Trolley -
9am-10pm - Jul-Aug 7 days, May&Sep - Sat&Sun only)* **OnCall:** Rental
Car *(Enterprise 395-0758)*, Taxi *(East Shore Cab 388-2819)*
Airport: Groton/Bradley *(17 mi./55 mi.)*

Medical Services
911 Service **OnCall:** Ambulance **Near:** Dentist **Under 1 mi:** Chiropractor
(Connaughty 388-2819) **1-3 mi:** Doctor *(Community Health Center 388-
4433)*, Holistic Services *(Essence 388-1002)*, Veterinarian *(Saybrook Vet
388-9681)* **Hospital:** Middlesex Hospital 358-3700 *(6 mi.)*

Setting -- At a narrow point in the Connecticut River, between the railroad bascule bride and the 81-ft. I95 bridge, this large, full-service, carefully maintained marina sprawls along the western shore. The contemporary, sharply-angled, cedar-sided and concrete shoreside buildings lend a bit of dramatic flair to the bucolic riverscape. A pool perches a few steps up from the parking lot and, a full flight up, is the Ocean's 11 restaurant deck - affording panoramic views of the marina, the River and both bridges.

Marina Notes -- In 1998 a consortium acquired Saybrook Marine Services and River Landing Marina, combined and renovated them into their current incarnation - creating North and South yards, about a quarter mile apart. Currently all transient activities are focused at the North Yard. 350 foot fuel dock. Full-service onsite boatyard with 65T travel lift. Inside rack storage - summer & winter- for boats to 50 ft. TowBoat US. North Yard,142 Ferry Road - 388-1431 South Yard, 2 Clark Street - 388-3614. The plan is for the BY services to be gradually migrated to the South Yard. *Group rates $2.00/1.50 per ft.

Notable -- Onsite Ocean's 11, a new eatery in '03, features a "rat pack" theme, vintage Sinatra music and Italian food. Old Saybrook Trolley stops onsite and offers hourly service to 22 stops throughout the town from 9am-10pm during summer. This provides access to all provisioning and general services as well as to restaurants, recreation and entertainment venues. The CofC publishes a walking tour of historic Old Saybrook. Katharine Hepburn's family home was on Fenwick Point and the original African Queen tours the river from the Saybrook Yacht Basin.

Old Lyme Dock Co.

Old Lyme Dock Co.

323 Ferry Road; Old Lyme, CT 06371

Tel: (860) 434-2267 **VHF: Monitor** 9 **Talk** 7
Fax: n/a **Alternate Tel:** n/a
Email: n/a **Web:** www.oldlymedock.com
Nearest Town: Old Lyme *(1 mi.)* **Tourist Info:** (860) 388-3266

Navigational Information

Lat: 41°18.881' **Long:** 072°20.668' **Tide:** 3 ft. **Current:** 3 kt. **Chart:** 12375
Rep. Depths *(MLW)*: **Entry** 16 ft. **Fuel Dock** 13 ft. **Max Slip/Moor** 13 ft./13 ft.
Access: LI Sound to Connecticut River, 2 miles north on eastern shore

Marina Facilities *(In Season/Off Season)*

Fuel: *Texaco* - Slip-Side Fueling, Gasoline, Diesel
Slips: 25 Total, 4 Transient **Max LOA:** 100 ft. **Max Beam:** n/a
 Rate *(per ft.)*: **Day** $1.25 **Week** Inq. **Month** Inq.
 Power: 30 amp Incl., **50 amp** Incl., **100 amp** Incl., **200 amp** n/a
 Cable TV: No **Dockside Phone:** No
 Dock Type: Fixed, Floating, Alongside
Moorings: 20 Total, 4 Transient **Launch:** No
 Rate: Day $25 **Week** Inq. **Month** Inq.
Heads: 1 Toilet(s), 1 Shower(s)
Laundry: None **Pay Phones:** No
Pump-Out: No **Fee:** n/a **Closed Heads:** No

Marina Operations

Owner/Manager: Herb Chambers/Dave Peterson **Dockmaster:** n/a
In-Season: Summer, 8am-Dusk **Off-Season:** Spring/Fall, 8am-Dark
After-Hours Arrival: Call ahead
Reservations: Preferred **Credit Cards:** Visa/MC, Dscvr, Din, Amex, Tex
Discounts: None
Pets: Welcome, Dog Walk Area **Handicap Access:** No

Marina Services and Boat Supplies

Services - Docking Assistance, Concierge, Dock Carts **Communication -** FedEx, Express Mail **Supplies - OnSite:** Ice *(Block, Cube)*, Ships' Store **OnCall:** Propane **1-3 mi:** Bait/Tackle *(Teds Bait & Tackle 388-4882)*, CNG *(Brewer Ferry Point Marina 388-3260)* **3+ mi:** Boat/US *(399-3170, 6 mi.)*

Boatyard Services

OnCall: Electrical Repairs, Electronics Repairs, Hull Repairs **Nearest Yard:** Between the Bridges (860) 388-1431

Restaurants and Accommodations

OnCall: Pizzeria *(Illiano's 434-1110)* **Near:** Restaurant *(Ocean's 11 395-0372, dinghy across the river)* **Under 1 mi:** Restaurant *(The Hideaway 434-3335, L $5-8, D $12-21, overlooking the Lieutenant River)*, *(Hong Kong II 434-3788)*, *(Anne's Kitchen & Bistro)*, Coffee Shop *(Bess Eaton)*, *(Coffee Works)*, Pizzeria *(Toby One)* **1-3 mi:** Restaurant *(The Bee & Thistle 434-1667, B $3-7, L $10-16, D $21-30, B Mon-Sat 8-10am, Sun 8-10:30am, L: Wed-Sat 11:30am-2pm; D Wed-Mon 6pm, Sun Brunch: 11am-2pm $14-18)*, *(Old Lyme Inn 434-2600, L $6-11, D $15-27)*, Inn/B&B *(Old Lyme Inn 434-2600, $100-180)*, *(Bee & Thistle Inn 395-1414, $80-220)*

Recreation and Entertainment

Near: Jogging Paths, Roller Blade/Bike Paths **Under 1 mi:** Fitness Center *(Curves)*, Video Rental *(Video Circuit 434-2112)*, Museum *(Florence Griswold Museum on 11 manicured acres 434-5542 $7/4 - Apr-Dec, Tue-Sat, 10-5, Sun 1-5; Jan-Mar, Wed-Sun, 1-5)*, Sightseeing *(Old Lyme Town Center)* **1-3 mi:** Beach *(Sound View Beach)*, Cultural Attract *(Lyme*

Academy of Fine Arts 434-5232), Galleries *(Lime Art Association 434-7802 $3 and along Lyme Street)* **3+ mi:** Bowling *(AMF Saybrook 388-3488, 4 mi.)*

Provisioning and General Services

Under 1 mi: Convenience Store *(Nicole's)*, Market *(Hadlyme Country Store 526-3188)*, Supermarket *(A&P 434-1433)*, Gourmet Shop, Health Food *(Grist Mill)*, Wine/Beer *(A&P)*, Liquor Store, Bakery, Farmers' Market *(Fri 3-6pm Hideaway Restaurant 713-2503)*, Bank/ATM *(Essex, Citizen)*, Post Office, Catholic Church, Protestant Church *(1668 Olde Congregational Church)*, Library *(Phoebe Griffin Noyes 434-1684)*, Beauty Salon *(Rob Rivers)*, Barber Shop, Dry Cleaners *(Starlett's)*, Bookstore *(The Happy Carrot 434-0380)*, Pharmacy *(Old Lyme 434-8111)*, Newsstand, Hardware Store *(Christiansen 434-7053)*, Florist, Clothing Store, Retail Shops *(Bowerbird gifts)*, Copies Etc. *(Office Express)* **1-3 mi:** Fishmonger, Lobster Pound, Laundry **3+ mi:** Department Store *(4 mi.)*

Transportation

OnSite: Courtesy Car/Van **OnCall:** Rental Car *(Enterprise 395-0758)*, Taxi *(East Shore Cab 388-2819)*, Airport Limo *(Essex Limo 767-2152)* **3+ mi:** Rail *(Saybrook Eastern Rail, 5 mi.)* **Airport:** Groton/Bradley *(16 mi./55 mi.)*

Medical Services

911 Service **OnCall:** Ambulance **Under 1 mi:** Doctor *(Old Lyme Family or Shoreline Family 434-1661)*, Dentist *(Old Lyme Dentist or Marshview Dental 434-5565)*, Holistic Services *(Faces 434-0100)*, Veterinarian *(Old Lyme Vet 434-8387)* **1-3 mi:** Chiropractor *(Natural Family Health Care 739-6259)* **Hospital:** Middlesex 358-3700 *(7 mi.)*

Setting -- Past the mouth of the Lieutenant River, on the eastern shore, is this small, secluded marina in a lovely residential area. The view directly across is of Between the Bridges North Yard, and to the north the 81-foot I95 bridge. Landside look for the small shingled fuel dockhouse and, on the shore, a new single-story, trellised and beautifully landscaped cape cod -- both a private home and, around back, the location of the head and small marina office. A beautiful estate with several outbuildings, rolling lawns, Clydesdale "sculptures" and, usually, a helicopter sits above the docks.

Marina Notes -- Few cruiser amenities but promises the lowest dockage and fuel prices on the river - gas & diesel 87 & 93 octane -- and a long, easy access fuel dock. Seasonal and transient slips, good docks, fairly new Italian tile full bathroom with glass shower door. Accommodating staff. Courtesy van to some of the local attractions and arrangements for transport to local eateries. Ask about the CT Tax Rebate. Closed Dec 1-Mar 31.

Notable -- Within a mile (actually 0.9 mi.) are two adjacent shopping centers with an A&P, several eateries and a variety of other shops and services. About a mile the other way is Old Lyme's Historic Town Center, on Lyme Street, which begins a charming thoroughfare lined with vintage homes interspersed with an occasional gallery or boutique. Shortly after Lyme Street joins Route One you'll find the Lyme Academy of Fine Arts, Old Lyme Inn, Florence Griswold Art Museum and the romantic Bee & Thistle Inn (jackets Sat night). The Griswold Museum was home base - from 1899 to the 30's - to the Lyme Art Colony - those painters who became known as American Impressionists. For bird and wild-life sighting, take a dinghy ride up the secluded Lieutenant River.

Navigational Information
Lat: 41°19.200' **Long:** 072°21.100' **Tide:** 3 ft. **Current:** 3 kt. **Chart:** 12375
Rep. Depths (MLW): Entry 22 ft. **Fuel Dock** 17 ft. **Max Slip/Moor** 17 ft./-
Access: From outer light, 3.5 mi. up the CT River, on western bank

Marina Facilities (In Season/Off Season)
Fuel: No
Slips: 100 Total, 10 Transient **Max LOA:** 100 ft. **Max Beam:** n/a
 Rate (per ft.): **Day** $1.00/Inq. **Week** Inq. **Month** Inq.
 Power: 30 amp Incl., **50 amp** Inq., **100 amp** Inq., **200 amp** n/a
 Cable TV: No **Dockside Phone:** No
 Dock Type: Fixed, Floating, Long Fingers, Short Fingers, Pilings
Moorings: 0 Total, 0 Transient **Launch:** None
 Rate: Day n/a **Week** n/a **Month** n/a
Heads: 4 Toilet(s), 3 Shower(s) (with dressing rooms)
Laundry: 1 Washer(s), 1 Dryer(s) **Pay Phones:** Yes, 2
Pump-Out: No **Fee:** n/a **Closed Heads:** No

Marina Operations
Owner/Manager: Scott Masse/David Chase **Dockmaster:** Tracy Guerin
In-Season: Apr-Oct, 8am-5:30pm **Off-Season:** Nov-Mar, 8am-5pm
After-Hours Arrival: Call ahead
Reservations: Yes, Preferred **Credit Cards:** Visa/MC, Dscvr, Amex
Discounts: None
Pets: Welcome, Dog Walk Area **Handicap Access:** Yes, Heads, Docks

Oak Leaf Marina

218 Ferry Road; Old Saybrook, CT 06475

Tel: (860) 388-9817; (800) 835-5323 **VHF: Monitor** 9 **Talk** 11
Fax: (860) 388-6131 **Alternate Tel:** n/a
Email: Oak.leaf@snet.net **Web:** www.oakleafmarina.com
Nearest Town: Old Saybrook (3 mi.) **Tourist Info:** (860) 388-3266

Marina Services and Boat Supplies
Services - Docking Assistance, Dock Carts **Communication -** Phone Messages, Fax in/out, FedEx, AirBorne, UPS, Express Mail **Supplies -** **OnSite:** Ice (Block, Cube), Ships' Store **Under 1 mi:** Bait/Tackle (Ted's Bait & Tackle 388-4882) **3+ mi:** West Marine (3.5 mi.), Boat/US (399-3170, 5.5 mi.), Propane (Lagasse's 399-6996, 6 mi.)

Boatyard Services
OnSite: Travelift (25T), Engine mechanic (gas, diesel), Electrical Repairs, Hull Repairs, Bottom Cleaning, Brightwork, Compound, Wash & Wax, Interior Cleaning, Woodworking, Painting, Awlgrip, Total Refits **OnCall:** Sail Loft, Air Conditioning, Refrigeration, Divers, Propeller Repairs, Inflatable Repairs, Life Raft Service, Yacht Broker **Near:** Launching Ramp. **1-3 mi:** Electronic Sales, Electronics Repairs, Rigger. **Dealer for:** Mercury Mercruisers. **Member:** ABBRA **Yard Rates:** $80/hr., Haul & Launch $7-8/ft. short haul, $14-$16 long haul. (blocking incl.), Power Wash Incl., Bottom Paint $18/ft. (paint incl.) **Storage:** On-Land $27/ft.

Restaurants and Accommodations
Under 1 mi: Restaurant (Saybrook Fish House 388-4836, L $5-10, D $12-22), (Ship To Shore 395-0611, B $2-6, L $4-9, D $10-19, 7 days, 7am-9pm), Hotel (Comfort Inn 388-5716, $60-140) **1-3 mi:** Restaurant (Zhang's 388-3999), Pizzeria (Pizza Works 388-1218), Motel (Liberty Inn 388-1777, $50-100) **3+ mi:** Restaurant (Dock & Dine 388-2010, L $5-13, D $10-22, 4 mi.), (Terra Mar Grille 388-1111, B $4-10, L $8-14, D $22-33, 4 mi., at Saybrook Point Inn), Motel (Saybrook Motor Inn 399-5926, $50-120, 5 mi.), Hotel (Saybrook Point Inn 395-2000, $180-330, 4 mi.)

Recreation and Entertainment
OnSite: Picnic Area, Grills **Near:** Jogging Paths **Under 1 mi:** Video Rental (Blockbuster 395-1580) **1-3 mi:** Fitness Center (Saybrook Fitness 388-6303), Fishing Charter, Park (Fort Saybrook Monument Park 388-2622 Don: $2), Sightseeing **3+ mi:** Beach (4 mi.), Golf Course (Fenwick G.C. 388-2516, 4 mi.), Bowling (Amf Saybrook 388-3488, 3.5 mi.), Museum (Florence Griswold Museum 434-5542, 4 mi.)

Provisioning and General Services
1-3 mi: Supermarket (A&P 434-1433/Stop & Shop 388-6166), Delicatessen (Cloud Nine 388-0800), Wine/Beer, Liquor Store (Old Colony Package Store 388-3820), Bakery, Farmers' Market (Cinema Plaza Sat 9am-12pm & Old Saybrook Shopping Plaza Wed 10am-2pm 633-1067), Bank/ATM, Post Office, Catholic Church, Library, Beauty Salon, Barber Shop, Dry Cleaners (48 hours), Laundry, Bookstore (The Happy Carrot 434-0380), Pharmacy (CVS 388-1045), Newsstand, Hardware Store (Beard Lumber 388-0817), Florist, Clothing Store, Retail Shops, Department Store (Walmart)

Transportation
OnSite: Local Bus (Old Saybrook Seasonal Trolley 395-0871)
OnCall: Rental Car (Enterprise 395-0758), Taxi (Essex Taxi 767-7433), Airport Limo (Essex Limo 767-2152) **1-3 mi:** Rail (Shoreline East Commuter 203-777-7433) **Airport:** Groton/Bradley (20 mi./55 mi.)

Medical Services
911 Service **OnSite:** Ambulance **1-3 mi:** Doctor (Shoreline Family 434-1661), Chiropractor (Connaughty 388-1654), Veterinarian (Old Lyme Vet 434-8387) **Hospital:** Middlesex 358-3700 (6 mi.)

Setting -- Just after passing under the I-95 81-foot bridge, on the western shore, the gray dock house and the small barn-red building signal the southern section of this full-service boatyard with docks. The environment is simple, well-maintained and competent. There are limited, but useful and quite nice, cruiser amenities, but it's mostly all about the boat -- good docks and extensive boat yard services.

Marina Notes -- Two sections - South and North. Most services are in the South: two sets of docks, most of the boatyard, the office, a very nice single shower and men's and ladies' single heads. At the North Docks is a single pier of slips, inviting heads, showers and the laundry. While close by water, the sections are about a 1/4 mile apart by land (if laundry is important request North Dock). A major MerCruiser dealer and repair shop - Oak Leaf stocks virtually every part that Mercury makes. Good size mail order operation, too. Most complete boatyard in Old Saybrook. Clean, protected 18,000 sq. ft. indoor storage facility. Also considerable outside storage. Outer docks have plenty of depth - but also plenty of current.

Notable -- Two restaurants are within a reasonable 0.6 mi walk - Ship to Shore at a Comfort Inn and The Saybrook Fish House. Most other services, restaurants and recreational venues are about 3 miles away, but are all still quite accessible - if you are here during July and August - or on the week-ends in June & September. The Old Saybrook Seasonal Trolley runs hourly 9am-10pm, Jul-Aug 7 days, May&Sep - Sat&Sun only. It starts at Oak Leaf (on the hour) and visits an additional 21 useful places - parks, beaches, museums, supermarket, malls, movie theaters, railroad station, restaurants and Comfort Inn.

Offshore East Marina

Offshore East Marina

26 4th Avenue; Old Saybrook, CT 06475

Tel: (860) 388-4532 **VHF: Monitor** n/a **Talk** n/a
Fax: n/a **Alternate Tel:** (860) 434-3741
Email: p.w.kolbe@snet.net **Web:** n/a
Nearest Town: Old Saybrook *(3 mi.)* **Tourist Info:** (860) 388-3266

Marina Services and Boat Supplies
Services - Docking Assistance, Dock Carts **Supplies - OnSite:** Ice *(Block, Cube)*, Ships' Store **Under 1 mi:** Bait/Tackle *(Teds Bait & Tackle 388-4882)*, Propane **3+ mi:** Boat/US *(399-3170, 5 mi.)*

Boatyard Services
OnSite: Travelift *(20T)*, Crane, Engine mechanic *(gas, diesel)*, Electrical Repairs, Hull Repairs, Rigger, Bottom Cleaning, Brightwork, Compound, Wash & Wax, Interior Cleaning, Propeller Repairs, Woodworking
OnCall: Electronic Sales, Electronics Repairs, Divers, Metal Fabrication
Under 1 mi: Sail Loft, Inflatable Repairs, Life Raft Service **1-3 mi:** Interiors
Yard Rates: $45/hr., Haul & Launch $6/ft., Power Wash $2, Bottom Paint $12/ft. *(paint incl.)* **Storage:** In-Water $26/ft., On-Land $22/ft.

Restaurants and Accommodations
Near: Restaurant *(Saybrook Fish House 388-4836, L $5-10, D $10-22)*, *(Ship To Shore 395-0611, B $2-6, L $4-9, D $10-19, 7 days, 7am-9pm)*
Under 1 mi: Motel *(Liberty Inn 388-1777, $50-100)*, Hotel *(Comfort Inn 395-1414, $60-140)* **1-3 mi:** Restaurant *(Benjamin's 395-4764)*, *(Wine and Roses 388-9646)*, *(Andriana's Italian Seafood 388-0408)*, Fast Food, Pizzeria *(Pizza Works 388-2218)*, Hotel *(Saybrook Point Inn & Spa 395-2000, $180-330)*, Inn/B&B *(Deacon Timothy Pratt 395-1229)*

Recreation and Entertainment
OnSite: Picnic Area, Grills **1-3 mi:** Fitness Center *(Saybrook Fitness And Aerobics 388-6303)*, Video Rental *(Video Circuit 434-2112)*, Park, Sightseeing *(Old Saybrook)*

Navigational Information
Lat: 41°19.270' **Long:** 072°21.480' **Tide:** 3 ft. **Current:** 2 kt. **Chart:** 12375
Rep. Depths *(MLW):* **Entry** 8 ft. **Fuel Dock** n/a **Max Slip/Moor** 8 ft./10 ft.
Access: West side of the river above Baldwin Bridge, to basin entrance

Marina Facilities *(In Season/Off Season)*
Fuel: No
Slips: 30 Total, 2 Transient **Max LOA:** 40 ft. **Max Beam:** 13 ft.
　Rate *(per ft.):* **Day** $1.00 **Week** $5.00 **Month** $15
　Power: 30 amp Incl., **50 amp** n/a, **100 amp** n/a, **200 amp** n/a
　Cable TV: No **Dockside Phone:** No
　Dock Type: Floating, Long Fingers, Wood
Moorings: 12 Total, 2 Transient **Launch:** None, Dinghy Dock
　Rate: Day $20 **Week** $80 **Month** $160
Heads: 2 Toilet(s), 1 Shower(s) *(with dressing rooms)*
Laundry: None **Pay Phones:** Yes, 1
Pump-Out: No **Fee:** n/a **Closed Heads:** No

Marina Operations
Owner/Manager: Harold Kolbe **Dockmaster:** Same
In-Season: Apr-Dec 15, 8am-5pm **Off-Season:** Dec 15- Mar 31, 10am-2pm
After-Hours Arrival: Call ahead
Reservations: Yes **Credit Cards:** Personal Check/Cash
Discounts: None
Pets: Welcome **Handicap Access:** No

3+ mi: Golf Course *(Fenwick G.C. 388-2516, 4 mi.)*, Bowling *(Amf Saybrook 388-3488, 3.5 mi.)*, Museum *(Conn. River Museum 767-8269 , 4 mi.)*

Provisioning and General Services
Under 1 mi: Copies Etc. *(Schaller Associates 388-1635)* **1-3 mi:** Convenience Store, Supermarket *(A&P 434-1433/Stop & Shop 388-6166)*, Delicatessen *(Cloud Nine 388-0800)*, Wine/Beer, Liquor Store *(Genes Package Store 388-9549)*, Bakery, Farmers' Market *(Cinema Plaza Sat 9-12 & Old Saybrook Shopping Plaza Wed 10-2 633-1067)*, Bank/ATM, Post Office, Catholic Church, Protestant Church, Library *(388-2622)*, Beauty Salon, Barber Shop, Dry Cleaners, Laundry, Pharmacy *(CVS 388-1145)*, Newsstand, Hardware Store *(Beard Lumber 388-0817)*, Retail Shops, Department Store *(Walmart 388-0583)* **3+ mi:** Bookstore *(The Happy Carrot 434-0380, Harbor Books 388-6850, 3.5 mi.)*

Transportation
OnCall: Rental Car *(Enterprise 395-0758/Ugly Duck)*, Taxi *(East Shore Cab 388-2819)*, Airport Limo *(Essex Limo 767-2152)* **Near:** Local Bus *(Old Saybrook Trolley)* **1-3 mi:** Rail *(Old Saybrook)*
Airport: Groton/Bradley *(20mi./53 mi.)*

Medical Services
911 Service Under 1 mi: Chiropractor *(Connaughty 388-1654)*, Ambulance
1-3 mi: Doctor *(Sound Medical Assoc. 434-8300; Old Lyme Family 439-8300)*, Dentist, Holistic Services, Veterinarian *(Saybrook Vet 388-9681)*
Hospital: Middlesex 358-3700 *(6 mi.)*

Setting -- A hard turn to port around Ferry Point, heading toward the River's western shore, leads to the entrance of a protected, almost land-locked basin -- identified by twin private red markers, a series of stakes and Island Cove Marina's large pavilion on the entrance bluff. Ferry Point Basin (North Cove) is home to three marinas; the second facility to starboard, just past Island Cove Marina, is Offshore East Marina. Together the three facilities literally fill the Basin with docks.

Marina Notes -- This mostly seasonal, very rustic, small marina has been in business for more than two decades. A small, quiet, friendly and helpful do-it-yourself yard -- with optional full services also available. Focus is on sailboats. The basin is completely placid with no current at docks. The two other marinas are Brewer Ferry Point and the elegant, seasonal rentals-only Island Cove (388-0029).

Notable -- Two casual restaurants are nearby: Saybrook Fish House and Ship to Shore, open 7 days for breakfast, lunch & dinner -- located in a Comfort Inn. The Old Saybrook Trolley stops at the same Comfort Inn and from there it makes an hourly loop through downtown, with 22 stops - including the RR station, the historic district, the malls, supermarket and the Saybrook Point marinas and beaches (9am-10pm - Jul-Aug 7 days, May&Sep - Sat&Sun only). Fort Saybrook Monument Park, at Saybrook Pt., is Connecticut's third oldest settlement - open year 'round; admission is free. The General William Hart House, built in 1767, is open Fri-Sun, 1-4pm, MemDay-LabDay; it is also home to the Old Saybrook Historical Society (388-2622).

Navigational Information
Lat: 41°19.250' **Long:** 072°21.280' **Tide:** 3 ft. **Current:** 2 kt. **Chart:** 12375
Rep. Depths *(MLW)*: **Entry** 8 ft. **Fuel Dock** 6 ft. **Max Slip/Moor** 6 ft./-
Access: West side, above Baldwin Bridge & Ferry Pt. to channel entrance

Marina Facilities *(In Season/Off Season)*
Fuel: Gasoline
Slips: 146 Total, 12 Transient **Max LOA:** 55 ft. **Max Beam:** 17 ft.
 Rate *(per ft.)*: **Day** $1.50/Inq. **Week** Inq. **Month** Inq.
 Power: 30 amp Incl., 50 amp Incl., 100 amp n/a, 200 amp n/a
 Cable TV: Yes **Dockside Phone:** No
 Dock Type: Fixed, Floating, Long Fingers, Pilings, Wood
Moorings: 0 Total, 0 Transient **Launch:** n/a
 Rate: Day n/a **Week** n/a **Month** n/a
Heads: 4 Toilet(s), 4 Shower(s) *(with dressing rooms)*
Laundry: Yes **Pay Phones:** Yes
Pump-Out: OnSite, 1 Central **Fee:** $5 **Closed Heads:** No

Marina Operations
Owner/Manager: David Cronin **Dockmaster:** Ed Wollook
In-Season: MemDay-LabDay, 8-5 **Off-Season:** LabDay-MemDay, 9-4
After-Hours Arrival: Call ahead
Reservations: Yes **Credit Cards:** Visa/MC, Dscvr, Amex
Discounts: Brewer Customer **Dockage:** n/a **Fuel:** n/a **Repair:** n/a
Pets: Welcome, Dog Walk Area **Handicap Access:** No

Brewer Ferry Point Marina

PO Box; 29 Essex Road; Old Saybrook, CT 06475

Tel: (860) 388-3260 **VHF: Monitor** 9 **Talk** 10
Fax: (860) 388-0502 **Alternate Tel:** n/a
Email: dccronin@byy.com **Web:** www.byy.com/oldsaybrook
Nearest Town: Old Saybrook *(3 mi.)* **Tourist Info:** (860) 376-7390

Marina Services and Boat Supplies
Services - Docking Assistance, Trash Pick-Up **Communication -** Mail &
Package Hold, Phone Messages, Fax in/out, FedEx, AirBorne, UPS, Express
Mail **Supplies -** OnSite: Ice *(Block, Cube)*, Ships' Store, CNG
OnCall: Propane **Under 1 mi:** Bait/Tackle *(Teds Bait & Tackle 388-4882)*
1-3 mi: West Marine **3+ mi:** Boat/US *(399-3170, 5.5 mi.)*

Boatyard Services
OnSite: Travelift *(30T)*, Forklift *(20T Hydraulic Trailer)*, Engine mechanic
(gas, diesel), Rigger, Bottom Cleaning, Brightwork, Propeller Repairs,
Woodworking, Metal Fabrication, Painting, Awlgrip **Yard Rates:** $65/hr.,
Haul & Launch $8/ft.

Restaurants and Accommodations
Near: Restaurant *(Ship To Shore 395-0611, B $2-6, L $4-9, D $10-19, 7
days, 7am-9pm next to Comfort Inn)*, *(Saybrook Fish House 388-4836, L $5-
10, D $12-22)*, Hotel *(Comfort Inn 395-1414, $60-140)* **1-3 mi:** Restaurant
(Pats Kountry Kitchen 388-4784, L $6-12, D $12-15), Pizzeria *(Pizza Works
388-2218)*, Motel *(Liberty Inn 388-1777, $50-100)*, Inn/B&B *(Deacon Timothy
Pratt 395-1229, $100-230)* **3+ mi:** Hotel *(Saybrook Point Inn & Spa 395-
2000, $180-330, 6 mi.)*

Recreation and Entertainment
OnSite: Pool, Picnic Area, Grills, Fishing Charter *(several - inquire)*
Near: Jogging Paths **1-3 mi:** Fitness Center *(Saybrook Fitness & Aerobics
388-6303)*, Video Rental *(Video Circuit 434-2112)*, Sightseeing *(Old
Saybrook Walking Tour)*, Special Events *(Crafts Fair, last weekend July)*

3+ mi: Golf Course *(Fenwick G.C. 388-2516, 6 mi.)*, Bowling *(Amf Saybrook
388-3488, 3.5 mi.)*, Museum *(Florence Griswold Museum 434-5542, 4 mi.)*

Provisioning and General Services
Near: Copies Etc. *(Schaller Associates 388-1635)* **1-3 mi:** Supermarket
(Stop & Shop 388-6166), Delicatessen *(Cloud Nine 388-0800)*, Wine/Beer,
Liquor Store *(Genes Package Store 388-9549)*, Farmers' Market *(Cinema
Plaza Sat 9-12 & Old Saybrook Shopping Plaza Wed 10-2 633-1067)*,
Bank/ATM *(New Haven Savings 388-5751)*, Post Office, Catholic Church,
Protestant Church, Library *(Acton PL 395-3184)*, Beauty Salon, Barber Shop,
Dry Cleaners, Pharmacy *(CVS 388-1045)*, Hardware Store *(Beard Lumber
388-0817)*, Retail Shops, Department Store *(Wal-Mart 388-0583)* **3+ mi:**
Bookstore *(The Happy Carrot 434-0380, Harbor Books 388-6850, 3.5 mi.)*

Transportation
OnSite: Local Bus *(Old Saybrook Trolley Jul-Aug, 7 days, 9am-10pm, May &
Sep Sat&Sun only 395-0871)* **OnCall:** Rental Car *(Enterprise 395-0758)*,
Taxi *(East Shore Cab 388-2819)*, Airport Limo *(Essex Limo 767-2152)*
3+ mi: Rail *(Old Saybrook Shoreline East, 5 mi.)*
Airport: Groton/Bradley *(20 mi./53 mi.)*

Medical Services
911 Service **OnCall:** Ambulance **Under 1 mi:** Chiropractor *(Connaughty
388-1654)* **1-3 mi:** Doctor *(Community Health Center 388-4433)*, Dentist,
Holistic Services, Veterinarian *(Saybrook Vet 388-9681)*
Hospital: Middlesex 358-3700 *6 mi.*

CT - CONNECTICUT RIVER

PHOTOS ON CD-ROM: 9

Old Lyme Marina

Old Lyme Marina

34 Neck Road; Old Lyme, CT 06371

Tel: (860) 434-1272 **VHF: Monitor** 9 **Talk** n/a
Fax: (860) 434-3068 **Alternate Tel:** n/a
Email: olmarina@oldlymemarina.com **Web:** www.oldlymemarina.com
Nearest Town: Old Lyme (0.75 mi.) **Tourist Info:** (860) 338-3266

Navigational Information
Lat: 41°19.506' **Long:** 072°20.513' **Tide:** 3 ft. **Current:** 2 kt. **Chart:** 12375
Rep. Depths (*MLW*): **Entry** 25 ft. **Fuel Dock** n/a **Max Slip/Moor** 20 ft./20 ft.
Access: Connecticut River past the I95 bridge, on the eastern shore

Marina Facilities (*In Season/Off Season*)
Fuel: No
Slips: 36 Total, 5 Transient **Max LOA:** 55 ft. **Max Beam:** n/a
 Rate (*per ft.*): **Day** $1.50 **Week** $9 **Month** Inq.
 Power: 30 amp Incl., **50 amp** Incl., **100 amp** n/a **200 amp** n/a
 Cable TV: No **Dockside Phone:** No
 Dock Type: Fixed, Floating, Long Fingers, Short Fingers
Moorings: 65 Total, 10 Transient **Launch:** None, Dinghy Dock
 Rate: Day $20 **Week** Inq. **Month** Inq.
Heads: 1 Toilet(s), 1 Shower(s)
Laundry: None **Pay Phones:** No
Pump-Out: No **Fee:** n/a **Closed Heads:** No

Marina Operations
Owner/Manager: Alan Abrahamson **Dockmaster:** Todd Abrahamson
In-Season: May-Sep, 8am-5pm **Off-Season:** Oct-Apr, 9am-4:30
After-Hours Arrival: Call ahead
Reservations: Yes **Credit Cards:** Visa/MC, Dscvr, Amex
Discounts: None
Pets: Welcome **Handicap Access:** No

Marina Services and Boat Supplies
Services - Docking Assistance, Dock Carts **Communication -** Mail & Package Hold, Phone Messages, Fax in/out, FedEx, AirBorne, UPS (*Sat Del*) **Supplies - OnSite:** Ice (*Block, Cube*) **Near:** Propane **Under 1 mi:** Bait/Tackle (*Teds Bait & Tackle 388-4882*) **1-3 mi:** CNG (*Brewer Ferry Point 388-3260*) **3+ mi:** West Marine (*10 mi.*), Boat/US (*399-3170, 7 mi.*)

Boatyard Services
OnSite: Travelift (*25T*), Forklift, Crane (*20T*), Engine mechanic (*gas, diesel*), Electrical Repairs, Electronics Repairs, Hull Repairs, Rigger, Bottom Cleaning, Brightwork, Compound, Wash & Wax, Interior Cleaning, Woodworking, Painting, Awlgrip, Yacht Design, Yacht Broker, Total Refits **OnCall:** Refrigeration, Divers, Propeller Repairs, Inflatable Repairs, Life Raft Service, Upholstery, Yacht Interiors, Metal Fabrication
Dealer for: Osprey Boats, Yanmar, Westerbeke, Universal, Atomic 4, Phasor
Member: ABBRA, ABYC, Other Certifications: Westerbeke / Universal Yanmar
Yard Rates: $65/hr., Haul & Launch $8/ft. (*blocking incl.*), Bottom Paint $12/ft.
Storage: In-Water POR, On-Land POR

Restaurants and Accommodations
Near: Restaurant (*Hong Kong II 434-3788*), (*Hideaway 434-3335, L $5-8, D $12-21*), (*Anne's Kitchen & Bistro*), Snack Bar (*Happy Carrot 434-0380*), Coffee Shop (*Koffee Works*), Pizzeria (*Toby One*) **Under 1 mi:** Restaurant (*Old Lyme Inn L $7-10, D $13-28*), (*Bee & Thistle Inn B $3-7, L $10-16, D $21-30*), Inn/B&B (*Bee & Thistle 434-1667, $80-200*), (*Old Lyme Inn 434-2600, $100-180*) **1-3 mi:** Restaurant (*Anne's Bistro 434-9837*), (*Illianos 434-1110*), Inn/B&B (*Peck Tavern House 434-8896*)

Recreation and Entertainment
OnSite: Picnic Area, Grills **Near:** Fitness Center (*Curves*), Jogging Paths, Video Rental (*Video Circuit 434-2112*) **Under 1 mi:** Museum (*Florence Griswold 434-5542 $5*), Sightseeing (*Lyme Street; 1655 Olde Congregational Church 434-8686 - one of CT's prettiest*), Galleries (*Lyme Art Assoc. 343-7802 $4; Lyme Academy of Fine Arts 434-5232*) **1-3 mi:** Beach **3+ mi:** Golf Course (*Hillside 526-9986, 9 mi.*), Bowling (*Amf 388-3488, 4 mi.*)

Provisioning and General Services
Near: Convenience Store (*Nicole's*), Supermarket (*A&P 434-1433*), Gourmet Shop (*Grist Mill 434-2990*), Health Food, Wine/Beer (*A&P*), Bakery (*Bess Eaton*), Farmers' Market (*Fri 3-6pm - Hideaway 713-2503*), Fishmonger (*Old Lyme 434-5134*), Meat Market, Bank/ATM (*Fleet, Essex*), Post Office, Catholic Church, Beauty Salon (*Rob Rivers*), Barber Shop, Dry Cleaners (*Shalett's*), Bookstore (*Happy Carrot 434-0380*), Pharmacy (*Old Lyme 434-8111*), Newsstand, Florist, Clothing Store, Copies Etc. (*Office Express*) **Under 1 mi:** Delicatessen (*Laysville 434-1801*), Protestant Church **1-3 mi:** Liquor Store, Library (*434-1684*), Hardware Store (*Christiansen 434-7053*)

Transportation
OnCall: Rental Car (*Enterprise 395-0758*), Taxi (*East Shore Cab 388-2819*), Airport Limo (*Essex Limo 767-2152*) **3+ mi:** Rail (*Old Saybrook, 10 mi.*)
Airport: Groton/Bradley (*20 mi./53 mi.*)

Medical Services
911 Service **Near:** Doctor (*Old Lyme Family Practice 434-8300*), Dentist (*Old Lyme*) **Under 1 mi:** Ambulance **1-3 mi:** Chiropractor (*Natural Family Health 739-6259*) **Hospital:** Middlesex 358-3700 (*6.5 mi.*)

Setting -- Nestled in a pretty, sheltered elbow of the River, between Calves Island and the river's bank - Old Lyme Marina is just above the I-95 bridge on the eastern shore. The surroundings are reminders that this is one of the most pristine estuaries in the northeast. The marina's moorings are spread throughout this secluded, protected spur and its grounds are well landscaped and carefully maintained. The two-story cedar-sided, green-trimmed main office sits at the head of the docks. At the rear of the grounds, a sweet, perfectly turned-out, 2-story early American private house with field stone foundation adds to the ambiance.

Marina Notes -- A friendly, family-run marina built in the early 1950's, it was bought by the Abrahamsson family in 1973 -- who still run it today. One of the largest engine parts inventories in the country. A full-service yard with complete repair capabilities including engine, generators, pumps, refrigeration, electric, rigging, props, carpentry, fiberglass, awl-grips, gelcoat, paint and varnish. Newest expansion is a 6,000 sq. ft. building complex which houses the carpenters' loft, a travel-lift accessible paint booth, and boat storage/work bays with state-of-the-art radiant floor heating. Dinghy dock. Located directly off an I-95 exit.

Notable -- The picturesque village of Old Lyme is a little less than a mile away. Local historians have suggested that every house in its historic district was, at one time, occupied by a sea captain - 60 confirmed so far! A 0.4 mile to 2 adjacent shopping centers. Old Lyme was the center of the early 20thC American impressionist landscape movement; exquisite evidence of this can be found at the elegant and quite fabulous 11 acre Florence Griswold Museum (1899-1937 the literal home of the Lyme Art Colony), at the Lyme Academy of Fine Arts and the Lyme Art Association Gallery.

Navigational Information

Lat: 41°20.980' **Long:** 072°23.100' **Tide:** 3 ft. **Current:** 3 kt. **Chart:** 12375
Rep. Depths (*MLW*): **Entry** 12 ft. **Fuel Dock** 12 ft. **Max Slip/Moor** 12 ft./30 ft.
Access: 5 miles up the CT River, just past marker 26 on the western shore

Marina Facilities (*In Season/Off Season*)

Fuel: Gasoline, Diesel
Slips: 44 Total, 10 Transient **Max LOA:** 120 ft. **Max Beam:** n/a
  Rate (*per ft.*): **Day** $2.50/1.50 **Week** $15.75 **Month** Inq.
  Power: 30 amp Incl., 50 amp Incl., 100 amp n/a, 200 amp n/a
  Cable TV: No **Dockside Phone:** No
  Dock Type: Floating, Long Fingers, Short Fingers, Pilings, Wood
Moorings: 55 Total, 10 Transient **Launch:** Yes (Free), Dinghy Dock
  Rate: Day $35 **Week** $210 **Month** $500
Heads: 5 Toilet(s), 5 Shower(s) (*with dressing rooms*)
Laundry: 2 Washer(s), 2 Dryer(s) **Pay Phones:** No
Pump-Out: OnSite, Full Service, 2 Central **Fee:** $5 **Closed Heads:** Yes

Marina Operations

Owner/Manager: John Lewis **Dockmaster:** Same
In-Season: May-Oct 31, 8am-8pm **Off-Season:** Nov 1- Apr 30, 8am-5pm
After-Hours Arrival: Call ahead
Reservations: Yes, Preferred **Credit Cards:** Visa/MC, Dscvr, Amex
Discounts: Nautical Miles **Dockage:** n/a **Fuel:** n/a **Repair:** n/a
Pets: Welcome **Handicap Access:** No

The Chandlery at Essex

19 Novelty Lane; Essex, CT 06426

Tel: (860) 767-8267 **VHF: Monitor** 68 **Talk** 68
Fax: (860) 767-0356 **Alternate Tel:** (860) 767-8267
Email: n/a **Web:** www.chandleryatessex.com
Nearest Town: Essex (*0 mi.*) **Tourist Info:** (860) 767-3904

Marina Services and Boat Supplies

Services - Docking Assistance, Trash Pick-Up, Dock Carts
Communication - Mail & Package Hold, Phone Messages, Fax in/out, Data Ports, FedEx, AirBorne, UPS, Express Mail (*Sat Del*) **Supplies - OnSite:** Ice (*Block, Cube*), Ships' Store, CNG **Under 1 mi:** Propane (*Sunoco*)

Boatyard Services

OnSite: Bottom Cleaning, Divers, Interior Cleaning **Near:** Travelift, Forklift, Crane, Engine mechanic (*gas, diesel*), Launching Ramp, Electrical Repairs, Electronic Sales, Electronics Repairs, Hull Repairs, Rigger, Sail Loft, Brightwork, Air Conditioning, Refrigeration, Compound, Wash & Wax, Propeller Repairs, Inflatable Repairs, Metal Fabrication, Painting, Awlgrip, Yacht Broker. **Nearest Yard:** Essex Boat Works (860) 767-8276

Restaurants and Accommodations

OnCall: Pizzeria (*Pizza Pub 767-1993*) **Near:** Restaurant (*Griswold Inn "The Griz" 767-1776, L $7-12, D $17-30, L 11:45am-3pm, D 5:30-9pm, S&S 10pm, Sun Hunt Break $17*), (*Black Seal Seafood Grille 767-0233, L $5-11, D $5-20, Kids' menu*), (*Gabrielle's 767-2440, L $9-13, D $18-25*), (*Oliver's Taverne 767-2633, L $7-12, D $7-19, Kids' menu*), Lite Fare (*Olive Oyl's L $5-8*), Inn/B&B (*Griswold Inn 767-1776, $105-225, 14 rooms*)
Under 1 mi: Inn/B&B (*Ivoryton Inn 767-6549*) **1-3 mi:** Restaurant (*Characters 767-0690*), (*Copper Beech Inn 767-0330, D $24-35, Very highly rated*), Inn/B&B *The Copper Beech Inn $135-325*)
3+ mi: Motel (*Comfort Inn 395-1414, $60-140, 5 mi.*)

Recreation and Entertainment

OnSite: Picnic Area, Grills, Fitness Center (*Fitness on the Waterfront*

767 3992 **Near:** Beach, Jogging Paths, Roller Blade/Bike Paths, Video Rental, Park (*Town Park*), Museum (*CT River 767-8269 -- Tue-Sun 10am-5pm $6/3*) **Under 1 mi:** Playground, Tennis Courts **1-3 mi:** Dive Shop, Cultural Attract (*Ivoryton Playhouse 767-8348*), Sightseeing(*Essex Steam Train 767-0103 $18.50/9.50*) **3+ mi:** Golf Course (*Hillside 526-9986, 10 mi.*), Bowling (*Amf 388-3488, 5 mi.*)

Provisioning and General Services

OnSite: Newsstand **Near:** Market (*Village Provision 767-7376, Sam's 767-9885*), Gourmet Shop (*Olive Oyls 767-4909*), Delicatessen (*Crow's Nest 767-3288*), Liquor Store (*That's the Spirit 767-8979*), Farmers' Market (*Village Green Fri 3-6pm Jun-Oct*), Bank/ATM, Post Office, Catholic Church, Protestant Church, Library (*Tue-Sat 10am-5pm, Sun to 4pm; Internet*), Beauty Salon, Florist, Retail Shops **Under 1 mi:** Pharmacy (*Brooks 767-2181*), Hardware Store (*Essex 767-0077*) **1-3 mi:** Supermarket (*Colonial IGA 767-9029*), Meat Market (*Cliff's 767-1539*), Dry Cleaners, Laundry, Copies Etc. (*Essex Mail 767-7743*)

Transportation

OnCall: Rental Car (*Enterprise 395-0758*), Taxi (*Essex 767-7433*), Airport Limo (*Essex 767-2152*) **Under 1 mi:** Bikes (*Village Prov 767-7376*) **3+ mi:** Rail (*Old Saybrook Shoreline, 4 mi.*) **Airport:** Groton/Bradley (*20 mi./53 mi.*)

Medical Services

911 Service **Near:** Doctor (*Family Practice 767-0098*), Holistic Services (*Miller-Dory 767-3915*) **Under 1 mi:** Dentist **1-3 mi:** Ambulance, Veterinarian (*Essex Vet 767-7976*) **Hospital:** Middlesex 358-3700 (*3 mi.*)

Setting -- This small, boutique marina sits right on the River's western bank, just past the entrance to Middle Cove. Its docks and mooring field offer panoramic views up and down the River. Landside the limited amenities are housed in the attractive brick chandlery building and a smaller out building -- all surrounded by well-tended grounds.

Marina Notes -- Vessels up to 45' at the floating docks; vessels to 125' at the stationary T-dock. Moorings for boats to 50'. Founded in 1920 as Essex Paint & Marine, it later became Brewers Chandlery, and has been the Chandlery at Essex since 1990. The Launch hours speak to their service-orientation: Mon-Thu 8am-9pm, Fri-Sat 8am-11pm, Sun 8am-10pm. The Chandlery is an exceptionally well-stocked ship's store. Heads, showers & laundry in a small building behind the store. On-site, too, are Connecticut Marine Instrument (767-8960), Venwest Yachts, Connecticut River Dock & Dredge, Fitness on the Waterfront - memberships 1 day-1 year, and the Essex Corinthian Yacht Club (767-3239) - which may have transient dockage available only to members of other clubs.

Notable -- The CT River Museum is a block away. Housed in an 1878 warehouse at the old Essex Steamboat Dock, it interprets early area life with an emphasis on maritime history. $5/3. Sam's Food Store is right next door. It's an easy walk to Main Street and downtown. Many of the buildings that line the lanes of Essex Village date back to the 17thC. River Quest cruises leave from the museum, too. A 46-sight, 1.5 mi. Walking Tour Map, starting at the Museum, is at www.essexct.com. Nearby, world-famous Griswold Inn (The Griz), is over 200 years old and continues to be a gathering spot for boaters.

Essex Boat Works

PO Box 37; 9 Ferry Street; Essex, CT 06426

Tel: (860) 767-8276 **VHF: Monitor** 9 **Talk** 10
Fax: (860) 767-1729 **Alternate Tel:** n/a
Email: sxboat@rcn.com **Web:** www.essexboatworks.com
Nearest Town: Essex *(0 mi.)* **Tourist Info:** (860) 767-3904

Navigational Information

Lat: 41°21.150' **Long:** 072°23.150' **Tide:** 4 ft. **Current:** 2 kt. **Chart:** 12375
Rep. Depths *(MLW):* **Entry** 8 ft. **Fuel Dock** n/a **Max Slip/Moor** 14 ft./14 ft.
Access: 5 miles north up CT River to North Cove Channel

Marina Facilities *(In Season/Off Season)*

Fuel: No
Slips: 30 Total, 10 Transient **Max LOA:** 100 ft. **Max Beam:** 22 ft.
  Rate *(per ft.):* **Day** $2.50/Inq. **Week** $14 **Month** $450
  Power: 30 amp Incl., 50 amp Incl., 100 amp n/a, 200 amp n/a
  Cable TV: No **Dockside Phone:** No
  Dock Type: Fixed, Floating, Long Fingers, Wood
Moorings: 14 Total, 6 Transient **Launch:** n/a, Dinghy Dock
  Rate: Day $30 **Week** $130 **Month** $480
Heads: 2 Toilet(s), 1 Shower(s)
Laundry: None **Pay Phones:** Yes, 1
Pump-Out: OnCall **Fee:** n/a **Closed Heads:** Yes

Marina Operations

Owner/Manager: Ted Lahey / Jim Greig **Dockmaster:** Same
In-Season: Year-Round, 7am-4:30pm **Off-Season:** n/a
After-Hours Arrival: n/a
Reservations: No **Credit Cards:** Visa/MC
Discounts: None
Pets: Welcome, Dog Walk Area **Handicap Access:** No

Marina Services and Boat Supplies

Services - Docking Assistance **Communication -** Mail & Package Hold, FedEx, AirBorne, UPS, Express Mail **Supplies - OnCall:** Propane **Near:** Ice *(Block, Cube)*, Ships' Store *(Chandlery at Essex 767-8267)*, CNG *(Chandlery)* **3+ mi:** Boat/US *(399-3170, 6 mi.)*

Boatyard Services

OnSite: Travelift *(50T, 20T)*, Railway, Forklift *(2)*, Crane, Engine mechanic *(gas, diesel)*, Electrical Repairs, Hull Repairs, Rigger, Bottom Cleaning, Brightwork, Air Conditioning, Refrigeration, Divers, Compound, Wash & Wax, Interior Cleaning, Propeller Repairs, Woodworking, Inflatable Repairs, Metal Fabrication, Painting, Awlgrip, Yacht Design, Yacht Building, Total Refits **OnCall:** Electronic Sales, Sail Loft, Life Raft Service, Yacht Interiors **Near:** Launching Ramp. **Dealer for:** Kohler, Yanmar, Westerbeke, Caterpillar, Marine Air, Detroit Diesel, Naiad Stabilizers. **Member:** ABBRA, ABYC **Yard Rates:** $70/hr., Haul & Launch $9/ft. *(blocking $3.50/ft.)*, Power Wash $2/ft. **Storage:** In-Water Inq., On-Land Inq.

Restaurants and Accommodations

OnCall: Pizzeria *(Pizza Public 767-1993)* **Near:** Restaurant *(Griswold Inn 767-1776, L $7-12, D $17-30, Sun Hunt Break $17)*, *(Gabrielle's 767-2440, L $9-13, D $18-25)*, *(Black Seal Seafood 767-0233, L $5-11, D $5-20)*, Lite Fare *(Essex Coffee & Tea 767-7804)*, *(Crows Nest Deli 767-3288)*, Inn/B&B *(Griswold Inn $105-225, 14 rooms)* **1-3 mi:** Inn/B&B *(Copper Beech Inn $135-325)* **3+ mi:** Motel *(Comfort Inn 395-1414, $60-140, 5 mi.)*

Recreation and Entertainment

Near: Picnic Area, Jogging Paths, Roller Blade/Bike Paths, Park *(Town Park)*, Museum *(CT River Museum)*, Special Events *(Wed nights Concerts in the Park)* **1-3 mi:** Fitness Center *(Fitness on the Waterfront 767-3992)*, Video Rental *(Valley Shore 767-1234)*, Cultural Attract *(Ivorytown Playhouse 767-8348)*, Sightseeing *(Essex Train & Steamboat 767-0103)* **3+ mi:** Golf Course *(Hillside 526-9986, 10 mi.)*, Bowling *(Amf 388-3488, 5 mi.)*

Provisioning and General Services

Near: Market *(Village Provision 767-7376)*, Gourmet Shop *(Olive Oyls)*, Wine/Beer, Liquor Store *(That's the Spirit 767-8979 delivers)*, Bakery, Farmers' Market *(Village Green Fri 3-6pm)*, Bank/ATM, Post Office, Catholic Church, Protestant Church *(3)*, Barber Shop, Newsstand, Florist, Clothing Store *(Talbots)* **Under 1 mi:** Library *(Internet)*, Beauty Salon, Hardware Store *(Essex 767-0177)* **1-3 mi:** Supermarket *(Colonial IGA 767-9029)*, Green Grocer *(Bennie's 767-8448)*, Meat Market *(Cliff's 767-1539)*, Synagogue, Dry Cleaners, Laundry, Pharmacy *(Brooks 767-2181)*, Copies Etc. *(Mail Mart 767-7743)*

Transportation

OnSite: Water Taxi **OnCall:** Rental Car *(Enterprise 395-0758)*, Taxi *(Essex Taxi 767-7433)*, Airport Limo *(Essex Limo 767-2152)* **Under 1 mi:** Bikes *(Essex Provisioning)* **3+ mi:** Rail *(Saybrook, 10 mi.)*
Airport: Chester/Bradley *(15 mi./50 mi.)*

Medical Services

911 Service **OnCall:** Ambulance **Near:** Doctor *(Family Practice 767-0098)*, Holistic Services *(Miller-Dory 767-3915)* **Under 1 mi:** Dentist *(Essex Fam 767-9403)* **1-3 mi:** Veterinarian *(Essex Vet 767-7976)*
Hospital: Middlesex 358-3700 *3 mi.*

Setting -- As you enter the channel to Essex's North Cove, Essex Boat Works' large red immaculate work sheds loom immediately to port. This is clearly a boat yard and the docks are secondary considerations - albeit very conveniently located ones. Landside there is little except the sheds and a small parking lot, usually filled with boats on the hard. Directly across the channel is Essex Island Marina.

Marina Notes -- A full service boatyard has been on this site, servicing Essex mariners, for more than fifty years. The current incarnation has 2 travelifts - 50 ton 4-sling hoist and 20 ton 2-sling hoist, a railway, a crane, 2 forklifts and virtually every required service either on-site or oncall. And they are open seven days a week! Home of sport fish boat the Essex 30.

Notable -- The boatyard is just one block from Essex's Main Street, so the town's many services and eateries are conveniently accessible. The Connecticut River Museum is a very short walk - it's housed in an 1879 steamboat dock and warehouse with panoramic views of the river and distant shore. Its exhibits cover the area's shipbuilding and maritime history, including steam boats and the first submarine - the 1775 American Turtle. Hrs: Tue-Sun 10-5pm, $6/3. The museum may also have some dockage available - 2 hr tie-up to see the museum. Admission and 1 night dockage is Free with $40 & up membership (767-8269). The Essex historic walking tour covers the whole area and starts from the museum - a map with descriptions of 46 sites is at www.essexct.com. The nearby legendary Griswold Inn (The Griz), an easy walk, has an interesting art collection and period furniture.

Navigational Information
Lat: 41°21.120' **Long:** 072°23.600' **Tide:** 3 ft. **Current:** 2 kt. **Chart:** 12375
Rep. Depths (*MLW*): **Entry** 7 ft. **Fuel Dock** 7 ft. **Max Slip/Moor** 9 ft./-
Access: 5 nm upriver from the breakwater, just north of North Cove Channel

Marina Facilities (*In Season/Off Season*)
Fuel: *Texaco* - Gasoline, Diesel
Slips: 135 Total, 60 Transient **Max LOA:** 200 ft. **Max Beam:** n/a
 Rate (*per ft.*): **Day** $3.95* **Week** Inq. **Month** Inq.
 Power: 30 amp Incl., 50 amp Incl., 100 amp Incl., 200 amp n/a
 Cable TV: Yes, Incl. **Dockside Phone:** No
 Dock Type: Fixed, Floating, Long Fingers, Alongside, Wood
Moorings: 0 Total, 0 Transient **Launch:** n/a
 Rate: Day n/a **Week** n/a **Month** n/a
Heads: 16 Toilet(s), 12 Shower(s) (*with dressing rooms*)
Laundry: 4 Washer(s), 3 Dryer(s), Book Exchange **Pay Phones:** Yes, 2
Pump-Out: OnCall, Full Service, 1 Central **Fee:** n/a **Closed Heads:** Yes

Marina Operations
Owner/Manager: Schieferdecker Family **Dockmaster:** Dawn Schieferdecker
In-Season: Jul-LabDay, 8am-7pm **Off-Season:** LabDay-Jun, 8am-5pm
After-Hours Arrival: Check in with office following AM.
Reservations: Yes **Credit Cards:** Visa/MC, Amex, Tex
Discounts: Off season rates **Dockage:** n/a **Fuel:** n/a **Repair:** n/a
Pets: Welcome, Dog Walk Area **Handicap Access:** Yes, Heads, Docks

Essex Island Marina
Foot of Ferry Street; Essex, CT 06426

Tel: (860) 767-1267 **VHF: Monitor** 9 **Talk** 68
Fax: (860) 767-0075 **Alternate Tel:** n/a
Email: info@essexislandmarina.com **Web:** www.essexislandmarina.com
Nearest Town: Essex (*0.1 mi.*) **Tourist Info:** (860) 767-3904

Marina Services and Boat Supplies
Services - Docking Assistance, Concierge, Security, Trash Pick-Up, Dock Carts **Communication -** Mail & Package Hold, Phone Messages, Fax in/out *(Yes)*, Data Ports *(Eagle's Roost)*, FedEx, AirBorne, UPS, Express Mail *(Sat Del)* **Supplies -** OnSite: Ice *(Block, Cube)* **Near:** Ships' Store *(Chandlery 767-8267)*, Propane *(Sunoco 767-0079)*, CNG *(Chandlery)*

Boatyard Services
OnSite: Travelift *(30T)*, Hull Repairs, Rigger, Bottom Cleaning, Brightwork, Compound, Wash & Wax **Near:** Engine mechanic *(gas, diesel)*, Launching Ramp, Electrical Repairs, Electronics Repairs, Air Conditioning, Refrigeration, Divers, Propeller Repairs, Awlgrip, Yacht Broker. **Yard Rates:** $69/hr. Haul & Launch $8/ft. *(blocking addl.)* **Storage:** In-Water $6/ft./mo. w/metered electr. (Nov-Apr), On-Land Outside $33/ft.

Restaurants and Accommodations
Near: Restaurant *(Gabrielle's 767-2440, L $9-13, D $18-25)*, *(Griswold Inn L $7-12, D $17-30, Sun Hunt Breakfast $17)*, *(Black Seal 767-0233, L $5-11, D $5-20, No Res., Kids' menu)*, *(Oliver's 767-2633)*, Lite Fare *(Essex Coffee &Tea 767-7804)*, *(Crows Nest 767-3288)*, Inn/B&B *(Griswold Inn 767-1776, $105-225)* **1-3 mi:** Restaurant *(Characters 767-0690)*, *(Copper Beech 767-0330, D $24-35)*, Pizzeria *(Pizza Pub 767-1993)*, Inn/B&B *(Copper Beach Inn 767-0330, $135-325)* **3+ mi:** Motel (Comfort Inn 395-1414, $60-140, 5 mi.)

Recreation and Entertainment
OnSite: Pool, Picnic Area, Grills *(charcoal)*, Playground *(also basketball, horseshoes)*, Volleyball, Video Arcade

Near: Beach *(Nott Island)*, Tennis Courts, Fitness Center *(Fitness on the Waterfront 767-3992)*, Jogging Paths, Video Rental, Park, Museum *(CT River Museum 767-8269 $6/3, Essex Historical Society 767-0681)*, Special Events, Galleries *(Antiques)* **Under 1 mi:** Dive Shop, Roller Blade/Bike Paths **1-3 mi:** Cultural Attract *(Ivoryton Playhouse 767-7318, Essex Steam Train 767-0103)* **3+ mi:** Golf Course *(Hillside Links 526-9986 , 4 mi.)*

Provisioning and General Services
OnSite: Convenience Store *(Ditty Bag)*, Newsstand **Near:** Gourmet Shop *(Olive Oyls 767-4909)*, Liquor Store *(That's the Spirit 767-8979, delivers)*, Farmers' Market *(Fri 3-6pm Village Green)*, Bank/ATM, Post Office, Catholic Church, Protestant Church, Library, Beauty Salon *(Society's)*, Florist **1-3 mi:** Supermarket *(IGA 767-9029)*, Green Grocer *(Benny's Farm 767-8448)*, Meat Market *(Cliff's 767-1539)*, Dry Cleaners, Pharmacy *(Brooks 767-2181)*, Hardware Store *(Essex Hardware 767-0077)*, Copies Etc. *(Essex Mail 767-7743)*

Transportation
OnCall: Rental Car *(Enterprise 395-0758, Thrifty 399-5146)*, Taxi *(Essex Taxi 767-7433)*, Airport Limo *(Essex Limo 767-2152)* **3+ mi:** Rail *(7 mi.)* **Airport:** Bradley/Groton *(50 mi./18mi.)*

Medical Services
911 Service **Near:** Doctor *(Family Practice 767-0098)*, Holistic Services *(Miller-Dory 767-3915)*, Veterinarian *(Essex Vet 767-7976)* **Under 1 mi:** Dentist *(Essex Fam 767-9403)*, Ambulance **1-3 mi:** Chiropractor *(Lower Valley 767-2119)* **Hospital:** Middlesex Shoreline Med Ctr 358-3700 *(3 mi.)*

Setting -- A thirteen acre bridgeless island has been thoughtfully transformed into a delightful, family-oriented boating resort. The grounds are secure and very well maintained -- with ready access to the "mainland" by private ferry. Docks surround three sides of the island - on the east they front on the River, on the south the channel, and on the west North Cove. A large activity building dominates the island with several smaller ones scattered about.

Marina Notes -- * 25 ft. min. This is a resort where guests stay on boats; extremely service-oriented staff, and real concierge service. Ask for the Port of Call booklet. Three sets of heads/showers open 24 hrs. A ferry crosses the 100 ft. to the Essex shore literally on-demand: 7:30am-11:30pm Sun-Thu, 7:30am-1:00am Fri-Sat & holidays (in season) . Eagle's Roost communication center has modem connections, weather and news updates. A large tented area is available for group functions to 100 - complimentary for rendezvous staying here. The Ditty Box has provisions and last minute necessities. Complimentary grocery store transportation twice daily (in season). Sea Bound Marine's boatyard services onsite (Lenny Lindh, Manager). Developed in 1955 by Louis W. Schieferdecker, family owned and operated for four generations. The best views are from the most northern slips on both the North Cove and River side.

Notable -- Swimming pool, billiards, ping pong, horseshoes, shuffleboard, volleyball, tetherball, bocce, croquet, and basketball all onsite. Air-conditioned lounges for kids (chaperoned) and for adults. In past years the Captain's Gig has served breakfast, lunch and "To Go Boats." As of publication, E.I.M. does not know if the deli will open for 2004. Historic 18thC Essex village is a one-minute ferry ride followed by a short walk - annotated tour maps: www.essexct.com.

Brewer Dauntless Shipyard

37 Pratt Street; Essex, CT 06426

Tel: (860) 767-0001 **VHF: Monitor** 9 **Talk** 12
Fax: (860) 767-3074 **Alternate Tel:** n/a
Email: bds@byy.com **Web:** www.byy.com/Essex
Nearest Town: Essex **Tourist Info:** (860) 767-3904

Navigational Information
Lat: 41°21.140' **Long:** 072°23.230' **Tide:** 3 ft. **Current:** n/a **Chart:** 12375
Rep. Depths (MLW): Entry 11 ft. **Fuel Dock** n/a **Max Slip/Moor** 12 ft./-
Access: 5 miles north of the breakwater, through Essex channel

Marina Facilities (In Season/Off Season)
Fuel: No
Slips: 108 Total, 10-15 Transient **Max LOA:** 125 ft. **Max Beam:** n/a
   Rate (per ft.): Day $3.00 **Week** $18 **Month** $40
   Power: 30 amp Incl., **50 amp** Incl., **100 amp** n/a, **200 amp** n/a
   Cable TV: Yes **Dockside Phone:** Yes
   Dock Type: Floating, Long Fingers, Pilings, Wood
Moorings: 5 Total, 0 Transient **Launch:** None, Dinghy Dock
   Rate: Day n/a **Week** n/a **Month** n/a
Heads: 4 Toilet(s), 4 Shower(s)
Laundry: 1 Washer(s), 1 Dryer(s) **Pay Phones:** No
Pump-Out: OnSite, Full Service, 1 Central **Fee:** n/a **Closed Heads:** Yes

Marina Operations
Owner/Manager: Doug Domenie **Dockmaster:** Same
In-Season: Summer, 7:30am-6pm **Off-Season:** Fall-Win-Sprg, 7:30am-5pm
After-Hours Arrival: Call ahead
Reservations: Yes **Credit Cards:** Visa/MC, Amex
Discounts: None
Pets: Welcome **Handicap Access:** No

Marina Services and Boat Supplies
Services - Docking Assistance, Dock Carts **Communication -** Mail & Package Hold, Phone Messages, Fax in/out, Data Ports (office or dockside), FedEx, AirBorne, UPS, Express Mail (Sat Del) **Supplies - OnSite:** Ice (Block, Cube), Ships' Store **Near:** Propane, CNG (Chandlery) **3+ mi:** Boat/US (399-3170, 6 mi.), Bait/Tackle (Rivers End 388-2283, 4 mi.)

Boatyard Services
OnSite: Travelift (35T), Forklift, Crane, Engine mechanic (gas, diesel), Electrical Repairs, Hull Repairs, Rigger, Sail Loft, Bottom Cleaning, Brightwork, Air Conditioning, Refrigeration, Compound, Wash & Wax, Interior Cleaning, Woodworking, Metal Fabrication, Painting, Awlgrip, Yacht Broker, Total Refits **OnCall:** Electronics Repairs, Divers **Near:** Launching Ramp, Electronic Sales, Inflatable Repairs, Upholstery, Yacht Interiors, Yacht Design. **Dealer for:** Westerbeke engines and generators, Yanmar & Universal diesel engines, Fischer Panda, Spurs, Marine Air, Grunert & Sea Frost, Espar, Sealand. **Yard Rates:** $70/hr., Haul & Launch $7/ft. to 30', $9/ft. 30-40', $11/ft. 40'+, Power Wash $2.25/ft., Bottom Paint $60/hr.

Restaurants and Accommodations
OnSite: Lite Fare (Crows Nest Gourmet Deli 767-3288, B $2-6, L $4-15, D $8-15) **OnCall:** Pizzeria (Pizza Public 767-1993) **Near:** Restaurant (Black Seal 767-0233, L $5-11, D $5-20, No Res.), (Griswold Inn 767-1776, L $7-12, D $17-30, Sun Hunt Break $17, D weekends), (Gabrielle's 767-2440, L $9-13, D $18-25) **Under 1 mi:** Restaurant (Characters 767-0690), (Debbies 767-8175), Inn/B&B (Griswold Inn $105-225) **1-3 mi:** Restaurant (Copper Beech 767-0330, D $24-35), Inn/B&B (Copper Beech $135-325)

Recreation and Entertainment
OnSite: Pool, Picnic Area, Grills **Near:** Fitness Center (Fitness on the Waterfront 767-3992), Roller Blade/Bike Paths, Video Rental, Park (Town Park), Sightseeing (Essex Train and Steam Boat 767-0103), Special Events (Village Green Wed night concerts) **Under 1 mi:** Museum (Connecticut River 767-8269) **1-3 mi:** Cultural Attract (Ivoryton Playhouse 767-7318) **3+ mi:** Golf Course (Hillside Links 526-9986, 5 mi.)

Provisioning and General Services
OnSite: Delicatessen **Near:** Convenience Store (Village Provision 767-7376), Market (Sam's 767-9885), Liquor Store (That's the Spirit 767-8979), Bakery, Farmers' Market (Fri 3-6pm Village Green), Bank/ATM, Post Office, Catholic Church, Library (767-1560), Beauty Salon, Newsstand, Florist, Clothing Store (Talbots) **Under 1 mi:** Fishmonger, Pharmacy (Brooks 767-2181), Hardware Store (Essex 767-0077), Copies Etc. (Essex Mail 767-7743) **1-3 mi:** Synagogue, Dry Cleaners, Laundry **3+ mi:** Supermarket (Adams, 4 mi.)

Transportation
OnCall: Rental Car (Enterprise 395-0758), Taxi (Essex Taxi 767-7433), Airport Limo (Essex Limo) **Near:** Bikes (Village Provision 767-7376) **1-3 mi:** Rail **Airport:** Bradley/Groton (16 mi/50 mi.)

Medical Services
911 Service **Near:** Doctor (Shoreline Emergency Clinic 767-3700), Holistic Services (Miller-Dory 767-3915), Ambulance **Under 1 mi:** Dentist (Essex Fam 767-9403) **1-3 mi:** Chiropractor (Lower Valley Chiropractic 767-2119), Veterinarian (Essex Vet 767-7976) **Hospital:** Middlesex 358-3700 (3 mi.)

Setting -- The most protected of the Essex marinas, Dauntless is tucked into the entrance to North Cove. Looking north, the last set of docks ("C") have views of the truly unspoiled cove and its marsh; looking east, the views are of Essex Island Marina's docks. Landside are two-story buildings that house a ships' store, small eatery, brokerage, and a variety of marine services - backed up by large boat sheds. A pool is nestled between the buildings and the grounds, although mostly paved, are enlivened by colorful mini-gardens tucked in here and there.

Marina Notes -- Onsite are a full-service boat yard, a marine surveyor and a finance company. In addition, several boat brokerage firms handle Grand Banks, Sabre, Sabreline, Caliber, Nonsuch, and Northeast. Brewer Preferred Customer Card Program good at all Northeast Brewer Yards. Onsite Internet access via dockside phone lines or in the office; access also at the Essex Library.

Notable -- The second floor Crow's Nest Gourmet Deli serves breakfast, lunch (year 'round, 7am-5pm)) and week-end dinners (Friday, Saturday, & Sunday BYOB - 5:30-9pm, Memorial Day - Labor Day) - casual inside seating and outside covered deck seating overlook the Cove. Within easy walking distance is charming, historic Essex village. A tour of its many restored 18thC. houses, interesting gift and antique shops, clothing stores and galleries is enhanced by the Essex Walking Tour - www.essexct.com. The Connecticut River Museum is a must for those with a passion for the sea and its history. And the world famous 200-year-old Griswold Inn ("the Griz") is a short walk-- yachting attire welcome.

Navigational Information

Lat: 41°23.448' **Long:** 072°25.468' **Tide:** 2 ft. **Current:** 3 kt. **Chart:** 12377
Rep. Depths (*MLW*): **Entry** 15 ft. **Fuel Dock** 10 ft. **Max Slip/Moor** 10 ft./-
Access: 7 miles north of LI Sound breakwater, behind Eustasia Island

Marina Facilities (*In Season/Off Season*)

Fuel: *Valvtect* - Gasoline, Diesel
Slips: 240 Total, 15 Transient **Max LOA:** 50 ft. **Max Beam:** n/a
  Rate (*per ft.*): **Day** $1.75 **Week** Inq. **Month** Inq.
  Power: 30 amp Incl., **50 amp** Incl., **100 amp** n/a, **200 amp** n/a
  Cable TV: Yes **Dockside Phone:** No
  Dock Type: Fixed, Floating, Long Fingers, Pilings, Wood, Composition
Moorings: 35 Total, 5 Transient **Launch:** None, Dinghy Dock
  Rate: Day $25 **Week** Inq. **Month** Inq.
Heads: 9 Toilet(s), 10 Shower(s)
Laundry: None **Pay Phones:** No
Pump-Out: OnSite, Full Service, 1 Central **Fee:** Free **Closed Heads:** Yes

Marina Operations

Owner/Manager: Brewer Group **Dockmaster:** Jim Brown
In-Season: Year-Round, 8am-4:30pm **Off-Season:** n/a
After-Hours Arrival: Notify Dockmaster one day in advance.
Reservations: Yes **Credit Cards:** Visa/MC, Dscvr, Amex, Tex
Discounts: Brewer Members **Dockage:** n/a **Fuel:** n/a **Repair:** n/a
Pets: Welcome, Dog Walk Area **Handicap Access:** No

Brewer Deep River Marina

50 River Lane; Deep River, CT 06417

Tel: (860) 526-5560 **VHF: Monitor** 9 **Talk** 68
Fax: (860) 526-2469 **Alternate Tel:** n/a
Email: drm@byy.com **Web:** www.byy.com/deepriver
Nearest Town: Deep River (0.7 mi.) **Tourist Info:** (860) 767-3904

Marina Services and Boat Supplies

Services - Docking Assistance, Security, Trash Pick-Up, Dock
Carts **Communication -** Phone Messages, Fax in/out, FedEx, AirBorne,
UPS, Express Mail (*Sat Del*) **Supplies - OnSite:** Ice (*Block, Cube*), Ships'
Store, CNG **OnCall:** Propane **Near:** Bait/Tackle **1-3 mi:** Boater's World
(767-3007)

Boatyard Services

OnSite: Travelift (*15T*), Forklift, Crane, Engine mechanic (*gas, diesel*),
Electrical Repairs, Hull Repairs, Rigger, Bottom Cleaning, Brightwork, Air
Conditioning, Compound, Wash & Wax, Woodworking, Upholstery, Painting,
Awlgrip, Yacht Broker, Total Refits **OnCall:** Electronic Sales, Propeller
Repairs, Inflatable Repairs **Near:** Launching Ramp, Electronics Repairs,
Refrigeration. **1-3 mi:** Life Raft Service, Metal Fabrication.

Restaurants and Accommodations

OnCall: Pizzeria (*Deep River Pizza 526-1348*) **Near:** Snack Bar
Under 1 mi: Restaurant (*Whistle Stop 526-4122, B $2-5, L $3-8*), (Great
Wall Chinese 526-8988), (*Shortstop 526-4146*), (*Ivory Restaurant & Pub
526-2528*), (*Fabled Foods 526-2666*), (*Pasta Unlimited 526-4026*), Inn/
B&B (*Riverwind Country Inn 526-2014, $95-175*) **1-3 mi:** Restaurant (*Rest-
aurant Du Village 526-5301, D $25-29, Tue-Sat 5:30-9pm, Zagats Best food
in CT*), Inn/B&B (*123 Main B&B 525-3456*) **3+ mi:** Motel (*Comfort Inn 395-
1414, $60-140, 6 mi.*), Inn/B&B (*Griswold Inn 767-1776, $125-200, 3.5 mi.*)

Recreation and Entertainment

OnSite: Pool, Picnic Area, Grills, Playground, Jogging Paths **Near:** Beach,
Boat Rentals, Roller Blade/Bike Paths, Park (*Selden Neck State Park -*

dingy 526-2336), Sightseeing (*Valley Railroad Steam Train to Essex
$10.50/5.50 or add the Riverboat trip $16.50/8.50 767-0103*) **Under 1 mi:**
Video Rental, Special Events (*Muster Weekend, third Sat. in July, celebrates
early American fife & drum corps 399-6665*) **1-3 mi:** Dive Shop, Tennis
Courts, Golf Course (*Hillside Links 526-9986*), Museum (*Gillette Castle 526-
2336 by dinghy $5/3*), Cultural Attract (*Ivoryton Playhouse 767-8348*)

Provisioning and General Services

Under 1 mi: Convenience Store, Supermarket (*Adams 526-2807*), Gourmet
Shop, Delicatessen, Wine/Beer, Liquor Store (*Shore Discount 526-5197*),
Bakery (*Our Daily Bread 526-2488*), Green Grocer, Fishmonger, Meat
Market, Bank/ATM, Post Office, Catholic Church, Library (*526-6039*), Beauty
Salon, Barber Shop, Dry Cleaners, Laundry, Hardware Store (*Deep River
526-2776*), Florist, Retail Shops **1-3 mi:** Farmers' Market (*Chester Center
Sat 8:30-12 526-9157*), Protestant Church, Synagogue, Bookstore (*Chester
Book 526-9887; Centerbridge 767-8943*), Pharmacy (*Doanes 767-1455*)

Transportation

OnCall: Rental Car (*Enterprise 395-0758*), Taxi (*Essex Taxi 767-7433*),
Airport Limo (*Corporate Connection 767-7004*) **3+ mi:** Rail (*3 mi.*)
Airport: Bradley (*48 mi.*)

Medical Services

911 Service **Near:** Dentist, Ambulance **1-3 mi:** Doctor (*Lower Valley 526-
4945*), Chiropractor (*Lower Valley 767-2119*), Holistic Services (*Hamel-Smith
526-4861*), Veterinarian (*Chester Vet 526-5313*)
Hospital: Middlesex 358-3700 *5 mi.*

Setting -- Tucked behind Eustasia Island, and surrounded by marshlands, Brewer Deep River's docks have views of the pristine Island and an unspoiled
stretch of river. The natural setting and the park-like grounds create a peaceful environment. There's a lovely free-form pool, with natural stone decking, set next
to the club house, and an inviting picnic area on a grassy knoll overlooking the river.

Marina Notes -- Well-protected, off the main channel, away from the wash of wakes. No laundry due to environmental restrictions. Brewer Yacht Yards
membership privileges. In addition to the docks, there are 16 moorings and 8 mooring floats (these are single 'private island' floating docks that can
accommodate two boats each). Continual upgrades. An additional 27 wider, roomier slips with "IPE" decking and new modern power centers were installed
2002 and one of the all-tile bath facilities was remodeled as well. A few years ago, the clubhouse was renovated, along with its heads and showers. A second
set of relatively new heads is at the North Yard.

Notable -- This is about the point at which the 410 mile-long Connecticut River turns "fresh." Just north are the Valley Railroad Steam Train depot and Becky
Thatcher Cruise Boats at Deep River's town landing. The train runs right beside the marina. Located less then a mile from Deep River village, 2 miles from
Chester and 2 miles from Essex. This is the place to get the dinghy out. Picnicking spots, accessible by boat, include Hamburg Cove, Selden Creek, Selden
Neck State Park and Pratt Cove -- plus untouched 11 acre Eustasia Island. Also dinghy to Gillette Castle's 184 acre park (free) and hilltop fieldstone mansion.

Navigational Information
Lat: 41°24.305' **Long:** 072°25.790' **Tide:** 4 ft. **Current:** n/a **Chart:** 12377
Rep. Depths *(MLW):* **Entry** 6 ft. **Fuel Dock** 6 ft. **Max Slip/Moor** 6 ft./-
Access: West from Buoy 37 into narrow cut just before Chester Creek

Marina Facilities *(In Season/Off Season)*
Fuel: Gasoline, Diesel
Slips: 145 Total, 25 Transient **Max LOA:** 40 ft. **Max Beam:** 16 ft.
  Rate *(per ft.):* **Day** $1.25/1.00 **Week** $5 **Month** Inq
  Power: 30 amp Incl., **50 amp** n/a, **100 amp** n/a, **200 amp** n/a
  Cable TV: Yes, Incl. **Dockside Phone:** No
  Dock Type: Floating, Short Fingers, Alongside, Wood
Moorings: 0 Total, 0 Transient **Launch:** n/a
  Rate: Day n/a **Week** n/a **Month** n/a
Heads: 6 Toilet(s), 4 Shower(s)
Laundry: None **Pay Phones:** Yes
Pump-Out: OnSite **Fee:** n/a **Closed Heads:** Yes

Marina Operations
Owner/Manager: Gil Bartlett **Dockmaster:** Same
In-Season: Year 'Round, 8am-5pm **Off-Season:** n/a, 8am-5pm
After-Hours Arrival: Tie up to available dock - contact office in the morning
Reservations: Yes, Preferred **Credit Cards:** Visa/MC
Discounts: None
Pets: Welcome, Dog Walk Area **Handicap Access:** No

Chester Marina

72 Railroad Avenue; Chester, CT 06412

Tel: (860) 526-2227 **VHF: Monitor** 16 **Talk** n/a
Fax: (860) 526-2111 **Alternate Tel:** (860) 526-3849
Email: n/a **Web:** www.chestermarina.com
Nearest Town: Chester *(1.5 mi.)* **Tourist Info:** (860) 767-3904

Marina Services and Boat Supplies
Services - Dock Carts **Supplies - OnSite:** Ice *(Block, Cube)*, Ships'
Store **1-3 mi:** Propane, CNG *(Brewer Deep River 526-5560)* **3+ mi:**
Boat/US *(399-3170, 10 mi.)*

Boatyard Services
OnSite: Travelift *(25T- 2)*, Engine mechanic *(gas, diesel)*, Launching Ramp,
Electrical Repairs, Hull Repairs, Bottom Cleaning, Compound, Wash & Wax,
Propeller Repairs **Yard Rates:** $70/hr., Haul & Launch $11/ft. *(blocking
$3/ft.)*, Power Wash $2/ft.

Restaurants and Accommodations
Under 1 mi: Inn/B&B *(123 Main B&B 526-3456, $95-145)*, *(Inn at Chester
526-9541, $105-215)* **1-3 mi:** Restaurant *(Restaurant Du Village 526-5301,
D $25-29, Zagats best food in CT)*, *(Fiddlers Seafood 526-3210, L $8-17,
D $19-34, Wed-Sun 11:30-2, Wed-Sat 5:30-9:30, Sun 4-8 specialty is
bouillabaisse)*, *(Pattaconk 1850 Bar & Grille 526-8143, L $6-13, D $8-19,
113 beers, 20 wines by glass - home of the hand-cut jigsaw puzzle)*, *(Post
and Beam 526-9541, D $17-32)*, *(River Tavern 526-9417, B, L, D $21-23,
(Sage American 526-9898, D $9-17)*, *(Inn at Chester D $17-26)*, Lite Fare
(The Lunch Box B, L) **3+ mi:** Inn/B&B *(Griswold Inn 767-1776,
$125-200, 5 mi.)*

Recreation and Entertainment
OnSite: Pool, Picnic Area, Grills, Playground **Under 1 mi:** Boat Rentals
(Down River Canoes 526-1966) **1-3 mi:** Golf Course *(Hillside Links 526-
9986)*, Park *(Selden Neck State Park 526-2336 - dinghy only)*, Cultural
Attract *(Goodspeed at Chester 873-8668)*, Sightseeing *(Gillette Castle*

526-2336; *Chester Airport plane rides 526-4321)*, Special Events *(Chester
Fair - Aug; Hands Tell Stores - Jun-Jul 2 weeks)* **3+ mi:** Museum
(Connecticut River Museum 767-8269, 5 mi.)

Provisioning and General Services
Under 1 mi: Newsstand, Florist, Clothing Store *(Sarah Kate 526-3811)*,
Retail Shops **1-3 mi:** Convenience Store, Supermarket *(Adams 526-2807)*,
Gourmet Shop *(Wheat Market 526-9347)*, Delicatessen *(Lunch Box 526-
9154)*, Wine/Beer, Liquor Store *(Chester Package Store 526-5305)*, Bakery
(Queen of Tarts 526-5024), Farmers' Market *(Chester Center Sat 8:30-noon
526-9157)*, Meat Market, Bank/ATM, Post Office, Catholic Church, Protestant
Church, Synagogue, Library *(Deep River PL 526-6039)*, Beauty Salon,
Barber Shop, Dry Cleaners, Laundry, Bookstore *(Chester Book Co 526-
9887, Naturally Books & Coffee 526-3212)*, Hardware Store *(Deep River
Hardware 526-2776)* **3+ mi:** Pharmacy *(Doanes 767-1455, 4 mi.)*

Transportation
OnCall: Rental Car *(Enterprise 395-0758)*, Taxi *(Essex Taxi 767-7433)*,
Airport Limo *(Essex Limo 767-2152)* **Near:** Ferry Service *(Chester-Hadlyme
- 5 min river crossing)* **3+ mi:** Rail *(Old Saybrook, 10 mi.)*
Airport: Bradley *(47 mi.)*

Medical Services
911 Service **OnCall:** Ambulance **1-3 mi:** Doctor *(Lower Valley Family 526-
4945)*, Dentist *(Kearns 526-4921)*, Holistic Services *(Hamel-Smith 526-
4861)*, Veterinarian *(Chester Vet 526-5313)* **3+ mi:** Chiropractor *(Lower
Valley Chiropractic 767-2119 , 4 mi.)* **Hospital:** Middlesex 358-3700 *(7 mi.)*

Setting -- Across from the Chester Creek Bar, just north of Brewer Deep River, is a narrow unmarked opening on the western shore of the River. This is the entrance to Chester Marina's large, almost land-locked basin. The surroundings are protected and relatively unspoiled -- with large stretches of grass dotted with picnic tables and gazebos.

Marina Notes -- Third generation family owned and managed. Full service boatyard or Do-It-Yourself. The basin is ringed with docks - mostly slips but some alongside. Trees help mitigate the views of the parking lots. A large grassy picnic area overlooks the River. Mostly seasonal, smaller boats. FYI: in '01 Chester Marina sold off their North Yard to Castle Marina.

Notable -- The charming and artistic river community of Chester is a mile and a half. Main Street, and its offshoots, are chock-a-block with interesting old houses occupied by antique shops, craft and fine art galleries, food shops and some very intriguing dining options -- one of which has been declared the best in the state (Restaurant Du Village). It's also home to Goodspeed at Chester's Norma Terris Theater which produces new musicals and experimental theater. Selden Neck State Park and campgrounds, located on the largest island in the river, is accessible only by dingy or kayak.

Navigational Information
Lat: 41°24.448' **Long:** 072°25.965' **Tide:** 2 ft. **Current:** 4 kt. **Chart:** 12377
Rep. Depths (*MLW*): **Entry** 10 ft. **Fuel Dock** n/a **Max Slip/Moor** 10 ft./-
Access: West from Buoy 37 in Chester Creek

Marina Facilities (*In Season/Off Season*)
Fuel: No
Slips: 82 Total, 2 Transient **Max LOA:** 55 ft. **Max Beam:** 16 ft.
  Rate (*per ft.*): **Day** $1.00/0.50 **Week** n/a **Month** n/a
  Power: 30 amp Inq., **50 amp** Inq., **100 amp** n/a, **200 amp** n/a
  Cable TV: Yes **Dockside Phone:** No
  Dock Type: Fixed, Floating, Short Fingers, Alongside, Wood
Moorings: 0 Total, 0 Transient **Launch:** n/a
  Rate: Day n/a **Week** n/a **Month** n/a
Heads: 7 Toilet(s), 4 Shower(s)
Laundry: None **Pay Phones:** No
Pump-Out: No **Fee:** n/a **Closed Heads:** No

Marina Operations
Owner/Manager: Bruce & Barbara MacLeod **Dockmaster:** Same
In-Season: Apr-Oct, 8am-8pm **Off-Season:** Nov-Mar, 9am-4pm
After-Hours Arrival: n/a
Reservations: Required **Credit Cards:** Visa/MC
Discounts: None
Pets: Welcome, Dog Walk Area **Handicap Access:** No

Castle Marina

61 Railroad Avenue; Chester, CT 06412

Tel: (860) 526-2735 **VHF: Monitor** n/a **Talk** n/a
Fax: (860) 526-3083 **Alternate Tel:** n/a
Email: castlemarina@juno.com **Web:** www.castle-marina.com
Nearest Town: Chester (*1.5 mi.*) **Tourist Info:** n/a

Marina Services and Boat Supplies
Supplies - OnSite: Ice (*Block, Cube*), Ships' Store **1-3 mi:** Propane (*Brewer Deep River 526-5560*), CNG **3+ mi:** West Marine (*664-4060, 15 mi.*), Boater's World (*399-3170, 10 mi.*)

Boatyard Services
OnSite: Travelift, Hydraulic Trailer, Engine mechanic (*gas*), Launching Ramp, Electrical Repairs, Hull Repairs, Bottom Cleaning, Brightwork, Compound, Wash & Wax, Interior Cleaning, Woodworking **OnCall:** Crane, Rigger, Propeller Repairs **Yard Rates:** $65/hr., Haul & Launch $10/ft. (*blocking $2/ft.*), Power Wash $2/ft. **Storage:** In-Water $22/ft., On-Land $22/ft.

Restaurants and Accommodations
Under 1 mi: Inn/B&B (*123 Main B&B 526-3456, $95-145*), (*Inn at Chester 526-9541, $105-215*) **1-3 mi:** Restaurant (*River Tavern 526-9417, D $21-23, B, L, D*), (*Sage American 526-9898, D $9-17*), (*Restaurant Du Village 526-5301, D $25-29, Zagats best food in CT*), (*Fiddlers Seafood 526-3210, L $8-17, D $19-34, Wed-Sun 11:30-2, Wed-Sat 5:30-9:30, Sun 4-8 - specialty is bouillabaisse*), (*Pattaconk 1850 Bar & Grille 526-8143, L $6-13, D $8-19, 113 beers, 20 wines by glass - home of the hand-cut jigsaw puzzle*), (*Post and Beam 526-9541, D $17-32*), (*Inn at Chester D $17-26*), Lite Fare (*The Lunch Box B, L*)

Recreation and Entertainment
OnSite: Pool, Picnic Area **Under 1 mi:** Horseback Riding **1-3 mi:** Golf Course (*Hillside Links 526-9986*), Cultural Attract (*Goodspeed at Chester 873-8668*), Sightseeing (*Gillette Castle 526-2336; Chester Airport plane rides 526-4321 $85/30min, $165/hr.*), Special Events (*Chester Fair - Aug; Hands Tell Stores - Jun-Jul 2 weeks*) **3+ mi:** Museum (*Connecticut River Museum 767-8269, 5 mi.*)

Provisioning and General Services
OnSite: Copies Etc. **Under 1 mi:** Newsstand, Florist, Clothing Store (*Sarah Kate 526-3811*), Retail Shops **1-3 mi:** Convenience Store, Supermarket (*Adams 526-2807*), Gourmet Shop (*Wheat Market 526-9347*), Delicatessen (*Lunch Box 526-9154*), Wine/Beer, Liquor Store (*Chester Package Store 526-5305*), Bakery (*Queen of Tarts 526-5024*), Farmers' Market (*Chester Center Sat 8:30-noon 526-9157*), Meat Market, Bank/ATM, Post Office, Catholic Church, Protestant Church, Synagogue, Library (*Deep River PL 526-6039*), Beauty Salon, Barber Shop, Dry Cleaners, Laundry, Bookstore (*Chester Book Co 526-9887, Naturally Books & Coffee 526-3212*), Hardware Store (*Deep River Hardware 526-2776*) **3+ mi:** Pharmacy (*Doanes 767-1455, 4 mi.*)

Transportation
OnCall: Rental Car (*Enterprise 395-0758*), Taxi (*Essex Taxi 767-7433*), Airport Limo (*Essex Limo 767-2152*) **Near:** Ferry Service (*Chester-Hadlyme - 5 min river crossing*) **3+ mi:** Rail (*Old Saybrook, 10 mi.*) **Airport:** Bradley (*47 mi.*)

Medical Services
911 Service **OnCall:** Ambulance **1-3 mi:** Doctor (*Lower Valley Family Physicians 526-4945*), Dentist (*Kearns 526-4921*), Holistic Services (*Hamel-Smith 526-4861*), Veterinarian (*Chester Vet 526-5313*) **3+ mi:** Chiropractor (*Lower Valley Chiro 767-2119, 4 mi.*) **Hospital:** Middlesex 358-3700 (*7 mi.*)

Setting -- Immediately north of the cut to Chester Marina is the entrance to well-protected Chester Creek. The first on the port side is Castle Marina, a small and relatively new operation. There is alongside dockage for larger boats as you enter the Creek and stern-to dockage -- with short finger piers -- that rings the marina's quiet, placid basin for smaller craft. Quite nice heads and showers are in the lower level of the owner's house.

Marina Notes -- Formerly Chester Marine's North Yard, Castle is now a totally separate enterprise owned and managed by Bruce Macleod, a local retired ships' carpenter and cabinet maker. The Macleods live on site and Bruce still does some boat interiors. There's a three-foot bar at the Creek entrance, a 2 foot tide swing and 3-4 knots of current. Half the boats are over 30 feet. Larger boats tend to be docked on the outside of the basin. A fenced pool and a couple of gazebos provide recreational options.

Notable -- The unique Essex Valley View Scenic Railway runs right alongside the marina -- the antique steam engine puffs by several times a day on sightseeing trips and, in the evening, on a dinner trip when the engine pulls a string of elegantly refurbished dining and parlor cars. The train begins in Essex and continues up to Ferry Point and Haddam. The marina's namesake Gillette Castle and Park is a dinghy ride away; there's a small dock on the eastern shore north of the ferry landing. The charming town of Chester, about a mile and a half walk, is a very worthwhile visit.

Hays Haven Marina

PO Box 236; 59 Railroad Avenue; Chester, CT 06412

Tel: (860) 526-9366 **VHF: Monitor** n/a **Talk** n/a
Fax: (860) 526-4186 **Alternate Tel:** (860) 526-9366
Email: n/a **Web:** n/a
Nearest Town: Chester *(1.5 mi.)* **Tourist Info:** (860) 388-3266

Navigational Information
Lat: 41°24.546' **Long:** 072°25.978' **Tide:** 3 ft. **Current:** 1 kt. **Chart:** 12377
Rep. Depths *(MLW):* **Entry** 6 ft. **Fuel Dock** 6 ft. **Max Slip/Moor** 6 ft./-
Access: Across from Buoy 37 off CT River in Chester Creek

Marina Facilities *(In Season/Off Season)*
Fuel: Gasoline, Diesel, High-Speed Pumps
Slips: 220 Total, 4 Transient **Max LOA:** 46 ft. **Max Beam:** 16 ft.
 Rate *(per ft.):* **Day** $1.25/Inq. **Week** Inq. **Month** Inq.
 Power: 30 amp Incl., **50 amp** n/a, **100 amp** n/a, **200 amp** n/a
 Cable TV: Yes, Incl. **Dockside Phone:** No
 Dock Type: Fixed, Floating, Long Fingers, Short Fingers, Wood
Moorings: 0 Total, 0 Transient **Launch:** n/a
 Rate: Day n/a **Week** n/a **Month** n/a
Heads: 4 Toilet(s), 6 Shower(s)
Laundry: None **Pay Phones:** No
Pump-Out: OnSite, Self Service, 1 Central **Fee:** Free **Closed Heads:** Yes

Marina Operations
Owner/Manager: James Hays Jr. **Dockmaster:** same
In-Season: Year-Round, 10am-4pm **Off-Season:** Same
After-Hours Arrival: Call ahead
Reservations: Preferred **Credit Cards:** Visa/MC, Dscvr
Discounts: None
Pets: Welcome, Dog Walk Area **Handicap Access:** No

Marina Services and Boat Supplies
Services - Security *(24 Hrs.)*, Dock Carts **Communication -** Phone Messages **Supplies - OnSite:** Ice *(Block, Cube)*, Ships' Store **1-3 mi:** Propane, CNG *(Brewer Deep River)* **3+ mi:** Boater's World *(Essex)*, Boat/US *(399-3170, 10 mi.)*

Boatyard Services
OnSite: Travelift *(25T)*, Launching Ramp, Bottom Cleaning **OnCall:** Engine mechanic *(gas, diesel)*, Electrical Repairs, Hull Repairs, Brightwork, Air Conditioning, Refrigeration, Divers, Compound, Wash & Wax, Interior Cleaning, Woodworking, Upholstery **Under 1 mi:** Painting, Awlgrip. **Yard Rates:** $40/hr., Haul & Launch $4/ft. *(blocking $6/ft.)*, Power Wash $1/ft. **Storage:** On-Land $23/ft.

Restaurants and Accommodations
Under 1 mi: Inn/B&B *(Inn at Chester 526-9541, $105-215)*, *(123 Main B&B 526-3456, $95-145, 5 rooms)* **1-3 mi:** Restaurant *(Sage American 526-9898, D $9-17)*, *(Pattaconk 1850 526-8143, L $6-13, D $8-19, remarkable beer & wine-by-the glass selections)*, *(Fiddlers Seafood 526-3210, L $8-17, D $19-34)*, *(Restaurant Du Village 526-5301, D $21-27)*, *(River Tavern 526-9417, D $21-23, B, L, D)*, *(Post & Beam 526-9541, D $17-32)*, Snack Bar *(Short Stop 526-4146)*, Lite Fare *(The Lunch Box 526-9154, B, L)*, Pizzeria *(Cozy Castle 526-3633)*, Inn/B&B *(Griswold Inn 767-1776, $125-200)*

Recreation and Entertainment
OnSite: Picnic Area, Grills, Volleyball *(Horseshoes, Basketball, too)* **Under 1 mi:** Video Rental, Video Arcade, Park, Cultural Attract *(Goodspeed-* at- *Chester Norma Terris Theater 873 8668* , Sightseein *(Gillette Castle; Essex-Chester Railroad; Open cockpit bi-plane rides 526-4321 $85/30min, $165/hr.)*, Special Events **1-3 mi:** Golf Course *(Hillside Links 526-9986)* **3+ mi:** Museum *(Connecticut River Museum 767-8269, 5 mi.)*

Provisioning and General Services
Under 1 mi: Gourmet Shop *(The Wheat Market 526-9347)*, Liquor Store *(Chester Package 526-5305)*, Bakery *(Queen of Tarts 526-5024)*, Farmers' Market *(Sat 8:30-12 Chester Center 526-9157)*, Meat Market, Bank/ATM, Post Office, Catholic Church, Protestant Church, Synagogue, Beauty Salon, Barber Shop, Dry Cleaners, Laundry, Bookstore *(Chester Book CO 526-9887, Naturally Books & Coffee 526-3212)*, Newsstand, Clothing Store *(Sarah Kate 526-3811)*, Retail Shops, Copies Etc. **1-3 mi:** Convenience Store *(Basic Goods & Services 526-8984)*, Supermarket *(Adams 526-2807)*, Delicatessen, Library *(Deep River PL 526-6039)*, Hardware Store *(Deep River Hardware 526-2776)* **3+ mi:** Pharmacy *(Doane's 767-1455, 4 mi.)*

Transportation
OnCall: Rental Car *(Enterprise 395-0758)*, Taxi *(Essex Taxi 767-7433)*, Airport Limo *(Corporate Connection)* **Near:** Ferry Service *(Chester-Hadlyme)* **3+ mi:** Rail *(Old Saybrook, 10mi.)* **Airport:** Bradley *(47 mi.)*

Medical Services
911 Service **OnCall:** Ambulance **Under 1 mi:** Doctor *(Lower Valley Family 526-4945)*, Holistic Services *(Hamel-Smith Massage 526-4861)*, Veterinarian *(Chester Vet 526-5313)* **1-3 mi:** Dentist **3+ mi:** Chiropractor *(Lower Valley Chiro 767-2119, 4 mi.)* **Hospital:** Middlesex 358-3700 *(7 mi.)*

Setting -- Just west of the Chester Creek Bar is a narrow cut in the river bank that is the entrance to Chester Creek. Hays Haven is the second facility in the creek, just past and around Castle Marina. The marina is tucked into a long narrow placid basin; the slips ring the perimeter - and trees ring the slips. Landscaping is well maintained -- and there are some unexpected and artistic touches.

Marina Notes -- Family owned and operated for over 20 years. Clearly there's a wood-worker and artist in the family -- the base of the flagpole is a nicely crafted lighthouse. This same attention to detail shows up in other places, too. Hauling capability but few on-site boatyard services. Very nice, recently renovated heads with card key access. Seasonal boats tend to be smaller, but some larger sport fishing boats make their home here.

Notable -- The Chester depot for the Essex Valley View Scenic Railway is nearby. The charming, sleepy river village of Chester is a mile and a half away. Its "untouristy" streets are lined with interesting old houses and restored buildings - occupied by antique shops, craft and fine art galleries, food shops and some very fine eateries. Check out the Connecticut River Artisans Cooperative 526-5575. Goodspeed at Chester's Norma Terris Theater, the branch of the Goodspeed Opera House which produces new musicals and experimental theater, is also in the village. Across the river is Gillette Castle and State Park; there's a small dinghy dock on the eastern shore, north of the ferry landing. Park access free, Castle Fri-Sun, MemDay-LabDay, 10am-5pm $5/3 526-2336.

Navigational Information
Lat: 41°25.496' **Long:** 072°26.268' **Tide:** 3 ft. **Current:** n/a **Chart:** 12377
Rep. Depths (*MLW*): **Entry** 5 ft. **Fuel Dock** 5 ft. **Max Slip/Moor** 8 ft./-
Access: CT River, past Hadlyme Ferry to cut on west shore

Marina Facilities *(In Season/Off Season)*
Fuel: Gasoline
Slips: 135 Total, 2 Transient **Max LOA:** 50 ft. **Max Beam:** 15 ft.
 Rate *(per ft.)*: **Day** $1.50 **Week** Inq. **Month** Inq.
 Power: 30 amp Incl., **50 amp** n/a, **100 amp** n/a, **200 amp** n/a
 Cable TV: Yes, Incl. **Dockside Phone:** No
 Dock Type: Floating, Long Fingers, Wood
Moorings: 0 Total, 0 Transient **Launch:** n/a
 Rate: Day n/a **Week** n/a **Month** n/a
Heads: 4 Toilet(s), 4 Shower(s) *(with dressing rooms)*, Hair Dryers
Laundry: None **Pay Phones:** No
Pump-Out: OnSite, Self Service, 1 Central **Fee:** Free **Closed Heads:** Yes

Marina Operations
Owner/Manager: Abbie Coderre **Dockmaster:** Lou Matz
In-Season: Apr-Oct, 9am-5pm **Off-Season:** Nov-Mar, 8am-4pm
After-Hours Arrival: Call ahead
Reservations: Yes, Required **Credit Cards:** Visa/MC
Discounts: None
Pets: Welcome **Handicap Access:** No

Chrisholm Marina

PO Box 306; 226 Route 154; Chester, CT 06412

Tel: (860) 526-5147 **VHF: Monitor** 9 **Talk** n/a
Fax: (860) 526-1473 **Alternate Tel:** n/a
Email: n/a **Web:** www.chrisholmmarina.com
Nearest Town: Chester *(2 mi.)* **Tourist Info:** (860) 767-3904

Marina Services and Boat Supplies
Communication - Phone Messages, UPS, Express Mail **Supplies -**
OnSite: Ice *(Block, Cube)*, Ships' Store **1-3 mi:** Propane, CNG *(Brewer Deep River Marina)* **3+ mi:** Boat/US *(399-3170, 10 mi.)*

Boatyard Services
OnSite: Travelift *(35T)*, Crane, Engine mechanic *(gas, diesel)*, Electrical Repairs, Electronic Sales, Electronics Repairs, Hull Repairs, Brightwork, Compound, Wash & Wax, Propeller Repairs, Woodworking, Painting
Dealer for: Sealand Vacuflush, Interlux, Interprotect, Tohutsu Outboards.
Yard Rates: $60/hr., Haul & Launch $7/ft. *(blocking $12/ft.)*, Power Wash $2/ft. **Storage:** On-Land $27.50/ft.

Restaurants and Accommodations
1-3 mi: Restaurant *(Restaurant Du Village 526-5301, D $21-27)*, *(Fiddlers Seafood 526-3210, L $9-17, D $20-36)*, *(Sage American Bar & Grill 526-9898)*, *(Post & Beam 526-1307, D $17-32, at Inn at Chester)*, Lite Fare *(Pattaconk 1850 526-8143, puzzles, beer & wine)*, *(Lunch Box 526-9145)*, Pizzeria *(Deep River Pizza 526-1348)*, *(Cozy Castle Pizza 526-3633)*, Inn/B&B *(123 Main B&B 526-3456, $95-145)*, *(Riverwind Inn 526-2014)*
3+ mi: Restaurant *(Inn at Chester D $17-26, 4 mi.)*, Inn/B&B *(Inn at Chester 526-9541, $105-215, 4 mi.)*, *(Griswold Inn 767-1776, $95-120, 5 mi.)*

Recreation and Entertainment
OnSite: Beach, Picnic Area, Grills, Playground **Near:** Jogging Paths **Under 1 mi:** Park **1-3 mi:** Golf Course *(Hillside Links 526-9986)*, Museum *(Gillette Castle 526-2336 10-5 Fri-Sun May-Sep $5/3 - closer by dink)*, Cultural Attract *(Goodspeed at Chester - The Norma Terris Theater 873-8668)*, Sightseeing *(Valley Railroad's Essex Steam Train & Riverboat Ride 767-0103 $16.50/8.50)*

Provisioning and General Services
1-3 mi: Convenience Store, Supermarket *(Adams 526-2807)*, Gourmet Shop *(The Wheatmarket 526-9347)*, Delicatessen *(Lunch Box 526-9154)*, Wine/Beer, Liquor Store *(Chester Package Store 526-5305)*, Bakery *(Queen of Tarts 526-5024)*, Farmers' Market *(Chester Center Sat 8:30-noon)*, Bank/ATM, Post Office, Catholic Church, Protestant Church, Synagogue, Library *(Deep River PL 526-6039)*, Beauty Salon, Barber Shop, Dry Cleaners, Bookstore *(Naturally Books & Coffee 526-3212)*, Pharmacy *(Westown Pharmacy 649-9946)*, Newsstand, Hardware Store *(Deep River Hardware 526-2776)*, Florist, Retail Shops

Transportation
OnCall: Rental Car *(Enterprise 537-0181)*, Taxi *(Essex Taxi 767-4733)*, Airport Limo *(Essex Limo)* **Near:** Ferry Service *(Chester-Hadlyme 566-7635)* **3+ mi:** Rail *(Old Saybrook, 10 mi.)* **Airport:** Bradley *(45 mi.)*

Medical Services
911 Service **OnCall:** Ambulance **1-3 mi:** Doctor *(Lower Valley Family Physicians 526-4945)*, Dentist *(Kearns 526-4921)*, Chiropractor *(McColl 345-5121)*, Holistic Services *(Hamel-Smith Massage 526-4921)*, Veterinarian *(Chester Vet 526-5313)* **Hospital:** Middlesex 358-3700 *(5 mi.)*

Setting -- Less than a mile north of the Hadlyme Ferry, well past Gillette Castle, is a cut on the western bank of the River. Inside is a protected, quiet basin filled with docks - Chrisholm Marina. The facility is nicely maintained with large grassed areas and the Connecticut Valley hills as a back drop. A perfectly sited gazebo and very nice wooden play gym share pretty views across the river.

Marina Notes -- Can accommodate boats to 65 ft. with 6 ft draft. Founded in 1961.Third generation family owned and managed. Full service boatyard with 35 Ton/17 ft. beam travelift. Good, recently renovated heads and showers with thoughtful touches. Attractive and well-stocked ship's store. Complimentary pump-out. Winter in-water storage - entire marina is "bubbled". Liveaboards welcome. Wooden boat specialists. Authorized Sealand Vacuflush dealer.

Notable -- The historic, unaffected town of Chester -- with its intriguing assortment of galleries, artists, artisans, antique shops, food purveyors and superb eateries -- is two miles away. Downriver, the 200 acre Gillette Castle State Park is home to an outrageous 24-room fieldstone mansion built in 1919 by thespian William Gillette (best known as Sherlock Holmes). Park open daily 8am-dusk, Free; Castle Fri-Sun, MemDay-LabDay, 10am-5pm $5/3 526-2336. A small dock just south for docking dinks. Up river is the Goodspeed Opera House, parent to Goodspeed at Chester. The 8-car Hadlyme Ferry departs less than a mile away for the 5 minute trip across - vehicles $2.25, people $0.75. An interesting dingy destination is Whalebone Creek, across the river just south of the ferry landing. It's a fresh-water tidal marsh (best accessed at high tide) and home to marsh grasses, wild rice and hundreds of birds - including the imperial great blue heron.

Goodspeed Opera House

Goodspeed Opera House

Goodspeed Landing, 6 Main Street; East Haddam, CT 06423

Tel: (860) 873-8664 **VHF: Monitor** n/a **Talk** n/a
Fax: (860) 873-2329 **Alternate Tel:** (860) 873-8668
Email: n/a **Web:** www.goodspeed.org
Nearest Town: East Haddam *(1 mi.)* **Tourist Info:** (860) 347-0028

Navigational Information
Lat: 41°27.097' **Long:** 072°27.720' **Tide:** 3 ft. **Current:** n/a **Chart:** 12377
Rep. Depths *(MLW)*: **Entry** 21 ft. **Fuel Dock** n/a **Max Slip/Moor** 9 ft./-
Access: 3 miles past Chester to just below the Eas Haddam Swing Bridge

Marina Facilities *(In Season/Off Season)*
Fuel: No
Slips: 3 Total, 3 Transient **Max LOA:** n/a **Max Beam:** n/a
  Rate *(per ft.)*: **Day** n/a **Week** n/a **Month** n/a
  Power: 30 amp n/a, **50 amp** n/a, **100 amp** n/a, **200 amp** n/a
  Cable TV: No **Dockside Phone:** No
  Dock Type: Fixed, Alongside, Wood
Moorings: 0 Total, 0 Transient **Launch:** n/a, Dinghy Dock
  Rate: Day n/a **Week** n/a **Month** n/a
Heads: None
Laundry: None **Pay Phones:** No
Pump-Out: No **Fee:** n/a **Closed Heads:** No

Marina Operations
Owner/Manager: Michael Price **Dockmaster:** Linda Benson *(Receptionist)*
In-Season: Mid-Apr-Mid-Dec, Noon-9pm **Off-Season:** n/a
After-Hours Arrival: Check in with the Box Office
Reservations: Yes **Credit Cards:** No Charge
Discounts: None
Pets: Welcome **Handicap Access:** No

Marina Services and Boat Supplies
Supplies - Near: Ice *(Block)*, Ships' Store *(Andrew's)* **Under 1 mi:** Bait/Tackle, Propane **1-3 mi:** CNG *(Brewer Deep River 526-5660)*

Boatyard Services
Nearest Yard: Chester Marina (860) 526-3849

Restaurants and Accommodations
OnSite: Restaurant *(Gelston House River Grill 873-1411, D $25-32, 125 seats with views of the River)*, *(Gelston House Tavern L $12-17, D $18-25)*, Lite Fare *(Beer Garden L $5-7, D $5-16, fun, outdoor cafe - lobster, too - MemDay-LabDay)*, Inn/B&B *(Gelston House 837-1411, $100-150, six guestroooms w/ bath)* **Near:** Restaurant *(Country Restaurant 345-4229, B $2-5, L $4-6.50)*, *(La Vita Gustosa 873-8999, L $8-15, D $9-26, Sunday Brunch $16, across the street, 11am-10pm)*, Inn/B&B *(Bishopsgate Inn 837-1677,$105-165)* **Under 1 mi:** Pizzeria *(Haddam Pizza 345-4472, L $3-13, D $3-13, grinders, salads & entrees, too Mon-Thu 11-9, Fri-Sat 11-10)* **1-3 mi:** Motel *(Klar Crest Resort & Motel 873-8649)*, Inn/B&B *(Granite Lodge 345-2482)*

Recreation and Entertainment
OnSite: Picnic Area, Cultural Attract *(Goodspeed Opera House, Wed-Sun, Apr-Dec)* **Near:** Jogging Paths, Museum *(Nathan Hale School House 873-9547 Week-ends MemDay-LabDay; Horse Drawn Carriage & Sleigh Museum 873-9658 - 4 mi.)*, Sightseeing *(Camelot Cruises of Ct. River at Marine Park In Haddam 345-8591; Eagle Aviation's secenic plane rides over the river valley 873-8568; St. Stephen's Episcopal church - home to world's oldest bell)*, Galleries

Under 1 mi: Fitness Center *(Unique Physique 345-2983)*, Special Events *(East Haddam Fair - Sep, 873-8878)* **1-3 mi:** Park *(Gillette Castle and Park 526-2336 $5/3 10am-5pm Fri-Sun May-Sep)* **3+ mi:** Golf Course *(Banner Leisure Country Club 873-9075, 5 mi.)*

Provisioning and General Services
Near: Liquor Store *(De Lorenzos Package Store 873-8553)*, Bakery, Bank/ATM, Post Office, Catholic Church, Protestant Church, Library *(Rathbun Memorial 873-8210)*, Florist, Retail Shops **Under 1 mi:** Convenience Store *(Tylerville BP Fast Fare 345-3775)*, Gourmet Shop *(Everyday Gourmet 345-9234)*, Delicatessen *(Cheeseboard Deli & Pizza 345-4418)*, Laundry **1-3 mi:** Green Grocer *(New Hope Farm 640-0342)*, Hardware Store *(Shagbark Lumber & Farms Supplies 873-1946)* **3+ mi:** Pharmacy *(Nathan Hale 873-1481, 4 mi.)*

Transportation
OnCall: Rental Car *(Enterprise 395-0758)*, Taxi *(Action 848-2233; Essex Taxi 767-7433)*, Airport Limo *(Corporate Connect 767-7004)*
Under 1 mi: Ferry Service *(Hadlyme-Chester)*
3+ mi: Rail *(Old Saybrook MetroNorth/Amtrak $20 cab ride 1/way, 14 mi.*
Airport: Bradley/Goodspeed *(46 mi./1 mi.)*

Medical Services
911 Service **OnCall:** Ambulance **Near:** Holistic Services *(Harmony Health Center & Massage 873-9630)* **Under 1 mi:** Chiropractor *(McColl 873-9630)* **3+ mi:** Doctor *(Higganum Family Medical Group 345-8535, 4 mi.)*, Veterinarian *(East Haddham Vet 873-8673, 4 mi.)*
Hospital: Middlesex 358-3700 *(9 mi.)*

Setting -- On the eastern shore, just south of the Rte 82 East Haddam swing bridge, an elegant mansard-roofed, 1876 Victorian jewel looms above the River: the Goodspeed Opera House. Directly downriver from the House is a lovely, grassy water-front park scattered with picnic tables. A 120 foot stationary dock runs parallel to the bank, offering inviting views of the park, the river and the Opera House.

Marina Notes -- *120 linear feet. There are no services on the dock or shoreside for boaters. Dockage is complimentary with performance tickets. Tickets: $57-61, partial views at $22. Sched: Wed 2pm & 7:30, Thur 7:30, Fri 8:00, Sat 4 & 8:30, Sun 2 & 6:30. Wed, Thur, & Sun, Student Rush tickets $10 for that night. In 1959 Goodspeed Musicals was formed to restore the 19th century Opera House which opened in 1963. Its mission, as the home of American Musical Theater, is to preserve and revitalize the past and create the future. Each Apr-Dec season it produces 3 musicals in East Haddam and 3 new musicals at The Norma Terris Theatre in Chester. The onsite Scherer Library of Musical Theatre is one of the most extensive theatre research facilities in the U.S.

Notable -- Arriving by boat for an evening at this lovingly restored Opera House -- with its exquisite lobby, staircase and main stage -- adds a "step-back-in-time" dimension to an already truly special event. Victorian Bar & Gum Drop Shoppe opens one hour before curtain and for intermission. Pre-order intermission cocktails; they will be waiting in the lobby. The adjacent 1853 Gelston House's River Grill's panoramic windows overlook the River. Casual dining in the Tavern and at the outdoor Beer Garden MemDay-LabDay. Nearby are galleries and a classic New England village. Note: Rte 82 bridge's surface is wide grating.

Navigational Information
Lat: 41°27.108' **Long:** 072°27.976' **Tide:** 2 ft. **Current:** 2 kt. **Chart:** 12377
Rep. Depths (*MLW*): **Entry** 6 ft. **Fuel Dock** 6 ft. **Max Slip/Moor** 8 ft./12 ft.
Access: 12 mi. north - just past Rte 82 bridge, on western bank

Marina Facilities (*In Season/Off Season*)
Fuel: *Mid Grade* - Gasoline, High-Speed Pumps
Slips: 75 Total, 5 Transient **Max LOA:** 50 ft. **Max Beam:** 16 ft.
  Rate (*per ft.*): **Day** $2.50/1.50 **Week** $10.50/7 **Month** $30
  Power: 30 amp $8, **50 amp** $15, **100 amp** n/a, **200 amp** n/a
  Cable TV: No **Dockside Phone:** No
Dock Type: Floating, Short Fingers, Pilings, Wood
Moorings: 9 Total, 2 Transient **Launch:** No, Dinghy Dock
  Rate: Day $40/20 **Week** $175/105 **Month** $450
Heads: 3 Toilet(s), 3 Shower(s) (*with dressing rooms*)
Laundry: None **Pay Phones:** No
Pump-Out: Full Service, 1 Central, 1 InSlip **Fee:** $10* **Closed Heads:** Yes

Marina Operations
Owner/Manager: David J. Papallo, JR **Dockmaster:** Same
In-Season: Jun-Sep 1, 8am-6pm **Off-Season:** Sep 1-Nov 1, 8am-5pm
After-Hours Arrival: Gas Dock
Reservations: Yes, Preferred **Credit Cards:** Visa/MC
Discounts: None
Pets: Welcome, Dog Walk Area **Handicap Access:** Yes, Heads, Docks

Andrews Marina

Harpers Landing Drive; Haddam, CT 06438

Tel: (860) 345-2286 **VHF: Monitor** 68 **Talk** 69
Fax: (860) 345-7547 **Alternate Tel:** (860) 690-5555
Email: djpapallo01@snet.net **Web:** n/a
Nearest Town: Essex (*4 mi.*) **Tourist Info:** (860) 347-0028

Marina Services and Boat Supplies
Services - Docking Assistance, Concierge, Room Service to the Boat, Security (*24 Hrs., Dockmaster lives on property*), Trash Pick-Up, Dock Carts **Communication** - Mail & Package Hold, Phone Messages, Fax in/out (*$5*), Data Ports (*Office*), FedEx, UPS **Supplies - OnSite:** Ice (*Block*), Ships' Store **Near:** Bait/Tackle, Propane

Boatyard Services
OnSite: Engine mechanic (*gas, diesel*), Launching Ramp, Air Conditioning, Refrigeration, Compound, Wash & Wax, Interior Cleaning **OnCall:** Divers **Under 1 mi:** Travelift, Electrical Repairs, Electronic Sales, Electronics Repairs, Hull Repairs, Rigger, Sail Loft, Bottom Cleaning, Brightwork, Propeller Repairs. **Nearest Yard:** Midway Marina (860) 345-4330

Restaurants and Accommodations
Near: Restaurant (*Gelston House River Room 873-1411, D $25-32, panoramic river views*), (*Country 345-4229, B $2-5, L $4-6.50*), (*Gelston Tavern L $12-17, D $12-17*), (*La Vita Gusta 873-8999, L $6-15, D $9-26, Sun Brunch $16*), Fast Food (*Subway*), Lite Fare (*Cooking Co. 345-8008*), (*Beer Garden L $5-7, D $5-16, snacks to lobsters*), Pizzeria (*Haddam 345-4472, L $3-13, D $3-13, grinders, salads, entrees, Mon-Thu 11-9, Fri-Sat 'til 10pm*), Inn/B&B (*Bishopsgate 873-1677, $105-165*), (*Gelston House 873-1411, $100-150*) **Under 1 mi:** Inn/B&B (*Chester Inn 526-9541, $105-215*)

Recreation and Entertainment
OnSite: Beach (*swimming float*), Picnic Area, Grills **Near:** Jogging Paths, Cultural Attract (*Goodspeed Opera House - Wed-Sun, Apr-Dec $22-61*), Sightseeing (*Camelot Cruises; Eagle Aviation 873-8568 - 0.8 mi. - plane rides over the valley*), Galleries (*East Haddam*) **Under 1 mi:** Horseback Riding, Museum (*Nathan Hale School House 873-9547*), Special Events (*East Haddam Fair - Sep 873-8878*) **1-3 mi:** Playground, Fitness Center (*Unique Physique 345-2983*), Video Rental, Park (*Gillette Castle and Park 526-2336 - Park free, Castle $5/3 Fri-Sun*) **3+ mi:** Golf Course (*Banner Liesure C.C. 873-9075, 5 mi.*)

Provisioning and General Services
Near: Convenience Store, Delicatessen (*Cooking Co. 345-8008*), Health Food, Wine/Beer, Liquor Store (*De Lorenzo's 873-8553*), Bakery, Green Grocer, Bank/ATM **Under 1 mi:** Supermarket (*IGA*), Gourmet Shop (*Everyday Gourmet 345-9234*), Fishmonger (*Spencer's Shad Shack*), Meat Market, Post Office, Hardware Store (*Shagbark 873-1946*) **1-3 mi:** Catholic Church, Protestant Church, Library, Beauty Salon, Barber Shop, Dry Cleaners, Laundry, Bookstore, Pharmacy, Florist, Copies Etc.

Transportation
OnSite: Courtesy Car/Van (*4 hrs. advance notice required*) **OnCall:** Rental Car (*Enterprise 395-0758*), Taxi (*Action 848-2233; Essex Taxi 767-7433*), Airport Limo (*Corporate Connect 767-7004*) **Under 1 mi:** Ferry Service (*Hadlyme-Chester*) **3+ mi:** Rail (*Old Saybrook Metro North & Amtrak $20 cab ride 1/way, 14 mi.*) **Airport:** Bradley/Goodspeed (*46 mi./1 mi.*)

Medical Services
911 Service **OnCall:** Ambulance **Near:** Chiropractor (*McColl 873-9630*), Holistic Services (*Swedish Body Works 345-7919*) **1-3 mi:** Doctor (*Higganum Family 345-8535*), Dentist **3+ mi:** Veterinarian (*East Haddham Vet 873-8673, 4 mi.*) **Hospital:** Middlesex 358-3700 (*9 mi.*)

Setting -- Tucked into a basin on the river's western shore, Andrew's Marina at Harper's Landing lies quietly in the shadow of the historic East Haddam Route 82 Swing Bridge. A sweet, park-like swath of well-tailored lawn borders the basin's northern edge and offers panoramic views of the unspoiled river and far bank. Picnic tables, strategically placed lighting and nicely pruned bushes are sheltered by stands of weeping willows. At the head of the basin, single-story gray buildings house this well maintained marina's amenities.

Marina Notes -- New ownership & management 2000. Very service oriented. Commodious heads with dressing rooms. Barbecue and picnic area with 7 tables and 6 grills -- each with wide-open views upriver -- plus a small beach and swimming float. Voted the "most photographed location in Connecticut." *Complimentary pump-out for marina customers. Closed Nov-May 1. Mailing address: PO BOX 458, East Haddam, CT 06423.

Notable -- Andrews is directly across the East Haddam Swing Bridge from the fabulous 19thC. Goodspeed Opera House and is the only marina within walking distance. The bridge was built in 1913 and was considered an engineering wonder at the time; today it is reputed to be the longest swing bridge in the world and the oldest operating one. If walking to Goodspeed or Gelston House or any of the other East Haddam attractions, note that the bridge's roadway consists of wide metal grating and there's no sidewalk -- wear boat shoes and walk gingerly. Several other restaurants are within walking distance.

Damar / Midway Marina

Haddam Dock Road; Haddam, CT 06438

Tel: (860) 345-4330; (800) 498-6838 **VHF: Monitor** n/a **Talk** n/a
Fax: (860) 345-4330 **Alternate Tel:** (860) 345-4330
Email: damarltd1@aol.com **Web:** n/a
Nearest Town: Haddam *(2 mi.)* **Tourist Info:** (860) 767-3904

Navigational Information
Lat: 41°28.028' **Long:** 072°28.615' **Tide:** 3 ft. **Current:** n/a **Chart:** 12377
Rep. Depths *(MLW)*: **Entry** 14 ft. **Fuel Dock** n/a **Max Slip/Moor** 14 ft./-
Access: 1 mile past the East Haddam Swing bridge on the western shore

Marina Facilities *(In Season/Off Season)*
Fuel: No
Slips: 63 Total, 4 Transient **Max LOA:** 40 ft. **Max Beam:** 14 ft.
  Rate *(per ft.)*: **Day** $1.00/$1.00 **Week** Inq. **Month** $12
  Power: 30 amp 110, **50 amp** n/a, **100 amp** n/a, **200 amp** n/a
  Cable TV: No **Dockside Phone:** No
  Dock Type: Floating, Short Fingers, Alongside, Wood
Moorings: 0 Total, 0 Transient **Launch:** n/a
  Rate: Day n/a **Week** n/a **Month** n/a
Heads: 2 Toilet(s), 2 Shower(s)
Laundry: None **Pay Phones:** No
Pump-Out: No **Fee:** n/a **Closed Heads:** No

Marina Operations
Owner/Manager: Scott or Elliot Davidson **Dockmaster:** Same
In-Season: Year-Round, 8am-4:30pm **Off-Season:** n/a
After-Hours Arrival: Call ahead for instructions
Reservations: Yes, Preferred **Credit Cards:** Visa/MC, Cash or Check
Discounts: No **Dockage:** n/a **Fuel:** n/a **Repair:** n/a
Pets: No **Handicap Access:** Yes, Docks

Marina Services and Boat Supplies
Services - Docking Assistance **Supplies - OnSite:** Ice *(Block, Cube)*, Ships' Store **3+ mi:** Propane *(Amerigas 663-1636, 10 mi.)*

Boatyard Services
OnSite: Travelift *(10T & 15T)*, Crane, Engine mechanic *(gas, diesel)*, Launching Ramp, Electrical Repairs, Hull Repairs *(fiberglass work)*, Rigger *(custom rigging work)*, Bottom Cleaning, Brightwork, Compound, Wash & Wax, Interior Cleaning, Woodworking *(ships carpentry)*, Painting *(Interspray preferred)*, Awlgrip, Yacht Design, Yacht Building *(Custom Downeast Style)*, Total Refits **OnCall:** Propeller Repairs **Dealer for:** MerCruiser engines.
Yard Rates: $48/hr., Power Wash $1/ft.

Restaurants and Accommodations
OnSite: Seafood Shack *(The Blue Oar 345-2994)* **1-3 mi:** Restaurant *(Gelston House 873-1411)*, *(Country Restaurant 345-4229, B $2-5, L $4-6.50)*, *(Cooking Company 345-8008)*, Fast Food *(Subway)*, Pizzeria *(Haddam Pizza 345-4472, L $3-13, D $3-13, grinders, salads, entree, too Sun-Thurs 11:30-9:30, Fri-Sat 11:30-10)*, Motel *(Klar Crest Resort & Motel 873-8649)*, *(Granite Lodge 119 345-2482)*, Inn/B&B *(Gelston House 873-8411, $100-150)*, *(Bishopsgate Inns 873-1677, $105-165)*, *(123 Main 526-3456, $95-145)*

Recreation and Entertainment
OnSite: Picnic Area, Grills, Volleyball **Near:** Jogging Paths **1-3 mi:** Fitness Center *(Unique Physique 345-2983)*, Horseback Riding *(Pleasant View Stables 621-6474)*, Cultural Attract *(Goodspeed Opera House)*, Sightseeing *(Gillette Castle St. Pk. 526-2336; Connecticut Yankee Info & Science Center 267-9279)* **3+ mi:** Golf Course *(Banner Leisure Country Club 873-9075, 4 mi.)*, Museum *(Thankful Arnold House 345-2400, 3 mi.; Horse Drawn Carriage & Sleigh Museum 873-9658, 5 mi.)*

Provisioning and General Services
1-3 mi: Convenience Store *(Tylerville Citgo 345-3775)*, Delicatessen *(Cheeseboard Deli & Pizza 345-4418)*, Wine/Beer, Liquor Store *(De Lorenzos Package Store 873-8553)*, Bank/ATM, Post Office, Library *(Brainerd Memorial 345-2204)*, Laundry

Transportation
OnCall: Rental Car *(Enterprise 537-0181)* **3+ mi:** Rail *(Old Saybrook, 15 mi.)* **Airport:** Bradley Int'l. *(44 mi.)*

Medical Services
911 Service **OnCall:** Ambulance **1-3 mi:** Doctor *(Higganum Family Medical Group 345-8535)*, Dentist *(Higganum Dental Associates 345-4538)*, Chiropractor *(McColl 345-5121)*, Holistic Services *(Swedish Body Works 345-7919)*, Veterinarian *(Higganum Clinic 345-3366)*
Hospital: Middlesex 358-3700 *(9 mi.)*

Setting -- Lining the river's western shore, about a mile above the Haddam swing bridge, across from the Salmon River's mouth, are the docks of Damar/Midway Marina. This unspoiled, secluded stretch of River bends slightly westward as it approaches the marina's well-maintained facility and 7 acres of grounds. The gray 2-story building and adjacent work and storage sheds are perched high above the water. The Blue Oar Restaurant sits on pilings at dock level.

Marina Notes -- Shore Power is 110v. Small, service-oriented, second generation. Slips are a combination of alongside, stern-to, and slips with finger piers. Wide, nicely constructed outer dock is a recent upgrade. Extensive boatyard services and facilities - although do-it-yourself is encouraged. The well-equipped ships' store is heavily discounted and will special order. Indoor & outdoor storage for over 200 boats (including covered mast racks) is located 30 feet above flood stages. Power and water throughout the yard. Home of Salmon River Boatworks. A no wake zone in front of marina helps somewhat to reduce the roll.

Notable -- The onsite Blue Oar Restaurant offers very casual outdoor dining directly on the riverfront -- choose from under cover porch dining, scattered brightly colored patio tables & chairs, or picnic tables. Open from Mid-April-Mid-October, 11am-9pm, 7 days, during the summer and Fri-Sun to 7pm in the shoulder season. It's BYOB with a focus on seafood. About a mile downstream is The Goodspeed Opera House -- it is not walking distance (since roads don't parallel the river) and cabs are generally not available. However, the Opera House does have a dinghy dock just south of its main dock. 2 miles up river the Connecticut Yankee Information & Science Center has nuclear power plant exhibits, a picnic area and dock.

IV. Connecticut: Eastern Long Island Sound

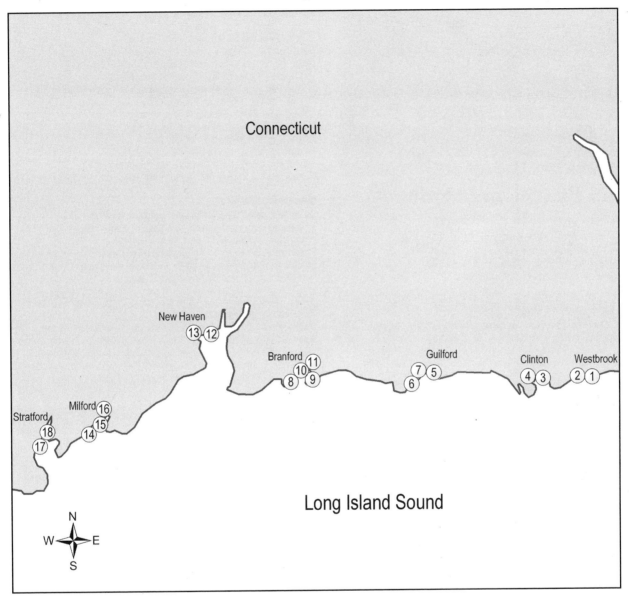

MAP	MARINA	HARBOR	PAGE	MAP	MARINA	HARBOR	PAGE
1	Brewer Pilot's Point Marina	Duck Island Rds/Patchogue Rvr	74	10	Dutch Wharf Marina	Branford River	83
2	Harry's Marine Repair	Duck Island Rds/Patchogue Rvr	75	11	Branford Landing	Branford River	84
3	Port Clinton Marina	Clinton Harbor	76	12	Oyster Point Marina	New Haven Harbor	85
4	Cedar Island Marina	Clinton Harbor	77	13	West Cove Marina	New Haven Harbor	86
5	Len Hubbard Municipal Marina	Guilford Harbor	78	14	Port Milford	Milford Hbr/Wepawaug Rvr	87
6	Brown's Boat Yard	Guilford Harbor/West River	79	15	Milford Boat Works	Milford Hbr/Wepawaug Rvr	88
7	Guilford Yacht Club	Guilford Harbor/West River	80	16	Milford Landing Marina	Milford Hbr/Wepawaug Rvr	89
8	Pier 66 Marina	Branford River	81	17	Brewer Stratford Marina	Housatonic River	90
9	Brewer Bruce & Johnson Marina	Branford River	82	18	Marina at The Dock	Housatonic River	91

Brewer Pilot's Point Marinas

63 Pilot's Point Drive; Westbrook, CT 06498

Tel: (860) 399-7906 **VHF: Monitor** 9 **Talk** 12
Fax: (860) 399-7259 **Alternate Tel:** n/a
Email: ppm @snet.net **Web:** www.byy.com/Westbrook
Nearest Town: Westbrook *(1 mi.)* **Tourist Info:** (860) 669-3889

Navigational Information
Lat: 41°16.250' **Long:** 072°28.250' **Tide:** 6 ft. **Current:** 1 kt. **Chart:** 12374
Rep. Depths *(MLW)*: **Entry** 10 ft. **Fuel Dock** 12 ft. **Max Slip/Moor** 15 ft./-
Access: Duck Island Roads to Patchogue & Menunketesuck Rivers

Marina Facilities *(In Season/Off Season)*
Fuel: *Texaco* - Gasoline, Diesel, High-Speed Pumps
Slips: 880 Total, 20 Transient **Max LOA:** 170 ft. **Max Beam:** 30 ft.
 Rate *(per ft.)*: **Day** $3.00 **Week** $15 **Month** $45
 Power: 30 amp Incl., **50 amp** Incl., **100 amp** n/a, **200 amp** n/a
 Cable TV: Yes **Dockside Phone:** Yes Through local tel co
 Dock Type: Floating, Long Fingers, Wood
Moorings: 0 Total, 0 Transient **Launch:** n/a, Dinghy Dock
 Rate: Day n/a **Week** n/a **Month** n/a
Heads: 7 Toilet(s), 14 Shower(s), Hair Dryers
Laundry: 1 Washer(s), 1 Dryer(s) **Pay Phones:** Yes, 7
Pump-Out: Full Service, 5 Central, 1 Port **Fee:** Free **Closed Heads:** Yes

Marina Operations
Owner/Manager: Todd R. Turcotte **Dockmaster:** Tom Lyon
In-Season: Summer, 7am-8pm **Off-Season:** Fall-Win-Sprg, 8am-4pm
After-Hours Arrival: Call on Ch. 09 for instructions
Reservations: Yes, Required **Credit Cards:** Visa/MC, Dscvr, Amex, Tex
Discounts: Group Price, 5+ boats **Dockage:** n/a **Fuel:** n/a **Repair:** n/a
Pets: Welcome, Dog Walk Area **Handicap Access:** Yes, Heads, Docks

Marina Services and Boat Supplies
Services - Docking Assistance, Concierge, Boaters' Lounge, Security, Trash Pick-Up, Dock Carts **Communication -** Mail & Package Hold, Phone Messages, Fax in/out, Data Ports *(South Clubhouse)*, FedEx, AirBorne, UPS, Express Mail **Supplies - OnSite:** Ice *(Block, Cube)*, Ships' Store, Propane, CNG **Near:** Boater's World *(399-9773)*, Bait/Tackle
1-3 mi: West Marine *(664-4060)*, Boat/US *(399-3170)*

Boatyard Services
OnSite: Travelift *(5, to 80T)*, Forklift, Crane, Engine mechanic *(gas, diesel)*, Electrical Repairs, Electronic Sales, Electronics Repairs, Hull Repairs, Rigger, Bottom Cleaning, Brightwork, Air Conditioning, Refrigeration, Divers, Compound, Wash & Wax, Interior Cleaning, Woodworking, Metal Fabrication, Painting, Awlgrip, Yacht Design, Yacht Broker, Yacht Building, Total Refits **OnCall:** Propeller Repairs, Inflatable Repairs **Near:** Launching Ramp, Sail Loft, Upholstery, Yacht Interiors. **Dealer for:** Volvo Penta, Caterpillar, Detroit Diesel, Perkins, Westerbeke, Yanmar, Xantrex, Grunnert, Naiad, Kohler, Crusader, Marine Power, Pleasurecraft, Universal, Vacuflush, Village Marine, Webasto, Waeco Adler Barbour, CruiseAir, Espar.

Restaurants and Accommodations
OnSite: Restaurant *(Boom 399-2322, L $5-13, D $15-23, Sun Brunch $6.50-16.50)* **OnCall:** Pizzeria *(Westbrook Pizza 399-7160)*
Under 1 mi: Restaurant *(Humphreys 399-0311)*, *(Frankies 399-5524)*, Seafood Shack *(Bill's Seafood 399-7224, or dinghy)*, Lite Fare *(Edd's Place 399-9498)*, Inn/B&B *(Westbrook 399-4777)*, *(Talcott House 399-5020)*, *(Angels Watch 399-8846)*, *(Capt Stannard 399-4634, $125-165)*
1-3 mi: Inn/B&B *(Beach Plum 399-9345)*, *(Water's Edge 399-5501)*

Recreation and Entertainment
OnSite: Pool (2), Picnic Area, Grills, Playground, Volleyball, Tennis Courts, Roller Blade/Bike Paths **Near:** Beach *(Town Beach)*, Boat Rentals, Park
Under 1 mi: Dive Shop, Video Rental *(Video Movie Time 664-4401)*
1-3 mi: Movie Theater *(Marquee Cinemas 399-9692)* **3+ mi:** Golf Course *(Hillside 526-9986, 14 mi.)*, Bowling *(Amf 388-3488, 5 mi.)*

Provisioning and General Services
Near: Catholic Church, Protestant Church, Synagogue, Dry Cleaners, Laundry *(Kenni's coin op, Better Cleaners - full-serve)*, Newsstand, Copies Etc. **Under 1 mi:** Convenience Store, Gourmet Shop, Delicatessen *(Westbrook Deli 399-5090)*, Liquor Store *(Good-Spirits 669-5821)*, Bakery, Farmers' Market, Bank/ATM, Post Office, Beauty Salon, Barber Shop, Bookstore *(Bargain Books 399-6652)*, Pharmacy *(Westbrook 399-9500)*
1-3 mi: Supermarket *(Westbrook Food Center 399-6915; Shaw's 669-0107 van service)*, Fishmonger, Lobster Pound *(Westbrook Lobster 664-9464)*, Library *(399-6422)*, Florist, Retail Shops *(Westbrook Factory Outlets 399-8656)*
3+ mi: Hardware Store *(Clinton Hardware 669-8255, 4 mi.)*

Transportation
OnSite: Courtesy Car/Van **OnCall:** Rental Car *(Enterprise 395-0758)*, Taxi *(East Shore 388-2819)* **3+ mi:** Rail *(Shore Line East 777-7433, 5 mi.)*
Airport: Tweed New Haven /Bradley *(30 mi./60 mi.)*

Medical Services
911 Service **OnCall:** Ambulance **Under 1 mi:** Dentist **1-3 mi:** Doctor *(Community Health Center 664-0787)*, Chiropractor *(Clinton Chiropractic 669-6790)* **Hospital:** Middlesex 358-3700 *(8 mi.)*

Setting -- 863 slips, many amenities, and major boatyard services -- divided into three yards and spread over 50 nicely landscaped and carefully tended acres -- make this one of the largest full-service marinas in the Northeast. The Pilot's Point Yards have protected locations, club-like amenities -- including pools, tennis courts, playgrounds, a restaurant and more -- and are attractively sited along two small rivers. The docks have been thoughtfully grouped into smaller, more intimate sectors that belie the extensiveness of the facility. Pots of flowers and cultivated annual and perennial borders add to the ambiance and, in some cases, the views from the slips are of unspoiled wildlife refuges.

Marina Notes -- A three-marina complex connected by courtesy vans - which also go to town. Two swimming pools, 2 sand volleyball courts, 2 basketball courts, 2 tennis courts, a putting green, 2 playgrounds, several gazebos, 2 clubhouses (TV, VCR and cooking facilities), 2 pavilions, a convenience and ships' store, Boom Restaurant (L, D & Sun Brunch, intriguing menu, great views), 3 picnic areas with grills (including dock decks), 2 dockmaster stations, and over 70 year-round staff members to make it all work. Large scale boatyard services with 5 travelifts, 7 inside storage buildings (up to 100 ft). Mega-yacht capabilities.

Notable -- Service! Ice and newspaper deliveries, restaurant reservations, etc. Local zoning forbids onsite laundry. Dinghy the meandering Menunketesuck and Patchogue Rivers to explore the protected wildlife refuge that adjoins the marina (or to get to Bill's). Nearby is a town beach, shops, restaurants - plus two major designer outlets - Westbrook Factory Stores and Clinton Crossings. NOTE: Above distances to various services are generalized from the 3 yards.

Navigational Information

Lat: 41°16.350' **Long:** 072°28.050' **Tide:** 4.5 ft. **Current:** 1 kt. **Chart:** n/a
Rep. Depths *(MLW)*: **Entry** 8 ft. **Fuel Dock** 8 ft. **Max Slip/Moor** 8 ft./4 ft.
Access: Follow federal channel in from red #2 bouy

Marina Facilities *(In Season/Off Season)*

Fuel: *Mobil* - Gasoline
Slips: 76 Total, 3 Transient **Max LOA:** 40 ft. **Max Beam:** 15 ft.
 Rate *(per ft.)*: **Day** $1.25/Inq. **Week** Inq. **Month** Inq.
 Power: 30 amp Incl., 50 amp Incl., 100 amp n/a, 200 amp n/a
 Cable TV: No **Dockside Phone:** No
 Dock Type: Floating, Long Fingers, Wood
Moorings: 0 Total, 0 Transient **Launch:** n/a
 Rate: Day n/a **Week** n/a **Month** n/a
Heads: 4 Toilet(s), 4 Shower(s) *(with dressing rooms)*
Laundry: None, Book Exchange **Pay Phones:** No
Pump-Out: OnCall, Full Service **Fee:** $5 **Closed Heads:** Yes

Marina Operations

Owner/Manager: Harry P. Ruppenicker Sr. **Dockmaster:** Same
In-Season: Year-Round, 8am-4:30pm **Off-Season:** Same
After-Hours Arrival: Tie up at fuel dock
Reservations: Yes, Preferred **Credit Cards:** Visa/MC
Discounts: None
Pets: Welcome **Handicap Access:** No

Harry's Marine Repair

38 Hammock Road SO.; Westbrook, CT 06498

Tel: (860) 399-6165 **VHF: Monitor** n/a **Talk** n/a
Fax: (860) 399-5724 **Alternate Tel:** n/a
Email: harmar38@snet.net **Web:** n/a
Nearest Town: Westbrook *(1.5 mi.)* **Tourist Info:** (860) 399-6479

Marina Services and Boat Supplies

Services - Docking Assistance, Boaters' Lounge, Dock Carts
Communication - Mail & Package Hold, Phone Messages, Fax in/out
Supplies - OnSite: Ice *(Block, Cube)*, Ships' Store **Near:** Boater's World *(399-9773)*, Propane *(Pilot's Point)*, CNG *(Pilot's Point)*
Under 1 mi: Boat/US, Bait/Tackle *(Paul's Custom Tackle & Bait 399-2271)*
1-3 mi: West Marine *(664-4060)*

Boatyard Services

OnSite: Travelift *(10T)*, Crane, Engine mechanic *(gas, diesel)*, Electrical Repairs, Hull Repairs, Rigger, Bottom Cleaning, Brightwork, Compound, Wash & Wax, Propeller Repairs, Woodworking, Yacht Broker *(Westbrook Sailing Center)* **Yard Rates:** $70/hr., Haul & Launch $7/ft., Power Wash $0.25/sq. ft. **Storage:** In-Water $25/ft., On-Land $3/sq. ft.

Restaurants and Accommodations

Near: Restaurant *(Edd's Place 399-9498)*, *(Porter's Bar & Grill 399-2233)*, *(Bill's Seafood 399-7224)*, *(New Deal Steakplace 399-0015)*, *(Boom 399-2322, L $5-13, D $15-23)* **Under 1 mi:** Inn/B&B *(Angels Watch 399-8846)*
1-3 mi: Restaurant *(Fish Tale 669-0767)*, Fast Food *(Dunkin Donuts)*, *(Subway)*, Pizzeria *(Westbrook Pizza 399-7160)*, Motel *(Village 669-8403)*, Hotel *(Water Edge)*, Inn/B&B *(Talcott House 399-5020)*
3+ mi: Motel *(Days Inn 388-3453, 4 mi.)*

Recreation and Entertainment

OnSite: Picnic Area, Grills **Under 1 mi:** Beach *(Westbrook Town Beach*

- by dinghy) **1-3 mi:** Fitness Center *(Curves for Women 399-0392)*, Movie Theater *(Westbrook Cinemas 399-9692)*, Video Rental *(Video Movie Time 664-4401)*, Park **3+ mi:** Golf Course *(Hillside Links 526-9986, 7 mi.)*, Bowling *(Amf Saybrook 388-3488, 6 mi.)*, Museum *(Connecticut River Museum 767-8269, 7 mi.)*

Provisioning and General Services

1-3 mi: Convenience Store, Supermarket *(Shaw's 669-0107)*, Delicatessen *(Westbrook Deli 399-5090)*, Wine/Beer, Liquor Store *(Good-Spirits 669-5821)*, Bakery, Farmers' Market, Fishmonger, Lobster Pound, Meat Market, Bank/ATM, Post Office, Catholic Church, Protestant Church *(Cong. Episc.)*, Library *(Westbrook 399-6422)*, Beauty Salon, Barber Shop, Dry Cleaners, Laundry, Florist, Clothing Store, Retail Shops, Copies Etc. *(Value Print 669-8614)* **3+ mi:** Hardware Store *(Stevens - Clinton 669-8441, 4 mi.)*

Transportation

OnCall: Rental Car *(Enterprise 395-0758 /Thrifty 399-5146 2 mi.)*, Taxi *(Essex Taxi 767-7433)*, Airport Limo *(Mr. Limousine 203-245-3465)*
1-3 mi: Rail *(Shore Line East Commuter Rail 777-7433)*
Airport: Tweed New Haven/Bradley *(30 mi./60 mi.)*

Medical Services

911 Service **OnCall:** Ambulance **1-3 mi:** Doctor, Dentist *(Shoreline Dental Associates 399-7971)*, Veterinarian *(Clinton Veterinary Hospital 669-5721)*
3+ mi: Chiropractor *(Clinton Chiropractic 669-6790, 4 mi.)*
Hospital: Middlesex 358-3700 *(5 mi.)*

Setting -- On the western shore of the Patchogue River, between Pilot's Point East and Pilot's Point South yards, is this small, bristol marina and boatyard. The docks are noticeably well cared for and regularly stained. A small, attractive two-story building by the water houses the dockmaster's office and a boaters' lounge. Views - both water and landside - are mostly, in this narrow waterway, of boats and buildings.

Marina Notes -- Family owned and operated since 1965, with a friendly and helpful staff. Designated a CT Clean Marina. Full boat yard services and onsite fuel. Pump-out boat on call. A separate building farther back houses a small ships' store, a work shed, and, in the rear, the restrooms. Picnic tables and grills are near the docks. Right next door is Westbrook Sailing School. Local zoning does not permit on-site laundry facilities but up the road at Kenni's is a coin operated laundromat, and downtown Westbrook Better Cleaners provides a full-service laundry.

Notable -- Its location, well up the river, provides not only excellent protection but also easy access to land services. A short walk up the hill takes you to Route One; Edd's Place, with a small deck by the water, and Porter's Bar and Grill are both right across the road. Or explore, by dinghy, farther up the Patchogue River - Bill's Seafood is just north of the Route 1 bridge and farther along there's lots of wildlife. Then head south toward the mouth where it joins the Menunketesuck River. Head north again as the Menunketesuck meanders through Pilot Point's North and a protected wildlife refuge. Nearby is the Westbrook town beach, shops, a number of eateries, plus, a little farther afield, two major designer outlets - Westbrook Factory Stores and Clinton Crossings.

Port Clinton Marina

33 Indian Drive; Clinton, CT 06413

Tel: (860) 669-4563 **VHF: Monitor** n/a **Talk** n/a
Fax: (860) 669-9905 **Alternate Tel:** (860) 669-6278
Email: n/a **Web:** n/a
Nearest Town: Clinton *(0.7 mi.)* **Tourist Info:** (860) 669-3889

Navigational Information

Lat: 41°16.149' **Long:** 072°31.508' **Tide:** 4.5 ft. **Current:** n/a **Chart:** 12374
Rep. Depths *(MLW)*: **Entry** 8 ft. **Fuel Dock** n/a **Max Slip/Moor** 7 ft./-
Access: Clinton channel at 7G, follow past R14 turn to starboard

Marina Facilities *(In Season/Off Season)*

Fuel: No
Slips: 110 Total, 10 Transient **Max LOA:** 50 ft. **Max Beam:** n/a
  Rate *(per ft.)*: **Day** $1.30/Inq. **Week** Inq. **Month** Inq.
  Power: 30 amp Incl., **50 amp** n/a, **100 amp** n/a, **200 amp** n/a
  Cable TV: No **Dockside Phone:** No
  Dock Type: Floating, Long Fingers, Wood
Moorings: 0 Total, 0 Transient **Launch:** n/a
  Rate: Day n/a **Week** n/a **Month** n/a
Heads: 4 Toilet(s), 4 Shower(s) *(with dressing rooms)*
Laundry: 2 Washer(s), 1 Dryer(s) **Pay Phones:** No
Pump-Out: No **Fee:** n/a **Closed Heads:** No

Marina Operations

Owner/Manager: Michael Mackey **Dockmaster:** n/a
In-Season: Apr-Nov, 8am-8pm **Off-Season:** Dec-Mar, 9am-5pm
After-Hours Arrival: Call ahead
Reservations: Yes **Credit Cards:** Visa/MC
Discounts: Boat/US; 25% **Dockage:** n/a **Fuel:** n/a **Repair:** n/a
Pets: Welcome **Handicap Access:** No

Marina Services and Boat Supplies

Services - Security *(24 Hrs.)*, Trash Pick-Up, Dock Carts **Communication** - FedEx, AirBorne, UPS, Express Mail **Supplies - Near:** Ships' Store, Bait/Tackle *(Jan's Tackle 669-1377)* **Under 1 mi:** Marine Discount Store **1-3 mi:** West Marine *(664-4060)*, Propane *(Sound Petroleum 669-8697)*

Boatyard Services

OnSite: Travelift *(50T)*, Engine mechanic *(gas)*, Launching Ramp, Electrical Repairs, Hull Repairs, Bottom Cleaning, Interior Cleaning, Painting
Yard Rates: $60/hr., Haul & Launch $7/ft. *(blocking $2/ft.)*, Power Wash $2/ft., Bottom Paint $11/ft.

Restaurants and Accommodations

Under 1 mi: Restaurant *(Chip's Pub Restaurant 669-3463)*, *(Aqua Restaurant 664-3788)*, *(Great Wall Chinese 664-4110)*, *(Bella Luna 669-9987)*, *(Ryan's Driftwood Café 669-5807)*, Coffee Shop *(Coffee Break 664-0808)*, Pizzeria *(Grand Apizza 669-1204)*, Motel *(Village Motel 669-8403)*, *(Clinton Motel 669-8850, $55-90)* **1-3 mi:** Seafood Shack *(Clam Castle 203-245-4911)*, Crab House *(Westbrook Lobster)*, Fast Food, Motel *(Lamp Lighter 669-7983)*

Recreation and Entertainment

OnSite: Picnic Area **Near:** Playground, Dive Shop, Jogging Paths, Video Arcade, Park, Special Events **Under 1 mi:** Cultural Attract *(Connecticut Opera at Andrews Memorial Hall)*, Sightseeing *(The Brickhouse)* **1-3 mi:** Beach *(Hammonasset State Park)*, Tennis Courts, Fitness Center *(Shoreline Health & Fitness 669-9456)*, Video Rental *(Blockbuster 664-1786)*

3+ mi: Golf Course *(Guilford Lakes 203-453-8214, 13 mi.)*, Movie Theater *(Madison Art Cinemas 203-245-3456, 5 mi.)*, Museum *(Madison Historical Society 203-245-4567, 5 mi.)*

Provisioning and General Services

Under 1 mi: Delicatessen *(Saldamarco's 669-3469)*, Liquor Store *(Bottle Shop 664-0570)*, Fishmonger, Bank/ATM, Post Office, Catholic Church, Protestant Church, Library *(Clinton 669-2342, Internet access)*, Beauty Salon, Barber Shop, Dry Cleaners, Laundry, Pharmacy *(CVS 664-9335)*, Newsstand, Hardware Store *(Cashman's 669-8441)*, Florist, Clothing Store, Retail Shops, Buying Club, Copies Etc. *(Mail Boxes Etc 664-0066)* **1-3 mi:** Convenience Store, Supermarket *(Shaw's 669-0107)*, Gourmet Shop, Wine/Beer, Bakery, Farmers' Market, Green Grocer, Lobster Pound *(Westbrook Lobster Market & Restaurant 664-9464)*, Bookstore *(Book Warehouse 669-9784)*, Department Store **3+ mi:** Health Food *(Madison Health Foods 203-245-8607, 5 mi.)*

Transportation

OnCall: Rental Car *(Enterprise 203-245-1920/Thrifty 203-562-3191, 3 mi.)*, Taxi *(Essex Taxi 767-7433)*, Airport Limo *(Mr. Limousine 245-3465)*
Under 1 mi: Rail *(Shore Line East Commuter Rail 777-7433)*
Airport: Tweed New Haven/Bradley Int'l. *(25 mi./52 mi.)*

Medical Services

911 Service **Under 1 mi:** Doctor *(Community Health Cntr. 664-0787)*, Dentist *(Clinton Family Dentistry 669-2700)*, Chiropractor *(Milone Chiropractic 664-3966)*, Veterinarian *(Shoreline Animal Hospital 669-9374)*
Hospital: Middlesex 358-3700 *(7 mi.)*

Setting -- The first of the marinas on the Hammonasset River off Clinton Harbor, this quite rustic boatyard usually has a number of conveniently located transient slips for boats up to 50 ft. The gray, two-story office building sits above 3 long piers with finger slips. Also overlooking the docks is a small platform that holds several picnic tables where you can enjoy the changing light on the marsh. Waterside, the pretty views are across to the harbor to the houses on Cedar Island.

Marina Notes -- Prides itself on friendly service. New bathrooms installed in 2001. Mostly modest size boats and a basic boat yard. Connecticut Power Marine is onsite, and has a small ships' store. One hundred foot wide entrance channel was dredged to a minimum depth of 8 feet, much of it 10-12 feet -- to east of Cedar Island -- in 2001. Nearby Old Harbor Marine (669-8361), up the Indian River, may also have transient dock space.

Notable -- Walk through the nearby neighborhood of 18thC houses and follow Commerce Street back to town. The center of Clinton, less than a mile away, has a pizzeria, pharmacy, post office, bank, and a few restaurants. Clinton Crossings designer discount outlet is 1.7 miles away and Shaw's supermarket is 2 miles. On the sound side of Cedar Island - via dinghy - you'll find large sand beaches with playground and picnic areas. A restaurant, fish market, and other services open to the public are also at Cedar Island Marina. Stop by the Visitors' Information Center on East Main Street to learn about "The Brickhouse."

Navigational Information
Lat: 41°16.133' **Long:** 072°32.880' **Tide:** 4.5 ft. **Current:** n/a **Chart:** 12372
Rep. Depths (MLW): Entry 8 ft. **Fuel Dock** 8 ft. **Max Slip/Moor** 8 ft./-
Access: Hammonasset River around Cedar Island

Marina Facilities *(In Season/Off Season)*
Fuel: Gulf - Gasoline, Diesel
Slips: 400 Total, 70 Transient **Max LOA:** 120 ft. **Max Beam:** n/a
 Rate *(per ft.):* **Day** $3.00/1.60* **Week** $15.50/7.50 **Month** $48.50/24.25
Power: 30 amp Incl., 50 amp $5, 100 amp $10, 200 amp n/a
Cable TV: Yes, $0 **Dockside Phone:** No
Dock Type: Floating
Moorings: 0 Total, 0 Transient **Launch:** n/a
 Rate: Day n/a **Week** n/a **Month** n/a
Heads: 10 Toilet(s), 14 Shower(s) *(with dressing rooms)*
Laundry: 3 Washer(s), 3 Dryer(s) **Pay Phones:** Yes, 2
Pump-Out: OnSite, Full Service **Fee:** Free **Closed Heads:** Yes

Marina Operations
Owner/Manager: Jeff Shapiro **Dockmaster:** Marc Tardiff
In-Season: Summer, 8am-8pm **Off-Season:** Winter, 8am-4pm
After-Hours Arrival: Service person on-site until 4am.
Reservations: Yes, Preferred **Credit Cards:** Visa/MC, Dscvr, Amex, Gulf
Discounts: Volume **Dockage:** n/a **Fuel:** n/a **Repair:** n/a
Pets: Welcome, Dog Walk Area **Handicap Access:** No

Cedar Island Marina

PO Box 181; 34 Riverside Drive; Clinton, CT 06413

Tel: (860) 669-8681 **VHF: Monitor** 9 **Talk** 68
Fax: (860) 669-4157 **Alternate Tel:** (860) 669-8681
Email: n/a **Web:** www.cedarislandmarina.com
Nearest Town: Clinton *(1 mi.)* **Tourist Info:** (860) 669-3889

Marina Services and Boat Supplies
Services - Docking Assistance, Security *(20 Hrs., Summer)*, Trash Pick-Up, Dock Carts **Communication -** Mail & Package Hold, Phone Messages, Fax in/out, FedEx, AirBorne, UPS, Express Mail **Supplies - OnSite:** Ice *(Block, Cube)*, Ships' Store *(Crew's Closet)*, Bait/Tackle *(Jan's Tackle Shop)*, Live Bait **Near:** Propane **1-3 mi:** West Marine *(664-4060)*

Boatyard Services
OnSite: Travelift, Forklift, Crane, Engine mechanic *(gas, diesel)*, Hull Repairs, Rigger, Bottom Cleaning, Brightwork, Refrigeration, Compound, Wash & Wax, Propeller Repairs, Woodworking, Upholstery, Yacht Interiors, Painting, Awlgrip, Yacht Broker, Total Refits **Near:** Launching Ramp, Electrical Repairs, Electronics Repairs. **1-3 mi:** Inflatable Repairs, Metal Fabrication. **Dealer for:** Westerbeke, Allison, Yanmar, Mercruiser. **Yard Rates:** $75/hr. mechanical, Haul & Launch $7.80-20/ft., Power Wash $2, Bottom Paint $8-14.50/ft. **Storage:** In-Water $25/ft., On-Land $34-41/ft.

Restaurants and Accommodations
OnSite: Restaurant *(Aqua Restaurant 664-3788)* **Under 1 mi:** Restaurant *(Great Wall Chinese 664-4110)*, *(Ryan's Driftwood Café 669-5807)*, Coffee Shop *(Coffee Break 664-0808)*, Fast Food, Pizzeria *(Grand Apizza 669-1204)* **1-3 mi:** Restaurant *(Log Cabin 669-6253, L $6-9, D $12-20)*, *(Clam Castle 203-245-4911)*, Motel *(Clinton Motel 669-8850)*, *(Lamp Lighter 669-7983)*, *(Village Motel 669-8403)*, Inn/B&B *(Tidewater Inn 245-8457)*

Recreation and Entertainment
OnSite: Heated Pool, Picnic Area, Grills, Playground *(with a multi-slide climbing structure)*, Volleyball **Near:** Beach *(Hammonasset)*

Under 1 mi: Fitness Center *(Curves 669-4068)*, Jogging Paths, Park **1-3 mi:** Video Rental *(Blockbuster 664-1786)*, Museum *(Clinton Historical Society)*, Cultural Attract *(Connecticut Opera at Andrews Mem. Hall)*, Galleries *(& antique shops)* **3+ mi:** Tennis Courts *(Madison Racquet & Swim Club 203-245-9444, 4 mi.)*, Golf Course *(Guilford Lakes 203-453-8214, 13 mi.)*, Movie Theater *(Madison Art 203- 245-3456, 4 mi.)*

Provisioning and General Services
OnSite: Fishmonger *(BB&G Lobster & Seafood)*, Lobster Pound, Copies Etc. **Under 1 mi:** Convenience Store, Gourmet Shop, Delicatessen *(Aunt Shirley's 669-3354)*, Liquor Store *(Bottle Shop 664-0570)*, Bakery, Farmers' Market, Bank/ATM, Post Office, Catholic Church, Protestant Church, Library *(Clinton 669-2342)*, Beauty Salon, Barber Shop, Dry Cleaners, Laundry, Bookstore *(Encore Books 664-3885)*, Pharmacy *(CVS 664-9335)*, Newsstand, Hardware Store *(Cashman's 669-8441)*, Florist, Clothing Store **1-3 mi:** Supermarket *(Shaw's 669-0107)*, Meat Market, Synagogue, Retail Shops **3+ mi:** Health Food *(Madison Health Foods 203-245-8607, 4 mi.)*

Transportation
OnSite: Courtesy Car/Van *(Shuttle to town & Clinton Crossings)*, Rental Car *(Enterprise 203 245-1920)* **OnCall:** Airport Limo *(Mr. Limo 203-245-3465)* **Under 1 mi:** Taxi, Local Bus, Rail *(Shore Line East Commuter 777-7433)* **Airport:** New Haven 203- 466-8833/Bradley Int'l. 292-2000 *(25 mi./53 mi.)*

Medical Services
911 Service **OnSite:** Doctor **OnCall:** Ambulance **Under 1 mi:** Dentist *(Clinton Family Dentistry 669-2700)*, Chiropractor *(Milone 664-3966)* **Hospital:** Middlesex 358-3700 *(8 mi.)*

Setting -- Through lovely, industry-free Clinton Harbor, up the meandering Hammonasset River, and halfway around Cedar Island, is this very protected, large scale, full-service marina resort. Landside are many amenities, including a new, heated 60 ft. pool, large whirlpool, playground, shuffleboard, volleyball, horseshoes, picnic areas, marine habitat center, full-service boatyard, snack bar and restaurant. The views are of the pristine marshes of Cedar Island.

Marina Notes -- * $65 min. Sizable and available (via intercom) dock help on staff. Newly renovated heads and showers. Excellent canvas shop onsite, plus marine hardware and tackle shop. Three picnic-barbecue areas, plus grills at the ends of the docks. Supervised kids' activity program and adult lounge with pool table, large TV, kitchen, fireplace and comfortable seating (also available for groups up to 50). Slip rates include all services, electric, cable. "L" dock offers "no-frills" rate with just water service. Storage includes haul, launch, wash. The 100-foot wide entrance channel was dredged to a minimum depth of 8 ft. (much of it 10-12 ft.) to east of Cedar Island in June 2001.

Notable -- Historically, this has been one of the most ecologically conscious marinas on LI Sound (a staff biologist monitors water quality and fish habitats and leads field trips to the state park). Consistently named one of the 25 cleanest marinas in the US. A 400 gal. aquarium displays more than 40 types of local fish. Marina shuttle bus (9am-7pm) to town, supermarket and to Clinton Crossing outlets. Onsite is a pool-side snack bar and the 275-seat Aqua Restaurant open 7 days May-Oct (Wed-Sun 11:30-10pm off-season). Club cruises accommodated. Home to Clinton Harbor Boat Show 3rd Week July and other events.

Len Hubbard Municipal Marina

31 Park Street; Guilford, CT 06437

Tel: (203) 453-8092 **VHF: Monitor** 9 **Talk** 11
Fax: n/a **Alternate Tel:** n/a
Email: n/a **Web:** n/a
Nearest Town: Guilford *(1 mi.)* **Tourist Info:** (203) 453-9677

Navigational Information

Lat: 41°16.327' **Long:** 072°39.931' **Tide:** 4 ft. **Current:** 2 kt. **Chart:** 12354
Rep. Depths (MLW): Entry 5 ft. **Fuel Dock** n/a **Max Slip/Moor** 8 ft./8 ft.
Access: Guilford Harbor to East River

Marina Facilities *(In Season/Off Season)*

Fuel: No
Slips: 130 Total, 2 Transient **Max LOA:** 38 ft. **Max Beam:** 14 ft.
 Rate *(per ft.):* **Day** $32.00* **Week** n/a **Month** n/a
 Power: 30 amp Incl., **50 amp** n/a, **100 amp** n/a, **200 amp** n/a
 Cable TV: No **Dockside Phone:** No
 Dock Type: Fixed, Floating, Alongside
Moorings: 14 Total, 2 Transient **Launch:** None, Dinghy Dock
 Rate: Day $16 **Week** Inq. **Month** Inq.
Heads: 2 Toilet(s)
Laundry: None **Pay Phones:** No
Pump-Out: No **Fee:** n/a **Closed Heads:** Yes

Marina Operations

Owner/Manager: Guilford Commission **Dockmaster:** Joe DesRochers
In-Season: Apr-Nov 1, 9am-4pm **Off-Season:** n/a
After-Hours Arrival: Honor system or call in advance
Reservations: Preferred **Credit Cards:** Cash or check only
Discounts: None
Pets: Welcome **Handicap Access:** Yes, Docks

Marina Services and Boat Supplies

Services - Docking Assistance, Security *(24 Hrs., Local police patrol)*, Trash Pick-Up, Dock Carts **Supplies - OnSite:** Ice *(Block, Cube)*, Bait/Tackle *(The Bait House; also fishing licenses)*, Live Bait **Under 1 mi:** Ships' Store *(Lewmar Marine 458-6200)* **1-3 mi:** Propane *(Hocon Gas 458-2790)* **3+ mi:** West Marine *(481-3465, 6 mi.)*, CNG *(Brewer Bruce & Johnson 488-8329, 10 mi.)*

Restaurants and Accommodations

OnSite: Restaurant *(The Stone House 458-7600, L $7-9, D $9-18, Sun Brunch $13/6.50)*, *(Guilford Mooring 458-2921, L $7-20, D $11-23, Pub $7-17; sandwiches to three-course meals)*, Snack Bar *(The Bait House 458-2554, B $1-2, L & D $3-8; views of Faulkner's Light)*
OnCall: Pizzeria *(Giuseppes 458-8676)* **Under 1 mi:** Restaurant *(Tastebuds of Guilford 453-1937)* **1-3 mi:** Fast Food, Motel *(Tower Suites 453-9069, $55-75)*, *(Crescent Motel 245-9145)* **3+ mi:** Restaurant *(Guilford Tavern 453-2216, 3.5 mi.)*, Motel *(Guilford Suites 453-0123, 4 mi)*, Inn/B&B *(Madison Post Road Bed & Breakfast 245-2866, 4 mi.)*

Recreation and Entertainment

OnSite: Picnic Area, Boat Rentals *(The Bait House 458-2554, 2 hrs. $25, 4 hrs. $35, day $40)*, Fishing Charter **Near:** Park *(Foote Memorial, West Point)* **Under 1 mi:** Beach *(East Point - dinghy)*, Museum *(Hyland House 453-947 - early colonial artifacts, Tue-Sun Jun-LabDay, Weekends 'til ColDay 10am-4:30pm, $2; Whitfield State Historical Museum 453-2457 $3.50/2.00, under 6 free)*, Sightseeing *(Guilford's 17th-19thC houses)*,
Galleries *(Guilford Handcraft Center - gallery Mon-Sat 10-5, Sun 12-4, shop open 'til 7 on Thu)* **1-3 mi:** Tennis Courts *(Guilford Racquet & Swim Club 453-4367)*, Video Rental *(Blockbuster 453-2666)* **3+ mi:** Golf Course *(Twin Lakes Golf 488-8778, 7 mi.)*, Movie Theater *(5 mi.)*

Provisioning and General Services

OnSite: Lobster Pound **Near:** Library *(Guilford Library 453-8282)*, Hardware Store *(Page Hardware 453-5267)* **Under 1 mi:** Supermarket *(Guilford Food Center 543-4849 - delivers)*, Gourmet Shop, Delicatessen *(Deli Unlimited 453-2473)*, Bakery, Meat Market, Bank/ATM, Post Office, Catholic Church, Protestant Church, Beauty Salon, Barber Shop, Dry Cleaners, Bookstore *(Breakwater Books 453-4141)*, Pharmacy *(Genovese 453-4310)*, Florist, Clothing Store, Retail Shops, Copies Etc. *(Mail Boxes Etc 453-8866)* **1-3 mi:** Wine/Beer, Liquor Store *(Franks Package Store 453-2259)*, Farmers' Market

Transportation

OnCall: Rental Car *(Enterprise 245-1920)*, Airport Limo *(Proto Limousine Service 245-9581)* **Under 1 mi:** Rail *(Shore Line East Commuter Rail 777-7433)* **Airport:** Bradley Int'l. *(55 mi.)*

Medical Services

911 Service Near: Chiropractor *(Seery 453-2205)* **Under 1 mi:** Doctor *(Family Practice Assoc. 453-0677)*, Dentist, Holistic Services, Ambulance **1-3 mi:** Veterinarian *(Marina Village Veterinary Clinic 245-8511)*
Hospital: Yale New Haven 458-2875 *(5 mi.)*

Setting --Just off Guilford Harbor's East River, this picturesque municipal marina occupies a modest basin that is anchored at its head by two attractive stone buildings - each well-regarded restaurant. The docks on the west side are devoted to commercial lobster and fishing craft which just adds to the charm. A 100 footwide federally-maintained channel leads into the basin. If you can squeeze in here, it's well worth the effort -- especially if you're hungry.

Marina Notes -- *Dockage rate is a flat $32. Small municipal marina for boats less than 38 ft. Floating slips for 140 recreational boats, a fixed pier for twelve commercial vessels, two transient spaces and river moorings for twelve pleasure boats. Formerly known as the Guilford Town Marina. Channel dredged to 6 feetevery 10 years -- but silts in, so call ahead for information on depths. Last dredging Spring 2003. Heads (no showers) are basic, with wood slatted floors, but clean and quite usable. Coast Guard station onsite. Free dockage for 2 hours for restaurants.

Notable -- Two quite differnt restaurants and a snack bar are onsite: The Stone House - D Tue-Sat 5-9pm, Sun brunch 11-2:30; Guilford Mooring, 7 days 11:30am-1am, entertainment Fri & Sat, dining room overlooking the town dock and harbor beyond; and The Bait House, 5am-8:30pm ('til 5pm spring/fall) with occasional entertainment, gifts, and views of Faulkner's Light. Guilford Lobster also has a pound onsite. About 1 mile walk to the train station and the charming New England town of Guilford, with blocks of enticing shops and services. Many historic homes, some from the 17thC, surround the Town Green. The Henry Whitfield State Museum, dating back to 1639, is a National Historic Landmark and the oldest house in the state of CT - Feb-Dec 14, Wed-Sun 10am-4:30pm.

Navigational Information
Lat: 41°16.025' **Long:** 072°40.680' **Tide:** 5 ft. **Current:** 2 kt. **Chart:** 12373
Rep. Depths (*MLW*): **Entry** 6 ft. **Fuel Dock** 5 ft. **Max Slip/Moor** 5 ft./-
Access: 1.25 NM from Guilford Harbor Buoy #3

Marina Facilities (*In Season/Off Season*)
Fuel: Gasoline, Diesel
Slips: 40 Total, 3 Transient **Max LOA:** 40 ft. **Max Beam:** n/a
  Rate (*per ft.*): **Day** $1.75/Inq. **Week** Inq. **Month** Inq.
  Power: 30 amp Incl., **50 amp** n/a, **100 amp** n/a, **200 amp** n/a
  Cable TV: No **Dockside Phone:** No
  Dock Type: Floating, Alongside, Wood
Moorings: 0 Total, 0 Transient **Launch:** n/a
  Rate: Day n/a **Week** n/a **Month** n/a
Heads: None
Laundry: None **Pay Phones:** No
Pump-Out: No **Fee:** n/a **Closed Heads:** Yes

Marina Operations
Owner/Manager: Dave North **Dockmaster:** Same
In-Season: Jun-Sep, 8am-5pm **Off-Season:** Sep-May, 8am-4:30pm
After-Hours Arrival: Tie at Fuel Dock
Reservations: Yes, Preferred **Credit Cards:** Visa/MC
Discounts: None
Pets: Welcome **Handicap Access:** No

Brown's Boat Yard

348 Chaffinch Island Road; Guilford, CT 06437

Tel: (203) 453-6283 **VHF: Monitor** 16 **Talk** 71
Fax: (203) 453-6283 **Alternate Tel:** (203) 415-4172
Email: bnbtyd@aol.com **Web:** www.guilfordct.com/brownsboatyard/
Nearest Town: Guilford (*2 mi.*) **Tourist Info:** (203) 453-9677

Marina Services and Boat Supplies
Services - Docking Assistance, Security **Communication -** FedEx, AirBorne, UPS, Express Mail **Supplies - OnSite:** Ships' Store **1-3 mi:** Bait/Tackle (*The Bait House 458-2554*), Propane (*Hocon Gas 458-2790*) **3+ mi:** West Marine (*481-3465, 7 mi.*), CNG (*Brewer Bruce & Johnson 488-8329, 10 mi.*)

Boatyard Services
OnSite: Travelift (*25T*), Engine mechanic (*gas, diesel*), Hull Repairs, Bottom Cleaning, Brightwork, Compound, Wash & Wax, Interior Cleaning, Propeller Repairs, Woodworking, Painting, Awlgrip **OnCall:** Electrical Repairs, Electronic Sales, Rigger **Near:** Electronics Repairs. **Dealer for:** Crusucher, Yanmar. **Member:** ABBRA **Yard Rates:** $70/hr., Haul & Launch $4/ft. (*blocking $9-11/ft.*), Power Wash $1.50/ft. **Storage:** On-Land $28-32/ft.

Restaurants and Accommodations
OnCall: Pizzeria (*Giuseppes 453-8676, closer by dinghy*) **1-3 mi:** Restaurant (*Guilford Mooring 458-2921, L $7-9, D $7-20, - Closer by dinghy*), (*The Stonehouse Restaurant 458-7600, L $7-9, D $10-19, Sun Brunch $13/6.50 - Closer by dinghy*), (*Nata's On the Green 453-3228*), (*Tastebuds of Guilford 453-1937*), Snack Bar (*The Bait House 458-2554*), Motel (*Tower Suites Motel 453-9069, $55-75*), (*Crescent Motel 245-9145*), (*Comfort Inn 453-5600*), Inn/B&B (*Cottage on Church Street 458-2598*)

Recreation and Entertainment
Near: Beach (*Dinghy to the Town Beach - Guilford Pt. or Grass Island*)
Under 1 mi: Picnic Area **1-3 mi:** Tennis Courts (*Guilford Racquet & Swim Club 453-4367*), Boat Rentals (*Kayaks at The Bait House*), Video Rental (*Blockbuster 453-2666*), Museum (*Hyland House 453-947 $2, early colonial artifacts; 1639 Whitfield State Historical Museum 453-2457, $3/2*), Sightseeing (*Guilford's many historic houses - 17th-19thC*), Special Events (*On the Guilford Village Green*) **3+ mi:** Golf Course (*Twin Lakes Golf 488-8778, 7 mi.*), Movie Theater (*5 mi.*)

Provisioning and General Services
1-3 mi: Convenience Store, Supermarket (*Guilford Food Center 543-4849v-delivers*), Gourmet Shop, Delicatessen (*Deli Unlimited 453-2473*), Health Food, Wine/Beer, Liquor Store (*Frank's Package Store 453-2259*), Bakery, Farmers' Market, Green Grocer, Fishmonger, Lobster Pound, Meat Market, Bank/ATM, Post Office, Catholic Church, Protestant Church, Library (*Guilford Library 453-8282*), Barber Shop, Bookstore (*Breakwater Books 453-4141*), Pharmacy (*Genovese 453-4310*), Hardware Store (*Page Hardware 453-5267*), Retail Shops, Copies Etc. (*Mailboxes Etc. 453-8866*)
 3+ mi: Synagogue (*5 mi.*)

Transportation
OnCall: Rental Car (*Enterprise 245-1920*), Airport Limo (*Proto Limo Service 245-9581*) **1-3 mi:** Rail (*Shoreline East Commuter 777-7433*) **3+ mi:** Ferry Service (*8 mi.*) **Airport:** Bradley (*55 mi.*)

Medical Services
911 Service **OnCall:** Ambulance **1-3 mi:** Doctor (*Family Practice Assoc. 453-0677*), Dentist, Chiropractor (*Seery 453-2205*), Veterinarian (*Marina Village Vet Clinic 245-8511*) **Hospital:** Yale-New Haven 245-3205 (*5 mi.*)

Setting -- At the mouth of the West River, just off Guilford Harbor, this small, rustic boatyard/marina offers limited transient dockage, no services for the cruiser, and panoramic views across the marsh and harbor and out to the Sound. The atmosphere is classic, old time, no frills New England "boat yard." The weathered sheds and out buildings, laid against the golden marsh grasses and the sparkling water, could be a Wyeth painting.

Marina Notes -- A family owned and operated boat yard since the late 50's. The docks are "alongside" and strung out along the bank of the River. Most expected BY services are onsite. Specializes in the maintenance, service and winter storage of vessels in the 20-35 foot range. Prides itself on fair prices and generations of service. No heads or showers or other amenities.

Notable -- It's two miles to the charming village of Guilford and an easy dinghy ride across the harbor and up the East River to the Town Marina (Len Hubbard Municipal Marina) -- where there are two good restaurants (Guilford Moorings & The Stone House), a great snack bar (The Bait House), and a lobster pound. The town marina offers 2 hours of free dockage for restaurant patrons. From there it's about a mile walk into town. The Guilford Town Beach and Grass Island are also easily accessible by dinghy. Downtown Guilford offers a delightful Town Green surrounded by many historic houses. Contemporary arts and crafts are on display and for sale at the Guilford Handcraft Center, open year 'round (453-5947).

Guilford Yacht Club

PO Box 644; 379 New Whitfield Street; Guilford, CT 06437

Tel: (203) 458-3048 **VHF: Monitor** 71 **Talk** 71
Fax: n/a **Alternate Tel:** n/a
Email: john@gyc.com **Web:** www.gyc.com
Nearest Town: Guilford *(0.75 mi.)* **Tourist Info:** (203) 453-9677

Navigational Information

Lat: 41°16.188' **Long:** 072°40.638' **Tide:** 6 ft. **Current:** 1.5 kt. **Chart:** 21175
Rep. Depths *(MLW):* **Entry** 6 ft. **Fuel Dock** 6 ft. **Max Slip/Moor** 6 ft./6 ft.
Access: Guilford Harbor to the West River - 0.25 mi. upriver

Marina Facilities *(In Season/Off Season)*

Fuel: Gasoline, Diesel
Slips: 150 Total, 5 Transient **Max LOA:** 50 ft. **Max Beam:** 18 ft.
  Rate *(per ft.):* **Day** $1.50/Inq. **Week** Inq. **Month** Inq.
  Power: 30 amp Incl., 50 amp Incl., 100 amp n/a, 200 amp n/a
  Cable TV: Yes, Incl. **Dockside Phone:** Yes Longer term only
  Dock Type: Fixed, Long Fingers, Concrete
Moorings: 0 Total, 0 Transient **Launch:** n/a
  Rate: Day n/a **Week** n/a **Month** n/a
Heads: 6 Toilet(s), 3 Shower(s) *(with dressing rooms)*
Laundry: None **Pay Phones:** No
Pump-Out: OnSite, Full Service **Fee:** $5 **Closed Heads:** Yes

Marina Operations

Owner/Manager: Doug Shaw, John Febbraio **Dockmaster:** Claude Rossetti
In-Season: May-Sep 15, 8am-8pm **Off-Season:** n/a
After-Hours Arrival: If reservation, Dock your vessel in open slip.
Reservations: Yes, Required **Credit Cards:** Visa/MC
Discounts: None
Pets: Welcome, Dog Walk Area **Handicap Access:** Yes, Heads, Docks

Marina Services and Boat Supplies

Services - Docking Assistance, Boaters' Lounge, Dock Carts
Communication - Mail & Package Hold, Phone Messages, FedEx, AirBorne, UPS, Express Mail *(Sat Del)* **Supplies - OnSite:** Ice *(Cube)*
Near: Ships' Store *(Lewmar Marine 458-6200)* **Under 1 mi:** Bait/Tackle
1-3 mi: Propane *(Hocon Gas 458-2790)* **3+ mi:** West Marine *(481-3465, 6 mi.)*, CNG *(Brewer Bruce & Johnson 488-8329, 10 mi.)*

Boatyard Services

Near: Travelift, Engine mechanic *(gas, diesel)*, Electrical Repairs.
1-3 mi: Hull Repairs, Bottom Cleaning, Brightwork, Air Conditioning, Divers.
3+ mi: Electronic Sales *(10 mi.)*, Electronics Repairs *(10 mi.)*, Rigger *(10 mi.)*.

Restaurants and Accommodations

OnCall: Pizzeria *(Giuseppes 458-8676)* **Near:** Restaurant *(The Stonehouse Restaurant 458-7600, L $7-9, D $10-19, Sun Brunch $13/6.50)*, *(Guilford Mooring 458-2921, L $7-9, D $6-20)*, Snack Bar *(The Bait House 458-2554, B $1-2, L & D $3-8)* **Under 1 mi:** Restaurant *(Tastebuds of Guilford 453-1937)* **1-3 mi:** Fast Food, Motel *(Guilford Motor Lodge)*, *(Tower Suites 453-9060, $55-75)*, *(Crescent Motel 245-9145)*, Inn/B&B *(Guilford Corners B&B 453-4129)* **3+ mi:** Restaurant *(Guilford Tavern 453-2216, 3.5 mi.)*, Inn/B&B *(Madison Post Road Bed & Breakfast 245-2866, 4 mi.)*

Recreation and Entertainment

OnSite: Pool, Picnic Area, Playground, Tennis Courts *(Har-Tru)*
Under 1 mi: Beach *(East Point - dinghy)*, Park *(West Point)*, Museum *(Hyland House 453-947, colonial artifacts, Tue-Sun Jun- LabDay, Weekends 'til ColDay 10am-4:30pm, $2; Whitfield State Historical Museum 453-2457,* *built 1639, Wed Sun 10am 4:30pm, $3.50/Kids $2.00)*, Sightseeing *(Guilford's 17th-19thC houses)* **1-3 mi:** Fitness Center, Video Rental *(Blockbuster 453-2666)* **3+ mi:** Dive Shop *(10 miles)*, Golf Course *(Twin Lakes Golf 488-8778, 7 mi.)*, Movie Theater *(5 mi.)*

Provisioning and General Services

Near: Bookstore *(Breakwater Books 453-4141)* **Under 1 mi:** Convenience Store, Supermarket *(Guilford Food Center 543-4849 - delivers)*, Gourmet Shop, Delicatessen *(Deli Unlimited 453-2473)*, Wine/Beer, Liquor Store *(Franks Package Store 453-2259)*, Bakery, Meat Market, Bank/ATM, Post Office, Catholic Church, Protestant Church, Library *(Guilford Library 453-8282)*, Barber Shop, Dry Cleaners, Pharmacy *(Genovese 453-4310)*, Newsstand, Hardware Store *(Page Hardware 453-5267)*, Florist, Clothing Store, Retail Shops, Copies Etc. *(Mail Boxes Etc 453-8866)* **1-3 mi:** Health Food, Farmers' Market, Fishmonger, Beauty Salon, Laundry, Department Store **3+ mi:** Synagogue *(5 mi.)*

Transportation

OnSite: Bikes *(Complimentary)* **OnCall:** Rental Car *(Enterprise 245-1920)*, Airport Limo *(Proto Limousine Service 245-9581)* **1-3 mi:** Rail *(Shore Line East Commuter Rail 777-7433)* **Airport:** Bradley *(55 mi.)*

Medical Services

911 Service **OnCall:** Ambulance **Under 1 mi:** Chiropractor *(Seery 453-2205)* **1-3 mi:** Doctor *(Family Practice Assoc. 453-0677)*, Dentist, Veterinarian *(Marina Village Veterinary Clinic 245-8511)*
Hospital: Yale-New Haven 245-3205 *(5 mi.)*

Setting -- Just off scenic Guilford Harbor, in a completely protected basin on the West River, this amenity-rich, very attractive 21 acre dockominium club welcomes transients. Guilford Yacht Club is set in a beautiful, virgin salt marsh with sweeping views from the docks and marina facilities across waves of marsh grass, out to the Sound and Faulkner's Light. The atmosphere is serene and tranquil. It's a quarter mile up the River.

Marina Notes -- Very quiet and family oriented, with excellent, top-of-the-line docks and services - all well maintained. Beautiful new contemporary multi-story club house with fireplace and cathedral ceilings opened in late 2002. Tiled heads and showers with dressing rooms and hair dryers. New, very inviting and well executed pool and bath house sit on a promontory overlooking the docks, the marshes and the sound. Har-Tru tennis courts. Children's playground. Tented picnic area with tables and grills. Banquet facility for events holds 180-200. Contact Jordan Caterers 453-5651.

Notable -- Three quarters of a mile is the charming town of Guilford and its quintessential New England Green; the village sports an engaging array of shops, summer activities, including the Guilford Fair, Handcrafts Show (Biggest in New England), and free concerts on Sunday nights on the Green. The streets are lined with more than 500 17th-19thC houses, including the 1639 Whitfield House, considered the oldest stone house in the U.S. It's a short dinghy ride to town, the beach on East Point or to the town park on West Point. 0.4 mile to Stone House Restaurant, Guilford Moorings, and Guilford Lobster Pound. 0.3 mi. to Shoreline East rail road station.

Navigational Information
Lat: 41°15.812' **Long:** 072°48.872' **Tide:** 6 ft. **Current:** n/a **Chart:** 12373
Rep. Depths (MLW): Entry 6 ft. **Fuel Dock** 10 ft. **Max Slip/Moor** 6 ft./6 ft.
Access: Western shore of Branford River - just past Branford YC

Marina Facilities (In Season/Off Season)
Fuel: Gulf - Gasoline, Diesel
Slips: 300 Total, 12 Transient **Max LOA:** 60 ft. **Max Beam:** n/a
 Rate (per ft.): Day $1.75 **Week** n/a **Month** n/a
 Power: 30 amp Incl., **50 amp** Incl., **100 amp** n/a, **200 amp** n/a
 Cable TV: No **Dockside Phone:** No
 Dock Type: Floating, Long Fingers, Wood
Moorings: 14 Total, 0 Transient **Launch:** None, Dinghy Dock
 Rate: Day $1.25/ft. **Week** n/a **Month** n/a
Heads: 2 Toilet(s), 2 Shower(s) (with dressing rooms)
Laundry: None **Pay Phones:** No
Pump-Out: OnSite, Full Service, 1 Central **Fee:** $5* **Closed Heads:** Yes

Marina Operations
Owner/Manager: Paul Kurzawa **Dockmaster:** Same
In-Season: Apr 15-Nov 15, 9am-5pm **Off-Season:** n/a
After-Hours Arrival: Pull-up to gas dock and phone office
Reservations: Yes, Preferred **Credit Cards:** Visa/MC, Amex, Gulf Gas
Discounts: None
Pets: Welcome **Handicap Access:** No

Pier 66 Marina

51 Goodsell Pt. Road; Branford, CT 06405

Tel: (203) 488-5613 **VHF: Monitor** 9 **Talk** n/a
Fax: (203) 483-0369 **Alternate Tel:** n/a
Email: n/a **Web:** n/a
Nearest Town: Branford (1.4 mi.) **Tourist Info:** (203) 483-4654

Marina Services and Boat Supplies
Services - Dock Carts Communication - FedEx, AirBorne, UPS, Express Mail **Supplies - OnSite:** Ice (Block, Cube), Ships' Store (Paul's Locker), Bait/Tackle, Propane **Near:** CNG (Special order only Bruce & Johnson dinghy) **1-3 mi:** West Marine (481-3465)

Boatyard Services
OnSite: Travelift (40T), Crane, Engine mechanic (gas), Launching Ramp, Electrical Repairs, Hull Repairs, Rigger, Bottom Cleaning, Compound, Wash & Wax, Interior Cleaning, Propeller Repairs **Near:** Metal Fabrication.
Yard Rates: $55/hr., Power Wash $1.75

Restaurants and Accommodations
OnCall: Pizzeria (Pacileos 481-5930) **Near:** Restaurant (Sam's Dockside 488-3007, L $3-16, D $3-16, dinghy across the river, Tue-Thu 11:30-9, Fri&Sat 11:30-9, Sun 11:30-8:30) **Under 1 mi:** Restaurant (Calypso River Grill 481-1211, L $6-8, D $5-18, dinghy up river) **1-3 mi:** Restaurant (Lenny's 488-1500, Will pick up at marinas), (LoMonaco's 488-1600), (Carmelas / Claudio's 481-3599), Fast Food (Wendy's, McDonalds, Burger King), Lite Fare (Main Street Lunch 481-5847), (Bagelicious Bagels 481-6728), Motel (Motel 6 483-5828), Inn/B&B (Abigails 483-1612), (By the Sea Inn & Spa 483-3333) **3+ mi:** Motel (Days Inn 488-8314, 5 mi.), Hotel (Holiday Inn Express 469-5321, 4.5 mi.)

Recreation and Entertainment
Near: Beach (Branford Point), Picnic Area (Branford Pt.), Playground (Branford Pt.), Jogging Paths, Fishing Charter, Video Arcade, Park (Foote Memorial), Special Events (Fireworks Branford Point) **Under 1 mi:** Tennis Courts (Foote Park), Video Rental (Blockbuster 488-6262), Sightseeing (Thimble Island Cruise) **1-3 mi:** Bowling (Amf Cherry Hill 488-2523), Movie Theater (Hoyts Cinema 481-2711) **3+ mi:** Golf Course (Twin Lakes Golf Course 488-8778, 5 mi.), Museum (Trolley Museum 467-6927, Connecticut Childrens Museum, 8 mi. 562-5437, 4 mi.)

Provisioning and General Services
Near: Library (Blackstone Memorial 488-1441) **Under 1 mi:** Health Food (Fields of Health 488-3462), Laundry (QWIK Wash 483-0547), Department Store (Wal-Mart 488-4106) **1-3 mi:** Market (Harbor St. Market 483-1612), Supermarket (A & P 481-9671), Gourmet Shop (Marketplace at Indian Neck 483-8220), Delicatessen (Serious Subs 488-8824), Wine/Beer (Wine & Spirit 488-7363), Bookstore (Branford Book 488-5975), Pharmacy (Branford Pharmacy 488-1631), Copies Etc. (Branford Printing 488-2431) **3+ mi:** Hardware Store (Country Paint & Hardware 481-5255, 5 mi.)

Transportation
OnCall: Taxi (Yellow Cab 777-5555), Airport Limo (Executive Express 488-1186) **Near:** Rental Car (Allie Auto Rental 483-6015), Local Bus, InterCity Bus **Under 1 mi:** Rail (Shore Line East Commuter Rail 777-7433) **Airport:** New Haven/Bradley Int'l. (7 mi./50 mi.)

Medical Services
911 Service **OnCall:** Ambulance **Under 1 mi:** Doctor (Cass 637-0186), Dentist, Chiropractor (Caldarone 488-1105) **1-3 mi:** Veterinarian (Branford Vet Associates 481-3411) **Hospital:** Yale New Haven 458-2875 (10 mi.)

Setting -- Primarily a smaller boat marina, this facility, the second to port at the mouth of the Branford River past Branford Yacht Club, can accommodate larger boats on its outer docks and T-heads. Good docks are coupled with more rustic landside facilities. A small picnic platform overlooks the docks and a vintage white three-story dwelling with multiple decks dominates the view. Across the River, the views are gently residential.

Marina Notes -- Standard wood docks with full fingers secured only at one point. Very attractively furnished small "Party Room" is available for $25 for a maximum of 25 people. A picnic table and grill are at the head of the docks. Some boat services are located on site including Marine Stainless Steel Fabricators and a chandlery, Paul's Locker. Gas & diesel on the docks. Nice tiled heads and showers are located on the ground floor of the 3-story low-rise apartment building at the rear of the property. *Pump-out, onsite, is free for marina guests and $5 for others - Apr-Oct, daily 9am-11am. Branford Y. C. (488-9798) may have slips for members of reciprocal clubs.

Notable -- Dinghyable restaurants are the most convenient: Calypso River Grill, upriver at Branford Landing and Sam's Dockside, across the River at Brewer Bruce & Johnson, are the only two on the River. The village, which offers modest provisioning and a number of dining possibilities, is about 1.4 miles. At Harbor and Maple Streets you'll find Pacileo's Apizza and Pasta as well as the Harbor St. Market. From there, follow Maple Street for about 0.3 mi. to downtown Branford for additional restaurants and major provisioning.

Brewer Bruce & Johnson Marina

145 South Montowese Street; Branford, CT 06405

Tel: (203) 488-8329 **VHF: Monitor** 9 **Talk** 65A
Fax: (203) 488-5010 **Alternate Tel:** n/a
Email: bjm@byy.com **Web:** www.byy.com/Branford
Nearest Town: Branford *(1.5 mi.)* **Tourist Info:** (203) 488-5500

Navigational Information
Lat: 41°15.764' **Long:** 072°48.516' **Tide:** 6 ft. **Current:** n/a **Chart:** 12373
Rep. Depths *(MLW)*: **Entry** 6 ft. **Fuel Dock** n/a **Max Slip/Moor** 10 ft./-
Access: Channel into Branford River, the first marina on eastern bank

Marina Facilities *(In Season/Off Season)*
Fuel: No
Slips: 500 Total, 30 Transient **Max LOA:** 60 ft. **Max Beam:** 18 ft.
  Rate *(per ft.)*: **Day** $2.75 **Week** Inq. **Month** Inq.
  Power: 30 amp Incl., **50 amp** Incl., **100 amp** n/a, **200 amp** n/a
  Cable TV: Yes, Incl. **Dockside Phone:** No
  Dock Type: Floating, Long Fingers, Concrete, Wood
Moorings: 0 Total, 0 Transient **Launch:** n/a
  Rate: Day n/a **Week** n/a **Month** n/a
Heads: 12 Toilet(s), 10 Shower(s)
Laundry: 2 Washer(s), 2 Dryer(s) **Pay Phones:** Yes
Pump-Out: OnSite, Full Service, 2 Central **Fee:** $5* **Closed Heads:** Yes

Marina Operations
Owner/Manager: John McMahon **Dockmaster:** Same
In-Season: Apr-Mid-Nov, 7am-7pm **Off-Season:** n/a
After-Hours Arrival: Call in advance
Reservations: Recommended **Credit Cards:** Visa/MC, Dscvr, Amex
Discounts: None
Pets: Welcome, Dog Walk Area **Handicap Access:** Yes, Heads

Marina Services and Boat Supplies
Services - Docking Assistance, Security, Trash Pick-Up, Dock Carts
Communication - Mail & Package Hold, Phone Messages, Fax in/out, FedEx, AirBorne, UPS, Express Mail *(Sat Del)* **Supplies - OnSite:** Ice *(Block, Cube)*, Ships' Store **3+ mi:** West Marine *(481-3465, 4 mi.)*, Propane *(Agway of N. Branford 483-7800, 4 mi.)*

Boatyard Services
OnSite: Travelift *(50T to 70 ft.)*, Forklift *(8000 lbs.)*, Crane *(15T)*, Engine mechanic *(gas, diesel)*, Electrical Repairs, Hull Repairs, Rigger, Bottom Cleaning, Brightwork, Refrigeration, Compound, Wash & Wax, Woodworking, Painting, Awlgrip **Near:** Launching Ramp.
Dealer for: Sealand, Yanmar, Caterpillar, Westerbeke. **Member:** ABYC

Restaurants and Accommodations
OnSite: Restaurant *(Sam's Dockside Restaurant 488-3007, L $7-20, D $7-20, $4 hot dog platters, too)*, Snack Bar **OnCall:** Pizzeria *(Indian Neck 488-5330)* **Near:** Restaurant *(Lenny's Indian Head 488-1500, great seafood, lobsters, steamers, steaks; casual, cash only)*, *(Marketplace at Indian Neck 483-8220, B, L & D)*, *(Pasta Cosi 483-9397)*
Under 1 mi Restaurant *(Calypso L $6-8, D $15-18, by dinghy or land)*, *(Citrus/Panevino 488-0077)*, Inn/B&B *(By the Sea Inn & Spa 483-3333)*
1-3 mi: Motel *(Motel 6 483-5828, $45-70)*, *(Days Inn 481-9900)*

Recreation and Entertainment
OnSite: Pool, Picnic Area, Grills, Playground **Near:** Jogging Paths, Cultural Attract, Sightseeing **Under 1 mi:** Park *(Foote Memorial)* **1-3 mi:** Fitness Center *(In Shape 481-0774)*, Bowling *(Amf 488-2523)*, Movie Theater

(Hoyts 481-2711), Video Rental *(Tommy K's 488-6262)*, Museum *(Harrison House 488-4828)* **3+ mi:** Golf Course *(Twin Lakes Golf 488-8778 , 5 mi.)*

Provisioning and General Services
Near: Gourmet Shop *(Marketplace 483-8220)*, Liquor Store *(Indian Neck Liquor 488-4990)*, Bakery *(Marketplace)*, Green Grocer *(The Stand)*, Fishmonger *(Bud's Fish Market 488-1019)*, Dry Cleaners, Laundry
Under 1 mi: Convenience Store, Market *(Caron's Corner 488-5857)*, Delicatessen, Lobster Pound *(Branford Landing Lobster)*, Pharmacy *(Walgreens 481-0387)*, Copies Etc. *(Branford Printing 481-9803)*
1-3 mi: Supermarket *(A &P 481-9671)*, Health Food *(Fields of Health 488-3462)*, Bank/ATM, Post Office, Catholic Church, Library *(Blackstone Memorial 488-1441)*, Beauty Salon, Bookstore *(Branford Book 488-5975)*, Newsstand Hardware Store *(Richlin 481-8081; Branford Lumber)*, Department Store *(Wal-Mart 488-4106)*

Transportation
OnCall: Rental Car *(Enterprise 488-1311/ National 481-8462 1 mi.)*, Taxi *(C & C Taxi 483-8901)*, Airport Limo *(Executive Express 488-1186)*
Under 1mi: Rail *(Shore Line East Commuter Rail 777-7433)* **1-3 mi:** Bikes *(Cycles of Madison 245-8735)* **Airport:** New Haven/Bradley Int'l. *(5 mi./50mi.)*

Medical Services
911 Service **OnCall:** Ambulance **Under 1 mi:** Dentist *(Branford Dental 488-7444)*, Veterinarian *(Pet Shield 481-1492)* **1-3 mi:** Doctor *(General Practitioners of Branford 483-2426)*, Chiropractor *(Caldarone 488-1105)*, Holistic Services *(Beyond Care - in town)*
Hospital: Yale-New Haven 688-2000 *(10 mi.)*

Setting -- Tucked into a safe, secure basin on the eastern bank of the Branford River, one mile from the center of Branford Harbor, Brewer Bruce & Johnson provides a large, nicely maintained stop mid-way to the Sound. The lovely surrounding area is residential; the marina and boatyard attractively rendered and pleasantly landscaped. Scattered throughout the grounds are a variety of inviting amenities - islands in the midst of what seem to be acres of pavement - a clean, grass-decked pool (with heads), an adjacent full-service restaurant, and particularly nice, treed, picnic areas with views of the docks and River.

Marina Notes -- *Pump-out free for customers, $5 for others. 2 excellent bath houses offer tiled heads and showers. Extensive and full-service boatyard. Onsite is Sam's Dockside Restaurant - open Mar-Oct, Mon-Thu 11:30am-9pm, Fri & Sat 'til 9:30pm, Sun 'til 8:30pm - inside and deck dining: seafood entrees, salads, sandwiches, and a raw bar - 12 prep options for each fish entree. The restaurant's raised deck has views of the docks and river, but across a large parking area. Beacon Wi-Fi offers high-speed wireless internet access - $39.99/mo. for 6 months; $29.99/mo. for 12 months (762-2657).

Notable -- A handful of eateries and some services -- a market, 3 restaurants, a pizzeria, snack bar, ice-cream shop, package store, full-serve laundry, cleaners, seafood market and farm stand -- are about 0.35 mile south at Indian Neck Point. About 1.5 miles northwest is downtown Branford, a very pleasant, good-sized classic Connecticut town with a village green, many more restaurants and a good selection of shops. Another 0.3 miles farther is a supermarket, fast food, and more shops. Branford Festival and Father's Day Weekend Picnic at the marina. The town has frequent firework displays.

Navigational Information
Lat: 41°16.247' **Long:** 072°49.092' **Tide:** 6 ft. **Current:** n/a **Chart:** 12372
Rep. Depths (MLW): Entry 10 ft. **Fuel Dock** n/a **Max Slip/Moor** 10 ft./-
Access: Channel into Branford River, midway up on the western shore

Marina Facilities *(In Season/Off Season)*
Fuel: No
Slips: 75 Total, 3 Transient **Max LOA:** 60 ft. **Max Beam:** n/a
  Rate *(per ft.)*: **Day** $1.65/Inq. **Week** Inq. **Month** n/a
  Power: 30 amp Incl., 50 amp Incl., **100 amp** n/a, **200 amp** n/a
  Cable TV: No **Dockside Phone:** No
  Dock Type: Floating
Moorings: 0 Total, 0 Transient **Launch:** n/a
  Rate: Day n/a **Week** n/a **Month** n/a
Heads: 2 Toilet(s), 2 Shower(s)
Laundry: None **Pay Phones:** No
Pump-Out: No **Fee:** n/a **Closed Heads:** Yes

Marina Operations
Owner/Manager: Paul Jacques **Dockmaster:** Abbey S. Mayer - Brokerage
In-Season: Year-Round, 9am-5pm **Off-Season:** n/a
After-Hours Arrival: Call ahead for instructions
Reservations: Preferred **Credit Cards:** Visa/MC, Amex
Discounts: None
Pets: Welcome **Handicap Access:** No

Dutch Wharf Marina & Boatyard

PO Box 2076; 70 Maple Street; Branford, CT 06405

Tel: (203) 488-9000; (203) 483-8642 **VHF: Monitor** n/a **Talk** n/a
Fax: n/a **Alternate Tel:** n/a
Email: n/a **Web:** n/a
Nearest Town: Branford *(0.6 mi.)* **Tourist Info:** (203) 488-5500

Marina Services and Boat Supplies
Services - Docking Assistance, Trash Pick-Up, Dock Carts
Communication - FedEx, AirBorne, UPS, Express Mail **Supplies -**
OnSite: Ships' Store **Near:** Ice *(Block, Cube)* **Under 1 mi:** CNG *(Special order only at Bruce & Johnson)* **1-3 mi:** West Marine *(481-3465)*
3+ mi: Bait/Tackle *(4 mi.)*, Propane *(Agway of N. Branford 483-7800, 5 mi.)*

Boatyard Services
OnSite: Travelift *(35T)*, Engine mechanic *(gas, diesel)*, Hull Repairs, Rigger, Sail Loft, Brightwork, Propeller Repairs, Woodworking

Restaurants and Accommodations
OnCall: Pizzeria *(Pacileo's Apizza & Pasta 481-5930)* **Near:** Restaurant *(Claudio's/Carmela's 481-3599)*, *(Calypso 481-1211, L $6-18, D $16-18, interesting Carribbean menu)*, *(Coral Reef 488-5573)* **Under 1 mi:** Restaurant *(Waiting Station 488-5176)*, *(Yooki Yama Japanese 481-5788)*, Motel *(Days Inn 481-9900)* **1-3 mi:** Restaurant *(Sam's Dockside 488-3007, L $3-16, D $3-16, or downriver by dinghy)*, Motel *(Motel 6 483-5828)*, *(Economy Inn 488-4035)* **3+ mi:** Hotel *(Ramada Inn 488-4991, 4 mi.)*

Recreation and Entertainment
Under 1 mi: Fitness Center *(In-Shape Fitness 481-0774)*, Boat Rentals *(Branford Kayak 483-0236)*, Video Rental *(Tommy K's Video 488-6262)*, Galleries **1-3 mi:** Bowling *(Amf Cherry Hill Lanes 488-2523)*, Movie Theater *(Hoyts Cinema 481-2711)*, Park *(Foote Memorial)*, Museum *(Harrison House 488-4828)*

3+ mi: Golf Course *(Twin Lakes Golf 488-8778, 7 mi.)*, Sightseeing *(Shoreline Trolley Museum 467-6927, 4 mi.)*

Provisioning and General Services
Near: Market *(Harbor St. Market 483-1612)*, Gourmet Shop *(P&M Fine Foods 488-6183)*, Delicatessen *(Serious Subs & Deli 488-8824/Palma's Deli 481-9778)*, Liquor Store *(Harbor Package Store 488-4048)* **Under 1 mi:** Supermarket *(A&P 481-9671)*, Health Food *(Fields of Health 488-3462)*, Bank/ATM, Post Office, Catholic Church, Library *(Blackstone Memorial 488-1441)*, Laundry *(QWIK Wash 483-0547)*, Bookstore *(Branford Book 488-5975)*, Pharmacy *(CVS 488-4372)*, Hardware Store *(Richlin 481-8081)*, Retail Shops, Copies Etc. *(Village Express 481-7426)* **1-3 mi:** Fishmonger *(Bud's Fish Market 488-1019)*, Protestant Church

Transportation
OnCall: Rental Car *(Enterprise 488-1311/ National 481-8462 1 mi.)*, Taxi *(C & C Taxi 483-8901)*, Airport Limo *(Executive Express 488-1186)* **Near:** Rail *(Shore Line East Commuter Rail 777-7433)* **1-3 mi:** Bikes *(Cycles of Madison 245-8735)* **Airport:** Tweed New Haven/Bradley Int'l. *(8 mi./50 mi.)*

Medical Services
911 Service **Under 1 mi:** Doctor *(General Practitioners of Branford 483-2426)*, Dentist *(Goldstein 481-5385)*, Chiropractor *(Peterson 481-6150)*, Veterinarian *(Branford Veterinary Associates 481-3411)*
Hospital: Yale New Haven 688-3333 *(10 mi.)*

Setting -- Tucked farther up the Branford River is this protected and "down home" boatyard/marina. An attractive, new two-story white building sits up on the bank. Waterside views are of the narrow river and docks belonging to the Indian Neck Yacht Club along the eastern shore.

Marina Notes -- Second generation family operation. The new 2-story office building also houses new heads and showers - two commodious full bathrooms - a very welcome addition. Extensive and full-service boat yard onsite with a clear bent toward wooden boat repair and restoration. The small bowed bridge, with meticulously varnished hand railings, which connects the docks to the river bank also reflects the staff's woodworking expertise. On an ebb tide, serious current could make docking difficult.

Notable -- The village of Branford is an easy 0.4 mile walk. Nearby Harbor St. Market has modest provisions, and a supermarket is a mile away. A number of galleries and glass studios are within a mile - stop by The Glass Hut for stained glass and glass blowing demos. Branford Canoe & Kayak (483-0236) is also within a mile. For a cruise to the Thimble Islands, call Captain Bob Milne at 481-3345. About 4 miles away, in East Haven, The Shore Line Trolley Museum is the oldest operating trolley museum in the U.S. A National Historic Site, it houses a collection of nearly 100 vintage vehicles, and offers trips aboard restored vintage trolley cars (467-6927).

Branford Landing

50 Maple Street; Branford, CT 06405

Tel: (203) 483-6544 **VHF: Monitor** n/a **Talk** n/a
Fax: n/a **Alternate Tel:** n/a
Email: n/a **Web:** n/a
Nearest Town: Branford (0.3 mi.) **Tourist Info:** (203) 488-5500

Navigational Information

Lat: 41°16.421' **Long:** 072°48.820' **Tide:** 6 ft. **Current:** n/a **Chart:** 12373
Rep. Depths (MLW): Entry 8 ft. **Fuel Dock** 8 ft. **Max Slip/Moor** 8 ft./-
Access: Branford River to the end of channel, before the fixed bridge

Marina Facilities (In Season/Off Season)

Fuel: No
Slips: 30 Total, 4 Transient **Max LOA:** 55 ft. **Max Beam:** n/a
Rate (per ft.): **Day** $2.00/Inq. **Week** Inq. **Month** n/a
Power: 30 amp Incl., **50 amp** n/a, **100 amp** n/a, **200 amp** n/a
Cable TV: No **Dockside Phone:** No
Dock Type: Floating, Long Fingers, Alongside, Wood
Moorings: 0 Total, 0 Transient **Launch:** n/a
Rate: Day n/a **Week** n/a **Month** n/a
Heads: 2 Toilet(s)
Laundry: None **Pay Phones:** No
Pump-Out: No **Fee:** n/a **Closed Heads:** Yes

Marina Operations

Owner/Manager: Chris Anderson **Dockmaster:** n/a
In-Season: May-Oct, 9am-8pm **Off-Season:** Nov-Apr, 9am-5pm
After-Hours Arrival: Call in advance for instructions
Reservations: Required **Credit Cards:** n/a
Discounts: None
Pets: Welcome **Handicap Access:** No

Marina Services and Boat Supplies

Services - Docking Assistance, Trash Pick-Up, Dock Carts
Communication - Mail & Package Hold, FedEx, AirBorne, UPS, Express
Mail **Supplies - Under 1 mi:** CNG (Special order at Bruce & Johnson)
3+ mi: Live Bait (4 mi.)

Boatyard Services

OnSite: Travelift (50T), Forklift, Crane, Engine mechanic (gas, diesel),
Electronics Repairs, Hull Repairs, Brightwork, Propeller Repairs,
Woodworking, Painting **Dealer for:** Crusader, MercCruiser, Volvo-Penta,
Cats, Detroits.

Restaurants and Accommodations

OnSite: Restaurant (Calypso River Grill 481-1211, L $6-8, D $15-18,
interesting Carribbean menu) **OnCall:** Pizzeria (Pacileo's Apizza & Pasta
481-5930) **Near:** Restaurant (Yooki Yama Japanese 481-5788), (Waiting
Station 488-5176), (Citrus/Panevino 488-0077), Lite Fare (Meadow Muffins
481-4198), Inn/B&B (By the Sea Inn & Spa 483-3333) **Under 1 mi:** Restaurant (Coral Reef 488-5573), Motel (Days Inn 481-9900) **1-3 mi:** Restaurant (Sam's Dockside 488-3007, L $3-16, D $3-16, or by dinghy -
burgers, seafood entrees, salads,), Motel (Motel 6 483-5828)

Recreation and Entertainment

Near: Beach (Parker Memorial), Picnic Area, Jogging Paths **Under 1 mi:**
Fitness Center (In-Shape Fitness 481-0774), Bowling (Amf Bowling Centers
488-2523), Movie Theater (Hoyts Cinema 481-2711), Museum (Branford
Historical Society's Branford House 488-4828) **3+ mi:** Golf Course

(Upper Green Golf Center 481-8400, 4 mi.), Cultural Attract (Branford Craft
Village - wood workers, glass blowers, potters, etc., 5 mi.), Sightseeing
(Shoreline Trolley Museum 467-6927, 4 mi.)

Provisioning and General Services

OnSite: Lobster Pound (Branford River Lobster Co.) **Near:** Gourmet Shop
(P & M Fine Foods 488-6183), Delicatessen (Serious Subs & Deli 488-
8824/Palma's Deli 481-9778), Wine/Beer (Shoreline Wine & Spirits 488-
5732), Liquor Store (Harbor Package Store 488-4048), Bank/ATM, Post
Office, Catholic Church, Library (Blackstone Memorial 488-1441), Bookstore
(Branford Book 488-5975), Pharmacy (CVS 488-4372), Retail Shops, Copies
Etc. (Village Express 481-7426) **Under 1 mi:** Supermarket (A & P 481-
9671), Health Food (Fields of Health 488-3462), Protestant Church, Laundry
(QWIK Wash 483-0547), Hardware Store (Richlin 481-8081; Branford
Lumber)

Transportation

OnCall: Rental Car (Enterprise 488-1311/ National 481-8462 1 mi.), Taxi (C
& C Taxi 483-8901), Airport Limo (Executive Express 488-1186) **Near:** Rail
(Shore Line East Commuter Rail 777-7433) **1-3 mi:** Bikes (Cycles of
Madison 245-8735) **Airport:** Tweed New Haven /Bradley Int'l. (8 mi./50 mi.)

Medical Services

911 Service **OnCall:** Ambulance **Near:** Holistic Services (By the Sea Spa)
Under 1 mi: Doctor (General Practitioners of Branford 483-2426), Dentist
(Goldstein 481-5385), Chiropractor (Peterson 481-6150), Veterinarian (East
Shore 488-1686) **Hospital:** Yale New Haven 688-3333 (10 mi.)

Setting -- On the western shore of the meandering Branford River, this is the last marina on the navigable, dredged channel. It is just south of the fixed bridge. Shoreside is an attractive waterfront restaurant with a patio right off the docks; a short promenade, with picnic tables, overlooks the docks. A series of re-purposed factory buildings provide extensive inside boat storage, facilities and work sheds. The river is quite narrow at this point and the waterside views are of the facilities on the eastern shore.

Marina Notes -- Note that only some of the docks have power and water. Fuel dock and mechanic onsite 7 days a week. The nicely maintained floating docks, a combination of "alongside" and slips with full finger piers, were built in the late 80's. Roomy, quite nice heads are in the most southern of the old brick buildings. Active dry stack operation uses a Coastal Marine boat rack storage system. The boat storage facility occupies the brick factory building. Inside storage customers are permitted to work on their own boats. Three lobster boats make their home here as does the Branford River Lobster Company.

Notable -- The Branford railroad station is practically next door (Shore Line connects to Metro North in New Haven). This is the closest marina to the pretty village of Branford and to provisioning and services. The village, which offers some interesting shops and eating possibilities, is about 0.3 mile and a supermarket is 0.9 mile away. Onsite Calypso River Grill is one of only two restaurants on the River (Sam's Dockside at Bruce & Johnson is the other). Inside, this modest but full-service restaurant is white table cloth and outside umbrellaed patio dining. Lunch 11:30-2:30pm, Light fare 2:30-5:30pm, Dinner after 5:30.

Navigational Information
Lat: 41°16.867' **Long:** 072°55.784' **Tide:** 6 ft. **Current:** n/a **Chart:** 12372
Rep. Depths (MLW): Entry 10 ft. **Fuel Dock** 8 ft. **Max Slip/Moor** 8 ft./20 ft.
Access: New Haven Harbor to eastern shore of West River Channel

Marina Facilities (In Season/Off Season)
Fuel: Gasoline, Diesel
Slips: 135 Total, 5 Transient **Max LOA:** 50 ft. **Max Beam:** 16 ft.
  Rate (per ft.): **Day** $1.50/Inq. **Week** $10.50 **Month** n/a
  Power: 30 amp $6, **50 amp** n/a, **100 amp** n/a, **200 amp** n/a
  Cable TV: No **Dockside Phone:** No
  Dock Type: Fixed, Wood, Aluminum
Moorings: 0 Total, 0 Transient **Launch:** None
  Rate: Day n/a **Week** n/a **Month** n/a
Heads: 4 Toilet(s), 4 Shower(s) (with dressing rooms)
Laundry: 2 Washer(s), 2 Dryer(s) **Pay Phones:** Yes
Pump-Out: OnSite, Full Service, 1 Central **Fee:** $5 **Closed Heads:** Yes

Marina Operations
Owner/Manager: n/a **Dockmaster:** Fran Adinelfi
In-Season: May-Nov 1, 8am-5pm **Off-Season:** Nov 1-May 1, 8am-5pm
After-Hours Arrival: Tie up at gas dock
Reservations: Yes, Preferred **Credit Cards:** Visa/MC, Amex
Discounts: Boat/US **Dockage:** 25% **Fuel:** $.10 **Repair:** n/a
Pets: Welcome **Handicap Access:** Yes, Heads

Oyster Point Marina
98 South Water Street; New Haven, CT 06519

Tel: (203) 624-5895 **VHF: Monitor** 9 **Talk** 11
Fax: (203) 934-6470 **Alternate Tel:** (203) 624-5895
Email: marinegen@aol.com **Web:** n/a
Nearest Town: New Haven (2 mi.) **Tourist Info:** (203) 787-6735

Marina Services and Boat Supplies
Supplies - OnSite: Ice (Cube) **Under 1 mi:** Ships' Store **1-3 mi:** Propane (National Propane 747-9868) **3+ mi:** West Marine (467-4436, 5 mi.), Boater's World (Orange 799-9774, 6 mi.)

Boatyard Services
OnSite: Travelift (10T)

Restaurants and Accommodations
OnSite: Restaurant (Sage American Grill 787-3466, D $9-26), Lite Fare (Dockside Deli & Market 562-4949) **Near:** Lite Fare (Nick's Luncheonette 937-9036), Pizzeria (Seaside Pizza 937-9740), Hotel (Marriott Residence Inn 777-5377, $140-200), Inn/B&B (Swan Cove 776-3240, $100-325), (Inn at Oyster Point 773-3334, $90-160) **Under 1 mi:** Restaurant (Lorenzos 932-5846), (Lucibello's 933-6142), (Rusty Scupper 777-5711, L $8-15, D $17-25), Fast Food **1-3 mi:** Seafood Shack (Stowes 934-1991, also a fish market), Motel (Best Western 933-0344, $80-180), Hotel (Omni New Haven 772-6664, $260-350), Inn/B&B (Three Chimneys Inn 789-1201, $190-260)

Recreation and Entertainment
OnSite: Beach, Picnic Area, Grills **Near:** Park (Bayview Park & Vietnam War Veterans Mem Park) **Under 1 mi:** Playground, Fitness Center (Quest Aerobic & Athletic 933-0052), Jogging Paths, Roller Blade/Bike Paths, Cultural Attract (Shubert Theatre 562-5666 - Broadway, Shakespeare & concerts; Long Wharf Theater 787-4282 - 2 stages - 8 plays each season Oct-May $30-55) **1-3 mi:** Dive Shop, Tennis Courts, Boat Rentals, Bowling (Woodlawn Duckpin 932-3202), Movie Theater (Forest 934-0370), Video Rental (Tommy K's 234-8110), Museum (Pardee-Morris House 772-7060;

Yale University), Sightseeing (Yale 432-2300 - tours M-F 10:30am & 2pm, Sat & Sun 1:30pm) **3+ mi:** Golf Course (Orange Hills 795-4161, 5 mi.)

Provisioning and General Services
OnSite: Delicatessen (Dockside) **Near:** Convenience Store (Eddy's Food Store), Liquor Store (Big Tom's 933-1383), Pharmacy (Rite Aid 933-5260) **Under 1 mi:** Market (Roses Supermarket 933-7065), Health Food (Nature's Garden 937-6905), Wine/Beer, Bank/ATM, Post Office, Catholic Church, Barber Shop, Dry Cleaners, Laundry, Bookstore (Follett College Bookstore 865-5614), Newsstand **1-3 mi:** Supermarket (Shop Rite 934-5660), Gourmet Shop, Bakery, Fishmonger, Lobster Pound, Meat Market, Other, Library (West Haven 933-9335), Beauty Salon, Hardware Store (True Value 934-0766), Florist, Retail Shops, Copies Etc. **3+ mi:** Department Store (Sears, J C Penney, 5 mi.), Buying Club (Sams, BJ's, 5 mi.)

Transportation
OnCall: Rental Car (Enterprise 931-4090/ 2 mi. Avis 624-2161), Taxi (Ecuamex Taxi 624-3333), Airport Limo (Prestige Limousine 867-3880) **Near:** Local Bus ("Z" route to downtown New Haven stops at the school, during arrival and departure times, much more frequently at the Long Wharf - $1 - 785-8930) **1-3 mi:** InterCity Bus (Greyhound 800-229-9424), Rail (Amtrak 800-USARAIL & MetroNorth 800-METROINFO)
Airport: Tweed /Bradley Int'l. (4 mi./52 mi.)

Medical Services
911 Service **Under 1 mi:** Doctor, Chiropractor (Chiropractic Associates of West Haven 937-7246) **1-3 mi:** Dentist (Elm Street Family Dental 933-2223) **Hospital:** Yale-New Haven 688-2222 (2 mi.)

Setting -- Conveniently located, right off New Haven Harbor on the West River channel, Oyster Point is part of a tiny, Victorian residential community that is now the Oyster Point National Historic district. There is a harborside boardwalk, a waterfront restaurant and a snack bar. Views are of the wide open harbor.

Marina Notes -- In 1998, new owner/managers made substantial renovations, including new heads and showers. The docks, boardwalk, and pedestals are still very shipshape. Limited cruiser services. Physically the Sage American Grille peninsula is the center of the marina. Along its south side are three piers with slips; on its north is the fuel dock and additional dockage, and further north is the main network of slips that radiate from the boardwalk. The well-regarded Sage American offers 1st & 2nd floor dining plus deck dining - all with fabulous harbor views - Dinner 5-10pm Mon-Sat, Lounge 4-11pm, Sun brunch 11-3, Happy Hour Mon-Fri 4-6pm. Live piano music - contemporary, jazz or classical. Monthly wine tastings. The onsite Dockside deli/market serves light meals.

Notable -- Next door are the attractive buildings that house the Sound (High) School, focused on maritime skills. Stroll gentrifying Oyster (City) Point's Howard Street to enjoy some lovely old turn-of-the-century houses. Famous Long Wharf Theater is less than a mile. Take the bus to the New Haven Green and Yale University's main campus (Chapel & Church Streets stop) - about 2 miles or 10 minutes away. Right there are the Yale Art Gallery (432-0600) and the Yale Center for British Art (432.2800). On nearby Hillhouse Avenue (described by Dickens as the "most beautiful street in America") is the Y.U. Collection of Musical Instruments (432-0822). On Sachem & Whitney is the Peabody Museum of Natural History - dinosaurs to Egyptian mummies $7/5 (432-5050).

West Cove Marina

13 Kimberly Avenue; West Haven, CT 06516

Tel: (203) 933-3000 **VHF: Monitor** n/a **Talk** n/a
Fax: (203) 933-3081 **Alternate Tel:** (203) 933-3000
Email: n/a **Web:** n/a
Nearest Town: New Haven *(3 mi.)* **Tourist Info:** (203) 787-6735

Navigational Information

Lat: 41°16.945' **Long:** 072°56.450' **Tide:** 8 ft. **Current:** n/a **Chart:** 12372
Rep. Depths *(MLW):* **Entry** 8 ft. **Fuel Dock** 8 ft. **Max Slip/Moor** 8 ft./-
Access: New Haven Harbor to West River past I-95 bridge

Marina Facilities *(In Season/Off Season)*

Fuel: Gasoline
Slips: 122 Total, 56 Transient **Max LOA:** 45 ft. **Max Beam:** n/a
  Rate *(per ft.):* **Day** $2.00 **Week** $9.00 **Month** $30
  Power: 30 amp Incl., **50 amp** Incl., **100 amp** n/a, **200 amp** n/a
  Cable TV: No **Dockside Phone:** No
  Dock Type: Floating, Wood
Moorings: 0 Total, 0 Transient **Launch:** n/a
  Rate: Day n/a **Week** n/a **Month** n/a
Heads: 4 Toilet(s), 2 Shower(s)
Laundry: 1 Washer(s), 1 Dryer(s) **Pay Phones:** Yes, 1
Pump-Out: OnSite, Full Service, 1 Central **Fee:** $5 **Closed Heads:** Yes

Marina Operations

Owner/Manager: n/a **Dockmaster:** Gene Pacapelli
In-Season: May 15-Oct 15, 8am-7pm* **Off-Season:** Oct 15-Apr 15, Closed
After-Hours Arrival: Call ahead
Reservations: No **Credit Cards:** Visa/MC, Amex
Discounts: None
Pets: Welcome **Handicap Access:** No

Marina Services and Boat Supplies

Services - Docking Assistance, Dock Carts **Communication -** Phone Messages, FedEx, AirBorne, UPS, Express Mail **Supplies - OnSite:** Ice *(Cube)* **Near:** Bait/Tackle *(Some-Things Fishy 933-2002)*
Under 1 mi: Ships' Store **1-3 mi:** Propane *(National Propane 747-9868)*
3+ mi: Boater's World *(Orange 799-9774, 6 mi.)*, Boat/US *(467-4436, 5 mi.)*

Boatyard Services

OnSite: Bottom Cleaning **Under 1 mi:** Launching Ramp.

Restaurants and Accommodations

OnSite: Motel *(Super 8 932-9000, $50-100)* **Near:** Restaurant *(Lorenzo's Ristorante 932-5846)*, *(Hazelnut 787-1088)*, *(Tropical Krust 868-6588)*, Fast Food, Lite Fare *(Nick's Luncheonette 937-9036)* **Under 1 mi:** Restaurant *(Burton's 933-9929)*, *(Sage American Bar & Grill 785-8086)*, Pizzeria *(Zuppardi's 934-1949, take-out available)* **1-3 mi:** Motel *(Econo Lodge 934-6611)*, Hotel *(Omni New Haven 772-6664, $260-350)*, *(Best Western 933-0344, $80-180)*, Inn/B&B *(Three Chimneys Inn 789-1201, $190-260)*, *(Historic Mansion Inn 865-8324)*

Recreation and Entertainment

OnSite: Heated Pool, Grills **Near:** Park *(Bayview Park - West Haven)*
Under 1 mi: Fitness Center *(Quest Aerobic & Athletic 933-0052)*, Video Rental *(Tommy K's 234-8110)* **1-3 mi:** Bowling *(Woodlawn Duckpin Bowling 932-3202)*, Movie Theater *(Forest Theatre 934-0370)*, Museum *(Yale Center for British Art 432-2800)*, Cultural Attract *(Long Wharf Theater 787-4282; Creative Arts Workshop 562-2329)*, Sightseeing *(Yale University 432-2300,*

free tours M-F 10:30am & 2pm, Sat&Sun 1:30am) **3+ mi:** Golf Course *(Orange Hills 795-4161, 5 mi.)*, Horseback Riding *(Tancreti Stables 234-7884, 5 mi.)*

Provisioning and General Services

Near: Delicatessen *(Paesano 937-6358)*, Liquor Store *(Big Toms 933-1383)*, Pharmacy *(Rite Aid 933-5260)*, Newsstand **Under 1 mi:** Convenience Store *(Corner Store 865-1468)*, Market *(West Haven Market & Deli 932-3335)*, Health Food *(Natures Garden 937-6905)*, Wine/Beer *(Rosette Wine & Liquor 562-2808)*, Meat Market, Bank/ATM, Post Office, Catholic Church, Protestant Church, Synagogue, Library *(West Haven 933-9335)*, Beauty Salon, Barber Shop, Dry Cleaners, Laundry, Florist, Clothing Store, Copies Etc. *(Ross Copy 933-8732)* **1-3 mi:** Supermarket *(Shop Rite 934-5660)*, Hardware Store *(True Value 934-0766)*, Buying Club **3+ mi:** Bookstore *(Barnes & Noble 799-1266, 4 mi.)*, Department Store *(K-mart 735-8850, 8 mi.)*

Transportation

OnCall: Rental Car *(Enterprise 931-4090/ 2 mi. Avis 624-2161)*, Taxi *(Meriden Yellow Cab 235-4434)*, Airport Limo *(First Class 787-3489)*
1-3 mi: InterCity Bus *(Greyhound 800-229-9424)*, Rail *(Amtrak 800-872-7245 & MetroNorth 800-638-7646)* **Airport:** Tweed/Bradley *(4 mi./54 mi.)*

Medical Services

911 Service **OnCall:** Ambulance **Near:** Dentist *(Elm Street Family Dental 933-2223)* **Under 1 mi:** Doctor, Chiropractor *(Chiropractic Assoc. of West Haven 937-7246)*, Veterinarian *(Angel Animal Hospital 934-3536)*
Hospital: Yale-New Haven 688-2222 *(2 mi.)*

Setting -- Located between the 23 foot fixed Elm Street bridge and the I-95 bridge, this largely residential marina is tucked into a protected cove on the West River. Views, in this semi-industrial area, are mostly of the large glass-front contemporary clubhouse, the docks, and the active bridges.

Marina Notes -- *Closed Mondays and Tuesdays. Wed-Sun open 8am-7pm; dock help available Wed-Fri 8am-3pm. All marina facilities (including the heads and laundry) are housed in a single-story, good sized contemporary-styled clubhouse. The main, all-glass room overlooks the marina on one side and on the other a small inviting pool with sunbathing area, surrounded by an attractive white fence. It has a nicely furnished party room with a bar, comfortable tables and chairs, a lounge and TV area and a well-equipped kitchen (all available to transients). Note: Pets must be leashed.

Notable -- Busy New Haven Harbor is the second largest commercial port in Connecticut and has limited recreational facilities. A two-story Super-8 motel is adjacent to the property. The surrounding area is commercial and industrial but there are some facilities and services nearby, including a restaurant, snack bar, and a couple of fast food eateries as well as a pharmacy and deli stores. Historic Yale University and New Haven's bustling central business district are about 3 miles across the Elm Street bridge. And the famous Long Wharf Theater is 2 miles away.

Navigational Information

Lat: 41°12.800' **Long:** 073°03.273' **Tide:** 6.7 ft. **Current:** n/a **Chart:** 12370
Rep. Depths (*MLW*): **Entry** 8 ft. **Fuel Dock** n/a **Max Slip/Moor** 8 ft./-
Access: The Gulf to Milford Harbor, 2nd facility to port

Marina Facilities (In Season/Off Season)

Fuel: No
Slips: 100 Total, 8 Transient **Max LOA:** 45 ft. **Max Beam:** 15 ft.
   Rate (*per ft.*): **Day** $1.75/Inq. **Week** Inq. **Month** Inq.
   Power: 30 amp Incl., 50 amp Incl., 100 amp n/a, 200 amp n/a
   Cable TV: No **Dockside Phone:** No
   Dock Type: Floating, Wood
Moorings: 0 Total, 0 Transient **Launch:** n/a
   Rate: Day n/a **Week** n/a **Month** n/a
Heads: 4 Toilet(s), 2 Shower(s)
Laundry: None **Pay Phones:** Yes
Pump-Out: No **Fee:** n/a **Closed Heads:** Yes

Marina Operations

Owner/Manager: Bruce Kuryla **Dockmaster:** n/a
In-Season: May-Sep 1, 8am-5pm **Off-Season:** Oct 1-Apr 30, 8am-5pm
After-Hours Arrival: Call ahead
Reservations: Yes, Required **Credit Cards:** Visa/MC
Discounts: None
Pets: Welcome **Handicap Access:** No

Port Milford

164 Rogers Avenue; Milford, CT 06464

Tel: (203) 877-7802 **VHF: Monitor** 9 **Talk** n/a
Fax: (203) 877-5809 **Alternate Tel:** (203) 877-7802
Email: n/a **Web:** n/a
Nearest Town: Milford (*1 mi.*) **Tourist Info:** (203) 878-0681

Marina Services and Boat Supplies

Services - Docking Assistance, Dock Carts **Communication -** Mail & Package Hold, Fax in/out (*$2*), FedEx, UPS **Supplies - OnSite:** Ice (*Cube*) **Under 1 mi:** Ships' Store (*Milford Boatworks 878-2900*) **1-3 mi:** Bait/Tackle (*Fisherman's Quarters 876-1495*), Propane (*Gloria's Garden 877-2776*) **3+ mi:** West Marine (*877-4004, 8 mi.*)

Boatyard Services

OnSite: Travelift (*35T*), Engine mechanic (*gas, diesel*), Electrical Repairs, Electronic Sales, Electronics Repairs, Hull Repairs, Rigger, Bottom Cleaning, Brightwork, Air Conditioning, Refrigeration, Divers, Compound, Wash & Wax, Interior Cleaning, Propeller Repairs, Woodworking, Inflatable Repairs, Upholstery, Yacht Interiors, Metal Fabrication, Awlgrip, Yacht Broker
Yard Rates: $60/hr., Haul & Launch $12/ft., Power Wash $1.50/ft., Bottom Paint $15/ft. (*paint incl.*)

Restaurants and Accommodations

OnCall: Pizzeria (*Francos 877-6180*) **Near:** Restaurant (*Rainbow Gardens 878-2500, L $7-10, D $14-18*), Fast Food (*Subway*) **Under 1 mi:** Restaurant (*Amberjack's*), (*Seven Seas 877-7327, voted best fish & chips*), (*Stonebridge 874-7947, L $8-14, D $13-27*), (*Citrus 877-1138*), (*Archie Moores 876-5088*) **1-3 mi:** Motel (*Shoreline Motel 876-8556*), (*Hampton Inn 874-4400, $90-120*), (*Comfort Inn 877-9411, $80-180*)

Recreation and Entertainment

OnSite: Picnic Area **Near:** Beach **Under 1 mi:** Tennis Courts (*Milford courts*), Golf Course (*Orchards GC 877-8200*), Boat Rentals (*Tony's 878-5380*), Movie Theater (*Milford Fourplex 878-3203*), Museum (*Milford*

Historical Society Wharf Lane 874-2664*) **1-3 mi:** Playground, Fitness Center (*Fitness Edge 874-3343*), Jogging Paths, Horseback Riding, Roller Blade/Bike Paths, Video Rental (*Blockbuster 876-0809*), Park (*Wilcox*)

Provisioning and General Services

Near: Convenience Store (*Speedy Mart*), Gourmet Shop (*Rainbow Gardens*), Delicatessen (*Food Fare 878-1551*), Wine/Beer, Bank/ATM, Post Office, Pharmacy (*Howes 878-2441*), Newsstand **Under 1 mi:** Liquor Store (*Friendly 874-9225*), Bakery, Farmers' Market, Green Grocer, Fishmonger, Lobster Pound, Meat Market, Catholic Church, Protestant Church, Synagogue, Library (*874-5675*), Beauty Salon, Barber Shop, Dry Cleaners, Laundry, Bookstore (*Waldenbooks 876-2258*), Hardware Store (*Harrison's 878-2491*), Florist, Clothing Store, Retail Shops **1-3 mi:** Supermarket (*Stop & Shop 876-0467*), Health Food (*Healthy Foods 882-9011*), Department Store (*Kmart 877-6036*), Buying Club (*Costco*)

Transportation

OnCall: Taxi (*East Haven 877-1460*), Airport Limo (*TC Airport Transp. 783-1135*) **Near:** Local Bus, Rail (*Metro North 874-4507*) **Under 1 mi:** Bikes (*Tony's 878-5380*), Rental Car (*Enterprise 874-7440/ Alamo 874-1759*), InterCity Bus (*Coastal Link 874-4507 Milford to Norwalk on Rte 1*)
Airport: Tweed/Bradley/Westchester (*11 mi./60 mi./50 mi.*)

Medical Services

911 Service **OnCall:** Ambulance **Near:** Doctor, Dentist
Under 1 mi: Chiropractor (*Cherry St. 874-2224*), Holistic Services (*Milford Body Therapy, Ruby Slippers Day Spa*) **1-3 mi:** Veterinarian (*Milford 882-8311*) **Hospital:** Milford 876-4000 (*1 mi.*)

Setting -- Right off the Gulf, on the western shore of lovely Milford Harbor (Wepawaug River), just past the usually very busy docks of Milford Yacht Club, is Port Milford. Its extensive network of docks are conveniently located and easily accessed. It also sports some wonderful restored antique buildings and great views down the harbor -- all quite quaint.

Marina Notes -- Port Milford is primarily a boatyard with a serious set of docks. It also has a very active dry stack storage operation. Virtually every boat service is available onsite. The heads are located at the rear of the property in one of those charming antique buildings touched with Victoriana. Milford Yacht Club (877-5598), next door, usually has a slip or mooring (with launch service), including use of their pool and facilities, for members of reciprocating yacht clubs.

Notable -- Many restaurants, as well as delightful downtown Milford, are within a mile. Fort Trumbull Beach - a large crescent - is an easy walk. Bikes and kayak rentals available at Tony's Bikes and Sports on Broad Street. Dinghy across the Gulf to Charles Island to observe nesting birds or to search for Capt. Kidd's treasure, supposedly buried on the south side. Or to Gulf Beach which has concessions, lifeguards and a fishing pier. Milford summer events: Summer Nights by Harbor Lights concerts, a very popular Sand Castle Contest, and the Milford Oyster Festival - third Sat. in August - with arts and crafts fair, canoe and kayak races, a classic car show and live entertainment. Call the CofC at 878-0681.

Milford Boat Works

1 High Street; Milford, CT 06460

Tel: (203) 877-1475 **VHF: Monitor** 68 **Talk** n/a
Fax: (203) 783-1678 **Alternate Tel:** n/a
Email: milfordboat@aol.com **Web:** www.milfordboatworks.com
Nearest Town: Milford *(0.1 mi.)* **Tourist Info:** (203) 878-0681

Navigational Information
Lat: 41°13.000' **Long:** 073°03.000' **Tide:** 6 ft. **Current:** .25 kt. **Chart:** 12370
Rep. Depths (MLW): Entry 8 ft. **Fuel Dock** 8 ft. **Max Slip/Moor** 8 ft./-
Access: The Gulf to Milford Harbor, 3rd facility to port

Marina Facilities *(In Season/Off Season)*
Fuel: *Texaco* - Gasoline, Diesel
Slips: 200 Total, 10 Transient **Max LOA:** 50 ft. **Max Beam:** n/a
  Rate *(per ft.):* **Day** $1.75/Inq. **Week** Inq. **Month** Inq.
  Power: 30 amp Incl., **50 amp** Incl., **100 amp** n/a, **200 amp** n/a
  Cable TV: No **Dockside Phone:** No
  Dock Type: Floating, Long Fingers, Wood
Moorings: 0 Total, 0 Transient **Launch:** n/a, Dinghy Dock
  Rate: Day n/a **Week** n/a **Month** n/a
Heads: 6 Toilet(s), 4 Shower(s) *(with dressing rooms)*
Laundry: 1 Washer(s), 1 Dryer(s), Book Exchange **Pay Phones:** Yes, 1
Pump-Out: OnSite, Full Service, 1 Central **Fee:** $10 **Closed Heads:** Yes

Marina Operations
Owner/Manager: Nancy Bodick **Dockmaster:** n/a
In-Season: May-Sep, 8am-7pm **Off-Season:** Sep-May, 9am-4:30pm
After-Hours Arrival: Cannot arrive after hours, call in advance.
Reservations: Yes, Required **Credit Cards:** Visa/MC, Dscvr, Amex, Tex
Discounts: None
Pets: Welcome **Handicap Access:** No

Marina Services and Boat Supplies
Services - Security, Dock Carts **Communication -** Fax in/out, FedEx, AirBorne, UPS, Express Mail **Supplies - OnSite:** Ice *(Block, Cube)*, Ships' Store **1-3 mi:** Bait/Tackle *(Fishermans Quarters 876-1495)*, Propane *(Gloria's Garden Center 877-2776)* **3+ mi:** West Marine *(877-4004, 8 mi.)*

Boatyard Services
OnSite: Travelift *(35T)*, Forklift, Crane, Engine mechanic *(gas, diesel)*, Electrical Repairs, Hull Repairs, Rigger, Bottom Cleaning, Brightwork, Air Conditioning, Refrigeration, Compound, Wash & Wax, Yacht Broker *(Tartan C&C Yachts of Milford)* **Member:** ABBRA, ABYC **Yard Rates:** $63/hr.

Restaurants and Accommodations
Near: Restaurant *(Seven Seas 877-7329)*, *(Milford Seafood 874-7947)*, *(Citrus)*, *(Stonebridge 874-7947, L $8-14, D $13-27, Sun-Thu 2 dinners $22 indoor-outdoor dining, formal deck, casual patio - also caters)*, *(Rainbow Gardens 878-2500, L $7-10, D $14-18)*, *(Archie Moore's 876-5088)*, *(Amberjack's)*, Pizzeria *(Peter Pan 878-9224)* **Under 1 mi:** Motel *(Hampton Inn 874-4400, $90-120)*, *(Red Roof 787-6060)*, Inn/B&B *(Rainbow Gardens 787-2500, $100-125)*

Recreation and Entertainment
Near: Tennis Courts *(Milford Municipal Courts)*, Golf Course *(Orchards G. C. 877-8200)*, Jogging Paths, Park *(Over the Footbridge - Wilcox Park)*, Special Events *(Concerts on the Green)*, Galleries *(Imagine That!)* **Under 1 mi:** Fitness Center *(Fitness Edge 874-3343)*, Movie Theater *(Milford Fourplex 878-3203)*, Video Rental *(Blockbuster 876-0809)*,

Museum *(Eells Stow House 874 2664, Downes House 877-9199)* **1-3 mi:** Bowling *(Devon Duckpin 882-1867)*

Provisioning and General Services
Near: Convenience Store, Delicatessen *(Harborwalk Deli 783-1627)*, Wine/Beer, Liquor Store *(TJ's Package Store 878-2649)*, Fishmonger, Bank/ATM, Post Office, Library, Beauty Salon, Barber Shop, Dry Cleaners *(Green's)*, Laundry, Pharmacy *(Howes 878-2441)*, Newsstand, Hardware Store *(Harrison's Ace 878-2491)*, Florist, Clothing Store, Retail Shops **Under 1 mi:** Health Food *(Healthy Foods Plus 882-9011)*, Catholic Church, Protestant Church *(Methodist, Baptist, Episcopal)*, Bookstore *(Waldenbooks 876-2258)* **1-3 mi:** Supermarket *(Shop Rite 876-7868/Stop & Shop 876-0467)*, Department Store *(Kmart 877-6036, Sears at Mall)*

Transportation
OnCall: Rental Car *(Enterprise 874-7440/ Alamo 874-1759, 1 mi.)*, Taxi *(East Haven Taxi 877-1460)*, Airport Limo *(TC Airport Transp. 783-1135)* **Near:** Bikes *(Tony's 878-5380)*, Local Bus, InterCity Bus *(Milford to Norwalk)*, Rail *(Metro North, Amtrak 10 mi.)*
Airport: Westchester/Bradley *(50 mi./60 mi.)*

Medical Services
911 Service OnCall: Ambulance **Near:** Holistic Services *(Ruby Slippers Day Spa, Milford Body Therapy)* **Under 1 mi:** Doctor, Dentist *(Helms 878-6699)*, Chiropractor *(Cherry Street Chiropractic 874-2224)* **1-3 mi:** Veterinarian *(Animal Clinic of Milford 882-8311)*
Hospital: Milford 876-4000 *(1 mi.)*

Setting -- Strung out along the western shore of Wepawaug River is very ship-shape Milford Boat Works. The first set of docks provide a more marina-like environment with picnic tables, chairs, and grills perched on the well-clipped grassy bank - a low gray building houses facilities and a chandlery. The second set of docks, mostly single, larger slips, are integrated into the boatyard part of the operation; the grass replaced by gravel. The main building is a particularly attractive 2-story gray shingled colonial. The surrounding area is residential.

Marina Notes -- Milford Boatworks incorporated Milford Harbor Marina into its operation in the late 90's. Now this large facility is divided by a road -- with most of the boatyard services and offices on the north side and the marina and ships' store on the south. All the grounds, docks and facilities demonstrate a caring hand. Founded in 1946 by the Bodick family; a well-trained 3rd generation now runs the operation. Immaculate and quite nice heads. Very few other cruiser services, but extensive ones for the yacht are onsite. Great place to look at boats -- a railed catwalk makes boarding those on the hard very easy. Note that Spencer Marina (874-4173), on the eastern shore -- identifiable by its brick-red 2-story headquarters - occasionally has a transient slip.

Notable -- Delightful downtown Milford begins a mere two blocks away, making a dozen eateries and most other required services an easy walk. First stop is Scooby Doo's Ice Cream shop. Milford's artistic ventures center around the Milford Fine Arts Council. Enjoy summer concerts on the classic New England green. Mid August brings the Oyster Festival. The unique Stonebridge Restaurant, within walking distance, offers views of the river and the waterfall.

Navigational Information

Lat: 41°13.250' **Long:** 073°03.290' **Tide:** 6 ft. **Current:** .25 kt. **Chart:** 12370
Rep. Depths *(MLW):* **Entry** 10 ft. **Fuel Dock** n/a **Max Slip/Moor** 9 ft./-
Access: The Gulf to Milford Harbor to head

Marina Facilities *(In Season/Off Season)*

Fuel: No
Slips: 40 Total, 35 Transient **Max LOA:** 65 ft. **Max Beam:** 20 ft.
  Rate *(per ft.):* **Day** $2.50/2.50* **Week** $12 **Month** Inq.
  Power: 30 amp $7.50-10, **50 amp** $10, **100 amp** n/a, **200 amp** n/a
  Cable TV: No **Dockside Phone:** No
  Dock Type: Floating, Short Fingers, Pilings, Wood
Moorings: 0 Total, 0 Transient **Launch:** n/a
  Rate: Day n/a **Week** n/a **Month** n/a
Heads: 4 Toilet(s), 4 Shower(s) *(with dressing rooms)*
Laundry: 1 Washer(s), 1 Dryer(s), Iron **Pay Phones:** Yes
Pump-Out: OnSite **Fee:** Free **Closed Heads:** Yes

Marina Operations

Owner/Manager: Dick Hosking **Dockmaster:** Barry Gallo
In-Season: Jun 15-Oct 15, 7am-11pm **Off-Season:** n/a, 7am-5pm
After-Hours Arrival: n/a
Reservations: Yes **Credit Cards:** Visa/MC
Discounts: None
Pets: Welcome, Dog Walk Area **Handicap Access:** Yes, Heads, Docks

Milford Landing Marina

37 Helwig Street; Milford, CT 06460

Tel: (203) 874-1610 **VHF: Monitor** 9 **Talk** 10
Fax: (203) 874-1619 **Alternate Tel:** (203) 874-1610
Email: mdf.landing@snet.net **Web:** n/a
Nearest Town: Milford *(0 mi.)* **Tourist Info:** (203) 878-0681

Marina Services and Boat Supplies

Services - Docking Assistance, Concierge, Boaters' Lounge, Security *(24 Hrs., T.V.)*, Trash Pick-Up **Communication -** Mail & Package Hold, Phone Messages, Fax in/out *(Free)*, Data Ports *(Marina)*, FedEx, AirBorne, UPS, Express Mail *(Sat Del)* **Supplies - OnSite:** Ice *(Cube)* **Near:** Ice *(Block)*, Ships' Store *(M. Boatworks 878-2900)* **1-3 mi:** Bait/Tackle *(Fishermans Quarters 876-1495)*, Live Bait, Propane *(Secondi 878-4687)*

Boatyard Services

OnSite: Launching Ramp **Nearest Yard:** Milford B. W. (203) 877-1475

Restaurants and Accommodations

OnSite: Snack Bar *(Scooby Doo's Ice Cream)* **OnCall:** Pizzeria *(Francos 877-6180)* **Near:** Restaurant *(Stonebridge 874-7947, L $8-14, D $13-27)*, *(Archie Moores 876-5088)*, *(Seven Seas Fish & Chips 877-7237, L $6, D $12)*, *(Amberjack's 882-9387)*, *(Rainbow Gardens 878-2500, L $7-10, D $14-18)*, *(Citrus New American 877-1138)*, Snack Bar *(Wayne's Place across the bridge, B&L, Lobster roll, fries, drink $10)*, Coffee Shop *(Dunkin Donuts)*, Fast Food *(Subway)*, Lite Fare *(Harborview Cafe B $3, L $6)*, *(Cafe Atlantique 882-1602)*, Pizzeria *(Peter Pan 878-9224)* **Under 1 mi:** Inn/B&B *(Rainbow Garden 878-2500, $110-125)* **1-3 mi:** Motel *(Hampton Inn 878-4400, $90-120)*

Recreation and Entertainment

OnSite: Picnic Area, Grills, Tennis Courts, Jogging Paths, Park *(Wilcox Park)* **Near:** Golf Course *(Orchards G. C. 877-8200)*, Museum *(Eells-Stow House 874-2664, Bryan-Downes House 877-9199, Stockade House)*, Cultural Attract *(Band Concerts - Fowler Field, Fri 7pm)*, Special Events

(Oyster festival - mid-Aug; Rotary Lobster Bake - mid-July) **Under 1 mi:** Fitness Center *(Fitness Edge 874-3343)*, Movie Theater *(Milford Fourplex 878-3203)*, Video Rental *(Blockbuster 876-0809)* **1-3 mi:** Beach, Bowling *(Duckpin Lanes 882-1867)*, Sightseeing *(Milford Jai Alai 877-4242)*

Provisioning and General Services

OnSite: Fishmonger **Near:** Convenience Store, Delicatessen *(Harborwalk Deli 783-1627; Park Lane Deli)*, Wine/Beer, Liquor Store *(Friendly Liquor 874-9225)*, Bakery, Bank/ATM *(Fleet)*, Post Office, Library, Beauty Salon *(Harbor Lites)*, Barber Shop, Dry Cleaners *(Green)*, Bookstore *(Waldenbooks 876-2258; The Wench)*, Pharmacy *(Howe's 878-2441)*, Newsstand, Hardware Store *(Harrison's Ace 878-2491)*, Florist, Clothing Store, Retail Shops **Under 1 mi:** Supermarket *(Shop Rite 876-7868)*, Health Food *(Healthy Foods Plus 882-9011)*, Catholic Church, Protestant Church, Laundry, Copies Etc. *(Mail Boxes Etc 783-1876)*

Transportation

OnCall: Rental Car *(Enterprise 874-7440/ Alamo 874-1759)*, Taxi *(East Haven Taxi 877-1460)*, Airport Limo *(TC Airport Transp. 783-1135)* **Near:** Bikes *(Tony's 878-5380)*, Local Bus *(Milford Transit)*, InterCity Bus *(Milford-Norwalk)*, Rail *(Metro North, or Amtrak 10 mi.)* **Airport:** Tweed/Westchester/Bradley *(11 mi./50 mi./60 mi.)*

Medical Services

911 Service **Near:** Holistic Services *(Ruby Slippers Day Spa 877-8809; Milford Body Therapy 874-3096)* **Under 1 mi:** Doctor, Dentist *(Helms 878-6699)*, Chiropractor *(Cherry St. 874-2224)*, Ambulance **1-3 mi:** Veterinarian *(Animal Clinic 882-8311)* **Hospital:** Milford 876-4000 *(1 mi.)*

Setting -- At the navigable head of Wepawaug River, Milford Landing is a perfect example of a municipal facility "done right". The small complex is really a beautifully landscaped, impeccably maintained maritime pocket-park. The 40 slips, with power and finger piers, line the park's shoreline with views across to Wilcox Park. Onshore, there's a large flagstone patio, populated by tables with market umbrellas. A raised rose garden blooms for an extended season, park benches line the walkway overlooking the River, and another group of picnic tables is next to the grills. Across the river is a large launching ramp and gazebo.

Marina Notes -- * Min. daily $70. Hourly $10 (under 30 ft.), $15 (30 ft.+), $40 after 6pm. This all-transient marina, built in 1996, was designed to draw traffic and cruisers to the area - and it works! The historic brick building houses nice heads, showers with dressing rooms, and a laundry. Complimentary coffee and newspapers every morning, charcoal for the grills, and lots of service. 24 hr. security cameras. Free pump-out. Just behind the rose garden, another small, restored brick house is an ice cream shop. Three commercial clam boats and a lobster boat are permanent residents and sell to cruisers at "boat prices".

Notable -- The burgeoning New England town of Milford - complete with a classic village green - has expanded down the hill to the Marina. Many charming shops and, at last count, 14 eateries are within a couple of blocks. A wrought-iron bridge crosses the River and leads to tennis courts, basketball courts, and a large pavilion with dozens of picnic tables - a good destination for club cruises and rendezvous. Milford's Fine Arts Council hosts 3 plays a year, a coffee house, a jazz concert series, and arts and crafts fair on the Green. Meet the Artists and Artisans is the 3rd weekend in May and the last weekend in September.

Brewer Stratford Marina

Brewer Stratford Marina

Foot of Broad Street; Stratford, CT 06615

Tel: (203) 377-4477 **VHF: Monitor** 9 **Talk** 10
Fax: (203) 375-8879 **Alternate Tel:** n/a
Email: std@byy.com **Web:** www.byy.com/Stratford
Nearest Town: Stratford *(0.25 mi.)* **Tourist Info:** (203) 335-3800

Navigational Information
Lat: 41°11.400' **Long:** 073°07.180' **Tide:** 7 ft. **Current:** 2 kt. **Chart:** 12370
Rep. Depths *(MLW):* **Entry** 12 ft. **Fuel Dock** 12 ft. **Max Slip/Moor** 15 ft./-
Access: Housatonic River, fifth facility on Western shore

Marina Facilities *(In Season/Off Season)*
Fuel: Gasoline, Diesel
Slips: 200 Total, 10 Transient **Max LOA:** 100 ft. **Max Beam:** n/a
Rate *(per ft.):* **Day** $2.00 **Week** $10/ft. **Month** Inq.
Power: 30 amp Incl., 50 amp Incl., 100 amp n/a, 200 amp n/a
Cable TV: Yes, $5 **Dockside Phone:** Yes Long term only
Dock Type: Floating, Long Fingers, Wood
Moorings: 0 Total, 0 Transient **Launch:** n/a
Rate: Day n/a **Week** n/a **Month** n/a
Heads: 7 Toilet(s), 7 Shower(s) *(with dressing rooms)*
Laundry: 2 Washer(s), 2 Dryer(s), Book Exchange **Pay Phones:** Yes, 1
Pump-Out: OnSite, Full Service, 1 Central **Fee:** $5* **Closed Heads:** Yes

Marina Operations
Owner/Manager: Rod Swift **Dockmaster:** n/a
In-Season: Summer, 8am-8pm **Off-Season:** Fall-Win-Sprg, 8am-5pm
After-Hours Arrival: Take any available slip; register in the morning.
Reservations: Yes **Credit Cards:** Visa/MC, Dscvr, Amex
Discounts: None
Pets: Welcome, Dog Walk Area **Handicap Access:** Yes, Heads, Docks

Marina Services and Boat Supplies
Services - Docking Assistance, Concierge, Dock Carts **Communication -** Mail & Package Hold, Phone Messages, Fax in/out, FedEx, UPS, Express Mail *(Sat Del)* **Supplies - OnSite:** Ice *(Block, Cube)*, Ships' Store **Under 1 mi:** Bait/Tackle *(Stratford Bait & Tackle 377-8091)*, Live Bait, Propane *(AmeriGas 330-9852)* **3+ mi:** West Marine *(877-4004, 4 mi.)*

Boatyard Services
OnSite: Travelift *(35T)*, Forklift, Crane, Engine mechanic *(gas, diesel)*, Launching Ramp, Electrical Repairs, Electronic Sales, Electronics Repairs, Hull Repairs, Rigger, Bottom Cleaning, Brightwork, Compound, Wash & Wax, Woodworking, Upholstery, Awlgrip, Total Refits **OnCall:** Propeller Repairs, Inflatable Repairs, Life Raft Service **Near:** Air Conditioning, Refrigeration. **Member:** ABYC - 3 Certified Tech(s) **Yard Rates:** $78/hr., Haul & Launch $14/ft. *(blocking incl.)*, Power Wash Incl., Bottom Paint $13-15/ft. + materials **Storage:** In-Water $38/ft., On-Land $44/ft.

Restaurants and Accommodations
OnSite: Restaurant *(Outriggers 377-8815, L $6-15, D $8-24)*, Snack Bar **Near:** Restaurant *(Agustyn's Blue Goose 375-9130, L Tue-Sat, D $13-20)*, *(Blue Sky Diner)*, *(Seven Seas 877-7327)*, Seafood Shack *(Ubert's Fish & Chips 377-2581, L & D 7 days $3-23)*, *(Lighthouse B, L, D)*, Pizzeria *(Pizza Works 348-4780)* **Under 1 mi:** Restaurant *(Wings 378-4000, at Sikiorsky Airport)*, *(Haborside Bar & Grille 375-3037, L $8-15, D $8-25, by dinghy)*, Motel *(HOJO Inn 375-5666)* **1-3 mi:** Hotel *(Ramada 375-8866, $85-110)*

Recreation and Entertainment
OnSite: Pool, Picnic Area, Grills **Near:** Beach, Fishing Charter

Under 1 mi: Playground, Tennis Courts, Fitness Center *(Fitness Edge 378-4242)*, Video Rental *(Blockbuster 377-6979)*, Museum *(Judson House 378-0630)* **1-3 mi:** Horseback Riding *(Circle B 526-4677)*, Bowling *(Barnum Duckpin 375-0621)*, Movie Theater *(Stratford Cinemas 381-1000)*, Cultural Attract *(Square One Theatre 375-8778)* **3+ mi:** Golf Course *(Orchards G. C. 877-8200, 6 mi.)*

Provisioning and General Services
Near: Convenience Store *(Citgo)*, Gourmet Shop *(Bountiful Baskets 381-0413)*, Delicatessen *(Armons 378-9442)*, Liquor Store *(Stratford Spirits 378-8636)*, Fishmonger *(Ubert's)*, Catholic Church, Barber Shop, Dry Cleaners, Newsstand, Copies Etc. *(DigiPrint)* **Under 1 mi:** Supermarket *(Stop & Shop; Shaw's 378-4296)*, Bakery, Bank/ATM, Post Office, Library *(Stratford PL 385-4161)*, Beauty Salon, Laundry, Bookstore *(Whistle Stop Book Shop 375-4146)*, Pharmacy *(Rotary Drug 378-9394)*, Hardware Store *(West & Langdon 378-9371; Home Depot)*, Retail Shops, Department Store *(Wal - Mart 502-7631)*

Transportation
OnSite: Courtesy Car/Van **OnCall:** Rental Car *(Enterprise 380-6070)*, Taxi *(Action Cab 579-4444)*, Airport Limo *(T C Airport Trans 783-1135)* **Under 1 mi:** Local Bus, InterCity Bus *(Coastal Link)*, Rail *(MetroNorth)* **Airport:** Tweed New Haven/Westchester/Bradley *(16 mi./45 mi./65 mi.)*

Medical Services
911 Service **Near:** Ambulance **Under 1 mi:** Doctor *(Covenant Family 377-3666)*, Dentist *(Aspen 378-9882)* **1-3 mi:** Chiropractor *(New Vision 380-1413)* **Hospital:** Bridgeport 384-3000 *(2.5 mi.)*

Setting -- About a mile and a half up the Housatonic River, Stratford's large, two-story, gray New England-style contemporary marina building appears on the western shore. Flower-filled planters and perennial beds are tucked in and around the docks and buildings. A raised pool deck and covered picnic area are enhanced by distant views of the boats, the Housatonic, and the expanse of marsh on the other side. All facilities are notably well tended. A two story yellow-brick building houses the boatyard operation and a restaurant with deck sits dockside right in the center.

Marina Notes -- *Pump-out free for Brewers Yacht Yard customers. Courtesy rides into town. Two sets of docks, each with its own set of particularly nice, large, family-style, full bathrooms. The large, inviting laundry room has a folding table, ironing board and sofa. The pool house, with 5 new individual bathrooms plus a recreation room, was built in the late nineties. Brewer signature fresh flowers are in each bath. This site has been the home of a shipyard since the 1700's. During the mid 1800's large schooners were built here -- most notably, the 280-ton Helen Mar. Stratford joined the Brewer chain in 1996.

Notable -- The onsite Outrigger Restaurant offers a choice of a bright, airy dining room or a deck overlooking the marina, river and marsh. It's open Mon-Thu 11:30-9, Fri & Sat 'til 10pm, Sun 11:30-8pm - everything from hamburgers to seafood entrées. A half mile north on Route 1 are two large shopping centers, with 2 supermarkets, a Wal-Mart, Home Depot, Staples, etc. plus several eateries. The Housatonic's water quality is very good and the river teems with wildlife. The Stratford Shakespeare Theater (a several block walk) may or may not be operating -- the deed was conveyed to the town in 2002.

Navigational Information
Lat: 41°12.205' **Long:** 073°06.722' **Tide:** 7 ft. **Current:** 2 kt. **Chart:** 12370
Rep. Depths *(MLW)*: **Entry** 20 ft. **Fuel Dock** n/a **Max Slip/Moor** 8 ft./-
Access: About two miles up the Housatonic opposite red nun 24

Marina Facilities *(In Season/Off Season)*
Fuel: No
Slips: 192 Total, 20 Transient **Max LOA:** 85 ft. **Max Beam:** n/a
  Rate *(per ft.)*: **Day** $1.50 **Week** Inq. **Month** n/a
  Power: 30 amp Incl., **50 amp** Incl., **100 amp** n/a, **200 amp** n/a
  Cable TV: Yes, Incl. **Dockside Phone:** Yes Longer term only
  Dock Type: Floating, Long Fingers, Wood
Moorings: 0 Total, 0 Transient **Launch:** n/a
  Rate: Day n/a **Week** n/a **Month** n/a
Heads: 4 Toilet(s), 4 Shower(s) *(with dressing rooms)*, Fitness Center
Laundry: 2 Washer(s), 2 Dryer(s) **Pay Phones:** Yes
Pump-Out: OnSite, Self Service, 1 Central **Fee:** Free **Closed Heads:** Yes

Marina Operations
Owner/Manager: Dick Speer **Dockmaster:** Same
In-Season: Year Round, 8am-5pm **Off-Season:** Closed weekends
After-Hours Arrival: Call ahead, or call pager
Reservations: Yes **Credit Cards:** Visa/MC
Discounts: None
Pets: Welcome **Handicap Access:** Yes, Heads, Docks

Marina at The Dock

PO Box 368; 955 Ferry Boulevard; Stratford, CT 06497

Tel: (203) 378-9300 **VHF: Monitor** 9 **Talk** n/a
Fax: (203) 377-5951 **Alternate Tel:** n/a
Email: spetrella@shopthedock.com **Web:** www.shopthedock.com
Nearest Town: Milford *(1 mi.)* **Tourist Info:** (203) 335-3800

Marina Services and Boat Supplies
Services - Security *(24 Hrs., Electronic security gate)*, Dock Carts
Communication - FedEx, AirBorne, UPS, Express Mail *(Sat Del)* **Supplies - OnSite:** Ice *(Block)* **Under 1 mi:** Ships' Store *(Hitchcock Landmark Marine 378-2270)* **1-3 mi:** West Marine *(877-4004)*, Bait/Tackle *(Stratford Bait & Tackle 377-8091)*, Propane *(Paraco 629-5627)*, CNG *(Brewer Stratford)*

Boatyard Services
OnSite: Travelift *(50T)* **Under 1 mi:** Launching Ramp **Yard Rates:** $50/hr. Haul & Launch $100 *(blocking incl.)*, Power Wash Incl., Bottom Paint $7/ft.
Storage: In-Water $22.5/ft., On-Land $34/ft. Sep-Jun

Restaurants and Accommodations
OnSite: Snack Bar *(Doug's Dockside Dogs B&L $2-4, 7-ppm Fri, 8-6 Sat & Sun)*, Pizzeria *(De Pizza Man 377-7888)* **Near:** Restaurant *(Harborside Bar & Grille 375-3037, L $9-15, D $9-25, L 11-4 & D 4-10:30, kids' menu $6; Sun Brunch 11-3pm $20/11)*, *(Ponderosa Steak House 377-8003)*, Fast Food *(Danny's Drive-In)* **Under 1 mi:** Restaurant *(Augustyn's Blue Goose 375-9130)*, *(Outrigger 377-8815, L $6-13, D $9-24, by dinghy - at Brewer Stratford Marina)*, Seafood Shack *(Ubert's Fish & Chips 377-2581, L&D $3-23)*, *(Lighthouse B, L, D)* **1-3 mi:** Restaurant *(Knapps Landing)*, Motel *(Red Roof Inns 877-6060)*, Hotel *(Hampton Inn 874-4400, $90-110)* **3+ mi:** Hotel *(Marriott 378-1400, 3.5 mi.)*

Recreation and Entertainment
OnSite: Picnic Area, Fitness Center, Video Rental *(Blockbuster 377-6979)*
Near: Jogging Paths **Under 1 mi:** Bowling *(Devon Duckpin Lanes 882-1867)*, Movie Theater *(Stratford Cinemas 381-1000)*, Cultural Attract *(Square One Theatre 375-8778)* **1-3 mi:** Tennis Courts *(Milford Tennis Club 261-2363)*, Museum *(Judson House, Stratford Historical Society 378-0630)* **3+ mi:** Golf Course *(Orchards G.C. 877-8200, 4 mi.)*, Horseback Riding *(Circle B Stables 526-4677, 4.5 mi.)*

Provisioning and General Services
OnSite: Supermarket *(Stop & Shop 375-8787; Shaws is nearby)*, Wine/Beer *(Captain's Keg 377-5025)*, Liquor Store, Bank/ATM *(Fleet 380-6640)*, Beauty Salon *(PK Salon 377-7699)*, Dry Cleaners *(Dockside 378-1811)*, Laundry *(Dockwash)*, Pharmacy *(Stop & Shop 375-5717, GNC 375-0034)*, Retail Shops, Copies Etc. *(Staples 375-1884)* **Near:** Bakery, Barber Shop, Newsstand, Hardware Store *(Home Depot 386-9815)*, Department Store *(Wal Mart)* **Under 1 mi:** Convenience Store, Delicatessen *(Devon News & Deli 877-8785)*, Fishmonger *(Ubert's)*, Post Office, Library *(Stratford PL 385-4161)*, Bookstore *(Whistle Stop Book Shop 375-4146)* **1-3 mi:** Health Food, Protestant Church, Synagogue

Transportation
OnCall: Rental Car *(Enerprise 874-7440)*, Taxi *(Orange Cab 877-1468)*, Airport Limo *(Airport Transport 783-1135)* **1-3 mi:** Rail **Airport:** Tweed New Haven/Westchester/Bradley *(16 mi./45 mi./65 mi.)*

Medical Services
911 Service **OnSite:** Dentist *(Aspen 378-9882)*, Veterinarian *(PetCo 378-9004)* **OnCall:** Ambulance **1-3 mi:** Doctor *(Covenant Family 377-3666)*, Chiropractor *(Family Life 377-4600)* **Hospital:** Milford 876-4000 *(3.5 mi.)*

PHOTOS ON CD-ROM: 9

Setting -- A little over two miles up the Housatonic, just above the bascule bridge and just south of the Route I-95 100-foot bridge, lies this relatively new, attractively executed, marina. It sits on the river's western shore and is an integral part of The Dock Shopping Center. The docks run almost from bridge to bridge. A wide wooden boardwalk, dotted with picnic tables, runs halfway along the docks and a grassy promenade continues to a 160-foot fishing pier.

Marina Notes -- Floating wood docks are fully lined with rubber fenders. Admiral's Association year round at discount fees. Individual, exceptionally nice, bathrooms with showers and hair dryers, a laundry room, and an adjacent small boaters' lounge and lending library complete the amenities. Low-level dock lighting provides good security and a welcome evening glow. Onsite is 50 ton travelift; boatyard services are limited to haul/launch operations and include extensive on the hard storage - out of sight of the docks. There's ample parking for crew changes.

Notable -- If you need services, supplies or provisions, it is well worth the trek up river. Nothing beats pushing the cart directly to the boat. The surrounding 2-part mall has a good assortment of stores, including a large Super Stop & Shop supermarket, Staples (copy center & UPS depot), fabric & craft store, PetCo (with vet) toys, bank, hair salon, commercial laundry, dry cleaner, GNC, Blockbuster, fast food and pizza parlor (an old Bradlees stands empty; a replacement is expected). Directly beyond are Wal-Mart, Shaw's Supermarket and Home Depot. A selection of eateries is nearby including upscale Harborside, across the street, with a river deck and a small municipal dinghy dock. The Stratford Shakespeare Theater may re-open soon -- the town now owns it.

V. Connecticut: Western Long Island Sound

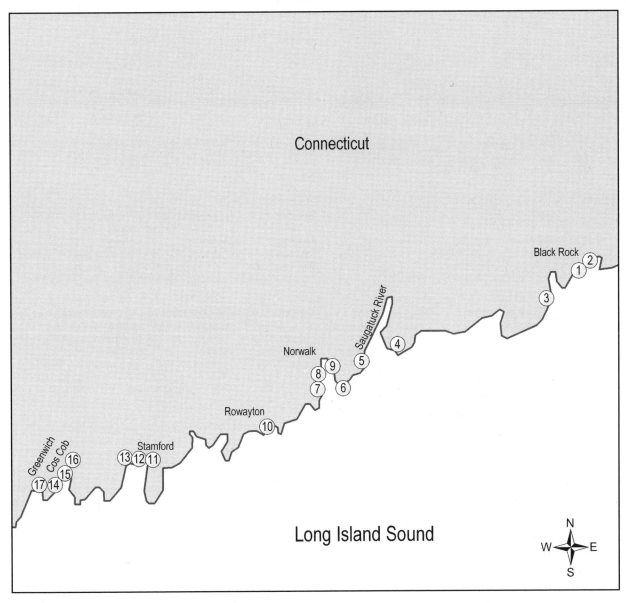

MAP	MARINA	HARBOR	PAGE	MAP	MARINA	HARBOR	PAGE
1	Captain's Cove Seaport	Black Rock Hbr/Burr Creek	94	10	The Boatworks	Five Mile River	103
2	Cedar Marina	Black Rock Hbr/Cedar Creek	95	11	Harbour Square Marina	Stamford Hbr/East Branch	104
3	South Benson Marina	Black Rock Hbr/Ash Creek	96	12	Brewer Yacht Haven Marina	Stamford Hbr/East and West Branch	105
4	Compo Yacht Basin	Saugatuck River	97	13	Stamford Landing Marina	Stamford Hbr/West Branch	106
5	Cedar Point Yacht Club	Saugatuck River	98	14	Palmer Point Marina	Mianus River	107
6	Norwalk Cove Marina	Norwalk Harbor/North Basin	99	15	Beacon Point Marina	Mianus River	108
7	Total Marine of Norwalk	Norwalk River	100	16	OMA Marine	Mianus River	109
8	Rex Marine Center	Norwalk River	101	17	Delamar Greenwich Harbor	Greenwich Harbor	110
9	Norwalk Visitors Dock	Norwalk River	102				

Captain's Cove Seaport

1 Bostwick Avenue; Bridgeport, CT 06605

Tel: (203) 335-1433 **VHF: Monitor** 18 **Talk** 18
Fax: (203) 335-6793 **Alternate Tel:** (203) 335-1433
Email: n/a **Web:** www.captainscoveseaport.com
Nearest Town: Black Rock (2 mi.) **Tourist Info:** (800) 866-7925

Navigational Information

Lat: 41°09.474' **Long:** 073°12.873' **Tide:** 8 ft. **Current:** n/a **Chart:** 12369
Rep. Depths (MLW): **Entry** 18 ft. **Fuel Dock** 13 ft. **Max Slip/Moor** 13 ft./-
Access: Long Island Sound to Black Rock Harbor/Cedar Creek

Marina Facilities (In Season/Off Season)
Fuel: Gasoline, Diesel
Slips: 350 Total, 50 - 100 Transient **Max LOA:** 200 ft. **Max Beam:** n/a
 Rate (per ft.): **Day** $1.50 **Week** Inq. **Month** Inq.
 Power: 30 amp Incl., **50 amp** Incl., **100 amp** n/a, **200 amp** n/a
 Cable TV: No **Dockside Phone:** No
 Dock Type: Floating, Long Fingers, Alongside, Wood
Moorings: 0 Total, 0 Transient **Launch:** n/a
 Rate: Day n/a **Week** n/a **Month** n/a
Heads: 2 Toilet(s), 2 Shower(s)
Laundry: 1 Washer(s), 1 Dryer(s) **Pay Phones:** Yes, 3
Pump-Out: OnSite **Fee:** n/a **Closed Heads:** Yes

Marina Operations
Owner/Manager: Joseph Savino **Dockmaster:** Jan Williams (Harbormaster)
In-Season: May-Oct, 7:30am-5:30pm **Off-Season:** Nov-Apr, 7:30am-4:30pm
After-Hours Arrival: VHF channel 18
Reservations: Call in advance 203-335-1433 **Credit Cards:** Visa/MC
Discounts: None
Pets: Welcome, Dog Walk Area **Handicap Access:** No

Marina Services and Boat Supplies
Services - Docking Assistance, Security, Dock Carts **Communication -** Mail & Package Hold, Phone Messages, Fax in/out, FedEx, AirBorne, UPS, Express Mail (Sat Del) **Supplies - OnSite:** Ice (Block, Cube), Ships' Store (Boathouse) **Under 1 mi:** Bait/Tackle (Ted's Bait & Tackle 366-7615) **1-3 mi:** West Marine (330-1100), Propane (AmeriGas 330-9852)

Boatyard Services
OnSite: Travelift (85T), Forklift, Crane, Engine mechanic (gas, diesel), Electrical Repairs, Hull Repairs, Rigger, Bottom Cleaning, Brightwork, Refrigeration, Compound, Wash & Wax, Painting, Awlgrip, Total Refits **OnCall:** Electronics Repairs, Air Conditioning, Divers, Interior Cleaning, Propeller Repairs, Woodworking, Inflatable Repairs, Life Raft Service **Dealer for:** Volvo Penta. Other Certifications: Yanmar, Westerbeake **Yard Rates:** $60/hr., Haul & Launch $9/ft. (blocking $5 per stand), Power Wash $1/ft., Bottom Paint $9.50/ft. **Storage:** In-Water $80/ft. summer, $30/ft. winter, On-Land $30/ft.

Restaurants and Accommodations
OnSite: Seafood Shack (The Restaurant 335-7104, L & D $5-15, kids' menu, Lobster market-priced; call ahead for take-out), Snack Bar, Lite Fare (Club Titanic at the Cove) **OnCall:** Pizzeria (Pizza & More 331-1100) **Under 1 mi:** Restaurant (Number 1 Chinese 368-2888), (Taqueria 576-8534), Coffee Shop (Dunkin Donuts) **1-3 mi:** Hotel (Holiday Inn 334-1234, $80-400)

Recreation and Entertainment
OnSite: Dive Shop (Orbit Divers 335-DIVE), Boat Rentals (866-4842 Black Rock Sailing - courses, charters, cruises), Fishing Charter (Carol Marie,

Daystar & Sometime), Group Fishing Boat, Museum (Dundon House Apr-Nov 335-1433), Sightseeing **Near:** Park (Seaside) **Under 1 mi:** Playground, Tennis Courts, Fitness Center (Sunshine Spa 366-6974), Movie Theater (Showcase Cinemas 339-7171), Video Rental (Video Plus 331-0101) **1-3 mi:** Beach, Horseback Riding (Circle B Stables 526-4677), Bowling (Amf Lanes 255-0408), Cultural Attract (Polka Dot Playhouse 333-3666) **3+ mi:** Golf Course (Fairchild Wheeler G.C. 373-5911, 4.5 mi.)

Provisioning and General Services
OnSite: Fishmonger, Retail Shops **Near:** Convenience Store (Mini-Rite 366-4684, Krauszer's) **Under 1 mi:** Market (Fairfield Market 368-6907), Supermarket (Gigante 367-9028), Delicatessen (Harry Marley's 366-5323), Liquor Store (West Side 333-2507), Bakery, Library (Bridgeport PL 576-7403), Beauty Salon, Pharmacy (Collins 576-8642) **1-3 mi:** Health Food (Sprouts 333-3455), Farmers' Market (Congregational Church Thu 2-6pm), Bank/ATM, Post Office, Bookstore (Black Sage 333-3889), Hardware Store (Madison 366-3865), Clothing Store (Syms 330-6700)

Transportation
OnCall: Rental Car (Enterprise 330-1399), Taxi (Yellow 334-2121), Airport Limo (Red Dot 330-1005) **Under 1 mi:** Local Bus **1-3 mi:** Rail (Metro North), Ferry Service (Port Jeff) **Airport:** Tweed/Westchester (25mi./40 mi.)

Medical Services
911 Service **OnCall:** Ambulance, Veterinarian (Vet HouseCall 929-7297) **Under 1 mi:** Chiropractor (Best Health 384-9999) **1-3 mi:** Doctor, Dentist (Family Dental 333-1841), Holistic Services (Alt Health Care 334-3660) **Hospital:** Bridgeport 384-3410 (1.5 mi.)

Setting -- One mile off Long Island Sound, in historic Black Rock Harbor, sits this truly unique maritime center and funky tourist attraction. Captain's Cove fills a protected basin on the west side of Cedar Creek. It is not missable. The docks are dominated by the 2-story main building, along with a Nantucket Lightship. Little Victorian-styled shops and "push carts" line the boardwalk giving the place a festive party atmosphere.

Marina Notes -- Additional, less expensive dockage across the basin is accessible by ferry. Showers & laundry in the rear of Pilot House building. Family founded, owned and operated since 1982. Full service boatyard, too. Heliport onsite. The 400-seat "Restaurant" is an overgrown seafood shack. Specialties are fried and steamed seafood, grills, wraps, ribs, hot dogs and a new cold bar. Tables are inside a cavernous, funky dockfront building, with a giant fish tank, or out on the large wharf-deck that overlooks the marina. Sunday afternoons feature bands on the boardwalk. Upstairs, The Club Titanic's bar is the former wheelhouse of a 19thC tugboat. Suspended above the dance floor are huge models of the Titanic & Excalibur, the Sikorsky flying boat. Big screen TV, too.

Notable -- Home to a Nantucket Lightship and an extensive collection of nautical memorabilia. At the end of the boardwalk is the Gustave Whitehead hangar which contains a half-scale model of Whitehead #21, an engine-powered aircraft that flew 28 months before the Wright Bros. Shops include a large fish market, Dave & Jeri's Ice Cream, Candy Land, a number of gift and craft shops, a dog bakery, photo shop, sailing center and yacht brokerage. Onsite, too, is Dundon House, a restored Queen Anne Victorian, with an exhibit on the area's maritime history, and Bridgeport Regional Vocational Aquaculture High School.

Navigational Information

Lat: 41°09.550' **Long:** 073°13.100' **Tide:** 6.5 ft. **Current:** n/a **Chart:** 12369
Rep. Depths (*MLW*): **Entry** 30 ft. **Fuel Dock** 8 ft. **Max Slip/Moor** 30 ft./-
Access: Black Rock Harbor to Cedar Creek channel

Marina Facilities *(In Season/Off Season)*

Fuel: No
Slips: 200 Total, 10 Transient **Max LOA:** 50 ft. **Max Beam:** 18 ft.
  Rate (*per ft.*): **Day** $1.50/Inq. **Week** Inq. **Month** Inq.
  Power: 30 amp $5, **50 amp** n/a, **100 amp** n/a, **200 amp** n/a
  Cable TV: Yes **Dockside Phone:** No
  Dock Type: Floating, Long Fingers, Short Fingers, Pilings, Wood
Moorings: 0 Total, 0 Transient **Launch:** n/a
  Rate: Day n/a **Week** n/a **Month** n/a
Heads: 3 Toilet(s), 2 Shower(s) *(with dressing rooms)*
Laundry: 1 Washer(s), 1 Dryer(s) **Pay Phones:** Yes, 1
Pump-Out: OnSite, Full Service, 1 Central **Fee:** $5 **Closed Heads:** Yes

Marina Operations

Owner/Manager: Frank Gulia **Dockmaster:** Same
In-Season: Year-Round, 8am-5pm **Off-Season:** n/a
After-Hours Arrival: Call ahead
Reservations: Yes, Required **Credit Cards:** Visa/MC, Dscvr
Discounts: Port Partners **Dockage:** 15% **Fuel:** n/a **Repair:** 10%
Pets: Welcome **Handicap Access:** Yes, Heads, Docks

Cedar Marina

86 Bostwick Avenue; Bridgeport, CT 06605

Tel: (203) 335-6262 **VHF: Monitor** 9 **Talk** 72
Fax: (203) 335-9159 **Alternate Tel:** (203) 335-6262
Email: n/a **Web:** n/a
Nearest Town: Black Rock *(2 mi.)* **Tourist Info:** (800) 866-7925

Marina Services and Boat Supplies

Services - Docking Assistance, Dock Carts **Communication -** FedEx,
AirBorne, UPS, Express Mail **Supplies - OnSite:** Ice *(Cube)* **Near:** Ice
(Block), Ships' Store *(Boat House at Captain's Cove)* **Under 1 mi:**
Bait/Tackle *(Teds Bait & Tackle 366-7615)* **1-3 mi:** West Marine *(330-1100)*, Boat/US, Propane *(AmeriGas 330-9852)*

Boatyard Services

OnSite: Travelift *(15T)*, Forklift, Crane, Engine mechanic *(gas, diesel)*,
Electrical Repairs, Hull Repairs, Bottom Cleaning, Brightwork, Divers,
Compound, Wash & Wax, Interior Cleaning, Propeller Repairs, Life Raft
Service **Yard Rates:** $55/hr., Haul & Launch $5/ft., Power Wash $1.50,
Bottom Paint $10/ft. *(paint incl.)* **Storage:** In-Water $20/ft., On-Land $30/ft.
incl. haul, wash, & launch

Restaurants and Accommodations

OnSite: Snack Bar **Near:** Seafood Shack *(Restaurant at Captains Cove
335-7104, L $5-15, D $5-15, Lobsters, Steamers Market-Priced, Kids
Menu)* **Under 1 mi:** Restaurant *(Boaters Restaurant 955-3100)*, *(Number
One Chinese 368-2888)*, *(Taqueria Mexicana 576-8534)*, *(Bloodroot
Feminist Bookstore 576-9168, Vegetarian Restaurant)*, Fast Food, Pizzeria
(Pizza & More 331-1100) **1-3 mi:** Restaurant *(Black Rock Castle 336-3990,
L $5-8, D $10-18)*, Motel *(Quality Motel 255-0491)*, Hotel *(Holiday Inn
334-1234, $80-400)*

Recreation and Entertainment

Near: Dive Shop, Jogging Paths, Park *(Seaside Park, by dinghy)*
Under 1 mi: Fitness Center *(Sunshine Spa 366-6974)*, Movie Theater

(Showcase Cinemas 339 7171 , Video Rental *(Video Plus 331 0101*
1-3 mi: Horseback Riding *(Circle B Stables 526-4677)*, Bowling *(Amf Lanes
255-0408)*, Museum *(Barnum Museum 331-1104)*, Cultural Attract *(Polka
Dot Playhouse 333-3666)* **3+ mi:** Golf Course *(Fairchild Wheeler Golf
Course 373-5911, 4.5 mi.)*

Provisioning and General Services

Near: Convenience Store *(Mini-Rite 366-4684)*, Fishmonger *(Captain's
Cove)*, Retail Shops *(Captain's Cove)* **Under 1 mi:** Delicatessen *(Harry
Marley's 366-5323)*, Liquor Store *(West Side 333-2507)*, Bakery, Meat
Market, Post Office, Library *(Bridgeport PL 576-7403)*, Dry Cleaners,
Laundry, Pharmacy *(Collins 576-8642)*, Newsstand **1-3 mi:** Supermarket
(Stop & Shop, Shaw's), Health Food *(Sprouts 333-3455)*, Wine/Beer *(Wine
Store 336-9199)*, Farmers' Market *(Congregational Church Thu 2-6pm)*,
Bank/ATM, Beauty Salon, Barber Shop, Bookstore *(Black Sage 333-3889)*,
Hardware Store *(Madison Hardware 366-3865)*, Clothing Store *(Sym's 330-6700)*, Buying Club *(BJ's)*, Copies Etc. *(Perfect Image 335-4443)*

Transportation

OnCall: Rental Car *(Enterprise 330-1399)*, Airport Limo *(Connecticut Town
Car 336-1633)* **1-3 mi:** Rail *(MetroNorth)*, Ferry Service *(Bridgeport - Port
Jefferson)* **Airport:** Tweed/Westchester *(25mi./40mi.)*

Medical Services

911 Service **OnCall:** Ambulance, Veterinarian *(Veterinary House Call 929-7297)* **1-3 mi:** Doctor, Dentist *(Family Dental 333-1841)*, Chiropractor *(Best
Health 384-9999)*, Holistic Services *(Alternative Health Care Center 334-3660)* **Hospital:** Bridgeport 384-3410 *(1.5 mi.)*

Setting -- Just past Captain's Cove Seaport Marina, on the western shore of Cedar Creek, is this well-protected marina that tends to cater to smaller boats. A large sand and gravel (aggregates) operation dominates the marina and also most of the views from the docks. The landside facilities and amenities are limited and housed in a one-story gray building.

Marina Notes -- Family owned and operated since 1965. Water and electric available, as well as cable TV. Security appears to be good, making this an interesting choice for "leaving the boat". One basic head. Train, ferry and bus transportation are a short cab ride away. Get some local advice before straying too far from the marinas. The area is in transition and the "lines" tend to move.

Notable -- Cedar Marina is just upriver from Captain's Cove Seaport, so all of its shops, services, activities and its restaurant are a short walk away. There, one will find a Nantucket Lightship, several fishing charter boats, a sailing school, a dozen small craft and gift shops, maritime memorabilia, and Dundon House, a restored Queen Anne Victorian that features an exhibit on the maritime history of the area. Also there is The Restaurant at Captain's Seaport -- a huge, overgrown seafood shack with a very wide and varied menu - inside and outside dining. Upstairs is a Bar and Dance Club decorated with a forty-foot model of the Titanic and a model of Excalibur; a Sikorsky flying boat. Bands play on the deck on Sundays. Farmers' Market at the United Congregational Church (Park Ave) Thu 2-6pm.

Navigational Information
Lat: 41°08.370' **Long:** 073°14.110' **Tide:** 7 ft. **Current:** 3 kt. **Chart:** 12369
Rep. Depths (MLW): Entry 6 ft. **Fuel Dock** 6 ft. **Max Slip/Moor** 6 ft./-
Access: West of Black Rock Harbor, northwest to private channel G1 & R2

Marina Facilities *(In Season/Off Season)*
Fuel: Gasoline
Slips: 635 Total, 4 Transient **Max LOA:** 36 ft. **Max Beam:** 13 ft.
  Rate *(per ft.):* **Day** $0.50 **Week** $3.50 **Month** n/a
  Power: 30 amp Incl., **50 amp** n/a, **100 amp** n/a, **200 amp** n/a
  Cable TV: No **Dockside Phone:** No
  Dock Type: Floating, Aluminum
Moorings: 0 Total, 0 Transient **Launch:** n/a
  Rate: Day n/a **Week** n/a **Month** n/a
Heads: 2 Toilet(s)
Laundry: None **Pay Phones:** Yes, 2
Pump-Out: OnSite, Self Service, 1 Central **Fee:** Free **Closed Heads:** Yes

Marina Operations
Owner/Manager: Robin Bimmel **Dockmaster:** Same
In-Season: Year Round, 8am-4pm **Off-Season:** Same
After-Hours Arrival: call in advance for instructions
Reservations: Yes, Required **Credit Cards:** Cash/Check
Discounts: None
Pets: Welcome, Dog Walk Area **Handicap Access:** No

South Benson Marina

552 Turney Road;* Fairfield, CT 06430

Tel: (203) 254-0068 **VHF: Monitor** 16 **Talk** n/a
Fax: (203) 256-3080 **Alternate Tel:** n/a
Email: n/a **Web:** n/a
Nearest Town: Fairfield *(1 mi.)* **Tourist Info:** (203) 255-1011

Marina Services and Boat Supplies
Services - Security *(24 Hrs., Gate guards)* **Supplies - OnSite:** Ice *(Cube)*,
Bait/Tackle *(Bait & Fuel)* **1-3 mi:** Ships' Store *(Marine Sport Center 335-8646)* **3+ mi:** West Marine *(330-1100, 5 mi.)*

Boatyard Services
OnSite: Launching Ramp **Nearest Yard:** Captain's Cove Seaport (203) 335-1433

Restaurants and Accommodations
OnSite: Snack Bar *(Bake & Fuel 254-0068, 8am-8pm)* **OnCall:** Pizzeria *(Captain's Pizza No 5 256-0688)* **Near:** Restaurant *(Circle Diner)*, *(Europa)*, *(Miko of Japan)*, *(Bombay Kitchen)*, *(Joe's American Bar & Grille)*, *(China Star)*, *(Reggiano's)*, Fast Food *(Duchess, McDonalds)*, Lite Fare *(Bagel Maven)*, *(Village Bagels)*, Motel *(Fairfield Inn 255-0491, $75-115)*
1-3 mi: Hotel *(Country Inn of Fairfield 367-4404)* **3+ mi:** Inn/B&B *(Westport Inn 259-5236, $100-280, 4.5 mi.)*

Recreation and Entertainment
OnSite: Beach, Picnic Area, Grills, Park **Near:** Playground, Fitness Center *(Curves)* **Under 1 mi:** Bowling *(Amf Circle Lanes 255-0408)*, Cultural Attract *(Fairfield Theatre 319-1404)*, Sightseeing *(Historical Society of Fairfield 259-1598)* **1-3 mi:** Tennis Courts *(Davis Cup 255-2421)*, Movie Theater *(Fairfield Cinemas 339-7151)*, Video Rental *(Media Wave 255-8643)*, Museum *(Connecticut Audubon Birdcraft Museum 259-0416, Ogden House 259-6356)* **3+ mi:** Golf Course *(Fairchild Wheeler Golf Club 373-5911, 5 mi.)*, Horseback Riding *(Salko Farm & Stables 255-5092, 3.5 mi.)*

Provisioning and General Services
Near: Convenience Store *(Mik Stop 256-8164)*, Newsstand
Under 1 mi: Market *(Harborview Market 367-7336)*, Supermarket *(Stop & Shop 254-8478)*, Delicatessen *(Gold's Delicatessen 259-2233)*, Wine/Beer *(Fairfield Spirits)*, Liquor Store *(Grasmere 256-9728)*, Bakery *(Dunkin Donuts, Doughnut Inn 256-1908)*, Bank/ATM *(Fleet)*, Post Office, Catholic Church, Library *(Fairfield PL 256-3155)*, Beauty Salon *(Scissors 259-6261)*, Barber Shop, Dry Cleaners *(Mona Lisa 259-2990)*, Laundry *(Post Plaza)*, Florist, Clothing Store *(Marshalls)*, Retail Shops, Copies Etc. *(Office Max)*
1-3 mi: Gourmet Shop *(Along Came Carol 254-0200)*, Health Food *(Mrs. Green's 255-4333)*, Protestant Church, Bookstore *(Borders 256-1619)*, Pharmacy *(Collins 576-8642)*, Hardware Store *(Village Hardware 259-0425)*
3+ mi: Farmers' Market *(Greenfield Hills Sat 1-4pm, Jul-Oct, 3.5 mi.)*

Transportation
OnCall: Rental Car *(Enterprise 330-1399, Hertz, Budget, Avis all w/in 0.4 mi.)*, Taxi *(Fairfield Cab 255-5797)*, Airport Limo *(New England Limo 367-8779)* **Under 1 mi:** Local Bus **1-3 mi:** Bikes *(Dons Cycle 255-4079)*, Rail *(MetroNorth)*, Ferry Service *(Bridgeport to Port Jefferson, L.I.)*
Airport: Tweed New Haven/Westchester *(27mi./36mi)*

Medical Services
911 Service **OnCall:** Ambulance **Near:** Holistic Services *(Deidras Health Salon 255-3610)* **Under 1 mi:** Doctor *(Basta 256-9249)*, Chiropractor *(Harrison 259-8072)* **1-3 mi:** Veterinarian *(Thackaberry-Becker 259-5295)*
Hospital: Hall-Brooke 227-1251 *(5.5 mi.)*

Setting -- Just west of Black Rock Harbor, up a private channel, this protected municipal facility is tucked into a pleasant but crowded basin that lies directly to port after entering Ash Creek. The basin is completely surrounded by land, except for that small entrance channel, and completely filled with very nice docks. Landside the views are mostly of unspoiled marsh and woods on two sides and a grassy strip dotted with benches on the parking lot side.

Marina Notes -- The Town of Fairfield's marina is exclusively for residents -- with the exception of a handful of transient docks. The docks are mostly "stern-to" without finger piers. Free pump-out & porta-potti dump. Dredging in 2000 has removed the shoals that made the approach difficult. Most of the basin is still only 4 feet at mean low water. Bait & Fuel is located in a low gray building - they provide ice cream, soda, juice, snacks, frozen bait, tackle and ice, as well as gasoline (not diesel). Pockets of picnic tables with grills. *The mailing address is 725 Old Post Road, the town administration office.

Notable -- Jennings Beach - a lovely, wide beach with long open views of the Sound, is virtually onsite. It is divided into two sections: swimming and boating. A large flotilla of small catamarans makes its home here (Jennings Beach Sailing Center). In the season, a concession stand offers basic snack bar food. There's also a long fishing pier. Adjacent is a new skateboard park, as well as basketball hoops and a large play area. Concerts throughout the summer at the Sherman Green Gazebo and the Penfield Pavilion. It's a pleasant 0.5 mile walk out Turney Road to Route 1 (Boston Post Rd.) - which is lined with eateries, services and supply stores. Turn either way and walk a tenth of a mile.

Navigational Information
Lat: 41°06.364' **Long:** 073°21.261' **Tide:** 7.5 ft. **Current:** 1 kt **Chart:** 12368
Rep. Depths *(MLW):* **Entry** 10 ft. **Fuel Dock** 9 ft. **Max Slip/Moor** 9 ft./-
Access: Mouth of the Saugatuck River, starboard side, to private channel

Marina Facilities *(In Season/Off Season)*
Fuel: *Texaco* - Gasoline
Slips: 90 Total, 6 Transient **Max LOA:** 50 ft. **Max Beam:** 20 ft.
 Rate *(per ft.):* **Day** $2.00/Inq. **Week** Inq. **Month** Inq.
 Power: 30 amp Incl., 50 amp n/a, 100 amp n/a, 200 amp n/a
 Cable TV: No **Dockside Phone:** No
 Dock Type: Floating, Long Fingers, Concrete
 Moorings: 0 Total, 0 Transient **Launch:** n/a
 Rate: Day n/a **Week** n/a **Month** n/a
Heads: 2 Toilet(s)
Laundry: None **Pay Phones:** No
Pump-Out: OnSite, Full Service, Self Service **Fee:** Free **Closed Heads:** Yes

Marina Operations
Owner/Manager: Town of Westport **Dockmaster:** Edward Frawley
In-Season: Apr-Nov 30, 8am-8pm **Off-Season:** n/a
After-Hours Arrival: Check in with the security guard 8am - 8pm
Reservations: Yes **Credit Cards:** Visa/MC, Dscvr, Din, Amex, Tex
Discounts: None
Pets: Welcome **Handicap Access:** No

Compo Yacht Basin

64 Compo Beach Road; Westport, CT 06880

Tel: (203) 227-9136 **VHF: Monitor** 9 **Talk** 11
Fax: n/a **Alternate Tel:** n/a
Email: n/a **Web:** n/a
Nearest Town: Westport *(2.5 mi.)* **Tourist Info:** (203) 866-2521

Marina Services and Boat Supplies
Services - Security *(12 Hrs., 8pm - 8am)* **Communication -** FedEx, AirBorne, UPS, Express Mail **Supplies - OnSite:** Ice *(Block, Cube)*
1-3 mi: Bait/Tackle *(Compact Fishing Gear 227-4377)* **3+ mi:** Boat/US *(866-4426, 4 mi.)*, Propane *(Hocon Propane 324-6512, 5 mi.)*

Boatyard Services
Nearest Yard: Norwalk Cove Marina (203) 838-2326

Restaurants and Accommodations
OnCall: Pizzeria *(Derosa's 221-1769)* **Near:** Snack Bar *(Joey's by the Beach B $2-4, L $2-6, D $2-10, 9am-9pm, 7 days)* **Under 1 mi:** Restaurant *(Splash 454-7798)*, *(Positano 454-4922)*, Inn/B&B *(Longshore Inn 226-3316, $120-150)* **1-3 mi:** Restaurant *(Tarantino 454-3188, L $12, D $19)*, *(Jasmine Restaurant 221-7777)*, *(Miramar 222-2267, D $18-30, at Inn at National Hall)*, Seafood Shack *(Mansion Clam House 454-7979, L $10, D $10)*, Motel *(Norwalk-Westport Motel 847-0065)*, Inn/B&B *(Inn at National Hall 221-1351, $275-850)*

Recreation and Entertainment
OnSite: Beach *(Compo Beach)*, Picnic Area, Grills, Playground, Volleyball *(basketball & soccer)*, Jogging Paths, Roller Blade/Bike Paths, Park **Under 1 mi:** Fitness Center *(Chi Fitness 226-1864)* **1-3 mi:** Tennis Courts *(Sylvan Tennis Club 227-8933)*, Movie Theater *(Crown Royale 846-8795)*, Video Rental *(World Video 226-6181)*, Sightseeing *(Nature Center for Environ-* -mental *Activities 227-7253* **3+ mi:** Golf Course *Oak Hills Park 838-0303, 6 mi.)*, Horseback Riding *(Salko Farm & Stables 255-5092, 5 mi.)*

Provisioning and General Services
Under 1 mi: Bookstore *(Remarkable Book Shop 227-1000)* **1-3 mi:** Market *(Peters Bridge Market 227-0602)*, Supermarket *(Shaw's 222-9594)*, Gourmet Shop *(Chef's Table 226-3663)*, Delicatessen *(Roly Poly Rolled Sandwiches 226-9376)*, Health Food *(Golds 227-0101)*, Wine/Beer *(Saugatuck Wine & Spirits 227-6672)*, Liquor Store, Fishmonger *(Harborside Seafood 221-9141)*, Post Office *(227-4212)*, Library *(Westport PL 227-8411)*, Beauty Salon, Barber Shop, Dry Cleaners, Laundry *(Minute Men 227-6153)*, Pharmacy *(Colonial Druggists 227-9538)*, Hardware Store *(Westport Hardware 227-1211)*, Retail Shops, Copies Etc. *(Baker Graphics 226-6928)*

Transportation
OnCall: Rental Car *(Enterprise 847-7963)*, Taxi *(Norwalk Yellow Cab 853-1267)*, Airport Limo *(First Class Driving 227-2327)* **1-3 mi:** Rail *(Metro North)* **Airport:** Westchester/White Plains *(30 mi.)*

Medical Services
911 Service **OnCall:** Ambulance **1-3 mi:** Dentist *(Westport Dental 227-3709)*, Chiropractor *(Marcus 226-2366)*, Holistic Services *(Westport Healing Center 226-2299)*, Veterinarian *(Kay 227-6869)* **3+ mi:** Doctor *(Immediate Care Center 846-4460, 5 mi.)* **Hospital:** Hall-Brooke 227-1251 *(3 mi.)*

Setting -- Right at the mouth of the Saugatuck River, on the eastern shore, Compo Yacht Basin is directly accessible from the Sound. It's Part of Westport's municipal facility, and is located in a very quiet, secure basin entered through a narrow channel. The surrounding area is secluded, residential, and pretty. If you can squeeze in here, it's a kid's paradise.

Marina Notes -- This Westport town facility has a long waiting list but there are some dedicated slips for transients. An attractive small white building with hunter green trim is home to the basic amenities, to the dockmaster (who is on duty seven days - 9am-8pm) and to the Minuteman Yacht Club. All facilities, both at the marina and the surrounding park, are available to marina guests. Good heads but no showers anywhere - even in the beach pavilion.

Notable -- There's a roller blading and skate boarding trick court (jumps, half pipes, railings, etc.), a roller hockey court, soccer field, basketball court, a huge crescent shape beach with real sand, a separate picnic beach with tables, beach volleyball nets, and a fantasy wooden playground that's a guaranteed magnet for the little ones -- and seems continally crawling with kids. Joey's By-the-Beach Snack Bar is open every day 7am-Sunset - hot dogs, burgers, salads, ice cream. There are two restaurants within hiking distance (about 0.7 mi.). "Downtown" Westport is about a $6 cab ride for provisions, a more substantial restaurant scene, or the Metro-North train station with regular commuter schedules into Manhattan.

Cedar Point Yacht Club

1 Bluff Point; Westport, CT 06880

Tel: (203) 226-7411 **VHF: Monitor** 78 **Talk** 78
Fax: (203) 226-6810 **Alternate Tel:** n/a
Email: cpyc@townline.com **Web:** www.cedarpointyachtclub.org
Nearest Town: Westport *(3 mi.)* **Tourist Info:** (203) 866-2521

Navigational Information
Lat: 41°05.969' **Long:** 073°22.090' **Tide:** 8 ft. **Current:** 0 kt. **Chart:** 12368
Rep. Depths *(MLW)*: **Entry** 10 ft. **Fuel Dock** 10 ft. **Max Slip/Moor** 10 ft./-
Access: Saugautuck River around Bluff Point

Marina Facilities *(In Season/Off Season)*
Fuel: No
Slips: 160 Total, 5 Transient **Max LOA:** 50 ft. **Max Beam:** n/a
 Rate *(per ft.)*: **Day** $2.00/Inq. **Week** $12.25 **Month** $30
 Power: 30 amp Incl., **50 amp** Incl., **100 amp** n/a, **200 amp** n/a
 Cable TV: No **Dockside Phone:** No
 Dock Type: Floating, Long Fingers, Wood, Composition
Moorings: 0 Total, 0 Transient **Launch:** n/a, Dinghy Dock
 Rate: Day n/a **Week** n/a **Month** n/a
Heads: 8 Toilet(s), 6 Shower(s) *(with dressing rooms)*, Hair Dryers
Laundry: None **Pay Phones:** Yes, 2
Pump-Out: OnCall, 1 Port **Fee:** n/a **Closed Heads:** Yes

Marina Operations
Owner/Manager: Stephen Shaw **Dockmaster:** Rick Hindle
In-Season: Apr-Oct 30, 7am-12pm **Off-Season:** Nov 2-Mar 30, 9am-5pm
After-Hours Arrival: Pick an empty slip and check in in the morning
Reservations: Yes **Credit Cards:** n/a
Discounts: None
Pets: Welcome, Dog Walk Area **Handicap Access:** Yes, Heads, Docks

Marina Services and Boat Supplies
Services - Docking Assistance, Boaters' Lounge, Security *(18 Hrs.)*, Dock Carts, 3 Phase **Communication -** Mail & Package Hold, Phone Messages, Fax in/out *(Free)*, FedEx, AirBorne, UPS, Express Mail *(Sat Del)* **Supplies -** OnSite: Ice *(Block, Cube)* **Under 1 mi:** Bait/Tackle *(Compact Fishing Gear 227-4377)*, Live Bait **1-3 mi:** Ships' Store, West Marine, Boat/US *(866-4426)*, Marine Discount Store *(Rex Marine)*, Propane *(Stew Leonard's)*

Boatyard Services
OnSite: Launching Ramp, Hull Repairs, Bottom Cleaning, Brightwork, Divers, Compound, Wash & Wax, Interior Cleaning **OnCall:** Engine mechanic *(gas, diesel)*, Sail Loft *(UK Shore, North Fairclough)*, Woodworking, Inflatable Repairs, Life Raft Service, Upholstery, Yacht Interiors, Metal Fabrication **Near:** Yacht Broker. **Under 1 mi:** Electrical Repairs *(Captain's Cove)*, Propeller Repairs, Painting, Awlgrip. **1-3 mi:** Travelift, Forklift, Crane, Electronic Sales *(West Marine)*, Electronics Repairs *(West Marine)*, Rigger *(Hathaway)*, Air Conditioning, Refrigeration. **Nearest Yard:** Norwalk Cove Marina (2 mi.) (203) 838-2326

Restaurants and Accommodations
OnSite: Snack Bar **OnCall:** Pizzeria *(Partners 853-7827)*, *(Little Nick's 341-0505)* **Near:** Fast Food **Under 1 mi:** Restaurant *(Tarrantino's 456-3188, L $12, D $19)*, Seafood Shack *(Mansion Clam House 454-7979, L $10, D $10)* **1-3 mi:** Restaurant *(Jasmine 221-7777)*, *(Miramar 222-2267, D $18-30, at National Hall)*, Hotel *(Westport Inn 259-2536)*, *(Longshore Inn 226-3316, $120-150)*, Inn/B&B *(Inn at National Hall 221-1351, $250-650)*

Recreation and Entertainment
OnSite: Beach, Picnic Area, Grills, Playground, Volleyball, Tennis Courts, Jogging Paths, Roller Blade/Bike Paths **Near:** Park **1-3 mi:** Dive Shop, Fitness Center *(Fitness Edge 226-1864)*, Boat Rentals *(Longshore Sailing School)*, Movie Theater *(Crown Royale 846-8795)*, Video Rental *(World Video 226-6181)*, Video Arcade, Museum, Cultural Attract *(Westport Play House)*, Sightseeing **3+ mi:** Golf Course *(Oak Hills Park 838-0303, 5 mi.)*

Provisioning and General Services
Under 1 mi: Convenience Store, Bank/ATM, Post Office, Catholic Church, Protestant Church **1-3 mi:** Supermarket *(Shaw's 222-9594)*, Gourmet Shop *(Chefs Table 226-3663)*, Delicatessen *(Roly Poly Rolled Sand 226-9376)*, Health Food, Liquor Store *(Saugatuck Wine & Spirits 227-6672)*, Fishmonger, Synagogue, Library *(227-8411)*, Beauty Salon, Dry Cleaners, Laundry, Bookstore *(Remarkable Book Shop 227-1000)*, Pharmacy *(CVS 750-6900)*, Hardware Store *(Westport Hardware 227-1211)*, Florist, Retail Shops, Copies Etc. *(Kinkos 847-7004)*

Transportation
OnCall: Rental Car *(Avis 227-1232)*, Taxi *(Norwalk Yellow 853-1267)*, Airport Limo *(Lexington Limo 341-0395)* **Near:** Local Bus **Under 1 mi:** InterCity Bus **1-3 mi:** Rail *(MetroNorth)* **3+ mi:** Ferry Service *(Port Jefferson, 5 mi.)* **Airport:** Westchester *(35 mi.)*

Medical Services
911 Service **OnCall:** Ambulance **1-3 mi:** Doctor *(Parnas 849-1222)*, Dentist, Chiropractor *(Marcus 226-2366)*, Holistic Services *(Westport Healing 226-2299)* **Hospital:** Norwalk 855-3578 *(5 mi.)*

Setting -- Cedar Point has a truly spectacular location at the mouth of the Saugatuck River. Just around Bluff Point, on the western shore, it's quickly and easily accessible from the Sound. The docks are tucked into a placid, protected basin while the Club House and amenities enjoy 360 degree views of the wild beauty of Saugatuck Island -- part of a narrow, pristine peninsula -- and the Sound, Harbor and River that surround it.

Marina Notes -- This is a private club that welcomes transient yachtsmen. Most slips have 30 amp service, a few have 50 amps. One of the oldest "one design" racing clubs in the country, founded in 1887. CPYC is home to six one-design fleets (Lasers, Vanguard - 15s, Lightnings, Thistles, Stars, and Atlantics), and an active PHRF fleet. Dry sail facilities include a wide launching ramp, beachfront launching, two high speed one-ton electric hoists, a large rigging dock and a floating "opti-condo". In addition to the 130 slips, there's space for more than 150 dry sailed boats. Very nice tiled heads and showers with private dressing rooms and hair dryers. Snack bar in season. They try to accommodate visiting fleets, making this an interesting group or club destination.

Notable -- The two-story contemporary clubhouse was designed to take full advantage of the club's remarkable location. The second floor lounge, encircled by decks, provides a relaxing place to watch the regattas out on the Sound or the boat traffic headed up the river. There are picnic tables, grills, a basketball hoop, and an inventive children's playground right next to the old tennis courts (please note that the club has disbanded its infrequently used tennis courts). Two small, rocky sand beaches complete the list of amenities available to the visiting boater.

Navigational Information

Lat: 41°05.240' **Long:** 073°23.635' **Tide:** 7 ft. **Current:** n/a **Chart:** 12368
Rep. Depths *(MLW)*: **Entry** 10 ft. **Fuel Dock** 8 ft. **Max Slip/Moor** 10 ft./-
Access: LI Sound to Norwalk Harbor to the eastern shore of the river

Marina Facilities *(In Season/Off Season)*

Fuel: *Gulf* - Gasoline, Diesel, High-Speed Pumps
Slips: 400 Total, 10 Transient **Max LOA:** 200 ft. **Max Beam:** 50 ft.
 Rate *(per ft.)*: **Day** $2.00 **Week** Inq. **Month** Inq.
 Power: 30 amp Inq., **50 amp** Inq., **100 amp** Inq., **200 amp** n/a
 Cable TV: No **Dockside Phone:** No
 Dock Type: Floating, Long Fingers, Wood
Moorings: 0 Total, 0 Transient **Launch:** n/a
 Rate: Day n/a **Week** n/a **Month** n/a
Heads: 8 Toilet(s), 8 Shower(s) *(with dressing rooms)*
Laundry: 2 Washer(s), 2 Dryer(s) **Pay Phones:** Yes
Pump-Out: OnSite, Full Service, 1 Central **Fee:** Free **Closed Heads:** Yes

Marina Operations

Owner/Manager: n/a **Dockmaster:** Valerie Morris
In-Season: Apr-Oct, 8am-6pm **Off-Season:** Nov-Mar, 8am-4:30pm*
After-Hours Arrival: Pull up to fuel dock
Reservations: Yes **Credit Cards:** Visa/MC, Amex
Discounts: None
Pets: Welcome, Dog Walk Area **Handicap Access:** No

Norwalk Cove Marina

Calf Pasture Beach Road; East Norwalk, CT 06855

Tel: (203) 838-2326 **VHF: Monitor** 9 **Talk** 72
Fax: (203) 838-9756 **Alternate Tel:** (203) 838-5899
Email: marina@norwalkcove.com **Web:** www.norwalkcove.com
Nearest Town: South Norwalk *(2 mi.)* **Tourist Info:** (203) 866-2521

Marina Services and Boat Supplies

Services - Docking Assistance, Concierge, Security *(10 Hrs., Guard 7pm - 5am)*, Trash Pick-Up, Dock Carts **Communication -** Mail & Package Hold, Fax in/out, FedEx, AirBorne, UPS, Express Mail *(Sat Del)* **Supplies - OnSite:** Ice *(Cube)*, Ships' Store, Bait/Tackle **1-3 mi:** Boat/US *(866-4426)*, Propane *(Hocon Gas 324-6512)* **3+ mi:** West Marine *(969-7727, 10 mi.)*

Boatyard Services

OnSite: Travelift *(Three: 15T, 70T, 160T)*, Forklift *(4)*, Crane *(2)*, Engine mechanic *(gas, diesel)*, Electrical Repairs, Electronics Repairs, Hull Repairs, Rigger, Brightwork, Refrigeration, Compound, Wash & Wax, Propeller Repairs, Woodworking, Painting, Yacht Broker *(3)* **OnCall:** Bottom Cleaning, Air Conditioning, Divers **Under 1 mi:** Launching Ramp.
Yard Rates: $75-80/hr.

Restaurants and Accommodations

OnSite: Restaurant *(Sunset Grill 866-4177, L $6-12, D $15-25)*, Snack Bar
Near: Snack Bar *(Stew Leonards Grill at Calf pasture Beach)* **Under 1 mi:** Restaurant *(Sandbar 866-8567)*, Seafood Shack *(Sharky's Fish & Chips 866-4622, L $4-10, D $4-10)*, Pizzeria *(Norwalk Pizza & Pasta 854-9788)*
1-3 mi: Restaurant *(Adams Rib Restaurant 838-5531, at Norwalk Inn)*, *(Sono Seaport Seafood 866-9083)*, *(Porterhouse 855-0441)*, Fast Food, Motel *(Norwalk Inn 838-5531)*, Hotel *(Legrand Hotel 849-1892)*

Recreation and Entertainment

OnSite: Group Fishing Boat *(Middlebank 655-5918)*, Special Events *(Norwalk Int'l Boat Show mid-Sep; Near: Oyster Fest, 1st weekend after LabDay, Arts Festival, 1st weekend Aug)* **Near:** Pool *(Ascension Beach Club pass for transients)*, Beach *(Calf Pasture)*, Picnic Area, Grills, Playground, Boat Rentals *(Calf Pasture)*, Park **Under 1 mi:** Dive Shop
1-3 mi: Tennis Courts *(Norwalk Health and Racquet Club 853-7727)*, Golf Course *(Oak Hills Park 838-0303)*, Movie Theater *(Crown Sono 899-7979)*, Video Rental *(Blockbuster 846-4220)*, Museum *(Maritime Aquarium 10-5 $8.25/6.75 and IMAX 852-9700 $6.50/4.75., Loockwood Mathews 838-9799)*, Cultural Attract **3+ mi:** Bowling *(AMF 838-7501, 4 mi.)*

Provisioning and General Services

Under 1 mi: Convenience Store *(Speedy Mart 866-4420)*, Liquor Store *(Liquor Center 866-3666)*, Bank/ATM, Beauty Salon, Dry Cleaners, Pharmacy *(Rite Aid 838-6141)*, Newsstand **1-3 mi:** Supermarket *(Stew Leonards 847-7213; Stop & Shop 299-1715 4 mi.)*, Delicatessen *(East Side 853-2680)*, Farmers' Market *(Wed 12-6 at Maritime Center)*, Fishmonger, Post Office, Catholic Church, Library *(838-0408)*, Copies Etc. *(Minuteman 838-2795)* **3+ mi:** Bookstore *(Barnes & Noble 866-2213, 4 mi.)*, Hardware Store *(Home Depot, 4 mi.)*, Buying Club *(Costco, 4 mi.)*

Transportation

OnCall: Rental Car *(Enterprise 847-0566, Avis 849-8147)*, Taxi *(Yellow Cab 853-1267)* **Under 1 mi:** Rail *(East Norwalk Metro-North to NYC; Amtrak 6 mi.)* **1-3 mi:** Bikes *(Smart Cycles 831-9144)*, Ferry Service *(Sheffield Island 854-4656 $15/10)* **Airport:** Westchester *(30 mi.)*

Medical Services

911 Service **OnCall:** Ambulance **1-3 mi:** Doctor *(Soundview 838-4000)*, Dentist *(Passero 853-3434)*, Chiropractor *(East Ave. 838-0388)*, Veterinarian *(Park Hosp. 849-7733)* **Hospital:** Norwalk 852-2000 *(4 mi.)*

Setting -- Located at the tip of Pasture Point, just off Norwalk Harbor at the entrance to the Norwalk River, sits this vast marina with new dockage for up to 200 foot yachts. Views are across the river to the densely built shore and of the marina's mostly paved landside facility; new landscaping has helped with some much-needed sprucing up. For panoramic views of the Sound and Norwalk Islands head next door to Calf Pasture Beach.

Marina Notes -- *Open off season weather permitting. Easy access fuel dock. 100 amp - single/three phase. 3 travelifts to 160 tons (one of the largest in Connecticut). Diesel engine overhauls, re-powers, refrigeration, air conditioning, heating & watermaker service. Full service parts department and large ships' store. Comprehensive long-term upgrade plan. Two sets of new tiled heads and showers sporting wainscoting, dressing rooms and shower doors. Newly refurbished miniature golf course is on-site; as is the Sunset Grille, a Mar-Oct seasonal restaurant that offers indoor dining and deck dining overlooking the docks and harbor entrance. Sound Sailing Center (838-1110) bases here. Transient dockage includes membership in the Ascension Beach Club next door.

Notable -- Adjacent 33-acre Calf Pasture Beach town park offers a picnic area, wide mile-lon beach, ball fields, volleyball court, good playground, and a newly refurbished snack bar: Stew Leonard's Grill (11am-8pm, Mon-Sat, 'til 6pm Sun) - burgers, lobster rolls, ice cream, seafood, and beach supplies. Historic South Norwalk - often referred to as SoNo, the suburban SoHo/TriBeCa - is a long dinghy ride up river or a short cab ride. Across the bridge from the Norwalk Visitors' Dock are galleries, restaurants and shops and the Maritime Center's Aquarium, exhibits & Imax shows. Train to NYC is less than a mile.

Total Marine of Norwalk

160 Water Street; Norwalk, CT 06854

Tel: (203) 838-3210 **VHF: Monitor** n/a **Talk** n/a
Fax: (203) 838-7809 **Alternate Tel:** n/a
Email: totalmarine@aol.com **Web:** www.totalmarine.com
Nearest Town: Norwalk *(0.25 mi.)* **Tourist Info:** (203) 866-2521

Navigational Information
Lat: 41°05.616' **Long:** 073°24.761' **Tide:** 7 ft. **Current:** 0.5 kt. **Chart:** 12368
Rep. Depths (*MLW*): Entry 8 ft. **Fuel Dock** n/a **Max Slip/Moor** 8 ft./-
Access: Norwalk Harbor to Western shore of Norwalk River

Marina Facilities *(In Season/Off Season)*
Fuel: No
Slips: 80 Total, 8 Transient **Max LOA:** 60 ft. **Max Beam:** 20 ft.
  Rate *(per ft.)*: **Day** $1.50 **Week** Inq. **Month** Inq.
  Power: 30 amp Incl., **50 amp** n/a, **100 amp** n/a, **200 amp** n/a
  Cable TV: No **Dockside Phone:** No
  Dock Type: Floating, Wood
Moorings: 0 Total, 0 Transient **Launch:** n/a
  Rate: Day n/a **Week** n/a **Month** n/a
Heads: 6 Toilet(s), 4 Shower(s) *(with dressing rooms)*
Laundry: 1 Washer(s), 1 Dryer(s) **Pay Phones:** No
Pump-Out: No **Fee:** n/a **Closed Heads:** Yes

Marina Operations
Owner/Manager: Gary Jacobs **Dockmaster:** n/a
In-Season: Year-Round, 8am-6pm **Off-Season:** n/a
After-Hours Arrival: Check in the next morning
Reservations: No **Credit Cards:** Visa/MC, Dscvr
Discounts: None
Pets: Welcome **Handicap Access:** Yes, Docks

Marina Services and Boat Supplies
Services - Docking Assistance, Trash Pick-Up, Dock Carts
Communication - FedEx, AirBorne **Supplies - Near:** Ice *(Block, Cube)*, Ships' Store *(Rex Marine 831-5234)*, Bait/Tackle *(Hiller 857-3474)* **Under 1 mi:** Boat/US *(866-4426)*, Propane *(Hocon Gas 324-6512)*

Boatyard Services
OnSite: Travelift *(35T)*, Engine mechanic *(gas, diesel)*, Electrical Repairs, Electronic Sales, Hull Repairs, Bottom Cleaning, Brightwork, Divers, Compound, Wash & Wax, Interior Cleaning, Propeller Repairs, Upholstery, Yacht Interiors, Painting, Awlgrip, Yacht Design, Yacht Building, Total Refits **OnCall:** Electronics Repairs, Air Conditioning, Refrigeration, Woodworking, Metal Fabrication **Near:** Launching Ramp, Inflatable Repairs, Life Raft Service, Yacht Broker *(Chuck Levert)*. **Dealer for:** Formula, Seastrike, C-Hawk. **Yard Rates:** $80/hr., Haul & Launch $10/ft. *(blocking $6/ft.)*, Power Wash $6/ft., Bottom Paint $15/ft. **Storage:** On-Land $45/ft.

Restaurants and Accommodations
OnCall: Pizzeria *(Pappa's Pizza 838-9921)* **Near:** Restaurant *(Donovan's 838-3430, L $7)*, *(Pasta Nostra 854-9700, D $15-30, home-made pasta)*, *(Harborview 838-5231)*, *(Porterhouse 855-0441)*, Seafood Shack *(Sono Seaport Seafood 866-9083)*, Snack Bar *(Caffeine 857-4224)* **Under 1 mi:** Restaurant *(Rattlesnake Grille 852-1716, L $10)*, *(Amber Jacks 853-4332, L $15)* **1-3 mi:** Hotel *(Doubletree 853-3477)*, Inn/B&B *(Norwalk Inn 838-5531)* **3+ mi:** Hotel *(Sheraton 849-9828, 4 mi.)*, *(Marriott 849-9111, 4 mi.)*

Recreation and Entertainment
OnSite: Picnic Area, Grills **Near:** Beach, Playground, Dive Shop *(Rex Dive Center 853-4148)*, Jogging Paths, Boat Rentals *(Small Boat Shop 854-5223)*, Roller Blade/Bike Paths, Fishing Charter, Park **Under 1 mi:** Tennis Courts, Movie Theater *(Crown Sono 899-7979)*, Video Arcade, Museum *(Norwalk Museum 847-0852, Lockwood Mathews Mansion 838-9799)*, Cultural Attract *(Maritime Aquarium and IMAX 852-0700)*, Sightseeing *(Sheffield Island Lighthouse Tours 838-9444)* **1-3 mi:** Golf Course *(Oak Hills Park 838-0303)* **3+ mi:** Bowling *(Amf 838-7501, 4 mi.)*

Provisioning and General Services
Near: Delicatessen *(Sono Deli Market 866-7211)*, Fishmonger *(Sono Seafood 854-9483)*, Lobster Pound, Bank/ATM, Post Office, Pharmacy *(SWC 899-0708)*, Retail Shops **Under 1 mi:** Gourmet Shop, Liquor Store *(Aponte 854-9102)*, Farmers' Market *(Maritime Aquarium Wed 12-6)*, Library *(East Norwalk 838-0408)*, Beauty Salon, Barber Shop, Dry Cleaners, Laundry, Newsstand, Hardware Store *(Dunne 866-0386)*, Florist, Copies Etc. *(Copy Source 972-7488)* **1-3 mi:** Market *(Stew Leonard's 750-9715)*, Supermarket *(Stop & Shop 299-1715)*, Health Food, Bakery, Bookstore *(Barnes & Noble 866-2213)* **3+ mi:** Buying Club *(Costco, 4 mi.)*

Transportation
OnCall: Rental Car *(Enterprise 847-0566)*, Taxi *(Yellow Cab 853-1267)*, Airport Limo *(Nutmeg Driving 579-8782)* **Under 1 mi:** Local Bus, Rail *(Metro-North)* **Airport:** Westchester *(30 mi.)*

Medical Services
911 Service **OnCall:** Ambulance **Near:** Veterinarian *(Neaderland 855-1533)* **1-3 mi:** Doctor *(Immediate Care Center 846-4460)*, Chiropractor *(East Ave. Chiropractic 838-0388)* **Hospital:** Norwalk 852-2160 *(2 mi.)*

Setting -- The second "big boat" recreational facility on the western shore of Norwalk Harbor/Norwalk River - just past the Norwalk Boat Club, revitalized Total Marine offers transient and seasonal dockage for boats up to 60 ft. Landside is an attractively renovated, 2-story building with a green roof that houses offices and facilities. Views across the narrow channel are of marsh.

Marina Notes -- The Caruso family purchased Vinco Marine in 1999 to add to their small chain - all named Total Marine (the others are in Neptune, NJ, Tuckerton, NJ, and Mamaroneck, NY). A full service marina with a mechanic on duty most of the time. Nice heads and showers are on the second floor of the renovated building - Italian tile floors with fiberglass dividers - showers have glass doors. The most northern dock is shared with Rex Marine.

Notable -- An easy six block walk to the heart of South Norwalk - "SoNo". This 19thC historic area, listed on the National Register, promises interesting, creative and one-of-a-kind shops, a wide range of restaurants, wine bars, museums and is also home to artists and galleries. Boat tours to the historic 1868 10-room Sheffield Island Lighthouse, that has guarded the harbor entrance for 125 years, leave from Hope Dock near the Maritime Center. (It's also possible to anchor off-shore and wait for dinghy service to visit). The Maritime Center's Aquarium represents all of Long Island Sound with over 125 species, a shark touch tank, seal pool, many interactive exhibits, a maritime museum ($8.25/6.75) and an IMAX Theater ($6.50/4.75) Combination Tickets $12/9.50. Oyster Festival every September. Arts Festival 1st weekend August.

Navigational Information

Lat: 41°05.653' **Long:** 073°24.794' **Tide:** 7 ft. **Current:** 0.5 kt. **Chart:** 12368
Rep. Depths (*MLW*): **Entry** 8 ft. **Fuel Dock** n/a **Max Slip/Moor** 10 ft./-
Access: Norwalk Harbor west bank, 0.25 mi. of draw bridge

Marina Facilities *(In Season/Off Season)*

Fuel: No
Slips: 60 Total, 3 Transient **Max LOA:** 50 ft. **Max Beam:** 15 ft.
  Rate *(per ft.):* **Day** $2.00/Inq. **Week** Inq. **Month** Inq.
  Power: 30 amp $5, **50 amp** n/a, **100 amp** n/a, **200 amp** n/a
  Cable TV: No **Dockside Phone:** No
  Dock Type: Floating, Long Fingers, Wood
Moorings: 0 Total, 0 Transient **Launch:** n/a
  Rate: Day n/a **Week** n/a **Month** n/a
Heads: 2 Toilet(s), 4 Shower(s)
Laundry: None **Pay Phones:** Yes, 1
Pump-Out: Full Service, Self Service, 1 Port **Fee:** n/a **Closed Heads:** Yes

Marina Operations

Owner/Manager: Bill Gardella Jr. **Dockmaster:** Same
In-Season: MemDay-LabDay, 8am-5pm **Off-Season:** Sep-May, 8am-4:30pm
After-Hours Arrival: Tie up on north dock, check-in next morning
Reservations: Yes, Preferred **Credit Cards:** Visa/MC, Dscvr, Amex
Discounts: None
Pets: Welcome **Handicap Access:** No

Rex Marine Center

144 Water Street; South Norwalk, CT 06854

Tel: (203) 866-5555 **VHF: Monitor** n/a **Talk** n/a
Fax: (203) 866-2518 **Alternate Tel:** (203) 984-1278
Email: wgardellajr@rexmarine.com **Web:** www.rexmarine.com
Nearest Town: South Norwalk *(0.25 mi.)* **Tourist Info:** (203) 866-2521

Marina Services and Boat Supplies

Services - Docking Assistance, Security *(10 Hrs., Evenings)*, Dock Carts
Communication - Mail & Package Hold, Phone Messages, Fax in/out *(Free)*, FedEx, AirBorne, UPS, Express Mail *(Sat Del)* **Supplies - OnSite:** Ice *(Block, Cube)*, Ships' Store **Near:** Bait/Tackle **Under 1 mi:** Boat/US *(866-4426)*, Propane *(Hocon Gas 324-6512)*

Boatyard Services

OnSite: Travelift *(35T)*, Forklift, Engine mechanic *(gas, diesel)*, Electrical Repairs, Hull Repairs, Bottom Cleaning, Compound, Wash & Wax, Interior Cleaning, Inflatable Repairs, Life Raft Service, Painting, Awlgrip, Yacht Broker *(Bill Deacy)*, Total Refits **OnCall:** Electronic Sales, Electronics Repairs, Rigger, Sail Loft, Divers, Propeller Repairs, Woodworking, Metal Fabrication **Dealer for:** Mercruiser, Mercury, Volvo, Yanmar, Crusader, Boston Whaler, Sea Ray. **Member:** ABYC, Other Certifications: Mercruiser and Mercury **Yard Rates:** $84/hr., Haul & Launch $10/ft. *(blocking $2/ft.)*, Power Wash $2.25, Bottom Paint $13/ft. *(paint incl.)* **Storage:** On-Land Indoor $58.50/ft, Outdoor $46/ft.

Restaurants and Accommodations

Near: Restaurant *(Porterhouse 855-0441)*, *(Rattlesnake 852-1716)*, Seafood Shack *(Sono Seaport 866-9083)*, Lite Fare *(Harborview 838-5231)* **Under 1 mi:** Restaurant *(Kazu 866-7492)*, *(Norwalk Brewhouse 853-9110)*, Pizzeria *(Famous Pizza 847-3187)* **1-3 mi:** Motel *(Round Tree Inn 847-5827)*, Hotel *(Marriott 849-9111, $125)*, Inn/B&B *(Norwalk 838-5531, $125)*

Recreation and Entertainment

OnSite: Dive Shop *(Rex Dive Ctr. 853-4148)*, Boat Rentals *(Small Boat Shop 854-5223 Kayaks, Canoes)* **OnCall:** Fishing Charter **Near:** Museum *(Maritime Center 852-0700)*, Sightseeing *(Sheffield Island Ferry)* **Under 1 mi:** Group Fishing Boat, Movie Theater *(Crown Sono 899-7979)*, Video Rental, Park **1-3 mi:** Pool, Beach, Picnic Area, Grills, Playground, Tennis Courts, Golf Course *(Oak Hills 838-0303)*, Fitness Center *(NYSC 847-2244)*, Video Arcade **3+ mi:** Bowling *(Amf Lanes 838-7501, 4 mi.)*

Provisioning and General Services

Near: Delicatessen *(El Samaritano 838-7211)*, Fishmonger *(Sono Seafood 854-9483)*, Catholic Church, Pharmacy *(SWC 899-0708)* **Under 1 mi:** Convenience Store, Liquor Store *(Woodward Ave. 838-6014)*, Bakery, Farmers' Market *(Maritime Center, Wed 12-6)*, Bank/ATM, Post Office, Protestant Church, Synagogue, Library *(838-0408)*, Beauty Salon, Barber Shop, Dry Cleaners, Laundry, Newsstand, Florist, Retail Shops, Copies Etc. *(Copy Source 972-7488)* **1-3 mi:** Supermarket *(Stop & Shop 299-1715)*, Gourmet Shop, Health Food, Bookstore *(Barnes & Noble 866-2213)*, Hardware Store *(Dunne 866-0386)* **3+ mi:** Buying Club *(Costco, 4 mi.)*

Transportation

OnCall: Rental Car *(Enterprise 847-0566)*, Taxi *(Columbia 853-1267)*, Airport Limo *(Gardella's Elite 356-8932)* **Near:** Rail *(Metro-North)* **Under 1 mi:** Local Bus, InterCity Bus **Airport:** Westchester *(30 mi.)*

Medical Services

911 Service **OnCall:** Ambulance **Under 1 mi:** Doctor *(Immediate Care Center 846-4460)* **1-3 mi:** Dentist *(Santorella 866-6658)*, Chiropractor *(Norwalk Chiropractic 838-5544)*, Holistic Services, Veterinarian *(Neaderland 855-1533)* **Hospital:** Norwalk 852-2160 *(3 mi.)*

Setting -- This is the third major facility on the western shore of Norwalk Harbor as it narrows into the Norwalk River. The environment is urban, and the shore is lined with docks and smaller boat facilities. The views across the channel are mainly of unspoiled marsh and landside they tend toward industrial. Rex is dominated by a very long, gray metal storage and work shed, behind which is a "mini-mall" of marine-oriented dealers and services.

Marina Notes -- Founded in 1936 by L.J. Gardella and still family owned and operated. This is a traditional full service boatyard coupled with a major dry stack storage operation for boats up to 30 ft. and seasonal and transient wet dockage for boats up to 48 ft. Small boaters' lounge at the head of the docks with good tiled heads and commodious individual shower rooms with 24 hr. combination access. Very large and very complete ships' store and parts department with knowledgeable staff dedicated to problem solving. Mercury Marine Master Dealer. Fiberglass repair specialists. Also on premises: Inflatable boat dealer and repair facility. Scuba dive shop, including air fills. Plus a kayak, rowing shell and small craft specialist - they also give kayak tours and lessons.

Notable -- Walk past the yard, past all of the shops and dealers, and out onto Water Street; this is about four blocks from the heart of downtown South Norwalk, known as SoNo -- the TriBeCa of Connecticut. Interesting shops and restaurants abound - more than a dozen within a mile. The wonderful Maritime Center at Norwalk occupies a 5 acre renovated 19thC brick factory and includes the Aquarium with interactive exhibits $8.25/6.75, Maritime Hall, boat building courses and an Imax Theater $6.50/4.75, Both $12/9.50. The Sheffield Island Ferry also leaves from Hope Dock next to the Maritime Center - $15/10 854-4656.

Norwalk Visitors Dock

125 East Avenue; Norwalk, CT 06851

Tel: (203) 866-8810 **VHF:** Monitor 9 **Talk** 9
Fax: (203) 849-8823 **Alternate Tel:** (203) 849-4858
Email: ctharbormaster@aol.com **Web:** www.norwalkct.org/HarborComm
Nearest Town: Norwalk *(0 mi.)* **Tourist Info:** (203) 866-2521

Navigational Information
Lat: 41°05.540' **Long:** 073°24.490' **Tide:** 6 ft. **Current:** n/a **Chart:** 12368
Rep. Depths *(MLW):* **Entry** 10 ft. **Fuel Dock** n/a **Max Slip/Moor** 8 ft./8 ft.
Access: Norwalk River to just south of the bascule bridge on the east side

Marina Facilities *(In Season/Off Season)*
Fuel: No
Slips: 20 Total, 20 Transient **Max LOA:** 60 ft. **Max Beam:** n/a
  Rate *(per ft.):* **Day** $1.25 **Week** n/a **Month** n/a
  Power: 30 amp n/a, **50 amp** n/a, **100 amp** n/a, **200 amp** n/a
  Cable TV: No **Dockside Phone:** No
  Dock Type: Floating, Alongside, Concrete
Moorings: 22 Total, 2 Transient **Launch:** n/a, Dinghy Dock (Free)
  Rate: Day $1.25/ft.ft. **Week** n/a **Month** n/a
Heads: 2 Toilet(s)
Laundry: None **Pay Phones:** Yes, 1
Pump-Out: OnSite, Self Service, 1 Central **Fee:** Free **Closed Heads:** Yes

Marina Operations
Owner/Manager: City of Norwalk **Dockmaster:** Michael Griffin (Hrbrmaster)
In-Season: Apr 20-Oct 15, 6am-9pm **Off-Season:** Oct 15-Apr 15, Closed
After-Hours Arrival: Register next morning
Reservations: Yes **Credit Cards:** Visa/MC, Cash
Discounts: None
Pets: Welcome, Dog Walk Area **Handicap Access:** No

Marina Services and Boat Supplies
Services - Security *(24 Hrs.)* **Communication -** FedEx, AirBorne, UPS, Express Mail *(Sat Del)* **Supplies - Near:** Ice *(Block, Cube, Shaved)*, Ships' Store, Bait/Tackle *(Hiller Sports 857-3474)* **Under 1 mi:** Propane *(Hocon Gas 324-6512)* **1-3 mi:** Boat/US *(866-4426)* **3+ mi:** West Marine *(969-7727, 10 mi.)*

Boatyard Services
OnSite: Launching Ramp **Near:** Travelift, Engine mechanic *(gas, diesel)*, Electrical Repairs, Electronic Sales, Electronics Repairs, Hull Repairs, Rigger, Sail Loft, Bottom Cleaning, Brightwork, Air Conditioning, Refrigeration, Divers, Compound, Wash & Wax, Propeller Repairs, Inflatable Repairs, Painting, Yacht Broker *(Norwalk Cove Marina)*, Total Refits.
Nearest Yard: Rex Marine (203) 831-5234

Restaurants and Accommodations
Near: Restaurant *(Sono Seaport Seafood 854-9483)*, *(Kazu Japanese 866-7492, great reviews)*, *(Pasta Nostra 854-9700)*, *(Cote d'Azur 855-8900)*, Seafood Shack *(Sharky's Fish & Chips 866-4662)*, Fast Food *(Subway)*, Pizzeria *(New York 866-9068)* **Under 1 mi:** Restaurant *(Streets of London 866-7552, Fish and Chips)*, *(Meson Galicia 866-8800, Spanish)*, Inn/B&B *(Norwalk Inn 838-5531)* **3+ mi:** Hotel *(Marriott 849-9111, 4 mi.)*, *(Sheraton 849-9828, 4 mi.)*, Inn/B&B *(Inn at the Longshore 226-3316, 4 mi.)*

Recreation and Entertainment
OnSite: Playground, Jogging Paths, Park, Special Events *(Oyster Festival)* **Near:** Dive Shop, Boat Rentals, Video Arcade, Museum *(The Norwalk Museum 847-0852)*, Cultural Attract *(Maritime Aquarium and IMAX 852-9700)*, Sightseeing *(Sheffield Island Lighthouse tours 838-9444)*, Galleries **Under 1 mi:** Beach, Picnic Area, Fishing Charter, Movie Theater *(Crown Sono 899-7979)* **1-3 mi:** Fitness Center **3+ mi:** Golf Course *(Oak Hills 838-0303, 4 mi.)*, Bowling *(Amf 838-7501, 4 mi.)*

Provisioning and General Services
Near: Convenience Store, Gourmet Shop *(Kaas & Co 838-6161)*, Farmers' Market *(Maritime Aquarium Wed 12-6)*, Fishmonger *(Sono Seafood 854-9483)*, Bank/ATM, Post Office, Beauty Salon, Dry Cleaners, Laundry, Newsstand, Hardware Store *(Dunne 866-0386)*, Florist **Under 1 mi:** Delicatessen *(Mikes 866-3772)*, Health Food, Wine/Beer *(Banner Wines 853-7535)*, Liquor Store *(Woodward Ave. 838-6014)*, Bakery, Green Grocer, Lobster Pound, Meat Market, Catholic Church, Library *(838-0408)*, Pharmacy *(Swc 899-0708)*, Clothing Store, Retail Shops, Department Store, Copies Etc. *(Preferred 838-1936)* **1-3 mi:** Market *(Stew Leonard's 750-9715)*, Supermarket *(Stop & Shop 299-1715)*, Bookstore *(Barnes & Noble 866-2213)* **3+ mi:** Buying Club *(Costco, 4 mi.)*

Transportation
OnCall: Rental Car *(Enterprise 847-3771, Avis 849-8147)*, Taxi *(Norwalk 855-1764)*, Airport Limo *(Dee Dee 855-7703)* **Near:** Local Bus **Under 1 mi:** Rail *(Metro North)* **Airport:** Westchester *(30 mi.)*

Medical Services
911 Service **OnCall:** Ambulance **Under 1 mi:** Doctor *(Norwalk Community Health 899-1770)*, Dentist *(Santorella 866-6658)*, Chiropractor *(East Ave. 838-0388)* **1-3 mi:** Holistic Services *(Executive Spa 853-9289)*, Veterinarian *(Neaderland 855-1533)* **Hospital:** Norwalk 852-2160 *(3 mi.)*

Setting -- On the east side of the Norwalk River, just south of the Bascule Bridge, the Norwalk Visitors Dock sits at the edge of Veterans Memorial Park. Just across the bridge is Washington Street, the heart of South Norwalk's historic district. SoNo's gas lit, restored 19thC streets are listed on the National Historic Register and house an intriguing assortment of quirky shops, interesting restaurants, clubs, bars, arts and crafts galleries, and home decorating resources.

Marina Notes -- Part of a municipal boat launch facility and the city's Veterans Memorial Park. There are long floating concrete docks, but no electric or other services, save water. Municipal toilets but no showers. Harbor and Visitors Dock dredged to 8 feet in spring 2002. The new Heritage Park Riverwalk runs from the Maritime Center to Oyster Shell Park -- which has a fishing pier and scenic overlook plus an "under-construction" amphitheater -- then under I95 to Mathews Park, home of the Lockwood Mathews Mansion and the Stepping Stones Children's Museum.

Notable -- The cornerstone of the gentrified, historic village of South Norwalk, SoNo, is the Maritime Center at Norwalk, a renovated 5 acre 19thC foundry, home to the Norwalk Aquarium and 6-story IMAX Theater. The Aquarium is devoted to L.I. Sound sea life -- touch & seal tanks, interactive displays, boat building, and history. The Norwalk Museum, a restoration of the former City Hall, is a hands-on showcase of period furniture and decorative Arts. The 8-plex Crown Movie Theater is nearby as is the old art film's SoNo Theater. A Ferry to the Sheffield Island Lighthouse leaves from Hope Dock, a little up river. Oyster Festival, 1st weekend after LabDay, at Veterans Memorial Park. Arts Festival 1st weekend in August, and Boat Show at Norwalk Cove in mid September.

Navigational Information
Lat: 41°03.348' **Long:** 073°26.782' **Tide:** 7 ft. **Current:** n/a **Chart:** 12368
Rep. Depths *(MLW)*: **Entry** 8 ft. **Fuel Dock** 8 ft. **Max Slip/Moor** 8 ft./8 ft.
Access: Mouth of Five Mile River

Marina Facilities *(In Season/Off Season)*
Fuel: Diesel
Slips: 65 Total, 2 Transient **Max LOA:** 50 ft. **Max Beam:** 14 ft.
  Rate *(per ft.)*: **Day** $1.50 **Week** n/a **Month** n/a
Power: 30 amp Incl., 50 amp Incl., 100 amp n/a, 200 amp n/a
Cable TV: No **Dockside Phone:** No
Dock Type: Floating, Short Fingers, Pilings, Wood
Moorings: 10 Total, Inq.* Transient **Launch:** n/a, Dinghy Dock (Free)
  Rate: Day $0.75/ft. **Week** n/a **Month** n/a
Heads: 1 Toilet(s)
Laundry: None **Pay Phones:** No
Pump-Out: Self Service **Fee:** n/a **Closed Heads:** No

Marina Operations
Owner/Manager: James Bildahl **Dockmaster:** David Campbell
In-Season: Year-Round, 8am-4:30pm **Off-Season:** n/a
After-Hours Arrival: Tie up to gas dock
Reservations: Yes **Credit Cards:** Visa/MC, Dscvr, Amex
Discounts: None
Pets: Welcome, Dog Walk Area **Handicap Access:** No

The Boatworks

PO Box 265; 95 Rowayton Avenue; Rowayton, CT 06853

Tel: (203) 866-9295 **VHF: Monitor** 68 **Talk** n/a
Fax: (203) 853-4910 **Alternate Tel:** (203) 866-9295
Email: BildahlBoatworks@aol.com **Web:** n/a
Nearest Town: Rowayton *(0.25 mi.)* **Tourist Info:** (203) 866-2521

Marina Services and Boat Supplies
Communication - FedEx, AirBorne, UPS, Express Mail **Supplies - OnSite:**
Ships' Store **Near:** Ice *(Block, Cube, Shaved)*, Bait/Tackle *(The Bait Shop 853-38110)*, Live Bait, Propane *(Rowayton Hardware)* **1-3 mi:** Boat/US *(866-4426)* **3+ mi:** West Marine *(969-7727, 8 mi.)*

Boatyard Services
OnSite: Crane, Engine mechanic *(gas, diesel)*, Electrical Repairs, Electronic Sales, Electronics Repairs, Hull Repairs, Rigger, Bottom Cleaning, Brightwork, Compound, Wash & Wax, Interior Cleaning, Woodworking, Painting, Awlgrip, Yacht Broker *(Boatworks Yacht Sales)*, Total Refits **OnCall:** Sail Loft, Air Conditioning, Refrigeration, Divers, Propeller Repairs, Inflatable Repairs, Life Raft Service, Upholstery, Yacht Interiors, Metal Fabrication **Dealer for:** East Bay, Grand Banks, Sabre, Blue Star, Caliber.
Yard Rates: $75/hr., Haul & Launch $12/ft. *(blocking $2.50/ft.)*, Power Wash $2.50, Bottom Paint $15.50/ft. **Storage:** In-Water $7.50/ft./mo., On-Land $7.50/ft./mo.

Restaurants and Accommodations
OnSite: Restaurant *(The Restaurant at Rowayton Seafood 866-4488, L $11-18, D $21-27)* **OnCall:** Pizzeria *(Rowayton Pizza 853-7555)* **Near:** Restaurant *(River Cat Grille 854-0860, L $10-14, D $15-22)*, Bistro Du Soleil *855-9469)*, Raw Bar *(Five Mile Oyster House 855-0025)*, Snack Bar *(101 B $4, L $7)* **Under 1 mi:** Restaurant *(Lucas Steak House 869-4403)*
1-3 mi: Raw Bar *(Overtons)*, Fast Food *(Duchess/KFC)*, Motel *(Howard Johnson 655-3933)*, *(Motel 6 621-7351)*, Hotel *(Doubletree 853-3477)*, Inn/B&B *(Three Stallion Inn 655-7010)* **3+ mi:** Inn/B&B *(Homestead Inn 869-7500, 5 mi.)*

Recreation and Entertainment
Near: Beach, Jogging Paths, Cultural Attract *(Shakespeare Festival)*, Galleries *(Rowayton Arts Center)* **Under 1 mi:** Video Arcade **1-3 mi:** Tennis Courts *(Cherry Lawn 655-7272)*, Bowling *(Amf 838-7501)*, Movie Theater, Video Rental, Park **3+ mi:** Golf Course *(Oak Hills Park 838-0303, 4 mi.)*, Museum *(Norwalk Aquarium 852-9700, 4 mi.)*

Provisioning and General Services
OnSite: Fishmonger *(Rowayton Seafood)* **Near:** Market *(Rowayton Market 852-0011)*, Gourmet Shop, Delicatessen *(Rowaytons 101 853-1050)*, Farmers' Market *(Summer Fridays)*, Lobster Pound, Meat Market, Bank/ATM, Post Office, Catholic Church, Library *(838-5038)*, Barber Shop, Dry Cleaners, Hardware Store *(Rowayton 853-9505)*, Florist **Under 1 mi:** Wine/Beer, Liquor Store *(White Bridge 655-0658)*, Protestant Church
1-3 mi: Supermarket *(Grand Union 656-2259)*, Health Food, Bakery, Synagogue, Beauty Salon, Laundry, Bookstore *(Gilann Books 655-4532)*, Pharmacy *(CVS 655-7165)*, Newsstand, Clothing Store, Retail Shops, Department Store, Copies Etc. **3+ mi:** Buying Club *(Costco, 6 mi.)*

Transportation
OnCall: Rental Car *(Budget 629-8500, Enterprise 622-1611)*, Taxi *(Darien 655-2266)*, Airport Limo *(Dee Dee 855-7703)* **1-3 mi:** Rail *(Metro-North)*
Airport: Westchester *(25 mi.)*

Medical Services
911 Service **OnCall:** Ambulance *(Norwalk)* **Near:** Dentist **1-3 mi:** Doctor *(Darien Medical 655-8701)*, Chiropractor *(Marsillo 656-2044)*, Veterinarian *(Duffy 838-8421)* **Hospital:** Norwalk 852-2000 *(5 mi.)*

Setting -- The first facility to starboard heading up the one-mile long Five Mile River, The Boatworks can be easily spotted by the unusual number of pristine Sabre and Grand Banks yachts hanging off its nicely maintained docks. Its attractive, well-marked two-story office building and the adjacent restaurant's blue awning (sheltering its alfresco porch) are also good markers. The River is literally chock-a-block with dockage along the Rowayton (eastern) shore and moorings, stem to stern, right down the center -- all brimming with attractive, well-maintained craft.

Marina Notes -- Limited Transient dockage, moorings, and services. *Moorings are allocated by the Harbormaster. Primarily a brokerage for Sabre, Grand Banks, Blue Star and Caliber yachts. Right next door is The Bait Shop which offers outboard engine repairs, bait, fishing tackle, and many, many fishing tournaments. Boatworks Boutique has, in addition to the standard chandlery supplies, a very nice yachty gift shop with high-end, useful and fun items. B&G Marine (853-9599) and Five Mile Riverworks (866-4226) down the road may also have transient dockage or moorings.

Notable -- Adjacent is The Restaurant at Rowayton Seafood, with a bustling dining room and an eating porch fronting the docks, which specializes in preparing the best that their companion shop - Rowayton Seafood - has to offer (including sushi). Wendell's ice cream shop and deli is down the road, along with Rowayton Pizza. Rowayton Market and liquor store is 0.25 mile. "Downtown" Rowayton sports cute shops that cater to this outdoor and fitness-oriented community - streets are clogged with runners, walkers, bikers, skateboarders, etc.. Annual Shakespeare on the Sound Festival.

Harbour Square Marina

860 Canal Street; Stamford, CT 06902

Tel: (203) 324-3331 **VHF: Monitor** 9 **Talk** 12
Fax: (203) 324-1921 **Alternate Tel:** n/a
Email: n/a **Web:** n/a
Nearest Town: Stamford (1 mi.) **Tourist Info:** (203) 359-4761

Navigational Information

Lat: 41°02.531' **Long:** 073°31.842' **Tide:** 8 ft. **Current:** 2 kt. **Chart:** 12368
Rep. Depths (MLW): Entry 15 ft. **Fuel Dock** 12 ft. **Max Slip/Moor** 12 ft./-
Access: LI Sound to east branch of Stamford Harbor, on port side

Marina Facilities (In Season/Off Season)

Fuel: Shell - Gasoline, Diesel, High-Speed Pumps
Slips: 75 Total, 20 Transient **Max LOA:** 175 ft. **Max Beam:** n/a
  Rate (per ft.): Day $1.75/1.50 **Week** Inq. **Month** Inq.
  Power: 30 amp Incl., **50 amp** Incl., **100 amp** Incl., **200 amp** n/a
  Cable TV: Yes, Incl. **Dockside Phone:** Yes
  Dock Type: Fixed, Floating, Long Fingers, Alongside, Wood
Moorings: 0 Total, 0 Transient **Launch:** n/a
  Rate: Day n/a **Week** n/a **Month** n/a
Heads: 2 Toilet(s), 2 Shower(s)
Laundry: None **Pay Phones:** Yes
Pump-Out: OnSite, Full Service **Fee:** $5 **Closed Heads:** Yes

Marina Operations

Owner/Manager: Vincent Ciaramello **Dockmaster:** Same
In-Season: May-Oct, 8am-8pm **Off-Season:** Nov 1-Apr, 9am-5pm
After-Hours Arrival: Tie up at the fuel dock.
Reservations: Yes **Credit Cards:** Visa/MC, Dscvr, Amex, Tex
Discounts: Nautical Miles **Dockage:** 15% **Fuel:** $.10 **Repair:** n/a
Pets: Welcome, Dog Walk Area **Handicap Access:** No

Marina Services and Boat Supplies

Services - Docking Assistance, Dock Carts **Communication -** Mail & Package Hold, Phone Messages, Fax in/out, FedEx, AirBorne, UPS, Express Mail (Sat Del) **Supplies - OnSite:** Ice (Cube), Ships' Store, Propane **Under 1 mi:** West Marine (969-7727), Bait/Tackle (Pete's Place 356-9383), CNG (Brewer Yacht Haven)

Boatyard Services

OnCall: Electrical Repairs, Electronics Repairs, Hull Repairs, Rigger, Bottom Cleaning, Brightwork, Refrigeration **Nearest Yard:** Brewer Yacht Haven (203) 359-4500

Restaurants and Accommodations

OnSite: Restaurant (Eclisse Restaurant 325-3773, L $8-15, D $18-30, Family style dinners, every entrée serves 2 or more), Snack Bar (Vinny's Dockhouse Deli B $2.50-4, L $4-6, 7:30am-5pm), Lite Fare (Xando Restaurant & Coffee Bar Mon-Wed 6:30am-8pm, Thu-Fri 6:30am-Mid - Wraps, sandwiches, coffee/tea) **OnCall:** Pizzeria (Planet Pizza 357-1101) **Under 1 mi:** Restaurant (John's Diner 325-3655), (Fiddlers Green 356-0906), Fast Food, Inn/B&B (Shippan Point Inn 323-1910) **1-3 mi:** Restaurant (Mortons Steakhouse 324-3939), (Bank St. Brewery 325-2739), (Cove Restaurant 353-8984), Motel (Westin 967-2222, $140-200), (Stamford Motor Inn 325-2655), Hotel (Holiday Inn 358-8400, $100-140), (Marriott 357-9555, $140-275)

Recreation and Entertainment

Under 1 mi: Beach, Tennis Courts (Shippan Racquet Club 323-3129), Movie Theater (Crown Landmark Square 324-3100), Video Rental (Video Plus 964-1900), Museum (Whitney Museum Of American Art 358-7630), Cultural Attract (The Palace & the Rich Forum 325-4466) **1-3 mi:** Bowling (Bowlarama 323-1041), Park **3+ mi:** Golf Course (Sterling Farms G. C. 461-9090, 5 mi.)

Provisioning and General Services

OnSite: Delicatessen, Newsstand **Under 1 mi:** Convenience Store, Supermarket (Shoprite 964-9500), Wine/Beer, Liquor Store (Star Wines & Spirits 323-7814), Bank/ATM, Post Office, Beauty Salon, Dry Cleaners, Pharmacy (Shoprite), Florist, Retail Shops, Copies Etc. (County Repro 348-3758) **1-3 mi:** Bakery, Farmers' Market (Columbus Park Mon & Thu 10-3), Fishmonger, Meat Market, Catholic Church, Protestant Church, Library (Ferguson 964-1000), Bookstore (Waldenbooks 358-8927), Hardware Store (Westside Hardware 348-2930), Clothing Store, Department Store **3+ mi:** Synagogue (4 mi.)

Transportation

OnCall: Rental Car (Budget 325-1535, National 425-9902, Enterprise 327-6500), Taxi (Eveeredy 967-3633) **Under 1 mi:** Rail (Metro-North & Amtrak) **Airport:** Westchester/LaGuardia (20 mi./32 mi.)

Medical Services

911 Service OnCall: Ambulance **1-3 mi:** Doctor (Cove Family Practice 326-2978), Dentist (Stamford Dental 969-0802), Chiropractor (Back & Neck 329-1143), Holistic Services, Veterinarian (Davis Animal Hosp. 327-0300) **Hospital:** Stamford 325-7000 (2 mi.)

Setting -- Tucked well up the East Branch of Stamford Harbor -- the only facility on the western shore -- Harbor Park is safely behind the closable Hurricane Barrier. This small facility, with mostly along-side dockage, caters to larger transient yachts. It's located in an office park complex with fairly industrial views on both sides of the channel. Onsite is a well-regarded restaurant and a small deli with tables.

Marina Notes -- Volume fuel discount. Heliport on-site. Downstream from a treatment facility. Basic heads. Onsite white table-cloth Eclisse Restaurant promises authentic Italian food and décor with a casually elegant atmosphere. Mon-Thu 12-3pm, 5-10:30pm, Fri 12-3pm, 5-11:30pm, Sat (no lunch) 5-11:30pm, Sun 3-10pm. Dockhouse deli also on-site. Nautical Miles members get 15% off transient dockage, 10% off food and drinks, 10-15 cents off per gallon of fuel over 200 gallons, 15 cents off with Texaco Credit Card.

Notable -- A nicely landscaped promenade, with benches, runs along the water just south of Harbor Park. It's a short cab ride to Stamford Town Center (a large, high-end mall anchored by Filene's, Macy's and Saks), and downtown Stamford, with restaurants, services, and two theaters - the Palace and the Rich Forum - featuring concerts and national Broadway tours. Also very convenient to transportation - nearby Stamford RR station is a stop for Metro-North and Amtrak, making this a great place to leave your boat.

Navigational Information
Lat: 41°02.193' **Long:** 073°32.479' **Tide:** 7 ft. **Current:** Var. **Chart:** 12368
Rep. Depths *(MLW):* **Entry** 13 ft. **Fuel Dock** 12 ft. **Max Slip/Moor** 12 ft./-
Access: Stamford Harbor to West Branch N2 or East Branch N12

Marina Facilities *(In Season/Off Season)*
Fuel: *Texaco* - Gasoline, Diesel, High-Speed Pumps
Slips: 625 Total, 100 Transient **Max LOA:** 140 ft. **Max Beam:** 40 ft.
 Rate *(per ft.):* **Day** $1.75/Inq. **Week** $10 **Month** $25
 Power: 30 amp Incl., 50 amp Incl., 100 amp n/a, 200 amp n/a
 Cable TV: No **Dockside Phone:** No
 Dock Type: Floating, Long Fingers, Concrete, Wood, Vinyl
Moorings: 0 Total, 0 Transient **Launch:** n/a, Dinghy Dock
 Rate: Day n/a **Week** n/a **Month** n/a
Heads: 20 Toilet(s), 10 Shower(s) *(with dressing rooms)*, Hair Dryers
Laundry: 7 Washer(s), 6 Dryer(s) **Pay Phones:** Yes, yes
Pump-Out: OnSite, Full Service, 1 Port **Fee:** $5* **Closed Heads:** Yes

Marina Operations
Owner/Manager: James O. Whitmore **Dockmaster:** Eric C. Symeon
In-Season: Apr 15-Nov, 8am-8pm **Off-Season:** Nov-Apr 15, 8am-5pm
After-Hours Arrival: See security then call office next morning
Reservations: Yes, Preferred **Credit Cards:** Visa/MC, Dscvr, Amex, Tex
Discounts: Brewer Customer Card **Dockage:** n/a **Fuel:** n/a **Repair:** n/a
Pets: Welcome, Dog Walk Area **Handicap Access:** Yes, Heads, Docks

Brewer Yacht Haven Marina

PO Box 931; Foot of Washington Boulevard; Stamford, CT 06904

Tel: (203) 359-4500 **VHF: Monitor** 9 **Talk** n/a
Fax: (203) 359-9522 **Alternate Tel:** (203) 395-4500
Email: byh@byy.com **Web:** www.byy.com
Nearest Town: Stamford *(1.5 mi.)* **Tourist Info:** (203) 359-4761

Marina Services and Boat Supplies
Services - Docking Assistance, Security *(24 Hrs.)*, Trash Pick-Up, Dock
Carts **Communication -** Mail & Package Hold, Phone Messages, Data
Ports, FedEx, AirBorne, UPS, Express Mail *(Sat Del)* **Supplies -**
OnSite: Ice *(Block, Cube)*, Ships' Store *(West Yard)* **OnCall:** CNG
Under 1 mi: West Marine *(969-7727 - East Yard)*, Bait/Tackle *(Pete's Place
356-9383)*, Live Bait, Propane *(U-Haul 324-3869)*

Boatyard Services
OnSite: Travelift *(30T & 60T)*, Forklift, Crane, Electrical Repairs, Electronic
Sales *(Maritech)*, Hull Repairs, Rigger, Sail Loft, Bottom Cleaning, Bright-
work, Air Conditioning, Refrigeration, Compound, Wash & Wax, Interior
Cleaning, Woodworking *(Erik's)*, Upholstery, Yacht Interiors, Metal
Fabrication, Painting, Awlgrip, Yacht Broker, Total Refits **OnCall:** Divers,
Propeller Repairs **Dealer for:** Yanmar, Westerbeke, Cruisair, Marine Air,
Espar, Webasto, Volvo, Adler-Barbour, Norcold, Sea Frost, Sea Recovery,
Marvel, Universal Aqua, Balmar, Pur, SeaLand, Ample Power, Cruising
Equipment, Amptech, Batt-Maxx, Heart, Trace Engineering, Stat Power,
Sent. **Member:** ABYC - 3 Certified Tech(s) **Yard Rates:** $68/hr., Haul &
Launch $16/ft. *(blocking incl.)*, Power Wash Incl., Bottom Paint $15/ft.
Storage: In-Water $28/ft., On-Land $40/season

Restaurants and Accommodations
OnSite: Restaurant *(Shore House D $18-30, East Yard)*, *(Lighthouse Grill
at Ponus Y.C. 975-0411, West Yard)* **OnCall:** Pizzeria *(Planet 357-1101)*
Near: Restaurant *(Crabshell 967-7229, L $7-13, D $9-30, across channel)*,
(Paradise Grill 323-1116, across channel) **1-3 mi:** Restaurant *(Zanghi 327-
3663)*, *(Bennetts Steak & Fish House 978-7995)*, Hotel *(Marriott 357-9555,*

$200-260), *(Westin 967-2222)*, *(Holiday Inn 961-8902)*

Recreation and Entertainment
OnSite: Picnic Area, Grills **Near:** Dive Shop, Jogging Paths
Under 1 mi: Beach, Tennis Courts *(Shippan Racquet 323-3129)*, Fitness
Center *(YMCA 357-7000)*, Movie Theater *(Crown 324-3100)*, Video Rental
(Video Plus 964-1900), Video Arcade, Park, Museum *(Whitney 358-7630)*,
Cultural Attract *(Rich Forum & Palace Theatre 325-4466)* **1-3 mi:** Bowling
(Bowlarama 323-1041) **3+ mi:** Golf Course *(Sterling Farms 461-9090, 4 mi.)*

Provisioning and General Services
Under 1 mi: Supermarket *(Bongiorno 324-1054 East Yard)*, Delicatessen
(Dockside Deli 325-3595), Wine/Beer, Liquor Store *(Star 323-7814)*, Bakery,
Fishmonger, Lobster Pound, Meat Market, Post Office, Catholic Church,
Protestant Church, Beauty Salon, Barber Shop, Dry Cleaners, Laundry,
Pharmacy *(CVS 325-2884)* **1-3 mi:** Farmers' Market *(Columbus Park Mon
& Thu 10-3)*, Library *(Ferguson 964-1000)*, Bookstore *(Waldenbooks)*,
Hardware Store *(Westside 348-2930)*, Retail Shops, Department Store
(Stamford Town Center)

Transportation
OnSite: Local Bus **OnCall:** Taxi *(Eveready 967-3633)* **Under 1 mi:** Rail
(MetroNorth/Amtrak) **Airport:** Westchester/Laguardia *(20 mi./32 mi.)*

Medical Services
911 Service **OnCall:** Ambulance **1-3 mi:** Doctor *(Cove Family Practice
326-2978)*, Dentist *(Fisher 964-8486)*, Chiropractor *(Back & Neck 329-
1143)*, Holistic Services **Hospital:** Stamford 325-7000 *(3 mi.)*

Setting -- From Stamford Harbor choose either the East or West Branch - both lead to Brewer Yacht Haven docks. The West slips surround a large work yard that juts out into the harbor -- it's loaded with sheds, services and boats on the hard -- and is closer to town. Views are best from the south and west docks; the east ones, on a narrow channel, are treed. The East slips occupy two spaces separated by a high-end office complex: on the harbor side protected by an earth berm and on the inside in a nearly enclosed basin. It has a restaurant onsite and delightful Picnic Island with tables, grills and a playground.

Marina Notes -- The West yard is a very large, active full-service boatyard with a well equipped chandlery and many independent marine services onsite: Soundings Publications, Z Sails Sailmakers, MacDonald Yacht Rigging, Nautor Swan New York, Prestige Yacht Sales, Tropical Tops, Colgate Offshore Sailing School, Boatmaster Detailing Service and Soundwaters. Originally home of Luders Marine Construction, builder of mine sweepers & 12-meter America's Cup boat, American Eagle. Both yards have good heads and showers - knotty-pine, tile, hairdryers & flowers. *Free pump-out for Brewer Customers.

Notable -- At the East Yard, casually elegant Shore House Restaurant (food designed by famed chef Michael Lomonaco) overlooks the boat-filled basin from both inside tables and dining deck- dinner 5:30-10pm, Sun Brunch 12-2:30 - also delivers to the boats! Next door to the West Yard, Ponus Y.C. welcomes all to its reasonably priced Lighthouse Grille - lunch Mon-Sat 11-3, Sun 10-5, dinner Thu-Sat, 5-9. Downtown Stamford is a little over a mile away with upscale Stamford Town Center (Filene's, Macy's & Sak's), many shops, restaurants, services. Live performances at The Palace concert hall and the Rich Forum theater.

Stamford Landing Marina

78 Southfield Avenue; Stamford, CT 06902

Tel: (203) 965-0065 **VHF: Monitor** 9 **Talk** 11
Fax: (203) 322-4505 **Alternate Tel:** n/a
Email: n/a **Web:** n/a
Nearest Town: Stamford *(3 mi.)* **Tourist Info:** (203) 359-4761

Navigational Information
Lat: 41°02.290' **Long:** 073°32.722' **Tide:** 8 ft. **Current:** n/a **Chart:** 12368
Rep. Depths *(MLW):* **Entry** 12 ft. **Fuel Dock** n/a **Max Slip/Moor** 9 ft./-
Access: L.I. Sound to Stamford Harbor West Branch

Marina Facilities *(In Season/Off Season)*
Fuel: No
Slips: 130 Total, 10 Transient **Max LOA:** 50 ft. **Max Beam:** 16.5 ft.
 Rate *(per ft.):* **Day** $2.00 **Week** $12.25 **Month** $45
 Power: 30 amp Incl., 50 amp Incl., 100 amp n/a, 200 amp n/a
 Cable TV: Yes Seasonal Only **Dockside Phone:** Yes Seasonal Only
 Dock Type: Floating, Long Fingers, Pilings, Aluminum
Moorings: 0 Total, 0 Transient **Launch:** n/a
 Rate: Day n/a **Week** n/a **Month** n/a
Heads: 4 Toilet(s), 2 Shower(s)
Laundry: 1 Washer(s), 1 Dryer(s), Book Exchange **Pay Phones:** Yes, 2
Pump-Out: OnSite, Self Service, 1 Central **Fee:** $15 **Closed Heads:** Yes

Marina Operations
Owner/Manager: Valerie Morris **Dockmaster:** Same
In-Season: May-Oct 31, 9am-5pm* **Off-Season:** Oct 1-Apr, 10am-3pm*
After-Hours Arrival: n/a
Reservations: Yes **Credit Cards:** Visa/MC
Discounts: Boat/US **Dockage:** 25% **Fuel:** n/a **Repair:** n/a
Pets: Welcome, Dog Walk Area **Handicap Access:** No

Marina Services and Boat Supplies
Services - Docking Assistance, Concierge, Security, Trash Pick-Up, Dock Carts **Communication -** Mail & Package Hold, Phone Messages, FedEx, AirBorne, UPS, Express Mail *(Sat Del)* **Supplies - OnSite:** Ice *(Block, Cube)* **Near:** Ships' Store **Under 1 mi:** West Marine (969-7727) **1-3 mi:** Bait/Tackle, Propane *(Propane Gas 869-4226)*, CNG *(Brewer Yacht Haven)*

Boatyard Services
OnCall: Bottom Cleaning, Divers *(Shippan Scuba 327-3723)*, Woodworking *(Erik's Boat Works 359-3657)*, Upholstery *(Royal Interiors)*, Painting, Awlgrip, Yacht Broker *(Prestige Yachts)* **Near:** Travelift, Crane, Engine mechanic *(gas, diesel)*, Launching Ramp *(West Beach)*, Electrical Repairs, Electronics Repairs, Hull Repairs, Rigger, Brightwork, Refrigeration
Nearest Yard: Brewer Yacht Haven Marina (203) 359-4500

Restaurants and Accommodations
OnSite: Restaurant *(Crab Shell 967-7229, L $8-12, D $14-20, Dockage & a lively atmosphere)*, *(Paradise Bar & Grill 323-1116, L $7-20, D $8-22, Sun Brunch $9-13, Pizza, too)* **OnCall:** Pizzeria *(Planet Pizza 357-1101)* **Near:** Restaurant *(Sunset Café 323-3477)*, *(Buddy and Pat's 969-2113)*, *(Lighthouse Grille 975-0411, at Ponus Yacht Club, by dinghy)* **Under 1 mi:** Restaurant *(Beamers 975-7707)*, Motel *(Super 8 324-8887, $70-90)*, Hotel *(Fairfield Inn by Marriott 357-7100)* **1-3 mi:** Restaurant *(New Orleans Au Bistro 324-5071)*, *(Bennigans 327-2801)*, *(Kujaku 357-0821)*, *(Southport Brewing Co. 327-2337)*, *(Zanghi 327-3663)*, Fast Food, Motel *(Old Saybrook 388-3463)*, Hotel *(Holiday Inn 961-8902, $100-150)*, *(Westin 967-2222, $140-200)*

Recreation and Entertainment
Under 1 mi: Park, Cultural Attract *(The Rich Forum & the Palace Theatre 325-4466)* **1-3 mi:** Beach, Playground, Dive Shop, Tennis Courts *(Shippan Racquet Club 323-3129)*, Fitness Center *(YMCA 357-7000)*, Jogging Paths, Boat Rentals, Movie Theater *(Crown Majestic 323-1690)*, Video Rental, Museum *(Whitney Museum Of American Art 358-7630)*, Galleries **3+ mi:** Golf Course *(Sterling Farms 461-9090, 5 mi.)*

Provisioning and General Services
OnSite: Bank/ATM **Near:** Post Office, Catholic Church, Newsstand, Florist **Under 1 mi:** Convenience Store, Supermarket *(Bongiorno 324-1054)*, Gourmet Shop, Delicatessen *(Dockside Deli 325-3595)*, Wine/Beer, Laundry, Pharmacy *(Brooks 327-6822)* **1-3 mi:** Liquor Store *(Star Wines & Spirits 323-7814)*, Bakery, Farmers' Market *(Columbus Park Mon & Thu 10-3)*, Fishmonger, Meat Market, Library *(Ferguson 964-1000)*, Beauty Salon, Dry Cleaners, Bookstore *(Waldenbooks 358-8927)*, Hardware Store *(Westside Hardware 348-2930)*, Copies Etc. *(Kinkos)*

Transportation
OnCall: Rental Car *(Enterprise 327-6500, Hertz 324-3131, Avis 964-3200)* **Near:** Local Bus **Under 1 mi:** Rail *(Metro-North to Manhattan or New Haven and Amtrak)* **Airport:** Westchester/LaGuardia *(20 mi./32 mi.)*

Medical Services
911 Service **OnCall:** Ambulance **1-3 mi:** Doctor, Dentist *(Dental Center of Stamford 969-0802)*, Chiropractor *(Back & Neck 329-1143)*, Holistic Services **Hospital:** Stamford 325-7000 *(2 mi.)*

Setting -- The first facility on the western shore of the West Branch of Stamford Harbor, Stamford Town Landing is located in an upscale office park and condominium complex -- an oasis in the midst of a semi-industrial area. A boardwalk runs the length of the marina. Landside views from the docks are of the two onsite restaurants and their active, outdoor dining scenes. Across the narrow channel is Ponus Yacht Club and some of the Brewer Yacht Haven docks. The atmosphere is generally fun and festive.

Marina Notes -- Cable TV and phone availability are seasonal. The marina has been dredged to nine feet. Boat/U.S. cooperating marina. Brewer Yacht Haven, a full-service yard, is located directly across the channel. Both the two-tiered, well-reviewed and always crowded Crab Shell (7 days L 11:30-3pm, D Sun-Thu 5-10pm, Fri & Sat 5-11pm), and the Paradise Bar and Grill (L 12-5pm, D Mon-Thu 5-10pm, Fri & Sat 5-11pm, Sun 3-10pm, Sun Brunch 11:30-3pm), are very good full-service white-tablecloth restaurants, each with inside and outside dining, that overlook the docks.

Notable -- Lovely waterfront pocket park. Downtown Stamford's very active "city scene" is about a three mile cab ride.. It offers just about every service and facility you could need: lots of restaurants, two breweries, movies, art galleries, the Stamford Town Center (a large high-end mall anchored by Filenes, Saks and Macy's), and two theaters -- the Rich Forum and The Palace -- which offer original live theater, concerts & Broadway national tours. An independent supermarket is within a mile, but the chains are farther away. Metro-North RR station to NYC is also less than a mile.

Navigational Information
Lat: 41°02.009' **Long:** 073°35.641' **Tide:** 6 ft. **Current:** 2 kt. **Chart:** 12367
Rep. Depths (*MLW*): **Entry** 6 ft. **Fuel Dock** 6 ft. **Max Slip/Moor** 6 ft./-
Access: LI Sound to Mianus River, past RR bridge on port side

Marina Facilities *(In Season/Off Season)*
Fuel: *Shell* - Slip-Side Fueling, Gasoline, Diesel, High-Speed Pumps
Slips: 130 Total, 2 Transient **Max LOA:** 59 ft. **Max Beam:** 16 ft.
 Rate *(per ft.):* **Day** $3.00/2.50 **Week** n/a **Month** n/a
 Power: 30 amp Incl., **50 amp** Incl., **100 amp** n/a, **200 amp** n/a
 Cable TV: Yes **Dockside Phone:** No
 Dock Type: Floating, Long Fingers
Moorings: 0 Total, 0 Transient **Launch:** n/a
 Rate: Day n/a **Week** n/a **Month** n/a
Heads: 4 Toilet(s), 4 Shower(s)
Laundry: None, Book Exchange **Pay Phones:** No
Pump-Out: OnCall **Fee:** Free **Closed Heads:** Yes

Marina Operations
Owner/Manager: Diane & James DeNardo **Dockmaster:** Ken Tenore
In-Season: May-Oct, 9am-5pm **Off-Season:** Oct-May, 9am-4pm*
After-Hours Arrival: Call and leave message
Reservations: Yes **Credit Cards:** Visa/MC, Tex, Shell
Discounts: Boat/US; Store 10% **Dockage:** 10% **Fuel:** 10% **Repair:** n/a
Pets: Welcome, Dog Walk Area **Handicap Access:** Yes, Heads, Docks

Palmer Point Marina

7 River Road, #311; Cos Cob, CT 06807

Tel: (203) 661-1243 **VHF: Monitor** n/a **Talk** n/a
Fax: (203) 661-1368 **Alternate Tel:** n/a
Email: ppm97@aol.com **Web:** n/a
Nearest Town: Greenwich *(2 mi.)* **Tourist Info:** (203) 869-3500

Marina Services and Boat Supplies
Services - Dock Carts **Supplies - OnSite:** Ice *(Block, Cube)*, Ships' Store,
Bait/Tackle *(Chandlery & Sportsman's Den 869-3234)* **Near:** Live Bait

Boatyard Services
OnSite: Travelift *(35T)*, Crane, Engine mechanic *(gas, diesel)*, Electrical
Repairs, Electronic Sales, Electronics Repairs, Hull Repairs, Bottom
Cleaning, Brightwork, Compound, Wash & Wax, Interior Cleaning,
Woodworking, Painting, Awlgrip, Yacht Broker *(Used boats)* **OnCall:** Air
Conditioning, Refrigeration, Propeller Repairs, Inflatable Repairs, Life Raft
Service, Metal Fabrication **Under 1 mi:** Launching Ramp, Divers.
1-3 mi: Rigger. **Yard Rates:** $85/hr., Haul & Launch $10/ft. *(blocking $3/ft.)*,
Power Wash $3.59/ft.

Restaurants and Accommodations
OnCall: Pizzeria *(Planet Pizza 622-4629)* **Near:** Snack Bar *(Darlene's
Heavenly Desires 622-7077, Sedutto ice cream & gourmet chocolates)*,
Inn/B&B *(Cos Cob Inn 661-5845)* **Under 1 mi:** Restaurant *(Angie's Mianus
Tavern 862-0640, L $15-20, D $15-20)*, *(The Good Life 698-2201, L $15-20,
D $15-20, at Howard Johnson)*, *(Cos Cob Grill 629-9029)*, *(Fonda La Paloma
661-9395, Mexican)*, *(Yangtze Riverside 698-0800)*, *(Tomaso's 698-2201)*,
(Glory Days Diner 869-0954), Motel *(Howard Johnson 637-3691)*
1-3 mi: Hotel *(Hyatt 637-1234)*, Inn/B&B *(Stanton House 869-2110)*

Recreation and Entertainment
Near: Tennis Courts *(Town courts)*, Video Rental, Park, Museum *(Bush-
Holly House 552-5329, Bruce Museum 869-0376)*

1-3 mi: Golf Course *(Town of Greenwich 531-7261, or Stamford Municipal
324-4185)*, Movie Theater *(Greenwich Crown Plaza 869-4030)*
3+ mi: Cultural Attract *(Stamford Rich Forum / Palace Theatre 325-4466)*

Provisioning and General Services
Near: Convenience Store, Delicatessen *(Cardillo's 661-3354)*, Liquor Store
(Cos Cob Liquor 661-3353), Green Grocer *(Sandy's Outdoor Farm Stand)*,
Fishmonger *(Fjord Fisheries 661-5006)*, Meat Market, Bank/ATM, Post
Office, Catholic Church, Library *(Greenwich - Cos Cob Branch 622-6883)*,
Beauty Salon, Barber Shop, Dry Cleaners, Laundry, Pharmacy *(Arrow 869-
3398)*, Newsstand, Hardware Store *(Center Hardware 869-9255)*, Florist
Under 1 mi: Market *(Food Mart 629-2100)*, Gourmet Shop *(Hay Day 637-
7600)*, Bakery, Clothing Store, Retail Shops, Copies Etc. *(Mail Boxes Etc
698-0016)* **1-3 mi:** Supermarket *(Fresh Fields/Whole Foods 661-0631)*,
Health Food *(Whole Foods)*, Protestant Church, Synagogue, Bookstore *(Just
Books 869-5023, Old Greenwich Bookstore 637-5106)*, Department Store

Transportation
OnCall: Rental Car *(Enterprise 622-1611/Hertz 622-4044 - 3 mi.)*, Taxi
(Greenwich Cab 869-6000) **Near:** Rail *(Amtrak, Metro North)*
 Under 1 mi: Local Bus **Airport:** Westchester / LaGuardia *(14 mi./30 mi.)*

Medical Services
911 Service **Near:** Dentist *(Greenwich Dental 661-4410)*, Chiropractor *(Cos
Cob Chiropractic 661-0582)* **Under 1 mi:** Doctor *(Convenient Medical Care
698-1419)*, Veterinarian *(Blue Cross Animal Hosp 869-7755)*
Hospital: Greenwich 863-3000 *2.5 mi.*

Setting -- Just north of the railroad bridge, and just south of the I-95 bridge, a nicely landscaped and carefully maintained luxury condominium complex provides a backdrop for Palmer Point's docks. Swaths of well tended flower beds and mature trees shelter the promenade that runs alongside the marina's basin. Across the River the sparsely populated and quite pretty eastern shore delivers tranquil, leafy views.

Marina Notes -- *Off-season closed Sundays. Boat US Members receive 10% discount on store items not on sale. Family run business for 27 years. Built on the site of famous Palmer Engine Factory. Good, well-maintained docks; a substantial number are owned by residents of the condominium complex and other boaters. Palmer Point, Inc owns 20 of the slips. Management is onsite on weekends. The well staffed onsite boatyard has considerable capability. The jammed packed large chandlery is well stocked and has lots of other fun and useful nautical stuff as well. There are quite nice tiled heads and showers. Sportsman's Den has bait (including live) & tackle plus hourly fly casting lessons, (hrs: Tue-Fri 9-5, Sat 8-5, Sun & Mon 8-2). The railroad bridge opens on demand but is on the main N.Y.C. commuter line so there is significant activity. Closed clearance 20 feet. The main channel runs very close to the docks.

Notable -- The enormous Chart House restaurant next door is now closed and has been converted into an office building. The Sound Shore Tennis Club is just up the block. A little under a mile north is Route One (the Boston Post Road). Some services are right at the crossroads; others are within easy reach, just another half a mile -- to Cos Cob one way or Old Greenwich the other.

Beacon Point Marina

49 River Road; Cos Cob, CT 06807

Tel: (203) 661-4033 **VHF: Monitor** 16 **Talk** n/a
Fax: (203) 661-2054 **Alternate Tel:** (203) 661-4033
Email: service@beaconpointmarine.com **Web:** beaconpointmarine.com
Nearest Town: Greenwich (2 mi.) **Tourist Info:** (203) 869-3500

Navigational Information
Lat: 41°02.134' **Long:** 073°35.733' **Tide:** 8 ft. **Current:** 1 kt. **Chart:** 12367
Rep. Depths (MLW): Entry 6 ft. **Fuel Dock** n/a **Max Slip/Moor** 4 ft./-
Access: Mianus River, just past the I95 Bridge, on port side

Marina Facilities (In Season/Off Season)
Fuel: Gasoline, Diesel
Slips: 300 Total, 5 Transient **Max LOA:** 70 ft. **Max Beam:** 17 ft.
  Rate (per ft.): **Day** $2.00/Inq. **Week** Inq. **Month** n/a
  Power: 30 amp Incl., **50 amp** Incl., **100 amp** n/a, **200 amp** n/a
  Cable TV: No **Dockside Phone:** Yes access avail.
  Dock Type: Floating, Long Fingers, Wood
Moorings: 0 Total, 0 Transient **Launch:** n/a
  Rate: Day n/a **Week** n/a **Month** n/a
Heads: 4 Toilet(s), 4 Shower(s) (with dressing rooms), Hair Dryers
Laundry: 2 Washer(s), 2 Dryer(s) **Pay Phones:** Yes, 2
Pump-Out: Full Service, 1 Central, 1 Port **Fee:** Free **Closed Heads:** Yes

Marina Operations
Owner/Manager: Richard Kral **Dockmaster:** n/a
In-Season: Year-Round, 9am-5pm **Off-Season:** n/a
After-Hours Arrival: Call ahead
Reservations: Preferred **Credit Cards:** Visa/MC, Din, Amex
Discounts: None
Pets: Welcome, Dog Walk Area **Handicap Access:** Yes

Marina Services and Boat Supplies
Services - Docking Assistance, Boaters' Lounge, Trash Pick-Up, Dock
Carts **Communication -** FedEx, AirBorne, UPS, Express Mail
Supplies - OnSite: Ice (Block), Ships' Store (Chandlery & Blue Lightening)
Near: Bait/Tackle, Live Bait **1-3 mi:** Propane (Paraco 629-5627)
3+ mi: West Marine (969-7727, 6 mi.)

Boatyard Services
OnSite: Travelift (35T), Forklift, Crane (15T), Hydraulic Trailer (to 15T),
Engine mechanic (gas, diesel), Electrical Repairs, Electronic Sales,
Electronics Repairs, Hull Repairs, Rigger, Bottom Cleaning, Brightwork, Air
Conditioning, Refrigeration, Divers, Compound, Wash & Wax, Interior
Cleaning, Propeller Repairs, Woodworking, Inflatable Repairs, Life Raft
Service, Painting, Awlgrip, Yacht Broker, Total Refits **OnCall:** Metal
Fabrication **Near:** Launching Ramp. **Member:** ABBRA - 4 Certified Tech
(s), ABYC - 1 Certified Tech(s) **Yard Rates:** $90/hr., Haul & Launch $8/ft.
(blocking $4), Power Wash $2/ft., Bottom Paint $14/ft.

Restaurants and Accommodations
OnCall: Pizzeria (Pizza Factory 661-5188) **Near:** Restaurant (Augies 862-
0640), (Fonda La Paloma 661-9393), (Arcuris 698-2201, pizza), Inn/B&B
(Cos Cob 661-5845, $119-249) **Under 1 mi:** Restaurant (Yangtze Riverside
698-0800), Motel (Howard Johnson 637-3691) **1-3 mi:** Restaurant (Boxing
Cat 869-6999), (Bella Nonna 869-4445), (Mackenzies 698-0223), Hotel
(Hyatt 637-1234, $220-280), Inn/B&B (Harbor House 698-0943, $170-285)

Recreation and Entertainment
Near: Beach, Picnic Area, Grills, Playground, Tennis Courts (Town Courts
5 min walk or Greenwich Racquet Club 661-0606), Jogging Paths, Roller
Blade/Bike Paths, Video Arcade, Park **Under 1 mi:** Fitness Center (YWCA
869-6501), Video Rental (Academy Video 629-3260) **1-3 mi:** Golf Course
(Town of Greenwich 531-7261), Movie Theater (Greenwich Crown Plaza
869-4030), Museum (Bruce Museum 869-0376)

Provisioning and General Services
Near: Convenience Store, Delicatessen (Cardillos 661-3354), Bakery, Green
Grocer (Sandy's Outdoor Farm Stand), Fishmonger (Fijord - fresh fish, sushi
and prepared foods), Bank/ATM, Post Office, Catholic Church, Protestant
Church, Synagogue, Library (622-6883), Beauty Salon, Barber Shop, Dry
Cleaners, Newsstand, Florist, Clothing Store, Retail Shops, Department
Store, Buying Club **Under 1 mi:** Gourmet Shop (Hay Day 637-7600),
Health Food (Fresh Fields/Whole Foods 661-0631), Liquor Store (Cos Cob
Liquor 661-2253), Pharmacy (Walgreens 637-7807), Hardware Store (Center
Hardware 869-9255), Copies Etc. (Mail Boxes Etc 698-0016) **1-3 mi:** Super-
market (Stop & Shop 625-0622), Bookstore (Just Books 869-5023)

Transportation
OnCall: Rental Car (Enterprise 622-1611/Hertz 622-4044 - 3 mi.), Taxi
(Eveready 869-1700) **Near:** Local Bus, Rail (Metro-North to NYC)
Airport: Westchester/LaGuardia (14 mi./30 mi.)

Medical Services
911 Service **OnCall:** Ambulance **Near:** Doctor (Convenient Medical Ctr
698-1419), Dentist (Greenwich Dental 661-4410), Chiropractor (Cos Cob
Chiro 661-0582), Holistic Services **Hospital:** Greenwich 863-3000 (1 mi.)

Setting -- This very large marina is just north of the I-95, 45 foot bridge on the western shore of the Mianus River. The landside views from the slips are of a boatyard and gravel parking lots; waterside views are of wide expanses of unspoiled marsh and green trees, and a small condo complex farther up.

Marina Notes -- Primarily a motor boat marina because of depths and bridge heights. New, very nice tiled heads and showers along with a small "boaters' lounge". A chandlery and Blue Lightning Marine are also onsite. Complete stock of paints, rope, cleaners and hardware, Mercury/Mercruiser/Yamaha Parts, Yanmar/Universal Atomic 4. Helpful and professional counter staff. Factory-trained techs: Mercury, Mercruiser, Yamaha, Crusaider. Tune-up to complete rebuilds - Inboard, I/O, Outboard, Small Diesel. Part of a small chain - other marinas are in Shelton and Old Saybrook. Nearby Sportsmen's Den (869-3234) is an International Game Fish Association Official Weigh Station.

Notable -- Across the street from the docks is the charming, 19thC, Victorian Cos Cob Inn with 14 rooms, each with private bath, TV, VCR, voice-mail, data port, hair dryer, iron/ironing board, coffee maker, refrigerator, ceiling fan, and air conditioning. Tennis courts and restaurants are a 5-10 minute walk, as are a market and fish market. The Bruce Museum, in Greenwich, is worth a visit; it's open Tue-Sat 10am-5pm, Sat 1-5pm. Nearby Fjord Charters offers Wednesday dinner or Sunday brunch cruises ($55/25) on its large yacht.

Navigational Information

Lat: 41°02.404' **Long:** 073°35.462' **Tide:** 8 ft. **Current:** 1 kt. **Chart:** 12367
Rep. Depths (MLW): Entry 5 ft. **Fuel Dock** n/a **Max Slip/Moor** 5 ft./-
Access: Greenwich Harbor to Mianus River, past I-95 bridge on port side

Marina Facilities (In Season/Off Season)
Fuel: No
Slips: 55 Total, 3 Transient **Max LOA:** 34 ft. **Max Beam:** 13 ft.
  Rate (per ft.): **Day** $2.50/Inq. **Week** Inq. **Month** Inq.
  Power: 30 amp Incl., **50 amp** n/a, **100 amp** n/a, **200 amp** n/a
  Cable TV: Yes, Incl. **Dockside Phone:** No
  Dock Type: Floating, Long Fingers, Alongside, Wood
Moorings: 0 Total, 0 Transient **Launch:** n/a
  Rate: Day n/a **Week** n/a **Month** n/a
Heads: 2 Toilet(s), 2 Shower(s), Hair Dryers
Laundry: None **Pay Phones:** No
Pump-Out: No **Fee:** n/a **Closed Heads:** No

Marina Operations
Owner/Manager: George Ward **Dockmaster:** n/a
In-Season: Year-Round, 9am-6pm **Off-Season:** n/a, Same
After-Hours Arrival: Call ahead
Reservations: Yes **Credit Cards:** n/a
Discounts: None
Pets: Welcome **Handicap Access:** No

OMA Marine

151 River Road; Cos Cob, CT 06807

Tel: (203) 661-4283 **VHF: Monitor** n/a **Talk** n/a
Fax: (203) 661-5217 **Alternate Tel:** n/a
Email: n/a **Web:** n/a
Nearest Town: Greenwich (2 mi.) **Tourist Info:** (203) 869-3500

Marina Services and Boat Supplies
Services - Dock Carts **Communication -** FedEx, AirBorne, UPS, Express Mail **Supplies - OnSite:** Ice (Block, Cube) **Near:** Ships' Store, Bait/Tackle **1-3 mi:** Propane (Paraco Gas 629-5627) **3+ mi:** West Marine (969-7727, 6 mi.)

Boatyard Services
OnSite: Travelift (30T), Engine mechanic (gas, diesel), Electrical Repairs, Hull Repairs, Bottom Cleaning, Brightwork, Divers, Compound, Wash & Wax, Interior Cleaning, Woodworking **OnCall:** Electronic Sales, Electronics Repairs, Rigger, Sail Loft, Air Conditioning, Refrigeration, Propeller Repairs, Inflatable Repairs, Life Raft Service, Upholstery, Yacht Interiors, Metal Fabrication, Painting, Awlgrip, Total Refits **Near:** Launching Ramp.
Dealer for: Mercury, Volvo. Other Certifications: Mercury, Volvo
Yard Rates: $60/hr., Haul & Launch $8/ft. (blocking $2/ft.), Power Wash $3, Bottom Paint $10/ft. **Storage:** In-Water $28/ft., On-Land $35/ft.

Restaurants and Accommodations
OnCall: Pizzeria (Planet Pizza 622-0999) **Near:** Restaurant (Fonda La Paloma 661-9395), (Augies 862-0640), (Landmark Diner 869-0954) **Under 1 mi:** Restaurant (Sevilla 629-9029), Snack Bar, Hotel (Howard Johnson 637-3691), Inn/B&B (Cos Cob Inn 661-5845) **1-3 mi:** Restaurant (Boxing Cat Grill 698-1995), Fast Food, Motel (Grand Chalet 357-7100), Hotel (Hyatt Regency 637-1234), Inn/B&B (Stanton House Inn 869-2110)

Recreation and Entertainment
OnSite: Grills **Near:** Fishing Charter **Under 1 mi:** Pool, Beach, Playground, Jogging Paths, Park **1-3 mi:** Tennis Courts (Greenwich Racquet Club 661-0606), Golf Course (Town Of Greenwich 531-7261), Fitness Center (YWCA 869-6501), Boat Rentals, Roller Blade/Bike Paths, Movie Theater, Video Rental (Academy Video 629-3260), Museum (Bruce Museum 869-0376)

Provisioning and General Services
Near: Delicatessen (B & B Deli 661-9866), Bakery (Fjord Fisheries), Green Grocer (Sandy's Outdoor Farm Stand), Fishmonger (Fjord Fisheries 661-5006), Lobster Pound, Bank/ATM, Post Office, Catholic Church, Protestant Church **Under 1 mi:** Convenience Store, Supermarket (Stop & Shop), Gourmet Shop (Hay Day 637-7600), Health Food (Fresh Fields/Whole Foods 661-0631), Wine/Beer, Liquor Store (Cos Cob Liquor 661-2253), Synagogue, Library (Greenwich Library 622-6883), Beauty Salon, Barber Shop, Dry Cleaners, Laundry, Pharmacy (Arrow Pharmacy 869-3398), Newsstand, Hardware Store (Center Hardware 869-9255), Florist, Retail Shops, Copies Etc. (Mail Boxes Etc 698-0016) **1-3 mi:** Meat Market, Bookstore (Old Greenwich Bookstore 637-5106), Clothing Store

Transportation
OnCall: Rental Car (Enterprise 622-1611, Hertz 622-4044 3 mi.), Taxi (Eveready 869-1700) **Near:** Local Bus **Under 1 mi:** Rail (Metro North) **Airport:** Westchester/ LaGuardia (14 mi./30 mi.)

Medical Services
911 Service **OnCall:** Ambulance **Near:** Dentist (Greenwich Dental 661-4410), Chiropractor (Cos Cob 661-0582) **Under 1 mi:** Doctor (Convenient Medical Care 698-1419) Holistic Services **1-3 mi:** Veterinarian (Davis Hospital 327-0300) **Hospital:** Greenwich 629-9490 (2.5 mi.)

Setting -- This very small marina/boat yard and engine repair facility on the Mianus River's western bank is north of the 45 foot I-95 bridge and just south of the Route One bridge. A large, white, wedge-shaped building overlooks its docks and is a highly visible landmark.

Marina Notes -- Caters to smaller power boats and specializes in outboard rebuilding. In addition it has a full-service marine facility, including a machine shop and mobile welding facility. It's a certified dealer for MerCruiser. Quite limited services and basic facilities. Next door Mianus Marine (869-2253) can handle boats up to 50 ft. and occasionally has a transient slip, as might Drenckhahn Boat Basin (869-1892) which can handle boats to 40 feet.

Notable -- This is a good provisioning stop because so many services are within walking distance. Just down the road, at Mianus Marine, is Fjord Fisheries (661-5006), 7am-7pm, 7 days. Wonderful assortment of very fresh fish and shellfish, an onsite sushi chef, prepared salads, rollups and good bread (and a picnic area for onsite snacking); call ahead to pre-order steamed lobster or clams on the half shell. Next to Fjord, Sandy's Outdoor Farm Stand features local corn and tomatoes -- and lots of other local and imported produce.

Delamar Greenwich Harbor

Delamar Greenwich Harbor

500 Steamboat Road; Greenwich, CT 06830

Tel: (203) 661-9800; (866) 335-2627 **VHF: Monitor** 9 **Talk** 78
Fax: (203) 661-2513 **Alternate Tel:** (203) 661-9800
Email: sales@thedelamar.com **Web:** www.thedelamar.com
Nearest Town: Greenwich *(1 mi.)* **Tourist Info:** (203) 869-3500

Navigational Information
Lat: 41°01.070' **Long:** 073°37.010' **Tide:** 7 ft. **Current:** n/a **Chart:** 12367
Rep. Depths *(MLW):* **Entry** 9 ft. **Fuel Dock** n/a **Max Slip/Moor** 9 ft./9 ft.
Access: Greenwich Harbor to the end of the channel on the east side

Marina Facilities *(In Season/Off Season)*
Fuel: No
Slips: 10 Total, 10* Transient **Max LOA:** 150 ft. **Max Beam:** n/a
 Rate *(per ft.):* **Day** $6.00 **Week** n/a **Month** n/a
 Power: 30 amp Inq., **50 amp** Inq., **100 amp** Inq., **200 amp** n/a
 Cable TV: Yes, Incl. **Dockside Phone:** Yes, Incl.
 Dock Type: Fixed, Alongside
Moorings: 3 Total, 3 Transient **Launch:** None
 Rate: Day $50 **Week** n/a **Month** n/a
Heads: Toilet(s)
Laundry: None **Pay Phones:** Yes, 1
Pump-Out: No **Fee:** n/a **Closed Heads:** Yes

Marina Operations
Owner/Manager: Klaus Peters **Dockmaster:** Robert M. Fenner
In-Season: Apr-Oct, 11am-7pm **Off-Season:** n/a
After-Hours Arrival: Call in advance.
Reservations: Required **Credit Cards:** Visa/MC, Din, Amex
Discounts: None
Pets: Welcome, Dog Walk Area **Handicap Access:** No

Marina Services and Boat Supplies
Services - Docking Assistance, Concierge, Trash Pick-Up, Megayacht Facilities, 3 Phase **Communication -** Fax in/out *($1)*, Data Ports, FedEx, AirBorne, UPS, Express Mail *(Sat Del)* **Supplies - OnSite:** Ice *(Cube)*
Under 1 mi: Ships' Store **1-3 mi:** Bait/Tackle, Propane *(Greenwich Propane 869-1881)* **3+ mi:** West Marine *(969-7727, 9 mi.)*

Boatyard Services
Nearest Yard: Brewer Yacht Haven (203) 359-4500

Restaurants and Accommodations
OnSite: Restaurant *(L'Escale 661-9800, L $9-25, D $17-35)*, Hotel *(Delamar 661-9800, $385-1500)* **OnCall:** Pizzeria *(Planet Pizza 862-2099)* **Near:** Restaurant *(Maneros 622-9684)*, *(Thataway Café 622-0947)*, *(ABIS Japanese 862-9100)*, *(de Paris 622-0018)* **Under 1 mi:** Restaurant *(Jean-Louis 622-8450, L $30-50 Prixe-Fixe, D $33-41 entrée)*, *(Thomas Henkelmann at Homestead Inn 869-7500, B $10-17, L $15-30, D $26-40)*, Lite Fare *(Organic Planet 861-9822)*, Motel *(Mews 869-9448)*, Inn/B&B *(Homestead Inn 869-7500, $250-500)* **1-3 mi:** Inn/B&B *(Howard Johnson 637-3691)*, *(Cos Cob Inn 661-5845)*

Recreation and Entertainment
OnSite: Fitness Center **Near:** Beach *(Island Beach 10 min ferry ride, leaves from across channel)*, Picnic Area, Grills, Playground, Volleyball, Tennis Courts *(Bruce Park)*, Jogging Paths, Movie Theater *(Crown Plaza 869-4030; Clearview 869-6030)*, Park *(Greenwich Park)*, Museum *(Bruce Museum 869-0376, US Tobacco Museum 869-5531)*, Cultural Attract *(Greenwich Symphony)*, Special Events *(Summer Outdoor Concerts)*

Under 1 mi: Roller Blade/Bike Paths, Fishing Charter, Video Rental *(Video Station 869-8543)* **1-3 mi:** Dive Shop, Golf Course *(Town Of Greenwich 531-7261)* **3+ mi:** Horseback Riding *(3.5 mi.)*

Provisioning and General Services
OnCall: Copies Etc. **Near:** Gourmet Shop, Bakery, Fishmonger, Meat Market, Bank/ATM, Beauty Salon, Barber Shop, Dry Cleaners, Laundry, Newsstand, Florist, Clothing Store, Retail Shops, Department Store
Under 1 mi: Delicatessen *(Olive Branch 622-9099)*, Wine/Beer, Liquor Store *(Quinns 869-0766)*, Farmers' Market *(Horse Neck parking lot, Sat 9:30-1pm)*, Post Office, Catholic Church, Protestant Church, Synagogue, Library *(Greenwich Library 622-6883)*, Bookstore *(Diane's Books 869-1515)*, Pharmacy *(Grannicks 869-3492)*, Hardware Store *(Greenwich 869-6750)* **1-3 mi:** Convenience Store, Supermarket *(Stop & Shop 625-0622, Food Emporium 622-0374)*, Health Food *(Fresh Fields 661-0631)*, Lobster Pound, Buying Club *(CostCo 914-937-3028)*

Transportation
OnCall: Taxi *(Greenwich Taxi 869-6000)*, Airport Limo *(Regency 869-9306; Rudy's 869-0014)* **Near:** Rental Car *(Budget 629-8500)*, Rail *(MetroNorth to NYC)*, Ferry Service *(to beach)* **1-3 mi:** Bikes *(Greenwich Bikes 869-4141)*
Airport: Westchester/LaGuardia *(7mi./27mi.)*

Medical Services
911 Service **OnCall:** Doctor, Ambulance **Near:** Dentist *(Greenwich Dental Assoc 661-4410)*, Chiropractor *(Cos Cob Chiropractic 661-0582)*, Holistic Services **Hospital:** Greenwich Hospital 863-3000 *(1 mi.)*

Setting -- At the head of Greenwich Harbor is a spectacular new luxury boutique hotel with 600 feet of big boat dockage. Securely snuggled up at the end of the channel, the dock is an integral part of this three-story, balconied, Tuscan-style villa with yellow stucco exterior and terracotta tile roof. The views, landside, are of the hotel, the walkway, and L'Escale Restaurant's alfresco dining terrace.

Marina Notes -- Former site of the Greenwich Harbor Inn. *Alongside dockage designed to accommodate megayachts. Hotel and Marina benefited from a $10 million renovation and re-opened in November 2002. Pump-out, gas & diesel are 1,000 feet away. Member of the prestigious Small Luxury Hotels of the World. 74 guest rooms and nine specialty suites (some with fireplaces) all have DVD/CD players, 900 MHz cordless phones, high-speed Internet access, two-line phones, and fax capability. Elegant 150 seat L'Escale serves breakfast, lunch, and dinner (3-course meals or bar food) and provides room service to the boats! Chef Frederic Kieffer's creations reflect Provençal influences and emphasize fresh seafood.

Notable -- Walking distance to fashionable, downtown Greenwich with many blocks of upscale shops, services, entertainment, and provisioning resources -- and to the world-class Bruce Museum. A couple of blocks from the Metro-North RR station (45 min. to NYC's Grand Central or 10 min. to Stamford). The Delamar is 20 min. from Westchester's White Plains Airport, 45 min. from LaGuardia, 60 min. from JFK. Hourly limo service to all three.

VI. New York: Western Long Island Sound

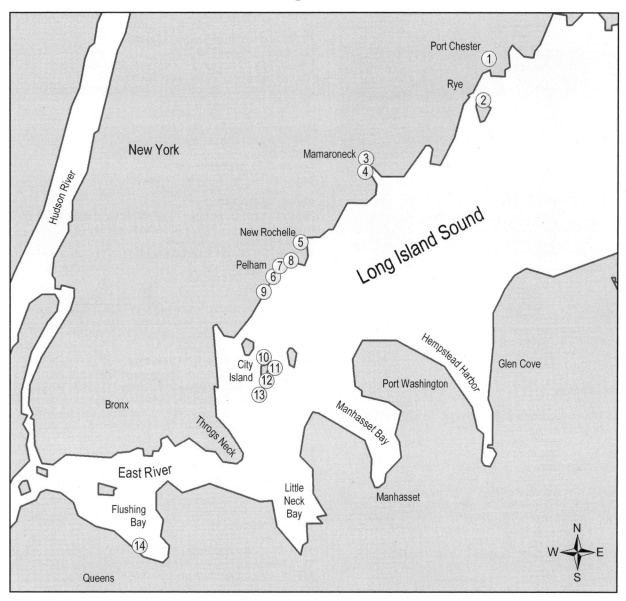

MAP	MARINA	HARBOR	PAGE	MAP	MARINA	HARBOR	PAGE
1	Ebb Tide Marina	Byram River	112	8	Castaways Yacht Club	New Rochelle Harbor	119
2	Tide Mill Yacht Basin	Port Chester Harbor	113	9	West Harbor Yacht Service	New Rochelle Harbor	120
3	Brewer Post Road Boat Yard	Mamaroneck Harbor	114	10	Barron's Marine Services	City Island Harbor	121
4	Harbor Island Municipal Marina	Mamaroneck Harbor	115	11	North Minneford Yacht Club	City Island Harbor	122
5	New Rochelle Municipal Marina	Echo Bay	116	12	South Minneford Yacht Club	City Island Harbor	123
6	Wright Island Marina	New Rochelle Harbor	117	13	Consolidated Yachts Inc.	City Island Harbor	124
7	Imperial Yacht Club	New Rochelle Harbor	118	14	World's Fair Marina	Flushing Bay	125

Ebb Tide Marina

1 Willett Avenue; Port Chester, NY 10573

Tel: (914) 939-4810 **VHF: Monitor** n/a **Talk** n/a
Fax: (914) 939-3474 **Alternate Tel:** n/a
Email: n/a **Web:** n/a
Nearest Town: Port Chester **Tourist Info:** (914) 939-1900

Navigational Information
Lat: 40°59.930' **Long:** 073°39.600' **Tide:** n/a **Current:** n/a **Chart:** 12367
Rep. Depths (*MLW*): Entry 16 ft. **Fuel Dock** n/a **Max Slip/Moor** 8 ft./-
Access: LI Sound up the Byram River, just past Costco, western shore

Marina Facilities (*In Season/Off Season*)
Fuel: Exxon - *In Byram* - Gasoline
Slips: 20 Total, 3 Transient **Max LOA:** 45 ft. **Max Beam:** n/a
 Rate (*per ft.*): **Day** $2.50/2.00 **Week** $15 **Month** n/a
 Power: 30 amp Incl., **50 amp** n/a, **100 amp** n/a, **200 amp** n/a
 Cable TV: No **Dockside Phone:** No
 Dock Type: Floating, Alongside, Wood
Moorings: 0 Total, 0 Transient **Launch:** n/a
 Rate: Day n/a **Week** n/a **Month** n/a
Heads: None
Laundry: None **Pay Phones:** No
Pump-Out: No **Fee:** n/a **Closed Heads:** No

Marina Operations
Owner/Manager: Tav Passarelli **Dockmaster:** Nunzio Raimo
In-Season: May-Oct, 7am-9pm **Off-Season:** Nov-Apr, 7am-7pm
After-Hours Arrival: Call in advance
Reservations: Yes **Credit Cards:** Visa/MC
Discounts: None
Pets: Welcome **Handicap Access:** No

Marina Services and Boat Supplies
Services - Docking Assistance **Communication -** FedEx, AirBorne, UPS, Express Mail (*Sat Del*) **Supplies - OnSite:** Bait/Tackle **1-3 mi:** Ships' Store, Propane (*Greenwich Propane 203-869-1881*) **3+ mi:** West Marine (*203-969-7727, 8 mi.*), Boater's World (*698-3686, 7 mi.*)

Boatyard Services
OnSite: Forklift, Engine mechanic (*gas, diesel*), Bottom Cleaning, Compound, Wash & Wax, Interior Cleaning, Painting **OnCall:** Hull Repairs, Brightwork, Air Conditioning, Refrigeration, Divers, Propeller Repairs, Inflatable Repairs, Upholstery **Dealer for:** Mercruiser, OMC, Volvo.
Yard Rates: $75/hr, Haul & Launch $5/ft., Power Wash $3/ft., Bottom Paint $14.50/ft. (*paint incl.*) **Storage:** In-Water $80/ft., On-Land $40/ft.

Restaurants and Accommodations
OnSite: Seafood Shack (*Ebb Tide all food home-made*) **Near:** Restaurant (*Willet House 939-7500, steak*), (*Castillo Rosa 939-9437*), (*Caribbean Affair 937-4885*), (*Shipwrecked Tavern 937-0333*), (*Miramar 939-0477, Indian*), (*La Bopusa Loca 935-0767*), (*Inca & Gaucho 939-2100*), (*Hakata Japan 939-7911*), (*Pasta Per Voi 937-3200*), (*Tandoori-Taste of India 937-2727*), (*That Little Italian Restaurant 531-7500*), Snack Bar (*Margots Signature 934-0087*), Pizzeria (*Vinnys Pizza 937-5120*) **1-3 mi:** Hotel (*Rye Town Hilton 939-6300*), (*Marriott Courtyard 921-1110*)

Recreation and Entertainment
OnSite: Fishing Charter **Near:** Video Rental (*State-Line 203-531-1141*), Cultural Attract (*Capitol Theatre 937-4126 - rock concerts*) **Under 1 mi:** Tennis Courts (*Sound Shore 939-1300*), Fitness Center (*YMCA 939-7800*), Movie Theater (*Rye Ridge Cinema 939-8177; nearby Cineplex summer '04*) **1-3 mi:** Museum (*Neuberger 251-6100, 939-0234*) **3+ mi:** Golf Course (*Doral Arrowwood 939-5500, 4 mi.*), Bowling (*AMF 946-8787, 7 mi.*)

Provisioning and General Services
OnSite: Fishmonger (*Ebb Tide*), Lobster Pound **Near:** Convenience Store (*LL Market 939-8756*), Delicatessen (*Deli Delight 937-5775; Biltmore 939-5749*), Bakery (*Kneaded Bread 937-9489 a fabulous artisanal bakery with coffee and sandwiches, too*), Bank/ATM, Post Office, Catholic Church, Protestant Church, Beauty Salon, Dry Cleaners, Laundry, Pharmacy (*Postiglione 939-2392/CVS 937-2301*), Newsstand, Hardware Store (*Feinsod 939-3872*), Retail Shops, Buying Club (*Costco*), Copies Etc. (*Graphic 939-0571*) **Under 1 mi:** Supermarket (*Pathmark 937-1400; nearby Stop & Shop summer '04*), Gourmet Shop (*Truffles Catering 203-629-2993*), Liquor Store (*Vaccaros 939-4104*), Library (*P.C. 939-6710*), Bookstore (*Readers Market 937-3370*) **1-3 mi:** Synagogue, Department Store (*Kohl's 690-0107*)

Transportation
OnCall: Rental Car (*Enterprise 937-4131 or 3 mi. Hertz 203-622-4044*), Taxi (*Village Taxi 937-4040*), Airport Limo (*Rye Brook Cab & Airport Service 939-0007*) **Near:** Local Bus, Rail (*MetroNorth to NYC or to Stamford for Amtrak*) **Airport:** Westchester/LaGuardia (*7 mi./25 mi.*)

Medical Services
911 Service **Near:** Doctor, Dentist (*Family Dental Center 939-6555*), Holistic Services (*Alternative Medicine Cntr 939-0003*) **Under 1 mi:** Chiropractor (*Port Chester Chiropractic 939-0101*), Veterinarian (*Port Chester Animal Hosp. 939-2388*) **Hospital:** New York United 934-3001 (*1 mi.*)

Setting -- Up the well protected and fairly industrial Byram River, this smaller boat marina has two facilities. The first, to starboard heading upriver, is in Byram, CT and has boatyard services and seasonal-only dockage. The second, to port, a little further upriver has some transients docks, an al fresco eatery and easy access to the interesting village of Port Chester, NY. The village and its waterfront are in the throes of a major redevelopment.

Marina Notes -- The Byram facility offers extensive, locally well-regarded, boatyard services. At the Port Chester facility, there are brand new stern-to docks - mostly seasonal but usually some transient slips available. Charter fishing boat onsite. The new seafood shack has limited, basic inside seating -- along with a fish market and a bait and tackle shop -- and a very inviting dining deck with umbrellaed tables overlooking the River.

Notable -- Emerging, gentrifying Port Chester is one block away. Dozens of diverse and creative restaurants populate Main Street. A substantial Latino population (Peruvian, Mexican and Brazilian) has joined the original Italian one and spawned some interesting small, store-front eateries, bodegas, and other provisioning sources - infusing the whole village with an interesting ethnic flair. Costco (with public dockage in front) is less than a block making it possible to push the cart right to EbbTide. G&S Investors is developing "The Waterfront at Port Chester," a $100-million downtown revitalization project that will rehabilitate a half-mile of the village's Byram River frontage. More restaurants, boat slips and, by mid 2004, a Bed, Bath & Beyond, Super Stop & Shop, Marshall's and Loews's Cineplex movie theater. The waterfront promenade and park connects the new shopping complex to Ebb Tide.

Tide Mill Yacht Basin

Navigational Information
Lat: 40°58.820' **Long:** 073°39.730' **Tide:** 8 ft. **Current:** n/a **Chart:** 12367
Rep. Depths (*MLW*): **Entry** 7 ft. **Fuel Dock** 7 ft. **Max Slip/Moor** 9 ft./-
Access: Inside breakwater, look to port for private TMYB marker

Marina Facilities (*In Season/Off Season*)
Fuel: *Citgo* - Gasoline, Diesel
Slips: 54 Total, 2-5 Transient **Max LOA:** 60 ft. **Max Beam:** n/a
  Rate (*per ft.*): **Day** $1.80 **Week** $10.50 **Month** $36
  Power: 30 amp $5, **50 amp** $5, **100 amp** n/a, **200 amp** n/a
  Cable TV: No **Dockside Phone:** No
  Dock Type: Floating, Long Fingers, Wood
Moorings: 0 Total, 0 Transient **Launch:** n/a
  Rate: Day n/a **Week** n/a **Month** n/a
Heads: 2 Toilet(s), 2 Shower(s)
Laundry: None **Pay Phones:** Yes
Pump-Out: No **Fee:** n/a **Closed Heads:** Yes

Marina Operations
Owner/Manager: Donahue Family **Dockmaster:** Peter Donahue
In-Season: May-Oct, 9am-5pm **Off-Season:** Nov-Apr, Closed
After-Hours Arrival: Call in advance
Reservations: Yes **Credit Cards:** Visa/MC, Amex
Discounts: None
Pets: Welcome **Handicap Access:** No

Tide Mill Yacht Basin

191 Kirby Lane; Rye, NY 10580

Tel: (914) 967-2995 **VHF: Monitor** 68 **Talk** 68
Fax: (914) 967-2999 **Alternate Tel:** n/a
Email: tidemill@aol.com **Web:** www.tidemill.com
Nearest Town: Rye *(1.25 mi.)* **Tourist Info:** (914) 939-1900

Marina Services and Boat Supplies
Services - Docking Assistance, Concierge, Security, Trash Pick-Up, Dock
Carts **Communication -** Mail & Package Hold, Phone Messages, Fax
in/out, FedEx, AirBorne, UPS, Express Mail *(Sat Del)* **Supplies -**
OnSite: Ice *(Cube)*, Ships' Store **1-3 mi:** Bait/Tackle *(Rudys 203-531-5928)*
Boater's World *(833-8349, 8 mi.)*, Marine Discount Store *(Landfall Navigation*
3+ mi: *203 661-3176, 9 mi.)*, Propane *(Brewers BY 698-0295, 4 mi.)*,
CNG *(Brewers, 4 mi.)*

Boatyard Services
OnSite: Travelift *(35T)*, Forklift, Engine mechanic *(gas, diesel)*, Electrical
Repairs, Electronics Repairs, Hull Repairs, Rigger, Bottom Cleaning,
Brightwork, Divers, Compound, Wash & Wax, Interior Cleaning,
Woodworking, Total Refits **OnCall:** Sail Loft, Air Conditioning, Refrigeration,
Propeller Repairs, Inflatable Repairs, Life Raft Service, Upholstery, Metal
Fabrication, Awlgrip **Member:** ABBRA, ABYC
Yard Rates: $69/hr., Haul & Launch $5/ft., Power Wash $2/ft.

Restaurants and Accommodations
OnCall: Pizzeria *(Antonios 939-5137)* **Under 1 mi:** Restaurant *(Belluscios*
967-5634), Lite Fare *(Kellys 967-0868)* **1-3 mi:** Restaurant *(Koo's 921-*
9888), *(Ruby's Oyster Bar 921-4166)*, *(Rye Grille 967-0332)*, *(Café Livorno*
967-1909), *(La Panetiere 967-8140, L $19-26, Prix Fixe $34, D $27-45 Prix*
Fixe $85-90), *(Frankie & Johnnie's 925-3900)*, *(Coyote Flaco 939-6969)*,
Hotel *(Marriott Courtyard 921-1110, $100-175)*, *(Rye Hilton 939-6300)*

Recreation and Entertainment
OnSite: Picnic Area, Grills **Under 1 mi:** Playground

1-3 mi: Pool, Beach, Tennis Courts *(Sound Shore 939-1300)*, Fitness Center
(YMCA 967-6363), Horseback Riding *(Stratford Stables 939-9294)*, Movie
Theater *(Rye Ridge 939-8177)*, Park *(Playland 925-2701)*, Museum *(Square
House 967-7588)*, Cultural Attract *(Capitol Theatre 937-4126)*, Special
Events *(Wed night fireworks, Playland)* **3+ mi:** Golf Course *(Doral's
Arrowood939-5500, 5 mi.)*, Bowling *(AMF 946-8787, 8 mi.)*

Provisioning and General Services
OnCall: Gourmet Shop *(Rye Country Store 967-3450)*, Wine/Beer, Meat
Market **Under 1 mi:** Delicatessen *(Midland Ave. 967-3947)*, Liquor Store
(Vaccaros 939-4104) **1-3 mi:** Convenience Store, Supermarket *(Pathmark
937-1400, A&P)*, Bakery, Green Grocer, Fishmonger *(June & Ho's 967-
1900)*, Bank/ATM, Post Office, Catholic Church, Protestant Church,
Synagogue, Library *(Rye Free Reading Room 967-0480)*, Beauty Salon, ,
Barber Shop, Dry Cleaners, Bookstore *(Lighthouse Bookstore 967-0966)*,
Pharmacy *(CVS 921-4192)*, Newsstand, Hardware Store *(Home Depot 690-
9745)*, Florist, Clothing Store, Retail Shops, Copies Etc. *(Staples 937-8193)*

Transportation
OnCall: Rental Car *(Enterprise 937-4131)*, Taxi *(Rye Cab 967-0500)*,
Airport Limo *(Rye Airport Svc 967-3003)* **Under 1 mi:** Local Bus
1-3 mi: Bikes *(Rye Bikes 967-2849)*, Rail *(MetroNorth)*
Airport: Westchester/ LaGuardia *(7 mi./25 mi.)*

Medical Services
911 Service **OnCall:** Ambulance **1-3 mi:** Doctor, Dentist *(Family Dental
939-6555)*, Chiropractor *(Rye Chiropractic 921-3331)*, Veterinarian *(Rye-
Harrison Vet 921-2000)* **Hospital:** NY United 934-3001 *(2 mi.)*

Setting -- Behind Manursing Island, just outside Kirby Pond, is historic, picturesque TMYB's small marina and boatyard. Its signaturedeep-red, 18thC grist mill, in its bucolic setting, looks like a greeting card. It's one of the prettiest spots on the Sound and usually ends up on local real estate brochures. The grounds are attractive and well-tended. Access from the Sound is up a privately maintained deep water channel. If you can get in here, it's a lovely stop.

Marina Notes -- Services are located in the actual Tide Mill, which was originally constructed in 1770, as were the three dams. Each tide managed 5-6 hours of grinding when the sluice gate was opened. It was an active mill until the turn of the 20thC and used primarily as a BY after that -- although tending the sluice gates continued (and still does today!). Jake Senf managed the original operation and then, in the 40's, his son Reggie bought the yard with the Boardman family. It was known as Jake's BoatYard. In 1972, it was bought by Frank Donahue and the name changed to Tide Mill Yacht Basin. The Donahue family still operates it today. Full boatyard services. Heads and showers in process of being renovated.

Notable -- Charming downtown Rye, a 1.25 mile walk, has 4 blocks of upscale shops (unique and chain), several gourmet provisioning resources, salons and a growing roster of higher-end restaurants. A classic New England green is bounded by the library and the Square House (an 18thC coach stop, the state's smallest museum). MetroNorth station 1.5 miles; 37 min to Manhattan. A Kohl's anchored shopping mall is 1.5 miles. Nat'l. Historic Landmark.270-acre Art Deco Rye Playland Amusement Park is also 1.5 miles (there's a bus) - beach, pool, mini golf, rides and an ice rink where the Rangers practice.

Brewer Post Road Boat Yard

Brewer Post Road Boat Yard

155 East Boston Post Road; Mamaroneck, NY 10543

Tel: (914) 698-0295 **VHF: Monitor** 19 **Talk** 19
Fax: (914) 698-6203 **Alternate Tel:** (914) 527-0782
Email: prb@byy.com **Web:** www.byy.com/Mamaroneck
Nearest Town: Mamaroneck *(0 mi.)* **Tourist Info:** (914) 698-4400

Navigational Information
Lat: 40°57.000' **Long:** 073°44.000' **Tide:** 7.2 ft. **Current:** n/a **Chart:** 25605
Rep. Depths *(MLW):* **Entry** 11 ft. **Fuel Dock** 11 ft. **Max Slip/Moor** 11 ft./-
Access: Mamaroneck Harbor to the East Basin's first set of docks

Marina Facilities *(In Season/Off Season)*
Fuel: Gasoline, Diesel
Slips: 48 Total, 2-5 Transient **Max LOA:** 60 ft. **Max Beam:** n/a
  Rate *(per ft.):* **Day** $3.00 **Week** $12 **Month** $28
  Power: 30 amp Incl., **50 amp** Incl., **100 amp** n/a, **200 amp** n/a
  Cable TV: No **Dockside Phone:** No
  Dock Type: Floating, Long Fingers, Alongside, Concrete
Moorings: 4 Total, 1 Transient **Launch:** n/a
  Rate: Day n/a **Week** n/a **Month** n/a
Heads: 2 Toilet(s), 2 Shower(s)
Laundry: None **Pay Phones:** No
Pump-Out: OnSite, Full Service, 1 Central **Fee:** $5 **Closed Heads:** Yes

Marina Operations
Owner/Manager: Paul Muenzinger **Dockmaster:** Same
In-Season: Summer, 8am-6pm **Off-Season:** Fall-Win-Sprg, 8am-5pm
After-Hours Arrival: Pull up at gas dock
Reservations: Preferred **Credit Cards:** Visa/MC, Dscvr, Amex
Discounts: None
Pets: No **Handicap Access:** No

Marina Services and Boat Supplies
Services - Docking Assistance, Security, Trash Pick-Up, Dock Carts
Communication - Mail & Package Hold, Phone Messages, Fax in/out, FedEx, AirBorne, UPS, Express Mail *(Sat Del)* **Supplies - OnSite:** Ice *(Block, Cube)*, Ships' Store *(698-3232)*, Propane, CNG **Near:** Bait/Tackle *(Mamaroneck B&T 381-1924)* **1-3 mi:** Boater's World *(833-8349)*

Boatyard Services
OnSite: Travelift *(50T)*, Crane, Engine mechanic *(gas, diesel)*, Electrical Repairs, Hull Repairs, Rigger, Bottom Cleaning, Brightwork, Interior Cleaning, Woodworking, Metal Fabrication, Painting, Awlgrip, Total Refits **OnCall:** Electronic Sales, Electronics Repairs, Sail Loft, Air Conditioning, Refrigeration, Divers *(allowed on moorings only)*, Propeller Repairs, Inflatable Repairs, Life Raft Service, Upholstery **Near:** Launching Ramp. **Dealer for:** Mercury, Sealand, Harken, Furlex, Caterpiller, Jabsco, Maxprop, Spurs. **Member:** ABBRA, ABYC - 1 Certified Tech(s), Other Certifications: Mercury, Diesel, BSME **Yard Rates:** $40-80/hr., Haul & Launch $15/ft. *(blocking incl.)*, Power Wash $3/ft., Bottom Paint $15-17/ft. **Storage:** In-Water $26/ft./6mo., On-Land Outside $49 ft./6 mo. Inside $84/ft.

Restaurants and Accommodations
Near: Restaurant *(Jolly Trolley 698-6610, L $6-18, D $6-18, 'til 12am 7 days)*, *(Piccolo Mulino 777-0481)*, *(Coachess 835-4125)*, *(Turquoise Mediterranean 381-3693)*, *(Café Mozart 698-4166)*, *(Lum Yen 698-6881)*, *(Abis Japanese 698-8777, L $6-11, D $10-37)*, Pizzeria *(Joes Pizza & Rest 698-2829)* **3+ mi:** Hotel *(Courtyard by Marriott 921-1110, 5 mi.)*, *(Marriott Residence - New Roc Inn 694-5400, 4 mi.)*

Recreation and Entertainment
OnSite: Picnic Area, Grills **Near:** Spa, Beach, Playground, Tennis Courts *(Harbour View 698-1634)*, Fitness Center *(NYSC 381-3282)*, Jogging Paths, Boat Rentals, Roller Blade/Bike Paths, Movie Theater *(Playhouse 698-2200)*, Video Rental *(Action Video 777-3500)*, Park *(Harbor Park; Playland Amusement Park 925-2701 3.5 mi.)*, Cultural Attract *(Emelin Theater 698-0098)* **Under 1 mi:** Dive Shop **3+ mi:** Golf Course *(Westchester County 779-9827, 7 mi.)*, Bowling *(New Roc 636-3700, 5 mi.)*

Provisioning and General Services
OnSite: Hardware Store **Near:** Convenience Store *(C&L 698-7368)*, Gourmet Shop, Delicatessen *(Mercurio 381-0348)*, Liquor Store *(Cloudy Bay 698-0582)*, Green Grocer, Fishmonger *(Imperial 698-4848)*, Bank/ATM, Post Office, Catholic Church, Library *(698-1250)*, Beauty Salon, Dry Cleaners, Laundry, Bookstore *(Waldenbooks 698-6303)*, Pharmacy *(R & R 777-0357)* **Under 1 mi:** Supermarket *(A&P 381-4336, Food Emporium 698-6224)*, Health Food *(Natures Cove 381-4506)*, Copies Etc. *(UPS Store 833-1955)*

Transportation
OnCall: Taxi *(Mamaroneck Taxi 698-2000)*, Airport Limo *(Larchmont Airport Svce 777-2666)* **Under 1 mi:** Rail *(MetroNorth - 35 min to NY)*
Airport: Westchester /LaGuardia *(11mi./17mi.)*

Medical Services
911 Service **OnCall:** Ambulance **Near:** Dentist *(Family Dental 698-4410)* **Under 1 mi:** Doctor, Chiropractor *(Harbor Family 835-4545)*, Veterinarian *(Mamaroneck 777-0398)* **1-3 mi:** Holistic Services *(Therapeutic Loft 835-1390)* **Hospital:** NY United 934-3001 *(5 mi.)*

Setting -- Deep into Mamaroneck Harbor, at the head of well protected East Basin, this service-oriented boatyard is easily recognizable by the large sheds which dwarf its docks. A mooring field fills the center of the basin. Views are mostly of boats - at the docks, in the water, on the hard, in the sheds. A small gazebo perched above the docks is the only concession to "amenities." Downtown Mamaroneck is less than a block.

Marina Notes -- This excellent, small, full-service boat yard -- where customer service reigns -- is the original Brewer facility; it's considered the flagship of the 22 marina chain, although it has the smallest footprint and fewest amenities. It also houses their administrative offices. Brewers Preferred Customer Card Program. Laundry is planned. Note: No pets allowed. Very nice tile heads - full bathrooms. Pump-out free to customers. Onsite is Brewer's Hardware -- one of the best-stocked chandleries on the Coast (as well as a regular hardware store); it's where mariners head for just the right latch and good advice. There's also a separate marine-oriented wood-working shop that both sells supplies and does the work. Next door are Derektor Shipyard and McMichaels Boatyard.

Notable -- Immediately adjacent is the Jolly Trolley restaurant (formerly Charlie Brown's); it keeps late hours and specializes in pub grub & sports TV. Brewer's is a perfect stop if you need anything - for boat or crew. Nearby Mamaroneck Avenue's Italian roots are evident in some of the specialty food stores and eateries. There's a spirited six block stretch of interesting restaurants, movies, boutiques, clothing shops, books, many antique galleries, services, delis, markets, and gourmet shops, more on the side streets -- plus 2 supermarkets are 0.8 mi. Great hiking trails at the Marshland Conservancy about 3 mi. north.

Navigational Information

Lat: 40°56.640' **Long:** 073°43.982' **Tide:** 7.9 ft. **Current:** 2 kt. **Chart:** 25605
Rep. Depths (*MLW*): **Entry** 8 ft. **Fuel Dock** n/a **Max Slip/Moor** 8 ft./15 ft.
Access: R42 to Mamaroneck Harbor's West Basin

Marina Facilities *(In Season/Off Season)*

Fuel: No
Slips: 400 Total, 4 Transient **Max LOA:** 50 ft. **Max Beam:** 20 ft.
  Rate *(per ft.)*: **Day** n/a **Week** n/a **Month** n/a
  Power: 30 amp n/a, **50 amp** n/a, **100 amp** n/a, **200 amp** n/a
  Cable TV: No **Dockside Phone:** Yes
  Dock Type: Floating, Pilings, Wood
Moorings: 250 Total, 4 Transient **Launch:** n/a, Dinghy Dock
  Rate: Day Free **Week** n/a **Month** n/a
Heads: 4 Toilet(s)
Laundry: None **Pay Phones:** No
Pump-Out: Self Service, 2 Central, 4 InSlip **Fee:** Free **Closed Heads:** Yes

Marina Operations

Owner/Manager: Mamaroneck **Dockmaster:** James Mancusi (Hrbrmaster)
In-Season: May-Nov 30, 9am-4pm **Off-Season:** Dec-May, 9am-4pm
After-Hours Arrival: Tie up to guest dock on either basin; call 777-7744
Reservations: First come, first served **Credit Cards:** n/a
Discounts: None
Pets: Welcome **Handicap Access:** No

Harbor Island Municipal Marina

PO Box 369; 123 Mamaroneck Avenue; Mamaroneck, NY 10543

Tel: (914) 777-7744 **VHF: Monitor** 16 **Talk** 8
Fax: (914) 777-7744 **Alternate Tel:** n/a
Email: n/a **Web:** n/a
Nearest Town: Mamaroneck *(0.1 mi.)* **Tourist Info:** (914) 698-4400

Marina Services and Boat Supplies

Supplies - OnSite: Bait/Tackle **Near:** Ships' Store *(Brewer's 698-3232)*, Propane *(Brewers)*, CNG *(Brewers)* **Under 1 mi:** Boater's World *(833-8349)*

Boatyard Services

OnSite: Launching Ramp **Nearest Yard:** Brewer Post Road Boat Yard (914) 698-0295

Restaurants and Accommodations

OnCall: Pizzeria *(Sal's 381-2022)* **Near:** Restaurant *(Mamaroneck Diner 698-3564, pizza also)*, *(Piccolo Mulino 777-0481)*, *(Jolly Trolley 698-6610, L & D $6-18, 7 days 'til midnight)*, *(Turquoise Mediterranean 381-3693)*, *(Il Castello 835-9066)*, *(Down By the Bay 381-6939)*, *(Café Mozart 698-4166)*, *(Le Provencal 777-2324, L $6-11, D $17-25)* **Under 1 mi:** Restaurant *(Nautilus Diner 833-1320)* **1-3 mi:** Seafood Shack *(Crab Shanty 698-1352)* **3+ mi:** Hotel *(Ramada 576-3700, 4 mi.)*, *(Renaissance 694-5400, 5 mi.)*, Inn/B&B *(Courtyard by Marriott 921-1110, 5 mi.)*

Recreation and Entertainment

OnSite: Beach, Playground, Tennis Courts *(Harbor Island 698-1634)*, Boat Rentals, Park, Special Events *(Holiday and Week-end Concerts)* **Near:** Fitness Center *(NYSC 381-3282)*, Movie Theater *(Mamaroneck Playhouse 698-2200)*, Cultural Attract *(Emelin Theater 698-0098)* **Under 1 mi:** Video Rental *(Blockbuster 833-1002)* **1-3 mi:** Horseback Riding *(Kentucky Stables 381-2825)*, Other *(Playland Amusement Park 925-2701)* **3+ mi:** Golf Course *(Westchester County 779-9827, 7 mi.)*, Bowling *(New Roc Bowling 636-3700, 5 mi.)*, Museum *(Rye Square House, 4 mi.)*

Provisioning and General Services

Near: Convenience Store *(C&L Grocery 698-7368)*, Gourmet Shop, Delicatessen *(Pisano Bros 381-4402)*, Health Food *(Natures Cove 381-4506)*, Wine/Beer, Liquor Store *(Cloudy Bay Wines & Spirits 698-0582)*, Bakery, Fishmonger *(Imperial 698-4848)*, Meat Market, Bank/ATM, Post Office, Catholic Church, Protestant Church, Library *(Mamaroneck 698-1250)*, Beauty Salon, Barber Shop, Dry Cleaners, Laundry, Bookstore *(Waldenbooks 698-6303)*, Pharmacy *(CVS 381-4550)*, Newsstand, Hardware Store *(Brewer's)*, Florist, Clothing Store, Retail Shops **Under 1 mi:** Supermarket *(A&P 381-4336, Food Emporium 698-6224)*, Farmers' Market *(Mangone's 698-3865)*, Green Grocer, Synagogue, Copies Etc. *(Pronto Printer 381-6404)*

Transportation

OnCall: Rental Car *(Enterprise 381-1199, Avis 834-8883 2 mi.)*, Taxi *(Mamaroneck Taxi 698-2000)*, Airport Limo *(Larchmont Airport Svce 777-2666)* **Near:** Local Bus, Rail *(Metro North to NY City)*
Airport: Westchester/LaGuardia *(11 mi./17 mi.)*

Medical Services

911 Service **OnCall:** Ambulance **Near:** Doctor *(Harbor Immediate Medical Care 381-2091)*, Dentist *(Family Dental 698-4410)*, Chiropractor *(Harbor Family 835-4545)* **Under 1 mi:** Veterinarian *(Mamaroneck Vet 777-0398)* **1-3 mi:** Holistic Services *(Therapeutic Loft 835-1390)*
Hospital: Sound Shore 637-5463 *(5 mi.)*

PHOTOS ON CD-ROM: 9

Setting -- As you enter Mamaroneck Harbor - down the main channel -- the peninsula known as Harbor Island is directly ahead. The Town of Mamaroneck maintains complimentary guest moorings in both the West Basin (on the port side of the peninsula) and in the East Basin (on the starboard side). There are also some guest slips in each basin. Harbor Island is a 45-acre municipal park with a beach. The town shares East Basin with 3 large boatyards and 4 yacht/beach clubs -- it's pretty crowded and feels commercial. West Basin is more open and prettier, home to some small boat marinas.

Marina Notes -- Moorings and slips are free -- first come, first served. The harbormaster (Ch.16) can be found east of the West Basin's floating dock -- where the majority of slips and moorings are located. Behind the Harbormaster's office is the Coast Guard Auxiliary. A "town pier", for short tie-ups, and a free, self-serve pump-out station are both located on the western side of Harbor Island in the East Basin. Harbor Island is also home to a state-of-the-art sewage treatment plant. The smaller boat marinas in West Basin may also have a free transient slip; try Nichols (698-6065) or McMichael Rushmore (381-2100).

Notable -- During the season, Harbor Park hosts free concerts and cultural events. Across the street, Down By the Bay Restaurant is housed in James Fenimore Cooper's early 19thC home. A short walk to Mamaroneck Avenue yields a six block stretch of restaurants, movies, boutiques, clothing shops, books, many antique galleries, services, delis, markets, and gourmet shops. If you need anything, this is the place. Brewer's Hardware is a maritime version of the classic, small-town shop - with very knowledgeable personnel. Two supermarkets are within a mile. MetroNorth station is half a mile away: 35 min. to NY.

New Rochelle Municipal Marina

22 Pelham Road; New Rochelle, NY 10805

Tel: (914) 235-6930 **VHF: Monitor** 16/9 **Talk** 9
Fax: (914) 235-8268 **Alternate Tel:** n/a
Email: sgugliar@ci.new-rochelle.ny.us **Web:** n/a
Nearest Town: New Rochelle *(0.4 mi.)* **Tourist Info:** (914) 632-5700

Navigational Information

Lat: 40°54.600' **Long:** 073°46.190' **Tide:** 8 ft. **Current:** 4 kt. **Chart:** 12366
Rep. Depths *(MLW):* **Entry** 8 ft. **Fuel Dock** 15 ft. **Max Slip/Moor** 12 ft./-
Access: Echo Bay to Beaufort Pt, RN 10, into the basin

Marina Facilities *(In Season/Off Season)*

Fuel: Gasoline, Diesel
Slips: 300 Total, 12 Transient **Max LOA:** 45 ft. **Max Beam:** n/a
 Rate *(per ft.):* **Day** $2.00 **Week** $5.00 **Month** $10.00
 Power: 30 amp Incl., **50 amp** n/a, **100 amp** n/a, **200 amp** n/a
 Cable TV: No **Dockside Phone:** No
 Dock Type: Floating, Wood
Moorings: 150 Total, 2 Transient **Launch:** None, Dinghy Dock
 Rate: Day $25 **Week** n/a **Month** n/a
Heads: 8 Toilet(s), 4 Shower(s)
Laundry: 3 Washer(s), 2 Dryer(s) **Pay Phones:** Yes, 2
Pump-Out: OnSite, 1 Central **Fee:** Free **Closed Heads:** Yes

Marina Operations

Owner/Manager: Capt. Sal Gugliara (Harbormaster) **Dockmaster:** Same
In-Season: Year-Round, 8am - 4pm **Off-Season:** n/a
After-Hours Arrival: Call in advance for instructions
Reservations: Yes **Credit Cards:** Visa/MC
Discounts: None
Pets: Welcome, Dog Walk Area **Handicap Access:** No

Marina Services and Boat Supplies

Services - Security *(24 Hrs.)* **Supplies - OnSite:** Ships' Store **Near:** Ice *(Block, Cube)*, Bait/Tackle *(Hudson Park Bait & Tackle 235-0050)*, Live Bait *(Worms, clams)* **Under 1 mi:** Marine Discount Store *(Post Marine 235-9800)* **1-3 mi:** Propane *(Almstead 576-3253)*

Boatyard Services

OnSite: Travelift *(20T)*, Forklift, Engine mechanic *(gas, diesel)*, Electrical Repairs, Electronic Sales, Electronics Repairs, Bottom Cleaning

Restaurants and Accommodations

OnSite: Restaurant *(On the Waterfront 632-9625, L $5-9, D $10-18, burgers, pasta, seafood, etc.)* **Near:** Restaurant *(Empire Work 632-5688)*, *(Frank & John's 636-6611)*, *(Brunello Trattoria 636-8237)*, *(Pizza Hut 576-0147)*, Fast Food *(Mc Donald's/Taco Bell)*, Lite Fare *(Dudley's Parkview 636-9491)*
Under 1 mi: Restaurant *(Mama Francasca 636-1229)*, *(Fratelli 633-1690)*, Pizzeria *(Centre Pizza 636-1817, no delivery)*, Hotel *(Ramada 576-3700, $150-180)*, *(Marriott Residence - New Roc 636-7888)*

Recreation and Entertainment

OnSite: Special Events *(Harbor Festival last week-end in Aug.)*
Near: Beach, Picnic Area, Playground, Fitness Center *(Bally)*, Park *(Hudson)*
Under 1 mi: Bowling *(New Roc Bowling 636-3700)*, Fishing Charter, Group Fishing Boat, Movie Theater *(New Roc City 18 Cinemas 235-3737/IMAX 576-5757)*, Video Rental *(Great American Video 633-4013)*, Video Arcade
1-3 mi: Tennis Courts *(Cliff Street Racquet Club 576-9000)*, Horseback Riding *(Pelham Bit Stables 718-885-9723)*, Boat Rentals, Museum *(Thomas Paine 632-5376)* **3+ mi:** Golf Course *(Split Rock 718-885-1258, 4 mi.)*

Provisioning and General Services

Near: Convenience Store *(DB Mart 636-5676)*, Supermarket *(A&P 636-9437)*, Delicatessen *(Loupinos Deli 654-1049)*, Wine/Beer, Green Grocer, Fishmonger, Meat Market, Bank/ATM, Post Office, Catholic Church, Synagogue, Beauty Salon, Barber Shop, Dry Cleaners, Laundry *(Laundry Connection 654-1295)*, Pharmacy *(CVS 654-8819)*, Newsstand **Under 1 mi:** Liquor Store *(Cloudy Bay Wines & Spirits 698-0582)*, Bakery, Farmers' Market *(Fridays 9am-1pm)*, Protestant Church, Library *(New Rochelle PL 632-7878)*, Bookstore *(Book Cafe 637-7092)*, Hardware Store *(Home Depot 712-0392)*, Florist, Retail Shops *(New Roc City)*, Buying Club *(Costco 632-3459)*, Copies Etc. *(Adrean Printing 636-0200)* **1-3 mi:** Health Food

Transportation

OnCall: Rental Car *(Enterprise 381-1199/ Budget 632-7400 1 mi.)*, Taxi *(Yellow Bird 235-5858)*, Airport Limo *(Bayview Airport Svces 834-0500)*
Near: Local Bus **Under 1 mi:** Rail *(MetroNorth & Amtrak)*
Airport: Westchester/La Guardia *(12 mi./17 mi.)*

Medical Services

911 Service **OnCall:** Ambulance **Near:** Doctor *(Metro Med 633-1020)*, Dentist *(Torres 235-7369)*, Chiropractor *(New Rochelle Chiropractic 636-4113)* **Under 1 mi:** Veterinarian *(New Rochelle Animal Hosp. 636-8106)*
1-3 mi: Holistic Services **Hospital:** Sound Shore 632-5000 *(1 mi.)*

Setting -- At the head of Echo Bay, around Beaufort Point to port, is this crowded, active municipal facility tucked into a well protected basin. The marina sits on 6 acres of shorefront; its most western edge is a cliff and ancillary services and a restaurant sit almost a story above the dock level. A large, white, 2-story concrete building houses the harbormaster's office and services; on its roof is a parking lot. The general ambience is urban.

Marina Notes -- New York State recently approved dredging approx. 30,000 cubic yards of sand, silt and sediment from the harbor; goal is 8 feet mlw. In 1945, the City bought this property, a local coal/lumber company, to develop the marina -- which may explain the "cliff". A number of marine-support services are located here, including G&R Marine (632-4020). Most heads are on the lower end of "municipal" but a brand new unisex, handicapped-accessible tile bath was installed in '02. Great strides are also being made with landscaping and a much needed spruce-up. Consider cabs after dark.

Notable -- New York Sailing School (235-6052 - nysailing@nyss.com) makes its home here. Pan Aqua's recreational dive boat leaves from here, too (800-434-0884). Across the harbor is very casual Dudley's which serves light fare and pub food. Within a mile are some good provisioning resources. The perfect rainy day retreat is just 0.6 mi: New Roc City -- a new 1.2 million sq. ft. multi-level shopping and entertainment mall -- fun house, 18-plex movie, IMAX, rides, Marriott Residence hotel, NHL size skating arena, Bally's fitness, restaurants, a supermarket, etc. It's a 0.8 mi. walk to the Costco Buying Club and Home Depot. The RR station is a 10-min walk - both Metro North commuter trains to Manhattan (31 min.) and Amtrak Northeast Corridor trains.

Navigational Information
Lat: 40°53.710' **Long:** 073°46.960' **Tide:** 7 ft. **Current:** n/a **Chart:** 12367
Rep. Depths (MLW): Entry 11 ft. **Fuel Dock** 11 ft. **Max Slip/Moor** 11 ft./-
Access: New Rochelle Harbor - starboard at Neptune Is., first docks to port

Marina Facilities *(In Season/Off Season)*
Fuel: *ATI 93 Octane* - Gasoline, Diesel, High-Speed Pumps
Slips: 150 Total, 50 Transient **Max LOA:** 65 ft. **Max Beam:** n/a
  Rate *(per ft.):* **Day** $1.50 **Week** Inq. **Month** Inq.
  Power: 30 amp Incl., **50 amp** Incl., **100 amp** n/a, **200 amp** n/a
  Cable TV: Yes, Incl. **Dockside Phone:** Yes Longer term only
  Dock Type: Fixed, Floating, Long Fingers, Pilings
Moorings: 0 Total, 0 Transient **Launch:** n/a
  Rate: Day n/a **Week** n/a **Month** n/a
Heads: 4 Toilet(s), 4 Shower(s)
Laundry: 4 Washer(s), 4 Dryer(s) **Pay Phones:** Yes, 2
Pump-Out: OnSite, Full Service, 1 Central **Fee:** Free **Closed Heads:** Yes

Marina Operations
Owner/Manager: n/a **Dockmaster:** Joey Aquino
In-Season: Year-Round, 8am-5pm **Off-Season:** n/a
After-Hours Arrival: Call ahead or pull up to gas dock.
Reservations: Yes **Credit Cards:** Visa/MC, Amex
Discounts: None
Pets: Welcome, Dog Walk Area **Handicap Access:** No

Wright Island Marina

290 Drake Avenue; New Rochelle, NY 10801

Tel: (914) 636-2628 **VHF: Monitor** n/a **Talk** n/a
Fax: (914) 633-8333 **Alternate Tel:** (914) 235-8014
Email: n/a **Web:** n/a
Nearest Town: New Rochelle *(0.5 mi.)* **Tourist Info:** (914) 632-5700

Marina Services and Boat Supplies
Services - Docking Assistance, Security, Trash Pick-Up, Dock Carts
Communication - Mail & Package Hold, Fax in/out, FedEx, AirBorne, UPS, Express Mail *(Sat Del)* **Supplies - Near:** Ice *(Cube)*, Ships' Store, Bait/Tackle **1-3 mi:** Marine Discount Store *(Post Marine 235-9800)*, Propane *(Almstead Propane 576-3253)*, CNG *(Brewers 698-0295)*

Boatyard Services
OnSite: Travelift *(50T)*, Engine mechanic *(gas, diesel)*, Electrical Repairs, Electronics Repairs, Hull Repairs, Bottom Cleaning, Brightwork, Refrigeration **OnCall:** Rigger

Restaurants and Accommodations
OnSite: Restaurant *(Marina Seafood Grille 235-5252, L $7-12, D $17-22, Sun Brunch $10)* **OnCall:** Pizzeria *(Happy Days 723-8855)* **Near:** Restaurant *(Hong Kong 576-7979)*, *(Mamma Francesca Trattoria 636-1229, D $13-19)*, *(Tokyo Bay 576-9838)* **Under 1 mi:** Restaurant *(Arlechino 472-1233)*, *(Italian Village 472-4400)*, *(Il Cigno 472-8484)*, Seafood Shack *(Leno's Clam Bar 636-9869)* **1-3 mi:** Hotel *(Ramada 576-3700, $80-125)*, *(Marriott New Roc. Residence Inn 636-7888, 124 suites)*, Inn/B&B *(Soundview Manor 421-9080)*

Recreation and Entertainment
OnSite: Pool, Beach, Picnic Area, Grills **Near:** Playground, Volleyball, Boat Rentals, Roller Blade/Bike Paths **Under 1 mi:** Dive Shop, Fitness Center *(Evolution Fitness 723-8006)*, Video Rental *(Great American Video 633-4013)* **1-3 mi:** Tennis Courts *(Cliff St. Racquet Club 576-9000)*, Golf Course

(Split Rock 718-885-1258), Horseback Riding *(Pelham Bit Stables 718-885-9723)*, Bowling *(New Roc Bowling 636-3700)*, Movie Theater *(New Roc City 18 Cinemas 235-3737/IMAX 576-5757)*, Park *(Pelham Bay Park)*, Museum *(Thomas Paine 632-5376)*

Provisioning and General Services
Near: Market *(Met Foods 636-0720)*, Gourmet Shop, Delicatessen *(New Marina Deli 576-8580)*, Wine/Beer, Liquor Store *(Shore Road Liquors 235-7762)*, Bakery *(Hacker's Bakery 654-1099)*, Fishmonger, Meat Market, Bank/ATM, Post Office, Catholic Church, Beauty Salon, Dry Cleaners, Laundry, Newsstand **Under 1 mi:** Supermarket *(A&P 636-9437)*, Library *(New Rochelle PL 632-7878)*, Bookstore *(Book Cafe 637-7092)*, Pharmacy *(CVS 235-7171)*, Hardware Store *(Modern 632-8060, Home Depot)*, Buying Club *(Costco 632-3459)*, Copies Etc. *(AMC Printing 632-3969)* **1-3 mi:** Farmers' Market *(Fri 9am-1pm)*, Green Grocer *(Viva Ranch 632-6496)*

Transportation
OnCall: Rental Car *(Enterprise 997-9484/ Avis 725-1941 - 2 mi.)*, Taxi *(Central Taxi 723-0016)*, Airport Limo *(Metro Airport & Limousine 654-0079)* **Near:** Local Bus **1-3 mi:** Bikes *(Pelham Bicycle Center 738-3338)*, Rail *(MetroNorth & Amtrak)* **Airport:** Westchester/LaGuardia *(25 mi./17 mi.)*

Medical Services
911 Service **Near:** Doctor *(Russell 654-0722)*, Ambulance **Under 1 mi:** Dentist *(Scarsdale Family Dental 722-7667)*, Chiropractor *(Chiropractic 636-5533)*, Veterinarian *(New Rochelle Animal 636-8106)* **Hospital:** Sound Shore 637-5463 *(2 mi.)*

Setting -- Enter New Rochelle Harbor at R 14 and bear to starboard at Neptune Island. Wright Island Marina is directly to port. While the views, as you enter, tend toward the urban, once inside, the views out to the Sound are really quite spectacular. The most noticeable landmark is the two story Marina restaurant building directly ahead as you turn into the basin. It sits on a peninsula -- shared with the pool and parking lot -- and is surrounded on two sides by docks.

Marina Notes -- A full-service boatyard is on-site. A number of marine services have offices on site. Large winter storage yard. Some liveaboards. This is a "cell phone" operation; they don't monitor VHF. The Marina Seafood Grill - inside and deck dining -- with wonderful water views (Tue-Thu 12-10pm, Fri-Sat 12-11pm, Sun 12-3, 4-9) has music and dancing on Fri & Sat, Sun Brunch and an outdoor Tiki bar on week-ends. Closed Jan-Mar. The pool is nicely done and is a good spot to watch the boat traffic and enjoy the scenery (although it is part of the scenery from the restaurant deck).

Notable -- Once out of the marina, the urban environment is real. Many services are quite close by. A small, but well-equipped strip mall is 0.25 mi. -- with Italian restaurant, ice cream shop, deli, Chinese restaurant, dry cleaners, liquor/wine store, stationery shop, nail salon, Met Supermarket, and a full-service laundromat. Anything else you might need is within a mile. 1.7 miles to New Roc City, a huge retail and entertainment center with an 18-plex movie theater, oversize ice rink, bowling, the Tower Space Shot ride, an assortment of eateries, a supermarket, retail shops, bowling, a Marriott, etc. Take cabs after dark. The Amtrak & MetroNorth stop is 1.5 mi. away - 30 min. to Manhattan

Imperial Yacht Club

583 Davenport Avenue; New Rochelle, NY 10805

Tel: (914) 636-1122 **VHF: Monitor** n/a **Talk** n/a
Fax: (914) 636-0842 **Alternate Tel:** n/a
Email: n/a **Web:** n/a
Nearest Town: New Rochelle *(2 mi.)* **Tourist Info:** (914) 632-5700

Navigational Information
Lat: 40°53.520' **Long:** 073°46.620' **Tide:** 6 ft. **Current:** n/a **Chart:** 13266
Rep. Depths *(MLW):* **Entry** 13 ft. **Fuel Dock** 9 ft. **Max Slip/Moor** 13 ft./-
Access: New Rochelle Harbor, a hard turn to starboard, at nun R14

Marina Facilities *(In Season/Off Season)*
Fuel: *Citgo* - Gasoline, Diesel
Slips: 90 Total, 5-10 Transient **Max LOA:** 70 ft. **Max Beam:** n/a
  Rate *(per ft.):* **Day** $2.00/1.00 **Week** Inq. **Month** Inq.
  Power: 30 amp $5, **50 amp** $5, **100 amp** n/a, **200 amp** n/a
  Cable TV: Yes, Incl.* **Dockside Phone:** No
  Dock Type: Floating, Long Fingers
Moorings: 0 Total, 0 Transient **Launch:** n/a, Dinghy Dock
  Rate: Day n/a **Week** n/a **Month** n/a
Heads: 2 Toilet(s), 5 Shower(s)
Laundry: 2 Washer(s), 2 Dryer(s), Book Exchange **Pay Phones:** Yes, 2
Pump-Out: No **Fee:** n/a **Closed Heads:** Yes

Marina Operations
Owner/Manager: Anthony Giacobbe **Dockmaster:** Johanna Giacobbe
In-Season: May-Sep, 8am-5pm **Off-Season:** Oct-Apr, 9am-5pm
After-Hours Arrival: Tie up at fuel dock
Reservations: Yes **Credit Cards:** Visa/MC
Discounts: None
Pets: Welcome, Dog Walk Area **Handicap Access:** No

Marina Services and Boat Supplies
Services - Security, Trash Pick-Up **Communication -** Mail & Package
Hold, Phone Messages, Fax in/out, FedEx, AirBorne, UPS, Express Mail
(Sat Del) **Supplies -** 1-3 mi: Ships' Store *(Post Marine 235-9800)*,
Bait/Tackle *(Hudson Park 235-0050)*, Propane *(Almstead 576-3253)*
3+ mi: CNG *(Brewer Hardware 698-3232, 5 mi.)*

Boatyard Services
OnSite: Travelift *(70T open end)*, Forklift *(30T Pos-Neg)*, Crane *(15T)*,
Engine mechanic *(gas, diesel)*, Electrical Repairs, Electronics Repairs, Hull
Repairs, Bottom Cleaning, Brightwork, Air Conditioning, Refrigeration,
Compound, Wash & Wax, Propeller Repairs **Dealer for:** Chrysler/Mercury.
Yard Rates: $85-90/hr. **Storage:** In-Water $50/ft., On-Land $50/ft.**

Restaurants and Accommodations
OnSite: Restaurant *(Sparky's L $6-13, D $14-22, Noon-9pm, seasonal
only)* **OnCall:** Pizzeria *(Modern)* **Near:** Restaurant *(Marina Restaurant
235-5252, L $7-12, D $17-22, by dinghy)*, *(Castaways 633-8900, L $6-13,
D$16-27)*, Pizzeria *(Pizza Centre 636-1817)* **Under 1 mi:** Restaurant
(Glen Island Harbour 636-6500), *(Frank and Johns 636-6611)*, *(Mamma
Francesca Trattoria 636-1229, D $13-19)*, Seafood Shack *(Lenos Clam Bar
636-9869)* **1-3 mi:** Motel *(Marriott New Roc Residence 636-7888)*,
Hotel *(Ramada 576-3600, $150-180)*

Recreation and Entertainment
OnSite: Pool, Tennis Courts **Near:** Jogging Paths, Roller Blade/Bike
Paths **Under 1 mi:** Playground, Video Rental *(Great American 633-4013)*,

1-3 mi: Golf Course *(Split Rock 718-885-1258)*, Fitness Center *(Ballys at
New Roc)*, Horseback Riding *(Pelham Bit Stables 718-885-9723)*, Bowling
(New Roc 636-3700), Fishing Charter, Movie Theater *(New Roc City 235-
3737)*, Video Arcade, Museum *(Thomas Paine 632-5376)*

Provisioning and General Services
OnSite: Laundry **Near:** Market *(Met Foods 636-0720)* **Under 1 mi:**
Supermarket *(A&P 636-9437)*, Delicatessen *(New Marina Deli 576-8580)*,
Liquor Store *(Shore Road Liquors 235-7762)*, Bank/ATM, Newsstand
1-3 mi: Gourmet Shop, Wine/Beer, Bakery, Farmers' Market *(Fri 9am-1pm)*,
Green Grocer, Post Office, Catholic Church, Protestant Church, Synagogue,
Library *(New Rochelle PL 632-7878)*, Beauty Salon, Barber Shop, Dry
Cleaners, Bookstore *(Book Cafe 637-7092)*, Pharmacy *(CVS or Rite Aid 235-
3400)*, Hardware Store *(Home Depot 235-7575)*, Florist, Buying Club
(Costco), Copies Etc. *(AMC Printing 632-3969)*

Transportation
OnCall: Rental Car *(Enterprise 637-9271, National 946-9080 1 mi.)*, Taxi
(City Taxi 633-4500), Airport Limo *(Metro Airport & Limousine 654-0079)*
Near: Local Bus **1-3 mi:** Rail *(Metro North & Amtrak)*
Airport: LaGuardia *(17 mi.)*

Medical Services
911 Service **OnCall:** Ambulance **Near:** Dentist *(McCosker/Reich 636-
3042)* **Under 1 mi:** Doctor *(Russell 654-0722)*, Veterinarian *(New Rochelle
Animal Hosp. 636-8106)* **1-3 mi:** Chiropractor *(New Rochelle Chiropractic
636-4113)*, Holistic Services *(Metro Med 633-1020)*
Hospital: Sound Shore Medical Center 632-5000 *2 mi.*

Setting -- New Rochelle Harbor is a long, narrow basin with an urban, built-up environment on its western shore and a chock-a-block line-up of marina
and club docks on its prettier residential eastern shore, known as Davenport Neck. The first set of docks to starboard belongs to the Imperial Yacht Club.
Its inviting pool, surrounded by umbrellaed tables, overlooks the docks. A two story restaurant building (with an alfresco terrace) overlooks the pool. A nicely
shrubbed tennis court is nearby. The overall effect is neat, tidy and well-cared; there's a thoughtful hand here.

Marina Notes -- *Not all docks have cable, so ask. **Dry storage rates include haul & launch, blocking, and power wash. Full-service boatyard with 24-hour
emergency haul-out and an active fuel dock. Family owned and operated since 1976; the Giacobbes live onsite! 75-ft. Olympic size pool and tennis court. The
views across the harbor are mostly of apartment buildings. Sparky's Restaurant has an Italian American menu, and serves lunch and dinner from noon 'til
9pm.

Notable -- Davenport Neck is home to clubs, marinas, and lovely homes. Many ethnic shops, markets and restaurants are a 5 minute cab ride in downtown
New Rochelle, and a well-supplied strip mall is on Shore Road a short dinghy ride across the harbor. Wright Island's Marina Restaurant encourages dock and
dine. It's 1.7 mi. to New Roc City, a new 1.2 million square-foot retail and entertainment center, also "downtown"; it promises a plethora of amusements from an
ice rink to bowling, an 18-screen theater, IMAX, retail shops, eateries, and the famous Tower Space Shot Ride -- plus a supermarket and a Marriott Hotel.

Navigational Information
Lat: 40°53.740' **Long:** 073°46.620' **Tide:** 7 ft. **Current:** n/a **Chart:** 12367
Rep. Depths *(MLW)*: **Entry** 14 ft. **Fuel Dock** 8 ft. **Max Slip/Moor** 8 ft./-
Access: New Rochelle Harbor, hard turn to starboard at R14

Marina Facilities *(In Season/Off Season)*
Fuel: Gasoline, Diesel
Slips: 100 Total, 2-3 Transient **Max LOA:** 65 ft. **Max Beam:** n/a
Rate *(per ft.)*: **Day** $2.00 **Week** Inq. **Month** Inq.
Power: 30 amp $5, **50 amp** $10, **100 amp** n/a, **200 amp** n/a
Cable TV: Yes, Incl. **Dockside Phone:** Yes
Dock Type: Floating, Long Fingers, Pilings
Moorings: 0 Total, 0 Transient **Launch:** n/a
Rate: Day n/a **Week** n/a **Month** n/a
Heads: 4 Toilet(s), 4 Shower(s)
Laundry: 2 Washer(s), 2 Dryer(s) **Pay Phones:** Yes
Pump-Out: OnSite, Full Service, 1 Central **Fee:** Free **Closed Heads:** Yes

Marina Operations
Owner/Manager: Alan Mechanic **Dockmaster:** Same
In-Season: Year-Round, 8am-6pm **Off-Season:** n/a
After-Hours Arrival: Call ahead
Reservations: Yes **Credit Cards:** Visa/MC, Amex
Discounts: None
Pets: Welcome, Dog Walk Area **Handicap Access:** No

Marina Services and Boat Supplies
Services - Docking Assistance, Trash Pick-Up, Dock Carts, 3 Phase
Communication - Mail & Package Hold, Phone Messages, Fax in/out,
FedEx, AirBorne, UPS, Express Mail *(Sat Del)* **Supplies - OnSite:** Ice
(Cube) **Under 1 mi:** Ships' Store, Bait/Tackle *(Hudson Park Bait & Tackle
235-0050)* **1-3 mi:** Marine Discount Store *(Post Marine 235-9800)*, Propane
(Almstead 576-3253), CNG *(Brewer 98-0295)*

Boatyard Services
OnSite: Travelift *(35T)*, Engine mechanic *(gas, diesel)*, Electrical Repairs,
Electronics Repairs, Hull Repairs, Bottom Cleaning, Brightwork, Propeller
Repairs **OnCall:** Rigger, Air Conditioning, Refrigeration **Near:** Electronic
Sales.

Restaurants and Accommodations
OnSite: Restaurant *(Castaways 633-8900, L $4-13, D $16-27)*
OnCall: Pizzeria *(Pete's 633-1777)* **Under 1 mi:** Restaurant *(Frank &
Johns 636-6611)*, *(Tokyo Bay 576-9838)*, *(Marina Restaurant 235-5252,
L $7-12, D $15-22)*, *(Waterfront 632-9625)*, *(Mamma Francesca Trattoria
636-1229, D $13-19, dinghy)* **1-3 mi:** Motel *(Marriott 367-7888)*, Hotel
(Ramada 763-3700, $150-180), Inn/B&B *(Wonder View Inn 288-3358)*

Recreation and Entertainment
OnSite: Pool, Picnic Area, Volleyball, Tennis Courts **Near:** Jogging Paths,
Roller Blade/Bike Paths **Under 1 mi:** Playground, Video Rental *(Great
American Video 633-4013)* **1-3 mi:** Fitness Center *(NYSC 834-7700)*,
Horseback Riding *(Pelham Bit Stables 718-885-9723)*, Bowling *(New Roc*

Castaways Yacht Club

425 Davenport Avenue; New Rochelle, NY 10805

Tel: (914) 636-8444 **VHF: Monitor** n/a **Talk** n/a
Fax: (914) 636-3130 **Alternate Tel:** n/a
Email: n/a **Web:** n/a
Nearest Town: New Rochelle *(2 mi.)* **Tourist Info:** (914) 632-5700

City 636-3700), Movie Theater *(New Roc City Cinemas 235-3737, IMAX
576-5757)*, Video Arcade, Park, Museum *(Thomas Paine 632-5376)*,
Cultural Attract **3+ mi:** Golf Course *(Split Rock 718-885-1258, 4 mi.)*

Provisioning and General Services
Near: Market *(Met Foods 636-0720)* **Under 1 mi:** Supermarket *(A&P 636-
9437)*, Delicatessen *(New Marina Deli 576-8580)*, Wine/Beer, Liquor Store
(Shore Road Liquors 235-7762), Bank/ATM, Pharmacy *(CVS 654-8819)*,
Newsstand, Hardware Store *(Modern 632-8060)*, Florist, Clothing Store,
Retail Shops, Copies Etc. *(AMC Printing 632-3969)* **1-3 mi:** Gourmet Shop,
Bakery, Farmers' Market *(Fri, 9am-1pm)*, Green Grocer *(Viva Ranch 632-
6496)*, Fishmonger, Meat Market, Post Office, Catholic Church, Protestant
Church, Synagogue, Library *(New Rochelle PL 632-7878)*, Beauty Salon,
Barber Shop, Dry Cleaners, Laundry, Bookstore *(Book Cafe 637-7092)*,
Buying Club *(Costco 632-3459)*

Transportation
OnCall: Rental Car *(Enterprise 381-1199, Budget 632-7400 1 mi.)*, Taxi
(Yellow Bird 235-5858), Airport Limo *(Bayview 834-0500)* **Near:** Local Bus
1-3 mi: Rail *(Metro North & Amtrak)* **Airport:** LaGuardia *(17 mi.)*

Medical Services
911 Service **OnCall:** Ambulance **Near:** Doctor *(Russell 654-0722)*, Dentist
(McCosker/Reich 636-3042), Chiropractor *(New Rochelle Chiropractic 636-
4113)* **Under 1 mi:** Veterinarian *(New Rochelle Animal Hosp. 636-8106)*
Hospital: Sound Shore 632-5000 *(2 mi.)*

Setting -- New Rochelle Harbor's third set of docks, to starboard, belong to Castaways Yacht Club, a well-maintained facility in a suburban environment but with urban views. The docks look either to the Castaway's nicely executed, club-like environment, or across the harbor to a series of apartment buildings. An attractive pool and restaurant complex, along with tennis courts, provides the recreational focus for seasonal members and transient boaters.

Marina Notes -- Service-oriented marina with boatyard facilities. Hauling to 60 feet. Three-phase service. Castaways Clubhouse has a bar and a full-service restaurant -- bar food to full meals, late breakfast, lunch and dinner, outside and inside dining. Nice heads and showers. All facilities are well-cared for and service is a focus. This is the New York area home of the Sunseekers Club.

Notable -- Castaways is located on Davenport Neck -- a peninsula sandwiched between L.I. Sound and New Rochelle Harbor. It is home to a string of large clubs, interspersed with large vintage houses. It's a five minute cab ride to Amtrak and MetroNorth: 35 minutes to Manhattan. Most other services are a short cab ride. A walk around the harbor to New Roc City is 1.7 mi.; this huge retail and entertainment center offers an 18-plex movie theater, oversize ice rink, bowling, the Tower Space Shot ride, an assortment of eateries, a supermarket, retail shops, bowling, a Marriott, and more. Dinghy across the harbor to Wright Island - their Marina Restaurant encourages dock and dine and there's also a string of nearby services within walking distance.

West Harbor Yacht Service

101 Harbor Lane West; New Rochelle, NY 10805

Tel: (914) 636-1524 **VHF: Monitor** n/a **Talk** n/a
Fax: (914) 636-1359 **Alternate Tel:** n/a
Email: whyssail@aol.com **Web:** n/a
Nearest Town: New Rochelle (2 mi.) **Tourist Info:** (914) 632-5700

Navigational Information
Lat: 40°53.342' **Long:** 073°47.070' **Tide:** 7 ft. **Current:** 1 kt. **Chart:** 12366
Rep. Depths (*MLW*): **Entry** 8 ft. **Fuel Dock** n/a **Max Slip/Moor** 8 ft./8 ft.
Access: NW from Execution Rocks Lighthouse to Huckleberry Island R2

Marina Facilities (*In Season/Off Season*)
Fuel: No
Slips: 32 Total, 2 Transient **Max LOA:** 60 ft. **Max Beam:** 15 ft.
 Rate (*per ft.*): **Day** $1.00 **Week** $5.00 **Month** $20
 Power: 30 amp Incl., **50 amp** n/a, **100 amp** n/a, **200 amp** n/a
 Cable TV: No **Dockside Phone:** No
 Dock Type: Floating, Long Fingers, Wood
Moorings: 0 Total, 0 Transient **Launch:** None, Dinghy Dock
 Rate: Day n/a **Week** n/a **Month** n/a
Heads: 1 Toilet(s), 1 Shower(s)
Laundry: 1 Washer(s), 1 Dryer(s) **Pay Phones:** No
Pump-Out: OnCall, Full Service **Fee:** n/a **Closed Heads:** Yes

Marina Operations
Owner/Manager: Arthur I. Karpf **Dockmaster:** Same
In-Season: May-Oct, 8am-7pm **Off-Season:** Nov-Apr, 9am-6pm
After-Hours Arrival: Tie up in work area
Reservations: Preferred **Credit Cards:** Cash or check
Discounts: None
Pets: Welcome, Dog Walk Area **Handicap Access:** No

Marina Services and Boat Supplies
Services - Dock Carts **Communication -** Mail & Package Hold, Phone Messages, Fax in/out, Data Ports (*Office*), FedEx, AirBorne, UPS, Express Mail (*Sat Del*) **Supplies - OnSite:** Ice (*Block, Cube*), Ships' Store **1-3 mi:** Marine Discount Store (*Post Marine 235-9800*), Bait/Tackle (*Hudson Park 235-0050*), Live Bait, Propane (*Almstead 576-3253*) **3+ mi:** CNG (*Brewer 698-3232, 5 mi.*)

Boatyard Services
OnSite: Travelift (*20T*), Crane, Engine mechanic (*gas, diesel*), Electrical Repairs, Hull Repairs, Rigger, Bottom Cleaning, Brightwork, Air Conditioning, Refrigeration, Divers, Compound, Wash & Wax, Interior Cleaning, Woodworking, Metal Fabrication, Painting, Yacht Broker **OnCall:** Propeller Repairs, Inflatable Repairs, Life Raft Service, Upholstery **Dealer for:** Volvo Auxiliaries. **Yard Rates:** $70/hr., Haul & Launch $7-11/ft., Power Wash $2, Bottom Paint $12/ft. **Storage:** In-Water $17.50/ft./mo., On-Land $6.50/ft./mo.

Restaurants and Accommodations
OnCall: Pizzeria (*Modern Pizza 733-9479*) **Near:** Restaurant (*Marina Restaurant 235-5252, L $7-12, D $17-22*), (*Glen Island Harbour 636-6500*), Seafood Shack (*Lenos Clam Bar 636-9869*) **Under 1 mi:** Restaurant (*Mama Francesca 636-1229, L $6, D $13-19*), (*Tokyo Bay 576-9838, L $6-9, D $12-20*), (*Paisano 632-6488*) **1-3 mi:** Fast Food (*Taco Bell, Mc Donalds*), Hotel (*Ramada Plaza 576-3600, $150-170*), (*Marriott 636-7888, $175*)

Recreation and Entertainment
Near: Beach, Picnic Area, Grills, Playground, Group Fishing Boat, Park

Under 1 mi: Horseback Riding (*Pelham Bit 718-885-9723*), Video Rental (*Great American 633-4013*) **1-3 mi:** Tennis Courts (*Cliff Street 576-9000*), Golf Course (*Split Rock 718-885-1258*), Fitness Center (*Bally or Omni Health 738-2200*), Bowling (*New Roc 636-3700*), Movie Theater (*New Roc City 235-3737*), Video Arcade **3+ mi:** Museum (*Thomas Paine 632-5376/Bill of Rights Museum at St Pauls Nat'l Historic Site 667-4116, 4 mi.*)

Provisioning and General Services
Near: Market (*Met Foods 636-0720*) **Under 1 mi:** Supermarket (*A&P 636-9437*), Delicatessen (*New Marina Deli 576-8580*), Liquor Store (*Shore Road Liquors 235-7762*), Bakery (*Hacker's Bakery 654-1099*), Bank/ATM, Pharmacy (*CVS 235-7171*), Newsstand, Hardware Store (*Modern 632-8060*), Florist, Buying Club (*Costco*) **1-3 mi:** Farmers' Market (*Fri, 9am-1pm*), Green Grocer, Post Office, Catholic Church, Protestant Church, Synagogue, Library (*New Rochelle 632-7878*), Beauty Salon, Barber Shop, Dry Cleaners, Laundry, Bookstore (*Collegiate Bookstore 633-3829*), Clothing Store, Retail Shops, Copies Etc. (*Budget Office 637-0740*) **3+ mi:** Health Food (*Mrs. Green's 834-6667, 4 mi.*)

Transportation
OnCall: Rental Car (*Enterprise 637-9271, National 946-9080*), Taxi (*City Taxi 633-4500*), Airport Limo (*Metro 654-0079*) **Near:** Local Bus **Under 1 mi:** InterCity Bus, Rail (*Metro North & Amtrak*) **Airport:** La Guardia (17 mi.)

Medical Services
911 Service **OnCall:** Ambulance **Under 1 mi:** Doctor (*Barnett 738-5058*), Dentist (*McCosker 636-3042*) **1-3 mi:** Chiropractor (*N.R. Chiro 636-4113*), Veterinarian (*New Roc 636-8106*) **Hospital:** Sound Shore 632-5000 (2 mi.)

Setting -- Just south of the bascule bridge, past the Huguenot Yacht Club docks, is West Harbor Yacht Service - a "sail only" facility. It sits on Neptune Island, on the western side of the Lower Harbor Channel. The surrounding area is a residential mix of private houses and apartment buildings and a very short walk over the bridge is lovely Glen Island Park.

Marina Notes -- This is a working boatyard with an all-sail marina - they are sailboat specialists and do not accept powerboats. The harbor is very well sheltered and has an on-call Pump-out Vessel Service. LaComte Yacht Brokerage is also on site.

Notable -- 105 acre Westchester County-owned Glen Island Park includes the landmark Glen Island Casino. Built in 1930, it became a mecca for big bands, especially Glenn Miller and Tommy Dorsey, and was known as Westchester's "Swing Palace." Today it's been renovated and is called the Glen Island Harbour Club; it's used for private functions, including weddings. The Park features a playground, picnic area, boat launch, bicycling, in-line skating, fishing, hiking/walking, a refreshment stand, swimming ($5/3) and an 18-hole mini golf course ($3/2) - a combined ticket for swimming and miniature golf is $7/5. Theoretically, only Westchester residents (with Park passes) are permitted on the Island, but when one arrives on foot there seems to be a bit more leeway (ask at the marina). Groups, with a Westchester County resident member, can also rent large picnic areas.

Navigational Information
Lat: 40°50.938' **Long:** 073°46.953' **Tide:** 8 ft. **Current:** 0.5 kt **Chart:** 12366
Rep. Depths (*MLW*): **Entry** 100 ft. **Fuel Dock** 10 ft. **Max Slip/Moor** -/30 ft.
Access: Between Hart Island and City Island 200 yards north of the ferry slip

Marina Facilities *(In Season/Off Season)*
Fuel: No
Slips: 0 Total, 0 Transient **Max LOA:** 60 ft. **Max Beam:** 15 ft.
  Rate *(per ft.)*: **Day** n/a **Week** n/a **Month** n/a
  Power: 30 amp n/a, 50 amp n/a, 100 amp n/a, 200 amp n/a
  Cable TV: No **Dockside Phone:** No
  Dock Type: n/a
Moorings: 15 Total, 3 Transient **Launch:** Yes (Free), Dinghy Dock
  Rate: Day $15 **Week** $105 **Month** n/a
Heads: 1 Toilet(s), 1 Shower(s)
Laundry: None **Pay Phones:** No
Pump-Out: No **Fee:** n/a **Closed Heads:** No

Marina Operations
Owner/Manager: John Barron **Dockmaster:** n/a
In-Season: All Summer, 8am-12am **Off-Season:** All Winter, 8am-5pm
After-Hours Arrival: Cll in advance
Reservations: No **Credit Cards:** Visa/MC
Discounts: None
Pets: Welcome, Dog Walk Area **Handicap Access:** No

Barron's Marine Services

350 Fordham Place; City Island, NY 10464

Tel: (718) 885-9802 **VHF: Monitor** n/a **Talk** n/a
Fax: (718) 885-3252 **Alternate Tel:** n/a
Email: barrons@cityisland.com **Web:** n/a
Nearest Town: City Island **Tourist Info:** (914) 738-7380

Marina Services and Boat Supplies
Services - Trash Pick-Up **Supplies - Near:** Ice *(Cube)*, Ships' Store *(Bridge Marine 885-2302)*, Propane *(No. Minneford YC 885-2000)* **Under 1 mi:** Bait/Tackle *(City Island Bait & Tackle 885-2153)*

Boatyard Services
OnSite: Travelift *(20T)*, Engine mechanic *(gas, diesel)*, Launching Ramp, Electrical Repairs, Electronic Sales, Electronics Repairs, Hull Repairs, Rigger, Sail Loft *(Doyle-Hild Sails)*, Bottom Cleaning, Brightwork, Air Conditioning, Compound, Wash & Wax, Interior Cleaning, Propeller Repairs, Woodworking, Metal Fabrication, Painting, Total Refits
Yard Rates: $60/hr. **Storage:** On-Land $35-38/ft.

Restaurants and Accommodations
Near: Restaurant *(Arties 885-9885, L $7-12, D $12-30)*, *(Tree House 885-0806)*, *(Black Whale 885-3657)*, *(City Island Diner 885-9867)*, *(King Lobster 885-1579, Rest. & Fish Mkt.)*, Seafood Shack *(Rhodes Seafood 885-1538)*, Crab House *(Crab Shanty 885-1810)*, Pizzeria *(Pizza Place 885-0744)* **Under 1 mi:** Inn/B&B *(Le Refuge Inn 885-2478, $65-140)*

Recreation and Entertainment
Near: Picnic Area, Playground, Dive Shop, Jogging Paths, Roller Blade/Bike Paths, Fishing Charter, Video Rental *(KVG Video 824-9796)*, Museum *(City Island Nautical Museum 885-0008; The North Wind Undersea Institute also helps nurse injured and ill marine animals)* **1-3 mi:** Beach *(mile long, man-made Orchard Beach)*, Golf Course *(Turtle Cove 885-2646)*, Horseback

Riding *(Pelham Bit Stables 885-9723)*, Park *(Pelham Bay Park offers hikes, beaches and the Barstow-Pell Mansion)*

Provisioning and General Services
Near: Provisioning Service, Convenience Store, Delicatessen *(Outward Bound Cafe & Deli 885-0947)*, Wine/Beer, Bakery, Farmers' Market, Green Grocer, Fishmonger, Meat Market, Bank/ATM, Post Office, Catholic Church, Protestant Church, Synagogue, Library *(City Island 885-1703 - NYC's largest maritime collection)*, Beauty Salon, Barber Shop, Dry Cleaners, Laundry, Bookstore *(Tea & Empathy Limited 885-3837)*, Pharmacy *(City Island Pharm. 885-3053)*, Newsstand, Florist, Retail Shops **Under 1 mi:** Supermarket *(City Island Supermarket 885-0881)*, Hardware Store *JJ Burke Hardware & Marine Supplies 885-1559)* **1-3 mi:** Liquor Store *(Big Three Liquors 824-9390)*

Transportation
OnCall: Rental Car *(Enterprise 824-0266)*, Taxi *(Ampere 824-6666)*, Airport Limo *(Ark Limousine 829-7900)* **Under 1 mi:** Local Bus *(NYC Transit)* **Airport:** LaGuardia *(11 mi.)*

Medical Services
911 Service **Near:** Doctor, Ambulance **1-3 mi:** Dentist *(East Tremont Dental 823-3000)*, Veterinarian *(MiddleTown Animal Clinic 824-8300)* **3+ mi:** Holistic Services *(Acupuncture Medical Center 671-6100, 4 mi.)* **Hospital:** Westchester Square 430-7300 *(4 mi.)*

Setting -- Heading south along the eastern shore of City Island, about a third of the way along the island, Barron's is the first boatyard facility. This venerable City Island establishment is pure "yard" with the addition of a small mooring field right off its service dock. Shoreside, it's at the end of a dead-end street about four short blocks from the main drag.

Marina Notes -- Family owned and operated, established in 1934. Two 60-foot floats with water and power for use by mooring guests. Patio and shower overlook the water. A working boatyard, it's equipped to do almost any type of repair and/or maintenance: carpentry, fiberglass, hauling, washing, painting, storage. Also encourages "do-it-yourselfers". The mooring field promises deep water even at low tide. Sail-away trips in summer. Next door is Fenton Marine which is also a working boatyard and winter boat storage facility. Mark Ploch's Doyle-Hild Sails and Island Nautical Canvas are in the same complex.

Notable -- City Island is just a mile and a half long, so from Barron's central location almost everything is within walking distance. There are about 30 eateries of varying descriptions on the island, some of which reflect the Island's Italian roots, and almost all of which specialize in seafood. There are also a fair number of interesting provisioning options. New restaurants and food sources catering to the newly arrived Latino population add to the culinary mix. Just off the island is Orchard Beach, a huge New York City Park. About 1.4 miles away, in the park, is Turtle Cove - a golf and baseball complex.

North Minneford Yacht Club

150 City Island Avenue; City Island, NY 10464

Tel: (718) 885-2000 **VHF: Monitor** 77 **Talk** 77
Fax: (718) 885-2015 **Alternate Tel:** n/a
Email: n/a **Web:** n/a
Nearest Town: City Island **Tourist Info:** (914) 738-7380

Navigational Information
Lat: 40°50.550' **Long:** 073°47.000' **Tide:** 7 ft. **Current:** 1 kt. **Chart:** 13266
Rep. Depths (MLW): Entry 17 ft. **Fuel Dock** 17 ft. **Max Slip/Moor** 17 ft./-
Access: South east side of City Island, opposite southern tip of Hart Island

Marina Facilities (In Season/Off Season)
Fuel: No
Slips: 380 Total, 35 Transient **Max LOA:** 100 ft. **Max Beam:** 21 ft.
 Rate (per ft.): Day $1.50* **Week** $1.00 **Month** Inq.
 Power: 30 amp Incl., **50 amp** Incl., **100 amp** n/a, **200 amp** n/a
 Cable TV: No **Dockside Phone:** No
 Dock Type: Floating, Long Fingers, Alongside, Wood
Moorings: 0 Total, 0 Transient **Launch:** n/a
 Rate: Day n/a **Week** n/a **Month** n/a
Heads: 4 Toilet(s), 4 Shower(s)
Laundry: None **Pay Phones:** Yes
Pump-Out: OnSite, Full Service, 1 Central **Fee:** n/a **Closed Heads:** No

Marina Operations
Owner/Manager: Capt. Jack Hammel **Dockmaster:** Same
In-Season: Year-Round, 9am-9pm **Off-Season:** Same
After-Hours Arrival: Call in advance
Reservations: Yes **Credit Cards:** Visa/MC, Dscvr, Amex
Discounts: Boat/US **Dockage:** 25% **Fuel:** n/a **Repair:** n/a
Pets: Welcome, Dog Walk Area **Handicap Access:** No

Marina Services and Boat Supplies
Services - Docking Assistance, Concierge, Security (24 Hrs.), Trash Pick-Up, Dock Carts **Communication -** Mail & Package Hold, Phone Messages, Fax in/out, FedEx, AirBorne, UPS, Express Mail (Sat Del) **Supplies - OnSite:** Ice (Block, Cube), Ships' Store, Propane **Under 1 mi:** Marine Discount Store (Bridge Marine 885-2302), Bait/Tackle (City Island Bait & Tackle 885-2153)

Boatyard Services
OnSite: Travelift (35T), Forklift, Engine mechanic (gas, diesel), Electrical Repairs, Electronic Sales, Electronics Repairs, Hull Repairs, Rigger, Bottom Cleaning, Brightwork, Refrigeration, Divers, Compound, Wash & Wax, Propeller Repairs, Painting, Yacht Broker

Restaurants and Accommodations
OnCall: Pizzeria (Pizza Place 885-0744) **Near:** Restaurant (Black Whale 885-3657), (Rhodes Seafood 885-1538), (Tree House 885-0806), (City Island Diner 885-9867), (Arties 885-9885, L $7-12, D $12-30), Seafood Shack (Johnn's Reef 885-2090, L & D $6-18), Crab House (Crab Shanty 885-1810) **Under 1 mi:** Restaurant (King Lobster 885-1579, Restaurant & Fish Market), Inn/B&B (Le Refuge 885-2478, $65-140)

Recreation and Entertainment
OnSite: Picnic Area, Grills **Near:** Playground, Dive Shop, Jogging Paths, Roller Blade/Bike Paths, Video Rental (KVG Video 824-9796), Park, Museum (City Island Nautical Museum 885-0008 features guided tours,

lectures, paintings, and memorabilia from the 18th century to the present) **Under 1 mi:** Sightseeing (just walk the island) **1-3 mi:** Golf Course (Split Rock 885-1258), Fitness Center (Golds Gym 863-3488), Horseback Riding (Pelham Bit Stables 885-9723) **3+ mi:** Bowling (Gun Post Lanes 994-8700, 4 mi.)

Provisioning and General Services
OnSite: Copies Etc. **OnCall:** Fishmonger, Meat Market **Near:** Convenience Store (Moe's Grocery & Deli 885-3179), Gourmet Shop, Delicatessen (Outward Bound Cafe & Deli 885-0947), Wine/Beer, Bakery, Bank/ATM, Post Office, Catholic Church, Synagogue, Library (City Island 885-1703), Beauty Salon, Barber Shop, Dry Cleaners, Laundry, Bookstore (Tea & Empathy Limited 885-3837), Pharmacy (City Island Pharm. 885-3053), Newsstand, Hardware Store (JJ Burke 885-1559), Retail Shops **Under 1 mi:** Supermarket (City Island Supermarket 885-0881) **1-3 mi:** Liquor Store (Big Three Liquors 824-9390)

Transportation
OnCall: Rental Car (Enterprise 824-0266), Taxi (Zeros 822-2222), Airport Limo (Ark Limo 829-7900) **Near:** Local Bus **Airport:** LaGuardia (11 mi.)

Medical Services
911 Service **Near:** Doctor, Ambulance **Under 1 mi:** Dentist (East Tremont Dental Assoc. 823-3000) **1-3 mi:** Veterinarian (MiddleTown Animal Clinic 824-8300) **3+ mi:** Holistic Services (Acupuncture Medical Center 671-6100, 4 mi.) **Hospital:** Westchester Square 430-7300 (4 mi.)

Setting -- The fourth boating facility, heading south, on the eastern shore of City Island, is North Minneford Yacht Club. It's a fairly recent addition to the Island's maritime scene and the handsome docking facilities reflect that. A wide wooden boardwalk, dotted with picnic tables, umbrellas and barbeque grills, runs the full length of the marina and provides an excellent vantage point for observing the passing scene.

Marina Notes -- *The rates reflect those of a "Club Membership". Basic boatyard services and excellent location. The heads and showers, housed in the Boatmax brokerage building, are very nice and well kept. 250 state-of the art slips for boats to 100 ft. Mostly a seasonal club. An active dry stack storage operation manages boats 27 ft. and shorter. This site has hosted a boatyard since 1920; Seven America's Cup Winners were built here. Brokerage listings can be seen at www.boatmax.com.

Notable -- Everything for the boat and crew is within a very easy walk. Located just about dead center on City Island, it is a perfect place to take full advantage of this completely boat-oriented seaside community within the borders of New York City. Dozens of restaurants line the main street, along with most every service that could possibly be needed. Two small supermarkets cater to boaters and to the varied requirements of the various ethnic groups that make this their home -- which makes for fun and interesting provisioning. Nearby little City Island Library houses a remarkable maritime collection. Bus to train service to Manhattan and all local NYC Airports.

Navigational Information
Lat: 40°50.586' **Long:** 073°46.850' **Tide:** 8 ft. **Current:** 2 kt. **Chart:** 12366
Rep. Depths (MLW): Entry 10 ft. **Fuel Dock** n/a **Max Slip/Moor** 8 ft./-
Access: Southeast side of City Island, opposite Hart Island

Marina Facilities *(In Season/Off Season)*
Fuel: No
Slips: 120 Total, 25 Transient **Max LOA:** 70 ft. **Max Beam:** 19 ft.
 Rate *(per ft.)*: **Day** $2.00 **Week** Inq. **Month** Inq.
 Power: 30 amp $5, **50 amp** $10, **100 amp** n/a, **200 amp** n/a
Cable TV: No **Dockside Phone:** No
 Dock Type: Floating, Long Fingers, Wood
Moorings: 0 Total, 0 Transient **Launch:** n/a
 Rate: Day n/a **Week** n/a **Month** n/a
Heads: 2 Toilet(s), 1 Shower(s) *(with dressing rooms)*
Laundry: None **Pay Phones:** No
Pump-Out: No **Fee:** n/a **Closed Heads:** No

Marina Operations
Owner/Manager: Edward Ge **Dockmaster:** Same
In-Season: Apr 15-Oct 15, 24 hrs. **Off-Season:** Oct 15-Apr 15, 8am-4pm
After-Hours Arrival: Call on VHF 69 prior to entering marina
Reservations: Yes, Preferred **Credit Cards:** Visa/MC
Discounts: Boat/US **Dockage:** 25% **Fuel:** n/a **Repair:** n/a
Pets: Welcome **Handicap Access:** No

South Minneford Yacht Club

PO Box 130; 150 City Island Avenue; City Island, NY 10464

Tel: (718) 885-3113 **VHF: Monitor** 69 **Talk** 69
Fax: (718) 885-0332 **Alternate Tel:** n/a
Email: n/a **Web:** n/a
Nearest Town: City Island **Tourist Info:** (914) 738-7380

Marina Services and Boat Supplies
Services - Docking Assistance, Security *(24 Hrs., guard)*, Trash Pick-Up, Dock Carts **Communication -** Mail & Package Hold, Phone Messages, Fax in/out, FedEx, AirBorne, UPS, Express Mail *(Sat Del)* **Supplies -**
OnSite: Ice *(Block, Cube)* **Near:** Ships' Store *(Bridge Marine 885-2302)*, Propane *(No. Minneford YC)* **Under 1 mi:** Bait/Tackle *(C.I. Bait & Tackle 885-2153)*

Boatyard Services
Near: Travelift *(40T)*, Forklift, Engine mechanic *(gas, diesel)*, Launching Ramp, Electrical Repairs, Electronic Sales, Electronics Repairs, Hull Repairs, Rigger, Sail Loft, Bottom Cleaning, Brightwork, Air Conditioning, Refrigeration, Divers, Compound, Wash & Wax, Interior Cleaning, Woodworking, Upholstery, Yacht Interiors, Yacht Broker *(Boat Max)*.
1-3 mi: Propeller Repairs. **Nearest Yard:** No. Minneford (718) 885-2000

Restaurants and Accommodations
OnCall: Pizzeria *(The Pizza Place 885-0744)* **Near:** Restaurant *(Arties 885-9885, L $7-12, D $12-30)*, *(Lobster Box 885-1953)*, *(Sammy's 885-0950)*, *(Tree House 885-0806)*, *(City Island Diner 885-9867)*, *(Crab Shanty 885-1810)*, *(Lido's)*, *(Rhodes)*, *(Portofino)*, *(Tito Puente)*, Seafood Shack *(Tony's Pier 885-1424)* **Under 1 mi:** Inn/B&B *(Le Refuge 885-2478, $65-140)*

Recreation and Entertainment
OnSite: Picnic Area, Grills **Near:** Playground, Dive Shop, Fishing Charter, Group Fishing Boat, Video Rental *(KVG Video 824-9796)*, Park
Under 1 mi: Boat Rentals, Museum *(City Island Nautical Museum 885-0008, North Wind Museum & Undersea Institute founded by '60s rocker*

Richie Havens and former Navy SEAL Michael Sandlofer 885-0701, CIAO Gallery and Art Center) **1-3 mi:** Golf Course *(Split Rock 885-1258)*, Fitness Center *(Golds Gym 863-3488)*, Jogging Paths, Horseback Riding *(Pelham Bit Stables 885-0551)*, Roller Blade/Bike Paths **3+ mi:** Bowling *(Pelham Lanes 994-8700, 4 mi.)*, Movie Theater *(Whitestone Multiplex 409-9030, 4 mi.)*

Provisioning and General Services
Near: Convenience Store *(Moe's Grocery 885-3179)*, Supermarket *(City Island Super 885-0881)*, Delicatessen *(Outward Bound Cafe 885-0947)*, Wine/Beer, Fishmonger, Lobster Pound, Meat Market, Bank/ATM, Post Office, Catholic Church, Protestant Church, Synagogue, Library *(City Island 885-1703)*, Beauty Salon, Barber Shop, Dry Cleaners, Laundry, Bookstore *(Tea & Empathy Limited 885-3837)*, Pharmacy *(C.I. Pharm. 885-3053)*, Newsstand, Florist, Retail Shops **Under 1 mi:** Hardware Store *(JJ Burke 885-1559)* **1-3 mi:** Liquor Store *(Big Three 824-9390)*, Copies Etc. *(Flier Factory 369-1215)*

Transportation
OnCall: Rental Car *(Enterprise 824-0266)*, Airport Limo *(Ark Limousine 829-7900)* **Near:** Local Bus *(NY Bus Service 994-5500)* **1-3 mi:** Taxi *(Zeros 822-2222)* **3+ mi:** Rail *(New Rochelle Amtrak, 10 mi.)*
Airport: La Guardia *(11 mi.)*

Medical Services
911 Service **Under 1 mi:** Doctor, Dentist *(East Tremont 823-3000)*
1-3 mi: Chiropractor, Holistic Services, Veterinarian *(MiddleTown Clinic 824-8300)* **Hospital:** Jacobi Hospital 918-5370 *(4 mi.)*

Setting -- Directly south of North Minneford Yacht Club, on City Island's eastern shore, this private, cooperative marina welcomes transients to its relatively new, high quality docks and central location. A small nicely-done brick patio is home to grills and park benches and provides an attractive entrance to the long boardwalk that skirts the southern edge of the marina. Round white tables with green and white striped umbrellas add a welcoming and festive touch. Look for the white steel pilings.

Marina Notes -- 24 hour security and 24 hour docking assistance. Shoreside is a large parking lot that is dominated by the racks from North Minneford's dry-stack storage operation. Limited amenities. Excellent docks. Directly next door is North Minneford/Boatwork's full service boatyard. Despite the similar names, these two facilities are distinctly separate operations.

Notable -- This is one of the island's narrowest points, so City Island Avenue - the main street that runs the length of the Island - is right outside the gates. There are three art galleries, several historical and maritime museums, antique shops, great seafood restaurants, and the only Auberge Francais in New York (Le Refuge B&B is owned by Pierre Saint-Denis of Manhattan's Le Refuge restaurant); the focus of everything here is the sea. Nearby is the library (with its highly regarded collection of nautical material) and the City Island Nautical Museum, housed in a former 19thC New York school building (885-0008, Sun 1-5pm or by appt; it's about 0.4 mi. walk). The justly famous New York Botanical Garden and Bronx Zoo are about an 8 mile cab ride.

Consolidated Yachts Inc.

Consolidated Yachts Inc.

157 Pilot Street; City Island, NY 10464

Tel: (718) 855-1900 **VHF: Monitor** 16 **Talk** n/a
Fax: (718) 885-1904 **Alternate Tel:** (718) 855-1900
Email: n/a **Web:** n/a
Nearest Town: City Island **Tourist Info:** (914) 738-7380

Navigational Information
Lat: 40°50.479' **Long:** 073°46.911' **Tide:** 8.5 ft. **Current:** 3 kt. **Chart:** 12366
Rep. Depths (MLW): Entry 10 ft. **Fuel Dock** n/a **Max Slip/Moor** 12 ft./-
Access: Southeast side of City Island

Marina Facilities (In Season/Off Season)
Fuel: No
Slips: 60 Total, 6 Transient **Max LOA:** 150 ft. **Max Beam:** 30 ft.
  Rate (per ft.): **Day** $1.75* **Week** $1.75 **Month** $1.50
  Power: 30 amp Inq., 50 amp Inq., **100 amp** n/a, **200 amp** n/a
  Cable TV: No **Dockside Phone:** No
  Dock Type: Fixed, Floating, Wood
Moorings: 0 Total, 0 Transient **Launch:** n/a
  Rate: Day n/a **Week** n/a **Month** n/a
Heads: 4 Toilet(s), 2 Shower(s)
Laundry: None **Pay Phones:** Yes, 1
Pump-Out: No **Fee:** n/a **Closed Heads:** No

Marina Operations
Owner/Manager: Wesley L. Rodstrom Jr. **Dockmaster:** Same
In-Season: Year-Round, 7:30am-4pm **Off-Season:** n/a
After-Hours Arrival: Call office ahead
Reservations: Yes, Preferred **Credit Cards:** Visa/MC
Discounts: None
Pets: Welcome, Dog Walk Area **Handicap Access:** No

Marina Services and Boat Supplies
Services - Trash Pick-Up, Dock Carts **Communication -** Mail & Package Hold, Phone Messages, Fax in/out, FedEx, AirBorne, UPS, Express Mail (Sat Del) **Supplies - OnSite:** Ice (Block, Cube), Ships' Store **Under 1 mi:** Bait/Tackle (Jack's 885-2042), Live Bait **3+ mi:** Marine Discount Store (Post Marine 914-235-9800, 5 mi.), Propane (Imperia Bros. 738-0900, 4 mi.)

Boatyard Services
OnSite: Travelift (60T), Forklift, Crane, Engine mechanic (gas, diesel), Electrical Repairs, Electronic Sales, Electronics Repairs, Hull Repairs, Rigger, Sail Loft, Bottom Cleaning, Brightwork, Air Conditioning, Refrigeration, Compound, Wash & Wax, Woodworking, Upholstery (Rick Urban), Metal Fabrication, Awlgrip, Yacht Broker **OnCall:** Divers, Propeller Repairs, Inflatable Repairs, Life Raft Service **Dealer for:** Yanmar.
Yard Rates: $70/hr., Haul & Launch $9/ft. (blocking $9/ft.), Power Wash $1.75/ft. **Storage:** On-Land $7/ft./mo.

Restaurants and Accommodations
OnCall: Pizzeria (Pizza Place 885-0740) **Near:** Restaurant (Black Whale 885-3657), (Artie's 885-9815, L $7-12, D $12-30), (Frans Place 885-0716, L $7-12, D $12-30), (Crab Shanty 885-1810), (Lobster Box 885-1952), Seafood Shack (Johnny's Reef L $6-18, D $6-18), (Tony's Pier 885-1424), Snack Bar (Island Café 885-0716, B $3-5, L $4-8, D $4-8, Delivers) **Under 1 mi:** Restaurant (JP'S 885-3364, L $7-10, D $12-30), Inn/B&B (Le Refuge 885-2478, $65-140) **3+ mi:** Motel (Holiday Motel 324-4200, 4 mi.)

Recreation and Entertainment
OnSite: Picnic Area, Grills **Near:** Playground **Under 1 mi:** Dive Shop, Jogging Paths, Boat Rentals, Roller Blade/Bike Paths, Fishing Charter, Group Fishing Boat, Video Rental (KVG Video 824-9796), Park, Museum (City Island Nautical Museum 885-0008) **1-3 mi:** Beach, Tennis Courts, Golf Course (Split Rock 885-1258), Fitness Center (Golds Gym 863-3488), Horseback Riding (Pelham Bit Stables 885-9723), Video Arcade

Provisioning and General Services
Near: Convenience Store (Moe's Grocery 885-3179), Fishmonger, Lobster Pound, Bank/ATM, Post Office, Protestant Church, Laundry, Bookstore (Tea & Empathy Limited 885-3837) **Under 1 mi:** Supermarket (City Island Super 885-0881), Gourmet Shop, Delicatessen (Outward Bound 885-0947), Health Food, Wine/Beer, Bakery, Farmers' Market, Meat Market, Catholic Church, Synagogue, Library (885-1703), Beauty Salon, Barber Shop, Dry Cleaners, Pharmacy (City Island 885-3053), Newsstand, Hardware Store, Florist, Retail Shops **1-3 mi:** Liquor Store (4101 Wines 824-7300), Department Store, Copies Etc. (Flier Factory 369-1215)

Transportation
OnCall: Rental Car (Enterprise 824-0266), Taxi (Crosby 824-1111), Airport Limo (Ark Limo 829-7900) **Near:** Local Bus (One block- To NYC)
Airport: LaGuardia (10 mi.)

Medical Services
911 Service **OnCall:** Ambulance **Near:** Dentist (Berman 885-1688) **Under 1 mi:** Doctor (Sander 885-0333) **1-3 mi:** Chiropractor (Guarino 636-4113), Holistic Services, Veterinarian (MiddleTown 824-8300)
Hospital: Sound Shore 632-5000 (5 mi.)

Setting -- Past the Minnefords, close to the foot of City Island, on the eastern shore, Consolidated has been providing services to yachts people for almost half a century. Tucked into a comfortable basin created by wave fences, the solid slips are home to an interesting mix of very nice boats. A cement patio with picnic tables and chairs overlooks the docks. This is generally considered the "social" part of City Island - directly across, on the western side, are all the yacht clubs and the most residential area.

Marina Notes -- Landside is a well maintained boatyard with a thorough assortment of services and a small-boat dry stack facility. Highly professional operation with good amenities. Stuyvesant Yacht Club (885-9840) may have a transient slip, and City Island Yacht Club (885-2487) and Morris Yacht and Beach Club (885-0574) may have a transient mooring for members of other clubs. (Non club members should ask, as well.)

Notable -- At the foot of the island are two fairly wild "seafood shacks" with great views. There's lots to do on a rainy day: 1 mile north is Focal Point Gallery, which showcases local photographers and handmade jewelry and crafts, City Island Nautical Museum with guided tours, lectures, paintings, and memorabilia from the 18th century to the present. The North Wind Undersea Institute nurses injured and ill marine animals and exhibits an eclectic mix of rare sea animals, old scrimshaws, whale and shark bones, and a 100-year-old tugboat; founded by musician Richie Havens and former Navy SEAL Michael Sandlofer. 6 miles to the world-famous Bronx Zoo and N.Y. Botanical Gardens.

PHOTOS ON CD-ROM: 5

Navigational Information
Lat: 40°46.000' **Long:** 073°51.500' **Tide:** 7.5 ft. **Current:** n/a **Chart:** 12339
Rep. Depths (*MLW*): **Entry** 12 ft. **Fuel Dock** 12 ft. **Max Slip/Moor** 9 ft./-
Access: Flushing Bay to RN2, follow channel until the end

Marina Facilities *(In Season/Off Season)*
Fuel: *Texaco* - Gasoline, Diesel
Slips: 320 Total, 25 Transient **Max LOA:** 200 ft. **Max Beam:** 80 ft.
Rate *(per ft.)*: **Day** $1.50 **Week** Inq. **Month** Inq.
Power: 30 amp $6, 50 amp $6, 100 amp Inq., 200 amp n/a
Cable TV: No **Dockside Phone:** No
Dock Type: Floating, Long Fingers, Wood
Moorings: 0 Total, 0 Transient **Launch:** n/a
Rate: Day n/a **Week** n/a **Month** n/a
Heads: 3 Toilet(s), 3 Shower(s)
Laundry: None **Pay Phones:** Yes, 2
Pump-Out: No **Fee:** n/a **Closed Heads:** No

Marina Operations
Owner/Manager: Michael O'Rourke **Dockmaster:** Greg Smith
In-Season: Year-Round, 9am-5pm **Off-Season:** Closed Sun
After-Hours Arrival: Call channel 71
Reservations: Preferred **Credit Cards:** Cash or check
Discounts: None
Pets: Welcome **Handicap Access:** Yes, Heads, Docks

World's Fair Marina

125-00 Northern Boulevard; Flushing, NY 11368

Tel: (718) 478-0480 **VHF: Monitor** 71 **Talk** 71
Fax: (718) 478-9487 **Alternate Tel:** (718) 478-9487
Email: n/a **Web:** n/a
Nearest Town: Flushing, Queens **Tourist Info:** (718) 898-8500

Marina Services and Boat Supplies
Services - Docking Assistance, Security (24 Hrs., Guard service)
Supplies - Near: Bait/Tackle (*Professional Fish & Tack 461-9612*)
Under 1 mi: Ice (*Block, Cube, Shaved*) **3+ mi:** Ships' Store (*Dover Marine, 899-3827, 5 mi.*), Propane (*Big Apple 204-1166, 4 mi.*)

Boatyard Services
OnSite: Travelift (*50T*), Forklift, Crane, Engine mechanic (*gas, diesel*), Launching Ramp, Electrical Repairs, Rigger, Bottom Cleaning, Brightwork, Compound, Wash & Wax, Propeller Repairs, Painting **OnCall:** Air Conditioning, Refrigeration, Divers **Yard Rates:** $55/hr., Haul & Launch $5/ft. (*blocking $2.50/ft.*), Power Wash $2.50/ft., Bottom Paint $14.75/ft. (*paint incl.*) **Storage:** In-Water $24/ft., On-Land $32/ft.

Restaurants and Accommodations
OnSite: Restaurant (*World's Fair Marina 898-1200, L $5-16, D $9-16*)
OnCall: Pizzeria (*T.J.'s 321-8571, Delivers*) **Near:** Restaurant (*Golden Pond Seafood 886-1628*), (*Union 888-2226*), (*Leflores 961-5600*), Hotel (*Ramada Plaza 672-1200*), (*Sheraton 460-6666*) **Under 1 mi:** Restaurant (*Full House Seafood 937-1717*), Coffee Shop (*Roosevelt 886-2888*)
1-3 mi: Motel (*Best Western 699-4400*), Hotel (*Marriott 505-0043*)

Recreation and Entertainment
OnSite: Boat Rentals (*699-9596*) **Near:** Picnic Area, Playground (*"For All Children"*), Tennis Courts (*U.S. Tennis Assoc 760-6200 8am-Mid 760-6200*), Fitness Center (*Pure Power 939-7382*), Jogging Paths, Roller Blade/Bike Paths, Park (*Flushing Meadows; Wildlife Center 271-1500*), Museum (*Queens Museum of Art 592-5555; NY Hall of Science 699-0005*), Cultural

Attract (*Queens Theatre in the Park 760-0064, Louis Armstrong's House 478-8274*), Special Events (*Shea Stadium*) **Under 1 mi:** Movie Theater (*College Point Multiplex 886-4900*), Video Rental (*Mega Video 672-9599*), Video Arcade **1-3 mi:** Golf Course (*Clearview 229-2570*), Bowling (*Big Apple 353-6300*) **3+ mi:** Horseback Riding (*Stanleys 261-7679 , 4 mi.*)

Provisioning and General Services
Near: Delicatessen (*Main Street 463-3426*), Pharmacy (*Genovese 886-8082*), Hardware Store (*Topware 460-6240*), Copies Etc. (*Scanning America 463-1900*) **Under 1 mi:** Convenience Store, Market (*Franks Grocery 476-9550*), Supermarket (*Pathmark 886-4488*), Gourmet Shop, Health Food, Liquor Store (*Roosevelt 426-7720*), Bakery, Green Grocer, Fishmonger, Bank/ATM, Post Office, Catholic Church, Protestant Church, Synagogue, Other, Beauty Salon, Barber Shop, Dry Cleaners, Laundry, Bookstore (*World Book Store 445-2277, Republic Book Co 457-3993*), Newsstand, Florist, Clothing Store, Retail Shops, Buying Club **1-3 mi:** Library (*426-2844*)

Transportation
OnSite: Ferry Service (*Basball ferry service to/from lower Manhattan*)
OnCall: Taxi (*Always Ready 275-1111*), Airport Limo (*Caprice Car Service 626-5100*) **Near:** Bikes (*or Flushing Meadow 699-9598*), Rental Car (*Enterprise 939-1500/ Avis 539-2424*), Local Bus (*also Subway to Manhattan*) **Airport:** Laguardia (*0.25 mi.*)

Medical Services
911 Service **OnCall:** Chiropractor, Ambulance **Under 1 mi:** Dentist (*Flushing Family 445-7030*), Veterinarian (*Flushing Med. Center 886-4416*)
1-3 mi: Doctor **Hospital:** Flushing 321-6000/Booth Mem (*1 mi.*)

Setting -- The marina is tucked into a basin off Flushing Bay, and surrounded by Flushing Meadows Corona Park, Shea Stadium (home of the NY Mets), and LaGuardia Airport. A large two-story white building sits at the foot of the docks. Currently, it houses the marina offices and facilities.

Marina Notes -- On the site of the 1939 & 1964 World's Fairs. Marina was founded in 1939 as part of the World's Fair Exhibition, then updated as part of the 1964-65 World's Fair's permanent installation. The marina has been run by the New York City Dept. of Parks and Recreation since late 1999. Worlds Fair Marina & Banquet has recently opened onsite; they serve Punjabi -style Indian cuisine (some with a Chinese twist), a la carte & a buffet, 7 days. On the second floor, it has expansive views of Flushing Bay. The first floor is a large banquet facility for up to 500. W.F.M. is home to the 120' Tri-Level luxury charter motor yacht Skyline Princess (446-1100). Note: the park is so large that all those amenities that might normally be listed as "on-site" are listed as "nearby".

Notable -- Part of 1,255 acre Flushing Meadows Corona Park - meadows, fields and lakes. Home to: Queens Museum of Art, New York Hall of Science (hands-on; one of the best), New York Mets' Shea Stadium (507-1000), Queens Theatre in the Park, USTA National Center, Queens Wildlife Center, World's Fair 18,000 sq.ft. indoor ice skating rink (271-1996), Pitch & Putt mini golf (271-8182) and 39-acre Botanical Garden (886-3800). The Unisphere (217-6034) was featured in the film "Men in Black." An antique Carousel is right next to a remarkable children's playground (592-6539). Nearby #7 subway heads to Grand Central station and Times Square in Manhattan. During the American Revolution, the Lent Farmhouse stood here; headquarters for British 37th Regiment.

VII. New York: Western Long Islands North Shore

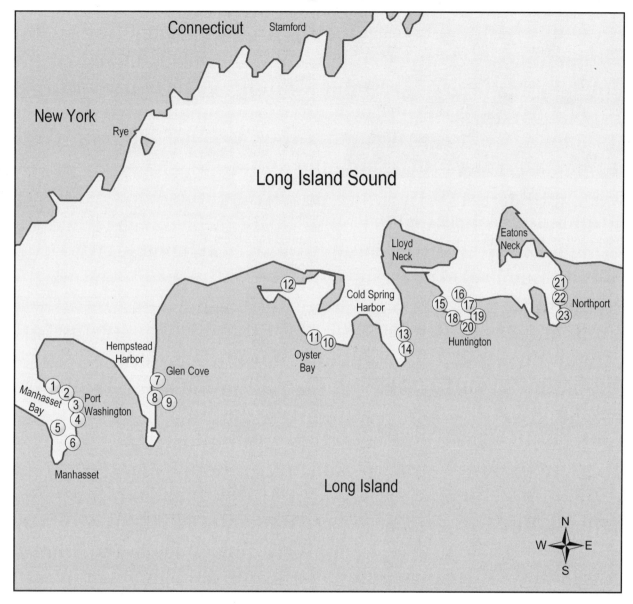

MAP	MARINA	HARBOR	PAGE	MAP	MARINA	HARBOR	PAGE
1	Brewer Capri Marina - East & West	Manhassett Bay	128	13	H & M Powles	Cold Spring Harbor	140
2	North Shore Yacht Club	Manhassett Bay	129	14	Whaler's Cove Yacht Club	Cold Spring Harbor	141
3	Toms Point Marina	Manhassett Bay	130	15	Wyncote Club	Huntington Harbor	142
4	Manhasset Bay Marina	Manhassett Bay	131	16	Huntington Yacht Club	Huntington Harbor	143
5	North Hempstead Town Moorings	Manhasset Bay	132	17	Knutson's Marine	Huntington Harbor	144
6	Port Washington Yacht Club	Manhasset Bay	133	18	West Shore Marina	Huntington Harbor	145
7	Hempstead Harbour Club	Hempstead Harbor	134	19	Coneys Marine	Huntington Harbor	146
8	Brewer Yacht Yard at Glen Cove	Hempstead Hbr/Glen Cove Cr	135	20	Willis Marine Center	Huntington Harbor	147
9	The Jude Thaddeus Glen Cove Marina	Hempstead Hbr/Glen Cove Cr	136	21	Seymour's Boat Yard	Northport Harbor	148
10	Oyster Bay Marine Center	Oyster Bay Harbor	137	22	Northport Village Dock	Northport Harbor	149
11	Sagamore Yacht Club	Oyster Bay Harbor	138	23	Britannia Yachting Center	Northport Harbor	150
12	Bridge Marina	Oyster Bay Hbr/Mill Neck Cr	139				

Brewer Capri Marina

15 Orchard Beach Boulevard; Port Washington, NY 11050

Tel: (516) 883-7800 **VHF:** Monitor 9 Talk 71
Fax: (516) 944-8770 **Alternate Tel:** (516) 883-7800
Email: BCM@BYY.com **Web:** www.BYY.com
Nearest Town: Manorhaven *(0.25 mi.)* **Tourist Info:** (516) 883-6566

Navigational Information
Lat: 40°50.236' **Long:** 073°43.258' **Tide:** 7 ft. **Current:** 0.5 kt. **Chart:** 12366
Rep. Depths *(MLW)*: **Entry** 6 ft. **Fuel Dock** 6 ft. **Max Slip/Moor** 10 ft./-
Access: Long Island Sound to Manhasset Bay around Plum Point

Marina Facilities *(In Season/Off Season)*
Fuel: BP - Gasoline, Diesel, High-Speed Pumps
Slips: 330 Total, 20 Transient **Max LOA:** 160 ft. **Max Beam:** n/a
Rate *(per ft.)*: **Day** $2.00/1.00* **Week** $12.60 **Month** $48
Power: 30 amp $7.50, **50 amp** $15, **100 amp** $40*, **200 amp** n/a
Cable TV: Yes, $6 Per day **Dockside Phone:** Yes Seasonal Only
Dock Type: Floating, Long Fingers, Pilings, Alongside, Wood
Moorings: 30 Total, 5 Transient **Launch:** Yes (Free), Dinghy Dock ($15/day)
Rate: Day $25 **Week** n/a **Month** n/a
Heads: 12 Toilet(s), 8 Shower(s) *(with dressing rooms)*
Laundry: 4 Washer(s), 4 Dryer(s), Book Exchange **Pay Phones:** Yes, 5
Pump-Out: OnSite, Self Service **Fee:** Free** **Closed Heads:** Yes

Marina Operations
Owner/Manager: Steve Wachter **Dockmaster:** Same
In-Season: May-Sep, 8am-10pm **Off-Season:** Oct-Apr, 8:30am-8pm
After-Hours Arrival: Call ahead.
Reservations: Yes **Credit Cards:** Visa/MC, Amex
Discounts: None
Pets: Welcome, Dog Walk Area **Handicap Access:** Yes, Heads

Marina Services and Boat Supplies
Services - Docking Assistance, Concierge, Boaters' Lounge, Trash Pick-Up, Dock Carts, Megayacht Facilities, 3 Phase **Communication -** Mail & Package Hold, Phone Messages, Fax in/out *(Yes)*, Data Ports *(Capri West & Wi-Fi)*, FedEx, AirBorne, UPS, Express Mail *(Sat Del)* **Supplies - OnSite:** Ice *(Block, Cube)*, Ships' Store **OnCall:** CNG **Under 1 mi:** West Marine *(944-1729)*, Bait/Tackle *(R&G 883-3958)* **1-3 mi:** Propane *(Shields)*

Boatyard Services
OnSite: Travelift *(3 travelifts, 20-70T)*, Forklift, Crane, Engine mechanic *(gas, diesel)*, Electrical Repairs, Electronics Repairs, Hull Repairs, Rigger, Bottom Cleaning, Brightwork, Air Conditioning, Refrigeration, Compound, Wash & Wax, Interior Cleaning, Propeller Repairs, Woodworking, Awlgrip, Yacht Broker **OnCall:** Divers, Inflatable Repairs, Life Raft Service, Yacht Interiors, Metal Fabrication **Near:** Launching Ramp. **Under 1 mi:** Sail Loft. **Dealer for:** Mercruiser, Northern Lights, Cat, Man, Volvo, Westerbeke. **Member:** ABBRA, ABYC **Yard Rates:** $55-75/hr., Haul & Launch $7-10/ft. *(blocking incl.)*, Power Wash $2.50, Bottom Paint $15/ft. (paint incl.) **Storage:** In-Water $35/ft., On-Land $34-40/ft.

Restaurants and Accommodations
OnSite: Restaurant *(Dimaggio's on the Bay 944-5900, L $6-18, D $15-28, Sun brunch $22 with cocktail)*, Lite Fare *(Senor Coco Waterfront Café 767-6505, L $5-10, salads, burgers, mexican)* **Near:** Restaurant *(Bill's Harbor Inn 883-3554)*, *(Mi Ranchito 94-479-26)*, Snack Bar *(Munchies 767-0269)* **Under 1 mi:** Restaurant *(Piccola Liguria 767-6490)*, *(Watersedge 767-2755)*, Fast Food, Lite Fare *(Yogurt & Such 883-8862)* **1-3 mi:** Seafood Shack *(Louie's 883-4242)*, Inn/B&B *(Inn of Port Washington 883-3122)*

Recreation and Entertainment
OnSite: Pool, Video Arcade **Near:** Picnic Area, Grills, Playground, Volleyball, Tennis Courts, Park *(Manorhaven Beach - tennis, ball fields, picnic pavilions)* **Under 1 mi:** Beach, Jogging Paths, Roller Blade/Bike Paths, Movie Theater *(Soundview 944-3900)*, Video Rental *(Blockbuster 883-5533)* **1-3 mi:** Golf Course *(N. Hempstead 767-4800)*, Museum *(Polish American 883-6542; North Shore Science 627-9400; American Merchant Marine 466-9696)*, Cultural Attract *(Cow Neck Historical Soc. 365-9074)*

Provisioning and General Services
OnSite: Copies Etc. **Near:** Convenience Store *(La Hispana 767-1600)*, Dry Cleaners, Laundry **Under 1 mi:** Gourmet Shop *(Razzanos 883-5033)*, Delicatessen *(Manorhaven Mkt 883-8130)*, Liquor Store *(Black Tie 767-9000)*, Bank/ATM, Post Office, Catholic Church, Protestant Church, Synagogue, Beauty Salon, Bookstore, Pharmacy *(Genovese 883-8830)*, Hardware Store *(Manorhaven 767-0068)*, Florist **1-3 mi:** Supermarket *(King Kullen 883-9733)*, Library *(Port Washington 883-4400)*, Retail Shops

Transportation
OnSite: Courtesy Car/Van *(weekends)* **OnCall:** Water Taxi *($6 RT, $25 unlimited Ch.9 /767-1691)*, Rental Car *(Enterprise 487-0055; Avis 944-8194 1 mi.)*, Taxi *(Delux 883-1900)*, Airport Limo *(N. Shore 627-0900)* **Under 1 mi:** Local Bus, Rail *(LIRR to NY)* **Airport:** LaGuardia/JFK *(15 mi./20 mi.)*

Medical Services
911 Service **OnCall:** Ambulance **Under 1 mi:** Doctor *(Webster 767-3774)*, Dentist *(Berglass 883-4477)* **1-3 mi:** Chiropractor, Veterinarian *(P.W. Animal Hosp. 883-2005)* **Hospital:** St Francis 562-6200 *(4 mi.)*

Setting -- Two large arms, populated with networks of docks, stretch out into Manhasset Bay just inside Plum Point. Brewer Capri East and Capri West are about a block apart and each has its own set of excellent facilities and superb service staff. They are separated by North Shore Yacht Club, Orchard Beach Bath Club, and a condo development. Wide open views of Manhasset Bay contrast nicely with the quiet and residential neighborhood setting.

Marina Notes -- *Under 50' $2/ft., 50-75' $2.75/ft., 75'+ $3/ft. **Fee for pump-out if service needed. Founded in the 1950's and acquired by Brewer in 1999, this is truly a full-service boatyard: mechanic 7 days, 24/7 dock help and security, plus megayacht facilities - 100'+ slips, and 3 phase, 100 amp electric ($40 per line). The pool, DiMaggio's Restaurant & Senor Coco Café (inside or deck dining), Capt's Quarters Library with Internet access, the dockmasters' office, and the Quarterdeck game room are at Capri West. The courtesy car (weekends) is at Capri East. Both yards have golf cart service to the slips. 2 sets of heads in West (1 with showers), 1 set in East. Seaplane dock. Bay Watch yacht broker onsite. Corporate and charter pick-up available. Beacon Wi-Fi (203-762-2657).

Notable -- Less than a mile away is Soundview Marketplace, a large shopping center with a bank, West Marine, supermarket, movie theater, Carvel, and many other services. Cheeburger Cheeburger offers "fast food" (burgers, grilled chicken, salads, shakes), and Rib Roost (944-3272) is in the new shopping mall a little farther away. Famous Louie's Shore Restaurant is next to Inspiration Wharf (seasonal dockage only) - call the water taxi. A waterfront town park with tennis and a ball field is a short walk away. Seasonal farmers' market at the Town Dock Sat 8am-Noon. Annual Port Washington Harborfest - June.

Navigational Information
Lat: 40°50.243' **Long:** 073°43.213' **Tide:** 7 ft. **Current:** 1 kt. **Chart:** 12366
Rep. Depths *(MLW)*: **Entry** n/a **Fuel Dock** n/a **Max Slip/Moor** -/10 ft.
Access: Manhasset Bay, past Brewer Capri, mooring field is off the gas dock

Marina Facilities *(In Season/Off Season)*
Fuel: No
Slips: 0 Total, 0 Transient **Max LOA:** n/a **Max Beam:** n/a
 Rate *(per ft.)*: **Day** n/a **Week** n/a **Month** n/a
 Power: 30 amp n/a, 50 amp n/a, 100 amp n/a, 200 amp n/a
 Cable TV: No **Dockside Phone:** No
 Dock Type: n/a
Moorings: 85 Total, 6 Transient **Launch:** Yes (Free), Dinghy Dock
 Rate: Day $30 **Week** $125 **Month** $500
Heads: 2 Toilet(s), 2 Shower(s) *(with dressing rooms)*
Laundry: None **Pay Phones:** No
Pump-Out: OnCall **Fee:** Free **Closed Heads:** Yes

Marina Operations
Owner/Manager: Capt. Vic Geryk **Dockmaster:** Same
In-Season: May 15-Sep, 9am-10:45pm **Off-Season:** Oct-May 14, 9am-6pm
After-Hours Arrival: Pick up mooring. See launch driver in the am
Reservations: Yes **Credit Cards:** Cash
Discounts: None
Pets: Welcome **Handicap Access:** No

North Shore Yacht Club

73 Orchard Beach Boulevard; Port Washington, NY 11050

Tel: (516) 883-9823 **VHF: Monitor** 78 **Talk** 78
Fax: (516) 883-7185 **Alternate Tel:** n/a
Email: n/a **Web:** www.nsyc.org
Nearest Town: Port Washington *(0.5 mi.)* **Tourist Info:** (516) 886-6566

Marina Services and Boat Supplies
Communication - Data Ports *(Beacon Wi-Fi)* **Supplies - OnSite:** Ice *(Block, Cube)* **Under 1 mi:** West Marine *(944-1729)*, Bait/Tackle *(R&G 883-3958)* **1-3 mi:** Propane *(Shields 767-0300)*

Boatyard Services
Nearest Yard: Brewer Capri Marina (516) 883-7800

Restaurants and Accommodations
Near: Restaurant *(DiMaggio's on the Bay 944-5900, L $6-18, D $16-28, Sun Brunch $22)*, *(Chowder House 767-7924)*, *(Bills Harbor Inn 883-3554)*, *(MiRanchito Grill B, L, D)*, Lite Fare *(Senor Coco's Waterfront Cafe 767-6505)* **Under 1 mi:** Restaurant *(La Mottas 944-7900, L $8-15, D $9-12, inside or outside)*, *(Romantico 767-0077)*, Pizzeria *(Lastella 883-4191)* **1-3 mi:** Restaurant *(Pomodoro 767-7164)*, Seafood Shack *(Seaport 883-3030)*, Inn/B&B *(Inn of Port Washington 883-3122)* **3+ mi:** Motel *(Royal Inn 627-5567, 4 mi.)*, Hotel *(Bayberry-Great Neck 482-2900, 4 mi.)*

Recreation and Entertainment
Near: Tennis Courts *(Manorhaven Beach or Wildwood Pool & Tennis Club 482-9447 - 1.5 mi.)*, Video Rental, Video Arcade, Park, Special Events *(Concerts all summer long at Bar Beach Park)* **1-3 mi:** Golf Course *(North Hempstead 767-4800)*, Fitness Center *(Kings Point Fitness 773-8778)*, Movie Theater *(Soundview Cinema 944-3900)*, Museum *(Polish American Museum 883-6542, US Merchant Marine Museum 466-9696, Science Museum of LI 627-9400)*, Cultural Attract *(Landmark On Main St. 767-6444)*, Sightseeing *(216-acre Sands Point Preserve, a former estate of the Guggenheims, the Hempstead House and the Falaise 571-7900 -*

nature trails and exhibits for all ages tours in the summer, call for hours), Galleries *(Sculpture Laboratory 883-2544)*

Provisioning and General Services
Near: Gourmet Shop *(Razzanos 883-5033)*, Delicatessen *(Munchies 767-0269)*, Wine/Beer, Bank/ATM, Hardware Store *(Manorhaven Hardware 767-0068)*, Florist **Under 1 mi:** Supermarket *(King Kullen 883-9733, Grand Union 883-9549)*, Liquor Store *(Black Tie 767-9000)*, Farmers' Market *(Town Dock Sat 8am-Noon, seasonal)*, Lobster Pound, Catholic Church, Protestant Church, Library *(Port Washington 883-4400)*, Beauty Salon, Barber Shop, Dry Cleaners, Laundry, Pharmacy *(Genovese 883-8830)*, Clothing Store, Retail Shops, Copies Etc. *(Finer Touch Printing 944-8000)* **1-3 mi:** Bakery *(St Honore Pastry Shop 767-2555)*, Bookstore *(Dolphin Bookshop 767-2650)*

Transportation
OnCall: Rental Car *(Enterprise 487-0055; Avis 944-8194 1 mi.)*, Taxi *(Red Arrow 621-4500)*, Airport Limo *(North Shore Airport Service 627-0900)* **Near:** Local Bus **Under 1 mi:** Rail *(LIRR to NYC)* **1-3 mi:** Bikes *(Port Washington Cyclery 883-8243)* **Airport:** La Guardia/JFK *(15 mi./20 mi.)*

Medical Services
911 Service **OnCall:** Ambulance **Under 1 mi:** Doctor *(Webster 767-3774)*, Dentist *(Berglass 883-4477)*, Holistic Services *(Therapeutic Massage 883-4869)* **1-3 mi:** Chiropractor *(Sandy Hollow Chiropractic 883-1305)*, Veterinarian *(Port Washington Animal Hosp. 883-2005)*, Optician *(Katims 767-2106)* **Hospital:** St Francis 562-6060 *(4 mi.)*

Setting -- Snuggled safely inside Plum Point, between Brewer Capri Marina West and Orchard Beach Bath Club, North Shore Yacht Club offers privacy in a very convenient location. The narrow two-story clubhouse is perched squarely above the head of the wide main pier. A work boat and comfortable club launch service the mooring field beyond. Views are of wide-open, spectacular Manhasset Harbor.

Marina Notes -- Established in 1871, this is the oldest yacht club on Long Island. Small and friendly, it welcomes all boaters; reciprocity not required. The clubhouse has a large, lovely second floor club room, with contemporary furnishings and a deck overlooking the harbor, a great kitchen. and attractively decorated fully-tiled heads and showers. All important Wi-Fi web/email access right on the dock or possibly on your boat through Beacon Wireless Broadband (203-762-2657). The launch runs mid-May to LabDay 8am-11pm, Mid-Apr to Mid-May and Sep-Nov weekdays Noon-4:45, weekends 9am -7:45. If they are full, try the Town of North Hempstead, which has 5 free moorings. Use the Town dinghy dock or water taxi service.

Notable -- Many restaurants and almost any service you might need are within easy reach. Walk next door to Brewer Capri's DiMaggio's for dinner or to Senor Coco Café for a light lunch. The Manhasset Bay Water Taxi (Ch.9) will take you to restaurants on the harbor, including Louie's next to Inspiration Wharf--which has been totally renovated with a new deck overlooking the harbor and new docks for customers. It's a relatively easy walk to Soundview Marketplace with a supermarket, movies, take-out, and other services. Tennis courts and picnic tables are nearby at Manorhaven Beach Park.

Toms Point Marina

1 Sagamore Hill Drive; Port Washington, NY 11050

Tel: (516) 883-6630 **VHF: Monitor** 68 **Talk** 17
Fax: (516) 767-0386 **Alternate Tel:** (516) 883-6630
Email: n/a **Web:** www.tomspointmarina.com
Nearest Town: Port Washington *(1 mi.)* **Tourist Info:** (516) 883-6566

Navigational Information
Lat: 40°50.090' **Long:** 073°42.462' **Tide:** 7 ft. **Current:** 2 kt. **Chart:** 13266
Rep. Depths *(MLW)*: **Entry** 6 ft. **Fuel Dock** n/a **Max Slip/Moor** 6 ft./-
Access: Long Island Sound to Manhasset Bay, just around Tom Pt.

Marina Facilities *(In Season/Off Season)*
Fuel: No
Slips: 135 Total, 1- Transient **Max LOA:** 42 ft. **Max Beam:** n/a
Rate *(per ft.)*: **Day** $1.50/Inq. **Week** Inq. **Month** Inq.
Power: 30 amp Incl., **50 amp** n/a, **100 amp** n/a, **200 amp** n/a
Cable TV: No **Dockside Phone:** No
Dock Type: Floating, Long Fingers, Alongside, Concrete, Wood
Moorings: 0 Total, 0 Transient **Launch:** n/a
Rate: Day n/a **Week** n/a **Month** n/a
Heads: 2 Toilet(s)
Laundry: 1 Washer(s), 1 Dryer(s) **Pay Phones:** No
Pump-Out: OnSite, Self Service **Fee:** Free **Closed Heads:** Yes

Marina Operations
Owner/Manager: Tony Luccaro **Dockmaster:** Same
In-Season: Year-Round, 8am-5pm **Off-Season:** n/a
After-Hours Arrival: Call in advance
Reservations: Yes, Preferred **Credit Cards:** Visa/MC
Discounts: Boat/US **Dockage:** 25% **Fuel:** n/a **Repair:** n/a
Pets: Welcome **Handicap Access:** No

Marina Services and Boat Supplies
Services - Docking Assistance, Dock Carts **Communication -** Data Ports *(Beacon Wi-Fi)*, FedEx, AirBorne, UPS, Express Mail *(Sat Del)* **Supplies - OnSite:** Ice *(Cube)* **Near:** Ships' Store, West Marine *(944-1729)* **Under 1 mi:** Bait/Tackle *(R&G 883-3958)*, Propane *(Shields 767-0300)*

Boatyard Services
OnSite: Crane, Engine mechanic *(gas)*, Electrical Repairs, Hull Repairs, Rigger, Bottom Cleaning, Brightwork, Air Conditioning, Refrigeration, Compound, Wash & Wax, Propeller Repairs, Woodworking, Painting, Awlgrip, Total Refits **Under 1 mi:** Launching Ramp. **Yard Rates:** $65/hr., Haul & Launch $6/ft. *(blocking $2/ft.)*, Power Wash $2, Bottom Paint $12/ft. **Storage:** In-Water $22/ft., On-Land $30/ft.

Restaurants and Accommodations
OnCall: Pizzeria *(Carlo's 944-4754)* **Near:** Restaurant *(Piccola Liguria 767-6490)*, *(Cheeburger 767-1144, L $5-11, D $5-11)*, *(LaMotta's 944-7900, L $8-15, D $9-22)*, Pizzeria *(Lastella 884-4191)* **Under 1 mi:** Restaurant *(Port Seafood)*, *(Latitudes 776-7400)*, *(Pastabilities 883-9067)*, *(Romantico 767-0077)*, *(Gum How Kitchen 944-8713)*, *(Louie's Shore Restaurant 883-4242)*, Lite Fare *(Yogurt & Such 883-8862)*, Inn/B&B *(Inn of Port Washington 883-3122)* **3+ mi:** Motel *(Royal Inn 627-5300, 3 mi.)*, Hotel *(Bayberry-Great Neck 482-2900, 4 mi.)*

Recreation and Entertainment
OnSite: Picnic Area, Grills **Near:** Video Rental *(Blockbuster 883-5533)*, Park *(Bar Beach Park, Manorhaven Beach)* **Under 1 mi:** Movie Theater *(Soundview Cinema 944-3900)*, Special Events *(Concerts, HarborFest)*

1-3 mi: Pool, Beach, Playground, Tennis Courts *(Wildwood Pool & Tennis Club 482-9447)*, Golf Course *(North Hempstead 767-4800)*, Fitness Center *(Fitness Express 944-2270)*, Museum *(Polish American Museum 883-6542, American Merchant Marine Museum 466-9696)*, Cultural Attract *(Landmark On Main St. 767-6444)*, Sightseeing *(Sands Point Preserve 571-7900)*

Provisioning and General Services
OnCall: Delicatessen **Near:** Supermarket *(Grand Union 883-9549)*, Wine/Beer, Liquor Store *(Village Wines & Liquors 883-7066)*, Bank/ATM, Post Office, Beauty Salon, Barber Shop, Dry Cleaners, Laundry, Newsstand, Copies Etc. *(Finer Touch Printing 944-8000)* **Under 1 mi:** Gourmet Shop *(Mediterranean Mkt Place 767-1400)*, Health Food *(Renaissance Natural Foods 883-1157)*, Farmers' Market *(summer only at Town Dock, Sat 8am-Noon)*, Pharmacy *(Genovese 883-8830)*, Hardware Store *(Manorhaven 767-0068)* **1-3 mi:** Catholic Church, Library *(Port Washington 883-4400)*, Bookstore *(Dolphin Bookshop 767-2650)*

Transportation
OnCall: Rental Car *(Enterprise 487-0055; Avis 944-8194 1 mi.)*, Taxi *(Delux 883-1900)*, Airport Limo *(North Shore 627-0900)* **Near:** Local Bus **Under 1 mi:** Rail *(LIRR to NY City)* **1-3 mi:** Bikes *(P.W. Cyclery 883-8243)* **Airport:** LaGuardia/JFK *(15 mi./20 mi.)*

Medical Services
911 Service **OnCall:** Ambulance **Near:** Dentist *(Berglass 883-4477)* **Under 1 mi:** Doctor *(Webster 767-3774)* **1-3 mi:** Chiropractor *(Sandy Hollow Chiropractic 883-1305)*, Veterinarian *(Port Washington Animal Hosp. 883-2005)* **Hospital:** St. Francis 562-6060 *(4 mi.)*

Setting -- About half way down the harbor, tucked behind Tom Point, is down-home, family-oriented Toms Point Marina. The surrounding area is quite industrial and the marina itself caters to a unique combination of smaller boats, larger seasonals and liveaboards. The rarely-seen collection of houseboats is certainly worth a stop. A flagpole announces the presence of a waterfront picnic deck with tables, chairs and grills adjacent to the marina office.

Marina Notes -- Family owned and operated by the Luccaro Family since 1970, this service-oriented marina offers protected docks, mostly for smaller boats; occasionally a 42 foot slip is available for transients. Engine mechanic on staff 8am-5pm Mon-Fri. Winter storage and lots of parking for boaters. An OMC dealer, and also home to Quantum Sails and a fishing charter operations. Beacon Wi-Fi broadband service available (203-762-2657).

Notable -- Conveniently located, Toms Point is about 0.4 mile from a large shopping center (supermarket, bank, West Marine, fast food, and more), parks, and other recreational facilities. Manhasset Bay Marina is just up the road making La Motta's restaurant a very easy walk. Hail the water taxi or dinghy across the cove to the town dock next to Inspiration Wharf for more restaurants, including Port Seafood Grille, or the all-new Louie's Shoreside which also has brand new docks. Visit Sands Point Preserve, home to impressive castles, a large collection of Wedgwood china, and wonderful nature trails. The Museum at the US Merchant Marine Academy has a great collection of maritime artifacts and ships models (Tue-Fri 10-3:30, Sat-Sun 1-4:30). On a rainy day, the Science Museum of LI, open daily, has great activities for children (627-9400).

Navigational Information
Lat: 40°50.170' **Long:** 073°42.317' **Tide:** 7 ft. **Current:** n/a **Chart:** 12366
Rep. Depths *(MLW)*: **Entry** 8 ft. **Fuel Dock** 6 ft. **Max Slip/Moor** 7 ft./-
Access: Long Island Sound to Manhasset Bay around Tom Point

Marina Facilities *(In Season/Off Season)*
Fuel: *Texaco* - Gasoline, Diesel
Slips: 285 Total, 50 Transient **Max LOA:** 110 ft. **Max Beam:** n/a
  Rate *(per ft.)*: **Day** $6.00 **Week** $42 **Month** $25
  Power: 30 amp Incl., **50 amp** Incl., **100 amp** n/a, **200 amp** n/a
  Cable TV: Yes **Dockside Phone:** Yes
  Dock Type: Floating, Long Fingers
Moorings: 25 Total, 25 Transient **Launch:** Yes (Free), Dinghy Dock
  Rate: Day $25 **Week** $100 **Month** $500
Heads: 4 Toilet(s), 2 Shower(s)
Laundry: 2 Washer(s), 2 Dryer(s) **Pay Phones:** Yes
Pump-Out: OnSite **Fee:** Free **Closed Heads:** Yes

Marina Operations
Owner/Manager: LaMotta Family **Dockmaster:** Guy LaMotta
In-Season: May-October, 8am-8pm **Off-Season:** Nov-Apr, 8am-5pm
After-Hours Arrival: Tie up at the fuel dock.
Reservations: Yes **Credit Cards:** Visa/MC, Dscvr, Amex, Tex
Discounts: Boat/US; Naut. Miles* **Dockage:** 25% **Fuel:** $.10 **Repair:** n/a
Pets: Welcome, Dog Walk Area **Handicap Access:** Yes

Manhasset Bay Marina

10 Matinecock Avenue; Port Washington, NY 11050

Tel: (516) 883-8411 **VHF: Monitor** 9 **Talk** 71
Fax: (516) 883-8957 **Alternate Tel:** (516) 767-9129
Email: mbmaria@msn.com **Web:** marinas.com/manhassetbaymarina
Nearest Town: Port Washington *(1 mi.)* **Tourist Info:** (516) 883-6566

Marina Services and Boat Supplies
Services - Docking Assistance, Concierge, Trash Pick-Up, Dock Carts **Communication -** Mail & Package Hold, Phone Messages, Fax in/out, Data Ports *(Beacon Wi-Fi)*, FedEx, AirBorne, UPS, Express Mail *(Sat Del)* **Supplies - OnSite:** Ice *(Cube)*, Ships' Store **OnCall:** Bait/Tackle, Propane **Near:** West Marine *(944-1729)*

Boatyard Services
OnSite: Travelift *(80T)*, Forklift *(10T)*, Crane *(20T)*, Engine mechanic *(gas, diesel)*, Electrical Repairs, Hull Repairs, Bottom Cleaning, Brightwork, Compound, Wash & Wax, Interior Cleaning, Metal Fabrication, Painting, Awlgrip, Yacht Broker **OnCall:** Electronics Repairs, Rigger, Refrigeration **Near:** Launching Ramp. **Dealer for:** Marine Power, MerCruiser Stern Drives, Volvo Penta, Crusader, Onan. **Yard Rates:** Haul & Launch $8/ft., Power Wash $2, Bottom Paint $15/ft. *(paint incl.)* **Storage:** In-Water $30/ft., On-Land $36/ft.

Restaurants and Accommodations
OnSite: Restaurant *(LaMotta's 944-7900, L $8-15, D $9-26, Inside/outside dining, seafood)*, Snack Bar **Near:** Restaurant *(Piccola Liguria 767-6490)*, *(Romantico 767-0077)*, Pizzeria *(Lastella 883-4191)* **Under 1 mi:** Restaurant *(Pastabilities 883-9067)*, *(Louie's Shore 883-4242)*, *(Shish-Kebab 883-9309)*, Seafood Shack *(Seaport 883-3030)*, Inn/B&B *(Inn of Port Washington 883-3122)* **3+ mi:** Motel *(Royal Inn 627-5300, 3 mi.)*, Hotel *(Bayberry-Great Neck 482-2900, 4 mi.)*

Recreation and Entertainment
OnSite: Picnic Area, Grills, Sightseeing *(Statue of Liberty cruise $65-95)*,

Special Events *(HarborFest, Fiesta Italiana, Pride in Port)* **Under 1 mi:** Pool, Beach, Playground, Dive Shop, Golf Course *(North Hempstead 767-4800)*, Jogging Paths, Boat Rentals, Roller Blade/Bike Paths, Movie Theater *(Port Washington 944-6200)*, Video Rental *(Blockbuster 883-5533)*, Park **1-3 mi:** Tennis Courts *(Wildwood Pool & Tennis Club 482-9447)*, Fitness Center *(Fitness Express 944-2270)*, Museum *(Polish American Museum 883-6542; Leeds Pond Preserve Science Museum 627-9400)*

Provisioning and General Services
Near: Delicatessen *(Bayview 883-7788)*, Copies Etc. *(Finer Touch 944-8000)* **Under 1 mi:** Supermarket *(Grand Union 883-9549)*, Gourmet Shop *(Mediterranean Mkt 767-1400)*, Health Food *(Renaissance 883-1157)*, Liquor Store *(Black Tie 767-9000)*, Bakery, Farmers' Market, Fishmonger, Bank/ATM, Post Office, Catholic Church, Protestant Church, Synagogue, Library *(Port Washington 883-4400)*, Beauty Salon, Dry Cleaners, Laundry, Pharmacy *(Genovese 883-8830)*, Hardware Store *(Alpers True Value 767-0508)*, Florist **1-3 mi:** Bookstore *(Dolphin Bookshop 767-2650)*

Transportation
OnSite: Courtesy Car/Van, Taxi **OnCall:** Rental Car *(Enterprise 487-0055, Avis 944-8194 1 mi.)*, Airport Limo *(North Shore 627-0900)* **Under 1 mi:** Bikes *(Port Washington Cyclery 883-8243)*, Water Taxi, Rail *(LIRR to NYC)* **Airport:** LaGuardia/JFK *(15 mi./20 mi.)*

Medical Services
911 Service **OnCall:** Ambulance **Under 1 mi:** Doctor, Dentist, Chiropractor **1-3 mi:** Veterinarian *(Port Washington Animal Hosp. 883-2005)* **Hospital:** St Francis 562-6060 *(4 mi.)*

Setting -- Located in a protected cove around Tom Point, off beautiful Manhasset Bay, this large, very active and nicely maintained marina is easily identified by the white lighthouse and the restaurant's red and white domed roof. It specializes in and caters primarily to power boats - particularly big racing boats.

Marina Notes -- Owned and operated by the LaMotta Family since 1970. Fuel, onsite ship's store, 24-hour security, and courtesy car service. The full-service boatyard provides all the support a boater might need, with 80 ton haul-out capacity and mechanics on staff. *Nautical Miles discounts: 15% off dockage, $0.10/gal on fuel, 10% off ship's store non-sale items, 15% off food & beverage. Individual, tiled heads and showers, and laundry onsite. Beacon Wi-Fi Network Service (203-762-2657). Home of the National Power Boat Association's Annual Manhasset Bay Gold Cup races (If "go fast" interests you - this is the place). Captain's Quarters Nautical Embroidery shop on premises. Water taxi services the whole bay.

Notable -- Onsite is a snack bar for breakfast and lunch, and the waterfront La Motta's Restaurant, overlooking the marina, for lunch (11:30-4pm), dinner (4:30-9pm, 'til 10pm Fri & Sat) and Sunday Brunch - a 24 foot buffet (11:30am-3pm). The unusual interior includes a hand-painted half round cathedral ceiling embellished with yachting flags. (The red & white dome is from Sinclair Oil's '64 World's Fair Exhibit - ask for details.) There's also live entertainment and a sports bar. Daily Lady Liberty lunch/dinner cruises to the Statue of Liberty. It's about 0.3 mile to a major shopping center with all services and supplies. Tennis courts, picnic tables, and a ball field are nearby at Manorhaven Beach Park. Organic farmers' market at the Town Dock Sat 8am-Noon in season.

North Hempstead Town Moorings

Town Dock, Main Street;* Port Washington, NY 11501

Tel: (516) 767-4622 **VHF: Monitor** 9/16 **Talk** 6
Fax: (516) 327-1900 **Alternate Tel:** n/a
Email: warrenschein@northhempstead.com **Web:** northhempstead.com
Nearest Town: Port Washington *(1 mi.)* **Tourist Info:** (516) 883-6566

Navigational Information
Lat: 40°49.880' **Long:** 073°42.630' **Tide:** 7 ft. **Current:** 1 kt. **Chart:** 12364
Rep. Depths *(MLW)*: **Entry** 15 ft. **Fuel Dock** n/a **Max Slip/Moor** 7 ft./15 ft.
Access: Manhasset Bay to center of harbor west of Inspiration Wharf

Marina Facilities *(In Season/Off Season)*
Fuel: No
Slips: 0 Total, 0 Transient **Max LOA:** 50 ft. **Max Beam:** n/a
 Rate *(per ft.)*: **Day** n/a **Week** n/a **Month** n/a
 Power: 30 amp n/a, 50 amp n/a, 100 amp n/a, 200 amp n/a
 Cable TV: No **Dockside Phone:** No
 Dock Type: n/a
Moorings: 5 Total, 5 Transient **Launch:** M.B. Water Taxi ($6/RT pp)
 Rate: Day Free **Week** n/a **Month** n/a
Heads: None
Laundry: None **Pay Phones:** No
Pump-Out: OnSite, Self Service **Fee:** Free **Closed Heads:** Yes

Marina Operations
Owner/Manager: Warren Schein (H.M.) **Dockmaster:** Mallory Nathan (B.C.)
In-Season: May-Oct, 8am-Mid **Off-Season:** n/a
After-Hours Arrival: n/a
Reservations: No **Credit Cards:** n/a
Discounts: None
Pets: Welcome, Dog Walk Area **Handicap Access:** No

Marina Services and Boat Supplies
Services - Trash Pick-Up **Supplies - Near:** Ice *(Cube)*, Ships' Store, Bait/Tackle *(R7G 883-3958)* **Under 1 mi:** West Marine *(944-1729)*, Propane *(Shields)*

Boatyard Services
Nearest Yard: Manhasset Bay Marina (516) 883-8411

Restaurants and Accommodations
Near: Restaurant *(Bongo Bay 767-2900, Dock)*, *(Louie's Shore 883-4242, Dock)*, *(LaMotta's 944-7900, L $8-15, D $9-22, Dock at Manhasset Bay Marina)*, *(Dynasty 883-4100, Dock)*, *(Nicole's 883-0091)*, *(Pomodoro 767-7164)*, *(Finn MacCool's 944-3439)*, *(Ayhan's Shish-Kebab 883-9309, L $7-10, D $12-20)*, Snack Bar *(Douglas & Jones Ice Cream)*
Under 1 mi: Restaurant *(DiMaggio's 944-5900, L $6-18, D $15-28, BrewerCapri)*, Lite Fare *(Senor Coco L $5-10, Brewer Capri)*

Recreation and Entertainment
OnSite: Park *(Sunset Park & Town Dock)*, Cultural Attract *(John Philip Sousa Memorial Bandshell Concerts in Sunset Park; also Bar Beach Park Summer Concerts Free; and nearby the Jeanne Rimsky Theater - a Landmark)*, Special Events *(HarborFest - weekend before MemDay)*
Near: Beach *(Bar Beach Park 327-3100)*, Picnic Area *(Sunset Park)*, Playground, Fitness Center *(P.W. Kung Fu Academy & Yoga Ctr 944-0832; Training Station 944-5009 1 mi.)*, Jogging Paths, Boat Rentals *(Inspiration Wharf)*, Galleries *(Graphic Eye 883-9668; Artists Studio 767-8702)*
Under 1 mi: Tennis Courts *(Port Washington Academy 883-6425)*, Golf Course *(North Hempstead 767-4800; Harbor Links 767-4800 2.5 mi.)*,

Movie Theater *(P.W. Cine 944 6200)*, Video Rental *(Blockbuster 883 5533)*
1-3 mi: Museum *(18 room 1735 Sands-Willets House Museum 365-9074)*, Sightseeing *(Sands Point Preserve 571-7900 218 acre Gould/Guggenheim estate - Castlegould $4/3, Falaise, a Norman manor house $6, no children; Hempstead House $4 and nature preserve $6/4)*

Provisioning and General Services
OnSite: Farmers' Market *(Sat 8am-noon, seasonal)* **Near:** Supermarket *(King Kullen 883-9733)*, Gourmet Shop *(Mediterranean Mkt Place 767-1400)*, Delicatessen *(Harbor 883-9597)*, Wine/Beer *(XTC 883-6488)*, Liquor Store, Bank/ATM, Synagogue, Library *(883-4400)*, Beauty Salon *(Diane's Spa)*, Newsstand, Retail Shops **Under 1 mi:** Health Food *(Renaissance 883-1157)*, Bakery *(Baked 944-5642)*, Fishmonger *(North Shore Farm 944-2205)*, Meat Market *(Main St. 767-1260)*, Post Office, Catholic Church, Protestant Church, Dry Cleaners *(Newman 883-8260)*, Laundry *(Coin-Op 883-9760)*, Bookstore *(Dolphin 767-2650)*, Pharmacy *(Beacon 883-1155)*, Hardware Store *(Alper's 767-0508)*, Copies Etc. *(Trotter's 944-6851)*

Transportation
OnCall: Water Taxi *(Manhasset Bay Water Taxi Ch.68, 767-1691)*, Taxi *(AA Madison 883-3800)*, Airport Limo *(Polo 944-2255)* **Under 1 mi:** Rental Car *(Avis 944-8194)*, Rail *(LIRR to NYC)* **Airport:** LaGuardia *(10 mi.)*

Medical Services
911 Service **OnCall:** Ambulance **Near:** Chiropractor *(Vitaglione 767-7220)*, Veterinarian *(Port Washington 883-2005)*, Optician *(Katims 767-2106)*
Under 1 mi: Doctor *(Bienenstock 767-3161)*, Holistic Services *(Body Works 767-6370)* **Hospital:** Long Island Jewish 365-1145 *(3 mi.)*

Setting -- West of Inspiration Wharf and the North Hempstead Town Docks at Sunset Park, are the conveniently-located, complimentary North Hempstead Moorings. They provide a perfect venue for enjoying beautiful, welcoming Manhasset Bay as well as its many handy waterfront eateries with docks.

Marina Notes -- The free North Hempstead Town Moorings have been installed as a gift to the boating community by the Manhasset Bay Water Taxi (Ch.68, 767-1691). The moorings are White with TNH imprinted on them and attached to a tallboy. Maximum stay is 24 hours (exceptions only for inclement weather). Please radio the Harbormaster (Warren Schein) or Bay Constable (Mallory Nathan) to inquire about availability or to notify them that you've found a vacant mooring. The North Hempstead Town Dock, just north of Louie's Shore Restaurant, has 7 feet at MLW and is staffed from 8am to midnight in the summer. There's a dinghy dock. Big boats can also tie up for 15 minutes. A brand new stationary vacuum-system pump-out station has been installed on the Town Dock's north side - it's easy to use, self-service, very fast and free! The Town's pump-out boat (Ch.9, 767-4622) is available to service vessels during the summer and fall. Note: the 5 mph speed limit is enforced. *Mailing Address: 1801 Evergreen Ave.; New Hyde Park, NY 11040.

Notable -- This is a boater-friendly harbor and great effort is made to create a positive experience. The Manhasset Bay Water Taxi will take you to any public waterfront location. Immediately surrounding the Town Dock (and dinghy landing) is a small satellite village that has grown up around Inspiration Wharf. There are eateries, services, and some provisioning options. "Downtown" Port Washington is about a mile and has a shop for just about anything you might need.

Navigational Information
Lat: 40°49.366' **Long:** 073°42.276' **Tide:** 7 ft. **Current:** 1 kt. **Chart:** 12364
Rep. Depths *(MLW):* **Entry** 9 ft. **Fuel Dock** n/a **Max Slip/Moor** -/7 ft.
Access: Manhasset Bay almost to head, last facility to port

Marina Facilities *(In Season/Off Season)*
Fuel: No
Slips: 0 Total, 0 Transient **Max LOA:** 100 ft. **Max Beam:** n/a
  Rate *(per ft.):* **Day** n/a **Week** n/a **Month** n/a
  Power: 30 amp n/a, 50 amp n/a, 100 amp n/a, 200 amp n/a
  Cable TV: No **Dockside Phone:** No
  Dock Type: n/a
Moorings: 250 Total, 20 Transient **Launch:** Yes (Included), Dinghy Dock
  Rate: Day $25 **Week** $150 **Month** n/a
Heads: 6 Toilet(s), 6 Shower(s) *(with dressing rooms)*
Laundry: None **Pay Phones:** No
Pump-Out: OnCall *(Ch.78)* **Fee:** Free **Closed Heads:** Yes

Marina Operations
Owner/Manager: Jorge Giribaldo **Dockmaster:** Keith Haberman
In-Season: MemDay-ColDay, 8-10 **Off-Season:** Apr-May, Sep-Oct, 9-7
After-Hours Arrival: Call in advance
Reservations: Yes **Credit Cards:** Cash
Discounts: None
Pets: Welcome **Handicap Access:** Yes, Heads

Port Washington Yacht Club

One Yacht Club Drive; Port Washington, NY 11050

Tel: (516) 767-1614 **VHF: Monitor** Ch.74 **Talk** n/a
Fax: (516) 767-3531 **Alternate Tel:** n/a
Email: info@pwyc.com **Web:** www.pwyc.com
Nearest Town: Port Washington *(1 mi.)* **Tourist Info:** (516) 883-6566

Marina Services and Boat Supplies
Services - Docking Assistance, Security *(24 hrs.)*, Dock Carts
Communication - Data Ports *(Beacon Wi-Fi)*, FedEx, AirBorne, UPS,
Express Mail *(Sat Del)* **Supplies - OnSite:** Ice *(Block, Cube)*
Under 1 mi: Bait/Tackle *(R&G 883-3958)*, Propane *(Shields 767-0300)*
1-3 mi: West Marine *(944-1729)*

Boatyard Services
Nearest Yard: Manhasset Bay Marina (516) 883-8411

Restaurants and Accommodations
OnSite: Restaurant *(PWYC dining room L $6-13, D $7-29, Kids' Menu $3-6
Members of other YC's only)* **Near:** Restaurant *(Louie's Shore 883-4242,
Dock)*, *(Dynasty 883-4100, Dock)*, *(Bongo Bay 767-2900, Dock)*, *(Nicole
883-0091)* **Under 1 mi:** Restaurant *(Pomodoro 767-7164)*, *(Luigi's
Pastabilities 883-9067)*, *(Finn MacCool 944-3439)*, *(Il Forno 944-0755)*,
(Tsuru No Mai 944-7492), *(Mi Ranchito Grill 767-1300)*, *(Port Seafood Grill
767-7878)*, *(Romantico 767-0077)*, *(Chez Noelle 883-3191)*, Pizzeria
(Lastella 883-4191) **3+ mi:** Inn/B&B *(Royal Inn 627-5300, 3 mi.)*, *(Inn At
Great Neck 773-2000, 5 mi.)*

Recreation and Entertainment
OnSite: Pool, Picnic Area, Playground **Near:** Jogging Paths
Under 1 mi: Beach, Fishing Charter, Movie Theater *(Soundview 944-3900)*,
Video Rental *(Blockbuster 883-5533)*, Park, Cultural Attract *(Jeanne Rimsky
Theatre at Landmark on Main St. 767-6444)* **1-3 mi:** Tennis Courts
(Wildwood Pool & Tennis Club 482-9447), Golf Course *(North Hempstead*

767-4800), Fitness Center *(Fitness Express 944-2270)*, Sightseeing
*(Sands Pt. Preserve 571-7900 - tours of The Hempstead House and
the Falaise; call for hours)*, Galleries *(Sculpture Laboratory 883-2544)*

Provisioning and General Services
Under 1 mi: Supermarket *(King Kullen 883-9733)*, Delicatessen *(Harbor
Delicatessen 883-9597)*, Health Food *(Renaissance Natural Foods 883-
1157)*, Wine/Beer, Liquor Store *(Village Wines & Liquors 883-7066)*,
Bank/ATM, Post Office, Catholic Church, Protestant Church, Synagogue,
Library *(Port Washington 883-4400)*, Dry Cleaners, Laundry, Hardware Store
(Manorhaven 767-0068), Retail Shops **1-3 mi:** Gourmet Shop, Bakery
(Baked To Perfection 944-5642), Farmers' Market *(Town Dock Sat 8am-
Noon, seasonal)*, Fishmonger, Bookstore *(Dolphin Bookshop 767-2650)*,
Pharmacy *(Port Chemists 883-7117)*, Clothing Store, Department Store,
Copies Etc.

Transportation
OnCall: Water Taxi *(Manhasset Bay, Ch.9)*, Rental Car *(Enterprise 487-
0055, Avis 944-8194 - 1 mi.)*, Taxi *(Red Arrow 621-4500)*, Airport Limo
(North Shore Airport Service 627-0900) **Under 1 mi:** Rail *(LIRR to Penn
Station NYC)* **1-3 mi:** Bikes *(Port Washington Cyclery 883-8243)*
Airport: LaGuardia/JFK *(15 mi./20 mi.)*

Medical Services
911 Service **OnCall:** Ambulance **Under 1 mi:** Dentist *(Josen/Ruben
944-2227)*, Veterinarian *(Port Washington Animal Hosp. 883-2005)*
1-3 mi: Doctor, Chiropractor *(Vitaglione 767-7220)*
Hospial: St. Francis 562-6060, *(3 mi.)*

Setting -- Gracious, private Port Washington Yacht Club is safely tucked near the head of Manhasset Bay on the eastern shore. The recently enlarged and beautifully renovated two-story, mostly-windowed, white clubhouse sits at the waterfront, surrounded by impeccably maintained grounds.

Marina Notes -- The moorings, launch service, heads and showers are open to all visiting boaters. The spacious new water-view Dining Room (flags flutter from the trusses of the cathedral ceiling), the outdoor bay-side dining area, and the elegant Commodore's Lounge are open to members of other recognized yacht clubs. Check with the manager regarding the availability (to visiting boaters) of the large, inviting pool with its new pavilion, sizeable well-furnished deck and full snack bar; guest use depends on club events, the day of the week, and member usage. Tennis courts not available to any non-member. Ice and soda machines on dock. Three well maintained launches ply the mooring field Mon-Fri 8am-5pm; Fri-Sun 8am-7pm. Pool 10-7 weekdays, 10-9 weekends. Dining room and patio open Wed-Sun 12-2:30 and 6-9pm. Beacon Wi-Fi Network Service (203-762-2657). Located at Yacht Club Drive and North Plandome Road.

Notable -- Founded in 1905, PWYC was instrumental in establishing the Star sail boat class and then the Meteor class. Continuing that tradition, club racing is Thursday nights & weekend days. The shops and eateries surrounding Inspiration Wharf are less than half a mile away. Famous Louie's Shore Restaurant, under new ownership, has been totally renovated and offers "dock 'n dine" at its new docks. For all waterfront restaurants, hail the Manhasset Bay water taxi on Ch.9. Manhasset's famous Miracle Mile shopping district is about a 5 mile cab ride. Americana Manhasset Mall sports Sephore, Prada, Polo, Tiffany's, etc.

Hempstead Harbour Club

PO Box 192; Garvies Point Road; Glen Cove, NY 11542

Tel: (516) 671-0600 **VHF:** Monitor 72 **Talk** 72
Fax: (516) 759-0369 **Alternate Tel:** n/a
Email: n/a **Web:** www.hempsteadharbourclub.com
Nearest Town: Glen Cove *(1.5 mi.)* **Tourist Info:** (516) 676-6666

Navigational Information

Lat: 40°51.433' **Long:** 073°39.035' **Tide:** 8 ft. **Current:** n/a **Chart:** 12366
Rep. Depths (MLW): Entry 20 ft. **Fuel Dock** n/a **Max Slip/Moor** -/20 ft.
Access: Hempstead Harbor to the breakwater in Mosquito Cove

Marina Facilities *(In Season/Off Season)*

Fuel: No
Slips: 0 Total, 0 Transient **Max LOA:** 44 ft. **Max Beam:** n/a
  Rate *(per ft.):* **Day** n/a **Week** n/a **Month** n/a
  Power: 30 amp n/a, **50 amp** n/a, **100 amp** n/a, **200 amp** n/a
  Cable TV: No **Dockside Phone:** No
  Dock Type: n/a
Moorings: 140 Total, 3 Transient **Launch:** Yes
  Rate: Day $30 **Week** $180 **Month** $650
Heads: 5 Toilet(s), 2 Shower(s) *(with dressing rooms)*
Laundry: None **Pay Phones:** No
Pump-Out: No **Fee:** n/a **Closed Heads:** No

Marina Operations

Owner/Manager: Mike Perito **Dockmaster:** Same
In-Season: May15-Oct15, 10am-10pm **Off-Season:** MidOct-MidMay, Closed
After-Hours Arrival: Call in advance
Reservations: Yes **Credit Cards:** Cash/Checks only
Discounts: None
Pets: Welcome **Handicap Access:** No

Marina Services and Boat Supplies

Services - Boaters' Lounge **Communication -** FedEx, AirBorne, UPS, Express Mail **Supplies - Near:** Ice *(Block, Cube)*, Ships' Store *(Jude Thaddeus Marina by dinghy 759-3129)*, CNG *(at Brewer by dinghy 671-5563)* **1-3 mi:** Propane *(Taylors 759-9646)*

Boatyard Services

Near: Travelift, Engine mechanic *(gas, diesel)*, Electrical Repairs, Electronics Repairs, Hull Repairs, Rigger, Bottom Cleaning, Refrigeration, Propeller Repairs. **Nearest Yard:** Brewer Yacht Yard at Glen Cove (516) 671-5563

Restaurants and Accommodations

OnCall: Pizzeria *(Dominick's 674-4743)* **Near:** Restaurant *(Steamboat Landing 759-3921, D $15-24, by dinghy)* **1-3 mi:** Restaurant *(Ruby Tuesdays 609-8378)*, *(Marra's 609-3335)*, *(Downtown Cafe 759-2233)*, *(American Cafe 656-0003)*, Motel *(Jin Jin 671-3464)*

Recreation and Entertainment

OnSite: Beach, Picnic Area, Grills **Near:** Jogging Paths, Museum *(Garvies Point Museum and Preserve 671-0300)* **1-3 mi:** Tennis Courts *(Cove Tennis Center 759-0505)*, Golf Course *(Glen Cove Golf Course 676-6534)*, Bowling *(Glen Cove Bowl 671-0028)*, Movie Theater *(Cineplex Odeon 671-0028)*, Video Rental *(Blockbuster 674-0690)*

Provisioning and General Services

Under 1 mi: Bank/ATM *(Citibank 627-3999)*, Post Office, Laundry *(B&CF Laundry 676-3383)* **1-3 mi:** Convenience Store *(7-11)*, Market *(Glen Cove Mini Mart 609-0252)*, Supermarket *(Edwards 671-9583)*, Delicatessen *(Welcome 676-8225)*, Health Food *(Rising Tide 676-7895)*, Wine/Beer, Liquor Store *(The Wine Basket 674-3763)*, Bakery, Catholic Church, Protestant Church, Synagogue, Library *(Glen Cove 676-2130)*, Beauty Salon, Barber Shop, Dry Cleaners *(Corniche 759-6530)*, Pharmacy *(Glen Cove 676-9111)*, Newsstand, Hardware Store *(Charles 671-3111)*, Florist, Retail Shops

Transportation

OnCall: Rental Car *(Enterprise 674-4300)*, Taxi *(Mid Island 671-0707)*, Airport Limo *(Arena 671-1848)* **1-3 mi:** Bikes *(Road Runners 671-8280)*, Rail *(LIRR to NYC)* **Airport:** LaGuardia *(15 mi.)*

Medical Services

911 Service **OnCall:** Ambulance **1-3 mi:** Doctor *(North Coast 676-1742)*, Dentist *(Ferris 674-4557)*, Chiropractor *(Village Square 759-2032)*, Holistic Services *(Complete Care 759-2032)*, Veterinarian *(Giordano 671-8780)*, Optician *(Glen Optics 674-4063)* **Hospital:** Community 674-7300 *(2 mi.)*

Setting -- Located below the breakwater in Mosquito Cove, is the mooring field of the gracious Hempstead Harbour Club. On the shore is the modest but bristol club house, a separate bath house, a small beach and a playground. The wide-open views of Hempstead Harbor are spectacular - particularly at sunset. Around the corner is the entrance to Glen Cove Creek.

Marina Notes -- Established in 1891, Hempstead Harbour Club is a private, membership club that welcomes all visiting boaters to its mooring field, launch and lovely facility. Launch Hours: Mon-Thu 10am-9:30pm, Fri 10am-11:30, Sat 9am-11:30pm, Sun 9:30am-9:30pm. A "Do it Yourself" Yacht Yard is onsite.

Notable -- At the intersection of Mosquito Cove and Glen Cove Creek is the 62-acre Garvies Point Museum and Preserve - natural history museum and nature preserve devoted to regional geology, Native American archaeology and ethnology. Five miles of nature trails wind through glacial moraine, including forests, thickets, and meadows with 48 species of trees and 140 species of birds (571-8010) $2/1. Steps leading to the Preserve are walking distance from H.H.C. Alternatively, consider dinghying north to the Garvies Point Boating Association's dock which is closer to the Preserve (call 596-9101 for permission). Down the road from H.H.C. is a park-like area that was once home to the temporarily defunct Glen Cove to New York Fast Ferry. Across Glen Cove Creek, Brewer's offers a full complement of boatyard services plus ice and CNG and the Steamboat Landing Restaurant, in the Jude Thaddeus Marina, offers "dock 'n dine." The town of Glen Cove is about a 1.5 mile walk, (Garvies Point Road to Glen Cove Avenue); it offers a selection of eateries and shops.

Navigational Information

Lat: 40°51.305' **Long:** 733°8..733' **Tide:** 3 ft. **Current:** 1.5 kt. **Chart:** 12366
Rep. Depths (*MLW*): **Entry** 7 ft. **Fuel Dock** 8 ft. **Max Slip/Moor** 8 ft./-
Access: Long Island Sound to just east of Execution Rocks

Marina Facilities *(In Season/Off Season)*

Fuel: *ValvTect* - Gasoline, Diesel
Slips: 325 Total, 10 Transient **Max LOA:** 75 ft. **Max Beam:** n/a
  Rate *(per ft.)*: **Day** $1.50 **Week** $7.50 **Month** $27
Power: 30 amp Incl., 50 amp Incl., 100 amp n/a, 200 amp n/a
Cable TV: No **Dockside Phone:** No
Dock Type: Floating, Long Fingers
Moorings: 0 Total, 0 Transient **Launch:** n/a
  Rate: Day n/a **Week** n/a **Month** n/a
Heads: 6 Toilet(s), 8 Shower(s)
Laundry: 2 Washer(s), 2 Dryer(s) **Pay Phones:** Yes, 1
Pump-Out: OnSite, Full Service **Fee:** n/a **Closed Heads:** Yes

Marina Operations

Owner/Manager: Kevin McMahon **Dockmaster:** n/a
In-Season: Apr-Oct, 24 hrs. **Off-Season:** Nov-Mar, 24 hrs
After-Hours Arrival: Call in advance
Reservations: Yes **Credit Cards:** Visa/MC, Dscvr, Amex, Tex
Discounts: None
Pets: Welcome **Handicap Access:** Yes, Heads, Docks

Brewer Yacht Yard at Glen Cove

128 Shore Road; Glen Cove, NY 11542

Tel: (516) 671-5563 **VHF: Monitor** 9 **Talk** 9
Fax: (516) 674-0113 **Alternate Tel:** n/a
Email: bgc@byy.com **Web:** www.byy.com/glencove
Nearest Town: Sea Cliff *(1 mi.)* **Tourist Info:** (516) 676-6666

Marina Services and Boat Supplies

Services - Docking Assistance, Security, Trash Pick-Up, Dock Carts
Communication - Mail & Package Hold, Phone Messages, Fax in/out,
FedEx, AirBorne, UPS, Express Mail *(Sat Del)* **Supplies -**
OnSite: Ice *(Block, Cube)*, Ships' Store, CNG **Near:** Bait/Tackle
Under 1 mi: Propane *(Moretto Supply 759-0722)*

Boatyard Services

OnSite: Travelift *(30T & 60T)*, Forklift, Crane, Engine mechanic *(gas, diesel)*,
Electrical Repairs, Electronics Repairs, Hull Repairs, Rigger, Bottom
Cleaning, Brightwork, Refrigeration, Compound, Wash & Wax, Interior
Cleaning, Propeller Repairs, Woodworking, Painting, Awlgrip, Yacht Broker,
Total Refits **OnCall:** Upholstery **Under 1 mi:** Launching Ramp.
Dealer for: Interlux, Awlgrip, Sealand, Edson, Yanmar, Westerbeke, Mer-
cruiser, Volvo, Tides Marine, Harken, Lewmar, Sailtec, OS Rod & Wire
Rigging Systems, New England Ropes, Yale Cordage, Schaefer, B & G,
Furlex,Navtec, Interlux, Awlgrip, Imron, 3M. **Member:** ABBRA, ABYC -
1 Certified Tech, Other Certifications: Many **Yard Rates:** $65-75/hr.,
Haul & Launch $81/hr. *(blocking $12-15)*, Power Wash $2, Bottom Paint
$12/ft. **Storage:** In-Water $25/ft., On-Land $35-38/ft.

Restaurants and Accommodations

Near: Restaurant *(Steamboat Landing 759-3921, D $16-24)*, *(Costellos Pub
676-9043)* **Under 1 mi:** Restaurant *(Gallaghers 656-0996)*, *(Cozy Corner
676-9651)*, *(Good Time Charlies 676-9846)*, *(Cactus Café 609-2621)*,
Pizzeria *(Village Pizza 671-5519)*, Hotel *(Jin Jin 671-4364)* **1-3 mi:** Motel
(North Shore Inn 759-7726) **3+ mi:** Motel *(Tides 671-7070, 4 mi.)*

Recreation and Entertainment

OnSite: Pool, Picnic Area, Grills, Playground **Near:** Beach, Tennis Courts
(Cove Tennis 759-0505) **Under 1 mi:** Dive Shop, Golf Course *(Glen Cove
676-6534)*, Movie Theater *(Cineplex 671-0028)*, Video Rental *(Blockbuster
674-0690)*, Park, Museum *(Sea Cliff Village 671-0090)* **1-3 mi:** Bowling
(Glen Cove 671-0028), Cultural Attract *(Garvies Point Preserve 671-0300)*

Provisioning and General Services

Under 1 mi: Convenience Store, Supermarket *(Waldbaums 676-9769)*,
Gourmet Shop *(Nordik Coast 671-7796)*, Delicatessen *(McCarthys 759-
9501)*, Liquor Store *(Capobianco 676-4586)*, Bakery, Farmers' Market,
Fishmonger, Meat Market, Bank/ATM, Post Office, Catholic Church,
Synagogue, Library *(Glen Cove 676-2130)*, Beauty Salon, Dry Cleaners,
Laundry, Bookstore, Pharmacy *(CVS 656-0305)*, Newsstand, Hardware
Store *(Sea Cliff 671-3195)* **1-3 mi:** Health Food *(Rising Tide 676-7895)*,
Protestant Church

Transportation

OnCall: Rental Car *(Enterprise 674-4300; Gold Coast Rental 671-8001-
1 mi.)*, Taxi *(Arena Taxi 676-1016)*, Airport Limo *(Anthonys Diamond 628-
8094)* **Under 1 mi:** Local Bus, Rail *(LIRR to NYC)* **1-3 mi:** Bikes *(Road
Runners 671-8280)* **Airport:** LaGuardia/JFK *(15 mi./20 mi.)*

Medical Services

911 Service **OnCall:** Ambulance **Near:** Dentist **Under 1 mi:** Chiropractor
(Sea Cliff Chiropractic 759-2424), Veterinarian *(Glen Animal Hosp. 671-
2800)* **1-3 mi:** Doctor *(the Med Station 759-5406)*
Hospital: North Shore University 674-7300 *(1.8 mi.)*

Setting -- Just after entering channel-like Glen Cove Creek, from Hempstead Harbor, the extensive network of docks that now compriseservice-oriented Brewer Yacht Yard is immediately to starboard. About half the docks are nestled in a large square basin and the remainder are strung along the creek-front. Landside views are of the large sheds somewhat blocked by an ever-increasing and welcome landscaping effort. Flower-filled planters and strategically sited beds of shrubs soften the boatyard atmosphere. The western shore of the basin has been left undisturbed which adds even more relief.

Marina Notes -- Acquired and incorporated the docks of Glen Cove Yacht Service several years ago which significantly expanded the facility. At the time new docks were added as was a new 60 ton travelift. A new building housing new heads, showers and offices is in production. As at all Brewer's, there are flowers in the heads - which are particularly nice wood, ceramic tile and stainless steel and have individual showers with dressing rooms. A full-service boat yard. Welcome package. Brewers Preferred Customer Card Program good at all Northeast Brewer Boat Yards.

Notable -- A large attractive pool is set in the middle of the yard and serves as the centerpiece of the "amenities area." Adjacent is a small, creative play-ground and a gazebo - all overlooking the docks. Another gazebo and set of picnic tables punctuate the yard. A hike up through the intriguing and very hilly Sea Cliff neighborhood could prove quite interesting. A cab ride into Glen Cove will net a wide assortment of restaurants: from pizza to a remarkable number of fine dining establishments. The Long Island Railroad goes to Manhattan.

Jude Thaddeus Glen Cove Marina

76 Shore Road; Glen Cove, NY 11542

Tel: (516) 759-3129 **VHF: Monitor** n/a **Talk** n/a
Fax: (516) 759-3306 **Alternate Tel:** n/a
Email: n/a **Web:** n/a
Nearest Town: Sea Cliff *(0.25 mi.)* **Tourist Info:** (516) 676-6666

Navigational Information
Lat: 40°51.417' **Long:** 073°38.491' **Tide:** 8 ft. **Current:** n/a **Chart:** 12366
Rep. Depths *(MLW)*: **Entry** 6 ft. **Fuel Dock** 6 ft. **Max Slip/Moor** 6 ft./-
Access: Long Island Sound to Hempstead Harbor

Marina Facilities *(In Season/Off Season)*
Fuel: *Gulf* - Gasoline, Diesel
Slips: 340 Total, 12 Transient **Max LOA:** 85 ft. **Max Beam:** n/a
  Rate *(per ft.)*: **Day** $2.50/1.50 **Week** Inq. **Month** Inq.
  Power: 30 amp Metered, 50 amp Metered, 100 amp n/a, 200 amp n/a
  Cable TV: No **Dockside Phone:** No
  Dock Type: Floating, Long Fingers
Moorings: 0 Total, 0 Transient **Launch:** n/a
  Rate: Day n/a **Week** n/a **Month** n/a
Heads: 4 Toilet(s), 4 Shower(s)
Laundry: None **Pay Phones:** Yes, 1
Pump-Out: No **Fee:** n/a **Closed Heads:** Yes

Marina Operations
Owner/Manager: n/a **Dockmaster:** Joseph Weiser
In-Season: Summer, 7:30am-Dusk **Off-Season:** Winter, 9am-5pm
After-Hours Arrival: n/a
Reservations: Required **Credit Cards:** Visa/MC
Discounts: None
Pets: Welcome **Handicap Access:** Yes, Heads

Marina Services and Boat Supplies
Services - Docking Assistance, Concierge, Security *(6 Hrs., 11pm - 5pm)*, Trash Pick-Up, Dock Carts **Communication -** Mail & Package Hold, Phone Messages, Fax in/out, FedEx, AirBorne, UPS, Express Mail *(Sat Del)*
Supplies - OnSite: Ice *(Cube)* **Near:** Ships' Store *(Brewer Glen Cove)*, Bait/Tackle, Propane *(Moretto Supply 759-0722)*, CNG *(Brewer)*
3+ mi: West Marine *(673-3910, 9 mi.)*

Boatyard Services
OnSite: Travelift *(35T)*, Electrical Repairs, Electronics Repairs, Hull Repairs, Rigger, Bottom Cleaning, Brightwork, Refrigeration, Painting
OnCall: Interior Cleaning, Propeller Repairs

Restaurants and Accommodations
OnSite: Restaurant *(Steamboat Landing 759-3921, L $8-13 D $15-24)*
OnCall: Pizzeria *(Village 671-5519)* **Near:** Restaurant *(Costellos Pub 676-9403)*, *(Tupelo Honey 671-8300)* **Under 1 mi:** Restaurant *(Crown Fried Chicken 676-5790)*, *(Terranova 676-3344)*, *(KC Gallaghers 656-0996)*
1-3 mi: Lite Fare *(Ice Cream Stop 671-8620)*, Motel *(Jin Jin 671-3464)*, *(North Shore Inn 759-7726)* **3+ mi:** Motel *(Tides 671-7070, 4 mi.)*

Recreation and Entertainment
OnSite: Picnic Area, Grills **Near:** Pool, Beach, Playground, Dive Shop, Volleyball, Tennis Courts *(Cove Tennis 759-0505)*, Jogging Paths, Boat Rentals, Roller Blade/Bike Paths, Park, Museum *(Sea Cliff Village Museum 671-0090)*, Sightseeing, Special Events **Under 1 mi:** Golf Course *(Glen Cove 676-6534)*, Fitness Center *(Glen Cove Health & Fitness 656-0515)*,
Movie Theater *(Cineplex Odeon 671-0028)*, Video Rental *(Blockbuster 674-0690)* **1-3 mi:** Bowling *(Glen Cove Bowl 671-0028)*, Cultural Attract *(Garvies Point Museum and Preserve 671-0300)*

Provisioning and General Services
Under 1 mi: Convenience Store, Gourmet Shop *(Nordik Coast Gourmet 671-7796)*, Delicatessen *(McCarthys 759-9501, Glen Cove Grocery & Deli 674-8310)*, Wine/Beer, Liquor Store *(Capobianco 676-4586)*, Bakery *(Albies Cookies 674-8115)*, Farmers' Market, Fishmonger, Bank/ATM, Post Office, Catholic Church, Protestant Church, Synagogue, Library *(Glen Cove 676-2130)*, Beauty Salon, Barber Shop, Dry Cleaners, Laundry, Bookstore *(Forest Value Books 759-1489)*, Pharmacy *(CVS 656-0305)*, Hardware Store *(Sea Cliff Paint & Hardware 671-3195)*, Copies Etc. *(LI Printing 671-7000)*
1-3 mi: Supermarket *(Waldbaums 676-9769; Stop & Shop 759-1440)*, Health Food *(Rising Tide 676-7895)*

Transportation
OnCall: Rental Car *(Enterprise 674-4300; Gold Coast Rental 671-8001 - 1 mi.)*, Taxi *(Mid-Island 671-0707)*, Airport Limo *(Arena 676-1848)*
Under 1 mi: Water Taxi, Local Bus **1-3 mi:** Bikes *(Road Runners 671-8280)*
Airport: LaGuardia/JFK *(15 mi./20 mi.)*

Medical Services
911 Service **OnCall:** Ambulance **Near:** Dentist **Under 1 mi:** Chiropractor *(Sea Cliff Chiro 759-2424)*, Veterinarian *(Glen Animal Hosp. 671-2800)*
1-3 mi: Doctor *(The Med Station 759-5406)*
Hospital: Glen Cove 674-7300 *(1.8mi.*

Setting -- The second facility to starboard after entering placid Glen Cove Creek, Jude Thaddeus is located beyond Brewer's and just before Steamboat Landing. On the port side of the Creek is a park with the cliffs of Garvies Point Preserve in the background; the starboard side is just non-stop docks.

Marina Notes -- Formerly Glen Cove Marina. New ownership in 1997 that is significantly upgrading the facility. A new main marina building will be completed by summer '04. It will contain new heads, showers, a "lite-fare" eatery for breakfast and lunch, and a bait and tackle shop and was well underway at press time. New and very welcome landscaping is already in place and suggests that, once the new building is completed, that this will be quite lovely. Well stocked ships store. Full-service boat yard.

Notable -- Expect to be greeted by a herd of well-mannered, delightful boxers; they seem to be in charge. Steamboat Landing is an elegant, nicely designed restaurant immediately adjacent to Jude Thaddeus (and for all intents and purposes onsite). The contemporary structure is surrounded by brick patios that overlook the docks and creek. Occasionally its namesake, the replica of 19C side-wheel paddle steamer, Thomas Jefferson, makes its home here. Across the Creek is the park-like Landing for the currently defunct Glen Cove to Manhattan Fast Ferry (hopefully it will soon revive). The intriguing community of Sea Cliff is an interesting hike. A cab ride into Glen Cove (a mile and a half) will net a wide assortment of restaurants: from pizza to a remarkable number of fine dining establishments.

Navigational Information
Lat: 40°52.648' **Long:** 073°31.716' **Tide:** 7 ft. **Current:** n/a **Chart:** 12365
Rep. Depths (*MLW*): **Entry** 13 ft. **Fuel Dock** 20 ft. **Max Slip/Moor** 20 ft./30 ft.
Access: Long Island Sound to Oyster Bay to southern shore

Marina Facilities (*In Season/Off Season*)
Fuel: *BP* - Gasoline, Diesel
Slips: 33 Total, 3 Transient **Max LOA:** 180 ft. **Max Beam:** n/a
 Rate (*per ft.*): **Day** $3.00 **Week** Inq. **Month** Inq.
 Power: 30 amp $5, 50 amp $10, 100 amp n/a, 200 amp n/a
 Cable TV: No **Dockside Phone:** No
 Dock Type: Floating
Moorings: 200 Total, 10 Transient **Launch:** Yes (Included)
 Rate: Day $1.50*/ft. **Week** n/a **Month** n/a
Heads: 2 Toilet(s), 2 Shower(s)
Laundry: None **Pay Phones:** Yes, 1
Pump-Out: OnSite, Self Service **Fee:** Free **Closed Heads:** No

Marina Operations
Owner/Manager: John McGrane **Dockmaster:** Charles Ferraris
In-Season: Summer, 7am-11pm **Off-Season:** Winter, 9am-5pm
After-Hours Arrival: Select slip/mooring; contact office in the morning
Reservations: Yes **Credit Cards:** Visa/MC
Discounts: None
Pets: Welcome **Handicap Access:** No

Oyster Bay Marine Center

Five Bay Avenue; Oyster Bay, NY 11771

Tel: (516) 922-6331 **VHF: Monitor** 71 **Talk** 71
Fax: (516) 922-3542 **Alternate Tel:** n/a
Email: OBMC@pipeline.com **Web:** www.obmc.com
Nearest Town: Oyster Bay (*0.2 mi.*) **Tourist Info:** (631) 922-6464

Marina Services and Boat Supplies
Services - Docking Assistance, Dock Carts **Communication -** Mail &
Package Hold, Phone Messages, Fax in/out (*Free*), FedEx, UPS, Express
Mail (*Sat Del*) **Supplies - OnSite:** Ice (*Block, Cube*), Ships' Store
Under 1 mi: Marine Discount Store (*OB Marine Supply 922-8010*),
Bait/Tackle (*OB Marine Supply*), Propane (*Dodds & Eder 922-4412*)

Boatyard Services
OnSite: Crane (*10T*), Engine mechanic (*gas, diesel*), Electrical Repairs,
Electronics Repairs, Hull Repairs, Rigger, Brightwork, Compound, Wash &
Wax, Woodworking, Painting, Awlgrip, Yacht Broker **OnCall:** Bottom
Cleaning, Refrigeration, Divers, Propeller Repairs, Upholstery, Metal
Fabrication **Dealer for:** Douglas Geill, Frederiksen, Schaeffer, Harken,
Leisure Furl, ProFurl, Navtec, Yanmar, Mercruiser. **Member:** ABYC, Other
Certifications: Mercruiser, Yanmar, Mercury, Navtech, Furlex
Yard Rates: $77.50/hr., Haul & Launch $12/ft., Power Wash $2.50/ft.

Restaurants and Accommodations
Near: Restaurant (*Bayville Landing 628-2309*), (*Railz 624-6911*), (*Café Al
Dente 922-2442*), (*Taste of Mexico 624-8740*), (*Homestead 624-7410*),
(*Fiddleheads 922-2999, L $7-13, D $16-28*), (*Canterbury Ales 922-3614,
L $6-15, D $9-22, Oyster bar*), (*Happy Garden 922-5791*), Lite Fare
(*Taby's 624-7781*), (*Book Mark Café 922-0036*), Pizzeria (*Anthony's Cafe
922-4279*), (*Ninos 922-0434*) **Under 1 mi:** Seafood Shack (*Fish & Clam
922-5522*), Motel (*East Norwich Inn 922-1089*)

Recreation and Entertainment
Near: Beach, Picnic Area, Grills, Playground, Tennis Courts, Fitness Center

(*Custom Physiques 922-8311*), Video Rental (*Video Connection 922-1331*),
Park (*Oyster Bay Park*), Museum (*Raynam Hall 922-6808 - $3/2*), Special
Events (*Oyster Festival, wknd after ColDay*), Galleries (*Dillon 922-1050*)
Under 1 mi: Boat Rentals (*Oyster Bay Sailing 624-7900*) **1-3 mi:** Horse-
back Riding (*Cedar Valley 624-2117*), Cultural Attract (*Planting Fields
Arboretum 922-9201*), Sightseeing (*Sagamore Hill 922-4447 - go early*)
3+ mi: Golf Course (*Glen Cove 671-0033 , 8 mi.*)

Provisioning and General Services
Near: Convenience Store (*Sajoma's 922-2047*), Market (*Verrellis IGA 624-
8989*), Delicatessen (*Harborside 922-2950; Olive Branch 624-6949 *), Health
Food (*Right Stuff 922-2604*), Wine/Beer (*VNS 922-0024*), Liquor Store (*De
Rosa 922-0024*), Bakery (*Page Two 922-7002 *), Bank/ATM, Post Office,
Catholic Church, Protestant Church, Library (*Oyster Bay 922-1212*), Beauty
Salon, Barber Shop, Dry Cleaners (*Bay 922-3269*), Bookstore (*Book Mark
922-0040*), Pharmacy (*Snouders Corner 922-4300*), Hardware Store
(*Nobmans 922-6233 *) **Under 1 mi:** Supermarket (*Stop & Shop 922-0800*),
Gourmet Shop, Fishmonger (*Rozzo 624-7640*), Synagogue, Laundry

Transportation
OnCall: Rental Car (*Enterprise 364-3300 *), Taxi (*Oyster Rides 624-8294 *),
Airport Limo (*Buzzys 922-1909*) **Near:** Rail (*LIRR to NYC 718-243-4999*)
Airport: LaGuardia/JFK (*25 mi./25 mi.*)

Medical Services
911 Service **Near:** Doctor (*North Shore 624-9225*), Dentist (*Krober 922-
0065*), Chiropractor (*O.B. 924-4606*), Optician (*Smith's 922-2533*) **1-3 mi:**
Veterinarian (*E. Norwich 922-7200*) **Hospital:** Glen Cove 674-7300 (*8 mi.*)

Setting -- Located near the historic town of Oyster Bay, on the southern shore of the "Queen of Harbors", OBMC offers a professional operation, basic
shoreside facilities and a very convenient location. Look for the small 1.5 story white building dwarfed by a large crane. Most everything is an easy walk.

Marina Notes -- *Transient mooring rate is $1.50/ft. Specializes in sailboat rigging, engine repair, re-powering, fiberglass and other composite repairs. Slips,
moorings, launch. On weekends, there's a snack bar out on the main fuel dock 9-5. From 1938-93, this site was home to Jakobson Shipyard, builders of
minesweepers, subs, and tugs. 3 Pump-out choices: (1.) Oyster Bay Pump-out Boat, 9am-6pm on weekends, CH. 9; (2.) automatic self-service pump-out at
Oyster Bay Town Marina, just west of OBMC and Sagamore YC - go in main channel (reportedly 8' MLW - call harbormaster) - Free; or (3.) manual self-service
pump-out on floating dock west of OBMC on edge of mooring field - also free. The L.I. Railroad is nearby for easy access to New York City.

Notable -- The hamlet of Oyster Bay, filled with restaurants, provisions, and services, is 0.2 mile away, and a great town park is practically across the street.
Raynham Hall (C. 1770's) a 20-room museum invokes the life of one of Oyster Bay's founding families. The 260-year-old saltbox (Tue-Sun 12-5) is equally
famous for its ghost-sightings (A&E documentary). 3 miles northeast around the harbor is 83-acre Sagamore Hill National Historic Site, the summer home of
Theodore Roosevelt from 1885-1919. The well-informed park rangers make this truly fascinating. 50-minute guided tours of the 23-room Queen Anne-styled
house every hour 10am-4pm - limited to 14 people, no reservations. Visitor's center, films, Old Orchard Museum and a walking tour. A cab's about $8/1way.

Sagamore Yacht Club

PO Box 327; Bay Avenue; Oyster Bay, NY 11771

Tel: (516) 922-0555 **VHF: Monitor** 78 **Talk** 78
Fax: n/a **Alternate Tel:** n/a
Email: n/a **Web:** www.sagamoreyc.com
Nearest Town: Oyster Bay *(0.2 mi.)* **Tourist Info:** (631) 922-6464

Navigational Information
Lat: 40°52.400' **Long:** 073°31.450' **Tide:** 7 ft. **Current:** n/a **Chart:** 12365
Rep. Depths *(MLW)*: **Entry** 9 ft. **Fuel Dock** 20 ft. **Max Slip/Moor** -/30 ft.
Access: Oyster Bay Harbor to mooring field across from Centre Island

Marina Facilities *(In Season/Off Season)*
Fuel: No
Slips: 0 Total, 0 Transient **Max LOA:** 50 ft. **Max Beam:** n/a
  Rate *(per ft.)*: **Day** n/a **Week** n/a **Month** n/a
  Power: 30 amp n/a, 50 amp n/a, 100 amp n/a, 200 amp n/a
  Cable TV: No **Dockside Phone:** No
  Dock Type: n/a
Moorings: 12 Total, 12 Transient **Launch:** Yes (Free), Dinghy Dock
  Rate: Day $40 **Week** n/a **Month** n/a
Heads: 6 Toilet(s), 2 Shower(s) *(with dressing rooms)*
Laundry: None **Pay Phones:** No
Pump-Out: OnCall *(Ch.9)* **Fee:** Free **Closed Heads:** Yes

Marina Operations
Owner/Manager: SYC **Dockmaster:** John Pokorny
In-Season: MidMay-MidOct, 7am-Mid **Off-Season:** Apr-May, Oct-Nov, 9-8
After-Hours Arrival: Call ahead
Reservations: Preferred **Credit Cards:** Visa/MC
Discounts: None
Pets: Welcome **Handicap Access:** No

Marina Services and Boat Supplies
Services - Security *(7am-Mid)*, Trash Pick-Up, Dock Carts
Communication - FedEx, AirBorne, UPS, Express Mail **Supplies - Under 1 mi:** Ships' Store *(OB Marine Supply 922-8010)*, Bait/Tackle *(OB Marine)*, Propane *(Dodds & Eder 922-4412)* **3+ mi:** West Marine *(673-3910, 9 mi.)*

Boatyard Services
OnCall: Bottom Cleaning *(624-DIVE)*, Divers *(624-DIVE)* **Near:** Crane *(OBMC)*, Engine mechanic *(gas, diesel)*, Launching Ramp, Electrical Repairs *(OBMC)*, Electronic Sales *(OBMC)*, Electronics Repairs *(OBMC)*, Hull Repairs *(OBMC)*, Rigger *(OBMC)*. **1-3 mi:** Travelift *(Seawanhaka YC)*.
Nearest Yard: Oyster Bay Marine Center (631) 922-6331

Restaurants and Accommodations
OnSite: Restaurant *(Sagamore Yacht Club - Wed eve, Sat & Sun, cash only; simple Italian food at very reasonable prices; Prix Fixe $7-12)* **OnCall:** Restaurant *(Anthony's Café 922-4279, Pizza & Italian)*, Pizzeria *(Mario's Pizza 922-9111)* **Near:** Restaurant *(Fiddleheads 922-2999, L $7-13, D $16-28)*, *(Canterbury Ales 922-3614, L $6-15, D $9-22, Oyster bar)*, *(Railz 624-6911)*, *(Café Al Dente 922-2442)*, *(Taste of Mexico 624-8740)*, *(Taby's 624-7781)*, *(Homestead 624-7410)* **Under 1 mi:** Restaurant *(Fish & Clam 922-5522)* **1-3 mi:** Restaurant *(Bayville Landing 628-2309)*, Motel *(East Norwich Inn 922-1089)* **3+ mi:** Motel *(Tides 671-7070, 4 mi.)*

Recreation and Entertainment
Near: Beach, Picnic Area, Grills, Playground, Tennis Courts, Fitness Center *(Custom Physiques 922-8311)*, Video Rental *(Video Connection 922-1331)*, Park *(O.B. Park - tennis, picnic pavilion, ball fields)*, Museum *(Raynam Hall 922-6808 - $3/2; Earl Wrightman House)*, Special Events *(Oyster Festival, wknd after ColDay; Beethoven Fest- Sep; Jazz Fest - Aug; Fall & Flower - Oct)*, Galleries *(Dillon 922-1050)* **Under 1 mi:** Boat Rentals *(O.B. Sailing 624-7900)* **1-3 mi:** Cultural Attract *(409 acre Planting Fields Arboretum 922-9201)*, Sightseeing *(Sagamore Hill 922-4447 50 min tours limited to 14 - be there early $5/Free)* **3+ mi:** Golf Course *(Glen Cove G.C. 671-0033, 8 mi.)*

Provisioning and General Services
Near: Convenience Store, Market *(Verrellis IGA 624-8989)*, Delicatessen *(Harborside 922-2950; Olive Branch 624-6949)*, Health Food *(Right Stuff 922-2604)*, Wine/Beer *(VNS 922-0024)*, Liquor Store *(De Rosa 922-0024)*, Bakery *(Page Two 922-7002)*, Bank/ATM, Post Office, Catholic Church, Protestant Church, Library *(Oyster Bay 922-1212)*, Beauty Salon *(Glamor Inn 922-1195)*, Barber Shop, Dry Cleaners *(Bay 922-3269)*, Laundry, Bookstore, Pharmacy *(Snouders Corner 922-4300)*, Hardware Store *(Nobmans 922-6233)*, Retail Shops **Under 1 mi:** Supermarket *(Stop & Shop 922-0800)*, Fishmonger, Synagogue, Florist **1-3 mi:** Copies Etc. *(QRC 921-5450)*

Transportation
OnCall: Rental Car *(Enterprise 364-3300)*, Taxi *(Syosset 921-2141)*, Airport Limo *(Buzzys 922-1909)* **Near:** Rail *(LIRR to NYC 718-243-4999)* **Airport:** LaGuardia/ JFK *(25 mi./25 mi.)*

Medical Services
911 Service **Near:** Doctor *(North Shore 624-9225)*, Dentist *(Krober 922-0065)*, Chiropractor *(O.B. 922-4606)*, Ambulance, Optician *(Smith's 922-2533)* **1-3 mi:** Veterinarian *(E. Norwich 922-7200)*
Hospital: Glen Cove 674-7300 *8 mi.*

Setting -- Sagamore Yacht Club's attractive, modest 2-story white clubhouse is easy to spot - look for the bright blue awning just west of the Oyster Bay Marine Center. The nicely landscaped and well-maintained waterfront sports a large patio populated with tables and chairs that overlooks the pier and harbor. On the second floor is a well furnished deck with fabulous harbor views.

Marina Notes -- The club has a first floor pub and small dining room with food service on week-ends. When weather permits, service is at the waterside patio tables. Three launches serve the mooring field. LateMay-Mid Sep 7am-midnight, diminishing during the shoulder seasons. Upstairs are nicely decorated, inviting heads/showers, a conference/party room and the aforementioned deck. 3 Free Pump-out choices: 1. Oyster Bay Pump-out Boat, 9am-6pm weekends, Ch. 9; 2. Automatic self-service pump-out at Oyster Bay Town Marina, just west of Sagamore - go in main channel (reportedly 8' MLW - call harbormaster); or 3. Manual self-service pump-out on floating dock west of OBMC on edge of mooring field. Beware of shoaling a quarter mile north of town marina.

Notable -- A local Italian Deli provides breakfast, lunch and dinner for members and guests on Sat & Sun, and dinner on Wed night after racing, on a cash basis. SYC enjoys a fabulously convenient location two tenths of a mile from the bustling town of Oyster Bay. A playground, very lovely park, tennis courts, baseball diamond, restaurants, picnic area and LIRR station are all a block away. Oyster Bay Historical Society offers several fascinating stops, including "Haunted" 22-room Rayham Hall (C. 1740) and the 1720 Earl Wightman house, a research library and interactive museum that welcomes children.

Navigational Information
Lat: 40°54.253' **Long:** 073°32.596' **Tide:** n/a **Current:** n/a **Chart:** 12365
Rep. Depths (*MLW*): **Entry** 8 ft. **Fuel Dock** n/a **Max Slip/Moor** 7 ft./12 ft.
Access: Oyster Bay Harbor to West Harbor to Mill Neck Creek

Marina Facilities *(In Season/Off Season)*
Fuel: No
Slips: 55 Total, 3 Transient **Max LOA:** 42 ft. **Max Beam:** n/a
  Rate (*per ft.*): **Day** $2.25 **Week** Inq. **Month** Inq.
  Power: 30 amp n/a, **50 amp** n/a, **100 amp** n/a, **200 amp** n/a
Cable TV: No **Dockside Phone:** No
Dock Type: Long Fingers, Wood
Moorings: 20 Total, 1-2 Transient **Launch:** Yes (Free)
  Rate: Day $25 **Week** n/a **Month** n/a
Heads: 2 Toilet(s)
Laundry: None **Pay Phones:** Yes, 1
Pump-Out: No **Fee:** n/a **Closed Heads:** Yes

Marina Operations
Owner/Manager: Warren Barteau **Dockmaster:** Same
In-Season: MemDay-ColDay, 7-5 **Off-Season:** ColDay-MemDay, 8-4
After-Hours Arrival: Call in advance
Reservations: Yes, Required **Credit Cards:** Visa/MC, Dscvr, Din, Amex
Discounts: Boat/US **Dockage:** 15% **Fuel:** n/a **Repair:** n/a
Pets: Welcome **Handicap Access:** No

Bridge Marina

40 Ludlam Avenue; Bayville, NY 11709

Tel: (516) 628-8688 **VHF: Monitor** n/a **Talk** n/a
Fax: (516) 628-3462 **Alternate Tel:** n/a
Email: n/a **Web:** n/a
Nearest Town: Bayville (*0.1 mi.*) **Tourist Info:** (631) 676-9501

Marina Services and Boat Supplies
Services - Security (*8 Hrs.*) **Supplies - OnSite:** Ice (*Block, Cube*),
Bait/Tackle, Live Bait (*Sandworms*) **Near:** Ships' Store (*Bridge Marine*)
Under 1 mi: Marine Discount Store (*Oyster Bay Marine Supply 922-8010*)
1-3 mi: Propane (*Dodds & Eder 922-4412*)

Boatyard Services
OnSite: Forklift, Engine mechanic (*gas, diesel*), Launching Ramp, Electrical
Repairs, Electronic Sales, Electronics Repairs, Hull Repairs, Bottom
Cleaning, Compound, Wash & Wax, Interior Cleaning, Propeller Repairs,
Inflatable Repairs, Painting, Yacht Broker **Near:** Upholstery.

Restaurants and Accommodations
OnSite: Seafood Shack (*Clam Bar 628-8688, L $6, D $10*) **Near:** Restaurant (*Crescent 628-1700*), (*A Taste of China 628-2288*), (*Pine Island
Grill 628-3000, L $11-23, D $20-36, Sun Brunch $28/12, raw bar*), (*Chantres
New American Bistro 628-0364*) **Under 1 mi:** Restaurant (*Homestead 624-
7410*), (*Coach Grill 624-0900*), (*Bayville Landing 629-2309*), Pizzeria (*Gus
628-9679*) **1-3 mi:** Motel (*Tides 671-7070*), (*East Norwich Inn 922-1089*)
3+ mi: Hotel (*Fairfield Inn by Marriott 921-1111, 5 mi.*)

Recreation and Entertainment
OnSite: Boat Rentals (*Skiffs, small powerboats, kayak & canoe rentals*)
Under 1 mi: Beach (*Centre Island Beaches 624-6124*), Picnic Area, Grills,
Playground, Fitness Center (*Waterfront Fitness 922-7884*), Video Rental
(*Village Video 628-2761*), Video Arcade, Park

1-3 mi: Tennis Courts (*Cove Neck 922-6055*), Golf Course (*Muttontown 922-
9842*), Museum (*Bayville Historical Museum 628-1720, Raynham Hall
Museum 922-6808*) **3+ mi:** Bowling (*6 mi.*), Movie Theater (*5 mi.*), Cultural
Attract (*Sagamore Hills 922-4447, 5 mi.*)

Provisioning and General Services
Near: Convenience Store, Delicatessen (*Bayville Deli 628-2063*), Wine/Beer
(*Bayville Beverage*), Liquor Store (*Our Hobby Liquors 628-8744*), Green
Grocer, Fishmonger, Lobster Pound, Meat Market (*Bayville Meat*), Post
Office, Beauty Salon, Barber Shop, Dry Cleaners (*Village Cleaners*),
Pharmacy (*Bayville 628-3640*), Newsstand, Hardware Store (*Bayville
Hardware 628-1488*), Florist, Retail Shops **Under 1 mi:** Catholic Church,
Protestant Church, Library (*Oyster Bay Library 922-1212*), Laundry
1-3 mi: Supermarket (*IGA/Stop & Shop 922-0800*), Bakery (*Page Two
922-7002*) **3+ mi:** Health Food (*5 mi.*)

Transportation
OnCall: Rental Car (*Enterprise 364-3300*), Taxi (*Oyster Bay Taxi 921-2141*),
Airport Limo (*Buzzys 922-1909*) **1-3 mi:** Rail (*LIRR to NYC 718-243-4999*)
Airport: Islip McArthur/Laguardia/JFK (*20 mi./20 mi./20 mi.*)

Medical Services
911 Service **OnCall:** Ambulance **Near:** Dentist (*Lippman & Valicenti 628-
1122*), Chiropractor (*Healthy Living 628-0535, Schauer 628-3300*)
Under 1 mi: Doctor (*Deschamps 628-8376, Milea 628-2566, Fullmer
628-2744*) **1-3 mi:** Veterinarian (*Bayville Animal Clinic 628-2634*)
Hospital: NSU at Glen Cove 674-7300 *6 mi.*

Setting -- Bridge Marina is in the farthest reaches of Oyster Bay Harbor. Once past Centre Island's Brickyard Point head back north; turn to port through the Bayville Bascule Bridge into little, but surprisingly deep Mill Neck Creek. The marina is just inside the bridge, on the north side; the environment is rustic boatyard, but the basin is very protected. The quiet little hamlet of Bayview is a couple blocks away.

Marina Notes -- 12-13' at low tide. The bridge opens on demand 7am-5pm 7 days a week, otherwise 4 hours notice is required. Primarily small boats, but can accommodate up to 42 ft. Docks, moorings, launch service. Basic heads, no showers. A take-out Clam Bar onsite with casual outdoor eating area, which overlooks the bay, serves fresh seafood, soups and burgers. The boatyard offers engine and fiberglass service & repair. Bridge Marine Sales & Tackle (628-8686) is up the street and offers Boat Us Discounts: 10% Off New Engine Sales Rigging Labor 5% Off in-stock Parts & Accessories. Closed Monday off season. (Called Soundview Marina before 1992.) Onsite Boat rentals: Skiff $25/day, skiff with motor $75/day, 18 ft powerboat $250/day.

Notable -- Small, laid-back Bayville has a stopped in time beachy atmosphere and a fairly complete number of necessary services and eateries (including the upscale Pine Island Grill) and three nail salons! Nearby Centre Island Beach offers swimming in Long Island Sound and Oyster Bay Harbor. Further west, Charles Ransome Beach (624-6160) has a playground, and a refreshment stand. Across the street from Charles Ransome Beach is the Bayville Boardwalk - with food, a batting cage, miniature golf and two game rooms.

H & M Powles

PO Box 495; 104 Harbor Road; Cold Spring Harbor, NY 11724

Tel: (631) 367-7670 **VHF: Monitor** 10 **Talk** 10
Fax: (631) 692-9379 **Alternate Tel:** n/a
Email: n/a **Web:** n/a
Nearest Town: Cold Spring Harbor *(0.3 mi.)* **Tourist Info:** (631) 367-2875

Navigational Information

Lat: 40°51.978' **Long:** 073°27.718' **Tide:** 7 ft. **Current:** n/a **Chart:** 12364
Rep. Depths *(MLW)*: **Entry** n/a **Fuel Dock** 4 ft. **Max Slip/Moor** -/-
Access: Cold Spring Harbor, past CS Beach, into inner harbor, east side

Marina Facilities *(In Season/Off Season)*

Fuel: Gasoline, Diesel
Slips: 0 Total, 0 Transient **Max LOA:** 60 ft. **Max Beam:** n/a
  Rate *(per ft.)*: **Day** n/a **Week** n/a **Month** n/a
  Power: 30 amp n/a, **50 amp** n/a, **100 amp** n/a, **200 amp** n/a
  Cable TV: No **Dockside Phone:** No
  Dock Type: Floating, Wood
Moorings: 60 Total, 10 Transient **Launch:** yes (Included), Dinghy Dock ($5)
  Rate: Day $30 **Week** $100 **Month** $300
Heads: 2 Toilet(s)
Laundry: None **Pay Phones:** Yes, 1
Pump-Out: OnSite, 1 Central **Fee:** Free **Closed Heads:** Yes

Marina Operations

Owner/Manager: Joe Powles **Dockmaster:** n/a
In-Season: Apr-MidNov, 7am-11pm **Off-Season:** Mid-Nov. to Mar, Closed
After-Hours Arrival: Call in advance
Reservations: Yes **Credit Cards:** Visa/MC, Dscvr, Amex
Discounts: None
Pets: Welcome **Handicap Access:** No

Marina Services and Boat Supplies

Services - Docking Assistance, Trash Pick-Up **Communication -** FedEx, AirBorne, UPS, Express Mail **Supplies - OnSite:** Ice *(Cube)*, Ships' Store, Bait/Tackle **1-3 mi:** Propane *(Village Fireplace 351-1499)* **3+ mi:** West Marine *(673-3910, 4 mi.)*

Boatyard Services

OnSite: Engine mechanic *(gas, diesel)*, Electrical Repairs, Bottom Cleaning, Compound, Wash & Wax, Interior Cleaning **Near:** Launching Ramp.
1-3 mi: Hull Repairs, Rigger, Sail Loft, Brightwork, Air Conditioning, Refrigeration, Propeller Repairs, Woodworking, Painting, Awlgrip, Total Refits. **Nearest Yard:** Oyster Bay Marine Service (516) 922-6331

Restaurants and Accommodations

Near: Restaurant *(Wyland's Country Cafe 692-5655)*, *(Inn On the Harbor 367-3166, L $16-30, D $18-33, Also Prix fixe 3- course Lunch $16, 3-course Sun Brunch with cocktails $23)*, *(Trattoria Grasso Due 367-6060, L $11-16, D $16-25, Bar menu Sun-Fri $5-13)*, Inn/B&B *(Swan View 367-2070)*
1-3 mi: Restaurant *(Brasserie 345 673-8084)*, *(Santa Fe Kitchen 423-3003)*, *(Golden Dolphin 351-9680)*, Pizzeria *(Rosas Pizza 425-7694)* **3+ mi:** Motel *(Abbey Motor Inn 423-0800, 4 mi.)*, *(East Norwich Inn 922-1500, 4 mi.)*, Hotel *(Marriott 423-1600, 3 mi.)*

Recreation and Entertainment

OnSite: Fishing Charter, Park *(also Cold Spring Harbor State Park on Rte 25A & Harbor Rd.)* **Near:** Picnic Area, Grills, Jogging Paths **Under 1 mi:** Tennis Courts *(CS Valley Tennis and Racquet Club 692-6480)*, Museum *(Cold Spring Harbor Whaling Museum 367-3418, 11am-5pm, $3/1.50)*,

Sightseeing *(CSH Fish Hatchery & Aquarium 692-6768 - witness the 6-pool trout hatching process)* **1-3 mi:** Fitness Center *(Huntington YMCA 421-4242)*, Movie Theater *(Cineplex Odeon 425-7680)*, Video Rental *(Double S 421-9228)* **3+ mi:** Golf Course *(Dix Hills 271-4788, 7 mi.)*, Cultural Attract *(Heckscher Art Museum 351-3250, Walt Whitman Birthplace 427-5240, 4 mi.)*

Provisioning and General Services

Near: Delicatessen *(CS Plaza Deli 367-3533)*, Bank/ATM, Post Office, Catholic Church, Protestant Church, Barber Shop, Newsstand, Clothing Store **Under 1 mi:** Gourmet Shop *(Gourmets Delight 692-6093)*, Library *(CSH 692-6820)* **1-3 mi:** Supermarket *(Waldbaums 421-0134)*, Health Food, Wine/Beer, Liquor Store *(Southdown Liquor 271-6380)*, Bakery *(Joelles 673-8888)*, Farmers' Market, Green Grocer, Fishmonger, Meat Market, Dry Cleaners, Laundry, Bookstore, Pharmacy *(Genovese 549-9558)*, Hardware Store *(Home Depot 424-9170)*, Florist, Copies Etc. *(Brittany Printing 692-4166)*

Transportation

OnCall: Rental Car *(Enterprise 424-2500; Hertz 427-6106 4 mi.)*, Taxi *(Orange and White 271-3600)*, Airport Limo *(Coachman 367-1500)*
3+ mi: Bikes *(Bicycle Buys 673-2211, 4 mi.)* **Airport:** Islip 467-3210 *(30 mi.)*

Medical Services

911 Service **1-3 mi:** Doctor, Dentist, Chiropractor *(Huntington Chiro Health 425-0500)*, Holistic Services, Ambulance, Veterinarian *(Animal Clinic at Wall Street 427-7479)* **Hospital:** Huntington 351-2000 *(4 mi.)*

Setting -- Exquisite 3 mile-long Cold Spring Harbor is bordered by wooded bluffs and un-named beaches. Almost to its head is Cold Spring Beach which, running west to east, creates a narrow entrance to the inner harbor. Here in a quiet protected stretch is the mooring field and along the eastern shore the landing dock of H & M Powles. The facility is book-ended by two well-tended town parks with swaths of lawn, picnic tables and grills.

Marina Notes -- Founded in 1940. Their new, recently completed, main building houses new heads, an office, a snack bar and bait and tackle. Only moorings - deep moorings, but quite shallow dockside (reportedly 4 ft). Launch service 7am-6pm Memorial Day-Labor Day. 24 Hours Pump-out. Self - Serve, May 1 - Oct. 31, Channel 10, free. Basic boatyard services - gas/diesel engine mechanic onsite.

Notable -- Directly across the street is the elegant and romantic Inn on the Harbor with water views and an interesting wine list. Innovative French cuisine is created by chef/owner Guy Peuch, formerly at Manhattan's Water Club (Lunch 11am-3pm, Dinner 4:30-11pm, Sun Brunch 11am-3pm). A very easywalk is the lovely 19th century village of Cold Spring Harbor with many shops, eateries and services. The Cold Spring Harbor Whaling Museum, whichcommemorates C.S.H.'s history as the busiest whaling port on Long Island, has an authentic whaleboat with its original gear along with some fine examples of scrimshaw and a "Wonder of Whales" exhibit. A bit further a field is the Cold Spring Harbor Laboratory, a leading molecular biology research and conference center with three noble laureates to its credit. It's an outgrowth of the Carnegie Institute's 1904 Center for Experimental Evolution.

Navigational Information

Lat: 40°51.781' **Long:** 073°27.748' **Tide:** n/a **Current:** n/a **Chart:** 12364
Rep. Depths (*MLW*): Entry 15 ft. **Fuel Dock** n/a **Max Slip/Moor** 25 ft./-
Access: Oyster Bay to Cold Spring Harbor past Cold Spring Beach to head

Marina Facilities *(In Season/Off Season)*

Fuel: No
Slips: 50 Total, 4 Transient **Max LOA:** 540 ft. **Max Beam:** 14 ft.
 Rate *(per ft.)*: **Day** $1.50 **Week** $2.25 **Month** Inq.
 Power: 30 amp Incl., **50 amp** n/a, **100 amp** n/a, **200 amp** n/a
 Cable TV: No **Dockside Phone:** No
 Dock Type: Floating, Long Fingers, Wood
Moorings: 0 Total, 0 Transient **Launch:** n/a
 Rate: Day n/a **Week** n/a **Month** n/a
Heads: 2 Toilet(s)
Laundry: None **Pay Phones:** Yes
Pump-Out: No **Fee:** n/a **Closed Heads:** No

Marina Operations

Owner/Manager: John Zapf **Dockmaster:** same
In-Season: Apr-Nov, 9am-5pm **Off-Season:** Dec-Mar, closed
After-Hours Arrival: Call in advance
Reservations: Yes **Credit Cards:** Cash or Check
Discounts: None
Pets: Welcome **Handicap Access:** Yes, Heads, Docks

Marina Services and Boat Supplies

Services - Docking Assistance, Security *(24 Hrs.)*, Dock Carts **Supplies -**
OnSite: Ice *(Cube)* **Near:** Bait/Tackle **3+ mi:** West Marine *(673-3910, 4 mi.)*, Propane *(Village Fireplace 351-1499, 4 mi.)*

Boatyard Services

Nearest Yard: Oyster Bay Marine Center (516) 922-6331

Restaurants and Accommodations

OnCall: Pizzeria *(Franks 692-5626)* **Near:** Restaurant *(Inn on the Harbor 367-3166, L $16-30, D $16-30, Prix fixe Lunch, Sun Brunch $23)* **Under 1 mi:** Restaurant *(Trattoria Grasso Due 367-6060, L $11-16, D $16-25, Bar menu Sun-Fri $5-13)*, *(Old Whaler 367-3166, L $8-15, D $18-30)*, Lite Fare *(Wylands 692-5655, L $7-10)*, Inn/B&B *(Inn On the Harbor 367-3166)* **1-3 mi:** Restaurant *(Brasserie 345 673-8084)*, *(Santa Fe Kitchen 423-3003)* **3+ mi:** Motel *(Best Western 921-6100, 4 mi., Woodbury)*, *(Quality Inn 921-6900, 4 mi., Woodbury)*, Hotel *(Marriott 423-1600, 4 mi., Huntington)*

Recreation and Entertainment

Near: Beach *(Cold Spring Beach)*, Park **Under 1 mi:** Tennis Courts *(CS Valley Tennis and Racquet Club 692-6480)*, Museum *(Whaling Museum 367-3418 11-5, $3/1.50)* **1-3 mi:** Fitness Center *(Huntington YMCA 421-4242)*, Movie Theater *(Cineplex 425-7680)*, Video Rental *(Double S 421-9228)*

Whaler's Cove Yacht Club

PO Box 293; 150 Harbor Road; Cold Spring Harbor, NY 11724

Tel: (631) 367-9822 **VHF: Monitor** 9 **Talk** n/a
Fax: n/a **Alternate Tel:** n/a
Email: n/a **Web:** n/a
Nearest Town: Cold Spring Harbor *(0.6 mi.)* **Tourist Info:** (631) 367-2875

3+ mi: Golf Course *(Dix Hills 271-4788, 7 mi.)*, Cultural Attract *(Heckscher Art Museum 351-3250, Walt Whitman Birthplace 427-5240, 3.5 mi.)*

Provisioning and General Services

Near: Delicatessen *(CS Plaza Deli 367-3533)*, Bank/ATM, Catholic Church, Barber Shop **Under 1 mi:** Gourmet Shop *(Gourmets Delight 692-6093)*, Post Office, Beauty Salon, Clothing Store, Retail Shops **1-3 mi:** Supermarket *(Westside 351-9660)*, Liquor Store *(Southdown Liquor 271-6380)*, Bakery *(Joelles 673-8888)*, Library *(CSH 692-6820)*, Bookstore, Pharmacy *(Genovese 549-9558)*, Hardware Store *(Home Depot 424-9170)* **3+ mi:** Department Store *(Kmart 421-5005, 4 mi.)*

Transportation

OnCall: Rental Car *(Enterprise 424-2500; Hertz 427-6106 2 mi.)*, Taxi *(Orange and White 271-3600)*, Airport Limo *(Coachman 367-1500)*
3+ mi: Bikes *(Bicycle Buys 673-2211, 4 mi.)*
Airport: Islip-MacArthur 467-3210 *(30 mi.)*

Medical Services

911 Service **Under 1 mi:** Dentist, Holistic Services *(Welcome Back Massage 692-4688)* **1-3 mi:** Doctor, Chiropractor *(Huntington Chiropractic Health 425-0500)*, Veterinarian *(Animal Clinic at Wall Street 427-7479)*
Hospital: Huntington 351-2000 *(4 mi.)*

Setting -- Set at the foot of a small rise, delightful and tiny Whaler's Cove Yacht Club promises a retreat-like setting amid trees and flowers. Although the main road is a short way up the W.C. Y.C.'s drive, there is a feeling of remoteness. The modest colonial-style black and white club house is surrounded by a ground-level covered porch; pots overflowing with trailing bouquets of flowers hang from the ceiling. More flowers punctuate the simple grounds. There is a mid- twentieth century feel which is rare. The views across the harbor are even more unspoiled. Fall is a particularly pretty time here.

Marina Notes -- Established in 1963, the club ambiance appears not to have changed, although the gate that guards the docks is probably recent. Very protected docks are tucked way up into the inner harbor. Maximum vessel is 45 feet. Limited services made up for by a great spot. Moorings may be available from Cold Spring Harbor Beach Club (692-6540).

Notable -- Cold Spring Harbor is one of the most picturesque, unspoiled villages on Long Island's very built-up "gold coast". It was one of NY's first custom ports and in the 1840's was the busiest whaling port on L.I. In the late 1800's, it was discovered by the wealthy leisured class (including Louis Comfort Tiffany, whose home overlooked the harbor) and grand hotels quickly dotted its hills and beaches. Happily, all that is now gone leaving a charming 19th century architectural legacy and abundant peace and quiet. A number of intriguing institutions also make their home here: Cold Spring Harbor Whaling Museum, Cold Spring Harbor Laboratories. The village of Cold Spring Harbor promises gift shops, galleries, a deli, a gourmet shop, a couple restaurants and boutiques.

Wyncote Club

PO Box 385; 311 West Shore Drive; Huntington, NY 11743

Tel: (631) 351-9521 **VHF: Monitor** 10 **Talk** n/a
Fax: n/a **Alternate Tel:** (631) 351-9521
Email: info@wyncoteclub.com **Web:** www.wyncoteclub.com
Nearest Town: Huntington *(2 mi.)* **Tourist Info:** (631) 423-6100

Navigational Information
Lat: 40°53.847' **Long:** 073°25.831' **Tide:** 7 ft. **Current:** 2 kt. **Chart:** 12365
Rep. Depths *(MLW):* **Entry** 20 ft. **Fuel Dock** 7 ft. **Max Slip/Moor** 7 ft./15 ft.
Access: L.I.S. to buoy #8 in Huntington Bay, then to Huntington Lighthouse

Marina Facilities *(In Season/Off Season)*
Fuel: Valvtect - Gasoline
Slips: 77 Total, 4 Transient **Max LOA:** 52 ft. **Max Beam:** 17 ft.
  Rate *(per ft.):* **Day** $2.00* **Week** n/a **Month** n/a
  Power: 30 amp Incl., 50 amp n/a, 100 amp n/a, 200 amp n/a
  Cable TV: No **Dockside Phone:** No
  Dock Type: Floating, Short Fingers, Pilings, Wood
Moorings: 9 Total, 6 Transient **Launch:** No, Dinghy Dock (Free)
  Rate: Day $10 **Week** n/a **Month** n/a
Heads: 2 Toilet(s), 2 Shower(s) *(with dressing rooms)*
Laundry: None **Pay Phones:** Yes
Pump-Out: No **Fee:** n/a **Closed Heads:** No

Marina Operations
Owner/Manager: Richard Van Stry **Dockmaster:** Same
In-Season: Apr 15-Nov 15, 7:30 am-8pm **Off-Season:** n/a
After-Hours Arrival: Tie up at fuel dock and meet night watchman
Reservations: Preferred **Credit Cards:** Visa/MC, Dscvr, Amex
Discounts: Boat/US **Dockage:** n/a **Fuel:** $0.10 **Repair:** n/a
Pets: Welcome, Dog Walk Area **Handicap Access:** No

Marina Services and Boat Supplies
Services - Docking Assistance, Boaters' Lounge, Security *(24 Hrs., Dock help and night watchman)*, Dock Carts **Communication -** Mail & Package Hold, Phone Messages **Supplies - OnSite:** Ice *(Block, Cube)*
Under 1 mi: Ships' Store *(Compass Rose 673-4144)*, Bait/Tackle *(Huntington Bait & Tackle 385-4200)* **1-3 mi:** Propane *(Village Grinding 421-5020)* **3+ mi:** West Marine *(673-3910, 5 mi.)*

Boatyard Services
Near: Electrical Repairs, Electronic Sales, Electronics Repairs.
Under 1 mi: Travelift, Railway, Forklift, Crane, Engine mechanic *(gas, diesel)*, Launching Ramp, Hull Repairs, Rigger, Sail Loft.
 Nearest Yard: Willis Marine (631) 421-3400

Restaurants and Accommodations
OnCall: Pizzeria *(DiRaimo 673-5755)* **Under 1 mi:** Restaurant *(Tutto Pazzo 271-2253, L $9-18, D $18-36, by dinghy)*, *(Coco Water Café 271-5700, L $10-20, D $17-22, by dinghy)*, *(Pomodorino 549-7074, L $15, D $25)*, *(Piccolo 424-5592)*, Seafood Shack *(Jeff's Seafood 427-5120)*, Snack Bar *(Golden Dolphin B $3, L $7, D $12)* **1-3 mi:** Motel *(Huntington County Inn 421-3900)*, Inn/B&B *(Centerport Harbor 754-1730)*, *(Swan View Manor 367-2070)* **3+ mi:** Hotel *(Sheraton 231-1100, 11 mi.)*, *(Hilton 845-1000, 9 mi.)*

Recreation and Entertainment
OnSite: Picnic Area, Grills **Near:** Beach, Playground, Fitness Center, Jogging Paths **Under 1 mi:** Fishing Charter, Video Rental *(Blockbuster 421-6850)*, Park **1-3 mi:** Dive Shop, Tennis Courts *(Huntington Racquet Club 351-9679)*, Horseback Riding, Movie Theater *(Cineplex Odeon 425-7680)*, Museum *(Heckscher Art Museum 351-3250/Cold Spring Whaling Museum 367-3418)* **3+ mi:** Golf Course *(Dix Hills 271-4788 , 6 mi.)*, Sightseeing *(Walt Whitman Birthplace, 5 mi.)*

Provisioning and General Services
Under 1 mi: Gourmet Shop *(Mr. Sausage 424-5248)*, Delicatessen *(Bay Deli 421-4250)*, Wine/Beer, Liquor Store *(Seaholm Wines & Liquors 427-0031)*, Green Grocer, Fishmonger, Bank/ATM, Post Office, Catholic Church, Protestant Church, Library *(Huntington 421-5053)*, Beauty Salon, Barber Shop, Dry Cleaners, Laundry, Pharmacy *(North Shore 427-6262)*, Newsstand, Hardware Store *(True Value 271-2774)* **1-3 mi:** Convenience Store, Supermarket *(Waldbaums 385-0145)*, Health Food *(Sweet Potatoes Organic Mkt. 423-6424)*, Bakery *(Cardinali 425-7424)*, Farmers' Market *(Elks Club, Sun 8-1 323-3653)*, Synagogue, Bookstore *(Polyanthos Park Ave Books 271-5558)*, Florist, Clothing Store, Retail Shops, Copies Etc. *(Dunlap Printing 427-5222)*

Transportation
OnCall: Rental Car *(Enterprise 424-8300)*, Taxi *(Crown Taxi 427-1166)*, Airport Limo *(Gold Coast Limousine 427-1684)* **Under 1 mi:** Local Bus *(Huntington Area Rapid Transit)* **1-3 mi:** Rail *(LIRR to NY City)*
Airport: Islip/Laguardia/JFK *(22 mi./26 mi./35 mi.)*

Medical Services
911 Service Under 1 mi: Doctor, Dentist, Chiropractor *(Waterfront Chiro Cntr 549-1490)*, Holistic Services, Ambulance **1-3 mi:** Veterinarian *(Harborside 549-1540)* **Hospital:** Huntington 351-2000 *(2 mi.)*

Setting -- After passing Wincome Point sand bar and entering Huntington Harbor, follow the channel straight ahead (due south) to the Wyncote Club's still perfect docks. This gracious private club, on the harbor's west side, welcomes all boaters to its new shorefront facility. The surrounding area is hilly, densely treed, almost rural and completely residential. The road cuts close to the water, separating the main clubhouse from the docks. At the foot of the docks is a bristol satellite club house and dockmaster's office. The view landside from the docks is of the Main Clubhouse perched high up on the hill.

Marina Notes -- *min $40. A private club, founded over 30 years ago, Wyncote welcomes all boaters - no reciprocity required. A small building on the water-side of the road houses a bright and airy, crisply decorated and furnished boaters' lounge with a small kitchen, and quite new, excellent full "family" bathrooms. The main club house, up the hill, overlooks the harbor. Member of the Yachting Club of America.

Notable -- Since Wyncote is very close to the mouth of the harbor, it's an easy overnight stop. But that also makes it a long way to town. Take a cab or dinghy to the head of the east side of the harbor. There you'll find one of the two Huntington Town Docks - Mill Dam Marina (the other is Halesite). It's the furthest, but the closest to town, and is next to the Ketoamoke Yacht Club (a little white house). Plan on a 15 minute walk to the center of Huntington Village. South of Mill Dam is CoCo's Waterfront Restaurant (and supper club) which offers dock 'n dine. The Halesite dock (also on the eastside) is closer; a few eateries, markets and services can be found nearby in the little burg of Halesite.

Navigational Information

Lat: 40°53.785' **Long:** 073°25.271' **Tide:** 7 ft. **Current:** 2 kt. **Chart:** 13264
Rep. Depths (*MLW*): **Entry** 13 ft. **Fuel Dock** 8 ft. **Max Slip/Moor** 13 ft./13 ft.
Access: Almost due South of Easton's Neck CG Station on the east side

Marina Facilities *(In Season/Off Season)*

Fuel: Gasoline, Diesel
Slips: 103 Total, 15 Transient **Max LOA:** 100 ft. **Max Beam:** n/a
  Rate *(per ft.)*: **Day** $2.50/Inq. **Week** Inq. **Month** Inq.
  Power: 30 amp $5, **50 amp** $10, **100 amp** n/a, **200 amp** n/a
  Cable TV: Yes, Incl. **Dockside Phone:** Yes Long Term
  Dock Type: Floating, Wood
Moorings: 54 Total, 20 Transient **Launch:** n/a
  Rate: Day $30 **Week** n/a **Month** n/a
Heads: 5 Toilet(s), 4 Shower(s) *(with dressing rooms)*
Laundry: None **Pay Phones:** Yes, 2
Pump-Out: OnSite, Self Service **Fee:** Free **Closed Heads:** Yes

Marina Operations

Owner/Manager: Harold Von Dolln **Dockmaster:** Vinny Marino
In-Season: MemDay-LabDay, 7am-7pm* **Off-Season:** Sep-May, 8am-5pm
After-Hours Arrival: Call in advance
Reservations: Yes, Preferred **Credit Cards:** Visa/MC, Amex
Discounts: None
Pets: No **Handicap Access:** Yes, Heads

Huntington Yacht Club

95 East Shore Road; Huntington, NY 11743

Tel: (631) 427-4949 **VHF: Monitor** 68 **Talk** 68
Fax: (631) 427-4995 **Alternate Tel:** (631) 427-4949
Email: huntyc@aol.com **Web:** www.huntingtonyachtclub.com
Nearest Town: Halesite *(1 mi.)* **Tourist Info:** (631) 423-6100

Marina Services and Boat Supplies

Services - Docking Assistance, Boaters' Lounge, Dock Carts
Communication - FedEx, AirBorne, UPS, Express Mail *(Sat Del)*
Supplies - OnSite: Ice *(Block, Cube, Shaved)* **Near:** Bait/Tackle
(Huntington Bait & Tackle 385-4200) **Under 1 mi:** Ships' Store *(Compass Rose 673-4144)* **1-3 mi:** Propane *(Village Grinding 421-5020)*
3+ mi: West Marine *(673-3910, 5 mi.)*

Boatyard Services

Near: Travelift, Crane, Hydraulic Trailer, Engine mechanic *(gas, diesel)*, Electrical Repairs, Electronic Sales, Electronics Repairs, Hull Repairs, Rigger, Sail Loft, Bottom Cleaning, Brightwork, Refrigeration, Divers, Compound, Wash & Wax, Propeller Repairs, Painting, Yacht Broker.
Under 1 mi: Launching Ramp. **Nearest Yard:** Knutson (631) 549-7842

Restaurants and Accommodations

OnSite: Restaurant *(Hungtington YC Dining Room 427-4961, L $7-9, D $17-26)*, Snack Bar, Lite Fare *(HYC Pub D $7-9)* **Near:** Restaurant *(Tutto Pazzo 271-2253, L $9-36, D $9-36)* **Under 1 mi:** Restaurant *(Coco's Water Café 271-5700, L $11-20, D $17-22)*, *(TK's Galley 351-8666)* **1-3 mi:** Pizzeria *(Southtown 421-2323)*, Motel *(Chalet 757-4600)*, Hotel *(Marriott 423-1600)*, Inn/B&B *(Centerport Harbor 754-1730)*

Recreation and Entertainment

OnSite: Pool, Picnic Area **Under 1 mi:** Beach, Video Rental *(Blockbuster 421-6850)* **1-3 mi:** Tennis Courts *(Huntington Racquet Club 351-9679)*, Fitness Center *(Village Gym 423-4418)*, Movie Theater *(Cinema Art 423-3456; Cineplex Odeon)*, Park, Museum *(Heckscher Art Museum 351-3250;*

Cold Spring Whaling Museum 367-3418), Sightseeing *(Huntington Village)*
3+ mi: Golf Course *(Dix Hills 271-4788 , 6 mi.)*

Provisioning and General Services

Near: Wine/Beer **Under 1 mi:** Convenience Store, Supermarket *(King Kullen 351-8400)*, Gourmet Shop *(Mr Sausage 424-5248)*, Delicatessen *(Brothers 261-4411; Bay 421-4250)*, Fishmonger, Bank/ATM, Post Office, Beauty Salon, Barber Shop, Dry Cleaners, Laundry, Newsstand, Florist, Copies Etc. *(Dunlap Printing 427-5222)* **1-3 mi:** Health Food *(Sweet Potatoes Organic Market 423-6424)*, Liquor Store *(Southdown Liquor 271-6380)*, Farmers' Market *(Elks Club, Sun 8-1 323-3653)*, Meat Market, Catholic Church, Protestant Church, Synagogue, Library *(Huntington 421-5053)*, Bookstore *(Polyanthos Park Ave 271-5558; Book Revue 271-1442)*, Pharmacy *(Genovese 549-9400)*, Hardware Store *(True Value 271-2774)*, Clothing Store, Retail Shops **3+ mi:** Department Store *(Walt Whitman Mall - Macys, Bloomingdales, Lord & Taylor, 5 mi.)*

Transportation

OnCall: Rental Car *(Enterprise 424-2500, or Hertz 427-6106, 2 mi.)*, Taxi *(AAA Taxi 271-3600)*, Airport Limo *(Gold Coast Limo 427-684)* **Under 1 mi:** Local Bus *(HART/SCT from Halesite to Village, RR & Whitman Mall)* **1-3 mi:** Rail *(LIRR)* **Airport:** Islip/Laguardia/JFK *(22 mi./26 mi./35 mi.)*

Medical Services

911 Service **OnCall:** Doctor, Ambulance **Under 1 mi:** Dentist, Chiropractor *(Waterfront Chiropractor Cntr 549-1490)*, Veterinarian *(Harborside Veterinary Hosp. 549-1540)* **1-3 mi:** Holistic Services *(Massage On the Run 351-9898)* **Hospital:** Huntington 351-2000 *(1 mi.)*

Setting -- As you wend your way through narrow, boat-packed Huntington Harbor, gracious, professional Huntington Yacht Club's extensive network of docks will appear off your port bow about mid-way. The club, with its excellent set of amenities, nestles in an upscale residential neighborhood far from the bustle and services of town. The water-face of the two story, beige-brick clubhouse, which hosts a fine-dining restaurant, is reminiscent of the stern of a ship.

Marina Notes -- *Week-end hours in season: 7am-10pm. This lovely private century-old club welcomes all transients. A small two-story dockhouse provides easy oversight of the 103 state-of-the-art slips (17 quite new), the 54 moorings that surround it, and the extensive and speedy launch service (in-season: Mon-Thu 7am-10pm, Fri-Sun 'til 12am; off season: 8am-6/8pm). There's even an "after-hours" courtesy dinghy. High speed fuel pumps; high speed free pump-put. Water, power, cable TV at every slip. The ceramic tile heads and showers are particularly inviting. Inquire about required dress in the clubhouse.

Notable -- All of HYC's facilities are available to the visiting mariner. A large, attractively furnished Olympic-size pool, adjacent to the clubhouse, overlooks the docks and harbor. A bath house and snack bar are east of the pool. An expansive first floor lounge and the polished second floor main dining room both have views up and down Huntington Harbor. A pub/bar at the rear of the second floor offers light fare. The restaurant also provides "room service" to the boat! A King Kullen Supermarket 0.7 mile. The little burg of Halesite is just under a mile (Nathan Hale landed here); there's a town dock (Halesite Marina), basic services and a few eateries. The wonderful shopping town of Huntington is about 1.8 miles. Farther out, the huge Walt Whitman Mall is about 5 miles by cab or bus.

Knutson's West Marine

41 East Shore Road; Huntington, NY 11743

Tel: (631) 549-7842 **VHF: Monitor** 9 **Talk** n/a
Fax: (631) 549-2375 **Alternate Tel:** n/a
Email: n/a **Web:** n/a
Nearest Town: Halesite *(0.4 mi.)* **Tourist Info:** (631) 423-6100

Navigational Information

Lat: 40°53.406' **Long:** 073°25.002' **Tide:** 8 ft. **Current:** 2 kt. **Chart:** 12364
Rep. Depths *(MLW)*: **Entry** 10 ft. **Fuel Dock** n/a **Max Slip/Moor** 10 ft./10 ft.
Access: About 3/4 of the way to head of harbor on east shore at RN 14

Marina Facilities *(In Season/Off Season)*

Fuel: No
Slips: 100 Total, 5 Transient **Max LOA:** 60 ft. **Max Beam:** n/a
  Rate *(per ft.)*: **Day** $2.00/$1.50 **Week** $12 **Month** n/a
  Power: 30 amp Incl., **50 amp** Incl., **100 amp** n/a, **200 amp** n/a
  Cable TV: No **Dockside Phone:** No
  Dock Type: Floating, Wood
Moorings: 75 Total, 5 Transient **Launch:** Yes (Free), Dinghy Dock
  Rate: Day $30 **Week** n/a **Month** n/a
Heads: 2 Toilet(s), 2 Shower(s) *(with dressing rooms)*
Laundry: 1 Washer(s), 1 Dryer(s) **Pay Phones:** No
Pump-Out: OnSite, Self Service **Fee:** $10 **Closed Heads:** Yes

Marina Operations

Owner/Manager: Peter Knutson **Dockmaster:** Same
In-Season: Apr-Oct, 8am-6pm **Off-Season:** Nov-Mar, 9am-4pm
After-Hours Arrival: Call in advance
Reservations: Yes **Credit Cards:** Visa/MC, Amex
Discounts: None
Pets: Welcome **Handicap Access:** Yes, Heads

Marina Services and Boat Supplies

Services - Docking Assistance, Trash Pick-Up, Dock Carts
Communication - Mail & Package Hold, FedEx, AirBorne, UPS, Express
Mail **Supplies - Near:** Bait/Tackle *(Huntington Bait & Tackle 385-4200)*
Under 1 mi: Ships' Store *(Compass Rose 673-4144)* **1-3 mi:** Propane
(Village Grinding 421-5020) **3+ mi:** West Marine *(673-3910, 5 mi.)*

Boatyard Services

OnSite: Travelift, Engine mechanic *(gas, diesel)*, Electrical Repairs, Hull
Repairs, Bottom Cleaning, Brightwork, Compound, Wash & Wax, Propeller
Repairs, Woodworking **OnCall:** Rigger, Sail Loft, Air Conditioning,
Refrigeration **Near:** Launching Ramp.

Restaurants and Accommodations

OnCall: Pizzeria *(Junior's 423-9006)* **Near:** Restaurant *(Tutto Pazzo
271-2253, L $9-36, D $9-36)*, *(Aix En Provence 549-3338)*, Lite Fare
(T.K.'sGalley 351-8666), *(Halesite Harbour Delicatessen 351-9340)*,
Condo/ Cottage *(Harbor Inn 385-2182)* **Under 1 mi:** Restaurant *(Si
Yuang 351-1833)*, *(Coco's Water Cafe 271-5700, L $11-20, D $17-22,
Lite fare for dinner, too, Kids' Menu, Dock 'n Dine)* **1-3 mi:** Motel *(Chalet
754-4600)*, *(Marriott 423-1600)*, Inn/B&B *(Centerport Harbor 754-1730)*

Recreation and Entertainment

Near: Jogging Paths **Under 1 mi:** Beach, Video Rental *(Blockbuster 421-
6850)* **1-3 mi:** Tennis Courts *(Huntington Racquet Club 351-9679)*, Fitness
Center *(Tonl Fitness 423-4545)*, Movie Theater *(Cinema Art 423-3456;
Cineplex Odeon)*, Park, Museum *(Heckscher Art Museum 351-3250; Cold
Spring Whaling Museum 367-3418)*, Sightseeing *(Huntington Village)*

3+ mi: Golf Course *(Dix Hills 271-4788, 6 mi.)*, Bowling *(Larkfield Lanes 368-
8788, 7 mi.)*

Provisioning and General Services

Near: Fishmonger *(Jeff's Seafood)*, Dry Cleaners *(Harbor)*, Laundry
(Halesite 351-9051) **Under 1 mi:** Convenience Store, Supermarket *(King
Kullen 351-8400)*, Gourmet Shop *(Mr. Sausage 424-5248)*, Delicatessen
(Brothers 261-4411, Bay 421-4250), Liquor Store *(Southdown Liquor 271-
6380)*, Bank/ATM, Post Office, Pharmacy *(North Shore Pharmacy 427-
6262)* **1-3 mi:** Health Food *(Sweet Potatoes Organic Mkt. 423-6424)*,
Wine/Beer *(Bottles & Cases 423-9463)*, Farmers' Market *(Elks Club, Sun 8-1
323-3653)*, Catholic Church, Protestant Church, Synagogue, Library
(Huntington 421-5053), Hardware Store *(Southdown True Value 271-2774)*,
Copies Etc. *(Dunlap Printing 427-5222)* **3+ mi:** Bookstore *(Waldenbooks
673-1176, Barnes & Noble 421-9886, 5 mi.)*, Department Store *(Walt
Whitman Mall - Macys, Bloomingdales, Lord & Taylor, 5 mi.)*

Transportation

OnCall: Rental Car *(Enterprise 424-2500 or Hertz 427-6106 2 mi.)*, Taxi
(AAA Taxi 271-3600), Airport Limo *(Gold Coast Limo 427-684)* **Near:** Local
Bus *(HART/SCT to Village, RR & Whitman Mall)* **1-3 mi:** Rail *(LIRR)*
Airport: Islip/Laguardia/JFK *(22 mi./26 mi./35 mi.)*

Medical Services

911 Service **OnCall:** Ambulance **Under 1 mi:** Doctor *(Stonybrook Family
Medicine 385-8200)*, Chiropractor *(Waterfront Chiropractor 549-1490)*
1-3 mi: Dentist *(Berg 271-2310)*, Holistic Services *(Massage On the Run
351-9898* **Hospital:** Huntington 351-2000 *(W/in 1 mi*

Setting -- About a tenth of a mile past Huntington Yacht Club, on the eastern shore, Knutson's docks, travelift and bright blue boat shed come into view. From here south, the shoreline becomes more commercial as do the landside environs. Knutson's is pure boatyard, with docks and a launch-serviced mooring field.

Marina Notes -- Formerly Dornic Marina. The Knutson family has been in the marine business in Huntington since the mid 1950's. Today, grandson Peter runs both locations in the harbor: this is the main office (Knutson's West), with docks, storage, haul-out, repair facilities and moorings. Across the harbor is a smaller power boat marina. There is a third, unrelated, Knutson's in Huntington. Excellent tile heads and showers with private dressing rooms and a laundry. Also onsite is a small chandlery, pump-out (8am-6pm and by appointment). Launch service to moorings is a very admirable 8am-11pm.

Notable -- A big, new King Kullen supermarket is an easy 0.2 mile walk. A little farther is the tiny burg of Halesite, where Nathan Hale went ashore, was arrested and ultimately hanged. There are a couple of eateries, a deli, 7-11, laundromat, cleaners, bank/ATM, and a marine supply. There's also the Halesite Huntington Town Dock for convenient dinghy tie-up. CoCo's, overlooking Huntington Harbor, offers a fine dining restaurant, a deck and a couple of bar/supper club options along with dockage (about 0.7 mi.). Upscale, downtown Huntington is 1.7 miles away and has block upon block of shops, restaurants, theaters, and historic sights. It's an easy cab ride or take the Huntington Area Rapid Transit/Suffolk County Transit bus into Huntington Village, the Long Island Railroad at Huntington Station or out to huge Walt Whitman Mall.

Navigational Information
Lat: 40°53.325' **Long:** 073°25.404' **Tide:** 8 ft. **Current:** 0 kt. **Chart:** 12365
Rep. Depths (*MLW*): **Entry** 15 ft. **Fuel Dock** n/a **Max Slip/Moor** 15 ft./-
Access: South off Long Island Sound Eaton's Neck to harbor's west shoe

Marina Facilities (*In Season/Off Season*)
Fuel: No
Slips: 308 Total, 20 Transient **Max LOA:** 120 ft. **Max Beam:** n/a
 Rate (*per ft.*): **Day** $3.00/$2.50* **Week** $12 **Month** $31
Power: 30 amp Inq., 50 amp Inq., 100 amp Inq., 200 amp n/a
Cable TV: No **Dockside Phone:** No
Dock Type: Floating, Long Fingers, Alongside, Wood
Moorings: 0 Total, 0 Transient **Launch:** n/a
 Rate: Day n/a **Week** n/a **Month** n/a
Heads: 8 Toilet(s), 4 Shower(s) (*with dressing rooms*)
Laundry: 2 Washer(s), 2 Dryer(s), Book Exchange **Pay Phones:** Yes, 3
Pump-Out: OnSite, Full Service, 1 Central **Fee:** $10 **Closed Heads:** Yes

Marina Operations
Owner/Manager: A. Gould & A. DeRose **Dockmaster:** Karl Almstrom
In-Season: Mar 16- Dec 14, 24 hrs. **Off-Season:** Dec 15-Mar 15, 8am-5pm
After-Hours Arrival: Check in at Guard Shed
Reservations: Yes **Credit Cards:** Visa/MC
Discounts: None
Pets: Welcome, Dog Walk Area **Handicap Access:** Yes, Heads, Docks

West Shore Marina

100 West Shore Road; Huntington, NY 11743

Tel: (631) 427-3444 **VHF: Monitor** 9 **Talk** 73
Fax: (631) 427-0009 **Alternate Tel:** (631) 427-3444
Email: n/a **Web:** n/a
Nearest Town: Huntington (*1.5 mi.*) **Tourist Info:** (631) 423-6100

Marina Services and Boat Supplies
Services - Docking Assistance, Security (*24 Hrs.*), Dock Carts
Communication - Mail & Package Hold, Phone Messages, FedEx, UPS,
Express Mail (*Sat Del*) **Supplies - OnSite:** Ice (*Block, Cube*), Ships' Store
OnCall: West Marine (*5 mi. 673-3910*) **Near:** Bait/Tackle (*Huntington Bait
& Tackle 385-4200*) **Under 1 mi:** Propane (*Village Grinding 421-5020*)
1-3 mi: Boat/US, Marine Discount Store

Boatyard Services
OnSite: Travelift (*35T*), Engine mechanic (*gas, diesel*), Electrical Repairs,
Electronic Sales, Electronics Repairs, Hull Repairs, Rigger, Sail Loft, Bottom
Cleaning, Brightwork, Air Conditioning, Refrigeration, Divers, Compound,
Wash & Wax, Interior Cleaning, Propeller Repairs, Woodworking, Painting,
Awlgrip, Yacht Broker (*Center Yacht*), Total Refits **OnCall:** Inflatable
Repairs, Life Raft Service, Upholstery, Metal Fabrication **Near:** Launching
Ramp. **Yard Rates:** $75/hr., Haul & Launch $7.50/ft. (*blocking $4.50/ft.*),
Power Wash $2.50/ft., Bottom Paint $9/ft. **Storage:** In-Water $105/ft. + slip
selection and electric hookup, On-Land $35/ft.

Restaurants and Accommodations
Near: Restaurant (*Coco's 271-5700, L & D $10-22*), Seafood Shack (*Jeff's
Seafood 427-5120*), Snack Bar (*TK's Galley 351-8666*), Fast Food (*Burger
King*), Pizzeria (*O'Raimo 673-5755*) **Under 1 mi:** Restaurant (*Piccolo 424-
5592*), (*Canterbury Ales 549-4404*) **1-3 mi:** Motel (*Chalet 757-4600, $75-
125*), Hotel (*Marriott 423-1600*)

Recreation and Entertainment
OnSite: Pool, Picnic Area, Grills, Playground **Near:** Beach, Tennis Courts,
Jogging Paths, Fishing Charter, Video Rental (*Blockbuster 421-6850*), Park
Under 1 mi: Movie Theater (*Cineplex 425-7680; Cinema Arts 423-FILM*)
1-3 mi: Fitness Center (*NYSC 424-7100*), Museum (*Heckscher Art Museum
351-3250*), Cultural Attract (*IMAC 549-ARTS, concerts*), Sightseeing
(*Downtown Huntington*) **3+ mi:** Golf Course (*Dix Hills 271-4788, 5 mi.*)

Provisioning and General Services
Near: Convenience Store, Gourmet Shop (*Mr. Sausage 424-5248*),
Delicatessen (*Bay Deli 421-4250*), Wine/Beer, Farmers' Market (*Elks Club,
Sun 8-1 323-3653*), Bank/ATM, Post Office, Barber Shop, Dry Cleaners,
Laundry, Pharmacy (*North Shore 427-6262*), Newsstand, Florist **Under
1 mi:** Supermarket (*King Kullen 351-8400*), Health Food, Liquor Store
(*Seaholm 427-0031*), Bakery (*Cardinale 425-7424*), Green Grocer, Catholic
Church, Protestant Church, Library (*Huntington 421-5053*), Beauty Salon,
Bookstore (*Book Revue*), Hardware Store (*True Value 271-2774*), Clothing
Store, Retail Shops **1-3 mi:** Synagogue, Copies Etc.

Transportation
OnCall: Rental Car (*Enterprise 424-2500; Hertz 427-6106 2 mi.*), Taxi
(*Orange & White 271-3600*), Airport Limo (*Bay Limo 547-5466*)
Near: Local Bus (*HART*) **1-3 mi:** Rail (*LIRR to NY City 718-243-4999*)
Airport: Islip/Laguardia/JFK (*22 mi./26 mi./35 mi.*)

Medical Services
911 Service **OnCall:** Ambulance **Under 1 mi:** Doctor (*Plaza Medeical 385-
0207*), Dentist (*Sims 549-4055*), Chiropractor (*Aslan-Stacey 549-1490*),
Optician (*Southdown 271-0550*) **1-3 mi:** Veterinarian (*Harborside 549-
1540*) **Hospital:** Huntington 351-2000 (*1 mi.*)

Setting -- On the western shore of Huntington Harbor, almost to the head, is this large, superbly outfitted and maintained, full-service marina. West Shore's
strikingly stylish contemporary main building acts as both a location beacon and a tone setter and dominates the extensive dockage facility. A large, grassy
area, furnished with picnic tables and grills, overlooks the harbor and an inviting pool is directly south.

Marina Notes -- *Memorial Day-Labor Day. Designed and constructed by owner/operators Arthur Gould & Armand DeRose. Built on the site of the old
historic Huntington commercial Wharfs. Three rows of widely spaced floating docks with full finger piers radiate from a central, fixed pier straight out from the
main building. Full service yard includes sailmaker, electronics, cleaning, broker. Friendly, helpful staff. Many nautical services in the marine center across the
road. Particularly nice heads and showers with private dressing rooms and laundry room.

Notable -- A beautiful pool is surrounded by chaises, tables & chairs with white market umbrellas-- all fronting the harbor. A manicured dock-sidelawn is
hosts picnic tables and grills. A 20 minute walk, Historical Huntington has a remarkable number of entertainment and cultural activities - as well as lots
of eateries and great shops. Beaux-arts style Heckscher Museum of Art, built in 1920 by philanthropist August Heckscher, houses over 1800 works spanning
500 years of American & European art (Tue-Fri 10am-5pm, Sat-Sun 1-5pm $3/1) - in Heckscher Park. The Old Town Hall National Register Historic District
includes 1882 Soldiers and Sailors Memorial Building (now a visitors' center), 1910 Old Town Hall and the 1905 Sewing and Trade School Building.

Coneys Marine

32 New York Avenue *; Huntington, NY 11743

Tel: (631) 421-3366 **VHF: Monitor** 9 **Talk** 9
Fax: (631) 549-7392 **Alternate Tel:** n/a
Email: info@coneys.com **Web:** www.coneys.com
Nearest Town: Huntington *(1.5 mi.)* **Tourist Info:** (631) 423-6100

Navigational Information
Lat: 40°53.245' **Long:** 073°25.008' **Tide:** 8 ft. **Current:** 2 kt. **Chart:** 12364
Rep. Depths *(MLW):* **Entry** 6 ft. **Fuel Dock** n/a **Max Slip/Moor** -/20 ft.
Access: Huntington Harbor, almost to head on eastern shore

Marina Facilities *(In Season/Off Season)*
Fuel: No
Slips: 0 Total, 0 Transient **Max LOA:** 50 ft. **Max Beam:** 12 ft.
  Rate *(per ft.):* **Day** n/a **Week** n/a **Month** n/a
  Power: 30 amp n/a, **50 amp** n/a, **100 amp** n/a, **200 amp** n/a
  Cable TV: No **Dockside Phone:** No
  Dock Type: n/a
Moorings: 50 Total, 5 Transient **Launch:** Yes (Free), Dinghy Dock
  Rate: Day $30 **Week** $145 **Month** $485
Heads: 2 Toilet(s), 2 Shower(s) *(with dressing rooms)*
Laundry: None **Pay Phones:** No
Pump-Out: OnSite **Fee:** Free **Closed Heads:** Yes

Marina Operations
Owner/Manager: Coneys Family **Dockmaster:** Jim & Tom Coneys
In-Season: Apr-Nov, 8am-11pm **Off-Season:** Dec-Mar, 8am-5pm
After-Hours Arrival: No arrivals after 11pm
Reservations: Yes **Credit Cards:** Visa/MC
Discounts: None
Pets: Welcome **Handicap Access:** No

Marina Services and Boat Supplies
Services - Docking Assistance, Security, Dock Carts **Supplies -**
OnSite: Ice *(Cube)* **Near:** Ships' Store *(Coney's Marine Supply)*,
Bait/Tackle *(Huntington Bait & Tackle 385-4200)* **Under 1 mi:** Propane
3+ mi: West Marine *(673-3910, 5 mi.)*

Boatyard Services
OnSite: Forklift, Crane *(40T)*, Engine mechanic *(gas, diesel)*, Electrical
Repairs, Hull Repairs, Rigger, Bottom Cleaning, Brightwork, Air Conditioning,
Compound, Wash & Wax, Painting, Yacht Broker *(Matt Grant 421-3366)*
OnCall: Sail Loft, Upholstery **Near:** Launching Ramp, Electronic Sales,
Electronics Repairs, Refrigeration, Divers, Propeller Repairs.
Dealer for: Catalina, Morgan, Vanguard, Jeanneau, Walker Day, Achilles.
Yard Rates: $75/hr., Haul & Launch $6.15-7.95/ft., Power Wash $3/ft.,
Bottom Paint $13/ft. **Storage:** In-Water $20/ft., On-Land $30/ft.

Restaurants and Accommodations
OnCall: Pizzeria *(Junior's 423-9006)* **Near:** Restaurant *(Coco's Water Cafe*
L $10-22, D $10-22, Kids' Menu), *(Tutto Pazzo 271-2253, L $9-36, D $9-36,*
Lunch & early dinner special $10), *(T.K.'s Galley 351-8666)*, Snack Bar
(Ralph's Italian Ices) **Under 1 mi:** Pizzeria *(Rosa's 425-7694)*, Hotel
(Marriott 351-8100) **3+ mi:** Motel *(Chalet 757-4600, $75-125, 3.5 mi.)*,
Inn/B&B *(Centerport Harbor 754-1730, 4 mi.)*

Recreation and Entertainment
Near: Video Rental *(Blockbuster 421-6850)* **Under 1 mi:** Beach,
Playground, Movie Theater *(Cineplex Odeon 425-7680)*, Video Arcade, Park
(18-acre Hecksher), Museum *(Heckscher Museum 351-3250)*, Cultural

Attract *(Inter-media Art Center 549-2787 - live music concerts)* **1-3 mi:**
Tennis Courts *(Park Avenue 271-1810)*, Fitness Center *(The Village Gym*
423-4418), Horseback Riding *(Sweet Hollow Stables 351-9696)* **3+ mi:** Golf
Course *(Dix Hills C.C. 271-4788, 7 mi.)*, Bowling *(Amf 271-1180, 7 mi.)*

Provisioning and General Services
Near: Convenience Store *(7-11)*, Supermarket *(King Kullen)*, Delicatessen
(Bay 421-4250), Green Grocer, Fishmonger *(Jeff's Seafood)*, Bank/ATM,
Post Office, Dry Cleaners *(Harbor)*, Laundry *(Halsite)* **Under 1 mi:** Gourmet
Shop *(Renaissance 549-2727)*, Health Food, Wine/Beer *(Seaholm 427-*
0031), Liquor Store *(Southdown 271-6380)*, Farmers' Market *(Elks Club, Sun*
8-1 323-3653), Meat Market, Catholic Church, Protestant Church,
Synagogue, Beauty Salon, Barber Shop, Bookstore *(Book Revue 271-1442)*,
Pharmacy *(King Kullen 385-7320)*, Newsstand, Hardware Store *(Southdown*
271-2774), Copies Etc. *(Minuteman Press 427-1155)* **1-3 mi:** Library *(427-*
5165), Department Store *(Kmart 421-5005)*

Transportation
OnSite: Local Bus *(HART/SCT to Village, RR & Whitman Mall)*
OnCall: Rental Car *(Enterprise)*, Taxi *(Henry's 822-3330)* **Under 1 mi:** Air-
port Limo *(NY City Lights 424-6868)* **1-3 mi:** Rail *(LIRR to NY City)*
Airport: Islip/ Laguardia/JFK *(22 mi./26 mi./35 mi.)*

Medical Services
911 Service **Near:** Dentist *(Sims 549-4055)*, Chiropractor *(Waterfront Chiro)*,
Veterinarian *(Harborside Vet 549-1540)* **Under 1 mi:** Doctor *(Cormier 351-*
3779) **1-3 mi:** Holistic Services *(Hands of Healing 271-5107)*
Hospital: Huntington 351-2000 *0.5 mi.*

Setting -- The southeastern corner of long, tongue-like Huntington Harbor is home base to Coneys Marine. The small red building , perched practically right on the water, is the working home of the fairly extensive Coneys sailing conglomerate. This is where its launch and work boats land.

Marina Notes -- *This is the main office address. The launch and dinghy landing is at the corner of New York Avenue and Ketewomoke Drive (all distances are from here). A family business since the early 1970's, run by eight Coneys "boys". Everyone you talk to will be named Coneys. Major sailboat yard; largest Catalina Dealer in U.S. Coneys Marine operates mooring and launch service at two convenient locations within Huntington Harbor but only the "in town" one has transient facilities. The Goldstar Battalion field and launch is seasonal only. Launch hours (Ch.9): Apr 15-May 2 8am-6pm, May 3-23, 8am-8pm, May 24-Sep 1 8am-11pm, Sept 2 - Oct 5 8am-8pm, Oct 6-16 8am-6pm.

Notable -- Nearby Coco's Water Cafe overlooks the harbor and mooring field; service is inside or waterside and its separate Supper Club offers DJ & live music (dock 'n dine, too). One of the closest facilities to downtown Huntington with its blocks and blocks of shops, restaurants, theaters, and just about whatever you might need. The Cinema Arts Center (one of L.I.'s 6 primary cultural organizations) showcases American independent features and outstanding American and European films. Huntington Arts Council sponsors the Summer Arts Festival (271-8423) with free concerts and shows in Heckscher Park. Also home to Heckscher Museum of Art, open Tue-Fri 10am-5pm, Sat-Sun 1-5pm, $3/1 (Family Gallery Guide to each exhibit).

Navigational Information

Lat: 40°53.148' **Long:** 073°25.239' **Tide:** 7 **Current:** 1 **Chart:** 12364
Rep. Depths (*MLW*)**: Entry** 10 ft. **Fuel Dock** 13 ft. **Max Slip/Moor** 15 ft./14 ft.
Access: Huntington Harbor to head - in center

Marina Facilities *(In Season/Off Season)*

Fuel: *Shell* - Gasoline, Diesel
Slips: 120 Total, 14 Transient **Max LOA:** 65 ft. **Max Beam:** 18 ft.
  Rate *(per ft.)*: **Day** $2.50/Inq. **Week** Inq. **Month** Inq.
  Power: 30 amp $10, **50 amp** $20, **100 amp** n/a, **200 amp** n/a
  Cable TV: No **Dockside Phone:** No
  Dock Type: Floating, Long Fingers, Alongside, Wood
Moorings: 85 Total, 15 Transient **Launch:** Yes
  Rate: Day $25.00 **Week** n/a **Month** n/a
Heads: 2 Toilet(s), 2 Shower(s) *(with dressing rooms)*
Laundry: Yes **Pay Phones:** Yes
Pump-Out: OnCall, 3 Central, 1 Port **Fee:** Free **Closed Heads:** No

Marina Operations

Owner/Manager: Jeff Willis **Dockmaster:** Dave Albert
In-Season: Jun-Sep, 8am-10pm **Off-Season:** Oct-May, 8am-6pm
After-Hours Arrival: Go to gas dock
Reservations: Preferred **Credit Cards:** Visa/MC, Amex, Shell
Discounts: None
Pets: Welcome **Handicap Access:** Yes, Heads

Willis Marine Center

17 Mill Dam Road; Huntington, NY 11743

Tel: (631) 421-3400 **VHF: Monitor** 9 **Talk** 72
Fax: (631) 421-3302 **Alternate Tel:** n/a
Email: info@willismarine.com **Web:** www.willismarine.com
Nearest Town: Huntington *(1 mi.)* **Tourist Info:** (631) 423-6100

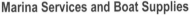

Marina Services and Boat Supplies

Services - Docking Assistance, Security (6), Dock Carts **Communication -** FedEx, AirBorne, UPS, Express Mail *(Sat Del)* **Supplies - OnSite:** Ice *(Block, Cube)*, Marine Discount Store *(Compass Rose)* **Near:** Ships' Store *(Huntington Marine Supply)* **Under 1 mi:** Bait/Tackle *(Huntington Bait & Tackle 385-4200)* **3+ mi:** West Marine *(673-3910, 4.5 mi.)*

Boatyard Services

OnSite: Travelift *(Three - to 35T)*, Crane *(Three - to 55 ft.)*, Engine mechanic *(gas, diesel)*, Electrical Repairs, Hull Repairs, Rigger, Bottom Cleaning, Brightwork, Air Conditioning, Refrigeration, Compound, Wash & Wax, Propeller Repairs, Woodworking, Painting, Awlgrip **Dealer for:** Sabre, Sabreline, Beneteau. **Yard Rates:** $75-85/hr., Haul & Launch Incl., Power Wash $2.75/ft. **Storage:** In-Water $24/ft., On-Land $34-$40/ft.

Restaurants and Accommodations

OnCall: Pizzeria *(Junior's)* **Near:** Restaurant *(T.K.'s Galley B, L, D)*, *(Aix en Provence 549-3338)*, *(Coco's Waterfront L $10-22, D $10-22, Kids' Menu)*, *(Harbor Inn 271-2253)*, Snack Bar *(Ralph's Italian Ices)* **Under 1 mi:** Hotel *(Marriott Hotels 351-8100)* **3+ mi:** Fast Food *(Taco Bell 427-7633, 4.5 mi.)*, Motel *(Chalet Motor Inn 757-4600, 3.5 mi.)*, Inn/B&B *(Centerport Harbor B & B 754-1730, 3.5 mi.)*

Recreation and Entertainment

Near: Video Rental *(Blockbuster Video 421-6850)* **Under 1 mi:** Fitness Center *(The Village Gym 423-4418)*, Park *(Heckscher)*, Museum *(Heckscher Art 351-3250 $5/1)* **1-3 mi:** Tennis Courts *(Huntington Indoor 421-0040)*, Movie Theater *(Cinema Art Centre 423-3456)*

3+ mi: Golf Course *(Dix Hills 271-4788, 7 mi.)*, Horseback Riding *(Sweet Hills 351-9168, 5.5 mi.)*, Bowling *(AMF 271-1180, 6.5 mi.)*, Sightseeing *(Walt Whitman's birthplace & Interpretive Center 427-5240 $3/1, 5 mi.)*

Provisioning and General Services

Near: Convenience Store *(7-11)*, Supermarket *(King Kullen)*, Delicatessen *(Bay Deli)*, Fishmonger *(Jeff's Seafood)*, Bank/ATM, Post Office, Dry Cleaners *(Harbor)*, Laundry *(Halsite 351-9051)* **Under 1 mi:** Gourmet Shop *(Renaissance Gourmet 549-2727)*, Health Food *(A Zone Diet 351-4005)*, Wine/Beer *(Seaholm Wines 427-0031)*, Liquor Store *(Southdown Liquor Store 271-6380)*, Farmers' Market *(Elks Club, Sun 8-1 323-3653)*, Library *(Huntington PL 427-5165)*, Pharmacy *(North Shore Pharmacy 427-6262)*, Hardware Store *(Southdown General Store 271-2774)*, Copies Etc. *(Minuteman Press 427-1155)* **1-3 mi:** Bookstore *(George Lenz Books 427-3744, Polyanthos Park Ave Books 271-5558)*, Department Store *(Kmart Stores 421-5005)*

Transportation

OnCall: Taxi *(Henry's Taxi/Limo 822-3330)*, Airport Limo *(NY City Lights Limousine Service 424-6868)* **Near:** Local Bus *(HART area shuttle)* **Under 1 mi:** Rail *(LIRR to NYC 718-243-4999)* **Airport:** Islip/LaGuardia/JFK *(22 mi./26 mi./35 mi.)*

Medical Services

911 Service **OnCall:** Ambulance **Near:** Doctor *(Callan 351-3766)*, Dentist *(Sims 549-4055)*, Chiropractor *(Waterfront Chiro)*, Veterinarian *(Harborside Vet)* **Under 1 mi:** Holistic Services *(Massage On The Run 487-1222)* **Hospital:** Huntington 351-2000 *(0.5 mi.)*

Setting -- Safely ensconced at the very head of Huntington Harbor, Willis' extensive network of docks lines the bulkhead and juts out into the inner harbor. Waterside views, from outside slips, are straight up the harbor past the Huntington Yacht Club. Landside, it's purely paved, well maintained, boatyard.

Marina Notes -- There are really no amenities to speak of. Nice tile heads and showers open to the office and to the outside. Here it's all about the boat. Full-service boatyard. Compass Rose Marine Supply is onsite. Willis Marine Center was established in 1975 by Jeff and Dick Willis and is a family owned and operated business with the second generation now running the show. Very large Sabre, Beneteau and Sabreline dealer with a major used boat brokerage on site as well. Two storage yards - one 5 acre waterfront and one 3-acre inland. Six sets of boat slips provide dockage for over 120 boats. Launch service to the 85 moorings.

Notable -- What Willis lacks in shoreside cruiser amenities, it makes up for in convenience. Willis and its neighbor Coneys Marine are the closest facilities to the large, upscale, full-service village of Huntington. It's 0.4 mile to a large shopping plaza and 0.8 miles to downtown Huntington with its plethora of restaurants, shops, and services. Whatever you need, you'll find here. The IMAC is an acoustically remarkable small concert hall. Two movie theaters - a first run multi-plex plus an independent and international film house. The 1819 house that was Walt Whitman's birthplace is a bit of a hike - but worth it for Whitman fans - portraits, artifacts, new interpretive center, film, readings, picnic area - take the S-1 bus or a cab; Mon-Fri 11am-4pm, Sat & Sun 12-5pm.

Seymour's Boat Yard

63 Bayview Avenue; Northport, NY 11768

Tel: (631) 261-6574 **VHF: Monitor** 68 **Talk** n/a
Fax: (631) 261-6084 **Alternate Tel:** (631) 261-6574
Email: seymours@optonline.net **Web:** n/a
Nearest Town: Northport Village *(0 mi.)* **Tourist Info:** (631) 261-3573

Navigational Information
Lat: 40°54.143' **Long:** 073°21.291' **Tide:** 7 ft. **Current:** n/a **Chart:** 12365
Rep. Depths (*MLW*): Entry 8 ft. **Fuel Dock** 5.5 ft. **Max Slip/Moor** 6 ft./9 ft.
Access: Huntington Bay to Northport Bay to Northport Harbor east side

Marina Facilities *(In Season/Off Season)*
Fuel: *Valvtect* - Gasoline, Diesel
Slips: 16 Total, 4 Transient **Max LOA:** 45 ft. **Max Beam:** 20 ft.
  Rate *(per ft.):* **Day** $2.00/$2.00 **Week** Inq. **Month** Inq.
  Power: 30 amp Incl., **50 amp** n/a, **100 amp** n/a, **200 amp** n/a
  Cable TV: No **Dockside Phone:** No
  Dock Type: Floating, Wood
Moorings: 600 Total, 40 Transient **Launch:** Yes (Included), Dinghy Dock
  Rate: Day $35 **Week** $150 **Month** n/a
Heads: 1 Toilet(s)
Laundry: None **Pay Phones:** No
Pump-Out: OnCall **Fee:** Free **Closed Heads:** Yes

Marina Operations
Owner/Manager: Dave Weber **Dockmaster:** Same
In-Season: Apr 15-Oct 30, 8am-12mid **Off-Season:** n/a
After-Hours Arrival: Call on VHF 68 or telephone
Reservations: Yes, Preferred **Credit Cards:** Visa/MC, Dscvr, Din, Amex
Discounts: Boat/US **Dockage:** 25% **Fuel:** n/a **Repair:** 15%*
Pets: Welcome **Handicap Access:** Yes

Marina Services and Boat Supplies
Services - Dock Carts **Communication -** Phone Messages, FedEx, AirBorne, UPS, Express Mail *(Sat Del)* **Supplies - OnSite:** Ice *(Block, Cube)* **Under 1 mi:** Ships' Store *(Snug Harbour Marine Supply 754-0777)*, Bait/Tackle *(Baitacular 261-3474)* **1-3 mi:** Propane *(Ace 261-0119)* **3+ mi:** West Marine *(673-3910, 7 mi.)*

Boatyard Services
OnSite: Railway *(50T)*, Crane, Engine mechanic *(gas, diesel)*, Hull Repairs, Bottom Cleaning, Brightwork, Compound, Wash & Wax, Interior Cleaning, Painting, Awlgrip **OnCall:** Electrical Repairs, Electronic Sales, Electronics Repairs, Rigger, Sail Loft, Air Conditioning, Refrigeration, Divers, Propeller Repairs, Woodworking, Inflatable Repairs, Life Raft Service, Upholstery, Metal Fabrication **Near:** Launching Ramp. **Yard Rates:** $60-80/hr., Haul & Launch $10.75/ft., Power Wash $2.10/ft., Bottom Paint $10.75/ft. **Storage:** On-Land $25/ft.

Restaurants and Accommodations
Near: Restaurant *(Skipper's Pub 261-3589, L $7-15, D $8-21)*, *(Tavern on Harbor 757-1225)*, *(Ritz 754-6348)*, *(Maronis 757-4500)*, *(Bayview Bistro 262-9744; L $8-16, D $19-34)*, Snack Bar *(Sweet Shop)*, Pizzeria *(Michelangelo 757-6700)* **1-3 mi:** Motel *(Chalet 757-4600)*, Inn/B&B *(Centerport Harbor B&B 754-1730)*

Recreation and Entertainment
OnSite: Playground, Park **Near:** Beach, Picnic Area, Grills, Cultural Attract, Sightseeing, Special Events **Under 1 mi:** Dive Shop, Museum *(Northport Museum 757-9859, Vanderbilt Museum & Planetarium 854-5555)*

1-3 mi: Tennis Courts *(Northport Club 754-9851)*, Golf Course *(Northport G.C. 261-8000)*, Fitness Center *(Thoroughfit 544-6408)*, Horseback Riding *(Stonyhill Farms 261-0907)*, Bowling *(Larkfield Lanes 368-8788)*

Provisioning and General Services
Near: Convenience Store, Gourmet Shop *(Northport Village - great prepared meals)*, Delicatessen *(Northport Harbor Deli 261-6808)*, Health Food *(Organically Yours 754-2150)*, Bakery, Bank/ATM, Post Office, Catholic Church, Library *(Northport 261-6930)*, Beauty Salon, Barber Shop, Dry Cleaners, Laundry *(Clothes Line 757-2548)*, Bookstore *(Dog-Eared Book Shop 262-0149)*, Pharmacy *(Jones 261-7070)*, Newsstand, Hardware Store *(Northport Hardware 261-4449)*, Florist, Clothing Store, Retail Shops, Copies Etc. *(Northport Copy 754-9030)* **Under 1 mi:** Wine/Beer, Liquor Store *(Port To Port 754-8282)*, Protestant Church, Synagogue **1-3 mi:** Supermarket *(King Kullen 754-9763)*

Transportation
OnCall: Rental Car *(Enterprise 424-2500, Hertz 427-6106 5 mi.)*, Taxi *(Quinlans 261-0235)*, Airport Limo *(S&J 912-9800)* **Near:** Bikes *(Centerport Cycles 262-0909)*, Local Bus *(SCT #H-4 to LIRR & Walt Whitman Mall 852-5200)* **Under 1 mi:** Rail *(LIRR to NYC's Penn Station 718-243-4999)* **Airport:** Islip/LaGuardia/JFK *(16 mi./36 mi./38 mi.)*

Medical Services
911 Service **Near:** Dentist *(Northport Fam. 754-1107)*, Chiropractor *(Wellness Alliance 262-8505)*, Holistic Services *(Universal Touch 754-7505)* **Under 1 mi:** Doctor *(Northport Fam. 261-4445)* **1-3 mi:** Veterinarian *(Fort Salonga 261-0610)* **Hospital:** Huntington 351-2000 *(5 mi.)*

Setting -- Seymour's is a marvelous anachronism. This full-service boatyard and marina, just north of the Northport Village Dock, looks like it's "stopped in time." Watch for the bright blue sign above the narrow 2 story shingled building, on the harbor's east side. Easy chairs dot the "front porch." Appearances can be deceiving - that narrow building, once an oyster house (C. 1923), is very deep and houses the boatyard services. Along its north side, a wooden walkway that harkens back to the original building, leads to the street. A vintage marine railway is adjacent. A stunning 1882 Eastlake Victorian is visible to the rear.

Marina Notes -- Owned and operated by the Weber Family since 1996. *Boat-US discount is 25% on dockage and 15% on parts only. The tiled head is in the lower level of the newly restored Victorian manse; an outside entrance faces the boatyard. The house faces the street and sports a large antique anchor and a "Seymour's" sign on its manicured lawn. An onsite mechanic and a staff of fifteen provide most needed services. A supporting vessel is the working tug "Active," built here in the 1950's. Two launches (Ebb and Flow) provide service from 8am-midnight.

Notable -- Seymour's is funky and fun, a pleasant respite from personality-free modern facilities. The delightful village of Northport is about a block away. Main Street runs east from the water and is home to most any shop or service one might need (save a supermarket - King Kullen is 1.4 mi. away). But there are lots of other provisioning resources and eateries around -- from the creative new-Italian at Maroni Cuisine (take-to-the-boat option) to lunch in the garden at Bayview Bistro to the venerable Sea Shanty for fried "baskets."

Navigational Information

Lat: 40°54.010' **Long:** 073°21.230' **Tide:** 7 ft. **Current:** n/a **Chart:** 12365
Rep. Depths *(MLW):* **Entry** 8 ft. **Fuel Dock** n/a **Max Slip/Moor** 6 ft./-
Access: LI Sound to Huntington Bay to Northport Bay to Northport Harbor

Marina Facilities *(In Season/Off Season)*

Fuel: No
Slips: 15 Total, 15 Transient **Max LOA:** 120 ft. **Max Beam:** n/a
  Rate *(per ft.):* **Day** $1.00* **Week** n/a **Month** n/a
  Power: 30 amp Incl., **50 amp** n/a, **100 amp** n/a, **200 amp** n/a
  Cable TV: No **Dockside Phone:** No
  Dock Type: Fixed, Pilings, Wood
Moorings: 0 Total, 0 Transient **Launch:** n/a
  Rate: Day n/a **Week** n/a **Month** n/a
Heads: 1 Toilet(s)
Laundry: None **Pay Phones:** Yes, 2
Pump-Out: OnCall *(Ch.9/10)* **Fee:** Free **Closed Heads:** Yes

Marina Operations

Owner/Manager: Reeves Gandy, Harbormaster **Dockmaster:** n/a
In-Season: May-Sep, 9am-8pm **Off-Season:** n/a
After-Hours Arrival: n/a
Reservations: No **Credit Cards:** n/a
Discounts: None
Pets: Welcome, Dog Walk Area **Handicap Access:** No

Northport Village Dock

Foot of Main Street; Northport, NY 11768**

Tel: (631) 261-7502 **VHF: Monitor** n/a **Talk** n/a
Fax: (631) 261-7521 **Alternate Tel:** n/a
Email: n/a **Web:** n/a
Nearest Town: Northport *(0 mi.)* **Tourist Info:** (631) 261-3573

Marina Services and Boat Supplies

Supplies - Near: Ice *(Block, Cube)*, Ships' Store *(Snug Harbour Marine 754-0777)*, Bait/Tackle **1-3 mi:** Propane *(Ace 261-0119)* **3+ mi:** West Marine *(673-3910, 7 mi.)*

Boatyard Services

Near: Travelift, Railway, Forklift, Crane, Engine mechanic *(gas, diesel)*, Electronic Sales, Electronics Repairs, Hull Repairs, Rigger, Bottom Cleaning, Air Conditioning, Refrigeration, Divers, Propeller Repairs, Woodworking.
Nearest Yard: Seymour's Boatyard (631) 261-6574

Restaurants and Accommodations

Near: Restaurant *(Ship's Inn 261-3000, B $4-14, L $6-12, D $13-24, Early Bird $12)*, *(Skippers Pub 261-3589)*, *(Bayview Bistro 262-9744, L $8-16, D $19-34)*, *(Shipwreck Diner 754-1797, B $4-7, L $3-9, D $10-14, Kids' $3-5)*, *(Maroni's Cuisine 757-4500)*, Snack Bar *(Harry's Frozen Custard)*, Lite Fare *(Main Street Cafe)*, Pizzeria *(Michelangelo 757-6700)*
1-3 mi: Motel *(Chalet 757-4600)*, Inn/B&B *(Centerport Harbor 754-1730)*

Recreation and Entertainment

OnSite: Picnic Area, Playground, Jogging Paths, Park, Cultural Attract *(Park Concerts Summer Thu)*, Special Events *(Cow Harbor Day, 3rd Sun in Sep; July 4th is particularly fun)* **Near:** Museum *(Northport Historical Society & Museum 757-9859, 1-4:30pm; 3 mi.: Vanderbilt Museum Complex 854-5555, Tue-Sat 10-5, Sun & Hols 12-5, $5/2 grounds, $8/5 Mansion incl. grounds, $7/4 Planetarium show, $10/7 combination - 3 mi.)*, Galleries *(Wilke's)*
Under 1 mi: Tennis Courts *(Northport Tennis 754-9851)*, Fitness Center *(Thoroughfit 544-6408)* **1-3 mi:** Golf Course *(Northport G.C. 261-8000)*, Horseback Riding *(Stonyhill Farms 261-0907)*, Bowling *(Larkfield Lanes 368-8788)*, Video Rental *(Blockbuster 912-9051)*

Provisioning and General Services

Near: Convenience Store, Gourmet Shop *(Northport Village - lots of perpared meals)*, Delicatessen *(Northport Harbor Deli 261-6808)*, Health Food *(Organically Yours 754-2150 - Great store!)*, Wine/Beer, Bakery, Bank/ATM, Post Office, Catholic Church, Beauty Salon, Barber Shop, Dry Cleaners *(Moy's)*, Laundry *(Clothesline)*, Bookstore *(Dog-Eared Bookstore)*, Pharmacy *(Jones 261-7070)*, Newsstand, Hardware Store *(Northport Hardware 261-4449, 4-Star)*, Florist, Clothing Store, Retail Shops *(Bowman's)*, Copies Etc. *(Northport Copy 754-9030)* **Under 1 mi:** Liquor Store *(Port To Port 754-8282)*, Library *(Northport 261-6930)*
1-3 mi: Supermarket *(King Kullen 754-9763)*, Fishmonger, Meat Market

Transportation

OnCall: Rental Car *(Enterprise 424-2500, Hertz 427-6106 5 mi.)*, Taxi *(Quinlans 261-0235)*, Airport Limo *(S&J 912-9800)* **Near:** Local Bus *(SCT #H-4 to LIRR & Walt Whitman Mall 852-5200)* **Under 1 mi:** Bikes *(Centerport Cycles 262-0909)*, Rail *(LIRR 718-243-4999)*
Airport: Islip/LaGuardia/JFK *(16 mi./36 mi./38 mi.)*

Medical Services

911 Service **OnCall:** Ambulance **Under 1 mi:** Doctor *(Northport Family 261-4445)*, Dentist *(Northport Family Dental 754-1107)*, Chiropractor *(Wellness Alliance 262-8505)*, Holistic Services *(Chiro & Wellness - Yoga 368-9642)*, Veterinarian *(Fort Salonga 261-0610)*
Hospital: Huntington 351-2000 *5 mi.*

Setting -- Located in the town park, at the foot of Main Street, the Northport Village Dock provides easy entrance to this quintessential slice of Americana. The charming small town atmosphere, inviting waterfront park, and a host of convenient restaurants and services make this a compelling destination.

Marina Notes -- This really is the village dock and the contact number listed above is for Northport Village Hall (for general information). There is no phone at the dock. Dockmaster onsite MemDay-LabDay. *Two hours of tie-up are free. 50% refund of overnight fee if you depart by 11pm (e.g., tie up just for the day). Since there are no reservations, getting a spot is hit or miss and boats tend to hang around just off the docks waiting for someone to leave. It's only 3 ft. on the inside. Note the 7' tidal range when setting lines to fixed docks. A public dinghy dock is right at the foot of the Village Dock. Pump-out boat 9am-5pm, MemDay-Mid-Oct. **Above address is physical; mail goes to Town Hall: 224 Main Street; Northport, NY 11768.

Notable -- Everything is within an easy walk. Lots of restaurants, shops, and provisioning opportunities. The attractive and nicely maintained Town Park has a band shell gazebo, a nice playground, trees and grass, and benches for observing the passing scene. Northport also provides a "small-town" experience on holidays with parades and events. The Northport Museum has changing photographic exhibits and a monthly "Parade Down Main" walking tour. Across the harbor (but 3 miles around by land) is the 43-acre Vanderbilt Museum complex with the 24-room Eagle's Nest Spanish Revival style mansion, Planetarium, and Natural History Museum with decorative arts, ethnographic exhibits and one of the largest private collections of marine specimens.

Britannia Yachting Center

81 C Fort Salonga Rd.; Northport, NY 11768

Tel: (631) 261-5600 **VHF: Monitor** 9 **Talk** n/a
Fax: (631) 261-5654 **Alternate Tel:** n/a
Email: info@brityacht.com **Web:** www.brityacht.com
Nearest Town: Northport *(1 mi.)* **Tourist Info:** (631) 261-3573

Navigational Information
Lat: 40°53.427' **Long:** 073°21.313' **Tide:** n/a **Current:** n/a **Chart:** 13265
Rep. Depths *(MLW):* **Entry** 6 ft. **Fuel Dock** n/a **Max Slip/Moor** 8 ft./-
Access: Head of Northport Harbor, past Bird Island, hard turn east into basin

Marina Facilities *(In Season/Off Season)*
Fuel: Gasoline, Diesel
Slips: 310 Total, 20 Transient **Max LOA:** 75 ft. **Max Beam:** n/a
 Rate *(per ft.):* **Day** $2.50 **Week** n/a **Month** n/a
 Power: 30 amp Incl., **50 amp** Incl., **100 amp** n/a, **200 amp** n/a
 Cable TV: No **Dockside Phone:** Yes
 Dock Type: Floating, Long Fingers
Moorings: 0 Total, 0 Transient **Launch:** n/a
 Rate: Day n/a **Week** n/a **Month** n/a
Heads: 12 Toilet(s), 8 Shower(s), Hair Dryers
Laundry: None **Pay Phones:** No
Pump-Out: OnSite, Full Service, 1 Central **Fee:** n/a **Closed Heads:** Yes

Marina Operations
Owner/Manager: Kim Gommermann **Dockmaster:** Peter Houmere
In-Season: Year Round, 9am-6pm **Off-Season:** n/a
After-Hours Arrival: Call in advance
Reservations: Yes **Credit Cards:** Visa/MC, Dscvr, Amex, Tex
Discounts: Nautical Miles **Dockage:** 15% **Fuel:** n/a **Repair:** n/a
Pets: Welcome, Dog Walk Area **Handicap Access:** Yes, Heads, Docks

Marina Services and Boat Supplies
Services - Docking Assistance, Security, Trash Pick-Up, Dock Carts
Communication - Mail & Package Hold, Phone Messages, Fax in/out, FedEx, AirBorne, UPS, Express Mail *(Sat Del)* **Supplies - OnSite:** Ice *(Block, Cube)*, Ships' Store, Marine Discount Store *(Tidewater 754-0160)*, Bait/Tackle *(also Northport B&T 368-7335)*, Live Bait **3+ mi:** West Marine *(673-3910, 8 mi.)*, Propane *(6 mi.)*

Boatyard Services
OnSite: Travelift *(55T)*, Forklift, Crane, Engine mechanic *(gas, diesel)*, Electrical Repairs, Electronics Repairs, Hull Repairs, Rigger, Bottom Cleaning, Brightwork, Air Conditioning, Refrigeration, Compound, Wash & Wax, Interior Cleaning, Painting, Awlgrip, Yacht Design, Yacht Broker *(Britannia 261-5614)* **OnCall:** Sail Loft, Divers, Propeller Repairs, Woodworking, Inflatable Repairs, Upholstery, Metal Fabrication
Member: ABBRA, ABYC - 2 Certified Tech(s) **Yard Rates:** $85, Haul & Launch $10/ft. *(blocking $10)*, Power Wash $3/ft., Bottom Paint $13/ft.

Restaurants and Accommodations
OnSite: Restaurant *(Mariner's Galley 262-1975, B $1.50-4, L $5-7, D $12-19, M-Th 8-5, Fri-Sun 8-8)* **Under 1 mi:** Restaurant *(Happy Wok 754-1688)*, *(Maroni's 757-4500)*, *(Skippers' Pub 261-3589, L $7-15, D $8-21)*, *(Ritz Cafe 754-6348)*, Seafood Shack *(Northport Ship's Inn 261-3000, B $4-14, L $6-12, D $13-24)*, Pizzeria *(Jimmy's Pizza Of Northport 757-6009)*, *(Vineddi's Trattoria 754-5577)*

Recreation and Entertainment
OnSite: Pool, Dive Shop *(North Shore Aquatics 262-7282)*, Tennis Courts,
Fitness Center, Boat Rentals *(Glacier Bay Kayaks 262-9116)* **Under 1 mi:** Video Rental *(Blockbuster Video 912-9051)*, Park, Museum *(Northport Historical Society 757-9859)* **1-3 mi:** Bowling *(Larkfield Lanes 368-8788)* **3+ mi:** Golf Course *(Dix Hills C.C. 271-4788, 5.5 mi.)*

Provisioning and General Services
Near: Supermarket *(King Kullen 754-9763)*, Copies Etc. *(Northport Copy 754-9030)* **Under 1 mi:** Convenience Store *(7-11 754-9371)*, Gourmet Shop *(Northport Village)*, Delicatessen *(Northport Harbor 261-6808)*, Health Food *(Organically Yours 754-2150)*, Wine/Beer, Liquor Store *(Port To Port 754-8282)*, Bakery *(Copenhagen 754-3256)*, Bank/ATM, Post Office, Catholic Church, Protestant Church, Library *(Northport 261-6930)*, Beauty Salon, Barber Shop, Dry Cleaners *(Moy's)*, Laundry *(Clothesline)*, Bookstore *(Dog-Eared 262-0149)*, Pharmacy *(Jones/Nothport 261-7070)*, Hardware Store *(Northport 261-4449; Four Star 261-7223)* **1-3 mi:** Fishmonger *(Fort Hill 427-2444)*, Synagogue *(East Northport 368-6474)*

Transportation
OnCall: Rental Car *(Enterprise 424-2500 or Hertz 427-6106 - 5 mi.)*, Taxi *(McRides 754-9495)*, Airport Limo *(D'Anna & Son 368-0079)* **Under 1 mi:** Rail *(LIRR to NYC)* **Airport:** Islip/LaGuardia/JFK *(16 mi./36 mi./38 mi.)*

Medical Services
911 Service **OnCall:** Ambulance **Under 1 mi:** Dentist *(Huberman/Letica 261-4477)*, Chiropractor *(Keidel 261-9396)*, Holistic Services *(Universal Touch Massage 754-7505)* **1-3 mi:** Doctor *(Thompson 754-4200)*, Veterinarian *(Fredericks 757-0522)* **Hospital:** Huntington 351-2000 *(4 mi.)*

Setting -- Tucked way up into a basin on the southeast corner of Northport Harbor, Britannia Yachting Center offers a high-end marina experience. After turning into the basin, the multi-level clubhouse and contemporary out-buildings, all perched above the docks, come into view. Decks and promenades, with railings reminiscent of vintage ocean liners, rim the basin.

Marina Notes -- Entry is under six feet. Stay in the center and watch the tides. The fuel dock is at the end of the most northerly set of docks. Onsite is an attractive pool that overlooks the docks and basin; its deck is nicely furnished with tables and chairs. Just off the pool deck is the Mariner's Galley, a modest eatery that serves breakfast & lunch 7-days (sandwiches, wraps and salads) and Friday - Sunday, during the season offers nightly dinner specials - lobsters, steaks, etc. $12-19. Good tennis courts are up the hill. On the lower level of the main building are the heads, showers, sauna, and a small exercise room (Note: no laundry). Onsite is a very complete boatyard and an extensively inventoried large chandlery. Home of Britannia Custom Yachts featuring Dorado boats.

Notable -- It's less than a mile to Northport's Main Street and all its services, restaurants and provisioning resources. And about 2.5 miles around the harbor is Centerport and the 43-acre Vanderbilt Museum complex with its 24-room Eagle's Nest Spanish Revival style mansion, Planetarium (with a 238-seat Sky Theater), and Natural History Museum with decorative arts, ethnographic (including a 3000-year-old mummy) and The Hall of Fishes -- one of the world's largest private collections of marine specimens, many of which are the only such specimens in existence. Tue-Sat 10am-5pm, Sun & Hold 12-5pm.

VIII. New York: Eastern Long Islands North Shore

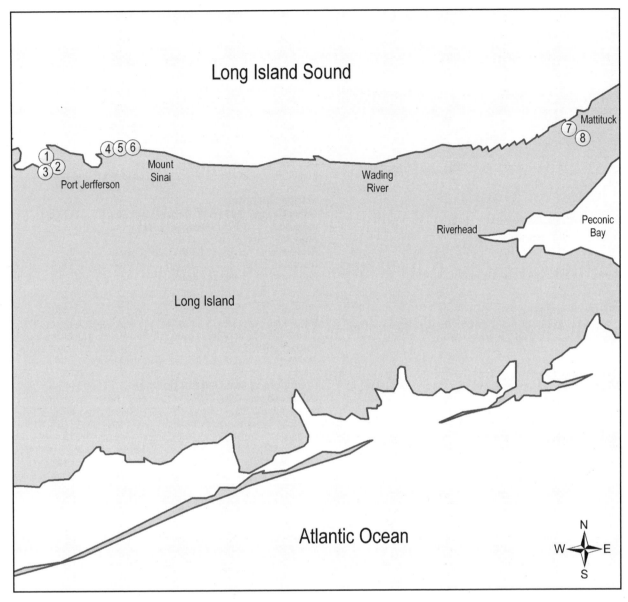

MAP	MARINA	HARBOR	PAGE	MAP	MARINA	HARBOR	PAGE
1	**Port Jefferson Moorings & Launch**	*Port Jefferson Hbr*	*152*	5	**Mount Sinai Yacht Club and Marina**	*Mt. Sinai Harbor*	*156*
2	**Danfords Marina & Inn on the Sound**	*Port Jefferson Hbr*	*153*	6	**Old Man's Boat Yard**	*Mt. Sinai Harbor*	*157*
3	**Port Jefferson Town Marina**	*Port Jefferson Hbr*	*154*	7	**Mattituck Inlet Marina & Shipyard**	*Mattituck Inlet*	*158*
4	**Ralph's Fishing Station & Marina**	*Mt. Sinai Harbor*	*155*	8	**Matt-A-Mar Marina**	*Mattituck Inlet*	*159*

Port Jefferson Moorings & Launch Service

Port Jefferson Moorings

West Broadway;* Port Jefferson, NY 11777

Tel: (631) 689-8262 **VHF: Monitor** 68 **Talk** 68
Fax: (631) 689-7014 **Alternate Tel:** (631) 642-0849
Email: n/a **Web:** n/a
Nearest Town: Port Jefferson **Tourist Info:** (631) 331-3334

Navigational Information
Lat: 40°57.154' **Long:** 073°04.282' **Tide:** 8 ft. **Current:** n/a **Chart:** 12362
Rep. Depths (MLW): Entry 32 ft. **Fuel Dock** 6 ft. **Max Slip/Moor** -/25 ft.
Access: Port Jeff Harbor to east side of the channel

Marina Facilities (In Season/Off Season)
Fuel: Gasoline, Diesel
Slips: 0 Total, 0 Transient **Max LOA:** n/a **Max Beam:** n/a
 Rate (per ft.): Day n/a **Week** n/a **Month** n/a
 Power: 30 amp n/a, **50 amp** n/a, **100 amp** n/a, **200 amp** n/a
 Cable TV: No **Dockside Phone:** No
 Dock Type: n/a
 Moorings: 25 Total, 25 Transient **Launch:** Yes (Included)
 Rate: Day $35 **Week** $175 **Month** n/a
Heads: 2 Toilet(s)
Laundry: None **Pay Phones:** No
Pump-Out: OnCall (Ch.73) **Fee:** Free **Closed Heads:** Yes

Marina Operations
Owner/Manager: Eddie Gatz **Dockmaster:** n/a
In-Season: Apr-Oct, 8am-10pm **Off-Season:** n/a
After-Hours Arrival: Call in advance
Reservations: Yes **Credit Cards:** Visa/MC, Cash
Discounts: None
Pets: Welcome **Handicap Access:** No

Marina Services and Boat Supplies
Supplies - Near: Ice (Block, Cube), Ships' Store (The Boat Place 473-0612; Islander Boat 473-6700), Bait/Tackle (Caraftis 473-2288) **1-3 mi:** West Marine (331-9280)

Boatyard Services
OnCall: Rigger, Bottom Cleaning, Brightwork, Divers, Inflatable Repairs, Upholstery **Near:** Travelift (25T), Engine mechanic (gas, diesel), Launching Ramp. **Nearest Yard:** The Boat Place (631) 473-0612

Restaurants and Accommodations
Near: Restaurant (25 East American Bistro 928-5200, L $9-17, D $19-32, Vegetarian 9-6), (Dockside 473-5656, L $7-17, D $13-19, Fish & Veg Sepcials $10, Kids' $5-8, Sun Brunch $16/8), (Pasta Pasta 331-5335, L $7-12, D $12-24), (Elk Street Grill), (Salsa Burrito 473-9700, L $4-8, D $4-8), (Portico 474-2233), (The Martha Jefferson 331-3333, L, D, & Brunch on an 85 ft. Mississippi River Paddle Cruiser), Seafood Shack (The Steam Room 928-6690, L $3-23, D $3-23), Snack Bar (P.J. Frigate Chocolatier 474-8888), Fast Food, Lite Fare (Admiral's Deck), Pizzeria (Pizza Supreme 474-0757), (San Remo 331-4646), Hotel (Danford's 928-5200, $160-320), Inn/B&B (Holly Berry 331-3123, $120-160), (Golden Pineapple 331-0706, $120-150)

Recreation and Entertainment
OnSite: Fishing Charter (Port Jefferson Prowler 689-7215) **Near:** Picnic Area, Playground (Rocketship Park), Tennis Courts, Fitness Center (Gold's 331-0030), Jogging Paths, Park (Harbourfront & Centennial), Museum (Mather House 473-2665 Tue, Wed, Sat, Sun 1-5), Cultural Attract (Theater Three 928-9100), Sightseeing (Walking Tour - map at CofC), Special Events

(Biatholon - Aug, Harborfest - Sep), Galleries (Soundview 473-9544)
Under 1 mi: Beach (dinghy out to Old Field Beach or Mt. Misey Cove)
1-3 mi: Golf Course (Village-owned P.J. Country Club 473-1440; public Heatherwood 473-9000 4 mi.), Bowling (Port Jeff Bowl 473-3300), Movie Theater (P.J. Cinema 928-3456), Video Rental (Blockbuster 331-0766)

Provisioning and General Services
OnSite: Farmers' Market (Thu 11-4 323-3653) **Near:** Convenience Store, Market (Mizra's Village Grocery 476-0107), Gourmet Shop (Moore's 928-1443), Delicatessen (Harbor 331-5877), Liquor Store (Pindar 331-7070), Bakery (Rachelle's 476-8245), Fishmonger (The Fish Co. 473-1764), Bank/ATM, Post Office, Catholic Church, Protestant Church, Library (473-0022), Beauty Salon, Dry Cleaners (Port View 473-8100), Laundry, Bookstore (Good Times 928-2664), Florist **Under 1 mi:** Pharmacy (Seaport 473-1144), Clothing Store **1-3 mi:** Supermarket (King Kullen 473-9186), Synagogue (North Shore 928-3737), Hardware Store (Fox's 751-7272)

Transportation
OnSite: Local Bus (Red Trolley MemDay-LabDay or SCT #60-62 to LIRR & Smith Haven Mall) **OnCall:** Water Taxi, Rental Car (Enterprise 474-2100), Taxi (Port 473-0707) **Near:** Ferry Service (Bridgeport - adjacent), Airport Limo (Genesis 473-0079) **Under 1 mi:** Rail (LIRR) **Airport:** Islip (20 mi.)

Medical Services
911 Service **OnCall:** Ambulance **Near:** Doctor (P.J. Fam Prac 473-0611), Dentist (P.J. Dental 473-1511), Holistic Services (Danford's Spa), Optician (Levine 473-6622) **1-3 mi:** Chiropractor (George 751-0900), Veterinarian (Countryside 473-0942) **Hospital:** St. Charles (0.25)

Setting -- In the southern half of the 2-mile deep harbor, east of the channel, lies Port Jeff's Mooring field. Views to the west are largely commercial, particularly L.I. Power's landmark twin red & white smoke stacks. The heavily treed bluffs along the east side hide large private homes, and at the head is an increasingly charming historic seaport village. The ferry wharf divides the shoreline - flanked by a matched set of docks - Danfords' and P.J. Town.

Marina Notes -- Silver Bay Marine Services manages the bright yellow moorings & launch, the P.J. Town fuel dock, and sells soda, ice, etc. Launch embarks/disembarks by the dockmaster house. Extensive launch hours. Service to anchored boats available. *Mailing address is P.O. Box 461; Stony Brook, NY 11790. Danford's offers a courtesy dinghy dock with a meal. (Note: to access their dinghy dock, literally circumnavigate the marina clockwise until you are below the outdoor café.) Town of Brookhaven's 2 free pump-out vessels operate mid-May to mid-Sep, Sat 10am-5pm, Sun & Hols 8am-5pm, plus Fri & Mon by app't. (Note: Diesel Marine Services - DMS - is no longer in business.) Setauket Y.C. (Ch.68, 473-9650) has 20 transient white moorings ($35) for members of other YCs; occasionally they welcome all boaters - so ask. Includes SYC Launch (9am-11pm), heads, showers, ice, & a bar.

Notable -- Port Jeff feels like a perpetual holiday. 30+ restaurants & many shops are crowded within a few blocks of the waterfront. Once the biggest shipbuilding town on Long Island; the Port Jeff Historical society has created three walking tours of the harbor area (www.portjeffhistorical.org). Some of the stops were originally homes of ship builders/captains - many are now charming shops. A Red Trolley loops from the Ferry, Main Street, Hospitals to RR Station.

Navigational Information
Lat: 40°56.880' **Long:** 073°04.133' **Tide:** 8 ft. **Current:** n/a **Chart:** 12362
Rep. Depths *(MLW)*: **Entry** 15 ft. **Fuel Dock** 12 ft. **Max Slip/Moor** 12 ft./-
Access: Long Island Sound to head of Port Jefferson Harbor

Marina Facilities *(In Season/Off Season)*
Fuel: *Gulf* - Gasoline, Diesel, High-Speed Pumps
Slips: 75 Total, 75 Transient **Max LOA:** 200 ft. **Max Beam:** n/a
  Rate *(per ft.)*: **Day** $3.75 **Week** n/a **Month** n/a
  Power: 30 amp $17.50, **50 amp** $17.50, **100 amp** $25, **200 amp** $25
  Cable TV: Yes **Dockside Phone:** Yes Inq.
  Dock Type: Fixed, Floating, Long Fingers, Pilings, Alongside, Wood
Moorings: 0 Total, 0 Transient **Launch:** n/a, Dinghy Dock
  Rate: Day n/a **Week** n/a **Month** n/a
Heads: 4 Toilet(s), 2 Shower(s) *(with dressing rooms)*
Laundry: None **Pay Phones:** Yes, 3
Pump-Out: OnSite **Fee:** Free **Closed Heads:** Yes

Marina Operations
Owner/Manager: Carrie Rubino **Dockmaster:** n/a
In-Season: Jul-Aug, 8am-8pm **Off-Season:** Sep-Oct & May-Jun, 8am-5pm
After-Hours Arrival: See front desk in the Inn.
Reservations: Yes, Preferred **Credit Cards:** Visa/MC, Dscvr, Din, Amex
Discounts: None
Pets: Welcome **Handicap Access:** Yes, Heads

Danfords Marina & Inn

25 East Broadway; Port Jefferson, NY 11777

Tel: (631) 928-5200; (800) 332-6367 **VHF: Monitor** 9 **Talk** 8
Fax: (631) 928-3598 **Alternate Tel:** n/a
Email: n/a **Web:** www.Danfords.com
Nearest Town: Port Jefferson *(0 mi.)* **Tourist Info:** (631) 473-1414

Marina Services and Boat Supplies
Services - Docking Assistance, Security *(24 Hrs.)*, Dock Carts, 300 amps, 3 Phase **Communication -** Mail & Package Hold, Phone Messages, Fax in/out *($2)*, FedEx, UPS *(Sat Del)* **Supplies - OnSite:** Ice *(Block, Cube)* **Near:** Ships' Store, Bait/Tackle, Live Bait **1-3 mi:** West Marine, Propane

Boatyard Services
OnSite: Compound, Wash & Wax *(East Coast Detailing 516-528-3098)*, Interior Cleaning **OnCall:** Crane, Engine mechanic *(gas, diesel)*, Electrical Repairs, Electronics Repairs, Rigger, Bottom Cleaning, Brightwork, Air Conditioning, Refrigeration, Divers *(Rent-a-Diver 476-1499)*, Propeller Repairs, Upholstery *(Amy Lund 928-8110)* **Near:** Launching Ramp, Inflatable Repairs. **Nearest Yard:** Port Jefferson Marine (631) 331-3567

Restaurants and Accommodations
OnSite: Restaurant *(25 East American Bistro 928-5200, B $3-10, L $9-17, D $19-32)*, Lite Fare *(The Admiral's Deck)*, Inn/B&B *(Danford's Inn 928-5200, $160-320)* **Near:** Restaurant *(Dockside 473-5656, L $7-17, D $13-19, Fresh fish + veggies $10, Kids' $5-8, Sun Brunch $16/8)*, *(Portico 474-2233)*, *(Pasta Pasta 331-5335, L $7-12, D $12-24)*, *(Sidewalk Grill/Backyard Cafe 331-9100)*, Seafood Shack *(The Steam Room 928-6690, L $3-23, D $3-23, mostly lower teens)*, Pizzeria *(San Remo 331-4646)*, Inn/B&B *(Holly Berry 331-3123, $120-160)*, *(Golden Pineapple 331-0706, $120-150)*

Recreation and Entertainment
OnSite: Spa, Fitness Center **Near:** Beach, Picnic Area, Playground, Tennis Courts, Jogging Paths, Boat Rentals, Roller Blade/Bike Paths, Fishing Charter *(P.J. Ace; P.J.Prowler 689-7215)*, Park *(Harborfront/Centennial)*,

Museum *(Mather House 473-2665)*, Cultural Attract *(Theater Three 928-9100)*, Sightseeing *(Walking Tour)*, Special Events, Galleries *(Soundview 473-9544)* **Under 1 mi:** Group Fishing Boat **1-3 mi:** Dive Shop, Golf Course *(Port Jeff C.C. 473-1440)*, Bowling, Movie Theater

Provisioning and General Services
OnSite: Beauty Salon, Copies Etc. **Near:** Market *(Mizra's Village Grocery 476-0107)*, Gourmet Shop *(Moore's 928-1443)*, Delicatessen *(Harbor 331-5877)*, Wine/Beer *(Pindar 331-7070)*, Liquor Store, Bakery *(Rachelle's 476-8245)*, Farmers' Market *(Thu 11-4 323-3653)*, Fishmonger *(The Fish Co. 473-1764)*, Bank/ATM, Post Office, Catholic Church, Protestant Church, Library *(473-0022)*, Barber Shop, Dry Cleaners *(Port View 473-8100)*, Laundry, Bookstore *(Good Times 928-2664)*, Newsstand, Florist *(Flower Garden 331-4950)*, Retail Shops **Under 1 mi:** Convenience Store, Pharmacy *(Seaport Chemists 473-1144)* **1-3 mi:** Supermarket *(King Kullen 473-9186)*, Synagogue, Hardware Store *(Fox's True Value 751-7272)*

Transportation
OnSite: Local Bus *(P.J. Trolley to LIRR)* **OnCall:** Water Taxi *(Ch.68 / 689-8262)*, Rental Car *(Entrprise 474-2100)*, Taxi *(Port 473-0707)*, Airport Limo *(Genesis 473-0079)* **Near:** Bikes, Ferry Service *(Bridgeport)* **1-3 mi:** Rail *(LIRR to NYC 718-243-4999)* **Airport:** Islip *(20 mi.)*

Medical Services
911 Service **OnSite:** Holistic Services *(Spa)* **Near:** Doctor *(P.J. Family Practice 473-0611)*, Dentist *(P.J. Dental 473-1511)*, Optician *(Levine 473-6622)* **Under 1 mi:** Ambulance **1-3 mi:** Chiropractor *(George 751-0900)*, Veterinarian *(Countryside 473-0942)* **Hospital:** St. Charles *(0.25 mi.)*

Setting -- Danford's dominates the head of long, protected Port Jeff Harbor - to the left of the ferry dock. The beautiful, historic facility is an amalgam of several white, vintage buildings which give it a crisp New England quality. On the northwest corner of the perimeter piers is the large dockmaster's office - action central for the heavy flow of traffic. The resort has lovely, antique-filled rooms, event and conference rooms, a spa, and a perfectly sited restaurant.

Marina Notes -- Closed Nov-Apr. *Hourly rates: up to 39 ft. $15, 40-59 ft. $20, 60-79 ft. $30. For overnight guests, check-out is 11am. Facility management is helpful and professional. The excellent docks are neat and well organized and megayachts regularly tie up here as do replica and tall ships. Add a full-service health spa (10% discount for marina guests) and salon, as well as two dining options: a recently upgraded but pricey restaurant and a very fun tavern and room service to the boats. Plus 85 individually decorated rooms with antiques, fireplaces, balconies and water views. Accommodates up to 150 for special events and conferences. Once called Bayle's Dock, this is the site of the original Bayle's Shipyard which built 140 wooden ships from 1830 to 1917.

Notable -- 25 East American Bistro's floor to ceiling glass walls create the feeling of literally sitting over the water (B 7-10:30, L 11:30-3, D 5-10, 'til 11 F&S). Al fresco dining on the Admirals Deck, MemDay-Oct. Danford's offers "Theater Three" dinner packages, too. Port Jeff really jumps on weekends so be prepared (kids love it), but Danford's provides a bit of an oasis. Along the waterfront, and a few blocks inland, are shops, pubs, art galleries, a theater, charter boats and a wide variety of restaurants and lobster/seafood "in-the-rough." The beach just east is the site of the new Harbourfront Park.

Port Jefferson Town Marina

East Broadway*; Port Jefferson, NY

Tel: (631) 331-3567 **VHF: Monitor** 9 **Talk** n/a
Fax: n/a **Alternate Tel:** (631) 331-3567
Email: n/a **Web:** www.brookhaven.gov
Nearest Town: Pt. Jefferson **Tourist Info:** (631) 473-1414

Navigational Information
Lat: 40°56.870' **Long:** 073°04.320' **Tide:** 8 **Current:** n/a **Chart:** 12362
Rep. Depths (*MLW*): **Entry** 25 ft. **Fuel Dock** 6 ft. **Max Slip/Moor** 4 ft./-
Access: Head of Port Jeff Harbor; line up with the large red landmarker panel

Marina Facilities (*In Season/Off Season*)
Fuel: Gasoline, Diesel
Slips: 120 Total, 10 Transient **Max LOA:** 45 ft. **Max Beam:** n/a
  Rate (*per ft.*): **Day** $3.00 **Week** n/a **Month** n/a
  Power: 30 amp Incl., **50 amp** n/a, **100 amp** n/a, **200 amp** n/a
  Cable TV: No **Dockside Phone:** No
  Dock Type: Fixed, Floating, Wood
Moorings: 0 Total, 0 Transient **Launch:** Port Jefferson Launch
  Rate: Day n/a **Week** n/a **Month** n/a
Heads: 3 Toilet(s)
Laundry: Yes **Pay Phones:** Yes, 1
Pump-Out: OnSite, Self Service **Fee:** Free **Closed Heads:** Yes

Marina Operations
Owner/Manager: Peter Koutrakos (Harbormaster) **Dockmaster:** Channel 9
In-Season: May-Nov1, 24 hrs. **Off-Season:** n/a
After-Hours Arrival: See dockmaster
Reservations: Yes **Credit Cards:** No credit cards; no out-of-state checks
Discounts: None
Pets: Welcome **Handicap Access:** No

Marina Services and Boat Supplies
Services - Docking Assistance, Dock Carts **Supplies - OnSite:** Ice (*Block, Cube*) **Near:** Ships' Store (*The Boat Place 473-0612; Islander Boat 473-6700*), Bait/Tackle (*Caraftis 473-2288*), Live Bait **1-3 mi:** West Marine (*331-9280*), Propane

Boatyard Services
OnCall: Engine mechanic (*gas, diesel*), Electrical Repairs, Electronics Repairs, Bottom Cleaning, Air Conditioning, Compound, Wash & Wax, Propeller Repairs **Near:** Launching Ramp, Electronic Sales, Hull Repairs, Rigger, Brightwork, Divers. **Nearest Yard:** P.J. Marine (631) 473-6416

Restaurants and Accommodations
Near: Restaurant (*Kimi Japanese 928-8868*), (*The Steamroom 928-6690, L $3-23, D $3-23, Picnic for 2 $25*), (*Portico 474-2233*), (*25 East American Bistro 958-5200*), Snack Bar (*P.J. Frigate Chocolatier 474-8888, Ice Cream & Dessert*), Fast Food (*McDonalds*), Lite Fare (*Tiger Lily 476-7080, vegetarian 9-6*), (*Salsa Salsa Burrito Bar 473-9700, L $4-8, D $4-8*), Pizzeria (*Pizza Supreme 474-0757*), Motel (*Heritage Inn 928-2400*), Hotel (*Danfords Inn 928-5200, $160-320*), Inn/B&B (*Holly Berry 331-3123, $120-160*), (*Golden Pineapple 331-0706, $120-150*)

Recreation and Entertainment
OnSite: Fishing Charter (*P.J. Ace/P.J.Prowler 689-7215*) **Near:** Playground, Tennis Courts, Fitness Center (*Bodydome @ Gold's 331-0030*), Jogging Paths, Park (*Harborfront Park*), Museum (*Mather House 473-2665 Tue-Wed, Sat-Sun 1-5*), Cultural Attract (*Theater Three 928-9100 - professioanl rep company in 400-seat historic Athena Hall + 100-seat cabaret theater + kids' theater*), Sightseeing (*Historical Soc's Walking Tour*), Galleries (*Soundview 473-9544*) **Under 1 mi:** Beach (*dinghy to Old Field or Mt. Misey Cove*) **1-3 mi:** Golf Course (*Village-owned Port Jeff Country Club 473-1440; Heatherwood 473-9000 4 mi.*), Movie Theater

Provisioning and General Services
OnSite: Farmers' Market (*Thu 11-4 323-3653*) **Near:** Convenience Store, Market (*Mizra's Village Grocery 476-0107*), Gourmet Shop (*Penne Lane 474-9300*), Delicatessen (*Harbor 331-5877*), Wine/Beer (*Pindar 331-7070*), Bakery (*La Bonne Boulangerie 473-7900*), Fishmonger (*The Fish Co. 473-1764*), Bank/ATM, Post Office, Protestant Church, Library (*473-0022*), Beauty Salon, Barber Shop, Dry Cleaners (*Port View 473-8100*), Bookstore (*Good Times 928-2664*), Pharmacy (*Seaport473-1144*), Newsstand, Florist (*Flower Garden 331-4950*), Clothing Store (*Gap*) **Under 1 mi:** Hardware Store (*Fox's True Value 751-7272*) **1-3 mi:** Supermarket (*King Kullen 473-9186*), Liquor Store, Synagogue (*North Shore 928-3737*)

Transportation
OnSite: Ferry Service (*to Bridgeport*) **OnCall:** Water Taxi (*Ch.68*), Rental Car (*Entrprise 474-2100*), Taxi (*Port 473-0707*), Airport Limo (*Genesis 473-0079*) **Near:** Local Bus (*P.J. Trolley & SCT to LIRR, Smithtown Mall, etc.*) **1-3 mi:** Rail (*Port Jefferson LIRR*) **Airport:** Islip (*20 mi.*)

Medical Services
911 Service **OnCall:** Ambulance **Near:** Doctor (*P.J. Family 473-0611*), Dentist (*P.J. Dental 473-1511*), Chiropractor (*George 751-0900*), Holistic Services (*Atlantis Spa 473-5560*), Optician (*Optical Outfitters 928-6401*) **1-3 mi:** Veterinarian (*Countryside 473 0942*) **Hospital:** St. Charles (*.5 mi.*

Setting -- Just west of the Ferry wharf, in the center of Port Jeff's harborfront, the well-protected Town Marina is recognizable by the dockmaster's brown two-story building. The surrounding historic seaport village is a block away. It's a tourist destination, by land or sea, and the Town Marina is right in the thick of it.

Marina Notes -- This basic municipal facility offers electricity, water, and heads in a spectacular location. Reported shoaling conditions in harbor may limit movement at low tides (estimates are 4 ft. on the outer docks during low tide, 8 plus at high). The docks are almost all newly constructed and populated mostly by Brookhaven town residents. The fuel dock on the outside is privately operated by Silver Bay Marine Services (689-8262), which operates P.J. Launch. Given traffic you may tie up alongside there, at the fueler's discretion. Note: the southwest side of the harbor has a power plant (with its infamous red & white striped stacks) and significant commercial loading/unloading which can get noisy at times. *Contact Address: 1130 Old Town Road; Coram, NY 11727

Notable -- Port Jeff has lots to do, see and eat. The Town Marina is a tourist favorite. Originally, Mather Shipbuilding occupied this site, building 54 vessels, including the earliest P.T. Barnum-sponsored ferries. The Bridgeport ferry has been operating since 1883. West of Danfords, the fabulous new Port Jefferson Harbourfront Park (on the old Mobil property) is under construction. A 350-foot recreation/maritime pier opened in '02. Nautically-themed Chandlery Park playground has a frog water spray and full size replica of a Long Island Skipjack. A 2,300 ft. promenade along the harbor is under way. And a modified and refurbished Bayles Shipyard Building will become Harbourfront Park's waterfront living room. Don't miss the very good Theater Three rep company.

Navigational Information
Lat: 40°57.809' **Long:** 073°02.546' **Tide:** 7 ft. **Current:** 2 kt. **Chart:** 12362
Rep. Depths *(MLW)*: **Entry** 25 ft. **Fuel Dock** 15 ft. **Max Slip/Moor** 15 ft./40 ft.
Access: Mt. Sinai Inlet, bear left to first set of docks on port side

Marina Facilities *(In Season/Off Season)*
Fuel: *BP* - Gasoline, Diesel
Slips: 53 Total, 2 Transient **Max LOA:** 50 ft. **Max Beam:** n/a
  Rate *(per ft.)*: **Day** $2.00 **Week** n/a **Month** n/a
  Power: 30 amp $5.00, **50 amp** n/a, **100 amp** n/a, **200 amp** n/a
  Cable TV: No **Dockside Phone:** No
  Dock Type: Floating, Wood
Moorings: 200 Total, 6 Transient **Launch:** Yes (Incl.), Dinghy Dock
  Rate: Day $40 **Week** $130 **Month** n/a
Heads: 2 Toilet(s)
Laundry: None **Pay Phones:** Yes, 1
Pump-Out: No **Fee:** n/a **Closed Heads:** Yes

Marina Operations
Owner/Manager: Jeff Corey **Dockmaster:** Same
In-Season: May-Sep, 6am-7pm **Off-Season:** Oct-Apr, 8am-5pm
After-Hours Arrival: Check in with Launch
Reservations: Yes, Preferred **Credit Cards:** Visa/MC, Dscvr, Amex
Discounts: None
Pets: Welcome **Handicap Access:** Yes, Docks

Ralph's Fishing Station

PO Box 381; 250 Harbor Beach Road; Mount Sinai, NY 11766

Tel: (631) 473-6655 **VHF: Monitor** 67 **Talk** n/a
Fax: (631) 331-6607 **Alternate Tel:** n/a
Email: n/a **Web:** n/a
Nearest Town: Port Jefferson *(5 mi.)* **Tourist Info:** (631) 473-1414

Marina Services and Boat Supplies
Services - Docking Assistance, Dock Carts **Communication -** UPS, Express Mail **Supplies - OnSite:** Ice *(Cube)*, Ships' Store, Bait/Tackle **3+ mi:** West Marine *(331-9280, 5 mi.)*, Boater's World *(751-8524, 9 mi.)*

Boatyard Services
OnSite: Forklift, Engine mechanic *(gas)*, Launching Ramp, Bottom Cleaning **OnCall:** Engine mechanic *(diesel)*, Electrical Repairs, Brightwork, Air Conditioning, Refrigeration, Divers, Compound, Wash & Wax, Interior Cleaning, Propeller Repairs, Woodworking **Member:** ABBRA
Yard Rates: Haul & Launch $7-8/ft. *(blocking $1.50 ea.)*, Power Wash $2/ft.

Restaurants and Accommodations
OnSite: Lite Fare *(The Roost 473-6655, Breakfast, Burgers, Salads, Sandwiches)* **OnCall:** Restaurant *(Over Pasta at Pizza Picasso 331-5554, L $3-22, D $11-22, $10 min, no delivery charge - large and varied menu, incl deisgner pizzas)* **Near:** Snack Bar *(Cedar Beach)*, Lite Fare *(Mt. Sinai Yacht Club 473-2993, lunch only)* **1-3 mi:** Restaurant *(Colucci's Ristorante 331-4848, D $7-18)*, *(Savino's Hide-A-Way 928-6510, L $7-13, D $9-19)*, *(Benten Japanese 473-7878)*, *(Wing Hing Kitchen 331-0333, L $4-5, D $7-9)*, Pizzeria *(Papa John 473-1119)*

Recreation and Entertainment
OnSite: Boat Rentals *(14-16 ft.skiffs w/motors, 20 Ft. runabouts $75-250/day; Kayaks $40/day)* **Near:** Beach *(Cedar Beach - right across the road)*, Picnic Area, Grills, Volleyball, Jogging Paths, Park, Museum *(Mount*

Sinai Marine Sanctuary & Nature Center 473-8346), Special Events *(Cedar Beach Blues Festival - May)* **1-3 mi:** Fitness Center *(Powerhouse Gym 928-4200)* **3+ mi:** Dive Shop *(Port Divers, 5 mi.)*, Golf Course *(Rolling Oaks C.C. 744-3200, 5 mi.)*, Bowling *(Jefferson Lanes 473-3300, 5 mi.)*, Movie Theater *(P.J. Cinema 928-3456, 4 mi.)*

Provisioning and General Services
1-3 mi: Market *(Town & Country Market & Deli 473-1222)*, Delicatessen *(Parkside Family 331-3066)*, Wine/Beer *(North Country Wine 744-6922)*, Liquor Store, Bakery *(Better On A Bagel 473-3030)*, Bank/ATM *(Suffolk Cty Nat'l 474-8400)*, Post Office *(Miller Place 928-0394)*, Protestant Church, Dry Cleaners, Laundry, Pharmacy *(Echo 642-8175)*, Copies Etc. *(Miller Place Printing 473-1158)* **3+ mi:** Supermarket *(Waldbaum's 476-2394, 4 mi.)*, Library *(Port Jefferson 473-0022, 5 mi.)*, Hardware Store *(Miller Place True Value 821-3567, 4 mi.)*, Department Store *(Kohl's 744-0017, 5 mi.)*

Transportation
OnCall: Rental Car *(Enterprise 472-2100)*, Taxi *(Abby's 732-3390)*, Airport Limo *(Genesis 473-0079)* **3+ mi:** Rail *(Port Jeff Station, 4 mi.)*
Airport: Islip MacArthur *(20 mi.)*

Medical Services
911 Service **OnCall:** Ambulance **1-3 mi:** Dentist *(Bean 928-6566)*, Chiropractor *(Chiropractic Ctr. of Mt. Sinai 476-4600)* **3+ mi:** Doctor *(L.I. Family Medical Group 821-0505, 4 mi.)*, Veterinarian *(Jefferson 473-0415, 4.5)* **Hospital:** Mather 473-1320 *(4 mi.)*

Setting -- After passing along the jetty that stabilizes Mount Sinai inlet, turn to port around the Cedar Beach sandspit that protects the Harbor. The first facility, immediately to port, is Ralph's Marina and Fishing Station. The prominent fuel dock, backed by a network of slips, makes it easy to spot. A one and a half story cedar shake building with brown trim provides a backdrop for an assortment of tables, chairs and benches shaded with red and white umbrellas and a red vinyl pavilion, providing a variety of venues for the on-site eatery. Raised beds and barrels of flowers soften the "fishing station" ambiance.

Marina Notes -- Ralph's is a full-service marina with fuel, parts, a modest ships' store, bait, tackle and ice. Reportedly, it has one of the easiest accessed fuel docks on the North Shore. A launch services the mooring field. The onsite Roost serves breakfast and casual "basket" food throughout the day - eat at their tables or take it to the beach or the boat. Fishing skiffs and comfortable 2-seat kayaks can be rented for perusing the nearby marsh. And, for more ambitious ventures, Ralph's rents 20 ft. center consoles with 115 hp. Johnson motors. A substantial fork lift provides boat hauling and storage capability.

Notable -- Mt. Sinai Harbor is a largely unspoiled embayment - one of the very few on Long Island's North Shore. It's 455 acres of salt marsh, mudflats, and open waters, except for the most northern stretch which houses marinas and mooring fields (which rent the rights). This stretch is a sandbar; the western end is the Cedar Beach Town Park with life guards, a snack bar, picnic area and the Cedar Beach Nature Center (451-6455). It has a 500-foot boardwalk, inside displays, touch tanks and a shellfish mariculture program Mon-Fri 10-4, Sat & Sun 11-4, Free. A number of commercial fishermen also work out of the harbor.

Mount Sinai Yacht Club

244 Harbor Beach Road; Mount Sinai, NY 11766

Tel: (631) 473-2993 **VHF: Monitor** n/a **Talk** n/a
Fax: (631) 473-3567 **Alternate Tel:** (631) 929-8120
Email: n/a **Web:** www.msyc.org
Nearest Town: Pt. Jefferson *(5 mi.)* **Tourist Info:** (631) 473-1414

Navigational Information

Lat: 40°57.809' **Long:** 073°02.348' **Tide:** n/a **Current:** n/a **Chart:** 12362
Rep. Depths *(MLW):* **Entry** 10 ft. **Fuel Dock** 20 ft. **Max Slip/Moor** 8 ft./20 ft.
Access: Mt. Sinai Inlet bear left to second set of docks, past Ralph's

Marina Facilities *(In Season/Off Season)*

Fuel: *Shell* - Gasoline, Diesel
Slips: 99 Total, 5 Transient **Max LOA:** 46 ft. **Max Beam:** 18 ft.
  Rate *(per ft.):* **Day** $1.00* **Week** $6 **Month** n/a
  Power: 30 amp Incl., 50 amp Incl., 100 amp n/a, 200 amp n/a
Cable TV: No **Dockside Phone:** No
Dock Type: Floating, Pilings, Wood, Aluminum
Moorings: 4 Total, 4 Transient **Launch:** yes (Included), Dinghy Dock
  Rate: Day $20 **Week** n/a **Month** n/a
Heads: 2 Toilet(s), 2 Shower(s)
Laundry: None **Pay Phones:** No
Pump-Out: No **Fee:** n/a **Closed Heads:** Yes

Marina Operations

Owner/Manager: Ron Prwivo, Fleet Captain **Dockmaster:** n/a
In-Season: Jul-Aug, 9am-10pm **Off-Season:** May-Jun, Sep-Oct, 10-10
After-Hours Arrival: Contact dockmaster next morning
Reservations: Pending availability **Credit Cards:** Visa/MC, Tex, Shell
Discounts: None
Pets: Welcome **Handicap Access:** Yes

Marina Services and Boat Supplies

Services - Trash Pick-Up, Dock Carts **Communication -** Mail & Package Hold, Fax in/out, FedEx, UPS, Express Mail **Supplies - OnSite:** Ice *(Cube)* **Near:** Ice *(Block)*, Ships' Store *(Ralph's Fishing Station)*, Marine Discount Store, Bait/Tackle, Live Bait *(Ralph's)* **1-3 mi:** Propane *(Audell-Bennett Bottled Gas 266-1333)* **3+ mi:** West Marine *(331-9280, 5 mi.)*

Boatyard Services

OnSite: Engine mechanic *(gas, diesel)*, Bottom Cleaning **Near:** Travelift, Forklift. **Nearest Yard:** Old Mans Boatyard (631) 473-7330

Restaurants and Accommodations

OnSite: Lite Fare *(MSYC Lunch only)* **OnCall:** Restaurant *(Over Pasta at Pizza Picasso 331-5554, L $3-22, D $11-22, pizzas, heros, too.)* **Near:** Lite Fare *(The Roost - dockside at Ralph's Breakfast, burgers, salads, sandwiches)*, *(Cedar Beach Snack Bar)* **1-3 mi:** Restaurant *(Savino's Hide-A-Way 928-6510, L $7-13, D $9-19)*, *(Colucci's Ristorante 331-4848, D $17-28)*, *(Benten Japanese 473-7878)*, *(Cafe Bada-Bing 474-4427)*, *(Wing Hing Kitchen 331-0333, L $4-5, D $7-$9)*, Fast Food *(Mc Donald's)*, Pizzeria *(Papa John 473-1119)*

Recreation and Entertainment

OnSite: Picnic Area, Playground **Near:** Beach *(Cedar - across the street)*, Volleyball, Jogging Paths, Boat Rentals *(Ralph's 473-6655 14-16 ft.skiffs w/motors, 20 Ft. runabouts $75-250/day; Kayaks $40/day)*, Roller Blade/Bike Paths, Park, Museum *(Mount Sinai Marine Sanctuary & Nature Center 473-8346)* **1-3 mi:** Fitness Center *(Powerhouse Gym 928-4200)*

3+ mi: Dive Shop *(Port Divers, 5 mi. , Golf Course (Rolling Oaks C.C. 744-3200, 5 mi.)*, Bowling *(Jefferson Lanes 473-3300, 5 mi.)*, Movie Theater *(P J Cinemas 928-3456, 4 mi.)*, Video Rental *(Blockbuster 331-0766, 4 mi.)*

Provisioning and General Services

1-3 mi: Market *(Town & Country Market & Deli 473-1222)*, Delicatessen *(Parkside Family Delicatessen 331-3066)*, Liquor Store *(North Country Wine 744-6922)*, Bank/ATM *(Suffolk Cty Nat'l 474-8400)*, Post Office, Protestant Church, Dry Cleaners, Laundry, Pharmacy *(Echo Pharmacy 642-8175)*, Copies Etc. *(Miller Place Printing 473-1158)* **3+ mi:** Supermarket *(Waldbaum's 476-2394, 4 mi.)*, Gourmet Shop *(Moore's Gourmet Mkt 928-1443, 5 mi.)*, Wine/Beer *(Pindar Wine Store 331-7070, 5 mi.)*, Hardware Store *(Miller Place True Value Hardware 821-3567, 4 mi.)*, Department Store *(Kohl's Department Store 744-0017, 5 mi.)*

Transportation

OnCall: Rental Car *(Enterprise 474-2100)*, Taxi *(Abby's Car Service 732-3390)*, Airport Limo *(Genesis Limousine Service 473-0079)* **3+ mi:** Rail *(LIRR, Pt. Jefferson Station to NYC, 4 mi.)*, Ferry Service *(Pt. Jefferson to Bridgeport, 6 mi.)* **Airport:** Islip *(20 mi.)*

Medical Services

911 Service **1-3 mi:** Dentist *(Bean 928-6566)*, Chiropractor *(Chiropractic Center of Mount Sinai 476-4600)* **3+ mi:** Doctor *(L.I. Family Medical 821-0505, 4 mi.)*, Holistic Services *(Port Jefferson Therapeutic Massage 331-7631, 4.5 mi.)*, Veterinarian *(Jefferson Animal Hospital 473-0415, 4.5 mi.)*
Hospital: Mather Memorial 473-1320 *(4 mi.)*

Setting -- In rural but quite crowded Mt. Sinai Harbor, Mount Sinai Yacht Club & Marina is conveniently situated on the north shore - just past Ralph's Fishing Station. Look for the very red fuel dock, under the M.S.Y.C. sign, and the brand new, lovely, gray cuppolaed club house. The docks curve gracefully in front and the mooring field is just beyond. Most of Mt. Sinai Harbor is a salt marsh nature preserve which creates unspoiled views and occasional wildlife sightings.

Marina Notes -- * Rates change often; call for updates. Founded in 1964, MSYC's memberships are limited to residents of the Township of Brookhaven. The result of a compromise, the town created the harbor in the '50s by dredging a third of the salt marsh; the remainder was left as a preserve. The club leases its land from Brookhaven. The current 225 members christened their brand new, very lovely club house, along with some new and upgraded infrastructure equipment, in November 2003. A porch, patios, and lovely, new heads and showers make this an even better stop. The 99 floating wood docks offer power and water. Visitors can get a light lunch at the club and several area restaurants will deliver (Over Pasta, 11:30am-9:30pm, 11pm weekends, designer pizza to full-course meals - $10 min, no del charge). The closest full-service town is Pt. Jefferson, about five miles away by land.

Notable -- MSYC is part of a large town recreation area which includes Sound-front Cedar Beach (directly across the street), a snack bar, fishing pier, playground, town moorings, docks and ramp, and more. Closeby Mount Sinai Marine Sanctuary & Nature Center, 10am-2pm, features walking trails along with indoor and outdoor displays of local freshwater and saltwater marine life. They have also mapped a bike tour of the Mt. Sinai area.

Navigational Information
Lat: 40°57.809' **Long:** 073°02.252' **Tide:** 7 ft. **Current:** 2 kt. **Chart:** 12362
Rep. Depths (*MLW*): Entry 12 ft. **Fuel Dock** n/a **Max Slip/Moor** 35 ft./20 ft.
Access: East-West Channel, east of entrance, last facility to port

Marina Facilities (*In Season/Off Season*)
Fuel: No
Slips: 60 Total, 3 Transient **Max LOA:** 15 ft. **Max Beam:** n/a
  Rate (*per ft.*): Day $1.00/Inq. **Week** $125 **Month** $500
  Power: 30 amp Incl., **50 amp** n/a, **100 amp** n/a, **200 amp** n/a
  Cable TV: No **Dockside Phone:** No
  Dock Type: Floating
Moorings: 600 Total, 3 Transient **Launch:** n/a
  Rate: Day $5 **Week** $20 **Month** $50
Heads: 1 Toilet(s)
Laundry: None **Pay Phones:** No
Pump-Out: No **Fee:** n/a **Closed Heads:** Yes

Marina Operations
Owner/Manager: Robert Zumft **Dockmaster:** n/a
In-Season: Year 'Round, 8am-4pm weekdays only **Off-Season:** Same
After-Hours Arrival: Any broadside space open
Reservations: Yes **Credit Cards:** Cash
Discounts: None
Pets: Welcome, Dog Walk Area **Handicap Access:** No

Old Man's Boat Yard

PO Box 317; Harbor Beach Road - Cedar Beach; Mount Sinai, NY

Tel: (631) 473-7330 **VHF: Monitor** n/a **Talk** n/a
Fax: (631) 928-6464 **Alternate Tel:** n/a
Email: n/a **Web:** n/a
Nearest Town: Port Jefferson (*5 mi.*) **Tourist Info:** (631) 473-1414

Marina Services and Boat Supplies
Services - Trash Pick-Up **Communication -** Mail & Package Hold, Phone Messages, Fax in/out, FedEx, UPS, Express Mail **Supplies - Near:** Ice (Block), Ships' Store, Bait/Tackle (*Ralph's*) **3+ mi:** West Marine (*5 mi.*)

Boatyard Services
OnSite: Travelift (*25T*), Electrical Repairs, Electronic Sales, Electronics Repairs, Hull Repairs, Rigger, Sail Loft, Bottom Cleaning, Brightwork, Air Conditioning, Refrigeration, Painting, Awlgrip **OnCall:** Divers, Compound, Wash & Wax, Interior Cleaning, Propeller Repairs, Woodworking, Upholstery, Yacht Interiors, Metal Fabrication **Near:** Launching Ramp (*Town resident or fee*). **Member:** ABBRA - 2 Certified Tech(s)
Yard Rates: $80/hr., Haul & Launch $10/ft., Power Wash $2/ft., Bottom Paint $12/ft. (*paint incl.*)

Restaurants and Accommodations
OnCall: Restaurant (*Over Pasta at Pizza Picasso 331-5554, L $3-22, D $11-22, Pizza, Subs, too $10 min, free delivery*) **Near:** Snack Bar (*Ralph's The Roost 473-6655, Cedar Beach*), Lite Fare (*Mount Sinai Yacht Club 473-2993, Lunch only*) **1-3 mi:** Restaurant (*Benten Japanese 473-7878, L $6-16, D $13-39*), (*Colucci's Ristorante 473-4848, D $17-28*), (*Savino's Hide-A-Way 926-6510, L $7-13, D $9-19*), (*Cafe Bada-Bing 474-4427*), Pizzeria (*Papa John's 473-1119*) **3+ mi:** Hotel (*Danford's Inn 928-5200, 5 mi.*)

Recreation and Entertainment
Near: Beach (*Cedar Beach*), Picnic Area, Grills, Volleyball, Jogging Paths, Boat Rentals (*Ralph's - Skiffs & Runabouts $75-250/day; Kayaks $40/day*), Roller Blade/Bike Paths, Fishing Charter (*Port Jeff*), Park, Museum (*Mt. Sinai Marine Sanctuary and Nature Center 473-8346*) **Under 1 mi:** Playground **3+ mi:** Dive Shop (*Port Scuba, 5 mi.*), Tennis Courts (*Port Jefferson Town, 5 mi.*), Golf Course (*Rolling Oaks G.C., 5 mi.*), Movie Theater (*P.J. Cinema 926-3456, 5 mi.*)

Provisioning and General Services
1-3 mi: Provisioning Service, Convenience Store, Delicatessen (*Parkside 331-3066*), Wine/Beer (*North Country 744-6922*), Liquor Store, Bank/ATM (*Suffolk Cty Nat'l 474-8400*), Post Office (*Miller Place*), Protestant Church, Beauty Salon, Dry Cleaners, Laundry, Pharmacy (*Echo 642-8175*), Hardware Store (*Miller Place True Value 821-3567*), Florist, Retail Shops, Copies Etc. (*Miller Place Printing 473-1158*) **3+ mi:** Supermarket (*Waldbaum's 476-2394, 4 mi.*), Gourmet Shop (*Moore's 928-1443, 5 mi.*)

Transportation
OnCall: Rental Car (*Enterprise 474-2100*), Taxi (*Abby's Car Service 732-3390*), Airport Limo **3+ mi:** Rail (*Port Jeff Station, 5 mi.*), Ferry Service (*Bridgeport, 6 mi.*) **Airport:** Islip (*20 mi.*)

Medical Services
911 Service **OnCall:** Ambulance **1-3 mi:** Dentist (*Bean 928-6566*), Chiropractor (*Chiro. Ctr of Mt. Sinai 476-4600*) **3+ mi:** Doctor (*Long Island Family Med of Mt. Sinai 476-4600, 4 mi.*), Holistic Services (*Port Jeff Massage 331-7631, 4 mi.*), Optician (*Port Jeff 473-0415, 4 mi.*)
Hospital: Mather Memorial 473-1320 *6 mi.*

Setting -- The third commercial facility on the north shore after entering the Inlet, Old Man's Boat Yard offers basic dockage and boatyard services in a convenient but very rural location. Mount Sinai Harbor was carved out of the Salt Marsh in the early 70's and is owned, in its entirety, by the Brookhaven Township. But, beware, there are over 1500 moorings and approximately 800 slips in a relatively small harbor. Old Man's dockage consists of 60 slips set in a 300 foot by 400 foot wood basin, with a travelift in the middle, and a small mooring field.

Marina Notes -- Founded 1959 - previously it was the Davis Island Boatyard. A friendly and knowledgeable owner provides basic boatyard services and can import most others. If your boat has a problem, they can get someone to fix it. Note: Marina staff leaves Friday pm and does not return until Monday am. Additional inland storage 5 miles from water. Only three transient docks, not specifically held for that purpose. The moorings come with a dinghy dock. Launch service is provided by Ralph's Fishing Station for a fee. Very basic head. "Old Man" was the original name of the town (after an early Native American inhabitant) before it was renamed Mt. Sinai (the stories about how that happened are legion).

Notable -- If you can get a slip or mooring, Mount Sinai is a very convenient spot to duck into for the night. It's purely fun-in-the-sun; there is a town fishing pier at the inlet, Cedar Beach with a snack bar, a marine nature center, and extensive tidal wetlands that are home to abundant wildlife. Several restaurants deliver. The area was a 'port' of sorts long before it was a harbor and was the landing site of Tallmadge's famous Revolutionary War raid on the British.

PHOTOS ON CD-ROM: 5

Mattituck Inlet Marina

PO Box 1408; 5780 W. Mill Rd.; Mattituck, NY 11952

Tel: (631) 298-4480 **VHF: Monitor** 68 **Talk** n/a
Fax: (631) 298-4126 **Alternate Tel:** n/a
Email: mimsboats@aol.com **Web:** n/a
Nearest Town: Mattituck *(1.5 mi.)* **Tourist Info:** (631) 298-5757

Navigational Information
Lat: 41°00.570' **Long:** 072°33.020' **Tide:** 5 ft. **Current:** 3 kt. **Chart:** 12358
Rep. Depths *(MLW):* **Entry** 6 ft. **Fuel Dock** 23 ft. **Max Slip/Moor** 6 ft./-
Access: L.I. Sound into Mattituck Inlet, about one mile on starboard side

Marina Facilities *(In Season/Off Season)*
Fuel: Gasoline, Diesel
Slips: 65 Total, 6 Transient **Max LOA:** 90 ft. **Max Beam:** n/a
  Rate *(per ft.):* **Day** $2.00/$1.50 **Week** $5.00/5.00 **Month** $12/12
Power: 30 amp Incl., **50 amp** Incl., **100 amp** n/a, **200 amp** n/a
Cable TV: No **Dockside Phone:** No
Dock Type: Floating, Long Fingers, Wood
Moorings: 0 Total, 0 Transient **Launch:** n/a
  Rate: Day n/a **Week** n/a **Month** n/a
Heads: 2 Toilet(s), 2 Shower(s)
Laundry: None **Pay Phones:** No
Pump-Out: No **Fee:** n/a **Closed Heads:** Yes

Marina Operations
Owner/Manager: Jim Pape **Dockmaster:** Same
In-Season: Year-Round, 8am-4:30pm **Off-Season:** n/a
After-Hours Arrival: Call in advance
Reservations: Yes, Required **Credit Cards:** Visa/MC, Dscvr, Amex
Discounts: None
Pets: Welcome, Dog Walk Area **Handicap Access:** Yes, Heads, Docks

Marina Services and Boat Supplies
Services - Docking Assistance, Security *(Southold Police Dept.)*, Trash Pick-Up, Megayacht Facilities **Communication -** Phone Messages, FedEx, AirBorne, UPS, Express Mail *(Sat Del)* **Supplies - OnSite:** Ships' Store **Near:** Bait/Tackle **Under 1 mi:** Ice *(Cube)*, Propane **1-3 mi:** Marine Discount Store *(Lewis Marine)*

Boatyard Services
OnSite: Travelift *(80T)*, Engine mechanic *(gas, diesel)*, Electrical Repairs, Electronic Sales, Electronics Repairs, Hull Repairs, Bottom Cleaning, Brightwork, Air Conditioning, Compound, Wash & Wax, Interior Cleaning, Propeller Repairs, Woodworking, Upholstery, Yacht Interiors, Metal Fabrication, Painting, Total Refits **Dealer for:** Viking. Other Certifications: Westerbeke, Detroit Diesel **Yard Rates:** $72/hr., Haul & Launch $10/ft., Power Wash $5/ft. **Storage:** In-Water $60/ft./6 mo., On-Land $60/ft./6 mo.

Restaurants and Accommodations
OnSite: Restaurant *(Daly's Old Mill Inn 298-8080, L $7-10, D $15-22, Kid's Menu)* **Near:** Pizzeria *(The Sicilian 298-1947)* **Under 1 mi:** Restaurant *'Do Littles Family 298-4000, dinghy)*, *(The Red Door 298-4800, D $17-28, dinghy)*, *(A Touch of Venice 298-5851, L $7-14, D $11-18, dinghy)*, *(Hong Kong 298-8088, dinghy)* **1-3 mi:** Motel *(Mattituck Motel 298-4131)*, *(Beachcomber Resort 734-6370)*, Inn/B&B *(James Creek B&B 298-5968)*

Recreation and Entertainment
OnSite: Pool **Near:** Group Fishing Boat *(50 passenger Captain Bob IV & V 298-5727)* **Under 1 mi:** Beach *(Bailie's or Breakwater)*, Boat Rentals

1-3 mi: Tennis Courts, Roller Blade/Bike Paths, Bowling *(Mattituck Lanes 298-8311)*, Movie Theater *(Mattituck 298-7469)*, Video Rental *(Movietech 298-5630)*, Video Arcade, Cultural Attract *(North Fork Comm. Theatre 298-4500)*, Sightseeing *(23 North Fork vineyards or Vintage Vineyard Tours 765-4689 will pick up)* **3+ mi:** Golf Course *(Cedars G.C. 734-6363, 5 mi.)*, Fitness Center *(Advanced Health & Racquet Club 734-2897, 5 mi.)*

Provisioning and General Services
Near: Fishmonger **Under 1 mi:** Delicatessen *(Wendy's Sound Ave. Deli 298-1500)*, Green Grocer *(Harbes Farms 298-2054)* **1-3 mi:** Convenience Store *(Village Market 298-8543)*, Supermarket *(Waldbaums 298-9797)*, Gourmet Shop *(Cheese Shop North 298-8556)*, Health Food, Wine/Beer, Liquor Store *(North Fork Liquor 298-8160)*, Bakery, Meat Market, Bank/ATM, Post Office, Catholic Church, Protestant Church *(Presbyterian, Episcopalian, Baptist, Lutheran)*, Library *(Mattituck 298-4134)*, Beauty Salon, Barber Shop, Dry Cleaners, Laundry, Bookstore, Pharmacy *(Genovese 298-5601)*, Newsstand, Hardware Store *(Raynor & Suter 298-8420)*, Florist, Retail Shops, Copies Etc.

Transportation
OnCall: Rental Car *(Enterprise 765-6600)*, Taxi *(Far East 298-9617)*, Airport Limo *(Sea Aire 298-4082)* **1-3 mi:** Bikes *(Country Time 298-8700, $22/day)*, Rail *(LIRR)* **Airport:** Mattituck/Islip *(3 mi./40 mi.)*

Medical Services
911 Service **OnCall:** Ambulance **1-3 mi:** Doctor *(Family Practice 298-2030)*, Dentist, Chiropractor *(Family Chiro 298-5333)*, Veterinarian *(Laurel 298-1177)* **Hospital:** Central Suffolk 369-2775 *(12 mi.)*

Setting -- Heading down narrow, quiet Mattituck Inlet for the first time can be a surprising experience; it is rife with incongruous vistas. The landscape hints more of Downeast than of Long Island. On the east side, the Inlet is lined with a small but colorful collection of active working boats. On the western shore you'll pass Capt. Bob's charter fleet, then the bright umbrellas of the red-shingled Old Mill Inn, and then, wedged into the slim creek, an astonishing congregation of large sport fishing boats and some super yachts. Apparently, the enticement, located at the base of the bluffs, is very neat and orderly Mattituck Inlet Marina.

Marina Notes -- A truly full service repair facility and marina, MIM&S tends to cater to larger motor yachts, but welcomes all. Short fingers, off the dock wall, hold a variety of boats with smaller craft located farther south in the marina. Extensive engine, fiberglass, carpentry skills onsite. Seven sheds for work and storage; 3 travelifts, inside storage, a very sizeable parts department - all managed by a proficient, quality-oriented staff. Indoor parking for cars, too. Attractive heads and showers. A nicely appointed pool, with a view of the marina, snuggles between two large sheds.

Notable -- Adjacent to the marina is Daly's Old Mill Inn (since 1960), a colonial-era mill literally suspended over Mattituck Creek. Casual food is served on the outside deck and inside in the Tap Room, with a huge original fireplace. If weather permits, eat outside, and watch the amazing amalgam of craft chug by. Inside, the Dining Room offers more serious food, local LI wines, large creek-front windows overlooking the fishing fleet, and live entertainment on weekends. A very nice town beach fronts on the Sound, an easy dinghy ride up the inlet. Lobsters and fish can be purchased directly from the work boats across the way.

Navigational Information

Lat: 40°59.773' **Long:** 072°32.295' **Tide:** 5 ft. **Current:** 2 kt. **Chart:** 12358
Rep. Depths (*MLW*): **Entry** 5 ft. **Fuel Dock** 10 ft. **Max Slip/Moor** 10 ft./-
Access: Mattituck Breakwater, follow inlet for 1.7 miles

Marina Facilities *(In Season/Off Season)*

Fuel: 93 Oct. - Gasoline, Diesel
Slips: 125 Total, 20 Transient **Max LOA:** 7065 ft. **Max Beam:** 20 ft.
 Rate *(per ft.)*: **Day** $2.00/1.50 **Week** $12 **Month** Inq.
 Power: 30 amp Incl., **50 amp** Incl., **100 amp** n/a, **200 amp** n/a
 Cable TV: No **Dockside Phone:** No
 Dock Type: Floating, Long Fingers, Wood
Moorings: 0 Total, 0 Transient **Launch:** n/a
 Rate: Day n/a **Week** n/a **Month** n/a
Heads: 6 Toilet(s), 4 Shower(s)
Laundry: None **Pay Phones:** Yes
Pump-Out: OnCall, Full Service, 1 Port **Fee:** $40 **Closed Heads:** Yes

Marina Operations

Owner/Manager: Michael & Monica Raynor **Dockmaster:** n/a
In-Season: Jun-Sep, 8am-5pm **Off-Season:** Sept-May, 8am-4pm
After-Hours Arrival: Night watchman on call
Reservations: Yes, Preferred **Credit Cards:** Visa/MC, Dscvr, Amex
Discounts: None
Pets: Welcome, Dog Walk Area **Handicap Access:** Yes, Heads, Docks

Matt-A-Mar Marina

2255 Wickham Avenue; Mattituck, NY 11952

Tel: (631) 298-4739 **VHF: Monitor** 68 **Talk** 10
Fax: (631) 298-4803 **Alternate Tel:** (631) 298-4739
Email: mammllc@aol.com **Web:** www.mattamar.com
Nearest Town: Mattituck *(0.1 mi.)* **Tourist Info:** (631) 298-5757

Marina Services and Boat Supplies

Services - Docking Assistance, Security, Dock Carts **Communication -** FedEx, AirBorne, UPS, Express Mail **Supplies - OnSite:** Ice *(Cube)*, Ships' Store **Under 1 mi:** Bait/Tackle, Propane

Boatyard Services

OnSite: Travelift *(50T)*, Engine mechanic *(gas, diesel)*, Hull Repairs, Rigger, Bottom Cleaning, Brightwork, Divers, Compound, Wash & Wax, Interior Cleaning, Woodworking, Yacht Interiors, Awlgrip, Yacht Broker *(Saber Yacht Sales)* **OnCall:** Electrical Repairs, Sail Loft, Canvas Work, Air Conditioning, Propeller Repairs, Inflatable Repairs, Life Raft Service, Metal Fabrication **Under 1 mi:** Launching Ramp. **Dealer for:** MAN, CAT, Volvo Penta.
Yard Rates: $65/hr., Haul & Launch $10/ft. *(blocking $2/ft.)*, Power Wash $3/ft., Bottom Paint $10/ft. *(paint incl.)*

Restaurants and Accommodations

OnSite: Restaurant *(A Touch of Venice 298-5851, L $7-14, D $11-18)*, Snack Bar *(L $3-9)* **Near:** Restaurant *(Do Littles 298-4000)*, *(Hong Kong 298-8088)*, *(Red Door 298-4800, D $17-28, Prix Fixe Sun-Thu $23)*, Lite Fare *(Bagel Café 298-8521)*, Pizzeria *(Angelo's 298-8910)*
Under 1 mi: Restaurant *(Old Mill Inn 298-8080, L $7-10, D $15-22, dinghy)*, *(1/2 Shell 298-4180)*, Motel *(Mattituck 298-4131)*

Recreation and Entertainment

OnSite: Pool, Picnic Area, Playground, Boat Rentals *(Kayaks)* **OnCall:** Sightseeing *(Vintage Vineyard Tours 765-4689)* **Near:** Tennis Courts, Fitness Center *(Synchronicity 298-0172)*, Jogging Paths, Movie Theater *(Mattituck Cinemas 298-7469)*, Video Rental *(Front Row Video 289-5151)*,

Park, Museum *(AAF Tank 588-0033 $6/5)*, Special Events *(Mattituck Street Fair, July)*, Galleries **Under 1 mi:** Beach, Horseback Riding, Bowling *(Mattituck Lanes 298-8311)*, Fishing Charter *(Strong Marine 298-4770)*, Group Fishing Boat *(Captain Bob's 298-5727)* **1-3 mi:** Dive Shop, Cultural Attract *(Macari Vineyards 298-0100Northfork Community Theater)* **3+ mi:** Golf Course *(Cedars Golf Club 734-6363, 4 mi.)*

Provisioning and General Services

OnSite: Green Grocer *(or Harbes Farms 298-2054; Hallock Farms 298-8969 w/in 1 mi.)* **Near:** Convenience Store *(Village Mkt. 298-8543)*, Supermarket *(Waldbaums 298-9797)*, Gourmet Shop *(Cheese Shop North 298-8556)*, Delicatessen *(LLL 298-4404)*, Bakery *(Connie's 298-9301)*, Meat Market, Bank/ATM, Post Office, Catholic Church, Protestant Church, Library *(Mattituck 298-4134)*, Beauty Salon, Barber Shop, Laundry, Bookstore, Pharmacy *(Barkers 298-8666)*, Newsstand, Hardware Store *(Raynor & Suter 298-8420)*, Florist, Retail Shops **Under 1 mi:** Wine/Beer, Fishmonger, Lobster Pound, Dry Cleaners **1-3 mi:** Liquor Store *(Murphy's 298-8400)*

Transportation

OnSite: Bikes *(or Country Time Cycle 298-8700, $22/day w/in 1 mi.)*
OnCall: Rental Car *(Enterprise 765-6600/Sensible Car Rental 298-1039)*, Taxi *(Far East 298-9617)*, Airport Limo *(Sea Aire 298-4082)* **Near:** Local Bus *(SCT)*, Rail *(LIRR)* **Airport:** Islip *(40 mi.)*

Medical Services

911 Service **OnCall:** Ambulance **Near:** Doctor *(Family Practice 298-2030)*, Dentist **Under 1 mi:** Chiropractor *(Family Chiro 298-5333)* **1-3 mi:** Veterinarian *(Laurel 298-1177)* **Hospital:** Central Suffolk 369-2775 *10 mi.*

Setting -- Matt-A-Mar is about 1.7 miles from the Inlet, at the head of continually surprising Mattituck Creek. En route, the waterway widens considerably, bellying out to a modest basin at the end. The sprawling family-oriented resort marina occupies a wide promontory that juts into the Creek's east side. The docks surround the peninsula and the extensive facilities occupy a small rise above them. The setting is park-like, reminiscent of the Adirondacks. Most of the slips are sheltered from the boatyard operation by thick stands of trees. The surrounding area is mostly grassland with North Highway visible to the south.

Marina Notes -- The docks are well kept and accessed by ramps, with views across the creek. There's a ships' store, outdoor storage ($26/ft. incl. haul, launch, wash, & block), 25,000 sq. ft. inside ($4.25/sq.ft.), 2 full-time mechanics (Yamaha-certified), and nice showers and heads. Matt-A-Mar offers lots to do: an Olympic-size pool with lifeguard and lessons, aqua aerobics, and a snack bar. Plus volleyball courts, playground, kayak & canoe rentals, sales, instruction and an interesting variety of tours. Tree-shaded picnic tables dot the grounds. A large Federal anchorage with dinghy dock is across the creek.

Notable -- Onsite is well-reviewed A Touch of Venice restaurant. Dine on the deck overlooking the marina or in the window-walled dining room. It's an easy 0.3 mile walk to the charming shopping strip Love Lane that runs form Route 25 to the Creek - services, antiques, ice cream, boutiques. It's a half mile straight out to the village center on Main Rd./Rte 25. Nearby American Armored Foundation Tank Museum, with 95 tanks and artillery pieces from 1800's-Desert Storm, is open 10:30am-5pm Wed-Sun MemDay-LabDay and Sundays year 'round. Macari Vineyards is 2 miles; 20 other vineyards are within easy reach.

PHOTOS ON CD-ROM: 9

IX. New York: Long Island's North Fork

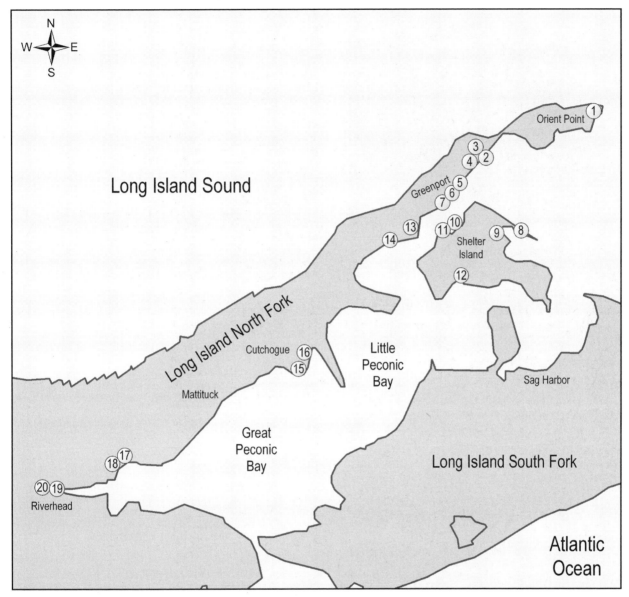

MAP	MARINA	HARBOR	PAGE	MAP	MARINA	HARBOR	PAGE
1	Orient-By-The-Sea Marina	Gardiners Bay	162	11	Jack's Marine at True Value	Dering Harbor	172
2	Brewer Yacht Yard at Greenport	Stirling Basin	163	12	The Island Boatyard & Marina	West Neck Harbor	173
3	Brewer Stirling Harbor Marina	Stirling Basin	164	13	Brick Cove Marina	Sage Beach	174
4	Townsend Manor Inn & Marina	Stirling Basin	165	14	Port of Egypt Marina	Southold Bay	175
5	S.T. Preston & Son	Greenport Harbor	166	15	New Suffolk Shipyard	Cutchogue Harbor	176
6	Claudio's Marina	Greenport Harbor	167	16	Cutchogue Harbor Marina	Cutchogue Harbor	177
7	Greenport Moorings & Dock	Greenport Hbr/Stirling Basin	168	17	Great Peconic Bay Marina	Flanders Bay	178
8	Ram's Head Inn	Coecles Harbor	169	18	Larry's Lighthouse Marina	Meetinghouse Creek	179
9	Coecles Harbor Marina	Coecles Harbor	170	19	Treasure Cove Marina Resort	Peconic River	180
10	Piccozzi's Dering Harbor Marina	Dering Harbor	171	20	Peconic Riverfront Marina	Peconic River	181

Orient-By-The-Sea Marina

PO Box 333; 40200 Main Road; Orient, NY 11957

Tel: (631) 323-2424 **VHF: Monitor** 9 **Talk** n/a
Fax: (631) 323-1332 **Alternate Tel:** (631) 323-2424
Email: OBTS@aol.com **Web:** orientbythesea.com
Nearest Town: Greenport *(8 mi.)* **Tourist Info:** (631) 765-3161

Navigational Information
Lat: 41°09.160' **Long:** 072°14.623' **Tide:** 3 ft. **Current:** n/a **Chart:** 12358
Rep. Depths *(MLW)*: **Entry** 6 ft. **Fuel Dock** 10 ft. **Max Slip/Moor** 10 ft./-
Access: 1 mile west of Plum Gut on Gardiners Bay

Marina Facilities *(In Season/Off Season)*
Fuel: Gasoline, Diesel
Slips: 90 Total, 10 Transient **Max LOA:** 55 ft. **Max Beam:** 16 ft.
 Rate *(per ft.)*: **Day** $30.00/Inq.* **Week** Inq. **Month** Inq.
 Power: 30 amp Inq., **50 amp** n/a, **100 amp** n/a, **200 amp** n/a
 Cable TV: No **Dockside Phone:** No
 Dock Type: Fixed, Floating, Long Fingers, Wood
Moorings: 0 Total, 0 Transient **Launch:** n/a
 Rate: Day n/a **Week** n/a **Month** n/a
Heads: 2 Toilet(s), Shower(s)
Laundry: None **Pay Phones:** Yes, 1
Pump-Out: No **Fee:** n/a **Closed Heads:** Yes

Marina Operations
Owner/Manager: Robert & George Haase **Dockmaster:** Same
In-Season: May-Nov, 8am-mid. **Off-Season:** Dec-Apr, Closed
After-Hours Arrival: n/a
Reservations: Preferred **Credit Cards:** Visa/MC, Dscvr, Din
Discounts: Boat/US; Naut. Miles **Dockage:** n/a **Fuel:** $.10 **Repair:** n/a
Pets: Welcome, Dog Walk Area **Handicap Access:** Yes, Heads, Docks

Marina Services and Boat Supplies
Services - Docking Assistance, Boaters' Lounge **Communication -** Phone Messages **Supplies - OnSite:** Ice *(Cube)* **3+ mi:** Ships' Store *(East End Marine 477-1900 , 8 mi.)*, Bait/Tackle *(Alices Fish Mkt, Greenport 477-8485, 8 mi.)*, Propane *(Van Duzer 765-3882, 10 mi.)*

Boatyard Services
OnSite: Launching Ramp, Divers **OnCall:** Engine mechanic *(gas, diesel)*, Electrical Repairs **Nearest Yard:** Brewer Greenport (516) 477-9594

Restaurants and Accommodations
OnSite: Restaurant *(Orient By The Sea L $6-14, D $12-24, Kids' menu; open daily May-October for lunch and dinner 11am+)* **Under 1 mi:** Restaurant *(Oyster Ponds Beach Café 323-0024, at the tip of Orient Beach State Park May-Oct 11am until park closing)*, Lite Fare *(Orient Ice Cream Parlour 323-0100)* **1-3 mi:** Motel *(Blue Dolphin 477-0907)*, *(Orient Inn 323-2300)*, Inn/B&B *(Treasure Island 477-2788)*, *(Arbor View House 477-8440)*

Recreation and Entertainment
OnSite: Fishing Charter *(Saxatilis Charters 323-1494, Sundowner 765-2227, Coyote Sports Fishing 734-6288, Celtic Horizon 734-4295, Rainbow Charters 765-4314, Black Rock Charters 516-819-5731, Fishy Business 722-4899, Casey J. 722-4407, Open Boat Prime Time III 323-2618, Brooklyn Girl 395-7055, Tautoga Charters 395-7055, K.J. Flyfishing 722-5453)*, Group Fishing Boat *(Orient Star II 785-6149, Nancy Ann 477-2337)*

Near: Beach *(Orient State Park)*, Picnic Area, Grills, Playground, Jogging Paths, Roller Blade/Bike Paths, Park *(Orient State)* **1-3 mi:** Museum *(Oysterponds Historical Society's restored buildings 323-2480)* **3+ mi:** Golf Course *(Island's End Golf and Country Club 477-8190, 6 mi.)*

Provisioning and General Services
OnCall: Fishmonger **1-3 mi:** Convenience Store *(Orient Country Store 323-2580)*, Farmers' Market, Post Office, Protestant Church **3+ mi:** Supermarket *(IGA Greenport 477-0101, 8 mi.)*, Liquor Store *(JB Liquor 477-0024 , 6 mi.)*, Pharmacy *(Colonial Drugs 477-1111, 6 mi.)*, Hardware Store *(White's 477-0317, 6 mi.)*

Transportation
OnSite: Local Bus **OnCall:** Rental Car *(Enterprise 765-6600)*, Taxi *(Maria's Taxi 477-0700)*, Airport Limo *(Fleetwood East 477-0078)* **Near:** Ferry Service *(Cross Sound to New London, 323-2525 - Auto Ferry 80 min $37 car & driver, passenger $16/8. Sea Jet 40 min. passenger only $25/12.50 RT same day)* **3+ mi:** Bikes *(Bike Stop 477-2432, 5 mi.)*, Rail *(LIRR to Penn Station NYC, 8 mi.)* **Airport:** Islip 467-3210 *(70 mi.)*

Medical Services
911 Service **OnCall:** Ambulance **3+ mi:** Doctor *(8 mi.)*, Dentist *(8 mi.)*, Chiropractor *(8 mi.)*, Holistic Services *(Center for Integrative HealthCare, 477-8236, 8 mi.)*, Veterinarian *(North Fork Animal Hosp. 765-2400, 8 mi.)*
Hospital: Eastern Long Island 477-1000 *(8 mi.)*

Setting -- Adjacent to the New London and Plum Island Ferries and Orient Beach State Park, close to the easternmost point of the North Fork, Orient-by-the-Sea is tucked into a small, man-made basin directly off Gardiners Bay. This is a large charter fishing port on the open beach.

Marina Notes -- *Flat dockage rate $30. Family owned by George and Robert Haase since 1979. Friendly, well run, with easy access for smaller craft (the entrance can be tight). If you've got a problem, the owner can get the right people to fix almost everything. The casual onsite bar and restaurant is all knotty pine and windows; patrons are mostly anglers and ocassional tourists. Homemade chowders, burgers, pastas, steaks, and lots of local seafood; Thursday is lobster night. 15% off food and beverages for Nautical Miles members. Home to the largest fleet of charter sport fishing boats on the North Fork. Basic heads and showers. Recently refurbished docks.

Notable -- Orient Beach State Park immediately next door is worth a look for the solitude and the pristine beach it offers. Greenport is the closest place for services and shops. Suffolk County Bus West stops in front and runs pretty much on the hour, making the 8 mile run to Greenport then on to Riverhead. The marina is located next to the Plum Island ferry; Plum Island is the US government's animal disease lab located on the island of the same name. Great fishing in the Plum Gut bewteen the mainland and Plum. Oysterponds Historical Society offers walking tours of the many buildings it has restored in the National Historic Landmark district depicting the maritime and rural past of Orient (Wed, Thu, Sat & Sun 2-5pm in the summer).

Navigational Information
Lat: 41°06.500' **Long:** 072°21.300' **Tide:** 3 ft. **Current:** n/a **Chart:** 12358
Rep. Depths (*MLW*): **Entry** 8 ft. **Fuel Dock** n/a **Max Slip/Moor** 10 ft./-
Access: Gardiners Bay to Stirling Basin

Marina Facilities (*In Season/Off Season*)
Fuel: *next door at Brewer Stirling Harbor -*
Slips: 207 Total, 20 Transient **Max LOA:** 60 ft. **Max Beam:** n/a
Rate (*per ft.*): **Day** $2.00 **Week** Inq. **Month** Inq.
Power: 30 amp Incl., 50 amp Incl., 100 amp n/a, 200 amp n/a
Cable TV: No **Dockside Phone:** No
Dock Type: Floating, Wood
Moorings: 0 Total, 0 Transient **Launch:** n/a, Dinghy Dock
Rate: Day n/a **Week** n/a **Month** n/a
Heads: 5 Toilet(s), 7 Shower(s)
Laundry: 2 Washer(s), 2 Dryer(s), Book Exchange **Pay Phones:** No
Pump-Out: Full Service, 1 Central, 1 Port **Fee:** $8 **Closed Heads:** Yes

Marina Operations
Owner/Manager: Mike Acebo **Dockmaster:** n/a
In-Season: Apr 15-Oct 15, 7:30-6 **Off-Season:** Oct 16-Apr 14, 7:30-4
After-Hours Arrival: Call for slip assignment, pay next morning
Reservations: Required **Credit Cards:** Visa/MC, Dscvr, Amex
Discounts: Brewers **Dockage:** n/a **Fuel:** n/a **Repair:** n/a
Pets: Welcome, Dog Walk Area **Handicap Access:** No

Brewer Yacht Yard at Greenport

500 Beach Road; Greenport, NY 11944

Tel: (631) 477-9594 **VHF: Monitor** 9 **Talk** 68
Fax: (631) 477-1150 **Alternate Tel:** n/a
Email: gre@byy.com **Web:** www.byy.com/Greenport
Nearest Town: Greenport (*1.5 mi.*) **Tourist Info:** (631) 765-3161

Marina Services and Boat Supplies
Services - Docking Assistance, Dock Carts **Communication -** Mail & Package Hold, Phone Messages, FedEx, AirBorne, UPS, Express Mail (*Sat Del*) **Supplies - OnSite:** Ice (*Block, Cube*), Ships' Store **OnCall:** Propane **Under 1 mi:** Bait/Tackle (*Alice's Fish Market*)

Boatyard Services
OnSite: Travelift (*70T*), Engine mechanic (*gas, diesel*), Electrical Repairs, Electronics Repairs, Hull Repairs, Rigger, Bottom Cleaning, Brightwork, Refrigeration, Compound, Wash & Wax, Propeller Repairs, Woodworking, Yacht Interiors, Painting, Awlgrip, Total Refits **OnCall:** Divers, Interior Cleaning, Inflatable Repairs, Life Raft Service, Metal Fabrication **Dealer for:** Scandvik, Vetus, Edson, Tides Marine, Furlex, Schaefer, Yanmar, Sealand, Awlgrip, Interlux, Westerbeke, Fischer Panda, Espar Heat, Seafrost. **Member:** ABYC - 4 Certified Tech(s) **Yard Rates:** $40-80, Haul & Launch $11-13.50/ft., Power Wash $3, Bottom Paint $11/ft.

Restaurants and Accommodations
OnSite: Restaurant (*Antares Café 477-8839, L $12-28, D $19-28, kids' items available*) **Near:** Restaurant (*Blue Water Grille 477-3583, L $8-25, D $16-25*) **Under 1 mi:** Restaurant (*Townsend Manor 477-2000, or dinghy*), (*252 Broadway 262-7200*), (*Ile de Beaute 477-2822*), (*Sandpiper 447-1154*), Lite Fare (*Not Just Ice Cream 447-2914*), Pizzeria (*Christie's 477-0787*), Inn/B&B (*Stirling House 477-0654*), (*Townsend Manor 477-2000, $60-175*), (*Morning Glory 477-3324*), (*Bartlett House 477-0371, $110-215*)

Recreation and Entertainment
OnSite: Pool, Picnic Area, Grills **OnCall:** Fishing Charter, Sightseeing

(*Vintage Vinyeyard Tours 765-4689*) **Near:** Beach (*Norman E. Kilp Marine Park*), Playground, Park **Under 1 mi:** Tennis Courts **1-3 mi:** Dive Shop, Golf Course (*Island's End 477-0777*), Jogging Paths, Movie Theater (*Village Cinema 477-8600*), Video Rental (*Desiderio 477-8120*), Museum (*East End Maritime 477-2100, Railroad M. of LI 477-0439*) **3+ mi:** Horseback Riding (*Hidden Lake 765-9896, 6mi.*)

Provisioning and General Services
Near: Fishmonger (*Alice's 477-8485*) **1-3 mi:** Supermarket (*IGA 477-0101*), Gourmet Shop (*Cheese Emporium 477-0023*), Delicatessen (*Sterlington, 477-8547*), Health Food, Wine/Beer, Liquor Store (*JB Liquor 477-0024*), Bakery, Farmers' Market (*Thu 3-8pm & Sat 8am-1pm*), Bank/ATM, Post Office, Catholic Church, Protestant Church, Synagogue, Library (*Floyd Mem. 477-0660*), Beauty Salon, Barber Shop, Dry Cleaners, Laundry, Bookstore (*Book Scout 477-8536, Burton's 477-1161*), Pharmacy (*Pharmco 477-1111*), Newsstand, Hardware Store (*White 477-0317*), Florist, Department Store (*Arcade 477-1440*), Copies Etc. (*North Fork Press 477-1250*)

Transportation
OnSite: Courtesy Car/Van **OnCall:** Rental Car (*Enterprise 765-6600*), Taxi (*Maria's Taxi 477-0700*), Airport Limo (*Fleetwood East 477-0078*) **1-3 mi:** Local Bus, InterCity Bus, Rail (*LIRR to NYC 477-5477*), Ferry Service (*to Shelter Island*) **Airport:** Islip (*60 mi.*)

Medical Services
911 Service **OnCall:** Ambulance **1-3 mi:** Doctor, Dentist (*A. Lamia 477-0123*), Holistic Services **3+ mi:** Veterinarian (*North Fork 765-2400, 5 mi.*) **Hospital:** Eastern LI 477-1000 (*1 mi.*)

Setting -- Tucked into protected, pristine Stirling Basin, Brewer's extensive set of docks is the first on the east side. The stair-step gray yard buildings are very visible beyond the docks. A large pool, furnished with chaises and tables and chairs, is separated from the docks by the parking lot. Adjacent is Antares Café. Picnic tables and gazebos are sprinkled around the perfectly kept grounds. Occasional pots of flowers and small beds break up the cement and gravel.

Marina Notes -- Bicycle rental no longer available. Welcome package. Discounts to those with Brewer's Preferred Customer Card. *Pump-out $8, Pump-out Boat Ch. 9 free. Courtesy van for provisioning and restaurants. A friendly, professional staff manages this full service boatyard and well-run, customer-oriented marina. Top rated Antares Café offers contemporary American fare in a small cathedral-ceilinged dining room with bright red stucco walls and white tablecloths. Fresh flowers in the heads. Brewer's Yacht Yard Time Warp Regattas are in June and October. Emergency phone: (800) 922-4821

Notable -- The Norman E. Kilp Marine Park is an easy walk on Manhasset Avenue - it has a wide beach, a playground, heads, and a boat ramp. Downtown bustling, revitalized Greenport -- with its dozens of shops, galleries, and restaurants -- is about a mile and a half by land (foot or courtesy van), or a quick dinghy ride. Preston's, the oldest and largest chandlery on the east coast, offers free dinghy dockage -- great stop for marine supplies and clothing, too. Don't miss the 1920's, 40 foot carousel in its spectacular contemporary glass house at Harbor Front Park and the East End Maritime Museum. About 25 vineyards are within easy cab distance. Or Vintage Vineyards Tours will pick you up for lunch and a three-vineyard overview ($48-55, 4-5 hrs., save $10 in off season).

Brewer Stirling Harbor Marina

1410 Manhanset Avenue; Greenport, NY 11944

Tel: (631) 477-0828 **VHF: Monitor** 9 **Talk** 9
Fax: (631) 477-0847 **Alternate Tel:** n/a
Email: bsh@byy.com **Web:** byy.com
Nearest Town: Greenport *(1.25 mi.)* **Tourist Info:** (631) 765-3161

Navigational Information
Lat: 41°06.661' **Long:** 072°21.547' **Tide:** 3 ft. **Current:** n/a **Chart:** 12358
Rep. Depths *(MLW)*: **Entry** 12 ft. **Fuel Dock** 12 ft. **Max Slip/Moor** 12 ft./-
Access: Gardiner's Bay to Stirling Basin

Marina Facilities *(In Season/Off Season)*
Fuel: *ValvTect* - Gasoline, Diesel
Slips: 189 Total, 5 Transient **Max LOA:** 100 ft. **Max Beam:** 23 ft.
  Rate *(per ft.)*: **Day** $2.50 **Week** n/a **Month** n/a
  Power: 30 amp Incl., **50 amp** Incl., **100 amp** n/a, **200 amp** n/a
  Cable TV: No **Dockside Phone:** No
  Dock Type: Fixed, Floating, Long Fingers, Pilings, Wood
Moorings: 0 Total, 0 Transient **Launch:** n/a
  Rate: Day n/a **Week** n/a **Month** n/a
Heads: 4 Toilet(s), 6 Shower(s), Hair Dryers
Laundry: 3 Washer(s), 3 Dryer(s), Iron, Iron Board **Pay Phones:** Yes, 2
Pump-Out: Full Service, Self Service **Fee:** *$5-8 **Closed Heads:** Yes

Marina Operations
Owner/Manager: Jeffrey Bubb **Dockmaster:** Anne Hall
In-Season: Apr 15-Oct 15, 7:30-7 **Off-Season:** Oct 16-Apr 14, 7:30-4
After-Hours Arrival: Check bulletin board at fuel dock
Reservations: Required **Credit Cards:** Visa/MC, Dscvr, Amex
Discounts: Brewer's Customer Card **Dockage:** n/a **Fuel:** n/a **Repair:** n/a
Pets: Welcome, Dog Walk Area **Handicap Access:** No

Marina Services and Boat Supplies
Services - Docking Assistance, Concierge, Security, Trash Pick-Up
Communication - Mail & Package Hold, Fax in/out, Data Ports *(Beacon Wi-Fi)*, FedEx, AirBorne, UPS, Express Mail *(Sat Del)* **Supplies - OnSite:** Ice *(Block, Cube)* **OnCall:** Propane **Near:** Bait/Tackle *(Alice's Fish Mkt)*
Under 1 mi: Ships' Store *(Brewer YY, Preston's 477-1990)*, Live Bait

Boatyard Services
OnSite: Travelift *(30 & 50T)*, Engine mechanic *(gas, diesel)*, Electrical Repairs, Hull Repairs, Rigger, Bottom Cleaning, Brightwork, Air Conditioning, Refrigeration, Divers, Compound, Wash & Wax, Interior Cleaning, Propeller Repairs, Woodworking, Inflatable Repairs, Upholstery, Painting, Awlgrip, Yacht Broker, Total Refits **OnCall:** Electronics Repairs, Life Raft Service, Metal Fabrication **Member:** ABYC - 2 Certified Tech(s) **Yard Rates:** $80/hr., Haul & Launch $11/ft., Power Wash $3, Bottom Paint $11/ft.

Restaurants and Accommodations
OnSite: Restaurant *(Blue Water Grille** 477-3582, B $3-7, L $8-25, D $16-25)* **Near:** Restaurant *(Antares Café 477-8839, L $12-28, D $19-28)* **1-3 mi:** Restaurant *(Townsend Manor 477-2000)*, *(252 Broadway 262-7200)*, *(Desiderio 477-2828)*, Pizzeria *(Christie's 477-0787)*, Motel *(Sound View 477-1910)*, Inn/B&B *(Townsend 477-2000, $60-175)*, *(Sterling Harbor 477-4814)*, *(Morning Glory 477-3324, $175-225)*, *(Bartlett 477-0371, $110-215)*

Recreation and Entertainment
OnSite: Pool, Picnic Area, Grills, Fitness Center, Special Events *(Wine tastings, Jewelery shows)* **Near:** Dive Shop, Jogging Paths, Roller Blade/Bike Paths **Under 1 mi:** Beach *(Norman E. Kilp Marine Park)*

1-3 mi: Golf Course *(Island's End 477-8190)*, Fishing Charter *(AP White 477-0008)*, Movie Theater *(Village Cinema 477-8600)*, Video Rental *(Desiderio 477-8120)*, Museum *(East End Maritime 477-2100, Railroad Museum of LI 477-0439)*, Sightseeing *(Mary E Schooner Cruises 477-8966)*

Provisioning and General Services
OnSite: Newsstand, Copies Etc. **OnCall:** Florist **Near:** Fishmonger *(Alice's/Greenport Seafood 477-8485)* **Under 1 mi:** Convenience Store, Protestant Church **1-3 mi:** Supermarket *(IGA 477-0101)*, Gourmet Shop *(Cheese Emporium 477-0023)*, Delicatessen *(Sterlington Deli 477-8547)*, Wine/Beer *(Ternhaven Cellars 477-8737)*, Liquor Store *(JB Liquor 477-0024)*, Farmers' Market *(Adams St. Thu 3-8pm & Sat 8am-1pm)*, Bank/ATM, Post Office, Catholic Church, Synagogue, Library *(Floyd Mem. 477-0660)*, Beauty Salon, Dry Cleaners, Laundry, Bookstore *(Book Scout 477-8536, Burton's 477-1161)*, Pharmacy *(Pharmco 477-1111)*, Hardware Store *(White 477-0317)*, Retail Shops, Department Store *(Arcade 477-1440)*

Transportation
OnSite: Courtesy Car/Van **OnCall:** Rental Car *(Enterprise 765-6600)*, Taxi *(Maria's Taxi 477-0700)*, Airport Limo *(Fleetwood East 477-0078)* **Near:** Bikes *(at Brewer Yacht Yard)* **1-3 mi:** Local Bus, Rail *(LIRR to NYC 477-5477)*, Ferry Service *(Shelter Island)* **Airport:** Islip 467-3210 *(60 mi.)*

Medical Services
911 Service **OnSite:** Holistic Services **OnCall:** Chiropractor, Ambulance *(masage therapist on weekends)* **Near:** Doctor **1-3 mi:** Dentist *(Lamia 477-0123)* **3+ mi:** Veterinarian *(North Fork Animal Hosp. 765-2400, 5 mi.)*
Hospital: Eastern LI 477-1000 *(1 mi.)*

Setting -- The thoughtfully designed, perfectly sited mature plantings give an intimate feel to this large facility set in the north-east corner of "storm-safe" Stirling Harbor. A tree-canopied, waterfront picnic patch is home to a half dozen tables with grills. On some docks, greenery arches above walkways creating graceful entrances. The lovely pool and fitness center is set in its own club-like enclave with views of the docks.

Marina Notes -- Recently acquired by Brewer Yacht Yard chain, this wonderful facility is getting the maintenance it deserves. A well-equipped and inviting exercise room and mini-spa open out onto the well-furnished pool deck (a massage therapist staffs the spa on weekends). Onsite book exchange. Mixture of floating and fixed slips - all with full finger piers. Full service boatyard onsite with emergency service 7 days. Free ice. Complimentary shuttle to Greenport "downtown." *Pump-out at Brewer Yacht Yard next door ($8) or call the village pump-out boat ($5).

Notable -- The new onsite Blue Water Grille opened for the '04 season - replacing Bistro Blue; it features Spanish cuisine and interesting turns on fresh seafood. The mostly glass dining room has a cobalt blue ceiling and great views of the docks. Serves breakfast, lunch and dinner, seven days a week in season -- reduced schedule in the shoulder months. **Price range is approximate as the menu was not set at press time. It's a 1.3 mile walk or courtesy van ride to "downtown" Greenport. Check out Ternhaven Cellars on the west side or hop the ferry to Shelter Island and its "Heights" historic district. The East End Seaport Museum (in the old 3rd St. train station) preserves the local maritime heritage Wed-Mon 11-5; the Blacksmith Shop (477-2100) is also nearby.

Navigational Information
Lat: 41°06.537' **Long:** 072°21.721' **Tide:** 3 ft. **Current:** n/a **Chart:** 12358
Rep. Depths (MLW): Entry 8 ft. **Fuel Dock** n/a **Max Slip/Moor** 8 ft./-
Access: Gardiner's Bay to Stirling Basin to western shore

Marina Facilities *(In Season/Off Season)*
Fuel: Gasoline
Slips: 50 Total, 40 Transient **Max LOA:** 55 ft. **Max Beam:** 17 ft.
  Rate *(per ft.):* **Day** $2.25/$1.25* **Week** n/a **Month** n/a
  Power: 30 amp Inq., 50 amp Inq., 100 amp n/a, 200 amp n/a
  Cable TV: Yes **Dockside Phone:** No
  Dock Type: Fixed, Floating, Pilings, Alongside, Wood
Moorings: 0 Total, 0 Transient **Launch:** n/a, Dinghy Dock
  Rate: Day n/a **Week** n/a **Month** n/a
Heads: 5 Toilet(s), 6 Shower(s)
Laundry: 3 Washer(s), 3 Dryer(s) **Pay Phones:** Yes
Pump-Out: OnCall, Full Service **Fee:** $5 **Closed Heads:** Yes

Marina Operations
Owner/Manager: Scott Gonzalez **Dockmaster:** Same
In-Season: Year-Round, 8am-7:30pm **Off-Season:** n/a
After-Hours Arrival: Call in advance
Reservations: Yes **Credit Cards:** Visa/MC, Dscvr, Amex
Discounts: None
Pets: Welcome, Dog Walk Area **Handicap Access:** No

Townsend Manor Inn & Marina

714 Main Street; Greenport, NY 11944

Tel: (631) 477-2000 **VHF: Monitor** 9 **Talk** n/a
Fax: (631) 477-2503 **Alternate Tel:** n/a
Email: n/a **Web:** www.townsendmanorinn.com
Nearest Town: Greenport *(0.25 mi.)* **Tourist Info:** (631) 765-3161

Marina Services and Boat Supplies
Services - Docking Assistance **Communication -** Mail & Package Hold, Fax in/out, FedEx, AirBorne, UPS, Express Mail **Supplies - OnSite:** Ice *(Cube)* **Near:** Ice *(Shaved)*, Bait/Tackle *(Alice's Fish Mkt)*, Live Bait *(White's)* **Under 1 mi:** Ships' Store *(Preston's 477-1990)*, CNG *(Brewer Yacht Yard)* **3+ mi:** Propane *(Van Duzer 765-3882, 6 mi.)*

Boatyard Services
OnCall: Engine mechanic *(gas, diesel)*, Electrical Repairs, Electronics Repairs, Hull Repairs, Bottom Cleaning, Refrigeration, Divers
Near: Electronic Sales. **Under 1 mi:** Travelift, Forklift, Launching Ramp.
Nearest Yard: Brewers (631) 477-9594

Restaurants and Accommodations
OnSite: Restaurant *(Townsend Manor Inn, $5-25 B $4-8, L $5-14, D $9-27)*, Snack Bar *(Towsend Manor B $3-10, Poolside snack bar)*, Inn/B&B *(Townsend Manor Inn $75-175, in season $60-200)* **OnCall:** Pizzeria *(Christie's 477-8707)* **Near:** Restaurant *(Ile de Beaute 477-2822, French rest. & Creperie, inside & outside dining)*, Inn/B&B *(Morning Glory Inn 477-3324)*, *(Sterling Harbor House 477-4814)*, *(Bartlett House 477-0371, $110-215)* **Under 1 mi:** Restaurant *(Desiderio 477-2828)*, *(Chowder Pot Pub 477-1345)*, *(Bay & Main 477-1442)*, *(Aldo's & Aldo's Too 477-2859)*, Lite Fare *(Greenport Tea Co. 477-8744, L, High Tea and weekend brunch in an enchanting Victorian room)*, Inn/B&B *(Watson's by the Bay Bed 477-0426)*

Recreation and Entertainment
OnSite: Pool, Picnic Area, Grills **Near:** Beach *(by dinghy to Norman E. Kilp Marine Park just east of the Greenport jetty)*, Playground, Boat Rentals, Movie Theater *(Village 477-8600)*, Video Rental *(Desiderio Video 477-8120)* Park, CulturAttract, Sightseeing *(Mary E Schooner Cruises 477-8966)* **Under 1 mi:** Jogging Paths, Horseback Riding, Roller Blade/Bike Paths, Museum *(East End Maritime Museum 477-2100, Railroad Museum of LI 477-0439)* **1-3 mi:** Dive Shop, Tennis Courts, Golf Course *(Island's End Golf and Country Club 477-0777)*, Fishing Charter *(AP White 477-0008)*

Provisioning and General Services
Near: Convenience Store, Supermarket *(IGA 477-0101)*, Gourmet Shop *(Cheese Emporium 477-0023)*, Delicatessen *(Sterlington Deli 477-8547)*, Liquor Store *(JB Liquor 477-0024)*, Bakery *(Salamander Bakery 477-3711)*, Farmers' Market *(Adams St. Thu 3-8pm, Sat 8am-1pm)*, Fishmonger *(Alice's Fish Mkt. 477-8485)*, Meat Market, Bank/ATM, Post Office, Catholic Church, Library *(Floyd Mem. 477-0660)*, Beauty Salon, Barber Shop, Dry Cleaners, Laundry, Bookstore *(Book Scout 477-8536, Burton's Book Store 477-1161)*, Pharmacy *(Colonial Drugs 477-1111)*, Newsstand, Hardware Store *(White 477-0317)*, Florist, Clothing Store, Retail Shops, Department Store *(Arcade 477-1440)*, Copies Etc. *(North Fork Press 477-1250)*

Transportation
OnCall: Rental Car *(Enterprise 765-6600)*, Taxi *(Maria's Taxi 477-0700)*, Airport Limo *(Fleetwood East 477-0078)* **Under 1 mi:** Bikes *(Bike Stop 477-2432)* **Airport:** Islip Macarthur 467-3210 *(60 mi.)*

Medical Services
911 Service **OnCall:** Ambulance **Under 1 mi:** Doctor **1-3 mi:** Dentist *(Lamia 477-0123)* **3+ mi:** Chiropractor *(4 mi.)*, Veterinarian *(North Fork Animal Hosp. 765-2400, 4 mi.)* **Hospital:** Eastern LI 477-1000 *(0.1 mi.)*

Setting -- Townsend Manor is an old-fashioned country inn and marina on the West side of Stirling Basin - close to downtown Greenport. A collection of refurbished 19thC buildings, recreational amenities, and docks ring a "basin within a basin" creating stern-to slips that are very, very protected. The views are of the upland buildings, the basin, the Brewer docks on the other side and the looming Eastern Long Island Hospital. There is a lively family atmosphere.

Marina Notes -- * In-season rates: Mon-Thu $2.25/ft., Fri-Sun $2.75/ft.; off-season Mon-Thu $1.25/ft., Fri-Sun $2. Pedestals have 30 & 50 amp, 125 volt service, and cable TV. The docks line the basin with stern-to slips (no finger piers). Good showers and heads. Easy fuel access on the outside south corner of the basin. There's a snack bar next to the Olympic-size pool, a children's pool, and chairs sprinkled about the lawn. The main restaurant, with two dining rooms and a cocktail lounge, specializes in local produce and seafood. Serves breakfast (8-11am), lunch (Mon-Fri Noon-2:30, Sat 'til 5pm), and dinner (Mon-Sat 5-9pm, Sat 'til 9:30pm, and Sun Noon-9pm). The sunken bar has great waterviews and a 35 inch TV tuned to the most popular sporting events. The Gingerbread House, Captain's House, and Waterfront Cottage have rooms and efficiency appartments - most of which have been updated over the past three years.

Notable -- The Inn's Main House was built in 1835 by whaling captain George Cogswell. Lillian Cook Townsend bought the property in 1916, converting it to an inn in 1926. In 1954, the Gonzales family bought and renovated the Inn; they still own it today. It's an easy half-mile stroll to the Greenport wharf - and less to the center of town. Preston's and the Town Dock host a number of replica and tall ships - including 1906 Mary E., 105 ft. Malabar, and electric powered Glory.

S.T. Preston & Son

102 Main Street; Greenport, NY 11944

Tel: (631) 477-1990 **VHF:** Monitor n/a **Talk** n/a
Fax: (631) 477-8541 **Alternate Tel:** n/a
Email: andrew@prestons.com **Web:** www.prestons.com
Nearest Town: Greenport *(0 mi.)* **Tourist Info:** (631) 765-3161

Navigational Information
Lat: 41°06.087' **Long:** 072°21.520' **Tide:** 4 ft. **Current:** 2 kt. **Chart:** 12358
Rep. Depths (*MLW*): Entry 15 ft. **Fuel Dock** n/a **Max Slip/Moor** 12 ft./-
Access: 3 miles W/NW of Gardiner's Bay, east side of Greenport waterfront

Marina Facilities *(In Season/Off Season)*
Fuel: No
Slips: 10 Total, 10 Transient **Max LOA:** 100 ft. **Max Beam:** 20 ft.
Rate *(per ft.)*: **Day** $0.75/Inq. **Week** Inq. **Month** Inq.
Power: 30 amp Incl., **50 amp** n/a, **100 amp** n/a, **200 amp** n/a
Cable TV: No **Dockside Phone:** No
Dock Type: Fixed, Alongside, Wood
Moorings: 0 Total, 0 Transient **Launch:** n/a, Dinghy Dock
Rate: Day n/a **Week** n/a **Month** n/a
Heads: None
Laundry: None **Pay Phones:** No
Pump-Out: OnCall, Full Service **Fee:** $5 **Closed Heads:** Yes

Marina Operations
Owner/Manager: Andrew Rowson **Dockmaster:** Same
In-Season: Jun-Aug 31, 9am-6pm **Off-Season:** Sep 1-May 30, 10am-5pm
After-Hours Arrival: See dockmaster next morning
Reservations: No **Credit Cards:** Visa/MC, Dscvr, Amex
Discounts: None
Pets: Welcome **Handicap Access:** Yes, Docks

Marina Services and Boat Supplies
Communication - Mail & Package Hold **Supplies - OnSite:** Ships' Store, Bait/Tackle **Near:** Ice *(Cube)* **Under 1 mi:** Propane *(Piccozzi's 749-0045)*, CNG *(Brewer Yacht Yard)*

Boatyard Services
OnSite: Electronic Sales **OnCall:** Rigger, Canvas Work, Air Conditioning, Refrigeration **Near:** Railway, Hull Repairs, Bottom Cleaning, Woodworking. **1-3 mi:** Metal Fabrication, Painting, Awlgrip, Total Refits.
Nearest Yard: Greenport Yacht & Ship (631) 477-2277

Restaurants and Accommodations
Near: Restaurant *(Claudio's 477-0627, L $8-14, D $17-26, Kid's $8)*, *(Rhumb Line 477-9883)*, *(Katsura Sushi 477-1566)*, *(Meson Ole)*, *(Aldo's, Too)*, *(Aldo's Sushi 477-1699)*, Seafood Shack *(Crabby Jerry's 477-8252, L $5-16, D $5-16, Kid's $5-6)*, Lite Fare *(Sterlington Deli 477-8547)*, *(Chowder Pot Pub)*, *(Cannery Row)*, Pizzeria *(La Capriciosa 477-1625)*, *(Christie's)*, Inn/B&B *(Watson's by the Bay Bed 477-0426)*, *(Victorian Lady 477-1837, $160-190)* **Under 1 mi:** Motel *(Silver Sands 477-0011)*, Inn/B&B *(Greenporter 477-0066, $90-150)*, *(Bartlett House 477-0371, $110-215)*, *(Harfbor Knoll 477-2352, $175-250)*

Recreation and Entertainment
OnSite: Sightseeing *(Mary E Schooner Cruises 477-8966; Glory Electric Boat Cruises 477-8966)* **Near:** Group Fishing Boat, Video Arcade, Park, Museum *(East End Maritime 477-2100 - Wed-Mon, 11-5, Free; Blacksmith Shop, Sat 11-5, Free; Railroad Museum of L.I. 477-0439, Sat, Sun & Hols $3/1.50)*, Cultural Attract *(Carousel 10am-10pm, $1)*, Special Events

(Maritime Festival - last weekend in Sep), Galleries **Under 1 mi:** Fishing Charter *(AP White 477-0008)* **1-3 mi:** Tennis Courts, Golf Course *(Islands End G.C. 477-0777)*, Horseback Riding *(Stable Hands 765-5201)*

Provisioning and General Services
Near: Supermarket *(IGA 477-0101)*, Gourmet Shop *(Aldos 477-1699)*, Delicatessen *(Harbourfront 477-3080)*, Health Food, Liquor Store *(Claudio's 477-1035)*, Bakery, Farmers' Market *(Adams St. Thu 3-8pm, Sat 8am-1pm)*, Green Grocer, Bank/ATM, Post Office, Beauty Salon, Barber Shop, Laundry, Bookstore *(Burton's 477-1161, Book Scout 477-8536)*, Pharmacy *(Colonial 477-1111)*, Newsstand, Hardware Store *(White 477-0317)*, Florist, Retail Shops, Department Store *(Arcade 477-1440)*, Copies Etc. *(North Fork Press 477-1250)* **Under 1 mi:** Convenience Store, Fishmonger *(Alice's Fish Mkt. 477-8485)*, Lobster Pound, Catholic Church, Protestant Church *(Epis/Method/Bapt)*, Synagogue, Library *(Floyd 477-0660)*, Dry Cleaners

Transportation
OnCall: Rental Car *(Enterprise 765-6600)*, Taxi *(Maria's 477-0700)*, Airport Limo *(Fleetwood East 477-0078)* **Near:** Bikes *(Bike Stop 477-2432)*, Local Bus *(SuffolkTransit 852-5200)*, InterCity Bus *(Sunshine - 477-1200 to NYC $16/1way)*, Rail *(LIRR to NYC 477-5477)*, Ferry Service *(Shelter Island North Ferry)* **Airport:** Islip 467-3210 *(60 mi.)*

Medical Services
911 Service **OnCall:** Ambulance **Under 1 mi:** Doctor, Dentist *(Lamia 477-0123)*, Holistic Services **3+ mi:** Chiropractor *(Southold Chiropractic 765-1191 , 4 mi.)*, Veterinarian *(North Fork Animal Hospital 765-2400, 4 mi.)*
Hospital: Eastern LI 477-1000 *(1 mi.)*

Setting -- Head for the controversial giant wire heron sculpture at the end of Greenport Yacht & Ship's dock. A little west, a slightly sagging roof, emblazoned with "S.T. Preston & Son", stands as an enduring testament to Greenport's maritime history. For over a century, Preston's docks and chandlery were a lynchpin of a bustling, working waterfront. Today, two old, but well-kept, finger piers offer basic alongside tie-ups right in the middle of a now revitalized tourist town.

Marina Notes -- Overnight fees are a remarkable $0.75 per foot for basic, do-it-yourself dockage. Electric and water but no heads or showers. Free dinghy dock. Afternoon dockage is free if you spend $10 at Preston's. Exposed to the south. Established in 1880, at the tail end of the whaling industry, Preston's is likely the oldest, best equipped chandlery on the East End (Nautical Miles 10% off). When whaling died, Preston's moved on to outfitting local fishing fleets and then pleasure boats. The staff is consistently helpful and cordial. Mary E, a refurbished schooner, and the Glory, an electric tour boat, call Preston's home.

Notable -- Today Greenport is shifting to an up-scale summer tourist town, with plenty of restaurants, shops, services, and things to do. The nearby East End Seaport Museum has exhibits on the fishing and oyster industries and the area's maritime heritage; from the 1800's to 1940's Greenport built over 550 ships. Check out the Blacksmith Shop and Railroad Museum of L.I. as well. The 40 foot Greenport Carousel, an authentic 1920's merry-go-round with brass ring, was moved to Harborfront/Mitchell Park in 1995 and housed in a striking, contemporary glass enclosure. Coming soon is an extensive network of 65 floating slips, enclosed within the arms of the current 600-foot stationary piers, new boater heads & showers, a playground, picnic area and a mist field.

Navigational Information

Lat: 41°06.095' **Long:** 072°21.552' **Tide:** 4 ft. **Current:** 3 kt. **Chart:** 12358
Rep. Depths *(MLW):* **Entry** 40 ft. **Fuel Dock** 25 ft. **Max Slip/Moor** 17 ft./-
Access: West of ferry crossing on Greenport's harborfront

Marina Facilities *(In Season/Off Season)*

Fuel: Gasoline, Diesel, High-Speed Pumps
Slips: 30 Total, 30 Transient **Max LOA:** 175 ft. **Max Beam:** 30 ft.
  Rate *(per ft.):* **Day** $2.50/$1.50 **Week** Inq. **Month** Inq.
  Power: 30 amp Incl., 50 amp Incl., 100 amp Incl., 200 amp n/a
  Cable TV: No **Dockside Phone:** No
  Dock Type: Fixed, Alongside, Wood, Composition
Moorings: 0 Total, 0 Transient **Launch:** n/a, Dinghy Dock
  Rate: Day n/a **Week** n/a **Month** n/a
Heads: 2 Toilet(s), 2 Shower(s)
Laundry: None **Pay Phones:** No
Pump-Out: OnSite **Fee:** $5 **Closed Heads:** Yes

Marina Operations

Owner/Manager: Jerry Tuthill **Dockmaster:** Lloyd Miller
In-Season: Apr-Oct, 7am-7pm **Off-Season:** Nov-Mar, closed
After-Hours Arrival: Call ahead to arrange
Reservations: Preferred **Credit Cards:** Visa/MC, Amex
Discounts: None
Pets: Welcome **Handicap Access:** Yes, Heads, Docks

Claudio's Marina

111 Main Street; Greenport, NY 11944

Tel: (631) 477-0355 **VHF: Monitor** 9 **Talk** 72
Fax: (631) 477-2948 **Alternate Tel:** (631) 477-0715
Email: marina@claudios.com **Web:** www.claudios.com
Nearest Town: Greenport *(0 mi.)* **Tourist Info:** (631) 765-3161

Marina Services and Boat Supplies

Services - Docking Assistance, Security, Trash Pick-Up, Dock Carts, Megayacht Facilities **Communication -** FedEx, AirBorne, UPS, Express Mail **Supplies - OnSite:** Ice *(Cube)*, Ships' Store, Bait/Tackle, Live Bait **Near:** Ice *(Block, Shaved)* **1-3 mi:** CNG *(Brewer Yacht Yard)* **3+ mi:** Propane *(Van Duzer 765-3882, 5 mi.)*

Boatyard Services

OnCall: Rigger, Divers **Near:** Travelift, Railway, Engine mechanic *(gas, diesel)*, Electrical Repairs, Electronic Sales, Electronics Repairs, Hull Repairs, Bottom Cleaning, Air Conditioning, Woodworking, Painting, Awlgrip. **Nearest Yard:** Brewer Stirling Harbor (631) 477-0828

Restaurants and Accommodations

OnSite: Restaurant *(Claudio's 477-0627, L $8-14, D $17-26, Kid's $8)*, *(Claudio's Clam Bar 477-1889, L $5-12, D $5-12, Kid's $5)*, *(Crabby Jerry's 477-8252, L&D $5-16, Kid's $5-6)* **Near:** Restaurant *(Rhumb Line 477-9883)*, *(Hans Wursthaus 477-3430)*, Lite Fare *(Coronet Lunchonette 477-9834)*, Inn/B&B *(Stirliing House 477-0654, $125-200)*, *(Victorian Lady 477-1837, $160-190)* **Under 1 mi:** Pizzeria *(G&S 477-2300)*, Inn/B&B *(Greenporter 477-0066, $90-150)*, *(Morning Glory 477-3995, $175-225)*, *(Bartlett House 477-0371, $110-215)*, *(Townsend Manor 477-2000, $60-175)*

Recreation and Entertainment

Near: Beach *(Norman E. Kilp Marine park)*, Picnic Area, Roller Blade/Bike Paths, Fishing Charter *(AP White 477-0008)*, Group Fishing Boat, Video Rental *(Desiderio Video 477-8120)*, Park, Museum *(East End Maritime Museum 477-2100 Wed-Sun, 11-5, Free; Blacksmith Shop Sat & Sun,* 11-5, Free; Railroad Museum of LI 477-0439 $3/1.5)*, Special Events, Galleries **Under 1 mi:** Sightseeing *(Mary E Schooner Cruises 477-8966)* **1-3 mi:** Golf Course *(Islands End 477-0777)*

Provisioning and General Services

Near: Provisioning Service, Convenience Store, Supermarket *(IGA 477-0101)*, Gourmet Shop *(Aldos 477-1699)*, Delicatessen *(Harbourfront Deli 477-3080)*, Health Food, Wine/Beer, Liquor Store *(Claudios Wines & Liquors 477-1035)*, Bakery, Farmers' Market *(Adams St. Thu 3-8pm, Sat 8am-1pm)*, Bank/ATM, Post Office, Catholic Church, Protestant Church *(Greek, Methodist, Baptist, Lutheran)*, Synagogue, Library *(Floyd Mem 477-0660)*, Beauty Salon, Barber Shop, Dry Cleaners, Laundry, Bookstore *(Burton's 477-1161, Book Scout 477-8536)*, Pharmacy *(Colonial 477-1111)*, Newsstand, Hardware Store *(White 477-0317)*, Florist, Clothing Store, Retail Shops, Department Store *(Arcade 477-1440)*, Copies Etc. *(North Fork Press 477-1250)* **Under 1 mi:** Fishmonger *(Alice's Fish Mkt. 477-8485)*

Transportation

OnCall: Rental Car *(Enterprise 765-6600)*, Taxi *(Maria's 477-0700)*, Airport Limo *(Fleetwood East 477-0078)* **Near:** Bikes *(Bike Stop 477-2432)*, Local Bus *(SCT)*, InterCity Bus *(Sunshine - 477-1200 to NYC $16/1way)*, Ferry Service *(Shelter Island North)* **1-3 mi:** Rail *(LIRR to NYC 477-5477 $10-15/1way)* **Airport:** Islip 467-3210 *(60 mi.)*

Medical Services

911 Service **OnCall:** Ambulance **Near:** Doctor, Dentist *(Lamia 477-0123)* **3+ mi:** Chiropractor *(Southold Chiro 765-1191, 4 mi.)*, Veterinarian *(North Fork 765-2400, 4 mi.)* **Hospital:** Eastern LI 477-1000 *(1 mi.)*

Setting -- Claudio's and the Greenport waterfront are practically synonymous. A deep basin, created by two wide, drive-on wharfs - each with a signature blue and white striped awning and one of the bustling Claudio's eateries at its end - delivers relatively protected alongside dockage. Additional tie-ups are on the outside of those piers. The mostly transient yachts are tourist attractions and part of the scenery. The prevailing atmosphere is busy, historic, and fun.

Marina Notes -- Founded in 1870, Claudio's is the oldest continuously owned family restaurant in the U.S. A Nat'l. Historic Registered 1845 building houses the main restaurant which sports a 10-foot high Victorian bar, stained and etched glass, carved ornaments rescued from a Manhattan hotel, and, reportedly, a secret trap door from its "rum running" days. All three restaurants and wharf bar specialize in fresh seafood; its Little Wheel Gift Shop in nautical items. The docks are old but beefy and solid -- a bit open to the southwest. Easy access fuel dock. Free afternoon tie-up if you eat at Claudio's, but no discount for overnight. Reasonable heads and showers next to ice cream shoppe. Note: the most western dock on Preston's side of the main wharf is also Claudio's.

Notable -- The Claudio complex puts boaters in the middle of Greenport's summer action with easy access to the more than 80 shops, dozen restaurants and maritime attractions in the vibrant business district. The carousel, taverns, galleries, provisioning resources, boutiques, antique shops, Arcade department store, East End Seaport Museum, Railroad Museum, festivals throughout the season, replica ships, tall ships and more, are all nearby. Gentrified Greenport was a seaport and ship building center for more than three centuries - after whaling came Menhaden fishing, then oystering, and, for about a decade, rum running.

Greenport Moorings & Dock

Mitchell Park/Front St. & Stirling Basin; Greenport, NY 11944

Tel: (631) 702-4381 **VHF:** Monitor 9 **Talk** 72
Fax: (631) 477-1877 **Alternate Tel:** (631) 477-1217
Email: n/a **Web:** n/a
Nearest Town: Greenport *(0 mi.)* **Tourist Info:** (631) 765-3161

Navigational Information

Lat: 41°06.076' **Long:** 072°21.658' **Tide:** 4 ft. **Current:** n/a **Chart:** 12358
Rep. Depths *(MLW)*: **Entry** 35 ft. **Fuel Dock** n/a **Max Slip/Moor** 35 ft./13 ft.
Access: Docks: harbor west of Claudios; Moorings: basin across from Brewer

Marina Facilities *(In Season/Off Season)*

Fuel: No
Slips: 15 Total, 10 Transient **Max LOA:** 150 ft. **Max Beam:** n/a
Rate *(per ft.)*: **Day** $25.00* **Week** n/a **Month** n/a
Power: 30 amp n/a, 50 amp n/a, 100 amp n/a, 200 amp n/a
Cable TV: No **Dockside Phone:** No
Dock Type: Fixed, Alongside, Wood
Moorings: 8 Total, 8 Transient **Launch:** n/a, Dinghy Dock
Rate: Day $25 **Week** n/a **Month** n/a
Heads: None
Laundry: None **Pay Phones:** No
Pump-Out: OnCall, Full Service **Fee:** Free **Closed Heads:** Yes

Marina Operations

Owner/Manager: Joe Angevine (Harbormaster) **Dockmaster:** n/a
In-Season: Year-Round, 8am-4pm **Off-Season:** n/a
After-Hours Arrival: n/a
Reservations: Hail the Harbormaster and inquire **Credit Cards:** Cash only
Discounts: None
Pets: Welcome **Handicap Access:** No

Marina Services and Boat Supplies

Communication - Data Ports *(Library)* **Supplies - Near:** Ice *(Block)*, Ships' Store *(East End Marine 477-1900; Preston's)*, Bait/Tackle *(AP White 477-0008)* **Under 1 mi:** CNG *(Brewer YY)*

Boatyard Services

Near: Travelift, Engine mechanic *(gas, diesel)*, Electrical Repairs, Electronics Repairs. **Nearest Yard:** Brewer Yacht Yard (631) 477-9594

Restaurants and Accommodations

Near: Restaurant *(La Cuvee 477-0066, French bistro & wine bar)*, *(Bay & Main Restaurant 477-1442)*, *(The Green Porter 477-8284)*, *(Chowder Pot Pub 477-1345)*, *(Katsura Sushi 477-1593)*, Lite Fare *(Sterlington Deli 477-8547)*, Pizzeria *(La Capricciosa 477-1625)*, Hotel *(Harborfront Inn)*, Inn/B&B *(thre Greenporter)*, *(Bartlett House 477-0371, $110-215)* **Under 1 mi:** Motel *(Silver Sands 477-0011)*, Inn/B&B *(Stirling House B&B 477-0654)*

Recreation and Entertainment

OnSite: Group Fishing Boat *(Island Star)*, Park, Cultural Attract *(1920 Grumman Carousel 447-3000 - 10am-10pm, $1 - an international design competition spawned the elegrant new glass domed pavilion; Ternhaven Cellars tasting room 477-8737)*, Special Events *(Last wknd Sept - Harbor Fest)* **Near:** Beach, Playground, Jogging Paths, Roller Blade/Bike Paths *(skate park)*, Movie Theater *(Greenport 477-8600 - 4 screens)*, Museum *(East End Maritime 477-2100, Railroad Museum of LI 477-0439)*, Sightseeing *(Mary E. Schooner Cruises 477-8966; Sea Island Seaplane Tours 477-3730 - 20 min. narrated excursions over the North Fork $36/21; Safari, 22-passenger tour boat)*, Galleries *(Island Artists 477-3070)*

Under 1 mi: Video Rental *(Desiderio Video 477-8120)* **1-3 mi:** Dive Shop *(Sound View 765-9515)*, Tennis Courts, Golf Course *(Island's End Golf and Country Club 477-0777 $34-40)* **3+ mi:** Horseback Riding *(Hidden Lake Farm 765-9896 , 5 mi.)*

Provisioning and General Services

Near: Gourmet Shop *(Aldos 477-1699)*, Delicatessen *(Harbourfront Deli 477-3080)*, Liquor Store *(JB Liquor 477-0024)*, Farmers' Market *(Adams St. Thu 3-8pm, Sat 8am-1pm)*, Bank/ATM, Post Office, Catholic Church, Protestant Church, Library *(Floyd Memorial 477-0660)*, Beauty Salon, Dry Cleaners, Laundry, Bookstore *(Book Scout 477-8536, Burton's 477-1161)*, Pharmacy *(Colonial Drugs 477-1111)*, Newsstand, Hardware Store *(White 477-0317)*, Retail Shops *(Front & Main are the major shopping streets chock a block with interesting shops)*, Department Store *(Arcade 477-1440)*, Copies Etc. *(North Fork Press 477-1250)* **Under 1 mi:** Supermarket *(IGA 477-0101)*, Fishmonger *(Alice's Fish Mkt. 477-8485)*

Transportation

OnSite: Water Taxi *(Safari)* **OnCall:** Rental Car *(Enterprise 765-6600, or Greenport Auto Rentals 477-9602 - nearby)*, Taxi *(Maria's Taxi 477-0700)*, Airport Limo *(Fleetwood East 477-0078)* **Near:** Bikes *(Bike Stop 477-2432)*, Local Bus *(SCT - Riverhead -Orient)*, InterCity Bus *(Sunshine - 477-1200 to NYC $16/1way)* **Airport:** Islip Macarthur 467-3210 *(60 mi.)*

Medical Services

911 Service **Near:** Dentist *(Lamia 477-0123)* **Under 1 mi:** Doctor **3+ mi:** Chiropractor *(Southold Chiro 765-1191 , 4 mi.)*, Veterinarian *(North Fork 765-2400, 4 mi.)* **Hospital:** Eastern LI 477-1000 *(0.5 mi.)*

Setting -- Greenport Village offers three municipal options: In almost land-locked Stirling Basin are very protected town moorings and a public dinghy dock. On Greenport Harbor, between Claudio's and the Shelter Island ferry terminal, is the "in-development" Mitchell ParkTown Dock at Harbourfront Park. West of the railroad station is the small-boat day-use only Greenport Visitor's Dock. A new Harbourfront Boardwalk connects the docks, museums, and the park.

Marina Notes -- In Stirling Creek are 8 transient moorings (lobster pot-style floats & yellow buoys) marked "T1-T8". Outside the Creek, near the breakwater, are 5 more (white balls with blue stripes). Two public dinghy docks are on the western shore, just inside the breakwater, next to the Sharkey's sign. It's a short walk into town. Greenport harbor is home to an exciting and extensive redevelopment - stage one moved the carousel to its spectacular new home. Next, two stationary 600 foot piers - one straight to 35 ft. depths, the other "L" shaped -- provide immediate alongside dockage for tall ships and transient pleasure boats (no services, $25 overnight flat rate, $10 daytime only). In '05, it is anticipated that those two arms will shelter 62 floating docks, with full services, to host a mix of transient pleasure craft, tall ships, excursion boats, party & charter fishing boats, water taxis and ferries. Upland, surrounding the carousel, will be a large park with picnic areas, a bathhouse (heads, showers laundry), visitors' center, "Mist Field" (ice skating in winter), an amphitheater, and a Camera Obscura.

Notable -- Homey, sleepy Greenport is blossoming into a major tourist magnet. One of the delights are its contradictions: classic, '50s Coronet Luncheonette and sailors' hangout Rhumbline rub shoulders with trendy eateries like Bruce's Café, upscale Ile de Beaute and enchantingly unique Greenport Tea.

Navigational Information
Lat: 41°04.848' **Long:** 072°17.874' **Tide:** 3 ft. **Current:** 0 **Chart:** 12358
Rep. Depths *(MLW):* **Entry** 8 ft. **Fuel Dock** n/a **Max Slip/Moor** 10 ft./-
Access: Gardiner's Bay to Coecles Harbor off Ram Island

Marina Facilities *(In Season/Off Season)*
Fuel: No
Slips: 0 Total, 0 Transient **Max LOA:** n/a **Max Beam:** n/a
  Rate *(per ft.):* **Day** n/a **Week** n/a **Month** n/a
  Power: 30 amp n/a, **50 amp** n/a, **100 amp** n/a, **200 amp** n/a
Cable TV: No **Dockside Phone:** No
Dock Type: Floating
Moorings: 9 Total, 9 Transient **Launch:** None, Dinghy Dock
  Rate: Day Free* **Week** n/a **Month** n/a
Heads: None
Laundry: None **Pay Phones:** No
Pump-Out: OnCall **Fee:** Free **Closed Heads:** Yes

Marina Operations
Owner/Manager: James Eklund **Dockmaster:** Linda Eklund
In-Season: Jun15-Sep15, 8am-10pm **Off-Season:** May-Jun14, Sep16-Oct*
After-Hours Arrival: Call in advance
Reservations: First come, first served **Credit Cards:** Visa/MC, Amex
Discounts: None
Pets: Welcome, Dog Walk Area **Handicap Access:** No

Ram's Head Inn

PO Box 638; 108 Ram Island Drive; Shelter Island, NY 11965

Tel: (631) 749-0811 **VHF: Monitor** n/a **Talk** n/a
Fax: (631) 749-0059 **Alternate Tel:** (631) 749-1134
Email: info@shelterislandinns.com **Web:** www.shelterislandinns.com
Nearest Town: Shelter Island *(3 mi.)* **Tourist Info:** (631) 749-0399

Marina Services and Boat Supplies
Services - Concierge **Communication -** Mail & Package Hold, Phone
Messages, Fax in/out, FedEx, AirBorne, UPS, Express Mail *(Sat Del)*
Supplies - Under 1 mi: CNG *(Coecles Harbor by dinghy)* **1-3 mi:** Ice
(Block, Cube, Shaved), Ships' Store *(Coecles Harbor Marina 749-0700)*,
Bait/Tackle *(Jack's Marine)*, Live Bait, Propane *(Piccozzi's 749-0045)*

Boatyard Services
OnCall: Divers **Under 1 mi:** Engine mechanic *(gas, diesel)*, Electronics
Repairs, Hull Repairs, Rigger, Bottom Cleaning, Brightwork, Refrigeration,
Propeller Repairs, Painting. **Nearest Yard:** Coecles Harbor *(631) 749-
0700*

Restaurants and Accommodations
OnSite: Restaurant *(Rams Head 749-0811, L $14-20, D $28-40)*, Inn/B&B
(Ram's Head $65-275) **1-3 mi:** Restaurant *(Lucida Roadhouse 749-1900)*,
(Pat & Steve's Family Rest. 749-1998), *(Chequit Inn 749-0018)*, *(John's Grill
749-0234)*, Seafood Shack *(Bob's Fishmarket 749-0830, dine in or take out)*,
Pizzeria *(Primo Pizza 749-2732)*, Inn/B&B *(Candlelite Inn 749-0676)*,
(Captain Bennet 749-0460), Condo/Cottage *(Dering Harbor Inn 749-0900)*

Recreation and Entertainment
OnSite: Beach, Playground, Volleyball, Tennis Courts, Fitness Center, Boat
Rentals *(also Island Kayak Tours across the Harbor 749-1990)* **Near:**
Jogging Paths **Under 1 mi:** Golf Course *(S.I. Country Club 749-0416)*,
Horseback Riding *(Paard Hill Farms 749-9462; Hampshire Farms 749-0156)*,
Video Rental *(Geojo Video 749-2324)*

1-3 mi: Picnic Area, Grills, Fishing Charter *(Light Tackle Challenge 749-
1906)*, Park, Museum *(Havens House & Manhanset Chappel Museum 749-
0025)*, Sightseeing *(Mashomack Nature Preserve 749-1001)*

Provisioning and General Services
1-3 mi: Convenience Store, Supermarket *(George's IGA 749-0382)*,
Gourmet Shop, Delicatessen *(Dockside Deli 749-3366)*, Health Food *(Planet
Bliss 749-0053)*, Wine/Beer, Liquor Store *(Dandy Liquors 749-3302)*, Bakery
(S.I. Bake Shop 749-2717), Fishmonger, Meat Market, Bank/ATM, Post
Office, Catholic Church, Library *(Shelter Island 749-0042)*, Beauty Salon, Dry
Cleaners, Laundry, Bookstore *(Books & Video 749-8925)*, Pharmacy *(Shelter
Island Heights 749-0445)*, Newsstand, Hardware Store *(Jack's True Value
749-0114)*, Department Store *(Bliss 749-0041)*, Copies Etc. *(Exec. Option
749-3101)*

Transportation
OnSite: Courtesy Car/Van **OnCall:** Taxi *($10-12 to town, Gofors Taxi 749-
4252; Flying Cow 749-3421 $10-12 to town)* **1-3 mi:** Bikes *(Piccozzi's)*
3+ mi: Rental Car *(Enterprise Southhold 765-6600, 5 mi.)*, Ferry Service
(No. Ferry to Greenport, 5 mi.), Airport Limo *(Fleetwood, Greenport
477-0078, 5 mi.)* **Airport:** Islip/East Hampton *(60 mi./10 mi.)*

Medical Services
911 Service **OnCall:** Ambulance **1-3 mi:** Doctor *(Kelt 749-3149)*, Dentist
(Moran 749-0539), Veterinarian *(North Fork 749-2506)*
Hospital: Eastern Long Island Greenport 477-1000 *(5 mi.)*

Setting -- Overlooking beautiful Coecles Harbor, five acres of sweeping, manicured lawn, furnished with gazebos, hammocks and lawn chairs, tumbles to the waterfront. The exquisite 1929 Inn, a gracious center-hall colonial, sits on a bluff at the top of a rise. Seventeen individually decorated, gracious rooms share the space with one of the East End's best restaurant - choose inside, patio or porch dining. Clearly this is a destination in itself.

Marina Notes -- *Moorings are complimentary for dinner or Inn guests. They are clearly marked with "R.H.I." The lat/long coordinates are for the dinghy dock, on the left side of the cove as you face the Inn (easily identified by the gazebo); it has a Ram's Head Inn sign. (The dock to the right is private.) Owned and operated by the Eklund Family since 1979, the facility has always been an Inn. The Eklund's also own the Chequit Inn in Shelter Island Heights. **Off-season open weekends only: 8am-10pm Fri-Sun. Closed November 16 - Apr 30. All of the Inn's facilities, including the small exercise room and sauna, are available to mooring guests, and most needed services are available within three miles. Popular site for weddings on summer weekends.

Notable -- The resort's 800 feet of beach, tennis court, two Sunfish sailboats, a paddle boat, a kayak, invitingly sited lawn chairs, hammocks and gazebo, or games on the broad wicker furnished porch -- all help fill the time between Chef Alan Batson's delightfully inventive meals. It's a short dinghy ride across the harbor to the Burns Road landing. This is the beginning of the 12-station Coecles Harbor Marine Water Trail (maps available onsite). Rent kayaks right there from Island Kayak, bring your own, or take the dink. It's a wonderful naturalists' introduction to the ecology of Shelter Island.

Coecles Harbor Marina

Coecles Harbor Marina

PO Box 1670; Hudson Avenue; Shelter Island, NY 11964

Tel: (631) 749-0700 **VHF: Monitor** 9 **Talk** 68
Fax: (631) 749-0593 **Alternate Tel:** n/a
Email: coecles@optonline.net **Web:** www.chmb.net
Nearest Town: Shelter Island *(0.5 mi.)* **Tourist Info:** (631) 749-0399

Navigational Information
Lat: 41°04.700' **Long:** 072°19.265' **Tide:** 3 ft. **Current:** n/a **Chart:** 12358
Rep. Depths (MLW): Entry 7 ft. **Fuel Dock** 7 ft. **Max Slip/Moor** 7 ft./-
Access: Gardiner's Bay to Coecles Harbor past Little Ram Is to west shore

Marina Facilities *(In Season/Off Season)*
Fuel: Gasoline, Diesel
Slips: 60 Total, 19 Transient **Max LOA:** 60 ft. **Max Beam:** n/a
  Rate (per ft.): Day $3.00/1.50* **Week** Inq. **Month** Inq.
  Power: 30 amp Inq., **50 amp** $10, **100 amp** n/a, **200 amp** n/a
  Cable TV: No **Dockside Phone:** No
  Dock Type: Fixed, Floating, Pilings, Wood
Moorings: 50 Total, 10 Transient **Launch:** None, Dinghy Dock
  Rate: Day $35-40/25 **Week** Inq. **Month** Inq.
Heads: 6 Toilet(s), 4 Shower(s)
Laundry: 4 Washer(s), 4 Dryer(s) **Pay Phones:** Yes, 1
Pump-Out: OnSite **Fee:** $5 **Closed Heads:** Yes

Marina Operations
Owner/Manager: John Needham **Dockmaster:** Same
In-Season: Year-Round, 8am-5pm **Off-Season:** n/a
After-Hours Arrival: Call in advance
Reservations: Yes **Credit Cards:** Visa/MC
Discounts: None
Pets: Welcome, Dog Walk Area **Handicap Access:** No

Marina Services and Boat Supplies
Services - Docking Assistance, Concierge, Dock Carts **Communication -** Mail & Package Hold, Phone Messages, Fax in/out, Data Ports *(at S.I. Library)*, FedEx, AirBorne, UPS, Express Mail **Supplies - OnSite:** Ice *(Block, Cube)*, Ships' Store, CNG **1-3 mi:** Bait/Tackle *(Jack's 749-0114; Donna's 749-3500)*, Propane *(Piccozzi's 749-0045)*

Boatyard Services
OnSite: Travelift *(30T)*, Engine mechanic *(gas, diesel)*, Launching Ramp, Electrical Repairs, Electronic Sales, Electronics Repairs, Hull Repairs, Rigger, Bottom Cleaning, Brightwork, Air Conditioning, Refrigeration, Compound, Wash & Wax, Woodworking, Painting, Awlgrip, Yacht Broker, Yacht Building, Total Refits **Member:** ABBRA, ABYC

Restaurants and Accommodations
Under 1 mi: Restaurant *(Ram's Head Inn 749-0811, Dinghy across the harbor to their dock)*, Inn/B&B *(Ram's Head Inn)*, *(Candle Lite Inn 749-0676)* **1-3 mi:** Restaurant *(Pat & Steve's Family Rest. 749-1998)*, *(Old Country Inn 749-1633)*, *(Michael Anthony's 749-3460)*, *(Two Eds 749-0261, dingy to Congdon Rd. town landing - 0.6 mi. walk)*, *(Captain Cody's Fish 749-1851)*, *(Sunset Beach 749-1843)*, *(Chequit Inn 749-0018)*, Pizzeria *(Primo 749-2732)*, Inn/B&B *(Azalea House 749-4252)*

Recreation and Entertainment
OnSite: Pool, Picnic Area, Grills, Boat Rentals *(Sailboat rentals; nearby Island Kayak Tours 749-1990)* **Near:** Beach, Park, Museum *(Hist. Society's Havens House & Manhanset Chappel Museum 749-0025)*, Cultural Attract *(Perlman Music Program 749-0740)* **1-3 mi:** Tennis Courts *(S.I. Tennis Courts 749-8897)*, Golf Course *(S.I. Country Club 749-0416)*, Horseback Riding *(Paard Hill Farms 749-9462; Hampshire Farms 749-0156)*, Fishing Charter *(Light Tackle Challenge 749-1906)*, Video Rental *(Geojo Video 749-2324)*, Sightseeing *(Mashomack Nature Preserve 749-1001)*

Provisioning and General Services
Under 1 mi: Convenience Store **1-3 mi:** Supermarket *(George's IGA 749-0382)*, Gourmet Shop *(Island Food 749-3558)*, Delicatessen *(Fedi's 749-1177)*, Health Food *(Planet Bliss 749-0053)*, Liquor Store *(Shelter Island Wines & Spirits 749-0305)*, Bakery *(S.I. Bakery 749-2717)*, Fishmonger *(Commander Cody's Fish Shoppe 749-1851)*, Bank/ATM, Post Office, Catholic Church, Protestant Church, Library *(Shelter Island 749-0042)*, Dry Cleaners, Bookstore *(Books & Video 749-8925)*, Pharmacy *(S.I. Heights Pharmacy 749-0445)*, Hardware Store *(S.I.Hardware/Ace 749-0097)*, Department Store *(Bliss 749-0041)*, Copies Etc. *(Exec. Option 749-3101)*

Transportation
OnSite: Courtesy Car/Van *(only at scheduled times)*, Bikes **OnCall:** Rental Car *(Electric Cars on island; Enterprise Southold 765-6600 at ferry)*, Taxi *(GoFors 749-4252; Flying Cow 749-3421)* **1-3 mi:** Ferry Service *("South Ferry" to North Haven 749-1200, "North Ferry" to Greenport 749-0139)* **3+ mi:** Airport Limo *(Fleetwood, Greenport 477-0078 , 5 mi.)* **Airport:** Islip/EastHampton *(60 mi./10 mi.)*

Medical Services
911 Service **Under 1 mi:** Veterinarian *(North Fork 749-2506)* **1-3 mi:** Doctor *(Kelt 749-3149)*, Dentist *(Moran 749-0539)* **Hospital:** Eastern LI, Greenport 477-1000 *(5 mi.)*

Setting -- An unpretentious, relaxed, but carefully maintained marina and boat yard, Coecles Harbor delivers engaging views and rural solitude coupled with quiet, well-protected dockage and a full-service facility. All conveniently located between the Ram Island peninsula and S.I. proper on the northwest side of Coecles Inlet. A pool and picnic cabana (with tables and grills) overlook the docks and harbor. Coecles is one of the prettiest harbors on a very pretty island.

Marina Notes -- *Dockage: $25 min. - Fri, Sat & Holiday nightly rate $3/ft.; Sun-Thurs $2.50/ft. Moorings: Fri, Sat & Hols $40/day; Sun-Thurs $35/day. Owned and operated by the service-oriented Needham family since 1973 - 2nd generation now at the helm. Courtesy transportation to grocery store at 10 am and 4 pm, and to restaurants in evening. Excellent new heads, showers with dressing rooms, and laundry facilities. Builder of Billy Joel's Shelter Island Runabout. Boatbuilding division, CH Marine, is just up the road. A large classic sail contingent, and an equal number of powerboats, seem committed to the sheer of a "downeast" hull. Some wonderful classic wooden vessels live here, too. Ice cream and soda in the office, plus bike and sailboat rentals onsite.

Notable -- About three miles to ferry services to either Greenport & North Haven. Near are many historic spots including Manhanset Chapel Museum, Quaker burial grounds, and Havens House. A 0.3 mile dinghy ride to Burns Road landing is the beginning of the 12-station Coecles Harbor Marine Water Trail (maps onsite). Rent kayaks right there from Island Kayak, bring your own, or take the dink. A short bike ride is the Nature Conservancy's Mashomack Preserve, with miles of interconnected trails. Four marked hikes range from 1.5 to 11 miles. Visitor's Center has maps, programs & guided hikes, Wed-Mon 9am-5pm.

Navigational Information
Lat: 41°05.041' **Long:** 072°21.094' **Tide:** 3 ft. **Current:** 1 kt. **Chart:** 12358
Rep. Depths *(MLW):* **Entry** 12 ft. **Fuel Dock** 12 ft. **Max Slip/Moor** 12 ft./12 ft.
Access: Gardiner's Bay to Dering Harbor

Marina Facilities *(In Season/Off Season)*
Fuel: *Mobil* - Gasoline, Diesel
Slips: 35 Total, 15-20 Transient **Max LOA:** 150 ft. **Max Beam:** n/a
  Rate *(per ft.):* **Day** $2.75/$2.75* **Week** $12.50 **Month** $44
  Power: 30 amp $0.25/ft. for 2, **50 amp** $0.25/ft., **100 amp** n/a, **200 amp** n/a
Cable TV: No **Dockside Phone:** No
Dock Type: Fixed, Floating, Long Fingers, Pilings
Moorings: 14 Total, 14 Transient **Launch:** None, Dinghy Dock
  Rate: Day $1.25/ft. $45 min **Week** $8/ft.-$250 min **Month** $25/ft.-$900 min
Heads: 2 Toilet(s), 2 Shower(s)
Laundry: None **Pay Phones:** Yes, 1
Pump-Out: OnCall *(Ch.73)* **Fee:** Free **Closed Heads:** Yes

Marina Operations
Owner/Manager: Angelo Piccozzi **Dockmaster:** Carolyn Shils
In-Season: May 15-Oct 15, 7:30am-7:30pm **Off-Season:** Oct-May, 7:30-6:30
After-Hours Arrival: Check in at fuel dock or call ahead
Reservations: Yes **Credit Cards:** Visa/MC, Dscvr, Din, Amex, Price Club
Discounts: None
Pets: Welcome, Dog Walk Area **Handicap Access:** No

Piccozzi's Dering Harbor

PO Box 3034; Bridge Street; Shelter Island Heights, NY 11965

Tel: (631) 749-0045 **VHF: Monitor** 9 **Talk** 7
Fax: (631) 749-0411 **Alternate Tel:** n/a
Email: n/a **Web:** n/a
Nearest Town: Shelter Island Heights *(0 mi.)* **Tourist Info:** (631) 749-0399

Marina Services and Boat Supplies
Services - Docking Assistance, Trash Pick-Up, Dock Carts
Communication - Mail & Package Hold, Phone Messages, Fax in/out, Data Ports *(at S.I. Library)*, FedEx, AirBorne, UPS, Express Mail *(Sat Del)*
Supplies - OnSite: Ice *(Block, Cube)*, Propane **Near:** Ships' Store *(Jack's Marine 749-0114)*, Marine Discount Store, Bait/Tackle *(Jack's)*, Live Bait **1-3 mi:** CNG *(Coecles Harbor)*

Boatyard Services
OnCall: Engine mechanic *(gas, diesel)*, Electrical Repairs, Electronics Repairs, Rigger, Air Conditioning, Refrigeration, Divers, Compound, Wash & Wax, Interior Cleaning, Propeller Repairs, Woodworking, Inflatable Repairs
Nearest Yard: Brewer Greenport (631) 477-6594

Restaurants and Accommodations
Near: Restaurant *(Chequit 749-0018)*, *(Michael Anthonys 749-3460, superb)*, *(The Dory 749-8871, L $6, D $16)*, *(Sweet Tomatoes 749-4114)*, Lite Fare *(Stars 749-3484)*, Inn/B&B *(Chequit Inn)*, *(House on Chase Creek 749-3479)*, *(Belle Crest 749-2041)*, *(Avalon Manor 749-2502)*, *(Dering Harbor 749-0900)* **Under 1 mi:** Restaurant *(Old Country Inn 749-1633, Exquisite fine dining)*, *(Planet Bliss 749-0053, organic)*, Seafood Shack *(Bob's 749-0830)*, Lite Fare *(Tuck Shop 749-1548, Ice cream, game room)*

Recreation and Entertainment
OnSite: Picnic Area, Grills, Fishing Charter *(28 ft. Albin)* **Near:** Volleyball, Tennis Courts *(S.I. Tennis 749-8897; Whale's Tale - Mini Golf, game room 749-1839)*, Jogging Paths, Video Rental *(Books & Videos 749-8925; Triple A 749-3347)*, Sightseeing *(Mashomack Preserve 749-1001)*, Galleries

(Whales Folly 749-1110; Peggy Mach 749-0247; Fallen Angel 749-0243)
Under 1 mi: Beach *(Crescent)*, Playground, Golf Course *(S.I. C.C. 749-0416)*, Fitness Center, Boat Rentals *(Island Kayak 749-1990)*, Museum *(Havens House; Manhanset Chappel 749-0025)*

Provisioning and General Services
Near: Market *(Island Food Ctr. 749-3558)*, Gourmet Shop *(The Market 749-34845; Stars 749-3984)*, Delicatessen, Liquor Store *(Manikas)*, Bank/ATM, Post Office, Catholic Church, Protestant Church *(Union Chapel 749-1164)*, Beauty Salon, Dry Cleaners, Laundry, Bookstore *(Books & Video 749-8925)*, Pharmacy *(S.I. Heights 749-0445)*, Newsstand, Hardware Store *(Jack's 749-0224; S.I. Hardware/Ace 749-0097)*, Florist, Department Store *(Bliss 749-0041)* **Under 1 mi:** Supermarket *(George's IGA 749-0382)*, Health Food *(Planet Bliss 749-0053)*, Bakery *(S.I. Bake 749-2717)*, Fishmonger *(Bob's 749-0830)*, Library *(S.I. 749-0042)*, Copies Etc. *(Exec. Option 749-3101)*

Transportation
OnSite: Courtesy Car/Van, Bikes *($23/day 749-0045)* **OnCall:** Taxi *(Gofors 749-4252; Flying Cow 749-3421)* **Near:** Water Taxi *(477-2307 to Greenport)*, Ferry Service *(No. Ferry to Greenport 749-0139)* **1-3 mi:** Rental Car *(Enterprise Southhold 765-6600 - to ferry terminal)*, Rail *(Greenport LIRR to NYC)*, Airport Limo *(Fleetwood, Greenport 477-0078)* **Airport:** Islip/East Hampton *(60 mi./10 mi.)*

Medical Services
911 Service **OnCall:** Ambulance **Near:** Doctor, Chiropractor **Under 1 mi:** Dentist *(Moran 749-0539)*, Veterinarian *(North Fork Animal Hosp. 749-2506* **Hospital:** Eastern LI, Green ort 477-1000 *5 mi.*

Setting -- Piccozzi's ambiance is a functional mix of incongruous elements -- the spectacular views of a beautiful harbor filled with beautiful boats (with Greenport in the distance) counterpoints the industrial landside with its gravel parking lot and huge white fuel and gas storage tanks -- which, in turn, anchors the east end of Shelter Island's charming main drag - Bridge Street. Folded into this brew is a full-service marina with a personal touch.

Marina Notes -- *Minimum dockage fee is $85. Courtesy van to white-sand Crescent Beach and local restaurants. The helpful staff provides concierge service for restaurant and golf reservations or for organizing your Shelter Island visit. This is the major fuel depot for the Island -- if you need any type, it's here. Basic head/shower facilities are housed in a small separate building near the tanks. Old wood docks. Town Dock adjacent. Across the harbor, Shelter Island Yacht Club has transient moorings, launch service, and a newly renovated and enlarged dining room open to members of recognized clubs.

Notable -- Two hardware stores, art and antique galleries, a few restaurants, a couple of gourmet provisioning options, clothing shops and most needed services are right up the street. The Shelter Island Heights historic district begins on the far side of "town". About a half mile walk is the North Ferry to Greenport. 600 foot Crescent Beach, also known as Louis' Beach, is located on the northwest corner of Shelter Island about 1.5 mi. The island's most popular beach, it has a lifeguard and food concession, a fantastic view of Southold and Greenport, and great sunsets. It's also home to a famous July 4th celebration, several restaurants and hotels -- including the exquisite Pridwin, The Peconic Lodge, and the hot, celebrity studded Sunset Beach Bar & Restaurant.

Jack's Marine at True Value Hardware

Jack's Marine at True Value

188 N. Ferry Road; Shelter Island Heights, NY 11965

Tel: (631) 749-0114 **VHF:** Monitor 9 **Talk** 10
Fax: (631) 749-3191 **Alternate Tel:** (631) 749-0114
Email: n/a **Web:** n/a
Nearest Town: Shelter Island *(0 mi.)* **Tourist Info:** (631) 749-0399

Navigational Information
Lat: 41°05.052' **Long:** 072°21.118' **Tide:** 3 ft. **Current:** 1 kt. **Chart:** 12358
Rep. Depths (MLW): Entry 12 ft. **Fuel Dock** 10 ft. **Max Slip/Moor** -/16 ft.
Access: Gardiners Bay to Dering Harbor

Marina Facilities *(In Season/Off Season)*
Fuel: No
Slips: 0 Total, 0 Transient **Max LOA:** 60 ft. **Max Beam:** n/a
Rate *(per ft.):* **Day** n/a **Week** n/a **Month** n/a
Power: 30 amp n/a, **50 amp** n/a, **100 amp** n/a, **200 amp** n/a
Cable TV: No **Dockside Phone:** No
Dock Type: Floating, Wood, Vinyl
Moorings: 40 Total, 10 Transient **Launch:** n/a, Dinghy Dock
Rate: Day $40/$30 **Week** $240/150 **Month** $720/430
Heads: 1 Toilet(s)
Laundry: None **Pay Phones:** Yes
Pump-Out: OnCall *(Ch. 73)* **Fee:** Free **Closed Heads:** Yes

Marina Operations
Owner/Manager: Michael P. Anglin **Dockmaster:** Same
In-Season: May 15-Oct 15, 8am-5pm **Off-Season:** n/a
After-Hours Arrival: Call for instructions
Reservations: Yes **Credit Cards:** Visa/MC, Dscvr, Amex
Discounts: None
Pets: Welcome, Dog Walk Area **Handicap Access:** No

Marina Services and Boat Supplies
Communication - Mail & Package Hold, Fax in/out, FedEx, AirBorne, UPS, Express Mail **Supplies - OnSite:** Ships' Store, Bait/Tackle **OnCall:** Ice *(Cube)*, Propane *(Piccozzi's)* **1-3 mi:** CNG *(Coecles Harbor 749-0700)*

Boatyard Services
OnCall: Divers, Interior Cleaning, Inflatable Repairs *(pick up service)*, Life Raft Service **1-3 mi:** Travelift, Engine mechanic *(gas)*, Launching Ramp, Hull Repairs, Bottom Cleaning, Brightwork, Air Conditioning, Refrigeration, Compound, Wash & Wax, Propeller Repairs, Woodworking, Metal Fabrication, Painting, Awlgrip, Yacht Design, Yacht Broker, Yacht Building, Total Refits. **Nearest Yard:** Brewer Yacht Yard Greenport (631) 477-9594

Restaurants and Accommodations
Near: Restaurant *(The Dory 749-8871, L $6-9, D $8-18)*, *(Michael Anthonys 749-3460)*, *(Chequit Inn & The Catchall 749-0018)*, *(Sweet Tomatoes 749-4114)*, Inn/B&B *(House on Chase Creek 749-3479)*, *(Chequit Inn 749-0018)*, *(Belle Crest Inn 749-2041)*, *(Dering Harbor Inn 749-0900)* **Under 1 mi:** Restaurant *(Pat & Steve's Family 749-1998)*, *(Old Country Inn 749-1633, reserve)*, Seafood Shack *(Bob's Fish 749-0830)* **1-3 mi:** Restaurant *(Sunset Beach 749-3000)*, Motel *(Sunset Beach 749-1843, Andre Balasz' high end boutique)*, Hotel *(Pridwin 749-0476, 50 rooms, 8 acres, Crescent Beach)*

Recreation and Entertainment
Near: Video Rental *(Books & Videos 749-8925; Triple A 749-3347)*, Galleries *(Island Gallery 749-0733; Whales Folly 749-1110)* **Under 1 mi:** Beach *(Cresecent)*, Tennis Courts *(S.I. Tennis Courts 749-8897)*, Golf Course *(S.I. Country Club 749-0416)*, Boat Rentals *(Island Kayak 749-1990)*

1-3 mi: Playground, Fitness Center, Horseback Riding *(Hampshire Farms 749-0156; Paard Hill Farms 749-9462)*, Fishing Charter *(Light Tackle 749-1906)*, Movie Theater *(Greenport Village Cinema 477-8600)*, Museum *(Havens House & Manhanset Chappel 749-0025)*, Cultural Attract *(Perlman Music Program 749-0740)*, Sightseeing *(Mashomack Preserve 749-1001)*

Provisioning and General Services
OnSite: Hardware Store **Near:** Market *(Island Food Ctr. 749-3558)*, Gourmet Shop *(The Market 749-3484; Virtual Chef catering 749-3577)*, Wine/Beer, Liquor Store, Bank/ATM, Post Office, Catholic Church, Protestant Church, Beauty Salon, Barber Shop, Laundry, Bookstore *(Books & Videos 749-8925)*, Pharmacy *(S.I. Heights 749-0445)*, Department Store *(Bliss 749-0041)* **Under 1 mi:** Bakery *(S.I. Bake 749-2717)*, Green Grocer, Fishmonger *(Bob's 749-0830)*, Lobster Pound, Library *(749-0042)*, Dry Cleaners, Copies Etc. *(Exec. Option 749-3101)* **1-3 mi:** Supermarket *(George's IGA 749-0382)*, Health Food *(Planet Bliss 749-0053)*

Transportation
OnCall: Taxi *(Gofors 749-4252; Flying Cow 749-3421)* **Near:** Bikes *(Piccozzi's)*, Water Taxi *(477-2307 to Greenport)*, Ferry Service *(No. Ferry 749-0139 $1)* **1-3 mi:** InterCity Bus, Rail *(Greenport to NYC)* **3+ mi:** Rental Car *(Enterprise Southhold 765-6600, 5 mi.)*, Airport Limo *(Fleetwood, Greenport 477-0078 , 5 mi)* **Airport:** Islip *(60 mi.)*

Medical Services
911 Service **OnCall:** Ambulance **Near:** Doctor, Dentist, Holistic Services
Under 1 mi: Veterinarian *(North Fork 749-2506)*
Hospital: Eastern Long Island, Greenport 477-1000 *(5 mi.)*

Setting -- Experience a little piece of small town New England in the midst of exclusive Shelter Island. Jack's dinghy dock is behind the hardware store and the mooring field is in the heart of lovely Dering Harbor. Views to the north are of Greenport Harbor, to the south of Shelter Island, and to the west of the Shelter Island Yacht Club. The picturesque harbor is home to an eclectic mix of beautiful yachts and classic working boats.

Marina Notes -- In the same family since the mid 1940s, Jack's Marine is part of the True Value Hardware Store and Bait & Tackle shop (if they don't have it, they'll get it!). Right on Bridge Street, the primary shopping block in "downtown" S.I. It's also a continuation of the island's main north-south Route 114 (Ferry Road) of Shelter Island. Open 7 days. Heads, no showers. The dinghy dock is located out back. Internet access is at the S.I. Library 1 mile inland.

Notable -- Many of Shelter Island's shops and restaurants are a very short walk. Bliss "Department" Store, clothing shops, laundry, ice cream, liquor, Island Food, and bike rentals are all within a block. Up the hill is the Shelter Island Heights historic district's wonderful 19th C "cottages" overlooking the harbor. Across the street, casual Dory restaurant, with indoor or patio dining overlooking Chase Creek, opens 7 days in season, lunch 12-5pm, dinner 5-10 pm. Charming, higher end Chequit Inn (same owners as the Ram's Head) offers indoor/outdoor dining for lunch and dinner and casual food in its lower level Catchall Bistro. Walk to the North Ferry for the quick shuttle over to downtown Greenport and movies, provisions, shops and restaurants, etc. A well-marked 25-mile double-loop bike path starts at either ferry landing. About 1.5 miles is the S.I. Whale's Tale (749-1839) ice cream, tennis court, game room, & 18 hole mini-golf.

Navigational Information
Lat: 41°03.182' **Long:** 072°20.673' **Tide:** 3 ft. **Current:** n/a **Chart:** 12358
Rep. Depths (*MLW*): **Entry** 6 ft. **Fuel Dock** n/a **Max Slip/Moor** 6 ft./-
Access: Gardiner's Bay to West Neck Harbor

Marina Facilities *(In Season/Off Season)*
Fuel: *Shell* - Gasoline, Diesel
Slips: 75 Total, 20 Transient **Max LOA:** 60 ft. **Max Beam:** n/a
 Rate *(per ft.)*: **Day** $3.00/$2.00* **Week** $15.75 **Month** Inq.
Power: 30 amp Incl., **50 amp** n/a, **100 amp** n/a, **200 amp** n/a
Cable TV: No **Dockside Phone:** No
Dock Type: Fixed, Floating, Long Fingers, Pilings
Moorings: 0 Total, 0 Transient **Launch:** n/a
 Rate: Day n/a **Week** n/a **Month** n/a
Heads: 8 Toilet(s), 5 Shower(s)
Laundry: 2 Washer(s), 2 Dryer(s) **Pay Phones:** Yes, 2
Pump-Out: OnSite **Fee:** $5 **Closed Heads:** Yes

Marina Operations
Owner/Manager: Don Cooks **Dockmaster:** same
In-Season: Jun-Sep 7, 8am-6pm **Off-Season:** Fall-Win-Sprg, 9am-5pm*
After-Hours Arrival: Call ahead
Reservations: Yes **Credit Cards:** Visa/MC
Discounts: None
Pets: Welcome, Dog Walk Area **Handicap Access:** No

The Island Boatyard & Marina

P.O.Box 938; 63 South Menantic Road; Shelter Island, NY 11964

Tel: (631) 749-3333 **VHF: Monitor** 9 **Talk** n/a
Fax: (631) 749-3361 **Alternate Tel:** n/a
Email: IBY938@aol.com **Web:** www.islandboatyard.com
Nearest Town: Shelter Island *(2 mi.)* **Tourist Info:** (631) 749-0399

Marina Services and Boat Supplies
Services - Docking Assistance, Dock Carts **Communication -** Mail &
Package Hold, Phone Messages, Fax in/out, FedEx, AirBorne, UPS, Express
Mail **Supplies - OnSite:** Ice *(Cube)* **1-3 mi:** Ships' Store *(Jack's Marine
749-0114)*, Bait/Tackle, Propane *(Piccozzi's 749-0045)*, CNG *(Coecles
Harbor Marina 749-0700)*

Boatyard Services
OnSite: Travelift *(25T)*, Engine mechanic *(gas, diesel)*, Electrical Repairs,
Electronic Sales, Hull Repairs, Bottom Cleaning, Brightwork, Compound,
Wash & Wax, Propeller Repairs, Yacht Broker **OnCall:** Electronics Repairs,
Rigger, Air Conditioning, Refrigeration, Divers, Woodworking, Inflatable
Repairs, Life Raft Service, Yacht Interiors, Metal Fabrication
Under 1 mi: Launching Ramp. **Yard Rates:** $75/hr., Haul & Launch $11/ft
(blocking incl.), Power Wash $3.50, Bottom Paint $13/ft. *(paint incl.)*

Restaurants and Accommodations
OnSite: Restaurant *(Alfred's Port Tavern L $6-13, D $13-19, Kids' $4-6)*
1-3 mi: Restaurant *(Planet Bliss 749-0053, organic)*, *(Pat & Steve's Family
Rest.)*, *(Lucida Roadhouse 749-1900)*, Seafood Shack *(Bob's Fish Market
749-0830)*, Hotel *(Pridwin Hotel 749-0476, on Crescent Beach)*, Inn/B&B
(Candlelite Inn 749-0676), *(Azalea House 749-4252)*, *(Olde Country Inn
491-1633)*

Recreation and Entertainment
OnSite: Pool, Picnic Area, Grills, Volleyball, Video Arcade *(Game Room)*
Near: Beach *(Wades & Shell)*, Playground, Jogging Paths **1-3 mi:** Tennis
Courts *(Shelter Island Tennis Courts 749-8897)*, Golf Course *(Shelter

Island C.C. 749 0416* , Horseback Riding *Paard Hill Farms 749-9462,
Boat Rentals (Island Kayak Tours 749-1990)*, Fishing Charter *(Light
Tackle Challenge 749-1906)*, Video Rental *(Geojo Video 749-2324)*,
Museum *(Havens House & Manhanset Chappel 749-0025)*, Cultural Attract
(Perlman Music Program 749-0740), Sightseeing *(Mashomack Nature
Preserve 749-1001)*

Provisioning and General Services
Under 1 mi: Market *(Westneck 749-2100)* **1-3 mi:** Convenience Store,
Supermarket *(George's IGA 749-0382)*, Health Food *(Planet Bliss 749-
0053)*, Wine/Beer, Liquor Store *(S.I. Wines & Spirits 749-0305)*, Bakery *(S.I.
Bakery 749-2717)*, Fishmonger *(Bob's 749-0830)*, Bank/ATM, Post Office,
Catholic Church, Library *(749-0042)*, Beauty Salon, Dry Cleaners, Bookstore,
Pharmacy *(S.I. Heights 749-0445)*, Newsstand, Hardware Store *(S.I. Hard-
ware/Ace 749-0097)*, Florist, Retail Shops, Department Store *(Bliss)*,
Copies Etc. *(Exec. Option 749-3101)*

Transportation
OnSite: Courtesy Car/Van *(Courtesy transportation to town and
restaurants)* **OnCall:** Taxi *(Gofors Taxi 749-4252)* **Near:** Bikes
1-3 mi: Ferry Service *(South Ferry to North Haven)* **3+ mi:** Rental Car
(Enterprise Southhold 765-6600, 5 mi. to ferry), Airport Limo *(Fleetwood,
Greenport 477-0078, 5 mi.)* **Airport:** East Hampton/Islip *(10 mi./60 mi.)*

Medical Services
911 Service **Near:** Ambulance **1-3 mi:** Doctor *(Kelt 749-3149)*,
Veterinarian *(North Fork Animal Hospital 749-2506)*
Hospital: Eastern Long Island, Greenport 477-1000 *(5 mi.)*

Setting -- Snuggled safely into rural West Neck Harbor (a large white contemporary house marks the entrance), comprehensive, well turned-out Island
Boatyard is a somewhat unexpected, pleasant surprise. Flowers punctuate every view. A boardwalk leads to a tree-shaded sitting area with views of the outer
harbor. Two basins house the docks - smaller boats on the inside, larger ones on the out. Add a pool, picnic area, restaurant, banquet hall, and boatyard to
create a delightful small "resort" surrounded by fields, flavored more with horse-ranch than with boatyard.

Marina Notes -- *Fri-Mon $3/ft.; Tue-Thu $2.50/ft. Built in 1990. Van transport to local shops. "The Outback" (behind the marina buildings) is the recreation
center with grills, picnic area and a swimming pool. The range of amenities defines "full-service" marina. Mostly stern-to dockage without finger piers. The staff
is helpful, friendly and laid back. The "Harbour Club," an onsite banquet facility, can accommodate 250 people. $3/trash bag. Dinghy dock affords all marina
amenities, for those anchoring out, for $25 per boat (two people). Take care at the harbor entrance - comfortable 6 feet but inquire first.

Notable -- The Shipwreck Bar, built from the hull of a 1920's oyster smack, occasionally features entertainment on weekends. Alfred's Port Tavern serves
lunch and dinner - inside or on the more casual patio. Two good sand beaches flank the harbor entrance: secluded, 600-foot Shell Beach overlooks West Neck
Harbor, Shelter Island Sound and the Peconics - it's usually uncrowded; across from Shell Beach, more popular 1500-foot Wades Beach is also located inside
West Neck Harbor and has heads and a lifeguard.

Navigational Information

Lat: 41°04.818' **Long:** 072°23.211' **Tide:** 3 ft. **Current:** n/a **Chart:** 12358
Rep. Depths (*MLW*): **Entry** 6 ft. **Fuel Dock** n/a **Max Slip/Moor** -/-
Access: Base of Conklins Pt. between Southold Bay & Pipes Cove

Marina Facilities (*In Season/Off Season*)

Fuel: No
Slips: 138 Total, 5 Transient **Max LOA:** 55 ft. **Max Beam:** n/a
  Rate (*per ft.*): **Day** $2.25 **Week** $2.00 **Month** $1.85
  Power: 30 amp Incl., **50 amp** N/C for transient, **100 amp** n/a, **200 amp** n/a
Cable TV: No **Dockside Phone:** No
  Dock Type: Floating, Long Fingers, Wood, Aluminum
Moorings: 0 Total, 0 Transient **Launch:** n/a
  Rate: Day n/a **Week** n/a **Month** n/a
Heads: 2 Toilet(s), 4 Shower(s) (*with dressing rooms*)
Laundry: 1 Washer(s), 1 Dryer(s), Book Exchange **Pay Phones:** No
Pump-Out: OnCall, Full Service, 2 Port **Fee:** $25 **Closed Heads:** Yes

Marina Operations

Owner/Manager: Bill Leverich **Dockmaster:** Diane Vail, Assistant
In-Season: Mar-Dec 1, 9am-4pm **Off-Season:** Dec 1-Mar 1, 9am-4pm
After-Hours Arrival: Tie up and secure until the morning
Reservations: Yes, Required **Credit Cards:** Visa/MC, Amex
Discounts: None
Pets: Welcome, Dog Walk Area **Handicap Access:** No

Brick Cove Marina

PO Box 455; Sage Boulevard; Southold, NY 11971

Tel: (631) 477-0830 **VHF: Monitor** 16 **Talk** 9
Fax: (631) 477-2996 **Alternate Tel:** n/a
Email: geninfo@brickcove.com **Web:** www.brickcove.com
Nearest Town: Greenport (*2 mi.*) **Tourist Info:** (631) 765-3161

Marina Services and Boat Supplies

Services - Security (*24 hrs., Owner lives on property*), Trash Pick-Up, Dock Carts **Communication -** Mail & Package Hold, Phone Messages, FedEx, AirBorne, UPS, Express Mail (*Sat Del*) **Supplies - OnSite:** Ice (*Block, Cube*), Ships' Store **1-3 mi:** Bait/Tackle (*Wego Fishing 765-3918*), Propane (*Van Duzer 765-3882*)

Boatyard Services

OnSite: Travelift (*30T*), Engine mechanic (*gas, diesel*), Launching Ramp (*$10*), Electrical Repairs, Electronic Sales, Electronics Repairs, Hull Repairs, Rigger, Bottom Cleaning, Brightwork, Compound, Wash & Wax, Interior Cleaning, Propeller Repairs, Woodworking, Inflatable Repairs, Painting, Awlgrip **OnCall:** Air Conditioning, Refrigeration, Divers, Yacht Interiors, Yacht Design, Yacht Building (*Bill Leverich*) **Near:** Metal Fabrication.
Under 1 mi: Sail Loft, Canvas Work. **Yard Rates:** $85/hr., Haul & Launch $15/ft., Bottom Paint $17/ft. (*paint incl.*)

Restaurants and Accommodations

OnCall: Pizzeria (*Paganos 765-6109*) **Under 1 mi:** Restaurant (*Journeys Inn 765-5113, L $8, D $18*), Snack Bar (*Drossos*), Motel (*Drossos 477-1344*) **1-3 mi:** Restaurant (*Seafood Barge 765-3010, L $13-18, D $18-26*), (*Pepi's Cucina di Casa 765-6373*), (*The Old Barge 765-4700*), Seafood Shack (*Half Shell 765-1010, L $8, D $18*), Inn/B&B (*Shorecrest 765-1570*)

Recreation and Entertainment

OnSite: Pool, Beach, Picnic Area, Tennis Courts **OnCall:** Sightseeing (*Vintage Vineyards Tours 765-4689*) **Near:** Jogging Paths, Horseback Riding (*Stable Hands 765-5201*)

Under 1 mi: Video Arcade (*Drossos 477-1339*) **1-3 mi:** Playground, Golf Course (*Island's End Golf & C.C. 477-0777*), Fitness Center, Boat Rentals, Roller Blade/Bike Paths, Fishing Charter, Movie Theater (*Village Cinema Greenport 477-8600*), Video Rental (*Front Row 765-6666*), Park, Museum (*East End Maritime 477-2100; Railroad of LI 477-0439*)

Provisioning and General Services

Under 1 mi: Convenience Store (*7-Eleven 477-2302*) **1-3 mi:** Supermarket (*IGA 477-0101*), Gourmet Shop (*Cheese Emporium 477-0023*), Delicatessen (*Sterlington 477-8547*), Health Food (*Market 477-8803*), Wine/Beer (*Claudio's 477-1035*), Liquor Store, Bakery, Green Grocer, Fishmonger, Meat Market, Bank/ATM, Post Office, Catholic Church, Protestant Church, Synagogue, Library (*Floyd Mem 477-0660*), Beauty Salon, Dry Cleaners, Laundry, Bookstore (*Burton's 477-1161, Book Scout 477-8536*), Pharmacy (*Colonial 477-1111*), Newsstand, Hardware Store (*Harts True Value 765-2122*), Florist, Retail Shops, Copies Etc.

Transportation

OnCall: Rental Car (*Enterprise 765-6600*), Taxi (*Marias 24 Hrs 477-0700*), Airport Limo (*Islander 765-5834*) **Near:** Local Bus (*SCT #92 along Rte 25 every hour - Riverhead to Orient Pt. Ferry*) **1-3 mi:** Rail (*LIRR to NYC 477-5477*) **3+ mi:** Ferry Service (*Cross sound to CT. Orient Pt., 8 mi.*)
Airport: Islip 467-3210 (*40 mi.*)

Medical Services

911 Service **OnCall:** Ambulance **1-3 mi:** Doctor, Dentist (*Kroepel 765-2860*), Chiropractor (*Southold Chiropractic 765-1191*), Holistic Services, Veterinarian (*North Fork 765-2400*) **Hospital:** Eastern LI 477-1120 (*5 mi.*)

Setting -- An almost land-locked basin protects Brick Cove's new floating docks and the good size boats that are berthed in its slips. The landmark Brick Cove Smoke Stack and brick building are the marina's keynotes. Its lovely, secluded, natural setting, hidden from both land and water view, coupled with the excellent amenities, creates a "best kept secret" atmosphere. A quiet picnic area overlooks Little Peconic Bay; plus there's a very inviting 500 foot beach and a separate recreation area that houses a pool and tennis courts.

Marina Notes -- The excellent docking facilities (aluminum and composite with super hard Lau Pau wood decking and 50amp/120 & 250 plus 30amp service) pair with old boatyard buildings that support the full service yard. Specializes in restorations. Good heads and showers with dressing rooms open 24 hrs. Friendly owners and staff create down-home comfort. The environment speaks more of sand dunes than of forest so there is little in the way of shade. On the north side of the yard is the "club" part of the facility -- a 25 ft. X 50 ft. pool and two quality tennis courts. There's a private beach on the south side.

Notable -- Brick Cove is all about peace and quiet; remarkably, the only sounds are boats and boaters -- even with a north wind. It's 0.35 mile along a wooded road to the main drag - Route 25 - and the hourly local bus. Drossos Mini Golf & Video Arcade is about a mile away. There are 4 restaurants around the Port of Egypt complex which is about 1.25 miles. About 4 miles away is Hortons Point Lighthouse; built in 1857, it's still active -- great views, picnic tables, and a weekend-only marine museum 11:30am-4pm. 3 miles to the Southold Indian Museum; Sat & Sun 1:30-4:30pm Jul-Aug, Sun only Sep-Jun (765-5577).

Navigational Information
Lat: 41°04.345' **Long:** 072°24.162' **Tide:** n/a **Current:** n/a **Chart:** 13258
Rep. Depths *(MLW)*: **Entry** 4.5 ft. **Fuel Dock** 4.5 ft. **Max Slip/Moor** 4 ft./-
Access: North End of Southold Bay near Hashamomuck Pond

Marina Facilities *(In Season/Off Season)*
Fuel: Gasoline, Diesel
Slips: 150 Total, 10 Transient **Max LOA:** 40 ft. **Max Beam:** 12 ft.
Rate *(per ft.)*: **Day** $2.50/Inq. **Week** Inq. **Month** n/a
Power: 30 amp Incl., **50 amp** n/a, **100 amp** n/a, **200 amp** n/a
Cable TV: No **Dockside Phone:** No
Dock Type: Floating, Long Fingers, Alongside
Moorings: 0 Total, 0 Transient **Launch:** n/a
Rate: **Day** n/a **Week** n/a **Month** n/a
Heads: 6 Toilet(s), 6 Shower(s) *(with dressing rooms)*
Laundry: 1 Washer(s), 1 Dryer(s) **Pay Phones:** No
Pump-Out: OnSite **Fee:** $5 **Closed Heads:** Yes

Marina Operations
Owner/Manager: Lieblein Family **Dockmaster:** Carly Neville
In-Season: Apr-Nov, 8am-5pm* **Off-Season:** Dec-Mar, 9am-4pm
After-Hours Arrival: Prior arrangement
Reservations: Yes **Credit Cards:** Visa/MC, Dscvr, Amex
Discounts: None
Pets: Welcome **Handicap Access:** No

Port of Egypt Marina

62300 Main Road; Southold, NY 11971

Tel: (631) 765-2445 **VHF: Monitor** n/a **Talk** n/a
Fax: (631) 765-2592 **Alternate Tel:** n/a
Email: info@poemarine.com **Web:** www.poemarine.com
Nearest Town: Southold *(1.7 mi.)* **Tourist Info:** (631) 298-5757

Marina Services and Boat Supplies
Services - Docking Assistance, Security, Trash Pick-Up, Dock Carts
Communication - FedEx, AirBorne, UPS, Express Mail **Supplies -**
OnSite: Ice *(Block, Cube)*, Ships' Store *(Albertson Marine)*, Bait/Tackle
(Wego Fishing) **1-3 mi:** Propane *(Van Duzer 765-3882)*

Boatyard Services
OnSite: Travelift *(25T)*, Forklift, Engine mechanic *(gas)*, Launching Ramp,
Bottom Cleaning, Compound, Wash & Wax, Interior Cleaning, Propeller
Repairs **1-3 mi:** Electronic Sales. **Dealer for:** Grady White, Cobalt
Boats, Yamaha Outboards, Volvo, Mercruiser.
Yard Rates: $98/hr., Power Wash $5.50/ft.

Restaurants and Accommodations
OnSite: Restaurant *(Seafood Barge 765-3010, L $13-18, D $18-26, M-Th
Noon-3, 5-9; Fri 'til 10; Sat 12-4, 4-10 & Sun 12-4, 4-9)*, Motel *(P.O.E. New)*
OnCall: Pizzeria *(Cheesy Charlies 765-3400)* **Near:** Restaurant *(Pepi's
Cucina Di Casa 765-3653, L $15, D $15-21)*, *(The Old Barge)*, *(Half Shell
765-1010)* **Under 1 mi:** Restaurant *(Rotisserie & Smokehouse of Southold
765-9655)*, *(Coeur Des Vignes 765-2652, D $19-35, Tasting $65)*, Motel
(Cawleys Southold Beach 765-2233), Inn/B&B *(Coeurs des Vignes 765-
2665, $175-200)*

Recreation and Entertainment
OnSite: Heated Pool, Picnic Area, Playground **1-3 mi:** Fitness Center
(Fitness Advantage 765-4015), Horseback Riding *(Arshamomaque Stables
765-5829)*, Fishing Charter *(Rainbow Charters 765-4314)*, Video Rental
(Front Row Video 765-6666), Museum *(Southold Hist. Society 765-5500 -*

they manage more than a half dozen 18thC & 19thC restored buildings in the
village; Southold Indian Museum 765-5577)*, Sightseeing *(Hortons Point
Lighthouse 765-2101; Vineyard Tours 369-5887 - will pick up)* **3+ mi:** Golf
Course *(Island's End Golf & Country Club 477-0777, 5 mi.)*

Provisioning and General Services
OnSite: Green Grocer *(Pete's Produce)*, Fishmonger *(Southold Fish Market
765-3200)* **Under 1 mi:** Convenience Store, Market *(Wayside Market 765-
3575)* **1-3 mi:** Supermarket *(IGA 765-3040)*, Gourmet Shop, Delicatessen
(One Stop Deli Market 765-2399), Health Food *(Earthtones 765-5153)*,
Wine/Beer, Liquor Store *(Village Liquors 765-5434)*, Bakery, Meat Market,
Bank/ATM, Post Office, Catholic Church, Protestant Church, Synagogue,
Library *(Southold 765-2077)*, Beauty Salon, Barber Shop, Dry Cleaners
(Southold Village Cleaners 765-5094), Laundry, Bookstore *(Burton's Book
Store 477-1161, Book Scout 477-8536)*, Pharmacy *(Southold Pharmacy 765-
3434)*, Newsstand, Hardware Store *(Harts True Value 765-2122)*, Florist,
Retail Shops

Transportation
OnCall: Rental Car *(Enterprise 765-6600)*, Taxi *(Marias 24 Hrs 477-0700)*,
Airport Limo *(Islander Limo 765-5834)* **Near:** Local Bus *(SCT #92 852-5200
$1.50/1)* **1-3 mi:** Rail *(LIRR to NYC 477-5477)* **Airport:** Islip *(40 mi.)*

Medical Services
911 Service **OnCall:** Ambulance **Under 1 mi:** Dentist *(Dubovick 765-
1160)* **1-3 mi:** Doctor *(Hamid 765-3480)*, Chiropractor *(Southold
Chiropractic 765-1191)*, Veterinarian *(North Fork Animal Hosp. 765-2400)*
Hospital: Eastern LI 477-1120 *(5 mi.)*

Setting -- Located where Hashamomuck Pond accesses Southold Bay, just west of Greenport, Port of Egypt Marina's sprawling facility encompasses two basins, a small recreation area and several very popular restaurants. Most of the facility is well-sheltered dock, boatyard, and parking with with an open, beachy feeling. But, an inviting, pocket-size grassy park provides a place for picnic tables and grills, while the pleasingly landscaped pool and playground are a welcome respite from the boatyard atmosphere and summer sun.

Marina Notes -- *Sunday 11-4. A North Fork fixture since 1946 when Bill, Herman & Herb Lieblein bought a little fishing station and built it into a big marina. Now run by second generation Bill, Peter & Elisa. Good ships' store, friendly and helpful staff. Primarily smaller and mid-size boats, in singled loaded slips, but docks along the outer perimeter can accommodate larger crafts. Plus 135 boat dry-stack operation. Fuel dock 7 days. Very busy sales and repair facility.

Notable -- If you can get in here, it's a true foodie's destination. The onsite Seafood Barge delivers Peconic Bay views and Chef Michael Meehan's inventive fresh seafood (including sushi) accompanied by the best L.I. wines. Ever since the NY Times named it the best restaurant on the North Fork in '01, it's been jammed. Adjacent to the marina on the east side is Pepi's Ristorante, next to that is the Old Barge Restaurant. Across the street is the Sea Shell. Adjacent to the marina on the west side are a fish market, produce market, and fish and tackle shop. P.O.E. fronts on Route 25, the main east/west road; access to Greenport or Southold towns is easy via cab or hourly local bus. Nearby is Southhold Historical Society's headquarters, gift shop and Treasure Exchange.

New Suffolk Shipyard

PO Box 276; 6775 New Suffolk Road; New Suffolk, NY 11956

Tel: (631) 734-6311 **VHF: Monitor** 9 **Talk** 12
Fax: (631) 734-6246 **Alternate Tel:** (516) 662-1431
Email: newsuffolkship@aol.com **Web:** n/a
Nearest Town: New Suffolk *(0.75 mi.)* **Tourist Info:** (631) 765-3161

Navigational Information

Lat: 40°59.686' **Long:** 072°28.499' **Tide:** 3.5 ft. **Current:** n/a **Chart:** 12358
Rep. Depths *(MLW):* **Entry** 4 ft. **Fuel Dock** 4 ft. **Max Slip/Moor** 6 ft./12 ft.
Access: Peconic Bay: School House Creek

Marina Facilities *(In Season/Off Season)*

Fuel: Gasoline
Slips: 70 Total, 5 Transient **Max LOA:** 42 ft. **Max Beam:** 12 ft.
  Rate *(per ft.):* **Day** $2.50/Inq. **Week** Inq. **Month** Inq.
  Power: 30 amp $2.50, **50 amp** n/a, **100 amp** n/a, **200 amp** n/a
  Cable TV: No **Dockside Phone:** No
  Dock Type: Floating, Short Fingers, Pilings, Wood
Moorings: 16 Total, 3 Transient **Launch:** n/a
  Rate: Day $35 **Week** n/a **Month** $350
Heads: 3 Toilet(s), 2 Shower(s) *(with dressing rooms)*, Hair Dryers
Laundry: None **Pay Phones:** Yes
Pump-Out: OnSite, Full Service **Fee:** $6.50 **Closed Heads:** Yes

Marina Operations

Owner/Manager: Michael Irving **Dockmaster:** Same
In-Season: Year-Round, 8am-5pm **Off-Season:** n/a
After-Hours Arrival: Call 662-1431
Reservations: Yes, Required **Credit Cards:** Visa/MC, Dscvr, Amex
Discounts: None **Dockage:** n/a **Fuel:** n/a **Repair:** n/a
Pets: Welcome, Dog Walk Area **Handicap Access:** No

Marina Services and Boat Supplies

Services - Docking Assistance, Boaters' Lounge, Security *(24 Hrs., on site)*, Trash Pick-Up, Dock Carts **Communication -** Phone Messages, Fax in/out, Data Ports, FedEx, AirBorne, UPS **Supplies - OnSite:** Ice *(Block, Cube)*, Ships' Store **Near:** Bait/Tackle *(Captain Marty's 734-6852)* **3+ mi:** Propane *(Van Duzer 765-3882, 6 mi.)*

Boatyard Services

OnSite: Travelift *(25T)*, Forklift, Crane, Engine mechanic *(gas)*, Electrical Repairs, Electronic Sales, Electronics Repairs, Hull Repairs, Rigger, Bottom Cleaning, Brightwork, Compound, Wash & Wax, Interior Cleaning, Woodworking, Painting, Awlgrip, Total Refits **OnCall:** Sail Loft, Air Conditioning, Refrigeration, Divers, Propeller Repairs, Inflatable Repairs, Life Raft Service, Upholstery, Yacht Interiors, Metal Fabrication **Near:** Engine mechanic *(diesel)*, Launching Ramp. **Dealer for:** Mercury Marine, Mako Boats, Honda. **Yard Rates:** $68/hr., Haul & Launch $9/ft., Power Wash $4.50, Bottom Paint $6.25/ft. **Storage:** In-Water $85/ft., On-Land $28/ft.

Restaurants and Accommodations

OnCall: Pizzeria *(Michelangelo 298-0230)* **Near:** Restaurant *(Legends 734-5123)*, *(Cafe Sant Trop)* **Under 1 mi:** Lite Fare *(Sip N Dip 734-9082)* **1-3 mi:** Restaurant *(Tin Hung 734-7062)*, Seafood Shack *(Fisherman's Rest 734-5155)*, Motel *(Alianos Beachcomber Resort 634-6370)*, *(Santorini Beach Resort 734-6370, $120-150)*, Inn/B&B *(Vintage B&B 734-2053)*

Recreation and Entertainment

OnSite: Picnic Area, Grills **OnCall:** Sightseeing *(Vintage Vineyards tours 765-4689 $48-55 4-5 hrs, 3 vineyards, lunch $10 less off-season)*

Near: Beach *(New Suffolk - Jackson & First Sts.)*, Playground, Jogging Paths, Boat Rentals, Roller Blade/Bike Paths, Special Events *(White Bread Race; PBSA World Nitro Racing)* **1-3 mi:** Golf Course *(Cedars Golf Club 734-6363)*, Fitness Center *(Advanced Health & Racquet Club 734-2897)*, Video Rental, Park, Cultural Attract **3+ mi:** Bowling *(Mattituck Lanes 298-8311, 5 mi.)*, Movie Theater *(Mattituck Cinemas 298-7469, 4 mi.)*

Provisioning and General Services

Under 1 mi: Convenience Store *(7-Eleven)*, Gourmet Shop, Wine/Beer, Bakery, Farmers' Market, Green Grocer, Fishmonger, Lobster Pound, Meat Market, Bank/ATM, Post Office, Barber Shop, Bookstore *(Buccaneer Books 734-5724)*, Pharmacy *(Cutchogue Drug 734-6796)* **1-3 mi:** Market *(Village Market 734-6541)*, Supermarket *(King Kullen 734-5737)*, Delicatessen *(Country Deli 734-2069)*, Liquor Store *(Peconic Liquor 734-5859)*, Library *(Cutchogue 734-6360)*, Dry Cleaners, Newsstand, Hardware Store *(Cutchogue Hardware 734-6584)*, Florist

Transportation

OnCall: Rental Car *(Enterprise 765-6600)*, Taxi *(Southold Taxi 765-6161)*, Airport Limo *(Double D 765-2313)* **1-3 mi:** Rail *(LIRR)* **3+ mi:** Bikes *(Country Time 298-8700, 4 mi.)* **Airport:** Islip MacArthur *(35 mi.)*

Medical Services

911 Service **OnCall:** Ambulance **1-3 mi:** Dentist, Chiropractor *(Scott Family Chiropractic 298-7450)*, Veterinarian *(Miller 734-2105)* **3+ mi:** Doctor *(North Fork Family Practice Associates 298-2030, 4 mi.)* **Hospital:** Eastern LI 477-1120 *(10 mi.)*

Setting -- Charming, down home, New Suffolk Shipyard lies on a small peninsula in a quiet, narrow inlet off Cutchogue Harbor. The docks, a series of single finger piers lined along the twisting creek, are well insulated from the boatyard operation and parking lot by a bank of dunes, marsh grass and shade trees. Each finger pier has its own ramp up the bank through the foliage.

Marina Notes -- This full service boatyard with docks promises high quality workmanship at down-to-earth prices and specializes in mechanical services and yacht refinishing; it caters to a friendly community of knowledgeable boaters. One of the oldest marinas on eastern Long Island, under new ownership since 2000. Same team as New Suffolk. The first US Navy submarine was built in New Suffolk in 1900; the base of operations was in what was the Cafe Sant Trop.

Notable -- Very rural New Suffolk isn't a town as much as it is a state of mind - with tree-shaded streets, sweet cottages, even a red schoolhouse, surrounded by farmland and vineyards. The town has a small, active harbor front, a beach, and a lot of sailboat racing. Wednesday night is beer can racing around Robins Island. Annually, the locally famous Whitebread (spelled correctly!) Race, a circumnavigation of Shelter Island, stages in the waters off Cutchogue Harbor and regularly draws over a hundred boats. After-race festivities center on Legends, a local bistro/restaurant with over 20 TV monitors in its sports bar and separate upscale dining with table cloths, flowers, candles and sports memorabilia (with all the North Fork wines and about 200 kinds of beer). Up the road is the private ferry terminal for access to Louis Moore Bacon's Robins Island. About 1.25 miles away is the little burg of Cutchogue: eateries, drug store, 7-11.

Navigational Information
Lat: 41°00.251' **Long:** 072°28.211' **Tide:** 4 ft. **Current:** 2 kt. **Chart:** 12358
Rep. Depths *(MLW)*: **Entry** 6 ft. **Fuel Dock** 9 ft. **Max Slip/Moor** 7 ft./-
Access: Gardiners Bay to Little Peconic Bay to Cutchogue Harbor

Marina Facilities *(In Season/Off Season)*
Fuel: *Gulf* - Gasoline, Diesel
Slips: 110 Total, 5 Transient **Max LOA:** 60 ft. **Max Beam:** 18 ft.
  Rate *(per ft.)*: **Day** $2.50/$2.50 **Week** $12/10.00 **Month** $27/20
  Power: 30 amp $2.50, 50 amp $5, 100 amp n/a, 200 amp n/a
  Cable TV: No **Dockside Phone:** Yes $35 hook-up
  Dock Type: Floating, Long Fingers, Short Fingers, Pilings, Alongside, Wood
Moorings: 0 Total, 0 Transient **Launch:** n/a
  Rate: Day n/a **Week** n/a **Month** n/a
Heads: 5 Toilet(s), 4 Shower(s) *(with dressing rooms)*
Laundry: 1 Washer(s), 1 Dryer(s) **Pay Phones:** No
Pump-Out: OnSite, Full Service, 1 Central **Fee:** n/a **Closed Heads:** Yes

Marina Operations
Owner/Manager: Sharon Johnston **Dockmaster:** Varies seasonally
In-Season: May-Nov, 9am-5pm **Off-Season:** Nov-May, 9am-5pm
After-Hours Arrival: Tie up to gas dock file paperwork in the morning
Reservations: Preferred **Credit Cards:** Visa/MC, Amex
Discounts: Boat/US; SeaTow **Dockage:** n/a **Fuel:** 10% **Repair:** n/a
Pets: Welcome **Handicap Access:** Yes, Heads, Docks

Cutchogue Harbor Marina

3350 West Creek Avenue; Cutchogue, NY 11935

Tel: (631) 734-6993 **VHF: Monitor** 9 **Talk** 9
Fax: (631) 743-7052 **Alternate Tel:** (631) 734-6993
Email: n/a **Web:** n/a
Nearest Town: Cutchogue *(1.7 mi.)* **Tourist Info:** (631) 298-5757

Marina Services and Boat Supplies
Services - Docking Assistance, Security *(20 Hrs., On site manager)* **Communication -** Mail & Package Hold, Phone Messages, Fax in/out *($1)*, Data Ports *(Office) (Sat Del)* **Supplies - OnSite:** Ice *(Cube)*, Ships' Store **Near:** Bait/Tackle *(Dinghy)* **Under 1 mi:** Ice *(Block, Shaved)* **3+ mi:** Propane *(Northfork Beverage 298-8971, 6 mi.)*

Boatyard Services
OnSite: Travelift, Engine mechanic *(gas, diesel)*, Launching Ramp, Electrical Repairs, Hull Repairs, Bottom Cleaning, Brightwork, Compound, Wash & Wax, Interior Cleaning, Propeller Repairs, Woodworking, Inflatable Repairs, Painting, Total Refits **OnCall:** Rigger, Sail Loft **Under 1 mi:** Electronic Sales. **1-3 mi:** Air Conditioning, Refrigeration, Divers, Upholstery, Yacht Interiors. **Yard Rates:** $55/hr., Haul & Launch $7/ft. *(blocking $4/ft.)*, Power Wash $3/ft. **Storage:** In-Water $18/ft., On-Land $25/ft.

Restaurants and Accommodations
Under 1 mi: Restaurant *(Fisherman's Rest 734-5155, L $9, D $14)*, Snack Bar *(Rudy's)*, Inn/B&B *(Rhinelander 734-4156, $175)*, *(Top 'O the Mornin' 734-5143, $150)* **1-3 mi:** Restaurant *(Wild Goose 734-4145, by way of Daniel & Le Bernadin, Chef Frank Cole's menu is distinctly French)*, *(Cutchogue Diner 734-9056)*, Inn/B&B *(Vintage B&B 734-2053, $200-250)*, *(Blue Iris 734-7126)*, *(Country House 734-5097, $135-150)* **3+ mi:** Restaurant *(Legends 631-734-5123, L $10, D $18, 5 mi.)*

Recreation and Entertainment
OnSite: Picnic Area, Playground **OnCall:** Sightseeing *(Vintage Vineyards*

Tours 765-4689) **Near:** Beach, Jogging Paths, Roller Blade/Bike Paths, Park **1-3 mi:** Dive Shop, Golf Course *(Cedars Golf Club 734-6363)*, Fitness Center, Fishing Charter *(Captain Marty's 734-6852)* **3+ mi:** Bowling *(Mattituck Bowling 298-8311, 6 mi.)*, Movie Theater *(5 mi.)*

Provisioning and General Services
Under 1 mi: Convenience Store *(7-Eleven)*, Market *(Village Market 734-6541)*, Gourmet Shop, Delicatessen *(Country Deli 734-2069)*, Wine/Beer, Bakery, Farmers' Market *(Wickham Fruit Farm)*, Green Grocer, Lobster Pound, Bank/ATM, Post Office, Catholic Church, Pharmacy *(Cutchogue Drug Store 734-6796)*, Newsstand, Hardware Store **1-3 mi:** Supermarket *(King Kullen 734-5737)*, Liquor Store *(Peconic Liquor 734-5859)*, Fishmonger *(George Braun Oyster Co 734-6700)*, Library *(Cutchogue 734-6360)*, Beauty Salon, Barber Shop, Dry Cleaners *(East End Cleaners 734-7050)*, Bookstore *(Certain Books 734-7656, Buccaneer Books 734-5724)*, Florist, Copies Etc. **3+ mi:** Protestant Church *(5 mi.)*

Transportation
OnSite: Courtesy Car/Van **OnCall:** Rental Car *(Enterprise 369-6300)*, Taxi *(Far East 298-9617)* **Under 1 mi:** Local Bus, InterCity Bus *(Sunrise Coach 800-527-7709)* **3+ mi:** Rail *(LIRR from Mattituck, 5 mi.)*
Airport: Islip *(40 mi.)*

Medical Services
911 Service **OnCall:** Ambulance **Under 1 mi:** Doctor, Dentist *(Lizewski 734-6290)* **1-3 mi:** Chiropractor *(Scott 298-7450)*, Veterinarian *(Miller 734-2105)* **Hospital:** Eastern L.I. 477-1000 or Central Suffolk 548-6200 *(10 mi.)*

Setting -- At the mouth of scenic, quiet Wickham Creek, small, well thought-out, and impeccably kept Cutchogue Harbor Marina occupies two basins -- divided by an almost invisible boatyard operation. Landside, evergreens shelter the docks from the road, parking lot and shipyard. Waterside are beautiful views of unsullied, protected wetlands (home to Osprey and many other species), Robins Island and Nassau Point. A park-like, grassy picnic area, populated with tables, overlooks the docks and marsh.

Marina Notes -- The marina has been here over 6 decades and is now owned by four partners, who also own New Suffolk. The north basin docks are newly renovated. The manager lives onsite and runs a service-oriented operation - they'll even take you to town for provisions. A small ships' store and substantial boat repair and dock building facility are also onsite - out of sight and mind. Large, comfortable showers and head. Boat US and SeaTow discounts. Many of the boats that take part in the Whitebread 100, a late summer circumnavigation race of Shelter Island, stage out from here.

Notable -- Truly far, far from the madding crowds. It's too far from the small town of Cutchogue to walk and even further from more "cosmopolitan" Mattituck, but the marina staff will help with local transportation. There are two swimming beaches nearby - one within a stone's throw of the gas dock and accessible by dinghy. Lots of annual events in the vicinity: strawberry festival, craft fairs, boat races. This is the heart of the North Fork vineyards and many offer tours - Vintage Vineyards tours will even pick you up from the marina $48-55 4-5 hrs, 3 vineyards, lunch ($10 less off-season).

Great Peconic Bay Marina

PO Box 326; Washington Avenue; South Jamesport, NY 11970

Tel: (631) 722-3565 **VHF: Monitor** n/a **Talk** n/a
Fax: (631) 722-3724 **Alternate Tel:** n/a
Email: info@greatpeconicbaymarina.com **Web:** greatpeconicbaymarina.com
Nearest Town: Jamesport *(1 mi.)* **Tourist Info:** (631) 298-5757

Navigational Information

Lat: 40°56.070' **Long:** 072°36.540' **Tide:** 3 ft. **Current:** 1 kt. **Chart:** 12354
Rep. Depths *(MLW):* **Entry** 8 ft. **Fuel Dock** 8 ft. **Max Slip/Moor** 8 ft./-
Access: Flanders Bay, half way between buoy 5 and 7 turn N to marina

Marina Facilities *(In Season/Off Season)*

Fuel: Gasoline, Diesel
Slips: 170 Total, 15 Transient **Max LOA:** 65 ft. **Max Beam:** 20 ft.
Rate *(per ft.):* **Day** $2.25/Inq. **Week** Inq. **Month** Inq.
Power: 30 amp Incl., **50 amp** Incl., **100 amp** n/a, **200 amp** n/a
Cable TV: No **Dockside Phone:** No
Dock Type: Floating, Wood
Moorings: 0 Total, 0 Transient **Launch:** n/a, Dinghy Dock
 Rate: Day n/a **Week** n/a **Month** n/a
Heads: 2 Toilet(s), 2 Shower(s)
Laundry: None **Pay Phones:** No
Pump-Out: OnSite, 1 Central **Fee:** $5 **Closed Heads:** Yes

Marina Operations

Owner/Manager: Shawn and Dawn Williams **Dockmaster:** Same
In-Season: Year-Round, 8am-5pm Tue-Sun* **Off-Season:** n/a
After-Hours Arrival: Call in advance
Reservations: Preferred **Credit Cards:** Visa/MC
Discounts: None **Dockage:** n/a **Fuel:** n/a **Repair:** n/a
Pets: Welcome **Handicap Access:** No

Marina Services and Boat Supplies

Services - Security *(Completely Fenced)* **Communication -** Phone
Messages, Fax in/out, FedEx, AirBorne, UPS, Express Mail **Supplies -**
OnSite: Ice *(Block, Cube)*, Ships' Store **Under 1 mi:** Bait/Tackle
(Jamesport B&T 722-3219), Propane *(O'Neils)* **3+ mi:** West Marine *(369-2628, 6 mi.)*

Boatyard Services

OnSite: Travelift *(50T & 25T)*, Forklift, Engine mechanic *(gas, diesel)*,
Electrical Repairs, Electronic Sales, Electronics Repairs, Hull Repairs,
Bottom Cleaning, Brightwork, Compound, Wash & Wax, Interior Cleaning,
Woodworking, Painting, Awlgrip, Yacht Design, Yacht Broker *(Great Peconic
Bay Marina)*, Yacht Building, Total Refits **OnCall:** Rigger, Sail Loft, Canvas
Work, Air Conditioning, Refrigeration, Propeller Repairs, Inflatable Repairs,
Life Raft Service, Upholstery, Yacht Interiors, Metal Fabrication **1-3 mi:**
Launching Ramp. **Dealer for:** Mercury, Mercruiser, Volvo Penta. Other
Certifications: Mercury Mercruiser **Yard Rates:** $80/hr., Haul & Launch
$5.50/ft. *(blocking $7.50/ft.)*, Power Wash $3.25, Bottom Paint $10/ft. *(paint
incl.)* **Storage:** In-Water $70/ft.

Restaurants and Accommodations

Near: Restaurant *(Bayview Inn 722-2659, L $8-14, D $19-25)*, Motel *(Motel
on the bay 722-3458)*, Inn/B&B *(Bayview $110-235)* **Under 1 mi:** Rest-
aurant *(Jamesport Country Kitchen 722-3537, L $5-9, D $15-19, kids'
menu $5-6 - one of the best with fabulous wine list)*, *(Cliffs Elbow Room 722-
3292, Great steaks)*, Pizzeria *(Lenny's 722-8589)*, Motel *(Dreamers Cove
722-3212)* **1-3 mi:** Restaurant *(Meeting House Creek 722-4220, L $6-10,
D $20, Seafood, Sun brunch)*, *(Do Littles 298-4000, L $5-7, D $13-20)*

Recreation and Entertainment

OnSite: Beach, Picnic Area, Grills, Playground **OnCall:** Sightseeing
*(Vintage Vineyards tours 765-4689 $48-55 4-5 hrs, 3 vineyards, lunch $10
less off season)* **Under 1 mi:** Horseback Riding *(BJ Farms 722-5434)*,
Park **1-3 mi:** Dive Shop, Tennis Courts, Golf Course *(Sandy Pond 727-
0909)*, Boat Rentals, Bowling *(Wildwood Lanes 727-6622)*, Movie Theater
(Village Cinema 477-8600), Video Rental *(Blockbuster 369-1122)*
3+ mi: Fitness Center *(Peconic Health & Racquet 727-2642, 4 mi.)*,
Cultural Attract *(Atlantic Aquarium 208-9200, 5 mi.)*

Provisioning and General Services

Near: Post Office, Hardware Store *(True Value 722-4414)*
Under 1 mi: Convenience Store, Gourmet Shop *(Jamesport 722-8977)*,
Delicatessen *(Duffys 722-2150)*, Lobster Pound, Beauty Salon, Newsstand
1-3 mi: Wine/Beer, Liquor Store *(Wine County 722-3350)*, Farmers' Market
*(Golden Earthworm Organic 722-3302, Wickham Fruit 734-6441; Woodside
298-8896)*, Florist, Retail Shops **3+ mi:** Supermarket *(Walbaums 298-9797,
4 mi.)*, Fishmonger *(4 mi.)*, Pharmacy *(CVS 727-9000, 4 mi.)*

Transportation

OnSite: Bikes **OnCall:** Rental Car *(Enterprise 369-6300/Toyota 727-7722)*,
Airport Limo *(Hampton Hills 324-0108)* **Near:** Local Bus **3+ mi:** Rail *(LIRR,
5 mi.)* **Airport:** Islip MacArthur *(30 mi.)*

Medical Services

911 Service **OnCall:** Ambulance **Under 1 mi:** Doctor, Dentist **1-3 mi:** Veterinarian *(Laurel Vet. Hosp. 298-1177)* **3+ mi:** Chiropractor *(Aquebogue
Chiropractic 722-4425 , 4 mi.)* **Hospital:** Central Suffolk 369-2775 *(4 mi.)*

Setting -- Directly off the north side of Flanders Bay, Great Peconic Bay Marina is set in a large, nearly land-locked, completely protected basin. This comfortable, family-oriented facility boasts a creative children's play area and an onsite beautiful, private, crescent-shaped sand beach.

Marina Notes -- *Closed on Mondays. The full service marina is buttressed by a short wall with the docks and finger piers extending from it. Picnic tables are placed at nearly every dock and barbecue grills abound (although most are privately owned). Neat, air-conditioned showers and bathrooms are labelled "Inboard" and "Outboard" (women & men, respectively) and located near the well-stocked ship's store. The gate is push-button coded for after hours entry and the entire marina is chain link fenced. Boats run the gamut from small cabin cruisers to large yachts. Hustler Powerboats docks their latest efforts here for testing; if go-fast interests you, keep your eyes open.

Notable -- Nice and quiet; the surrounding area is low key residential. There's a tavern within walking distance (Finnegan's Wake 722-8911, Wed-Sun) and Bayview Inn and Restaurant. A gas station with mini-mart and excellent hardware store are located less than a mile walk, but the nearest towns -- Riverhead and Mattituck - are both miles beyond walking. Nearby Jamesport Country Kitchen is a delightful surprise and features the North Fork's wines and produce; this is a great place to sample the output of the local vineyards (wine range from $15-45). Cutchogue-New Sofflok Historical Council (734-7122) has restored many buildings now on the village green: 1649 Old House, 1704 Wickham Farmhouse, 1840 Old Schoolhouse and several others. Tanger Outlet Center is 8 miles.

Navigational Information
Lat: 40°56.190' **Long:** 072°37.022' **Tide:** 3 ft. **Current:** n/a **Chart:** 12553
Rep. Depths (*MLW*): **Entry** 6 ft. **Fuel Dock** 10 ft. **Max Slip/Moor** 12 ft./-
Access: North side of Flanders Bay at the mouth of Peconic River

Marina Facilities (In Season/Off Season)
Fuel: Gasoline, Diesel
Slips: 180 Total, 12 Transient **Max LOA:** 65 ft. **Max Beam:** 18 ft.
  Rate (per ft.): **Day** $3.00 **Week** n/a **Month** n/a
  Power: 30 amp $5, **50 amp** $10, **100 amp** n/a, **200 amp** n/a
  Cable TV: Yes for longer stays **Dockside Phone:** Yes for longer stays
  Dock Type: Floating, Long Fingers, Wood
Moorings: 0 Total, 0 Transient **Launch:** n/a, Dinghy Dock
  Rate: Day n/a **Week** n/a **Month** n/a
Heads: 12 Toilet(s), 10 Shower(s)
Laundry: 2 Washer(s), 2 Dryer(s) **Pay Phones:** Yes, 1
Pump-Out: 2 Central, 1 Port, 1 InSlip **Fee:** n/a **Closed Heads:** Yes

Marina Operations
Owner/Manager: Alex Galasso **Dockmaster:** Chris Galasso
In-Season: Apr-Nov, 8am-6pm; Sat 8-5; Sun 9-4 **Off-Season:** Dec-Mar, 8-5
After-Hours Arrival: Proceed to fuel dock for slip #
Reservations: Yes, Preferred **Credit Cards:** Visa/MC, Dscvr, Amex, Checks
Discounts: None **Dockage:** n/a **Fuel:** n/a **Repair:** n/a
Pets: Welcome, Dog Walk Area **Handicap Access:** Yes, Heads, Docks

Larry's Lighthouse Marina

PO Box 1250; Meetinghouse Creek Road; Aquebogue, NY 11931

Tel: (631) 722-3400 **VHF: Monitor** n/a **Talk** n/a
Fax: (631) 722-3417 **Alternate Tel:** n/a
Email: info@lighthousemarina.com **Web:** www.lighthousemarina.com
Nearest Town: Riverhead *(3 mi.)* **Tourist Info:** (631) 727-7600

Marina Services and Boat Supplies
Services - Docking Assistance, Boaters' Lounge, Security, Trash Pick-Up, Dock Carts **Communication -** Mail & Package Hold, Phone Messages, Fax in/out *(Free)*, Data Ports, FedEx, AirBorne, UPS, Express Mail *(Sat Del)* **Supplies - OnSite:** Ice *(Block, Cube)*, Ships' Store **Near:** Marine Discount Store *(Lighthouse 722-5700)* **Under 1 mi:** Bait/Tackle *(Warrens 722-4898)*, Live Bait *(Eels, killes, crabs)* **1-3 mi:** West Marine *(369-2628)* **3+ mi:** Propane *(AmeriGas 727-2424, 4 mi.)*

Boatyard Services
OnSite: Travelift *(40T)*, Forklift, Engine mechanic *(gas, diesel)*, Electrical Repairs, Electronic Sales, Electronics Repairs, Hull Repairs, Bottom Cleaning, Brightwork, Compound, Wash & Wax, Interior Cleaning, Inflatable Repairs, Yacht Broker *(Lighthouse Yacht Sales)* **OnCall:** Air Conditioning *(Starke Marine)*, Propeller Repairs *(Bossler & Sweezy)* **Dealer for:** Egg Harbor, Shamrock, Century. **Member:** ABBRA, ABYC - 2 Certified Tech(s), Other Certifications: Merc, Cat, Yahama **Yard Rates:** $64-104*, Haul & Launch Incl. *(blocking incl.)*, Power Wash Incl. **Storage:** On-Land Outside $50/ft; Inside $80/ft.

Restaurants and Accommodations
OnSite: Restaurant *(Meetinghouse Creek Inn 722-4220, L $7-10, D $15-22, Kids' menu, Sun Brunch $13)* **Near:** Restaurant *(John Wittmeier 722-3655)*, *(Modern Snack Bar 722-3655, great lobster rolls and great local food in humble surroundings)* **Under 1 mi:** Motel *(Dreamers Cove 722-3212)* **1-3 mi:** Restaurant *(Peconic Bay Diner 369-7758)*, *(Bayview L $8-14, D $19-25)*, Fast Food *(Mc Donalds, Taco Bell, KFC)*, Motel *(On the Bay 722-3458)*, Inn/B&B *(Bayview Inn 722-2659, $110-235)*

Recreation and Entertainment
OnSite: Pool, Picnic Area, Grills, Boat Rentals *(kayaks)* **Near:** Jogging Paths **1-3 mi:** Bowling *(Wildwood Lanes 727-6622)*, Cultural Attract *(Vision Theater 369-4115)*, Sightseeing *(Atlantis Aquarium 208-9200)* **3+ mi:** Golf Course *(Cherry Creek 369-6500, 5 mi.)*, Horseback Riding *(North Quarter Farm 369-4310 , 3.5 mi.)*, Video Rental *(Blockbuster 369-1122, 4 mi.)*

Provisioning and General Services
Near: Delicatessen *(Petes 722-2222)* **Under 1 mi:** Convenience Store *(Mini-Mart)* **1-3 mi:** Liquor Store *(Michaels 727-7410)*, Green Grocer *(Skelly's 722-3796; Farmer John's 727-3272)*, Post Office *(722-4368)*, Protestant Church, Library *(727-3228)*, Beauty Salon *(A Cut Above 722-3399)*, Dry Cleaners *(Vojvoda's 727-2432)*, Pharmacy *(CVS 727-9000)* **3+ mi:** Supermarket *(Walbaums 298-9797, King Kullen 727-9325, 4 mi.)*, Health Food *(Green Earth 369-2233, 4 mi.)*, Catholic Church *(4 mi.)*, Synagogue *(4 mi.)*, Bookstore *(Suffolk 369-1023, Book Whrhse 369-9763,- 4 mi.)*, Hardware Store *(Jamesport 722-4414; Griffing 727-2805, 4 mi.)*, Department Store *(Walmart 369-1041, 4 mi.)*, Buying Club *(BJ's, 4 mi.)*

Transportation
OnSite: Bikes **OnCall:** Rental Car *(Enterprise 369-6300)*, Taxi *(Hampton Coach 727-6088)*, Airport Limo *(All EH 369-7770; Hampton 324-0108)* **Under 1 mi:** Local Bus **1-3 mi:** Rail *(LIRR to NYC)* **Airport:** Islip *(30 mi.)*

Medical Services
911 Service **1-3 mi:** Doctor *(East End 722-4400)*, Dentist, Chiropractor *(Aquebogue Chiro 722-4425)*, Veterinarian *(Aquebogue 722-4242)* **Hospital:** Central Suffolk 548-6000 *(4 mi.)*

Setting -- Strung along the eastern shore of picturesque Meetinghouse Creek are the impeccable docks, boatyard, pool, restaurant, storage sheds and nicely landscaped grounds of Larry's Lighthouse Marina. At one end, the namesake faux lighthouse is surrounded by a picnic area. At the other, there's a quite new, well shrubbed pool with deck - attractively furnished with tables and umbrellas. Waterside views are of the unspoiled marsh and recently dredged creek.

Marina Notes -- *1st time service $124/hr. Second generation, family owned and operated for 30 years. Well kept, well run, full service marina. Meetinghouse Creek Inn serves lunch and dinner and also serves pool-side. The land-side space is tight, but the docks extend into the creek and are nicely constructed and in perfect shape (new transient docks 2001). They house a mixture of large and small boats. Full service boatyard with manufacturers' dealerships, and a small ship store with large parts department. Nice, fully tiled heads and showers -- most are new or have been replaced over the past four years. Nearby neighborhood is residential. Anglers note: A 33 pound striped bass was caught off the fuel dock in Spring '03.

Notable -- This convenient location provides easy, straightforward entry from Peconic Bay and it's a quick jaunt from Shinnecock Canal. Access to the town of Riverhead is simple by main craft or dinghy. (Fixed Rte 105 bridge has mlw 25 foot clearance; river dredged to reported 6 ft. mlw almost to dam). Tie up at the town dock; within 50-100 yards are West Marine, restaurants, taverns, diners, ice cream shops, churches, Sears, pizzeria, photo shop, drug store, jewelry shop and the only McDonalds with a dock. Peconic Waterfront Park is the site of many special events and docks fill up quickly.

Treasure Cove Marina Resort

469 East Main Street; Riverhead, NY 11901

Tel: (631) 727-8386 **VHF: Monitor** 9 **Talk** n/a
Fax: (631) 727-8370 **Alternate Tel:** n/a
Email: n/a **Web:** www.treasurecoveresortmarina.com
Nearest Town: Riverhead *(0 mi.)* **Tourist Info:** (631) 727-7600

Navigational Information

Lat: 40°52.910' **Long:** 072°30.070' **Tide:** 4 ft. **Current:** 1 kt. **Chart:** 12358
Rep. Depths *(MLW)*: **Entry** 6 ft. **Fuel Dock** n/a **Max Slip/Moor** 8 ft./-
Access: Flanders Bay to Peconic River's northern shore

Marina Facilities *(In Season/Off Season)*

Fuel: *Shell* - Gasoline
Slips: 150 Total, 30 Transient **Max LOA:** 65 ft. **Max Beam:** 18 ft.
Rate *(per ft.)*: **Day** $2.75/Inq. **Week** $16 **Month** $40
Power: 30 amp Yes, 50 amp Yes, 100 amp n/a, 200 amp n/a
Cable TV: Yes **Dockside Phone:** No
Dock Type: Floating, Long Fingers, Alongside, Wood
Moorings: 0 Total, 0 Transient **Launch:** n/a, Dinghy Dock
Rate: Day n/a **Week** n/a **Month** n/a
Heads: 10 Toilet(s), 7 Shower(s) *(with dressing rooms)*
Laundry: 2 Washer(s), 2 Dryer(s), Book Exchange **Pay Phones:** Yes, 1
Pump-Out: OnSite, 1 Central **Fee:** n/a **Closed Heads:** Yes

Marina Operations

Owner/Manager: Lorna Smith **Dockmaster:** Same
In-Season: Jun-Sep 10, 7:30am-8pm **Off-Season:** Nov- Apr 1, 7:30am-4pm
After-Hours Arrival: Call in advance
Reservations: Yes, Preferred **Credit Cards:** Visa/MC, Amex, Shell
Discounts: Sea Tow **Dockage:** n/a **Fuel:** n/a **Repair:** n/a
Pets: Welcome, Dog Walk Area **Handicap Access:** Yes, Heads, Docks

Marina Services and Boat Supplies

Services - Docking Assistance, Security *(24 Hrs.)*, Dock Carts
Communication - Mail & Package Hold, Phone Messages, Fax in/out *($1)*
Supplies - OnSite: Ice *(Cube)*, Ships' Store, Bait/Tackle **Near:** West Marine *(369-2628)* **Under 1 mi:** Live Bait, CNG *(National)* **1-3 mi:** Ice *(Block, Shaved)*, Propane *(Presto Peconic 727-1516)*

Boatyard Services

OnSite: Engine mechanic *(gas, diesel)*, Launching Ramp, Hull Repairs, Bottom Cleaning, Divers, Woodworking **OnCall:** Electrical Repairs, Electronics Repairs, Air Conditioning, Propeller Repairs
Yard Rates: $80/hr., Haul & Launch $6/ft., Power Wash $2.50, Bottom Paint $12.50/ft. *(paint incl.)* **Storage:** On-Land Winter only. Inq.

Restaurants and Accommodations

OnSite: Restaurant *(Jerry & the Mermaid 727-8489, L $5-9, D $5-21, $7 lunch specials, Kid frientdy $3+)* **OnCall:** Pizzeria *(Carlos 924-8760)*
Near: Restaurant *(Digger O'Dells 369-3200)*, *(Rondezvous - HyTing 727-1557)*, *(The Little Guppy 369-3635)*, Pizzeria *(Ramos 369-1510)*
Under 1 mi: Restaurant *(Tuscan House 727-2330)*, Hotel *(Ramada Inn)*
1-3 mi: Hotel *(Best Western 369-2200)*, Inn/B&B *(Dreamers Cove)*

Recreation and Entertainment

OnSite: Pool, Picnic Area, Grills, Playground, Volleyball, Boat Rentals *(canoes & kayaks)*, Cultural Attract *(Atlantis Marine World $12/9 208-9200)*
Near: Jogging Paths, Movie Theater, Park, Museum *(Suffolk County Hist. Soc 727-2881 Free; Railroad Museum 727-7920 Sat, Sun, Hols $3/1.50)*, Sightseeing *(Atlantis Explorer eco tours $17/15 369-3700)*, Special Events

(Polish Fest, Blues Fest), Galleries *(East End Arts)* **Under 1 mi:** Beach, Roller Blade/Bike Paths, Bowling *(Wildwood Lanes 727-6622)* **1-3 mi:** Dive Shop, Tennis Courts, Golf Course *(Sandy Pond 727-0909, Cherry Creek 369-8553; Indian Island 727-7776)*, Fitness Center *(Peconic 727-2642)*, Horseback Riding, Fishing Charter, Video Rental

Provisioning and General Services

OnSite: Bank/ATM **Near:** Convenience Store, Gourmet Shop, Delicatessen *(Riverhead Deli 369-7302, John's 727-1052)*, Health Food *(Green Earth 369-2233)*, Liquor Store *(Michaels 727-7410)*, Farmers' Market *(Thur 11-3)*, Post Office, Catholic Church, Bookstore *(Suffolk Bookstore 369-1023)*, Pharmacy *(Barth Drug 727-2125)* **Under 1 mi:** Supermarket *(King Kullen 727-9325, Walbaums 758-9216)*, Bakery *(Briermere Farm)*, Green Grocer *(Briermere Farm 722-3931)*, Lobster Pound, Meat Market, Protestant Church, Synagogue, Library *(Riverhead 727-3228)*, Beauty Salon, Barber Shop, Dry Cleaners, Laundry, Newsstand, Hardware Store *(Griffing Hardware 727-2805)*, Florist, Retail Shops, Department Store *(Wal-Mart 467-4825)*, Buying Club *(BJ's)*, Copies Etc.

Transportation

OnCall: Rental Car *(Enterprise 369-6300, Sensible 208-4000)*, Taxi *(McRides 727-0707)* **Near:** Local Bus *(SCT 852-5200)* **Under 1 mi:** Rail *(LIRR to NYC)* **Airport:** Islip *(27 mi.)*

Medical Services

911 Service **OnCall:** Veterinarian *(Petcalls 727-3775)* **Near:** Doctor *(Wasserman 727-8353)* **Under 1 mi:** Dentist *(Miller 727-0103)*, Chiropractor *(Hall 727-3795)* **Hospital:** Central Suffolk 369-2775 *(1 mi.)*

Setting -- Well up the Peconic River, Treasure Cove's handsome and thoughtfully designed grounds blend with the peacefulness of the surrounding natural wetlands. Yet, a short walk, through the marina, yields Riverhead's Main Street. Adjacent Atlantis Aquarium's red "sky needle" ride makes a good landmark.

Marina Notes -- Built in 1986 as Peconic Yacht Basin, Treasure Cove since 1994. Inviting tree-shaded picnic area, volleyball court, serendipitous hammocks. The 30 x 50 ft. pool (with brick deck, chaises and umbrellaed tables) is adjacent to Jerry and the Mermaid's Restaurant & Clam Bar (11:30am-10pm 7 days, 'til 4am Fri & Sat with Karyoke) -- take-out and catering, too. Sunday morning complimentary bagels & coffee. Nicely done ship store. Fairly spread out, with several long finger piers in reasonable shape; wide range of boats - larger ones on the outer perimeter. Manager Lorna Smith, who lives onsite, is an invaluable local resource. Also owns the Atlantis Aquarium. Peconic River Queen paddleboat berths here. Route 105 Bridge has 25 ft. max vertical at mlw.

Notable -- Treasure Cove offers downtown convenience wth privacy. An easy walk is Riverhead's shopping and restaurants - ice cream, diners, pubs, and delis - plus blocks of shops. Next door Atlantis Marine World's live coral reef, seal shows, and touch tanks are in an environment intended to evoke the lost continent of Atlantis. With partner Riverhead Foundation for Marine Research and Preservation, it also treats and releases wounded marine life. Walk west through town to the East End Art Council and restored Vail Leavit Theater where Thomas Edison showed films. Festivals at the Peconic Riverfront Park on weekends (walking is the easiest way to get there). Tanger Outlet Mall & Splish Splash Water Park (727-3600) $25/17 are a $6 cab ride.

Navigational Information
Lat: 40°55.089' **Long:** 072°39.400' **Tide:** 6 ft. **Current:** 1 kt. **Chart:** 12358
Rep. Depths *(MLW)*: **Entry** 3 ft. **Fuel Dock** n/a **Max Slip/Moor** 3 ft./-
Access: Peconic River almost to the navigational head

Marina Facilities *(In Season/Off Season)*
Fuel: No
Slips: 60 Total, 60 Transient **Max LOA:** 60 ft. **Max Beam:** 20 ft.
 Rate *(per ft.)*: **Day** $1.00* **Week** n/a **Month** n/a
 Power: 30 amp Incl., **50 amp** $5, **100 amp** n/a, **200 amp** n/a
 Cable TV: Yes, $10 **Dockside Phone:** No
 Dock Type: Fixed, Floating, Concrete
Moorings: 0 Total, 0 Transient **Launch:** n/a
 Rate: Day n/a **Week** n/a **Month** n/a
Heads: None
Laundry: None **Pay Phones:** No
Pump-Out: OnSite, Self Service, 1 Central **Fee:** Free **Closed Heads:** Yes

Marina Operations
Owner/Manager: Jim Janacek **Dockmaster:** n/a
In-Season: Year 'Round, 24 hrs **Off-Season:** n/a
After-Hours Arrival: n/a
Reservations: No **Credit Cards:** n/a
Discounts: None
Pets: Welcome, Dog Walk Area **Handicap Access:** No

Peconic Riverfront Marina

200 Howell Avenue; ** Riverhead, NY 11901

Tel: (631) 727-3200 **VHF: Monitor** n/a **Talk** n/a
Fax: (631) 369-7739 **Alternate Tel:** n/a
Email: n/a **Web:** n/a
Nearest Town: Riverhead *(0 mi.)* **Tourist Info:** (631) 727-7600

Marina Services and Boat Supplies
Services - Security *(Police Patrol)*, Trash Pick-Up **Supplies - Near:** Ice *(Cube)*, Ships' Store *(Treasure Cove 727-8386)*, West Marine *(369-2628)* **Under 1 mi:** CNG *(National)* **1-3 mi:** Propane *(Presto 727-1516)*

Boatyard Services
OnCall: Electrical Repairs, Electronics Repairs, Bottom Cleaning, Air Conditioning, Refrigeration, Divers, Propeller Repairs **Near:** Engine mechanic *(gas, diesel)*, Launching Ramp, Hull Repairs.
Nearest Yard: Treasure Cove Resort (631) 727-8386

Restaurants and Accommodations
OnSite: Lite Fare *(Fryer & Ice L $4-5, burgers, wraps, soup, melts, ice cream, salads, gyros 11am-5pm, Mon-Sat)* **Near:** Restaurant *(Riverhead Grill 727-8495)*, *(Boardwalk on Main 369-4445)*, *(Main Street Cafe 727-8668, B $3-5, L $3-11, D $8-11)*, *(Digger O'Dell's 369-3200)*, *(Tweed's & Buffalo Bar)*, Coffee Shop *(Eastender's 727-2656)*, Pizzeria *(Julia's 369-8332)*, *(Parto's 727-4828)* **Under 1 mi:** Restaurant *(Indian Island G.C. 727-0788, L $5-12, D $9-15, 11am-Dusk, Sun Brunch $5-12 7am-3pm)*, *(One Fish, Too Fish 208-9737)*, Inn/B&B *(Bayview 722-2659)*

Recreation and Entertainment
OnSite: Picnic Area, Park, Special Events *(Festivals, Tournaments: Snapper- mid Sep, Fluke Tournament-late Jul)* **Near:** Playground, Boat Rentals *(Peconic Paddlers 727-9895 kayaks $30-70/day)*, Movie Theater, Museum *(Suffolk County 727-2881, Free)*, Cultural Attract *(Vail-Leavitt Music Hall 727-2656; Atlantic Marine World 208-9200 $12/9)*, Sightseeing *(Atlantic Explorer eco tours 369-3700 $17/15)*, Galleries *(East End Arts)*

Under 1 mi: Beach, Golf Course *(Indian Island County Club 727-7776)*, Bowling *(Wildwood Lanes 727-6622)* **1-3 mi:** Tennis Courts, Fitness Center *(Peconic 727-2642)*, Video Rental *(Blockbuster 369-1122)*

Provisioning and General Services
OnSite: Farmers' Market *(Thurs 11am-4pm)* **Near:** Gourmet Shop *(Only for U)*, Delicatessen *(Riverhead 369-7302; El Caracol 369-0840)*, Health Food *(Green Earth 369-2233)*, Liquor Store *(Michael's 727-7410)*, Bakery *(Bagel Lovers 727-5080)*, Bank/ATM *(North Fork 727-6353)*, Post Office, Catholic Church, Protestant Church, Library *(727-3228)*, Beauty Salon *(Image)*, Barber Shop, Dry Cleaners, Laundry *(Riverside 369-1701)*, Bookstore *(Suffolk 369-1023)*, Pharmacy *(Barth 727-2125)*, Newsstand, Hardware Store *(MCM 727-3002; Griffing 727-2805)*, Florist, Retail Shops *(Camera, Ben Franklin Crafts, Safari Pets)*, Department Store *(Sears 727-3118)*, Copies Etc. *(PIP)* **Under 1 mi:** Fishmonger *(Danowski's 727-3990)*, Synagogue **1-3 mi:** Supermarket *(King Kullen 727-9325)*, Green Grocer *(Best Yet 208-9170)*, Buying Club *(BJ's 369-9421)*

Transportation
OnCall: Rental Car *(Enterprise 369-6300; Sensible 208-4000)*, Taxi *(Riverhead Town 369-5522)* **Near:** Local Bus *(SCT 852-5200 anywhere on north/south fork.)* **Under 1 mi:** Rail *(LIRR to NYC)* **Airport:** Islip *(27 mi.)*

Medical Services
911 Service **Near:** Doctor *(Scherzer 727-6785)*, Dentist *(All Dental 727-2827)*, Chiropractor *(Hall 727-3795)*, Optician *(Allied 727-4411)* **1-3 mi:** Holistic Services *(Schwartz 369-9099)*, Veterinarian *(Riverhead 727-2009)* **Hospital:** Central Suffolk 369-2775 *(1 mi.)*

Setting -- Peconic Waterfront Park stretches along the northern shore of the River and hosts this very appealing town dock. A serpentine, concrete bulkhead offers 1,000 linear feet of alongside dockage. There's a boardwalk, bike path and, a few steps from the bulkhead, a cafe, snack bar, Sears and West Marine. A few more steps is the delightful, flower-bedecked town of Riverhead - a resource for just about anything a cruiser might need.

Marina Notes -- *6am-6pm free; rates apply for 12 hours or more. **Address is City Hall. Historically, the town has not enforced these rates but a new administration has indicated that will change. Twenty very recent, quality pedestals have 30 & 50 amp power, water and cable TV. 10 day maximum stay. Dinghies must be on deck or davits. No heads or showers. Also called "Riverhead Town Dock". Reportedly, but unconfirmed, the river is dredged to 6 ft. mlw.

Notable -- If you can make it up the river, Riverhead is a worthy destination. On Main Street, flowers ring the base of shade trees and overflowing pots hang from lamp posts. Beautifully restored, historic 1880 Vail Leavitt Music Hall re-opened in Spring of '03. Attractive, well attended Atlantis Aquarium, adjacent to the Park, has a sea lion show every two hours, many interesting exhibits, and is expanding again. Throughout the season, Peconic Waterfront Park hosts festivals and events. Across the narrow river, is a McDonalds with a dock. Nearby Peconic Paddlers offers an 8-mile, 3-hour canoe trip ($45) on the Peconic above the bridge. About 1.5 miles, on Old Country Rd, are BJ's, King Kullen, Wal-Mart and Kmart; about 3 miles is the enormous Tanger Designer Outlet Center. Take a bus! You can get practically anywhere from here on an SCT bus - Riverhead is the transportation hub for the East End. (Swezey's has closed.)

X. New York: Long Island's South Fork

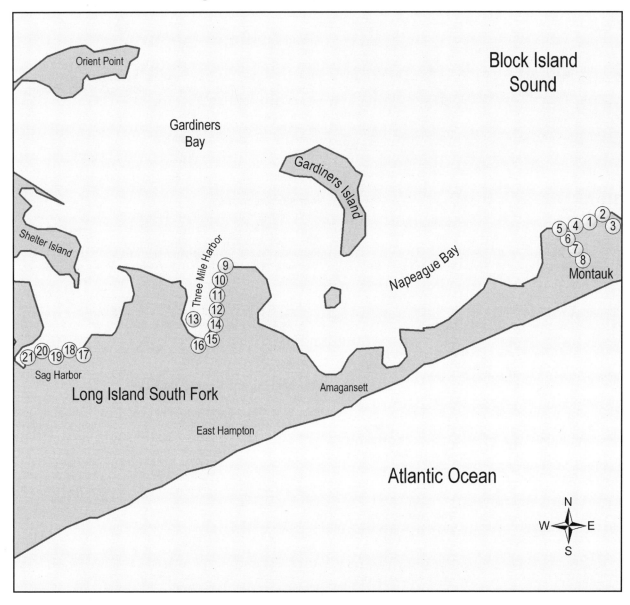

MAP	MARINA	HARBOR	PAGE	MAP	MARINA	HARBOR	PAGE
1	Montauk Yacht Club Resort & Marina	Lake Montauk	184	12	Shagwong Marina	Three Mile Harbor	195
2	Gone Fishing Marina	Lake Montauk	185	13	East Hampton Town Moorings	Three Mile Harbor	196
3	Montauk Lake Club & Marina	Lake Montauk	186	14	Halsey's Marina	Three Mile Harbor	197
4	Star Island Yacht Club	Montauk Harbor	187	15	Gardiner's Marina	Three Mile Harbor	198
5	Montauk Marine Basin	Montauk Harbor	188	16	Three Mile Harbor Boatyard	Three Mile Harbor	199
6	Offshore Sports Marina	Montauk Harbor	189	17	Sag Harbor Yacht Club	Sag Harbor	200
7	Westlake Marina	Montauk Harbor	190	18	Sag Harbor Marine Park	Sag Harbor	201
8	Snug Harbor Resort & Marina	Montauk Harbor	191	19	Malloy's Waterfront Marina	Sag Harbor	202
9	Harbor Marina of East Hampton	Three Mile Harbor	192	20	Malloy's Sag Harbor Cove East Marina	Sag Harbor Cove	203
10	Maidstone Harbor Marina	Three Mile Harbor	193	21	Malloy's Sag Harbor Cove West Marina	Sag Harbor Cove	204
11	East Hampton Point Marina & Boatyard	Three Mile Harbor	194				

Montauk Yacht Club

PO Box 5048; 32 Star Island Road; Montauk, NY 11954

Tel: (631) 668-3100 **VHF: Monitor** 9 **Talk** 11
Fax: (631) 668-6181 **Alternate Tel:** (516) 443-6059
Email: marina@montaukyachtclub.com **Web:** montaukyachtclub.com
Nearest Town: Montauk *(4 mi.)* **Tourist Info:** (631) 668-2428

Navigational Information

Lat: 41°04.281' **Long:** 071°55.950' **Tide:** 4 ft. **Current:** 2 kt. **Chart:** 12309
Rep. Depths *(MLW):* **Entry** 10 ft. **Fuel Dock** n/a **Max Slip/Moor** 12 ft./-
Access: B.I Sound to Montauk Lake, then leave Star Island to starboard

Marina Facilities *(In Season/Off Season)*

Fuel: No
Slips: 232 Total, 132 Transient **Max LOA:** 175 ft. **Max Beam:** n/a
  Rate *(per ft.):* **Day** $3.75/Inq.* **Week** Inq. **Month** $90/70 (electr incl.)
  Power: 30 amp $17.50, **50 amp** $17.50, **100 amp** $17.50, **200 amp** n/a
Cable TV: Yes, Incl. **Dockside Phone:** No
Dock Type: Fixed, Long Fingers, Pilings, Wood
Moorings: 0 Total, 0 Transient **Launch:** n/a
  Rate: Day n/a **Week** n/a **Month** n/a
Heads: 8 Toilet(s), 8 Shower(s) *(with dressing rooms)*, Sauna
Laundry: 4 Washer(s), 4 Dryer(s) **Pay Phones:** Yes, 4
Pump-Out: OnCall, Full Service **Fee:** Free **Closed Heads:** Yes

Marina Operations

Owner/Manager: James Stephens **Dockmaster:** n/a
In-Season: May-Oct 20, 7am-9pm **Off-Season:** Oct 21-Apr, 8am-4:30pm
After-Hours Arrival: Check in at front desk
Reservations: Yes **Credit Cards:** Visa/MC, Dscvr, Din, Amex
Discounts: None **Dockage:** group **Fuel:** n/a **Repair:** n/a
Pets: Welcome, Dog Walk Area **Handicap Access:** Yes

Marina Services and Boat Supplies

Services - Docking Assistance, Concierge, Security, Trash Pick-Up, Dock Carts, Megayacht Facilities **Communication -** Mail & Package Hold, Phone Messages, Fax in/out, FedEx, AirBorne, UPS, Express Mail **Supplies - OnSite:** Ice *(Cube)* **OnCall:** Live Bait **Near:** Ships' Store, Bait/Tackle **Under 1 mi:** Ice *(Shaved)* **1-3 mi:** Ice *(Block)*, Propane, CNG

Boatyard Services

OnCall: Divers **Near:** Travelift, Forklift, Crane, Engine mechanic *(gas, diesel)*, Launching Ramp, Electrical Repairs, Electronic Sales, Electronics Repairs, Hull Repairs, Rigger, Bottom Cleaning, Brightwork, Air Conditioning, Refrigeration, Compound, Wash & Wax, Interior Cleaning, Propeller Repairs, Woodworking, Metal Fabrication, Painting, Awlgrip, Yacht Broker. **Nearest Yard:** Star Island Yacht Club 0.25 mi. (631) 668-5052

Restaurants and Accommodations

OnSite: Restaurant *(Il Mare D $18-46)*, Seafood Shack *(Breeze's Café Break Buffet $13, Sun Brunch $ Kids' Menu)*, Snack Bar, Hotel *(Montauk Yacht Club $80-460)* **Near:** Restaurant *(Star Deck 668-5052, L $5-15, D $5-20)* **Under 1 mi:** Restaurant *(Salivar's 668-2555)*, Pizzeria *(Sausages 668-1144)* **1-3 mi:** Seafood Shack *(Gosman's 668-2549)*, Motel *(Harborside 668-2511, $65-130)*, Inn/B&B *(Kennys Tipperary Inn 668-2010, $85-200)*

Recreation and Entertainment

OnSite: Heated Pool *(3)*, Spa, Beach, Picnic Area, Grills, Playground, Volleyball, Tennis Courts *(lighted)*, Fitness Center, Video Arcade **OnCall:** Fishing Charter **Near:** Horseback Riding *(Rita's 668-5453)*, Group Fishing Boat **Under 1 mi:** Golf Course *(Montauk Downs 668-1234)*, Boat Rentals

(Uihlen's) **1-3 mi:** Dive Shop, Movie Theater *(Montauk Movie 668-2393)*, Video Rental *(Montauk Video 668-4824)*, Park, Museum *(Montauk Lighthouse 668-2544, Third House Museum 852-7878)*, Cultural Attract *(Montauk Theatre 668-5656)*, Sightseeing *(Whale Watching)*, Special Events *(Shakespeare Festival 267-0105)*

Provisioning and General Services

OnSite: Laundry, Retail Shops **OnCall:** Liquor Store *(White's 668-2426)* **Near:** Bank/ATM **1-3 mi:** Convenience Store, Market *(Gaviolas 668-1031)*, Supermarket *(IGA 668-4929)*, Gourmet Shop, Delicatessen *(Continental 668-6060)*, Health Food *(Naturally Good 668-9030)*, Bakery *(Bake Shoppe 668-2439)*, Green Grocer *(Ocean View 668-2900)*, Fishmonger *(Gosman's Dock)*, Lobster Pound, Post Office, Catholic Church, Protestant Church, Library *(668-3377)*, Beauty Salon, Barber Shop, Dry Cleaners, Bookstore *(Book Shoppe 668-4599)*, Pharmacy *(White's 668-2994)*, Hardware Store *(Beckers 668-2994)*, Florist, Department Store *(White's 668-2994)*

Transportation

OnSite: Courtesy Car/Van, Bikes **OnCall:** Rental Car *(Enterprise 668-3464)*, Taxi *(Montauk 668-2468)*, Airport Limo *(Eastern Limo 668-2702)* **Near:** Local Bus **Under 1 mi:** Rail *(LIRR to NYC)*, Ferry Service *(to Block Is. & New London)* **1-3 mi:** InterCity Bus *(Hampton Jitney)* **Airport:** Montauk/Islip *(5 mi./70 mi.)*

Medical Services

911 Service **OnSite:** Holistic Services *(Zeigfield Day Spa)* **1-3 mi:** Doctor *(Lighthouse Med 668-3696)*, Dentist *(Vasti 668-5959)*, Chiropractor *(Family 668-4535)* **Hospital:** Southampton 726-8335 *(30 mi.)*

Setting -- At the southern end of spectacular Star Island, on Lake Montauk's western shore, Montauk Yacht Club announces itself with the extraordinary number of megayachts gathered around its outer docks and the 60 foot replica of Montauk Lighthouse beyond. This complete and elegant resort offers a variety of accommodations, three pools (one indoor), nine lighted tennis courts, two restaurants, a snack bar, two lounges and a 232-slip marina.

Marina Notes -- *$4.00 on weekends & holidays, $17.50 utilities per day. A courtesy van makes hourly trips to Montauk Village and the ocean beaches. The docks were renovated by new owners in the late nineties and the boardwalk, pilings and railings were recently refurbished -- along with the heads and showers. There are saunas in the dockside heads. All the hotel rooms were completely renovated in 2000-02. A guest of the marina is a guest of the resort -- and of the well trained, service-oriented staff. A Day Spa is located at the resort's Ziegfield Estates - most treatments $90-245, some salon services for less.

Notable -- Wonderful family atmosphere. The fitness center, indoor pool, & spa are good bad-weather sanctuaries. The main outdoor pool overlooks the marina and a small, usually undiscovered, beach is at the southern end of the property. The restaurants, Il Mare (new world Italian), Breezes Cafe (more casual with frequent entertainment), and a poolside snack bar offer a range of alternatives to the galley. The Cohi Bar and the Lighthouse Bar host their share of yachties. Three restored 1920s facilities anchor the compound: Carl Fisher's Montauk Yacht Club, Montauk Island Club and the Zeigfield Estate. Fisher, who established Miami Beach, tried to replicate that success in Montauk. He lost everything in the '29 crash. Montauk Downs Golf Course was part of that effort.

Navigational Information
Lat: 41°04.359' **Long:** 071°55.650' **Tide:** 3 ft. **Current:** 2 kt. **Chart:** 12309
Rep. Depths (*MLW*): **Entry** 6 ft. **Fuel Dock** 8 ft. **Max Slip/Moor** 7 ft./-
Access: Block Island Sound to Montauk Lake's eastern shore

Marina Facilities (*In Season/Off Season*)
Fuel: *Gulf* - Gasoline, Diesel
Slips: 180 Total, 20 - 40 Transient **Max LOA:** 50 ft. **Max Beam:** n/a
  Rate (*per ft.*): **Day** $2.50* **Week** n/a **Month** n/a
  Power: 30 amp Incl., **50 amp** Incl.*, **100 amp** n/a, **200 amp** n/a
  Cable TV: Yes **Dockside Phone:** No
  Dock Type: Fixed, Floating, Long Fingers, Pilings
Moorings: 0 Total, 0 Transient **Launch:** n/a
  Rate: Day n/a **Week** n/a **Month** n/a
Heads: 12 Toilet(s), 5 Shower(s)
Laundry: 1 Washer(s), 1 Dryer(s) **Pay Phones:** Yes
Pump-Out: Onsite (*Slipside**) **Fee:** n/a **Closed Heads:** Yes

Marina Operations
Owner/Manager: n/a **Dockmaster:** T. J. Jordan
In-Season: Year-Round, 6am-6pm **Off-Season:** Dec-Apr, 8am-5pm
After-Hours Arrival: Call in advance
Reservations: Required May-Nov **Credit Cards:** Visa/MC, Amex, Gulf
Discounts: None
Pets: Welcome, Dog Walk Area **Handicap Access:** Yes, Heads, Docks

Marina Services and Boat Supplies
Services - Docking Assistance, Security, Dock Carts **Communication -** Phone Messages, Fax in/out, FedEx, AirBorne, UPS, Express Mail (*Sat Del*) **Supplies - OnSite:** Ice (*Block, Cube, Shaved*), Ships' Store, Bait/Tackle, Live Bait

Boatyard Services
OnSite: Travelift (*25T*), Forklift, Engine mechanic (*gas, diesel*), Launching Ramp, Electrical Repairs, Electronic Sales, Electronics Repairs, Hull Repairs, Rigger, Bottom Cleaning, Brightwork, Refrigeration, Compound, Wash & Wax, Interior Cleaning, Propeller Repairs, Inflatable Repairs, Painting, Awlgrip

Restaurants and Accommodations
OnSite: Restaurant (*After Fishing Bar & Grill B $2-6, L $6-13, D $8-17*)
OnCall: Pizzeria (*Pizza Village 668-2232*) **Near:** Restaurant (*Crabby Cowboy 668-3200, B, L, D 7-days, kids' menu, docks*) **Under 1 mi:** Motel (*Outrigger Cottages 668-4728*) **1-3 mi:** Restaurant (*Crow's Nest 668-2077*), Inn/B&B (*Crows Nest Inn 668-3700, $60-175*) **3+ mi:** Motel (*Sandy Acres 668-9293, 5 mi.*)

Recreation and Entertainment
OnSite: Fishing Charter **Near:** Beach, Picnic Area, Grills, Jogging Paths, Roller Blade/Bike Paths, Park **1-3 mi:** Horseback Riding (*Deep Hollow Beach & Trail Rides 668-2744*), Boat Rentals, Group Fishing Boat, Museum (*Montauk Lighthouse Museum 668-2544/Third House Museum 852-7878*), Sightseeing (*Harbor tours, whale watching*)

Gone Fishing Marina

467 East Lake Drive; Montauk, NY 11954

Tel: (631) 668-3232 **VHF: Monitor** 19 **Talk** 19
Fax: (631) 668-3293 **Alternate Tel:** n/a
Email: n/a **Web:** n/a
Nearest Town: Montauk (*6 mi.*) **Tourist Info:** (631) 668-2428

3+ mi: Golf Course (*Montauk Downs 668-1234, 5 mi.*), Movie Theater (*Montauk Movie 668-2393, 6 mi.*), Video Rental (*Montauk Video 668-4824, 6 mi.*), Cultural Attract (*Montauk Theatre 668-5656, 6 mi.*), Special Events (*Shakespeare Festival 267-0105*)

Provisioning and General Services
1-3 mi: Convenience Store **3+ mi:** Supermarket (*IGA 668-4929, 6 mi.*), Gourmet Shop (*4 mi.*), Delicatessen (*4 mi.*), Health Food (*Naturally Good 668-9030, 6 mi.*), Liquor Store (*White's Liquor 668-2426, delivers, 6 mi.*), Green Grocer (*Ocean View Market 668-2900, 6 mi.*), Fishmonger (*5 mi.*), Bank/ATM (*5 mi.*), Post Office (*6 mi.*), Catholic Church (*6 mi.*), Library (*Montauk 668-3377, 6 mi.*), Beauty Salon (*6 mi.*), Laundry (*Laundromat 668-4349, 6 mi.*), Bookstore (*The Book Shoppe 668-4599 , 6 mi.*), Pharmacy (*White's 668-2994, 6 mi.*), Hardware Store (*Beckers ACE 668-2368, 6 mi.*), Florist (*6 mi.*), Clothing Store (*6 mi.*), Retail Shops (*6 mi.*), Department Store (*White's, 6 mi.*)

Transportation
OnCall: Rental Car (*Enterprise 668-3464*), Taxi (*Montauk Taxi 668-2468, Pink Tuna 668-3838*), Airport Limo (*Eastern Limousine 668-2702*)
3+ mi: Bikes (*Bike Shop 668-8975, 6 mi.*), Rail (*LIRR to NYC, 6 mi.*)
Airport: Montauk/Islip (*0.25 mi./75 mi.*)

Medical Services
911 Service **OnCall:** Ambulance **Under 1 mi:** Chiropractor (*Sayers 668-4535*) **3+ mi:** Doctor (*Mountauk Med. Cntr. 668-3705, 6 mi.*), Dentist (*Vasti 668-5959, 4 mi.*) **Hospital:** Southampton 726-8335 (*35 mi.*)

Setting -- Well past the Coast Guard station, on Montauk Lake's eastern shore, Gone Fishing is home to a cadre of serious anglers who regularly do "just that." This very active sportfishing center and full-service marina is easy to spot -- a wood sided, two-story contemporary clubhouse, with a boldly striped awning, is surrounded by good sized off-shore fishing boats - with nary a mast in sight.

Marina Notes -- *Limited 50 amp pedestals, so reserve in advance. Family owned and operated since 1978. Caters to the sport fishing community. Very nice, basic but well maintained heads and showers. Extremely well-stocked ships' store, with extensive inventory of fishing tackle. Well known throughout the Long Island area by serious anglers. Good staff, excellent repair facility - with mechanics on staff. **Slip-side pump-out which is currently inoperative. The onsite, open air "After Fishing" Bar & Grill features fresh grilled fish, burgers and fried seafood in a casual atmosphere overlooking the marina (May-Oct) 5-9pm, 'til 10pm Fri & Sat. Plus Breakfast Mon-Fri 5am-10am, 'til 11am Sat & Sun and Lunch (salads, appetizers, burgers & beer-battered seafood) 11:30am-5pm.

Notable -- It's a half-mile to public Montauk Park which has a long, sandy beach on Block Island Sound, picnic facilities, and also offers some great hikes. Gone Fishing is on the eastern side on the Lake so almost all services, save a few restaurants, are a cab-ride away in Montauk. Montauk Airport is right next door. For the Montauk Point State Park and Lighthouse, either hike to Route 27 and then take the seasonal shuttle bus to the end, or call a cab. Completed in 1796, this is the oldest lighthouse in the state of New York. The museum is open daily during the summer, weather permitting $6/3 (668-2544).

Montauk Lake Club & Marina

Montauk Lake Club & Marina

P.O.Box 760; 211 East Lake Drive; Montauk, NY 11954

Tel: (631) 668-5705 **VHF: Monitor** 68 **Talk** n/a
Fax: (631) 668-3404 **Alternate Tel:** n/a
Email: n/a **Web:** n/a
Nearest Town: Montauk *(6 mi.)* **Tourist Info:** (631) 668-2428

Navigational Information
Lat: 41°03.703' **Long:** 071°54.693' **Tide:** 3 ft. **Current:** None **Chart:** 13209
Rep. Depths *(MLW)*: **Entry** 6 ft. **Fuel Dock** 7 ft. **Max Slip/Moor** 7 ft./-
Access: Block Island Sound to Montauk Lake, 1.5 miles on eastern shore

Marina Facilities *(In Season/Off Season)*
Fuel: *Texaco* - Gasoline, Diesel
Slips: 70 Total, 10 Transient **Max LOA:** 70 ft. **Max Beam:** n/a
  Rate *(per ft.)*: **Day** $2.00 **Week** $12 **Month** Inq.
  Power: 30 amp Yes, **50 amp** Yes, **100 amp** n/a, **200 amp** n/a
  Cable TV: Yes **Dockside Phone:** Yes
  Dock Type: Fixed, Floating, Long Fingers, Pilings
Moorings: 0 Total, 0 Transient **Launch:** n/a
  Rate: Day n/a **Week** n/a **Month** n/a
Heads: 6 Toilet(s), 8 Shower(s) *(with dressing rooms)*, Hair Dryers
Laundry: 3 Washer(s), 3 Dryer(s) **Pay Phones:** Yes
Pump-Out: No **Fee:** n/a **Closed Heads:** Yes

Marina Operations
Owner/Manager: Montauk Lake Club **Dockmaster:** Bob Van Mater
In-Season: Summer, 7am-4pm **Off-Season:** Winter, 9am-3pm
After-Hours Arrival: n/a
Reservations: No **Credit Cards:** Visa/MC, Dscvr, Amex
Discounts: None
Pets: Welcome, Dog Walk Area **Handicap Access:** No

Marina Services and Boat Supplies
Services - Docking Assistance, Trash Pick-Up, Dock Carts
Communication - Mail & Package Hold, Phone Messages, Fax in/out, FedEx, AirBorne, UPS, Express Mail *(Sat Del)* **Supplies -**
OnSite: Ice *(Cube)* **Under 1 mi:** Ships' Store, Bait/Tackle, Propane

Boatyard Services
Under 1 mi: Launching Ramp, Electrical Repairs, Electronics Repairs, Hull Repairs, Rigger, Bottom Cleaning, Brightwork, Refrigeration.
Nearest Yard: Gone Fishing Marina (631) 668-3232

Restaurants and Accommodations
OnSite: Restaurant *(Montauk Lake Club L $8-14, Lunch only Sat & Sun. Kids' menu)* **OnCall:** Pizzeria *(Pizza Village 668-2232)* **Under 1 mi:** Restaurant *(After Fishing 668-6535, B $2-6, L $6-13, D $8-17)*, *(Crabby Cowboy 668-3200, B, L, D 7-days, kids' menu, docks)* Condo/Cottage *(Outrigger Cottages 668-4728)* **1-3 mi:** Restaurant *(Crow's Nest 668-2077, Sunday brunch available)*, *(Shagwong 668-3050)*, *(Ruschmeyers 668-2877, D $18-26)*, Inn/B&B *(Crow's Nest 668-3700, $60-175)* **3+ mi:** Motel *(Harborside 668-2511, $65-130, 5 mi.)*, *(Royal Atlantic 668-5103, 5 mi.)*

Recreation and Entertainment
OnSite: Pool **Near:** Fitness Center, Jogging Paths, Roller Blade/Bike Paths **Under 1 mi:** Beach, Horseback Riding *(Deep Hollow Beach & Trail Rides 668-2744)*, Park, Sightseeing *(Harbor tours, whale watching)* **1-3 mi:** Playground, Dive Shop, Boat Rentals, Museum *(Montauk Lighthouse Museum 668-2544/Third House Museum 852-7878)*

3+ mi: Tennis Courts *(Harborside Tennis 668-2511, 5 mi.)*, Golf Course *(Montauk Downs 668-1234, 5 mi.)*, Movie Theater *(Montauk Movie 668-2393, 6 mi.)*, Video Rental *(Montauk Video 668-4824, 6 mi.)*, Cultural Attract *(Montauk Theatre 668-5656, 6 mi.)*, Special Events *(Shakespeare Festival 267-0105)*

Provisioning and General Services
1-3 mi: Convenience Store **3+ mi:** Supermarket *(IGA 668-4929, 6 mi.)*, Gourmet Shop *(4 mi.)*, Delicatessen *(4 mi.)*, Health Food *(Naturally Good 668-9030, 6 mi.)*, Liquor Store *(White's Liquor 668-2426, delivers, 6 mi.)*, Green Grocer *(Ocean View Market 668-2900, 6 mi.)*, Lobster Pound *(5 mi.)*, Bank/ATM *(5 mi.)*, Post Office *(6 mi.)*, Catholic Church *(6 mi.)*, Library *(Montauk 668-3377, 6 mi.)*, Laundry *(Montauk Laundromat 668-4349, 6 mi.)*, Bookstore *(The Book Shoppe 668-4599 , 5 mi.)*, Pharmacy *(White's 668-2994, 6 mi.)*, Hardware Store *(Beckers ACE 668-2368, 6 mi.)*, Department Store *(White's, 6 mi.)*

Transportation
OnCall: Rental Car *(Enterprise 668-3464)*, Taxi *(Montauk Taxi 668-2468)*, Airport Limo *(Eastern Limousine 668-2702)* **1-3 mi:** Local Bus **3+ mi:** Rail *(LIRR to Penn Station-NYC, 6 mi.)* **Airport:** Montauk/Islip *(1.5 mi./75 min.)*

Medical Services
911 Service **Near:** Chiropractor *(Family Chiropractic 668-4535)* **1-3 mi:** Ambulance **3+ mi:** Doctor *(Mountauk Medical 668-3705, 5 mi.)*, Dentist *(D. Vasti 668-5959, 4 mi.)* **Hospital:** Southampton 726-8335 *(35 mi.)*

Setting -- About a mile south of Gone Fishing Marina and the Montauk Yacht Club, on the eastern, more rural, side of Lake Montauk, this marina is part of an elegant and beautifully landscaped 1920s-style brick Tudor estate that has been converted into a private club. Manicured lawns run down to the water's edge and to the docks; a lovely pool and clubhouse patio look out over the Lake.

Marina Notes -- This private club graciously opens its facilities to transient boaters. Most club amenities available to marina guests, including pool and restaurant (Lunch only on weekends; kid's menu available). Very nice tiled heads and showers, dressing rooms, plugs for hair dryers above each sink. Gas and diesel available, but no pump-out. Dockmaster and staff are very helpful, but availability of dockhands is limited. Onsite rooms are available to members only.

Notable -- An elegant spot, definitely worth a stop. Montauk Lake Club is quite distant from town so all shopping, services, restaurants, boat supplies, etc. are a cab or dinghy ride away. Great town beach about 1.5 miles north just to the East of the Lake Montauk entrance channel. One mile from Montauk Airport. Nearby an unmarked nature trail winds through 1,000 acre Theodore Roosevelt Park around fresh-water Big Reed Pond to Shagwong Point for a view of the entire Montauk headland. Longer trek is around beautiful land-locked Oyster Pond on to Montauk Pt. State Park to magnificent Montauk Point. The Park office is in the opposite direction, almost to Montauk Highway, in historic 1797 Third House at Deep Hollow Ranch. Built in 1658, it is the oldest cattle ranch in U.S. and considered the birthplace of the American cowboy.

Navigational Information
Lat: 41°04.290' **Long:** 071°56.090' **Tide:** 3.5 ft. **Current:** 2 kt. **Chart:** 12309
Rep. Depths (*MLW*): **Entry** 7 ft. **Fuel Dock** 5 ft. **Max Slip/Moor** 7 ft./-
Access: Block Island Sound to Montauk Lake west into Montauk Harbor

Marina Facilities (*In Season/Off Season*)
Fuel: *Texaco/Shell* - Slip-Side Fueling, Gasoline, Diesel, High-Speed Pumps
Slips: 165 Total, 85 Transient **Max LOA:** 150 ft. **Max Beam:** n/a
  Rate (*per ft.*): **Day** $3.75* **Week** $22.50 **Month** Inq.
  Power: **30 amp** $17.50, **50 amp** $17.50, **100 amp** $17.50, **200 amp** n/a
  Cable TV: Yes, Inc. in utility charge **Dockside Phone:** No
  Dock Type: Floating, Long Fingers, Pilings, Alongside, Wood
Moorings: 0 Total, 0 Transient **Launch:** n/a
  Rate: Day n/a **Week** n/a **Month** n/a
Heads: 10 Toilet(s), 8 Shower(s)
Laundry: 4 Washer(s), 4 Dryer(s) **Pay Phones:** Yes, 3
Pump-Out: OnCall (*Ch. 73*) **Fee:** n/a **Closed Heads:** Yes

Marina Operations
Owner/Manager: Richard Janis **Dockmaster:** Josh Frazier
In-Season: May-Oct, 5am-9pm **Off-Season:** Oct-Apr, 6am-6pm
After-Hours Arrival: Tie up at fuel dock
Reservations: Yes **Credit Cards:** Visa/MC, Dscvr, Amex, Tex, Shell
Discounts: Fuel **Dockage:** n/a **Fuel:** volume **Repair:** n/a
Pets: Welcome, Dog Walk Area **Handicap Access:** No

Star Island Yacht Club

PO Box 2180; Star Island Road; Montauk, NY 11954

Tel: (631) 668-5053 **VHF: Monitor** 9 **Talk** 10
Fax: (631) 668-5503 **Alternate Tel:** n/a
Email: strislyc@aol.com **Web:** www.starislandyc.com
Nearest Town: Montauk (*4 mi.*) **Tourist Info:** (631) 668-2428

Marina Services and Boat Supplies
Services - Docking Assistance, Trash Pick-Up, Dock Carts, Megayacht
Facilities **Communication** - Mail & Package Hold, Phone Messages, Fax
in/out, FedEx, AirBorne, UPS, Express Mail **Supplies - OnSite:** Ice (*Block,
Cube*), Ships' Store, Bait/Tackle, Live Bait

Boatyard Services
OnSite: Travelift (*30T, 75T*), Engine mechanic (*gas, diesel*), Electrical
Repairs, Hull Repairs, Bottom Cleaning, Brightwork, Air Conditioning,
Refrigeration, Compound, Wash & Wax, Interior Cleaning, Propeller Repairs,
Yacht Broker **OnCall:** Electronics Repairs **Yard Rates:** $95/hr., Haul &
Launch $10/ft. (*blocking $2.50/ft.*), Power Wash $2.50/ft., Bottom Paint
$14/ft. + paint

Restaurants and Accommodations
OnSite: Restaurant (*Star Deck Grill L $5-15, D $5-20*) **OnCall:** Pizzeria
(*Pizza Village 668-2232*) **Near:** Restaurant (*Il Mare 668-3100, L $7-15, D
$19-38*), (*Breezes Cafe 668-3100*), Hotel (*Montauk Yacht Club 668-3100,
$110-560*) **Under 1 mi:** Restaurant (*The Dock 668-9778*), (*Salivar's 668-
2555*), (*Clam & Chowder House 668-6252, B $3-8, L $5-12, D $6-20*), Motel
(*Blue Haven 668-5943*), (*West Lake Drive 668-2545*) **1-3 mi:** Lite Fare
(*Anthony's Pancakes 668-9705*), Motel (*Seawind 668-4949*), Inn/B&B
(*Culloden House 668-9293, $60-150*)

Recreation and Entertainment
OnSite: Pool, Picnic Area, Grills, Jogging Paths, Fishing Charter
Near: Beach, Playground, Tennis Courts (*Harborside Tennis 668-2511*),
Fitness Center, Roller Blade/Bike Paths **Under 1 mi:** Boat Rentals (*boats,

jet skis and kayaks* **1-3 mi:** Golf Course (*Montauk Downs 668-1234* ,
Horseback Riding (*Deep Hollow Beach & Trail Rides 668-2744*), Group
Fishing Boat, Movie Theater (*Montauk Movie 668-2393*), Video Rental
(*Montauk Video 668-4824*), Video Arcade, Park, Museum (*Montauk
Lighthouse Museum 668-2544/Third House Museum 852-7878*), Cultural
Attract (*Montauk Theatre 668-5656*), Sightseeing (*Harbor tours, whale
watching*), Special Events (*Shakespeare Festival 267-0105*)

Provisioning and General Services
OnSite: Convenience Store, Newsstand, Clothing Store **Near:** Dry
Cleaners, Laundry **1-3 mi:** Market (*Gaviola's 668-1031*), Supermarket (*IGA
668-4929*), Gourmet Shop, Delicatessen (*Four Oaks 668-3872*), Health
Food (*Naturally Good 668-9030*), Wine/Beer, Liquor Store (*White's Liquor
668-2426, delivers*), Bakery (*Bake Shoppe 668-2439*), Fishmonger, Meat
Market, Bank/ATM, Post Office (*668-7043*), Catholic Church, Library
(*Montauk 668-3377*), Beauty Salon, Bookstore (*The Book Shoppe 668-
4599*), Pharmacy (*White's 668-2994*), Hardware Store (*Beckers ACE 668-
2368*), Florist, Retail Shops, Department Store (*White's*), Copies Etc.

Transportation
OnCall: Rental Car (*Enterprise 668-3464*), Taxi (*Montauk Taxi 668-2468*),
Airport Limo (*Eastern Limousine 668-2702*) **1-3 mi:** Bikes (*Bike Shop 668-
8975*), Local Bus, Rail (*LIRR to NYC*) **Airport:** Montauk/Islip (*5 mi./70 mi.*)

Medical Services
911 Service **OnCall:** Ambulance **1-3 mi:** Doctor (*Mountauk Medical 668-
3705*), Dentist (*Vasti 668-5959*), Chiropractor (*Family Chiropractic 668-
4535*) **Hospital:** Southampton 726-8335 (*30 mi.*)

Setting -- Well-executed, full-service Star Island is the first marina to port after the Coast Guard Station. Landward views are of the main two-story marina building and a string of flag poles streaming international colours. An attractive brick promenade, dotted with tables, chairs and potted flowers, runs along the edge of the four main docks. Waterside views are across the protected basin to other marinas and boatyards.

Marina Notes -- *Thurs-Sat to 60 ft $3.75/ft; 61 ft+ $4/ft. Sun-Wed to 60 ft. $3.25/ft. 61 ft. + $3.50/ft. Holiday & tounament rates higher. Memorial Day - 2 night min, July 4 & Labor Day - 3 night min. Focuses on meeting the needs of off-shore fishermen with live bait, tackle, slip-side diesel fueling on each dock. Full service boatyard onsite. An enormous, very well-stocked ships' store features boat supplies & parts, clothing, provisions, and bait & tackle. Winter storage available. Tournaments: Shark - early June, Shark Charity - mid July, and Mako Mania - mid August. Huge fish fillet table. Home to many club rendezvous. Steps from the docks is a nice size pool with brick and wood planked deck furnished with several rows of chaises plus tables and chairs.

Notable -- The casual, outdoor Star Deck Grill adjacent to the pool serves breakfast, lunch and dinner (good burgers and fresh fish - reportedly right off the charter boats) seven days a week, and features a band on weekends. The eatery is also available for private parties. Star Island Y.C. is home base for 18 six-passenger sport fishing charter boats ranging in size from 28-42 feet - Rates: $450/half day, $775-950/full day. The marina shares Star Island with the Coast Guard Station and Montauk Yacht Club. Generally quiet surroundings within a dinghy ride or a walk of restaurants and other diversions.

Montauk Marine Basin

PO Box 610; 426 West Lake Drive; Montauk, NY 11954

Tel: (631) 668-5900 **VHF: Monitor** 19 **Talk** 18
Fax: (631) 668-5659 **Alternate Tel:** (631) 668-5032
Email: n/a **Web:** www.montaukmarine.com
Nearest Town: Montauk (2.5 mi.) **Tourist Info:** (631) 668-2428

Navigational Information
Lat: 41°04.348' **Long:** 071°56.370' **Tide:** 2 ft. **Current:** 0 ft. **Chart:** 12309
Rep. Depths (MLW): **Entry** 7 ft. **Fuel Dock** 7 ft. **Max Slip/Moor** 8 ft./-
Access: Hard to starboard at Coast Guard Station, second facility west shore

Marina Facilities (In Season/Off Season)
Fuel: Yes* - Gasoline, Diesel, High-Speed Pumps
Slips: 104 Total, 25 Transient **Max LOA:** 75 ft. **Max Beam:** n/a
　Rate (per ft.): **Day** $2.25/$1.50 **Week** $15.50 **Month** n/a
　Power: 30 amp Incl., **50 amp** Incl., **100 amp** n/a, **200 amp** n/a
　Cable TV: Yes, Incl. **Dockside Phone:** No
　Dock Type: Fixed, Floating, Wood
Moorings: 0 Total, 0 Transient **Launch:** n/a
　Rate: Day n/a **Week** n/a **Month** n/a
Heads: 8 Toilet(s), 5 Shower(s) (with dressing rooms), Hair Dryers
Laundry: 2 Washer(s), 2 Dryer(s) **Pay Phones:** Yes, 3
Pump-Out: OnCall (Ch.73), 2 Port **Fee:** Free **Closed Heads:** Yes

Marina Operations
Owner/Manager: Tom Edwardes **Dockmaster:** Richard Schoen
In-Season: Jun-Sep, 5am-8pm **Off-Season:** Oct-Jun, 8am-5pm
After-Hours Arrival: Cal in advance
Reservations: Preferred **Credit Cards:** Visa/MC, Dscvr, Din, Amex
Discounts: Cash **Dockage:** n/a **Fuel:** $0.5g **Repair:** n/a
Pets: Welcome **Handicap Access:** No

Marina Services and Boat Supplies
Services - Docking Assistance, Trash Pick-Up, Dock Carts, Megayacht Facilities **Communication -** FedEx, AirBorne, UPS, Express Mail
Supplies - OnSite: Ice (Block, Cube, Shaved), Ships' Store, Bait/Tackle
OnCall: Propane

Boatyard Services
OnSite: Travelift (70T), Engine mechanic (gas, diesel), Electrical Repairs, Electronic Sales (Seatronics 728-8100), Electronics Repairs, Hull Repairs, Bottom Cleaning, Brightwork, Air Conditioning, Refrigeration, Compound, Wash & Wax, Interior Cleaning, Propeller Repairs, Woodworking, Painting, Awlgrip **OnCall:** Rigger, Sail Loft (80 +), Canvas Work, Inflatable Repairs, Life Raft Service, Upholstery, Yacht Interiors, Metal Fabrication
Near: Launching Ramp. **Yard Rates:** $85/hr., Power Wash $2.50/ft.

Restaurants and Accommodations
OnCall: Snack Bar , , Pizzeria (Pizza Village 668-2232) **Near:** Restaurant (Tipperary Inn 668-2010, D $12-22, Kids $6), (Clam & Chowder House 668-6252), (Salivar's 668-2555), (Dave's Grill 668-9190), (Lakeside Sunset Bar & Grill 668-6900), (Lenny's On The Dock 668-2500, D $7-19, Kids' $4-5), (Gosman's Inlet Café 668-2549), Motel (Harborside Motel 668-2511, $65-130), (Montauk Soundview 668-5500), (Seawind 668-4949), (Culloden House 668-2828, $60-150), (Tipperary Inn 668-2010, $65-195)

Recreation and Entertainment
OnSite: Picnic Area, Grills, Fishing Charter, Special Events (Shark Tournament) **OnCall:** Group Fishing Boat (Viking 668-5700) **Near:** Horseback Riding (Rita's Stable 668-5453 $30/hr.), Boat Rentals (Uihlein's - jet skis, etc.

668-3799 , Sightseeing (Whale Watching) **Under 1 mi:** Pool (Montauk Downs), Golf Course (Montauk Downs 668-1234) **1-3 mi:** Tennis Courts (Harborside 668-2511), Movie Theater (Montauk 668-2393), Video Rental (Montauk Vid 668-4824), Video Arcade, Museum (Second House)

Provisioning and General Services
Near: Convenience Store (Four Oaks 668-2534), Market (Gaviola's 668-1031), Gourmet Shop, Delicatessen (Country Kitchen 668-3872), Bakery, Fishmonger, Lobster Pound (Gosman's 668-5645) **Under 1 mi:** Bank/ATM
1-3 mi: Supermarket (Montauk IGA 668-4929), Health Food (Naturally Good 668-9030), Liquor Store (Montauk Lqrs & Wines 668-5454), Green Grocer (Ocean View 668-2900), Post Office (668-7043), Catholic Church, Protestant Church, Library (668-3377), Beauty Salon, Barber Shop, Dry Cleaners, Laundry (668-4349), Bookstore (Book Shoppe 668-4599), Pharmacy (White's 668-2994), Newsstand, Hardware Store (Montauk 668-2456)

Transportation
OnCall: Rental Car (Enterprise 668-3464), Taxi (Celtic 668-4747; Montauk 668-2468), Airport Limo (Hampton Jitney) **Near:** Local Bus (Suffolk Transit 852-5200 $1.50/1), Ferry Service (Viking to Block Is/New London)
1-3 mi: Bikes (Montauk Bike 668-8975), InterCity Bus (Hampton Jitney to NYC 283-4600 1/way $24/20), Rail (LIRR $10-15 one/way)
Airport: Montauk/Islip (5 mi./70 mi.)

Medical Services
911 Service **OnCall:** Ambulance **1-3 mi:** Doctor (Lighthouse Medical 668-3696), Dentist (Vasti 668-3398), Chiropractor (Montauk Chiropractic 668-4848) **Hospital:** Southhampton 726-8282 (30 mi.)

Setting -- This active, professional, buttoned-up sport fishing operation is Montauk Harbor's third facility -- leave the red-roofed Coast Guard station to port then pass the busy charter docks and Uihlein's to starboard. Find it on the west side across from the Star Island inlet in a very busy corner of the Harbor.

Marina Notes -- Family owned and operated since 1955. Significant shipyard operation can handle boats to 70 T/75 ft. with 2 travelifts. * Low sulfur fuel w/Cetane booster & fungicide additive; discount for cash purchases - $0.5/gal. 30/gal per min pumps. Extremely comprehensive, recently renovated ships' store with large bait and tackle section - including complete selection of inshore and off shore live bait, plus clothing, beverages and some groceries. Solid amenities, including very nice all tile heads, showers with dressing rooms and hair dryers. All in the context of a working yard marina. Seasonal rates $80-125/ft. Docks see a lot of early morning and late night action as serious anglers head out and return. International Game Fish Association Official Weigh Station.

Notable -- Annual onsite $50,000 Shark Tournament is late June (150 boat limit). Fishing Charters: El Bravo (Henriques 48), Dorado (Topaz 42), Karen Sue (Hattaras 41), Nora John (Bertram 42) - mostly $375/half day, $650+ full day. Within walking distance are Gosman's Dock, the Viking Ferry Fleet, many restaurants and the general Montauk Harbor action. For easy provisioning, Gaviola's market is nearby. Ocean View Farmers Market on Main St. has fresh local produce and gourmet provisions. Puff N Putt Family Fun Center (668-4473) across from the IGA. Local bus 10C goes to the Village & the RR station 9 times a day - and connects to # 94 out to Montauk Point (Jul & Aug only).

Navigational Information
Lat: 41°04.275' **Long:** 071°56.277' **Tide:** 2 ft. **Current:** 0 kt. **Chart:** 12309
Rep. Depths (MLW): Entry 10 ft. **Fuel Dock** 7 ft. **Max Slip/Moor** 8 ft./-
Access: Hard starboard at Coast Guard Station, 4th facility on western shore

Marina Facilities *(In Season/Off Season)*
Fuel: Gasoline, Diesel
Slips: 46 Total, 22 Transient **Max LOA:** 65 ft. **Max Beam:** n/a
  Rate *(per ft.)*: **Day** $2.00/1.40 **Week** $12 **Month** $25
  Power: 30 amp Incl., **50 amp** Incl., **100 amp** n/a, **200 amp** n/a
  Cable TV: No **Dockside Phone:** No
  Dock Type: Fixed, Short Fingers, Wood
Moorings: 0 Total, 0 Transient **Launch:** n/a
  Rate: Day n/a **Week** n/a **Month** n/a
Heads: 2 Toilet(s), 2 Shower(s)
Laundry: 1 Washer(s), 1 Dryer(s) **Pay Phones:** No
Pump-Out: OnCall *(Ch.73)* **Fee:** Free **Closed Heads:** Yes

Marina Operations
Owner/Manager: Vincent Carillo **Dockmaster:** Same
In-Season: May-Oct, 5am-7pm **Off-Season:** Nov-Apr, 8am-4pm
After-Hours Arrival: Call in advance
Reservations: Preferred **Credit Cards:** Visa/MC, Dscvr, Amex
Discounts: None
Pets: Welcome **Handicap Access:** No

Marina Services and Boat Supplies
Services - Docking Assistance, Security, Trash Pick-Up, Dock Carts
Communication - Fax in/out, FedEx, AirBorne, UPS, Express Mail
Supplies - OnSite: Ice *(Block, Cube, Shaved)*, Ships' Store, Bait/Tackle *(also Montauk Marine Basin)* **OnCall:** Propane

Boatyard Services
OnSite: Travelift *(50T)*, Engine mechanic *(gas, diesel)*, Electrical Repairs, Hull Repairs, Bottom Cleaning, Propeller Repairs **OnCall:** Electronics Repairs, Rigger, Brightwork, Air Conditioning, Refrigeration, Compound, Wash & Wax

Restaurants and Accommodations
OnSite: Lite Fare *(The Liar's Saloon 668-9597)* **Near:** Restaurant *(Gosman's 668-5330, L $14-22, D $14-22)*, *(Gosman's Inlet Cafe 668-2549, L $9-19, D $14-35, Kids' $9)*, *(Tipperary Inn 668-2010, D $12-20, Kids' $6)*, Seafood Shack *(Gosman's Clam Bar 668-2549)*, Motel *(Harborside Motel 668-2511, $65-130)*, *(Sea Wind 668-4949)*, *(Tipperary Inn 668-2010, $65-195)*, *(Gosman's Culloden House 668-9293)*

Recreation and Entertainment
OnSite: Picnic Area, Grills, Fishing Charter *(Sea Venture)* **Near:** Jogging Paths, Horseback Riding *(Rita's Stable 668-5453 $30/hr.)*, Boat Rentals *(Uihlein's - jet skis, etc. 668-3799)*, Group Fishing Boat *(Lazybones 668-5671, Flying Cloud 668-2026, Marlin 668-5852)*, Sightseeing *(Whale Watching - Viking)*, Special Events *(Shark Tournaments)*

Offshore Sports Marina

PO Box 2054; 408 West Lake Drive; Montauk, NY 11954

Tel: (631) 668-2406 **VHF: Monitor** 7 **Talk** 19
Fax: (631) 668-2423 **Alternate Tel:** n/a
Email: n/a **Web:** n/a
Nearest Town: Montauk *(3 mi.)* **Tourist Info:** n/a

Under 1 mi: Pool *(Montauk Downs 668-1234)*, Golf Course *(Montauk Downs)* **1-3 mi:** Tennis Courts, Movie Theater *(Montauk 668-2393)*, Video Rental *(Montauk Video 668-4824)*, Museum *(Second House)*

Provisioning and General Services
Near: Convenience Store *(Four Oaks 668-2534)*, Market, Gourmet Shop, Delicatessen *(Country Kitchen 668-3872)*, Bakery, Fishmonger, Lobster Pound *(Gosman's Continental Shelf 668-5645)* **Under 1 mi:** Bank/ATM **1-3 mi:** Supermarket *(Montauk IGA 668-4929)*, Liquor Store *(Montauk Lqrs & Wines 668-5454)*, Green Grocer *(Ocean View 668-2900)*, Post Office *(668-7043)*, Catholic Church, Protestant Church, Library *(668-3377)*, Beauty Salon, Barber Shop, Dry Cleaners, Laundry *(668-4349)*, Bookstore *(Book Shoppe 668-4599)*, Pharmacy *(White's 668-2994)*

Transportation
OnCall: Rental Car *(Enterprise 668-3464)*, Taxi *(Celtic 668-4747; Montauk 668-2468)*, Airport Limo *(Eastern Limo 668-2702)* **Near:** Local Bus *(Suffolk Transit 852-5200 $1.50/1)* **1-3 mi:** Bikes *(Montauk Bike 668-8975)*, InterCity Bus *(Hampton Jitney to NYC 283-4600 1/way $24/20)*, Rail *(LIRR $10-15 one/way)* **Airport:** Montauk/slip *(5 mi./70 mi.)*

Medical Services
911 Service **Under 1 mi:** Holistic Services **1-3 mi:** Doctor *(Lighthouse Medical 668-3696)*, Dentist *(Vasti 668-3398)*, Chiropractor *(Montauk Chiro 668-4848)* **Hospital:** Southampton 726-8282 *(30 mi.)*

Setting -- Nestled among the battery of docks that cover the western side of Montauk Harbor, about halfway along the shore, is down home, comfortable Offshore Sports Marina. The large "Liar's Saloon" sign on the two-story gray building makes it easy to find. A grassy strip along the docks is sprinkled with wooden picnic tables - most occupied by anglers trading stories, relaxing, and sharing food.

Marina Notes -- Owner operated, Offshore caters to a wide variety of sport fishing pleasure boats, particularly those looking for solid basics without the frills. Full boatyard services including a 50 ton travelift and most basic services. Mostly stationary stern-to dockage with pilings - few alongside - ask if this is important. Onsite is the infamous Liar's Saloon - a pub with food - where it's almost impossible to sort fact from fiction.

Notable -- A number of sport fishing charter boats make Offshore Sports Marina their home port. Among them is Sea Venture, a 37 ft. Topaz Sport Fish (Peter Stassi 631-987-3446), which specializes in fishing the Canyon - one and 2-day trips. Many restaurants are nearby and the Sea Wind Motel is right across the street. Located about a half mile from the entrance to Montauk Lake and the whole Gosman restaurant, fish market and gift shop complex and about two miles from the center of Montauk village. The Suffolk County bus #10C stops nearby and goes to the village, the Long Island railroad station, and the Ditch Plains ocean beach.

Westlake Marina

Westlake Marina

PO Box 5022; Westlake Drive; Montauk, NY 11954

Tel: (631) 668-5600 **VHF: Monitor** 19 **Talk** 19
Fax: (631) 668-5614 **Alternate Tel:** (631) 668-5600
Email: n/a **Web:** n/a
Nearest Town: Montauk *(2.5 mi.)* **Tourist Info:** (631) 668-2428

Navigational Information
Lat: 41°04.060' **Long:** 071°56.240' **Tide:** 2 ft. **Current:** 0 kt. **Chart:** 12309
Rep. Depths *(MLW)*: **Entry** 5 ft. **Fuel Dock** n/a **Max Slip/Moor** 5 ft./-
Access: Starboard at Coast Guard Station almost to harbor's head

Marina Facilities *(In Season/Off Season)*
Fuel: No
Slips: 100 Total, 15 Transient **Max LOA:** 65 ft. **Max Beam:** 20 ft.
  Rate *(per ft.)*: **Day** $2.00/1.75 **Week** $12/10 **Month** $36/30
  Power: 30 amp Incl., 50 amp Incl., 100 amp n/a, 200 amp n/a
  Cable TV: No **Dockside Phone:** No
  Dock Type: Fixed, Floating, Wood, Vinyl
Moorings: 0 Total, 0 Transient **Launch:** n/a
  Rate: Day n/a **Week** n/a **Month** n/a
Heads: 2 Toilet(s), 4 Shower(s) *(with dressing rooms)*
Laundry: None, Book Exchange **Pay Phones:** Yes, 2
Pump-Out: OnCall *(Ch. 73)* **Fee:** Free **Closed Heads:** Yes

Marina Operations
Owner/Manager: Chris Miller **Dockmaster:** Same
In-Season: Mar 15-Dec 15, 5am-6pm **Off-Season:** Dec-16-Mar14, Closed
After-Hours Arrival: Call ahead
Reservations: Yes, Preferred **Credit Cards:** Visa/MC, Dscvr
Discounts: None
Pets: Welcome, Dog Walk Area **Handicap Access:** No

Marina Services and Boat Supplies
Services - Docking Assistance, Trash Pick-Up, Dock Carts
Communication - Fax in/out, FedEx, AirBorne, UPS, Express Mail
Supplies - OnSite: Ice *(Block, Cube, Shaved)*, Ships' Store, Bait/Tackle
1-3 mi: Propane *(Beckers ACE 668-2368)*

Boatyard Services
OnCall: Bottom Cleaning, Brightwork, Divers, Compound, Wash & Wax, Interior Cleaning **Near:** Travelift, Engine mechanic *(gas, diesel)*, Launching Ramp, Electrical Repairs, Electronic Sales, Electronics Repairs, Hull Repairs, Air Conditioning, Refrigeration, Propeller Repairs, Metal Fabrication. **Nearest Yard:** Star Island YC (631) 668-5053

Restaurants and Accommodations
OnSite: Restaurant *(Clam & Chowder House B $3-8, L $5-12, D $6-20, Sandwiches, soups, and a sushi bar)* **OnCall:** Pizzeria *(Pizza Village 668-2232)* **Near:** Motel *(Seawind 668-4949, $140)*, *(Harborside 668-2511, $65-130)* **Under 1 mi:** Restaurant *(The Dock 668-9778)*, *(Sunset Bar & Grill 668-6900)*, *(Gosman's 668-5330)*, *(Lenny's 668-2500, D $7-19, Kids' $4-5)*, Motel *(Blue Haven 668-5943)*, *(Sandy Acre 668-9293)*, *(Soundview 668-5500)* **1-3 mi:** Seafood Shack *(West Cove Seafood 668-2705)*

Recreation and Entertainment
OnSite: Picnic Area, Grills, Playground, Fishing Charter *(Daybreaker)*
Near: Beach, Group Fishing Boat *(Viking 668-5700)* **1-3 mi:** Tennis Courts *(Harborside Tennis 668-2511)*, Golf Course *(Montauk Downs 668-1234)*, Movie Theater *(Montauk Movie 668-2393)*, Video Rental *(Montauk Video*

668-4824), Park, Museum *(Montauk Lighthouse Museum 668-2544, Third House Museum 852-7878)*, Cultural Attract *(Montauk Theatre 668-5656)*, Sightseeing *(Harbor tours, whale watching)*, Special Events *(Shakespeare Festival 267-0105)*

Provisioning and General Services
Under 1 mi: Convenience Store, Market *(Gaviola's 668-1031)*, Delicatessen *(Continental 668-6060)*, Wine/Beer, Bakery *(Bake Shoppe 668-2439)*, Fishmonger *(Gosman's)*, Lobster Pound, Bank/ATM, Bookstore *(The Book Shoppe 668-4599)* **1-3 mi:** Supermarket *(IGA 668-4929)*, Health Food *(Naturally Good 668-9030)*, Liquor Store *(White's Liquor 668-2426, delivers)*, Green Grocer *(Ocean View 668-2900)*, Meat Market, Post Office, Catholic Church, Protestant Church, Library *(Montauk 668-3377)*, Beauty Salon, Barber Shop, Laundry *(Montauk Laundromat 668-4349)*, Pharmacy *(White's 668-2994)*, Newsstand, Hardware Store *(Beckers ACE 668-2368)*, Florist, Retail Shops, Department Store *(White's)*, Copies Etc.

Transportation
OnCall: Rental Car *(Enterprise 668-3464)*, Taxi *(Montauk 668-2468, Celtic 668-4747)*, Airport Limo *(Eastern Limo 668-2702)* **Under 1 mi:** Bikes *(Bike Shop 668-8975)* **1-3 mi:** Rail *(LIRR to NYC)*
Airport: Montauk/Islip *(5 mi./70 mi.)*

Medical Services
911 Service **OnCall:** Ambulance **1-3 mi:** Doctor *(Mountauk Med 668-3705)*, Dentist *(Vasti 668-5959)*, Chiropractor *(Family Chiro 668-4535)*, Holistic Services **Hospital:** Southampton 726-8335 *(30 mi.)*

Setting -- On the south end of Montauk Harbor, tucked in between Diamond Cove and Snug Harbor, Westlake Marina is a warm homeport for many anglers with boats in the under forty foot category. The landside is dominated by the Clam & Chowder House and water views are mostly of the neighboring docks. Landscaping consists largely of beige gravel and stones.

Marina Notes -- Family owned and operated. Used to be called Westlake Fishing Lodge. A well-known Montauk anglers port, with decent heads, plenty of bait and tackle. Boats tend to be mid-range 25-40 feet -- rather than big offshore boats. Helpful, friendly staff with a good reputation among fishers. Traffic will be busy in the marina when the fishing is on. Picnic tables sit on the gravel right off the docks. Six-passenger charter boat Daybreaker makes its home here (668-5070).

Notable -- The Clam & Chowder House is practically on the dock and open for breakfast, lunch and dinner - with sandwich platters, pasta, appetizers, salads and a wide variety of very fresh sushi (try the crisp soft shell crab sushi with wasabi and pickled ginger). It will also prepare lunch sandwiches to go. Eat inside in the very casual, windowed dining room or at umbrellaed tables outside. A bar and raw bar open directly on the marina front. It's an easy stroll to the entire West Lake Drive/Gosmans/Montauk Harbor nexus, but you'll need a taxi or the local bus to get to the village and "The Plaza". Take the bus to the Montauk Lighthouse, or head to the ocean beaches and watch the surfers if there's a swell on (Ditch Plains is most popular).

Navigational Information
Lat: 41°04.027' **Long:** 071°56.200' **Tide:** 3 ft. **Current:** n/a **Chart:** 12309
Rep. Depths (*MLW*): **Entry** 8 ft. **Fuel Dock** n/a **Max Slip/Moor** 8 ft./-
Access: Block Island Sound to Montauk Harbor to the head

Marina Facilities *(In Season/Off Season)*
Fuel: No
Slips: 84 Total, 20 Transient **Max LOA:** 45 ft. **Max Beam:** 16 ft.
  Rate *(per ft.)*: **Day** $3.00* **Week** Inq. **Month** Inq.
  Power: 30 amp Inc., 50 amp Inc., 100 amp n/a, 200 amp n/a
  Cable TV: Yes Some slips **Dockside Phone:** No
  Dock Type: Fixed, Floating, Long Fingers, Pilings
Moorings: 0 Total, 0 Transient **Launch:** n/a
  Rate: Day n/a **Week** n/a **Month** n/a
Heads: 4 Toilet(s), 4 Shower(s)
Laundry: 1 Washer(s), 1 Dryer(s), Book Exchange **Pay Phones:** Yes
Pump-Out: OnCall *(Ch. 73)* **Fee:** Free **Closed Heads:** Yes

Marina Operations
Owner/Manager: n/a **Dockmaster:** Loretta DeRose
In-Season: May-Nov, 8:30 am-10 pm **Off-Season:** Dec-Apr, Closed
After-Hours Arrival: Call for slip assignment
Reservations: No **Credit Cards:** Visa/MC, Dscvr, Amex
Discounts: None
Pets: Welcome, Dog Walk Area **Handicap Access:** No

Snug Harbor Resort & Marina

3 Star Island Road; Montauk, NY 11954

Tel: (631) 668-2860 **VHF: Monitor** 9 **Talk** 8
Fax: (631) 668-9068 **Alternate Tel:** n/a
Email: n/a **Web:** www.MontaukSnugHarbor.com
Nearest Town: Montauk *(2.5 mi.)* **Tourist Info:** (631) 668-2428

Marina Services and Boat Supplies
Services - Docking Assistance, Trash Pick-Up, Dock Carts
Communication - Mail & Package Hold, Phone Messages, Fax in/out *($2)*, FedEx, AirBorne, UPS, Express Mail *(Sat Del)* **Supplies - Near:** Ice *(Block, Cube)*, Ships' Store, Bait/Tackle *(Star Island Y. C.)*, Live Bait
1-3 mi: Propane

Boatyard Services
OnCall: Electrical Repairs, Electronics Repairs, Bottom Cleaning
Near: Launching Ramp. **Under 1 mi:** Hull Repairs.
Nearest Yard: Star Island YC (631) 668-5053

Restaurants and Accommodations
OnSite: Motel *(Snug Harbor $110-260, Off season $55-185)* **Near:** Restaurant *(Il Mare at Montauk YC)*, Seafood Shack *(Clam & Chowder)*
Under 1 mi: Restaurant *(The Dock 668-9778)*, *(Sunset Bar & Grill 668-6900)*, Seafood Shack *(West Cove Seafood 668-2705)*, Pizzeria *(Sausages 668-1144)*, Motel *(Harborside 668-2511, $65-130)*, *(Blue Haven 668-5943)*, Inn/B&B *(Kennys Tipperary Inn 668-2010, $85-200)*, *(Culloden House 668-9293, $60-150)* **1-3 mi:** Lite Fare *(Munch Box 668-5009)*

Recreation and Entertainment
OnSite: Pool, Beach, Picnic Area, Grills, Playground, Volleyball
Near: Tennis Courts *(Harborside Tennis 668-2511)*, Horseback Riding *(Rita's Stable 668-5453 $30/hr.)*, Roller Blade/Bike Paths, Fishing Charter *(Star Island 668-5052)*, Group Fishing Boat *(Lazybones 668-5671, Flying Cloud 668-2026, Marlin 668-5852)* **Under 1 mi:** Dive Shop, Golf Course

(Montauk Downs 66 1234 , Boat Rentals *(Uihlens boats, kayaks & jet skis*
1-3 mi: Jogging Paths, Movie Theater *(Montauk Movie 668-2393)*, Video Rental *(Montauk Video 668-4824)*, Video Arcade, Park, Museum *(Montauk Lighthouse Museum 668-2544/Third House Museum 852-7878)*, Cultural Attract *(Montauk Theatre 668-5656)*, Sightseeing *(Harbor tours, whale watching)*, Special Events *(Shakespeare Festival 267-0105)*

Provisioning and General Services
Under 1 mi: Convenience Store, Gourmet Shop, Delicatessen *(Herb's Market 668-3908)*, Fishmonger, Bookstore *(The Book Shoppe 668-4599)*
1-3 mi: Supermarket *(IGA 668-4929)*, Health Food *(Naturally Good 668-9030)*, Wine/Beer, Liquor Store *(White's Liquor 668-2426, delivers)*, Bakery *(Bake Shoppe 668-2439)*, Green Grocer *(Ocean View 668-2900)*, Meat Market, Bank/ATM, Post Office, Catholic Church, Library *(Montauk 668-3377)*, Beauty Salon, Dry Cleaners, Laundry, Pharmacy *(White's 668-2994)*, Newsstand, Hardware Store *(Beckers ACE 668-2368)*, Florist, Retail Shops, Department Store *(White's)*, Copies Etc.

Transportation
OnCall: Taxi *(Celtic Cabs 668-4747)*, Airport Limo *(Eastern Limousine 668-2702)* **Near:** Bikes *(Bike Shop 668-8975)*, Local Bus **1-3 mi:** Rail *(LIRR to Penn Station-NYC)* **Airport:** Montauk/Islip *(5 mi./70 mi.)*

Medical Services
911 Service **OnCall:** Ambulance **1-3 mi:** Doctor *(Lighthouse Medical 668-3696)*, Dentist *(Vasti 668-5959)*, Chiropractor *(Family Chiropractic 668-4535)*, Holistic Services **Hospital:** Southampton 726-8335 *(30 mi.)*

Setting -- Snug Harbor is at the end of the channel to the west of Star Island -- at the head of Montauk Harbor. Star Island Road forms one boundary of this mini-resort. Landward views are of grass, picnic tables, playgrounds, the contemporary waterfront two-story motel and the marina buildings. Views to the north and east are of nearby marinas and Star Island.

Marina Notes -- *Dockage rate is $2.50/ft. with a room. Snug Harbor offers two stories of large, comfortable, well-equipped efficiency units with large kitchenettes, dining tables, 2 double beds and patios directly overlooking the docks, plus motel rooms that open onto the waterfront. Daily and weekly rates. Tucked into a private shrubbed oasis is a small, inviting kidney shaped pool surrounded by a brick patio and chaises. A somewhat less-inviting beach lies just east of the docks. In the marina, Snug Harbor offers well maintained docks with 30 and 50 amp shore power. No fuel or pump-out, but hail pump-out boat on Channel 73.

Notable -- All of Montauk Harbor is located on the edge of some of the best fishing grounds in the Atlantic and Snug Harbor caters to families drawn to that reputation. Adjacent Westlake Clam Chowder and Sushi Bar serves breakfast, lunch and dinner. Plenty of activity to keep everyone amused in the Montauk Harbor/Gosman's Dock area, virtually all within walking distance. Town requires a taxi or local bus, but you can literally access the rest of Long Island from there by train, light plane or bus. Puff & Putt miniature golf is 3 miles away (668-4473).

PHOTOS ON CD-ROM: 9

Harbor Marina

423 Three Mile Harbor HC Road; East Hampton, NY 11937

Tel: (631) 324-5666 **VHF: Monitor** 9 **Talk** 10
Fax: (631) 324-3366 **Alternate Tel:** n/a
Email: info@harbormarina.com **Web:** www.harbormarina.com
Nearest Town: East Hampton *(4.5 mi.)* **Tourist Info:** (631) 324-0362

Navigational Information
Lat: 41°01.700' **Long:** 072°10.800' **Tide:** 3 ft. **Current:** 2 kt. **Chart:** 13209
Rep. Depths *(MLW):* **Entry** 13 ft. **Fuel Dock** 11 ft. **Max Slip/Moor** 11 ft./-
Access: Gardiner's Bay to Three Mile Harbor around Penny Sedge Is.

Marina Facilities *(In Season/Off Season)*
Fuel: *ValvTect* - Gasoline, Diesel
Slips: 95 Total, 3 Transient **Max LOA:** 67 ft. **Max Beam:** 20 ft.
  Rate *(per ft.):* **Day** $4.25/$2-4* **Week** $19.50 **Month** Inq.
  Power: 30 amp $5.50, **50 amp** $11, **100 amp** n/a, **200 amp** n/a
  Cable TV: No **Dockside Phone:** No
  Dock Type: Fixed, Floating, Long Fingers, Pilings, Wood
  Moorings: 0 Total, 0 Transient **Launch:** n/a
  Rate: Day n/a **Week** n/a **Month** n/a
Heads: 2 Toilet(s), 4 Shower(s)
Laundry: None **Pay Phones:** Yes
Pump-Out: OnCall **Fee:** Free **Closed Heads:** Yes

Marina Operations
Owner/Manager: Lynn Mendelman **Dockmaster:** Same
In-Season: May-Oct, 8am-5pm **Off-Season:** Nov-Apr, 8am-4:30pm**
After-Hours Arrival: Call ahead
Reservations: Yes **Credit Cards:** Visa/MC, Amex
Discounts: Fuel **Dockage:** n/a **Fuel:** $.10 **Repair:** n/a
Pets: Welcome, Dog Walk Area **Handicap Access:** Yes, Heads, Docks

Marina Services and Boat Supplies
Services - Docking Assistance, Security, Dock Carts **Communication -** Mail & Package Hold, Phone Messages, Fax in/out, Data Ports *(Marina office; will accept e-mails)*, FedEx, AirBorne, UPS, Express Mail *(Sat Del)*
Supplies - OnSite: Ice *(Block, Cube)*, Ships' Store, Bait/Tackle
1-3 mi: Propane *(Riverhead Building Supply 324-0300)*

Boatyard Services
OnSite: Travelift *(10T, 15T)*, Forklift *(7500 lb.)*, Electrical Repairs, Rigger, Bottom Cleaning, Brightwork **OnCall:** Electronics Repairs, Hull Repairs, Refrigeration **Near:** Launching Ramp. **Dealer for:** Cummins, Volvo Penta, Mercury MerCruiser, Johnson/Evinrude, Yamaha, Crusader, Yanmar, Westerbeke. **Member:** ABYC, Other Certifications: Mercruiser, Volvo Penta, Cummins, Yanmar, Yamaha, Johnson/Evinrude
Yard Rates: $75-105, Bottom Paint $12-13 *(paint incl.)*

Restaurants and Accommodations
OnSite: Restaurant *(Bostwick's Seafood Grill & Oyster Bar 324-1111, D $10-24, 5:30-10pm weeknights, 'til 11 Fri & Sat)*, Snack Bar **OnCall:** Pizzeria *(Pizza & Things 324-7974)* **Near:** Restaurant *(Michael's at Maidstone 324-0725)*, Condo/Cottage *(Maidstone Park Cottages 324-2837)* **Under 1 mi:** Restaurant *(E. H. Point 329-2800, L $7-15, D $20-40)*, *(Riccardo's Seafood 324-0000, D $18-30)*, Condo/Cottage *(E.H. Point 324-8400, $295-495)*

Recreation and Entertainment
OnSite: Beach *(Penny Sedge Island)* **Near:** Picnic Area, Grills, Museum *(Marine Museum's EH Boat Shop 324-6393, 267-6544; Pollack-Krasner House 324-4929 - 1mi.)* **Under 1 mi:** Video Rental *(Springs Video

324-5980)* **3+ mi:** Golf Course *(E.H. Golf Club 267-8810, 4 mi.)*, Bowling *(E.H. Bowl 324-1950, 5 mi.)*, Movie Theater *(EH Cinema 324-0448, 5 mi.)*, Cultural Attract *(John Drew Theater 324-4050, 5 mi.)*

Provisioning and General Services
OnSite: Newsstand **Near:** Convenience Store *(Maidstone 329-2830)*, Delicatessen, Bakery, Lobster Pound *(Commercial Docks)*, Beauty Salon *(Springs 329-3129)* **Under 1 mi:** Market *(Springs General Store 325-5065)*, Farmers' Market *(Round Swamp Farm 324-4438)*, Fishmonger, Meat Market, Protestant Church **1-3 mi:** Gourmet Shop *(Food & Co 329-1000)*, Liquor Store *(Franey's 324-0322)*, Bank/ATM, Post Office, Copies Etc. *(EH Bus 324-0405)* **3+ mi:** Supermarket *(Waldbaum's 324-6215, IGA 267-3556, 4 mi.)*, Health Food *(Second Nature 324-5257, 4 mi.)*, Library *(East Hampton 324-0222, 5 mi.)*, Bookstore *(Book Hampton 324-4939, 5 mi.)*, Pharmacy *(CVS 324-8587, 5 mi.)*, Hardware Store *(Village Hardware 324-2456, 4 mi.)*

Transportation
OnCall: Rental Car *(Enterprise 324-5050, Hertz 537-3987 - 2 mi.)*, Taxi *(Easthampton Taxi 329-0011)*, Airport Limo *(East Hampton 324-5466)* **Near:** Local Bus **1-3 mi:** Rail *(LIRR to NYC)* **3+ mi:** Bikes *(Bermuda Bikes 324-6688, 5 mi.)*, InterCity Bus *(Hampton Jitney 283-4600 to NYC, 5 mi.)* **Airport:** East Hampton/Islip *(7 mi./60 mi.)*

Medical Services
911 Service **OnCall:** Ambulance **1-3 mi:** Doctor *(Wainscott Walk-in 537-1892)*, Holistic Services *(Massage Associates 324-2201)* **3+ mi:** Dentist *(EH Dental 324-6800, 4 mi.)*, Chiropractor *(4 mi.)*, Veterinarian *(Disunno 324-0089, 4 mi.)* **Hospital:** Southampton 726-8200 *(19 mi.)*

Setting -- The first marina on the east side of Three Mile Harbor's entrance channel, Harbor Marina is partially tucked behind Penny Sedge Island. Views from the docks, in all directions other than east, are of natural, untouched beach and expanses of water. Landside is a well maintained boatyard and restaurant.

Marina Notes -- * Rates listed are for MemDay-LabDay. Offseason and shoulder season rates vary significantly, please call. ** In-season weekend hours 8am-6pm; Off-season closed Sat & Sun. Harbor's Mobile Marine Repair Service covers the South Fork (Sag Harbor to Montauk) for $75 plus reg charges. Fuel over 200 gals, $0.10 discount. Member ABYC, ESMTA, and AMI. Channel dredged to min. 18 foot depths; easy access from Gardiner's Bay. Well built and designed docks in excellent condition. Operated by the Mendleman Family, as are Gardiner's & Halsey's. While lacking the manicured aura of the latter, the same professionalism and helpfulness are apparent. Clientele is a mix of anglers and recreational boaters - serious sailors and powerboaters. Dry stack storage operation, too. Well-equipped ship's store (plus their www.seastore.net) can get you almost anything nautical. Onsite Bostwick's Restaurant offers casual dining inside and even less formal on the open air porch (with glorious sunsets) May-Jun,Thu-Sun; Jul-LabDay 7days; Thu-Sun 'til ColDay.

Notable -- Great beaches are an easy walk or dinghy ride. Penny Sedge is practically right off the docks - the island is owned by the marina and the Nature Conservancy. Maidstone has life guards, heads, picnic area, pavilion, and a ball field. "Three Mile Harbor", a fascinating new book on the history of the area, was written by co-owner Sylvia Mendelman. Nearby, Marine Museum's Boat Shop preserves traditional boatbuilding techniques with workshops & exhibits.

Navigational Information
Lat: 41°01.275' **Long:** 072°10.754' **Tide:** 3 ft. **Current:** 2 kt. **Chart:** 13209
Rep. Depths (*MLW*): **Entry** 8 ft. **Fuel Dock** n/a **Max Slip/Moor** 7 ft./-
Access: End of the channel leading into the harbor, hard turn to port

Marina Facilities *(In Season/Off Season)*
Fuel: No
Slips: 100 Total, 10 Transient **Max LOA:** 80 ft. **Max Beam:** n/a
  Rate (*per ft.*): **Day** $3.50 **Week** $19 **Month** Inq.
  Power: 30 amp Inc., **50 amp** Inc., **100 amp** n/a, **200 amp** n/a
  Cable TV: No **Dockside Phone:** No
  Dock Type: Floating, Long Fingers, Wood
Moorings: 0 Total, 0 Transient **Launch:** n/a
  Rate: Day n/a **Week** n/a **Month** n/a
Heads: 4 Toilet(s), 4 Shower(s)
Laundry: 2 Washer(s), 2 Dryer(s) **Pay Phones:** Yes
Pump-Out: OnCall (*Ch.73*), 1 Port **Fee:** Free **Closed Heads:** Yes

Marina Operations
Owner/Manager: Doug Dinizio **Dockmaster:** Same
In-Season: Jun-Sep, 8am-7pm **Off-Season:** Oct-May, 10am-4pm
After-Hours Arrival: Call in advance
Reservations: Preferred **Credit Cards:** n/a
Discounts: None
Pets: Welcome **Handicap Access:** No

Maidstone Harbor Marina
PO Box 3070; 313 3-Mile Harbor Rd; East Hampton, NY 11937

Tel: (631) 324-2651 **VHF: Monitor** 9 **Talk** 72
Fax: (631) 329-2536 **Alternate Tel:** n/a
Email: n/a **Web:** n/a
Nearest Town: East Hampton (*4 mi.*) **Tourist Info:** (631) 324-0362

Marina Services and Boat Supplies
Services - Docking Assistance, Trash Pick-Up, Dock Carts
Communication - FedEx, AirBorne, UPS, Express Mail (*Sat Del*)
Supplies - OnSite: Ice (*Block, Cube*) **Near:** Ships' Store (*East Hampton Pt. or Harbor Marina 324-5666 - 1 mi.*) **1-3 mi:** Bait/Tackle (*Sams 324-8686*)
3+ mi: Propane (*Pulver Gas 267-3700, 4 mi.*)

Boatyard Services
OnCall: Divers, Propeller Repairs **Near:** Travelift (*38T*), Forklift, Crane, Engine mechanic (*gas, diesel*), Electrical Repairs, Hull Repairs, Rigger, Bottom Cleaning, Air Conditioning, Refrigeration, Inflatable Repairs, Painting. **Nearest Yard:** East Hampton Point (631) 324-8400

Restaurants and Accommodations
OnSite: Restaurant (*Riccardo's D $20-40, Sun Brunch & Kids' Menu $6*)
Near: Restaurant (*East Hampton Point 329-4800, L $7-15, D $20-40*), Condo/Cottage (*East Hampton Point 329-2800*) **Under 1 mi:** Restaurant (*Michaels 324-0725*), Seafood Shack (*Bostwicks 324-1111, D $10-24*), Inn/B&B (*Getaway House 324-6422*)

Recreation and Entertainment
OnSite: Pool, Picnic Area, Grills **Near:** Beach (*Maidstone or Sammy's by dinghy*), Tennis Courts (*East Hampton Point*), Jogging Paths, Special Events (*Bastille Day fireworks*) **Under 1 mi:** Park (*Maidstone*), Museum (*Marine Museum's E.H. Boat Shop 324-6393, 267-6544; Polack-Krasner House 324-4929*) **1-3 mi:** Golf Course (*East Hampton Golf Club 267-2100*), Video Rental (*Springs Video 324-5980 631-324-5980*) **3+ mi:** Horseback Riding (*Stony Hill 267-3203, 4 mi.*), Bowling (*East Hampton Bowl 324-1950 , 4 mi.*),

Movie Theater (*EH Cinema 324-0448, 4 mi.*), Cultural Attract (*John Drew Theater 324-4050, 4 mi.*), Galleries (*in East Hampton, 4 mi.*)

Provisioning and General Services
Near: Convenience Store, Green Grocer (*Round Swamp Farm 324-4438*), Lobster Pound (*Commerical Docks*) **Under 1 mi:** Market (*Maidstone Market 329-2830 7am-7pm, 7days*), Gourmet Shop (*Food & Co. 329-3777*), Delicatessen (*Damarks 324-0691*) **1-3 mi:** Wine/Beer (*Franey's 324-0322 1.2 mi.*), Liquor Store (*East Hampton 324-5757*), Bank/ATM, Post Office, Protestant Church, Library, Beauty Salon, Dry Cleaners, Laundry, Pharmacy (*CVS 324-8587*), Retail Shops **3+ mi:** Supermarket (*Waldbaum's 324-6215, 4 mi.*), Health Food (*Mother Natures Garden 329-4745, 4 mi.*), Catholic Church (*4 mi.*), Synagogue (*4 mi.*), Bookstore (*Book Hampton 324-4939, 4 mi.*), Hardware Store (*Village Hardware 324-2456, 4 mi.*)

Transportation
OnCall: Rental Car (*Enterprise 324-5050/Hertz 537-3987 - 2 mi.*), Taxi (*Easthampton Taxi 329-0011*), Airport Limo (*East Hampton Limousine 324-5466*) **Near:** Local Bus (*Suffolk Transit $1.50/1*) **3+ mi:** Bikes (*Bermuda Bikes 324-6688, 4 mi.*), Rail (*LIRR to Penn Station NYC, 4 mi.*)
Airport: East Hampton/Islip (*5 mi./60 mi.*)

Medical Services
911 Service **1-3 mi:** Chiropractor (*Hampton Medical 324-1037*), Holistic Services (*Massage Associates 324-2201*), Veterinarian (*Disunno 324-0089*) **3+ mi:** Doctor (*Amagansett Health Cntr. 267-6987, 4 mi.*), Dentist (*Katz 324-5015, 4 mi.*), Optician (*Gruen 324-5441, 4 mi.*)
Hospital: Southampton 726-8200 15 mi.

Setting -- Hidden away in a placid basin, just before the most outer docks of East Hampton Point, Maidstone is a very well done, pretty and quiet small marina. The mature plantings and swaths of lawn that slope up from the docks artfully enhance the sense of seclusion. The views are mostly of the basin itself and the mature stands of trees and shrubs that ring it.

Marina Notes -- Completely rebuilt in 1993. The pedestals and docks are still in excellent shape. The docks line the large rectangular basin with an additional set of docks marching up the center. The configuration provides privacy to the crew and verdant views. Heads and showers are well maintained with combination locks.

Notable -- A cement patio with chaises surrounds a small, kidney shaped pool that looks out over the basin (and has a part-time life guard). At the head of the basin, surrounded by carefully tended perennial borders, is Riccardo's Seafood House - inside it's fine dining; outside a more casual covered porch, protected by a low hedge, has views of the basin to the entrance. The chef puts a South American twist on local bounty; in season it's open 7 nights a week Sun-Thu 6-10pm, Fri & Sat 6-11pm for dinner and on Sat and Sun from Noon to 3pm for brunch. They also offer a kids' menu. Right next door is East Hampton Point with more restaurants, services, and a complete boatyard and ships' store. Beaches are an easy dinghy ride or a hike and the local bus into town (and to the beach) runs past the door every 90 minutes (check the bulletin board for schedule).

East Hampton Point

PO Box 847; 295 Three Mile Harbor Rd.; East Hampton, NY 11937

Tel: (631) 324-8400 **VHF:** Monitor 9 **Talk** 10
Fax: (631) 324-3751 **Alternate Tel:** (631) 324-9191
Email: marina@easthamptonpoint.com **Web:** easthamptonpoint.com
Nearest Town: East Hampton *(4 mi.)* **Tourist Info:** (631) 324-0362

Navigational Information
Lat: 41°01.215' **Long:** 072°10.850' **Tide:** 3 ft. **Current:** 2 kt. **Chart:** 13209
Rep. Depths *(MLW)*: **Entry** 8 ft. **Fuel Dock** 7 ft. **Max Slip/Moor** 7 ft./-
Access: Follow the channel into the harbor, just past Maidstone Marina

Marina Facilities *(In Season/Off Season)*
Fuel: Gasoline, Diesel
Slips: 57 Total, 12 Transient **Max LOA:** 110 ft. **Max Beam:** n/a
   Rate *(per ft.)*: **Day** $3.75* **Week** n/a **Month** n/a
   Power: 30 amp $5, 50 amp $10, 100 amp $20, 200 amp n/a
   Cable TV: Yes, $5 /night **Dockside Phone:** No
   Dock Type: Fixed, Floating, Short Fingers, Pilings, Alongside
Moorings: 0 Total, 0 Transient **Launch:** Yes, Dinghy Dock ($10/day)
   Rate: Day n/a **Week** n/a **Month** n/a
Heads: 4 Toilet(s), 4 Shower(s) *(with dressing rooms)*, Hair Dryers
Laundry: 2 Washer(s), 2 Dryer(s) **Pay Phones:** Yes
Pump-Out: OnSite, OnCall, Full Service **Fee:** Free **Closed Heads:** Yes

Marina Operations
Owner/Manager: Tim Treadwell **Dockmaster:** Same
In-Season: May-Oct, 8am-6pm **Off-Season:** Nov-Apr, 9am-5pm
After-Hours Arrival: Contact Dockmaster
Reservations: Yes **Credit Cards:** Visa/MC, Amex
Discounts: None
Pets: Welcome **Handicap Access:** Yes, Heads, Docks

Marina Services and Boat Supplies
Services - Docking Assistance, Concierge, Boaters' Lounge, Security *(On site)*, Dock Carts **Communication -** Phone Messages, Fax in/out, Data Ports, FedEx, AirBorne, UPS, Express Mail *(Sat Del)* **Supplies - OnSite:** Ice *(Block, Cube)*, Ships' Store **Near:** Propane *(Three Mile Harbor Boatyard 324-1320)* **1-3 mi:** Ice *(Shaved)*, Bait/Tackle *(Sams 324-8686)*, Live Bait

Boatyard Services
OnSite: Travelift *(38T)*, Forklift, Crane, Engine mechanic *(gas, diesel)*, Electrical Repairs, Electronics Repairs, Hull Repairs, Rigger, Bottom Cleaning, Brightwork, Air Conditioning, Refrigeration, Inflatable Repairs, Painting, Yacht Broker, Total Refits **OnCall:** Divers, Compound, Wash & Wax, Propeller Repairs, Woodworking, Upholstery, Metal Fabrication **Dealer for:** Yanmar Diesel. **Member:** ABYC **Yard Rates:** $75/hr., Haul & Launch $8/ft. *(blocking incl.)*, Power Wash $3/ft., Bottom Paint $15/ft. *(paint incl.)* **Storage:** On-Land Winter $29.75 / $65 Indoor

Restaurants and Accommodations
OnSite: Restaurant *(East Hampton Point 329-2800, L $7-15, D $20-40)*, Condo/Cottage *(Individual townhouse cottages $295-495)* **Near:** Restaurant *(Riccardo's 324-0000, D $18-30)* **Under 1 mi:** Restaurant *(Michaels at Maidstone 324-0725)*, *(Bostwicks 324-1111, D $10-24)*, Pizzeria *(Pizza & Things 324-7974)*, Inn/B&B *(Getaway House 324-9024)* **1-3 mi:** Inn/B&B *(Mill House Inn 324-9766, $150-650)*

Recreation and Entertainment
OnSite: Heated Pool, Picnic Area, Grills, Playground, Tennis Courts, Fitness Center, Fishing Charter *(Fly fishing)* **Under 1 mi:** Beach *(Maidstone Park)*, Video Rental *(Springs Video 324-5980)*, Museum *(Marine Museum's EH Boat Shop 324-6393, 267-6544)* **1-3 mi:** Golf Course *(East Hampton G.C. 267-2100)* **3+ mi:** Horseback Riding *(Stony Hill 267-3203, 4 mi.)*, Bowling *(EH Bowl 324-1950, 4 mi.)*, Movie Theater *(EH Cinema 324-0448, 4 mi.)*, Cultural Attract *(John Drew Theater 324-4050, 4 mi.)*

Provisioning and General Services
OnSite: Copies Etc. **Near:** Convenience Store, Wine/Beer, Green Grocer *(Round Swamp 324-4438)* **Under 1 mi:** Market *(Maidstone 329-2830)*, Gourmet Shop *(Food & Co 329-3777)*, Delicatessen *(Damarks 324-0691)*, Bakery, Beauty Salon *(Springs 329-3129)* **1-3 mi:** Liquor Store *(Franeys 324-0322)*, Bank/ATM, Post Office, Protestant Church, Dry Cleaners, Pharmacy *(CVS 324-8587)* **3+ mi:** Supermarket *(Waldbaum's 324-6215, 4 mi.)*, Health Food *(Mother Natures 329-4745, 4 mi.)*, Fishmonger *(Citeralla 329-1004, 4 mi.)*, Catholic Church *(5 mi.)*, Synagogue *(5 mi.)*, Library *(324-0222, 4 mi.)*, Bookstore *(Book Hampton 324-4939, 4 mi.)*, Hardware Store *(Village 324-2456, 4 mi.)*

Transportation
OnSite: Courtesy Car/Van **OnCall:** Rental Car *(Enterprise 324-5050)*, Taxi *(East End 324-8800)*, Airport Limo *(East Hampton 324-5466)* **Near:** Local Bus **3+ mi:** InterCity Bus *(Hampton Jitney 283-4600, 5 mi.)*, Rail *(LIRR to NYC, 5 mi.)* **Airport:** East Hampton/Islip *(5 mi./60 mi.)*

Medical Services
911 Service **OnCall:** Ambulance **1-3 mi:** Doctor *(EH Prime Care 907-9086)*, Dentist *(Nelson 324-6800)*, Chiropractor, Holistic Services, Veterinarian *(Disunno 324-0089)* **Hospital:** Southampton 726-8200 *(13 mi.)*

Setting -- Directly on Three Mile Harbor, luxurious East Hampton Point is a magnet for larger cruising craft. This very pleasant, upscale resort, all beautifully maintained by a service-oriented staff, is a destination in itself. The recreational facilities and cottages are nestled in a woodland setting away from the water.

Marina Notes -- *$135 per ft. seasonal. Full service marina and boatyard - second largest travelift in the Harbor. Excellent dockage - many single slips with some alongside. High end quarry tile heads with private dressing rooms and saunas. A TV lounge for the kids. All recreational facilities are an easy walk from the docks and available free to marina guests. Fully equipped, handsomely decorated, rental "cottages" are two-story, one or two bedroom townhouse units with kitchens, dining and living areas. Onsite East Hampton Point Restaurant has five dining "rooms" and a bar. Fine dining in the elegant indoor main room or adjacent porch and casual outdoor dining on one of The Decks or at the Bar (which sports a full size, dressed, wooden sail boat). The upstairs room and deck serves private functions. All promise breathtaking sunsets. This was formerly Wings Point and acquired by the current owners in the early nineties.

Notable -- A guest of the marina is a guest of the resort. Between the docks and Three Mile Harbor Road is a fairly narrow mini resort with carefully manicured mature plantings. Shrubbery secludes the inviting pool which is surrounded by chaises, tables and chairs, and market umbrellas. The tennis courts, almost adjacent to the road, sport comfortable shaded seating. In between, closeted in greenery, are the cottages. A courtesy van makes regular runs to the beach and to the East Hampton shopping district with its block after block of high-end shops, boutiques, restaurants, gourmet shops and myriad services.

Navigational Information
Lat: 41°00.881' **Long:** 072°10.810' **Tide:** 3 ft. **Current:** 2 kt. **Chart:** 13209
Rep. Depths (*MLW*): **Entry** 6 ft. **Fuel Dock** n/a **Max Slip/Moor** 6 ft./-
Access: Three Mile Harbor Channel, about half way up Harbor on east side

Marina Facilities (*In Season/Off Season*)
Fuel: No
Slips: 40 Total, 3 Transient **Max LOA:** 50 ft. **Max Beam:** 20 ft.
  Rate (*per ft.*): **Day** $3.25 **Week** $20 **Month** n/a
  Power: 30 amp n/a, 50 amp n/a, 100 amp n/a, 200 amp n/a
  Cable TV: No **Dockside Phone:** No
  Dock Type: Fixed, Long Fingers, Short Fingers, Wood
Moorings: 0 Total, 0 Transient **Launch:** n/a
  Rate: Day n/a **Week** n/a **Month** n/a
Heads: 2 Toilet(s), 2 Shower(s) (*with dressing rooms*)
Laundry: 2 Washer(s), 2 Dryer(s) **Pay Phones:** No
Pump-Out: OnCall (*Ch.73*) **Fee:** Free **Closed Heads:** Yes

Marina Operations
Owner/Manager: Tim Treadwell **Dockmaster:** n/a
In-Season: May-Oct, 8am-6pm **Off-Season:** Nov-Apr, 9am-5pm
After-Hours Arrival: Call in advance
Reservations: Required **Credit Cards:** Visa/MC, Amex
Discounts: None
Pets: Welcome **Handicap Access:** Yes, Heads

Shagwong Marina

219 Three Mile Harbor HC Road; East Hampton, NY 11937

Tel: (631) 324-8400 **VHF: Monitor** 9 **Talk** 10
Fax: (631) 324-3751 **Alternate Tel:** n/a
Email: marina@easthamptonpoint.com **Web:** easthamptonpoint.com
Nearest Town: East Hampton (*4 mi.*) **Tourist Info:** (631) 324-0362

Marina Services and Boat Supplies
Services - Docking Assistance, Dock Carts **Communication -** FedEx, UPS, Express Mail **Supplies - Near:** Ice (*Block, Cube*), Ships' Store (*East Hampton Point*) **Under 1 mi:** Bait/Tackle (*Three Mile Harbor BY and Sams 324-8686*) **3+ mi:** Propane (*Pulver Gas 267-3700, 4 mi.*)

Boatyard Services
OnCall: Rigger, Canvas Work, Bottom Cleaning, Divers, Compound, Wash & Wax, Interior Cleaning **Near:** Travelift (*38T*), Forklift, Crane, Hydraulic Trailer, Engine mechanic (*gas, diesel*), Launching Ramp, Electrical Repairs, Electronics Repairs, Hull Repairs, Brightwork, Air Conditioning, Refrigeration, Propeller Repairs, Woodworking, Inflatable Repairs, Upholstery, Metal Fabrication, Painting. **Nearest Yard:** East Hampton Point (631) 324-8400

Restaurants and Accommodations
Near: Restaurant (*Riccardo's 324-0000, D $18-30*), (*East Hampton Point 329-2800, L $7-15, D $20-40*), Condo/Cottage (*East Hampton Point $295-495*) **Under 1 mi:** Restaurant (*Bostwicks 324-1111, D $10-24*), Inn/B&B (*Getaway House 324-6422*) **1-3 mi:** Restaurant (*Nick & Toni's 324-3550, D $15-29*), (*Michaels 324-0725*)

Recreation and Entertainment
OnSite: Picnic Area, Grills **OnCall:** Fishing Charter **Near:** Heated Pool (*East Hampton Point*), Playground, Tennis Courts (*East Hampton Point*), Fitness Center (*E. H. Point*), Jogging Paths, Special Events (*Bastille Day fireworks*) **Under 1 mi:** Beach (*Maidstone by dinghy*), Video Rental (*Springs Video 324-5980 631-324-5980*), Park (*Maidstone*)

1-3 mi: Golf Course (*East Hampton G.C. 267-2100*), Museum (*Pollack/Krasner House 324-4929; Osborn Jackson House 324-6850 4 mi.*) **3+ mi:** Bowling (*East Hampton Bowl 324-1950 , 4 mi.*), Movie Theater (*E.H. Cinema, 4 mi.*), Cultural Attract (*John Drew Theater 324-4050, 4 mi.*)

Provisioning and General Services
Near: Green Grocer (*Round Swamp Farm 324-4438*), Copies Etc. (*E.H. Point*) **Under 1 mi:** Convenience Store, Market (*Maidstone Mkt. 329-2830*), Gourmet Shop, Delicatessen (*Damark's 324-0691*), Wine/Beer, Lobster Pound, Beauty Salon (*Springs 329-3129*) **1-3 mi:** Liquor Store (*Franeys Wines & Liquors 324-0322*), Bakery (*Plain & Fancy 324-7853; Jessie's 907-8735*), Bank/ATM, Post Office, Protestant Church, Barber Shop, Dry Cleaners, Laundry, Pharmacy (*CVS 324-8587*) **3+ mi:** Supermarket (*Waldbaum's 324-6215 , 4 mi.*), Health Food (*Mother Natures Garden 329-4745, 4 mi.*), Catholic Church (5 mi.), Synagogue (5 mi.), Library (*324-0222, 4 mi.*), Bookstore (*BookHampton 324-4939, 4 mi.*), Hardware Store (*Village 324-2456, 4 mi.*)

Transportation
OnCall: Rental Car (*Enterprise 324-5050*), Taxi (*Easthampton 329-0011*), Airport Limo (*East Hampton Limo 324-5466*) **Near:** Local Bus (*Suffolk County to town or beach*) **1-3 mi:** InterCity Bus (*Hampton Jitney to NYC*), Rail (*LIRR to Penn station NYC*) **Airport:** East Hampton/Islip (*5mi./60mi.*)

Medical Services
911 Service **OnCall:** Ambulance **1-3 mi:** Doctor (*Amagansett Health 267-6987*), Dentist, Chiropractor, Holistic Services (*Massage Assoc 324-2201*), Veterinarian (*Disunno 324-0089*) **Hospital:** Southampton 726-8200 (*13 mi.*)

Setting -- High bulkheads guard the entrance to this quiet basin ringed with docks. A small beach with mini dunes and beach grass sits on the north side of the approach and a variety of chairs populate the grassy knoll behind it. A picnic area with tables and grills sits on the south side of the entry benefiting from the spectacular views across the harbor to the hilly, wooded shoreline and the undisturbed marsh.

Marina Notes -- As a result of a recent change in ownership, Shagwong is now managed by East Hampton Point Marina, a little over a quarter mile north. All the services of East Hampton Point are available to guests of Shagwong - the lovely secluded pool, tennis courts, laundry, full-service boat yard, ships store, restaurant, and courtesy van service into East Hampton town or the beach. It's an easy walk and E.H.P. also has a dinghy dock for use by Shagwong guests making those services quite convenient. Brand new heads and showers were installed at Shagwong during the Summer of '03 - along with other improvements. Docks have short or long finger piers.

Notable -- This is a quieter, more secluded alternative to East Hampton Point, where the docks are part of the restaurant scenery. This more private, off-the-beaten track location may have a distinct appeal to some. A large, waterfront stretch of lawn adjacent to the docks is, on occasion, the site of tented weddings or club cruise events (site still owned by the Shagwong's former owner, ask E.H. Point for contact information). The marina is about center in the two-mile long harbor - equidistant north to Maidstone Beach or south to Three Mile Harbor Boatyard's dinghy dock (the closest landing to East Hampton village).

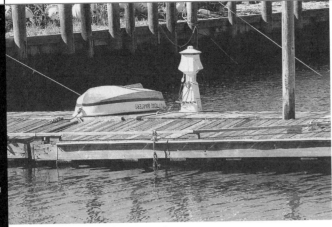

Navigational Information

Lat: 41°01.107' **Long:** 072°11.458' **Tide:** 3 ft. **Current:** 2 kt. **Chart:** 13209
Rep. Depths (*MLW*): Entry 13 ft. **Fuel Dock** n/a **Max Slip/Moor** -/10 ft.
Access: Gardiner's Bay to Three-Mile Harbor past Red 24

Marina Facilities *(In Season/Off Season)*

Fuel: No
Slips: 0 Total, 0 Transient **Max LOA** 50 ft. **Max Beam:** n/a
  Rate *(per ft.)*: **Day** n/a **Week** n/a **Month** n/a
  Power: 30 amp n/a, 50 amp n/a, 100 amp n/a, 200 amp n/a
  Cable TV: No **Dockside Phone:** No
  Dock Type: n/a
Moorings: 8 Total, 8 Transient **Launch:** None, Dinghy Dock
  Rate: Day $25 **Week** Inq. **Month** n/a
Heads: 2 Toilet(s)
Laundry: None **Pay Phones:** No
Pump-Out: OnCall *(Ch.73)* **Fee:** Free **Closed Heads:** Yes

Marina Operations

Owner/Manager: E.H.Town Trustees **Dockmaster:** Don Bousson (Hrbrmstr)
In-Season: May-October **Off-Season:** n/a
After-Hours Arrival: n/a
Reservations: First come, first served **Credit Cards:** cash only
Discounts: None
Pets: Welcome **Handicap Access:** No

East Hampton Town Moorings

159 Pantigo Road*; East Hampton, NY 11937

Tel: (631) 267-8688 **VHF: Monitor** Ch. 73 **Talk** n/a
Fax: (631) 267-2064 **Alternate Tel:** (631) 329-3078
Email: n/a **Web:** n/a
Nearest Town: East Hampton *(3 mi.)* **Tourist Info:** (631) 324-3366

Marina Services and Boat Supplies

Communication - Data Ports *(At East Hampton Public Library)* **Supplies -**
Near: Ice *(Block, Cube)*, Ships' Store *(Three Mile Harbor BY)*, Bait/Tackle
(Three Mile Harbor BY & & Mrs. Sam's 324-8686), Propane

Boatyard Services

Near: Travelift, Engine Mechanic (gas, diesel), Elecrical Repairs, Rigger
Nearest Yard: East Hampton Point Boatyard (631) 324-8400

Restaurants and Accommodations

Near: Restaurant *(East Hampton Point 324-8400, L $7-15, D $20-40, by
dinghy)*, *(Bostwick's 324-4111, by dinghy)*, *(Riccardo's 324-4000, D $18-30,
Seafood with a South American flair - by dinghy)*, Condo/Cottage *(Three Mile
harbor cottages 329-1431)* **Under 1 mi:** Inn/B&B *(Getaway House 324-
4622, $100-270)* **1-3 mi:** Restaurant *(Della Femina 329-6666)*, *(Maryjane's
324-8008)*, *(Nick & Toni's 324-3550, D $15-29, Sun Brunch $15)*

Recreation and Entertainment

Near: Beach *(Sammy's & Maidstone by dinghy)*, Picnic Area, Special Events
(Boys Harbor Fireworks display normally one week after July 4th.)
Under 1 mi: Tennis Courts *(Dunes Racquet Club 267-8508)*, Fitness Center
(East Hampton Gym 324-4499) **1-3 mi:** Golf Course *(East Hampton Golf
Club 267-2100)*, Horseback Riding *(East End Stables 324-9568)*, Bowling
(East Hampton Bowl 324-1950), Video Rental *(Springs Video 324-5980)*,
Museum *(Osborn Jackson House 324-6850; Marine Museum 267-6544)*,
Galleries *(in East Hampton)* **3+ mi:** Cultural Attract *(Playwrights Theatre
329-3909 , 4 mi.)*

Provisioning and General Services

Near: Delicatessen *(Damark's 324-0691)*, Hardware Store **Under 1 mi:**
Convenience Store, Wine/Beer *(E.H. Wine & Spirit 324-5757)*, Bakery
(Jessie's Bake Shop 907-8735), Pharmacy *(CVS 324-8587)*, Copies Etc.
(Town & Country Photo 324-4048) **1-3 mi:** Supermarket *(Waldbaum's
324-6215)*, Gourmet Shop *(Golden Pear 329-1600)*, Health Food *(Second
Nature Mkt 324-5257)*, Green Grocer *(Round Swamp Farm 324-4438)*,
Fishmonger *(Claws on Wheels 324-5090)*, Lobster Pound, Bank/ATM, Post
Office, Protestant Church, Library *(East Hampton 324-0222)*, Beauty Salon,
Barber Shop, Dry Cleaners, Bookstore *(BookHampton 324-4939; East End
324-8680)*, Newsstand, Florist, Retail Shops **3+ mi:** Catholic Church
(4 mi.), Synagogue *(4 mi.)*

Transportation

OnCall: Rental Car *(Enterprise 324-5050)*, Taxi *(East End 324-0077)*, Airport
Limo *(East Hampton Limousine 324-5466)* **Near:** Local Bus *(Suffolk
Country Transit to beach, East Hampton Village and LIRR 852-5200)*
1-3 mi: InterCity Bus *(Hampton Jitney 283-4600)*, Rail *(LIRR)* **3+ mi:** Bikes
(Bermuda Bikes 324-6688, 4 mi.) **Airport:** East Hampton/Islip *(3 mi./55 mi.)*

Medical Services

911 Service OnCall: Ambulance **Under 1 mi:** Dentist *(A. Katz 324-5015)*,
Holistic Services *(Naturopathica 329-2525)*, Veterinarian *(Disunno 324-
0089)* **1-3 mi:** Doctor *(Suffolk Health Care at East Hampton)*
Hospital: Southhampton *(15 mi.)*

Setting -- In the center of Three Mile Harbor, on the right side of the channel, just past red nun # 24, are the eight East Hampton Town Moorings. The location is quiet and the views of the western shore are remarkably bucolic - only a very occasional structure interrupts the wild, unsullied expanses of green.

Marina Notes -- Well-mudded 500 lb. mushroom moorings, reportedly good for a 4 boat raft, are managed by the E.H. Town Trustees - not the Harbormaster. Fee (per mooring not per boat) is collected by the pump-out boat. *Address is for East Hampton Town Hall. Three Mile Harbor Boatyard's dinghy dock is open to all - find ice and supplies there, too. (Above distances are calculated from this dock - except for beaches & marina restaurants). Heads, telephones plus additional dinghy tie-ups (if dock space is available) at the E.H.Town Marina in the Harbor's southeast corner, wedged between Gardiner's Marina on the north and Three Mile Harbor BY on the west. Free pump-out 8am-4pm Thu-Sun, Ch.73. Three Mile Harbormaster: Don Bousson, Ch.12.

Notable -- East Hampton Point has a dinghy dock ($10/day), and makes its superb facilities available to boats moored in the harbor - $25 daily pass for access to all the facilities: van service, pool, etc. Harbor Marina provides dinghy access to Bostwick's and Maidstone Marina to Riccardo's. Inquire about landing charges. Two dinghy accessible Gardiner's Bay beaches frame the Harbor entrance: Maidstone on the east side - pull up your dinghy on the harbor side and walk across to the Bay (life guards & heads); crescent-shaped Sammy's on the west side has a sharp drop-off so boats pull right up. Suffolk County bus 10B runs along Three Mile Harbor Rd. - north to the beach; south to E.H. town and LIRR $1.50/1 (at the E.H.Town Marina about every 90 min, 7am-6:30pm).

Navigational Information
Lat: 41°00.324' **Long:** 072°10.942' **Tide:** 3 ft. **Current:** 2 kt. **Chart:** 13209
Rep. Depths (*MLW*): **Entry** 8 ft. **Fuel Dock** n/a **Max Slip/Moor** 7 ft./-
Access: South End of Three Mile Harbor on east side

Marina Facilities *(In Season/Off Season)*
Fuel: No
Slips: 43 Total, 2 Transient **Max LOA:** 105 ft. **Max Beam:** 20 ft.
  Rate (*per ft.*): **Day** $4.25/$2-4* **Week** $19.50 **Month** n/a
  Power: 30 amp $5.50, **50 amp** $11, **100 amp** $22, **200 amp** n/a
  Cable TV: Yes, Inq. **Dockside Phone:** Yes, Inq.
  Dock Type: Fixed, Long Fingers, Wood
Moorings: 0 Total, 0 Transient **Launch:** n/a
  Rate: Day n/a **Week** n/a **Month** n/a
Heads: 2 Toilet(s), 2 Shower(s) *(with dressing rooms)*
Laundry: 1 Washer(s), 1 Dryer(s) **Pay Phones:** No
Pump-Out: OnCall *(Ch. 73)*, 1 Port **Fee:** n/a **Closed Heads:** Yes

Marina Operations
Owner/Manager: Peter Mendelman **Dockmaster:** Casey Jackson
In-Season: May-Oct, 8am-5pm **Off-Season:** Closed
After-Hours Arrival: Ch. 9
Reservations: Required **Credit Cards:** Visa/MC, Amex
Discounts: None
Pets: Welcome, Dog Walk Area **Handicap Access:** No

Halsey's Marina

73 Three Mile Harbor HC Rd.; East Hampton, NY 11937

Tel: (631) 324-5666 **VHF: Monitor** 9 **Talk** 10
Fax: (631) 324-3366 **Alternate Tel:** n/a
Email: info@halseysmarina.com **Web:** www.halseysmarina.com
Nearest Town: East Hampton *(3 mi.)* **Tourist Info:** (631) 324-0362

Marina Services and Boat Supplies
Services - Docking Assistance, Boaters' Lounge, Security, Trash Pick-Up, Dock Carts **Communication -** Phone Messages, Fax in/out, Data Ports *(Marina office)*, FedEx, AirBorne, UPS, Express Mail *(Sat Del)* **Supplies -** **OnSite:** Ice *(Block, Cube)* **Near:** Bait/Tackle *(Mrs. Sam's 324-8686)* **Under 1 mi:** Ships' Store *(Harbor Marina/Three Mile Harbor BY)* **1-3 mi:** Propane *(Riverhead Building Supply 324-0300)*

Boatyard Services
OnCall: Electrical Repairs, Electronic Sales, Electronics Repairs, Rigger, Canvas Work, Brightwork, Air Conditioning, Refrigeration, Divers, Propeller Repairs **Near:** Travelift *(40T)*, Engine mechanic *(gas, diesel)*, Launching Ramp, Hull Repairs, Bottom Cleaning. **Nearest Yard:** Three Mile Harbor Boatyard (631) 324-1320

Restaurants and Accommodations
Under 1 mi: Restaurant *(Riccardo's 324-0000, D $18-30)*, *(Bostwick's Seafood Grill & Oyster Bar 324-1111, D $10-24, by dinghy; check on landing fee)*, *(East Hampton Point 329-2800, L $7-15, D $20-40)*, Pizzeria *(Pepperonis 329-1800, delivers)*, Inn/B&B *(Getaway House 324-4622, $100-270)*, *(Mill House Inn 324-9766, $150-650)* **1-3 mi:** Restaurant *(Nick & Toni's 324-3550, D $15-29, Sun Brunch $15)*, *(Della Femina 329-6666)*, *(Turtle Crossing 324-7166)*, *(Rowdy Hall 324-8555)*

Recreation and Entertainment
OnSite: Picnic Area, Grills **Near:** Jogging Paths, Boat Rentals **Under 1 mi:** Tennis Courts *(Dunes Racquet Club 267-8508)*, Park **1-3 mi:** Beach *(East Hampotn's main beach)*, Golf Course *(E.H. G.C. 267-2100)*, Fitness Center, Bowling *(East Hampton Bowl 324-1950)*, Movie Theater *(E. H. Cinema 324-0448)*, Video Rental *(Springs Video 324-5980)*, Museum *(Osborn Jackson House 324-6850; Pollack/Krasner House 324-4929)*, Cultural Attract *(John Drew Theater 324-4050)*, Galleries *(East Hampton)*

Provisioning and General Services
Under 1 mi: Delicatessen *(Damarks 324-0691)*, Farmers' Market *(Round Swamp Farm 324-4438)*, Bank/ATM, Post Office, Protestant Church, Pharmacy *(CVS 324-2693)*, Newsstand **1-3 mi:** Supermarket *(Waldbaum's 324-6215; IGA 267-3556)*, Health Food *(Second Nature 324-5257)*, Liquor Store *(Franey's 324-0322, EH Wines & Spirits 324-5757)*, Catholic Church, Synagogue, Library *(East Hampton)*, Beauty Salon, Barber Shop, Dry Cleaners *(North Main 324-1640)*, Bookstore *(Book Hampton 324-4939)*, Hardware Store *(Village 324-2456)*, Copies Etc. *(EH Business 324-0405)*

Transportation
OnCall: Taxi *(Midway Taxi 324-9111)*, Airport Limo *(East Hampton Limousine 324-5466)* **1-3 mi:** InterCity Bus *(Hampton Jitney 283-4600)*, Rail *(LIRR to Penn Station NYC)* **3+ mi:** Bikes *(Bermuda Bikes 324-6688, 4 mi.)*, Rental Car *(Enterprise 324-5050/Hertz 537-3987, on call/2 mi.)* **Airport:** East Hampton/Islip *(3/60)*

Medical Services
911 Service **OnCall:** Ambulance **Near:** Chiropractor *(Kavanaugh 329-5994)* **Under 1 mi:** Veterinarian *(Disunno 324-0089)* **1-3 mi:** Doctor *(Wainscott Walk-in Clinic 537-1892)*, Dentist *(EH Dental 324-6800)*, Holistic Services *(Naturopathica 329-2525)*, Optician **Hospital:** Southampton 726-8200 *(18 mi.)*

Setting -- A peninsula carpeted with carefully-tended lawn juts into Three Mile Harbor and next to it a basin cuts into the shore - together these provide the bones for this perfect small oasis on the eastern shore. The best description of Halsey Marina is impeccable and manicured - and this applies to the craft docked there as well as the plant itself. Shade trees, flowers and grassy expanses, populated by picnic tables and grills, provide an idylic dockside setting.

Marina Notes -- **Rates listed are for MemDay-LabDay. Shoulder and off season rates can get complicated, call the office for details. This intimate big boat marina is managed the Mendelman Family, which owns Gardiners and Harbor Marina as well. A whitewashed club room, excellent heads and showers, plus a barbecue area shadowed by ancient trees make this a special place. The docks are old but well maintained. Yet the pedestal services are state-of-the-art. Boatyard services are available across the harbor at Three Mile Harbor B.Y. Or pick up a phone and a technician from Harbor Marina will be right down.

Notable -- The marina property is bordered on three sides by preserves providing unexpected quiet right off Three Mile Harbor Road -- just a couple of miles from upscale, vibrant East Hampton village. The head of Three Mile Harbor provides the closest boat access to the South Fork's literati and glitterati summer residence. Take the art, entertainment and political world's best and brightest and mix in locals, anglers, commercial fishermen, surfers and casual tourists for a people watching feast. The local bus - up to the beach or into town - runs by the door about every 90 minutes 'til 6pm. Or hike in and taxi back.

Gardiner's Marina

Navigational Information
Lat: 41°00.183' **Long:** 072°10.872' **Tide:** 3 ft. **Current:** 2 kt. **Chart:** 13209
Rep. Depths (*MLW*): **Entry** 13 ft. **Fuel Dock** n/a **Max Slip/Moor** 7 ft./-
Access: Gardiner's Bay to Three Mile Harbor

Marina Facilities *(In Season/Off Season)*
Fuel: No
Slips: 45 Total, 2-3 Transient **Max LOA:** 105 ft. **Max Beam:** 30 ft.
  Rate (*per ft.*): **Day** $4.25/$2-4** **Week** $19.50 **Month** Inq.
  Power: 30 amp $5.50, **50 amp** $11, **100 amp** $22, **200 amp** n/a
  Cable TV: Yes, Inq **Dockside Phone:** Yes
  Dock Type: Fixed, Floating, Pilings, Alongside, Wood
Moorings: 0 Total, 0 Transient **Launch:** n/a, Dinghy Dock
  Rate: Day n/a **Week** n/a **Month** n/a
Heads: 2 Toilet(s), 2 Shower(s)
Laundry: None **Pay Phones:** No
Pump-Out: OnCall *(Ch.73)*, Full Service **Fee:** Free **Closed Heads:** Yes

Marina Operations
Owner/Manager: Peter Mendelman **Dockmaster:** Casey Jackson
In-Season: May-Oct, 8am-5pm **Off-Season:** Closed
After-Hours Arrival: Call in advance
Reservations: Yes **Credit Cards:** Visa/MC, Amex
Discounts: None
Pets: Welcome, Dog Walk Area **Handicap Access:** Yes, Heads, Docks

Gardiner's Marina

35 Three Mile Harbor HC Road; East Hampton, NY 11937

Tel: (631) 324-5666 **VHF: Monitor** 9 **Talk** 10
Fax: (631) 324-3366 **Alternate Tel:** n/a
Email: info@gardinersmarina.com **Web:** www.gardinersmarina.com
Nearest Town: East Hampton *(2 mi.)* **Tourist Info:** (631) 324-0362

Marina Services and Boat Supplies
Services - Docking Assistance, Boaters' Lounge, Security *(24 hrs., Camera, May-Oct)*, Trash Pick-Up, Dock Carts **Communication -** Phone Messages, Data Ports *(Marina office)*, FedEx, UPS, Express Mail *(Sat Del)* **Supplies - OnSite:** Ice *(Block, Cube)* **Near:** Ships' Store *(Three Mile Harbor BY)*, Bait/Tackle *(Mrs. Sam's 324-8686)* **1-3 mi:** Propane *(Riverhead Building Supply 324-0300)*

Boatyard Services
OnCall: Electronic Sales, Electronics Repairs, Rigger, Canvas Work, Brightwork, Air Conditioning, Refrigeration, Divers, Propeller Repairs **Near:** Travelift *(40T)*, Engine mechanic *(gas, diesel)*, Launching Ramp, Electrical Repairs, Hull Repairs, Bottom Cleaning.
Nearest Yard: Three Mile Harbor Boat Yard (631) 324-1320

Restaurants and Accommodations
Near: Inn/B&B *(Mill House Inn 324-9766, $150-650)*, *(Getaway House 324-4622, $100-270)*, Condo/Cottage *(Three Mile Harbor Cottages 329-1431)* **Under 1 mi:** Restaurant *(East Hampton Point 329-2800, L $7-15, D $20-40, by dinghy)*, *(Bostwick's Seafood Grill 324-1111, D $10-24, by dinghy)*, *(Riccardo's 324-4000, D $18-30, by dinghy)* Pizzeria *(Pepperonis 329-1800, delivers)* **1-3 mi:** Restaurant *(Rowdy Hall 324-8555)*, *(Nick and Toni's 324-3550)*, *(Della Feminas 329-6666)*, *(Turtle Crossing 324-7166)*

Recreation and Entertainment
OnSite: Beach **Near:** Picnic Area, Grills, Playground, Jogging Paths, Boat Rentals, Fishing Charter, Video Rental *(EH Video 324-2441)* **Under 1 mi:** Tennis Courts *(Dunes Racquet Club 267-8508)*, Movie Theater *(EH Cinema 324-0448)* **1-3 mi:** Golf Course *(EH G.C. 267-2100)*, Fitness Center, Bowling *(EH Bowl 324-1950)*, Museum *(Marine Museum 267-6544; Pollack-Krasner House 324-4929)*, Cultural Attract *(John Drew Theater 324-0806)*

Provisioning and General Services
Near: Convenience Store, Bank/ATM **Under 1 mi:** Delicatessen *(Damarks 324-0691)*, Farmers' Market *(Round Swamp Farm 324-4438)*, Post Office, Protestant Church, Beauty Salon, Dry Cleaners *(North Main 324-1640)*, Pharmacy *(CVS 324-8587)*, Copies Etc. *(Town & Country 324-4048)* **1-3 mi:** Supermarket *(IGA 267-3556, Waldenbaums 324-6215)*, Gourmet Shop *(Barefoot Contessa 324-0240)*, Health Food *(Second Nature 324-5257)*, Liquor Store *(Franey's 324-0322)*, Bakery *(Hampton Bagels 324-5411)*, Fishmonger, Catholic Church, Synagogue, Library *(324-0222)*, Bookstore *(Book Hampton 324-4939)*, Hardware Store *(Village 324-2456)*, Florist

Transportation
OnCall: Rental Car *(Enterprise 324-5050 or N. Main Rental 329-1010, nearby)*, Taxi *(Easthampton Taxi 329-0011)*, Airport Limo *(EH Limousine 324-5466)* **Near:** Local Bus *(Suffolk Cty bus to beach or town; SCT 852-5200)* **1-3 mi:** InterCity Bus *(Hampton Jitney)*, Rail *(LIRR to NYC)*
Airport: East Hampton/Islip *(3 mi./60 mi.)*

Medical Services
911 Service **OnCall:** Ambulance **Near:** Chiropractor *(Kavanaugh 329-5994)* **Under 1 mi:** Veterinarian *(Disunno 324-0089)* **1-3 mi:** Doctor *(Wainscott Clinic 537-1892)*, Dentist *(EH Dental 324-6800)*, Holistic Services *(Naturopathica 329-2525)* **Hospital:** Southampton 726-8200 *(18 mi.)*

Setting -- Almost to the head of Three Mile Harbor, in its southeast corner, Gardiners sits just north of the East Hampton Town Docks. This well maintained, conveniently located marina offers deep water dockage for vessels to 105 feet. There is a very secure basin ringed with slips and an additional set of docks on the otutside. Cement tables with umbrellas dot the grass strip that separates the docks from the parking spaces

Marina Notes -- *Rates listed are for MemDay to LabDay. Off season and shoulder season vary significantly; call the marina for details. Under the same management as Halsey and Harbor Marina. Neat and basic, it offers a secure docking area, with manicured surroundings. A small dockmaster's office provides restrooms, showers, beverages & ice. Plenty of room on the docks and gravel parking lot by your boat for relaxing. Located about 100 feet from Three Mile Harbor Road, but a natural hedge blocks the traffic noise. Only amenities are picnic tables. If you don't need more than the basics, this is pretty ideal.

Notable -- Gardiner's and Three Mile Harbor B.Y. are the closest facilities to Easthampton Road and all the arts, galleries, restaurants, shopping and people watching that it offers. A public bus travels the 2.5 miles to the edge of EH's shopping district, to the beach, and to the East Hampton Railroad Station to NYC. Bostwick's, Ricardo's, and East Hampton Point restaurants are all easy dinghy rides (ask about tie-up fees) or are walkable. Or dinghy to the harbor's mouth to Maidstone Beach. Hampton's International Film Festival (324-4600) in late October is held in East Hampton and Southhampton.

Navigational Information
Lat: 41°00.045' **Long:** 072°10.973' **Tide:** 3 ft. **Current:** 2 kt. **Chart:** 13209
Rep. Depths (*MLW*): **Entry** 7 ft. **Fuel Dock** n/a **Max Slip/Moor** 7 ft./-
Access: Gardiner's Bay to Three Mile Harbor

Marina Facilities (*In Season/Off Season*)
Fuel: No
Slips: 71 Total, 8 Transient **Max LOA:** 65 ft. **Max Beam:** n/a
  Rate (*per ft.*): **Day** $2.25 **Week** $15 **Month** $45.00
  Power: 30 amp Incl., **50 amp** Incl., **100 amp** n/a, **200 amp** n/a
  Cable TV: No **Dockside Phone:** Yes
  Dock Type: Floating, Long Fingers, Pilings
Moorings: 0 Total, 0 Transient **Launch:** n/a, Dinghy Dock
  Rate: Day n/a **Week** n/a **Month** n/a
Heads: None
Laundry: None **Pay Phones:** Yes, 1
Pump-Out: OnCall, Full Service **Fee:** Free **Closed Heads:** Yes

Marina Operations
Owner/Manager: R. C. Story **Dockmaster:** Same
In-Season: Summer, 8am-4:30pm **Off-Season:** Winter, 9am-4:30pm
After-Hours Arrival: Call in advance
Reservations: Preferred **Credit Cards:** Visa/MC, Dscvr, Din, Amex
Discounts: None
Pets: Welcome, Dog Walk Area **Handicap Access:** Yes, Docks

Marina Services and Boat Supplies
Services - Docking Assistance, Security, Dock Carts **Communication -** Phone Messages, Fax in/out, FedEx, AirBorne, UPS, Express Mail (*Sat Del*) **Supplies - OnSite:** Ice (*Block, Cube*), Ships' Store, Bait/Tackle (*& Mrs. Sam's 324-8686 0.5 mi.*), Propane

Boatyard Services
OnSite: Travelift (*40T*), Forklift (*Up to 10T*), Engine mechanic (*gas, diesel*), Electrical Repairs, Electronic Sales, Electronics Repairs (*Limited*), Hull Repairs, Rigger (*Incl. swaging*), Bottom Cleaning, Brightwork, Air Conditioning, Refrigeration, Compound, Wash & Wax, Interior Cleaning, Propeller Repairs, Inflatable Repairs, Metal Fabrication, Painting, Awlgrip **Dealer for:** Yanmar, Onan, Avon. **Yard Rates:** $55-85/hr., Haul & Launch Short: $8-12/ft.; long $8-11 (*blocking incl.*), Power Wash $3/ft., Bottom Paint $9 **Storage:** On-Land Outside $30.50/ft. Inside $46/ft.

Restaurants and Accommodations
Near: Condo/Cottage (*Three Mile Harbor Cottages 329-1431*)
Under 1 mi: Restaurant (*Riccardos 324-0000, or by dinghy*), Pizzeria (*Pepperoni's 329-1800*), Inn/B&B (*Mill House Inn 324-9766*), (*Getaway House 324-4622*) **1-3 mi:** Restaurant (*Nick & Toni's 324-3550, D $15-29, Sun Brunch $15*), (*East Hampton Point 329-2800, L $7-15, D $20-40, or by dinghy*), (*Della Famina 329-6666*), (*Maryjane's 324-8008*)

Recreation and Entertainment
OnSite: Picnic Area, Grills, Playground **Under 1 mi:** Tennis Courts (*Dunes Racquet Club 267-8508*), Fitness Center (*East Hampton Gym 324-4499*), Video Rental (*Springs 324-5980; E.H 324-2441*), Sightseeing

Three Mile Harbor Boatyard

PO Box 31; 3 Three Mile Harbor Road; East Hampton, NY 11937
Tel: (631) 324-1320 **VHF: Monitor** 9 **Talk** n/a
Fax: (631) 324-9185 **Alternate Tel:** n/a
Email: 3mile@optonline.net **Web:** www.threemile.net
Nearest Town: East Hampton (*2.5 mi.*) **Tourist Info:** (631) 324-0362

1-3 mi: Beach (*Maidstone Park*), Golf Course (*East Hampton Golf Club 267-2100*), Horseback Riding (*East End Stables 324-9568*), Bowling (*East Hampton Bowl 324-1950*), Movie Theater (*E.H.Cinema 324-0448*)
3+ mi: Cultural Attract (*Playwrights Theatre 329-3909, 4 mi.*)

Provisioning and General Services
OnSite: Hardware Store **Near:** Convenience Store, Delicatessen (*Damarks's 324-0691*) **Under 1 mi:** Liquor Store, Bakery (*Jessie's 907-8735*), Farmers' Market (*Round Swamp Farm 324-4438*), Fishmonger, Meat Market, Bank/ATM, Post Office, Protestant Church, Beauty Salon, Barber Shop, Dry Cleaners (*North Main 324-1640*), Pharmacy (*CVS 324-8587*), Copies Etc. (*Town & Country Photo 324-4048*) **1-3 mi:** Supermarket (*Waldbaum's 324-6215*), Gourmet Shop (*Golden Pear 329-1600; Barefoot Contessa 324-0240*), Health Food (*Second Nature 324-5257*), Wine/Beer (*E.H. Wine & Spirits 324-5757*), Catholic Church, Synagogue, Library (*E.H. 324-0222*), Laundry, Bookstore (*BookHampton 324-4939*), Florist

Transportation
OnCall: Rental Car (*Enterprise 324-5050/Hertz 537-3987 - 1 mi.*), Taxi (*East End Taxi 324-0077*), Airport Limo (*East Hampton Limousine 324-5466*) **Near:** Local Bus (*To East Hampton village*) **1-3 mi:** InterCity Bus (*Hampton Jitney 283-4600*), Rail (*LIRR to Penn Station NYC*) **3+ mi:** Bikes (*Bermuda Bikes 324-6688, 4 mi.*) **Airport:** East Hampton/Islip (*3 mi./60 mi.*)

Medical Services
911 Service **OnCall:** Ambulance **Under 1 mi:** Doctor, Dentist (*A. Katz 324-5015*), Holistic Services (*Naturopathica 329-2525*), Veterinarian (*T. Disunno DVM 324-0089*) **Hospital:** Southampton 726-8200 (*15 mi.*)

Setting -- Southern-most marina on Three Mile Harbor, at end of the channel across from Gardiner's marina and the East Hampton Town Docks, TMHBY offers convenience and good boatyard services in a down-home environment. Landward, the view is of weathered boatyard buildings and docks. Waterside view is of the channel, Three Mile Harbor-Hog Creek Road, and the Town Docks.

Marina Notes -- The focus here is on the boatyard, although the marina has undergone some significant sprucing up recently -- new pedestals, satellite TV, etc.-- and is slated for more, including new heads and showers, in '04 & '05. Some slips have finger piers, but many are bow- or stern-to between pilings. Ask if this is important. Pump-out boat on Channel 73 in-season is free. A well-equipped Ships' store, hardware and parts department are also onsite. Full boatyard services including the largest Travelift on Three Mile Harbor. Owned and operated by the Story family since 1951.

Notable -- While the Town of East Hampton does not provide dedicated dinghy dockage for anchored and moored boats, Three Mile Harbor Boatyard graciously signs its dinghy dock "Open to All" - and there's no charge! That speaks volumes and should be appreciated. This is the closest marina to the town of East Hampton, making it a very convenient stop - especially if town is one of your reasons for being here. The local bus stops at the Town docks - 7am-6pm, every 90 minutes $1.50/1. The edge of "downtown" East Hampton is 2.5 miles away. Boys Harbor fireworks display is here on Bastille Day, one week after July 4. Hampton Film Festival in October (324-4600).

Sag Harbor Yacht Club

PO Box 1988; 27 Bay Street; Sag Harbor, NY 11963

Tel: (631) 725-0567 **VHF: Monitor** 9 **Talk** n/a
Fax: (631) 725-7126 **Alternate Tel:** n/a
Email: info@sagharboryc.com **Web:** www.sagharboryc.com
Nearest Town: Sag Harbor *(0.1 mi.)* **Tourist Info:** (631) 725-0011

Navigational Information
Lat: 41°00.110' **Long:** 072°17.513' **Tide:** 3 ft. **Current:** 1 kt. **Chart:** 12358
Rep. Depths *(MLW)*: **Entry** 11 ft. **Fuel Dock** 10 ft. **Max Slip/Moor** 12 ft./-
Access: Gardiner's Bay, past Sag Harbor breakwater to the most easterly set

Marina Facilities *(In Season/Off Season)*
Fuel: Gulf - Gasoline, Diesel
Slips: 100 Total, 15 Transient **Max LOA:** 200 ft. **Max Beam:** 30 ft.
Rate *(per ft.)*: **Day** $4.00/Inq. **Week** Inq. **Month** Inq.
Power: 30 amp $10, **50 amp** $20, **100 amp** $30, **200 amp** $40
Cable TV: Yes, $10 **Dockside Phone:** Yes with advance notice
Dock Type: Fixed, Long Fingers, Pilings, Alongside, Wood
Moorings: 0 Total, 0 Transient **Launch:** n/a
Rate: Day n/a **Week** n/a **Month** n/a
Heads: 2 Toilet(s), 4 Shower(s) *(with dressing rooms)*
Laundry: None, Book Exchange **Pay Phones:** Yes, 2
Pump-Out: OnCall, Full Service, 1 Central **Fee:** Free **Closed Heads:** Yes

Marina Operations
Owner/Manager: Les Black **Dockmaster:** Same
In-Season: Apr 1-Nov 1, 8am-6pm **Off-Season:** n/a
After-Hours Arrival: Call ahead. Happy to stand-by if possible
Reservations: Yes, Preferred **Credit Cards:** Visa/MC, Amex
Discounts: None **Dockage:** n/a **Fuel:** Bulk **Repair:** n/a
Pets: Welcome, Dog Walk Area **Handicap Access:** No

Marina Services and Boat Supplies
Services - Docking Assistance, Concierge, Boaters' Lounge, Dock Carts, Megayacht Facilities **Communication -** Mail & Package Hold, Phone Messages, Fax in/out *(Yes)*, Data Ports *(Club House)*, FedEx, AirBorne, UPS, Express Mail *(Sat Del)* **Supplies - OnSite:** Ice *(Block, Cube)* **Near:** Ships' Store *(Sag Harbor Ships Store 725-2458)*, Bait/Tackle *(Tight Line Tackle 725-0740)* **1-3 mi:** Propane *(Schiavoni Gas 725-8595)*

Boatyard Services
OnCall: Engine mechanic *(gas, diesel)*, Electrical Repairs, Electronics Repairs, Rigger, Compound, Wash & Wax, Interior Cleaning, Propeller Repairs **Near:** Travelift *(35T)*, Forklift, Launching Ramp, Hull Repairs.
Nearest Yard: Sag Harbor Yacht Yard (631) 725-3838

Restaurants and Accommodations
Near: Restaurant *(Paradise Diner 725-6080)*, *(Dockside Bar & Grill 725-7100, Sag Harbor Comm Band, Tues, 8pm)*, *(Magnolia 725-0101, D $19-25)*, *(Peter Miller's 725-9100)*, *(Sen Japanese 725-1774)*, *(Anna's By the Bay)*, *(All Seasons Café 725-9613)*, *(American Hotel D $15-45)*, Lite Fare *(Ice Cream Club)*, *(Espresso B&L)*, Hotel *(American Hotel 725-3535, $155-325)*, Inn/B&B *(Baron's Cove Inn 725-2100, $75-365)*, *(Sag Harbor Inn 725-2949, $85-385)* **Under 1 mi:** Restaurant *(The Beacon 725-7088)*, Pizzeria *(Conca D'oro 725-3167)*

Recreation and Entertainment
OnSite: Picnic Area, Grills **Near:** Beach *(Havens)*, Playground, Volleyball, Fitness Center *(American Fitness 725-0707)*, Jogging Paths, Boat Rentals, Roller Blade/Bike Paths, Video Rental *(Sag Harbor 725-7025)*, Park,

Museum *(Custom House 725-0250, Whaling Museum 725-0770)*, Cultural Attract *(Bay St. Theatre 725-9500)*, Sightseeing, Special Events **Under 1 mi:** Movie Theater *(Sag Harbor Theatre 725-0010)* **1-3 mi:** Tennis Courts *(Sag Harbor Park 725-4018)*, Golf Course *(Sag Harbor G.C. 725-9739)*

Provisioning and General Services
Near: Convenience Store, Gourmet Shop *(Espresso 725-4433 - great Itlaian deli)*, Delicatessen *(Harbor Deli 725-7398)*, Health Food *(Provisions 725-3636)*, Liquor Store *(Long Wharf 725-2400)*, Bakery, Fishmonger *(Bayview Seafood 725-0740)*, Bank/ATM, Post Office, Catholic Church, Protestant Church, Synagogue, Library *(John Jermain 725-0049)*, Beauty Salon, Barber Shop, Dry Cleaners, Laundry *(Sag Harbor 725-5830)*, Bookstore *(Black Cat Books 725-8654, BookHampton 725-1114)*, Pharmacy *(Sag Harbor 725-0074)*, Newsstand, Hardware Store *(Emporium 725-0103)*, Florist, Clothing Store, Retail Shops, Copies Etc. **Under 1 mi:** Supermarket *(Schiavoni's IGA 725-0366)*

Transportation
OnCall: Rental Car *(Enterprise 537-4800)*, Taxi *(725-9000)*, Airport Limo *(Midway 537-1800)* **Near:** Bikes *(Bike Hampton 725-7329)*, Local Bus, InterCity Bus *(Hampton Jitney 800-936-0440)* **Airport:** Islip *(60 mi.)*

Medical Services
911 Service **OnCall:** Ambulance **Near:** Doctor *(Oppenheimer 725-4600)*, Chiropractor *(Simunek 725-3215)*, Holistic Services *(Center For Hollistic Healing 725-3215)* **Under 1 mi:** Dentist *(Goodstein 725-2000)*
1-3 mi: Veterinarian **Hospital:** Southampton 726-8335 *(7 mi.)*

Setting -- Intimate, upscale, impeccably maintained Sag Harbor Yacht Club has an excellent, very private gated location. It's just beyond the bustle of Sag Harbor's high-season tourist traffic, directly east of the Sag Harbor Marine Park, but within very easy walking distance of the best this wonderful, elegant little town has to offer. Everything at SHYC appears to be spanking new and in Bristol condition from the resident boats to the pilings and the docks.

Marina Notes -- S.H.Y.C. was established in 1899; the dockhouse was originally New York Yacht Club's station #5 on Shelter Island. While lacking in a full range of traditional amenities, it can cater to almost every boating need with a professional and helpful staff. Megayachts are welcome (up to 200 amp, 3-phase service); concierge service is available. Shirts required on the dock. Adjacent to the entrance, a lovely, awninged picnic pavilion, with 6 tables and chairs and two gas grills, overlooks the docks; it provides a welcome gathering spot overlooking the docks. The small, well-furnished and inviting club house sits on the main wharf and sports an abundant array of club burgees. Fresh flowers in clubhouse and the men's and ladies' rooms reflect the standard of service.

Notable -- The traditional Sag Harbor Fireworks show on July 5 is visible from the docks and there's a Harborfest featuring classic boats in September. Directly across the street, in the American Legion Building, is the Dockside Bar and Grille with a charming sidewalk cafe. The Whaling and Historical Museum is housed in the 1845 home of Benjamin Hutting II, a whaling captain. It's open from 10am-5 pm Mon-Sat, 1-5pm on Sun (weekends only in winter). Many other historic buildings and churches are nearby on Union Street. Goat on a Boat Puppet Theatre (725-4193) has year 'round shows.

Navigational Information
Lat: 41°00.140' **Long:** 072°17.630' **Tide:** 3 ft. **Current:** 1 ft. **Chart:** 12358
Rep. Depths (*MLW*): Entry 11 ft. **Fuel Dock** n/a **Max Slip/Moor** 10 ft./10 ft.
Access: Gardiners Bay past Sage Harbor breakwater to docks in center

Marina Facilities *(In Season/Off Season)*
Fuel: No
Slips: 310 Total, 25 Transient **Max LOA:** 200 ft. **Max Beam:** 16 ft.
  Rate *(per ft.)*: **Day** $2.75/Inq.* **Week** Inq. **Month** Inq.
  Power: 30 amp $10, **50 amp** $15, **100 amp** n/a, **200 amp** n/a
  Cable TV: No **Dockside Phone:** No
  Dock Type: Fixed, Floating, Pilings, Alongside, Wood
Moorings: 100 Total, 10+/- Transient **Launch:** Yes ($3pp/1way)
  Rate: Day $30-50 **Week** n/a **Month** n/a
Heads: 2 Toilet(s), 2 Shower(s)
Laundry: None **Pay Phones:** Yes, 2
Pump-Out: OnCall *(Ch.73)*, 1 Central **Fee:** Free **Closed Heads:** Yes

Marina Operations
Owner/Manager: Ed. Barry & Ed. Swensen (Hrbmstrs) **Dockmaster:** n/a
In-Season: Apr-Oct, 6am-9pm **Off-Season:** Nov-Mar, Closed
After-Hours Arrival: Anchor outside the breakwater
Reservations: No **Credit Cards:** Visa/MC
Discounts: None
Pets: Welcome, Dog Walk Area **Handicap Access:** No

Sag Harbor Marine Park

PO Box 660; 55 Main & 3 Bay Street; Sag Harbor, NY 11963

Tel: (631) 725-2368 **VHF: Monitor** 9 **Talk** 10
Fax: (631) 725-5693 **Alternate Tel:** (631) 725-0222
Email: n/a **Web:** n/a
Nearest Town: Sag Harbor *(0 mi.)* **Tourist Info:** (631) 725-0011

Marina Services and Boat Supplies
Services - Docking Assistance, Megayacht Facilities **Communication** - FedEx, AirBorne, UPS, Express Mail *(Sat Del)* **Supplies - Near:** Ice *(Cube, Shaved)*, Ships' Store, Bait/Tackle *(Tight Line Tackle 725-0740)*
Under 1 mi: Marine Discount Store *(Sag Harbor Ships Store 725-2458)*
1-3 mi: Propane *(Schiavoni Gas 725-8595)*

Boatyard Services
OnSite: Launching Ramp **OnCall:** Rigger, Bottom Cleaning, Air Conditioning **Near:** Engine mechanic *(gas, diesel)*, Electrical Repairs, Electronics Repairs, Hull Repairs, Sail Loft, Refrigeration, Propeller Repairs. **Nearest Yard:** Sag Harbor Yacht Yard (631) 725-3838

Restaurants and Accommodations
Near: Restaurant *(Phao 725-0055, French-Thai bistro food)*, *(Anna's by the Bay 725-9613)*, *(B Smiths 725-5858)*, *(Il Capuccino 725-2747, D $14-20)*, *(The Beacon 725-7088)*, *(Searfina 725-0101, one of the very best)*, Seafood Shack *(Dockside 725-7100)*, Pizzeria *(Conca D'Oro 725-3167)*, Motel *(American Hotel 725-3535)*, Inn/B&B *(Sag Harbor Inn 725-2949)*, *(Barrons Cove Inn 725-7100)*, *(1891 Guest House 725-1396)*

Recreation and Entertainment
OnSite: Grills **Near:** Spa, Beach *(Havens)*, Picnic Area, Dive Shop, Fitness Center *(Hamptons Gym 725-0707)*, Boat Rentals, Movie Theater *(Sag Harbor Theatre 725-0010)*, Video Rental *(Sag Harbor Video 725-7025)*, Park, Museum *(Custom House 725-0250, Whaling Museum 725-0770)*, Cultural Attract *(Bay St. Theatre Festival 725-1108/9500 $10-42)*, Sightseeing *(45 ft. wooden powerboat American Beauty tours the harbor 725-0397 $19-25)*, Special Events *(Summer Carnival, Aug; Harborfest, Sep)*, Galleries *(Grenning 725-8469)* **Under 1 mi:** Tennis Courts *(Sag Harbor Park 725-4018)* **1-3 mi:** Golf Course *(Sag Harbor State G.C. 725-2503)*

Provisioning and General Services
Near: Convenience Store, Gourmet Shop *(Espresso 725-4433)*, Delicatessen *(Harbor Deli 725-7398)*, Health Food *(Provisions 725-3636)*, Wine/Beer, Liquor Store *(Long Wharf 725-2400)*, Bakery, Green Grocer, Fishmonger *(Bayview 725-0740)*, Lobster Pound, Meat Market, Bank/ATM, Post Office, Catholic Church, Protestant Church, Synagogue *(Temple Adas Israel 725-0904 - oldest on L.I.)*, Library *(John Jermain 725-0049)*, Beauty Salon, Barber Shop, Dry Cleaners, Laundry *(Sag Harbor 725-5830)*, Bookstore *(Black Cat 725-8654, Book Hampton 725-1114, Canio's 725-4926)*, Pharmacy *(Sag Harbor 725-0074)*, Newsstand, Hardware Store *(Emporium Hardware 725-0103)*, Florist, Clothing Store, Retail Shops, Copies Etc. **Under 1 mi:** Supermarket *(Schiavoni's IGA 725-0366)*

Transportation
OnCall: Rental Car *(Enterprise 537-4800)*, Taxi *(Sag Harbor Taxi 725-6969)*, Airport Limo *(Midway Limousine 537-1800)* **Near:** Bikes *(Bike Hampton 725-7329 $6/hr, $25/day)*, Local Bus, InterCity Bus *(Hampton Jitney 800-936-0440)* **Airport:** Islip *(60 mi.)*

Medical Services
911 Service **OnCall:** Veterinarian *(Village Mobile 725-0815)* **Near:** Doctor *(Oppenheimer 725-4600)*, Chiropractor *(Simunek 725-3215)*, Holistic Services *(Center for Holistic Healing 725-3215)*, Ambulance **Under 1 mi:** Dentist *(Benincasa 725-1240)* **Hospital:** Southampton 726-8335 *(7 mi.)*

Setting -- A grassy haborfront promenade is the centerpiece of Sag Harbor's Marine Park. Strung along the bulkhead are stern-to slips, their pedestals marching along a wooden boardwalk. Benches line the path and picnic tables, with grills, are scattered under the trees. Old fashioned street lights add an elegant touch. Right in town, it's between Malloy's and Sag Harbor Yacht Club. Just north of Malloys' is Long Wharf and the new set of floating Town Docks.

Marina Notes -- Marine Park has basic "stern-to" dockage without finger piers for boats to 50 ft. Heads and showers are in the two-story gray Harbormasters' building overlooking the marina. Grills, picnic tables and benches serve both boaters and non-boaters. The Town Docks are a few blocks north at Long Wharf, attended by a satellite harbormaster's office. The 250 ft. steel wharf, once home to whaling ships, serves megayachts; the 15 floating slips that radiate from it accommodate craft to 40 ft. Moorings are managed by Capt. Don Heckman's Sag Harbor Launch (725-0397). The Tourist Windmill has local info.

Notable -- The Dock has easy access to Sag Harbor's historic, arts, and culinary facilities: 25-year-old Corner Bar & Restaurant has fresh seafood and steaks with bay views; B.Smith's has indoor and outdoor dining in a casual atmosphere, with great harborviews; The Ice Cream Club and Bagel Buoy, reportedly, the best bagels in the Hamptons plus 20 varieties of cream cheese. Main St. offers more eateries, plus galleries, bookstores, and boutiques. The diminutive Whaling Museum has exhibits and programs for all ages. Sag Harbor Variety (725-9706) is a "stopped-in-time" five and dime. Bay Street Theater (725-9500) also presents a series of children's concerts - "Kidstreet". Nearby sandy Haven Beach has restrooms, picnic tables, grills, playground, and life guard.

Malloy's Waterfront Marina

PO Box 1979; Bay Street at Long Wharf; Sag Harbor, NY 11963

Tel: (616) 725-3886; (800) MAL-LOY4 **VHF: Monitor** 9 **Talk** n/a
Fax: (631) 725-0334 **Alternate Tel:** (631) 725-0033
Email: n/a **Web:** n/a
Nearest Town: Sag Harborf *(0 mi.)* **Tourist Info:** (631) 725-0011

Navigational Information

Lat: 41°00.205' **Long:** 072°17.707' **Tide:** 3 ft. **Current:** n/a **Chart:** 12358
Rep. Depths *(MLW):* **Entry** 10 ft. **Fuel Dock** n/a **Max Slip/Moor** 12 ft./-
Access: Gardiners Bay to Sag Harbor

Marina Facilities *(In Season/Off Season)*

Fuel: No
Slips: 75 Total, 10 Transient **Max LOA:** 195 ft. **Max Beam:** 38 ft.
 Rate *(per ft.):* **Day** $4.00* **Week** $28 **Month** $120
 Power: 30 amp $15, **50 amp** $20, **100 amp** Inq., **200 amp** n/a
 Cable TV: Yes, $10.00 **Dockside Phone:** No
 Dock Type: Fixed, Floating, Long Fingers, Short Fingers, Pilings, Wood
Moorings: 0 Total, 0 Transient **Launch:** n/a
 Rate: Day n/a **Week** n/a **Month** n/a
Heads: 6 Toilet(s), 4 Shower(s)
Laundry: None, Book Exchange **Pay Phones:** Yes, 2
Pump-Out: OnCall *(Ch.73)* **Fee:** Free **Closed Heads:** Yes

Marina Operations

Owner/Manager: Nancy Haynes **Dockmaster:** Same
In-Season: May 20-Sep 20, 8am-6pm **Off-Season:** Apr & Oct*, 9am-5pm
After-Hours Arrival: Call ahead.
Reservations: Yes **Credit Cards:** Visa/MC, Amex
Discounts: None
Pets: Welcome, Dog Walk Area **Handicap Access:** No

Marina Services and Boat Supplies

Services - Docking Assistance, Dock Carts, Megayacht Facilities, 3 Phase
Communication - Mail & Package Hold, Phone Messages, FedEx,
AirBorne, UPS, Express Mail *(Sat Del)* **Supplies - OnSite:** Ice *(Block, Cube)* **Near:** Ships' Store, Bait/Tackle *(Tight Line Tackle 725-0740)*
1-3 mi: Marine Discount Store *(Sag Harbor Ships Store 725-2458)*, Propane *(Schiavoni Gas 725-8595)*

Boatyard Services

OnSite: Yacht Broker **Near:** Travelift, Forklift, Launching Ramp, Hull
Repairs, Rigger, Bottom Cleaning, Brightwork. **3+ mi:** Refrigeration *(6 mi.)*. **Nearest Yard:** Sag Harbor Yacht Yard (631) 725-3838

Restaurants and Accommodations

OnSite: Restaurant *(B. Smith's Restaurant & Bar 725-5858, L $10-20, D $14-34)*, Seafood Shack *(Dockhouse 725-7555)* **Near:** Restaurant *(Anna's by the Bay 725-9613)*, *(Roccos 725-4925)*, *(The Beacon 725-7088)*, *(The American Hotel D $15-45)*, *(Paradise Cafe 725-6080, B, L, D part of BookHampton- casual during the day, serious at night)* Pizzeria *(Conca D'Oro 725-3167)*, Hotel *(The American Hotel 725-3535, $155-325)*, Inn/B&B *(Baron's Cove Inn 725-2100)*, *(Sag Harbor Inn 725-2949)*

Recreation and Entertainment

OnSite: Fitness Center *(American Fitness Factory 725-0707)* **Near:** Beach *(Havens)*, Picnic Area, Grills, Playground, Tennis Courts *(Mashashimuet 725-4018 $20-25/hr.)*, Jogging Paths, Boat Rentals, Roller Blade/Bike Paths, Movie Theater *(Sag Harbor Cinema 725-0010)*, Video Rental *(Harbor*

725-7025)*, Park, Museum *(Custom House 725-0250, Whaling Museum 725-0770)*, Cultural Attract *(Bay St. Theatre 725-9500)*, Special Events *(Arts & Crafts Fair, Summer Carnival - Aug. Harborfest - Sep)*, Galleries *(Grenning 725-8469)* **1-3 mi:** Golf Course *(Sag Harbor G.C. 725-2503)*

Provisioning and General Services

Near: Convenience Store, Gourmet Shop *(Sylvester & Co. 725-5012 kitchenware, too)*, Delicatessen *(Cove Deli 725-0216)*, Health Food *(Provisions 725-3636)*, Liquor Store *(Long Wharf 725-2400)*, Fishmonger *(Bayview 725-0740)*, Meat Market, Bank/ATM, Post Office, Catholic Church, Protestant Church, Synagogue, Library *(John Jermain 725-0049)*, Beauty Salon, Dry Cleaners, Laundry *(Sag Harbor 725-5830)*, Bookstore *(BookHampton 725-1114, Canio's 725-4926)*, Pharmacy *(Sag Harbour 725-0074)*, Newsstand, Hardware Store *(Emporium 725-0103)*, Florist, Retail Shops, Copies Etc. **Under 1 mi:** Supermarket *(IGA 725-0366)*

Transportation

OnCall: Rental Car *(Enterprise 537-4800)*, Taxi *(Sag Harbor Car 725-9000)*, Airport Limo *(Hampton Beach Limo 800-287-5757)* **Near:** Bikes *(Bike Hampton 725-7329)*, Local Bus, InterCity Bus *(Hampton Jitney to NYC)*
Airport: Islip/East Hampton *(60 mi./6 mi.)*

Medical Services

911 Service **OnCall:** Veterinarian *(Browning 725-6500)* **Near:** Doctor *(Oppenheimer 725-4600)*, Chiropractor *(Simunek 725-3215)*
Under 1 mi: Dentist *(Benincasa 725-1240)*, Holistic Services *(Center for Holistic Healing 725-3215)* **Hospital:** Southampton 726-8335 *(7 mi.)*

Setting -- The most centrally located marina in town, Malloy's Waterfront is easy to find - just look for a gaggle of mega yachts clustered on its outermost docks. An integral part of the well-polished Sag Harbor scene, it is "the place" for people and boat watching. Views seaward are of big yachts and the harbor; views landside are of B. Smith's restaurant and the buffed and polished diners on its covered veranda. While the docks are just a few steps off the main tourist path, they are also surrounded by it. Everything - including restaurants, boutiques, galleries and antique shops - is within a stone's throw.

Marina Notes -- *Dockage is a minimum $120. This is home port for many large yachts and a magnet for visiting ones. Three-phase service available: $125/day. Dockmaster Nancy Haynes is knowedgeable, friendly and helpful. Heads and showers are about 50 yards away. Closed head harbor; free pump-out boat Ch. 73. Off-season is Apr 15-May 20 and Sep 20-Oct 15. Closed Oct 15 - Apr 15. A complete onsite fitness facility is operated separately; daily and weekend memberships available (725-0707). If heading to, or coming from the east, follow the chart/channel carefully; there are serious rockpiles outside.

Notable -- B. Smith's Restaurant spans most of the width of the marina's waterfront; myriad French doors take the inside "outside" or there's real patio dining. This has been called the most spectacular restaurant location on the East End. The views are of stunning boats rocking in a beautiful harbor -- and of their inhabitants (making you part of the scenery). More casual fare can be found at the famed Dock House, also adjacent to the docks. The highly regarded Bay Street Theater is next door. The Windmill Tourist Office has lots of maps and local event information.

Navigational Information
Lat: 41°00.085' **Long:** 072°17.914' **Tide:** 4 ft. **Current:** 1 kt. **Chart:** 12358
Rep. Depths (*MLW*): **Entry** 9 ft. **Fuel Dock** n/a **Max Slip/Moor** 7 ft./-
Access: Sag Habor then just under the Sag Harbor Bridge, first to port

Marina Facilities (*In Season/Off Season*)
Fuel: No
Slips: 75 Total, 20 Transient **Max LOA:** 75 ft. **Max Beam:** n/a
Rate (*per ft.*): **Day** $3.75/Inq.* **Week** Inq. **Month** n/a
Power: 30 amp $15, **50 amp** $20, **100 amp** n/a, **200 amp** n/a
Cable TV: Yes, $10 **Dockside Phone:** No
Dock Type: Fixed, Floating, Wood
Moorings: 0 Total, 0 Transient **Launch:** n/a
Rate: Day n/a **Week** n/a **Month** n/a
Heads: 4 Toilet(s), 4 Shower(s)
Laundry: 3 Washer(s), 3 Dryer(s) **Pay Phones:** Yes
Pump-Out: OnCall (*Ch. 73*) **Fee:** Free **Closed Heads:** Yes

Marina Operations
Owner/Manager: Malloy's **Dockmaster:** Kevin Burton
In-Season: April 15 - Oct. 15, 8am - 6pm **Off-Season:** Closed
After-Hours Arrival: n/a
Reservations: No **Credit Cards:** Visa/MC, Amex
Discounts: None
Pets: Welcome, Dog Walk Area **Handicap Access:** Yes, Docks

Malloy's Sag Harbor Cove East

PO Box 1979; 8 West Water Street; Sag Harbor, NY 11963

Tel: (613) 725-1605; (800) 625-5694 **VHF:** Monitor 9 **Talk** n/a
Fax: n/a **Alternate Tel:** n/a
Email: n/a **Web:** n/a
Nearest Town: Sag Harbor (*0.2 mi.*) **Tourist Info:** (631) 725-0011

Marina Services and Boat Supplies
Services - Docking Assistance, Dock Carts **Communication -** Mail & Package Hold, FedEx, AirBorne, UPS, Express Mail (*Sat Del*)
Supplies - OnSite: Ice (*Cube*) **OnCall:** Ice (*Block*) **Near:** Bait/Tackle (*Bayview Seafood Market 725-0740*), Propane (*Ace Hardware 725-1900*)
Under 1 mi: Marine Discount Store (*Sag Harbor Ships Store 725-2458*)

Boatyard Services
Near: Travelift, Railway, Forklift, Crane, Engine mechanic (*gas, diesel*), Launching Ramp, Hull Repairs, Rigger, Bottom Cleaning, Brightwork, Divers, Compound, Wash & Wax, Interior Cleaning.
Nearest Yard: Ship Ashore (631) 725-3755

Restaurants and Accommodations
OnSite: Restaurant (*The Beacon 725-7088, seafood with a French-Asian touches*) **Near:** Restaurant (*Roccos Brazilian-Cuban 725-4925*), (*Sugar Reef 725-7500*), (*Peter Millers 725-9100*), (*Sag Harbor Grill 725-6060*), (*B. Smith's 725-5858, southern*), Fast Food (*The Corner 725-9760*), Pizzeria (*Conca D'Oro 725-3167*), Hotel (*Sag Harbor Inn 725-2949*) **Under 1 mi:** Hotel (*Baron's Cove Inn 725-2100*), Inn/B&B (*American Hotel 725-3535*)

Recreation and Entertainment
OnSite: Picnic Area, Grills **Near:** Beach (*Havens*), Fitness Center (*In Studio Balance Pilates 725-8282*), Jogging Paths, Roller Blade/Bike Paths, Movie Theater (*Sag Harbor Theatre 725-0010*), Video Arcade, Museum (*Custom House 725-0250, Whaling Museum 725-0770*), Cultural Attract (*Bay St.Theatre 725-9500*)

Under 1 mi: Playground, Video Rental (*Harbor 725-7025; Long Wharf 725-9090*) **1-3 mi:** Golf Course (*Atlantic Golf Club 537-1818*) **3+ mi:** Bowling (*East Hampton Bowl 324-1950, 6 mi.*)

Provisioning and General Services
Near: Provisioning Service, Convenience Store, Supermarket (*Schiavoni's IGA 725-0366*), Gourmet Shop, Delicatessen (*Harbor Delicatessen 725-7398*), Health Food, Wine/Beer (*Water Street*), Liquor Store (*Sag Harbor Liquor 725-8854*), Bakery (*Bagel Buoy 725-8103*), Fishmonger, Bank/ATM, Post Office, Catholic Church, Library (*John Jermain 725-0049*), Beauty Salon (*New Creative*), Barber Shop, Dry Cleaners, Laundry (*Sag Harbor 725-5830*), Bookstore (*BookHampton 725-1114, Canio's Books 725-4926; Paradise Books 725-1114*), Pharmacy (*Sag Harbor Pharmacy 725-0074*), Newsstand, Hardware Store (*Emporium 725-0103*), Florist, Clothing Store, Retail Shops, Department Store, Copies Etc. **1-3 mi:** Meat Market (*Cromers Country Market 725-9004*) **3+ mi:** Buying Club (*BJ's, 20 mi.*)

Transportation
OnCall: Rental Car (*Enterprise 537-4800*), Taxi (*Sag Harbor 725-6969*)
Near: Bikes (*Bike Hampton 725-7329*), InterCity Bus (*Hampton Jitney 800-936-0440*) **Airport:** Islip (*60 mi.*)

Medical Services
911 Service **OnCall:** Veterinarian (*Village Mobile Vet 725-0815*)
Near: Doctor, Dentist (*Benincasa 725-1240*), Chiropractor (*Kirby 725-3215*), Holistic Services (*Center for Holistic Healing 725-3215*)
Hospital: Southam ton 726-8335 *7 mi.*

Setting -- The first marina under the 21 foot bridge, Malloy Sag Harbor Cove East is barely a quarter mile west of downtown Sag Harbor. From both the land and water side, look for The Beacon, a restaurant on the second floor of the marina building; its prominent location (and spiraling reputation) makes it easy to spot. The smallest of the three Malloy marinas, this basic tie-up has good docks that put you within viewing distance of the Sag Harbor traffic circle - while still offering privacy and being out of the major tourist traffic.

Marina Notes -- The marina office and amenities are downstairs -- below the restaurant. So it's a bit hard to find from the street side. Good showers and heads plus a small deck for watching the harbor complete the amenities. The grounds are well tended and the dockmaster is helpful.

Notable -- The Beacon is a small, casual bistro, open Thursday through Monday for dinner, with striking views of the harbor and spectacular sunsets - dine inside or on the covered deck. Chef Paul LaBue's (formerly of Nick & Tony's) light menu features seafood, with an occasional Asian touch. The NY Times called it the best restaurant in Sag Harbor. Reservations are not accepted, so being dockside would seem a real advantage. Visit the Sag Harbor Whaling Museum or head over to Long Wharf to check out the latest megayacht arrivals. Or just stroll the side streets with their perfectly restored old sea captains' homes - some are even open to the public. Get a map from the Tourist Info booth in the windmill on Long Wharf.

Malloy's Sag Harbor Cove West

PO Box 1979; 50 West Water Street; Sag Harbor, NY 11963

Tel: (631) 725-3939 **VHF: Monitor** 9 **Talk** n/a
Fax: (631) 725-3939 **Alternate Tel:** n/a
Email: n/a **Web:** n/a
Nearest Town: Sag Harbor *(0.4 mi.)* **Tourist Info:** (631) 725-0011

Navigational Information
Lat: 41°00.056' **Long:** 072°18.098' **Tide:** 4 ft. **Current:** 1 kt. **Chart:** 12358
Rep. Depths (MLW): Entry 9 ft. **Fuel Dock** n/a **Max Slip/Moor** 8 ft./-
Access: Sag Harbor then under Sag Harbor Bridge on the port side

Marina Facilities *(In Season/Off Season)*
Fuel: Gulf - Gasoline
Slips: 90 Total, 5 Transient **Max LOA:** 80 ft. **Max Beam:** 20 ft.
Rate *(per ft.):* **Day** $3.75* **Week** Inq. **Month** Inq.
Power: 30 amp $15, **50 amp** $20, **100 amp** n/a, **200 amp** n/a
Cable TV: Yes, $10 Family basic **Dockside Phone:** No
Dock Type: Fixed, Floating, Long Fingers, Short Fingers, Pilings, Wood
Moorings: 0 Total, 0 Transient **Launch:** n/a
Rate: Day n/a **Week** n/a **Month** n/a
Heads: 7 Toilet(s), 4 Shower(s) *(with dressing rooms)*
Laundry: 2 Washer(s), 2 Dryer(s) **Pay Phones:** Yes, 2
Pump-Out: OnCall *(Ch.73)* **Fee:** Free **Closed Heads:** Yes

Marina Operations
Owner/Manager: Malloy's **Dockmaster:** Raymond Crescio
In-Season: Jun-Sep 7, 8am-6pm **Off-Season:** Sep-Oct; Apr-May, 9am-5pm
After-Hours Arrival: Call in advance
Reservations: Yes, Required **Credit Cards:** Visa/MC, Amex
Discounts: None
Pets: Welcome **Handicap Access:** Yes, Docks

Marina Services and Boat Supplies
Services - Docking Assistance, Boaters' Lounge, Dock Carts
Communication - Mail & Package Hold, Phone Messages, FedEx,
AirBorne, UPS, Express Mail *(Sat Del)* **Supplies - OnSite:** Ice *(Cube)*
Near: Ice *(Block, Shaved)*, Ships' Store, Bait/Tackle *(Bayview Seafood Market 725-0740)*, Propane *(Ace Hardware 725-1900)* **Under 1 mi:** Marine
Discount Store *(Sag Harbor Ships Store 725-2458)* **1-3 mi:** Live Bait

Boatyard Services
OnCall: Engine mechanic *(gas, diesel)*, Electrical Repairs, Electronics
Repairs, Hull Repairs, Bottom Cleaning, Brightwork, Air Conditioning,
Refrigeration, Divers, Compound, Wash & Wax, Interior Cleaning, Yacht
Interiors, Total Refits **Near:** Travelift, Forklift, Launching Ramp, Electronic
Sales, Propeller Repairs, Woodworking, Inflatable Repairs.
Nearest Yard: Ship Ashore 0.5 mi. (631) 725-3755

Restaurants and Accommodations
Near: Restaurant *(The Beacon 725-7088)*, *(Roccos 725-4925)*, *(Anna's by the Bay 725-6913)*, *(B Smiths 725-5858)*, *(Sen Japanese 725-1774)*,
Seafood Shack *(Dock House 725-7100)*, Lite Fare *(Bagel Buoy 725-8103)*,
Inn/B&B *(Sag Harbor Inn 725-2949)*, *(Barron's Cove Inn 725-2100)*
Under 1 mi: Pizzeria *(Conca D'Oro 725-3167)*, Hotel *(American Hotel 725-3535)*, Inn/B&B *(1891 Guest House 725-1396)*

Recreation and Entertainment
OnSite: Picnic Area, Grills **Near:** Fitness Center *(Hamptons Gym 725-0707)*, Jogging Paths, Movie Theater *(Sag Harbor 725-0010 - art & foreign films)*, Park *(Marina Park)*, Museum *(Whaling Museum 725-0770 $3/1,*

Custom House 725-0250), Cultural Attract *(Bay St.Theatre 725-9500)*,
Special Events **Under 1 mi:** Beach *(Havens)*, Video Rental *(Harbor Video 725-7025)* **1-3 mi:** Playground, Tennis Courts *(Sag Harbor Park 725-4018)*,
Golf Course *(Sag Harbor G.C. 725-2503)*

Provisioning and General Services
Near: Convenience Store *(7-Eleven)*, Supermarket *(IGA 725-0366)*, Gourmet
Shop, Delicatessen *(Cove Deli 725-0216)*, Health Food *(Provisions 725-3636)*, Liquor Store *(Long Wharf Wines & Spirits 725-2400)*, Bakery,
Fishmonger *(Bayview Seafood 725-0740)*, Lobster Pound, Bank/ATM, Post
Office, Catholic Church *(St. Andrews)*, Protestant Church, Synagogue
(Temple Adas Israel), Library *(John Jermain 725-0049)*, Barber Shop, Dry
Cleaners, Laundry *(Sag Harbor 725-5830)*, Bookstore *(Book Hampton 725-1114, Canio's Books 725-4926)*, Pharmacy *(Sag Harbor Pharmacy 725-0074)*, Newsstand, Hardware Store *(Emporium 725-0103)*, Florist, Clothing
Store, Retail Shops, Copies Etc. **Under 1 mi:** Beauty Salon

Transportation
OnCall: Rental Car *(Enterprise 537-4800)*, Taxi *(Sag Harbor Taxi 725-6969)*,
Airport Limo *(Midway 537-1800)* **Near:** Bikes *(Bike Hampton 725-7329 $6/hr., $25/day)*, Local Bus *(Suffolk County Transit)*, InterCity Bus *(Hampton Jitney)* **Airport:** Islip/East Hampton *(60 mi./6 mi.)*

Medical Services
911 Service **OnCall:** Ambulance, Veterinarian *(Village Mobile Vet. 725-0815)* **Near:** Chiropractor *(Kirby 725-3215)* **Under 1 mi:** Doctor *(Umana 725-4329)*, Dentist *(Goodstein/Heinze 725-2000)*, Holistic Services *(Center for Holistic Healing 725-3215)* **Hospital:** South Hampton 726-8335 *(6 mi.)*

Setting -- Just west of Sag Harbor under the North Sea/Sag Harbor Bridge, Malloy's Sag Harbor Cove West is easy to spot if you just head to one o'clock. It promises a bit of quiet and privacy, well out of the tourist hub-bub that attacks Sag Harbor in the season. Landside it fronts on Water Street across from several condominium complexes, and is less than a half mile walk into town. A restaurant is just east of the docks.

Marina Notes -- Entrance to the eastern most section of the marina is for smaller boats (under 35) and is well protected on all sides but fronts on the street. The remaining slips are in the inner harbor and fairly well protected. The small club house is attached to the dockmaster's office. Bathroom/shower combinations are clean and neat with the ladies' facility considerably more attractive than the men's. There's a laundry in the dockmaster's building, and barbecue grills and picnic tables are scattered about. This is a conveniently located basic marina with easy access to town and friendly help. Originally Baron's Cove, it's been part of the 3-marina Malloy group since the early '90s. Pump-out boat Ch. 73.

Notable -- Sag Harbor's Whaling Museum is housed in an 1845 Greek Revival Mansion - the entrance is through the jaws of a Right Whale (Mon-Sat 10am-5pm, Sun 1-5pm.) The same architect, Minard Lafever, also built the magnificent 1844 Whaler's Church (725-0894) - the 185 foot steeple will soon be restored. Temple Adas Israel (725-0904) built in 1900 is the oldest synagogue on Long Island.

XI. New York: Long Island's South Shore Inlets

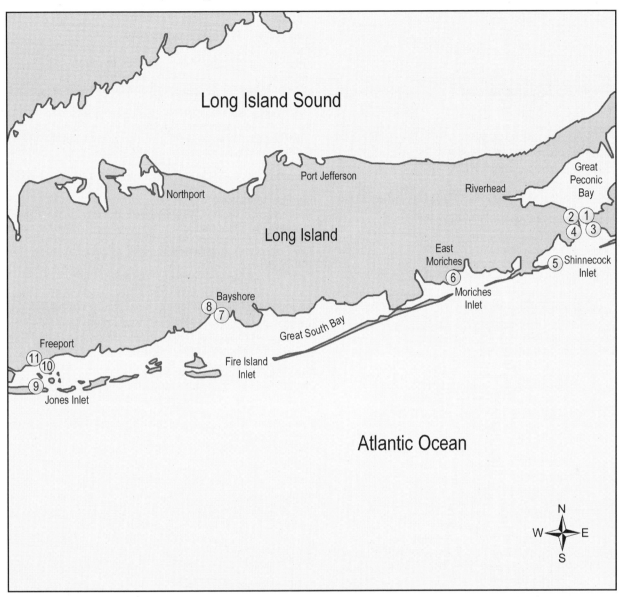

MAP	MARINA	HARBOR	PAGE	MAP	MARINA	HARBOR	PAGE
1	**Shinnecock Canal County Marina**	*Shinnecock Canal*	206	7	**Bay Shore Marina**	*Fire Island Inlet*	212
2	**Hampton Watercraft & Marine**	*Shinnecock Canal*	207	8	**Captain Bill's Marina**	*Fire Island Inlet*	213
3	**Jackson's Marina**	*Shinnecock Canal*	208	9	**Hempstead Town Marina — West**	*Jones Inlet*	214
4	**Mariner's Cove Marine**	*Shinnecock Canal*	209	10	**Guy Lombardo Marina**	*Jones Inlet*	215
5	**Oaklands Restaurant & Marina**	*Shinnecock Inlet*	210	11	**Jones Inlet Marine**	*Jones Inlet*	216
6	**Windswept Marina**	*Moriches Inlet*	211				

Shinnecock Canal County Marina

Canal Road at Bishop Place; Hampton Bays, NY 11946

Tel: (631) 323-2660 **VHF: Monitor** n/a **Talk** n/a
Fax: n/a **Alternate Tel:** (631) 854-4949
Email: n/a **Web:** www.co.suffolk.ny.us/exec/parks
Nearest Town: Hampton Bays *(1.5 miles)* **Tourist Info:** (631) 728-2211

Navigational Information
Lat: 40°53.610' **Long:** 072°30.090' **Tide:** 3 ft. **Current:** 5 kt. **Chart:** 12352
Rep. Depths *(MLW):* **Entry** 8 ft. **Fuel Dock** n/a **Max Slip/Moor** 8 ft./-
Access: South from Peconic Bay, north from Shinnecock Bay

Marina Facilities *(In Season/Off Season)*
Fuel: No
Slips: 62 Total, 20 Transient **Max LOA:** 45 ft. **Max Beam:** 15 ft.
Rate *(per ft.):* **Day** $55.00* **Week** n/a **Month** n/a
Power: 30 amp Incl., 50 amp n/a, 100 amp n/a, 200 amp n/a
Cable TV: No **Dockside Phone:** No
Dock Type: Fixed, Floating, Alongside, Wood, Composition
Moorings: 0 Total, 0 Transient **Launch:** n/a
Rate: Day n/a **Week** n/a **Month** n/a
Heads: 2 Toilet(s), 2 Shower(s)
Laundry: None **Pay Phones:** Yes, 2
Pump-Out: OnCall *(Ch.73)* **Fee:** Free **Closed Heads:** No

Marina Operations
Owner/Manager: Suffolk **Dockmaster:** John Donahue; Maureen Schamus
In-Season: n/a **Off-Season:** n/a
After-Hours Arrival: Check in in the morning.
Reservations: Yes **Credit Cards:** Visa/MC
Discounts: None
Pets: Welcome, Dog Walk Area **Handicap Access:** No

Marina Services and Boat Supplies
Services - Trash Pick-Up **Communication -** FedEx, AirBorne, UPS, Express Mail **Supplies - Near:** Ice *(Cube)* **1-3 mi:** Ships' Store, Bait/Tackle *(East End 728-1744)*, Propane

Boatyard Services
Near: Travelift, Engine mechanic *(gas)*, Hull Repairs, Rigger, Bottom Cleaning, Brightwork, Compound, Wash & Wax, Propeller Repairs, Painting. **Under 1 mi:** Launching Ramp, Electronic Sales, Electronics Repairs. **1-3 mi:** Canvas Work, Refrigeration.
Nearest Yard: Modern Yachts (631) 728-2266

Restaurants and Accommodations
OnSite: Lite Fare *(Meshutt Beach Hut Raw Bar & Grill 728-2988, B $1-4, L $2-9, D $7-11, 8am on)* **Near:** Restaurant *(Pasta Paisan 728-8704)*
Under 1 mi: Restaurant *(Indian Cove 728-5366, $23 3-course prix fixe)*, *(Michaelangelo Family Style Restaurant 728-7254)*, Seafood Shack *(Edgewater's 723-2323, Very good, reasonably priced, water views & deck dining)*, Lite Fare *(Hampton Maid 728-4166, Just Breakfast - best in the Hamptons - Cash Only)*, Motel *(Hampton Maid)*, *(Hampton Star Motel 728-6051)* **1-3 mi:** Pizzeria *(Francesca's 728-8979)*, Motel *(Allens Acres Motel 728-4698)*

Recreation and Entertainment
OnSite: Beach *(Meschutt 852-8205 - 7 acres of protected beach)*
Near: Picnic Area, Volleyball, Jogging Paths **Under 1 mi:** Fishing

Charter **1-3 mi:** Golf Course *(private Southampton G.C. 283 0623 , Movie Theater (UA Hampton Bays 728-8251)* **3+ mi:** Fitness Center *(World Gym Hampton Bays 723-3174, 4.5 mi.)*, Horseback Riding *(Sears Bellows Stables 723-3554, 3.5 mi.)*, Video Rental *(Blockbuster Video 723-3600, 4 mi.)*

Provisioning and General Services
Near: Fishmonger **Under 1 mi:** Wine/Beer *(Gimar Liquors 728-0024)*, Meat Market, Bank/ATM, Bookstore *(Oak Tree 723-3137)* **1-3 mi:** Supermarket *(King Kullen 728-9621)*, Delicatessen *(Kate's Old Country Deli 728-2983)*, Liquor Store *(Hampton Bays Wines 728-8595)*, Bakery, Post Office, Catholic Church, Protestant Church, Library *(728-6241)*, Beauty Salon, Barber Shop, Dry Cleaners, Pharmacy *(Bayman 723-2203)*, Newsstand, Hardware Store *(Shinnecock Hardware 728-4602)*, Florist, Retail Shops, Department Store *(Macy's 728-5500)*

Transportation
OnCall: Rental Car, Taxi *(Surf Taxi 723-1400)*, Airport Limo *(Gold Star Limousine 728-1100)* **Near:** Local Bus *(SCT Routes 10E, 92 852-5200 $1.50)* **1-3 mi:** InterCity Bus *(Hampton Jitney to NYC or airports 283-4600 $23-27 1/way)*, Rail *(LIRR to NYC 231-5477)*
Airport: Spadaro/Islip *(15 mi./45 mi.)*

Medical Services
911 Service **1-3 mi:** Doctor *(Prime Care 728-4500)*, Dentist *(Spinner 728-0251)*, Chiropractor *(Donohue 723-0613)*, Ambulance, Veterinarian *(Shinnecock Animal Hospital 723-0500)* **Hospital:** Southhampton *(8 mi.)*

Setting -- Shinnecock Canal County Marina is the first facility on the Canal's east side after entering from Peconic Bay. Its large square basin offers good, basic "stern-to" dockage in a protected environment away from the wash and current of the canal. It also provides easy access to one of Southampton Town's most popular and pretty Peconic Bay beaches.

Marina Notes -- *Flat rate weekday $55.00/day, weekends $65.00/day. This is a basic county owned and run marina in a great location. New floating stern-to docks down center of basin with some pedestals (no finger piers) will get most of the transient boats - some along-side dockage on the outside. Max 30 amp. Reasonable municipal heads and showers accessed by a combination code. Maximum stay 2 weeks (3 weekends). Seasonal also available. Free pump-out Ch.73. No repair facilities in the marina, but Mariner's Cove and Modern Yacht are located just across the canal. Lots of activity and events here during the summer. Town, county, and state marine patrols base out of here so security problems are moot. Weekday Dockmaster John Donahue is extremely helpful.

Notable -- Meschutt Beach County Park on the Shinnecock Canal is part of the same complex as the marina so it is considered "onsite". It's 1000 feet of protected, lifeguarded white sand beach fronting Peconic Bay -- with a picinic area, volleyball court, heads and a "snack bar". Meshutt Beach Shack sports attractive tables under green market umbrellas, and serves breakfast, lunch and dinner - sandwiches, grilled & fried "baskets" plus a raw bar. There's frequent nightly entertainment and special events like vintage car rallies, lobster feasts every Tues & Thur with live music, and sculpture contests.

Navigational Information
Lat: 40°53.550' **Long:** 072°30.210' **Tide:** 3 ft. **Current:** 4 kt. **Chart:** 12352
Rep. Depths (*MLW*): **Entry** 12 ft. **Fuel Dock** 12 ft. **Max Slip/Moor** 12 ft./-
Access: Shinnecock Inlet North to Canal; Peconic Bay South to Canal

Marina Facilities (*In Season/Off Season*)
Fuel: *Shell* - Gasoline, Diesel
Slips: 100 Total, 5 Transient **Max LOA:** 65 ft. **Max Beam:** 20 ft.
  Rate (*per ft.*): **Day** $3.00 **Week** Inq. **Month** Inq.
  Power: 30 amp Incl., **50 amp** n/a, **100 amp** n/a, **200 amp** n/a
  Cable TV: No **Dockside Phone:** No
  Dock Type: Fixed, Short Fingers, Pilings, Wood
Moorings: 0 Total, 0 Transient **Launch:** n/a
  Rate: Day n/a **Week** n/a **Month** n/a
Heads: 2 Toilet(s), 4 Shower(s) (*with dressing rooms*)
Laundry: None **Pay Phones:** No
Pump-Out: OnCall, Full Service **Fee:** Free **Closed Heads:** Yes

Marina Operations
Owner/Manager: Tony Villareale **Dockmaster:** Same
In-Season: Year 'Round, 8am-5pm **Off-Season:** n/a
After-Hours Arrival: See office personnel in the morning
Reservations: No **Credit Cards:** Visa/MC, Dscvr, Din, Amex, Tex
Discounts: None
Pets: Welcome, Dog Walk Area **Handicap Access:** No

Hampton Watercraft & Marine

PO Box 1010; 44 Newtown Road; Hampton Bays, NY 11946

Tel: (631) 728-8200 **VHF: Monitor** 68 **Talk** 68
Fax: (631) 728-0019 **Alternate Tel:** n/a
Email: info@hamptonwatercraft.com **Web:** www.hamptonwatercraft.com
Nearest Town: Hampton Bays (*2 mi.*) **Tourist Info:** (631) 728-2211

Marina Services and Boat Supplies
Services - Docking Assistance, Trash Pick-Up, Dock Carts
Communication - Mail & Package Hold, FedEx, AirBorne, UPS, Express Mail **Supplies** - OnSite: Ice (*Cube*), Ships' Store **Near:** Bait/Tackle, Live Bait **1-3 mi:** Marine Discount Store (*All Points Marine Supply 728-0012*), Propane (*Synergy 287-1150*)

Boatyard Services
OnSite: Travelift (*15T & 30T*), Forklift (*18,000 lb*), Hydraulic Trailer (*to 35 ft.*), Engine mechanic (*gas, diesel*), Launching Ramp, Electrical Repairs, Electronic Sales, Electronics Repairs, Hull Repairs, Air Conditioning, Refrigeration, Compound, Wash & Wax, Interior Cleaning, Painting, Yacht Broker **OnCall:** Rigger, Canvas Work, Bottom Cleaning, Brightwork, Divers, Propeller Repairs, Inflatable Repairs, Upholstery, Metal Fabrication
Dealer for: Boston Whaler, Sea Craft, Yamaha Jetboats & Waverunners, Monterey, Rampage, Lund, Novurania, Mercury, Envirude, Sportboats, Honda Outboards. Other Certifications: Mercury OptiMax, Yamaha
Yard Rates: $85/hr., Haul & Launch $5/ft. (*blocking $2.50/ft.*), Power Wash $4/ft., Bottom Paint $13/ft. (*paint incl.*) **Storage:** On-Land $39/ft.

Restaurants and Accommodations
OnSite: Restaurant (*Dock 75* 723-1275) **OnCall:** Pizzeria (*John's Pizza 728-9411*) **Under 1 mi:** Restaurant (*Hampton Bays Diner 728-0840*), (*Indian Cove 728-5366, $23 3-course prix fixe*), Coffee Shop (*Starbucks*), Motel (*Hampton Maid 728-4166, great breakfasts!*)

Recreation and Entertainment
OnSite: Picnic Area, Grills **Near:** Beach, Playground **Under 1 mi:** Park

1-3 mi: Dive Shop, Tennis Courts (*Southampton Bays 283-2406*), Jogging Paths, Horseback Riding (*Sears Bellows Stables 723-3554*), Boat Rentals, Roller Blade/Bike Paths, Bowling, Fishing Charter (*Shinnecock Star 728-4563*), Movie Theater (*Hampton Bays 728-8676*), Video Rental (*Video Kingdom 723-1000*) **3+ mi:** Golf Course (*Shinnecock Hills 283-1310, 5 mi.*), Fitness Center (*World Gym 723-3174, 4 mi.*)

Provisioning and General Services
Under 1 mi: Convenience Store, Supermarket (*King Kullen 723-3071*), Health Food, Liquor Store (*Purrfect 728-0740*), Green Grocer, Fishmonger (*Indian Cove 728-3474*), Bank/ATM, Post Office, Catholic Church, Library (728-6241), Beauty Salon, Barber Shop, Newsstand **1-3 mi:** Gourmet Shop, Delicatessen (*Baymens 728-8815*), Wine/Beer, Bakery (*Kriegs 728-6524*), Lobster Pound, Meat Market, Protestant Church, Dry Cleaners, Laundry (*Tony's Tubs 728-1046*), Bookstore (*Oak Tree 723-3137*), Pharmacy (*Bayman 723-2203*), Hardware Store (*Shinnecock 728-4602*), Florist, Retail Shops, Copies Etc. (*Stone 728-7065*)

Transportation
OnCall: Rental Car (*Enterprise 283-0055*), Taxi (*Hampton Coach 728-0050*), Airport Limo (*East Hampton Limo 723-2918*) **Near:** Local Bus (*SCT #10 D-E to town, train runs past the door*) **Airport:** Islip (*45 mi.*)

Medical Services
911 Service **Under 1 mi:** Doctor (*Prime Care 728-4500*), Ambulance **1-3mi:** Dentist (*Hampton Dental 728-8400*), Chiropractor (*Hampton Bays 728-8545*), Holistic Services, Veterinarian (*Shinnecock 723-0500*)
Hospital: Southampton 726-8200 (*10 mi.*)

PHOTOS ON CD-ROM: 9

Setting -- The first marina on the northwest side of the Shinnecock Canal, as you enter from Peconic Bay, Hampton Watercraft is north of the highway and railroad bridges (22 foot vertcal clearance). Its six and a half acres are primarily devoted to boatyard pursuits, but recent landscaping efforts and major construction have upgraded the ambiance considerably.

Marina Notes -- Primarily a boat dealership and boatyard, with mostly seasonal dockage, it has a mix of serious sport fishing boats and recreational boats among its regular clientele. Easy fuel accessibility. Major Boston Whaler certified "gold dealer" with a full service, knowledgeable boatyard operation. New owner in 1998 embarked on a serious upgrading process with new offices and very nice full bathrooms in '00 and a new restaurant in '01. The process continues with landscaping. It's neat, but still more boatyard than yacht club. Specializes in boat electronics rigging. Indoor 5800 sq ft Rigging Building. Storage for over 300 boats. Attractive proshop & ships store devoted primarily to water sports. Sponsors annual Offshore, Inshore and Kid's Fishing Tournaments. Closed Mondays in off season. *It is anticipated that the onsite eatery Dock 75 will open for the '04 season but check first.

Notable -- The 1,000 foot Meshutt Beach is a short dinghy ride - just east of the canal's entrance. The town of Hampton Bays is almost two miles. A new shopping plaza (about 0.8 mi. across the Montauk bridge) has a King Kullen supermarket, Starbucks and more. Many marine-oriented businesses in the area. Plus infamous and venerable CPI Canoe Place Inn (72804121), the largest club in the Hamptons (1,000 people in 3 lounges) $20 - 10pm on is nearby.

Jackson's Marina

PO Box 998; 6 Tepee Street; Hampton Bays, NY 11946

Tel: (631) 728-4220 **VHF: Monitor** 68 **Talk** n/a
Fax: (631) 728-4504 **Alternate Tel:** n/a
Email: info@jacksonsmarina.com **Web:** www.jacksonsmarina.com
Nearest Town: Hampton Bays *(2 mi.)* **Tourist Info:** (631) 728-2211

Navigational Information
Lat: 40°52.930' **Long:** 072°30.010' **Tide:** 4 ft. **Current:** 4 kt. **Chart:** 12352
Rep. Depths (*MLW*): Entry 8 ft. **Fuel Dock** 15 ft. **Max Slip/Moor** 15 ft./-
Access: East side of canal right off Shinnecock Bay

Marina Facilities *(In Season/Off Season)*
Fuel: *Valvetec* - Slip-Side Fueling, Gasoline, Diesel
Slips: 200 Total, 10 Transient **Max LOA:** 75 ft. **Max Beam:** 20 ft.
 Rate *(per ft.):* **Day** $1.75/Inq. **Week** $8.00 **Month** $28
 Power: 30 amp Incl., **50 amp** Incl., **100 amp** n/a, **200 amp** n/a
 Cable TV: Yes **Dockside Phone:** Yes
 Dock Type: Fixed, Floating, Long Fingers, Short Fingers, Pilings, Wood
Moorings: 0 Total, 0 Transient **Launch:** n/a, Dinghy Dock
 Rate: Day n/a **Week** n/a **Month** n/a
Heads: 2 Toilet(s), 5 Shower(s) *(with dressing rooms)*
Laundry: None **Pay Phones:** No
Pump-Out: OnCall *(Channel 73)*, 1 Port **Fee:** Free **Closed Heads:** No

Marina Operations
Owner/Manager: Charles Jackson **Dockmaster:** n/a
In-Season: Jun 1-Oct 1, 6am-6pm **Off-Season:** Oct 1-Jun 1, 7am-5pm
After-Hours Arrival: Tie up + register in the morning
Reservations: Yes **Credit Cards:** Visa/MC, Dscvr, Amex
Discounts: None
Pets: Welcome **Handicap Access:** Yes, Heads, Docks

Marina Services and Boat Supplies
Services - Docking Assistance, Security *(Electronic gate)*, Trash Pick-Up, Dock Carts **Communication -** Phone Messages **Supplies - OnSite:** Ice *(Block, Cube, Shaved)*, Ships' Store, Bait/Tackle *(Frozen)* **1-3 mi:** Propane *(Shinnecock Hardware)*

Boatyard Services
OnSite: Travelift *(18T, 35T & 75T)*, Forklift *(15,000 lb negative capacity)*, Hydraulic Trailer, Engine mechanic *(gas, diesel)*, Hull Repairs, Bottom Cleaning, Brightwork, Compound, Wash & Wax, Interior Cleaning, Propeller Repairs, Woodworking, Painting, Awlgrip, Yacht Broker *(Jacksons' & Jones Brothers)* **OnCall:** Electrical Repairs, Electronic Sales, Electronics Repairs, Rigger, Canvas Work, Air Conditioning, Refrigeration, Divers
Yard Rates: $65/hr. **Storage:** In-Water $30/ft., On-Land $22/ft.

Restaurants and Accommodations
Near: Restaurant *(Indian Cove 728-5366, 3-course prixe fixe $23)*, *(Edge Water 723-2323)*, *(Tide Runner 728-7373, L&D)*, Motel *(Hampton Maid 728-4166, Great breakfasts; cash only)*, *(Hampton Star 728-6051)* **Under 1 mi:** Restaurant *(Margarita Island 723-3200)*, *(Sunset Deck 728-3618)*, *(Paisons Pasta House 728-8704)*, Motel *(Shinnecock Mist 728-7200)*, *(Bowen's by The Bays 728-1158, small resort w/ motel rooms, cottages, tennis)* **1-3 mi:** Pizzeria *(Francescas 723-8979)*, Motel *(Ocean View Terrace 728-4036)*

Recreation and Entertainment
OnSite: Beach, Picnic Area, Grills, Group Fishing Boat *(Shinnecock Star 728-4563)* **Near:** Boat Rentals **1-3 mi:** Playground, Tennis Courts *(Southhampton Bays Tennis 283-2406)*, Horseback Riding *(Sears Bellows*

Stables 723-3554), Movie Theater *(Hampton Bays Theatre 728-8676)*, Video Rental *(Video Kingdom 723-1000)*, Park, Museum *(Shinnecock Nation Cultural Center & Museum 287-7153)* **3+ mi:** Dive Shop *(5 mi.)*, Golf Course *(Shinnecock Hills 283-1310 , 5 mi.)*

Provisioning and General Services
Near: Supermarket *(King Kullen 723-3071)*, Fishmonger, Lobster Pound, Florist **Under 1 mi:** Convenience Store, Delicatessen *(Baymens Deli 728-8815)*, Wine/Beer, Farmers' Market, Meat Market **1-3 mi:** Liquor Store *(Purrfect Liquors 728-0740)*, Bakery *(Kreig's 728-6524)*, Bank/ATM, Post Office, Catholic Church, Protestant Church, Library *(Hampton Bays 728-6241)*, Beauty Salon, Barber Shop, Dry Cleaners, Laundry *(Tony's Tubs 728-1046)*, Bookstore *(Oak Tree 723-3137)*, Pharmacy *(Bayman 723-2203)*, Newsstand, Hardware Store *(Shinnecock 728-4602)*, Copies Etc.
 3+ mi: Synagogue

Transportation
OnSite: Courtesy Car/Van *(to town or beach)* **OnCall:** Rental Car *(Enterprise 283-0055)*, Taxi *(Hampton Coach 728-0050)*, Airport Limo *(East Hampton Limo 723-2918)* **1-3 mi:** InterCity Bus *(Hampton Jitney to NYC and Airports)*, Rail *(LIRR to NYC)* **3+ mi:** Local Bus *(5 mi.)*
Airport: East Hampton/Islip *(15 mi./30 mi.)*

Medical Services
911 Service **Under 1 mi:** Holistic Services, Ambulance **1-3 mi:** Doctor *(Prime Care 728-4500)*, Dentist, Chiropractor *(HB Chiropractic 728-8545)*, Veterinarian *(Shinnecock Animal Hosp. 723-0500)*
Hospital: Southampton 726-8200 *6 mi.*

Setting -- Heading north, Jackson's is right off Shinnecock Bay, in the southeast corner of the Shinnecock Canal, before the bridges. It'a a full-service, rustic shipyard's shipyard on a half-circle peninsula. Five main docks radiate like spokes and two deep basins provide work space. Heading south, look for the two huge plastic quonset hut-style storage sheds on a promontory well south of the canal locks.

Marina Notes -- Owned and operated by the Jackson family since 1957. The outermost docks are in the current. As the docks round the circle into the basin, they are more protected. Mostly stationary docks with either stern-to with pilings or short finger piers. Very well stocked 50's style ships' store. 125 ft. easy access Fuel Dock. This is really a shipyard and it makes no bones about it; its 200 docks are strung around one of the largest yards on the Island. It maintains at least four travel lifts, an untold number of forklifts and cranes, and services virtually every type of boat from jumbo multihulls to offshore sport fish. In '03 the new bulkheading project along the south side of the main basin added new docks with electric and water. OK heads with *outdoor* showers.

Notable -- While Jackson's seems to be all about the boat - it provides some very useful people services. Notably a courtesy van to the beach or into town and cable and telephones on the docks. Easy access from Shinnecock Bay and the inlet, coupled with the boatyard services and no bridges, makes this a favorite of sportfishing boats. Capt. John Capuano's Shinnecock Star berths here - 47 ft. open boat carries 45 passengers. Nearby Tide Runners (formerly White Water Grill) overlooks the Canal lock -a mostly seafood menu in a nautically inspired room. 0.4 mile north is the new King Kullen shopping plaza.

Navigational Information

Lat: 40°52.918' **Long:** 072°30.147' **Tide:** 3 ft. **Current:** 5 kt. **Chart:** 12352
Rep. Depths (*MLW*): **Entry** 8 ft. **Fuel Dock** n/a **Max Slip/Moor** 6 ft./-
Access: North from Shinnecok Inlet via channels

Marina Facilities *(In Season/Off Season)*

Fuel: No
Slips: 250 Total, 6 Transient **Max LOA:** 65 ft. **Max Beam:** 20 ft.
  Rate *(per ft.)*: **Day** $2.50/$2.00 **Week** Inq. **Month** Inq.
  Power: 30 amp $10, **50 amp** n/a, **100 amp** n/a, **200 amp** n/a
  Cable TV: No **Dockside Phone:** No
  Dock Type: Fixed, Floating, Short Fingers, Pilings, Alongside, Wood
Moorings: 0 Total, 0 Transient **Launch:** n/a
  Rate: Day n/a **Week** n/a **Month** n/a
Heads: 6 Toilet(s), 8 Shower(s) *(with dressing rooms)*
Laundry: None **Pay Phones:** Yes, 1
Pump-Out: OnSite, Full Service **Fee:** n/a **Closed Heads:** No

Marina Operations

Owner/Manager: Robert Arcate **Dockmaster:** Same
In-Season: Apr-Oct, 8am-6pm **Off-Season:** Oct-Apr, 8am-5pm
After-Hours Arrival: Call first
Reservations: Yes, Required **Credit Cards:** Visa/MC, Dscvr
Discounts: None
Pets: Welcome, Dog Walk Area **Handicap Access:** Yes, Heads

Mariner's Cove Marine

9 Canoe Place Road; Hampton Bays, NY 11946

Tel: (631) 728-0286 **VHF: Monitor** n/a **Talk** n/a
Fax: (631) 728-0608 **Alternate Tel:** n/a
Email: eejetski@aol.com **Web:** n/a
Nearest Town: Hampton Bays *(1 mi.)* **Tourist Info:** (631) 728-2211

Marina Services and Boat Supplies

Services - Docking Assistance, Concierge, Trash Pick-Up **Communication** - FedEx, UPS, Express Mail *(Sat Del)* **Supplies - OnSite:** Ships' Store **Near:** Ice *(Block, Cube)*, Bait/Tackle *(East End 728-1744)*, Live Bait **Under 1 mi:** Propane *(Shinnecock Hrdwr 728-4602)* **1-3 mi:** Ice *(Shaved)*, West Marine, Marine Discount Store *(All Points Marine Supply 728-0012)*

Boatyard Services

OnSite: Travelift *(6T)*, Forklift, Engine mechanic *(gas, diesel)*, Launching Ramp, Electrical Repairs, Hull Repairs, Rigger, Bottom Cleaning, Brightwork, Compound, Wash & Wax, Interior Cleaning, Propeller Repairs, Woodworking, Inflatable Repairs **OnCall:** Air Conditioning, Refrigeration **Near:** Electronic Sales, Electronics Repairs, Canvas Work, Upholstery, Yacht Interiors, Metal Fabrication, Painting, Awlgrip. **Dealer for:** Celebrity Boats. **Yard Rates:** $75/hr., Haul & Launch $6/ft. *(blocking $3/ft.)*, Power Wash $3/ft., Bottom Paint $9/ft. *(paint incl.)* **Storage:** On-Land $30/ft.

Restaurants and Accommodations

Near: Restaurant *(Indian Cove 728-5366, 3-course prix fixe - $23; Raw bar)*, *(Margarita Island 723-3200)*, Motel *(Hampton Maid 728-4166, Great breakfasts - cash only)*, *(Hampton Star 728-6051)* **Under 1 mi:** Restaurant *(Tide Runner 723-7373)*, *(Gators 728-4100)*, Seafood Shack *(Fat Lucys 728-0304)*, Pizzeria *(Papa John's 728-9411)*, Motel *(Shinnecock Mist 728-7200)* **1-3 mi:** Restaurant *(Villa Paul's 728-3261, local institution)*

Recreation and Entertainment

OnSite: Beach, Picnic Area, Grills, Playground, Volleyball, Boat Rentals *(East End Polaris 728-8060 - Jet skis)* **OnCall:** Fishing Charter

Near: Fitness Center, Jogging Paths, Roller Blade/Bike Paths
Under 1 mi: Video Arcade, Park **1-3 mi:** Tennis Courts *(Southhampton Bays 283-2406)*, Horseback Riding *(Sears Bellows Stables 723-3554)*, Movie Theater *(Hampton Bays 728-8676)*, Video Rental *(Video Kingdom 723-1000)* **3+ mi:** Golf Course *(Shinnecock Hills 283-1310, 5 mi.)*

Provisioning and General Services

Near: Convenience Store, Gourmet Shop, Fishmonger, Lobster Pound, Bank/ATM **Under 1 mi:** Supermarket *(King Kullen 723-3071)*, Delicatessen *(Baymens 728-8815)*, Health Food, Wine/Beer, Liquor Store *(Purrfect Liquors 728-0740)*, Green Grocer, Meat Market, Post Office, Catholic Church, Protestant Church, Beauty Salon, Barber Shop, Bookstore *(Flos Carmeli 728-1280)*, Pharmacy *(Bayman 723-2203)*, Newsstand, Florist, Retail Shops **1-3 mi:** Bakery *(Kriegs 728-6524)*, Library *(Hampton Bays 728-6241)*, Dry Cleaners, Laundry *(Tony's Tubs 728-1046)*, Hardware Store *(Shinnecock Hardware 728-4602)*, Department Store *(Macy's)*, Copies Etc.

Transportation

OnSite: Bikes *(East End 728-8060)* **OnCall:** Rental Car *(Enterprise 283-0055)*, Taxi *(Surf 723-1400)*, Airport Limo *(East Hampton 723-2918)* **Near:** Local Bus *(SCT #10E 852-5200)* **Under 1 mi:** InterCity Bus *(Hampton Jitney to NYC & Airports)*, Rail *(LIRR)* **Airport:** Islip *(40 mi.)*

Medical Services

911 Service **OnCall:** Dentist, Chiropractor, Ambulance **1-3 mi:** Doctor *(Prime Care 728-4500)*, Veterinarian *(Shinnecock 723-0500)* **Hospital:** Southampton 726-8200 *(5 mi.)*

Setting -- On the southwest side of the Shinnecock Canal entrance, south of the locks and bridges, Mariner's Cove provides easy access to Shinnecock Bay and the Inlet beyond. Two basins, one behind the other, provide dockage for larger boats outside and for many, many personal watercraft inside. Adjacent to the basins, funky blue cottages and trailers sit at the edge of a private beach with a volleyball court.

Marina Notes -- A basic marina with room for boats up to 50 feet on its newer outside docks. The rear basin and interior docks house smaller boats and mostly personal watercraft (PWC/jetboats). Mariner's Cove is well known among the jetboat and PWC crowd and is a major purveyor and caterer of/to both. Good code-locked heads and showers. Easy access directly north to Peconic Bay. Bridges call for 22 feet vertical clearance.

Notable -- Hampton Bays hosts the second largest commercial fishing fleet in the state, hundreds of recreational boats, as well as some of the most vibrant nightlife. The town caters to serious mariners and manages serious partiers. It's a quick taxi ride or a long walk to Hampton Bays town and nightlife. On summer weekends, large crowds of young people fill the local bistros. Nearby Canoe Place Inn (CPI) packs in 1500 revelers on a Saturday night. What was once an historic, elegant inn (C. 1920), frequented by celebrities and politicians, is now a multi-stage, multi-bar dance nightclub. An appealing alternative is Chef Bernard Miny's window-wrapped Indian Cove restaurant. It overlooks the Canal and promises a fabulous Lyonaise take on the local seafood at wonderful prices (Miny grew up in Lyon and trained with Bocuse!).

Oaklands Restaurant & Marina

PO Box 6317; Dune Road & Road H; Hampton Bays, NY 11946

Tel: (631) 728-6900 **VHF: Monitor** 68 **Talk** n/a
Fax: (631) 728-6903 **Alternate Tel:** n/a
Email: info@oaklandsrestaurant.com **Web:** www.oaklandsrestaurant.com
Nearest Town: Hampton Bays (5 mi.) **Tourist Info:** (631) 728-2211

Navigational Information

Lat: 40°50.570' **Long:** 072°28.778' **Tide:** 4 ft. **Current:** 4 kt. **Chart:** 12352
Rep. Depths (MLW): Entry 12 ft. **Fuel Dock** 20 ft. **Max Slip/Moor** 7 ft./-
Access: through Atlantic Ocean to west side Shinnecock Inlet

Marina Facilities *(In Season/Off Season)*

Fuel: *Texaco* - Slip-Side Fueling, Gasoline, Diesel
Slips: 42 Total, 4 Transient **Max LOA:** 55 ft. **Max Beam:** 19 ft.
Rate *(per ft.):* **Day** $2.00/Inq. **Week** $9.00 **Month** Inq.
Power: 30 amp Inq., **50 amp** Inq., **100 amp** n/a, **200 amp** n/a
Cable TV: Yes **Dockside Phone:** No
Dock Type: Fixed, Short Fingers, Pilings, Wood
Moorings: 0 Total, 0 Transient **Launch:** n/a
Rate: Day n/a **Week** n/a **Month** n/a
Heads: 4 Toilet(s), 4 Shower(s)
Laundry: None **Pay Phones:** Yes
Pump-Out: OnCall, Full Service **Fee:** n/a **Closed Heads:** No

Marina Operations

Owner/Manager: Doug Oakland **Dockmaster:** Corol Sussner
In-Season: Apr-LabDay, 6am-mid **Off-Season:** Mar-Apr, LabDay-Nov, 7-9
After-Hours Arrival: Tie to fuel dock. Check with restaurant
Reservations: Preferred **Credit Cards:** Visa/MC, Dscvr, Din, Amex, Tex
Discounts: None
Pets: Welcome, Dog Walk Area **Handicap Access:** Yes, Heads, Docks

Marina Services and Boat Supplies

Services - Docking Assistance, Security *(Midnight to 5am)*, Dock Carts
Supplies - OnSite: Ice *(Cube)*, Bait/Tackle *(bait - wide variety)*, Live Bait
3+ mi: Ships' Store *(All Points Marine Supply 728-001, 4 mi.)*, Propane *(Shinnecock Hardware, 4 mi.)*

Boatyard Services

OnCall: Electrical Repairs, Electronics Repairs, Rigger, Canvas Work, Air Conditioning, Refrigeration, Divers **1-3 mi:** Travelift, Engine mechanic *(gas, diesel)*, Hull Repairs, Propeller Repairs.
Nearest Yard: Jackson's Marine- 631 728-4220

Restaurants and Accommodations

OnSite: Restaurant *(Oaklands 728-6900, L $9-18, D $16-32, Kids' Menu, Sun Brunch, Thur & Sun "Prix Fixe" $25, Mon & Fri "Lobster Bash" $22)*
Near: Restaurant *(Sunwater's Grill 728-1722, at Soleau's Wharf - entertainment nightly)* **Under 1 mi:** Restaurant *(Bayview House 728-1200, Breakfast & Dinner)*, *(Harbor Restaurant at Tully's 728-9111)*, Seafood Shack *(Tully's 728-9111)*, Motel *(Bel-Aire Cove 728-0416)*, *(Allens Acres 728-4698)*, *(Baywatch 728-4550)*, Inn/B&B *(Bayview House $170-500)*
1-3 mi: Pizzeria *(Francescas 728-8979)*

Recreation and Entertainment

OnSite: Beach *(Ponquoge)*, Picnic Area, Grills, Fishing Charter *(6 charter boats on site, includng Oakland's own "Reel Action" - 44 ft. Custom*

Henriques), Special Events *(Wally Oakland Memorial Tournament - Spring)*
Near: Park *(Shinnecock County Park West)* **3+ mi:** Golf Course *(Shinnecock Hills 283-1310 , 8 mi.)*, Boat Rentals *(4 mi.)*, Movie Theater *(Hampton Bays Theatre 728-8676, 5 mi.)*, Video Rental *(Blockbuster 723-3600, 5 mi.)*

Provisioning and General Services

OnSite: Wine/Beer **Near:** Fishmonger *(Soleau's Wharf or Tully's Seafood 728-9111- 1 mi.)* **3+ mi:** Convenience Store *(5 mi.)*, Supermarket *(King Kullen 723-3071, 5 mi.)*, Delicatessen *(Kates 728-2983 , 5 mi.)*, Liquor Store *(Bays Liquors 728-6111 , 5 mi.)*, Bank/ATM *(5 mi.)*, Post Office *(5 mi.)*, Pharmacy *(Bayman 723-2203, 5 mi.)*, Hardware Store *(Shinnecock Hardware 728-4602, 5 mi.)*, Department Store *(Macy's, 5 mi.)*

Transportation

OnCall: Rental Car *(Enterprise 283-0055)*, Taxi *(Surf Taxi 723-1400)*, Airport Limo *(East Hampton Limo 723-2918)* **3+ mi:** Rail *(LIRR to NYC, 4 mi.)*
Airport: Islip *(20 mi.)*

Medical Services

911 Service **OnCall:** Ambulance **1-3 mi:** Doctor *(Prime Care 728-4500)*
3+ mi: Chiropractor *(Hampton Bays 728-8545 , 4 mi.)*, Veterinarian *(Shinnecock Animal Hosp. 723-0500, 4 mi.)*
Hospital: Southampton 726-8200 *(10 mi.)*

Setting -- The first (non-commercial) marina west of the Shinnecock Inlet entrance, upscale Oaklands caters to larger sportfishing boats and anglers. The large and very attractiv, contemporary, shingle-style restaurant - with a wide, well appointed, deck and tiki bar -- dominates the landside view. The docks are protected on three sides with wave attenuators. The environment is pure, unadulterated beach - the nearest town is five miles away.

Marina Notes -- Built in the late 80's by the Oakland Family. A professionally run marina with a remarkably good restaurant. Although it is definitely oriented to the sport fish crowd, non-anglers are made right at home. Relatively new docks and pedestals - still in perfect shape. Lovely heads and showers with dressing rooms. International Game Fish Association Official Weigh Station (certified 1200 lb.). Rare summer north wind can make the small basin a bit choppy. Good access to the Atlantic or the Shinnecock Canal (mind the channels). Since the 1938 Hurricane this is now known familiarly as Dune Road.

Notable -- Oaklands is the quintessential upscale beachy restaurant. Eat inside in the cool, expansive, windowed dining room or outside on the deck with fabulous views of the marina and the bay beyond -- especially at sunset. Great tiki bar, too. Chef John Hill's own eclectic spin on local seafood has garnered some impressive reviews ("Dan's" named it one of the 7 best in all the Hamptons '03). Walk 100 feet south and you're on a spectacular, uncrowded ocean beach. Great surfing, beach fishing, and easy to find solitude - even on weekends, if you walk a bit. Great clam chowder just over the bridge at Tully's (one mile). Superb diving and fishing on the slack at the old bridge/fishing pier to the west (3/4 mile). Soleau's next-door offers fresh fish plus bait & tackle.

Navigational Information
Lat: 40°47.445' **Long:** 072°45.195' **Tide:** 2.5 ft. **Current:** n/a **Chart:** n/a
Rep. Depths (*MLW*): **Entry** 4 ft. **Fuel Dock** 4 ft. **Max Slip/Moor** 4 ft./-
Access: East Moriches to Coast Guard Station

Marina Facilities *(In Season/Off Season)*
Fuel: Gasoline
Slips: 145 Total, 5 Transient **Max LOA:** 38 ft. **Max Beam:** 12 ft.
  Rate *(per ft.)*: **Day** $2.00 **Week** $6.00 **Month** $25
  Power: 30 amp n/a, 50 amp n/a, 100 amp n/a, 200 amp n/a
  Cable TV: No **Dockside Phone:** No
  Dock Type: Fixed, Floating, Short Fingers, Alongside, Wood, Vinyl
Moorings: 0 Total, 0 Transient **Launch:** n/a
  Rate: Day n/a **Week** n/a **Month** n/a
Heads: Toilet(s)
Laundry: None **Pay Phones:** No
Pump-Out: OnSite, 1 Central **Fee:** Free **Closed Heads:** No

Marina Operations
Owner/Manager: Ian Hope **Dockmaster:** n/a
In-Season: May-Sep, 7am-7pm **Off-Season:** Oct-Apr, 8am-4pm
After-Hours Arrival: Call in advance
Reservations: No **Credit Cards:** Visa/MC
Discounts: Boat/US **Dockage:** 15% **Fuel:** n/a **Repair:** 5-10%
Pets: Welcome, Dog Walk Area **Handicap Access:** Yes, Heads, Docks

Marina Services and Boat Supplies
Services - Docking Assistance, Trash Pick-Up, Dock Carts
Communication - FedEx, UPS, Express Mail **Supplies - OnSite:** Ice
(Cube), Ships' Store **1-3 mi:** Bait/Tackle *(Harts Cove Bait & Tackle Plus
878-7514)*, Propane *(Bay Gas Service 399-3620)*

Boatyard Services
OnSite: Travelift, Forklift, Engine mechanic *(gas)*, Launching Ramp *($15)*,
Electrical Repairs, Electronic Sales, Electronics Repairs, Hull Repairs,
Rigger, Bottom Cleaning, Air Conditioning, Refrigeration, Compound, Wash
& Wax, Interior Cleaning, Propeller Repairs, Upholstery, Total Refits

Restaurants and Accommodations
OnSite: Restaurant *(Atlantic on the Bay 878-0700, seafood)*
Under 1 mi: Pizzeria *(Pizza Island II 874-0478)* **1-3 mi:** Restaurant
(Michelangelo 325-1314), *(White Truffle Inn 874-0757)*, Seafood Shack
(Atlantic Seafood Fish 878-8406), *(Seacove Restaurant 878-1820)*,
Fast Food *(McDonalds)*, Hotel *(Seatuck Cove House Inc 325-3300)*,
Inn/B&B *(White Truffle Inn 874-0757)*

Recreation and Entertainment
OnSite: Picnic Area, Playground **Under 1 mi:** Beach *(Great Bunn by boat -
docks, heads)* **1-3 mi:** Golf Course *(Rock Hill Golf Club 878-2250)*, Video
Rental *(Star Video 325-1229)* **3+ mi:** Tennis Courts *(East Side Tennis Club
288-1540, 4 mi.)*, Bowling *(Westhampton Bowling Lanes 288-4244, 6.5 mi.)*,

Windswept Marina

215 Atlantic Avenue; East Moriches, NY 11940

Tel: (631) 870-2100 **VHF: Monitor** 68 **Talk** n/a
Fax: (631) 870-6023 **Alternate Tel:** n/a
Email: n/a **Web:** n/a
Nearest Town: Center Moriches *(2 mi.)* **Tourist Info:** (631) 874-3849

Movie Theater *(Movieland Cinema of Mastic 281-8586, 5.5 mi.)*, Museum
(Moriches Bay Historical Society 878-1776, 4 mi.)

Provisioning and General Services
OnSite: Convenience Store **Under 1 mi:** Delicatessen *(Moriches Bay Deli
878-0254)*, Health Food *(Wholly Natural 878-1007)*, Liquor Store *(Kelley's
Wine & Liquor Shoppe 878-9463)*, Post Office, Catholic Church, Protestant
Church, Newsstand, Florist, Retail Shops **1-3 mi:** Supermarket *(King Kullen
325-9698)*, Wine/Beer *(Eastport Liquor 325-1388)*, Synagogue, Library
(Center Moriches 878-0940), Beauty Salon, Barber Shop, Dry Cleaners,
Laundry *(One Step Laundromat 878-9690)*, Pharmacy *(Genovese 325-
0646)*, Hardware Store *(Kostuk's 325-0616)* **3+ mi:** Bookstore *(Oak Tree
399-1012, 6 mi.)*, Copies Etc. *(Empire Publishing 288-6800, 5 mi.)*

Transportation
OnSite: Courtesy Car/Van **OnCall:** Taxi *(Check It Out Taxi 878-4118)*,
Airport Limo *(Alexbri Limo 399-7556)* **Under 1 mi:** Local Bus *(SCT Routes
90 & 66)* **Airport:** Spadaro/Islip *(1 mi./15 mi.)*

Medical Services
911 Service **OnCall:** Ambulance **Under 1 mi:** Dentist *(Campbell/Curtis
874-4747)* **1-3 mi:** Doctor *(Sound Medical Care 874-2900)*, Chiropractor
(Cirrone 325-3354), Holistic Services *(Lazy Day Spa 874-5998)*,
Veterinarian *(South Bay Animal Clinic 874-2615)*
Hospital: Peconic Bay Primary Medical Care 288-2273 *6.5 mi.*

Setting -- On Moriches Bay, near the Moriches Inlet and four miles west of Westhampton Beach, due north of buoy 23, Windswept Marina is safely ensconced right behind the US Coast Guard's East Moriches Station. This is a full service yard and marina with a restaurant on the property.

Marina Notes -- Established in the early 1940s. Closed Dec-Jan. The docks are well done (no electric, but there is water); the south facing dock area is a complicated series of walkways and walkovers that may leave you puzzled. Wetlands are the reason. Small boats dock behind the restaurant in a small basin, while larger boats have access to several areas. Game room for kids, car service to town (you'll need it), a barbecue area, slip-side parking, exceptionally clean heads and showers. Very helpful owner is onsite much of the time. Also outdoor wet or dry storage, a reasonably equipped ships' store, plus bait and tackle. The Boat-US discount is 15% on dockage, 10% on parts, and 5% on labor. International Game Fish Association Official Weigh Station.

Notable -- Moriches Inlet is great for fishing but is considered a "non-navigable inlet" due to shoaling. Shoaling is problematic in this area, even for the Coast Guard. Pay attention, take your time, and heed the water color. Windswept is in a wonderfully wild and isolated area. Nearby are intriguing nature trails and, a bit farther, a golf course. Consider dinghying to Great Bunn Beach on Fire Island's eastern tip, about a mile west of Windswept - it's part of the National Seashore. The town of Moriches is 5 miles west, with most services you might require. Westhampton is 5 miles east, with plenty of "Hamptons" atmosphere. Fortunately there is a courtesy car.

Bay Shore Marina

End of South Clinton Avenue ; Bay Shore, NY 11706

Tel: (631) 665-1184 **VHF: Monitor** 72 **Talk** 68
Fax: (631) 206-1486 **Alternate Tel:** n/a
Email: n/a **Web:** n/a
Nearest Town: Bay Shore *(1 mi.)* **Tourist Info:** (631) 665-7003

Navigational Information
Lat: 40°42.779' **Long:** 073°14.245' **Tide:** 2 ft. **Current:** 0 kt. **Chart:** 12352
Rep. Depths *(MLW)*: **Entry** 15 ft. **Fuel Dock** 5 ft. **Max Slip/Moor** 5 ft./-
Access: Fire Island Inlet to Great Cove to Watchogue Creek

Marina Facilities *(In Season/Off Season)*
Fuel: *Shell* - Gasoline, Diesel
Slips: 4 Total, 4 Transient **Max LOA:** 55 ft. **Max Beam:** n/a
 Rate *(per ft.)*: **Day** $50.00* **Week** n/a **Month** n/a
 Power: 30 amp n/a, **50 amp** n/a, **100 amp** n/a, **200 amp** n/a
 Cable TV: No **Dockside Phone:** No
 Dock Type: Fixed, Alongside, Wood
Moorings: 0 Total, 0 Transient **Launch:** n/a
 Rate: Day n/a **Week** n/a **Month** n/a
Heads: 2 Toilet(s)
Laundry: None **Pay Phones:** No
Pump-Out: OnSite, Self Service **Fee:** Free **Closed Heads:** Yes

Marina Operations
Owner/Manager: Dave Robinson **Dockmaster:** Same
In-Season: Apr 15-Nov 15, 6am-10pm **Off-Season:** Closed
After-Hours Arrival: Call in advance
Reservations: No **Credit Cards:** Visa/MC, Dscvr, Din, Amex, Shell
Discounts: Boat/US **Dockage:** n/a **Fuel:** $0.10 **Repair:** n/a
Pets: Welcome **Handicap Access:** No

Marina Services and Boat Supplies
Services - Docking Assistance, Security *(24 hrs)*, Trash Pick-Up
Communication - FedEx, AirBorne, UPS, Express Mail **Supplies -**
OnSite: Ice *(Cube)* **Near:** Bait/Tackle *(Burnett's Marina -Bait & Tackle 665-9050)* **1-3 mi:** Propane *(BGS Appliance Sales 581-4342)*
3+ mi: West Marine *(669-8585, 5 mi.)*, Boat/US *(422-9780, 6.5 mi.)*

Boatyard Services
Nearest Yard: Capt. Bill's (631) 666-4407

Restaurants and Accommodations
OnSite: Seafood Shack *(Lighthouse Landing 665-1184, B $2-4, L $3-22, D $3-22)* **Near:** Restaurant *(Captain Bill's 665-6262, L $6-14, D $18-30, Sun brunch 11:30am-2pm)*, *(Molly Malone's Pub & Restaurant 969-2232)*, Seafood Shack *(Nicky's 665-6621, Dinghy)*, *(Chowder Bar 665-9859, Dinghy)*, *(Porky's & Glenn's Seafood Restaurant 666-2899)*
Under 1 mi: Restaurant *(Bay Shore Palace Diner 665-2919)*, *(Sandella's Cafe 666-1074)*, Pizzeria *(Gino's Pizzeria 665-6350)*, Hotel *(Maple Bay Hotel 665-4433)* **1-3 mi:** Restaurant *(Siam Lotus Thai Restaurant 968-8196)*, Fast Food *(McDonald's)*, Pizzeria *(Carolina's 666-4400)*, Motel *(Bay Shore Summit Motor Lodge 666-6000)*

Recreation and Entertainment
Near: Fishing Charter **1-3 mi:** Tennis Courts *(Amritraj Racquet & Health Spa 968-8668)*, Fitness Center *(Bally 666-5533)*, Bowling *(AMF Bayshore Lanes 666-7600)*, Video Rental *(Blockbuster Video 666-0089)*

3+ mi: Golf Course *(Timber Point Country Club 581-2401, 3.5 mi.)*, Horseback Riding *(Babylon Riding Center 587-7778, 6 mi.)*, Movie Theater *(Islip Triplex 581-5200, 4 mi.)*

Provisioning and General Services
Under 1 mi: Market *(El Vincinito Grocery 206-0651)*, Delicatessen *(Eds South Bay Deli 969-9831)*, Bank/ATM, Post Office, Beauty Salon, Dry Cleaners, Pharmacy *(Bay Shore Chemists 665-3059)*, Retail Shops
1-3 mi: Supermarket *(Stop and Shop 666-2842)*, Health Food *(Galloping Greens 206-0874, Nutritious Creations 666-9815)*, Wine/Beer *(Bay Shore Beer Beverage Barn 665-0320)*, Liquor Store *(Bright Shore Wines & Liquors 665-4984)*, Catholic Church, Protestant Church, Library *(Bay Shore-Brightwaters PL 665-4350)*, Bookstore *(Waldenbooks 968-1867)*, Hardware Store *(Brightwaters 666-6422)*, Department Store *(Macy's 665-8400)*, Copies Etc. *(Sir Speedy 666-0900)*

Transportation
OnCall: Rental Car *(Enterprise 669-5500 or Budget 666-7777, 3 mi.)*, Taxi *(David Brothers 665-1515)*, Airport Limo *(Emerald Palace 968-4353)*
Near: Water Taxi, Ferry Service *(to Saltair and Ocean Beach on Fire Island)*
1-3 mi: Rail *(LIRR to NYC)* **Airport:** Islip *(14 mi.)*

Medical Services
911 Service **Under 1 mi:** Dentist *(Suffolk Dental Center 666-1440)*
1-3 mi: Doctor *(Immediate Family Care 968-0800)*, Chiropractor *(All Island Chiropractic Care 665-3714)*, Holistic Services *(Hands On Health Massage 665-0082)*, Veterinarian *(Bay Shore Animal Hospital 665-0004)*
Hospital: Southside 968-3000 *(2 mi.)*

Setting -- Just off Great South Bay's Great Cove, right at the mouth of Watchogue Creek, Bay Shore Marina fills a protected basin with town residents' boats at floating docks. Along the fuel dock and the stationary wharf is 150 feet of transient alongside dockage. A long, curved arm sweeps into the Cove. Inside the arm is the basin, in the center is a parking lot, at the end is the dockhouse and Lighthouse Landing, and along the outside is a bulkheaded beach.

Marina Notes -- *$50 flate rate up to 50 ft. The onsite, very casual Lighthouse Landing is open from 6am-10pm, seven days a week from mid-April through mid-November, for a cup of coffee to a complete clam bake ($22) - including homemade soups, wings, seafood platters ($6-20), steamers and lobsters, too. Good docks. This is a municipal marina and does not have transient slips. However, the concessionaire, which manages the fuel dock and the eatery, has alongside dockage for several boats, as well as a small, well equipped bait and tackle shop with live bait and shaved ice. Heads are surprisingly pleasant single men and women. Good fuel prices and very attentive dockmaster. The contact information above is directly to the concession.

Notable -- The 65-foot paddle wheeler Lauren Kristy lives here along with a couple of charter boats (321-9005 for information and reservations). It's a little less than a mile out to Bay Shore's main drag and the beginning of the town's shopping district. Captain Bill's, an elegant, upscale seafood restaurant (and wedding or event venue) is a few blocks away as is Porky's & Glenn's Seafood. For additional eateries, walk about a mile to West Main Street or dinghy over to the ferry docks on Maple Ave. There you'll find Nicky's Clam Bar (665-6621) and The Chowder Bar (665-9859).

Navigational Information
Lat: 40°42.805' **Long:** 073°14.482' **Tide:** 2 ft. **Current:** 0 kt. **Chart:** 12352
Rep. Depths (MLW): Entry 15 ft. **Fuel Dock** n/a **Max Slip/Moor** 6 ft./-
Access: Fire Island Inlet to Great Cove to Watchogue Creek

Marina Facilities *(In Season/Off Season)*
Fuel: No
Slips: 450 Total, 2 Transient **Max LOA:** 60 ft. **Max Beam:** n/a
 Rate *(per ft.)*: **Day** $2.00 **Week** n/a **Month** n/a
 Power: 30 amp Incl., **50 amp** Incl., **100 amp** n/a, **200 amp** n/a
 Cable TV: No **Dockside Phone:** No
 Dock Type: Fixed, Floating, Long Fingers, Wood
Moorings: 0 Total, 0 Transient **Launch:** n/a
 Rate: Day n/a **Week** n/a **Month** n/a
Heads: 3 Toilet(s), 3 Shower(s) *(with dressing rooms)*
Laundry: None **Pay Phones:** No
Pump-Out: No **Fee:** n/a **Closed Heads:** Yes

Marina Operations
Owner/Manager: Pete Sindone **Dockmaster:** Same
In-Season: Apr-Dec, 8am-4pm **Off-Season:** Jan-Mar, closed
After-Hours Arrival: Call ahead
Reservations: Preferred **Credit Cards:** Visa/MC, Amex
Discounts: Port Partners **Dockage:** 15% **Fuel:** n/a **Repair:** 10%
Pets: Welcome **Handicap Access:** Yes, Heads, Docks

Captain Bill's Marina

PO Box ; 133 Ocean Avenue; Bay Shore, NY 11706

Tel: (631) 666-4407 **VHF: Monitor** n/a **Talk** n/a
Fax: (631) 666-4407 **Alternate Tel:** n/a
Email: captnbillsmarina@aol.com **Web:** www.captainbillsmarina.com
Nearest Town: Bay Shore *(1 mi.)* **Tourist Info:** (631) 665-7003

Marina Services and Boat Supplies
Services - Docking Assistance, Security *(24 hr.)*, Trash Pick-Up
Communication - Phone Messages, Fax in/out *(Free)*, FedEx, AirBorne, UPS, Express Mail *(Sat Del)* **Supplies - Near:** Ice *(Block, Cube)*, Ships' Store *(Seaborn 665-0037)*, Bait/Tackle *(Burnett's Marina - Bait & Tackle 665-9050)* **3+ mi:** West Marine *(669-8585, 4.5 mi.)*, Boat/US *(422-9780, 6 mi.)*, CNG *(4.5 mi.)*

Boatyard Services
OnSite: Travelift *(50T)*, Forklift, Hydraulic Trailer, Engine mechanic *(gas, diesel)*, Electrical Repairs, Hull Repairs, Rigger, Bottom Cleaning, Brightwork, Compound, Wash & Wax, Interior Cleaning, Painting, Awlgrip
OnCall: Electronics Repairs, Air Conditioning, Refrigeration, Divers, Propeller Repairs, Woodworking, Upholstery, Metal Fabrication
Near: Canvas Work. **Yard Rates:** $85/hr., Haul & Launch $3/ft. *(blocking incl.)*, Power Wash $1.50/ft., Bottom Paint $10/ft. *(paint incl.)* **Storage:** In-Water $25/ft., On-Land $35/ft.

Restaurants and Accommodations
OnSite: Restaurant *(Captain Bill's 665-6262, L $6-14, D $18-34, Sun Brunch 11:30am-2:30pm)* **Near:** Seafood Shack *(Nicky's 665-6621, by dinghy)*, *(Chowder Bar 665-8859, by dinghy)*, *(Porky's & Glenn's Seafood 666-2899)*, Lite Fare *(Lighthouse Landing 665-1184, B $2-4, L $3-22, D $3-22, open 6am-10pm, 7 days)* **Under 1 mi:** Restaurant *(Speares Fair-Vu 665-9854)*, Pizzeria *(Gino's 665-6350)*, Motel *(Maple Bay Hotel 665-4433)* **1-3 mi:** Restaurant *(Siam Lotus Thai 968-8196)*, Fast Food *(McD's)*, Pizzeria *(Carolina's 666-4400)*, Motel *(Bay Shore Summit 666-6000)*, Inn/B&B *(Bayshore Inn 666-7275)*

Recreation and Entertainment
Near: Jogging Paths, Fishing Charter **1-3 mi:** Tennis Courts *(Amritraj Racquet & Health Spa 968-8668)*, Fitness Center *(Bally 666-5533; Point Set 968-8668)*, Bowling *(AMF Bayshore Lanes 666-7600)*, Movie Theater *(Islip Triplex 581-5200)*, Video Rental *(Blockbuster 666-0089)* **3+ mi:** Golf Course *(Timber Point C.C. 581-2401, 3.5 mi.)*

Provisioning and General Services
Near: Delicatessen *(Eds South Bay 969-9831)* **Under 1 mi:** Market *(El Vicinito 206-0651)*, Health Food *(Galloping Greens 206-0874, Nutritious Creations 666-9815)*, Liquor Store *(Bright Shore 665-4984)*, Bank/ATM, Post Office, Library *(665-4350)*, Beauty Salon, Dry Cleaners, Pharmacy *(Bay Shore 665-3059)*, Retail Shops, Copies Etc. *(Suffolk 665-0570)* **1-3 mi:** Supermarket *(Stop & Shop 666-2842)*, Catholic Church, Protestant Church, Bookstore *(Waldenbooks 968-1867)*, Hardware Store *(Brightwaters 666-6422)*, Department Store *(Kohl's 666-1152)*

Transportation
OnSite: Water Taxi *(South Bay to Fire Island - Kismet)* **OnCall:** Rental Car *(Enterprise 669-5500 or Budget 666-7777, 3 mi.)*, Taxi *(David Bros 665-1515)*, Airport Limo *(Emerald Palace 968-4353)* **Near:** Ferry Service *(to Ocean Beach & to Saltaire - across channel)* **Airport:** Islip *(14 mi.)*

Medical Services
911 Service **Under 1 mi:** Doctor *(Immediate Care 968-0800; McGrath 665-3710)*, Dentist *(Suffolk Dental 666-1440)*, Chiropractor *(All Island 665-3714)*, Veterinarian *(Bay Shore 665-0004)* **1-3 mi:** Holistic Services *(Hands On Massage 665-0082)* **Hospital:** Southside 968-3290 *(2 mi.)*

Setting -- After leaving Great Cove, passing the Bay Shore marina and entering Watchogue Creek, Captain Bill's is the first marina to port. It sports a substantial boatyard operation and a large, eye-catching, contemporary shingle-styled waterfront restaurant with multiple rooms and great decks with views of the basin. Marinas and other nautically oriented facilities line the reminder of the creek.

Marina Notes -- An extensive network of decent quality wood docks accompanied by a large full-service boatyard with a 55 ton travelift. All in a relatively convenient location relative to the inlet. Closed in the winter. Home to several tournaments, notably the Bay Shore Tuna Club's Mako Tournament in June and Long Island's Marlin and Tuna Tournament in July. Most required services can be found here or at nearby Seaborne (665-0037) - just a little further up the creek - which may also have an occasional transient slip.

Notable -- Large multi-room Captain Bill's Restaurant is a fine dining eatery with wide open vistas of the Great South Bay. It specializes in seafood and serves lunch and dinner seven days, and a famous Sunday Brunch buffet. Decks line the waterfront and a couple of function rooms and tented deck can serve up to 250 for parties and weddings. One of the Fire Island ferries leaves from an adjacent dock along with a water taxi service; other Fire Island ferries are within walking distance. The seafood shack and snack bar at Bayshore Marina is an easy walk out onto the point. It's about 0.6 miles to Bay Shore's Main Street; the town is teeming with services, shops, and interesting things to do.

Hempstead Town Marina - West

Lido Blvd. & Seaspray; Point Lookout, NY 11569

Tel: (516) 897-4127 **VHF: Monitor** 16 **Talk** 68
Fax: n/a **Alternate Tel:** n/a
Email: n/a **Web:** n/a
Nearest Town: Point Lookout *(0.03 mi.)* **Tourist Info:** (516) 431-1000

Navigational Information
Lat: 40°35.614' **Long:** 733°5..582' **Tide:** n/a **Current:** n/a **Chart:** n/a
Rep. Depths *(MLW)*: **Entry** 8 ft. **Fuel Dock** n/a **Max Slip/Moor** 6 ft./-
Access: Jones Inlet, channel to hard port around Pt. Lookout

Marina Facilities *(In Season/Off Season)*
Fuel: No
Slips: 155 Total, 5 Transient **Max LOA:** 45 ft. **Max Beam:** 15 ft.
  Rate *(per ft.)*: **Day** $1.00/1.00 **Week** n/a **Month** n/a
  Power: 30 amp Incl., **50 amp** n/a, **100 amp** n/a, **200 amp** n/a
  Cable TV: No **Dockside Phone:** No
  Dock Type: Floating, Short Fingers, Pilings, Wood
Moorings: 0 Total, 0 Transient **Launch:** n/a
  Rate: Day n/a **Week** n/a **Month** n/a
Heads: 6 Toilet(s), 2 Shower(s)
Laundry: None **Pay Phones:** Yes, 1
Pump-Out: OnSite, Self Service **Fee:** Free **Closed Heads:** Yes

Marina Operations
Owner/Manager: Frank Guma **Dockmaster:** n/a
In-Season: Apr-Nov, 7am-3pm **Off-Season:** Dec-Mar, Closed
After-Hours Arrival: Call 516-897-4127
Reservations: No **Credit Cards:** Cash or Check
Discounts: None
Pets: Welcome, Dog Walk Area **Handicap Access:** Yes, Heads

Marina Services and Boat Supplies
Services - Security *(24)*, Trash Pick-Up **Supplies -**
Under 1 mi: Bait/Tackle *(Atlantic Bait & Tackle 223-4406)*
3+ mi: West Marine *(431-0399, 5 mi.)*, Propane *(Island Park 431-1111, 6 mi.)*

Boatyard Services
OnSite: Launching Ramp
Nearest Yard: Jones Inlet Marine (516) 623-8115

Restaurants and Accommodations
Near: Restaurant *(Fisherman's Catch 670-9717)*, *(Lazy Pelican 889-3995)*, *(Capt. Joe's Anchor Inn 423-9335)*, Seafood Shack *(Point Lookout Clam Bar 897-4024)*, *(Ted's Clam Bar 431-4193)*, Snack Bar *(Jo Jo Apples 432-6494)*, Pizzeria *(Olive Oil's 432-9600)* **1-3 mi:** Pizzeria *(Pizzeria Del Mare 432-4600)* **3+ mi:** Fast Food *(Taco Bell, McDonalds 5 mi.)*, Motel *(Long Beach Motor Inn 431-5900, 5 mi.)*, *(Plantation 889-9500, 5 mi.)*, Hotel *(Brighton Hotel 431-0200, 4.5 mi.)*, *(Jackson Hotel 431-3700, 4 mi.)*

Recreation and Entertainment
OnSite: Picnic Area **Near:** Beach, Golf Course *(Town of Hempstead Golf Course 889-8181)*, Park **Under 1 mi:** Playground, Boat Rentals *(Ted's Fishing Station 431-4193)*, Group Fishing Boat *(Miss POint Lookout 546-5568; Super Hawk & Princess Marie 481-2841; Capt. Al's 623-2248; Lady JV 825-5727)* **3+ mi:** Tennis Courts *(Clay-Time Indoor Tennis 432-3040, 4.5 mi.)*, Fitness Center *(5 mi.)*, Bowling *(Nassau County Womens Bowling Association 379-2234 R 7.5 mi., 10 mi.)*, Movie Theater *(Long Beach Cinemas 431-2400, 4 mi.)*, Video Rental *(Blockbuster 897-5580, 4 mi.)*

Provisioning and General Services
Near: Supermarket *(Merola's Point Lookout IGA 431-2145)*, Delicatessen *(Point Look-Out Deli 889-0247)*, Liquor Store *(Point Lookout Liquor 432-3492)*, Fishmonger *(Doxsee Clams-Offshore Seafood 432-0529; Pt. Lookout Fish Dock 432-0034)*, Lobster Pound, Bank/ATM, Post Office *(431-0062)*, Library *(Long Beach PL - Point Lookout Branch 432-3409)*, Pharmacy *(Geo's Point Pharmacy 889-3444)*, Retail Shops **Under 1 mi:** Catholic Church, Protestant Church *(Community 432-5990)*, Beauty Salon, Barber Shop, Dry Cleaners *(Fashion 432-6377)*, Laundry, Newsstand, Florist **1-3 mi:** Synagogue, Hardware Store *(O'Rourke 432-5490)* **3+ mi:** Gourmet Shop *(Trader Joe's 771-1012, 6 mi.)*, Bakery *(5 mi.)*, Buying Club *(BJ's, 5 mi.)*

Transportation
OnCall: Taxi *(Long Beach Taxi 432-7500, Five Two Hundred Taxi 431-5200)*, Local Bus *(from Pt. Lookout to Long Beach)*, Airport Limo *(All County Limousine of LI 678-1166)* **1-3 mi:** Rail *(Long Beach LIRR)*
Airport: JFK *(18 mi.)*

Medical Services
911 Service **OnCall:** Ambulance **Under 1 mi:** Dentist *(Hagamen 431-2121)* **1-3 mi:** Doctor, Holistic Services *(New Alternatives Physical Therapy & Massage 889-5719)* **3+ mi:** Chiropractor *(East Park Chiro 431-7972, 4 mi.)*, Veterinarian *(Island Park Animal Hospital 431-4300, 5 mi.)*
Hospital: Long Beach Medical Center 897-1000 *4 mi.*

Setting -- Situated very conveniently at the entrance to Jones Inlet, in the channel between Point Lookout and Alder Island, are two Hempstead Town Marinas - East and West. The first one to port is "East", home to charter and party boats as well as many seasonal slip holders. Under the 20 foot fixed bridge is "West" which offers transient dockage in a protected, convenient and unsullied environment.

Marina Notes -- "East" will accommodate boats in trouble - but has no transient dockage. If your boat can't get under the 20 foot fixed bridge to get to "West", it is possible to get there by going straight up the Inlet channel, through the draw bridge and back around Alder Island through the well-marked course. Fair amount of traffic on week-ends. Bulkhead in need of replacement. Docks are currently stern-to with no finger piers but new docks with finger piers are scheduled for summer 2004. Heads are standard cinderblock but with tile floors plus showers have dressing rooms. There's a helpful dockmaster onsite .

Notable -- The entrance to Point Lookout Park Beach parking lot is directly across the street - then it's a 0.2 mile walk to the actual ocean beach. But if you like ocean beaches, it's worth it. The village of Point Lookout is a 0.3 mile walk; there you'll find a quarter mile long shopping district with most services and a nice selection of eateries and provisioning resources, including an IGA grocery.

Navigational Information
Lat: 40°37.625' **Long:** 073°34.497' **Tide:** n/a **Current:** n/a **Chart:** 12352
Rep. Depths (*MLW*): **Entry** 7 ft. **Fuel Dock** n/a **Max Slip/Moor** 6 ft./-
Access: Jones Inlet to Hudson Channel

Marina Facilities *(In Season/Off Season)*
Fuel: No
Slips: 260 Total, 30 Transient **Max LOA:** 60 ft. **Max Beam:** n/a
  Rate *(per ft.):* **Day** $1.00 **Week** n/a **Month** n/a
  Power: 30 amp Incl., **50 amp** Incl., **100 amp** n/a, **200 amp** n/a
  Cable TV: No **Dockside Phone:** No
  Dock Type: Floating, Wood
Moorings: 0 Total, 0 Transient **Launch:** n/a
  Rate: Day n/a **Week** n/a **Month** n/a
Heads: 6 Toilet(s), 6 Shower(s)
Laundry: None **Pay Phones:** No
Pump-Out: OnSite, Self Service **Fee:** Free **Closed Heads:** Yes

Marina Operations
Owner/Manager: Don Scarandino **Dockmaster:** Steve Dahlam
In-Season: Apr-Nov, 7am-3pm **Off-Season:** Dec-Mar, Closed
After-Hours Arrival: Call in advance
Reservations: No **Credit Cards:** Cash
Discounts: None
Pets: Welcome **Handicap Access:** No

Guy Lombardo Marina

Guy Lombardo Avenue at Tyler Street; Freeport, NY

Tel: (516) 378-3417 **VHF: Monitor** 16 **Talk** 68
Fax: (516) 431-0088 **Alternate Tel:** n/a
Email: n/a **Web:** n/a
Nearest Town: Freeport *(1 mi.)* **Tourist Info:** (516) 223-8840

Marina Services and Boat Supplies
Supplies - OnSite: Ice *(Block, Cube)* **Near:** Bait/Tackle *(Atlantic Bait & Tackle 223-4406)* **3+ mi:** Propane *(U-Haul Center Of Rockville 764-3703, 3.5 mi.)*

Boatyard Services
Near: Electronic Sales. **Under 1 mi:** Travelift, Engine mechanic *(gas, diesel)*, Electronics Repairs, Hull Repairs, Rigger, Air Conditioning, Refrigeration, Propeller Repairs. **Nearest Yard:** Jones Inlet Marina (516) 623-8115

Restaurants and Accommodations
Near: Restaurant *(Pier 95 867-9632)* **Under 1 mi:** Restaurant *(Happy Family 867-1699)*, *(El Tejadito 377-6263)*, *(Schooner 378-7575, D $14-30)*, *(Steve's Riptide Inn 771-5983)*, *(Helm Restaurant 378-9615)*, Seafood Shack *(Margo & Frank's Mermaid Restaurant 546-3393)*, Snack Bar *(Rosie's Ice Cream)*, *(Ralph's Italian Ices)*, Fast Food *(McDonald's)*, Pizzeria *(Domino's 867-3030)*, Hotel *(Freeport Motor Inn & Boatel 623-9100)*, *(Yankee Clipper Motor Lodge 379-2005)* **1-3 mi:** Inn/B&B *(Diplomat Motor Inn 678-1100)*

Recreation and Entertainment
OnSite: Picnic Area, Grills, Special Events *(Long Island In-Water Boat Show 691-7050 Apr)* **Near:** Jogging Paths **Under 1 mi:** Tennis Courts *(Freeport Indoor Tennis Inc 623-2929)*, Fishing Charter, Group Fishing Boat *(Super Spray, many others along Woodcleft Canal)*, Museum *(Freeport Historical Museum 623-9632)*, Cultural Attract *(South St. Seaport's LI Marine Education Center 771-0399 $3/2)*

1-3 mi: Fitness Center *(Synergy Fitness of Baldwin 771-1717)*, Movie Theater *(Grand AV Cinema 223-2323)*, Video Rental *(Blockbusters 546-4060)* **3+ mi:** Golf Course *(Merrick Road Park GC 868-4650, 4 mi.)*, Bowling *(Rockville Lanes 678-3010, 5 mi.)*

Provisioning and General Services
Under 1 mi: Convenience Store *(Felos Minimarket 868-0562)*, Delicatessen *(Central Deli 377-2122)*, Health Food *(ABC's of Nutrition and Wellness 935-6347)*, Wine/Beer, Liquor Store *(Atlantic Bayview Wines & Liquors 378-9421)*, Library *(Freeport Memorial 379-3274)*, Pharmacy *(CVS 378-2400)*, Hardware Store *(Richmond 378-4240)* **1-3 mi:** Supermarket *(Stop & Shop 868-8400)*, Bookstore *(Oak Tree Book Store 377-3226, Ship To Shore 623-1900)*, Copies Etc. *(Minuteman Press 546-2312)* **3+ mi:** Department Store *(Merrick Mall, 4 mi.)*

Transportation
OnCall: Taxi *(Taxi-America 377-3600)*, Local Bus *(N62 to the Freeport LIRR station, downtown, & Nautical Mile 228-4000)* **Under 1 mi:** Airport Limo *(Crosswinds Limo 867-4870)* **1-3 mi:** Rail **Airport:** JFK Int'l. *(14.5 mi.)*

Medical Services
911 Service **Under 1 mi:** Doctor *(Louis-Charles 608-6777)*
1-3 mi: Dentist *(Freeport Dental 377-3803)*, Chiropractor *(Freeport Communit 377-7213)*, Holistic Services *(Body Shoppe Therapeutic Massage Center 867-3960)*, Veterinarian *(Baldwin Harbor 379-5010)*
Hospital: South Nassau 632-3000 *3.5 mi.*

Setting -- After entering Jones Inlet, make a sharp turn to starboard at Red 10 and another to port just before Green Q1, and head into the narrow, stick-straight Hudson Channel. The very first facility on the port side is the Town of Hempstead's Guy Lombardo Marina. It is tucked into a very protected large square basin and is surrounded on three sides by pristine, preserved marsh.

Marina Notes -- The marina reserves dedicated transient slips. Heads and showers are standard issue municipal. Onsite you'll find: personnel, ice, fuel, and self-service pump-out.

Notable -- If you take the dinghy back around the point and head into Woodcleft Canal, you'll find Freeport's famous bustling, fun, and charming Nautical Mile. Tie up at the Esplanade, which has benches, a fountain, and heads. Alternatively, Guy Lombardo Avenue follows the Woodcleft Canal up its East side; walk to the canal's head and then stroll down the west side (where all the action is). Or take the N62 bus. The delightful Nautical Mile has recently undgone a complete renovation with a new promenade, pier, brick sidewalks, old-fashioned lighting and refurbished and renovated shops and restaurants. The strip is chock-a-block with seafood shacks, clam bars and fine dining spots (most offer "dock 'n dine"). Tucked among the eateries are many charter fishing and party, casino boats, dinner cruise "ships", plus tons of gift shops and lots of music. The Nautical Mile is also home to the Long Island Marine Education Center which is part of South Street Seaport Museum. It has year-round education programs, exhibitions, demonstrations, and workshops - Wed-Sun, 11am-4pm.

Jones Inlet Marine

710 South Main Street; Freeport, NY 11520

Tel: (516) 623-8115 **VHF:** Monitor 16 **Talk** 68
Fax: (516) 623-8298 **Alternate Tel:** n/a
Email: jinlet@goldfarbproperties.com **Web:** www.jonesinletmarine.com
Nearest Town: Freeport *(2 mi.)* **Tourist Info:** (516) 223-8840

Navigational Information
Lat: 40°38.203' **Long:** 073°34.471' **Tide:** n/a **Current:** n/a **Chart:** 12352
Rep. Depths *(MLW)*: **Entry** 5 ft. **Fuel Dock** 12 ft. **Max Slip/Moor** 12 ft./-
Access: Long creek to Hudson channel past Cow Meadow Park

Marina Facilities *(In Season/Off Season)*
Fuel: *Texaco* - Gasoline, Diesel
Slips: 175 Total, 10 Transient **Max LOA:** 120 ft. **Max Beam:** n/a
  Rate *(per ft.)*: **Day** $2.00 **Week** n/a **Month** n/a
  Power: 30 amp $4, 50 amp $6, 100 amp $15, 200 amp n/a
  Cable TV: Yes **Dockside Phone:** Yes
  Dock Type: Floating, Long Fingers, Wood
Moorings: 0 Total, 0 Transient **Launch:** n/a
  Rate: Day n/a **Week** n/a **Month** n/a
Heads: 1 Toilet(s), 2 Shower(s)
Laundry: None **Pay Phones:** No
Pump-Out: OnCall **Fee:** $5 **Closed Heads:** Yes

Marina Operations
Owner/Manager: Mike O'Rourke **Dockmaster:** Bryon Knoth
In-Season: Apr 15-Oct 14, 8am-5pm **Off-Season:** Oct 15-Apr 14, 7am-4pm
After-Hours Arrival: None
Reservations: Yes, Preferred **Credit Cards:** Visa/MC, Amex
Discounts: None
Pets: Welcome, Dog Walk Area **Handicap Access:** Yes, Docks

Marina Services and Boat Supplies
Services - Docking Assistance, Security *(24, gate)*, Trash Pick-Up, Dock Carts, Megayacht Facilities **Communication -** Mail & Package Hold, Fax in/out *($2)*, Data Ports *(On pedestal)*, FedEx, AirBorne, UPS, Express Mail
Supplies - OnSite: Ice *(Block, Cube)*, Ships' Store **Under 1 mi:** Bait/Tackle *(Freeport B&T 378-4988)* **3+ mi:** Propane *(U-haul 764-3703, 5 mi.)*

Boatyard Services
OnSite: Travelift *(88T)*, Forklift, Engine mechanic *(gas, diesel)*, Electrical Repairs, Electronics Repairs, Hull Repairs, Rigger, Bottom Cleaning, Brightwork, Air Conditioning, Refrigeration, Divers, Compound, Wash & Wax, Interior Cleaning, Propeller Repairs, Woodworking, Inflatable Repairs, Metal Fabrication, Painting, Awlgrip, Total Refits **OnCall:** Canvas Work, Life Raft Service, Upholstery, Yacht Interiors **Near:** Electronic Sales.
Member: ABBRA - 2 Certified Tech(s), ABYC - 7 Certified Tech(s), Other Certifications: M.A.N. & CAT **Yard Rates:** $50/hr., Haul & Launch $8/ft. *(blocking $50/hr.)*, Power Wash $3/ft., Bottom Paint $13/ft. *(paint incl.)*

Restaurants and Accommodations
Near: Restaurant *(Pier 95 Restaurant 379-9898)*, *(Bedell's at West Wind 546-4545)*, *(Sue's Place 868-2788)* **Under 1 mi:** Fast Food *(Boston Market 377-4220)*, Pizzeria *(Montana Pizzeria 379-3053)*, Motel *(Freeport Motor Inn 623-9100)*, *(Yankee Clipper Motor Lodge 397-2005)* **1-3 mi:** Restaurant *(Nautilus Cafe 379-2566)*, *(E B Elliot's 378-8776)*, Lite Fare *(Hanse Ave. Hero's 867-5587)* **3+ mi:** Hotel *(Holiday Inn Rockville 678-1300, 5 mi.)*

Recreation and Entertainment
OnSite: Pool *(New - Aug 2004)*, Picnic Area, Special Events *(Marine World's Fluke and Bass Fishing Tournament, Sep; 625-9351 $150)* **Near:** Grills, Playground, Tennis Courts *(Cow Meadow)*, Jogging Paths, Park *(Cow Meadow Park & Preserve)* **Under 1 mi:** Dive Shop, Museum *(Freeport Historical 623-9632)*, Galleries *(Frank's Art Shack 223-1399)* **1-3 mi:** Beach *(Jones Beach State Park)*, Golf Course *(Merrick Road Park GC 868-4650)*, Fitness Center *(Titans Fitness 623-5770)*, Group Fishing Boat *(Capt. Lou's Fleet 766-5716)*, Movie Theater *(Merrick 623-1177)*, Cultural Attract *(South St. Seaport's Marine Education 771-0399)* **3+ mi:** Bowling *(Rockville Lanes 678-3010, 5 mi.)*, Video Rental *(Blockbuster 868-4263, 4 mi.)*

Provisioning and General Services
Under 1 mi: Convenience Store *(7-Eleven)*, Delicatessen *(Atlantic Avenue Deli 378-0203, A's Deli 223-4385)* **1-3 mi:** Market *(M & B Food Market 379-9078)*, Supermarket *(Stop & Shop 868-8400)*, Gourmet Shop *(Trader Joe's 771-1012)*, Liquor Store *(N & J Wines & Liquors 867-5469)*, Library *(Freeport 379-3274)*, Laundry *(Freeport Station 623-7944)*, Bookstore *(Oak Tree Book Store 377-3226, Ship To Shore 623-1900)*, Pharmacy *(Walgreen 623-9673)*, Hardware Store *(Richmond 378-4240)*, Department Store *(Merrick Mall)*

Transportation
OnCall: Rental Car *(Enterprise 377-7600, Sensible Car Rental 867-6954 3 mi.)*, Taxi *(Taxi-America 377-3600)*, Airport Limo *(Crosswinds 867-4870)* **1-3 mi:** Rail *(LIRR)* **Airport:** JFK *(15 mi.)*

Medical Services
911 Service **OnCall:** Ambulance **1-3 mi:** Doctor, Dentist, Chiropractor *(Freeport Community Chiro 377-7213)*, Veterinarian *(Meadowbrook Animal Hosp. 546-3700)* **Hospital:** South Nassau 632-3000 *(3 mi.)*

Setting -- Head up Hudson Channel, past the acres and acres of unspoiled marsh that comprise Cow Meadow Preserve, to the first facility to starboard. Jones Inlet's immaculate, first class docks, with their bright blue entrance awnings, and its humongous travelift are hard to miss. A strip of grass, punctuated by pots of flowers and picnic tables, separates the docks from the boatyard operation.

Marina Notes -- *Rate is $3/ft. for T-Heads (End Ties). "D" dock, which handles the largest vessels, was new in 2003 as are the power pedestals (to 100 amps, cable, phone and modems). Largest (88 ton) travelift on Long Island, carrying up to a 100 foot yacht (26 ft. beam). Telephone, cable TV, and computer modem hook-up. Remarkable number of certified and factory-trained technicians (Engine, Carpenters, Fiberglass, Welders, and Painters) wield a one-million-dollar tool inventory and manage a completely computerized boatyard - from parts management to estimates. New pool - 2004.

Notable -- Cow Meadow Park & Preserve, literally adjacent, is a combination recreational facility (22 acres) and nature preserve (150 acres). The Park features a playground area (including swings, slides), 1-mile jogging course, chess and checker tables, tennis, basketball, handball/paddleball, shuffleboard courts, softball, football & soccer fields, a fishing pier and 2 picnic areas. 150 bird species and 15 mammals inhabit the salt marsh, mud flat, tidal creek habitats, and the surrounding uplands; a quarter mile nature trail winds through. Pier 95 restaurant is directly across the Channel. Freeport's Nautical Mile runs the length of Woodcleft Canal; it's a short dinghy ride (or a much longer walk or cab ride) north from the Channel into the Canal. Dock at the new Esplanade.

XII. New York/New Jersey: New York Harbor

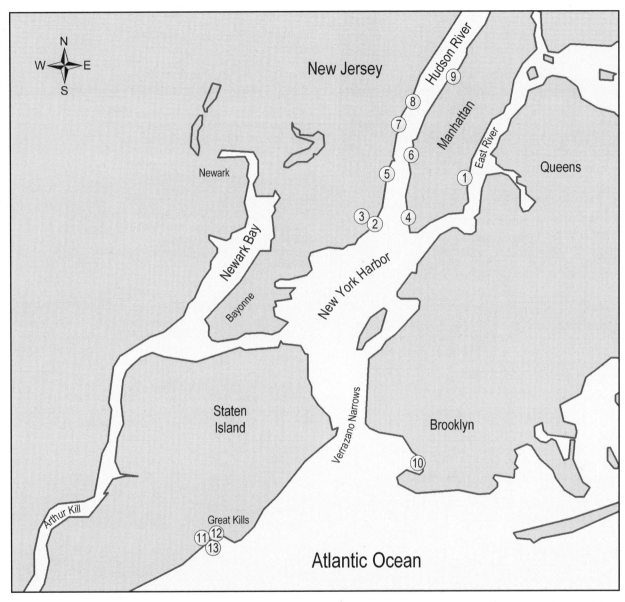

MAP	MARINA	HARBOR	PAGE	MAP	MARINA	HARBOR	PAGE
1	New York Skyports Marina	East River	218	8	Port Imperial Marina	Hudson River	225
2	Liberty Landing Marina	NY Harbor	219	9	West 79th Street Boat Basin	Hudson River	226
3	Liberty Harbor Marina	NY Harbor	220	10	Marine Basin Marina	Gravesend Bay	227
4	North Cove Marina	NY Harbor	221	11	Atlantis Marina & Yacht Sales	Great Kills Harbor	228
5	Newport Yacht Club & Marina	Hudson River	222	12	Mansion Marina	Great Kills Harbor	229
6	Surfside 3 Marina at Chelsea Piers	Husdon River	223	13	Nichols Great Kills Park Marina	Great Kills Harbor	230
7	Lincoln Harbor Yacht Club	Hudson River	224				

New York Skyports Marina

New York Skyports Marina

23rd Street & East River; New York, NY 10010

Tel: (212) 686-4548 **VHF: Monitor** 9 **Talk** 69
Fax: (212) 686-1371 **Alternate Tel:** (212) 686-4546
Email: n/a **Web:** n/a
Nearest Town: New York City *(0 mi.)* **Tourist Info:** (212) 484-1222

Navigational Information
Lat: 40°44.090' **Long:** 073°58.450' **Tide:** 5 ft. **Current:** n/a **Chart:** 12327
Rep. Depths (*MLW*): Entry 15 ft. **Fuel Dock** 9 ft. **Max Slip/Moor** 9 ft./-
Access: Long Island Sound or New York Harbor to East River

Marina Facilities *(In Season/Off Season)*
Fuel: No
Slips: 1236 Total, 2 Transient **Max LOA:** 120 ft. **Max Beam:** 10 ft.
  Rate *(per ft.)*: **Day** $3.00 **Week** Inq. **Month** Inq.
  Power: 30 amp Inq., **50 amp** Inq., **100 amp** Inq., **200 amp** n/a
  Cable TV: No **Dockside Phone:** No
  Dock Type: Fixed, Floating, Long Fingers, Pilings
Moorings: 0 Total, 0 Transient **Launch:** n/a
  Rate: Day n/a **Week** n/a **Month** n/a
Heads: 1 Toilet(s)
Laundry: None **Pay Phones:** Yes
Pump-Out: No **Fee:** n/a **Closed Heads:** No

Marina Operations
Owner/Manager: V. Rawaoyi **Dockmaster:** Don Wheathers
In-Season: Apr-Oct, 8am-8pm **Off-Season:** Nov-Mar, Closed
After-Hours Arrival: Call in advance
Reservations: Required **Credit Cards:** Visa/MC, Dscvr, Amex
Discounts: None
Pets: No **Handicap Access:** No

Marina Services and Boat Supplies
Services - Docking Assistance, Security (10 Hrs., 8pm - 6am), Dock Carts, Megayacht Facilities, 3 Phase **Communication -** Mail & Package Hold, FedEx, AirBorne, UPS, Express Mail *(Sat Del)* **Supplies - OnSite:** Ice *(Cube)* **1-3 mi:** Ships' Store, West Marine *(W 37th St. 594-6065)*, Bait/Tackle *(Urban Angler 979-7600)*, Propane

Boatyard Services
Nearest Yard: Liberty Landing, N.J. 6 mi. South

Restaurants and Accommodations
Near: Restaurant *(Eden 505-1300)*, Snack Bar *(Tamarind 674-7400)*, Lite Fare *(Kebab King 475-7575)*, *(Zoop Soups 614-7224)*, Hotel *(Marcel $110 - $240)* **Under 1 mi:** Restaurant *(Novita 677-2222)*, *(Alva 228-4399)*, *(Mayrose 533-3663)*, *(Pete's Tavern 473-7676, oldest bar in NYC, where O'Henry wrote "Gift of the Magi")*, *(Verbena 260-5454)*, Pizzeria *(Park Pizza 473-7784)*, Hotel *(The Inn at Irivng Place $325-475)*, *(Madison 532-7373)*, *(Gramercy Park 475-4320, $145-240)*

Recreation and Entertainment
Near: Pool *(Asser Levy Municipal Indoor & Outdoor Pool 447-2020 - 7am-9pm M-F; 9-5 S&S)*, Playground *(Asser Levy)*, Fitness Center *(X-Fit 725-7991; Asser Levy)*, Jogging Paths *(Stuyvesant Cove)*, Roller Blade/Bike Paths, Park *(new Stuyvesant Cove)*, Cultural Attract *(Morgan Library; National Arts Club)*, Galleries *(School of Visual Arts 592.2010)* **Under 1 mi:** Tennis Courts *(Crosstown Tennis 947-5780)*, Video Rental

(Island Video 86 1001 , Video Arcade, Museum *(Police Academy Museum 477-9753; Theodore Roosevelt Birthplace 28 E. 20th, 260-1616; South Street Seaport Museum)*, Sightseeing *(Gramercy Park Historic District)* **1-3 mi:** Golf Course *(NYC Golf Club 692-4653)*, Bowling *(Bowlmor Lanes 305-1354)*, Movie Theater *(Murray Hill Cinemas 689-6548)*

Provisioning and General Services
Near: Convenience Store, Supermarket *(D'Agostino 777-6719)*, Gourmet Shop, Delicatessen *(Lenzs Deli 979-2859)*, Health Food *(Organic Traditions 420-9247)*, Wine/Beer, Liquor Store *(Gramercy Park Wines & Spirits 505-0550)*, Bakery, Green Grocer, Bank/ATM, Post Office, Catholic Church, Synagogue, Beauty Salon, Barber Shop, Dry Cleaners, Laundry, Bookstore, Pharmacy *(Duane Reade 674-7704)*, Newsstand, Hardware Store *(Lumber Boys 683-0411)*, Florist, Copies Etc. **Under 1 mi:** Protestant Church **1-3 mi:** Fishmonger, Meat Market, Library *(NYPL 679-2645)*, Buying Club

Transportation
OnSite: Local Bus **OnCall:** Taxi *(All Star Taxi 563-9696; Just hail one)*, Airport Limo *(Car 24 677-7777; Carmel 666-6666)* **Near:** Rental Car *(Enterprise 647-9777; Dollar Rent A Car 253-9377)* **1-3 mi:** Ferry Service *(Staten Island)* **3+ mi:** Rail *(Penn Station; Grand Central, 2 mi.)* **Airport:** LaGuardia, Kennedy, or Newark *(20 mi.)*

Medical Services
911 Service **Near:** Doctor, Dentist, Chiropractor *(Metropolitan 260-0707)*, Ambulance **Under 1 mi:** Veterinarian *(Rivergate Vet. Clinic 213-9885)* **1-3 mi:** Holistic Services **Hospital:** Bellevue Hospital 562-3000 *(0.2 mi.)*

Setting -- The only marina on the East River, small New York Skyports sits in the shadow of a four story parking garage (with the same name) to the south, the UN School and Waterside apartment complex to the north, and the elevated FDR Drive to the west. The marina is an active base for commercial charter ventures (dinner cruises, etc) as well as seaplanes. Transients are welcome if the marina has space available.

Marina Notes -- Renovated in 2000 and 2001 when new steel floating docks were installed to accommodate large commercial vessels. A smaller floating dock, with good pedestals, hosts recreational boats. Although this appears "municipal", it is operated by a privately owned management company. Facilities for overnight guests are basic, and the dockmaster notes that the East River's wakes and chop can make the marina rolly. The location, however, East 23rd St. & FDR Drive, makes it a very useful and very convenient stop. Onsite is also the New York Skyport Seaplane Base; ten blocks north at 34th Street is a heliport.

Notable -- Adjacent is the new Stuyvesant Cove Park that runs south along the East River starting at 23rd Street. Walk west past Peter Cooper Village, a large upscale apartment complex, and Asser Levy Recreation Center, which boasts a dramatic indoor pool, with a marble fountain and newly restored sky lights, a basic outdoor pool, basketball & handball courts, a fitness center and playground. On 1st Avenue are most supplies and services (many deliver) and the edge of the Gramercy Park area (1st to Park Ave. & 24th to 17th Sts). Take the First Ave. bus north to the U.N. Or head further west to Third Ave. Crosstown 23rd Street bus heads west; transfer on Third or Madison for uptown or Lexington, Broadway or Fifth for downtown. Midtown is about a mile. Hail a cab.

Navigational Information

Lat: 40°42.606' **Long:** 074°02.600' **Tide:** 5 ft. **Current:** None **Chart:** 12327
Rep. Depths (*MLW*): **Entry** 18 ft. **Fuel Dock** 18 ft. **Max Slip/Moor** 18 ft./-
Access: New York Harbor / Hudson River to Morris Canal

Marina Facilities *(In Season/Off Season)*

Fuel: No
Slips: 620 Total, 50 Transient **Max LOA:** 200 ft. **Max Beam:** n/a
  Rate *(per ft.)*: **Day** $3.00/$2.50 **Week** $15/10 **Month** n/a
  Power: 30 amp $.18-.25/ft., **50 amp** $.18-.25/ft, **100 amp** $.18-.25/ft,
  Cable TV: No **Dockside Phone:** Yes
  Dock Type: Floating, Wood
Moorings: 0 Total, 0 Transient **Launch:** n/a
  Rate: Day n/a **Week** n/a **Month** n/a
Heads: 6 Toilet(s), 6 Shower(s)
Laundry: 2 Washer(s), 2 Dryer(s) **Pay Phones:** Yes, 2
Pump-Out: OnSite, Self Service **Fee:** $5 **Closed Heads:** Yes

Marina Operations

Owner/Manager: Bruce Boyle **Dockmaster:** Edward Cleslak (Harbormaster)
In-Season: Apr 15-Oct, 7:30am-7:30pm **Off-Season:** Oct 16-Apr, 9am-5pm
After-Hours Arrival: Tie up at fuel dock; contact Security at 201-324-0088
Reservations: Recommended **Credit Cards:** Visa/MC, Dscvr, Amex
Discounts: Nautical Miles **Dockage:** 15% **Fuel:** n/a **Repair:** n/a
Pets: Welcome, Dog Walk Area **Handicap Access:** No

Liberty Landing Marina

80 Audrey Zapp Drive/Liberty State Park; Jersey City, NJ 07305

Tel: (201) 985-8000 **VHF: Monitor** n/a **Talk** 72
Fax: (201) 985-9866 **Alternate Tel:** (201) 333-6755
Email: llmarina@aol.com **Web:** www.libertylandingmarina.com
Nearest Town: Jersey City **Tourist Info:** (201) 435-7400

Marina Services and Boat Supplies

Services - Docking Assistance, Concierge, Boaters' Lounge, Security *(24 Hrs.)*, Trash Pick-Up, Dock Carts, Megayacht Facilities **Communication -** Data Ports *(Wi-Fi)*, FedEx, AirBorne, UPS, Express Mail *(Sat Del)*
Supplies - OnSite: Ice *(Cube)* **Near:** Ships' Store **Under 1 mi:** Bait/Tackle *(MM Tackle & Bait 451-6272)* **1-3 mi:** Propane *(Liberty Strg 451-6939)*

Boatyard Services

OnSite: Travelift *(60T)*, Forklift, Crane, Engine mechanic *(gas, diesel)*, Compound, Wash & Wax, Interior Cleaning, Yacht Broker **OnCall:** Electrical Repairs, Electronics Repairs, Hull Repairs, Rigger, Sail Loft, Bottom Cleaning, Brightwork, Air Conditioning, Refrigeration, Divers, Propeller Repairs, Woodworking **Near:** Launching Ramp. **Yard Rates:** $50-85/hr., Haul & Launch $10/ft. *(blocking incl.)*, Power Wash $3/ft., Bottom Paint $8-15/ft. *(paint incl.)* **Storage:** In-Water $135-145/ft., On-Land Winter $56/ft.; Annual $155/ft.

Restaurants and Accommodations

OnSite: Restaurant *(Lightship Barge & Grill 200-4500, L & D, 11am-11pm)*, *(Liberty House 395-0300, L $9-28, D $11-17, D Tue-Sun, Brunch/L Sat & Sun)* **OnCall:** Pizzeria *(Stellas 436-4650)* **Near:** Restaurant *(La Gran Aventura 395-4595)* **Under 1 mi:** Restaurant *(Arties Tavern 435-9210)*, *(Prestos 433-6639)*, *(Ibbys Falafel 432-2400)* **1-3 mi:** Motel *(Regency 792-9500)*, Hotel *(Courtyard by Marriott 626-6600)*, *(Doubletree 499-2400)*

Recreation and Entertainment

OnSite: Picnic Area, Playground, Jogging Paths, Boat Rentals, Roller Blade/Bike Paths, Fishing Charter, Group Fishing Boat, Park *(Liberty)*,

Sightseeing *(Liberty & Ellis Island)*, Special Events *(NY-NJ In-Water Boat Show three times a year; Jul 4th Fireworks over New York Harbor; Sep Superboat Race)* **Near:** Museum *(Liberty Science M. 200-1000)*
Under 1 mi: Video Rental *(Rickys Video 2 432-8836)* **1-3 mi:** Bowling *(Roosevelt Lanes 432-3535)*, Movie Theater *(Cineplex Odeon 626-3200)*

Provisioning and General Services

OnSite: Bank/ATM **Near:** Fishmonger **Under 1 mi:** Convenience Store, Supermarket *(Shop-Rite 333-2345)*, Gourmet Shop, Delicatessen *(Ruggieros 433-4412)*, Liquor Store *(Communipaw Liquors 434-5889)*, Bakery *(Anns Schneider 653-8584)*, Catholic Church, Hardware Store *(Ace 435-0979)*, Copies Etc. *(EZ Office Supplies 333-3644)* **1-3 mi:** Health Food, Post Office, Library, Beauty Salon, Dry Cleaners, Laundry, Bookstore *(Barnes & Noble 435-6607)*, Pharmacy *(Carry Drug 332-4488)*

Transportation

OnSite: Water Taxi *(Little Lady to North Cove in NYC 232-5337, Mon-Thu 6am-7:45pm, Fri- 'til 8:45pm, Sat 9am-8:45pm, Sun 9am-7:45pm $5/3-1 way)* **OnCall:** Rental Car *(Enterprise 216-0400, Avis 217-3050)*, Taxi *(Yellow Taxi 309-0522)*, Airport Limo *(Newport Car 332-6868)* **Near:** Local Bus *(Light Rail)*, Ferry Service *(To Ellis Island and Statue of Liberty $8/4 RT to both incl. admission, 435-9499)* **3+ mi:** Rail *(Newark, 7 mi.)*
Airport: Newark *(5 mi.)*

Medical Services

911 Service **OnCall:** Ambulance **1-3 mi:** Doctor *(Jersey City Medical 915-2000)*, Dentist, Chiropractor *(Exchange Place Chiro 434-6678)*, Veterinarian *(Jersey City 435-6424)* **Hospital:** Pollack 432-1000 *(1.5 mi.)*

Setting -- Just off New York Harbor, directly across the Hudson from lower Manhattan, Liberty Landing stretches along most of the length of Morris Canal. It is quiet - save for the wash of the water taxis - with spectacular views of the NY skyline. A bright red, retired Lightship serves as the marina's base.

Marina Notes -- Opened in 1996, it is still in development. There are two sets of facilities: the original ones, in the handsomely renovated Lightship: heads, showers, conference room, lounge, and laundry. Also housed there is the Lightship Barge & Grill which has a large outside patio, a small enclosed outside "room" and a small cafe inside on the first floor of the ship. The second set of facilities is at the opposite end of the marina in the new "West Building" - a small white house with a blue roof. There are individual heads (sinks and toilets) as well as shower rooms. Beacon Wi-Fi Service (203-762-2657). Onsite, too, is the new and inviting Liberty House Restaurant - Dinner Tue-Sun, Lunch Sat & Sun - inside dining in two rooms or on the terrace. The upstairs banquet room, with views of the NY skyline, can accommodate up to 400. Two first floor patio rooms can manage catered events up to 135. Note: Marina will not hold packages.

Notable -- Onsite is the Little Lady Yellow Water Taxi which makes regular trips (every 30 min.) to North Cove in Manhattan's Battery Park (from there you can transfer to other water taxis). Nearby is the terminal for boats going to Ellis Island Immigration Museum and the Statue of Liberty - RT $8/4 to both including admission - 435-9499. The grounds of Liberty Island are open and, reportedly, the statue will re-open mid-2004. The Liberty Science Center is about half a mile walk through Liberty Landing Park - $10-16.50/$8-14.50, Tue-Sun 9:30-5:30. It boasts extensive hands-on exhibits, two IMAX theaters, and a laser show.

Liberty Harbor Marina

11 Marin Boulevard; Jersey City, NJ 07302

Tel: (201) 386-7500; (800) 646-2066 **VHF: Monitor** 68 **Talk** 68
Fax: (201) 386-7508 **Alternate Tel:** n/a
Email: linda.howard@libertyharbor.com **Web:** n/a
Nearest Town: Jersey City **Tourist Info:** (201) 435-7400

Navigational Information

Lat: 40°42.480' **Long:** 074°02.360' **Tide:** 7 ft. **Current:** n/a **Chart:** 12327
Rep. Depths (MLW): Entry 12 ft. **Fuel Dock** 12 ft. **Max Slip/Moor** 30 ft./-
Access: New York Harbor to Morris Canal to private channel on North side

Marina Facilities (In Season/Off Season)

Fuel: *Coastal/Exxon* - Gasoline, Diesel, High-Speed Pumps
Slips: 150 Total, 12 Transient **Max LOA:** 100 ft. **Max Beam:** 18 ft.
  Rate (per ft.): Day $2.50 **Week** $12.00 **Month** $35
  Power: 30 amp $3, **50 amp** $5, **100 amp** n/a, **200 amp** n/a
  Cable TV: No **Dockside Phone:** No
  Dock Type: Floating, Long Fingers, Pilings, Wood
Moorings: 0 Total, 0 Transient **Launch:** from travel lift to water
  Rate: Day n/a **Week** n/a **Month** n/a
Heads: 10 Toilet(s), 12 Shower(s) *(with dressing rooms)*
Laundry: 6 Washer(s), 6 Dryer(s) **Pay Phones:** Yes, 4
Pump-Out: OnSite, Full Service **Fee:** By gallon **Closed Heads:** Yes

Marina Operations

Owner/Manager: Linda Howard **Dockmaster:** Marc Freedman, Yard Mngr
In-Season: MidApr -MidOct, 8:30am-7pm **Off-Season:** MidOct-MidApr, 9-5
After-Hours Arrival: See security guard
Reservations: Required **Credit Cards:** Visa/MC, Dscvr, Amex, Trvlr Checks
Discounts: None
Pets: Welcome, Dog Walk Area **Handicap Access:** No

Marina Services and Boat Supplies

Services - Docking Assistance, Boaters' Lounge, Crew Lounge, Security *(24 hrs., 2 on patrol)*, Trash Pick-Up **Communication -** Mail & Package Hold, Phone Messages, Fax in/out *($1)*, Data Ports *(Marina Office, Wi-Fi, too)*, FedEx, AirBorne, UPS, Express Mail *(Sat Del)* **Supplies - OnSite:** Ice *(Cube)*, Ships' Store *(Tru World)*, Bait/Tackle *(TW Tackle & Bait)*, Live Bait *(TW)* **1-3 mi:** Propane *(Gary's Propane)*

Boatyard Services

OnSite: Travelift *(60T)* **OnCall:** Crane, Hydraulic Trailer, Engine mechanic *(gas, diesel)*, Electrical Repairs, Electronic Sales *(Chandlery 946-7955)*, Electronics Repairs *(Roberto's 304-1345)*, Hull Repairs *(Master Marine 451-0010)*, Rigger *(Veddar)*, Bottom Cleaning, Brightwork *(Roberto's)*, Air Conditioning *(Roberto's)*, Refrigeration, Divers *(Davidson 732-870-3711)*, Compound, Wash & Wax *(All Yacht 973-420-4049)*, Interior Cleaning *(All Yacht)*, Propeller Repairs *(S&S Prop 718-359-3393)*, Woodworking, Inflatable Repairs, Life Raft Service, Upholstery *(H. Parker)*, Yacht Interiors, Metal Fabrication, Painting, Awlgrip **Dealer for:** Petit. **Yard Rates:** Haul & Launch $15/ft. *(blocking incl.)*, Power Wash Incl., Bottom Paint $20/ft.
Storage: In-Water Year $155/ft., On-Land Year $165/ft.

Restaurants and Accommodations

OnSite: Restaurant *(Sand Dollar 386-7535, D $6-12)* **Near:** Restaurant *(Liberty House 395-0300, L $9-22, D $11-17, Brunch/Lunch Sat & Sun, by dinghy)*, *(Presto's 433-6639)*, *(Arties 435-9210)*, *(Komegashi 333-8946)*, *(White Horse Tavern)*, Seafood Shack *(Golden Crab 432-6886)*, Fast Food *(Blimpie 434-4558)*, Lite Fare *(Smilers 938-0020)*, Pizzeria *(Helen's 435-1507)*, Motel *(Quality Inn 653-0300)*, Hotel *(Double Tree 499-2400)*

Recreation and Entertainment

OnSite: Picnic Area, Fishing Charter, Group Fishing Boat *(Master Marine)*, Sightseeing *(NYC Tour)* **Near:** Video Rental *(Video Rent All 985-0477)*, Park *(Liberty State Park by dinghy)* **Under 1 mi:** Movie Theater *(Cineplex Odeon, Newport Mall 626-3200)*, Video Arcade *(Newport Mall)*
1-3 mi: Dive Shop *(Hoboken)*, Bowling *(Bowl Rite Lanes 864-2667)*

Provisioning and General Services

OnSite: Copies Etc. **Near:** Convenience Store, Supermarket *(Shop-Rite 333-2345)*, Delicatessen *(Port Side Deli 432-4442)*, Liquor Store *(Liberty 200-0020)*, Green Grocer, Fishmonger, Bank/ATM, Post Office, Catholic Church, Library, Beauty Salon, Barber Shop, Dry Cleaners, Bookstore, Pharmacy *(Rite Aid 659-9055)*, Florist, Retail Shops *(Newport Mall)*, Buying Club *(BJ's)* **Under 1 mi:** Bakery *(Bagels & More 433-8082)*, Farmers' Market *(Christopher Columbus Dr. & Hudson St., Mon 12-7)*, Protestant Church, Synagogue, Hardware Store *(Borinquen 432-9524)*
1-3 mi: Health Food *(Farmboy 656-0581)*

Transportation

OnSite: Ferry Service *(NY Waterway to Wall St.)* **OnCall:** Rental Car *(Enterprise 330-3307; Avis 217-3050)*, Taxi *(Yellow 309-0522)* **Near:** Rail *(Newark/NY-Penn Station via PATH train; NJ Lightrail)* **Under 1 mi:** Local Bus, InterCity Bus **Airport:** Newark Int'l *(15 mi.)*

Medical Services

911 Service **OnCall:** Ambulance **Near:** Doctor, Dentist *(Jersey Ave 433-8600)*, Chiropractor **Under 1 mi:** Veterinarian *(Jersey City 435-6424)*
Hospital: Jersey City 915-2000 *(1 mi.)*

Setting -- Liberty Harbor Marina is located just off New York Harbor on the Morris Canal, across from Liberty Landing. The fuel dock and a few alongside slips are right on the Canal. A narrow channel leads to a very protected, virtually enclosed basin. The imposing Sand Club, which is on the marina grounds, makes a good landmark. A quickly gentrifying neighborhood of new, high-end low-rise apartments surrounds the basin on two sides. The Sand Bar is on the third and an R-V park is on the fourth side. A set of stern-to single docks runs along entrance to the basin and has views of the NY skyline.

Marina Notes -- This constantly improving facility promises a "down-home" environment on an 80-acre site with marina and RV park and the only truly protected dockage on New York Harbor. If "a quiet night's sleep" is important, this is a good bet. Family owned and operated since 1988; accommodating and helpful staff. Slip holders get 10% fuel discount, others 5% over 500 gallons. Security is good; the basin is surrounded by fences; the docks require entry through individual "buildings" with massive gates. Some docks need work and some have been replaced. Basic heads and showers but a nice laundry room with relatively new machines. Beacon Wi-Fi (203-762-2657) provides wireless hotspot. Haulout only on weekdays. All other BY services on call.

Notable -- The Sand Bar nightclub has outdoor deck dining in the season and room for 1,000 cars. Onsite NY Waterway taxi runs to lower Manhattan at Pier 11, foot of Wall Street. Four blocks walk to the PATH station for easy access to Manhattan. The Light Rail stops at the end of the block and goes into Jersey City and Hoboken one way and to Bayonne, Liberty State Park (directly across the canal) and the NJ Transit Shuttle the other way. Newport Mall is nine blocks.

Navigational Information
Lat: 40°42.756' **Long:** 074°01.007' **Tide:** 7 **Current:** * **Chart:** 12327
Rep. Depths (*MLW*): **Entry** 24 ft. **Fuel Dock** n/a **Max Slip/Moor** 24 ft./-
Access: New York Harbor/Hudson River to Southern end of Manhattan

Marina Facilities (*In Season/Off Season*)
Fuel: No
Slips: 50 Total, 18 Transient **Max LOA:** 150 ft. **Max Beam:** n/a
  Rate (*per ft.*): **Day** $5.00 **Week** $28 **Month** $90
  Power: 30 amp $20, **50 amp** Metered, **100 amp** Metered, **200 amp** Metered
  Cable TV: No **Dockside Phone:** No
  Dock Type: Floating, Long Fingers, Wood
Moorings: 0 Total, 0 Transient **Launch:** n/a
  Rate: Day n/a **Week** n/a **Month** n/a
Heads: None
Laundry: None **Pay Phones:** No
Pump-Out: No **Fee:** n/a **Closed Heads:** No

Marina Operations
Owner/Manager: BPC Parks Conservancy **Dockmaster:** Ted Wallace
In-Season: Year-Round, 8am-8pm **Off-Season:** n/a
After-Hours Arrival: Call ahead.
Reservations: Preferred **Credit Cards:** Visa/MC, Dscvr, Amex
Discounts: None
Pets: Welcome, Dog Walk Area **Handicap Access:** Yes, Docks

North Cove Marina

2 South End Avenue; New York, NY 10280

Tel: (646) 210-5005 **VHF: Monitor** 69 **Talk** 69
Fax: (212) 267-9707 **Alternate Tel:** (212) 267-9700
Email: VMcGowan@bpcparks.org **Web:** www.northcove.org
Nearest Town: New York City (*0 mi.*) **Tourist Info:** (212) 839-8051

Marina Services and Boat Supplies
Services - Docking Assistance, Concierge, Security (*24 hours, Park Police; Guard Service*), Trash Pick-Up, Dock Carts, Megayacht Facilities
Communication - FedEx, AirBorne, UPS, Express Mail (*Sat Del*)
Supplies - Near: Ice (*Block, Cube*) **3+ mi:** West Marine (*594-6065, 4 mi.*)

Boatyard Services
OnCall: Engine mechanic (*gas, diesel*), Electrical Repairs, Electronics Repairs, Air Conditioning, Refrigeration, Divers, Interior Cleaning, Propeller Repairs, Inflatable Repairs **Nearest Yard:** Marine Basin (718) 372-5700

Restaurants and Accommodations
Near: Restaurant (*Steamer's Landing 432-1451*), (*American Park 809-5508, D $19-26*), (*Fraunces Tavern 968-1776, L $11-32, D $16-32*), (*PacRim Sushi 945-0900*), (*Unity 769-4200*), (*Zen 432-3634*), (*Yangtze On Hudson 964-8848*), (*GiGino's Cafe' 528-2228*), (*Church & Dey 312-2000, B,L,D*), (*Liquid Assets B,L,D*), (*2 West 917-790-2525*), (*Lili's Noodle 786-1300*), (*Applebee's 945-3277*), (*Chevy's Fresh-Mex 78-611-11*), Pizzeria (*Picasso 321-2616*), Hotel (*Ritz Carlton 344-0800, $450-850*), (*Embassy Suites 945-0100, $160-320*), (*Millennium Hilton 693-2001, $170-370*) **Under 1 mi:** Restaurant (*Nobu 219-0500, L $12-30, D $18-30, Prix Fixe L $20, D $70*)

Recreation and Entertainment
OnSite: Picnic Area, Playground, Volleyball, Jogging Paths **Near:** Heated Pool, Tennis Courts, Fitness Center (*NY Sports Club 945-3535*), Boat Rentals, Movie Theater (*U.A.B.P.C.*), Video Rental (*Video Room 962-6400*), Museum (*Skyscraper; American Indian 514-3720; Jewish Heritage*) **1-3 mi:** Bowling (*Bowlmor 255-8188*) **3+ mi:** Golf Course (*NYGC 692-4653, 4 mi.*)

Provisioning and General Services
OnSite: Convenience Store, Supermarket (*Gristedes 233-7770*), Bank/ATM, Post Office, Catholic Church (*St. Joseph's*), Beauty Salon, Barber Shop, Dry Cleaners (*Gateway 321-1010*), Pharmacy (*Eckerd 912-0555*), Newsstand, Florist, Retail Shops **Near:** Gourmet Shop (*Eighth Ave. 290-2374; Samantha 945-5555*), Delicatessen (*Cafe Maru 566-7050*), Wine/Beer (*West Street 383-8300*), Liquor Store (*Bulls & Bears 912-0890*), Bakery (*Ceci-Cela 566-8933*), Farmers' Market (*Liberty & Church Sts, Tue & Thu 8-5*), Green Grocer (*J.J. 432-3634*), Fishmonger (*Fulton Fish Market*), Meat Market, Protestant Church (*St. Paul's Chapel; Trinity Church*), Synagogue, Library (*732-8186*), Laundry, Bookstore (*Trinity 349-0376, Borders 964-1988*), Copies Etc. (*Kinkos 786-1666*) **Under 1 mi:** Hardware Store (*Whitehall 269-02698*), Department Store (*Century 21 227-9092*)

Transportation
OnSite: Rental Car, Local Bus (*Subway, PATH*) **OnCall:** Taxi
Near: Water Taxi (*N.Y. Water Taxi 742-1969 to Hoboken; South St. Seaport to Shea & Yankee Stadiums $16/12; Round Manhattan $24/12*)
Under 1 mi: Ferry Service (*Staten Island -64 trips/day; Liberty & Ellis Islands - via Liberty Landing 800-600-1600, 9am-6:15pm, $10/4*), Airport Limo (*Millennium 619-1700*) **3+ mi:** Rail (*Pennsylvania or Grand Central, 5 mi.*) **Airport:** Newark/LaGuardia/JFK (*12 mi./15 mi./18 mi.*)

Medical Services
911 Service **OnCall:** Ambulance **Near:** Dentist (*B.P. 945-0600*), Chiropractor (*B.P. Chiro 321-1922*), Veterinarian (*B.P. Vet 786-4444*) **Under 1 mi:** Holistic Services (*Studio Massage 587-2439; Heaven 785-0330*) **Hospital:** N.Y. Downtown 801-1710 (*W/in 1 mi*)

Setting -- Located at the World Financial Center in downtown Manhattan, North Cove occupies a man-made inlet off the Hudson River and is surrounded by a 3.5 acre public park and plaza fronting the Hudson River. Great views of the Hudson, the Statue of Liberty, and downtown Manhattan. The glass-enclosed Winter Garden, filled with shops, restaurants, and seating areas, opens directly onto the attractively landscaped plaza. North Cove hosts a variety of tourist and ferry vessels as well as the Manhattan Sailing School. The surrounding area is quickly recovering from the devastation of 9-11.

Marina Notes -- Currently managed by the Battery Park City Parks Conservancy and still a little "in transition." No heads/showers or dock office yet, although there is a nearby health club available for $15 per day. Dockmasters work with cell phones and VHF; hail them before entering the marina. A floating dock with slips is dedicated to 30-40' recreational cruising vessels. Megayachts tie up to the wharf or commercial piers. Ferry and other river traffic can make the marina waters choppy. *Up to 5 kt. current at the entrance. On-call mechanics available, but major repairs while in the marina are discouraged. 200 amp service; no phone or cable TV at slips yet. Concierge services through Ritz-Carlton; Ritz, Hilton & Embassy, each with several eateries, are virtually adjacent.

Notable -- The Hudson River Festival lasts all summer. A block away, on Liberty St., is the viewing area of Ground Zero - the 16-acre site of the former World Trade Center Towers (9am-9pm) and the temporary Memorial. Historical Walking Tour of the area Sat & Sun at 9am 888 692-8701 $15/7.50. Within a mile, are over 30 museums, including South Street Seaport (732-8257) 10-9, Sun 11-8 with fascinating, boardable tall ships and a maritime museum (748-8600) $5.

Newport Yacht Club & Marina

500 Washington Boulevard; Jersey City, NJ 07310

Tel: (201) 626-5550 **VHF: Monitor** 16 **Talk** 72
Fax: (201) 626-5558 **Alternate Tel:** n/a
Email: n/a **Web:** n/a
Nearest Town: Jersey City **Tourist Info:** (201) 465-7400

Navigational Information
Lat: 40°44.636' **Long:** 074°01.381' **Tide:** 6 ft. **Current:** 4 kt. **Chart:** 12327
Rep. Depths *(MLW)*: **Entry** 10 ft. **Fuel Dock** n/a **Max Slip/Moor** 10 ft./-
Access: New York Harbor

Marina Facilities *(In Season/Off Season)*
Fuel: No
Slips: 167 Total, 35 Transient **Max LOA:** 200 ft. **Max Beam:** n/a
  Rate *(per ft.)*: **Day** $2.40/$2.00* **Week** $12.40-15.60 **Month** $38-45
  Power: 30 amp $6, **50 amp** $12, **100 amp** $24, **200 amp** n/a
  Cable TV: Yes **Dockside Phone:** No
  Dock Type: Floating, Long Fingers, Alongside
Moorings: 0 Total, 0 Transient **Launch:** n/a, Dinghy Dock
  Rate: Day n/a **Week** n/a **Month** n/a
Heads: 8 Toilet(s), 6 Shower(s)
Laundry: 6 Washer(s), 4 Dryer(s), Book Exchange **Pay Phones:** Yes, 2
Pump-Out: OnSite, Full Service **Fee:** $15-25 **Closed Heads:** No

Marina Operations
Owner/Manager: Iris Hirsch **Dockmaster:** Same
In-Season: Apr 15-Oct 31, 8am-7pm** **Off-Season:** Nov 1-Apr 15, 8am-4pm
After-Hours Arrival: n/a
Reservations: Preferred **Credit Cards:** Visa/MC, Amex
Discounts: None
Pets: Welcome, Dog Walk Area **Handicap Access:** Yes, Heads, Docks

Marina Services and Boat Supplies
Services - Docking Assistance, Security *(24 Hrs.)*, Trash Pick-Up, Dock Carts, Megayacht Facilities, 3 Phase **Communication -** Mail & Package Hold, Phone Messages, Fax in/out, FedEx, AirBorne, UPS, Express Mail *(Sat Del)* **Supplies - OnSite:** Ice *(Block, Cube)*, Ships' Store *(Limited)* **1-3 mi:** Marine Discount Store *(Marine Wholesalers 963-4334)*, Bait/Tackle *(MM Tackle & Bait 451-6272)* **3+ mi:** West Marine *(212-594-6065, NY City)*, Propane *(U-Haul, 3 mi.)*

Boatyard Services
OnCall: Engine mechanic *(gas, diesel)*, Electrical Repairs, Electronics Repairs, Sail Loft, Bottom Cleaning, Brightwork, Air Conditioning, Refrigeration, Divers, Compound, Wash & Wax, Propeller Repairs, **Under 1 mi:** Launching Ramp, Hull Repairs, Rigger. **1-3 mi:** Travelif
Nearest Yard: Liberty Harbor Marina 1 mile (201) 451-1000

Restaurants and Accommodations
OnSite: Restaurant *(Café Newport 626-7200, L $17-23, D $17-23, same menu L&D,)* **OnCall:** Pizzeria *(TP Pizza 653-3700)*, *(Bertucci's 222-8088)* **Near:** Restaurant *(South City Grille 610-9225, great fish)*, *(Dorrian's Irish Pub 626-6660)*, *(Cosimo's Brick Oven 626-4455)*, *(Cafe Spice Newport 533-0111, Indian)*, Fast Food *(Food Court Newport Mall)*, Lite Fare *(First Street Café & Deli 963-2229)*, *(Cosi 963-0533)*, *(Deli Plus)*, *(Seattle Coffee Roaster 659-6668, soups, sandwiches, wraps)*, Hotel *(Courtyard by Marriott 626-6600)*, *(Doubletree 499-2400)* **Under 1 mi:** Raw Bar *(Piccolos 653-0564)* **1-3 mi:** Motel *(Econo Lodge 420-9040)*, Hotel *(Sheraton 617-5600)*

Recreation and Entertainment
OnCall: Fishing Charter **Near:** Heated Pool, Spa, Playground, Tennis Courts, Fitness Center, Jogging Paths, Movie Theater *(Cineplex Odeon, Newport Mall 626-3200)*, Video Rental, Park, Museum **Under 1 mi:** Roller Blade/Bike Paths, Cultural Attract **1-3 mi:** Dive Shop **3+ mi:** Bowling *(Bowl Rite Lanes 864-2667, 3 mi.)*

Provisioning and General Services
Near: Convenience Store, Supermarket *(A&P 217-9228)*, Gourmet Shop, Delicatessen *(Manhattan Express Deli 795-4669)*, Wine/Beer, Liquor Store, Bank/ATM, Beauty Salon, Dry Cleaners, Laundry, Pharmacy *(CVS Newport Mall 656-8082)*, Newsstand, Florist, Clothing Store, Retail Shops, Department Store, Buying Club, Copies Etc. **Under 1 mi:** Bakery, Farmers' Market *(Christopher Columbus Dr. & Hudson St., Mon 12-7)*, Fishmonger, Meat Market, Post Office, Catholic Church, Hardware Store *(City Paint & Ace Hardware 659-0061)* **1-3 mi:** Health Food, Protestant Church, Synagogue, Library, Bookstore *(Barnes and Noble 267-3474)*

Transportation
OnCall: Rental Car *(Enterprise 798-8499; Avis 217-3050 near)*, Taxi *(Grove Taxi 434-8566)*, Airport Limo *(Airport Taxi 792-2000)* **Under 1 mi:** Rail *(Newark/NY-Penn Station (via PATH train))* **Airport:** Newark Int'l *(10 mi.)*

Medical Services
911 Service **Near:** Doctor, Dentist, Chiropractor *(Hudson Family Chiropractic 656-5600)* **Under 1 mi:** Ambulance **1-3 mi:** Veterinarian *(Hoboken Animal Hosp. 963-3604)* **Hospital:** Bon Secours 418-1000 *(1 mi.)*

Setting -- Just south of the candy cane lighthouse which marks the NY Waterway terminal, Newport Yacht Club sits on a wide pier with dockage in front and along the more protected sides. The docks have spectacular close-up views of the lower Manhattan skyline which is just minutes away. Located in a self-contained community of high-end hi-rise residential and corporate buildings, the marina offers easy access to a fitness center, tennis courts, the 100-shop Newport Mall, numerous small shops, a PATH station and a plethora of eateries.

Marina Notes -- *In-season slip rates: $2.40-3.60. ** In-season open 8am-9pm Fri and Sat. Security 24/7. Three-phase. The entire basin is protected by a new 700 foot wave attenuator installed Spring '04. 28-60' craft are at floating slips and larger yachts -- to 200 ft. -- are docked alongside in the inner basins' fixed docks. HeliStop onsite. Daily passes to Swim & Fitness Center available for additional fee. Brick walled and tiled heads and showers. Docks are broadside to the swell, but the new wave fence significantly reduces the roll. It is, by comparison, relatively calm. The marina is part of the large Newport Mall complex.

Notable -- The onsite Waterfront Café offers upscale indoor & outdoor dining from pasta to a four-course Italian/Continental meal --all overlooking the docks. Restaurants abound - name an ethnicity; there's a restaurant to match. It's a short walk to a mall anchored by Macy's, Penney's, Sears, & BJ's. Farmers' market is at Christopher Columbus Dr. & Hudson St. Mondays. Very close-by PATH trains go to lower Manhattan, W. 33rd St. & Newark's Penn Station. The NY Water Taxi leaves from the adjacent pier (to minimize wakes in the marina) and stops in NYC at 38th Street, World Financial Center (transfer at Pier 11, Water Street).

Navigational Information
Lat: 40°44.700' **Long:** 074°00.700' **Tide:** 4.5 ft. **Current:** n/a **Chart:** 12327
Rep. Depths *(MLW)*: **Entry** 11 ft. **Fuel Dock** n/a **Max Slip/Moor** 15 ft./-
Access: Hudson River to the eastern shore

Marina Facilities *(In Season/Off Season)*
Fuel: No
Slips: 60 Total, 20 Transient **Max LOA:** 300 ft. **Max Beam:** n/a
Rate *(per ft.)*: **Day** $4.00 **Week** $25 **Month** $75
Power: 30 amp $10, 50 amp $15-20, 100 amp n/a, 200 amp n/a
Cable TV: Yes, Incl. **Dockside Phone:** Yes, Incl.
Dock Type: Floating, Long Fingers
Moorings: 0 Total, 0 Transient **Launch:** n/a
Rate: Day n/a **Week** n/a **Month** n/a
Heads: 4 Toilet(s), 4 Shower(s)
Laundry: None **Pay Phones:** Yes
Pump-Out: No **Fee:** n/a **Closed Heads:** No

Marina Operations
Owner/Manager: Scott Seisler **Dockmaster:** Ray Pinsky
In-Season: Apr 15-Nov, 8am-12mid **Off-Season:** Nov 16-Apr, 10am-6pm
After-Hours Arrival: Call in advance for slip number
Reservations: Required **Credit Cards:** Visa/MC, Amex
Discounts: None
Pets: Welcome, Dog Walk Area **Handicap Access:** No

Marina at Chelsea Piers

Pier 59, Chelsea Piers, W. 23rd St.; New York, NY 10011

Tel: (212) 336-7873 **VHF: Monitor** 16 **Talk** 68
Fax: (212) 824-4092 **Alternate Tel:** n/a
Email: n/a **Web:** www.chelseapiers.com
Nearest Town: New York City *(0 mi.)* **Tourist Info:** (212) 484-1222

Marina Services and Boat Supplies
Services - Docking Assistance, Concierge, Security (24 Hrs.), Trash Pick-Up, Dock Carts **Communication -** Mail & Package Hold, Phone Messages, FedEx, AirBorne, UPS, Express Mail *(Sat Del)* **Supplies - OnSite:** Ice *(Cube)*, Ships' Store **OnCall:** Propane **Under 1 mi:** West Marine *(W. 37th St. 594-6065)*, Bait/Tackle *(Capitol Fishing Tackle 929-6132)*

Boatyard Services
OnSite: Electrical Repairs, Brightwork **OnCall:** Divers, Compound, Wash & Wax, Propeller Repairs **Under 1 mi:** Travelift, Engine mechanic *(gas, diesel)*, Launching Ramp, Electronics Repairs, Hull Repairs, Rigger, Bottom Cleaning. **Nearest Yard:** Liberty Harbor (201) 386-7500

Restaurants and Accommodations
OnSite: Restaurant *(Chelsea Brewing Co. 336-6440, L $9-22, D $9-22, 2-story glass wall, inside or waterfront al fresco dining, onsite brewery plus catering)*, *(Pier 60 & Lighthouse event halls 336-6144, Abigail Kirsch catering)*, *(Spirit Cruises 727-7735, L $28, D $60, Eat while circling Manhattan)*, *(Bateaux New York 727-7735, L $37-, D $80-123, cruise)*, Snack Bar *(Chelsea Lanes 835-2695)*, Lite Fare *(Ruthy's Bakery & Cafe 336-6333)*, Pizzeria *(Famous Famiglia at Sky Rink 803-5552)* **Near:** Hotel *(Chelsea Savoy 929-9353)*, Inn/B&B *(Inn On 23rd 463-0330)*

Recreation and Entertainment
OnSite: Pool *(Chelsea Pier Sports Center)*, Picnic Area *(Pier Park 336-6666)*, Playground, Golf Course *(Driving range 336-6400 6am-Mid $20 80-118 balls)*, Fitness Center *(336-6000 6am-11pm)*, Jogging Paths, Boat Rentals *(C.P. Yacht Charters power & sail megayachts 645-6626;*

35-45 ft. Sea Rays), Roller Blade/Bike Paths, Bowling *(Amf Chelsea Piers 835-2695 $7.50)*, Fishing Charter *(Surfside 3)*, Video Arcade, Sightseeing *(all of NYC)*, Special Events *(Atlantic Cup Challenge, NY In-Water Boat Show)* **Near:** Movie Theater *(Quad Cinema 255-8800)*, Video Rental *(Koryo Video 643-1935)* **Under 1 mi:** Dive Shop, Tennis Courts *(Midtown T.C. 989-8572)*, Horseback Riding *(Claremont 724-5100)*

Provisioning and General Services
OnSite: Bakery *(Ruthys 463-8670)*, Bank/ATM **OnCall:** Dry Cleaners **Near:** Convenience Store *(Lyla 627-8594)*, Supermarket *(D'Agostinos 366-4474)*, Gourmet Shop *(Garden of Eden 675-6300)*, Delicatessen *(Kings 924-4489)*, Health Food *(at Chelsea Market)*, Wine/Beer, Liquor Store *(North Village 627-2009)*, Farmers' Market *(Chelsea Market)*, Green Grocer, Fishmonger, Meat Market, Post Office, Catholic Church, Beauty Salon, Barber Shop, Laundry, Bookstore, Pharmacy *(Duane Reade 463-8873)*, Newsstand, Hardware Store *(Halmor 675-0277)* **Under 1 mi:** Protestant Church, Synagogue, Library *(924-1585)*

Transportation
OnSite: Water Taxi, Local Bus *(M23, cross-town)* **OnCall:** Rental Car *(Enterprise 647-9777; Manhattan 244-2255)*, Taxi, Airport Limo *(First Class 304-1111)* **Near:** Bikes **Under 1 mi:** InterCity Bus *(Port Authority)*, Rail *(Penn Station)* **Airport:** LaGuardia/JFK/Newark *(10 mi./12 mi./15 mi.)*

Medical Services
911 Service **Near:** Doctor, Dentist *(Dental Assoc.691-2112)*, Chiropractor *(Chelsea 741-9660)*, Ambulance, Veterinarian *(Chelsea Dog & Cat 929-6963)* **Hospital:** Chelsea Clinic of St Vincents 594-2200 *(0.25 mi.)*

Setting -- Part of Chelsea Piers family entertainment complex, Surfside includes an esplanade & park, roller rinks, field house, indoor ice skating rink, driving range, several full service restaurants, and a large sports center. The recent docks fill three basins divided by huge piers that have been re-purposed as driving ranges and other recreational centers. At night, views across the Hudson to the New Jersey skyline are magical. And all of Manhattan is at your door.

Marina Notes -- *Electric rates 36-45 ft. $15/day, 46 ft.+ $20/day. Holiday weekends 2 night min. Group/Yacht Club rates. Equipment for all activities can be rented: 4-level Golf Driving Range, Indoor Ice Sky Rink ($13/9.50), Roller Rink ($7/6, extreme park $7-10), Field House (batting cages, basketball, & classes), Bowling Lanes, enormous Sports & Fitness Center with track, pool, workout, volleyball, rock climbing wall - Day pass $26 6am-11pm weekdays, 8pm Sat & Sun. Steve & Doris Colgate's Offshore Sailing School (888 454-8002). Chelsea Screamer's speedboat tours around Manhattan (924-6262) $15/8. Charter truly amazing classic craft: 85 ft. Eastern Star (800 454-5942), 110 ft. 1926 Mariner III (645-8813) & 80 ft. replica schooner Adirondack (646-336-5270).

Notable -- On the southwestern edge of midtown Manhattan, this is the most convenient NYC marina. The 23rd Street cross-town bus ($2) stops here - take it east to a major N/S street and transfer (free - just ask on boarding). Gentrified, artsy nearby Chelsea is always fun. Restaurants abound - get a copy of the newest Zagats. An easy walk is Chelsea Market, a million sq. ft one-stop culinary food wonder (and flower market), down on 10th Ave. & 16th St. (Mon-Fri 8am-8pm, Sat & Sun 10-8). Free Wi-Fi hotspot, too! The famous Chelsea Flea Market happens at 25th St. & 6th Ave. on weekends 9am-5pm $1.

Lincoln Harbor Yacht Club

1500 Harbor Boulevard; Weehawken, NJ 07086

Tel: (201) 319-5100; (800) 205-6987 **VHF: Monitor** 74 **Talk** 74
Fax: (201) 319-5111 **Alternate Tel:** (201) 319-5100
Email: mgr@lincolnharbor.com **Web:** www.lincolnharbor.com
Nearest Town: Hoboken *(0.5 mi.)* **Tourist Info:** (201) 688-2777

Navigational Information
Lat: 40°45.603' **Long:** 074°01.330' **Tide:** 4.3 ft. **Current:** 2 kt. **Chart:** 12327
Rep. Depths *(MLW)*: **Entry** 15 ft. **Fuel Dock** 7 ft. **Max Slip/Moor** 15 ft./-
Access: Hudson River - Directly across from the Empire State Building

Marina Facilities *(In Season/Off Season)*
Fuel: *Fuel Barge* - Diesel
Slips: 250 Total, 100 Transient **Max LOA:** 200 ft. **Max Beam:** 60 ft.
Rate *(per ft.)*: **Day** $2.00 **Week** $11 **Month** $39*
Power: 30 amp Inq., 50 amp Inq., 100 amp Inq., 200 amp n/a
Cable TV: Yes **Dockside Phone:** Yes
Dock Type: Floating, Long Fingers, Wood
Moorings: 0 Total, 0 Transient **Launch:** n/a
Rate: Day n/a **Week** n/a **Month** n/a
Heads: 4 Toilet(s), 2 Shower(s)
Laundry: 1 Washer(s), 1 Dryer(s) **Pay Phones:** Yes, 2
Pump-Out: OnSite, Full Service, 1 Port **Fee:** n/a **Closed Heads:** No

Marina Operations
Owner/Manager: Gerard Rokosz **Dockmaster:** Janer Vazquez
In-Season: May-Oct 31, 8am-9pm **Off-Season:** Nov-Apr, 8am-5pm
After-Hours Arrival: Radio channel 74.
Reservations: Yes **Credit Cards:** Visa/MC, Dscvr, Amex
Discounts: None
Pets: Welcome, Dog Walk Area **Handicap Access:** Yes, Heads, Docks

Marina Services and Boat Supplies
Services - Docking Assistance, Concierge, Trash Pick-Up, Dock Carts, Megayacht Facilities **Communication -** Mail & Package Hold, Phone Messages, Fax in/out, Data Ports *(Wi-Fi)*, FedEx, AirBorne, UPS, Express Mail *(Sat Del)* **Supplies - OnSite:** Ice *(Cube)* **OnCall:** Ice *(Block)* **Near:** Ships' Store **Under 1 mi:** Bait/Tackle *(Creative Lure 617-8143)*, Propane *(P&D Amoco 864-0907)* **3+ mi:** West Marine *(212-594-6065, W. 37th St. New York City)*

Boatyard Services
OnSite: Electrical Repairs, Electronics Repairs, Bottom Cleaning, Brightwork, Yacht Broker **OnCall:** Engine mechanic *(gas, diesel)*, Hull Repairs, Air Conditioning, Refrigeration, Divers, Compound, Wash & Wax, Interior Cleaning, Propeller Repairs, Woodworking, Inflatable Repairs, Life Raft Service, Upholstery, Yacht Interiors, Metal Fabrication, Yacht Design, Total Refits **Near:** Launching Ramp *(Liberty Harbor 201 386-7500)*, Rigger. **Under 1 mi:** Travelift, Painting, Awlgrip.

Restaurants and Accommodations
Near: Restaurant *(Chart House 348-6628, D $20)*, *(Ruth's Chris Steak House 863-5100)*, *(Spirit Grill 867-0101)*, *(Houlihans 863-4000)*, *(Oscars 867-0204)*, Lite Fare *(LIncoln Harbor Food Court Lite & Natural, Golden Egg Roll, gourmet Chicken, Bravo Pizza, 3rd Ave. Deli, The dog House)*, Pizzeria *(Bravo Pizza 865-3817)*, Hotel *(Sheraton Suites 617-5600)* **1-3 mi:** Motel *(Super 8 864-4500)*, *(Lincoln Tunnel Motel 867-3211)*

Recreation and Entertainment
OnSite: Fitness Center, Jogging Paths, Roller Blade/Bike Paths, Fishing

Charter, Other *(Horizon Cruises 319-0008)* **Near:** Picnic Area, Playground, Dive Shop, Golf Course **Under 1 mi:** Video Rental *(Hollywood Video 325-8070)*, Park, Cultural Attract, Sightseeing **1-3 mi:** Movie Theater *(Century Cinemas 854-7847)*, Museum

Provisioning and General Services
OnSite: Bank/ATM, Beauty Salon, Pharmacy *(CVS 867-6003)*, Newsstand **OnCall:** Provisioning Service, Liquor Store, Farmers' Market, Fishmonger, Meat Market, Dry Cleaners, Laundry, Florist **Near:** Convenience Store, Delicatessen *(Third Ave. Deli 865-3817)*, Post Office, Catholic Church, Library, Clothing Store, Retail Shops **Under 1 mi:** Gourmet Shop *(River View Gourmet 271-0060 - free delivery 7 days)*, Health Food, Wine/Beer *(Maple & Palisade Liquors & Deli 867-8020)*, Bakery *(Sabrina's 902-0600)*, Hardware Store *(Model Hardware 865-1732, Dykes Lumber)*, Copies Etc. *(Right Away Printing 348-8555)* **1-3 mi:** Supermarket *(Pathmark 867-8778)*, Bookstore, Department Store *(Kmart 868-1960)*, Buying Club

Transportation
OnSite: Ferry Service *(To Manhattan)* **OnCall:** Rental Car *(Enterprise 319-9090 / Budget 867-2700)*, Taxi *(Best Taxi 865-3456)*, Airport Limo *(Kiwee Airport Limo 662-4500)* **Near:** Water Taxi, Local Bus, InterCity Bus **Airport:** Newark *(15 mi.)*

Medical Services
911 Service **OnCall:** Chiropractor, Ambulance **Under 1 mi:** Doctor, Dentist *(Park Ave Dental Associates 864-4730)*, Veterinarian *(North Bergen Animal Hosp. 868-3753)* **Hospital:** Palisades Medical Center 854-5099 *(1 mi.)*

Setting -- Two high rise complexes, built on the footprint of old piers, form a basin that holds the Lincoln Harbor Yacht Club's extensive network of docks. The facilities for the marina are located out on the end of the north pier. The entire 66 acre residential/ commercial waterfront community has spectacular views of the midtown Manhattan skyline.

Marina Notes -- Lovely heads and showers with dressing rooms, sauna, steam shower. A conference room with long table surrounded by "fish fighting" chairs is available to visiting boaters. A couple of fitness machines are tucked into a corner. 24-hr. security. Complimentary continental breakfast served 8am-11am week-ends. *Float Plan offers monthly rate for "any" 30 days. Land/Sea pkg: two-night dockage & accommodations. Slips are perpendicular to the swells and face directly into them. Some rolling problem from the ferry wash but a bit more protected. Season $120/ft., Annual $152/ft. Beacon Wi-Fi Network Service (203-762-2657)

Notable -- Across the street is a mini-mall with services, shops and a food court. Several restaurants, including Ruth Chris and Spirito Grill in the Sheraton Suites, are very nearby and the Chart House occupies the pier directly north. On the next pier south is a ferry to Manhattan's West 38th Street 6am-9:50pm, (800-53-FERRY) every 15 minutes weekdays. 3/4 miles to NY Waterway's main ferry terminal (seven days, 'til midnight) - Sheraton Suites runs a jitney. $12 cab ride to Manhattan. Factory outlet center short ride.

Navigational Information

Lat: 40°46.299' **Long:** 074°00.768' **Tide:** 5 ft. **Current:** n/a **Chart:** 12327
Rep. Depths (MLW): **Entry** 10 ft. **Fuel Dock** 6 ft. **Max Slip/Moor** 4 ft./-
Access: Hudson River

Marina Facilities (In Season/Off Season)

Fuel: *Hess* - Gasoline, Diesel, High-Speed Pumps
Slips: 300 Total, 100 Transient **Max LOA:** 200 ft. **Max Beam:** n/a
  Rate *(per ft.):* **Day** $2.00 **Week** $11 **Month** $32
Power: 30 amp Inq., 50 amp Inq., 100 amp Inq., 200 amp n/a
Cable TV: No **Dockside Phone:** No
Dock Type: Fixed, Floating, Long Fingers, Pilings, Concrete, Wood
Moorings: 0 Total, 0 Transient **Launch:** n/a
  Rate: **Day** n/a **Week** n/a **Month** n/a
Heads: 6 Toilet(s), 8 Shower(s)
Laundry: 3 Washer(s), 3 Dryer(s) **Pay Phones:** Yes, 3
Pump-Out: OnSite **Fee:** $10 **Closed Heads:** No

Marina Operations

Owner/Manager: Alfredo Gamarra **Dockmaster:** Same
In-Season: May-Sep, 8am-8pm **Off-Season:** Oct 1-Apr, 8am-5pm
After-Hours Arrival: Must call in advance.
Reservations: Yes **Credit Cards:** Visa/MC, Dscvr, Amex
Discounts: Boat/US; Naut. Mil. **Dockage:** 25% **Fuel:** $.10 **Repair:** n/a
Pets: Welcome, Dog Walk Area **Handicap Access:** No

Port Imperial Marina

1 Pershing Circle; Weehawken, NJ 07087

Tel: (201) 902-8787 **VHF:** **Monitor** n/a **Talk** 88
Fax: (201) 974-0523 **Alternate Tel:** n/a
Email: n/a **Web:** www.portimperial.com
Nearest Town: Weehawken **Tourist Info:** (201) 688-2777

Marina Services and Boat Supplies

Services - Docking Assistance, Concierge, Security *(24 Hrs.)*, Trash Pick-Up, Dock Carts **Communication -** Mail & Package Hold, Phone Messages, Fax in/out, FedEx, AirBorne, UPS, Express Mail *(Sat Del)* **Supplies -** **OnSite:** Ice *(Cube)*, Ships' Store **Near:** Bait/Tackle *(Creative Lure 617-8143)* **1-3 mi:** Propane *(P&D Amoco 864-0907)*

Boatyard Services

OnSite: Electrical Repairs, Electronics Repairs, Hull Repairs, Bottom Cleaning, Brightwork **Near:** Rigger. **Yard Rates:** N/A **Storage:** In-Water $35/ft.

Restaurants and Accommodations

OnSite: Restaurant *(Arthur's Landing 867-0777, L $10-15, D $18-35, Sun Brunch $25; Lunch: 11:30-2:30, Dinner: 5-10pm, 7 days)* **OnCall:** Pizzeria *(Presto 854-9482)* **Near:** Snack Bar *(NY Waterway)* **Under 1 mi:** Restaurant *(Spirito Grill 867-0101)*, *(Kennedys 864-9999)*, *(Havana 866-5705)*, *(Riverside 868-5655)*, *(Hudson Kitchen 54 223-1195)*, Hotel *(Sheraton Suites On The Hudson 617-5600)* **1-3 mi:** Motel *(Rays Old Mill Inn 863-9504)* **3+ mi:** Motel *(Comfort Inn 943-3131, 4 mi.)*

Recreation and Entertainment

OnSite: Picnic Area, Grills, Playground **Near:** Park *(NY Waterway)* **Under 1 mi:** Video Rental *(West Coast Video 865-4515)* **1-3 mi:** Bowling *(Bowl Rite Lanes 864-2667)*, Movie Theater *(Mayfair Theatre 869-3333)*

, Museum, Cultural Attract, Sightseeing *(Spirit Cruises 866-211-3805, NTY Waterway Cruises 800-53-ferry)*

Provisioning and General Services

OnSite: Liquor Store, Bank/ATM, Post Office, Dry Cleaners **Near:** Convenience Store, Gourmet Shop, Delicatessen *(Lindas Place 392-8208)*, Fishmonger, Meat Market, Pharmacy *(Rite Aid 866-8582)*, Newsstand, Hardware Store *(Rojo Hardware 867-3375)*, Florist **Under 1 mi:** Supermarket *(Pathmark 867-8778)*, Wine/Beer *(Paradise Wine & Liquor 867-7077)*, Bakery *(Gran Via 348-4322)*, Catholic Church, Bookstore, Clothing Store, Retail Shops, Department Store *(Target's)* **1-3 mi:** Protestant Church

Transportation

OnSite: Water Taxi *(NY Waterway 800-53-FERRY)*, Ferry Service *(To New York City)* **OnCall:** Rental Car *(Enterprise 319-9090/Alamo 330-0046)*, Taxi *(Best Taxi 867-4137)*, Airport Limo *(Aero-Link 223-5512)* **Near:** Local Bus, InterCity Bus *(Light Rail system from Weehawken to Bayonne)* **3+ mi:** Rail *(Newark, 30mi.)* **Airport:** Newark *(30mi.)*

Medical Services

911 Service **Near:** Dentist, Ambulance **Under 1 mi:** Doctor *(Union City Medical Center 583-1600)* **1-3 mi:** Chiropractor *(Chiropractic Cntr of Union City 330-7575)*, Veterinarian *(Ambassador Vet Hosp. 863-4072)* **Hospital:** Palisades Medical Center. 854-6300 *(2 mi.)*

Setting -- Wedged in next to the New York Waterway docks, Port Imperial's extensive network of docks provides dramatic views across the Hudson to Manhattan and the Intrepid Air & Space Museum. Landside is well-known Arthur's Landing restaurant, with its al fresco deck, a new high end, low-rise condo development and adjacent are the lovely pocket gardens created by New York Waterway.

Marina Notes -- Modern, nicely maintained facilities. Fuel dock. Floating docks now take up to 35 feet; the fixed piers can manage larger vessels. This part of the Harbor has been silting in, diminishing depths to 3 and 4 feet. The constant flow of water taxis can create a significant roll. Arthur's Landing Restaurant offers a varied menu. Indoor/ Outdoor dining: high-end three-course meals, bar menu, brunch, kids' menu. $55 package: dinner, parking & RT ferry. Free dockage while dining. The aging docks will be rejuvenated once the onsite condo complex is completed in late '04.

Notable -- The adjacent US Waterway Ferry has created a particularly attractive, flower bedecked landside facility which is easily accessible to marina guests. It's a four minute, $5/2.50 water taxi ride to West 38th Street in Midtown Manhattan 6am - 1am weekdays, from 8am Sat & Sun - $7/3.50; to Pier 11 at Wall Street 6am-8pm weekdays - $7/3.50; and to World Financial Center 6am-7:53pm weekdays. Broadway Bound package (dinner, theater, ferry) call 800-53FERRY. In the Ferry terminal is a snack bar - 7am-9pm, 8am-8pm week-ends, plus a bar. Also a one-day dry cleaner and photo shop. Climb the "million" switch-back steps to the town of Weehawken up on the Palisades for all kinds of shopping.

West 79th Street Boat Basin

W. 79th Street Boat Basin; New York, NY 10024

Tel: (212) 496-2105 **VHF: Monitor** 9 **Talk** 9
Fax: (212) 496-2157 **Alternate Tel:** n/a
Email: nyccdm@aol **Web:** n/a
Nearest Town: New York City *(0 mi.)* **Tourist Info:** (212) 484-1222

Navigational Information

Lat: 40°47.161' **Long:** 073°59.140' **Tide:** 7 ft. **Current:** 6 kt. **Chart:** 12327
Rep. Depths *(MLW):* **Entry** 30 ft. **Fuel Dock** n/a **Max Slip/Moor** 5 ft./30 ft.
Access: Hudson River eastern shore - Nautical River Mile 1.9

Marina Facilities *(In Season/Off Season)*
Fuel: No
Slips: 115 Total, 6 Transient **Max LOA:** 140 ft. **Max Beam:** 40 ft.
   Rate *(per ft.):* **Day** $2.00 **Week** Inq. **Month** Inq.
   Power: 30 amp Inq., 50 amp Inq., 100 amp n/a, 200 amp n/a
   Cable TV: Yes **Dockside Phone:** Yes
   Dock Type: Fixed, Floating, Long Fingers, Pilings, Alongside, Wood
Moorings: 60 Total, 25 Transient **Launch:** None, Dinghy Dock
   Rate: Day $15 **Week** $90 **Month** $300
Heads: None
Laundry: None, Book Exchange **Pay Phones:** Yes
Pump-Out: OnSite, Self Service **Fee:** Free **Closed Heads:** Yes

Marina Operations
Owner/Manager: Michael O'Rourke **Dockmaster:** n/a
In-Season: Year-Round, 24 hrs. **Off-Season:** n/a
After-Hours Arrival: n/a
Reservations: No **Credit Cards:** Cash, check or money order
Discounts: None
Pets: Welcome, Dog Walk Area **Handicap Access:** Yes

Marina Services and Boat Supplies
Services - Docking Assistance, Concierge, Dock Carts **Communication -** Mail & Package Hold, Phone Messages, Fax in/out, FedEx, AirBorne, UPS, Express Mail *(Sat Del)* **Supplies - OnCall:** Ice *(Block, Cube)* **Near:** Ships' Store **1-3 mi:** West Marine *(W. 37th St. 594-6065)*, Bait/Tackle *(Universal Angler 398-1932)*, Live Bait

Boatyard Services
OnCall: Bottom Cleaning, Divers, Interior Cleaning, Propeller Repairs, Inflatable Repairs **1-3 mi:** Travelift, Engine mechanic *(gas, diesel)*, Electronic Sales. **Nearest Yard:** Liberty Harbor (201) 386-7500

Restaurants and Accommodations
OnSite: Restaurant *(W 79 St. Boat Basin Café 796-5542, L $3-11, D $13-19, Kids' menu, Mid Apr-Mid Nov)* **Near:** Restaurant *(Zagat's N.Y. Restaurant Guide)*, *(Isabellas 724-2100)*, *(Scaletta 769-9191)*, *(Assaggio 877-0170)*, *(Fujiyama 769-1144)*, Pizzeria *(Pizzeria Uno 595-4700)*, Hotel *(Lucerne 875-1000)*, *(Excelsior 362-9200)*, *(The Beacon 787-1100)*, *(The Belleclaire 362-7700)*, *(On the Avenue 362-1100)*

Recreation and Entertainment
OnSite: Picnic Area, Playground, Jogging Paths, Roller Blade/Bike Paths **Near:** Volleyball, Fitness Center *(Equinox 721-4200)*, Horseback Riding *(Claremont 724-5100)*, Video Arcade, Park, Museum *(Childrens' Museum 721-4862, American Museum of Natural History 873-4225, Metropolitan Museum of Art 535-7710 - 1 mi.)*, Galleries **Under 1 mi:** Dive Shop, Tennis Courts *(Eastside 737-0185)*, Movie Theater *(Lincoln Plaza 757-2280)*, Video Rental *(Blockbuster 580-8822)*, Cultural Attract *(Lincoln Center 877-1800 -*

Metropolitan Opera 362-6000, NYC Ballet & NYC Opera 870-5570, Avery Fisher Hall 875.5350) **1-3 mi:** Golf Course *(Chelsea Piers Driving Range 336-6400)*, Bowling *(Amf Chelsea Piers 835-2695)*, Sightseeing *(Gray Line 397-2620 $15/7-50/8; NY Apple 876-9868 $25/16 2-days)*

Provisioning and General Services
Near: Convenience Store, Gourmet Shop *(world famous Zabars 787-2000)*, Delicatessen *(Andy 799-3355)*, Health Food *(Blanches Organic Take Away 579-3179)*, Wine/Beer, Liquor Store *(Beacon 877-0028)*, Bakery *(Columbus 724-6880)*, Farmers' Market *(77th St & Columbus Sun 10am)*, Green Grocer *(Fairway - and so much more -595-1889)*, Fishmonger *(Citarella 874.0383 pricey but impeccable)*, Lobster Pound, Meat Market, Bank/ATM, Post Office, Catholic Church, Protestant Church, Synagogue, Library, Beauty Salon, Barber Shop, Dry Cleaners, Laundry, Bookstore, Pharmacy *(Park West 721-3883)*, Newsstand, Hardware Store *(True Value 874-1910)*, Florist **Under 1 mi:** Supermarket *(Food Emporium 873-4032)*

Transportation
OnCall: Taxi *(Hail a cab the street or call Carmel 666-6666)*, Airport Limo *(First Class 304-1111)* **Near:** Bikes *(Eddies 580-2011; Central Park 861-4137)*, Rental Car *(Alamo 875-1255; Budget 501-7669; Avis 362-6865)*, Local Bus **1-3 mi:** Rail *(Penn Station/Grand Central)*
Airport: JFK/LaGuardia /Newark *(7 mi./12 mi./12 mi.)*

Medical Services
911 Service **OnCall:** Ambulance **Near:** Doctor, Dentist, Chiropractor, Holistic Services, Veterinarian *(Riverside 787-1993)*
Hospital: Mount Sinai 579-1520 *(1 mi.)*

Setting -- About midway along Manhattan Island, on the eastern shore of the Hudson, the West 79th Street Boat Basin is an integral part of 315 acre active Riverside Park. Its views are across the river to the New Jersey Palisades and landside to the Park and the vaulted arches of the Marina Cafe. It is conveniently located at the foot of 79th St. near Riverside Drive.

Marina Notes -- Owned by NYC Parks & Recreation. Limited services and limited depth (Some slips 3' at low tide) - reflected in the remarkable rates. Moorings are in deeper water. A dinghy dock for going ashore, but no launch. 24-hr security. Delightful, reasonable onsite Boat Basin Cafe is set beneath vaulted arches, designed by Guastavino, that are an integral part of a many-tiered landside structure (including an underground cave-like parking garage). Quite a few liveaboards. A short walk to retail-oriented upper Broadway. For the best restaurant info, pick up the most current Zagat's Guide. Take care at night.

Notable -- Riverside Park runs from 59th St. to 152nd St. along the Hudson, and was originally designed by Frederick Law Olmsted in the 1870s and renovated by Robert Moses in the 1930's. Three walkways at three levels - road, river and in between - wind along the River. In the spring, cherry trees line the paths. Lots to see & do and easy to get there and back -- buses (along Riverside Dr., Broadway, Amsterdam, Columbus & Central Park West) subways (79th & Broadway) and taxis (just hail one). Easy access to attractions: Lincoln Center - 12 blocks. Museum of Natural History - four blocks. Great shopping and provisioning - three blocks to Broadway: Zabar's, Citarella, Fairway, Food Emporium. Most restaurants and services deliver, including the supermarkets.

Navigational Information
Lat: 40°35.348' **Long:** 073°59.708' **Tide:** 8 **Current:** 0 **Chart:** n/a
Rep. Depths (MLW): Entry 6 ft. **Fuel Dock** 15 ft. **Max Slip/Moor** 20 ft./-
Access: Go to Gravesend Bay Bouy C-3

Marina Facilities *(In Season/Off Season)*
Fuel: Gasoline, Diesel
Slips: 250 Total, 30 Transient **Max LOA:** 110 ft. **Max Beam:** 20 ft.
  Rate *(per ft.):* **Day** $1.25 **Week** $10.75 **Month** $30
  Power: 30 amp $5, **50 amp** $10, **100 amp** n/a, **200 amp** n/a
  Cable TV: No **Dockside Phone:** No
  Dock Type: Floating, Long Fingers, Short Fingers, Pilings, Wood
Moorings: 0 Total, 0 Transient **Launch:** n/a
  Rate: Day n/a **Week** n/a **Month** n/a
Heads: 2 Toilet(s), 1 Shower(s)
Laundry: None **Pay Phones:** Yes, 1
Pump-Out: No **Fee:** n/a **Closed Heads:** No

Marina Operations
Owner/Manager: Carmelo Gagliano **Dockmaster:** n/a
In-Season: Year 'Round, 7am-7pm **Off-Season:** n/a
After-Hours Arrival: Call in daytime
Reservations: Required **Credit Cards:** Visa/MC, Amex
Discounts: Boat/US; Nautical Miles **Dockage:** 25% **Fuel:** n/a **Repair:** n/a
Pets: Welcome, Dog Walk Area **Handicap Access:** No

Marine Basin Marina

1900 Shore Parkway at Bay 41 St.; Brooklyn, NY 11214

Tel: (718) 372-5700 **VHF: Monitor** 16 **Talk** 69
Fax: (718) 372-1265 **Alternate Tel:** (718) 265-4226
Email: mbmboats@aol.com **Web:** n/a
Nearest Town: Brooklyn *(0 mi.)* **Tourist Info:** (718) 785-1000

Marina Services and Boat Supplies
Services - Docking Assistance, Concierge, Boaters' Lounge, Security *(24, fences/electric gate)*, Dock Carts **Communication -** Mail & Package Hold, Fax in/out, Data Ports *(Office)*, FedEx, AirBorne, UPS, Express Mail *(Sat Del)* **Supplies - OnSite:** Ice *(Cube)*, Ships' Store *(small store, next-day delivery)*, Bait/Tackle **Under 1 mi:** Propane

Boatyard Services
OnSite: Crane *(10T & 50T)*, Engine mechanic *(gas, diesel)*, Electrical Repairs, Electronic Sales, Electronics Repairs, Hull Repairs, Rigger, Bottom Cleaning, Brightwork, Divers, Propeller Repairs **OnCall:** Canvas Work, Air Conditioning, Refrigeration, Compound, Wash & Wax, Interior Cleaning, Woodworking, Inflatable Repairs, Life Raft Service, Upholstery, Metal Fabrication, Painting, Awlgrip **1-3 mi:** Sail Loft. **Dealer for:** J.C. Marine, authorized MerCruiser mechanic. **Yard Rates:** $60, Haul & Launch $6/ft., Power Wash $1/ft., Bottom Paint $10/ft. *(paint incl.)*

Restaurants and Accommodations
OnCall: Pizzeria *(Pizza D'Amore 266-4433, in Toys R Us shopping center)* **Near:** Restaurant *(Villa Vivolo 372-9860, 8829 26th Avenue)*, Fast Food *(Burger King)*, Motel *(Harbor Motor Inn 946-9200)* **3+ mi:** Motel *(Comfort Inn Gregory 238-3737, 3 mi.)*

Recreation and Entertainment
OnSite: Picnic Area, Grills, Fishing Charter **Near:** Playground, Dive Shop, Tennis Courts, Park *(Dreier Offerman Park)*, Cultural Attract *(Nellie Bly Amusement Park, Coney Island, New York Aquarium)*, Sightseeing, Special Events *(Brooklyn Cyclones Baseball - check with management for tickets)*

Under 1 mi: Beach, Fitness Center *(Exercise Studio 373-3747)*, Jogging Paths, Video Rental, Video Arcade, Museum **1-3 mi:** Horseback Riding, Boat Rentals, Roller Blade/Bike Paths, Bowling, Movie Theater **3+ mi:** Golf Course *(Marine Park G.C. 338-7113, 6 mi.)*

Provisioning and General Services
Near: Provisioning Service, Convenience Store, Market, Gourmet Shop, Delicatessen, Bank/ATM, Bookstore, Pharmacy, Newsstand, Hardware Store, Florist, Clothing Store, Retail Shops, Department Store, Copies Etc. **Under 1 mi:** Health Food, Wine/Beer, Liquor Store, Bakery, Farmers' Market, Fishmonger, Post Office, Catholic Church, Protestant Church, Synagogue, Other, Beauty Salon, Barber Shop, Dry Cleaners, Laundry *(Cropsey Ave. between 25 & 26 St.)* **1-3 mi:** Supermarket, Library **3+ mi:** Green Grocer

Transportation
OnCall: Rental Car *(265-3000 or Rafy's 946-8327 - 1 mi.)*, Taxi *(Carmel 666-666; Harmony 714-1200, 996-2636)*, Airport Limo *(Isabell 251-8000)* **Under 1 mi:** Rail *(Subway to NYC - station at 25th Ave & 86th Street)* **Airport:** JFK Int'l *(14 mi.)*

Medical Services
911 Service Near: Dentist *(Carli 372-3535)*, Chiropractor *(Pedri 996-2214)* **Under 1 mi:** Holistic Services *(Exercise Studio - massage, yoga 373-3747)*, Ambulance, Veterinarian *(Animal Clinic of Bath Beach 373-5126)*, Optician *(Pearle 372-1212)* **1-3 mi:** Doctor *(Brooklyn Family 331-6600)* **Hospital:** Maimonides Medical Center 259-8800 *1.5 mi.*

Setting -- A welcome port in this part of New York Harbor, deep-water, very protected Marine Basin is located in Gravesend Bay, Brooklyn between the Verrazano Bridge and Coney Island. The docks are snuggled within a basin surrounded by tall bulkheads created from massive granite blocks. The office is in a very long single-story gray metal building perched atop that granite bulkhead. The landscape is basic, rustic "boatyard".

Marina Notes -- Friendly and helpful, Marine Basin has been family owned and operated for 45 years. There is minimal roll even in a blow-- the berths are very sheltered. Security is tight; there's a guard 24 hours. Some boatyard services -- hauling for boats to 35' -- and an onsite mechanic. Three heads, one sink and one shower. A deck right off the docks, with a grill, is home to boater gatherings. For inclement weather, there's a glass walled, open-air room also on the dock level. Bright blue steps and ramps lead up to the "road" level. Ask the marina management for guidance before venturing out after dark.

Notable -- A very short distance off the typical north-south course, MBM is extremely convenient. Once there, taxis are readily available and famous Coney Island is a short ride away - you can see the parachute jump from the marina. Alternatively, at the end of the marina "driveway" is Nelly Bly Amusements - a small (compared to Coney Island) but very active amusement park with lots of rides and a good size miniature golf course. Less than half a mile is a waterfront Toys R Us - you'll see it coming in -- a Modells, an HSBC Bank, and a Best Buy. A two block walk is Cropsey Avenue - it's a residential area with some pockets of stores, including a medium size food market and some additional shopping. It's 8 blocks to a subway; Manhattan is a twenty minute ride.

Atlantis Marina & Yacht Sales

PO Box; 180 Mansion Avenue; Staten Island, NY 10308

Tel: (718) 966-9700 **VHF: Monitor** 72 **Talk** n/a
Fax: (718) 966-5827 **Alternate Tel:** n/a
Email: sales@atlantismarinasi.com **Web:** www.atlantismarinasi.com
Nearest Town: Great Kills *(0.5 mi.)* **Tourist Info:** (718) 608-0174

Navigational Information
Lat: 40°32.593' **Long:** 074°08.454' **Tide:** n/a **Current:** n/a **Chart:** 12327
Rep. Depths *(MLW)*: **Entry** 12 ft. **Fuel Dock** n/a **Max Slip/Moor** 12 ft./-
Access: 305 from Buglight (light on rocks)

Marina Facilities *(In Season/Off Season)*
Fuel: Gasoline, Diesel
Slips: 100 Total, 4 Transient **Max LOA:** 100 ft. **Max Beam:** n/a
 Rate *(per ft.)*: **Day** $4.00/3.00 **Week** n/a **Month** n/a
 Power: 30 amp Metered, **50 amp** n/a, **100 amp** n/a, **200 amp** n/a
 Cable TV: No **Dockside Phone:** No
 Dock Type: Floating, Long Fingers, Wood
Moorings: 0 Total, 0 Transient **Launch:** n/a
 Rate: Day n/a **Week** n/a **Month** n/a
Heads: Toilet(s), Shower(s)
Laundry: None **Pay Phones:** No
Pump-Out: OnCall, 1 InSlip **Fee:** $30 **Closed Heads:** No

Marina Operations
Owner/Manager: Bianca Formica **Dockmaster:** Nicholas Ingrassia
In-Season: Apr 15-Oct 15, 9am-5pm **Off-Season:** Winter, 9am-4pm
After-Hours Arrival: Call in advance
Reservations: Yes **Credit Cards:** Visa/MC, Amex
Discounts: None
Pets: No **Handicap Access:** Yes, Heads, Docks

Marina Services and Boat Supplies
Services - Docking Assistance, Concierge, Room Service to the Boat, Boaters' Lounge, Security *(24, Security guard)*, Dock Carts, Megayacht Facilities **Communication -** Mail & Package Hold, Phone Messages, Fax in/out *($2)*, FedEx, AirBorne, UPS, Express Mail *(Sat Del)* **Supplies -** **OnSite:** Ice *(Block, Cube)*, Ships' Store, West Marine, Boat/US, Bait/Tackle **Near:** Propane

Boatyard Services
OnSite: Travelift *(35T)*, Engine mechanic *(gas, diesel)*, Electrical Repairs, Electronic Sales, Electronics Repairs, Hull Repairs, Canvas Work, Bottom Cleaning, Compound, Wash & Wax, Interior Cleaning, Propeller Repairs, Woodworking, Inflatable Repairs, Yacht Broker *(Bianca Formica)* **Near:** Brightwork, Air Conditioning, Refrigeration, Divers. **Dealer for:** Dawson, Seaview. **Yard Rates:** $25, Haul & Launch $10, Power Wash $4/ft.

Restaurants and Accommodations
OnSite: Restaurant *(Marina Cafe 967-3077, L $14-26, D $14-26, dockside dining, will deliver to boat noon to midnight 7 days)* **OnCall:** Pizzeria *(Benvenuti 967-6560)* **Near:** Restaurant *(Harborview Steakhouse)*, *(Marina Grande)*, Lite Fare *(Portabello 608-1900, deli, pizza, delivery too)* **Under 1 mi:** Hotel *(Hilton)*, *(Staten Island Hotel)* **1-3 mi:** Fast Food

Recreation and Entertainment
OnSite: Picnic Area, Grills **Near:** Beach, Playground, Jogging Paths, Roller Blade/Bike Paths, Park, Sightseeing, Special Events

Under 1 mi: Dive Shop, Volleyball, Tennis Courts, Golf Course *(La Tourette G.C. 351-1889, South Shore G.C. 984-0101)*, Fitness Center *(Breakthrough 987-8930)*, Bowling *(Bowling on the Green 351-4000)*, Movie Theater, Video Rental *(Blockbuster 966-5208)*, Museum *(Staten Island Historical Society 351-1611)*

Provisioning and General Services
Near: Convenience Store, Supermarket *(Waldbaums 948-9734)*, Gourmet Shop, Delicatessen *(Nelboy 227-1242; Michael's 356-4162)*, Health Food, Wine/Beer **Under 1 mi:** Liquor Store *(Super 984-8500; Aloa's 987-0044)*, Bakery, Green Grocer, Bank/ATM, Post Office, Catholic Church, Protestant Church, Library *(N.Y.P.L. 984-6670)*, Beauty Salon, Barber Shop, Dry Cleaners, Laundry *(Clothes Line 984-8423)*, Pharmacy *(CVS 317-2211)*, Newsstand, Hardware Store *(Southside 984-0796)*, Florist, Department Store *(K-Mart 351-8500)*, Buying Club *(Costco)*, Copies Etc. *(Luke's 667-3258)* **1-3 mi:** Meat Market, Synagogue, Bookstore

Transportation
OnCall: Taxi *(Silver Express 983-9828)*, Airport Limo *(Action 356-6390)* **3+mi:** Ferry Service *(to Manhattan, 5 mi.)* **Airport:** Newark Int'l *(14 mi.)*

Medical Services
911 Service **Under 1 mi:** Doctor *(Gazzara 966-3700)*, Dentist *(Hoffman 948-7103)*, Chiropractor *(Banas 227-6400)*, Veterinarian *(South Richmond 227-1313)* **1-3 mi:** Holistic Services *(Alobano Massage 356-8890)* **Hospital:** Staten Island *4 mi.*

Setting -- On the west shore of Great Kills Harbor, protected by the Crookes Point Peninsula, Atlantis Marina is an interesting stop. A two-story octagonal building with a turret provides an imposing landmark for this attractive and very nicely executed facility. Brick pavers surface patios furnished with tables, chairs and benches; pots of flowers add to the effect.

Marina Notes -- Pets not allowed. Closed on Sunday in winter. Family owned and operated. Formerly Canyons Marina, the property and docks were destroyed by the 1992 Nor'easter. In 1993, the Formica family purchased the marina, and renovated it into a state of the art facility with 100 floating wet slips and 20 personal watercraft flotation slips. Full service boatyard. 35T travelift and 2 mechanics on staff. Marine Supply Store onsite. A facilities building at the back of the parking lot houses the heads and showers (open 24 hrs.). An additional pair of heads (open only during office hours), along with a very nicely furnished boaters' lounge area, are in the wood paneled office in the octagonal building -- its wide expanse of windows overlooks the docks and patios.

Notable -- In the season - Memorial Day to Labor Day - the Marina Cafe operates "Dockside Dining" on the patio right in front of the marina's octagonal home. A raw bar and cocktail bar, along with umbrellaed tables makes this an inviting spot. Directly adjacent the main Marina Cafe is open all year, and serves the same menu for lunch & dinner entrees: $14-26. They also offer party platters to go plus, during the week, they serve a complete lobster dinner for under $20. The Atlantis fishing boat goes out twice a day in season, once in shoulder season.

Navigational Information
Lat: 40°32.000' **Long:** 070°00.000' **Tide:** 5 ft. **Current:** 1 kt. **Chart:** 12327
Rep. Depths (*MLW*): **Entry** 10 ft. **Fuel Dock** 12 ft. **Max Slip/Moor** -/20 ft.
Access: 305 from Buglight to Great Kills Harbor far shore

Marina Facilities *(In Season/Off Season)*
Fuel: Gasoline, Diesel
Slips: 217 Total, 5 Transient **Max LOA:** 70 ft. **Max Beam:** 20 ft.
  Rate *(per ft.)*: **Day** $1.75/1.00 **Week** n/a **Month** n/a
Power: 30 amp Incl., 50 amp Incl., 100 amp n/a, 200 amp n/a
Cable TV: No **Dockside Phone:** No
Dock Type: Fixed, Floating, Wood
Moorings: 0 Total, 0 Transient **Launch:** n/a
  Rate: Day n/a **Week** n/a **Month** n/a
Heads: 2 Toilet(s), 2 Shower(s)
Laundry: 1 Washer(s), 1 Dryer(s) **Pay Phones:** No
Pump-Out: No **Fee:** n/a **Closed Heads:** Yes

Marina Operations
Owner/Manager: Ed Corbo **Dockmaster:** n/a
In-Season: Apr-Oct, 7am-7pm **Off-Season:** Nov-Mar, 9am-3pm
After-Hours Arrival: Tie up to floating fuel dock
Reservations: Required **Credit Cards:** n/a
Discounts: None
Pets: Welcome **Handicap Access:** Yes, Docks

Mansion Marina

112 Mansion Ave; Staten Island, NY 10308

Tel: (718) 984-6611 **VHF: Monitor** n/a **Talk** n/a
Fax: (718) 984-0325 **Alternate Tel:** (718) 356-4620
Email: n/a **Web:** n/a
Nearest Town: Great Kills *(0.5mi.)* **Tourist Info:** (718) 608-0174

Marina Services and Boat Supplies
Services - Docking Assistance **Communication -** Fax in/out *($1/pg)*, FedEx, AirBorne, UPS, Express Mail **Supplies - OnSite:** Ice *(Block, Cube)*, Bait/Tackle *(and Michael's Bait & Tackle 984-9733 nearby)* **Near:** Ships' Store **3+ mi:** West Marine *(442-5700, 12 mi.)*

Boatyard Services
OnSite: Travelift *(15T)*, Engine mechanic *(gas, diesel)*, Canvas Work, Bottom Cleaning, Divers, Compound, Wash & Wax, Interior Cleaning, Propeller Repairs

Restaurants and Accommodations
OnCall: Lite Fare *(Chicken Holiday 356-9191)*, Pizzeria *(Benvenuti Pizzeria 967-6560)* **Near:** Restaurant *(Harbor Lights 948-5772)*, *(Marina Cafe 967-3077, L $14-26, D $14-26)*, *(Harbor Lights 948-5772)*, *(Harbor Rose 227-8500)*, *(Black Sea Cafe 984-0800)*, Fast Food *(Subway 227-7979)*
Under 1 mi: Restaurant *(Casa Perla Restaurant 356-5540)*, *(Buona Pasta Restaurant 967-9385)*, Seafood Shack *(Alfredo's Italian Seafood 984-3983)*, Pizzeria *(Alfredo's 984-3784)*, Motel *(Cosmopolitan Motel)*
1-3 mi: Inn/B&B *(Hilton Garden Inn 477-2400)*
3+ mi: Inn/B&B *(Midland Motor Inn 987-8322, 4 mi.)*

Recreation and Entertainment
Near: Jogging Paths, Roller Blade/Bike Paths, Fishing Charter
Under 1 mi: Beach *(dinghy across the harbor)*, Playground, Tennis Courts

1-3 mi: Golf Course *(La Tourette Golf Course 351-1889)*, Fitness Center *(Breakthrough Fitness 987-8930)*, Bowling *(Bowling On the Green 351-4000)*, Video Rental *(Blockbuster Video 966-5208)*, Museum *(Staten Island Historical Society 351-1611)* **3+ mi:** Movie Theater *(Movies at Staten Island 983-9600, 8 mi.)*

Provisioning and General Services
Near: Delicatessen *(Nelboy 227-1242 Michael's Deli 356-4162)*, Liquor Store *(Super Liquor Market 984-8500)*, Library *(New York Public Library 984-6670)*, Pharmacy *(CVS 317-2211)*, Hardware Store *(South Side Hardware 984-0796)* **Under 1 mi:** Bank/ATM, Post Office, Catholic Church, Protestant Church, Barber Shop, Dry Cleaners, Laundry *(Clothes Line 984-8423)*
1-3 mi: Supermarket *(Waldbaum's 948-9734; Pathmark 351-0862)*, Gourmet Shop *(Planet Dana - Fine Foods 351-0976)*, Health Food *(Dr Browne's Health Food Store 667-4765)*, Wine/Beer *(Aida's World of Liquors 987-0044)*, Department Store *(Kmart Stores 351-8500)*, Copies Etc. *(Luke's Copy Shop 667-3258)*

Transportation
OnCall: Taxi *(Silver Express 983-9828)*, Airport Limo *(Action Limousines 356-6390)* **Airport:** Newark 527-1600 *(14 mi.)*

Medical Services
911 Service **Under 1 mi:** Doctor *(Gazzara 966-3700)*, Dentist *(Hoffman 948-7103)*, Chiropractor *(Banas 227-6400)*, Veterinarian *(South Richmond 227-1313)* **1-3 mi:** Holistic Services *(Albano Massage 356-8890)*
Hospital: Staten Island Universit - South 226-2000 *4 mi.*

Setting -- The well-marked channel from Raritan Bay leads into very protected Great Kills Harbor. On the western shore, a large comfortable covered fuel dock-house, with a Citgo sign, sits out at the end of the main boardwalk-like pier. The extensive network of docks radiates from the pier. Two additional piers with docks sit on either side of the central one. A built-in seating area is landside of the boardwalk. Pots of flowers brighten the well-maintained facility,

Marina Notes -- Only other fuel in Great Kills is Staten Island Boat Sales - gas and diesel. Very nice docks and good pedestals. Heads and one shower. Full service boatyard with haul-out. All the moorings on this side of the harbor are privately owned and the only launch in the harbor is at Richmond County Yacht Club (356-4120 & 948-9648) -- which also has 40 slips and an occasional open one for members of other clubs.

Notable -- A fair number of north/south transients stop for a night in this convenient, protected harbor. Across the street from Mansion Marina is the Mansion caterers and several of restaurants are within an easy walk. A grocey store is about 1 mile; taxis are available.

Nichols Great Kills Park Marina

PO Box; 3270 Hylan Blvd.; Staten Island, NY 10308

Tel: (718) 351-8476 **VHF: Monitor** n/a **Talk** n/a
Fax: (718) 351-8771 **Alternate Tel:** (718) 351-8476
Email: n/a **Web:** n/a
Nearest Town: Great Kills *(4 mi.)* **Tourist Info:** (718) 727-1900

Navigational Information
Lat: 40°32.272' **Long:** 074°07.864' **Tide:** 6ft. **Current:** n/a **Chart:** n/a
Rep. Depths *(MLW):* **Entry** 15 ft. **Fuel Dock** n/a **Max Slip/Moor** 20 ft./-
Access: Sandy Hook Narrows Area

Marina Facilities *(In Season/Off Season)*
Fuel: No
Slips: 350 Total, 10 Transient **Max LOA:** 70 ft. **Max Beam:** 20 ft. ft.
  Rate *(per ft.):* **Day** $2.00 **Week** n/a **Month** n/a
  Power: 30 amp Incl., **50 amp** n/a, **100 amp** n/a, **200 amp** n/a
  Cable TV: No **Dockside Phone:** No
  Dock Type: Floating, Wood
Moorings: 0 Total, 0 Transient **Launch:** n/a, Dinghy Dock
  Rate: Day n/a **Week** n/a **Month** n/a
Heads: 4 Toilet(s), 4 Shower(s) *(with dressing rooms)*
Laundry: None **Pay Phones:** No
Pump-Out: No **Fee:** n/a **Closed Heads:** No

Marina Operations
Owner/Manager: Edward Tomanek **Dockmaster:** n/a
In-Season: all year, 8am-4:30pm **Off-Season:** n/a
After-Hours Arrival: see guard
Reservations: preferred **Credit Cards:** Visa/MC, Dscvr
Discounts: None
Pets: Welcome, Dog Walk Area **Handicap Access:** Yes, Heads

Marina Services and Boat Supplies
Services - Security *(24hrs.),* Dock Carts **Communication -** Mail & Package Hold *(Sat Del)* **Supplies - OnSite:** Ice *(Block, Cube),* Ships' Store
1-3 mi: Marine Discount Store, Propane *(Richmond Gas 761-8101)*
3+ mi: Bait/Tackle *(Michael's B&T 984-9733, 3.5 mi.)*

Boatyard Services
OnSite: Travelift *(25T),* Forklift, Crane, Bottom Cleaning, Compound, Wash & Wax, Interior Cleaning, Propeller Repairs, Painting **Near:** Launching Ramp. **Under 1 mi:** Engine mechanic *(gas, diesel),* Electrical Repairs, Electronic Sales, Electronics Repairs, Hull Repairs, Rigger. **1-3 mi:** Canvas Work, Brightwork, Air Conditioning, Refrigeration, Divers, Woodworking, Inflatable Repairs, Life Raft Service, Upholstery, Metal Fabrication, Awlgrip, Yacht Design, Yacht Building. **Yard Rates:** $65/hr., Haul & Launch $10/ft., Power Wash $4/ft., Bottom Paint $14/ft. *(paint incl.)*

Restaurants and Accommodations
OnSite: Snack Bar **Near:** Restaurant *(Sage 351-0977),* Pizzeria *(Villa Ponte 668-0468)* **Under 1 mi:** Fast Food *(Wendy's 668-9203),* Pizzeria *(Boulevard Bagels & Pizza 477-7752), (Jennie's Pizzeria 342-2188)*
1-3 mi: Restaurant *(Peking Taste 494-9393), (El Pollo Restaurant 815-4928), (Chan's Red Apple 667-3100),* Seafood Shack *(The Road House 447-0033),* Hotel *(The S.I. Hotel 698-5000), (Hilton Garden 477-2400)*

Recreation and Entertainment
OnSite: Beach, Jogging Paths, Park *(Gateway National Recreation Area 351-6970)* **Near:** Picnic Area, Grills, Roller Blade/Bike Paths

1-3 mi: Dive Shop, Tennis Courts *(Westerleigh Tennis Club 273-2462),* Golf Course *(La Tourette Golf Course 351-3318),* Fitness Center *(Savage Fitness 370-8484),* Horseback Riding, Boat Rentals, Bowling *(Big Apple Bowling & Fun Center 698-2695),* Fishing Charter, Group Fishing Boat, Movie Theater *(Atrium Cinemas 317-8300),* Video Rental *(Blockbuster Video 982-6130),* Museum *(Jacques Marchais Museum of Tibetan 987-3500)*

Provisioning and General Services
Under 1 mi: Market *(Dong Yang Market 761-9507),* Supermarket *(Pathmark 351-0862),* Hardware Store *(Mermaid 266-8295)* **1-3 mi:** Provisioning Service, Convenience Store, Gourmet Shop *(Jardines 494-0359),* Delicatessen *(Richmond Deli 967-3460),* Health Food *(Tastebud's 351-8693),* Liquor Store *(Wine Hut 761-3344),* Bakery, Green Grocer, Fishmonger, Bank/ATM, Post Office, Catholic Church, Protestant Church, Synagogue, Library *(New York PL 442-8562),* Beauty Salon, Barber Shop, Dry Cleaners, Bookstore *(B.Dalton 698-3500),* Pharmacy *(CVS370-1160, 370-0365),* Newsstand, Florist, Department Store *(Kmart 698-0900),* Copies Etc. *(Reliable Office 979-6000)*

Transportation
OnCall: Taxi *(Silver Express 983-9828)* **Under 1 mi:** Airport Limo *(D'elegance Limo 494-0969)* **Airport:** Newark Int'l *(10.5 mi.)*

Medical Services
911 Service **Under 1 mi:** Dentist *(Fisher 494-0421),* Chiropractor *(Bracco 494-9390)* **1-3 mi:** Doctor *(Alternative Medical 494-0675),* Holistic Services *(S.I.Massage 667-3333),* Veterinarian *(Animal Hospital of S.I. 698-1400)* **Hospital:** Staten Island University *(5 mi.)*

Setting -- Great Kills Harbor is a deep-water, nearly landlocked basin that's 3.75 square miles. On the east side Nichols Great Kills Park Marina, located in the Gateway National Recreation Area, dominates the shoreline. An extensive series of docks radiates from the gangplanks that tie them to the bulkhead. Landside is a single story building that houses the offices; behind it looms the large seashore pavilion that services the adjacent beach.

Marina Notes -- While Nichols Great Kills Park Marina is located within the GNRA, it is a private franchise, managed by Nichols Boatyard in Mamaroneck, N.Y. 24/7 security. Limited boatyard services include a 25T travelift, haul & launch, bottom paint, wash & wax, and winter storage. This section of the Harbor is a federal anchorage with moorings controlled by the Parks Department.

Notable -- Nearly land-locked Great Kills Harbor is well protected from the worst storms and Nichols is very close to the channel as you arrive. The beach is virtually onsite - miles of pristine, untouched sand and grass. In season there's a snack bar in the beach pavilion plus additional heads and a nice playground. Gateway National Recreation Area, which covers about two-thirds of the harbor, offers fishing, boating, sports, swimming, and ranger-led walks. Trails start right near the marina and go through ocean dunes, grasslands, marshes and a swamp oak forest to Crookes Point. In mid September, it's also a stopping place for Monarch butterflies on their way to Mexico. The S78 bus stops nearby; it's a 30 minute ride to the St. George Terminal, home to the Staten Island Ferry to Manhattan. Or take the S79 to the 86th Street subway in Bay Ridge, Brooklyn.

XIII. New Jersey: Upper Atlantic Inlets

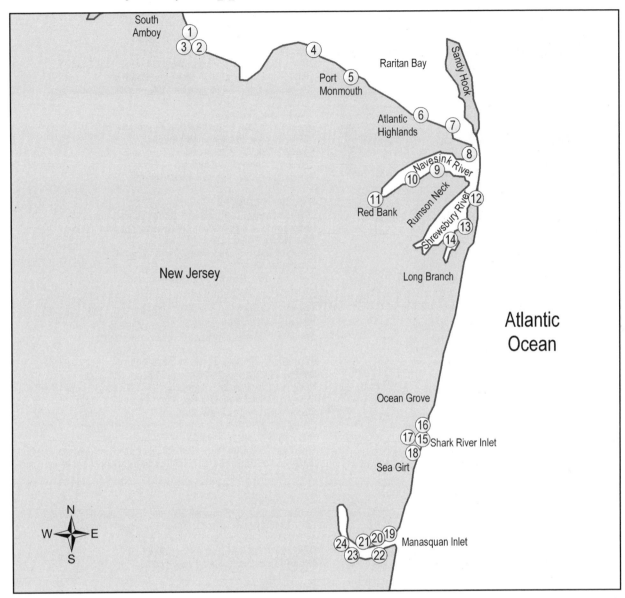

MAP	MARINA	HARBOR	PAGE	MAP	MARINA	HARBOR	PAGE
1	Vikings Marina	Raritan Bay/Stump Creek	232	13	Channel Club	Shrewsbury River	244
2	Lockwood Boat Works	Raritan Bay/Cheesequake Canal	233	14	Mariner's Emporium	Shrewsbury River	245
3	Morgan Marina	Raritan Bay/Cheesequake Canal	234	15	Shark River Yacht Club	Shark River	246
4	Lentze Marina	Raritan Bay/Thorns Creek	235	16	Bry's Marine	Shark River	247
5	Monmouth Cove Marina	Raritan Bay/Pews Creek	236	17	Shark River Hills Marina	Shark River	248
6	Atlantic Highlands Municipal Marina	Sandy Hook Bay	237	18	Belmar Marina	Shark River	249
7	Sandy Hook Bay Marina	Sandy Hook Bay	238	19	Hoffman's Marina	Manasquan River	250
8	Bahrs Landing Restaurant & Marina	Shrewsbury River	239	20	Brielle Marine Basin	Manasquan River	251
9	Oceanic Marina	Navesink River	240	21	Brielle Yacht Club	Manasquan River	252
10	Fair Haven Yacht Works	Navesink River	241	22	Southside Marina	Manasquan River	253
11	Molly Pitcher Inn & Marina	Navesink River	242	23	Clark's Landing Marina	Manasquan River	254
12	Navesink Marina	Shrewsbury River	243	24	Crystal Point Yacht Club	Manasquan River	255

Vikings Marina

1707 State Route 35; South Amboy, NJ 08879

Tel: (732) 566-5961 **VHF: Monitor** n/a **Talk** n/a
Fax: (732) 566-5963 **Alternate Tel:** n/a
Email: www.fishbox.tv/vikings **Web:** n/a
Nearest Town: Laurence Harbor *(0.75 mi.)* **Tourist Info:** (732) 442-7400

Navigational Information
Lat: 40°27.679' **Long:** 074°15.437' **Tide:** 3 ft. **Current:** 4 kt. **Chart:** 12327
Rep. Depths (*MLW*): Entry 4 ft. **Fuel Dock** 4 ft. **Max Slip/Moor** 6 ft./-
Access: Raritan Bay to entrance to Morgan Creek (Cheesequake Cr.)

Marina Facilities *(In Season/Off Season)*
Fuel: Gasoline
Slips: 165 Total, 10 Transient **Max LOA:** 45 ft. **Max Beam:** n/a
  Rate *(per ft.):* **Day** $20.00* **Week** n/a **Month** n/a
  Power: 30 amp Incl,, **50 amp** n/a, **100 amp** n/a, **200 amp** n/a
  Cable TV: No **Dockside Phone:** No
  Dock Type: Floating, Wood
Moorings: 0 Total, 0 Transient **Launch:** n/a
  Rate: Day n/a **Week** n/a **Month** n/a
Heads: 2 Toilet(s), 2 Shower(s)
Laundry: None **Pay Phones:** No
Pump-Out: OnSite **Fee:** n/a **Closed Heads:** No

Marina Operations
Owner/Manager: Larry Johnson **Dockmaster:** Same
In-Season: n/a, 8am-4:30pm **Off-Season:** n/a, 8am-4:30pm
After-Hours Arrival: Call in advance
Reservations: Required **Credit Cards:** Visa/MC
Discounts: None
Pets: Welcome **Handicap Access:** No

Marina Services and Boat Supplies
Services - Docking Assistance, Trash Pick-Up, Dock Carts
Communication - FedEx, AirBorne, UPS, Express Mail **Supplies -**
OnSite: Ice *(Cube)*, Ships' Store, Bait/Tackle *(or Freds 721-4747 - 1 mi.)*,
Live Bait *(Clams, squid, etc.)* **Under 1 mi:** West Marine *(525-2221)*
1-3 mi: Propane *(Industrial Welding - 721-1150)*

Boatyard Services
OnSite: Travelift *(25T)*, Hull Repairs, Bottom Cleaning, Brightwork,
Compound, Wash & Wax, Interior Cleaning **OnCall:** Air Conditioning,
Propeller Repairs **Under 1 mi:** Canvas Work. **1-3 mi:** Launching Ramp.
Dealer for: Mercruiser. **Yard Rates:** $82.50, Haul & Launch $6 *(blocking
$10)*, Power Wash Incl., Bottom Paint $12 *(paint incl.)* **Storage:** In-Water
Inq., On-Land Inq.

Restaurants and Accommodations
OnCall: Pizzeria *(Santino's 721-3163)* **Under 1 mi:** Restaurant *(China
Royal 290-7700, take out)*, Coffee Shop *(Dunkin Donuts)*, *(Reddy's 316-
5520)*, Lite Fare *(Pepperheads Pub)*, *(Harborside Pub)*, *(Stewarts 721-8914)*,
Pizzeria *(Lisa's 290-1313)*, Motel *(Gallery 727-2134)* **1-3 mi:** Restaurant
(Martini's Romantic Italian restaurant 727-9486) **3+ mi:** Motel *(Hampton Inn
855-6900, 4 mi.)*

Recreation and Entertainment
OnSite: Fishing Charter *(Misbehavin - 1-6 passengers - Capt. Dave Janas -
251-8793; Fishing Frenzy - 1-6 Passengers - Capt. Chris Munn - 642-7796)*
Near: Beach *(Morgan Beach, Old Harbor Waterfront Park)*, Picnic Area,
Playground, Jogging Paths, Park **1-3 mi:** Fitness Center *(Synergy
553-0500)*, Movie Theater *(Amboy Multiplkex 721-3400)*, Video Rental
(Blockbuster 727-2600), Museum *(Kearny Cottage 826-1826)*
3+ mi: Golf Course *(Glenwood C.C. 607-2582, 5 mi.)*

Provisioning and General Services
Near: Protestant Church, Library *(Old Bridge 566-2227)*
Under 1 mi: Delicatessen *(Morgan Bridge 721-2606)*, Bakery *(Dunkin'
Donuts)*, Bank/ATM *(Amboy Nat. Bank)*, Post Office, Catholic Church, Dry
Cleaners *(Sayreville Cleaners/Laundry 727-3455)*, Laundry, Pharmacy
(United 566-3304), Newsstand **1-3 mi:** Convenience Store *(Reddy's 316-
5520)*, Market *(Baranowski's 721-0650)*, Supermarket *(Foodtown 721-0276)*,
Wine/Beer *(Sayreville Plaza 7231-8800)*, Liquor Store *(Morgan 721-4631)*,
Beauty Salon *(Head Hunter 727-1100)*, Barber Shop, Department Store
(Wal-Marts 525-8685)

Transportation
OnCall: Rental Car *(Enterprise 888-7990; Econo Rental 271-6300 - .7 mi.)*,
Taxi *(South Amboy-Old Bridge 727-5569)*, Airport Limo *(Academy 727-
7575)* **Near:** InterCity Bus *(NJ Transit to NYC)* **1-3 mi:** Water Taxi *(Auto
Team 727-7272; Rent-A-Wreck 525-0505)*
Airport: Old Bridge/Newark *(7 mi./18 mi.)*

Medical Services
911 Service **OnCall:** Holistic Services *(OnSite Massage Therapy 316-0249)*,
Ambulance **Near:** Dentist *(Crain & Klemons 727-5000)*
Under 1 mi: Doctor *(Quano 727-7470)*, Chiropractor *(AC Center 727-3335)*
1-3 mi: Veterinarian *(Chiosi 727-1303)*, Optician *(Old Bridge 727-1811)*
Hospital: South Amboy Memorial 721-1000 *(2.5 mi.)*

Setting -- Just beyond the Route 35 drawbridge at the entrance to Morgan Creek (called Cheesequake Creek on the charts) is this rustic, service-oriented, friendly sport fishing marina. The docks are in two groups - the first set are stern-to along a single bulkhead, the second set, with the larger sport fish boats, line a series of piers that jut out from the dry storage land base.

Marina Notes -- Marina services all fishing needs with a tackle shop and an extensive live bait stock (call in advance and they will get you anything you want). *Ask about discount packages. Family owned and operated by the Johnsons since the 50s. Heads are remarkably nice - full tile baths with brick floors. Quite a current in the creek but less in the marina. Two fishing charters onsite: Capt. Dave James' Misbehavin (251-8793) and Capt. Chris Munn's Fishing Frenzy (642 7796). Zuback's across the creek often has a transient slip available.

Notable -- Directly across Route 35 is the Old Harbor Waterfront Park - a newly developed beach with services. Three quarters of a mile east is the little burg of Laurence Harbor with basic supplies - liquor store, deli, Dunkin Donuts, post office, pharmacy, bank satellite and a Chinese take-out. An interesting diversion might be to dinghy further up Morgan (Cheesequake) Creek to the Cheesequake State Park. Reportedly excellent crabbing in the Creek but watch the green flies (take lot of Cutters and don't wear perfume). About three miles west is a good size shopping center with a Home Depot, Wal-Mart, Radio Shack, Marshalls, Modells GNC, R&S Auto, fast food and a Pathmark. Worth a cab if you need supplies.

Navigational Information
Lat: 40°27.670' Long: 074°15.600' Tide: 6 Current: n/a Chart: 12327
Rep. Depths (*MLW*): Entry 6 ft. Fuel Dock 10 ft. Max Slip/Moor 10 ft./-
Access: G17 to marker #2 at canal entrance, past Rte 35 bridge

Marina Facilities (*In Season/Off Season*)
Fuel: Gasoline, Diesel
Slips: 178 Total, 5 Transient Max LOA: 60 ft. Max Beam: 16 ft.
  Rate (*per ft.*): Day $2.00 Week n/a Month n/a
Power: 30 amp Incl, 50 amp n/a, 100 amp n/a, 200 amp n/a
Cable TV: No Dockside Phone: No
Dock Type: n/a
Moorings: 0 Total, 0 Transient Launch: n/a
  Rate: Day n/a Week n/a Month n/a
Heads: 8 Toilet(s), 4 Shower(s) (*with dressing rooms*)
Laundry: 1 Washer(s), 1 Dryer(s) Pay Phones: Yes, 1
Pump-Out: OnSite, Self Service Fee: $5.00 Closed Heads: Yes

Marina Operations
Owner/Manager: The Lockwood Family Dockmaster: n/a
In-Season: Year Round, 8am-5pm Off-Season: Mon-Sat, 8am - 5pm
After-Hours Arrival: Tie up at service dock
Reservations: Required Credit Cards: Visa/MC, Dscvr, Amex
Discounts: None
Pets: Welcome Handicap Access: No

Lockwood Boat Works

1825 Highway 35; South Amboy, NJ 08879

Tel: (732) 721-1605 VHF: Monitor 72 Talk 72
Fax: (732) 525-8209 Alternate Tel: n/a
Email: mail@lockwoodboatworks.com Web: www.lockwoodboatworks.com
Nearest Town: South Amboy (*0.5 mi.*) Tourist Info: (732) 442-7400

Marina Services and Boat Supplies
Services - Dock Carts Communication - FedEx, AirBorne, UPS, Express Mail Supplies - OnSite: Ice (*Block, Cube, Shaved*), Ships' Store (*Lockwood Boat Works*), CNG Under 1 mi: West Marine (*525-2221*), Bait/Tackle (*Fred's Bait & Tackle 721-4747*) 3+ mi: Propane (*Suburban Propane 566-6200, 6 mi.*)

Boatyard Services
OnSite: Travelift (*2- 35T*), Engine mechanic (*gas, diesel*), Electrical Repairs, Electronic Sales, Hull Repairs, Rigger, Bottom Cleaning, Brightwork, Compound, Wash & Wax, Interior Cleaning, Woodworking, Metal Fabrication, Painting, Awlgrip, Total Refits OnCall: Canvas Work, Air Conditioning, Refrigeration, Divers, Propeller Repairs, Inflatable Repairs, Life Raft Service Under 1 mi: Launching Ramp. Dealer for: Mercruiser, Universal, Yanmar, Kohler, Volvo, Velvet Drives, Westerbeke.
Member: ABBRA, ABYC Yard Rates: $75/hr., Haul & Launch $11/ft., Power Wash $2.50/ft.

Restaurants and Accommodations
OnCall: Pizzeria (*Santino's 721-3163*) Near: Fast Food (*Stewarts 721-8914*), Lite Fare (*Reddy's Convenience Store, Deli & Coffee Shop*), (*SubMarina*), Hotel (*Sayreville Motor Lodge 721-0476*) Under 1 mi: Restaurant (*Martini's A Romantic Italian Restaurant 727-9466*), Pizzeria (*Lisa Restaurant & Pizza 290-1313*) 1-3 mi: Coffee Shop (*Dunkin Donuts*), Fast Food, Motel (*Welleslay 888-2800*) 3+ mi: Motel (*Hampton Inn 4 mi.*)

Recreation and Entertainment
OnSite: Picnic Area Near: Beach (*Old Harbor Waterfront*)

1-3 mi: Fitness Center (*Synergy Fitness Club 553-0500*), Video Rental (*Blockbuster 727-2600*), Park 3+ mi: Golf Course (*Monmouth County Golf Center 536-7272, 11.5 mi.*), Bowling (*Woodbridge Bowling 634-4520, 7.5 mi.*), Movie Theater (*Amboy Multiplex Cinemas 721-3400, 5.5 mi.*), Museum (*Kearny Cottage Museum 826-1826, 6mi.*)

Provisioning and General Services
Near: Convenience Store (*Reddy's 316-5520*), Delicatessen (*Budge's Deli 727-3222*), Fishmonger Under 1 mi: Liquor Store (*Buy Rite Liquors Old Bridge 727-3537*), Meat Market, Library (*Sadie Pope Dowdell Library 721-6060*), Pharmacy (*CVS 607-2940*) 1-3 mi: Market (*Krauszer's 525-9228*), Supermarket (*Pathmark*), Health Food (*International Health Food 721-0301*), Bank/ATM, Post Office, Catholic Church, Beauty Salon, Barber Shop, Dry Cleaners, Laundry, Newsstand, Hardware Store (*Home Depot 727-1417*), Florist, Clothing Store, Retail Shops (*Modell's, Marshall's*), Department Store (*Wal-Mart*), Copies Etc. (*Copyshop Office Supply 721-5700*)

Transportation
OnCall: Rental Car (*Enterprise 888-7990*), Taxi (*South Amboy-Old Bridge 727-5569; ABC 721-8101*) 1-3 mi: Airport Limo (*Altima Limo Plus 727-9690; ABC Limo 721-8101*) Airport: Old Bridge/Newark Int'l (*7.5 mi./18 mi.*)

Medical Services
911 Service Under 1 mi: Doctor (*Ramchandani 525-0600*), Dentist (*Sohoni 553-1313*) 1-3 mi: Chiropractor (*A C Chiro Center 727-3335*), Holistic Services (*On-Site Massage 316-0249*), Veterinarian (*Sayrebrook 727-1303*)
Hospital: Memorial Medical Center at South Amboy 721-1000 (*2 mi.*)

Setting -- A channel, lined with docks, leads off the Cheesequake Canal through stretches of untouched marsh into a rectangular basin. There are three sets of docks in the channel, the first, for smaller power boats, has finger piers and older pedestals, the second, for medium size powerboats, has stern-to slips with pilings, and new pedestals, and the third set, for larger sport fish boats, also has stern-to slips with pilings and new pedestals. A left turn into the basin reveals two sets of docks, with finger piers, which hosts sailboats. Landside is a 37-acre, full-service professional boatyard operation with extensive services.

Marina Notes -- Owned & operated by the Lockwood Family. Founded in 1946 by boat builder Bill Lockwood Sr. Large work sheds, covered rigging and mast storage. Area's only custom stainless steel and aluminum fabricator. Environmentally-safe awlgrip spray-booth. Sailboat and sport fish specialists. The yard office, with attractive steps and small patio, shares a buiilding with older, but well-maintained heads and showers (nice wooden flooring grates and dressing areas). Washer and dryer are outside. A small island of grass at the yard's entrance hosts a picnic table.

Notable -- A short walk up the hill, on busy Route 35, is the main office and the large Lockwood Marine Supply - an extraordinarily well-equipped chandlery with aisles and aisles of ships' store and marine inventory. Down the street is a West Marine. Across Route 35 are three casual eateries and a convenience store - there's a tall cement divider so it's necessary to walk a block either way to cross over. There is little else within walking distance. A cab to the train gets you to New York City in 45 minutes.

Navigational Information
Lat: 40°27.314' **Long:** 074°16.339' **Tide:** 8 ft. **Current:** 3 kt. **Chart:** 12327
Rep. Depths (MLW): Entry 8 ft. **Fuel Dock** 10 ft. **Max Slip/Moor** 8 ft./8 ft.
Access: Raritan Bay G17 to Cheesequake Creek

Marina Facilities (In Season/Off Season)
Fuel: Gasoline
Slips: 270 Total, 10 Transient **Max LOA:** 45 ft. **Max Beam:** 14 ft.
  Rate (per ft.): **Day** $1.50 **Week** n/a **Month** n/a
  Power: 30 amp Incl., **50 amp** n/a, **100 amp** n/a, **200 amp** n/a
  Cable TV: No **Dockside Phone:** No
  Dock Type: Floating, Wood
Moorings: 27 Total, 2 Transient **Launch:** n/a, Dinghy Dock
  Rate: Day $20 **Week** n/a **Month** n/a
Heads: 2 Toilet(s), 2 Shower(s) (with dressing rooms)
Laundry: Yes **Pay Phones:** Yes, 1
Pump-Out: OnCall **Fee:** $15 **Closed Heads:** Yes

Marina Operations
Owner/Manager: Peter M. Schultz Sr. **Dockmaster:** same
In-Season: Mar-MidDec, 8am-5pm **Off-Season:** MidDec-Feb, 9am-5pm
After-Hours Arrival: Stay on the gas dock until morning
Reservations: Preferred **Credit Cards:** Visa/MC, Dscvr, Amex
Discounts: None
Pets: Welcome, Dog Walk Area **Handicap Access:** No

Morgan Marina

8000 Gondeck Drive; Parlin, NJ 08859

Tel: (732) 727-2289 **VHF: Monitor** n/a **Talk** n/a
Fax: (732) 316-1950 **Alternate Tel:** n/a
Email: n/a **Web:** www.morganmarina.com
Nearest Town: Sayreville (2 mi.) **Tourist Info:** (732) 442-7400

Marina Services and Boat Supplies
Services - Docking Assistance, Trash Pick-Up **Communication -** Mail &
Package Hold, Phone Messages, Fax in/out, FedEx, UPS **Supplies -**
OnSite: Ice (Cube), Ships' Store, Bait/Tackle (Frozen)
Under 1 mi: West Marine (525-2221), Propane, CNG

Boatyard Services
OnSite: Travelift (2 - 35T), Crane (35T), Hydraulic Trailer (Up to 34'), Engine
mechanic (gas, diesel), Electrical Repairs, Electronic Sales, Electronics
Repairs, Hull Repairs, Rigger, Canvas Work, Bottom Cleaning, Brightwork,
Air Conditioning, Compound, Wash & Wax, Interior Cleaning, Woodworking,
Upholstery, Yacht Interiors, Metal Fabrication, Painting, Yacht Broker
(Morgan), Total Refits **OnCall:** Sail Loft (Eggers), Refrigeration, Propeller
Repairs **Near:** Launching Ramp. **Dealer for:** Interlux, Petitt, West System,
Volvo, Evinrude & Johnson, MerCruisers, OMC. **Member:** ABYC, Other
Certifications: NJ Marine Trades Assoc., MOAA **Yard Rates:** $25-75, Haul
& Launch $8/ft. (blocking $2/ft.), Power Wash $2/ft., Bottom Paint $12/ft.
(paint incl.) **Storage:** In-Water $22/ft., On-Land $18-29/ft. incl. haul,
power wash and launch

Restaurants and Accommodations
OnCall: Pizzeria (Santinos Restaurant & Pizza 721-3163) **1-3 mi:**
Restaurant (RajPoot India 525-2055), (Hong Kong House 525-2929),
(Chingari Indian 316-5599), (Szechuan Garden 727-6620), (Martini's
Romantic Italian 727-9486), Fast Food (Wendy's), (Stewarts), Lite Fare
(Parlin Bagels & More) **3+ mi:** Motel (Hampton Inn 855-6900, 4 mi.)

Recreation and Entertainment
OnSite: Picnic Area, Grills, Fishing Charter **OnCall:** Boat Rentals (Sailing
Charters in the fall.), Group Fishing Boat (Misty Morn) **Near:** Jogging
Paths **Under 1 mi:** Beach, Park **1-3 mi:** Movie Theater (Amboy Multiplex
721-3400), Video Rental (Blockbuster 727-2600) **3+ mi:** Golf Course
(Monmouth CountyG.C. 536-7272, 13 mi.)

Provisioning and General Services
Near: Bank/ATM **Under 1 mi:** Fishmonger **1-3 mi:** Convenience Store
(Quick-Chek; Reddy's), Market (Patel Food Market 721-7122), Supermarket
(Pathmark 721-8822), Wine/Beer, Liquor Store (Express LIquor 525-9463),
Bakery (Bagels & More 721-5454), Green Grocer, Meat Market, Post Office,
Catholic Church, Protestant Church, Synagogue, Library (Sadie Pope
Dowdell 721-6060), Beauty Salon, Barber Shop, Dry Cleaners, Laundry,
Pharmacy (CVS 607-2940), Newsstand, Hardware Store (Home Depot 727-
1417), Department Store (Walmart)

Transportation
OnCall: Taxi (So. Amboy Taxi 732-727-5569), Airport Limo (Altima Limo
Plus 727-9690; ABC Limo 721-8101) **1-3 mi:** InterCity Bus (New Jersey
Transit to NYC 973-762-5100), Rail (NJ Transit to NYC)
Airport: Old Bridge/Newark Int'l (7 mi./18 mi.)

Medical Services
911 Service **OnCall:** Ambulance (EMT) **1-3 mi:** Doctor (Remchandani
525-0600), Dentist (Sohoni 553-1313), Chiropractor (AC Chiro 727-3335),
Holistic Services (OnSite Massage 318-0249)
Hospital: Memorial Medical Center 721-1000 (4 mi.)

Setting -- Up quiet Cheesequake Creek, almost to the Garden State Parkway overpass, this large boatyard and well protected marina is surrounded by the
  pristine marsh of Cheesequake State Park. A long row of docks, mostly stern-to with pilings, line the basin. Views are of the marsh on one side and a boatyard,
  with all its detritus, on the other. A small pavilion with 2 picnic tables overlooks the most northern set of docks.

Marina Notes -- A friendly, family owned and operated marina for over 40 years. Home to some good sized vessels - both in the water and on the hard --
  including many sailboats and sport fishing boats. Good winter storage rates and facilities for do it yourselfers. Basic heads, no showers. Small well-supplied
  ship's store. Maiing address: P.O. Box 235; South Amboy, N.J. 08879

Notable -- A great spot for bird watching and crabbing - bait and crab traps are available at the chandlery. There are no services nearby, so bait a trap or drop
  a chicken neck and catch a dozen blue crabs for dinner. To get to the main road, it's about mile walk on Gondek Drive through Spinnaker Point (a new adult
  community) and the Harbor Club (a townhouse complex). Once on the main road (Lorraine Avenue), it's 3/4 mile north to Route 35 with Lockwood Marine
  Store, a West Marine and a handful of very casual eateries. Alternatively, a mile south, there are two small strip malls containing a half dozen restaurants, a
  number of useful services, and a mid-size market - many focusing on Asian and Indian cuisine. The entrance to the Garden State Parkway is less than half a
  mile.

Navigational Information
Lat: 40°26.499' **Long:** 076°08.433' **Tide:** 6 ft. **Current:** 3 kt. **Chart:** 12327
Rep. Depths *(MLW)*: **Entry** 11 ft. **Fuel Dock** n/a **Max Slip/Moor** 7 ft./-
Access: Lower New York Bay to Raritan Bay to Thorns Creek

Marina Facilities *(In Season/Off Season)*
Fuel: No
Slips: 115 Total, 5 Transient **Max LOA:** 42 ft. **Max Beam:** 14 ft.
 Rate *(per ft.)*: **Day** $1.25 **Week** n/a **Month** n/a
 Power: 30 amp Incl., 50 amp n/a, 100 amp n/a, 200 amp n/a
 Cable TV: No **Dockside Phone:** No
 Dock Type: Floating, Long Fingers, Wood
Moorings: 0 Total, 0 Transient **Launch:** n/a
 Rate: Day n/a **Week** n/a **Month** n/a
Heads: 2 Toilet(s), 3 Shower(s) *(with dressing rooms)*
Laundry: 1 Washer(s), 1 Dryer(s) **Pay Phones:** Yes
Pump-Out: OnSite **Fee:** $10 **Closed Heads:** Yes

Marina Operations
Owner/Manager: The Lentze Family **Dockmaster:** Patty Lentze
In-Season: May-Nov, 8am-5pm **Off-Season:** Nov-Apr, 9am-5pm
After-Hours Arrival: Call in advance
Reservations: Required **Credit Cards:** Visa/MC
Discounts: None
Pets: Welcome **Handicap Access:** No

Lentze's Marina

75 1st St.; West Keansburg, NJ 07734

Tel: (732) 787-2139 **VHF: Monitor** 16 **Talk** 78
Fax: (732) 495-2921 **Alternate Tel:** n/a
Email: n/a **Web:** n/a
Nearest Town: Hazlet **Tourist Info:** (732) 264-3626

Marina Services and Boat Supplies
Services - Docking Assistance, Trash Pick-Up, Dock Carts
Communication - FedEx, AirBorne, UPS, Express Mail **Supplies - OnSite:**
Ice *(Cube)*, Ships' Store, Bait/Tackle **1-3 mi:** Boat/US *(739-8890)*, Propane
(Heritage 787-0633), CNG **3+ mi:** West Marine *(872-8100, 5.5 mi.)*

Boatyard Services
OnSite: Travelift *(12.5T closed-end)*, Forklift, Crane, Engine mechanic *(gas, diesel)*, Electrical Repairs, Electronic Sales, Hull Repairs, Rigger, Bottom Cleaning, Brightwork, Air Conditioning, Compound, Wash & Wax, Interior Cleaning, Woodworking, Painting **OnCall:** Sail Loft, Canvas Work, Divers, Propeller Repairs, Inflatable Repairs, Upholstery, Metal Fabrication
Under 1 mi: Launching Ramp. **Dealer for:** Mercruiser. **Member:** ABBRA, ABYC, Other Certifications: Mercury Mercruiser OMC

Restaurants and Accommodations
OnCall: Pizzeria *(Domino's 495-5200)* **Near:** Restaurant *(Captain's Cove Family Restaurant 495-0101)* **Under 1 mi:** Restaurant *(Happy Family Chinese Restaurant 471-8887)*, Seafood Shack *(Shore Point Fishery 495-5925)*, Fast Food *(Stewart's 495-5969)*, Pizzeria *(Dolce 471-9004)* **1-3 mi:** Motel *(Days Inn Woodbridge 634-3200)*, *(Howard Johnson 671-3400)*

Recreation and Entertainment
OnSite: Picnic Area, Boat Rentals **Near:** Beach, Playground, Jogging Paths, Roller Blade/Bike Paths, Video Arcade, Park *(Keansburg Amusement Park 495-1400)* **Under 1 mi:** Pool *(Runaway Rapids Waterpark 495-1400)*, Video Rental *(Blockbuster 264-9255)* **1-3 mi:** Dive Shop, Fitness Center *(Study Hall 495-9590)*, Horseback Riding, Fishing Charter, Movie Theater

(Hazlet Multiplex 264-2200), Cultural Attract *(PNC Banks Arts Center 335-0400)*, Sightseeing *(Viet Nam Veterans Memorial 335-0033)* **3+ mi:** Golf Course *(Cruz Golf Club 938-3378, 6.5 mi.)*, Bowling *(Middletown Harmony 671-2100, 3.5 mi.)*, Museum *(Keyport Hist. Soc's Steamboat Dock Museum 739-6390, 3.5 mi.)*

Provisioning and General Services
OnSite: Convenience Store **Near:** Delicatessen *(Big Belli Deli 787-6311, Dena's 495-3708)*, Farmers' Market **Under 1 mi:** Market *(Laurel Market 495 1665)*, Supermarket *(A&P)*, Gourmet Shop *(Dearborn Farms 264-0256)*, Wine/Beer *(Smith's 264-4470)*, Liquor Store *(Sheehan's 787-0063)*, Bakery, Meat Market, Bank/ATM, Post Office, Catholic Church, Beauty Salon, Barber Shop, Dry Cleaners, Laundry, Pharmacy *(Rite Aid 471-9044; Eckerd Store 495-0156)*, Newsstand, Hardware Store *(AGIS Enterprises 787-1191)*, Florist, Clothing Store, Retail Shops, Department Store *(Kohl's)*, Copies Etc. *(Staples 671-1100)* **1-3 mi:** Fishmonger, Lobster Pound, Protestant Church, Synagogue, Buying Club *(CostCo)*

Transportation
OnCall: Rental Car *(Enterprise 471-8880)*, Taxi *(Goodfellow's 787-8877)*, Airport Limo *(New Concepts 787-3013)*
Airport: Newark Int'l/Old Bridge *(26mi./16.5 mi.)*

Medical Services
911 Service **OnCall:** Ambulance **Under 1 mi:** Doctor **1-3 mi:** Dentist, Chiropractor, Veterinarian *(Community 739-2111)* **3+ mi:** Holistic Services *(Intouch Massages 671-4430, 5 mi.)*
Hospital: Bayshore Community 739-0084 *3.5 mi.*

Setting -- Just after entering Thorns Creek (off Raritan Bay), Lentze's is visible at the mouth of a basin just off to the left. This small, rustic boatyard with slips provides a protected harbor surrounded by a combination of marshland and small houses.

Marina Notes -- 12.5T closed end travelift - max 35-40 foot boats. Cinder block heads with a separate coin-operated shower. Floating wood docks. Safe Harbour provides mechanical and lifting services. Forklift Dry Rack Service for 170 vessels on Single Tier Racks. Family owned and operated for 31 years. Closed Friday through Monday off-season.

Notable -- Three quarters of a mile away is the retro Keansburg Amusement Park with arcades, carousel, roller coaster, a wide assortment of rides, and the usual funky beach shops and eateries. Just 100 years old, this bit of Jersey Shore nostalgia is being reclaimed by the founder's grandsons who have added some high tech rides along with safety features - while preserving the old time ambiance. (Opens at 10am Mid-June through August and at noon April through Mid-June and September.) Rates vary - $13-20/day for all rides or various coupons book options. A separate Go-Cart Track has adult and kids tracks, $7/3. Adjacent Runaway Rapids Water Park is a contemporary tropically landscaped combination of high speed slides and lazy river floats (June-early September, opens 10am), $7-19, lockers $3. Combination Tickets $28-30. Check www.keansburgamusementpark.com for specials and times. A wide, well maintained yellow-sand beach is adjacent to the amusement strip.

Navigational Information
Lat: 40°26.360' **Long:** 074°06.260' **Tide:** 6 ft. **Current:** n/a **Chart:** 12327
Rep. Depths (MLW): Entry 3 ft. **Fuel Dock** n/a **Max Slip/Moor** 4 ft./-
Access: Steer 250 degrees from the U.S. Naval Earle Pier

Marina Facilities *(In Season/Off Season)*
Fuel: Gasoline, High-Speed Pumps
Slips: 153 Total, 5 Transient **Max LOA:** 40 ft. **Max Beam:** 13 ft.
  Rate *(per ft.)*: **Day** $1.25 **Week** Inq. **Month** n/a
  Power: 30 amp Incl., **50 amp** n/a, **100 amp** n/a, **200 amp** n/a
  Cable TV: No **Dockside Phone:** No
  Dock Type: Floating, Concrete
Moorings: 0 Total, 0 Transient **Launch:** n/a
  Rate: Day n/a **Week** n/a **Month** n/a
Heads: 3 Toilet(s), 2 Shower(s)
Laundry: None **Pay Phones:** No
Pump-Out: OnSite **Fee:** Free **Closed Heads:** Yes

Marina Operations
Owner/Manager: Terry Normand **Dockmaster:** n/a
In-Season: May-Oct 30, 8am-4pm **Off-Season:** Nov 1-Apr 30, 8am-4:30pm
After-Hours Arrival: Cll in advance to arrange
Reservations: No **Credit Cards:** Cash/Local Checks
Discounts: None
Pets: Welcome **Handicap Access:** Yes, Heads, Docks

Monmouth Cove Marina

200 Port Monmouth Road; Port Monmouth, NJ 07758

Tel: (732) 495-9440 **VHF: Monitor** n/a **Talk** n/a
Fax: (732) 495-9570 **Alternate Tel:** (732) 842-4000
Email: info@monmouthcountyparks.com **Web:** monmouthcountyparks.com
Nearest Town: Middeltown *(3 mi.)* **Tourist Info:** (732) 291-7870

Marina Services and Boat Supplies
Services - Docking Assistance, Dock Carts **Supplies - OnSite:** Ice *(Cube)* **Under 1 mi:** Bait/Tackle *(T & A Tackle 787-3853)* **1-3 mi:** Ice *(Block, Shaved)*, Live Bait, Propane *(Shoreway Services 787-0633)*, CNG **3+ mi:** West Marine *(872-8100, 5 mi.)*, Boat/US *(739-8890, 4 mi.)*

Boatyard Services
OnSite: Travelift *(5T Acme Marina Hoist)*, Forklift *(15T)*, Bottom Cleaning
OnCall: Sail Loft, Air Conditioning, Divers, Compound, Wash & Wax, Interior Cleaning, Woodworking, Life Raft Service, Upholstery, Metal Fabrication, Yacht Broker **3+ mi:** Propeller Repairs *(10 mi.)*.
Yard Rates: $60/hr., Haul & Launch $5/ft.*

Restaurants and Accommodations
Under 1 mi: Restaurant *(Pirates Cove 787-6581)*, Pizzeria *(Domino's 495-5200)* **1-3 mi:** Restaurant *(Jade Garden Chinese 495-0095)*, *(Happy Garden 495-3388)*, Seafood Shack *(Navesink Fishery 291-8017)*, Motel *(Holly Hill 787-6776)*, Hotel *(Cappuccio's 787-4333)* **3+ mi:** Fast Food *(Wendy's 4 mi.)*.

Recreation and Entertainment
OnSite: Beach *(Bayshore Waterfront Park 842-4000)*, Picnic Area, Grills
Near: Park *(Bayshore Waterfront Park 842-4000)* **Under 1 mi:** Playground **1-3 mi:** Dive Shop, Tennis Courts, Fitness Center *(Gold's Gym 671-4800)*, Boat Rentals, Roller Blade/Bike Paths, Fishing Charter, Group Fishing Boat, Video Rental, Video Arcade **3+ mi:** Golf Course *(Cruz Golf Club 938-3378, 7.5 mi.)*, Bowling *(Middletown Harmony Bowl 671-2100, 4 mi.)*, Museum *(Keyport Steamboat Dock Museum 739-6390, 5 mi.)*

Provisioning and General Services
Near: Delicatessen *(Charlie's 495-1180)* **Under 1 mi:** Fishmonger *(Belford Seafood 787-6508)*, Lobster Pound *(Shoal Harbor)* **1-3 mi:** Convenience Store *(Round the Clock 495-1108)*, Supermarket *(Foodtown)*, Wine/Beer *(Wine Sellers of Holmdel 706-9463)*, Liquor Store *(Lunney's 787-0135)*, Bakery, Green Grocer, Meat Market, Bank/ATM, Post Office, Catholic Church, Protestant Church, Library *(Middletown 787-1568)*, Beauty Salon, Barber Shop, Dry Cleaners, Laundry, Pharmacy *(Keansburg 787-1414)*, Newsstand, Hardware Store *(Township 787-4060)*, Florist, Clothing Store, Retail Shops, Department Store *(Eckerd Store 495-0156)*, Copies Etc. *(Mr Jiffy 787-2222)* **3+ mi:** Health Food *(Nu Generation 615-9300, 4.5 mi.)*, Bookstore *(Barnes & Noble 615-3933, 3.5 mi.)*, Buying Club *(Costco, 5 mi.)*

Transportation
OnCall: Taxi *(Tri State Car Service 495-0517)*, Airport Limo *(McKee 787-5827)* **Under 1 mi:** Local Bus *(Weekdays Only)*, Ferry Service *(NY Waterways Ferry about every half hour during rush hour to Manhattan's Pier 11 $15 one-way, or West 38th St.- connecting service to Hoboken, Jersey City, Brooklyn & Queens $15-16)*
Airport: Newark/Old Bridge 446-4189 *(40 mi./18mi.)*

Medical Services
911 Service OnCall: Ambulance **Under 1 mi:** Dentist *(Dental Care Center 495-8600)*, Chiropractor *(Chiro Specific 787-1450)* **1-3 mi:** Doctor *(Family Practice of Middletown 671-0860)*, Veterinarian *(Bayshore)* **3+ mi:** Holistic Services *(Shore Hands 495-1224, 4.5 mi.)*
Hospital: Bayshore Community 739-5912 *(6 mi.)*

Setting -- Just off Raritan Bay, this tidy county marina is snuggled into a tight basin, its entrance protected by stone jetties. Surrounding it are saltwater wetlands, the Bayshore Waterfront Park, and a suburban residential neighborhood. The mostly stern-to docks are strung in two rows around two sides of a large dry stack storage area and parking lot. A large blue and white work shed dominates the facility.

Marina Notes -- The Monmouth Cove Marina was purchased by Monmouth County in 1990. No bridge restrictions to bay or ocean. While the marina can accommodate up to 40 feet, there is limited turning room in the basin. Very nice floating concrete docks. 50-boat rack storage operation. Winter storage available. A small picnic pavilion, with awning, overlooks the docks. The stone jetties doubles as a fishing pier. Heads are a little better than municipal. *Haul & Launch rates: Forklift $100 one-way. Travelift $5/ft. one-way.

Notable -- On the far side of the parking lot is a beach - adjacent to the entry jetties -- and it continues down the block as part of the 145 acre Bayshore Waterfront Park and Shoal Harbor Homestead. A few blocks away (Wilson & Rt. 36) is access to the Henry Hudson Trail - Aberdeen to Atlantic Highlands - 10 mi. of paved trail along a former railroad right-of-way for use by walkers, bikers, in-line skaters, and equestrians. Belford Seafood Co-op (and its sister restaurant) is less than a mile walk - the co-op is reportedly a provisioning must. Also in Belford is the high-speed catamaran ferry - 40 min. to NYC's Pier 11 at Wall Street (near South Street Seaport) or 55 min. to West 38th Street in Midtown (sometimes requires a boat change) - 20 departures weekdays, 8 weekends.

Navigational Information
Lat: 40°24.956' **Long:** 074°01.924' **Tide:** 6 ft. **Current:** 2 kt. **Chart:** 12327
Rep. Depths (*MLW*): **Entry** 9 ft. **Fuel Dock** 8 ft. **Max Slip/Moor** 9 ft./9 ft.
Access: Raritan Bay, 3 miles south of Sandy Hook to Sandy Hook Bay

Marina Facilities (*In Season/Off Season*)
Fuel: *Gulf* - Gasoline, Diesel
Slips: 480 Total, 12 Transient **Max LOA:** 140 ft. **Max Beam:** 40 ft.
  Rate (*per ft.*): **Day** $2.00/Inq. **Week** n/a **Month** n/a
  Power: 30 amp Incl., **50 amp** $10/5, **100 amp** $25, **200 amp** n/a
  Cable TV: No **Dockside Phone:** No
  Dock Type: Fixed, Floating
Moorings: 50 Total, 6 Transient **Launch:** Yes (Incl.), Dinghy Dock ($12/nt.)
  Rate: Day $25** **Week** n/a **Month** n/a
Heads: 22 Toilet(s), 10 Shower(s)
Laundry: None, Book Exchange **Pay Phones:** Yes
Pump-Out: OnSite **Fee:** $5 **Closed Heads:** Yes

Marina Operations
Owner/Manager: Carol Cassese **Dockmaster:** Bill Bate
In-Season: Year-Round, 8:30am-4:30pm **Off-Season:** n/a
After-Hours Arrival: Call ahead
Reservations: Yes, Preferred **Credit Cards:** Visa/MC, Dscvr, Amex
Discounts: over 200gl. **Dockage:** n/a **Fuel:** $.05 **Repair:** n/a
Pets: Welcome, Dog Walk Area **Handicap Access:** Yes, Heads, Docks

Atlantic Highlands Marina

2 Simon Lake Drive; Atlantic Highlands, NJ 07716

Tel: (732) 291-1670 **VHF: Monitor** 9 **Talk** 9
Fax: (732) 291-9657 **Alternate Tel:** n/a
Email: n/a **Web:** n/a
Nearest Town: Atlantic Highlands (*0 mi.*) **Tourist Info:** (732) 872-8711

Marina Services and Boat Supplies
Services - Security (*24 Hrs., Live Person*), Trash Pick-Up, Dock Carts, Megayacht Facilities, 3 Phase **Communication** - Mail & Package Hold, Phone Messages, Fax in/out ($5), Data Ports (*Office*), FedEx, UPS, Express Mail (*Sat Del*) **Supplies** - OnSite: Ice (*Block*), Bait/Tackle (*Atlantic Highlands 291-4500, ice cream too*), Live Bait **Near:** Ships' Store (*Skippers' Shop 872-2600*), Propane (*Jasper 291-1500, Fitzgerald's 291-1883*) **1-3 mi:** West Marine (*872-8100*)

Boatyard Services
OnSite: Travelift (*50T*), Launching Ramp **Yard Rates:** Haul & Launch $8/ft., Power Wash $1.50/ft. **Storage:** In-Water $32/ft., On-Land $850

Restaurants and Accommodations
OnSite: Snack Bar (*Dot & Dan Hot Dog Stand*) **Near:** Restaurant (*Town Cafe*), (*Orleans 872-2400*), (*Memphis Pig Out*) **Under 1 mi:** Restaurant (*Davinci Pizzeria & Restaurant 291-8385*), Fast Food (*Burger King*), Pizzeria (*Frederico's 291-0300*) **1-3 mi:** Restaurant (*Doris & Ed's 872-1565, D $21-30, Kid's $10+ Gourmet's top NJ choices*), (*Harborside Grill 291-0066*), Hotel (*Conners 872-1500, $42-77*) **3+ mi:** Inn/B&B (*Seascape Manor 291-8467, $90-160, 4 mi.*)

Recreation and Entertainment
OnSite: Playground, Fishing Charter, Group Fishing Boat, Cultural Attract (*Band Concerts, Sun Jul-Aug, First Avenue Playhouse 291-7552 nearby - dessert & dinner theater*) **Near:** Jogging Paths, Boat Rentals, Roller Blade/Bike Paths, Movie Theater (*Atlantic Cinema 5*), Galleries (*Atlantic Artisans 291-0100*) **Under 1 mi:** Tennis Courts, Fitness Center

(*Supreme Fitness 291-7888*), Museum (*Strauss House Victorian Mansion Museum Sun 1pm-4pm, free 291-0074*) **1-3 mi:** Video Rental (*RST Video Inc 291-5354*), Park (*Gateway National Recreation Area - Sandy Hook 872-5970*) **3+ mi:** Golf Course (*Monmouth County 842-4000, 7.5mi.*)

Provisioning and General Services
OnSite: Bank/ATM **Near:** Convenience Store, Delicatessen (*Center Avenue 291-1006*), Wine/Beer, Liquor Store (*Buy-Rite Liquors 291-0517*), Bakery, Post Office, Beauty Salon, Barber Shop, Laundry, Bookstore (*Books Once Read - Internet access, too 708-0827*), Newsstand, Florist, Retail Shops **Under 1 mi:** Supermarket (*Foodtown 291-4079*), Catholic Church, Protestant Church, Dry Cleaners, Pharmacy (*CVS 872-2226*), Copies Etc. (*Simple Solution 872-2971*) **1-3 mi:** Library (*Atlantic Highlands 291-1956*), Hardware Store (*Jaspan Bros 291-1500*) **3+ mi:** Gourmet Shop (*Le Bon Panier 842-9496, 4 mi.*)

Transportation
OnSite: Ferry Service (*Seastreak to NYC 872-2600 $28RT*) **OnCall:** Rental Car (*Enterprise 471-8880, also Chevrolet 671-6200*), Taxi (*671-4600, Sea Bright Shore 345-9099, Eatontown Yellow 544-1111*), Airport Limo (*Aggressive 747-7998*) **1-3 mi:** Local Bus (*Red Bank or Highlands*), InterCity Bus (*Academy 291-1300 to NYC*) **Airport:** Newark (*36 mi.*)

Medical Services
911 Service **OnCall:** Ambulance **Near:** Holistic Services (*Gemini Touch 872-0272*) **Under 1 mi:** Doctor (*Commentucci 291-0692*), Chiropractor (*Shore Hands 872-8009, Page 291-5575*), Veterinarian (*Atlantic High. 291-4400*) **1-3 mi:** Dentist (*Fallon 291-1555*) **Hospital:** Riverview (*7 mi.*)

Setting -- Right on Sandy Hook Bay, Atlantic Highlands is tucked behind a three-quarter mile stone seawall enclosing the whole harbor. Across the Bay is Gateway National Park's Sandy Hook Area. Landside is new promenade, dotted with boat-shaped "window boxes", which runs along the bulkhead. Behind it is a very busy operation, with many boats on the hard and a large and active launching ramp, all managed from a two story, mostly glass control tower.

Marina Notes -- *$2/ft. up to 59 ft., $2.50 over 60 ft. Founded in 1941; owned by the Borough of Atlantic Highlands. 7 long fixed piers, 3 floating piers; limited transient floating docks. Large travelift for haul-out but no onsite repairs. Management suggests that transients not leave their boats unattended overnight due to weather. **Onsite Atlantic Highland Yacht Club (291-1118) manages the moorings and provides launch service. Many group fishing boats: Prowler 291-4904, Atlantic Star 291-5508, Sea Fox 291-4222, Fisherman 872-1925 Teal 872-0744, Emerald Tide 254-8509 and sport fishing charters. FYI: The onsite Shore Casino (291-4306) no longer serves meals on a regular basis; the more casual eatery is also in transition.

Notable -- The closest to the ocean of the Sandy Hook Bay marinas. Band concerts on Sunday nights in July and August. The Seastreak luxury catamaran to Manhattan makes 7 trips weekdays right from the marina with stops at Pier 11 Wall Street and East 34th Street. A short walk is the interesting town of Atlantic Highlands with several restaurants, two theaters and useful shops. The Bayshore Trail and the Henry Hudson Trail run along the marina. Consider a cab to hike the Mt. Mitchill Scenic Overlook - 12 acres overlooking Raritan Bay and the NYC skyline (playground, too).

Sandy Hook Bay Marina

One Willow Street; Highlands, NJ 07732

Tel: (732) 872-1511 **VHF: Monitor** 16 **Talk** 7
Fax: (732) 872-8122 **Alternate Tel:** n/a
Email: drew@ederagster.com **Web:** www.sandyhookbaymarina.com
Nearest Town: Highlands *(0.5 mi.)* **Tourist Info:** (732) 872-8711

Navigational Information
Lat: 40°24.584' **Long:** 074°00.013' **Tide:** 6 ft. **Current:** 5 kt. **Chart:** 12324
Rep. Depths *(MLW):* **Entry** 16 ft. **Fuel Dock** n/a **Max Slip/Moor** 8 ft./-
Access: G17 180 degrees 2.5 mi.; slow at G6, entrance at G7

Marina Facilities *(In Season/Off Season)*
Fuel: No
Slips: 95 Total, 4 Transient **Max LOA:** 90 ft. **Max Beam:** 18 ft. ft.
  Rate *(per ft.):* **Day** $3.00 **Week** n/a **Month** n/a
  Power: 30 amp Incl., 50 amp Incl., 100 amp n/a, 200 amp n/a
  Cable TV: No **Dockside Phone:** No
  Dock Type: Floating, Wood
Moorings: 0 Total, 0 Transient **Launch:** n/a
  Rate: Day n/a **Week** n/a **Month** n/a
Heads: 4 Toilet(s), 4 Shower(s)
Laundry: None **Pay Phones:** Yes
Pump-Out: OnCall, Full Service **Fee:** n/a **Closed Heads:** Yes

Marina Operations
Owner/Manager: Drew de Ganahl **Dockmaster:** Same
In-Season: May-Oct, 8am-6pm **Off-Season:** Nov-Apr, Closed
After-Hours Arrival: Call Oyster Restaurant 732 872-1450
Reservations: Yes, Preferred **Credit Cards:** Visa/MC, Amex
Discounts: Boat/US **Dockage:** 5% **Fuel:** n/a **Repair:** n/a
Pets: Welcome, Dog Walk Area **Handicap Access:** No

Marina Services and Boat Supplies
Services - Docking Assistance, Security *(24 hrs., Camera System)*, Trash Pick-Up, Dock Carts, Megayacht Facilities **Communication -** Mail & Package Hold, Fax in/out *($2pp)*, Data Ports *(Wi-Fi)*, FedEx, UPS, Express Mail **Supplies - OnSite:** Ice *(Cube)* **OnCall:** Ice *(Block)* **Under 1 mi:** Ships' Store, Bait/Tackle, Live Bait **1-3 mi:** West Marine *(872-8100)*, Propane *(Fitzgerald's RV 291-1883)* **3+ mi:** Boat/US *(739-8890, 8 mi.)*

Boatyard Services
OnSite: Travelift *(30T)*, Forklift *(8T)*, Engine mechanic *(gas, diesel)*, Electrical Repairs, Electronic Sales, Electronics Repairs, Bottom Cleaning, Brightwork, Propeller Repairs **OnCall:** Hull Repairs, Rigger, Sail Loft, Air Conditioning, Refrigeration, Divers, Compound, Wash & Wax, Interior Cleaning, Woodworking, Life Raft Service **1-3 mi:** Launching Ramp, Inflatable Repairs, Upholstery, Metal Fabrication. **Yard Rates:** $85/hr., Haul & Launch $10/ft. *(blocking incl.)*, Power Wash $6/ft., Bottom Paint $18/ft. *(paint incl.)* **Storage:** In-Water $8/ft./mo

Restaurants and Accommodations
OnSite: Restaurant *(The Original Oyster 872-1450, L $10-15, D $17-25)*
Near: Restaurant *(Doris & Eds 872-1565, D $21-30, Kid's $10+ a Gourmet's Top NJ choice)*, *(Lorenzo's Clam Hut)* **Under 1 mi:** Restaurant *(Hofbrauhaus 291-0224, D $11-16)*, *(Bahr's Landing 872-1241, L $6-15, D $15-29, Kids' Menu)*, Seafood Shack *(Lusty Lobster 291-1548)*, Pizzeria *(Francesco's 291-4729, Delivers)*, Inn/B&B *(Grandlady by the Sea 708-1900)*, Condo/Cottage *(Sandy Hook Cottages 708-1923, $100+)*
1-3 mi: Fast Food *(Burger King, McD)*, Motel *(Leonardo 291-9527, $80+)*, Inn/B&B *(Seascape Manor 291-8467, $90-160)*

Recreation and Entertainment
OnSite: Beach, Fishing Charter **Near:** Cultural Attract *(Seastreak Ferry concerts Tue 7pm July BBQ, too 872-2852)* **Under 1 mi:** Picnic Area *(Hartshorne Park)*, Playground, Fitness Center *(Sculpt Fitness 872-6595)*, Boat Rentals *(Hartshorne Park)*, Park *(Hartshorne)* **1-3 mi:** Group Fishing Boat, Movie Theater, Sightseeing *(Sandy Hook Nat'l Seashore)* **3+ mi:** Golf Course *(Monmouth County 842-4000, 8 mi.)*

Provisioning and General Services
Near: Convenience Store, Wine/Beer *(Bay Spirits 291-2300)*, Liquor Store *(Driftwood 291-2095)*, Bank/ATM **Under 1 mi:** Delicatessen *(J & R Gourmet Kitchen 291-2700)*, Farmers' Market *(Cornwall St & Bay Ave, Sat 10-2 291-4713)*, Fishmonger, Lobster Pound, Post Office, Catholic Church, Protestant Church, Beauty Salon, Barber Shop, Dry Cleaners, Laundry, Bookstore, Pharmacy *(CVS 872-2226)*, Newsstand, Hardware Store *(Highlands 872-1481)* **1-3 mi:** Supermarket *(Foodtown 291-4079)*, Synagogue, Library *(291-1956)*, Copies Etc. *(Simple Solution 872-2971)*

Transportation
OnSite: Ferry Service *(Seastreak to NYC $15-18/7 1-way, $25-33/12 RT)*, Airport Limo *(Monmouth 829-3883)* **OnCall:** Rental Car *(Enterprise 471-8880)*, Taxi *(Shore 345-9099; Red Bank 671-4600)* **Near:** Local Bus **Airport:** Newark Int'l/Monmouth *(40mi./22.5 mi.)*

Medical Services
911 Service **1-3 mi:** Doctor *(Commentucci 291-0692)*, Dentist *(Fallon 291-1555)*, Holistic Services *(Shore Hands 614-4974)*, Veterinarian *(Atlantic Highlands 291-4400)* **Hospital:** Riverview Medi 530-2273 *(7 mi.)*

Setting -- Just off Sandy Hook Bay, beneath the imposing Navesink Highlands, Sandy Hook Bay Marina sits just inside the mouth of the Shrewsbury River. Views are across the Shrewsbury to the Sandy Hook area of the Gateway National Park. Landside is dominated by a single highrise on the hill and The Original Oyster restaurant below. The covered dock for the Seastreak Ferry to Manhattan borders the southern edge.

Marina Notes -- New management as of '04; the marina is under renovation (stay tuned). Two wharfs with slips sit behind a wooden wave attenuator. Most transients are on the T-Heads. Standard group heads with showers. S&S Marine Mechanic on-site. The Original Oyster serves dinner Mon-Sat 5:30-10pm and a Sunday seafood Buffet ($29) from 3-8pm (a la carte dinner menu also available). Inside is "white tablecloth" fine dining or outside deck dining under the umbrellas - both options offer great views overlooking the docks. They will also prepare take-out for the boat. Tiki Bar, too. Cable TV coming in '05.

Notable -- Onsite and a couple of blocks south, at the former NY Waterway docks, are the two homes of the Seastreak high speed (35 minute) catamaran Ferry to Manhattan - Between the 2 terminals - 10 trips weekdays, 4 weekends - to Pier 11, Wall St or East 34 St.. From SHBM, it's 7:30am weekdays returning 5:30 & 6pm. The Marina staff will watch your boat while you're in NYC. This is the furthest north of the Highland marinas, making it the most convenient by boat but also the most distant from the services of "downtown" Highland. The village main drag, Bay Avenue with its antique shops, boutiques and restaurants, is walkable but the famous Twin Lights are a bit of a hike. Reportedly great Fluke and Bass fishing.

Navigational Information
Lat: 40°23.848' **Long:** 073°58.901' **Tide:** 6 ft. **Current:** 6 kt. **Chart:** 12324
Rep. Depths *(MLW)*: **Entry** 16 ft. **Fuel Dock** 10 ft. **Max Slip/Moor** 10 ft./15 ft.
Access: Shrewsbury River between Sandy Hook Bridge

Marina Facilities *(In Season/Off Season)*
Fuel: *Mobil* - Gasoline, Diesel, High-Speed Pumps
Slips: 35 Total, 4 Transient **Max LOA:** 180 ft. **Max Beam:** 25 ft.
 Rate *(per ft.)*: **Day** $3.00/Inq. **Week** $7.00 **Month** $15
 Power: 30 amp incl., **50 amp** incl., **100 amp** n/a, **200 amp** n/a
 Cable TV: No **Dockside Phone:** No
 Dock Type: Fixed, Floating
Moorings: 0 Total, 0 Transient **Launch:** n/a
 Rate: Day n/a **Week** n/a **Month** n/a
Heads: 2 Toilet(s)
Laundry: None **Pay Phones:** Yes, 2
Pump-Out: OnCall, Full Service, 1 Port **Fee:** $5 **Closed Heads:** Yes

Marina Operations
Owner/Manager: Jay Cosgrove **Dockmaster:** Big Ed Misiewicz
In-Season: Apr-Nov, 6am-9pm **Off-Season:** Dec-Mar, 7am-9am
After-Hours Arrival: Call in advance
Reservations: Preferred **Credit Cards:** Visa/MC, Amex, Mobil / Exxon
Discounts: Boat/US; SeaTow **Dockage:** 25% **Fuel:** $0.08* **Repair:** n/a
Pets: Welcome, Dog Walk Area **Handicap Access:** No

Bahrs Landing Restaurant

PO Box 436; 2 Bay Avenue; Highlands, NJ 07732

Tel: (732) 872-1245 **VHF: Monitor** 65 **Talk** 65
Fax: (732) 872-0495 **Alternate Tel:** (732) 291-7545
Email: Jay@Bahrs.com **Web:** www.Bahrs.com
Nearest Town: Highlands *(0 mi.)* **Tourist Info:** (732) 872-8711

Marina Services and Boat Supplies
Services - Docking Assistance **Communication -** FedEx, AirBorne, UPS,
Express Mail **Supplies - OnSite:** Ice *(Block)*, Bait/Tackle, Live Bait *(kellies, worms)* **Near:** Ships' Store **Under 1 mi:** Propane *(Fitzgerald's 291-1883)* **3+ mi:** West Marine *(872-8100, 5 mi.)*

Boatyard Services
Near: Engine mechanic *(gas, diesel)*, Electrical Repairs, Electronic Sales,
Electronics Repairs, Bottom Cleaning, Air Conditioning, Refrigeration.
1-3 mi: Launching Ramp **Nearest Yard:** Gateway Marina (732) 291-4440

Restaurants and Accommodations
OnSite: Restaurant *(Bahrs Landing 872-2124, L $6-15, D $15-29, Kid's $7)*,
Seafood Shack *(Mobys L $5-24, D $5-24)* **Near:** Restaurant *(Lorenzo's
Clam Hut)*, Seafood Shack *(Lusty Lobster 291-1548)*, Pizzeria *(Nunzio's 291-
5520)* **Under 1 mi:** Restaurant *(Bolero Cafe)*, *(Doris & Eds 8-721-5654, D
$21-30, Kids' $10)*, *(The Original Oyster 872-1450, L $10-15, D $17-25)*,
Pizzeria *(Francesco's 291-4729)*, Motel *(Fairbanks 842-8450)*, Inn/B&B
(Seascape Manor 291-8467, $90-160), Condo/Cottage *(Sandy Hook
Cottages 708-1923, $100+)*

Recreation and Entertainment
OnSite: Picnic Area, Fishing Charter **Near:** Beach, Playground, Jogging
Paths, Boat Rentals, Movie Theater **Under 1 mi:** Park *(park west of the
Twin Lights)*, Museum *(Twin Lights Historic Site - MemDay-LabDay,
10am-5pm 872-1814, Free; Ft. Hancock & Sandy Hook Museum at the*

tip of Sandy Hook , Sightseein *(Sandy Hook Gateway National Park*
1-3 mi: Fitness Center *(Sculpt)*, Video Rental *(Moondog Video 450-0076)*
3+ mi: Tennis Courts *(Little Silver 741-0200, 8 mi.)*, Golf Course *(Monmouth
County 842-4000, 8.5 mi.)*

Provisioning and General Services
OnSite: Bank/ATM, Clothing Store **Near:** Convenience Store, Wine/Beer
(Bay Spirits 291-2300), Fishmonger *(Lusty Lobster 291-1548)*, Lobster
Pound, Post Office, Catholic Church, Barber Shop, Dry Cleaners, Laundry,
Newsstand **Under 1 mi:** Delicatessen *(J & R Gourmet Kitchen 291-2700)*,
Liquor Store *(Driftwood 291-2095)*, Bookstore, Hardware Store *(Highlands
872-1481)* **1-3 mi:** Library *(Atlantic Highlands PL 291-1956)*, Pharmacy
(Sea Bright 842-1917) **3+ mi:** Supermarket *(Food town 291-4079, 3.5 mi.)*,
Copies Etc. *(Simple Solution 872-2971, 3..5 mi.)*

Transportation
OnSite: Local Bus, InterCity Bus **OnCall:** Taxi *(Shore Cab of Sea Bright
345-9099)*, Airport Limo *(State Shuttle 542-6505)* **Under 1 mi:** Ferry
Service *(Seastreak)* **Airport:** Newark Int'l/Monmouth *(40mi./21 mi.)*

Medical Services
911 Service **Near:** Dentist *(Pearl Dental Studio 872-6300)*, Chiropractor
(Highlands 291-1515), Ambulance **1-3 mi:** Doctor *(Commentucci 291-
0692)*, Veterinarian *(Atlantic Highlands 291-4400)* **3+ mi:** Holistic Services
(Rumson Therapeutic 842-2555, 4.5 mi.) **Hospital:** Riverview *(7.5 mi.)*

Setting -- Just before the Route 36 bascule bridge, this historic waterfront seafood restaurant with dockage sits at the base of the 200 foot Navesink Highlands with views across the river to the Sandy Hook portion of Gateway National Park. The landside environment is dominated by the multi-tiered restaurant and, behind it, the famous Twin Lights.

Marina Notes -- *Power on the docks for the first time in summer '03. The well-regarded onsite restaurant offers several attractive inside dining rooms and deck and patio options. Eat at the restaurant and there's 10% off dockage. **SeaTow gas discount $0.08 Tue & Thu. Family owned and operated since its founding in 1917; currently Ray and Jay Cosgrove, the 4th generation, are the owners. Heads shared with the restaurant. Moby's seafood shack next door is also owned by the Cosgroves.

Notable -- Walk directly across the Route 36 bridge to the Gateway National Recreation Area which includes Sandy Hook National Park, with its 5 mile stretch of wide, sandy beach. A 0.4 mile steep, but worthwhile hike, is straight up the hill to the park-like Twin Lights Historic Site - there is an interesting maritime museum (focusing on the US LIfesaving Service), the site of Marconi's first telegraph transmission, and truly spectacular views of the Shrewsbury and Sandy Hook. If you have the energy, climb the north tower for even better views. A mile north is the Seastreak high speed catamaran Ferry to Manhattan - 10 trips weekdays, 4 weekends - to Wall St or E. 34 St. $28RT.

Oceanic Marina

8 Washinghton Street; Rumson, NJ 07760

Tel: (732) 842-1194 **VHF: Monitor** n/a **Talk** n/a
Fax: (732) 758-0144 **Alternate Tel:** n/a
Email: oceanicmarina@comcast.net **Web:** www .oceanicmarina.com
Nearest Town: Rumson *(.5 mi.)* **Tourist Info:** n/a

Navigational Information
Lat: 40°22.632' **Long:** 074°00.762' **Tide:** 5 ft. **Current:** 1 kt. **Chart:** 12324
Rep. Depths *(MLW):* **Entry** 6 ft. **Fuel Dock** n/a **Max Slip/Moor** 5 ft./-
Access: Navisink past the Oceanic bascule bridge first facility on south shore

Marina Facilities *(In Season/Off Season)*
Fuel: No
Slips: 110 Total, 2 Transient **Max LOA:** 45 ft. **Max Beam:** n/a
  Rate *(per ft.):* **Day** $1.25 **Week** n/a **Month** n/a
  Power: 30 amp Inc., **50 amp** n/a, **100 amp** n/a, **200 amp** n/a
  Cable TV: No **Dockside Phone:** No
  Dock Type: Floating, Wood
Moorings: 0 Total, 0 Transient **Launch:** n/a
  Rate: Day n/a **Week** n/a **Month** n/a
Heads: 1 Toilet(s)
Laundry: None **Pay Phones:** No
Pump-Out: OnSite, 1 Central **Fee:** n/a **Closed Heads:** Yes

Marina Operations
Owner/Manager: Peter Pawlikowski **Dockmaster:** n/a
In-Season: Apr-Nov, 7am-5pm **Off-Season:** Dec-Mar, 8am-4:30pm
After-Hours Arrival: Call in advance
Reservations: Required **Credit Cards:** Visa/MC, Amex
Discounts: None
Pets: Welcome **Handicap Access:** No

Marina Services and Boat Supplies
Services - Docking Assistance, Dock Carts **Communication -** FedEx, AirBorne, UPS, Express Mail **Supplies - OnSite:** Ice *(Cube)*, Live Bait **1-3 mi:** Bait/Tackle *(Giglio's Bait & Tackle Shop 741-0480)*, Propane *(Jaspan Bros South Servistar 291-1500)* **3+ mi:** West Marine *(872-8100, 3.5 mi.)*

Boatyard Services
OnSite: Travelift *(20T)*, Forklift *(2)*, Engine mechanic *(gas, diesel)*, Electrical Repairs, Electronic Sales, Electronics Repairs, Bottom Cleaning *(Preasure washing)*, Air Conditioning *(Minor)*, Refrigeration *(Minor)*, Compound, Wash & Wax, Interior Cleaning, Inflatable Repairs *(Minor)*, Painting, Awlgrip **OnCall:** Propeller Repairs **Dealer for:** Mercury Marine. Other Certifications: Mercruiser, Optimax, Mercury **Yard Rates:** $110/hr., Haul & Launch $5/ft. *(blocking $2/ft.)*, Power Wash $4/ft.

Restaurants and Accommodations
Near: Restaurant *(Salt Creek Grille 933-9272, Kids' menu)*, *(What's Your Beef)*, *(Barnacle Bill's)*, Snack Bar *(Crazies)*, Lite Fare *(Savory Faire Carry Out)* **1-3 mi:** Seafood Shack *(Thompson's Fish N Chips 219-0888)*, Fast Food *(Burger King)*, Pizzeria *(Umberto Restaurant & Pizza 747-6522)* **3+ mi:** Hotel *(The Oyster Point 530-8200, 4 mi.)*, *(Molly Pitcher Inn 747-2500, 4 mi.)*, Inn/B&B *(Sandy Hook Cottage 708-1923, 3.5 mi.)*

Recreation and Entertainment
OnSite: Beach, Boat Rentals **Near:** Playground **Under 1 mi:** Video Rental *(Rumson Video 741-7401)* **1-3 mi:** Fitness Center *(Kick Fitness & Dance 212-1322)*, Museum *(New Jersey Audubon Society 872-2500)*

3+ mi: Tennis Courts *(Little Silver 741-0200, 5.5 mi.)*, Golf Course *(Old Orchard Country Club 542-7666, 9.5 mi.)*, Bowling *(Red Bank Lanes 747-6880, 4.5 mi.)*

Provisioning and General Services
Near: Delicatessen *(Brennan's Delicatessen 530-1801)*, Wine/Beer, Liquor Store *(Rumson Buy-Rite 842-0552)*, Bank/ATM, Post Office, Dry Cleaners, Pharmacy *(Rumson Pharmacy)*, Florist **Under 1 mi:** Market *(Rumson Market 842-0560)*, Gourmet Shop *(Rumson)*, Catholic Church, Protestant Church, Synagogue **1-3 mi:** Supermarket *(Acme 530-7481)*, Health Food *(BHealthE 758-0870)*, Other, Beauty Salon, Laundry, Bookstore *(Fair Haven Books 747-9455)*, Newsstand, Hardware Store *(Fair Haven Hardware 747-9500)* **3+ mi:** Library *(Monmouth County Library 842-5995, 6 mi.)*, Department Store *(Funk & Standard Variety Store 219-5885, 3.5 mi.)*, Copies Etc. *(Harper's Copy Center 741-9300, 3.5 mi.)*

Transportation
OnCall: Rental Car, Taxi *(Shore Cab of Sea Bright 345-9099; Eatontown 544-1111)*, Airport Limo *(Accutime Car Service 219-8993)* **Near:** Local Bus *(NJ Transit)* **Airport:** Newark Int'l *(42 mi.)*

Medical Services
911 Service **Near:** Holistic Services *(Rumson Therapeutic 842-2555)* **Under 1 mi:** Chiropractor *(Rumson Chiropractic Center 741-7888)* **1-3 mi:** Dentist *(Two River 741-4422)*, Veterinarian *(Fair Haven Animal 758-9797)* **3+ mi:** Doctor *(Pavilion Medical Associates 576-9990, 5 mi.)* **Hospital:** Riverview Medical 530-2229 *(3.5 mi.)*

Setting -- Just west of the Oceanic bascule bridge, on the Navesink's southern shore, is friendly, down-home Oceanic Marina. Landside it's pure boatyard, but the vistas across and up the river, which bellies out a bit at this point, are expansive and uncommercial.

Marina Notes -- Site of the former Paul's Boats. March to Thanksgiving they're open 7 days from 7am-5pm. The onsite snack bar shares the same hours. 8 & 40 lb bags of ice. Oceanic's Bait & Tackle shop offers advice and supplies for local fishermen - rigs for local species, crabbing supplies, plugs & lures, umbrella rigs, spoons, etc. - plus killies, spearing, sandeels, squid and whole bunker. Ship's Store with large inventory and fast turnaround (including new and re-conditioned propellors) -- Service center & parts department. Oceanic is a warranty center for Mercury and Mercruiser engines, drive & outboard repairs (Tom Kowalsky has 35 years experience).

Notable -- This stretch of river has a reputation as a great crabbing and fishing area. If you want to try your luck, Oceanic rents a fleet of 17 16-foot fiberglass skiffs with 8 HP outboards that make great crabbing boats. Alternatively, the nearby Oceanic Bridge is reportedly a great fishing spot. There's also a wading beach just east of the Bridge. Very close by is a waterfront park with tennis courts, bocce, a play ground and a gazebo. This stretch of the Navesink is well known for its sprawling waterfront estates and beautiful homes - particularly the north shore near Middletown and Rumson. A tour of the area in your dinghy or big boat makes for a delightful afternoon. Nearby Salt Creek Grille features Monday Prme Rib and Tuesday Lobster specials $20, Sunday Brunch $25/10.

Navigational Information

Lat: 40°22.133' **Long:** 074°02.232' **Tide:** 5 ft. **Current:** 1 kt. **Chart:** 12325
Rep. Depths (*MLW*): **Entry** 6 ft. **Fuel Dock** n/a **Max Slip/Moor** 6 ft./6 ft.
Access: Navesink River - South Shore off R18

Marina Facilities *(In Season/Off Season)*

Fuel: No
Slips: 82 Total, 1 Transient **Max LOA:** 50 ft. **Max Beam:** 16 ft.
Rate *(per ft.)*: **Day** $1.50/Inq. **Week** Inq. **Month** Inq.
Power: 30 amp Incl., 50 amp Incl., 100 amp n/a, 200 amp n/a
Cable TV: No **Dockside Phone:** No
Dock Type: Fixed, Floating, Long Fingers, Short Fingers, Pilings, Wood
Moorings: 60 Total, 5-10 Transient **Launch:** Yes (Incl.)
Rate: Day $35 **Week** n/a **Month** n/a
Heads: 2 Toilet(s), 2 Shower(s) *(with dressing rooms)*
Laundry: None **Pay Phones:** No
Pump-Out: OnSite, Full Service **Fee:** $5 **Closed Heads:** Yes

Marina Operations

Owner/Manager: Jim Cerruti **Dockmaster:** Mark Modderman
In-Season: May-Oct 15, 7am-6pm **Off-Season:** Oct 16-Apr 30, 8am-5pm
After-Hours Arrival: Call in advance
Reservations: Yes, Required **Credit Cards:** Visa/MC, Dscvr, Amex
Discounts: None
Pets: Welcome, Dog Walk Area **Handicap Access:** Yes, Heads, Docks

Fair Haven Yacht Works

75 DeNormandie Avenue; Fair Haven, NJ 07704

Tel: (732) 747-3010 **VHF: Monitor** n/a **Talk** 9
Fax: (732) 747-3019 **Alternate Tel:** n/a
Email: yachtworks@aol.com **Web:** n/a
Nearest Town: Fair Haven **Tourist Info:** (732) 741-0055

Marina Services and Boat Supplies

Services - Docking Assistance, Security *(24 Hrs., Camera/patrol)*, Trash Pick-Up, Dock Carts **Communication -** Mail & Package Hold, Phone Messages, Fax in/out *($3)*, FedEx, AirBorne, UPS, Express Mail *(Sat Del)*
Supplies - OnSite: Ice *(Block, Cube)*, Ships' Store **Under 1 mi:** Propane *(747-1212)* **1-3 mi:** Bait/Tackle *(Sea Land 741-5753)* **3+ mi:** West Marine *(542-8282, 4 mi.)*

Boatyard Services

OnSite: Travelift *(2/15T)*, Forklift, Engine mechanic *(gas)*, Electrical Repairs, Hull Repairs, Rigger, Bottom Cleaning, Brightwork, Compound, Wash & Wax, Interior Cleaning, Woodworking, Painting, Awlgrip, Total Refits
OnCall: Engine mechanic *(diesel)*, Electronic Sales, Electronics Repairs, Air Conditioning, Refrigeration, Divers, Propeller Repairs, Metal Fabrication
Under 1 mi: Launching Ramp. **Yard Rates:** $70/hr., Haul & Launch $7.50/ft. *(blocking incl.)*, Power Wash $4.50, Bottom Paint $16.50/ft. *(paint incl.)* **Storage:** In-Water $100/ft. summer, On-Land $35/ft. winter

Restaurants and Accommodations

Near: Restaurant *(Raven & Peach 747-4666, D $22-32)*, *(McGowens 741-5579)*, *(Navoo Grill)*, Snack Bar *(Java Stop)*, Lite Fare *(Fair Haven Cafe)*, Pizzeria *(Umbertos 747-6522)* **Under 1 mi:** Restaurant *(Salt Creek Grill 933-9272)*, *(No 1 Chinese 530-5888)*, Pizzeria *(Umberto Restaurant 747-6522)* **1-3 mi:** Seafood Shack *(Little Silver Seafood 758-8166)*, Hotel *(Molly Pitcher Inn 747-2500)*, *(Oyster Point 530-8200)*, *(Marriott 530-5552)*

Recreation and Entertainment

OnSite: Picnic Area **Under 1 mi:** Grills, Playground, Park

1-3 mi: Beach, Dive Shop *(Dosils, RT 36)*, Fitness Center *(On the Ball 576-8081)*, Horseback Riding *(Highland Stables 576-8911)*, Boat Rentals, Bowling *(Memory Lanes 747-6880)*, Video Rental *(Video On the Ritz 747-8080)* **3+ mi:** Tennis Courts *(Little Silver 741-0200, 4.5 mi.)*, Golf Course *(Monmouth County 842-4000, 5 mi.)*

Provisioning and General Services

Near: Gourmet Shop *(Fair Haven Cafe, La Jalisto 571-2246)*, Beauty Salon, Barber Shop, Dry Cleaners *(Flair)*, Bookstore *(Fair Haven 747-9455)*, Hardware Store *(Fair Haven 747-9500)*, Clothing Store, Retail Shops
Under 1 mi: Convenience Store, Supermarket *(Acme 530-7481)*, Delicatessen *(Brennan's 530-0302)*, Liquor Store *(Cellar 741-4847)*, Bakery, Fishmonger, Bank/ATM, Post Office, Catholic Church, Protestant Church, Synagogue, Library *(Fair Haven 747-5031)*, Laundry, Pharmacy *(Acme 936-0558)*, Newsstand, Florist **1-3 mi:** Health Food *(Second Nature 747-6448)*, Wine/Beer *(Fair Haven; Red Bank 747-1111)*, Green Grocer, Department Store *(Bon Ton 212-1568)*, Copies Etc. *(Harper's 741-9300)*

Transportation

OnCall: Taxi *(Eatontown 544-1111)*, Airport Limo *(Arrow Limo)* **Near:** Rental Car *(Avis)*, Local Bus *(NJ Transit)*, InterCity Bus **3+ mi:** Ferry Service *(Fast Ferry to NYC, 5 mi.)* **Airport:** Newark/Marlboro *(45 mi./12mi.)*

Medical Services

911 Service OnCall: Ambulance **Near:** Dentist *(Two River 741-4422)*, Veterinarian *(Fair Haven Animal Hosp. 758-9797)* **Under 1 mi:** Chiropractor *(Fair Haven 741-8668)* **1-3 mi:** Doctor *(Simon 842-3050)*, Holistic Services *(Alternative Health 747-9444)* **Hospital:** Riverview 741-2700 *(2 mi.)*

Setting -- About half way up the Navesink River, on the south side, Fair Haven Yacht Works' purely boatyard environment is clearly a desirable home judging by the very nice vessels that berth here. Landside is an attractive residential neighborhood with some shops and services within walking distance, and from the docks are beautiful, pristine views across a fairly wide stretch of river.

Marina Notes -- Very professional operation with a service and family-oriented staff. Founded in 1928, it was bought by its fourth set of owners, Jim and Molly Cerruti, in 1998. They immediately embarked on a long-range renovation plan -- new and reconditioned docks and bulkheads and dredging were the first items attended to. The main building will be renovated over time. 40 ft. courtesy dock for mooring guests and 7-day launch service from May 1- Oct 15.

Notable -- Jon Bon Jovi's classic HackerCraft makes its home here and demonstrates the boatyard's brightwork talent. This area of Fair Haven is called "Old Village" and maintains much of its original 19thC atmosphere and house and communal structures. Part of the Historic District, it invites a stroll along Fair Haven, Clay, DeNormandie and Gillespie streets. In the 1850's, Charles Williams, a free black person, built his home at the foot of DeNormandie Avenue. The residence is occupied today by his descendants, and is one of the oldest continuously inhabited houses in the Borough. Fair Haven was also a stop on the New York to Red Bank steamboat runs during summers in the later 19thC. The New Jersey Audubon Society is about 4 miles away (872-2500).

▲▲▲▲

Molly Pitcher Inn & Marina

88 Riverside Avenue; Red Bank, NJ 07701

Tel: (732) 747-2500; (800) 221-1372 **VHF: Monitor** 9 **Talk** 71
Fax: (732) 842-8289 **Alternate Tel:** n/a
Email: info@mollypitcher-oysterpoint.com **Web:** mollypitcher-oysterpoint.co
Nearest Town: Red Bank *(0.5 mi.)* **Tourist Info:** (732) 741-0055

Navigational Information
Lat: 40°21.198' **Long:** 074°04.334' **Tide:** 4 ft. **Current:** 1 kt. **Chart:** 12324
Rep. Depths *(MLW)*: **Entry** 5 ft. **Fuel Dock** n/a **Max Slip/Moor** 6 ft./-
Access: Sandy Bay - Shrewsbury River

Marina Facilities *(In Season/Off Season)*
Fuel: No
Slips: 70 Total, 10 Transient **Max LOA:** 60 ft. **Max Beam:** n/a
Rate *(per ft.)*: **Day** $2.00/Inq. **Week** Inq. **Month** Inq.
Power: 30 amp Inc., 50 amp Inc., 100 amp n/a, 200 amp n/a
Cable TV: Yes **Dockside Phone:** No
Dock Type: Floating, Long Fingers, Short Fingers
Moorings: 0 Total, 0 Transient **Launch:** None
Rate: Day n/a **Week** n/a **Month** n/a
Heads: 4 Toilet(s), 2 Shower(s)
Laundry: None **Pay Phones:** Yes, 1
Pump-Out: OnSite, Full Service **Fee:** Free **Closed Heads:** Yes

Marina Operations
Owner/Manager: Molly Pitcher Inn **Dockmaster:** Mickey Mendien
In-Season: Apr 15-Oct 15, 9am-5pm **Off-Season:** Oct 16-Apr 14, Closed
After-Hours Arrival: Call in advance
Reservations: Yes, Required **Credit Cards:** Visa/MC, Amex, Cash, Check
Discounts: None
Pets: No **Handicap Access:** No

Marina Services and Boat Supplies
Services - Docking Assistance, Concierge, Trash Pick-Up, Dock Carts
Communication - Fax in/out, FedEx, AirBorne, UPS, Express Mail
Supplies - OnSite: Ice *(Block)* **Near:** Bait/Tackle *(Sea Land 741-5753)*
1-3 mi: West Marine *(872-8100)* **3+ mi:** Propane *(U-Haul 671-1102, 4 mi.)*

Boatyard Services
OnCall: Engine mechanic *(gas, diesel)*, Electrical Repairs, Electronic Sales, Electronics Repairs, Hull Repairs, Rigger, Sail Loft, Bottom Cleaning, Brightwork, Air Conditioning, Refrigeration, Divers, Compound, Wash & Wax, Interior Cleaning **Under 1 mi:** Travelift *(30T)*, Launching Ramp.
Nearest Yard: Irwin Marine (731) 741-0003

Restaurants and Accommodations
OnSite: Restaurant *(Molly Pitcher 747-2500, B $6-10, L $8-12, D $16-30)*, Hotel *(Oyster Point Hotel 530-8200, $160-320)*, *(Molly Pitcher Inn 747-2500, $110-250)* **OnCall:** Pizzeria *(Danny's Pizza 842-2277)* **Near:** Restaurant *(Chiafullo's 824-2831)*, *(Siam Garden 224-1233)*, *(Basil T's Italians Grill)*, *(Old Union House 747-3444)*, Coffee Shop *(Einstein Bagels)*, Fast Food *(Cluck-U Chicken 530-2000)*, Pizzeria *(Brothers' Pizza 530-3356)*, *(Red Bank Pizza 741-9868)* **1-3 mi:** Seafood Shack *(Little Silver 758-8166)*, Inn/B&B *(Kelly's Celtic 898-1999)*

Recreation and Entertainment
OnSite: Pool **Near:** Picnic Area, Playground, Golf Course *(Monmouth County 842-4000)*, Fitness Center *(Parker Creek 758-1669)*, Movie Theater, Cultural Attract *(Count Basie Theatre 842-9000)*, Galleries **Under 1 mi:** Park *(Riverside)*

1-3 mi: Tennis Courts, Bowling *(Memory Lanes 747-6880)*, Video Rental *(Rumson Video 741-7401)*, Museum *(Shrewsbury Historical Soc. 530-7974)*

Provisioning and General Services
OnSite: Laundry **Near:** Delicatessen *(Victory 747-0508)*, Health Food *(Red Bank 842-5666)*, Liquor Store *(Red Bank 747-1111)*, Farmers' Market *(Shrewsbury Ave., Sun 9-2)*, Bank/ATM, Library *(Red Bank 842-0690)*, Beauty Salon, Dry Cleaners *(White Dove)*, Pharmacy *(Rite Aid 747-3727)*, Florist, Copies Etc. *(Alphagraphics 758-0095)* **Under 1 mi:** Convenience Store *(7-Eleven)*, Market *(Gonzalez Grocery II 345-9660)*, Wine/Beer *(On the Rocks 747-0380)*, Bakery, Retail Shops, Department Store *(Steinbachs, Funk & Standard 219-5885)* **1-3 mi:** Supermarket *(A&P 530-7449)*, Gourmet Shop *(Well Bred Basket 530-5880)*, Meat Market, Post Office, Catholic Church, Protestant Church, Synagogue, Bookstore *(Fair Haven 747-9455)*, Hardware Store *(Thompson 747-3205)*

Transportation
OnCall: Taxi *(Red Bank Yellow 747-0747)*, Airport Limo *(Airport Economy 741-4600)* **Near:** Rail *(To NYC and other shore points)* **1-3 mi:** Rental Car *(Avis 747-0308)* **Airport:** Newark/Monmouth County *(40 mi/15 mi.)*

Medical Services
911 Service **OnCall:** Ambulance **Near:** Dentist *(Santo 530-1003)*, Chiropractor *(Kutschman 741-4777)*, Optician *(Brigadoon 758-0606)* **Under 1 mi:** Doctor *(Simon 842-3050)* **1-3 mi:** Holistic Services *(Spa 500 530-5030)*, Veterinarian *(Red Bank Vet 747-3636)* **Hospital:** Riverview 741-2700 *0.5 mi.*

Setting -- About seven miles up the Navesink - at the navigable head of the river - the Molly Pitcher Inn and Marina's two major piers offer good berths with wonderful views all the way down the River and up to the multi-tiered outdoor spaces of the resort-style inn. The small city of Red Bank is close at hand.

Marina Notes -- *Weekends: 40 ft. minimum charge & 2 night minimum stay; Weekdays: 30 ft. minimum charge. Use of the pool is included in dockage for the captain and children, additional guests are $20/each. Dock'n Dine: 2 hrs. free while dining at the hotel. The Inn's rooms are large and luxuriously appointed with 18thC. reproductions. Those in the Navesink Wing have balconies that overlook the pool, river and marina. Under the same management, the Oyster Point Hotel/Marina, a block north, also offers waterfront rooms with balconies. At Oyster Point, there are two docks -- one for larger boats -- and the atmosphere is a little quieter.

Notable -- The Inn's Main Dining Room, with a wall of windows that provide truly breathtaking vistas down the length of the Navisink, offers Mon-Fri Breakfast 6:30am - 10:30am, Sat 8-10:30, Sun 8-10, Lunch Mon-Sat 11:30-3pm, Dinner Sun-Thu 5-9pm, Fri & Sat 'til 10pm, renowned Sun Brunch 11-1:15 or 1:30-3pm (Jackets are required after 5 pm in the Dining Room). The Grand Ballroom shares the spectacular view and can accommodate a sizeable crowd. Villa Eduard, Billiardes for pool, and delightful Red Bank's lovely collection of boutiques and antique shops, and the train station to NYC are all within easy walking distance. So is the 1400 seat, restored (circa 1926) Count Basie Theater, home to an electic set of top shelf concerts and programs.

Navigational Information
Lat: 40°21.470' **Long:** 073°58.370' **Tide:** n/a **Current:** n/a **Chart:** 12324
Rep. Depths (MLW): Entry 15 ft. **Fuel Dock** 8 ft. **Max Slip/Moor** 8 ft./-
Access: Two miles from entrance to Sandy Hook Bay

Marina Facilities (In Season/Off Season)
Fuel: Gulf - Gasoline, Diesel
Slips: 120 Total, 1 Transient **Max LOA:** 60 ft. **Max Beam:** n/a
Rate (per ft.): Day $1.75 **Week** n/a **Month** Inq.
Power: 30 amp Incl., **50 amp** Incl., **100 amp** n/a, **200 amp** n/a
Cable TV: Yes **Dockside Phone:** No
Dock Type: Fixed, Floating
Moorings: 0 Total, 0 Transient **Launch:** n/a
Rate: Day n/a **Week** n/a **Month** n/a
Heads: 6 Toilet(s), 6 Shower(s)
Laundry: 2 Washer(s), 2 Dryer(s) **Pay Phones:** Yes
Pump-Out: OnSite, Self Service **Fee:** n/a **Closed Heads:** Yes

Marina Operations
Owner/Manager: n/a **Dockmaster:** Earl Buchanan
In-Season: Apr 15-Oct, 8am-4:30pm **Off-Season:** Nov-Mar, 8am-4:30pm*
After-Hours Arrival: Call in advance
Reservations: Requested **Credit Cards:** Visa/MC, Amex, Gulf
Discounts: None
Pets: Welcome, Dog Walk Area **Handicap Access:** No

Navesink Marina

1410 Ocean Avenue; Sea Bright, NJ 07760

Tel: (732) 842-3700 **VHF: Monitor** 16 **Talk** 72
Fax: (732) 842-7618 **Alternate Tel:** n/a
Email: navesink@aol.com **Web:** n/a
Nearest Town: Sea Bright **Tourist Info:** (732) 222-0400

Marina Services and Boat Supplies
Services - Docking Assistance, Dock Carts **Communication -** Mail &
Package Hold, Fax in/out, FedEx, AirBorne, UPS, Express Mail (Sat Del)
Supplies - OnSite: Ice (Cube), Bait/Tackle (Giglio's 741-0480) **Near:** Ships'
Store **3+ mi:** West Marine (872-8100, 7 mi.), Boat/US (739-8890, 14 mi.),
Propane (Jaspan Bros 291-1500, 5 mi.)

Boatyard Services
OnSite: Travelift (35T), Forklift (38 ft.), Hull Repairs **OnCall:** Electrical
Repairs, Electronics Repairs, Bottom Cleaning, Brightwork, Refrigeration

Restaurants and Accommodations
OnSite: Restaurant (Waterfront Resteraunt 741-2244), Inn/B&B (Seascape
Manor 291-8467, $90 to $160) **Near:** Restaurant (Cove Restaurant 842-
4499) **Under 1 mi:** Restaurant (Harry's Lobster House 842-0205),
(Angelica's 842-2800), (McLoone's Riverside 84-228-94 , L $7-18, D $20-
30), Seafood Shack (Thompson's Fish N Chips 219-0888), Snack Bar
(Dave's Ice Cream), Lite Fare (Mad Hatter Pub 530-7861), (Steve's
Breakfast & Lunch 747-9598), (Subs 'n' More 224-9149), (McLoones'
Boathouse Deck L $7-13, D $11-22), Hotel (Ocean Hotel 571-4000, 4 mi.)
1-3 mi: Motel (Fairbanks Motel 842-8450) **3+ mi:** Seafood Shack
(Rooney's Crab House 870-1200, 3.5 mi.)

Recreation and Entertainment
OnSite: Picnic Area **Near:** Beach **1-3 mi:** Fitness Center (Curves 936-
0073) **3+ mi:** Golf Course (Old Orchard Country Club 542-7666, 6 mi.),

Bowling (Brunswick Monmouth Lanes 229-1414, 5 mi.), Museum (Long
Branch Historical 222-9879, 7 mi.)

Provisioning and General Services
Near: Bank/ATM, Post Office, Beauty Salon, Dry Cleaners **Under 1 mi:**
Delicatessen (Andy K'S Deli & Dairy 741-3222), Liquor Store (The Liquor
Store 842-8010), Protestant Church (Sea Bright Methodist), Library (Borough
of Sea Bright 758-9554), Pharmacy (Sea Bright 842-1917), Hardware Store
(Bain's Hardware 530-9425) **1-3 mi:** Market (Rumson Market 842-0560),
Catholic Church (Holy Cross - just across the bridge) **3+ mi:** Supermarket
(A&P 530-7449, 4 mi.), Wine/Beer (Buy-Rite Pleasure Bay 222-1555, 3.5
mi.), Bookstore (Fair Haven Books 747-9455, 5 mi.), Department Store
(Kmart Stores 542-5747, 5 mi.)

Transportation
OnCall: Taxi (Long Branch Yellow Cab 222-2200), Airport Limo
(Dependable Limousines 229-5357) **Near:** Rental Car
Airport: Newark/ Monmouth County (45 min.)

Medical Services
911 Service **Near:** Dentist (Brucker-Collier 530-5566) **1-3 mi:** Chiropractor
(Rumson Chiropractic Center 741-7888), Veterinarian (Veterinary Surgical
245-6622) **3+ mi:** Doctor (Jersey Shore Internal Medical 263-7965, 3.5 mi.),
Holistic Services (Rumson Therapeutic 842-2555, 3.5 mi.)
Hospital: Monmouth Medical Center 222-5200 **4 mi.**

Setting -- After traversing the narrow Rumson Reach of the Shrewsbury River, interrupted by the bascule bridge, the channel takes a sharp turn westward. If instead, you continue straight ahead, the Navesink docks appear on the east side. The views to the west are across the marshes of Sedge Island and the still rural landscape of Rumson Neck beyond. The approach to the marina itself is dominated by the red and green Waterfront Restaurant, which sits at the foot of the docks (2 dock 'n dine slips to 36 ft.). A plethora of flower-filled window boxes steps up the whole atmosphere.

Marina Notes -- *Closed week-ends off-season. This professional facility promises a friendly atmosphere with a helpful staff. Boat sales and brokerage on-site. Basic, well maintained facilities with good docks and pedestals. Small dry-stack storage operation. The bascule bridge opens on the hour & half.

Notable -- The inviting, onsite Waterfront Café is popular with locals and boaters alike; indoor or outdoor dining - under the sun or under the enclosed awning. Raw bar to bar food to three-course meals; white table cloth or casual - it responds to every mood. Open 'til 10pm Sun-Thurs, and 11pm Friday & Saturday. Walk out of the marina to Ocean Avenue (Route 36). This is the central thorofare of long, skinny Sea Bright -- 0.6 square mile stretched along 3.5 miles of sand bar wedged between the Shrewsbury and the Atlantic. Head north about 3/4 of a mile to a small gaggle of restaurants and a convenience store - including venerable Harry's Lobster. Or head south to McLoone's - a combination of local watering hole (with live entertainment and dancing) and a cozy fine dining restaurant - both overlooking the river. Straight across the Sea Bright sandbar from the marina are the Atlantic Ocean and the Jersey Shore beach.

Channel Club

PO Box 99; 33 West Street; Monmouth Beach, NJ 07750

Tel: (732) 222-7717 **VHF: Monitor** 9 **Talk** 8
Fax: (732) 229-0810 **Alternate Tel:** n/a
Email: ccmarina@worldnet.att.net **Web:** n/a
Nearest Town: Monmouth Beach *(0.1 mi.)* **Tourist Info:** (732) 222-0400

Navigational Information

Lat: 40°20.210' **Long:** 073°58.900' **Tide:** 2 ft. **Current:** n/a **Chart:** 12325
Rep. Depths *(MLW):* **Entry** 7 ft. **Fuel Dock** n/a **Max Slip/Moor** 7 ft./-
Access: Sandy Hook Inlet to the Shrewsbury past G29 to a private channel

Marina Facilities *(In Season/Off Season)*

Fuel: Gasoline, Diesel
Slips: 150 Total, 4 Transient **Max LOA:** 115 ft. **Max Beam:** n/a
  Rate *(per ft.):* **Day** $3.00* **Week** Inq. **Month** Inq.
  Power: 30 amp Incl., **50 amp** Incl., **100 amp** n/a, **200 amp** n/a
  Cable TV: Yes **Dockside Phone:** Yes
  Dock Type: Fixed, Long Fingers, Pilings, Wood
Moorings: 0 Total, 0 Transient **Launch:** n/a
  Rate: Day n/a **Week** n/a **Month** n/a
Heads: 4 Toilet(s), 4 Shower(s)
Laundry: None **Pay Phones:** Yes, 1
Pump-Out: OnSite, Full Service, 2 Central **Fee:** n/a **Closed Heads:** Yes

Marina Operations

Owner/Manager: n/a **Dockmaster:** Arnie D'Ambrosa
In-Season: Year-Round, 8am-5pm **Off-Season:** n/a
After-Hours Arrival: Call in Advance
Reservations: Required **Credit Cards:** Visa/MC, Dscvr, Amex
Discounts: None
Pets: Welcome **Handicap Access:** No

Marina Services and Boat Supplies

Services - Docking Assistance, Concierge, Dock Carts **Communication -** Mail & Package Hold, Phone Messages, Fax in/out, Data Ports *(Office)*, FedEx, UPS, Express Mail *(Sat Del)* **Supplies - OnSite:** Ice *(Cube)*, Ships' Store, Bait/Tackle **OnCall:** Ice *(Block)*

Boatyard Services

OnSite: Travelift *(60T)*, Forklift, Engine mechanic *(gas, diesel)*, Electrical Repairs, Electronics Repairs, Hull Repairs, Rigger, Bottom Cleaning, Brightwork, Compound, Wash & Wax, Interior Cleaning, Metal Fabrication, Painting, Yacht Broker **OnCall:** Sail Loft, Air Conditioning, Refrigeration, Divers, Propeller Repairs, Woodworking, Inflatable Repairs, Life Raft Service, Upholstery, Yacht Interiors, Awlgrip **Near:** Launching Ramp.
Yard Rates: $84/hr., Haul & Launch $9.50-10.50/ft. *(blocking incl.)*, Power Wash $3.50/ft., Bottom Paint $13-15/ft. *(paint incl.)*
Storage: In-Water Nov-Mar $25/ft., On-Land Nov-Mar $35/ft

Restaurants and Accommodations

OnSite: Restaurant *(Sallee Tee's Grille 870-8999, L $10-13, D $16-23)*, Snack Bar *(Channel Club Pool B $3-5, L $3-6)* **OnCall:** Pizzeria *(Michael Angelo's)* **Near:** Restaurant *(King Star 728-1918)* **Under 1 mi:** Restaurant *(Michael Angelo's 222-6910, L $6-16, D $6-16, Kid's menu $4.50, pizza & delivery)* **1-3 mi:** Restaurant *(Waterfront Cafe 741-2244)*, Seafood Shack *(Rooney's Ocean Crab 870-1200)*, *(Thompson's Fish N Chips 219-0888)*, Motel *(McIntosh 542-7900)*, *(Fountains Motel 222-7200)*, Hotel *(Ocean Place Resort 571-4000)*, Inn/B&B *(Cedars & Beeches 571-6777)*

Recreation and Entertainment

OnSite: Heated Pool, Picnic Area, Grills **Near:** Beach, Playground, Tennis Courts, Fitness Center *(Body Design 263-1625)*, Jogging Paths, Roller Blade/Bike Paths, Fishing Charter, Park **1-3 mi:** Video Rental *(Moondog 450-0076)* **3+ mi:** Golf Course *(Old Orchard Country Club 542-7666, 5 mi.)*, Bowling *(Brunswick 229-1414, 4 mi.)*, Museum *(Long Branch 222-9879, 5 mi.)*

Provisioning and General Services

OnSite: Delicatessen *(Sallee Tee's)* **Near:** Convenience Store *(Andy K'S Dairy & Deli 483-1210)*, Market *(Krauser's Food Store 728-1727, Rumson Market 842-0560)*, Wine/Beer *(Camelot 229-9100)*, Bank/ATM, Post Office, Catholic Church, Library *(Monmouth 229-1187)*, Beauty Salon, Dry Cleaners, Laundry **1-3 mi:** Health Food *(Stevens 222-6040)*, Liquor Store *(Buy-Rite 222-1555)*, Pharmacy *(Sea Bright 842-1917)*, Newsstand, Hardware Store *(Bain's 530-9425)*, Florist, Retail Shops, Copies Etc. *(JAMM 870-1999)*
3+ mi: Supermarket *(A&P 530-7449, 4 mi.)*, Department Store *(KMart, 5 mi.)*

Transportation

OnCall: Taxi *(Shore 345-9099)*, Airport Limo *(State Shuttle 542-6505, Dependable 229-3700)* **Near:** Rental Car
Airport: Newark/ Monmouth *(48 mi./16.5 mi.)*

Medical Services

911 Service OnCall: Ambulance **1-3 mi:** Doctor *(Jersey Shore 263-7965)*, Dentist *(Broadway 923-9559)*, Chiropractor *(Monmouth Chiro 229-3344)*, Holistic Services *(Wavelengths 229-4004)*, Veterinarian *(Long Branch 571-4100)* **Hospital:** Monmouth Med 222-5200 *(3 mi.*

Setting -- The 4 acre Channel Club family resort and marina is in a wide basin well off the Shrewsbury's main waterway and accessed by a private channel. The extensive grounds, festooned with flower beds, are carefully maintained and dominated by a two-story high-end banquet facility of the same name. There are 4 piers of slips connected by a boardwalk which runs the length of the marina and is punctuated by attractive groupings of white tables and chairs.

Marina Notes -- *$3.50 weekends and holidays. Winter storage. Service, service, service!! Dock hands who really help. Established in the 1930's by the Mihm family, it is now under new ownership. Channel & West Yacht Sales (870-0100) located onsite. Complete onsite repair facility with a 60-ton travel-lift, full-time certified technicians, ship store, and a fiberglass and wood shop managed by blue Water Marine Repairs (229-1166). Atlantis Yacht Club (222-9693) right next door also offers transient dockage but only to members of reciprocating clubs.

Notable -- The Channel Club features a heated pool with lifeguards, pool-side snack bar with beverage service, Sallee Tee's Grille - a full service restaurant -- and the Fagedaboudit Lounge - and great sunsets. Sallee Tee's is open 7 days for lunch and dinner. Plus they have a deli, an appetizing take-out menu and an extensive selection of catering platters, party subs, and other options. The active Channel Club establishment is home to many weddings. An ocean beach is only a few blocks, 0.2 mile walk. And a small shopping center, with a couple of restaurants, an independent supermarket, hairdresser, post office and ATM is less than a mile through a lovely, residential neighborhood.

Navigational Information

Lat: 40°19.600' **Long:** 073°59.740' **Tide:** 2 ft. **Current:** n/a **Chart:** 12324
Rep. Depths (*MLW*): **Entry** 6 ft. **Fuel Dock** n/a **Max Slip/Moor** 6 ft./-
Access: Sandy Hook to the Shrewbury to R 42 on Branchport Creek

Marina Facilities *(In Season/Off Season)*

Fuel: No
Slips: 86 Total, 3 Transient **Max LOA:** 48 ft. **Max Beam:** 16 ft.
  Rate *(per ft.)*: **Day** $1.50* **Week** n/a **Month** n/a
  Power: 30 amp Incl., **50 amp** n/a, **100 amp** n/a, **200 amp** n/a
  Cable TV: No **Dockside Phone:** No
  Dock Type: Floating, Pilings, Wood
Moorings: 0 Total, 0 Transient **Launch:** n/a, Dinghy Dock
  Rate: Day n/a **Week** n/a **Month** n/a
Heads: Toilet(s), Shower(s)
Laundry: None **Pay Phones:** No
Pump-Out: OnSite, Full Service **Fee:** $5.00 **Closed Heads:** Yes

Marina Operations

Owner/Manager: Michael Sosnowicz **Dockmaster:** Same
In-Season: Year round, 9am - 5pm **Off-Season:** n/a
After-Hours Arrival: n/a
Reservations: No **Credit Cards:** Visa/MC, Dscvr, Amex
Discounts: None
Pets: Welcome, Dog Walk Area **Handicap Access:** No

Mariner's Emporium

14 Renwick Pl.; Long Branch, NJ 07740

Tel: (732) 870-2542; (732) 870-1910 **VHF: Monitor** n/a **Talk** n/a
Fax: (732) 870-1910 **Alternate Tel:** n/a
Email: n/a **Web:** n/a
Nearest Town: Long Branch *(2 mi.)* **Tourist Info:** (732) 222-0400

Marina Services and Boat Supplies

Services - Docking Assistance, Security *(owner lives onsite)*, Trash Pick-Up, Dock Carts **Communication -** Mail & Package Hold, Phone Messages, Fax in/out, FedEx, AirBorne, UPS, Express Mail *(Sat Del)* **Supplies - OnSite:** Ships' Store **OnCall:** Ice *(Block)* **1-3 mi:** Bait/Tackle *(Jim's 229-9690)*

Boatyard Services

OnSite: Travelift *(to 47 ft.)*, Forklift *(to 28 ft.)*, Hydraulic Trailer *(15T)*, Engine mechanic *(gas, diesel)*, Electrical Repairs, Electronic Sales, Electronics Repairs, Bottom Cleaning, Brightwork, Air Conditioning, Refrigeration, Divers, Compound, Wash & Wax, Interior Cleaning **OnCall:** Rigger, Sail Loft, Propeller Repairs, Inflatable Repairs, Upholstery, Metal Fabrication **Near:** Launching Ramp. **Dealer for:** Mercruiser. **Yard Rates:** $75/ft., Haul & Launch $4/ft. *(blocking $100)*, Power Wash $3/ft., Bottom Paint $12/ft. *(paint incl.)* **Storage:** In-Water $25/ft., On-Land $35/ft.

Restaurants and Accommodations

Under 1 mi: Restaurant *(Michael Angelos 222-6910, L&D $6-16, del)*, Lite Fare *(Liberty Fried Chicken 263-1044)*, Pizzeria *(Bella's 229-7102, del)* **1-3 mi:** Restaurant *(King Star 728-1918)*, *(Acuna's 229-3033)*, *(Charley's Ocean222-4499)*, *(Sallee Tee's 870-8999)*, *(North Beach 229-5599)*, *(Reef Club 229-6004)*, Motel *(Fountains 222-7200, $50-60)*, Hotel *(Ocean Place Hilton 571-4000, $90-150)*, Inn/B&B *(Bradley Beach 774-0414)*

Recreation and Entertainment

OnSite: Pool, Picnic Area, Grills **Near:** Playground, Dive Shop, Volleyball, Special Events *(Oceanfest - July 4)* **Under 1 mi:** Beach, Fitness Center *(Body Design 263-1625)*, Boat Rentals, Fishing Charter, Group Fishing

Boat, Video Arcade **1-3 mi:** Bowling *(Brunswick 229-1414)*, Video Rental *(International 229-6995)*, Park *(Seven Presidents' Oceanfront Pavilion)*
3+ mi: Tennis Courts *(Little Silver 741-0200, 4 mi.)*, Golf Course *(Old Orchard C.C. 542-7666, 4 mi.)*, Museum *(Church of the Presidents 222-9879, 5 mi.)*

Provisioning and General Services

Under 1 mi: Convenience Store, Wine/Beer *(Buy-Rite 222-1555)*, Liquor Store *(Suburban 229-9158)*, Bakery, Farmers' Market, Lobster Pound, Bank/ATM, Post Office, Catholic Church, Protestant Church, Beauty Salon, Barber Shop, Dry Cleaners, Laundry, Newsstand **1-3 mi:** Market *(Andy K'S Dairy & Deli 483-1210)*, Delicatessen, Health Food *(Stevens 222-6040)*, Fishmonger, Synagogue, Library *(Long Branch PL 222-3900)*, Pharmacy *(Ace 222-1481)*, Hardware Store *(Coast 222-8200)*, Florist, Retail Shops, Department Store *(Newberry's 229-1296)*, Buying Club, Copies Etc. *(JAMM 870-1999)* **3+ mi:** Supermarket *(A&P 530-7449, 4 mi.)*, Gourmet Shop *(Rumson Market 842-0560, 5 mi.)*

Transportation

OnCall: Taxi *(Paramount 222-5300; Shore Cab 222-6688)*, Airport Limo *(Dependable 229-3700; State Shuttle 542-6505)* **Near:** Local Bus
Under 1mi: Rental Car *(Top Line 578-9700)*
Airport: Newark Int'l/Monmouth *(45 mi./15.5 mi.)*

Medical Services

911 Service **OnCall:** Ambulance **1-3 mi:** Doctor *(Jerey 263-7965)*, Dentist *(Monmouth 923-6585, Kindya 870-9658)*, Chiropractor *(Monmouth 229-3344)*, Holistic Services *(Wavelengths 229-4004)*, Veterinarian *(Rottenberg 571-4723)* **Hospital:** Monmouth 222-5200 *(2 mi.)*

Setting -- Located in a residential area on the scenic Shrewsbury River, Mariner's Emporium is safely tucked up Branchport Creek and offers a low-key, family-oriented atmosphere focused on "forty foot and under" boats. Views across the creek and out to the river are open and restful. Here, it is all about the boat with minimal landscaping and a mostly boatyard environment.

Marina Notes -- Best for shallower draft boats. The onsite, well equipped shop focuses on smaller boats; mechanic onsite as well. Small dry-stack operation. A pleasant pool, surrounded by a hurricane fence, sits off by itself overlooking the parking lot. Four reasonable heads and four showers sport dressing rooms. A small picnic area with 2 tables overlooks the parking area.

Notable -- An ocean beach, with a wood and cement boardwalk, is within walking distance. The agressive waves often attract more surfers than families; an ongoing renourishment effort compensates for the inevitable beach erosion. A little over a mile, across the Patten Avenue Bridge, is the burg of Monmouth Beach with restaurants (Kings Star & Acuna Cafe) and services (Andy K's). In its heyday, Long Branch was one of the 19thC's preeminent seaside resorts - its racetrack (now Monmouth Park) and gambling casinos attracted trainloads of fashionable, affluent visitors. A slow decline began in the '20's and it is now in the throes of a resurgence. Seven US Presidents, beginning with Grant, vacationed here. The 33-acre Seven Presidents Waterfront Park (2 miles away) keeps that history fresh. 3 miles further the Church of the Presidents, one of the few intact reminders of this era, is now the Long Branch Historical Museum.

Shark River Yacht Club

Seaview Circle North; Neptune, NJ 07753

Tel: (732) 502-0094 **VHF: Monitor** 10 **Talk** 10
Fax: (732) 502-9149 **Alternate Tel:** n/a
Email: n/a **Web:** www.sharkriveryachtclub.com
Nearest Town: Belmar (0.4 mi.) **Tourist Info:** (732) 775-7676

Navigational Information

Lat: 40°11.223' **Long:** 074°01.635' **Tide:** 6 ft. **Current:** 4 kt. **Chart:** 12324
Rep. Depths (MLW): **Entry** 10 ft. **Fuel Dock** n/a **Max Slip/Moor** 8 ft./-
Access: Shark River Inlet; Seaview/Shark Island to port to North Channel

Marina Facilities (In Season/Off Season)

Fuel: No
Slips: 166 Total, 10 Transient **Max LOA:** 55 ft. **Max Beam:** 16 ft.
  Rate (per ft.): **Day** $2.00/$1.50 **Week** n/a **Month** n/a
  Power: 30 amp Incl., 50 amp Incl., 100 amp n/a, 200 amp n/a
  Cable TV: Yes **Dockside Phone:** No
  Dock Type: Floating, Pilings, Alongside, Wood
Moorings: 0 Total, 0 Transient **Launch:** n/a
  Rate: Day n/a **Week** n/a **Month** n/a
Heads: 4 Toilet(s), 4 Shower(s) (with dressing rooms)
Laundry: 1 Washer(s), 1 Dryer(s) **Pay Phones:** No
Pump-Out: OnSite, 1 Central **Fee:** n/a **Closed Heads:** Yes

Marina Operations

Owner/Manager: Seth Frankel **Dockmaster:** same
In-Season: March-Nov, 8am-5pm **Off-Season:** Dec-Feb, 9am-3pm
After-Hours Arrival: Call in Advance
Reservations: Required **Credit Cards:** Visa/MC, Amex
Discounts: None
Pets: Welcome **Handicap Access:** Yes, Heads

Marina Services and Boat Supplies

Services - Docking Assistance, Trash Pick-Up **Communication -** FedEx, AirBorne, UPS, Express Mail **Supplies - OnSite:** Ships' Store
Near: Propane (Shark River Tackle 774-4360) **Under 1 mi:** Bait/Tackle (Shark River Tackle 774-4360) **3+ mi:** West Marine (542-8282, 10 mi.)

Boatyard Services

OnSite: Travelift, Engine mechanic (gas, diesel), Electrical Repairs, Electronic Sales, Electronics Repairs, Hull Repairs, Bottom Cleaning, Air Conditioning, Refrigeration, Divers, Compound, Wash & Wax, Interior Cleaning, Propeller Repairs, Painting, Awlgrip **3+ mi:** Life Raft Service (5 mi.). **Yard Rates:** $65/hr., Haul & Launch $6/ft. (blocking $6/ft.), Power Wash $2/ft., Bottom Paint $8/ft. **Storage:** On-Land $4/ft.

Restaurants and Accommodations

OnCall: Pizzeria (Pizza Etc. 775-1800, Delivers) **Near:** Restaurant (Belmar Café 681-5800), Pizzeria (Frederico's Pizzeria & Restaurant 681-7066)
Under 1 mi: Restaurant (Jack's Ribs & Ale House 774-9600), (Sunsets on the Water Front 775-9911), Lite Fare (Al's Subs & Deli 988-7703), Motel (Belmar Motor Lodge), Inn/B&B (Cashelmara B&B 776-8727) **1-3 mi:** Fast Food (Subway), Motel (Comfort Inn 449-6146), (Quaker Inn 775-7525)

Recreation and Entertainment

OnSite: Fishing Charter **Near:** Dive Shop, Jogging Paths, Boat Rentals, Group Fishing Boat **Under 1 mi:** Beach (Belmar), Tennis Courts (Good Sports 681-3366), Fitness Center (Belmar Core Four 681-8098), Roller Blade/Bike Paths, Video Rental (Belmar 681-6227), Park, Museum (Children's Museum of Monmouth Co 280-8000)

1-3 mi: Horseback Riding, Bowling (Shore Lanes 775-6050), Movie Theater (Spring Lake 449-4530), Video Arcade **3+ mi:** Golf Course (Quail Ridge Golf Course 681-1800, 4 mi.)

Provisioning and General Services

Near: Delicatessen (Italian Delight 681-5444), Liquor Store (Hanley's 681-7788), Pharmacy (Rite Aid 681-4101), Hardware Store (Taylor 681-0511)
Under 1 mi: Convenience Store, Market (LA Costena Grocery 556-1156), Health Food (Natural Nutrition 74-2016), Bakery, Farmers' Market, Green Grocer, Fishmonger (Capt Bill's 775-0222 or Belmar Marina when the boats come in), Lobster Pound, Bank/ATM, Post Office, Catholic Church, Library (Belmar 681-0775, Internet access), Beauty Salon, Barber Shop, Dry Cleaners, Laundry, Bookstore, Newsstand, Florist, Clothing Store, Retail Shops, Copies Etc. (Hoffman Press 502-0110) **1-3 mi:** Supermarket (A&P 974-9090, Shoprite 681-0900), Gourmet Shop (Cassoulet 774-1100), Wine/Beer (Bradley 775-8976), Protestant Church

Transportation

OnCall: Rental Car (Enterprise 556-0666, Hertz 280-2166 - near), Taxi (Vet's Cab 774-7711) **Near:** Bikes (DJ's 681-8228) **Under 1 mi:** Rail **1-3 mi:** Ferry Service (NY Fast Ferry), Airport Limo (Savannah's Limo 282-1666) **Airport:** Newark (40 mi.)

Medical Services

911 Service **Under 1 mi:** Doctor, Dentist (Avon 775-3531), Chiropractor (Caruso Family 280-8646) **1-3 mi:** Holistic Services (Alpha Massage 449-2763), Veterinarian (Belmar Wall 681-5040)
Hospital: Jersey Shore 775-5500 (3 mi.)

Setting -- On the north channel of the Shark River on Seaview (aka Shark) Island, Shark River Yacht Club's attractive and imposing two-story contemporary neo-Victorian structure is easy to spot. The gray shingled club house is a modern take on early Jersey Shore "cottages" and sports dormers and a full-le second-story porch. This less traveled stretch of the river, accessed by rounding part of the island, is narrow, protected and quiet.

Marina Notes -- The main building was completed in December 2001. It boasts inviting, fresh, new two-tone tile heads and showers, a small lounge area, and a laundry. Mostly seasonal slipholders, but there is room for more than a few transients. 6 feet at the T-head but shallower toward shore. Good docks with full service pedestals. A fairly well-supplied ships' store with tackle is also on the premises.

Notable -- The Shark River Yacht Club's second floor is a spacious, bright, well designed, cathedral ceilinged event facility with a private chef/caterer and a party planner. The room, which can accommodate 50-140 people, opens out onto a long veranda that overlooks the marina and River - perfect for yacht club cruises or rendezvous, as well as the weddings it was designed for. It is BYO. The bustling burg of Belmar is less than a half mile walk, across the Route 35 bridge, putting all of its services, resturants, events, attractions and provisioning options easily at hand.

Navigational Information
Lat: 40°11.358' **Long:** 074°01.736' **Tide:** 8 ft. **Current:** 4 kt. **Chart:** 12324
Rep. Depths (*MLW*): **Entry** 10 ft. **Fuel Dock** n/a **Max Slip/Moor** 6 ft./6 ft.
Access: Shark River Inlet leave Seaview/Shark Island to port to North Channe

Marina Facilities (*In Season/Off Season*)
Fuel: No
Slips: 20 Total; 2 Transient **Max LOA:** 40 ft. **Max Beam:** 14 ft.
  Rate (*per ft.*): **Day** $1.00/Inq. **Week** Inq. **Month** Inq.
  Power: 30 amp n/a, 50 amp n/a, 100 amp n/a, 200 amp n/a
  Cable TV: No **Dockside Phone:** No
  Dock Type: Fixed, Alongside, Wood
Moorings: 0 Total, 0 Transient **Launch:** n/a
  Rate: Day n/a **Week** n/a **Month** n/a
Heads: 1 Toilet(s)
Laundry: None **Pay Phones:** No
Pump-Out: No **Fee:** n/a **Closed Heads:** Yes

Marina Operations
Owner/Manager: Jim Bry **Dockmaster:** Same
In-Season: Apr 1-Dec 15, 8am-5pm **Off-Season:** closed
After-Hours Arrival: Call in advance - before 5pm
Reservations: Required **Credit Cards:** Visa/MC
Discounts: None
Pets: Welcome **Handicap Access:** No

Bry's Marine

100 S. Concourse; Neptune, NJ 07753

Tel: (732) 775-7364 **VHF: Monitor** n/a **Talk** n/a
Fax: (732) 774-1922 **Alternate Tel:** n/a
Email: brysmarine@aol.com **Web:** n/a
Nearest Town: Belmar (*0.75 mi.*) **Tourist Info:** (732) 681-2900

Marina Services and Boat Supplies
Services - Docking Assistance **Supplies - OnSite:** Marine Discount Store
Near: Ships' Store, Bait/Tackle (*Mac's 774-4360, Capt Bill's 775-0222*), Live
Bait (*Capt Bill's*) **Under 1 mi:** Propane (*Taylor's 681-0511*)

Boatyard Services
OnSite: Travelift (*15T*), Engine mechanic (*gas*), Launching Ramp, Electrical
Repairs, Electronic Sales, Hull Repairs, Rigger, Bottom Cleaning, Propeller
Repairs **Dealer for:** HydraSports, Maycraft, Lowe, Stratas, Javelin,
Johnson, Evinrude. Other Certifications: OMC Master Tech's
Yard Rates: $68/hr., Haul & Launch $10/ft., Power Wash $2.50/ft.,
Bottom Paint $9.50/ft. (*paint incl.*) **Storage:** On-Land $4.50/ft./mo.

Restaurants and Accommodations
Near: Restaurant (*Jack's Ribs & Ale House 774-9600*), (*Kellys Tavern 775-
9517*), (*Sunsets on the Water Front 775-9911*), Lite Fare (*Al's Subs & Deli
988-7703*), Hotel (*Neptune Motor Lodge 988-8059*) **Under 1 mi:** Restaurant
(*Zucconi's 502-0077*), Seafood Shack (*Klein's Fish Market and Waterside
Cafe 681-1177, cash only M*), Motel (*Belmar Motor 681-6600*)
1-3 mi: Restaurant (*Blue Marlin 988-7997*), Fast Food (*Subway*), Pizzeria
(*Carmen's Famous 774-6010*), Inn/B&B (*House by the Sea 681-8386*)

Recreation and Entertainment
Near: Picnic Area, Playground, Park (*Memorial*) **Under 1 mi:** Fitness
Center (*Yoga Anjali 681-7660, Belmar Intelligent Exercise 681-8098 - 1.5
mi.*), Fishing Charter (*Belmar Marina 681-3700*), Group Fishing Boat (*Belmar
Marina*), Video Rental (*Video Shop 681-6227*), Museum (*Children's Museum
of Monmouth 280-8000*), Cultural Attract (*Belmar's Fri night concerts & Thu

Night Socials), Special Events (*Seafood fest mid-June*) **1-3 mi:** Beach,
Tennis Courts (*Good Sports 681-3366*), Boat Rentals (*Midway jet ski and
kayak rentals 610-8562*), Bowling (*Shore Lanes 775-6050*), Movie Theater
(*Spring Lake Community House Theater 449-4530*) **3+ mi:** Golf Course
(*Colonial Terrace or Quail Ridge 681-1800, 4.5 mi.*)

Provisioning and General Services
Near: Convenience Store, Delicatessen (*Beth Kelly's Deli 988-6746*),
Wine/Beer, Fishmonger (*Capt Bill's 775-0222 or Belmar Marina when the
boats come in*), Lobster Pound (*Capt Bill's*), Bank/ATM, Post Office, Catholic
Church, Florist **Under 1 mi:** Market, Health Food (*Natural Nutrition 774-
2016*), Protestant Church, Library (*Belmar 681-0775, Internet access*),
Laundry, Bookstore (*Earth Haven Natural 681-8600*), Pharmacy (*Eckerd
681-3722*), Hardware Store (*Taylor 681-0511*) **1-3 mi:** Supermarket (*A&P
974-9090, Shoprite 681-0900*), Gourmet Shop (*Cassoule't Gourmet 774-
1100*), Liquor Store (*Corlies 775-7578*), Copies Etc. (*Maclearie 681-2772*)

Transportation
OnCall: Rental Car (*Enterprise 556-0666, Hertz 280-2166*), Taxi (*Vet's Cab
774-7711*), Airport Limo (*Pmc 280-0900*) **Near:** Bikes (*DJ's 681-8228*),
Local Bus **1-3 mi:** Rail (*Belmar*) **Airport:** Newark (*40 mi.*)

Medical Services
911 Service **OnCall:** Ambulance **1-3 mi:** Dentist (*Jersey Shore Dental 774-
5772*), Chiropractor (*Empire Chiropractic and Wellness 776-2400*), Holistic
Services (*Alpha Massage Therapy 449-2763*), Veterinarian (*Shark River
775-2444*) **3+ mi:** Doctor (*Jersey Shore 974-1980 , 3 mi.*)
Hospital: Jersey Shore 775-5500 *2 mi.*

Setting -- Located on the north Channel of the Shark River, directly across from Shark River (aka Seaview) Island, Bry's offers very convenient dockage for
smaller boats just 15 minutes from the Ocean. Amenties are few; here, it is all about the boat. A grass strip, dotted with picnic tables and benches, and concrete
walkways separate the docks from the road. Across the road are low-rise apartment complexes and the boatyard.

Marina Notes -- Founded in 1956, Bry's has been family owned and operated ever since. It services mostly smaller boats, with a few spots for 35 - 40
footers. A boatyard with haul-out, basic services, plus summer and winter dry storage. A port-a-john serves as the head. Note that, because of dredging and
bridge construction, Total Marine at Seaview is closed until 2006.

Notable -- It's a 0.7 mile walk across the Railroad Avenue bridge to the heart of the bustling village of Belmar with all its services and activities plus good
lodging, a dozen restaurants and provisioning options. Belmar's municipal marina is home to the state's largest collection of party fishing boats and sport
fishing charters. The ocean beach is a little over a mile walk. The convenient New Jersey Transit station with trains to Penn Station in NYC and to Newark
Airport make this an interesting place to leave the boat or change crews. The R.R. also a convenient method of visiting other Jersey shore communities. Two
stops to delightful, Victorian Ocean Grove (try the Secret Garden Restaurant at the Manchester Inn (775-0616) or a concert at The Stone Pony (294-8989)
made famous by Bruce Springsteen.

PHOTOS ON CD-ROM: 5

Shark River Hills Marina

149 South Riverside Drive; Neptune, NJ 07753

Tel: (732) 775-7400 **VHF: Monitor** n/a **Talk** n/a
Fax: (732) 775-0448 **Alternate Tel:** n/a
Email: sharkmari@infionline.net **Web:** www.sharkrivermarine.com
Nearest Town: Belmar *(5 mi.)* **Tourist Info:** (732) 775-7676

Navigational Information
Lat: 40°22.520' **Long:** 074°02.340' **Tide:** 6 ft. **Current:** 4 kt. **Chart:** 12324
Rep. Depths (*MLW*): **Entry** 10 ft. **Fuel Dock** n/a **Max Slip/Moor** 4 ft./-
Access: Inlet to Channel on north side of Shark River Island, straight ahead

Marina Facilities *(In Season/Off Season)*
Fuel: No
Slips: 200 Total, 8-10 Transient **Max LOA:** 45 ft. **Max Beam:** 14 ft.
  Rate *(per ft.)*: **Day** $1.00 **Week** n/a **Month** n/a
  Power: 30 amp Incl., **50 amp** n/a, **100 amp** n/a, **200 amp** n/a
  Cable TV: No **Dockside Phone:** No
  Dock Type: Fixed, Floating, Long Fingers, Wood
Moorings: 0 Total, 0 Transient **Launch:** n/a
  Rate: Day n/a **Week** n/a **Month** n/a
Heads: 4 Toilet(s), 2 Shower(s) *(with dressing rooms)*
Laundry: None **Pay Phones:** Yes
Pump-Out: No **Fee:** n/a **Closed Heads:** Yes

Marina Operations
Owner/Manager: Mark Oliver **Dockmaster:** same
In-Season: Mar-Nov, 8am-5pm **Off-Season:** Dec-Feb, 9am-5pm
After-Hours Arrival: Tie up and see watchman
Reservations: Yes **Credit Cards:** Visa/MC, Dscvr, Amex, Cash/Check
Discounts: None
Pets: Welcome **Handicap Access:** No

Marina Services and Boat Supplies
Services - Docking Assistance, Boaters' Lounge, Security *(12 Hrs., Watchman)*, Trash Pick-Up **Communication -** Phone Messages, FedEx, Express Mail **Supplies - OnSite:** Ice *(Cube)*, Ships' Store
1-3 mi: Bait/Tackle *(Shark River Tackle 774-4360)*, Propane *(Taylor Hardware 681-0511)* **3+ mi:** West Marine *(542-8282, 9 mi.)*

Boatyard Services
OnSite: Travelift *(15T)*, Engine mechanic *(gas)*, Electrical Repairs, Bottom Cleaning, Compound, Wash & Wax, Interior Cleaning, Propeller Repairs
1-3 mi: Divers, Metal Fabrication, Painting, Awlgrip. **Dealer for:** Chris Craft Key West Glaston. Other Certifications: NJ Marine Trade
Yard Rates: $70/hr., Haul & Launch $5/ft. *(blocking $5/ft.)*, Power Wash $1.50, Bottom Paint $12/ft. *(paint incl.)* **Storage:** On-Land $2/ft./mo.

Restaurants and Accommodations
OnSite: Snack Bar *(Bistro-by-the-Sea 775-9040, L $4-11, D $7-12)*, Pizzeria *(Bistro-by-the-Sea)* **Near:** Lite Fare *(Thomas's Crackerbarrel 774-9746)*, Inn/B&B *(House by the Sea 681-8386)* **Under 1 mi:** Restaurant *(Zucconi's 502-0077)* **1-3 mi:** Restaurant *(Joe Eng's Fortune House 775-3423)*, *(Molinari's 775-7733)*, Seafood Shack *(Blue Marlin Restaurant 988-7997)*, Fast Food *(Subway)*, Pizzeria *(Santino's 775-1800)*, Motel *(Belmar Motor Lodge 681-6600)*, *(Quaker Inn 775-7525)*, *(Neptune Motor Lodge)*

Recreation and Entertainment
OnSite: Beach *(For jet skis)* **Near:** Playground, Volleyball, Park *(Riverside)* **Under 1 mi:** Dive Shop, Boat Rentals, Fishing Charter, Video Rental *(Video Shop 681-6227)*, Video Arcade

1-3 mi: Tennis Courts *(Good Sports Racquet Club 681-3366)*, Fitness Center, Roller Blade/Bike Paths, Movie Theater, Museum *(Children's Museum of MON CTY 280-8000)*, Sightseeing **3+ mi:** Golf Course *(Colonial Terrace 775-3636 or Quail Ridge 681-1800, 5 mi.)*, Horseback Riding *(Wall Equestrian 681-6828, 5 mi.)*, Bowling *(Shore Lanes 775-6050, 4 mi.)*

Provisioning and General Services
Near: Convenience Store, Market *(WAWA)*, Delicatessen *(Thomas's 774-9647)*, Barber Shop *(Current Trends)*, Newsstand **Under 1 mi:** Gourmet Shop *(Cassoule't Gourmet 774-1100)*, Bakery *(Bread & Beyond 776-5938)*, Fishmonger, Lobster Pound, Post Office, Catholic Church, Protestant Church, Synagogue, Beauty Salon, Dry Cleaners, Laundry, Pharmacy *(Avon 774-0461)*, Clothing Store **1-3 mi:** Supermarket *(Shoprite 681-0900; East & West Grocery 988-7171)*, Health Food *(Natural Nutrition 774-2016)*, Liquor Store *(Corlies 775-7578)*, Library *(Neptune 988-8866)*, Hardware Store *(Hardware Enterprises 988-3401)*, Copies Etc. *(Hoffman Press 502-0110)*

Transportation
OnCall: Rental Car *(Enterprise 556-0666, Hertz 280-2166)*, Taxi *(Coast City Cab 774-1414)*, Airport Limo *(Always On Time 280-6779)*
1-3 mi: Bikes *(DJ's 681-8228)*, **3+ mi:** Rail *(Belmar to NYC, 5 mi.)*
Airport: Newark *(40 mi.)*

Medical Services
911 Service **Under 1 mi:** Doctor, Chiropractor *(Misner Chiropractic775-5050)*, Ambulance **1-3 mi:** Dentist *(Jersey Shore Dental 774-5772)*, Veterinarian *(Shark River Vet 775-2444)* **3+ mi:** Holistic Services *(Sea Girt Massage 974-1590, 4 mi.)* **Hospital:** Jersey Shore 775-5500 *(1.5 mi.)*

Setting -- Across the Shark River from the towns of Belmar and Neptune, Shark River Hills is in a quiet, residential setting. It straddles both sides of a 2-lane road and the docks are strung out along the roadway. However, its protected location, on the back side of the river, is also away from the bustle of the shore crowds.

Marina Notes -- Family owned and operated for 40 years by the Olivers, and also family-oriented. Oldest Chris Craft dealer in the nation. Home to mostly sport fishing boats and smaller runabouts - there are only four feet of water at low tide. 15 ton travelift onsite for major/minor engine repairs. Bistro-by-the-Sea pizzeria and snack bar onsite. Very nicely maintained full bathroom heads are shared with the snack bar. Discount on weekly and monthly if available. 4 bascule bridge from the ocean to the marina.

Notable -- Across the street is a pleasantly landscaped park. Bistro-by-the-Sea is open 11am-9pm Sun-Thu, to 10pm Fri-Sat and also offers an extensive Southern Italian catering menu - full pans of appetizers, dinners and pastas plus various platters. The downside of the quiet setting is that very few services or amenities are within walking distance - a couple of restaurants are about a mile away. Most other services are across the bridge.

Navigational Information
Lat: 40°10.845' **Long:** 074°01.774' **Tide:** 8 ft. **Current:** n/a **Chart:** 12324
Rep. Depths *(MLW):* **Entry** 12 ft. **Fuel Dock** 7 ft. **Max Slip/Moor** 7 ft./-
Access: One mile up the Shark River from the Atlantic inlet

Marina Facilities *(In Season/Off Season)*
Fuel: Gasoline, Diesel
Slips: 315 Total, 9 Transient **Max LOA:** 120 ft. **Max Beam:** n/a
  Rate *(per ft.):* **Day** $2.00 **Week** $1.25 **Month** Inq.
  Power: 30 amp Incl., 50 amp Incl., 100 amp n/a, 200 amp n/a
Cable TV: Yes **Dockside Phone:** No
Dock Type: Floating, Long Fingers, Concrete
Moorings: 0 Total, 0 Transient **Launch:** n/a
  Rate: Day n/a **Week** n/a **Month** n/a
Heads: 12 Toilet(s), 6 Shower(s)
Laundry: 2 Washer(s), 2 Dryer(s) **Pay Phones:** Yes
Pump-Out: OnSite, Full Service, 2 Central **Fee:** $5 **Closed Heads:** Yes

Marina Operations
Owner/Manager: Teddy King **Dockmaster:** John Provenzo (maintenance)
In-Season: Apr-Oct, 6am-6pm **Off-Season:** Nov-Mar, 7am-4pm
After-Hours Arrival: Call ahead
Reservations: Yes **Credit Cards:** Visa/MC, Amex
Discounts: None
Pets: Welcome **Handicap Access:** Yes, Heads, Docks

Belmar Marina

PO Box A, 601 Main St.; Belmar, NJ 07719

Tel: (732) 681-2266 **VHF: Monitor** 16 **Talk** 12
Fax: (732) 681-3434 **Alternate Tel:** n/a
Email: marina@belmar.com **Web:** www.belmar.com
Nearest Town: Belmar **Tourist Info:** (732) 681-3700

Marina Services and Boat Supplies
Services - Docking Assistance, Concierge, Boaters' Lounge, Security *(24 hrs., 8 cameras)* **Communication -** Mail & Package Hold, Phone Messages, Data Ports *(at the Library)*, FedEx, AirBorne, UPS, Express Mail **Supplies - OnSite:** Ice *(Cube)*, Bait/Tackle *(Fisherman's Den 681-5005)*
1-3 mi: Ships' Store *(Consumers Marine 681-9025)*, Propane *(A's 528-6909)*

Boatyard Services
OnSite: Launching Ramp **OnCall:** Electrical Repairs, Electronics Repairs, Hull Repairs, Rigger, Bottom Cleaning, Brightwork, Refrigeration

Restaurants and Accommodations
OnSite: Snack Bar *(Belmar Marina Deli 681-3282, B $2-5, L $2-8, 5am-7pm)* **Near:** Restaurant *(Princess Maria Diner 282-1722)*, *(Acropolis Diner 556-0050)*, *(Atlantic BBQ 681-8811, take-out)*, *(Ragin Cajun 280-6828)*, *(Klien's Grill Room & Sushi Bar 681-1177, cash only)*, *(Porta Romana 681-4785)*, *(Armadillo Crossing 280-8017)*, *(Veggie Works 280-1141)*, *(Oyama Japanese 280-5983)*, Pizzeria *(Frederico's 681-7066)*, Motel *(Belmar Motor Lodge 681-6600)* **Under 1 mi:** Hotel *(Sea Girt Lodge 974-2323)*, Inn/B&B *(Belport Inn 681-7894)*, *(Inn at the Shore 681-3762, $65-125)*

Recreation and Entertainment
OnSite: Dive Shop *(Boats 298-4519, 988-5455)*, Boat Rentals *(Fishman's Den 681-6677 motor boats $30)*, Fishing Charter *(18 boats)*, Group Fishing Boat *(8 boats $27-45)* **Near:** Beach, Picnic Area, Grills, Playground, Tennis Courts, Fitness Center *(Training Room 681-5009, Yoga 681-7660)*, Jogging Paths, Video Rental *(Belmar 681-6227)*, Park, Museum *(Children's Museum 280-8000)*, Cultural Attract *(Fri Night Concerts Pyanoe Plaza; Thu Socials*

Taylor Pavilion), Special Events *(Seafood Fest mid-Jun; Fieman's Canival, Sand Castles)* **1-3 mi:** Golf Course *(Quail Ridge 681-1800)*, Movie Theater *(Spring Lake 449-4530)* **3+ mi:** Bowling *(Lanes 775-6050, 3.5 mi.)*

Provisioning and General Services
OnSite: Fishmonger *(or Klien's 681-1177)*, Bank/ATM **Near:** Convenience Store, Delicatessen *(Italian Delight 681-5444)*, Wine/Beer *(Little Red Barn 681-4030)*, Liquor Store *(Hanley's 681-7788)*, Bakery *(Freedman's 681-2334; Belmar Bagels 681-2019)*, Post Office, Catholic Church, Protestant Church, Synagogue, Library *(681-0775 Internet)*, Beauty Salon *(Shampoo)*, Barber Shop *(Bruno's)*, Dry Cleaners, Laundry, Bookstore, Hardware Store *(Taylor's 681-0511)*, Florist, Copies Etc. *(Quikie 974-0220)* **Under 1 mi:** Supermarket *(Pathmark 449-6611)*, Health Food *(Nature's Corner 449-4950)*, Pharmacy *(Eckerd 681-3722)* **1-3 mi:** Gourmet Shop *(Barlow 449-9189)*, Green Grocer *(Welsh Farms 223-9517)*, Buying Club *(Costco, BJ's)*
3+ mi: Department Store *(Monmouth Mall, 6 mi.)*

Transportation
OnCall: Taxi *(280-1414)*, Airport Limo *(Belmar 681-8294)* **Near:** Bikes *(Skate Rental 681-7767 $20, DJ's 681-8228)*, Rental Car *(Enterprise 556-0666, Hertz 280-2121)*, Local Bus, Rail *(800-772-2222 Coast Line to Penn Station, NYC & Newark Airport)* **Airport:** Newark/Monmouth *(40mi./6mi.)*

Medical Services
911 Service **OnCall:** Ambulance **Near:** Doctor *(Wall Family Medical 974-1980)*, Dentist *(Belmar Dental 681-2393)*, Chiropractor *(NJ Chiro 449-9393)*, Holistic Services *(Body Basics Wellness 280-5505)*, Veterinarian *(Sea Girt Animal Hosp. 449-9224)* **Hospital:** Jersey Shore Medical 775-5500 *(3 mi.)*

Setting -- Overlooking scenic Shark River, this newly expanded and impeccably renovated municipal facility is a haven for anglers and fishing vessels - both private and commercial. The docks line two sides of a large parking area - pleasure boats down one side and charter and party vessels down the other. Fresh bright blue awnings mark the entryway to the six secure piers that host the floating recreational docks.

Marina Notes -- A $5 million renovation makes this municipal facility one of the state's nicest recreational, and its largest, commercial marina. 6 new state-of-the art floating concrete docks in '00, 2 more new in '03, and one with 57 new all-transient slips (26 ft.-90 ft.) scheduled for Fall '04. Now transients mostly on T-heads. An old time snack bar and large, well-equipped tackle shop are onsite. Attractive new clubhouse with rattan-furnished boaters lounge and lovely all-tile heads and showers, a baby-changing table and laundry. Note: 4 bridges to/from the ocean. The Acme supermarket closed; a replacement is promised.

Notable -- The well-appointed town of Belmar begins a block away and offers most of what a visitor might need, including dozens of restaurants. Its dual reputation as a pub-crawling party town for the twenty-something groupers and as home to dozens of charter and group fishing (head or party) boat operations makes for a fun and interesting mix. Boats go out daily for bluefish, weakfish, fluke and shark; when they return with their catch, there's a little pandemonium and a great scene. Crowds of people and gulls gather around each boat to barter for fish, bones, or just to watch the fillet knives flash. Eight festivals keep things hopping during the season. Across the street is the N.J. Transit's Coastline to NYC, Newark Airport and other points. Walk to the beach.

Hoffman's Marina

602 Green Avenue; Brielle, NJ 08730

Tel: (732) 528-6160 **VHF: Monitor** n/a **Talk** 65
Fax: (732) 223-0211 **Alternate Tel:** (732) 528-6160
Email: hoffmansmarina@aol.com **Web:** www.hoffmansmarina.com
Nearest Town: Brielle *(0.5 mi.)* **Tourist Info:** (732) 899-2424

Navigational Information
Lat: 40°06.457' **Long:** 074°02.964' **Tide:** 6 ft. **Current:** 2 kt. **Chart:** n/a
Rep. Depths *(MLW):* **Entry** 6 ft. **Fuel Dock** 6 ft. **Max Slip/Moor** 20 ft./-
Access: Manasquan Inlet - straight ahead, past R2

Marina Facilities *(In Season/Off Season)*
Fuel: *Texaco* - Slip-Side Fueling, Gasoline, Diesel
Slips: 48 Total, 2 Transient **Max LOA:** 80 ft. **Max Beam:** 21 ft.
 Rate *(per ft.):* **Day** $2.00/1.75 **Week** Inq. **Month** Inq.
 Power: 30 amp Incl., **50 amp** Incl., **100 amp** n/a **200 amp** n/a
 Cable TV: No **Dockside Phone:** No
 Dock Type: Fixed, Wood
Moorings: 0 Total, 0 Transient **Launch:** n/a
 Rate: Day n/a **Week** n/a **Month** n/a
Heads: 3 Toilet(s), 3 Shower(s) *(with dressing rooms)*
Laundry: None **Pay Phones:** Yes
Pump-Out: OnCall, Self Service, 1 InSlip **Fee:** $5 **Closed Heads:** Yes

Marina Operations
Owner/Manager: Art Colabella **Dockmaster:** Same
In-Season: Apr 18-Dec 19, Dawn-Dusk **Off-Season:** Dec 20-Apr 17, closed
After-Hours Arrival: Call in Advance
Reservations: Yes **Credit Cards:** Visa/MC, Dscvr, Din, Amex, Tex
Discounts: None
Pets: Welcome, Dog Walk Area **Handicap Access:** Yes, Heads, Docks

Marina Services and Boat Supplies
Services - Docking Assistance, Trash Pick-Up, Dock Carts
Communication - Mail & Package Hold, Phone Messages, Fax in/out,
FedEx, AirBorne, UPS, Express Mail *(Sat Del)* **Supplies - OnSite:** Ice
(Block, Cube), Ships' Store **Near:** Bait/Tackle *(Reel Seat 23-5353)*,
Propane *(Across the Street-Dickson's 528-9300)*

Boatyard Services
OnSite: Travelift *(35T)*, Engine mechanic *(gas, diesel)*, Electrical Repairs,
Hull Repairs, Bottom Cleaning, Brightwork, Air Conditioning, Refrigeration,
Compound, Wash & Wax, Interior Cleaning, Propeller Repairs **OnCall:**
Inflatable Repairs, Life Raft Service, Upholstery, Yacht Interiors, Metal
Fabrication **Dealer for:** Atlantic Detroit Diesel-Allison, Mercury.

Restaurants and Accommodations
OnCall: Pizzeria *(First Avenue 528-5754)* **Near:** Restaurant *(Union Landing
528-6665)*, *(Sand Bar 528-7750)*, *(Anthony's 528-7833)*, *(River Club 528-
7000, D $18-29)*, *(La Perla at the Riverhouse 528-7000)*, Snack Bar
(Eloise's), Lite Fare *(The River House Deck 528-7000, L $7-13, D $7-13)*,
Pizzeria *(Salernos 528-5566)* **Under 1 mi:** Hotel *(Beachcomber 223-2988)*,
(Osprey Hotel 528-1800), Inn/B&B *(Nathaniel Morris 223-7826)*
 1-3 mi: Fast Food *(Mc Donalds, Burger King)*, Motel *(Surf Side 899-1109)*,
 Hotel *(Harbor Lights Resorts 295-3440)*

Recreation and Entertainment
OnSite: Picnic Area, Grills, Fishing Charter **Near:** Playground, Park,
Special Events **Under 1 mi:** Beach, Dive Shop, Jogging Paths, Boat
Rentals, Video Arcade **1-3 mi:** Fitness Center *(Premier 295-1212)*, Video

Rental *(Blockbuster714-9153)*, Cultural Attract *(Algonquin Arts Theater 528-
9211)* **3+ mi:** Tennis Courts *(Atlantic 223-2100, 4 mi.)*, Golf Course *(Quail
Ridge G.C. 681-1800, 6 mi.)*, Bowling *(Highway 35 Lanes 449-4942, 5 mi.)*,
Movie Theater *(Spring Lake 449-4530, 4 mi.)*

Provisioning and General Services
Near: Convenience Store, Gourmet Shop *(Brielle Country 292-9888)*, Liquor
Store *(Jonathan 528-8166)*, Bakery, Green Grocer, Fishmonger, Lobster
Pound **Under 1 mi:** Bank/ATM, Post Office, Catholic Church, Protestant
Church, Library *(Brielle PL 528-9381)*, Beauty Salon, Barber Shop, Dry
Cleaners, Pharmacy *(Brielle 528-5400)*, Newsstand, Clothing Store **1-3 mi:**
Supermarket *(Acme, Foodtown, Quick-Pik 528-9542)*, Delicatessen *(Plaza
Deli 899-9551)*, Health Food *(Monmouth 223-4900)*, Wine/Beer *(Goodloe
223-3180)*, Laundry, Bookstore *(Book Bin 892-3456)*, Hardware Store *(A's
Home Center 528-6909)*, Florist, Copies Etc. *(Beta 292-9003)* **3+ mi:**
Department Store *(Kmart 840-0800, 4 mi.)*, Buying Club *(Costco, 6 mi.)*

Transportation
OnCall: Taxi *(Shore 223-8294, Sandy's 223-0060)* **Near:** Water Taxi *(Bar
Screen)*, Local Bus **Under 1 mi:** Bikes *(Brielle Cyclery 528-9121)*, Rail *(NJ
Transit to NYC & Phil.)* **1-3 mi:** Rental Car, Airport Limo *(Able 528-2253)*
Airport: Newark Int'l/Monmouth *(40 mi./7mi)*

Medical Services
911 Service **OnCall:** Ambulance **Under 1 mi:** Dentist *(Murray 528-5656)*,
Chiropractor *(Adio Chiro 528-6644)*, Veterinarian *(Brielle Clinic 528-7800)*
1-3 mi: Doctor *(Wall Family 974-1980)*, Holistic Services *(Integrated
Massage 681-8508)* **Hospital:** Brick Medical 840-2200 *(6 mi.)*

Setting -- Just past the River Club and before the railroad bridge, bold red pilings signal the docks of Hoffman Marine. Right off the channel, the docks have views across the river to the marsh on the unspoiled south shore, to the Gull Island reserve and out to the open inlet.

Marina Notes -- Family owned and operated, in business since 1964. Dedicated to fishing, it caters primarily to sport fishing boats. Basic, but quite nice, full cinderblock bathrooms. Fuel & bait for fisherman, fuel and dockage for transients. Bait & tackle shop and fish cleaning station. Onsite charter fleet offers inshore, offshore, bottom fishing, and tournament fishing for tuna, mako shark, marlin, dolphin, striped bass, bluefish, blackfish, sea bass, and fluke: Big Mac 388-5891, Blue Chip 528-7223, Egg Me On 908-203-0069, Fear No Fish 223-6383, Mary Lou 884-9093, Sherri Berri 223-5729.

Notable -- Adjacent is the River House (under new ownership) with a wide variety of dining options: River Club for a la carte dinning 5pm-midnight Tue-Sun; The Deck, for more casual al fresco dining on the 2 level veranda Tue-Thu & Sun Noon-10pm, Fri & Sat 11am on; The River Watch banquet room overlooking the inlet for groups 35-100; and the upstairs Ocean View Room for 100-200. The train runs right next to the marina and the town of Brielle is a reasonable walk. Brielle Day is the 1st Saturday after Labor Day - races, fine arts & crafts fair.

Navigational Information
Lat: 40°06.468' **Long:** 074°03.057' **Tide:** 4.5 ft. **Current:** 1.5 kt. **Chart:** 123;
Rep. Depths (*MLW*): **Entry** 15 ft. **Fuel Dock** 12 ft. **Max Slip/Moor** 8 ft./-
Access: 1/2 mile to Atlantic Ocean

Marina Facilities *(In Season/Off Season)*
Fuel: *Mobil* - Slip-Side Fueling, Gasoline, Diesel
Slips: 80 Total, 15 Transient **Max LOA:** 85 ft. **Max Beam:** 24 ft.
 Rate *(per ft.)*: **Day** $2.50/$1.50-$2.00* **Week** Inq. **Month** Inq.
 Power: 30 amp Incl., 50 amp Incl., 100 amp n/a, 200 amp n/a
 Cable TV: No **Dockside Phone:** No
 Dock Type: Fixed, Long Fingers, Pilings, Wood
Moorings: 0 Total, 0 Transient **Launch:** n/a
 Rate: Day n/a **Week** n/a **Month** n/a
Heads: 3 Toilet(s), 2 Shower(s)
Laundry: None **Pay Phones:** No
Pump-Out: OnSite, Self Service **Fee:** $5 **Closed Heads:** Yes

Marina Operations
Owner/Manager: Fred Ziemba & Joan Paslowski **Dockmaster:** same
In-Season: Apr-Oct, 7am-5pm **Off-Season:** Nov-Mar, 8am-4pm
After-Hours Arrival: Call on phone or VHF.
Reservations: Yes **Credit Cards:** Visa/MC
Discounts: None
Pets: Welcome, Dog Walk Area **Handicap Access:** No

Brielle Marine Basin

608 Green Avenue; Brielle, NJ 08730

Tel: (732) 528-6200 **VHF: Monitor** 16 **Talk** 9
Fax: (732) 528-6225 **Alternate Tel:** n/a
Email: service@briellemarine.com **Web:** www.briellemarine.com
Nearest Town: Manasquan *(1 mi.)* **Tourist Info:** (732) 528-0377

Marina Services and Boat Supplies
Services - Docking Assistance, Concierge, Dock Carts **Communication** - Mail & Package Hold, Phone Messages, Fax in/out, FedEx, AirBorne, UPS, Express Mail *(Sat Del)* **Supplies - OnSite:** Ice *(Cube)*, Ships' Store, Bait/Tackle *(Reel Seat 223-5353)* **Near:** Ice *(Block)*, Live Bait **Under 1 mi:** Propane *(Dickson's 528-9300)*

Boatyard Services
OnSite: Travelift *(30 & 70T)*, Forklift *(9T)*, Engine mechanic *(gas)*, Electrical Repairs, Hull Repairs, Bottom Cleaning, Brightwork, Yacht Broker **OnCall:** Electronics Repairs, Air Conditioning, Compound, Wash & Wax, Interior Cleaning, Propeller Repairs **Under 1 mi:** Engine mechanic *(diesel)*, Launching Ramp, Metal Fabrication. **1-3 mi:** Railway, Rigger, Sail Loft. **Dealer for:** Mercruiser Marine. **Yard Rates:** $80/hr., Haul & Launch $8/ft.-$10/ft. *(blocking $60 to 120')*, Power Wash $5 per ft., Bottom Paint $7.50-$9/ft. **Storage:** In-Water $115-$140/ft., On-Land Call for price

Restaurants and Accommodations
Near: Restaurant *(Sand Bar 528-7750, L $6-12, D $9-25, local award winning)*, *(Union Landing 528-6665, L $6-10, D $8-20)*, *(La Perla 528-7000)*, *(Alexus Steakhouse)*, *(Due Amici's 528-0666)*, *(Eloise's Cafe 223-6363)*, Lite Fare *(Shipwreck Grill 292-9380)* **Under 1 mi:** Pizzeria *(Salerno's)*, *(Squan Pizza)*, Hotel *(Beachcomber 223-2988)*, Inn/B&B *(Nathaniel Morris 223-7826)* **1-3 mi:** Fast Food *(McDonalds, Burger King)*, Lite Fare *(Mariner's Cove Diner 528-6023, B, L 6am-3pm)*, Motel *(Surfside 899-1109)*, Inn/B&B *(Steepleview 899-8999)*

Recreation and Entertainment
OnSite: Fishing Charter **Near:** Picnic Area, Playground, Group Fishing Boat **Under 1 mi:** Beach, Boat Rentals, Video Arcade, Park **1-3 mi:** Dive Shop, Tennis Courts *(Atlantic Club 223-2100)*, Video Rental *(Blockbuster 701-1009)* **3+ mi:** Golf Course *(Bel-Aire GC 449-6024, 5 mi)*, Bowling *(Sea Girt 449-4942, 4 mi.)*, Movie Theater *(Spring Lake 449-4530, 4 mi.)*

Provisioning and General Services
OnSite: Clothing Store *(Boutique)* **Near:** Convenience Store, Gourmet Shop *(Brielle Country 292-9888)*, Liquor Store *(Jonathan Ron 528-8166)*, Bakery, Farmers' Market, Bank/ATM, Post Office, Dry Cleaners, Pharmacy *(Brielle 528-5400)* **Under 1 mi:** Market *(Quick-Pik 528-9542)*, Delicatessen *(Jon Anthony's 223-0769)*, Fishmonger, Meat Market, Catholic Church, Protestant Church, Library *(Brielle 528-9381)*, Beauty Salon, Barber Shop, Laundry, Florist **1-3 mi:** Supermarket *(Acme 223-9622, Center Food Market 223-4556)*, Health Food *(Monmouth 223-4900)*, Wine/Beer *(Goodloe 223-3180)*, Hardware Store *(Jaspan 223-1667)*, Copies Etc. *(Beta 292-9003)*

Transportation
OnCall: Rental Car *(Enterprise)*, Taxi *(Sandy's Taxi)*, Airport Limo *(Able 528-2253, Olympic)* **Near:** Water Taxi **Under 1 mi:** Bikes *(Brielle Cyclery 528-9121)*, Local Bus, Rail **Airport:** Newark Int'l/Monmouth *(40 mi./8 mi.)*

Medical Services
911 Service **Near:** Ambulance **Under 1 mi:** Doctor *(Wall Family 974-1980)*, Dentist *(Brielle Hills 223-2334)*, Chiropractor *(Adio Chiro 528-6644)*, Holistic Services *(Di Napoli 528-5860)*, Veterinarian *(Brielle Clinic 528-7800)* **Hospital:** Ocean County 840-2200 *(6 mi.)*

Setting -- Brielle Marine Basin, one of the larger marinas on the Manasquan, is the first set of docks just past the open railroad bridge, about a half mile after entering the inlet. Its slips have peaceful views across to the Gull Island reserve and surrounding marsh and landside of the tidy full-service boatyard.

Marina Notes -- *Overnight rate: $2.00 w/ fuel purchase ($50 min.) $2.50/ft.without. Founded in the early 1950's by the Ziemba family, it is still a family operation; siblings Fred Ziemba and Joan Paslowski create a friendly, helpful atmosphere. Ask for their local map - it's very useful. Seven-day operation. Fuel, bait, ice, tackle, and in-slip fueling. Both charter and private sport fishing boats. Winter dockage, on-land storage and dry rack service. Fully stocked ships' store with an extensive MerCruiser parts department, charts and Racor filters. Propeller and shaft service. Coin-operated showers - 2 quarters for 7 minutes. A cute little clothing shop with nautical gear overlooks the docks. No laundry.

Notable -- The lovely little town of Manasquan is less than a mile walk. And it's about half a mile to an ocean beach. The Shoprite supermarket is now closed; the closest large market is Acme, 1.5 miles. The train runs along side the marina which could create some sound issues; the NJ Transit RR station is less than a mile with service to New York and Philadelphia. The Greywolf Fitness Gym is next door. Manasquan Water Taxi service runs up and down the river connecting the restaurants ($8) and offering special event cruises (292-1159). The New Jersey Museum of Boating (859-4767), founded in 2000, is located about 2.5 miles at Johnson Bros Boat Works.

Brielle Yacht Club

201 Union Lane; Brielle, NJ 08730

Tel: (732) 528-6250 **VHF: Monitor** 16 **Talk** 9
Fax: (732) 528-1865 **Alternate Tel:** (732) 892-3000
Email: n/a **Web:** n/a
Nearest Town: Manasquan *(0.6 mi.)* **Tourist Info:** (732) 899-2424

Navigational Information

Lat: 40°06.457' **Long:** 074°03.149' **Tide:** 4 ft. **Current:** 2 kt. **Chart:** 12324
Rep. Depths *(MLW):* **Entry** 8 ft. **Fuel Dock** 8 ft. **Max Slip/Moor** 8 ft./-
Access: Manasquan Inlet, past the railroad bridge, third set of docks

Marina Facilities *(In Season/Off Season)*

Fuel: *Mobil* - Slip-Side Fueling, Gasoline, Diesel, High-Speed Pumps
Slips: 0 Total, 0 Transient **Max LOA:** 108 ft. **Max Beam:** 28 ft.
 Rate *(per ft.):* **Day** $1.50/$1.50 **Week** Inq. **Month** Inq.
 Power: 30 amp Incl., 50 amp Incl., 100 amp n/a, 200 amp n/a
 Cable TV: No **Dockside Phone:** No
 Dock Type: Fixed, Long Fingers, Short Fingers, Wood
Moorings: 0 Total, 0 Transient **Launch:** n/a
 Rate: Day n/a **Week** n/a **Month** n/a
Heads: 4 Toilet(s), 4 Shower(s)
Laundry: None **Pay Phones:** Yes
Pump-Out: OnCall, Full Service **Fee:** $7 **Closed Heads:** Yes

Marina Operations

Owner/Manager: Arnold J. D'Ambrosa **Dockmaster:** Scott Roberts
In-Season: May 15-Nov 15, 6am-7pm **Off-Season:** Apr 15-Oct 15, 8am-6pm
After-Hours Arrival: Check in at Sandbar restaurant
Reservations: Preferred **Credit Cards:** Visa/MC, Amex, Mobil
Discounts: None
Pets: Welcome **Handicap Access:** No

Marina Services and Boat Supplies

Services - Docking Assistance, Trash Pick-Up, Dock Carts, Megayacht Facilities **Communication -** Phone Messages, FedEx, AirBorne, UPS, Express Mail *(Sat Del)* **Supplies - OnSite:** Ice *(Block, Cube, Shaved)*, Bait/Tackle *(Reel Seat 223-5353)*, Live Bait *(Killies)* **Under 1 mi:** Ships' Store, Propane *(Across the Street 528-9300)*

Boatyard Services

OnSite: Yacht Broker *(Laviola)* **OnCall:** Engine mechanic *(gas, diesel)*, Electrical Repairs, Electronic Sales, Electronics Repairs, Rigger, Sail Loft, Brightwork, Air Conditioning, Refrigeration, Divers, Compound, Wash & Wax, Interior Cleaning, Propeller Repairs, Inflatable Repairs, Life Raft Service, Yacht Interiors **Under 1 mi:** Launching Ramp.
Nearest Yard: Brielle Marine Basin (732) 528-6250

Restaurants and Accommodations

OnSite: Restaurant *(Sandbar 232-528-7750, L $6-8, D $11-16, Kids $5)*, *(Union Landing 528-6665, D $13-21, Kids $5-6)*, Seafood Shack *(Sand Bar)*, Lite Fare *(Union Landing Patio L $6-14, D $6-14)* **Near:** Restaurant *(River House 232-528-7000, L $6-9, D $12-25)*, *(La Perla 528-7000)* **Under 1 mi:** Inn/B&B *(Nathaniel Morris 223-7826)* **1-3 mi:** Fast Food *(Burger King)*, Pizzeria *(Maria's 223-2033)*, Motel *(Beachcomber 223-2988)*, *(Surfside 899-1109)*, *(Point Beach Motel 892-5100)*, Inn/B&B *(Steepleview 899-8999)*

Recreation and Entertainment

OnSite: Fishing Charter, Sightseeing *(Treasure Is. Tours $13, Salt Water Safari Narrow Bird Sanctuary 292-1159)* **Near:** Playground, Fitness Center *(Grey Wolf Fitness Gym)* **Under 1 mi:** Beach, Picnic Area, Grills, Cultural

Attract *(Algonquin Arts 528-9211)* **1-3 mi:** Dive Shop, Tennis Courts *(Atlantic Club 223-2100)*, Video Rental *(Blockbuster 714-9153)*, Museum *(NJ Boating Museum 859-4767)* **3+ mi:** Pool, Golf Course *(Bel-Aire G.C. 449-6024, 4 mi.)*, Bowling *(Lanes at Sea Girt 449-4942, 4 mi.)*, Movie Theater *(Spring Lake 449-4530, 4 mi.)*

Provisioning and General Services

Near: Convenience Store *(Quick-Pik 528-9542)*, Gourmet Shop *(Brielle 292-9888)*, Wine/Beer *(Manasquan)*, Liquor Store *(Jonathan Ron 528-8166)*, Farmers' Market, Green Grocer, Pharmacy *(Eckerd, Brielle 528-5400)*, Newsstand **Under 1 mi:** Delicatessen *(Jon Anthony's 223-0769)*, Bakery *(Freedman's)*, Bank/ATM, Post Office, Catholic Church, Protestant Church, Library *(Brielle PL 528-9381)*, Beauty Salon, Dry Cleaners, Laundry, Bookstore **1-3 mi:** Supermarket *(Acme 223-9622)*, Health Food *(Monmouth 223-4900)*, Fishmonger, Lobster Pound, Meat Market, Barber Shop, Hardware Store *(Jaspan 223-1667)*, Florist, Copies Etc. *(Ahern 223-1476)*

Transportation

OnSite: Water Taxi *(292-1159)* **OnCall:** Taxi *(Sandy's 223-0060)*, Airport Limo *(Able 528-2253)* **Under 1 mi:** Bikes *(Brielle Cyclery 528-9121)*, Rental Car *(Rent-a-Wreck 528-6668)*, Rail *(NJ transit to NYC & Phil.)*
Airport: Newark Int'l/Allaire *(40 mi./9 mi.)*

Medical Services

911 Service **Near:** Doctor *(Makowski Medical 528-5626)*, Chiropractor *(Adio 528-6644)* **Under 1 mi:** Holistic Services *(Coastal Massage Therapy 528-0896)*, Veterinarian *(Brielle Clinic 528-7800)* **1-3 mi:** Dentist *(Brielle Hills 223-2334)*, Ambulance **Hospital:** Ocean County 840-2200 *(6 miles)*

Setting -- Brielle Yacht Club Marina's 125 slips are the second set just past the railroad bridge. An easy 0.6 mile from the inlet, it is the centerpiece of Brielle Landing, a high-end contemporary condo and town house complex. The fancifully designed two-story octagonal main building, perched high on the river bank, has half-barrel windows that light the second floor of the onsite Sand Bar Restaurant.

Marina Notes -- Owner operated well maintained facility with a friendly, knowledgable staff. A small tree-shaded courtyard behind the restaurant serves as the axis point of the marina facilities. On the docks are Fish cleaning stations and a charter sport fishing operator. "A" dock is a second set of slips that are actually the very first set of docks one passes when heading in from the Inlet - before the River House. There is occasional transient dockage here, too; it is a little quieter but the heads and showers are quite a distance at the main Marina.

Notable -- The Sand Bar Restaurant and the adjacent Union Landing Restaurant and Marina combine to create a lively party atmosphere that spills out onto the docks. The Sandbar has two stories of eating options including cozy decks off the elevated first floor (11am-1pm, 7 days. Wed - DJ, Fri & Sat - live music, Mon & Thu - Lobster specials $16). Union Landing has a wonderful multi-tiered patio that tumbles to the docks (L&D 7 days) and a more formal inside dining room (Wed-Sun, 4:30 on for dinner). Its grounds include a perfectly executed Koi pond and waterfall. Manasquan Water Taxi connects many of the restaurants on the river, also offers bar-hopping and Treasure Island tours. The surrounding neighborhood features well maintained suburban homes.

Navigational Information
Lat: 40°06.076' **Long:** 074°02.781' **Tide:** 4 ft. **Current:** 3 kt. **Chart:** 12324
Rep. Depths (*MLW*): **Entry** 6 ft. **Fuel Dock** 5 ft. **Max Slip/Moor** 5 ft./-
Access: Manasquan Inlet, past Lake Louise channel to south side of Gull Islan

Marina Facilities (*In Season/Off Season*)
Fuel: Diesel
Slips: 43 Total, 4 Transient **Max LOA:** 50 ft. **Max Beam:** n/a
  Rate (*per ft.*): **Day** $1.50/Inq. **Week** Inq. **Month** Inq.
  Power: 30 amp $5, **50 amp** $5, **100 amp** n/a, **200 amp** n/a
  Cable TV: No **Dockside Phone:** No
  Dock Type: Fixed
Moorings: 0 Total, 0 Transient **Launch:** n/a
  Rate: Day n/a **Week** n/a **Month** n/a
Heads: 2 Toilet(s), 1 Shower(s)
Laundry: None **Pay Phones:** Yes, 1
Pump-Out: OnSite, Self Service **Fee:** $5 **Closed Heads:** Yes

Marina Operations
Owner/Manager: Rick Fischer **Dockmaster:** Same
In-Season: May-Oct, 8:30am-5pm **Off-Season:** Oct-Apr, Closed
After-Hours Arrival: Use haul out slip
Reservations: Preferred **Credit Cards:** Visa/MC, Dscvr, Amex
Discounts: None
Pets: Welcome **Handicap Access:** No

Southside Marina

PO Box 521; 311 Channel Drive; Pt. Pleasant, NJ 08742

Tel: (732) 892-0388 **VHF: Monitor** 16 **Talk** 17
Fax: (732) 892-8156 **Alternate Tel:** n/a
Email: Tunar@bytheshore.com **Web:** n/a
Nearest Town: Pt. Pleasant (*0.5 mi.*) **Tourist Info:** (732) 899-2424

Marina Services and Boat Supplies
Services - Docking Assistance **Communication -** Fax in/out, FedEx, AirBorne, UPS, Express Mail **Supplies -** OnSite: Ice (*Block*), Bait/Tackle (*Bogans 892-8822, too*) **Near:** Marine Discount Store (*USA Marine*) **1-3mi:** Propane (*Dickson's 528-9300*) **3+ mi:** West Marine (*262-8899, 9 mi.*)

Boatyard Services
OnSite: Travelift (*15T*), Engine mechanic (*gas, diesel*) **OnCall:** Electrical Repairs, Electronic Sales, Electronics Repairs, Hull Repairs, Rigger, Sail Loft, Bottom Cleaning, Brightwork, Air Conditioning, Refrigeration, Divers, Compound, Wash & Wax, Interior Cleaning

Restaurants and Accommodations
OnCall: Pizzeria (*Luigies 892-4848*) **Near:** Restaurant (*Tesauros 892-2090, D $10-18*), (*Off Shore 892-2848, D $18*), (*Barmore's Shrimp Box 899-1637*), Seafood Shack (*Spike's Fishery 295-9400*), Snack Bar (*Cottage*), Lite Fare (*Portofino's Lunch only Wed-Sun 11-4*), Motel (*Harbor Lights 295-3440*), (*Surfside Motel 899-1109*) **Under 1 mi:** Restaurant (*Sand Bar*), (*Ferrara's 899-3900*), (*Isohama 892-1600*), Seafood Shack (*Jack Baker's 899-6700*), Lite Fare (*Frankie's Grill 892-6000*), Pizzeria (*Stubby's Boardwalk 899-1060*), Hotel (*White Sands 899-3370, $150-260*) **1-3 mi:** Restaurant (*Clark Landing*), Fast Food (*Burger King*), Hotel (*Grenville Hotel 892-3100*), (*Sea Girt Lodge*), Inn/B&B (*Bay Head Gables 892-9844, $180-230*)

Recreation and Entertainment
OnSite: Fishing Charter **Near:** Dive Shop, Sightseeing (*River Belle Cruises 892-3377*), Special Events (*Brielle Day, 1st Sat after LabDay*) **Under 1 mi:** Beach, Fitness Center (*Meridian 295-1778*), Video Arcade (*Jenkinson's 899-09555*), Cultural Attract (*Jenkinson's Aquarium 899-1212 $8/5; Algonquin Arts 528-9211*) **1-3 mi:** Tennis Courts (*Atlantic Club 223-2100*), Bowling (*Playdrome 88 Lanes 892-0888*), Movie Theater, Video Rental (*Blockbuster 714-9153*), Museum (*NJ Museum of Boating 859-4767*) **3+ mi:** Golf Course (*Quail Ridge GC 681-1800, 7 mi.*)

Provisioning and General Services
Near: Convenience Store (*7-11*), Liquor Store, Fishmonger (*Spike's*), Lobster Pound (*Point Lobster 892-1792*), Copies Etc. (*C & D Printing 892-8044*) **Under 1 mi:** Supermarket (*Foodtown 899-8485*), Gourmet Shop (*Brielle 292-9888*), Delicatessen (*Plaza Deli 899-9551*), Health Food (*Health Matters 899-3353*), Wine/Beer (*Liquor Chain 899-8007*), Bakery, Meat Market, Bank/ATM, Post Office, Catholic Church, Protestant Church, Library (*Pt Pleasant 892-4575*), Beauty Salon, Barber Shop, Dry Cleaners, Laundry, Hardware Store (*Jaeger 899-9663*), Florist, Clothing Store, Retail Shops, Buying Club **1-3 mi:** Bookstore (*The Bookshop 892-1235*), Pharmacy (*Brielle 528-5400*) **3+ mi:** Department Store (*Kmart 840-0800, 4 mi.*)

Transportation
OnCall: Rental Car (*Enterprise 223-6400*), Taxi (*All City 477-5039*), Airport Limo (*WSAA 942-4400*) **Under 1 mi:** Rail (*NJ Transit to NYC & Phil*) **Airport:** Newark Int'l/Monmouth (*45 mi./8 mi.*)

Medical Services
911 Service **Under 1 mi:** Dentist (*Affiliated Ocean 840-3030*), Chiropractor (*Pt. Pleasant Chiro 892-1131*), Holistic Services (*Minding Body Wellness 892-7566*), Veterinarian (*Vet Depot 892-6470*) **1-3 mi:** Doctor (*Makowski Med 528-5626*) **Hospital:** Ocean County 840-2200 (*6.5 mi.*)

Setting -- After passing the Lake Louise Inlet, bear left to the channel on the southern side of Gull Island. Southside is a small, 43-slip rustic marina on the left side of the narow passage in a very convenient location. Views are of the backside of pristine Gull Island; landside is of a beachy, working waterfront area.

Marina Notes -- First marina inside the inlet. New owners in '98 add personal service that supports the basic boatyard operation. Several sport fishing charters and a dive boat make their home here (Miss Diane 899-FISH and 473-6382). The area has an appealing working waterfront feel. A short way up the road is a small gaggle of services - a 7-Eleven, Spike's Fishery, Portofino's restaurant, Point Lobster, a liquor store and Tsarro's restaurant.

Notable -- The proximity to the beach and Pt. Pleasant boardwalk makes Southside an even more interesting stop. The northern terminus of the Point Pleasant boardwalk is at the Manasquan Inlet, less than a half mile walk from the marina; the commercial part begins about a half mile south. The town of Point Pleasant has both public and private beaches: on the northern end, access tends to be private - Martells Tiki Bar has a beach, as does Jenkinson's Aquarium and Nightclub (beach -$6.50/1.50) which also has a large food court. South of this is private Bradshaw Beach, with lifeguard, which also requires the purchase of a beach badge. And further south is a free public beach with access on Ocean Avenue across from the Dunes Motel. NJ Transit rail station is less than a mile away, with service to NY City, Philadelphia, Newark and other shore points.

Navigational Information
Lat: 40°05.506' **Long:** 074°03.481' **Tide:** 4 ft. **Current:** 3 kt. **Chart:** 12324
Rep. Depths (*MLW*): **Entry** 5 ft. **Fuel Dock** n/a **Max Slip/Moor** 6 ft./-
Access: Manasquan Inlet, past Rt. 35 drawbridge, left at G7

Marina Facilities (*In Season/Off Season*)
Fuel: Gasoline, Diesel
Slips: 195 Total, 6 Transient **Max LOA:** 60 ft. **Max Beam:** n/a
  Rate (*per ft.*): **Day** $2.00/Same* **Week** Inq. **Month** Inq.
  Power: 30 amp Incl., **50 amp** Incl., **100 amp** n/a, **200 amp** n/a
  Cable TV: Yes **Dockside Phone:** Yes
  Dock Type: Fixed
Moorings: 0 Total, 0 Transient **Launch:** n/a
  Rate: Day n/a **Week** n/a **Month** n/a
Heads: 5 Toilet(s), 5 Shower(s) (*with dressing rooms*)
Laundry: None **Pay Phones:** Yes, 2
Pump-Out: OnSite, Full Service **Fee:** $5 **Closed Heads:** Yes

Marina Operations
Owner/Manager: Susan Brown **Dockmaster:** n/a
In-Season: May-Oct, 9am-5pm Sun-Sat **Off-Season:** Nov-Apr, 9am-4pm
After-Hours Arrival: Call in Advance
Reservations: Preferred **Credit Cards:** Visa/MC, Dscvr, Amex
Discounts: None
Pets: Welcome, Dog Walk Area **Handicap Access:** Yes, Heads, Docks

Clark's Landing Marina

847 Arnold Avenue; Pt. Pleasant, NJ 08742

Tel: (732) 899-5559 **VHF: Monitor** 5 **Talk** n/a
Fax: (732) 899-5572 **Alternate Tel:** n/a
Email: clpp@bellatlantic.net **Web:** www.clarkslanding.com
Nearest Town: Pt. Pleasant (*0.5 mi.*) **Tourist Info:** (732) 899-2424

Marina Services and Boat Supplies
Services - Docking Assistance, Security, Trash Pick-Up, Dock Carts
Communication - Mail & Package Hold, FedEx, AirBorne, UPS, Express
Mail (*Sat Del*) **Supplies - OnSite:** Ice (*Block, Cube*), Ships' Store,
Bait/Tackle (*or Bogans 892-8822 1 mi.*) **1-3 mi:** Propane (*Beaver Dam 899-4218*) **3+ mi:** West Marine (*262-8899, 6 mi.*), Boat/US (*477-9661, 5 mi.*)

Boatyard Services
OnSite: Travelift (*35T*), Forklift, Engine mechanic (*gas, diesel*), Hull Repairs,
Rigger, Bottom Cleaning, Brightwork, Divers **OnCall:** Electrical Repairs,
Electronic Sales, Electronics Repairs, Sail Loft, Air Conditioning,
Refrigeration, Compound, Wash & Wax **Yard Rates:** $85/hr., Haul &
Launch $7.75-8.75/ft. (*blocking incl.*), Power Wash $2.75/ft., Bottom Paint
$11-13/ft. (*paint incl.*) **Storage:** On-Land Inq. Winter Storage Pkg.

Restaurants and Accommodations
OnSite: Restaurant (*Clarks Landing Bar + Grill 899-1111, L $7-11,
D $13-40, L 11:30-4, D 'til 9:30*) **OnCall:** Pizzeria (*Luigi's 899-4848*)
Near: Restaurant (*Dennis Foys 295-0466*), (*Christy's 892-8553*), (*Capt'n
Ed's Steak & Seafood 892-4121*), Seafood Shack (*Beach Bar-Be-Que 899-8828*), Fast Food (*Jersey Mike's subs 892-9546*), (*Burger King, KFC, McD's*),
Pizzeria (*Pizza Plus 295-8908*) **Under 1 mi:** Motel (*Point Beach Motel 892-5100, $130-160*) **1-3 mi:** Hotel (*Bay Head Gables 892-9844, $180-225*),
(*White Sands Resort 899-3370, $150-260*)

Recreation and Entertainment
OnSite: Picnic Area, Grills, Fishing Charter **Near:** Beach, Fitness Center
(*Meridian 295-1778*), Special Events (*Festival by the Sea in Sep*)

Under 1 mi: Video Rental (*Blockbuster 701-1009*), Museum (*Pt. Pleasant
Hist. Soc.*), Cultural Attract (*Jenkinson's Aquarium 892-0600*)
1-3 mi: Playground, Bowling (*11th Frame 892-0888*), Movie Theater
(*Spring Lake449-4530*), Video Arcade **3+ mi:** Golf Course (*Forge Pond
County GC 920-8899, 6 mi.*)

Provisioning and General Services
OnSite: Convenience Store **Near:** Delicatessen (*Polish American 295-1707*), Health Food (*Sea Maiden 714-7100*), Wine/Beer (*Spirit Shoppe 899-7779*), Liquor Store (*C J'S 295-1707*), Bakery, Beauty Salon, Barber Shop,
Hardware Store (*Point 892-5200*), Clothing Store, Retail Shops, Buying
Club **Under 1 mi:** Supermarket (*Foodtown 899-8485*), Green Grocer,
Fishmonger, Lobster Pound (*Point 892-1729*), Bank/ATM, Post Office,
Library (*Pt. Pleasant 892-4575*), Dry Cleaners, Laundry, Bookstore,
Pharmacy (*CVS 295-9111*), Newsstand, Florist, Copies Etc. (*Precision
Copiers 458-0130*) **1-3 mi:** Gourmet Shop (*Brielle Country 292-9888*),
Meat Market, Catholic Church

Transportation
OnCall: Water Taxi (*Manasquan 292-1159*), Rental Car (*Enterprise 223-6400*), Taxi (*All City 477-5039*), Airport Limo (*Anthony's 295-3379*)
Under 1 mi: Rail (*to NY, Phil*) **Airport:** Newark Int'l/Monmouth (*45 mi./8 mi.*)

Medical Services
911 Service Near: Dentist (*Campbell 899-3363*), Holistic Services (*Minding
the Body 892-7566*) **Under 1 mi:** Chiropractor (*Pt Pleasant Chiror 892-1131*), Veterinarian (*Pt Pleasant Vet 892-4647*) **1-3 mi:** Doctor (*Makowski
528-5626*) **Hospital:** Ocean County 840-2200 (*4.5 mi.*)

Setting -- On the south side of the Manasquan, upriver from the Route 35 draw bridge, Clark's Landing's extensive network of docks and well-turned out
campus is hard to miss. Teal green mulit-level rooves top attractive beige contemporary buildings and a high energy party atmosphere counterpoints the
thoroughly professional, rock solid operation.

Marina Notes -- *Nightly rates include power: $1.75/ft. for 30 amp, $2/ft 50 amp. In 1878, Roderick Clark, a local boat builder, purchased this waterfront
property on Arnold Avenue. Clark's Landing's electric carousel, dance floor and steam orgran made it one of the area's first tourist destinations and was a big
draw at the turn of the 20th Century. Now it's known as "New Jersey's Tournament Center" because of the large fleet of over 20 sport fishing charters located
onsite. A full-service boatyard, yacht sales and a good ships' store with free-flowing coffee - all onsite. Clark's Landing Restaurant, open Wed-Sun, has live
entertainment Fri & Sat nights, Sun brunch, a Tiki bar, and a patio overlooking the Manasquan. A banquet room can hold up to 150.

Notable -- The Point Pleasant boardwalk and ocean beach is about a mile due east (commercial part begins half mile south of the Inlet). Along the way, you'll
pass through Pt. Pleasant's business district with some notable historic buildings (Pt. Pleasant Historical Society publishes a guide, 892-3091). Beaches are
both public and private; those closest to the marina are private (i.e. Bradshaw Beach, Martells, Jenkinson's) and require purchase of a beach badge - approx.
$5-6/2. Jenkinson's Boardwalk has rides, arcades, an aquarium, mini golf and a beach. The public beach is farther south with acess on Ocean Avenue.

Navigational Information
Lat: 40°05.726' **Long:** 074°05.222' **Tide:** 4 ft. **Current:** 2 kt. **Chart:** 12324
Rep. Depths *(MLW)*: **Entry** 8 ft. **Fuel Dock** n/a **Max Slip/Moor** 8 ft./-
Access: Manasquan Inlet

Marina Facilities *(In Season/Off Season)*
Fuel: *Gulf* - Gasoline, Diesel, High-Speed Pumps
Slips: 197 Total, 3 Transient **Max LOA:** 100 ft. **Max Beam:** n/a
 Rate *(per ft.)*: **Day** $1.75 **Week** n/a **Month** n/a
 Power: 30 amp $10, **50 amp** $10, **100 amp** n/a, **200 amp** n/a
 Cable TV: No **Dockside Phone:** No
 Dock Type: Floating, Short Fingers, Pilings, Wood
Moorings: 0 Total, 0 Transient **Launch:** n/a
 Rate: Day n/a **Week** n/a **Month** n/a
Heads: 4 Toilet(s), 4 Shower(s)
Laundry: None **Pay Phones:** Yes
Pump-Out: OnSite, Self Service **Fee:** $5 **Closed Heads:** Yes

Marina Operations
Owner/Manager: Thomas P. DeLotto **Dockmaster:** Bill Kanaris
In-Season: May-Oct, 8am - 4:30pm **Off-Season:** closed
After-Hours Arrival: Call in advance
Reservations: Required **Credit Cards:** Visa/MC, Dscvr, Amex, Gulf
Discounts: None
Pets: Welcome, Dog Walk Area **Handicap Access:** No

Crystal Point Yacht Club

3900 River Road; Point Pleasant Beach, NJ 08742

Tel: (732) 892-2300 **VHF: Monitor** 16 **Talk** 9
Fax: (732) 892-2828 **Alternate Tel:** n/a
Email: n/a **Web:** www.thecrystalpoint.com
Nearest Town: Point Pleasant *(1 mi.)* **Tourist Info:** (732) 899-2424

Marina Services and Boat Supplies
Services - Docking Assistance, Security *(8 hrs. at night)*, Trash Pick-Up,
Dock Carts **Supplies - OnSite:** Ice *(Cube)* **1-3 mi:** Bait/Tackle *(Reel-Life
899-3506)*, Propane *(Robert James Florist 840-2242)* **3+ mi:** West Marine
(262-8899, 5 mi.), Boat/US *(477-9661, 4 mi.)*

Boatyard Services
Nearest Yard: Manasquan River Club (732) 840-0300

Restaurants and Accommodations
OnSite: Motel *(Crystal Point Inn 899-3444, $50-180, 3 night min on holiday
week-ends)* **Under 1 mi:** Restaurant *(New China 88 89-215-15)*,
(Grazianos Italian 899-6336), Snack Bar *(Rita's Italian Ices 892-2244)*, Fast
Food *(Wendy's)*, Lite Fare *(Bob & Loris Cozy Kitchen 458-6110)*, Pizzeria
(Vinnies 840-9144) **1-3 mi:** Restaurant *(The Idle Hour Restaurant 899-
2102)*, Motel *(Wenke's Motel 899-0152)*, Inn/B&B *(Steepleview 899-8999)*

Recreation and Entertainment
OnSite: Pool **Under 1 mi:** Fitness Center *(Golds Gym 905-0999)*, Video
Rental *(Herbertsville 206-5555; Video C 458-8727)* **1-3 mi:** Beach, Bowling
(Playdrome 88 Lanes 892-0888), Museum *(NJ Museum of Boating at
Johnson Bros 892-9000)*, Cultural Attract *(Premier Theatre Co. 223-7122)*
3+ mi: Tennis Courts *(Atlantic Club 223-2100, 4 mi.)*, Golf Course *(Forge
Pond 920-8899, 5 mi.)*, Horseback Riding *(Howell Equestrian Center 751-
8500, 5 mi.)*

Provisioning and General Services
Under 1 mi: Market *(Country Farm 836-9205)*, Delicatessen *(Pat's Little
Deli 528-0853)*, Bakery *(Manhattan Bagel 528-4545)*, Pharmacy
(Herbertsville 840-0220), Hardware Store *(Home Repair 840-9133)*, Florist
(Purple Iris 899-8175) **1-3 mi:** Convenience Store *(7-11 295-3619)*,
Supermarket *(A&P 920-6001, WaWa 295-3734; Foodtown 223-1930)*,
Gourmet Shop, Health Food *(Shore 295-4770)*, Wine/Beer *(Buy Rite 892-
6161)*, Liquor Store *(C J'S Liquors 295-1707)*, Bookstore *(Book Bin 892-
3456)*, Department Store *(Kmart Stores 840-0800)*, Copies Etc. *(J M Printing
Service 899-2555)* **3+ mi:** Library *(Point Pleasant Beach Branch Ocean
County Library 892-4575, 4 mi.)*

Transportation
OnCall: Rental Car *(Enterprise 223-6400; Pt. Pleasant 451-1325)*, Taxi *(All
City 477-5039; Ace 899-1900)*, Airport Limo *(Meuerle's 836-1234)* **1-3 mi:**
Rail *(NJ Transit)* **Airport:** Newark Int'l/Monmouth County *(53 mi./7.5 mi.)*

Medical Services
911 Service **Near:** Dentist *(Navarro 295-8181)* **Under 1 mi:** Veterinarian
(Beach Animal 714-1516) **1-3 mi:** Doctor *(Shore Health 892-7687)*,
Chiropractor *(Coleman Chiro 892-8488)* **3+ mi:** Holistic Services *(Body
Kneads 292-1222, 4 mi.)* **Hospital:** Ocean County 840-3399 *(1 mi.)*

Setting -- Past the railroad and Route 35 draw bridges, and past Osborn Island (known locally as Treasure Island), Crystal Point is on the south side of the river just before the Route 70 drawbridge. The very long white two-story Crystal Point event and catering establishment rises above the equally long stretch of docks that sits at its feet.

Marina Notes -- The complex is home to the marina, a motel and a banquet hall - all separate operations. The marina is a sport fishing center and has limited transient dockage - so advanced reservations are critical. Very nice all-tile head and showers with dressing rooms. Service-oriented staff.

Notable -- Quite a way up the river, this location offers significantly quieter surroundings than the stretches closer to the Inlet. Up on the bank, running perpendicular to the docks, is the attractive 2-story Crystal Point Inn. An inviting pool, open to marina guests, sits high on the bank in front of the motel with great views of the docks and River. The Crystal Point Yacht Club catering hall, owned and managed by Clark's Landing, is very active with weddings and other luncheon and dinner functions on weekends in season. Little is immediately nearby, but shops, services and restaurants are within a mile walk and cabs are available.

XIV. New Jersey: Lower Atlantic Inlets

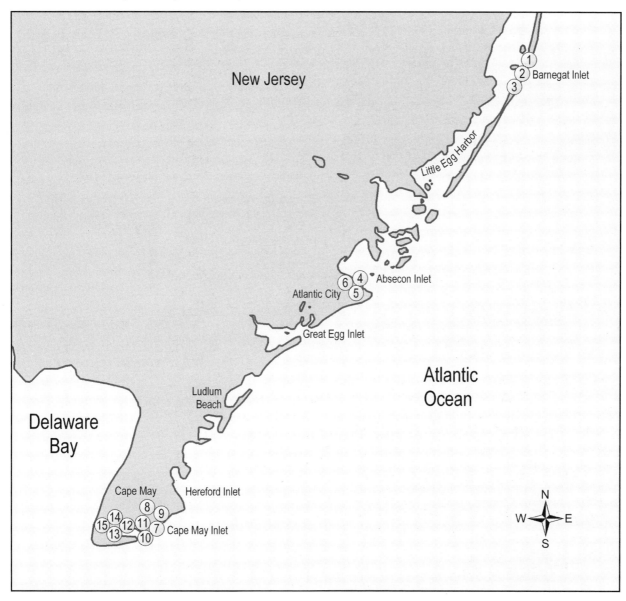

MAP	MARINA	HARBOR	PAGE	MAP	MARINA	HARBOR	PAGE
1	Lighthouse Marina	Barnegat Inlet	258	9	Schooner Island Marina	Grassy Sound Channel	266
2	Marina at Barnegat Light	Barnegat Inlet	259	10	Bree-Zee-Lee Yacht Basin	Cape May Harbor	267
3	Barnegat Light Yacht Basin	Barnegat Inlet	260	11	Canyon Club Resort Marina	Cape May Hbr/Cape May Canal	268
4	Historic Gardner's Basin	Absecon Inlet/Gardner's Basin	261	12	Utsch's Marina	Cape May Harbor	269
5	Les Kammerman's Marina	Absecon Inlet/Clam Creek	262	13	South Jersey Marina	Cape May Harbor	270
6	Farley State Marina	Absecon Inlet/Clam Creek	263	14	Miss Chris Marina	Cape May Hbr/Spicer Creek	271
7	Two Mile Landing Marina	Cape May Hbr/Lower Thorofare	264	15	Cape May Marine	Cape May Hbr/Spicer Creek	272
8	Lighthouse Pointe Marina	Grassy Sound Channel	265				

Navigational Information
Lat: 39°45.664' **Long:** 074°06.593' **Tide:** 4 ft. **Current:** n/a **Chart:** 12324
Rep. Depths *(MLW):* **Entry** 7 ft. **Fuel Dock** 8 ft. **Max Slip/Moor** 8 ft./-
Access: Inlet left past Lighthouse; before Coast Guard radio tower

Marina Facilities *(In Season/Off Season)*
Fuel: Gasoline, Diesel
Slips: 55 Total, 3 Transient **Max LOA:** 65 ft. **Max Beam:** n/a
  Rate *(per ft.):* **Day** $1.25 **Week** n/a **Month** n/a
  Power: 30 amp Incl., **50 amp** Incl., **100 amp** n/a, **200 amp** n/a
  Cable TV: No **Dockside Phone:** No
  Dock Type: Fixed, Wood
Moorings: 0 Total, 0 Transient **Launch:** n/a
  Rate: Day n/a **Week** n/a **Month** n/a
Heads: 2 Toilet(s)
Laundry: None **Pay Phones:** Yes
Pump-Out: OnSite, Self Service **Fee:** $5 **Closed Heads:** No

Lighthouse Marina

6th Street; Barnegat Light, NJ 08006

Tel: (609) 494-2305 **VHF: Monitor** 16 **Talk** n/a
Fax: (609) 494-1267 **Alternate Tel:** n/a
Email: n/a **Web:** n/a
Nearest Town: Barnegat Light *(0.5 mi.)* **Tourist Info:** (609) 693-8312

Marina Operations
Owner/Manager: Brian McMahon **Dockmaster:** Same
In-Season: Year 'Round, 8am-5pm **Off-Season:** n/a
After-Hours Arrival: Call ahead
Reservations: Yes **Credit Cards:** Visa/MC
Discounts: None
Pets: Welcome **Handicap Access:** No

Marina Services and Boat Supplies
Supplies - OnSite: Ships' Store *(and down the road at Finest Kind 494-4866)* **Near:** Ice *(Cube)*, Bait/Tackle *(Eric's 494-2447)*, Live Bait *(Ernie's B&T)* **Under 1 mi:** Propane *(Getty Station)*

Boatyard Services
OnSite: Travelift *(35T)*

Restaurants and Accommodations
Near: Restaurant *(Mustache Bills Diner 494-0155)*, *(Kubels 494-8592, since 1927 for seafood)*, *(Cassidy's Fish Tales 494-7719)*, *(Kelly's Old Barney 494-5115, ice cream, too.)*, Snack Bar *(Carousel Ice Cream Parlor 494-6752)*, Coffee Shop *(Andy's)*, Inn/B&B *(The Sand Castle 494-6555, $135-375, a contemporary Victorian with myriad amentities, one of the most luxurious on the NJ shore)*, *(North Shore Inn 494-5001)*, *(White Whale Revisited 494-3020)* **Under 1 mi:** Restaurant *(Rick's American Cafe & Clam Bar Pasta night Thu, Steak nite Tue)*, *(Eighteenth Street Cafe 494-6009)*, Fast Food *(Burger King)* **3+ mi:** Seafood Shack *(Red Lobster 493-2404, 4.5 mi.)*

Recreation and Entertainment
Near: Beach, Picnic Area, Video Rental *(Ive's Five Seasons; Island Video 494-4466)*, Park *(Edith Duff Gwinn Gardens behind the museum)*, Museum *(Barnegat Light Historical Museum in an old school house 494-8578)*
Under 1 mi: Video Arcade *(Mr. T's 492-5540)*
3+ mi: Movie Theater *(Hoyts Colony 4 Cinema 494-3330, 10 mi.)*

Provisioning and General Services
Near: Market *(White S Market 494-2752)*, Delicatessen *(Inlet Deli 494-3049, Barnegat Light 494-2444)*, Liquor Store *(Barnegat Light Liquor 494-2489)*, Green Grocer *(Foster's Farm Market 492-1360; Frank's Produce 494-2992- 1 mi.)*, Fishmonger *(Viking Village Fish Fri & Sat 9:30-6:30, Sun 9:30-3 - right off the boats)*, Bank/ATM *(Fleet 841-4000)*, Catholic Church *(St Peter's At- the-Light 494-2398)*, Protestant Church, Retail Shops *(Viking Village, including nautical clothing, or Islanders Store 494-1753)*
Under 1 mi: Pharmacy *(Medicap 698-2200)* **3+ mi:** Laundry *(4mi.)*

Transportation
OnCall: Rental Car *(Enterprise 597-2277)*, Taxi, Airport Limo *(Instant Limo 548-0052, Anchor 492-2287, Ace Cab & Livery 607-1600; Beach Haven Taxi 494-8606)* **Near:** Bikes *(Ive's Five Seasons, Surf Buggy Centers of Long Beach Island 361-3611 - 6 mi.)*
Airport: Monmouth County/Atlantic City, *(52 mi./45 mi.)*

Medical Services
911 Service **Near:** Doctor *(Dimant 494-6709, Shayer 494-8002)*
Under 1 mi: Dentist *(LBI 494-1880)* **1-3 mi:** Veterinarian *(Rubin 494-4463)*
Hospital: Southern Ocean County 978-8900 - has heliport *(15 mi.)*

Setting -- Located close to the tip of 18-mile Long Beach Island, this largely commercial, rustic marina provides a protected berth just inside Barnegat Inlet. It is the closest facility to the ocean. The views are of the truly unspoiled marsh that appears in every direction.

Marina Notes -- Mostly commercial fishing boats with a few private transient slips. No heads or showers. Home to a Boat-US towboat (494-0989). Winter storage $20/ft. Onsite are sport fishing charters: Hammerhead 494-4078; Lady Fran 494-5228 can carry over 6 people for charter, Mary M III 978-0673, Stingray 296-9191. Also LBI Parasail 361-6100.

Notable -- Wonderful old Victorian houses, great beaches, and a quiet, "barefoot" ambiance mark this relatively isolated beach community - it's nine miles south to the Rte 72 Causeway Bridge to the mainland (or two miles across by water). A little less than half a mile north is Barnegat Lighthouse (known as Old Barney), circa 1859, the second tallest in the U.S.; it's also the centerpiece of a 32 acre state park. Climb the 217 steps to the top, then visit the original Fresnel lens at the nearby Barnegat Light Historical Museum (Park:10am-10pm, daily, Memorial Day-September, closes at 4pm Nov-Apr; Lighthouse: 9am-4:30 and some evenings May-Oct, week-ends only Nov-Apr $1). Have a picnic or hike one of the trails (lighthouse closed in '03 for renovation, promised re-opening is '04). Three blocks south of the marina is Viking Village, a charming collection of beach shacks creating a shore version of a mini-mall.

Navigational Information
Lat: 39°45.151' **Long:** 074°06.719' **Tide:** 4 ft. **Current:** n/a **Chart:** 12324
Rep. Depths (*MLW*): **Entry** 7 ft. **Fuel Dock** n/a **Max Slip/Moor** 8 ft./12 ft.
Access: Barnegat Inlet south past lighhouse and coast guard station

Marina Facilities (*In Season/Off Season*)
Fuel: No
Slips: 61 Total, 1 Transient **Max LOA:** 40 ft. **Max Beam:** 12 ft.
  Rate *(per ft.)*: **Day** $1.00* **Week** n/a **Month** n/a
  Power: 30 amp Incl., **50 amp** Incl., **100 amp** n/a, **200 amp** n/a
  Cable TV: Yes, Incl. **Dockside Phone:** No
  Dock Type: Floating, Long Fingers, Short Fingers, Pilings, Alongside, Wood
Moorings: 0 Total, 0 Transient **Launch:** n/a
  Rate: Day n/a **Week** n/a **Month** n/a
Heads: 2 Toilet(s), 2 Shower(s) *(with dressing rooms)*
Laundry: None **Pay Phones:** No
Pump-Out: No **Fee:** n/a **Closed Heads:** No

Marina Operations
Owner/Manager: Tom Pimm **Dockmaster:** Same
In-Season: Apr15-Nov15, 6am-6:30pm **Off-Season:** Nov15-Apr15, 8am-4:30
After-Hours Arrival: Call in advance
Reservations: Yes, Required **Credit Cards:** Visa/MC, Dscvr, Amex
Discounts: None
Pets: Welcome, Dog Walk Area **Handicap Access:** Yes, Heads, Docks

Marina at Barnegat Light
PO Box 848; 1501 Bayview Avenue; Barnegat Light, NJ 08006

Tel: (609) 494-6611; (877) 648-7827 **VHF: Monitor** n/a **Talk** n/a
Fax: (609) 494-3266 **Alternate Tel:** (609) 494-6611
Email: blmarina@hotmail.com **Web:** www.fishgear.net
Nearest Town: Barnegat Light *(0 mi.)* **Tourist Info:** (609) 693-8312

Marina Services and Boat Supplies
Services - Docking Assistance, Dock Carts **Communication -** Mail &
Package Hold, Phone Messages, Fax in/out, FedEx, AirBorne, UPS, Express
Mail *(Sat Del)* **Supplies - OnSite:** Ice *(Cube)*, Ships' Store *(and down the
road at Finest Kind 494-4866)*, West Marine, Bait/Tackle *(and Barnegat Light
Bait & Tackle 494-4366)*, Live Bait *(Eel, minows, herring, crabs, clams,
worms, etc.)* **Near:** Propane *(Getty Station)*

Boatyard Services
OnSite: Forklift, Engine mechanic *(gas, diesel)*, Hull Repairs, Rigger, Bottom
Cleaning, Brightwork, Air Conditioning, Refrigeration, Compound, Wash &
Wax, Interior Cleaning, Woodworking, Inflatable Repairs, Painting, Awlgrip
OnCall: Divers, Propeller Repairs, Metal Fabrication **Near:** Launching
Ramp, Electrical Repairs, Electronic Sales, Electronics Repairs.
1-3 mi: Upholstery, Yacht Interiors.

Restaurants and Accommodations
OnCall: Pizzeria *(Domino's Pizza 698-7966)* **Near:** Restaurant *(Kubels
494-8593)*, *(Mustache Bills Diner 494-0155)*, *(Cassidy's Fish Tales 494-
7719)*, *(Kelly's Old Barney 494-5115, Ice cream, too)*, Snack Bar *(Carousel
Ice Cream Parlor 494-6752)*, Coffee Shop *(Andy's overlooking the inlet)*,
Inn/B&B *(Sand Castle 494-6555, $135-375)* **Under 1 mi:** Restaurant
(Carriage House 698-3578), *(Rick's American Cafe & Clam Bar Pasta night
Thu, Steak nite Tue)*, *(Eighteenth Street Cafe 494-6009)*, Fast Food *(Burger
King)*, Inn/B&B *(Arbor Rose 607-0743)* **1-3 mi:** Restaurant *(Point Resturant
242-4200)*, Seafood Shack *(Harvey Cedar's Shellfish)*, *(Red Lobster 493-
2404)*, Motel *(Quarter Deck Motel 494-3334)*, Hotel *(Ellas Motel 494-3200)*,
Inn/B&B *(North Shore Inn 494-5001)*, *(White Whale 494-3020)*

Recreation and Entertainment
Near: Beach, Picnic Area, Playground, Tennis Courts, Jogging Paths, Boat
Rentals, Roller Blade/Bike Paths, Fishing Charter *(Barnegat Light Marina)*,
Group Fishing Boat *(Lighthouse Marina)*, Video Rental *(Ive's Five Seasons;
Island Video 494-4466)*, Park *(Edith Duff Gwinn Gardens)*, Museum
(Barnegat Light Historical Soc 494-8578), Sightseeing *(Barnegat
Lighthouse)* **Under 1 mi:** Video Arcade *(Mr. T's 492-5540)* **3+ mi:** Movie
Theater *(Hoyts Colony 4 494-3330, 10 mi.)*

Provisioning and General Services
OnSite: Convenience Store, Bank/ATM, Newsstand **Near:** Market *(White S
Market 494-2752)*, Delicatessen *(Barnegat Light 494-2444; Inlet 494-3049)*,
Wine/Beer, Liquor Store *(Barnegat Light 494-2489)*, Green Grocer *(Foster's
492-1360; Frank's 494-2992 - 1 mi.)*, Fishmonger *(Viking Village)*, Post
Office, Hardware Store, Retail Shops *(Viking Village)* **Under 1 mi:** Beauty
Salon, Pharmacy *(Medicap 698-2200)* **1-3 mi:** Catholic Church *(St. Peter's
At-the-Light 494-2398)*, Barber Shop, Laundry, Bookstore

Transportation
OnCall: Rental Car *(Enterprise 597-2277)*, Taxi *(Beach Haven 494-8606)*,
Airport Limo *(Instant 548-0052; Anchor 492-2287; Ace 607-1600)*
Near: Bikes *(Ive's Five Seasons, Surf Buggy 361-3611, 6 mi.)*
Airport: Monmouth County/Atlantic City *(52 mi./45 mi.)*

Medical Services
911 Service **Under 1 mi:** Dentist *(LBI Dental 494-1880, under 1 mi.)* **1-3
mi:** Doctor *(Dimant 494-6709; Shayer 494-8002)*, Veterinarian *(Rubin 494-
4463)* **Hospital:** Southern Ocean County 978-8900 has heliport *(15 mi.)*

Setting -- After entering the inlet, bear south past famous "Old Barney" - the Barnegat Lighthouse, then past the Coast Guard station and the radio tower to
the very end of the basin. The wooden wave attenuators make this solid, well-equipped facility easy to spot - as does the large gray metal boat shed.

Marina Notes -- * $30 per night flat rate. 61 protected Slips. The marina was designed for smaller vessels but it can usually find an alongside berth to handle
the occasional forty footer. Very well equipped ships' store, deli and grocery, ATM, plus bait and tackle shop right at the marina. Sport fishing charter and party
boats are all onsite. Also insite is a mechanic for marine repairs, including fiberglass, engine repair. Commercial fishermen's discounts. Good docks with
relatively new pedestals. A wave attenuator protects the slips from the inlet traffic.

Notable -- Long Beach Island's wonderful ocean beaches are a very short hop across this very narrow barrier island. Walk north to the Barnegat Lighthouse,
its museum and 36 acre park. Or south to the Viking Village for a little shopping in a charming nest of re-purposed fishing shacks. They sell fish right off the
boats Fri & Sat 9:30-6:30, Sun 9:30-3pm. There are turn of the last century homes still standing and a remarkable amount of history for a sand bar. Barnegat
Light is about as far away as you can get from the crush of summer at the Jersey Shore - it's charming and a welcome relief.

Barnegat Light Yacht Basin

603 18th Street & Bayview; Barnegat Light, NJ 08006

Tel: (609) 494-2094 **VHF: Monitor** 16 **Talk** n/a
Fax: (609) 361-9536 **Alternate Tel:** (609) 494-2369
Email: n/a **Web:** n/a
Nearest Town: 0.25 mi. *(Barnegat Light)* **Tourist Info:** (609) 693-4554

Navigational Information
Lat: 39°45.039' **Long:** 074°06.812' **Tide:** 4 ft. **Current:** n/a **Chart:** 12324
Rep. Depths (*MLW*): Entry 6 ft. **Fuel Dock** 5 ft. **Max Slip/Moor** 5 ft./-
Access: Barnegat Inlet past the Lighthouse and the coast guard station

Marina Facilities *(In Season/Off Season)*
Fuel: Diesel
Slips: 85 Total, 5 Transient **Max LOA:** 40 ft. **Max Beam:** n/a
 Rate *(per ft.)*: **Day** $1.00 **Week** n/a **Month** n/a
 Power: 30 amp Incl., **50 amp** Incl,, **100 amp** n/a, **200 amp** n/a
 Cable TV: No **Dockside Phone:** No
 Dock Type: Fixed, Wood
Moorings: 0 Total, 0 Transient **Launch:** n/a
 Rate: Day n/a **Week** n/a **Month** n/a
Heads: None
Laundry: None **Pay Phones:** No
Pump-Out: No **Fee:** n/a **Closed Heads:** Yes

Marina Operations
Owner/Manager: Charles Eble **Dockmaster:** same
In-Season: Apr 1-Nov 30, 6am-7pm **Off-Season:** Dec 1-Mar. 31, Closed
After-Hours Arrival: Call in advance
Reservations: Yes **Credit Cards:** n/a
Discounts: None
Pets: Welcome **Handicap Access:** No

Marina Services and Boat Supplies
Communication - FedEx, AirBorne, UPS, Express Mail **Supplies -
Near:** Ice *(Cube)*, Ships' Store *(Finest Kind 494-4866 & Marina at Barnegat Light)*, Bait/Tackle *(Eric's 494-2447)*, Live Bait *(Ernie's B&T)*, Propane *(Getty Station)*

Boatyard Services
Nearest Yard: Bayview Marina (609) 494-7450

Restaurants and Accommodations
Near: Restaurant *(Kubels 494-8592)*, *(Cassidy's Fish Tales 494-7719)*, *(Kelly's Old Barney 494-5115)*, *(Rick's American Cafe & Clam Bar)*, *(Eighteenth Street Cafe 494-8578)*, Seafood Shack *(Off The Hook seafood take-out)*, Snack Bar *(Carousel Ice Cream Parlor 494-6752)*, Inn/B&B *(White Whale Revisited 494-3020)*, *(North Shore Inn 494-5001)*, *(Sand Castle 494-6555)* **Under 1 mi:** Coffee Shop *(Andy's)* **1-3 mi:** Restaurant *(Carriage House Restaurant 698-3578)*, *(Mustache Bills Diner 494-0155)*, Fast Food *(Burger King)*, Inn/B&B *(Arbor Rose B&B 607-0743)*

Recreation and Entertainment
OnSite: Fishing Charter, Group Fishing Boat **Near:** Beach *(right across the narrow island)*, Picnic Area, Playground, Tennis Courts *(St Francis Center Tennis Courts 494-3882)*, Boat Rentals, Video Rental *(Ive's Five Seasons; Island Video 494-4466)*, Park *(Edith Duff Gwinn Gardens behind the museum)*, Museum *(Barnegat Light Historical Museum in an old school*

house 494-8578)*, Sightseeing *(Barnegat Light)* **Under 1 mi:** Video Arcade *(Mr. T's 492-5540)* **3+ mi:** Bowling *(Thunderbird Lanes 978-9300, 7 mi.)*, Movie Theater *(Hoyt's Colony 4 494-3330, 10 mi.)*

Provisioning and General Services
OnSite: Fishmonger *(Cassidy's Viking Village Fish Fri & Sat 9:30-6:30, Sun 9:30-3 - right off the boats)*, Retail Shops *(Viking Village)* **Near:** Market *(White S. Market 494-2752)*, Delicatessen *(Barnegat Light Deli 494-2444; Inlet 494-3049)*, Wine/Beer, Liquor Store *(Barnegat Light 494-2489)*, Farmers' Market, Green Grocer *(Foster's Farm Market 492-1360; Frank's Produce 494-2992, 1 mi.)*, Bank/ATM *(Fleet 841-4000)*, Protestant Church **Under 1 mi:** Gourmet Shop *(Fat Cat's Café 494-7800)*, Post Office, Catholic Church *(St Peter's At-the-Light 494-2398)*, Pharmacy *(Medicap 698-2200)* **1-3 mi:** Library **3+ mi:** Health Food *(Franklin Vitamins 971-6737, 7 mi.)*

Transportation
OnCall: Rental Car *(Enterprise 597--2277)*, Taxi *(Beach Haven 978-4714)*, Airport Limo *(Instant 548-0052; Anchor 492-2287; Ace 607-1600)* **Near:** Bikes *(Ives Five Seasons; Surf Buggy Ctrs. of L BI 361-3611, 6 mi.)* **Airport:** Monmouth County/Atlantic City *(52 mi./45 mi.)*

Medical Services
911 Service **Near:** Doctor *(Dimant 494-6709; Shayer 494-8002)* **Under 1 mi:** Dentist *(L BI Dental 494-1800)*, Veterinarian *(Rubin 494-4463)* **Hospital:** Southern Ocean County 978-8900 has heliport *(15 mi.)*

Setting -- South of the Barnegat Inlet, past the Barnegat Lighthouse and the Coast Guard Station, is this homespun facility teeming with activity. The waterfront is lined with sport charter boats and party boats, each with a large sign announcing its presence and touting its benefits. Past the boats is appealing Viking Village, a beachy mini-mall of tiny restored fishing shacks.

Marina Notes -- Barnegat Light Yacht Basin is the clear winner among Barnegat Light marinas for the sheer number of charter boats it houses. Sport Fishing Charters include: Skirt Chaser 800-917-3034; Superchic 296-4480; T2 494-0500; Fleet King 693-3321. Party (or head) Fishing Boats include: Hunter 597-8739; Little Chic 758-7422; Pirate King II 628-3474; Searcher II; Barnegat Light Catamaran 494-2094; Doris Mae IV 693-4283; Carolyn Ann III 693-4283. It is also home to a number of commercial fishing boats.

Notable -- Funky and fun Viking Village is a collection of tiny re-purposed and somewhat restored fishing shacks that are now home to a variety of shops: Viking Outfitters (which has some good nautical wear), Fillet of Soles (shoes), Wink's Beachwear, Sugar Shock, Wooden You Love It (wood crafts and gifts), Viking Seafood Exchange (frozen and smoked seafood to go), Seaman's Landing (gifts), A La Carte (gifts and flowers), Iron Butterfly (antiques), Seawife Antiques and Cassidy's Viking Village Fish Market - buy fish right off the boats Fri-Sat 9:30-6:30, Sun 9:30 'til sold out. The nearby Getty station has an ATM, propane exchange, ice and a convenience store.

Navigational Information

Lat: 39°22.593' **Long:** 074°25.174' **Tide:** 4 ft. **Current:** n/a **Chart:** 12316
Rep. Depths *(MLW)*: **Entry** 6 ft. **Fuel Dock** n/a **Max Slip/Moor** 6 ft./-
Access: Absecon Inlet to Clam Creek, left into Gardner's Basin

Marina Facilities *(In Season/Off Season)*

Fuel: No
Slips: 35 Total, 6-10 Transient **Max LOA:** 60 ft. **Max Beam:** 16 ft.
  Rate *(per ft.)*: **Day** $1.25 **Week** $7.50 **Month** Inquire
  Power: 30 amp n/a, **50 amp** n/a, **100 amp** n/a, **200 amp** n/a
Cable TV: No **Dockside Phone:** No
Dock Type: Floating, Long Fingers, Wood
Moorings: 0 Total, 0 Transient **Launch:** n/a
  Rate: **Day** n/a **Week** n/a **Month** n/a
Heads: 2 Toilet(s)
Laundry: None **Pay Phones:** No
Pump-Out: OnSite, Full Service **Fee:** $5 **Closed Heads:** No

Marina Operations

Owner/Manager: Jack Kieth **Dockmaster:** Trish Marion
In-Season: May - Oct., 9am - 10pm **Off-Season:** Nov. - April, 9am - 5pm
After-Hours Arrival: Call ahead
Reservations: Preferred **Credit Cards:** Visa/MC
Discounts: None
Pets: Welcome, Dog Walk Area **Handicap Access:** Yes, Heads

Historic Gardner's Basin

800 North New Hampshire Avenue; Atlantic City, NJ 08401

Tel: (609) 348-2880 **VHF: Monitor** 9 **Talk** 9
Fax: (609) 345-4238 **Alternate Tel:** n/a
Email: n/a **Web:** n/a
Nearest Town: Atlantic City *(0.5 mi.)* **Tourist Info:** (609) 345-5600

Marina Services and Boat Supplies

Services - Docking Assistance, Security *(8, Evening Dockmaster)*, Trash Pick-Up **Communication -** Mail & Package Hold, Fax in/out, Data Ports *(Office)*, FedEx, AirBorne, UPS, Express Mail **Supplies - OnSite:** Ice *(Cube)* **Under 1 mi:** Bait/Tackle *(Big Bass 344-9823)*

Boatyard Services

Nearest Yard: M.W. Boat & Engine Worls (609) 345-1131

Restaurants and Accommodations

OnSite: Restaurant *(Back Bay Ale House 449-0006, L $5-10, D $5-16, B, too)*, *(Flying Cloud 345-8222, L $7-12, D $16-25, B, too & Kid's Menu)*, Snack Bar *(Frosty Bites ice cream)* **OnCall:** Pizzeria *(Chelsea 646-0860)* **Under 1 mi:** Restaurant *(El Nuevo Latino 340-0070)*, *(Knife & Fork Inn 344-1133)*, Lite Fare *(Corbin's Chicken Soulfood and Seafood 348-8200)*, Pizzeria *(Mike's 345-0055)*, Hotel *(Flagship All-Suite 343-1608, $130-170)*, *(Resorts Atlantic City 344-6000, $100-225)* **1-3 mi:** Seafood Shack *(Captain Youngs 344-2001, D $14-20)*, Fast Food *(Burger King)*, Motel *(Comfort Inn 348-4000)*, Hotel *(Trump Marina 441-8500, or dinghy across)*

Recreation and Entertainment

OnSite: Picnic Area, Fishing Charter, Group Fishing Boat *(High Roller- 4 hrs. 8am/1pm 348-3474 Back Bay, Capt. Applegate - 4 hrs. 8am/1pm $25)*, Cultural Attract *(Ocean Life Center 348-2880 $7/4; AC Cruises - Dolphin Watch 347-7600 $17.50/12.50)* **Near:** Beach, Playground *(McClinton)*, Roller Blade/Bike Paths, Park *(McClinton Waterfront Park)*, Sightseeing *(Absecon Lighthouse 449-1360 $5/2, Trolley Tours 884-7392 $16/8)*

1-3 mi: Golf Course *(Brigantine Golf Links 266-1388 R 5 mi.)*, Fitness Center *(Brigantine Fitness 266-0099)*, Video Rental *(Videoland 348-6566)*, Museum *(Atlantic City Historical Museum 347-5839)* **3+ mi:** Bowling *(King Pin 641-5117, 9 mi.)*, Movie Theater *(Ventnor 487-5800, 4 mi.)*

Provisioning and General Services

OnSite: Lobster Pound *(Buddy's Lobster Shanty)*, Retail Shops **OnCall:** Laundry *(Wise 348-6300)* **Near:** Convenience Store *(Ralph & Son 347-6002; 7-11 345-7691)*, Market *(Harbor Point 345-6774)*, Bakery, Green Grocer, Fishmonger *(Seasonal)*, Bank/ATM, Catholic Church, Protestant Church, Beauty Salon *(Aigner's)*, Dry Cleaners **Under 1 mi:** Delicatessen *(Lighhouse Deli 348-0303)*, Wine/Beer, Liquor Store *(Allstar Liquors 344-5010)*, Pharmacy *(Eckerd 344-2700)* **1-3 mi:** Supermarket *(Thriftway 340-8577, Charlie's Groceries 347-7747)*, Health Food *(Interhealth 345-3711)*, Post Office, Library *(Atlantic City 345-2269)*, Bookstore *(Atlantic City News & Book Store 344-9444)*, Hardware Store *(Smith Brothers 344-0046)*, Department Store, Copies Etc. *(Triangle 348-2805)*

Transportation

OnCall: Rental Car *(Enterprise 272-0099)*, Airport Limo *(Jonathan's 344-7535)* **Near:** Local Bus *(Jitney #1 & #3 344-8642 $1.50)* **1-3 mi:** Taxi *(M Mutual Taxi 345-6111)*, Rail *(To NY, Phil)* **Airport:** Atlantic City Int'l *(8 mi.)*

Medical Services

911 Service **OnCall:** Ambulance **Under 1 mi:** Holistic Services *(Oriental Accupressure 348-6565)* **1-3 mi:** Doctor *(Health Net 345-6000)*, Dentist *(Mainland Dental 345-1155)*, Chiropractor *(Atlantic Health 347-1999)*, Veterinarian *(Bayview 646-7195)* **Hospital:** Atlantic City 345-4000 *(1 mi.)*

Setting -- A short distance inside Absecon Inlet, at the mouth of Clam Creek, Historic Gardner's Basin, with its stretch of neatly lined up docks, offers a welcome counterpoint to the glitz of Atlantic City. The active, working harbor, and this nicely restored complex on its shore, is a destination in itself. Landside, the marina offers a compelling variety of attractions, restaurants, and shops. Seaward views include funky houses perched on piers over the water, the Farley State Marina (with Trump Hotel & Casino behind it), and working boats in various stages of dress. Surrounding area is an upscale housing development.

Marina Notes -- Onsite eateries include Flying Cloud, Back Bay Ale House, and Frosty Bites. Buddy's Lobster Shanty 11am-7pm, Fri-Sat has fresh lobsters, clams, and stone crab. If closed, then try the lobster boat that arrives between 1 and 2pm and is "open" for about an hour. Several attractions operate from here: Capt. Applegate and High Roller Party Fishing boats, Atlantic Parasail, Atlantic City Cruises 347-700 and Tall Ship Young America. Courtesy dockage is provided, as available, call ahead. Marina heads less than stellar; use the ones in the Ocean Life Center when it's open.

Notable -- The 3-level Ocean Life Center (7 days, 10am-5pm) promises a hands-on experience for all ages. Explore the 8 tank aquarium, including a 23,000 gallon one with sea life from the Jersey coast, a Touch Tank, Computer Leaning Center and 16 frequently changing exhibits. The Trump Marina Casino & Hotel is a long walk or quick dinghy ride. A small beach is nearby and the beginning of the famous boardwalk a little farther. And the Atlantic City Jitney, which stops about three blocks away, makes most everything very accessible, $1.50.

Les Kammerman's Atlantic City Marina

Kammerman's A.C. Marina

447 Carson Avenue; Atlantic City, NJ 08401

Tel: (609) 348-8418; (800) 353-8418 **VHF: Monitor** 16 **Talk** 9
Fax: (609) 348-1965 **Alternate Tel:** n/a
Email: kammermansmarina@comcast.net **Web:** atlanticstarcharters.com
Nearest Town: Atlantic City *(0.5 mi.)* **Tourist Info:** (609) 345-5600

Navigational Information
Lat: 39°22.600' **Long:** 074°25.500' **Tide:** 6 ft. **Current:** n/a **Chart:** 12316
Rep. Depths (*MLW*): **Entry** 9 ft. **Fuel Dock** 10 ft. **Max Slip/Moor** 5 ft./-
Access: Absecon Inlet into Clam Creek. Fuel dock on Port Side

Marina Facilities *(In Season/Off Season)*
Fuel: *Shell* - Slip-Side Fueling, Gasoline, Diesel, High-Speed Pumps
Slips: 13 Total, 5 Transient **Max LOA:** 200 ft. **Max Beam:** 25 ft.
  Rate *(per ft.)*: **Day** $2.00/$1.50 **Week** Inq. **Month** Inq.
  Power: 30 amp $5, **50 amp** $5, **100 amp** n/a, **200 amp** n/a
  Cable TV: No **Dockside Phone:** No
  Dock Type: Fixed, Floating, Wood
Moorings: 0 Total, 0 Transient **Launch:** n/a
  Rate: Day n/a **Week** n/a **Month** n/a
Heads: 2 Toilet(s), 2 Shower(s) *(with dressing rooms)*
Laundry: None **Pay Phones:** No
Pump-Out: OnSite, Full Service, 1 Central **Fee:** $5 **Closed Heads:** Yes

Marina Operations
Owner/Manager: Susan Hobson **Dockmaster:** Same
In-Season: Apr-Nov, 7am-8pm **Off-Season:** Dec-Apr, 9am-5pm
After-Hours Arrival: Call ahead for docking location
Reservations: Yes **Credit Cards:** Visa/MC, Dscvr, Din, Amex, Shell
Discounts: Boat/US **Dockage:** n/a **Fuel:** $0.10 **Repair:** n/a
Pets: Welcome **Handicap Access:** No

Marina Services and Boat Supplies
Services - Docking Assistance, Trash Pick-Up **Communication** - Mail &
Package Hold, FedEx, AirBorne, UPS, Express Mail **Supplies - OnSite:** Ice
(Block, Cube), Ships' Store, Bait/Tackle **Under 1 mi:** Propane

Boatyard Services
OnCall: Engine mechanic *(gas, diesel)*, Electrical Repairs, Electronic Sales,
Electronics Repairs, Bottom Cleaning, Brightwork, Air Conditioning,
Refrigeration, Divers, Compound, Wash & Wax, Interior Cleaning, Propeller
Repairs, Woodworking, Metal Fabrication **Near:** Hull Repairs, Rigger,
Painting, Awlgrip. **Under 1 mi:** Launching Ramp.
Nearest Yard: A. C.Wescoat (609) 345-1974

Restaurants and Accommodations
OnCall: Pizzeria *(Chelsea 646-0860)* **Near:** Restaurant *(Gilchrist 345-8278)*, *(Flying Cloud Cafe 345-8222, L $7-12, D $16-25, Breakast, Kids'
menu)*, *(Portofinos-Trump Marina 441-8300, by dinghy)*, *(High Steaks -
Trump 441-8300, by dinghy)*, *(Harbor View - Trumps)*, *(The Deck at Farley
Marina)*, *(Back Bay Ale House 449-0006, L $5-10, D $5-16, or dinghy)*
Under 1 mi: Restaurant *(Angelo's Fairmount Tavern 344-2439, L $6-12,
D $16-30)*, *(Babalu Grill 572-9898, L $6-11, D $16-30, Cuban cuisine)*,
Hotel *(Trump Marina 441-8321)* **1-3 mi:** Motel *(Comfort Inn 348-4000)*,
Hotel *(Resorts A.C. 344-6000, $70-225)*, *(Flagship All-Suite 343-7447)*

Recreation and Entertainment
OnSite: Fishing Charter *(Atlantic Star plus 4 smaller sport fish boats)*
Near: Boat Rentals **Under 1 mi:** Beach, Playground, Fitness Center
(Brigantine266-0099), Park, Cultural Attract *(Multiple Casino shows;*

BoardwalkArt Show Jul Aug; AC Art Center at Garden Pier 347 5837 Free,
Sightseeing *(Absecon Lighthouse 449-1360 $5/2; Ocean Life Center 348-2800 $7/4; Trolley Tours 884-7392 $16/8)* **1-3 mi:** Golf Course *(Brigantine
Links 266-1388, Blue Heron Pines 965-1800)*, Video Rental *(Videoland
348-6566)*, Video Arcade, Museum *(African American Heritage 345-1010)*
3+ mi: Movie Theater *(Ventnor 487-5800, 4 mi.)*

Provisioning and General Services
Near: Convenience Store *(Ralph & Son 347-6002; 7-11)* **Under 1 mi:**
Market *(Harbor Point 345-6774)*, Delicatessen *(Lighhouse Deli 348-0303)*,
Liquor Store *(Allstar Liquors 344-5010)*, Bakery, Fishmonger, Lobster Pound
(Buddy's Lobster Shanty), Bank/ATM, Post Office, Catholic Church,
Synagogue, Beauty Salon, Barber Shop, Dry Cleaners, Laundry, Pharmacy
(Eckerd 344-2700), Hardware Store *(Smith Bros 344-0046)*, Florist, Retail
Shops *(The Walk - designer outlet shops)* **1-3 mi:** Supermarket *(Shop N'
Bag 264-004)*, Library *(A.C. 345-2269)*, Bookstore *(Atlantic City News &
Book Store 344-9444)*, Buying Club *(Sam's)*, Copies Etc.

Transportation
OnCall: Taxi *(Economy344-6600)*, Airport Limo *(Royal 748-9777)*
Near: Local Bus *(Jitney #3344-8642 $1.50)* **Under 1 mi:** Bikes *(biking on
boardwalk 6-10am)*, InterCity Bus **1-3 mi:** Rail **Airport:** A.C. Int'l *(8 mi.)*

Medical Services
911 Service **OnCall:** Ambulance **Under 1 mi:** Holistic Services *(Oriental
Accupressure 348-6565)* **1-3 mi:** Doctor *(Health Net 345-6000)*, Dentist
(Mainland 345-1155), Chiropractor *(Atlantic Health 347-1999)*, Veterinarian
(Bayview 646-7195) **Hospital:** Atlantic City 345-4000 *(1.5 mi.)*

Setting -- At the end of Clam Creek, just past the coast guard station, Kammerman's is settled into the "other" Atlantic City. Picturesque tumbledown shacks on pilings, working fishing boats and restored historic structures combine to make this funky and appealing neighborhood a welcome relief from the glitz. Kammerman's big gray boat shed looms above its attractive new office which sports an octagonal room. Right across the creek is the enormous Frank Farley State Marina. Rising above its docks is the Trump Marina Hotel and Casino; at night it's a blaze of lights, providing a dramatic evening view.

Marina Notes -- Largest Fuel Dock in Atlantic City. Bulk fuel discounts; off hour fueling. Friendly atmosphere and dock attendants. Quite nice full bathrooms. A fish cleaning station. The spectacular 46 ft. luxury yacht Atlantic Star (348-8418) makes its home here. One of Vikings most opulent vessels, it is certified to carry up to 18 passengers when chartered. Marina can arrange charters for 2 to 200 guests. International Game Fish Association Official Weigh Station.

Notable -- The Farley Marina and Trump's is about a 2.5 miles walk by road or a quick dinghy ride across the creek (there is 2 hour courtesy tie-up). There one will find a half dozen restaurants (call the upscale ones in advance - some are not always open), shops and shows. A shorter walk around the basin or another brief dinghy ride takes you to Gardner's Basin with a good variety of restaurants and attractions. A 2-block walk to the 24-hr. A.C. route #3 Jitney makes all of the casinos, attractions and services easy to get to (including relatively close Trump's Marina and Harrah's) -- it runs the length of Pacific Ave., one block parallel to the famous Boardwalk. The "ArtShow on the Boardwalk" runs during July & August. Web URL: www.atlanticstarcharters.com

Navigational Information
Lat: 39°22.440' **Long:** 074°25.420' **Tide:** 4 ft. **Current:** None **Chart:** 12316
Rep. Depths (*MLW*): **Entry** 12 ft. **Fuel Dock** 12 ft. **Max Slip/Moor** 12 ft./-
Access: Absecon Inlet, left into Clam Creek, right into Marina

Marina Facilities *(In Season/Off Season)*
Fuel: *Texaco* - Gasoline, Diesel, High-Speed Pumps
Slips: 640 Total, 140 Transient **Max LOA:** 300 ft. **Max Beam:** 40 ft.
 Rate *(per ft.)*: **Day** $4.00/$2.00* **Week** Inq. **Month** $50
 Power: 30 amp Incl., **50 amp** Incl., **100 amp** Incl., **200 amp** n/a
 Cable TV: Yes, Incl. **Dockside Phone:** Yes, Incl.**, Switchboard
 Dock Type: Floating, Long Fingers, Pilings, Wood
Moorings: 0 Total, 0 Transient **Launch:** n/a
 Rate: Day n/a **Week** n/a **Month** n/a
Heads: 12 Toilet(s), 20 Shower(s) *(with dressing rooms)*
Laundry: 8 Washer(s), 8 Dryer(s) **Pay Phones:** Yes
Pump-Out: OnSite, Full Service **Fee:** $5 **Closed Heads:** Yes

Marina Operations
Owner/Manager: Deidre James **Dockmaster:** Dee Brown
In-Season: May-LabDay, 8am-10pm **Off-Season:** Sep-Apr, 9am-5pm
After-Hours Arrival: Security, Check in at front desk
Reservations: Yes **Credit Cards:** Visa/MC, Dscvr, Din, Amex, Shell
Discounts: MarinaLife **Dockage:** 25%*** **Fuel:** # Gals **Repair:** n/a
Pets: Welcome, Dog Walk Area **Handicap Access:** Yes, Heads, Docks

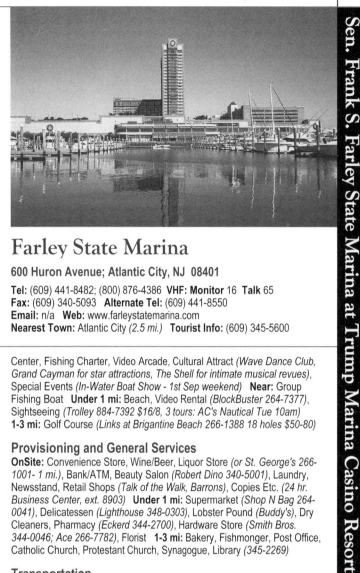

Farley State Marina

600 Huron Avenue; Atlantic City, NJ 08401

Tel: (609) 441-8482; (800) 876-4386 **VHF: Monitor** 16 **Talk** 65
Fax: (609) 340-5093 **Alternate Tel:** (609) 441-8550
Email: n/a **Web:** www.farleystatemarina.com
Nearest Town: Atlantic City *(2.5 mi.)* **Tourist Info:** (609) 345-5600

Marina Services and Boat Supplies
Services - Docking Assistance, Concierge, Room Service to the Boat, Security *(24 Hrs., N.J. Police HQ onsite)*, Dock Carts, Megayacht Facilities, 3 Phase **Communication -** Mail & Package Hold, Phone Messages, Fax in/out *($2)*, Data Ports *(Hotel Business Center)*, FedEx, AirBorne, UPS, Express Mail *(Sat Del)* **Supplies - OnSite:** Ice *(Block, Cube)*, Ships' Store, Bait/Tackle **3+ mi:** Propane *(BarbeClean 646-5560, 6 mi.)*

Boatyard Services
OnCall: Engine mechanic *(gas, diesel)*, Electrical Repairs, Electronics Repairs, Hull Repairs, Rigger, Bottom Cleaning, Brightwork, Air Conditioning, Refrigeration, Divers, Compound, Wash & Wax, Interior Cleaning, Propeller Repairs, Woodworking, Inflatable Repairs, Upholstery, Yacht Interiors, Metal Fabrication, Painting **Near:** Travelift, Railway, Launching Ramp.
Nearest Yard: M & W Boatworks (In harbor) (609) 345-1131

Restaurants and Accommodations
OnSite: Restaurant *(The Harbor View D $23-40, Sun Brunch, 10-3 $32, Kids half)*, *(Upstairs Cafe B, L, D $6-18)*, *(Hooters)*, *(Bayside Buffet L&D $16)*, *(Imperial Court Hunan, Catonese, Szechuan)*, *(Portofino's)*, *(High Steaks D $18-48, southwest fine dining)*, Snack Bar *(Poolside)*, Coffee Shop *(Horn & Hardart's)*, Lite Fare *(The Deck - live bands nightly)*, Pizzeria *(Cosimo's Pizza)*, Hotel *(Trump Marina 441-2000, $150-275)* **OnCall:** Pizzeria *(Carmine's 266-5400)* **Near:** Hotel *(Harrah's 441-5000, $80-280)*
1-3 mi: Restaurant *(The Links Grille 266-1388, L $5-20, D $10-20)*

Recreation and Entertainment
OnSite: Pool *(Seasonal)*, Spa, Picnic Area, Tennis Courts, Fitness

Center, Fishing Charter, Video Arcade, Cultural Attract *(Wave Dance Club, Grand Cayman for star attractions, The Shell for intimate musical revues)*, Special Events *(In-Water Boat Show - 1st Sep weekend)* **Near:** Group Fishing Boat **Under 1 mi:** Beach, Video Rental *(BlockBuster 264-7377)*, Sightseeing *(Trolley 884-7392 $16/8, 3 tours: AC's Nautical Tue 10am)*
1-3 mi: Golf Course *(Links at Brigantine Beach 266-1388 18 holes $50-80)*

Provisioning and General Services
OnSite: Convenience Store, Wine/Beer, Liquor Store *(or St. George's 266-1001- 1 mi.)*, Bank/ATM, Beauty Salon *(Robert Dino 340-5001)*, Laundry, Newsstand, Retail Shops *(Talk of the Walk, Barrons)*, Copies Etc. *(24 hr. Business Center, ext. 8903)* **Under 1 mi:** Supermarket *(Shop N Bag 264-0041)*, Delicatessen *(Lighthouse 348-0303)*, Lobster Pound *(Buddy's)*, Dry Cleaners, Pharmacy *(Eckerd 344-2700)*, Hardware Store *(Smith Bros. 344-0046; Ace 266-7782)*, Florist **1-3 mi:** Bakery, Fishmonger, Post Office, Catholic Church, Protestant Church, Synagogue, Library *(345-2269)*

Transportation
OnSite: Local Bus *(Trolley #3)* **OnCall:** Rental Car *(Just 4 Wheels 652-8611)*, Taxi *(DJs 572-9366; Island 264-1900; Brigantine 266-1300)*, Airport Limo *(Jonathan's 344-7535)* **1-3 mi:** Rail *(NJ Transit to NY & Phil)* **Airport:** Atlantic City *(7 mi.)*

Medical Services
911 Service **OnCall:** Ambulance **1-3 mi:** Doctor, Dentist *(Mainland 345-1155)*, Chiropractor *(Brigantine Chiro 266-5555)*, Holistic Services *(Oriental Accupressure 348-6565)*, Veterinarian *(Brigantine 266-0700)*
Hospital: Atlantic City 345-4000 *(2 mi.)*

Setting -- On Clam Creek just off the Absecon Inlet, the Frank S. Farley Marina is a large, state of the art facility that fills the basin at the foot of the Trump Marina Hotel & Casino. A marina guest is a hotel guest making all the services and facilities of this 4-star resort hotel available - many 24 hours a day.

Marina Notes -- *Nov-Mar $2/ft., Apr-Mid-May $3.50/ft., Mid-May-LabDay $4/ft., LabDay-Nov 1 $3/ft. Midweek, pay for 2 nights, get 3. Holiday weekends 2-night min. Group rates. Stay for 20 consecutive nights, @$2.50/night, get 10 nights free. **Free Dockside telephone must be reserved in advance. ***25% MarinaLife discount Sun-Thur only. Owned by New Jersey Division of Parks & Forestry, managed by Trump's Marina Assoc. 2 sets of quite nice tile heads, showers and laundry, located at opposite ends of the marina. Trump's excellent full-service health club & recreation deck is included in the dockage fees: tennis, basketball, ping pong, jogging track, free weights, and a roof-top outdoor pool -- plus spa services (i.e. 50 min Massage $60).

Notable -- The pricey and elegant Harbor View Restaurant is on the second floor of the marina building. On the dock level, The Deck, a bay-front alfresco patio bar, serves light fare with nightly entertainment.. There are 8 more eateries and three night spots across the enclosed bridge in the hotel; call ahead for hours at the more upscale ones. The hotel's first floor appears to be one massive, very busy casino; there are more intimate rooms on the second floor. The famous boardwalk and most other casinos & hotels are on the beach side, at least 2 miles away. A 24 hour jitney ($1.50 pp) has 3 convenient loops. For major provisioning, call a Brigantine cab and go over the bridge (just under a mile). Note: Generally, it's inadvisable to walk outside the marina grounds at night.

Two Mile Landing Marina

PO Box 1528; Ocean Dr.; Lower Township, NJ 08260

Tel: (609) 522-1341 **VHF: Monitor** 16 **Talk** 69
Fax: (609) 523-1751 **Alternate Tel:** n/a
Email: twomile@eclipse.net **Web:** www.twomilelanding.com
Nearest Town: Wildwood Crest *(1 mi.)* **Tourist Info:** (609)465-7181

Navigational Information
Lat: 38°57.564' **Long:** 074°51.968' **Tide:** 6 ft. **Current:** 3 kt. **Chart:** 12316
Rep. Depths (*MLW*): Entry 17 ft. **Fuel Dock** n/a **Max Slip/Moor** 18 ft./-
Access: Atlantic Ocean to Cape May Inlet, 1/2 mile north Two Mile Bridge

Marina Facilities *(In Season/Off Season)*
Fuel: No
Slips: 60 Total, 15 Transient **Max LOA:** 130 ft. **Max Beam:** n/a
 Rate *(per ft.)*: **Day** $2.00/Inq.* **Week** $7.50 **Month** $18.50
 Power: 30 amp Incl., **50 amp** Incl., **100 amp** n/a, **200 amp** n/a
 Cable TV: Yes Included to Trans. **Dockside Phone:** No
 Dock Type: Floating, Long Fingers, Short Fingers, Pilings, Alongside, Wood
Moorings: 2 Total, 2 Transient **Launch:** Yes ($10/trip)
 Rate: Day $30 **Week** $180 **Month** n/a
Heads: 6 Toilet(s), 4 Shower(s) *(with dressing rooms)*
Laundry: 1 Washer(s), 1 Dryer(s) **Pay Phones:** Yes
Pump-Out: OnSite, Full Service **Fee:** n/a **Closed Heads:** Yes

Marina Operations
Owner/Manager: Jim Salasin **Dockmaster:** Dick O'Donnell
In-Season: Apr-Oct, 8am-6pm **Off-Season:** Nov-Mar, Closed
After-Hours Arrival: Call 609-522-1341
Reservations: Yes, Preferred **Credit Cards:** Visa/MC, Dscvr, Din, Amex
Discounts: None
Pets: Welcome, Dog Walk Area **Handicap Access:** No

Marina Services and Boat Supplies
Services - Docking Assistance, Security, Trash Pick-Up, Dock Carts **Communication -** Mail & Package Hold, Phone Messages, Fax in/out *($1.00)*, FedEx, UPS **Supplies - OnSite:** Ice *(Block, Shaved)* **Under 1 mi:** Ships' Store, Bait/Tackle *(Carlson's Fish & Ice 522-3400)*, Propane *(North Wildwood Citgo 522-4023)* **1-3 mi:** West Marine *(898-8245)*

Boatyard Services
OnCall: Engine mechanic *(gas)*, Electrical Repairs, Electronic Sales, Electronics Repairs, Divers **Under 1 mi:** Travelift, Engine mechanic *(diesel)*, Launching Ramp. **Nearest Yard:** Utsch's Marina (609) 884-2051

Restaurants and Accommodations
OnSite: Restaurant *(Two Mile Landing 522-1341, D $15-23, Kids $6-13)*, *(Crab House 522-1341, L $5-18, D $14-19, Kids $5-9)* **Under 1 mi:** Restaurant *(Axelsson's Blue Claw 884-5878, D $24-30)*, *(Marie Nicole's 522-5425, D $15-36, also light menu & desserts 'til midnight)*, Lite Fare *(Crest Tavern 522-1200)*, Pizzeria *(Corini's 522-7304)*, Motel *(Suitcase Motel 522-7208)*, Hotel *(Surf Side 7 522-7647)* **1-3 mi:** Restaurant *(Triangle 729-9314)*, Seafood Shack *(Wharf 522-6336)*, Fast Food *(Burger King)*, Pizzeria *(Dolce Italia 522-6228)*, Inn/B&B *(Sea Gypsy 522-0690)*

Recreation and Entertainment
OnSite: Picnic Area, Grills, Video Arcade **Under 1 mi:** Beach *(Diamond Beach)* **1-3 mi:** Golf Course *(Cape May National Golf Club 884-1563)*, Fitness Center *(Cape Fitness Center 898-1515; Ultimate Fitness Gym 729-2050)*, Horseback Riding *(Jajas Pony Rides 886-6305)*, Fishing Charter, Movie Theater *(Sea Theatre 729-0337)*, Video Rental *(Collector's Corner &*

Twilight Video 523-8260), Park, Museum *(George F Boyer Historical Museum 523-0277)* **3+ mi:** Tennis Courts *(Cape May Tennis Club 884-8986, 4 mi.)*, Bowling *(3 J'S Wildwood Bowl 729-0111, 4 mi.)*

Provisioning and General Services
Near: Convenience Store *(WAWA)*, Delicatessen, Bakery
Under 1 mi: Wine/Beer *(Green's 729-9463)*, Liquor Store *(Bubba's 522-5142)*, Bank/ATM *(Crest Savings 522-3225)*, Laundry, Newsstand
1-3 mi: Supermarket *(Acme Markets 884-1203; Super Fresh Food 522-5697-4 mi.)*, Post Office, Catholic Church, Protestant Church, Synagogue, Library *(Wildwood Crest 522-0564)*, Beauty Salon, Barber Shop, Dry Cleaners, Bookstore *(Shore Personalized 729-3848)*, Pharmacy *(Eckerd 729-1050)*, Hardware Store *(South Jersey 522-8395; Thompson Hardware 729-4063)*, Florist, Clothing Store, Retail Shops, Department Store *(Kmart Stores 886-1122)*, Copies Etc. *(Office Services 522-1666)*

Transportation
OnCall: Taxi *(Caribbean 523-8000, Cape 884-2273, Checker 522-1431)*, Airport Limo *(Chuck's 522-6088)* **3+ mi:** Ferry Service *(Cape May - Lewes, 5 mi.)* **Airport:** Atlantic City/Cape May *(40 mi./6 mi.)*

Medical Services
911 Service **OnCall:** Ambulance **Under 1 mi:** Dentist *(Holly Beach Dental 522-1471)* **1-3 mi:** Doctor *(Farooqui 522-6779)*, Chiropractor *(Back To Health Family Chiropractic 522-7557)*, Holistic Services *(Met Massage Therapy 522-7120)* **3+ mi:** Veterinarian *(Baysea Veterinary Hospital 886-229, 7.5 mi.)* **Hospital:** Burdette Tomlin Memorial 463-2000 *(12 mi.)*

Setting -- After entering the Cape May Inlet, turn north into the ICW at the flashing buoy and cruise half a mile beyond the Cape May Bridge. There are wide open vistas of pristine marsh punctuated by The Two Mile Landing complex that rises from the mist. A series of connected one and two story funky, re-purposed buildings looms over a network of contemporary docks. Bright green awnings shade the dining decks.

Marina Notes -- *$40 min. Rate hike in mid Aug. In business for more than 25 years. Rigid Extra Wide Floating Dock System with mostly single loaded slips. Alongside docking to 130 ft., private seasonal charter and sport fishing boats. Spacious heads plus laundry facilities. Private picnic area with gas grills. Two onsite restaurants: Two Mile Inn offers casual waterfront dining, dinner only from 4:30 on and specializes in seafood and steak. The Crab House is more casual and family oriented; brown paper covers the tables on the enclosed porch overlooking the docks. BBQ chicken, ribs and burgers are an alternative to crabs - lunch and dinner, from noon on. Both have take-out and Kids' Menus, and views of the docks. There's a raw bar at the dockside Tiki Bar. Located between Cape May and Wildwood Crest at the cross roads of Ocean Drive and Country Road #630.

Notable -- The west facing docks and restaurants promise spectacular sunsets over the pristine marsh and Waterway, especially from the upper level lounge. There is much to do at the marina including Atlantic Parasailing (522-1869), sportfish charters, and a Game Room. Within walking distance are: Harbor Light Putting miniature golf (522-1221), a few additional restaurants and a bank. But mostly it's quiet, undeveloped stretches.

Navigational Information
Lat: 38°59.393' **Long:** 074°50.213' **Tide:** 7 ft. **Current:** 3 kt. **Chart:** 12316
Rep. Depths (MLW): Entry 3 ft. **Fuel Dock** n/a **Max Slip/Moor** 4 ft./-
Access: West side of ICW

Marina Facilities *(In Season/Off Season)*
Fuel: No
Slips: 173 Total, 0 Transient **Max LOA:** 40 ft. **Max Beam:** 15 ft.
  Rate *(per ft.):* **Day** $40.00* **Week** n/a **Month** n/a
  Power: 30 amp $5, **50 amp** $5, **100 amp** n/a, **200 amp** n/a
  Cable TV: Yes, Incl. **Dockside Phone:** Yes Phone hookup at each slip
  Dock Type: Floating, Long Fingers, Wood, Aluminum
Moorings: 0 Total, 0 Transient **Launch:** n/a
  Rate: Day n/a **Week** n/a **Month** n/a
Heads: 8 Toilet(s), 8 Shower(s) *(with dressing rooms)*, sauna
Laundry: 2 Washer(s), 2 Dryer(s) **Pay Phones:** Yes, 2
Pump-Out: Full Service, 3 Central, 1 Port **Fee:** Free **Closed Heads:** Yes

Marina Operations
Owner/Manager: Bob Dilossie **Dockmaster:** Blake Dietrich
In-Season: Apr 15-Nov 15, 8am-9:30pm **Off-Season:** n/a, 8am-5pm
After-Hours Arrival: Call in advance
Reservations: Yes, Preferred **Credit Cards:** Visa/MC, Amex
Discounts: None
Pets: Welcome, Dog Walk Area **Handicap Access:** Yes, Heads, Docks

Marina Services and Boat Supplies
Services - Docking Assistance, Boaters' Lounge, Security *(24, Survaillence, locked gates)*, Dock Carts **Communication -** Fax in/out *($5)*, Data Ports *(Magic Brain Cyber Café)*, FedEx, AirBorne, UPS, Express Mail **Supplies -**
OnSite: Ice *(Block, Cube)* **Near:** Bait/Tackle *(Sterling Harbor 729-5222)*
Under 1 mi: Ships' Store, Marine Discount Store **3+ mi:** West Marine *(898-8245, 7 mi.)*, Propane *(U S Gas 408-0675, 4 mi.)*

Boatyard Services
OnCall: Engine mechanic *(gas, diesel)* **Under 1 mi:** Travelift.
Nearest Yard: Shawcrest Marina (609) 522-0350

Restaurants and Accommodations
OnSite: Restaurant *(Lighthouse Point 502-7447, L $9, D $17)* **Under 1 mi:**
Restaurant *(Beach Creek 522-1062, D $15-26, + Raw Bar)*, *(Urie's 522-4189, D $15-30, kid's)*, *(Boathouse 729-5301, D $13-22, Kid's $4-9 + Early bird $10-14)*, Seafood Shack *(Russo's 522-7038)*, *(Wharf 522-6336)*, Fast Food *(McDonalds)*, Lite Fare *(Marina Deck 729-5301, L $4-17, D $4-17, + Raw Bar)*, Pizzeria *(Pizza Hut 729-4833)*, Motel *(Holly Beach 522-9033)*

Recreation and Entertainment
Under 1 mi: Fishing Charter, Video Rental *(Wildwood Video 522-7227)*
1-3 mi: Beach, Picnic Area, Grills, Playground, Dive Shop, Tennis Courts, Fitness Center *(Ultimate Fitness 729-2050)*, Jogging Paths, Boat Rentals, Bowling *(3 J'S Wildwood Bowl 729-0111)*, Movie Theater *(Sea Theatre 729-0337; Strand Movie Theater 523-0288 6 mi.)*, Video Arcade, Park, Museum *(Boyer Historical Museum 523-0277)*, Cultural Attract, Sightseeing *(Doo-Wop*

Lighthouse Pointe Marina
5100 Shawcreast Road; Wildwood, NJ 08260

Tel: (609) 729-2229 **VHF: Monitor** 16 **Talk** 9
Fax: (609) 522-1451 **Alternate Tel:** n/a
Email: pointe@bellatlantic.net **Web:** www.members.bellatlantic.net/~pointe/
Nearest Town: Wildwood *(1 mi.)* **Tourist Info:** (609) 729-1934

Historical District & Doo Wop Museum 729-4000), Special Events *(Wildwood Nat'l Saltwatr Fly Fishing Tourn - Oct 888-729-0033; Classic Car shows May & Sep)* **3+ mi:** Golf Course *(Sand Barrens 465-3555, 5 mi.)*

Provisioning and General Services
Under 1 mi: Market *(WaWa 729-6339)*, Supermarket *(Acme 729-9601)*, Delicatessen *(Bonellis' 522-5118)*, Wine/Beer *(Cork 'n Bottle 522-8313)*, Liquor Store *(Mulligan's 522-4810)*, Bakery *(Manna from Heaven 846-9199)*, Fishmonger *(Carlsons 522-3100)*, Protestant Church, Beauty Salon, Barber Shop, Dry Cleaners *(Bob's 729-3737)*, Laundry, Bookstore *(Atlantic 522-7298)*, Newsstand, Hardware Store *(Ace 522-8395)*, Florist *(Wagon Wheel 522-0136)*, Retail Shops, Department Store *(Kmart 886-1122)* **1-3 mi:** Health Food *(Back To Nature 886-4027)*, Bank/ATM, Post Office, Catholic Church, Library *(Wildwood Crest 522-0564)*, Pharmacy *(Eckerd 729-1050)*

Transportation
OnCall: Rental Car *(Enterprise 522-1119, Just 4 Wheels 522-0019)*, Taxi *(Caribbean Cab 523-8000)*, Airport Limo *(A-1 Chucks 522-6088)*
Near: Local Bus *(Trolley 800-4trolly $2)* **Under 1 mi:** Bikes *(FJC 522-9191)*
1-3 mi: InterCity Bus *(NJ Transit to Cape May, Phil. & Atlantic City)*, Rail *(Seashore Lines)* **Airport:** Atlantic City/Cape May *(40 mi./6 mi.)*

Medical Services
911 Service **Under 1 mi:** Doctor *(Farooqui 522-6779)*, Chiropractor *(Back To Health 522-7557)*, Holistic Services *(Met Massage Therapy 522-7120)*
1-3 mi: Dentist *(Community Dental 729-0088)*, Veterinarian *(Baysea Veterinary 886-2292)* **Hospital:** Burdette Tomlin Memorial 463-2000 *(9 mi.)*

Setting -- The Intracoastal Waterway provides easy water access to wild and funky Wildwood and its ocean beach and boardwalk. Lighthouse Point Marina is on the western side of the channel. Watch for a group of low, sand colored contemporary buildings, punctuated by a faux bell tower, that anchors five piers with floating docks - all strung along a nicely landscaped shoreline. The integral dockside restaurant sports bright yellow awnings with a large, reversed "Lighthouse Pointe Restaurant" sign above.

Marina Notes -- *Flat Rate $30 per day for 30', $40 for 40' plus $5 electric. Relatively new and well maintained docks that are part of a condoinimum complex. Pump-out available in all slips. A large, sparsely furnished, clubhouse offers a big screen TV and sauna along with its very nice indoor bath and laundry facilities. There are also five outside showers. The onsite Lighthouse Pointe Restaurant has a greenhouse window wall for inside "outside" fine dining plus a casual outside dining deck, bar, raw bar (half price Tue) with entertainment Thu-Mon.

Notable -- The Wildwood beach and boardwalk are 1.3 miles. The super ocean beach is free and off the main boardwalk are three amusement piers with roller coasters and newer "thrill" rides (MemDay-LabDay) one day passes range from $25-39 depending on age and day (522-3900). The famous Doo-Wop Historic District is a do not miss. It will preserve for eternity the garish, uniquely American, neon-studded motels of the 50's and early 60's. The DWPL has an "Official Guide to Doo Wop Architecture" (729-4000) - self-guided, walking or on a trolley; or visit the Mid Atlantic Center for the Arts (884-5404) $8/4.

Schooner Island Marina

Schooner Island Marina

5100 Lake Road; Wildwood, NJ 08260

Tel: (609) 729-8900; (888) 823-8470 **VHF: Monitor** 16 **Talk** 9
Fax: (609) 729-0525 **Alternate Tel:** n/a
Email: marina@schoonerislandmarina.com **Web:** schoonerislandmarina.com
Nearest Town: Wildwood *(1 mi.)* **Tourist Info:** (609) 729-0639

Navigational Information
Lat: 38°59.263' **Long:** 074°49.940' **Tide:** 4 ft. **Current:** 1 kt. **Chart:** n/a
Rep. Depths *(MLW)*: **Entry** 10 ft. **Fuel Dock** 9 ft. **Max Slip/Moor** 11 ft./-
Access: North ICW 3 miles from Cold Springs Inlet (Cape May) to day marker

Marina Facilities *(In Season/Off Season)*
Fuel: *Valv Tect* - Gasoline, Diesel, High-Speed Pumps
Slips: 330 Total, 50 Transient **Max LOA:** 110 ft. **Max Beam:** 22 ft.
 Rate *(per ft.)*: **Day** $2.25/$2.25 **Week** $1.75/1.25 **Month** $1.50/1.50
 Power: 30 amp Included, **50 amp** Included, **100 amp** n/a, **200 amp** n/a
 Cable TV: Yes **Dockside Phone:** No
 Dock Type: Floating, Long Fingers, Wood
Moorings: 0 Total, 0 Transient **Launch:** n/a
 Rate: Day n/a **Week** n/a **Month** n/a
Heads: 11 Toilet(s), 6 Shower(s)
Laundry: 3 Washer(s), 3 Dryer(s), Book Exchange **Pay Phones:** Yes, 1
Pump-Out: OnSite, 2 Central **Fee:** $5 **Closed Heads:** Yes

Marina Operations
Owner/Manager: Paul K. Hoffman III **Dockmaster:** Charlie Langan
In-Season: May-Oct, 7am-8pm **Off-Season:** Nov-Apr, 8am-5pm
After-Hours Arrival: Call prior to arrival
Reservations: Preferred **Credit Cards:** Visa/MC, Dscvr, Amex, Tex
Discounts: None
Pets: Welcome, Dog Walk Area **Handicap Access:** Yes, Heads, Docks

Marina Services and Boat Supplies
Services - Docking Assistance, Concierge, Security, Trash Pick-Up, Dock Carts, Megayacht Facilities **Communication -** Mail & Package Hold, Phone Messages, Fax in/out *($3)*, Data Ports *(Office)*, FedEx, AirBorne, UPS, Express Mail **Supplies - OnSite:** Ice *(Block, Cube)*, Ships' Store **Near:** Propane *(Ed's Citgo 522-3998)* **Under 1 mi:** Bait/Tackle *(Island Bait & Tackle 729-3533)*

Boatyard Services
OnSite: Travelift *(55T)*, Forklift, Engine mechanic *(gas, diesel)*, Electrical Repairs, Electronics Repairs, Bottom Cleaning, Brightwork, Air Conditioning, Refrigeration, Compound, Wash & Wax, Interior Cleaning, Propeller Repairs, Woodworking, Yacht Broker *(McKee)* **OnCall:** Hull Repairs, Divers, Metal Fabrication **Dealer for:** Mako, Jersey Cape, Rampage, Seacraft, Jasper, Honda, MerCruiser. **Member:** ABBRA, Other Certifications: IMI Member **Yard Rates:** $69/hr., Haul & Launch $7.50/ft. *(blocking $2/ft.)*, Power Wash $2.50, Bottom Paint Inq. *(paint incl.)* **Storage:** In-Water $375/mo., On-Land $375

Restaurants and Accommodations
Near: Restaurant *(Urie's 522-4189, D $15-30, "all you can eat" crabs)*, *(Beach Creek Oyster Bar & Grille 522-1062, D $15-26, Deck dining Wed-Sun, live jazz Fri)*, *(Boat House 729-5301, D $13-22, Kids' $4-9, Early Bird $$10-14)*, *(Tom Cat 522-8586)*, Seafood Shack *(Wharf 522-6336)*, *(Marina Deck at the Boat House 729-5301, L $$4-17, D $4-17, + Raw Bar)*, Snack Bar *(Dockside)*, Fast Food *(KFC, Mc Donalds)*, Motel *(Sea Edge 522-3100)*, *(Marina Bay 522-7762)* **Under 1 mi:** Seafood Shack *(Russo's 522-7038)*, Pizzeria *(3 B's Pizzeria 846-0500)*, Inn/B&B *(Gibson House 729-7125)*

Recreation and Entertainment
OnSite: Heated Pool, Picnic Area, Grills, Fishing Charter, Group Fishing Boat **Near:** Boat Rentals, Video Arcade **Under 1 mi:** Beach *(Wildwood)*, Tennis Courts, Bowling *(J'S Wildwood Bowl 729-0111)*, Movie Theater *(Sea Theatre 729-0337)*, Video Rental *(Wildwood Video 522-7227)*, Museum *(Doo Wop 729-4000)*, Sightseeing *(Doo Wop District)*, Special Events *(Christmas in July)* **3+ mi:** Golf Course *(Sand Barrens 465-3555 - 27 holes, 5 mi.)*

Provisioning and General Services
Near: Convenience Store, Supermarket *(Acme 729-9601)*, Liquor Store *(Mulligan's 522-4810)*, Bakery, Fishmonger *(Carlson's 522-3100)*, Bank/ATM, Bookstore *(Atlantic 522-7298)* **Under 1 mi:** Delicatessen *(Polonez 846-9400)*, Post Office, Catholic Church, Protestant Church, Synagogue, Beauty Salon, Dry Cleaners, Pharmacy *(Eckerd 729-1050)*, Hardware Store *(South Jersey 522-8395)*, Department Store *(Kmart 886-1122)* **1-3 mi:** Library *(522-0564)*

Transportation
OnCall: Rental Car *(Enterprise 522-1119)*, Taxi *(Yellow 522-0555)*, Airport Limo *(A-1 522-6088)* **Near:** Local Bus *(Trolley 800-4-trolly $2, Boardwalk Tram $2.25)* **Under 1 mi:** InterCity Bus *(973-762-5100, to Atlantic City, Phil. & Cape May)* **Airport:** Atlantic City/Cape May *(40 mi./6 mi.)*

Medical Services
911 Service **Under 1 mi:** Doctor *(Catona & Corrado 523-1331)*, Dentist *(Community 729-0088)*, Chiropractor *(Back To Health 522-7557)*, Holistic Services *(Met Massage 522-7120)*, Ambulance **1-3 mi:** Veterinarian *(Baysea 886-2292)* **Hospital:** Burdette 463-2000 *(9 mi.)*

Setting -- On Grassy Sound, four miles north of the Cape May Inlet, the crumbling Wildwood Yacht Basin gave way to this high-end marina in the late '90s. Schooner Island's delightful gray and turquoise neo-Victorian two-story turreted dock house overlooks the 300 docks and their impeccably executed and maintained surroundings. The centerpiece of the marina is a peninsula that juts out into the Waterway. A short bridge connects the marina island to the Wildwood mainland. Metaphorically, the design of this welcome facility also connects the 21st century to Wildwood's funky '50s architecture.

Marina Notes -- In May 1999, the McKee Group, a family operation, opened the first phase of this very professional facility. By May 2000 the entire marina was operational, including a ships' store, full service boatyard, and an inviting, nicely furnished swimming pool. On the drawing board is a 10,000 sq. ft. boat showroom. Yacht Club and Rendezvous friendly. Fishing tournaments & sport fishing charters - Adventurer 4 hr (729-7777) & Sea Raider 6 hr (522-1032).

Notable -- Eateries abound in the surrounding Marina District with several literally adjacent. Nearby are Silver Bullet speedboat rides, dolphin watching, Delta Lady Dinner Cruises, Magic Brain Cyber Café & Duffer's Miniature Golf. Wildwood's famous boardwalk and free beach are just 0.7 mile; it's quintessential Jersey Shore with 3 huge Morey's Amusement Piers and 2 water parks (522-3900 - $25-39/pp). Rendezvous Beach has 3 tented picnic pavilions for groups; the refurbished Amphitheater holds 3,000. Pink and turquoise are alive and well in the Doo Wop Historic District; blocks of perfectly preserved '50s motels light up the town at night with their gaudy neon signs. Do not miss! On your own or on MCA's nighttime Trolley (884-5404) $8/4 - Mon-Thu, late Jun-Aug, Sat in Sep.

Navigational Information

Lat: 38°57.260' **Long:** 074°53.090' **Tide:** 3 ft. **Current:** n/a **Chart:** 12316
Rep. Depths (*MLW*): **Entry** 4 ft. **Fuel Dock** 6 ft. **Max Slip/Moor** 6 ft./6 ft.
Access: First Marina off Cape May Inlet

Marina Facilities *(In Season/Off Season)*

Fuel: *Mobil* - Gasoline, Diesel, High-Speed Pumps
Slips: 1100 Total, 10 Transient **Max LOA:** 46 ft. **Max Beam:** 16 ft.
  Rate *(per ft.)*: **Day** $1.00 **Week** 6 **Month** n/a
  Power: 30 amp Incl., **50 amp** n/a, **100 amp** n/a, **200 amp** n/a
  Cable TV: No **Dockside Phone:** No
  Dock Type: Floating, Short Fingers, Pilings, Wood, Vinyl
Moorings: 0 Total, 0 Transient **Launch:** n/a
  Rate: Day n/a **Week** n/a **Month** n/a
Heads: 20 Toilet(s), 14 Shower(s) *(with dressing rooms)*
Laundry: Yes **Pay Phones:** Yes
Pump-Out: OnSite, Full Service **Fee:** n/a **Closed Heads:** Yes

Marina Operations

Owner/Manager: Harry Olson (Owner) **Dockmaster:** John Olsen (Mgr)
In-Season: Apr-Nov, 5am-7pm **Off-Season:** Dec-Mar, 8am-4:30pm
After-Hours Arrival: Call in Advance
Reservations: Preferred **Credit Cards:** Visa/MC, Dscvr, Mobil
Discounts: None
Pets: Welcome **Handicap Access:** No

Bree-Zee-Lee Yacht Basin

PO Box 299; 976 Ocean Drive; Cape May, NJ 08204

Tel: (609) 884-4849 **VHF: Monitor** n/a **Talk** n/a
Fax: n/a **Alternate Tel:** n/a
Email: n/a **Web:** n/a
Nearest Town: Cape May *(2.5 mi.)* **Tourist Info:** (609) 884-5508

Marina Services and Boat Supplies

Services - Dock Carts **Communication -** FedEx, AirBorne, UPS, Express
Mail **Supplies - OnSite:** Ice *(Block, Cube, Shaved)*, Ships' Store, Boat/US,
Bait/Tackle *(plus Harbor View Marina 884-0808)*, Live Bait *(Minnows)*
1-3 mi: West Marine *(898-8245)*, Propane *(Port Texaco 884-1278)*

Boatyard Services

OnSite: Travelift *(85T)*, Engine mechanic *(gas)*, Launching Ramp, Hull
Repairs, Bottom Cleaning, Brightwork, Compound, Wash & Wax, Propeller
Repairs **1-3 mi:** Engine mechanic *(diesel)*, Electrical Repairs, Electronic
Sales, Electronics Repairs, Air Conditioning, Refrigeration, Divers.

Restaurants and Accommodations

OnCall: Pizzeria *(Tony's 884-2020)* **Near:** Restaurant *(Axelsson's Blue
Claw 884-5878, D $24-30)* **Under 1 mi:** Restaurant *(Crab House 522-1341,
L $5-18, D $14-19, Kids $5-9)*, *(Two Mile Landing 522-1342, D $15-23, Kids
$6-13)* **1-3 mi:** Seafood Shack *(Waters Edge Restaurant 884-1717, D $22-
33)*, Pizzeria *(Carini's Pizza 522-7304)*, Hotel *(Grand Hotel of Cape May
884-5611, $136-195)*, Inn/B&B *(Angel of Sea 884-3369, $135-285)*,
(Mainstay Inn 884-8690, $110-350) **3+ mi:** Fast Food *(Burger King 4 mi.)*

Recreation and Entertainment

OnSite: Picnic Area, Grills, Fishing Charter **Under 1 mi:** Boat Rentals
1-3 mi: Beach *(Cape May & Wildwood Beaches)*, Tennis Courts *(Cape May
Tennis Club 884-8986)*, Golf Course *(Cape May Nat'l G.C. 884-1563)*,
Fitness Center *(Cape Fitness 898-1515)*, Video Rental *(Blockbuster Video
884-7741)*, Museum *(Physick Estate 884-5404)*, Sightseeing *(Cape May
Historic District)*, Galleries

3+ mi: Jogging Paths, Horseback Riding *(Sea Horse Farm 884-5354, 4 mi.)*,
Bowling *(J'S Wildwood Bowl 729-0111, 4.5 mi.)*, Movie Theater *(Bayshore 8
Theatre 889-8800, 4 mi.)*

Provisioning and General Services

Under 1 mi: Fishmonger, Lobster Pound **1-3 mi:** Convenience Store *(Wa-
Wa)*, Market *(Sun Crest 522-6811)*, Gourmet Shop *(Love the Cook 884-
9292)*, Delicatessen *(Polonez Deli 846-9400 R 3.5 mi.)*, Wine/Beer *(Green's
Liquors 522-9463 4 mi.)*, Liquor Store *(Cape 884-7676, Green's 522-9463 4
mi.)*, Meat Market, Bank/ATM, Dry Cleaners, Laundry, Bookstore *(Garden of
Verses 884-6275)*, Pharmacy *(CVS 263-1030)*, Newsstand, Hardware Store
(Swain's 884-8578), Retail Shops *(Dellas General Store 884-4568)*, Copies
Etc. **3+ mi:** Supermarket *(Acme, 5 mi.)*, Health Food *(Bayshore Nutrition
886-8008, 4.5 mi.)*, Farmers' Market *(Tue 3-8pm 884-4858 West Cape May
Boro Hall, 4 mi.)*, Post Office *(5 mi.)*, Library *(884-9568, 4 mi.)*, Beauty Salon
(4 mi.), Barber Shop *(4 mi.)*, Department Store *(K-Mart, 5 mi.)*

Transportation

OnCall: Rental Car *(Enterprise 522-1119)*, Taxi *(Yellow 522-0555)*, Airport
Limo *(A-1 Chucks 522-6088)* **1-3 mi:** Bikes, Ferry Service *(Cape May)*
Airport: Atlantic City/Cape May *(40 mi./3 mi.)*

Medical Services

911 Service **1-3 mi:** Doctor *(Tenenbaum 884-3606)*, Dentist *(Spevak 522-
3145)*, Chiropractor *(Rizzo 884-2162)*, Veterinarian *(Cape May Veterinary
Hospital 884-1729)* **3+ mi:** Holistic Services *(Met Massage Therapy 522-
7120, 4 mi.)* **Hospital:** Burdette Tomlin Memorial 463-2000 *(12.5 mi.)*

Setting -- After entering the Cape May Inlet, turn to port into Cape May Harbor and Bree-Zee-Lee's extensive network of docks will be somewhat immediately
on your right side. A long boardwalk, along a variegated marsh, interspersed with tufts of tall grasses, anchors its three basins. One has the limited-service
boatyard as its centerpiece, another claims one of the attractive, contemporary gray bath houses, and a third sports a cute awninged picnic area on the dock.

Marina Notes -- Family owned business for over 30 years. Friendly service and reasonable prices - "where everybody knows your name". In '99, a 439 slip
expansion of the existing marina facilities was constructed between the Mill Creek and the original facility including new pedestals and vinyl edged floating
docks. As part of that project, two lovely head/shower buildings - each with seven very nice fully tiled bathrooms, were also added. A laundry is on the drawing
board. A large 85 ton travel lift onsite along with Jodi Lee Canvas. Nearby Harborview (884-0808) has an occasional transient space on the fuel dock.

Notable -- Surrounded by saltwater meadows, a natural habitat of migrating waterfowl, Bree-Zee-Lee is a bird-watcher's paradise and ideal for early morning
bike rides if you tote your own. Its proximity to the Ocean also puts it fairly far from the Cape May historic and restaurant district, and even further from supplies
and services. It's about equidistant to the Cape May & Wildwood beaches. Cabs are the best way to navigate whether heading into town or to the many other
attractions - including a large free Zoo in lovely Cape May County Park, train, trolley and horse & buggy rides. Tours of indoor and outdoor museums. Cape
May hosts a plethora of events and festivals, including Victorian Week, Fireman's Week, Hogs Week and Sand Sculpting contests.

PHOTOS ON CD-ROM: 9

Canyon Club Resort Marina

900 Ocean Drive; Cape May, NJ 08204

Tel: (609) 884-0199 **VHF: Monitor** 16 **Talk** 9
Fax: (609) 884-2995 **Alternate Tel:** n/a
Email: dockmaster@canyonclubmarina.com **Web:** canyonclubmarina.com
Nearest Town: Cape May *(2 mi.)* **Tourist Info:** (609) 884-9345

Navigational Information
Lat: 38°57.337' **Long:** 074°54.039' **Tide:** 5 ft. **Current:** 0 kt. **Chart:** 12316
Rep. Depths *(MLW):* **Entry** 12 ft. **Fuel Dock** 8 ft. **Max Slip/Moor** 8 ft./-
Access: Cape May Canal from Ocean or Delaware Bay

Marina Facilities *(In Season/Off Season)*
Fuel: *Shell* - Slip-Side Fueling, Gasoline, Diesel, High-Speed Pumps
Slips: 260 Total, 50 Transient **Max LOA:** 125 ft. **Max Beam:** n/a
  Rate *(per ft.):* **Day** $2.45 **Week** Inq. **Month** $2.00
  Power: 30 amp Incl., 50 amp Incl., **100 amp** n/a, **200 amp** n/a
  Cable TV: Yes Incl. **Dockside Phone:** No
  Dock Type: Floating, Long Fingers, Pilings, Alongside, Concrete
Moorings: 0 Total, 0 Transient **Launch:** n/a
  Rate: Day n/a **Week** n/a **Month** n/a
Heads: 6 Toilet(s), 6 Shower(s)
Laundry: 2 Washer(s), 2 Dryer(s), Book Exchange **Pay Phones:** No
Pump-Out: OnSite, 2 Central **Fee:** Free* **Closed Heads:** Yes

Marina Operations
Owner/Manager: Mike Weber **Dockmaster:** Mike Weber
In-Season: Summer, 8am-8pm **Off-Season:** Fall-Win-Sprg, 9am-5pm
After-Hours Arrival: Call in advance
Reservations: Recommended **Credit Cards:** Visa/MC, Dscvr, Amex, Shell
Discounts: Fuel **Dockage:** n/a **Fuel:** volume & cash **Repair:** n/a
Pets: Welcome, Dog Walk Area **Handicap Access:** Yes, Heads, Docks

Marina Services and Boat Supplies
Services - Docking Assistance, Dock Carts **Communication -** Phone
Messages, Fax in/out *(Free)*, Data Ports *(Ship store)*, FedEx, AirBorne, UPS,
Express Mail *(Sat Del)* **Supplies - OnSite:** Ice *(Block, Cube)*, Ships' Store,
Bait/Tackle *(plus dead bait)* **Under 1 mi:** West Marine *(898-8245)*, Live Bait
(Cold Spring 884-2248), Propane *(Port Texaco 884-1278)*

Boatyard Services
OnSite: Travelift *(60T)*, Forklift, Engine mechanic *(gas, diesel)*, Electrical
Repairs, Electronic Sales, Electronics Repairs, Hull Repairs, Bottom
Cleaning, Brightwork, Air Conditioning, Refrigeration, Compound, Wash &
Wax, Woodworking, Metal Fabrication, Painting, Awlgrip, Yacht Broker
(South Jersey Yacht Sales) **OnCall:** Interior Cleaning, Propeller Repairs,
Life Raft Service **Under 1 mi:** Launching Ramp. **Dealer for:** Cat, Furuno,
Northstar, Cabo, Viking, Albemarle, Ocean Yachts. **Yard Rates:** $75/hr.,
Haul & Launch $5/ft. *(blocking $4/ft.)*, Power Wash $3, Bottom Paint
$12-15/ft. *(paint incl.)* **Storage:** In-Water $20/ft.mo., On-Land $25/ft.

Restaurants and Accommodations
OnCall: Pizzeria *(Tony's Pizza)* **Near:** Restaurant *(Lobster House 884-
8296, L $5-13 + lobsters, D $12-40)* **Under 1 mi:** Restaurant *(Captains
Cove 884-7288)*, *(Anchorage Inn 884-1174)*, Lite Fare *(Dock Mike's Pancake
House 884-2855, B $3-13, L $4-9, cash only)*, Inn/B&B *(Primrose Inn 884-
8288)* **1-3 mi:** Seafood Shack *(Waters Edge 884-1717, D $22-33)*, Fast
Food *(McDonalds, Burger King, KFC)*, Motel *(Lido 884-4098)*, Hotel
(Bacchus 884-2129), Inn/B&B *(Angel of Sea B&B 884-3369, $135-285)*,
(Queen Victoria 884-8702, $80-290) **3+ mi:** Restaurant *(Cactus Grill 898-
0354, Tex-Mex, Early Bird, Kids)*, Fast Food *(Burger King 5 miles)*

Recreation and Entertainment
OnSite: Pool, Tennis Courts **Near:** Fishing Charter, Group Fishing Boat
Under 1 mi: Boat Rentals *(C.M. Water Sports 884-8646)*, Video Rental
(Blockbuster 884-7741) **1-3 mi:** Beach, Golf Course *(C.M. Nat'l G.C. 884-
1563)*, Fitness Center *(Cape 898-1515)*, Horseback Riding *(Sea Horse Farm
884-5354)*, Movie Theater *(Bayshore-8 889-8800)*, Video Arcade, Museum
(Physick Estate 884-5404), Cultural Attract *(C.M.Point Bird Observatory)*

Provisioning and General Services
Near: Fishmonger *(Lobster House)*, Crabs/Waterman *(McDuells 884-0404)*
1-3 mi: Market *(Depot Market Cafe 884-8030)*, Supermarket *(Acme 463-
9106; SuperFresh 465-4140)*, Gourmet Shop *(Love the Cook 884-9292)*,
Health Food *(Bayshore 886-8008)*, Liquor Store *(Cape 884-7676)*, Bakery,
Farmers' Market, Green Grocer *(No Frills Farm 884-8209)*, Bank/ATM, Post
Office, Catholic Church, Protestant Church, Library *(884-9568)*, Beauty
Salon, Dry Cleaners, Laundry, Bookstore *(Book Shoppe 884-7878)*,
Pharmacy *(CVS 263-1030)*, Newsstand, Hardware Store *(Swain's Ace 884-
8578)*, Department Store *(Dellas 884-4568)*

Transportation
OnCall: Rental Car *(Enterprise 522-1119)*, Taxi *(AART 884-2273)*, Airport
Limo *(High Roller 425-5819)* **Under 1 mi:** Rail *(C.M.Seashore)*
Airport: Cape May/Atlantic City *(3 mi./40 mi.)*

Medical Services
911 Service **Under 1 mi:** Chiropractor *(Rizzo 884-2162)* **1-3 mi:** Doctor
(Tenenbaum 884-3606), Dentist *(Feldman 884-4260)*, Veterinarian *(Cape
May 884-1729)* **Hospital:** Burdette Tomlin Mem 463-2000 *(11.5 mi.)*

Setting -- Almost to the head of Cape May Harbor, just before the Canal, is this family-oriented sport fish country club. The contemporary, three story gray condominium complex that surrounds the impeccable docks provide an easy signpost. The grounds are professionally landscaped with winding paths interrupted by rock-bordered perennial gardens. The trapezoidal-shaped pool, furnished with tables and rows of chaises, overlooks the docks.

Marina Notes -- Caters to private sport fishing yachts. Service-focused. International Game Fish Association Official Weigh Station. Built in 1960 as Cape Island Marina; present ownership purchased it in 1984. Now family owned/operated together with South Jersey Marina. *Free full-serve pump-out for guests & volume fuel purchasers. $5 for others. Excellent ships' store has internet access - plug-in your laptop. Stable cement, low-profile floating docks, side-to docking, corrugated vinyl bulkheads, in-slip fueling, volume discounts for fuel & multiple 50 amp hook-ups. Good heads/showers. Full service boatyard. Dredged in 2003 for deeper draft vessels. Ocean Yachts, Viking Yachts, Cabo, Albemarle dealer. Winter dry storage. MemDay, LabDay picnics, pool/theme parties for all.

Notable -- Canyon Club hosts numerous off-shore world-class sport fishing tournaments for shark, tuna, and marlin, including the annual Viking/Ocean Showdown and the "Mid-Atlantic $500,000" (which pays out more than a $1 million) is in August. It's also a frequent flotilla or club cruise destination. The wonderfully preserved Victorian seaside resort of Cape May is about 2.5 miles. It has been designated one of only three National Historic Landmark Cities. There's also the Farmers Market on Tuesdays, 3-8pm (884-4858) at West Cape May Borough Hall. Sadly, the local CAT bus no longer operates.

Navigational Information

Lat: 38°57.120' **Long:** 074°54.381' **Tide:** 5 ft. **Current:** n/a **Chart:** 12316
Rep. Depths (*MLW*): **Entry** 7 ft. **Fuel Dock** 7 ft. **Max Slip/Moor** 12 ft./-
Access: Head of Cape May Harbor next to Cape May Canal

Marina Facilities *(In Season/Off Season)*

Fuel: *Texaco* - Gasoline, Diesel, High-Speed Pumps
Slips: 375 Total, 25 Transient **Max LOA:** 80 ft. **Max Beam:** n/a
Rate *(per ft.)*: **Day** $2.00 **Week** n/a **Month** n/a
Power: 30 amp Incl., **50 amp** Incl., **100 amp** n/a, **200 amp** n/a
Cable TV: Yes, Incl. **Dockside Phone:** No
Dock Type: Floating, Long Fingers, Alongside, Concrete, Wood
Moorings: 0 Total, 0 Transient **Launch:** n/a, Dinghy Dock
Rate: Day n/a **Week** n/a **Month** n/a
Heads: 14 Toilet(s), 14 Shower(s) *(with dressing rooms)*
Laundry: 3 Washer(s), 6 Dryer(s), Iron, Iron Board **Pay Phones:** No
Pump-Out: Self Service, 1 Central **Fee:** $35 **Closed Heads:** Yes

Marina Operations

Owner/Manager: Ernest & Charles Utsch **Dockmaster:** Same
In-Season: LateMar-Nov 30, 6am-7pm* **Off-Season:** Dec 25-Jan1, Closed
After-Hours Arrival: Call for special arrangements if possible
Reservations: Yes **Credit Cards:** Visa/MC, Dscvr, Tex
Discounts: Fuel **Dockage:** n/a **Fuel:** 500 gl or more **Repair:** n/a
Pets: Welcome, Dog Walk Area **Handicap Access:** Yes, Heads, Docks

Utsch's Marina

1121 Route 109; Cape May, NJ 08204

Tel: (609) 884-2051 **VHF: Monitor** 16 **Talk** 9
Fax: (609) 898-0136 **Alternate Tel:** n/a
Email: utschm@eticomm.net **Web:** www.capemayharbor.com
Nearest Town: Cape May *(1.2 mi.)* **Tourist Info:** (609) 884-9345

Marina Services and Boat Supplies

Services - Docking Assistance, Boaters' Lounge, Dock Carts, Megayacht Facilities **Communication -** Mail & Package Hold, Phone Messages, Fax in/out *($1)*, Data Ports *(Marina , Free)*, FedEx, AirBorne, UPS, Express Mail *(Sat Del)* **Supplies - OnSite:** Ice *(Block, Cube)*, Marine Discount Store, Bait/Tackle **Near:** Propane *(Texaco 884-1278)* **Under 1 mi:** West Marine *(898-8245)*, Live Bait *(Hand's B&T 898-3744)*

Boatyard Services

OnSite: Travelift *(25 & 35T)*, Forklift, Crane, Engine mechanic *(gas)*, Electrical Repairs, Hull Repairs, Bottom Cleaning, Brightwork, Compound, Wash & Wax, Woodworking, Yacht Broker **OnCall:** Engine mechanic *(diesel)*, Electronics Repairs, Divers, Interior Cleaning, Propeller Repairs, Inflatable Repairs, Upholstery, Metal Fabrication **Near:** Railway *(Tony's)*, Launching Ramp *(Hinche's)*. **Dealer for:** Mercruiser, Chrysler, Crusader, PCM, Volvo Penta, Yanmarl, Honda. **Member:** ABBRA **Yard Rates:** $70, Haul & Launch $2.50/ft. *(blocking $2/ft.)*, Power Wash $2/ft.

Restaurants and Accommodations

OnCall: Pizzeria *(Tony's 884-2020)* **Near:** Restaurant *(Lobster House 884-8296, L $5-13 + lobsters, D $12-40)*, *(Captain's Cove 884-5878, B $2-5, L $2-9, D $9-15 + lobster Tail)*, *(Anchorage 898-1154)*, Coffee Shop *(Dock Mike's 884-2855, B $3-13, L $4-9)* **Under 1 mi:** Restaurant *(Washington Inn 884-5697, D $20-32)*, Lite Fare *(Twinings Tea Room 884-5404, L $16.50, Tea $13.50)*, Hotel *(Thomas Webster 898-9248)*, Inn/B&B *(Primrose Inn 884-8288)* **1-3 mi:** Restaurant *(Waters Edge 884-1717, D $22-33)*, *(Cactus Grill 898-0354, Tex-Mex, Early Bird, Kids)*, Fast Food *(Burger King)*, Motel *(LA Mer 884-9000, $136-195)*, Inn/B&B *(Queen Victoria 884-8702, $80-290)*

Recreation and Entertainment

OnSite: Picnic Area, Grills, Fishing Charter, Group Fishing Boat **Near:** Boat Rentals, Video Arcade **Under 1 mi:** Beach, Tennis Courts *(Cape May Tennis 884-8986)*, Video Rental *(Blockbuster 884-7741)*, Museum *(Physick Estate 884-5404 $8/4)* **1-3 mi:** Golf Course *(Cape May Natl 884-1563; Ponder Lodge 886-8065)*, Horseback Riding *(Sea Horse Farm 884-5354)*, Movie Theater *(Bayshore-8 889-8800)*, Sightseeing *(CM Historical District)*

Provisioning and General Services

Near: Wine/Beer, Fishmonger *(Lobster House 884-3064)*, Beauty Salon, Barber Shop, Dry Cleaners **Under 1 mi:** Convenience Store *(WaWa 884-67-63)*, Crabs/Waterman *(McDuells 884-0404)*, Bank/ATM, Library, Newsstand **1-3 mi:** Supermarket *(Acme 463-9106; SuperFresh 465-4140)*, Liquor Store *(Cape 884-7676; Collier's 884-8488 delivers)*, Bakery, Post Office, Catholic Church, Protestant Church, Bookstore *(Book Shoppe 884-7878)*, Pharmacy *(CVS 263-1030)*, Hardware Store *(Swain's 884-8578)*, Florist, Department Store *(Kmart, Dellas 884-4568)*

Transportation

OnSite: Bikes *($10 day/$40 wk)*, InterCity Bus **OnCall:** Rental Car *(Enterprise 522-1119)*, Taxi *(AART's Cape 884-2273)* **Under 1 mi:** Ferry Service *(CM to Lewes)* **1-3 mi:** Airport Limo *(CM Limo 884-1171)* **Airport:** Cape May/Atlantic City *(5 mi./40 mi.)*

Medical Services

911 Service **Under 1 mi:** Chiropractor *(Rizzo 884-2162)* **1-3 mi:** Doctor *(Bayshore Med 886-3636)*, Dentist *(Cape May 884-5335)*, Veterinarian *(Cape May 884-1729)* **Hospital:** Burdette Tomlin 463-2000 *(11 mi.)*

Setting -- Located on Schellenger's Landing (RN Island) at the entrance to the Cape May Canal, venerable Utsch's has been a Cape May landmark since 1951. A successful landscaping effort softens the boatyard atmosphere with pretty raised flower beds and appealing plantings along the docks - interrrupted by the occasional gazebo. On the northwest corner of the property, a wonderfullly restored early summer cottage houses the superb boaters' services.

Marina Notes -- *All hours vary with the season. Founded by Ernest Utsch, Sr. & Jr., and still being operated by octegenarian Ernest Jr. and his sons Ernest III and Charles. Serious boatyard with 3 travelifts. Ships store with large parts inventory open 8-5. Thoughtfully renovated Gertrude M. Wagner building, once the Utsch's summer home & marina office, now shelters eight perfect, immaculate full bathrooms (two handicapped accessible with roll-in showers), a comfortable teak & wicker furnished boaters' lounge, wide multi-station desk for lap-top plug in and internet access and a spacious laundromat with commercial quality dryers. Late October sees Utsch's Annual $100,000 Striper Classic. $0.10 discount over 500 gals fuel. Bicycles rented on site!

Notable -- The famous Lobster House is just a block away. At West Cape May Borough Hall every Tuesday 3-8pm (884-4858) is the Farmer's Market. A mile walk is the 1879 Emlen Physick Estate, an 18-room mansion on 4 acres, home to the Mid-Atlantic Center for the Arts. Take a tour, view the gallery exhibits or lunch or take tea at Twinings Tea Room. MCA (884-5404) also offers 4 trolley tours of the CM Historic district $6/3 a walking tour $10/5, and a self-guided audio tour $6. The Cape Area Transit Shuttle into Cape May no longer operates.

South Jersey Marina

PO Box 641; 1231 U. S. Hwy. 109; Cape May, NJ 08204

Tel: (609) 884-2400 **VHF: Monitor** 16 **Talk** 9
Fax: (609) 884-0039 **Alternate Tel:** n/a
Email: admin@sjmarina.com **Web:** www.sjmarina.com
Nearest Town: Cape May *(1 mi.)* **Tourist Info:** (609) 884-5508

Navigational Information
Lat: 38°56.530' **Long:** 074°55.120' **Tide:** 4 ft. **Current:** 2 kt. **Chart:** 12316
Rep. Depths *(MLW):* **Entry** 12 ft. **Fuel Dock** 10 ft. **Max Slip/Moor** 10 ft./-
Access: Atlantic Ocean/Delaware Bay to Cape May Harbor

Marina Facilities *(In Season/Off Season)*
Fuel: *Texaco* - Slip-Side Fueling, Gasoline, Diesel, High-Speed Pumps
Slips: 170 Total, 25 Transient **Max LOA:** 140 ft. **Max Beam:** n/a
   Rate *(per ft.):* **Day** $2.45* **Week** n/a **Month** $77.50
   Power: 30 amp Incl., **50 amp** Incl., **100 amp** $10 add'l, **200 amp** n/a
   Cable TV: Yes, Incl. 48 channels **Dockside Phone:** No
   Dock Type: Floating, Long Fingers, Short Fingers, Pilings, Alongside, Wood
Moorings: 0 Total, 0 Transient **Launch:** n/a
   Rate: Day n/a **Week** n/a **Month** n/a
Heads: 6 Toilet(s), 4 Shower(s) *(with dressing rooms)*
Laundry: 1 Washer(s), 1 Dryer(s), Book Exchange **Pay Phones:** Yes, 4
Pump-Out: OnSite, Self Service, 9 Central **Fee:** Free** **Closed Heads:** Yes

Marina Operations
Owner/Manager: Rick Weber **Dockmaster:** Chris Booth
In-Season: May-Oct, 7am-9pm **Off-Season:** Nov-Apr, 8am-5pm
After-Hours Arrival: Call ahead for slip assignment
Reservations: Preferred **Credit Cards:** Visa/MC, Dscvr, Din, Amex, Tex
Discounts: Fuel **Dockage:** n/a **Fuel:** vol discount **Repair:** n/a
Pets: Welcome, Dog Walk Area **Handicap Access:** No

Marina Services and Boat Supplies
Services - Docking Assistance, Concierge, Trash Pick-Up, Dock Carts
Communication - Mail & Package Hold, Phone Messages, Fax in/out *($1/p)*, Data Ports *(Store)*, FedEx, AirBorne, UPS, Express Mail *(Sat Del)*
Supplies - OnSite: Ice *(Block, Cube)*, Ships' Store, Bait/Tackle *(or nearby Hand's B&T 898-3744)* **Near:** Live Bait *(Jim's Bait & Tackle)*, Propane *(Texaco 884-1278)* **Under 1 mi:** West Marine *(898-8245)*

Boatyard Services
OnSite: Yacht Broker **OnCall:** Engine mechanic *(gas, diesel)*, Electrical Repairs, Air Conditioning, Refrigeration, Divers, Compound, Wash & Wax, Interior Cleaning **Nearest Yard:** Utsch's Marina (609) 884-2051

Restaurants and Accommodations
OnSite: Restaurant *(Lobster House L $5-13 + Lobsters, D $12-40, also lite fare counter)*, Coffee Shop *(Dock Mike's B $3-13, L $4-9)* **Near:** Restaurant *(Anchorage Inn 898-1174)*, *(Captain's Cove B $2-5, L $2-9, D $9-15)*, Snack Bar *(Dry Dock 884-3434)*, Pizzeria *(Tony's Pizza 884-2020)* **Under 1 mi:** Inn/B&B *(Thomas Webster House 898-9248)*, *(Primrose Inn B & B 884-8288)*, Condo/Cottage *(Bill Mae Cottage 898-8558)* **1-3 mi:** Restaurant *(Ebbitt Room 884-5700, D $24-30)*, *(Waters Edge 884-1717, D $22-33)*, Fast Food *(Burger King)*, Hotel *(Virginia Hotel 884-5700, $145-345)*, *(La Mer 884-9000, $136-195)*, Inn/B&B *(Southern Mansion 898-0492, $185-350)*

Recreation and Entertainment
OnSite: Picnic Area, Fishing Charter, Group Fishing Boat **Near:** Video Rental *(Blockbuster 884-7741)* **Under 1 mi:** Beach, Playground, Volleyball, Video Arcade, Museum *(Physick House 884-5404 $8/4)*, Cultural Attract

(Elaine's Dinner Theater 884-1198), Sightseeing *(Great American Trolley 884-0450; MCA's trolley & walking tours 884-5404)* **1-3 mi:** Tennis Courts *(CM T.C. 884-8986)*, Golf Course *(CM Natl 884-1563; Ponder Lodge 886-8065)*, Movie Theater *(Bayshore-8 889-8800)*

Provisioning and General Services
Near: Convenience Store *(Wawa)*, Fishmonger *(Lobster House 609-884-8296)*, Bank/ATM, Beauty Salon *(Pauline's 884-3011)*, Barber Shop, Dry Cleaners *(Model 884-8446)*, Laundry **Under 1 mi:** Bakery, Post Office, Catholic Church, Protestant Church, Library, Pharmacy *(CVS 391-0070.)*, Newsstand, Clothing Store, Retail Shops **1-3 mi:** Supermarket *(Acme 463-9106; SuperFresh 465-4140)*, Delicatessen *(Depot Market Café 884-8030)*, Liquor Store *(Cape 884-7676 Delivers)*, Farmers' Market *(Tuesday 3-8pm 884-4858)*, Bookstore *(Book Shoppe 884-7878)*, Hardware Store *(Swain's 884-8578)*, Florist, Department Store *(Dellas 884-4568)*

Transportation
OnSite: Local Bus *(CAT $2)* **OnCall:** Rental Car *(Enterprise 522-1119)*, Taxi *(High Roller 884-5711)*, Airport Limo *(CM Limo 884-1171)* **Under 1 mi:** Bikes *(Village 884-8500)*, InterCity Bus *(NJ Transit to Wildwood, Phil, AC)* **1-3 mi:** Rail *(CM Seashore 884-2675)*, Ferry Service *(to Lewes)* **Airport:** CapeMay/Atlantic City *(5 mi./40 mi.)*

Medical Services
911 Service **Near:** Chiropractor *(Rizzo 884-2162)* **Under 1 mi:** Dentist *(CM Dental 884-5335)*, Holistic Services *(CM Day Spa 898-1003)* **1-3 mi:** Doctor *(Bayshore Med 886-3636)*, Veterinarian *(CM 884-1729)*, Optician *(Atlantic 465-1616)* **Hospital:** Beebe Med Ctr 645-3149 *(6 mi.)*

Setting -- Tucked into a protected basin right off the western edge of Cape May Harbor, South Jersey Marina delivers convenience and service-oriented dockage with delightful views of restored classic boat houses and cottages, the Lobster House schooner and an onsite archtecture remeniscent of the historic district. Swaths of attractive pavers collide with rock-walled raised beds overflowing with flowers, greenery and potted trees. Abundant flowering hanging plants trim the main building's second floor veranda. Umbrellaed tables and benches dot the area; out on the wharf is an inviting picnic spot.

Marina Notes -- *Rates include 50 Amp electric. **Pump-out free for overnight guests, $5 for others. Cash & volume discounts on fuel. Buy 2 nights, get 1 free from May-Jun & Sep-Oct. Side-to dockage at high profile floating piers. High speed in-slip fueling. Uniformed dock staff and concierge services set the tone. Very well supplied ships' store. Excellent, carpeted heads/showers. Formerly Cape Island Marina. Owned by the Weber family since 1980; they also own Canyon Club. Int'l Game Fish Association Official Weigh Station. Home of SEVEN fishing tournaments: Spring Striper, Annual $150,00 Shark, Viking/Ocean Showdown, Mid-Atlantic Tuna, Mid-Atlantic $500,000, Offshore Team Challenge & Big Bass. South Jersey Yacht Sales - Albemarle, Cabo, Ocean & Viking.

Notable -- Onsite South Jersey Fishing Center hosts the largest fleet in southern New Jersey - 16 sportfishing charters for inshore, canyon, overnight canyon, shark, stripers, & drum, 4-24 hrs, (884-3800) $300-2500. Plus 4 partyboats: Sea Star, Miss Cape May, Porgy & Fiesta (884-3421) for 4, 6 & 8 hrs. inshore adventures $25/15 to $35/25. Also here is Atlantic Parasail (898-1600). Cape May was named "The Restaurant Capital of New Jersey" - so while here indulge!

Navigational Information
Lat: 38°57.000' **Long:** 074°54.630' **Tide:** 4 ft. **Current:** 1 kt. **Chart:** n/a
Rep. Depths (MLW): Entry 8 ft. **Fuel Dock** 8 ft. **Max Slip/Moor** 8 ft./-
Access: CM Canal under 52 ft bridge, south into Spicer Creek

Marina Facilities *(In Season/Off Season)*
Fuel: *Mobil* - Slip-Side Fueling, Gasoline, Diesel, High-Speed Pumps
Slips: 12 Total, 2 Transient **Max LOA:** 85 ft. **Max Beam:** n/a
  Rate *(per ft.)*: **Day** $1.60 **Week** Inq. **Month** Inq.
  Power: 30 amp Incl., **50 amp** Incl., **100 amp** n/a, **200 amp** n/a
  Cable TV: No **Dockside Phone:** No
  Dock Type: Floating
Moorings: 0 Total, 0 Transient **Launch:** None
  Rate: Day n/a **Week** n/a **Month** n/a
Heads: 2 Toilet(s), 1 Shower(s)
Laundry: None **Pay Phones:** Yes
Pump-Out: OnSite **Fee:** $5 **Closed Heads:** Yes

Marina Operations
Owner/Manager: Bob Lubberman **Dockmaster:** Same
In-Season: May-Aug, 6am-7pm **Off-Season:** Sep-Apr, 6am-5pm
After-Hours Arrival: Call number on door
Reservations: Preferred **Credit Cards:** Visa/MC, Dscvr, Din, Amex, Mobil
Discounts: Boat/US; Port Partners **Dockage:** 25% **Fuel:** $.10 **Repair:** n/a
Pets: Welcome, Dog Walk Area **Handicap Access:** No

Miss Chris Marina

1218 Wilson Drive; Cape May, NJ 08204

Tel: (609) 884-3351 **VHF: Monitor** 16 **Talk** 19
Fax: n/a **Alternate Tel:** n/a
Email: n/a **Web:** www.misschrismarina.com
Nearest Town: Cape May *(1 mi.)* **Tourist Info:** (609) 884-5508

Marina Services and Boat Supplies
Services - Docking Assistance, Trash Pick-Up **Communication** - UPS
Supplies - OnSite: Ice *(Block, Cube)*, Bait/Tackle *(crabbing supplies + nearby Hand's Bait & Tackle 898-3744)*, Live Bait *(incl. eels, minnows)*
Near: Ships' Store **Under 1 mi:** West Marine *(898-8245 R 1.5 mi.)*, Marine Discount Store, Propane *(P & J Gas Service 886-6749 R 5.5 mi.)*

Boatyard Services
OnSite: Yacht Broker **OnCall:** Electronic Sales, Electronics Repairs, Air Conditioning, Refrigeration, Divers, Metal Fabrication **Near:** Railway.
Nearest Yard: Cape May Mairne (609) 884-0262

Restaurants and Accommodations
OnSite: Restaurant *(Captain's Cove 884-5878, B $2-5, L $2-9, D $9-15)*, Lite Fare *(Mayer's Tavern pub fare, outdoor porch overlooks marina buildings)*
Near: Restaurant *(Lobster House 884-8296, L $5-13 + lobster, D $12-40)*, *(C-View Inn)*, *(Anchorage Inn 898-1154)*, Snack Bar *(Dry Dock 884-3434, ice cream, etc.)*, Coffee Shop *(Dock Mike's 884-2855, B $3-13, L $4-9)*, Pizzeria *(Tony's)* **Under 1 mi:** Restaurant *(Cactus Grill 898-0354, Tex-Mex)*, Lite Fare *(Twinings Tea Room 884-5404, L $16.50, At Physick House - Tea $13.50)*, Inn/B&B *(Primrose Inn 884-8288)*, *(Thomas Webster House 898-9248)*, *(Jeramiah Hand House 884-1135)*, *(Duke of Windsor 884-1355)*, Condo/Cottage *(Bill Mae 898-8558)* **1-3 mi:** Restaurant *(Waters Edge Restaurant 884-1717, D $22-33)*

Recreation and Entertainment
OnSite: Boat Rentals *(Kayaks 884-3351 Old Town & Cobra)*, Fishing Charter, Group Fishing Boat **Near:** Video Rental *(Blockbuster 884-7741)* **Under 1 mi:** Picnic Area, Grills, Playground, Tennis Courts *(CMTennis 884-8986)*, Museum *(E. Physick Estate 884-5404 $8/4)*, Cultural Attract, Sightseeing *(Trolley & walking tours of historic district - MCA)*
1-3 mi: Beach, Golf Course *(CM Natl 884-1563; Ponder Lodge 886-8065)*, Fitness Center *(CM Fitness Ctrr 898-1515)*, Horseback Riding, Movie Theater *(Bayshore-8 889-8800)*

Provisioning and General Services
Near: Convenience Store, Market *(Wawa 884-6368)*, Delicatessen, Fishmonger, Bank/ATM **Under 1 mi:** Wine/Beer, Bakery, Dry Cleaners, Laundry **1-3 mi:** Supermarket *(Acme 463-9106; SuperFresh 465-4140)*, Gourmet Shop *(Love the Cook 898-9292)*, Liquor Store *(Collier's 884-8488)*, Farmers' Market, Post Office, Catholic Church, Protestant Church, Library, Beauty Salon, Barber Shop, Bookstore *(Book Shoppe 884-7878)*, Pharmacy *(CVS 263-1030)*, Newsstand, Hardware Store *(Swain's Ace 884-8578)*, Florist, Department Store *(Dellas 884-4568)*

Transportation
OnCall: Rental Car *(Enterprise 522-1119)*, Taxi *(AART's 884-2273)*, Airport Limo *(CM Limo 884-1171)* **Near:** Bikes *(Utsch's)* **Under 1 mi:** Rail *(Seashore Line)* **3+ mi:** Ferry Service *(to Lewes, 5 mi.)* **Airport:** Cape May/Atlantic City *(5 mi./40 mi.)*

Medical Services
911 Service **Near:** Chiropractor *(Rizzo 84-2162)*, Optician *(Dorn & Drake 884-2010)* **Under 1 mi:** Holistic Services *(CM Day Spa 898-1003)* **1-3 mi:** Doctor *(Bayshore Med 886-3636)*, Dentist *(Foster 898-0404)*, Veterinarian *(CM Vet 884-1729)* **Hospital:** Burdette Tomlin 463-2000 *(11 mi.)*

Setting -- Tucked up quiet Spicer Creek, Miss Chris Marina is anything but. A constant flow of activity spins from the tourist operations, the sport fish charter fleet, the party boats, the kayak rentals, the private seasonal boats, and the overnight transients. The atmosphere is tinged with a bit of funky, old-time Jersey Shore and it's rather fun. Coolers, bait boxes, traps and hoses sprawl across the solid by time-worn wharf that leads to the recently renovated docks. An occassional umbreallaed table or garden bench provides a good vantage point to take in all the action and enjoy the view across the salt marsh.

Marina Notes -- Docks recently renovated; water access moved to the ends. A new heads building was completed mid-summer 2003 (laundry on the drawing board). Easy access fuel dock with pump-out accommodates craft to 100 ft. Entrance to Spicer Creek is between 2 fixed 52 ft. bridges. Daily Party boats: Miss Chris II 8 hrs. day & night, Lady Chris 4 hrs. morning & afternoon (884-3939), Sea Hunt (884-0909) 6 hrs. Charter Sport Fish Fleet: Lone Star (782-1562), Canyon Clipper (374-4660), Hooked Up (861-1697), Mary Kaella (884-3351), Miss Andrea II (884-3351).

Notable -- It's a little under a mile to the historic district and beach, but there's so much to do onsite that you might not get there. Pub fare at adjacent Mayer's Tavern (noon-1am). Explore the tidelands and abundant wildlife in Spicer Creek and CM Harbor from a kayak - onsite rentals (1-3 passsengers). Whale and dolphin watching on 110 ft. "Cape May Whale Watcher" (786-5445), 10am $23/12, 1pm $30/18, Sunset $23/12 + $10/8 for optional dinner. Historic Lighthouse Cruises $65 & $45. Salt Marsh Safari on 40 ft pontoon boat - wildlife & birding (884-3100) Fri-Tue 10am, 1:30 & 6pm. Dancing Dolphin gift shop is onsite.

PHOTOS ON CD-ROM: 8

⛩ ⛩ 🔔 🔔

Cape May Marine

1263 Lafayette Street; Cape May, NJ 08204

Tel: (609) 884-0262 **VHF: Monitor** 68 **Talk** 9
Fax: (609) 884-7338 **Alternate Tel:** n/a
Email: cmmarine@yahoo.com **Web:** www.capemaymarine.com
Nearest Town: Cape May *(0.75 mi.)* **Tourist Info:** (609) 884-5508

Navigational Information
Lat: 38°56.819' **Long:** 074°55.782' **Tide:** 4 ft. **Current:** 1 kt. **Chart:** 12316
Rep. Depths *(MLW)*: **Entry** 8 ft. **Fuel Dock** 10 ft. **Max Slip/Moor** 12 ft./-
Access: CM Canal, under 52 ft. Bridge, south down Spicer Creek 1/4 mile

Marina Facilities *(In Season/Off Season)*
Fuel: Slip-Side Fueling, Gasoline, Diesel
Slips: 200 Total, 10 Transient **Max LOA:** 85 ft. **Max Beam:** 22 ft.
Rate *(per ft.)*: **Day** $2.00/Inq. **Week** Inq. **Month** Inq.
Power: 30 amp Incl., **50 amp** Incl., **100 amp** n/a, **200 amp** n/a
Cable TV: Yes 40' and larger **Dockside Phone:** No
Dock Type: Floating, Long Fingers, Pilings, Wood
Moorings: 0 Total, 0 Transient **Launch:** n/a
Rate: Day n/a **Week** n/a **Month** n/a
Heads: 4 Toilet(s), 6 Shower(s) *(with dressing rooms)*
Laundry: None **Pay Phones:** No
Pump-Out: OnSite, Self Service, 2 Central **Fee:** n/a **Closed Heads:** Yes

Marina Operations
Owner/Manager: Bill Kocis **Dockmaster:** Same
In-Season: Apr-Dec, 8am-5pm **Off-Season:** Dec-Apr, 9am-5pm
After-Hours Arrival: Call in advance
Reservations: Preferred **Credit Cards:** Visa/MC
Discounts: None
Pets: Welcome **Handicap Access:** No

Marina Services and Boat Supplies
Services - Concierge, Security *(24, Owner lives on site.)*, Dock Carts
Communication - Mail & Package Hold, Phone Messages, Fax in/out, FedEx, UPS, Express Mail *(Sat Del)* **Supplies - OnSite:** Ice *(Block, Cube)*, Bait/Tackle *(Hand's 898-3744)*, Live Bait **Near:** Propane *(Texaco 884-1278)* **Under 1 mi:** West Marine *(898-8245)*

Boatyard Services
OnSite: Travelift *(30T & 70T)*, Forklift, Engine mechanic *(gas)*, Electrical Repairs, Hull Repairs, Rigger, Bottom Cleaning, Brightwork, Compound, Wash & Wax, Interior Cleaning, Propeller Repairs, Yacht Broker
OnCall: Engine mechanic *(diesel)*, Electronic Sales, Electronics Repairs, Air Conditioning, Refrigeration, Woodworking, Upholstery, Metal Fabrication
Yard Rates: $84, Haul & Launch $8-10/ft. *(blocking $3/ft.)*, Power Wash $3/ft., Bottom Paint 8.50-12.50/ft. *(paint incl.)*

Restaurants and Accommodations
Near: Restaurant *(C View Inn 884-4712)*, *(Lobster House 884-8296, L $5-13, D $12-40)*, *(Captain's Cove 884-5878, B $2-5, L $2-9, D $9-15)*, *(Anchorage Inn 898-1174)*, *(Cactus Grill 898-0354)*, Snack Bar *(Dry Dock 884-3434, Ice Cream)*, Coffee Shop *(Dock Mike's 884-2855, B $3-13, L $4-9)*, Lite Fare *(Twinings Tea Room 884-5404, L $16.50, Tea $13.50)*, Pizzeria *(Tony's 884-2020)*, Inn/B&B *(Primrose Inn 884-8288)* **Under 1 mi:** Inn/B&B *(Dormer House 884-7446)*, Condo/Cottage *(Bill Mae Cottage 898-8558, Reserve)*

Recreation and Entertainment
OnSite: Fishing Charter **Near:** Video Rental *(Blockbuster 884-7741)*, Museum *(E. Physick Estate 884-5404 $8/4)* **Under 1 mi:** Beach,
Playground, Volleyball, Tennis Courts *(Cape May 884-8986)*, Golf Course *(CM Nat'l GC 884-1563)*, Cultural Attract *(Elaine's Dinner Thtr 884-1198)*, Sightseeing *(MCA's Tours Historic District, 1859 Light House 884-5404 $6/3-$10/5)* **1-3 mi:** Fitness Center *(Cape Fitness 898-1515)*, Horseback Riding *(Sea Horse 884-5354)*, Movie Theater *(Bayshore-8 889-8800)*

Provisioning and General Services
Near: Market *(WaWa 884-6753)*, Fishmonger *(Lobster House)*, Beauty Salon *(Pauline's 884-3011)*, Barber Shop, Dry Cleaners *(Model 884-8446)*, Laundry, Newsstand **Under 1 mi:** Gourmet Shop *(Love the Cook 884-9292)*, Delicatessen *(Depot 884-8030)*, Liquor Store *(Vance's 884-4704)*, Bakery, Meat Market, Bank/ATM, Post Office, Catholic Church, Protestant Church, Library, Bookstore *(Book Shoppe 884-7878)*, Pharmacy *(CVS 391-0070.)*, Hardware Store *(Swain's 884-8578)*, Retail Shops, Department Store *(Dellas 884-4568)* **1-3 mi:** Supermarket *(Acme 463-9106; SuperFresh 465-4140)*, Wine/Beer *(Cape 884-7676 Del.)*, Farmers' Market *(Tue 3-8pm 884-4858 West CM Boro Hall)*, Green Grocer *(Duckies 898-9191)*

Transportation
OnCall: Rental Car *(Enterprise 522-1119)* **Near:** InterCity Bus *(to Phil, A.C.)* **Under 1 mi:** Bikes *(Village 884-8500)*, Taxi *(AAART 884-2273)*, Rail *(Seashore Line)*, Airport Limo *(CM 884-1171)* **3+ mi:** Ferry Service *(Lewes, 5 mi.)* **Airport:** CM/Atlantic City *(5 mi./40 mi.)*

Medical Services
911 Service **Near:** Doctor *(Bayshore 886-3636)*, Chiropractor *(Rizzo 994-2162)* **Under 1 mi:** Dentist *(CM 884-5335)*, Holistic Services *(CM Spa)* **1-3 mi:** Veterinarian *(CM 884 1729* **Hospital:** Burdette 463-2000 *(11 mi.)*

Setting -- On Spicer Creek, off the Cape May Canal, CMM's very well protected docks sprawl along the grassy shoreline. The landside ambiance is strictly boatyard and the facilities tend toward basic but the quality docks, refreshing views of pristine marsh, and truly breathtaking sunsets more than compensate. Boats in the 25-35 foot range predominate, but those up to 85 feet can be comfortably accommodated if they draw less than 8 feet.

Marina Notes -- Founded in 1985, family owned and operated. Formerly Pharo's Marine. Full service boatyard. Slipside fueling over 50 ft. Quality wood docks, recent pedestals, 25 ft. vinyl-edged finger piers. Tiled heads with varnished wood doors; showers have dressing rooms. Onsite bait & tackle shop has live bait. Extensive charter operation; 11 sport fish boats base here: Trashman Too (856-297-2086), Big Game (463-0857), Tremendous (926-9656), Shadow (296-0066), Off Duty (425-8859), Hellraiser (856-297-4352), Tail Dancer (457-0115), Just Released (374-4969), First Light (884-2903), Bucktail (465-4369), Wits End (587-3589). Entrance to Spicer Creek is between 2 fixed 52 ft. bridges. Internet access at Magic Brain (884-8188) at Carpenter Square in town.

Notable -- A short walk is the famous Lobster House Restaurant and Fish Market which offers several dining options. Cape May Marine is the closest facility to downtown, affording a reasonable walk to the Physick Estate and quaint Cape May's Victorian Historic District - chock a block with great shopping and dining. Also walkable (or a short cab ride) are its beaches (1 mile) and the C.M. Shopping Mall. The Cape May Music Festival is mid June (800 275-4278). Trolley tours abound - to the restored Cape May Lighthouse or the Wildwood Doo-Wop District. The Seashore Railway goes to Cape May Courthouse & Cold Spring Village.

ATLANTIC CRUISING CLUB'S

GUIDE TO
LONG ISLAND SOUND MARINAS

ADDENDA

WWW.ATLANTICCRUISINGCLUB.COM

Suggested Reading List

SPECIFIC REGIONAL CRUISING GUIDES

Northern Waterway Guide — Annual; by Waterway Publishing
Comprehensive coverage — New Jersey through the Canadian Maritimes, extremely thorough and complete — just keeps getting bigger and better — includes advertising

Maptech's Embassy Guide — Long Island Sound — 9th Edition
Helpful and useful with extensive coverage for every harbor — includes advertising

The Cruising Guide to the New England Coast: Including the Hudson River, Long Island Sound, and the Coast of New Brunswick — 12th Edition by Robert C. Duncan, W. Wallace Fenn, Paul W. Fenn, Roger S. Duncan
The original cruising guide to New England — published for more than half a century & written by two generations of cruisers. An uncompromising, highly detailed and complete editorial work — no advertising

GENERAL CRUISING GUIDES

Cruising for Cowards — 2nd Edition by Liza & Andy Copeland
A terrific "how-to" guide to cruising anywhere; it's funny and filled with details and great information

Voyaging Under Power by Robert Beebe
A little dated, but it's still filled with important and useful info

Stapleton's Powerboat Bible: The Complete Guide to Selection, Seamanship, and Cruising by Sid Stapleton
Comprehensive and current, it's written for larger cruising powerboats

Comfortable Cruising Around North and Central America by Liza & Andy Copeland
A cruising guide to destinations that don't require ocean crossings; the sections on the North American seaboard will be of particular interest

Sail Book of Common Sense Cruising by Patience Wales
A collection of interesting articles from Sail Magazine

Voyager's Handbook, the Essential Guide to Blue Water Cruising by Beth Leonard
Lots of really useful info even if you're just planning a coastal cruise

Nigel Calder's Cruising Handbook by Nigel Calder
From the basics for a coastal cruise to readying for an off shore passage, this is a good place to start

The Perfect First Mate: A Woman's Guide to Recreational Boating by Joy Smith
Provisioning and organizing for comfort afloat

PROVISIONING GUIDES

All have something to contribute and most are filled with great ideas — you can't have too many cookbooks — at home or afloat ...

The Cruising Chef Cookbook By Michael Greenwald
Thorough and practical for a weeklong cruise or an ocean voyage

Cruising Cuisine: Fresh Food from the Galley
by Kay Pastorius, Hal Pastorius (Illustrator)
Lots of really good recipes

Dining on Deck: Fine Foods for Sailing & Boating by Linda Vail, Loretta Braren (Illustrator)
Encourages a little style and panache at anchor

Feasts Afloat: 150 Recipes for Great Meals from Small Spaces
by Jennifer Trainer Thompson, Elizabeth Wheeler
A new version of the Yachting Cookbook, a long-time favorite

The Care and Feeding of Sailing Crew by Lin Pardey, Larry Pardey
A true classic — tells you everything & lots we'd never think of ourselves

Cooking Under Pressure by Lorna J. Sass
The basics and sophisticated possibilities of pressure cooking — one of the safest and most fuel efficient methods of cooking under way

Guilt Free Gourmet by megayacht chef Sam Miles
Over 1200 low-fat recipes in one easily stowable volume — get the "70 Days of Menus," too

Natural Gourmet by Annemarie Colbin
Healthy cooking and provisioning concepts that are easily applicable to the galley

Food and Healing — 10th Anniversary Edition by Annemarie Colbin
Not a cookbook, but an indispensable guide to natural healing using natural remedies — many stowed in most galleys

CONNECTICUT SHORE TRAVEL GUIDES

Guide to the Connecticut Shore — 3rd Edition by Doe Boyle
The most specific and useful guide to this region

Connecticut Off the Beaten Path: A Guide to Unique Places — 5th Edition by Deborah Ritchie
About 25% of the book deals with coastal Connecticut and the river towns.

Food Lovers' Guide to Connecticut: Best Local Specialties, Shops, Recipes, Restaurants, Events, Lore, and More
by Patricia Brooks and Lester Brooks
From farm stands to fishmongers, and a lot of it is near the shore

The Connecticut Guide by Amy Ziffer
Geology, history and local culture plus the standard "travel guide" info — this book is packed with interesting lore and useful specifics

ZagatSurvey Connecticut Restaurants edited by Catherine Bigwood, Julie Wilson, and Lynn Hazelwood
Get the most recent edition — it's an invaluable resource

Connecticut: An Explorer's Guide — 5th Edition
by Barnett D. Laschever and Andi Marie Fusco
Hartford Courant says it's the most comprehensive guide to Connecticut in more than 50 years

Moon Handbooks: Connecticut — 1st Edition by Andrew Collins
This covers the whole state, not just the coastal and river regions, but the thoroughness of the information will make it a good buy

NEW YORK COASTAL TRAVEL GUIDES

ZagatSurvey New York City Restaurants by Curt Gathie and Carol Diuguid
A must have that slips easily into your pocket or boat bag

The New York Times Guide to New York City Restaurants 2004
by Eric Asimov & William Grimes
Combine this with Zagat's for the best advice on NYC restaurants

Moon Handbooks: New York State by Christiane Bird
While only about 25% of this book will be useful for the coastal cruiser, the depth of detail and useful information will make it worthwhile

Fodor's Around New York City with Kids — 2nd Edition: 68 Great Things to Do Together

New York's 50 Best Places to Take Children — 2nd Edition
by Allan Ishac

The Cool Parents' Guide to All of New York: Excursions and Activities in and Around Our City That Your Children Will Love and You Won't Think Are Too Bad Either by Alfred Gringold & Helen Rogan

Frommer's New York City by Brian Silverman

Nosh New York: The Food Lover's Guide to New York City's Most Delicious Neighborhoods by Myra Alperson
An in-depth look at the resources in all the New York City boroughs

New York Eats (More): The Food Shopper's Guide To The Freshest Ingredients, The Best Take-Out & Baked Goods, & The Most Unusual Marketplaces In All Of New York by Ed Levine
Covers all the NYC neighborhoods plus the Hamptons

Long Island Alive! By Francine Silverman

Where to Go and What to Do on Long Island — 3rd Edition by SCOPE

A Guide to Long Island Wine Country by Peter M. Gianotti

ZagatSurvey Long Island Restaurants Guide
Get the most recent edition — it comes out annually

The Hamptons Book: Including the North Fork and Shelter Island — 5th Edition by Suzi Forbes Chase
If you're cruising Long Island's East End, this book is indispensable

The Hamptons Survival Guide by Phil Keith
A handy little tome with the best in over 300 categories — each reviewed and rated

NEW JERSEY SHORE TRAVEL GUIDES

Insiders' Guide to the Jersey Shore by Lillian Africano & Nina Africano
The best all-around guide to the shore — it's very readable and useful

The Best of Everything at The Jersey Shore by Jeff Edelstein
A handy guide to the best in each N.J. shore town

Guide to the Jersey Shore — 6th Edition by Robert Santelli
Covers the northern towns in a bit more depth than other books

New Jersey Off the Beaten Path — 6th Edition: A Guide to Unique Places by Kay Scheller
About 50 pages on the Coast plus the New York Harbor area

ZagatSurvey New Jersey Restaurants edited by Andrea Clurfeld and Daniel Simmons
Be sure to pick up the most recent edition

ZagatSurvey New Jersey Shore
More in-depth coverage of just the Shore region — an absolute must have

HISTORY and CULTURAL PERSPECTIVES

For rainy days and long passages — the first three books should be of interest to everyone who cruises these waters

This Fine Piece of Water: An Environmental History of Long Island Sound by Tom Andersen (intro by Robert Kennedy, Jr.)
The definitive work on the ecology of the Sound and what's being done about it

The Long Island Sound: A History of Its People, Places, and Environment by Marilyn Weigold
Brand new, the advances look compelling — an historical, ecological and anthropological look at Long Island Sound and the people and communities that line its shore (originally published as The American Mediterranean)

Margins: A Naturalist Meets Long Island Sound
by Mary Parker Buckles
An exploration of and introduction to the natural wonders that still exist in this overcrowded "pond" that still teems with life

Crossing the Sound: The Rise of Atlantic American Communities in Seventeenth-Century Eastern Long Island
by Karen R. Simioff
A fascinating account for history buffs

Lights & Legends: A Historical Guide to Lighthouses of Long Island Sound, Fishers Island Sound and Block Island Sound by Harlon Hamilton

Outer Lands: A Natural History Guide to Cape Cod, Martha's Vineyard, Nantucket, Block Island, and Long Island by Dorothy Sterling

BLOCK ISLAND BACKGROUND

Images of America: Block Island, RI by Donald D'Amato & Henry Brown
Historical photos, prints and narratives

Block Island Geology: History Processes & Field Excursions by Les Sirkin

Block Island: The Land by Robert M. Downie
An in-depth investigation of this isolated, unique little island by an historian who has studied it for over 30 years

Seasons at Sea Meadow, Gardening and other Pleasures on Block Island by Jane B. Foster
A chronicle of life on Block that starts with the garden

Block Island Trivia by Robert Ellis Smith
Fun facts to consider as you cross Block Island Sound

Surfcaster's Quest: Seeking Stripers, Blues, and Solitude at the Edge of the Surging Sea by Roy Rowan
Fishing the waters around Block Island

She's Not There: A Poppy Rice Novel by Mary-Ann Tirone Smith
A fun who-done-it set on Block Island

CONNECTICUT SHORE BACKGROUND

Long River Winding: Life, Love, and Death Along the Connecticut by Jim Bissland

This American River: Five Centuries of Writing About the Connecticut by W.D. Wetherell

River Days: Exploring the Connecticut River and its History from Source to Sea by Michael Tougias

The Captain from Connecticut by C.S. Forester
A fictional account of a Yankee frigate on Long Island Sound breaking a British blockade in 1812 in the middle of a blizzard

Fishing the Connecticut and Rhode Island Coasts by Bob Sampson

Connecticut Curiosities: Quirky Characters, Roadside Oddities & Other Offbeat Stuff by Susan Campbell, Bill Heald
Fun, interesting, and a little weird

The Cos Cob Art Colony: Impressionists on the Connecticut Shore by Susan G. Larkin

NEW YORK and LONG ISLAND BACKGROUND

Heaven and Earth: The Last Farmers of the North Fork by Steve Wick

Long Island: An Illustrated History by Robert B. Mackay & Richard F. Welch

The Hamptons: Life Behind the Hedges by Ellen Susan & Harris Meisel

Hamptons Bohemia: Two Centuries of Artists and Writers on the Beach by Helen A. Harrison

Studios By the Sea: Artists of Long Island's East End by Bob Colacello

The Hamptons: Long Island's East End by Ken Miller
A photographer's "insider" look at the East End

Three Mile Harbor by Sylvia Mendelman
A history of East Hampton's harbor by a long-time resident and an owner of Harbor Marina

The Moon Pulled Up an Acre of Bass: A Flyrodder's Odyssey at Montauk Point by Peter Kaminsky

Walt Whitman's New York: From Manhattan to Montauk by Henry Christman
The perfect companion for exploring Long Island's North Shore

Long Island by Bernie Bookbinder
A cultural history and travel guide with a focus on the North Shore "Gold Coast" and the North and South Forks

The End: Montauk, N.Y. by Michael Dweck
Anthropological look at the surfing community that has grown up around Ditch Plains, the best surfing beach on the East Coast

Plum Island by Nelson Demille
A fun read; a suspense yarn set on an island that's off-limits to boaters

NEW JERSEY SHORE BACKGROUND

Guarding New Jersey's Shore: Lighthouses and Life-Saving Stations by David Veasey

Sentinels of the Shore: A Guide to the Lighthouses and Lightships of New Jersey by Bill Gately

Wreck Valley, A Record of Shipwrecks off Long Island's South Shore and New Jersey by Daniel Berg
A little out of date but nonetheless compelling

To The Shore Once More: A Portrait Of The Jersey Shore; Prose, Poetry, and Works Of Art — Vols I & II by Frank Finale
A commendable cruising companion

Down the Jersey Shore by Russell Roberts
A history of the Jersey shore towns and all the kitsch, elegance and events that made them famous — written in the early 90's

New Jersey's Coastal Heritage: A Guide by Mark Di Ionno
Filled with stories and information on the history of all the towns that line famous Jersey Shore — a little out of date but still a good read

The Jersey Shore Uncovered: A Revealing Season on the Beach by Peter Genovese
A chronicle of a summer exploring the whole Jersey shore by a local newspaper columnist

CHILDREN'S BOOKS — Pre-School

Little Toot and the Lighthouse by Linda Gramatky-Smith

You Can't Take a Balloon into the Metropolitan Museum by Robin Preiss Glasser & Jacqueine Preiss Weitzman
A balloon chase becomes a tour of Manhattan

September Roses by Jeanette Winter

CHILDREN'S BOOKS — Ages 4 – 8

Mary Had a Little Ham by Margie Palatini
A pig is drawn to the lights of Broadway and spawns a season of pork puns

Journey Around New York from A to Z by Martha Zschock, Heather Zschock

Maxi, the Hero and **The Adventures of Taxi Dog** both by Debra Barracca, Sal Barracca, Mark Boehner
Maxi, the Taxi dog, in Manhattan

A Gull's Story: A Tale of Learning about Life, the Shore, and the ABCs by Frank Finale, Margie Moore

Nellie the Lighthouse Dog by Jane Scarpino, Robert Ensor, Jane Weinberger

Mabel Takes a Sail by Emily Chetkowski, Dawn Peterson

Keep the Lights Burning, Abbie by Connie Roop, Peter Geiger Roop, Peter E. Hanson

Birdie's Lighthouse by Deborah Hopkinson, Kimberly Bucklen Root

The Colorful Connecticut Coloring Book, The Big Connecticut Activity Book & My First Book about Connecticut All by Carole Marsh

The Declaration of Independence and Roger Sherman of Connecticut by Kathy Furgang

CHILDREN'S BOOKS — Ages 9 – 12

Shutting Out the Sky: Life in the Tenements of New York, 1880 - 1924 by Alice Turner Curtis

A Little Maid of Old Connecticut by Alice Turner Curtis

The Forgotten Flag: Revolutionary Struggle in Connecticut by Frances Y. Evan
Set in Fairfield, this short novel describes the roles played by two young teens as their town stands against the British

From the Mixed-Up Files of Mrs. Basil E. Frankweiler by E. L. Konigsburg
Two girls run away to the Metropolitan Museum of Art

Tagger, Alone Along the Mystic River by J.A. Louthain
In 1687, a young girl from Barbados adjusts to colonial life and the threat of a "witch hunt".

Horrible Harry Goes to Sea by Suzy Kline
Harry and his classmates take a riverboat ride on the Connecticut

Stuart Little by E. B. White
A mouse, born to a family of New York City humans, finds adventure

Abigail Takes the Wheel by Avi & Don Bolognese
1880's Abigail helms her family's freight boat across New York Harbor from New Jersey to Manhattan

The Cricket in Times Square by George Selden

September 11, 2001: The Day That Changed America by Jill C. Wheeler

I Spy Treasure Hunt: A Book of Picture Riddles by Walter Wick, Jean Marzallo
A book of picture riddles set in "I Spy" Harbor

Close to Shore: The Terrifying Shark Attacks of 1916 by Michael Capuzzo

Liberty by Lynn Curlee
The story behind the Statue of Liberty by an impassioned art historian

Behind the Scenes of Home Alone 2: Lost in New York by Jordan Horowitz

CHECK THE WEBSITE FOR MORE COMMENTARY AND MORE SUGGESTIONS

WWW.ATLANTICCRUISINGCLUB.COM

Pump-Out and No Discharge Areas:

Each state, and its waterfront communities, continues to grapple with the issues of harbor clean-up, no discharge areas, and pump-out services. Some states are underwriting, frequently in tandem with an EPA grant, the construction of pump-out facilities and then requiring that these be made available to all comers at affordable rates. Other states are simply creating no discharge areas and leaving it up to the marina operators to provide the required mechanisms. This leads to a wide variety of services, facilities and rates. In committed communities, pump-out boats ply the waters and the services are usually free (tip appreciated!). In areas where facilities have been underwritten, the services are frequently land-based, costs are either free or nominal, and "self-service" is the rule. In areas where it's left up to the marinas, the quality and costs vary widely. Ecologically committed facilities will often charge very modest fees, take responsibility for the proper functioning of their systems, and provide assistance when needed. Others will charge outrageous fees, hours will be inconvenient, and systems will be frequently "out of order." Fortunately, this is becoming increasingly rare as the need has become clearer. But call ahead to confirm the rate, the operating hours and the current "availability" of the pump-out system. If it isn't working or the hours are absurd or the rate exorbitant, you might consider choosing another facility.

Pump-out is probably the least fun part of boating. No one wants to have anything to do with it, but it is critical to the well-being of Long Island Sound, as well as Fishers Island Sound, Block Island Sound, the Peconics and the New Jersey inland waterways. Rick Huntley of the Connecticut office of Long Island Sound Programs cited a recent USEPA document noting that "dumping a single 20-gallon waste holding tank has the same impact as discharging several thousand gallons of sewage from an efficiently run sewage treatment plant." Many of us have long operated under the presumption that the seemingly minor discharge from our own holding tanks was fairly irrelevant — but, clearly, that is not the case. As both the Federal government and the local states have determined, the only way that pumpout will become standard operating procedure is to make it easily available, not too unpleasant, inexpensive — and to make not doing it illegal.

Soundkeeper, a nonprofit group dedicated to "protecting and preserving the Sound," offers an excellent booklet "Soundkeeper: Clean Boating Guide." It can be downloaded from its website at http://www.soundkeeper.org.

No Discharge Areas (NDA's) are specified and regulated by both Federal and state law:

▸ **Federal Law:** According to the Environmental Protection Agency, a "No Discharge Area" is a designated body of water that prohibits the discharge of *treated and untreated* boat sewage. Boats with Type I (for vessels under 65 feet) and Type II (for vessels 65 feet and over) Marine Sanitation Devices may discharge treated effluent in coastal waters UNLESS they are in a "No Discharge Area." It is illegal to discharge the contents of Type III MSDs (which are standard holding tanks) in any U.S. territorial waters within three nautical miles from shore. For Type III MSDs one must find a pump-out facility — boat, stationary self-serve pump, or a full-service station.

The EPA is working with the states to advance the spread of "no discharge areas" as rapidly as possible. The main limiting factor is the existence of adequate pumpout facilities to service all of the boats in a given region. Once that is achieved conversion of those regions into "NDA"s will become virtually automatic. The Clean Vessel Act of 1992 authorized $40 million to be administered by the U.S. Fish and Wildlife Service in that cause. Each May grants are awarded for projects and priority is given to new pump-out boats or stations. Systems constructed with grant money cannot charge more than $5. Look for the Logo: "Keep our Water Clean — Use Pump-Out".

▸ **Rhode Island:** As of 1998, the state of Rhode Island designated all of its marine waters as "No Discharge Areas." According to the EPA, as of this publication date, RI has 43 pump-out facilities, with more on the way. *Great Salt Pond* on Block Island was one of the very first NDAs and regulation and enforcement is very strict.

▸ **Connecticut:** The state of Connecticut has several "No Discharge Areas," and petitions each year for legislation to increase the waters protected by that designation. As of 2004, the following areas have been designated as "NDA"s:

> *Pawcatuck River, Little Narragansett Bay, Stonington Harbor and Fishers Island Sound to the New York state line.*

An application has been submitted to extend the "No Discharge Area" to the east side of the Thames River, and it is expected to become law by Memorial Day 2004. Another application, to extend the NDA to include all of the Thames River and Connecticut coastal waters to the mouth of the Connecticut River, is expected to be submitted by October '04 with the expectation that it will be implemented in early 2005.

▸ **New York:** As of March, 2004, New York State has designated the following waters, covered by this Guide, as No Discharge Areas:

> *Mamaroneck Harbor, East Hampton (7 water bodies, including Three Mile Harbor), Greater Huntington-Northport Harbors, Port Jefferson Harbor Complex, the Peconic Estuary including all of the water within the two Long Island forks, plus stretches of the Hudson River*

▸ **New Jersey:** The state of New Jersey has designated the following areas "No Discharge," as of March 2004:

> *Barnegat Bay, Shark River, Manasquan River, Shrewsbury River, Navesink River*

The EPA's "No Discharge Area" website is http://www.epa.gov/owow/oceans/regulatory/vessel_sewage/vsdmsd.html

The Long Island Sound Study

Millions of people swim, boat, and fish in Long Island Sound or just enjoy the shoreline view. But a large population near the Sound also can contribute to serious threats, including pollution that affects marine plants and animals and water quality for swimming.

Realizing that challenges such as these are not easy to solve and that they cross political boundaries, the United States Environmental Protection Agency and the states of New York and Connecticut created the Long Island Sound Study. Since its formation in the mid-1980s, the Study's mandate has been to work toward restoring and protecting the Sound.

Since drafting a Comprehensive Conservation and Management Plan in 1994, the Study's efforts have included:

- Creating bi-state and federal support to reduce nitrogen pollution through upgrades to sewage treatment plants. Excess nitrogen results in over-enrichment of the Sound's waters, which leads to nuisance algal blooms and a harmful depletion of oxygen in the water (a process called "eutrophication"). Since the peak year of 1994, 55,000 fewer pounds of nitrogen a day enter the Sound.

- Creating a Habitat Restoration Initiative in 1998 that has led to the opening of 42.9 miles of rivers draining to LIS to anadromous fish (fish that swim up river to spawn) and restoring 465 acres of coastal habitats.

- Creating a Stewardship Initiative to help manage some of Long Island Sound's most sensitive sites.

The Long Island Sound Study continues to work as a partnership of federal, state, and local agencies and organizations to restore and protect one of the most densely developed watersheds in the U.S. To learn more about Long Island Sound and the Long Island Sound Study, contact the following agencies:

▸ **EPA Long Island Sound Office:** CT (203) 977-1541; NY (631) 632-9216; www.longislandsoundstudy.net

▸ **CT Dept. of Environmental Protection:** (860) 424-3020 www.dep.state.ct.us

▸ **CT DEP Oil and Chemical Spill Response (24-hour hotline):** (860) 424-3338

▸ **Connecticut Sea Grant:** (860) 405-9127 www.seagrant.uconn.edu

▸ **NYS Dept. of Environmental Conservation Bureau of Marine Resources:** (631) 444-0430; www.dec.state.ny.us

▸ **NYS DEC Spill Hotline:** (800) 457-7362

▸ **New York Sea Grant:** (631) 632-6905 www.seagrant.sunysb.edu/

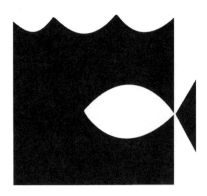

Programs in education, research, and advocacy are the means through which STS strives to accomplish its mission: saving Long Island Sound.

Save the Sound®

18 Reynolds Street
East Norwalk, CT 06855

Phone: 203-354-0036
Fax: 203-354-0041
Email: savethesound@savethesound.org
Web: www.savethesound.org

Habitat Projects

Brides Brook Salt Marsh & Fishway

Clark Pond Fishwat & Eelpass

Five Mile River Salt Marsh

Gorham's Pond

Johnsonville Pond Fishway

Lee'sPond Fishway & Eelpass

Manursing Lake

Merwin Meadows Dam

Old Field Creek & Cove River

Rippowam/Mill River Fishway

Soundview Salt Marsh

Twin Ponds Fishway

West River Tide Gate

Wilson Cove Salt Marsh

Mission

Save the Sound is a bi-state, non-profit membership organization dedicated to the restoration, protection, and appreciation of Long Island Sound and its watershed through advocacy, education and research.

History

Save the Sound is a non-profit 501(c)(3) organization funded by its membership contributions, individual and corporate donations, foundations and government grants. The organization was originally founded in 1972 as the Long Island Sound Taskforce and was first affiliated with the Sierra Club, then the Oceanic Society. It has been an independent organization since 1989. The name was changed to Save the Sound, Inc. in 1995 to better express the organization's mission and as a call to action. Save the Sound, Inc. is headquartered in South Norwalk, CT and has offices on Long Island at Garvies Point Museum, Glen Cove, NY and at UCONN's Marine Technology and Research Center in Groton, CT.

Programs in education, research, and advocacy are the means through which Save the Sound strives to accomplish its mission: saving Long Island Sound.

Current Advocacy Issues

- NYC Sewage Treatment Upgrades
- Dredging: Dredged Materials Disposal
- Long Island Sound Utility Crossing
- Solid Waste Agency of Northern Cook County (SWANCC) and the Clean Water Act
- Long Island Sound Stewardship Initiative
- Long Island Sound Municipal Report Cards
- Long Island Sound Watershed Alliance
- CT Siting Council: Overland Transmission
- Endangered Lands Coalition
- Ocean Zoning
- Environmental Assessment
- Citizen's Advocacy Guide
- Sunrise Storage Facility
- Madison Landing Development
- Pesticide Spraying
- Non-Point Source Pollution Campaign: What Goes On The Ground Goes In The Sound
- Federal TMDL Program
- Federal Energy Bill
- International Coastal Clean-up

Wi-Fi: Wireless Broad Band Network Services

Access Point

USB Antenna

PC Card

The ability to access both the web and email while cruising has become increasingly important to many boaters. Marinas, and their surrounding communities, are providing a variety of solutions — some more useful than others. As noted earlier, each Marina Report in this Guide details the existence and location of data-ports — either at the marina or its environs — and also notes the availability of Wi-Fi — potentially the most useful solution to the access problem. Wi-Fi, or Wireless Fidelity, allows one to connect to the Internet from anywhere on the boat. It's a wireless technology, like a cell phone, that can send and receive data indoors and out; anywhere within the range of a base station (called "hotspots"). It's fast and doesn't require expensive and cumbersome installation.

To access a Wi-Fi broadband system, one needs a portable PC card or built-in wireless modem that operates on the chosen network, a mobile computer (laptop, handheld, or PDA type device), and a subscription to the wireless network that hosts the "hotspots" you've identified. Unfortunately, there are many hotspot providers and they are not all working together — but cooperation is inevitable. LinkSys and D-Link are the most popular PC-Card Wi-Fi modem brands, and, unlike the providers, all Wi-Fi hardware is compatible.

Increasingly, larger marinas are installing Wi-Fi wireless systems. While Wi-Fi is a tremendous convenience and advantage, it's still quite new and marinas are handling delivery of the service in a variety of ways. Most are sub-contracting the installation to the subscription provider, which deals directly with the boater. Log-on procedures vary widely, too. Some marinas, or their sub-contractor, even have Wi-Fi PC cards available for nightly rental for those who don't have either a PC card or internal card. The standard is 802.11 — the first version was "b" (11 mbps), the current generation, as of publication, is the newer and faster "g." These versions are downward compatible and wireless modems will work with either system.

Since the requisite PC cards (or internal cards) are relatively inexpensive ($50-75, or much less for the "b" generation), buying your own, even if you don't have a wireless network elsewhere, could make sense. Airports, hotels, coffee shops, like Starbucks, and other public spaces, including some McDonalds, are also installing these systems. If you travel with more than one computer on board, you can also easily network your boat by installing "80211" "b" or "g" PC cards (or USB antennas) on each computer and then adding an inexpensive Router/Access Point to tie them together. If you're buying a new computer, have an 802.11 Wi-Fi card installed internally.

Beacon Wi-Fi Technologies (www.beaconwifi.com) is the leading provider of Wi-Fi hotspots to marinas in the Long Island Sound region. In the Northeast, the Brewer chain is, once again, leading the pack and has installed Wi-Fi hotspots in most of its marinas. Beacon installed the systems and is selling access at a variety of price points. Their rates are $39.95 a month for a 6 month seasonal contract, $29.95 for an annual contract or $19.95 for 3 days of access including a pc card rental.

If the marina you've selected doesn't have a Wi-Fi system check out the local coffee houses and hotels. A search on www.80211hotspots.com will help in locating Wi-Fi access points. T-Mobile is currently the largest hot-spot provider with almost 2500 Starbucks and airport lounges at press time. Their rates are $29.99/month on a yearly basis; there are also monthly ($39.99) and pay-as-you-go plans ($2.99 for the first 15 minutes, then $.10 cents for each additional minute). Hotels are also a major focus. Wayport has wired over 500 hotspots, and Boingo has wired over 1,200. Everyone's numbers are growing daily. Hopefully there will be greater sharing among the providers in the near future.

Deciphering the Marine Industry Alphabets and Certifications

There are a number of trade organizations that assist the professional boating industry. They each serve a variety of purposes — some of greater interest to the boating services consumer than others. But knowledge is power, so we have listed the most prevalent ones — preceded by the initials by which each is known.

In addition to the certifications provided by the manufacturers, there are several marine industry certifications. They are listed below as part of the description of their sponsoring organization. Facilities' memberships in these organizations, as well as the number of on-site employees which have been certified by each, is included under "Boatyard Services" in the Marina Reports — if we are aware of them. We have focused more specifically on ABBRA and ABYC as these relate directly to technicians who may work on your boat. It is, however, quite possible that a facility may hold these, or other, certifications but did not, for a variety of reasons, relay that information to ACC. Exactly what is required to achieve each of these certifications is generally disclosed on the organization's website. In a number of cases, certification programs are offered jointly by two of these organizations. If such certifications are a deciding factor in choosing a marina or boatyard, it might be helpful to inquire.

- **ABBRA** is the American Boat Builders & Repairers Association located in Warren, Rhode Island — (401) 247-0318; www.abbra.org. ABBRA is a 250-member network of boatyards, repairers and associated industries that, among other functions, trains its members' management and employee craftsmen. It offers a series of Technician certificate programs (fiberglass, bottom paint, basic and advanced diesel repair) and management training programs.

- **ABYC** is the American Boat and Yacht Council in Edgewater, Maryland — (410) 956-1050; www.abycinc.org. ABYC develops the consensus safety standards for the design, construction, equipage, maintenance, and repair of small craft. It offers a variety of workshops, seminars and a Marine Technician Certification program.

- **IMI** is the International Marina Institute in Jupiter, Florida — (561) 741-0626; www.imimarina.org. IMI is a non-profit membership marine trade organization which offers management training, education and information about research, legislation and environmental issues affecting the marina industry. It offers a variety of workshops, training and certifications in marina management and equipment operations — particularly the Certified Marina Manager Program.

- **NMMA** is the National Marine Manufacturers' Association in Chicago, Illinois — (312) 946-6200; www.nmma.org. NMMA is the primary trade organization for producers of products used by recreational boaters. It devotes its resources to public policy advocacy, promoting boating as a lifestyle, enhancing the consumer experience, education and training, and building partnerships and strategic alliances. To serve the needs of its 1400 members, NMMA provides a variety of programs and services related to technical expertise (some include certification), standards monitoring, government relations avocation, and industry statistics. They also produce recreational boat shows in key North American markets and two trade shows, BoatBuilding and Marine Aftermarket Accessories. NMMA certifications that would be of most interest are the Yacht and Boat Certification Programs (based on ABYC guidelines) that help manufacturers comply with established standards and safety regulations. (To obtain a Yacht Certification, all components used must be on the NMMA "Type Accepted" list.)

- **MOAA** is the Marina Operators' Association of America in Washington, DC — (866) 367-6622; www.moaa.com. MOAA is the national trade association of the marina industry. It represents over 950 marinas, boatyards, yacht clubs, and public/private moorage basins across the United States. These companies provide slip space for over 240,000 recreational watercraft and employment for over 13,000 marine tradesmen and women. Suppliers of equipment and services to this industry complete MOAA's membership. Their mission is to provide critical legislative and regulatory support, serve as a communication base and to offer practical, money saving programs.

- **MITAs** are the Marine Industry Trade Associations, not-for-profit groups that represent the recreational boating and related marine industries in their particular states. Their collective mission is to promote the general welfare of the marine industry and advance the safe and proper use of boats, marine accessories, and facilities through means consistent with the public interest and welfare.

  RIMTA — Rhode Island Marine Trade Association: P.O. Box 4468, Middletown, RI 02842
  Tel: (401) 885-5044 • Fax: (401) 848-9790 • Email: info@rimta.org • www.rimta.org

  CMTA — Connecticut Marine Trades Association: 20 Plains Road, Essex, CT 06426
  Tel: (860) 767-2645 • Fax: (860) 767-3559 • Email: info@ctmarinetrades.org • www.ctmarinetrades.org

  ESMTA — Empire State Marine Trades Association: 119 Washington Avenue, Suite 100 • Albany, NY 12210
  Tel: (518) 694-3107 • Fax: (518) 427-9495 • Email: esmta@adgcommunications.com • www.boatnys.com

  NYMTA — New York Marine Trades Association (Long Island and NYC): 194 Park Avenue; Amityville, NY 11701
  Tel: (631) 691-7050 • Fax: (631) 691-2724 • Email: csqueri@nymta.com • www.nymta.com

  MTANJ — Marine Trades Association of New Jersey: 1451 Route 88, Suite 11; Brick, NJ 08724
  Tel: (732) 206-1400 • www.boatingnj.com

Alphabetical Listing of Marinas, Harbors and Cities

Alphabetical Listing of Marinas, Harbors and Cities

INDEX ET AL.

WWW.ATLANTICCRUISINGCLUB.COM

About the Authors: Beth and Richard Smith

Richard and Beth have been "messing about in boats" at various times throughout their lives, individually and together. The last two decades have seen a move up to "big boats." Coastal cruises have included numerous trips up and down the Eastern seaboard including the ICW — where they've perfected the art of "achievable cruising" — a one or two week cruise, leave the boat, go home, and come back two weeks or a month or two later. Other cruising adventures have taken them to Bermuda, the Bahamas, the Caribbean, the South Pacific and the Mediterranean. They have shared many of these experiences with three superb crew members — their now-grown children, Jason and Amanda, and their sea-dog, Molly. They are firm believers in "going" even if it means taking the office along. Technology has made that not only possible, but amazingly easy. Even their boat is networked. They are also committed to wonderful food along the way — on board and ashore. Provisioning, they've discovered, may be the most entertaining and useful of all cruising skills (bested, perhaps, only by sail trim, engine mechanics and a clear understanding of navigation) and they seek out the best resources at every landfall. Along the way, they've also visited more than 1,700 marinas on the East coast as both cruisers and authors.

ELIZABETH ADAMS SMITH

Elizabeth Adams Smith, Ed.D., is Editor-in-Chief of Jerawyn Publishing, Inc. (JPI) and one of the primary writer/photographers of the *Guides to Marinas*. She is also a new media designer/producer focused on developing electronic methods of delivering large quantities of unique information in ways that are readily understood and manipulated.

In addition to her marine-oriented publishing work (nurturing the growth of the *Atlantic Cruising Club's Guides to Marinas* and incubating the Coastal Communities, Healthy Boat and Wandering Mariner series), she has produced video documentaries and multiple media projects in the areas of complementary and integrative medicine, holistic living, ecology, peace-making, technology, and food and health (including the award-winning "Children of War," the Mellon-funded "Students at Work," and "EarthFriends"). She created and developed the first, and largest, full-text and image database on complementary medicine, "Alt-HealthWatch," and is an advisor/consultant to firms focused on healthy living and integrative medicine.

Beth received a Doctorate from Columbia University in Educational Technology and New Media, Masters degrees in both Health Education (with a Nutrition focus) and Ed Tech from Columbia, and a B.S. in Broadcast Journalism from Boston University. She is a Certified Health Education Specialist and a graduate of James Gordon's Advanced Mind-Body Professional Training Program and the Natural Gourmet Institute for Food and Health. She is also Past President of the Board of Trustees and current Honorary Trustee of Wainwright House, an educational institution focusing on the integration of body, mind and spirit, a former Trustee of the Rye Free Reading Room, Co-Chair of the American Yacht Club Cruise Committee and is a member of the International Food, Wine and Travel Writers Association, Boating Writers International, and Society of American Travel Writers.

RICHARD Y. SMITH

Richard Y. Smith is Publisher of Jerawyn Publishing Inc. and President of Evergreen Capital Partners Inc. JPI is an umbrella company for the Atlantic Cruising Club and other publishing imprints. In addition to marine facilities, JPI focuses on coastal lifestyles, maritime-oriented travel and holistic living. JPI's activities involve data collection and publication using Datastract™, a proprietary data input and publishing program that permits the creation, maintenance, and direct publication of extensive databases of both factual and editorial information.

Evergreen Capital Partners Inc. undertakes merchant banking and private capital transactions both as an advisor and as a principal. As an advisor, the firm offers private financing, merger, acquisition, and divestiture advice to managements, directors, private investors, and institutional funds. As a principal, Evergreen Capital invests its own funds, often in conjunction with other individual or institutional private equity investors.

Prior to establishing Evergreen Capital in 1993, Richard was a Managing Director of Chemical Bank (now JP Morgan Chase) with responsibility for several investment and merchant banking groups. He was also a Senior Vice President of Rothschild Inc., an investment banking, venture capital, and money management firm. Richard received a B. A. degree from Wesleyan University and an M.B.A. from Harvard Business School. He has also been awarded the Chartered Financial Analyst (CFA) designation. When not reviewing marinas, editing books, attempting to close private equity deals, or out sailing, Richard is active in a number of not-for-profit activities including service as a former Chair of the Rye Arts Center, Inc., Past Chair of the Wesleyan (University) Annual Fund, current Fleet Captain of the American Yacht Club, and, occasionally, bass player in the venerable 60's rock 'n' roll band, "Gary and the Wombats."

Cruiser Comments Rate the marinas you've visited

Marina Name _____ Manager or Dockmaster _____

Address _____ City _____ State _____ Zip _____

Tel: _____ Fax: _____ Email _____ WebAddress _____

Date of visit _____ Number of Nights _____ Slip _____ Alongside _____ Mooring _____ Launch? _____

PLEASE RATE THE FOLLOWING ON A SCALE OF 1 to 10

From 1 (just awful) to 10 (best we've ever experienced) — write n/a if it doesn't apply, and please add as many comments as you wish ...

Dockage: Docks _____ Pedestals _____ Fuel Dock _____ Docking Help _____ Reservations _____

Heads, etc: Toilets _____ Showers _____ Laundry _____ Other Amenities _____ Fitness Center _____

Setting: Landscaping _____ Maintenance _____ Service _____ Overall Ambiance _____

Amenities: Pool/Beach _____ Eatery _____ Picnic/Grill Area _____ Boaters Lounge _____ Other _____

Services: Internet Access _____ Pump Out _____ Ships Store _____ Local info _____ Concierge _____

Transportation: Courtesy Car _____ Water Taxi _____ Bikes _____ Taxis _____ Rental Cars _____ Bus/Train _____ Airport _____

Provisioning: Convenience _____ Supermarket _____ Gourmet/Prepared food _____ Local Produce _____ Seafood _____

Nearby: Recreation _____ Entertainment _____ Restaurants _____ Shops & Services _____

What was the best part of this experience? _____

_____

What was the worst part of this experience? _____

_____

Your Name _____ Boat Name _____

Address _____ City _____ State _____ Zip _____

Tel _____ Fax _____ Email _____

Sail _____ Power _____ Megayacht _____ Sportfish _____ Length _____ Draft _____ Manufacturer _____ Year _____

This form can be found online at http://www.AtlanticCruisingClub.com

Or make copies and send the completed forms to:

Atlantic Cruising Club
PO Box 978; Rye, New York 10580
Fax: 914-967-5504

Order Form

Please ask for the *Guides* at your local book store or chandlery or order directly.

☐ **Please register me as a member of the Atlantic Cruising Club**

☐ **Please send me the following *Atlantic Cruising Club's Guides to Marinas* — as soon as each is available.**
Each Book, with bound-in CD-ROM, is US $24.95* (CN $34.95*)

*Quantity Discounts Available *(Titles may be mixed for maximum discount; Contact ACC for larger quantities)*
For orders of 2 books or more, deduct 10% — 4 books or more, deduct 17% — 6 books or more, deduct 25%.

_____ ***Atlantic Cruising Club's Guide to New England Marinas*** *(2003)*
Bar Harbor, ME to Block Island, RI *(Including Buzzards Bay, Narragansett Bay, Martha's Vineyard and Nantucket)*

_____ ***Atlantic Cruising Club's Guide to Long Island Sound Marinas*** *(2004)*
Block Island, RI to Cape May, NJ *(Including Connecticut River, New York Harbor and New Jersey Shore)*

_____ ***Atlantic Cruising Club's Guide to Florida East Coast Marinas*** *(2004)*
Fernandina, FL to Key West FL *(Including St. John's River, the Okeechobee Waterway and the Florida Keys)*

_____ ***Atlantic Cruising Club's Guide to Pacific Northwest Marinas*** *(2004)*
Point Roberts, WA to Brookings, OR *(Including the San Juan Islands, Puget Sound, Lake Union, Lake Washington, the Strait of Juan de Fuca, and the mouth of the Columbia River)*

_____ ***Atlantic Cruising Club's Guide to Mid-Atlantic & ICW Marinas*** *(2004)*
Hampton Roads, VA to St. Mary's, GA *(Including the Virginia Coast, the ICW, Bermuda and the North Carolina Sounds)*

_____ ***Atlantic Cruising Club's Guide to Gulf Coast Marinas*** *(2005)*
Everglades City, FL to Padre Island, TX *(Including the Gulf Coast ICW, the Caloosahatchee River, and Mobile Bay)*

_____ ***Atlantic Cruising Club's Guide to Chesapeake Bay Marinas*** *(2005)*
Cape May, NJ to Hampton Roads, VA *(Including the C&D Canal and the Delmarva Peninsula)*

_____ ***Atlantic Cruising Club's Guide to California Coast Marinas*** *(2005)*
Crescent City, CA to Chula Vista, CA *(Including San Francisco Bay, Newport Bay, Mission Bay, San Diego Bay and Catalina Island)*

_____ *Sub-Total x US $24.95 (CN $34.95)*

_____ *Quantity Discount Percentage (see above)**

_____ *Tax (New York State Residents only add 6.75%)*

_____ *Shipping & Handling (USPS — add $4.00 for first book and $2.00 for each subsequent book)*

Final Total	Note: Credit cards will not be charged until books are shipped.

Please Charge the following Credit Card: Amex ☐   MasterCard ☐   Visa ☐   Discover ☐   Check Enclosed ☐

Number: _____   Four-Digit Security Number: _____

Expiration Date: _____   Signature: _____

Name: _____   Email: _____

Address: _____   City: _____   State or Province: _____   Zip: _____

Home Phone: _____   Office Phone: _____   Fax: _____

Boat Name: _____   Length: _____   Manufacturer: _____

Boat Type: Sail Mono-Hull ☐   Sail Multi-Hull ☐   Power ☐   Trawler ☐   Megayacht ☐

Home Port: _____   Cruising Grounds: _____

Please mail, fax. email, or call-in your order to: **Atlantic Cruising Club at Jerawyn Publishing, Inc.** PO Box 978; Rye, New York 10580
Tel: (914) 967-0994 or (888) 967-0994;   Fax: (914) 967-5504;   Email: Orders@AtlanticCruisingClub.com